THE
MARKANDEYA PURANA

BIBLIOTHECA INDICA:
A
COLLECTION OF ORIENTAL WORKS,
PUBLISHED BY
THE ASIATIC SOCIETY OF BENGAL.
NEW SERIES, NOS. 700, 706, 810, 872, 890, 947, 1058, 1076, & 1104

THE MARKANDEYA PURANA

TRANSLATED WITH NOTES.

BY

F. EDEN PARGITER, B.A.
Indian Civil Service;
Judge of the High Court of Judicature, Calcutta;
Late Boden Sanskrit Scholar, Oxford.

GYAN

Published by

GYAN

Gyan Publishing House
5, Ansari Road
Daryaganj, New Delhi-110002
Phone: 011-47034999, 9811692060
E-mail: books@gyanbooks.com

Distribution Network
gyanbooks.com
India, USA, Canada, UK, Australia, France

ISBN : 978-81-212-2225-9 (PB)
First Published, 1904

2nd Impression 2021

Printed at: Gyan Press, Delhi.

The
Markandeya Purana
Translated by: F. Eden Pargiter

BIBLIOTHECA INDICA:

A

COLLECTION OF ORIENTAL WORKS,

PUBLISHED BY

THE ASIATIC SOCIETY OF BENGAL.

NEW SERISE, NOS. 700, 706, 810, 872, 890, 947, 1058, 1076, & 1104.

THE

MĀRKANDEYA PURĀNA

TRANSLATED WITH NOTES.

BY

F. EDEN PARGITER, B.A.

Indian Civil Service;

Judge of the High Court of Judicature, Calcutta;

Late Boden Sanskrit Scholar, Oxford.

CALCUTTA:

PRINTED AT THE BAPTIST MISSION PRESS,

AND PUBLISHED BY

THE ASIATIC SOCIETY, 57, PARK STREET.

1904.

PREFACE.

This translation of the Mārkaṇḍeya Purāṇa was undertaken by me for the Asiatic Society of Bengal many years ago, when I hoped to be able to carry it through in no long period; but onerous official duties left little leisure, and for years removed me to a distance from the Society's Library and other means of reference. The Society was reluctant that the translation should be dropped, and it has therefore been continued as well as leisure permitted. It is hoped that in spite of these difficulties the translation may be of service to scholars, and the notes with all their shortcomings not unwelcome.

CALCUTTA:
3rd December, 1904. F. E. P.

INTRODUCTION.

This translation of the Mārkaṇḍeya Purāṇa being made for the Asiatic Society of Bengal naturally follows the edition of this work prepared by the Rev. Dr. K. M. Banerjea, and published in the Bibliotheca Indica in 1862; yet other editions and some MSS. have been consulted and are referred to. The translation has been kept as close to the original as possible, consistently with English sense and idiom; for a translation loses some of its interest and much of its trustworthiness, when the reader can never know whether it reproduces the original accurately or only the purport of the original. The time during which the work has been in hand has rendered it difficult to maintain one system of transliteration throughout; but, in order to place the whole in a consistent state, the system established by the Royal Asiatic Society and approved by the Asiatic Society of Bengal has been adopted in the Index and in this Introduction.

The general character of this Purāṇa has been well summed up by Prof. Wilson in his preface to his Translation of the Viṣṇu Purāṇa, except that his description hardly applies to the Devī-māhātmya. "This Purāṇa has a character different from that of all the others. It has nothing of a sectarial spirit, little of a religious tone; rarely inserting prayers and invocations to any deity; and such as are inserted are brief and moderate. It deals little in precepts, ceremonial or moral. Its leading feature is narrative; and it presents an uninterrupted succession of legends, most of which when ancient are embellished with new circumstances, and when new partake so far of the spirit of the old, that they are disinterested creations of the imagination, having no particular motive, being designed to recommend no special doctrine or observance. Whether they are derived from any other source, or whether they are original inventions, it is not possible to ascertain. They are most probably, for the greater part at least, original; and the whole has been narrated in the compiler's own manner; a manner superior to that of the Purāṇas in general, with exception of the Bhāgavata."

Composition.

The Purāṇa is clearly divisible (as Dr. Banerjea noticed) into five distinct parts, namely :—

1. Cantos 1-9, in which Jaimini is referred by Mārkaṇḍeya to the wise Birds, and they directly explain to him the four questions that perplexed him and some connected matters.

2. Cantos 10-44, where, though Jaimini propounds further questions to the Birds and they nominally expound them, yet the real speakers are Sumati, nicknamed Jaḍa, and his father.

3. Cantos 45-81 : here, though Jaimini and the Birds are the nominal speakers, yet the real speakers are Mārkaṇḍeya and his disciple Krauṣṭuki.

4. Cantos 82-92, the Devī-māhātmya, a pure interpolation, in which the real speaker is a ṛṣi named Medhas, and which is only repeated by Mārkaṇḍeya.

5. Cantos 93-136, where Mārkaṇḍeya and Krauṣṭuki carry on their discourse from canto 81.

The 137th canto concludes the work; it is a necessary corollary to the first part.

There can be no doubt that only the third and fifth of these parts constituted the Purāṇa in its original shape as Mārkaṇḍeya's Puraṇa. The name would imply that originally Mārkaṇḍeya was the chief figure, and it is only in the third part that he appears as the real teacher. There is, however, clearer evidence that the Purāṇa began with the third part originally, for this is asserted almost positively in canto 45, verses 16 to 25. There Mārkaṇḍeya, after declaring that this Purāṇa, equally with the Vedas, issued from Brahmā's mouth, says—"I will now tell it to thee ...... Hear all this from me ...... as I formerly heard it when Dakṣa related it." These words plainly mean that the true Purāṇa began here ; or, if the necessary words of introduction be prefixed, that it began at verse 16 or 17, which verses have been slightly modified since in order to dovetail them into the preceding portion.

The first and second parts were composed afterwards and then prefixed to the Purāṇa proper. That they were later compositions is implied by the fact that the Birds recite the Purāṇa proper as an authority, and is indeed indicated by the origin attributed to them. While the original Purāṇa was proclaimed to be a revelation from Brahmā himself, no higher authority is claimed for the first and second parts than Mārkaṇḍeya and the unknown brahman Sumati Jaḍa. Further, mention is made in canto 20, verse 33, of Purāṇas which narrate Viṣṇu's manifestations. This expression is vague. If it means lengthy descriptions of some of the incarnations, such Purāṇas might be the Viṣṇu, Brahma-vaivarta, Brahma and Bhāgavata; but the last two were pronounced by Prof. Wilson to be late compositions, and the reference here may be to the former two only, to which he assigned about an equal date with this Purāṇa. There is nothing definite to show whether the first and second parts had been united before they were prefixed to the Purāṇa proper, or whether the second part was inserted after the first had been prefixed; yet it would seem more probable that they had been united before they were prefixed. There is a marked similarity between them.

The prefixing of the discourses delivered by the Birds to the Purāṇa proper raised the Birds to the primary and chief position and tended to derogate from Mārkaṇḍeya's pre-eminence; but clashing was avoided and Mārkaṇḍeya's supremacy was preserved by two expedients; *first*, he was introduced at the very beginning in order that he might expressly declare the wisdom and authority of the Birds; and *secondly*, the original Purāṇa was interfered with as little as possible by making the Birds repeat it in its entirety as Mārkaṇḍeya's teaching, conclusive upon the subjects dealt with in it. The Birds on beginning it retire from further notice, but reappear with Jaimini in the final canto to conclude their discourse and give consistency to the combined instruction. This was a termination rendered necessary by the prefixing of the first two parts to the original Purāṇa.

The second part appears to have been amplified beyond its primary scope. It discourses about birth and death, about the hells, about sins and their punishments and about yoga or religious devotion. All these subjects are briefly dealt with, though the description of the different hells is ampler than in other Purāṇas, but the last subject leads to a discursive exposition. If dealt with like the other subjects, the exposition would pass from canto 16, verse 12 immediately to canto 37, where king Alarka is driven by adversity to seek Dattātreya's advice and that ṛṣi expounds the doctrines of yoga to him in cantos 38 to 43, and the story naturally closes with canto 44. But the reference to that king and that ṛṣi was considered to require some elucidation at canto 16, verse 13, hence the story of Dattātreya and the story of Alarka's parents Ṛtadhvaja and Madālasā are made the introduction to the direct exposition of yoga, with the result that the digression is so long that, when the subject of yoga is reached, its connexion with Jaimini's questions has been lost to sight; and even the passage from the story of Dattātreya to that of Alarka at the end of canto 19 is inapt and abrupt.

Both these stories moreover appear in their turn to have been expanded beyond their natural course. The story of the brahman and his devoted wife in canto 16, which furnishes an unnecessary explanation of the birth of Dattātreya, is a story of common town life, an absurd anachronism compared with what it explains; and it seems with its reference to a temple dedicated to Anasūyā during her life-time to be an interpolation intended for her glorification. The story of Ṛtadhvaja and Madālasā is a charming one of simple marvel and runs its natural course in cantos 20 to 27 as far as Madālasā's instruction of her son Alarka in kingly duties; but the following cantos 28 to 35, in which she expounds the laws regarding brahmans, śrāddhas, custom, &c., hardly accord with the story or with her position and knowledge, and seem to be an interpolation. Some teaching on such matters being deemed desirable, here was the only place where the addition was possible.

The Devī-māhātmya stands entirely by itself as a later interpolation. It is a poem complete in itself. Its subject and the character attributed to the goddess shew that it is the product of a later age which developed and took pleasure in the sanguinary features of popular religion. The praise of the goddess Mahā-māyā in canto 81 is in the ordinary style. Her special glorification begins in canto 82, and is elaborated with the most extravagant laudation and the most miraculous imagination. Some of the hymns breathe deep religious feeling, express enthusiastic adoration, and evince fervent spiritual meditation. On the other hand, the descriptions of the battles abound with wild and repulsive incidents, and revel in gross and amazing fancies. The Devī-māhātmya is a compound of the most opposite characters. The religious out-pourings are at times pure and elevated: the material descriptions are absurd and debased.

The ending of the Purāṇa deserves notice. It closes with the exploits of king Dama. According to the Gauḍiya or Bengal MSS., which Dr. Banerjea followed, the Purāṇa ends abruptly in canto 136, leaving Dama acquiescing tamely in the flight of his father's murderer Vapuṣmat. The up-country version (the ending of which he placed in an appendix) is found in the Bombay and Poona editions and carries the story on till Dama takes vengeance on Vapuṣmat. Dr. Banerjea considered the abruptness and incompleteness were strong evidence of the genuineness of the Bengal ending; and no doubt that is a fair argument, but it overlooks the character of the two endings. The pusillanimity which that ending ascribes to Dama jars with the whole tone of his threat in canto 135 which both versions account genuine. On the other hand the up-country ending narrates the fulfilment of that threat, and the savage and even inhuman incidents which it mentions are hardly explicable if it is spurious, for Dama after killing Vapuṣmat used Vapuṣmat's blood and flesh for the oblations due to his murdered father, and also (it is implied) gave certain degraded brahmans a cannibal feast. A forger would not wish nor dare to invent in his eulogy of one of the kings such repulsive incidents, desecrating the most sacred rites and tenets of his religion, nor if we can imagine such a forgery did occur, could it have ever obtained even tolerance. It is impossible, therefore, to think that the up-country ending is a forgery; and if it be the true original, one can easily understand why such an ending should have been struck out, and how the reviser, unable to invent or palm off a new ending, had to bring the story to the abrupt and jejune conclusion of the Bengal version. The up-country ending has, therefore, been adopted as the true version in this translation, and the Bengal ending has been noticed separately. The former discloses, like stray passages elsewhere, that savagery was not absent from the earliest memories of the Aryans in India.

For the purpose of discussing the Purāṇa further, it will be convenient to consider the first and second parts as composing one Section, and the third and fifth parts as composing another Section;

and this division will be observed in what follows. The Devī-māhātmya constitutes a Section by itself.

Place of Origin.

With regard to the question of the place of its origin, the Purāṇa in both its Sections professes to have emanated from Western India.

The second Section as the oldest may be considered first. In canto 45, vs. 24 and 25, Mārkaṇḍeya says positively that Cyavana was the ṛṣi who first declared it: Cyavana obtained it from Bhṛgu and declared it to the ṛṣis, they repeated it to Dakṣa and Mārkaṇḍeya learnt it from Dakṣa. Now Cyavana is intimately associated with the west of India, especially with the region about the mouths of the rivers Narmadā and Tapti. His father Bhṛgu and their descendants Ṛcīka, Jamadagni and Paraśu Rāma are connected in many a legend with all the country north, east and south of that region. That was the territory of the Bhārgava race (see pp. 310 and 368). As Cyavana settled near the mouths of those rivers, the Purāṇa itself claims to have been first declared by him in that region.

Mārkaṇḍeya himself was a Bhārgava. This is stated in canto 45, v. 18 and canto 52 vs. 14-17; and also in the Mahā-bhārata, Vana-p. ccxvi. 14104-5. The Bhārgavas spread from Cyavana's region, especially eastward along the valleys of the Narmadā and Tapti, as those valleys were gradually wrested from the hill races by the Yādavas and Haihayas, the most famous conquerors of which race were Arjuna Kārtavīrya and Jyāmagha. The former reigned in Māhiṣmatī on the Narmadā; and the latter apparently conquered further eastward (see M. Bh., Vana-p. cxvi., S'ānti-p. xlix; Hari-V., xxxiii. 1850-90, and xxxvii. 1930-87; Viṣṇu P., cli-clxxiv; and Matsya P. xliii.-13-51 and xliv. 28-36). Mārkaṇḍeya is said to have paid visits to the Pāṇḍavas and to have had a tīrtha at the junction of the Ganges and Gomatī (M. Bh., Vana-p. lxxxiv. 8058-9), but his special abode appears to have been on the river Payoṣṇī (the modern Purnā and its continuation in the Tapti, see p. 299) (*id.* lxxxviii. 8330). Both by lineage and by residence therefore he belonged to that western country, and the original Purāṇa must have been composed there. Bhārgavas are continually alluded to throughout the Purāṇa.

As regards the first Section, it is said the Birds, to whom Jaimini was referred, were living in the Vindhya mountains, and it was there that they delivered the Purāṇa to him. They are explained of course to be four brahman brothers in a state of transmigration, and it appears to be implied in canto 3, vs. 22-24, that their father, the muni Sukṛṣa, dwelt on or near the Vindhyas. He had a brother named Tumburu. There were other persons of this name, such as Tumburu who was a guru among the Gandharvas (see pp. 571, 647, 648, and 118 as corrected; and M. Bh., Sabhā-p. li. 1881.); but it seems permissible to connect this brother Tumburu with the tribes of the names Tumbura and Tumbula who dwelt on the slopes of the Vindhyas (p. 343).

The Birds are said to have dwelt in the Vindhyas in a cave, where the water was very sacred (p. 17), and which was sprinkled with drops of water from the river Narmadā (p. 19); and it is no doubt allowable to infer the situation from these indications, namely, some cliffs of the Vindhya hills where those hills abut on the river Narmadā at a very sacred tīrtha. Such a spot cannot be sought above the modern Hoshangabad, for the river above that was encompassed in early times by hills, dense forest and wild tribes. Among the very sacred places where the Vindhya hills on the north approach close to the river, none satisfies the conditions better that the rocky island and town of Mandhāta, which is to be identified with Māhiṣmatī, the ancient and famous Haihaya capital. The modern town of Mahesar, some fifty miles lower down the river, claims to be the ancient Māhiṣmatī, but does not satisfy the allusions. Māhiṣmatī was situated on an island in the river and the palace looked out on the rushing stream (Raghu-V., vi. 43). This description agrees only with Mandhāta. Māhiṣmatī was sacred to Agni in the earliest times (M. Bh., Sabhā-p. 1125-63). Mandhāta has special claims to sanctity; it has very ancient remains; it has become sacred to S'iva, and the famous shrine of Oṁkāra and other temples dedicated to him are here (Hunter, Impl. Gaz., "Mandhāta."). The hills close in on the river here, and on the north bank are Jain temples. In these hills on the north bank overlooking the river at Mandhāta we may place the alleged cave where the first part of the Purāṇa professes that it was delivered; and this identification will be found to explain many further features of the Purāṇa

With regard to the second part it may be noticed that Sumati Jaḍa, whose words the Birds repeat, belonged also to the family of Bhṛgu (p. 63). Hence this part belonged to the same region where the Bhārgavas predominated. With this view agrees the statement that the rainy season lasts four months and the dry season eight months (p. 147), as I understand is the rule in this region. It is further worthy of note that eyes of blue colour, like the blue water-lily (*nīlotpala*) are given to Lakṣmī (p. 104) and to Madālasā (p. 114); and such a comparison is rare, I believe, in Sanskrit. It was (may it be inferred?) in Western India that people with blue eyes could have been seen as visitors in circumstances of such appreciation that their features became a model of beauty.

There are some other matters that might have been expected to yield information of a local character, such as the lists of various trees, plants, birds and animals (pp. 24-31, 164-6 and 244-5) and the peculiar exposition of the construction and nomenclature of fortresses (pp. 240-2). I have, however, been unable to deduce any definite conclusion from the latter, and the lists betray no special local character, but rather aim at being as comprehensive in their way as the geographical cantos (57 and 58).

Both the first and second Sections, therefore, plainly emanated from Western India, and indicate the middle portion of the Narbadā and Tapti valleys as their place of origin. It remains to consider the Devī-māhātmya, and the following considerations point to the same place of origin, especially to Mandhāta.

The Devī-māhātmya must have originated in some place dedicated to the goddess in her terrible form. The poem has now become a text-book of the worshippers of Kālī throughout Northern India and in Bengal, especially at the great Durgā-pūjā festival, but it did not originate in Bengal. The goddess whom the poem glorifies is a goddess formed by the union of the vigours or energies (*tejas*, not *śakti*) of all the gods (p. 473), and she is called Mahā-māyā, Caṇḍikā, Ambikā, Bhadra-kālī and Mahā-kālī (pp. 469, 476, &c. and 521). Though identified with S'rī once (p. 484), yet she is generally identified in the hymns with S'iva's consort as Durgā, Gaurī, S'iva-dūtī and Mahā-kālī (pp. 484-5, 494-6, and 521). The goddess Kālī, however, who is also called Cāmuṇḍā (p. 500), is made a separate goddess who issued from Caṇḍikā's forehead (p. 499); and Caṇḍikā gave her the name Cāmuṇḍā, because (as it is expressed in a *bon mot)* she had killed two great demons Caṇḍa and Muṇḍa (p. 500). Whether this derivation has any imaginary truth or not must be very doubtful, because fanciful derivations are common in this Purāṇa and elsewhere. The S'aktis of the gods are made separate emanations from the gods, and are called the Mothers, *mātṛ-gaṇa* (pp. 502, 504). The poem is therefore a glorification of Durgā in her terrible aspect, with Kālī as an emanation from her.

One would therefore look among the strongholds of S'iva worship for the birth-place of this poem. Now it is remarkable that of the great liṅga shrines (which are reckoned to be twelve), no less than six are situated in or near the very region of Western India where the Purāṇa originated; *viz*, Oṁkāra at Mandhāta, Mahākāla at Ujjain, Tryambak at Nasik, Ghṛṇeśvara at Ellora, Nāganāth east of Ahmadnagar, and Bhīma-śaṅkar at the sources of the river Bhīma. Mandhāta was doubly distinguished, for another famous liṅga was Amreśvara on the south bank of the river there. At none of them however, except at Oṁkāra, was S'iva or Durgā worshipped with sanguinary rites, as far as I can find.

In the Mahā-bhārata Durgā has the names Mahākālī, Bhadrakālī, Caṇḍā and Caṇḍī; and she is also called Kālī, no distinction being made (Virāṭa-p. vi. 195; Bhīṣma-p. xxiii. 796-7). The name Cāmuṇḍā does not apparently occur there. Cāmuṇḍā was worshipped with human sacrifices, for she is mentioned in the fifth Act of the Mālatī-mādhava, where her temple is introduced and her votaries tried to offer a human sacrifice at the city Padmāvatī. Padmāvatī was a name of Ujjain; but some scholars would identify it with Narwar which is on the R. Sindh, though that town seems to be too distant to suit the description at the beginning of the ninth Act. Whether Padmāvatī was Ujjain or not, there can be no doubt from that description that it was situated in the region north of the Vindhyas between the upper portions of the rivers Chambal and Parbati, that is, in the region immediately north of Mandhāta.

The only local allusion in the poem is that the goddess is Mahākālī at Mahākāla (p. 521), which is a shrine of S'iva at Ujjain; and it is possible the poem may have been composed to proclaim the māhātmya or glory of that place. But this is hardly probable, because the allusion is very brief, and the worship there was not apparently of the kind to originate this poem. Moreover, if Padmāvatī was Ujjain, the Mālatī-mādhava distinguishes between the temple of Cāmuṇḍā and the shrine of Mahākāla, for the temple is described as being adjacent to a field which was used as a burning-ground for corpses and which must have lain outside the city; and if Padmāvatī was some other town, the allusion here to Mahākāla has no connexion with Cāmuṇḍā or Caṇḍikā at Padmāvatī. It is hardly probable that, if this poem originated at Ujjain, the goddess at the shrine of Mahākāla would have been referred to in this manner. Hence this passage more probably conveys only a commendatory allusion; and it seems more natural and appropriate to connect the poem with Mandhāta, where this phase of sanguinary worship was particularly strong.

The worship of Cāmuṇḍā points to the same conclusion. Human sacrifices had long been abolished in the civilized countries of India, and the offering of such sacrifices at Padmāvatī could hardly have been a survival but must have been introduced from elsewhere. Such a practice would naturally be clandestine. Human sacrifices were offered in those times only among the rude tribes of Central India, among whom such sacrifices survived till the last century; hence it may be inferred that such offerings to Cāmuṇḍā at Padmāvatī must have been introduced from places which bordered on those tribes and were affected by their rites. The middle portion of the Narbada valley was eminently such a place. Pointing in the same direction is the statement in the Mahā-bhārata that Durgā had her eternal abode on the Vindhyas and was fond of intoxicating liquor, flesh and cattle (Virāṭa-p. vi. 195). It seems reasonable then to conclude that the Devī-māhātmya is earlier than the Mālatī-mādhava; and if so, the name Cāmuṇḍā and the form Caṇḍikā occur apparently the first time in this poem.

Mandhāta was a famous ancient tīrtha and appears to have fallen into neglect and been almost deserted in the 11th and 12th centuries A.D., but its glory was revived. About the year 1165 "a Gosáin, named Daryáo Náth, was the only worshipper of Omkár on the island, which pilgrims could not visit for fear of a terrible god called Kál

Bhairava and his consort Káli Deví, who fed on human flesh. At last Daryáo Náth by his austerities shut up Káli Deví in a cave, the mouth of which may yet be seen, appeasing her by erecting an image outside to receive worship; while he arranged that Kál Bhairava should, in future, receive human sacrifices at regular intervals. From that time devotees have dashed themselves over the Bírkhala cliffs at the eastern end of the island on to the rocks by the river brink, where the terrible god resided; till in 1824 the British officer in charge of Nimár witnessed the last such offering to Kál Bhairava." (Hunter, Impl. Gaz., "Mandhāta"). There does not appear to be any information, what kind of worship was offered there before the 11th century, yet the facts suggest strongly that such sanguinary rites were not a new ordinance but had prevailed there before.

Both S'iva and his consort in their most terrible forms were thus worshipped at Mandhāta, which was almost exclusively devoted to their service; and it is easy to understand how such a sanguinary form of religion could take shape here. This region of the Narbadā valley was specially connected with demon legends, such as the demon stronghold of Tripura and the demon Mahiṣa, after which the towns Tewar and Mahesar are said to be named. It also bordered on the Nāga country. Mandhāta, with such associations, would be the most probable birth-place of this poem, and the brief allusion to Mahākāla would then be only a collateral one; yet, even if the poem was composed at Ujjain, the conclusion would still remain good that the poem originated in this region of Western India.

Date of the Purāṇa.

The question of the date of the Purāṇa is more difficult, since all questions of chronology in Sanskrit writings are most uncertain. One definite and important date may be first noticed. Mahāmahopādhyāya Haraprasād S'āstrī found a copy of the Devī-māhātmya in old Newari characters in the Royal Library in Nepal, and it is dated 998 A.D. (See his Catalogue). It may be safely inferred therefrom, that this poem must have been composed before the beginning of the 10th century at the latest. The Devī-māhātmya cannot therefore be later than the 9th century and may be considerably earlier. Since it is the latest part of the Purāṇa, the other parts must have been composed earlier, and the question for consideration is, how much earlier?

Prof. Wilson in his preface to his Translation of the Viṣṇu Purāṇa pointed out that this Purāṇa is later than the Mahā-bhārata but anterior to the Brahma, Padma, Nāradīya and Bhāgavata Purāṇas, and conjectured that it may be placed in the ninth or tenth century A.D. This, as already noticed, is too recent, moreover it has been discovered since that his estimates of the composition of the several Purāṇas under-reckon their age, and that the periods assigned by him should be moved some centuries earlier. For instance, he conjectured the collective writings known as the Skanda Purāṇa to be modern and "the greater part of the contents of the Kāśī Khaṇḍa anterior to the first attack upon Benares by Mahmud of Ghizni" (Preface, p. lxxii)—which must mean that the Kāśī Khaṇḍa is earlier than the 11th century A.D. But Mahāmahopādhyāya Haraprasād S'āstrī found in the Royal Library in Nepal a copy of the "Skanda Purāṇa" written in the later Gupta characters of the 6th or 7th century A.D. From that it is obvious that the composition of the Skanda Purāṇa must have taken place four or five centuries earlier than Prof. Wilson's estimate. Hence it is possible that a corresponding modification of his estimate regarding the Mārkaṇḍeya Purāṇa should be made, and that would place it about the 4th century A.D.

Further evidence is obtained from Jain writings that the Purāṇas are much earlier than Prof. Wilson estimated. Thus the Padma Purāṇa of the Jains, which was written by Raviṣena in imitation of the Hindu Padma Purāṇa, contains, I understand, a couplet showing that it was composed in the year 678 A.D; and that Purāṇa mentions all the Purāṇas. All are mentioned again in the Jain Ādi Purāṇa of Jinasena who lived about a century later. This evidence would demonstrate that all the Hindu Purāṇas had been composed before the end of the sixth and probably by the end of the fifth century A.D.; though of course it leaves room open for subsequent additions and interpolations in them.

A common method of estimating the age of a Sanskrit composition is to consider the religious and philosophical ideas embodied in it; yet to discuss questions of chronology on the basis of such ideas seems to be more interesting than convincing. Such ideas have passed along a course of development in India, but it is doubtful how far general inferences therefrom can be safely applied to fix the date of a particular work. Where such ideas are founded on sacred compositions, which are the subject of reverent study, there must be flows, eddies and intervals of stagnation, and even rapids and back currents, in the stream of such ideas. Their course may be compared with similar speculations, not in a single European country, but in the whole of Europe, for India has always comprised many countries; and the history of Europe during the last four hundred years shews, whether it would be easy to determine the date of a writing on such subjects in Latin solely from its contents, for the progress of thought in the different countries has been neither simultaneous nor uniform. Similarly in India, there can be no doubt that, while religion and philosophy have had their general course of development, the course has been very unequal in the different countries, so that it would not be unreasonable to suspect that at the same time one country was advancing, another was stationary, and a third was even degenerating under political adversity. The development of religion and philosophy in India then is not so clear that one can do more than venture to conjecture upon such grounds, at what period or periods this Purāṇa, which was written in Western India, was composed. And, as already mentioned, it has so little of a sectarian spirit or of special doctrines that the basis for conjecture is meagre. Subject to this caution the following features may be noticed.

Among the deities, Indra and Brahmā are mentioned oftenest; next stand Viṣṇu and S'iva; then the Sun and Agni; and lastly Dharma and others. Indra is mentioned most often in the first and fifth parts, and Brahmā in the third and fifth parts; while Viṣṇu and S'iva do not show any particular preponderance. If the Devī-māhātmya is put aside, the Sun is the deity that receives the most special adoration, and his story is related twice, first, briefly in cantos 77 and 78, and afterwards with fullness in cantos 102-110. To this may be added the cognate worship of Agni in cantos 99 and 100. Such marked reverence for Agni and the Sun would be natural in such a place as Māhiṣmatī, which (as already mentioned) was specially sacred to Agni before the worship of S'iva obtained supremacy there. Kāmarūpa, the modern Gauhāṭi in Assam, is mentioned as specially appropriate for the worship of the Sun (p. 581), and why it should have been so characterized seems unintelligible unless it was considered to be an *udaya-giri*.

The prominent notice of the great Vedic god Indra, and of Brahmā the earliest of the post-Vedic gods, would indicate a fairly high antiquity for the Purāṇa, especially for the second Section, which boldly claims to have issued from Brahmā's mouth equally with the Vedas (p. 219) and thus to stand almost on an equality with them—an honour which none of the other Purāṇas ventures to arrogate for itself. Such an antiquity would also explain the high position assigned to the Sun and Agni, who are also among the chief Vedic gods; yet the special praise offered to the Sun may, as Dr. Banerjea hinted, be perhaps attributable in part to Persian influences.

The first Section of the Purāṇa is certainly later than the Mahā-bhārata, for the four questions that Jaimini propounds to the Birds arose expressly out of that work. These questions are, *first*, a religious enigma, Why did Vāsudeva (Viṣṇu) though devoid of qualities assume human shape with its qualities of goodness, passion and ignorance? *secondly*, a social perplexity, Why was Draupadī the common wife of the five Pāṇḍava brothers? *thirdly*, a moral incongruity, Why did Baladeva expiate the sin of brahmanicide by pilgrimage? and *fourthly*, a violation of natural justice, Why did Draupadī's five sons all perish in their youth? The obtrusion of these questions implies that the Mahā-bhārata was firmly established as an unimpeachable authority, so that difficulties involved in it could not be disputed and must admit of reconciliation with the laws of Righteousness.

The explanations offered by the Birds appear to be these. Vāsudeva (Viṣṇu) existed in quadruple form; the first form was devoid of qualities, but each of the others was characterized by one of the three qualities, so that in his assuming human and other shapes with all the qualities no violation occurred to his nature. The second question is solved by the assertion, that because of Indra's transgressions five portions of his essence became incarnate in the Pāṇḍavas, and his wife became incarnate as Draupadī, so that she was still the wife of only one person. The third question seems to turn on the ideas, that brahmanicide was a heinous sin expiable by death and that pilgrimage was a pious undertaking; how therefore could such a sin be expiated by such action? The answer seems to be that the sin was unintentional, being due to overpowering sensual influences, and did not call for the full rigour of punishment, while the real penance consisted in *confession*. The fourth question is solved by a story of transmigration; Draupadī's sons were five Viśve Devās who were cursed by Viśvāmitra to assume human form for a brief period.

The first two questions and answers call for some notice and throw some light on the age of the first Section of the Purāṇa.

With regard to the first question, Dr. Banerjea has remarked in his Introduction that the description of Vāsudeva belongs to the school Nārada-pañcarātra, to which S'aṅkarācārya has given an elaborate reply in his commentary on the Brahma Sūtras; while no trace of this doctrine is to be found in the second Section of the Purāṇa. As S'aṅkara lived in the 8th century A.D., that school existed before him. The first part of this Purāṇa was, therefore, probably prior to his time; yet it may possibly have been later. This comparison then yields nothing definite.

The second answer presents some remarkable peculiarities when compared with the Mahā-bhārata. That work gives two explanations about Draupadī's wifehood, *first*, why she was destined to have five husbands, and *secondly*, why the five Pāṇḍavas became her husbands.

The first explanation is given twice in the Ādi-parvan, *viz.*, in clxix. 6426-34 and in cxcvii. 7319-28. She had been a ṛṣi's daughter and unmarried; in order to obtain a husband she propitiated S'iva with austerities, and he offered her a boon. She begged for a husband, and in her eagerness made the request five times, hence he promised her five husbands, and in spite of her objection adhered to his word and promised them to her in another life. Hence she was born as Drupada's daughter. In the latter of these two passages and in line 7310 she is made an incarnation of Lakṣmī.

The second explanation is given in Ādi-parvan cxcvii. 7275-7310. Indra went to S'iva on Mount Himavat and accosted him rudely, but S'iva awed him and pointed to a cave in the mountain wherein were four prior Indras. S'iva said that Indra and those four prior Indras should be born in human shape in order to reduce the over-population of the world, and that Lakṣmī should be born and be their common wife. Accordingly Indra was born as Arjuna and the prior Indras as the other Pāṇḍavas, and Lakṣmī was born as Draupadī.

Now these stories in the Mahā-bhārata itself furnished some explanation, and why Jaimini should have felt any perplexity, if he had these explanations before him, is at first sight strange. This suggests a doubt whether they were then in the Mahā-bhārata, or whether they were inserted there afterwards to meet this very question. On the other hand, it may be noted that these explanations did not really solve the difficulty, for the five Indras who became the Pāṇḍavas were not the same deity, and thus Draupadī's husbands were still separate persons. On this point, therefore, the difficulty remained, and the answer given by the Birds removes it (though at variance with the Mahā-bhārata) by declaring that the Pāṇḍavas were all incarnations of portions of the same deity, Indra, and were thus really only one person. The Mahā-bhārata, however, presented a further difficulty, for why should Lakṣmī have become incarnate to be the wife of incarnations of Indra? The Birds alter this by declaring (again at variance with the Mahā-bhārata) that it was Indra's own wife who became incarnate as Draupadī. Both these contradictions are left unnoticed; yet it is said very truly that there was very great perplexity about this matter (p. 19).

This incongruity of Lakṣmī's becoming incarnate to be wife to incarnations of other deities suggests a further speculation. In the Mahā-bhārata as it now stands, Kṛṣṇa is an incarnation of Viṣṇu, and it was proper that Lakṣmī should become incarnate to be his queen. Nevertheless that work states that she became the wife of five persons all distinct from Viṣṇu. May it be surmised that these explanations in the Mahā-bhārata were fashioned before Kṛṣṇa had been deified, and before it was perceived that they could have any bearing on his story? If so, it is quite intelligible that it was deemed necessary, after Kṛṣṇa was deified, to remove the incongruity by asserting that Draupadī was an incarnation, not of Lakṣmī, but of Indrāṇī. This view, that the revised explanations here given regarding Draupadī and the Pāṇḍavas were necessitated by the deification of Kṛṣṇa, seems not improbable. If so, the revision and the name

Vāsudeva, by which Viṣṇu is specially addressed in the first part, would indicate that the first part was composed, when the Kṛṣṇa legend had become so well established that it was needful to bring other stories into harmony with it.

The Purāṇa contains little reference to the political condition of India; yet it may be pointed out that all the stories narrated in the first Section relate to Madhya-deśa, the Himālayas and Western India, while no mention occurs of Southern, Eastern or North-Western India. In the second Section, few illustrative stories occur apart from the main discourse on the Manus and the royal genealogies. Only one dynasty is treated of, that in which the chief princes were Vatsaprī, Khanitra, Karandhama, Avīkṣit and Marutta. These were famous kings, especially Marutta who was a universal monarch. I have not been able to find anything which indicates where their kingdom was, yet it must have been somewhere in the Middle-land or North-West, because of Marutta's relations with Vṛhaspati and Saṁvartta (M. Bh., Aśvam -p. iii-vi); the Middle-land here comprising the country as far east as Mithilā and Magadha. In the second Section the only allusions to other parts of India are one to the river Vitastā in the Panjab (p. 438), one to an unknown town in South India (p. 412), and several to Kāmarūpa, the modern Gauhāṭi in Assam; but the author's knowledge of Eastern India was so hazy that he treats Kāmarūpa as being easy of access from the Middle-land (p. 581). Is it reasonable to draw any inference from the mental horizon here disclosed? It agrees with the state of India in the third century A.D.

The geographical cantos 57 and 58 are no doubt special compilations and may to a certain degree stand apart. They appear to aim at being comprehensive, and to enumerate all the countries, races and tribes till then known, whether ancient or mediæval. This comprehensive character rather prevents the drawing of any large definite conclusions from them, yet two points may be noticed.

The Huṇas are placed among the peoples in the north in canto 58, though the context is not very precise. The Huns in their migrations from the confines of China appear to have arrived to the north of India about the beginning of the third century A.D., and one branch, the White Huns, established a kingdom afterwards in the

Oxus valley. India had no actual experience of them until their first invasion, which was made through the north-western passes in the middle of the fifth century (Mr. V. Smith's *Early History of India*, pp. 272, 273). The allusion to the Huns therefore, with the position assigned to them in the north, in canto 58, is plainly earlier than their invasion, and is what a writer in the third century or the early part of the fourth century would have made.

In these two cantos Prāgjyotiṣa is placed in the east, and no mention is made of Kāmarūpa. Prāgjyotiṣa was the ancient kingdom that comprised nearly all the north and east of Bengal (p. 328); later on it dwindled and seems to have lingered and perished in the east of Bengal; and after that Kāmarūpa came into prominence in its stead. In the Mahā-bhārata and Rāmāyaṇa Prāgjyotiṣa alone is named; Kāmarūpa is never, I believe, mentioned there, and it occurs in later writings only. In the Second Section however Kāmarūpa is mentioned, and no allusion is made to Prāgjyotiṣa. This difference tells in favour of the antiquity of these cantos.

With regard to the Devī-māhātmya, if the comparison made above between it and the Mālatī-mādhava is reasonable, it would follow that, since Bhavabhūti who wrote that play lived about the end of the seventh century A.D., this poem must be anterior. It would represent the incorporation of barbarous practices borrowed from the rude tribes of Central India into brahmanic doctrines, and might be assigned to the sixth or perhaps the fifth century.

From all these considerations it seems fair to draw the following conclusions. The Devī-māhātmya, the latest part, was certainly complete in the 9th century and very probably in the 5th or 6th century A.D. The third and fifth parts, which constituted the original Purāṇa, were very probably in existence in the third century, and perhaps even earlier; and the first and second parts were composed between those two periods.

Other matters of interest.

Certain other matters may be mentioned, which are of great interest in the Purāṇa.

In the first part Jaimini, though a disciple of Vyāsa and a famous ṛṣi (Mahā-bh., S'ānti-p. cccli. 13647), is yet made, when perplexed by four difficult questions in Vyāsa's own work, the Mahā-bhārata, to seek instruction, not from Vyāsa but from Mārkaṇḍeya; and this raises a presumption that there was an intention to make Mārkaṇḍeya equal with, if not superior to, Vyāsa. Further, Mārkaṇḍeya does not himself explain the questions but, declining with a transparent excuse, refers Jaimini to the Birds. The Birds, though said no doubt to be brahmans undergoing a transmigration, were inferior in education and fame to Jaimini, yet they were deemed fully capable of authoritatively answering the questions that puzzled him. It seems hard to avoid suspecting again in this construction of the story, that there was an intention to exalt the instruction given by the munis of the Vindhyas to equality with, if not superiority over, that given in Madhya-deśa. It may be mentioned that according to certain legends Vaiśampāyana's pupils were transformed into partridges (*tittiri*) in order to pick up the Black Yajus verses disgorged by one of their companions; but it does not seem reasonable to ascribe the introduction of these Birds as *dramatis personæ* in this Purāṇa to any imitation of those legends, because the nature of the stories is wholly different. The use of the Birds seems rather to be the application of a class of ideas common in the animal-tales of folk-lore to religious teaching, and to be similar to the machinery employed by Bāṇa in his story of Kādambarī.

In the second part it is worthy of note that indulgence in spirituous liquor and in sensual enjoyments is viewed with little or no disapprobation in the story of Dattātreya; and meat and strong drink are mentioned as most acceptable offerings in the worship of Dattātreya (p. 106), as an incarnation of Viṣṇu (p. 99). Meat of various kinds, including even hog's flesh, is declared to be most gratifying to the pitṛs. Such food was not unknown in ancient times, for it is said that during a severe famine king Triśaṅku supported Viśvāmitra's wife with the flesh of deer, wild pigs and buffaloes (Hari-V., 724–731).

A most extraordinary passage may be noticed in conclusion. It is related of king Dama that, after taking vengeance on prince Vapuṣmat, "with Vapuṣmat's flesh he offered the cakes to his [murdered] father, he feasted the brāhmans who were sprung from families of Rākṣasas" (p. 683 with 679). Brahmans at times lost their caste and became degraded, but here the position is reversed and certain descendants of Rākṣasas were reckoned as brahmans. Such cannibalism is, I believe, unparalleled in Sanskrit, and it is almost incredible that there should have been brahmans of any kind whatever who would have participated in it. Eating human flesh was not unknown in ancient times (p. 427), yet a story is told in the Mahā-bhārata where Rākṣasas and even flesh-eating Dasyus disdained the flesh of a true though degraded brahman (S'ānti-p. clxxii. 6420–29). This story of king Dama would seem to imply that it is of real antiquity, and that the account of the dynasty in which he occurred, and which is the only dynasty described, must be a purāṇa in the full meaning of the term.

CONTENTS.

CANTO. *Introduction.* PAGE.

1 Jaimini applied to Mārkaṇḍeya for instruction on four 1
questions. Mārkaṇḍeya referred him to four learned Birds,
sons of Droṇa and the Apsaras Vapu who was cursed by the
2 ṛṣi Durvāsas to be a bird; and narrated the story of their 6
3 birth, and of their education by S'amīka; and explained 11
that they were four brāhmans, who were so born, because
cursed by their father Sukṛṣa for not offering their bodies
as food to a famished bird.

The Birds' discourse on Jaimini's four questions.

4 Jaimini visited the Birds at the Vindhya Mts. and they 17
answered his four questions thus :—Viṣṇu assumed bodily
5 forms in order to accomplish good; Draupadī became the 21
joint wife of the five Pāṇḍavas because they were all
6 emanations of Indra; Baladeva committed brahmanicide 23
7 during intoxication and expiated it by pilgrimage; and five 32
Viśve Devās, who, on seeing Viśvāmitra's brutality to king
Hariścandra, censured Viśvāmitra, incurred his curse thereby
and were born as the five sons of Draupadī to die young and
unmarried.

8 This story led the Birds at Jaimini's request to narrate 38
the whole story of king Hariścandra's sufferings and
9 ultimate beatitude; and the terrible fight which resulted 59
therefrom between Vasiṣṭha and Viśvāmitra as gigantic
birds.

The Birds' discourse on Jaimini's further questions.

Discourse on life, death and action.

10 Jaimini propounded further questions regarding concep- 62
tion, fœtal life, birth, growth, death and the consequences
of action; and the Birds answered them by reproducing

CANTO. PAGE.

the instruction that a brāhman Sumati, nick-named Jaḍa,
once gave to his father (cantos x—xliv).

Thus the Birds gave in Jaḍa's words a description of
11 death, after-existences and certain hells; of human concep- 69
12 tion and birth, and the evils of all existence; of certain other 71
13 hells and the various terrible torments inflicted there; and 74
they narrated the story of king Vipaścit's descent into hell,
14 with a discourse regarding actions and the specific punish- 76
15 ments for a long list of various sins, and of his deliverance 83
from hell together with other persons confined there.

Stories illustrating religious devotion (yoga).

16 The Birds, continuing Jaḍa's discourse, broached the sub- 91
ject of *yoga* or religious devotion, but prefaced it with a long
narrative (cantos xvi to xliv). A brāhman Māṇḍavya was
saved from a curse by his devoted wife, who stopped the rising
17 of the sun and gained a boon from Atri's wife Anasūyā; the 99
gods in consequence blessed Anasūyā, and Brahmā, Viṣṇu and
S'iva were born as her three sons Soma, Dattātreya and Durvā-
18 sas; Dattātreya indulged in sensual pleasures; Arjuna Kār- 101
tavīrya, however, being advised by his minister Garga to
propitiate Dattātreya, because Dattātreya (being an incar-
nation of Viṣṇu) had once saved the gods from the demons,
19 did so and by Dattātreya's blessing reigned gloriously. 106
This led on to the story of Alarka, which is used to convey
political, religious and social instruction (cantos xx to xliv).

Alarka's birth and education.

20 King Satrujit's son Ṛtadhvaja lived in intimate friend- 109
ship with two Nāga princes; they told their father Aśva-
tara—how Ṛtadhvaja had succoured the brāhman Gālava
21 with the help of a wondrous horse named Kuvalaya, and 113
descending to Pātāla, had killed the demon Pātāla-ketu there,
and had rescued and married the Gandharva princess Madā-
22 lasā, and was famed as Kuvalayāśva; and also how a 121
demon had caused Madālasā to die on a false report of

CANTO. PAGE.

23 Kuvalayāśva's death. King Aśvatara, by propitiating Sa- 125
rasvatī then, gained perfect skill in poetry and music
(which are described), and by propitiating S'iva received
24 Madālasā restored to life; he invited Kuvalayāśva to 136
25 Pātāla and gave Madālasā back to him. Kuvalayāśva had 140
26 a son by her, and she prattled to the infant; they had 142
three other sons and she named the youngest Alarka.

Political, religious and social instruction.

27 Then followed an exposition of political, religious and social 145
doctrine in the guise of instruction given by Madālasā to
Alarka. She instructed him in the duties and conduct
28 of a king; in the duties of the four castes and of a brāh- 148
29 man's life; in the general duties of a gṛhastha and various 151
30 religious matters; in the duties of a gṛhastha in detail; 155
31 in the śrāddha ceremonies; in the performance of the Pār- 157
32 vaṇa S'rāddha and the persons to be excluded; in the par- 164
ticular foods, periods, sites and ordinances to be observed in
33 the śrāddha; in the Voluntary śrāddhas and their benefits 168
34 and proper occasions; in the rules of Virtuous Custom, 170
35 generally and with much detail; about diet, purification, 180
conduct, holy days and various religious ceremonies.

Exposition of religious devotion (yoga).

36 Ṛtadhvaja then resigned his kingdom to Alarka and de- 186
37 parted to the forest. Alarka lived in pleasure, but, being 187
reduced to great straits by his brother and the king of
38 Kāśi, sought relief from Dattātreya. Dattātreya spoke 191
about the soul and, on Alarka's asking about religious devotion
39 (yoga), expounded the method, conditions and signs of its 193
40 proper performance; the attendant ailments and the stages 198
41 which lead to final emancipation from existence; the way 202
in which a yogī should live, beg, eat and reach his end;
42 the composition, meaning and efficacy of the word "Om"; 205
43 ill omens and their signification; and the seasons for, and 207
the importance of, yoga. Alarka then relinquished the

CANTO. PAGE.
44 kingdom, but his brother, glad at Alarka's conversion, de- 213
clined it and departed. Alarka gave it to his son and de-
parted to the forest. This ends Jaḍa's exposition.

The Birds' discourse on Jaimini's further questions.

Discourse on Creation.

45 Jaimini put further questions, and the Birds answered 217
them by repeating what Mārkaṇḍeya had taught Krauṣṭuki.
This discourse runs on to the end of the Purāṇa.

Mārkaṇḍeya, after extolling this Purāṇa, described the
course of creation from Brahmā through Pradhāna, &c., and
46 the mundane egg; he discoursed about Brahmā, and ex- 224
47 plained divine and human time and the four ages. He de- 228
48 scribed the creation of the earth and all it contains; the 232
gods, demons, pitṛs, mankind, &c., and the positions assign-
49 ed them; the origin of the primeval human race and its 237
50 social and moral evolution; the birth of the nine Sages, 246
Rudra, Manu Svāyambhuva and his descendants, Dakṣa and
his offspring; A-dharma and his progeny, especially the
51 goblin Duḥsaha and his powers, whose brood of goblins and 257
52 hags are named with their particular functions; the crea- 268
tion of the Rudras; and the wives and offspring of the
ṛṣis and pitṛs.

Account of the Manus.

53 Mārkaṇḍeya next discoursed of the Manus and man- 271
vantaras. He told of the *first* Manu, Svāyambhuva, and
his descendants who peopled the seven Continents. Jambu-
dvīpa was occupied by Agnīdhra, and his descendant Bharata
gave his name to India. This introduced the subject of
geography.

Geography.

54 Mārkaṇḍeya described the earth and its continents, espe- 275
cially Jambu-dvīpa; and also Mount Meru, first briefly, and
55 then with full mention of neighbouring forests, lakes and 278
56 mountains; and the course of the Ganges in the sky and on 280

CANTO. PAGE.
57 the earth. He mentioned the nine divisions of Bhārata, 283
and then dealt with India in detail; naming its seven 284
mountain ranges and its scattered hills; and its rivers, dis- 290
tinguishing them according to their sources, in the Himā-
laya, the Pāripātra, the Vindhya, the Ṛkṣa, the Sahya, 293
the Malaya, the Mahendra and the S'uktimat ranges. 303
He named the various peoples inhabiting India and its 307
confines, according as they dwelt in the Middle Land
(Madhya-deśa), in the north-west, outside northwards, 311
in the north, in the east, in the south, in the west, 324
around the Vindhya mountains and beneath the Himālayas. 340
58 Next representing India as resting upon Viṣṇu in the form 348
of a tortoise, Mārkaṇḍeya named the various peoples (with
the corresponding lunar constellations) as they were dis- 349
tributed over the middle of the tortoise's body, over its 358
face, its right fore-foot, its right flank, its right hind-foot, 370
its tail, its left hind-foot, its left flank and its left fore-foot; 384
and he added some astrological, religious and political
59 comments. He then described the countries Bhadrāśva, 387
60 Ketumāla, the Northern Kurus, Kimpuruṣa, Hari-varṣa, 390
Ilāvṛta, Ramyaka, and Hiraṇmaya.

Account of the Manus (resumed).

61 Mārkaṇḍeya related the birth of the *second* Manu. A 391
brāhman visited Himavat and met an Apsaras Varūthinī;
62 a Gandharva Kali by personating him gained her affection; 399
63 and she bore a son Svarocis. Svarocis delivered a maiden 401
64 Manoramā from a curse and married her, and also rescued 406
65 her two girl-companions and married them; after living 408
66 long in heedless pleasure with them, he had three sons 411
whom he established in separate kingdoms by the know-
ledge called Padminī; and he had by a forest goddess
67 another son Dyutimat who became the *second* Manu, 415
68 Svārociṣa; and his period is noticed. The allusion to the 415
knowledge Padminī introduced a discourse on its supporters,
the Nidhis.

CANTO. PAGE.
69 Continuing, Mārkaṇḍeya related how king Uttama 419
banished his queen for bad temper, and helped a brāhman
to find his ill-tempered wife who had been carried off; he
70 was rebuked by a ṛṣi for his own conduct; he recovered the 425
brāhman's wife, whose bad temper a Rākṣasa consumed.
71 A Nāga king had taken the queen to Pātāla, and she was 429
72 hidden; the brāhman changed her nature and the Rākṣasa 432
restored her to king Uttama; she bore a son, who became
73 the *third* Manu, Auttama, and his period is noticed. 436
74 Mārkaṇḍeya related how king Svarāṣṭra when driven 438
from his kingdom, met his deceased queen, and had a son
who became the *fourth* Manu, Tāmasa; his period is noticed.
75 The ṛṣi Ṛtavāc made the constellation Revatī fall; a maiden 443
was born therefrom; she married king Durgama and bore
a son, who became the *fifth* Manu, Raivata; his period is
76 noticed. Cākṣuṣa, being changed when an infant by a hag, 449
became king Vikrānta's son, but turned an ascetic and became the *sixth* Manu, Cākṣuṣa; his period is noticed.
77 Continuing the manvantaras, Mārkaṇḍeya said the Sun 455
married Tvaṣṭṛ's daughter Sañjñā and had two sons Vaivasvata and Yama; Sañjñā quitted him, leaving her Shadow
78 behind, because his splendour was excessive; Tvaṣṭṛ pared 458
his splendour down while the gods hymned the Sun; the Sun
regained Sañjñā; he had by the Shadow a son who will be the
79 *eighth* Manu, Sāvarṇi. Vaivasvata is the *seventh and present* 461
80 Manu; his period is noticed. The future period of Sāvarṇi 463
with its ṛṣis, gods, &c., is prophesied.

The Devī-māhātmya.

81 The mention of Sāvarṇi introduced the Devī-māhātmya. 465
Mārkaṇḍeya related that king Suratha, being ousted from his kingdom, met a vaiśya driven from his family, and both consulted a ṛṣi about their longings for home; the ṛṣi ascribed their feelings to the goddess Mahā-māyā (Great Illusion), and related how, when she was lauded by Brahmā, Viṣṇu slew the demons Madhu and Kaiṭabha.

CANTO. PAGE.

82 The ṛṣi then recited her exploits. Here begins the Devī- 473
mahātmya properly. The demons under Mahiṣa vanquish-
ed the gods, and the goddess was formed as Caṇḍikā (Am-
83 bikā) out of their special energies combined; she began a 478
great battle and destroyed the demons, all the demon chiefs
84 and finally Mahiṣa himself. The gods praised her in a 482
hymn, and she promised to befriend them always. Again
the gods were vanquished by the demons S'umbha and
Niśumbha, and invoked her; she appeared, and S'umbha
86 wanted to marry her but she declined; he sent an army 497
and she destroyed it; he sent another with Caṇḍa and Muṇḍa;
87 the goddess Kālī destroyed them and Caṇḍikā gave her the 499
88 combined name Cāmuṇḍā; S'umbha sent all his armies; 501
89 Caṇḍikā killed the chief Raktavīja, then Niśumbha in spite 506
90 of S'umbha's aid, and many demons, and finally S'umbha 509
91 himself; whereat the universe was filled with joy. The 511
gods praised her in a hymn and she promised to deliver them
92 always. She descanted on the merits of this poem. The 519
gods regained their supremacy; and she is extolled. Here
ends the Devī-māhātmya properly.

93 After hearing this poem king Suratha worshipped Caṇḍi- 522
kā, and she promised he should be the *eighth* Manu, Sāvarṇi.

Account of the Manus (resumed).

94 Mārkaṇḍeya, continuing, mentioned the other future 524
Manus, the *ninth*, *tenth*, *eleventh* and *twelth* named Sāvarṇa,
95 and the *thirteenth* named Raucya; and their periods. He 526
narrated the story of Raucya. A prajāpati Ruci was urged
96 by the Pitṛs to marry; he propitiated Brahmā and praised 529
97 the Pitṛs in a hymn; they appeared and promised him a 534
98 wife and extolled his hymn; he married an Apsaras and had 538
99 a son who will be the *thirteenth* Manu Raucya. S'ānti, the 539
disciple of an irascible ṛṣi Bhūti, finding the sacred fire ex-
100 tinguished, offered a hymn to Agni. Agni restored the fire 546
and promised to Bhūti a son who should be the *fourteenth*

CANTO. PAGE.

Manu, Bhautya. Bhautya's period is noticed. This account
of the manvantaras is extolled.

Commencement of the Genealogies.

101 At Krauṣṭuki's request Mārkaṇḍeya began the genealo- 550
gies. Brahmā created Dakṣa, from whom came Mārtaṇḍa,
the Sun. Then mentioning that Brahmā was born from
the mundane egg, and produced the lokas (worlds), and
next the four Vedas with their merits—Mārkaṇḍeya di-
verged into a laudation of the Sun.

The majesty of the Sun.

102 The gods and the Vedas are declared to be manifesta- 553
103 tions of the Sun. The Sun's glory was at first too great, 556
and Brahmā with a hymn induced him to contract it
104 and then finished the creation. Marīci's son Kaśyapa 558
begot the gods, demons, mankind, &c. The demons over-
came the gods and Aditi sought help of the Sun in a
105 hymn. He became her son as Mārtaṇḍa and destroy- 563
106 ed the demons. The story of the Sun and his wife Sañ- 566
jñā (as told in cantos lxxvii and lxxviii) is re-told here
with more detail regarding the Shadow-Sañjñā, the curse on
107 Yama, the paring down of the Sun's splendour, the hymns 572
108 offered to the Sun, and the Sun's offspring and the sta- 574
tions alloted them.

109 Further Mārkaṇḍeya related that king Rājya-vardhana 577
when old resolved to resign the kingdom, but his people in
110 grief propitiated the Sun, and the Sun granted him great 583
length of life; the king similarly obtained the same boon
for them. This story is extolled.

The Genealogies resumed.

111 Mārkaṇḍeya mentioned Manu Vaivasvata's seven sons 587
112 and Ilā-Sudyumna, Purūravas, &c. Manu's son Pṛṣadhra 590
killed a brāhman's cow and being cursed became a śūdra.
113 Karūṣa's descendants were mentioned. 593
Diṣṭa's son Nābhāga married a vaiśya maiden wilfully

CANTO. PAGE.
114 and became a vaiśya; their son Bhanandana conquered the 597
earth, but Nābhāga declined to reign. Then Nābhāga's
wife explained that she was not really a vaiśya, but that her
father was a king who became a vaiśya under a ṛṣi's curse
115 with a promise of recovery, and that she was a princess and 601
had become a vaiśya under Agastya's curse.
116 Bhanandana became king. His son Vatsaprī rescued a 604
princess Sunandā from Pātāla after killing a demon king
117 who had a magic club, and married her. His son was 610
Prāṁśu, and Prāṁśu's son Prajāti. Prajāti's son Khani-
tra was beneficent; his brothers' ministers practised magic
118 to dethrone him but destroyed themselves; Khanitra re- 615
119 signed the kingdom in grief and went to the forest. His 617
son Kṣupa performed sacrifices for the harvests. His son
120 was Vīra and grandson Viviṁśa. Viviṁśa's son Khanīne- 619
tra while hunting met two deer eager to be sacrificed, and
121 by Indra's favour obtained a son Balāśva. Balāśva was called 623
Karandhama because of a fanciful victory.
122 His son Avīkṣit married many princesses and carried off 256
123 princess Vaiśālinī at her svayamvara: the suitor kings 628
conquered and captured him, but she refused them all:
124 Karandhama rescued Avīkṣit, but Avīkṣit refused to marry 631
the princess after his discomfiture; she turned to austerities
125 and obtained an assurance from the gods: Avīkṣit's mother 637
by a ruse obtained a promise from him to beget a son:
126 while hunting he rescued the princess from a demon and 641
127 pleased the gods: she proved to be a Gandharva maiden and 645
Avīkṣit married her in the Gandharva world; she bore a son
128 Marutta there. Avīkṣit returned but refused the kingdom 649
129 because of his discomfiture. Marutta became king, and was 653
a universal monarch, a great sacrificer, and liberal benefactor
130 to brāhmans. The Nāgas gave great trouble, and he at- 658
tacked them, but Avīkṣit interposed in favour of the Nāgas;
131 a battle was averted by the ṛṣis, and the Nāgas made repara- 660
tion. Marutta's wives are named.
132 His son Nariṣyanta enriched the brāhmans permanently 665

CANTO. PAGE.

133 at a great sacrifice. His son Dama was chosen by the 668
Daśārṇa princess, and defeated the suitor kings, who, in vio-
134 lation of marriage laws, opposed him. Dama became king. 674
Nariṣyanta was murdered in the forest by Vapuṣmat one of
135 those kings. Dama bewailed, and vowed vengeance against 678
136 the murderer ; he slew Vapuṣmat and celebrated his father's 680
obsequies with Vapuṣmat's flesh and blood.

Conclusion.

137 The Birds closed their long repetition of Mārkaṇḍeya's 684
instruction to Krauṣṭuki, with an encomium on the Purāṇas
and this Purāṇa in particular. Jaimini thanked them.

ADDITIONS AND CORRECTIONS.

P. 2, l. 23, *after* sacred *add* customs.

P. 20, l. 19, *for* Sáma *read* Sáman.

l. 26, *for* nára *read* nárá.

P. 25, l. 6, *dele* *-phul.*

P. 26, l. 21, *for* Ásoka *read* Aśoka.

P. 27, l. 25, *for* Peninsular *read* Peninsula.

P. 29, l. 18, *add* unless it is the same as the bird 'putra-priya" which was so named because its note resembled 'putra ;putra.' Rámáy., Ayodh.-k. (Ed. Gorr.) cv. 11, (Ed. Bom.) xcvi. 12.

P. 29, l. 24, *for* btween *read* between.

P. 29, l. 33, *add* See Raghu-V., vi. 36.

P. 31, l. 8, *for* famalies *read* families.

Cantos VII, VIII & IX *for* Hariś-ćandra *read* Hariścandra.

P. 42, l. 15, *for* back *read* bark.

P. 44, l. 11, *for* compassionate *read* passionate.

P. 55. l. 13, *for* Bráhman *read* Brahman.

l. 17, *for* Bráhman *read* the Prajápati.

P. 65, l. 29, *for* the *read* thee.

P. 89, l. 33, *for* not therefore long *read* therefore ; dele not.

P. 93, l. 15, *for* etcetera *read* et cetera.

P. 99, l. 6, for *Dattatreya* read *Dattátreya.*

P. 100, l. 12, *for* yogi *read* yogí.

P. 102, l. 35, *for* Bála-khilyas *read* Válakhilyas.

PP. 100-107, *passim for* Lakshmi *read* Lakshmí.

P. 108, heading, *for* XX *read* XIX.

P. 109, l. 1-3 *read instead* And the doctrine of religious devotion was indeed declared by Dattátreya to that high-souled royal ṛishi Alarka who was faithful to his father.

P. 113, l. 2, *for* excedingly *read* exceedingly.

P. 118, l. 5, *for* him, the large-thighed* hero, the chief of his race, *read* Tumburu*, the spiritual preceptor of her family.

l. 7, *for* accepted her *read* arrived.

note*, *cancel the note and substitute* See canto cxxvii, verses 13 and 26.

P. 122, l. 15, *dele* funeral.

P. 124, last line, *for* son and daughter *read* son's wife.

P. 125, l. 33, *after* anxiety *add* "

P. 133, l. 30, *after* inspirer *add* "

P. 136, l. 12, *for* atru-jit's *read* S'atru-jit's.

P. 143, l. 14, *for* religion *read* righteousness.

P. 159, l. 34, *for* begun *read* begin.

P. 173, bottom, *for* Kámatás *read* Kámatas.

P. 174, l. 14, *for* carry *read* use.

l. 15, *for* are carrying *read* have used.

P. 177, l. 20, *read instead* the wise man should bathe, keeping his clothes on; and so also after resorting to a place where bodies are burnt.

P. 179, l. 34, *for* guru *read* gurus.

P. 181, l. 2, for *holidoys* read *holidays.*

P. 182, l. 3, *for* screened by many *read* concealed within many *things.*

P. 197, l. 34, *for* practice *read* practise.

P. 201, l. 7, *for* Gandarvas *read* Gandharvas.

P. 236, l. 3, *for* aptor *read* áptor.

P. 239, l. 8, *for* is *read* are.

P. 241, l. 21, *add* The Bombay edition reads instead "the kharvaṭaka and the dramí."

P. 242, l. 1, *to* varma-vat *add note* The Bombay edition reads "kharvaṭa" instead.

l. 21, *add* The Bombay edition reads "jana" instead of "jala."

l. 38, *add* The Bombay edition reads "dramí" instead.

P. 245, l. 27, *for* mentioueed *read* mentioned.

P. 269, l. 21, *for* Dhúṃravatí *read* Dhúmravatí.

P. 288, l. 23, *dele the words from* In a list *to* Nága-ráṭ.

P. 293, l. 3, *for* Vritra-ghní *read* Vṛitra-ghní.

P. 300, l. 40 *for* S'ilāvatí *read* S'ilavatí.

P. 332, l. 4, *add* May this name be identified with the town Kodungalūr (the modern Cranganore) north of Cochin? It is a place of sanctity, and was formerly an important town and harbour.

P. 366, l. 6, *add* See p. 445.

P. 368, l. 13, *for* Badavá *read* Baḍavá.

P. 403, l. 12, *for* mightly *read* mighty.

P. 445, l. 35, *add* and p. 365.

P. 469, l. 9, *for* universel *read* universal.

P. 486, l. 25, *for* my *read* may.

P. 581, l. 27, *for* ungnents *read* unguents.

P. 636, last line, *for* om *read* from.

THE

MÁRKAṆḌEYA PURÁṆA.

ADDENDA AND CORRIGENDA.

Page 2, line 24, *insert* customs *before* and.
In cantos VII, VIII and IX *for* Hariś-c'andra *read* Hari-śc'andra.

May He protect you, who is skilled to save
In every kind of sin impure; whose form
Within the bosom of the sea of milk
Upon the hooded snake reclines; and at
Whose touch the sea grows mountainous, its spray
Up-tossing from its waters by his breath
Disturbed, and into seeming dancing breaks!

CANTO I.

The Curse on Vapu.

Jaimini applies to Márkaṇḍeya for instruction regarding certain difficulties in the Mahábhárata—Márkaṇḍeya refers him to four learned Birds, the sons of Droṇa, and narrates their history—Their

THE

MÁRKAṆḌEYA PURÁṆA.

OM! REVERENCE TO THE ADORABLE VISHNU!

May Vishnu's lotus-feet, which power have
To dissipate the woes wrought by the fear
Of existence, and which are lauded high
By ascetics, assidnous, whose minds
From all things else are rapt—may those same feet,
Whose steps the earth, the sky, and heaven o'erpassed,
To sight appearing, purify your souls!

May He protect you, who is skilled to save
In every kind of sin impure; whose form
Within the bosom of the sea of milk
Upon the hooded snake reclines; and at
Whose touch the sea grows mountainous, its spray
Up-tossing from its waters by his breath
Disturbed, and into seeming dancing breaks!

CANTO I.

The Curse on Vapu.

Jaimini applies to Márkaṇḍeya for instruction regarding certain difficulties in the Mahábhárata—Márkaṇḍeya refers him to four learned Birds, the sons of Droṇa, and narrates their history—Their mother Vapu, an Apsaras, was condemned by the Muni Durvásas to become a bird for tempting him.

Having adored Náráyana, and Nara the best of men, the goddess Sarasvati, and then Vyása, let him utter the verse of Victory!

1 The illustrious Jaimini, the disciple of Vyása, interrogated
the great Muni Márkaṇḍeya, who was engaged in the per-
formance of austerities and the study of the Veda.
2 "Sir! the high-souled Vyása related the story of the Mahá-
bhárata, which is replete with splendid spotless collections
3 of various S'ástras, which is characterized by accuracy regard-
ing the different classes, is embellished with beautiful words,
and contains complete knowledge of *primâ facie* assertions, and
4 established conclusions. As Vishṇu is chief among the gods,
as the brahman *chief* among men, and as the crest-jewel *chief*
5 among all decorations, as the axe* is the best among weapons,
as the mind *best* among the organs, so in this world is the
6 Mahábhárata the best among all the S'ástras. Here are des-
cribed both Wealth and Virtue, Love, and Final emancipation
from transmigration; these have both reciprocal and peculiar
7 consequences. It is the best Dharma-śástra, it is the most
eminent Artha-śástra; it too is the foremost Káma-śástra, as
8 well as the noblest Moksha-śástra. It has been declared, Sir,
by Veda-Vyása the wise, to be the authority for the sacred
and maxims of the laws of the four periods of *a brahman's*
9 life. For this Mahá-śástra has been so constructed, dear
Sir, by Vyása the noble in deeds, that *although* beset with
10 difficulties it is not overthrown by them. The earth has
been freed from the dust of passion by the stream of Vyása's
words, which has descended from the mountain of the Veda,
11 and has swept away the trees of bad reasoning. Therefore
have I come to thee, Sir, being desirous to know truly the
story of Vyása, in which melodious sounds are the geese, the
12 noble story is the splendid lotus, the words are the expanse
of water, and the Vedas are the great lake—this precious
13 and long story of the Mahábhárata. Why was Janárdana

* *Or* Indra's thunderbolt.

Vásudeva, who is the cause of the creation preservation and
destruction of the world, although devoid of qualities, endued
14 with humanity? And why was Drupada's daughter Kṛishṇá
the common wife of the five sons of Páṇḍu? for on this point
15 we feel great perplexity. Why did the mighty Baladeva
Haláyudha expiate his brahmanicide by engaging in a pilgri-
16 mage? And how was it that the unmarried heroic high-souled
sons of Draupadí, whose protector was Páṇḍu, were slain, as
17 if they had no protector? Deign to recount all this to me here
at length; for sages like thee are ever the instructors of the
ignorant."

18 Having thus heard his speech, the great Muni Márkaṇḍeya,
devoid of the eighteen* defects, began to speak.

Márkaṇḍeya spoke.

19 "The time for my engaging in religious rites has now arrived,
most virtuous Muni! and this is not esteemed the season
20 for a long discourse. But I will now tell thee, O Jaimini,
of those birds who will speak to thee and so resolve thy
21 doubts. *They are* Pingáksha and Vibodha, Supatra, and Su-
mukha, the sons of Droṇa, the noblest of birds, versed in the
principles of philosophy, and meditators on the S'ástras.
22 Their mind is unclouded in the knowledge of the meaning of
the Veda and S'ástras. They dwell in a cave of the Vindhya
mountains, visit and question them."

23 Then, thus addressed by the wise Márkaṇḍeya, replied the
Muni pre-eminent, his eyes wide open with astonishment.

Jaimini spoke.

24 "Very wonderful is this, O brahman! that those birds have
gained knowledge most difficult to be acquired, as if birds

* The 18 defects are said, in a translation begun by the late Rev. K. M. Banerjea, to be these—palpitation, fear, thickness in speech, indistinctness, speaking through the nose, discordancy, want of emotion, disconnectedness, roughness, hoarseness, high pitch, inaccuracy in pronunciation, perturbation, want of cadence, sing-song, shaking the head, weakness of voice, and unmeaningness.

25 possessed human speech. If their birth is of the brute creation,
whence have they the knowledge? And how is it that those
26 winged ones are called the children of Droṇa? And who was
this famous Droṇa, who had those four sons. Do those virtuous
high-souled birds possess the knowledge of righteousness?"

Márkaṇḍeya spoke.

27 "Listen attentively to what happened of yore in Nandana
at the meeting of Indra and the Apsarases and Nárada.
28 Nárada saw Indra the king of the gods in Nandana, sur-
rounded by a band of those wanton maidens, with eyes fasten-
29 ed on their faces. S'ac'í's lord, immediately he was seen by
that best of Ṛishis, rose up, and respectfully gave him his own
30 seat. Those heavenly maidens, on seeing him, the slayer of
Bala and Vṛitra, rise up, prostrated themselves before the
31 Devarshi and stood reverently bending. He then, worshipped
by them, duly greeted Indra, when he had seated himself, and
conversed pleasantly with him.
32 "Then in the course of their talk, Indra said to the great
Muni—'Declare, which of these dancers pleases thee most. Is
33 it Rambhá, or Karkaśá, or Urvasí, Tilottamá, Ghṛitác'í, or
34 Menaká? or whichever delights thee.' Nárada, best of dvijas,
hearing this speech of Indra, pondered and then addressed
35 the reverently bending Apsarases:—'She, of you all here
present, who thinks herself pre-eminent in beauty, nobility
36 and good qualities, let her dance before me. There is indeed
no success in dancing for one who is destitute of good qualities
and beauty. *Good* dancing implies graceful comportment:
other dancing is vexation.'

Márkaṇḍeya spoke.

37 "And immediately on that speech, each one of those bowing
ones thus exclaimed—'I excel in good qualities; not you, nor
38 you!' The lord Indra seeing their agitation said, 'Let the Muni
be asked, he will say which of you excels in good qualities.'
39 What Nárada, sought by those followers of Indra's will,
40 then said, hear that from me, O Jaimini! 'She among you

who by her power perturbs the most noble Muni Durvásas, who is performing austerities, dwelling on the mountain, her among you I deem pre-eminent in good qualities.'

Márkaṇḍeya spoke.

41 "Having heard that his sentence, they all exclaimed, with trembling necks, 'this is impossible for us!'
42 "Among them an Apsaras named Vapu, confident of perturbing the Muni, replied, 'I will follow where the Muni dwells;
43 now will I make that tamer of his body, who has yoked
the horses of his organs, but a poor charioteer whose reins
44 drop before the weapons of love. Whether it be Brahmá, or
Janárdana or the purple *S'iva*, his heart will I now pierce
with the arrow of love.'
45 "Having thus spoken Vapu departed then to the Snowy
mountain to the Muni's hermitage, where the beasts of prey
46 were quelled by the might of his austerities. Stopping at the
distance of a call from where the great Muni is seated,
47 the lovely Apsaras sang the cuckoo's melody. Hearing
the strains of her song, the Muni astonished in mind went
48 to where sits that beauteous-faced maiden. On seeing
her, beautiful in every limb, the Muni, summoning his
resolution, was filled with anger and resentment, knowing
49 that she had come to perturb him. Then the great Ṛishi, the
performer of mighty austerities, pronounced this sentence.
50 'Since thou hast come here, O maiden! intoxicated with pride,
to cause me pain by obstructing my austerities, which are ac-
51 complished with difficulty, O Apsaras, therefore shalt thou,
polluted by my wrath, be born in the foolish race of birds
52 for the space of sixteen years, losing thine own form, and
taking the form of a bird; and four sons shall be born to
53 thee, O vilest of Apsarases; and without having gained affection
among them, absolved from guilt by dying in the field of
battle, thou shalt regain thy dwelling in the sky. Never
make any reply.'
54 The Bráhman, red-eyed with anger, having pronounced this
grievous sentence on that proud maiden, whose tinkling

bracelets were trembling, abandoned the earth, whose waves were very tremulous, and departed to the heavenly Ganges whose stream consists of a multitude of renowned qualities."

CANTO II.

The Birth of the Sparrows.

The story of the Birds continued—Kandhara, king of the birds killed a Rákhasa Vidyud-rúpa for killing his brother, and, marrying the Rákhasa's wife, had a daughter by her named Tárkshí who was the Apsaras Vapu—She married Droṇa—When pregnant by him she was killed at the battle of the Kauravas and Páṇḍavas, and there laid four eggs from which the four Birds were born—The Birds were nourished by the Muni S'amíka.

Márkaṇḍeya spoke.

1 The king of the birds, Garuda by name, was the son of
2 Arishṭanemi: Garuda's son was renowned as Sampáti: and
his son was Supárśva, heroic, mighty as Váyu: Supárśva's son
3 was Kunti; Kunti's son was Pralolupa. And he had two sons
Kanka and Kandhara.

4 On the top of Kailása, Kanka saw the Rákshasa famed as
Vidyud-rúpa, whose eyes were like a lotus leaf, a follower
5 of Kuvera, who was busied in a banquet, clad with strings of
bright garlands, sitting in company with his wife on a beau-
6 tiful clean rocky seat. Then the Rákshasa, immediately he
was seen by Kanka, filled with anger, said, "Wherefore hast
7 thou come hither, O vilest of the egg-born? Why hast thou
approached me when I am in company with my wife? Such
is not the rule of the wise in matters that must be accom-
plished in secret."

Kanka spoke.

8 "This mountain is common both to you and me and to other creatures also; what special ownership then canst thou, Sir, have here?"

Márkaṇḍeya spoke.

9 The Rákshasa with his sword slew Kanka, while he was thus
speaking, *who fell* defiled with the streaming blood, quivering
and senseless.
10 Having heard that Kanka was slain, Kandhara the king of
the birds, bewildered with anger, resolved speedily to slay
11 Vidyud-rúpa. Having gone to the mountain-top, where Kanka
lay slain, the king of the birds, his eyes swollen with anger
and resentment, and sighing like the king of the Nágas
12 performed the Sankalana for his elder brother. Where sits
the slayer of his brother, there he went, rocking the lofty
13 mountains with the mighty wind from his wings. He, with
blood-red eyes, overtopping the mountains, and forcibly hurling down masses of clouds with his wings, used to destroy
14 his enemies suddenly. There he saw that demon, whose
thoughts were intent on drinking, whose face and eyes were of
a copperish colour, and who was seated on a golden couch,
15 whose crest was covered with strings of garlands, who was
adorned with yellow sandal, whose face was very horrible
with teeth that resembled the inside of the Ketakí leaf.
16 And he saw, seated on the Rákshasa's left thigh his long-eyed
wife, named Madaniká, whose voice was soft as the cuckoo's.
17 Then Kandhara, whose mind was filled with wrath, addressed
that inmate of the cave, "O thou of utterly evil soul! come
18 forth and fight with me. Since thou hast murdered my
trustful elder brother, therefore I will bring thee, while en-
19 grossed in drunkenness, down to Yama's abode. To-day, slain
by me, shalt thou go to all those hells that are the abodes of
the murderers of those who trust in them, and of the murderers of women and children."

Márkaṇḍeya spoke.

20 Addressed even thus by the king of the birds in his wife's
presence, the Rákshasa, filled with anger, then answered the
21 bird. "If thy brother has been slain, then have I displayed
my valour; thee, too, to-day, will I slay with this sword, O

22 bird. Stay a moment, thou shalt not move here alive, O
vilest of birds."

Thus he spoke and seized his bright sword that resembled
23 a mass of collyrium. Then took place a marvellous battle
between the king of the birds and Kuvera's warrior, such
24 as between Garuḍa and Indra. Then the Rákshasa, in anger
swiftly hurling his sword, black as charcoal, flung it against
25 the king of the birds. And then the king of the birds, slightly
springing up from the ground, seized it with his beak, as
26 Garuḍa seizes a serpent; and the egg-born one broke it with
his beak and talons, and shook it. Thereupon, the sword
27 being broken, they began to fight with their arms. Then the
Rákshasa, being attacked in the breast by the king of the
birds, was speedily deprived of arms, feet, hands and head.

28 When he was killed, his wife besought protection of the
29 bird: somewhat fearful, she said, "I am thy wife." That
noblest of birds, taking her, returned to his abode, having
obtained a recompense for his brother by the slaughter of
30 Vidyud-rúpa. And she, the daughter of Menaká, with beauti-
ful eyebrows, capable of assuming forms at pleasure, on reach-
ing the house of Kandhara, took a form resembling Garu-
31 ḍa's. Of her, he then begat a daughter named Tárkshí,
(*namely* Vapu the loveliest of the Apsarases, who was consumed
by the fire of the Muni's curse). Then the bird gave her the
name Tárkshí.

32 And Mandapála had four sons of boundless intellect, Jari-
33 tári the eldest and Droṇa the youngest, best of dvijas. The
youngest of them, righteous in soul, thoroughly read in the
Vedas and Vedángas, married her the beauteous Tárkshi,
34 with the consent of Kandhara. And after a while Tárkshí
conceived; when she had gone seven fortnights in her preg-
35 nancy, she went to Kurukshetra. The very terrible battle
between the Kurus and Paṇḍavas was then being fought, and,
in consequence of her action being predestined, she entered into
36 the battle. There, then, she beheld the contest between Bha-
gadatta and Arjuna. The sky was thick filled with arrows,
37 as if with locusts. Discharged from the bow of Arjuna an

arrow, black as a serpent, fell with great force and pierced
38 the skin of her belly. Her belly being pierced, four moon-like
eggs fell on the ground as if on a heap of cotton, from the
39 fact that their allotted period of life was not ended. At the
same time that they fell, fell the great bell, the cord of which
was cut by an arrow, from the noble elephant Supratíka.
40 It reached *the ground* evenly all around, cutting into the
surface of the ground, and covering the eggs of the bird which
lay upon flesh.

41 And after king Bhagadatta, ruler of men, was slain, the
fight between the armies of the Kurus and Páṇḍavas went on
42 many days. At the end of the battle, when Dharma's son
Yudhishṭhira approached the son of S'ántanu to hear the high-
43 souled Bhíshma proclaiming the entire laws, a sage named
S'amíka came to the spot where, O best of dvijas, lay the eggs
44 within the bell. There he heard the voice of the little birds
chirping, whose voices were inarticulate on account of their
45 infancy, although they had transcendant knowledge. Then the
Ṛishi, accompanied by his disciples, lifted up the bell and
saw with surprise the young motherless and fatherless birds.
46 The venerable Muni S'amíka, having so seen them on the
ground there, filled with astonishment, addressed his attendant
dvijas.

47 "Well was it said by the chief of the dvijas, Uśanas himself,
the regent of the planet Venus, when he saw the army of
48 the Daityas intent on fleeing, hard-pressed by the gods. 'Ye
must not go, turn ye back; why run ye away, ye feeble ones?
Abandoning valour and glory, where have ye gone? Ye shall
49 not perish. Whether one perishes or whether one fights,
one possesses life as long as God originally created, not as
50 long as one's mind desires. Men perish, some in their
homes, some in flight; so, too, do they meet their death when
51 eating food and drinking water. So, too, others, when
sporting themselves, seated in the chariot of Love, free from
sickness, their bodies unpierced by arrows, fall into the power
52 of the King of the departed. Others, when intent on aus-
terities, are led off by the servants of the King of the departed:

2

and others occupied in meditation and study have not gained
53 immortality. Of yore, Indra hurled his thunderbolt against
S'ambara, yet that demon, though pierced thereby to the heart,
54 did not perish. By that very thunderbolt, indeed, and by
the same Indra, when their time was come, the Dánavas
55 were slain, the Daityas forthwith perished. Perceiving
this, ye should not fear: return ye.' Then those Daityas, aban-
56 doning the fear of death, turned back. This speech of
Uśanas is proved true by these most noble birds, which even
in the superhuman battle did not meet with destruction.
57 Whence comes the laying of the eggs, O brahmans? Whence
comes the even fall of the bell? And how comes it that the
58 ground is covered with flesh, fat, and blood? Certainly these
must be some brahmans; they are not ordinary birds. The
favour of destiny shows great good-fortune in the world."

59 Having spoken thus he looked at them and spoke again,
"Return, go to the hermitage, taking the young birds *with you.*
60 Where these egg-born may have no fear of cat, or rat, of
61 hawk or ichneumon, there let the birds be placed. O dvijas,
what is the use of great care? All creatures are destroyed
or preserved by their own actions, as have been these young
62 birds. Nevertheless men must exert themselves in all matters;
he who does a manly act gains commendation from us, the
good."

63 Thus urged by that illustrious Muni, those young Munis,
taking those birds, went then to their own hermitage, delight-
ful to ascetics, where clusters of bees settled on the boughs of
64 the trees. And he, the noblest of dvijas, gathering wild
roots, flowers, fruits, grasses, such as his mind loved, perform-
65 ed the various religious ceremonies ordained by the Veda to
all the deities, to Vishṇu, Rudra, and the Creator, to Indra,
Yama, and Agni, to Varuṇa, to Vṛihaspati and Kuvera, and
also to Vayu, to Dhátṛi and Vidhátṛi.

Canto III.

The Visit to the Vindhya Mountain.

The Story of the Birds continued—The Birds, when full-grown, were endowed with speech, and explained that wonder to the Muni Samíka—They were the four sons of a Ṛishi Sukṛisha—Indra appeared to the Ṛishi in the form of an aged bird, and asked for human flesh—The Ṛishi ordered his four sons to sacrifice themselves —They refused, and he cursed them to be born in the brute creation, but, moved with compassion at their entreaty, bestowed on them perfect knowledge—Hence they were born as birds.

Márkaṇḍeya spoke.

1 Thus he, the most virtuous Muni, O princely brahman,
nourished them day by day with food and water, and in safety.
2 After a month they resorted to the sun's chariot-road, being
gazed at by the Munis' sons, whose eyes were tremulous
3 with curiosity. After seeing the earth, with its cities, and
with its ocean and noble rivers, which appeared of the size
4 of a chariot wheel, they returned to the hermitage. The
spirited birds were wearied in their souls with their toil: and
their knowledge was developed there through their energy.
5 They all performed the reverential circumambulation around
the Ṛishi, who was expounding the truths of the law in compassion for his disciples, and respectfully saluted his feet
6 and said, "We have been delivered by thee, O Muni! from
dreadful death; thou hast given us shelter, food, and water;
7 thou art our father and spiritual guide. Our mother died,
when we were still in the womb; nor have we been nourished
by a father: thou, by whom we were preserved when young,
8 hast given us life. Thou, of perfect splendour on the earth,
lifting high up the elephant's bell, didst purge away evil
9 from us who were withering like worms. 'How may *these*
strength-less ones grow? When shall I see them flying
in the sky? When shall I see them alighting on a tree of the
10 earth, settling within the trees? When shall my natural
colour be obliterated by the dust which the wind from their

11 wings raises, as they flit about near me?' Thou, dear Sir,
thus thinking, didst nourish us; now we, those *very birds*, are
grown up and have become wise, what ought we to do?"
12 Having clearly heard this their perfectly articulated speech,
the Ṛishi, surrounded by all his disciples, and accompanied
13 by his son S'ṛingin, being full of eager curiosity, and covered
with horripilation as with a garment, said, "Tell *me* truly the
14 cause of your power of speech. Through whose curse did
you incur this wondrous transformation both in form and
speech? Deign here to tell me that."

The birds spoke.

15 "There was of yore a most virtuous Muni named Vipulasvat.
16 To him were born two sons Sukṛisha and Tumburu. We are
the four sons of soul-subdued Sukṛisha; to that Ṛishi we were
ever submissive in reverence, religious practices and faith.
17 As he desired, who was diligent in the performance of
austerities, and who constantly kept his organs under control,
18 we at once produced fuel, flowers and everything else, and
whatever was needed for sustenance.
19 "Now while he and we thus dwelt in the forest, there came
the king of the gods in the appearance of a bird, mighty in
size, with broken wings, stricken with age, with eyes of a
20 copperish colour, down-cast in soul; desirous to prove that
venerable Ṛishi, who practised truth, purity, and patience,
and who was exceedingly lofty in mind; and for the coming of
the curse upon us.

"The bird spoke.

21 "'O exalted dvija, deign here to save me, who am consumed
with hunger. I seek for food, noble Sir! be thou my in-
22 comparable refuge. As I was standing on a summit of the
Vindhya Mountains, I fell, Sir, at an exceedingly swift blast sent
23 by the wings of a bird. So there I *lay* on the ground, lost
in unconsciousness, without memory, for seven days; with the
24 eighth day I regained consciousness. Now fully conscious,
pressed by hunger, I have come for help to thee; I am seek-

ing for food, deprived of all pleasure, and with a mind in
25 pain. Therefore turn, pure-minded *sage*, thy steadfast mind
to my rescue; give me, O Brahmarshi, food suitable to
support my life.'

26 "He, thus invoked, answered him, Indra in bird-like shape,
'I will give thee the food thou desirest for the support of thy
27 life.' Thus having spoken, that best of dvijas further asked
him, 'What food shall I prepare for thy use?' and he replied,
'My chiefest delight is in human flesh.'

"The Ṛishi spoke.

28 "'Thy childhood is past; thy youth, too, gone; thou art as-
29 suredly in the decline of life, O egg-born. Why art thou
most malign-hearted even in old age, thou in whom of all
30 mankind every desire has ceased? What has thy last stage
of life to do with human flesh? Assuredly no one is created
31 foremost among evil-beings! Or what need hast thou to ad-
dress me, being what I am? One should always give when
one has promised—such is our professed opinion.'

32 "Having thus spoken to him, the Brahmarshi resolved that
it should be so. Calling us quickly and commending us accord-
33 ing to our good qualities, the Muni, agitated at heart, ad-
dressed a most severe speech to us all, who were respectfully
34 bowing, full of faith, with hands reverently joined. 'Ye noble
dvijas, whose minds are improved, are bound by obligations
equally with me. A glorious progeny has sprung from you, just
35 as ye, O twice-born, have sprung from me. If a father is
deemed by you a guru worthy of reverence and most exalted,
perform ye then my promise with cheerful mind.'

36 "Whilst he so spoke we exclaimed respectfully, 'What thou
shalt say, consider that in truth as already accomplished.'

"The Ṛishi spoke.

37 "'Of me has this bird sought protection oppressed with
hunger and thirst; wherefore let him be straightway satisfied
38 with your flesh, and let his thirst be quickly assuaged with
your blood.

"Then we, afflicted, our terror visible in our trembling, ex-
39 claimed, 'Alas, alas!' and said, 'not this deed! How for
the sake of another's body can a wise man destroy or injure
40 his own body? for a son is even as one's own self. A son
pays those debts, indeed, that have been declared due to the
pitṛis, the gods, and men; a son does not offer up his body.
41 Therefore we will not do this; we have done as has been
done by men of old. While alive one receives good things,
42 and while alive one does holy acts. When one is dead, the
body perishes, and there is an end of righteousness, &c.
Men skilled in holy law have declared that one ought by all
means to preserve one's self.'

43 "Having heard us speak thus, the Muni, burning as it were
with anger, again addressed us, scorching us, as it were, with
44 his eyes. 'Since ye will not perform this my plighted word
for me, therefore, blasted by my curse, ye shall be born among
the brute creation!'

45 "Having thus addressed us, he next said to that bird, 'When
I have performed for myself the final sacrifice, and my obsequies,
46 according to the S'ástras, do thou unhesitatingly eat me
here, (O best of dvijas): this my body I here grant thee for
47 food. The brahmanhood of a brahman is deemed such, so far
indeed as he maintains his truthfulness, O chief of the feather-
48 ed race. Not by sacrifices accompanied with presents, nor by
any other act, do brahmans acquire such great virtue as by the
observance of truth.'

49 "Having thus heard the Ṛishi's speech, Indra, in bird-like
form, his soul filled with astonishment, then replied to the
50 Muni, 'Applying thyself to deep meditation, O lord of brah-
mans, quit this thy body; for living thing I never eat, O lord
of brahmans.'

51 "Having heard this his speech, the Muni concentrated himself
in deep meditation. Perceiving that his fixed resolution, Indra,
52 further, resuming his own form said, 'Ho! princely brah-
man, understand with thy understanding what is to be under-
stood, O man of understanding! To prove thee have I thus
53 transgressed, O sinless one! Pardon me then, O pure-minded

one: and what wish is there of thine that may be granted?
Pleased most highly am I with thee, for maintaining thy true
54 word. Henceforth, knowledge like Indra's shall be revealed
to thee, and no obstacle shall withstand thee in austerities and
holy law.'
55 "But when Indra after speaking thus had departed, we pros-
trate on our faces thus implored our father, the renowned
56 Muni, who was filled with anger. 'Dear father, high-minded,
deign to pardon us miserable ones who dread death; for life
57 is dear to us. In an aggregate of skin bones and flesh, filled
with pus and blood, wherein one should take no delight, therein
58 do we find this delight. Hear too, Sir, how people are be-
guiled when overcome by those powerful enemies, their faults,
59 love, anger and so forth. Great is the fortress which has
Wisdom for its rampart, the bones for its pillars, the skin for
60 its walls and banks, the flesh and blood for its plaster. Nine
gates it has; it is capable of great effort; it is enclosed on all
sides with sinews; and there the Sentient Soul* sits firm as
61 king. He has two rival ministers, the Intelligence† and the
Understanding‡; those two strive to destroy each other as
62 foes. Four enemies desire the destruction of that king, Desire,§
63 Anger, and Covetousness; and Folly|| is the other enemy. But
when that king closes those gates and stands firm, then he
becomes indeed both happily strong and free from alarm;
64 he displays his affections; he is not overcome by his enemies.
65 But when he leaves all the gates open, then the enemy named
66 Passion¶ assails the gates of the eyes, etc. Gaining an entrance
by the five gates, he penetrates everywhere and spreads widely:
then indeed enter, following on his track, the three *other*
67 terrible enemies. That very *enemy*, Passion, having entered
there, forms a close union with the Understanding, together

* Purusha.

† Buddhi, *perceptive faculty.*

‡ Manas, *cognitive faculty.*

§ Káma, *love, desire, affection.*

|| Moha, *folly, infatuation.*

¶ Rága, *passion, emotion;* used as equivalent to Káma.

68 with the other gates which are known as the organs. He,
difficult to be approached, having reduced into subjection the
organs and the Understanding, and having reduced into sub-
69 jection the gates, then destroys the rampart. The Intelligence,
seeing the Understanding the dependent of that enemy, perishes
forthwith. And there, deprived of his ministers and abandoned
70 by his subjects, the king, his strategetical points gained by
the enemies, perishes. Even so Passion, Folly, Covetousness and
71 Anger prevail, evil in their nature, wrecking the memory of
mankind. From Passion springs Anger; from Anger is born
72 Covetousness; from Covetousness arises Folly; from Folly errors
of memory; from loss of memory loss of the intellect; through
73 loss of the intellect man perishes. Shew favour, O thou most
virtuous! to us who have thus lost our intellects, who are
compliant to Passion and Covetousness, and who covet life.
74 And let not this curse take effect, which thou hast pronounced,
Sir! Let us not tread the miserable path of darkness, O best
of Munis!'

" The Ṛishi spoke.

75 " 'What I have uttered, will never become false; my voice
76 has not spoken untruth hitherto, O sons! Fate is here supreme,
I think. Fie on worthless manhood, whereby I have been
thoughtlessly forced to do a deed that ought not to be done!
77 And since I am besought reverently by you, therefore, when
endowed with the nature of brutes, ye shall obtain the highest
78 knowledge. And ye, having your paths illuminated by
knowledge, with the stains of pain removed, free from doubt,
shall through my favour gain the highest perfection.'
79 " Thus, Sir, we were cursed of old by our father through the
power of destiny; hence we have descended to a lower grade of
80 created beings for a long time; and we were born on the
field of battle; we were nourished by thee: thus have we
acquired the nature of birds, O bráhman. There is no man
in this world who is not bound by fate."

Márkaṇḍeya spoke.

81 Having heard this their speech, the venerable and eminent

Muni S'amíka answered those dvijas who stood near him.
82 "Even before did I make this remark in your presence, 'These
are not ordinary birds; these must be some bráhmans, who
even in the superhuman battle escaped destruction.'"
83 Then they, permitted by that affectionate high-souled *Muni*,
went to the Vindhya, the goodliest of mountains, clad with
84 trees and creepers. Hitherto have the righteous birds re-
mained on that mountain, engaged in austerities and the study
85 of the Vedas, and resolute in meditation. Thus those Muni's
sons gained the hospitality of the noble Muni, acquired the
shape of birds, *and* are dwelling on the Vindhya range, in a
cave of the noble mountain, where the water is very sacred,
with their minds subdued.

Canto IV.

The Incarnation of the Four-formed God.

Jaimini visits the Birds, and explaining the reason of his visit, puts them the four questions that perplexed him—After invoking Vishṇu, Brahmá and S'iva, they explain the first question, why Vishṇu, though devoid of qualities, is endued with humanity.

Márkaṇḍeya spoke.

1 Thus those birds, the sons of Droṇa, became learned; and
they dwell on the Vindhya mountain: visit them and ask
them.
2 Jaimini, having heard this speech of the Ṛishi Márkaṇḍeya,
went to the Vindhya mountain, where dwelt those righte-
3 ous birds. And when Jaimini reached that mountain, he
heard their voices as they were reading, and having heard
4 filled with surprise, he reflected. 'The bráhmans are read-
ing, observing the beauties of the *various* passages, regu-
lating their breath, without any intermission, distinctly and
5 without faults: wondrous is this, methinks, that Sarasvatí
does not forsake these Muni's sons, although they are born in
6 the brute creation. One's circle of relatives and a friend and
whatever else is desired in one's home—all that forsakes one

7 and departs; Sarasvatí does not abandon one.' Thinking even
thus, he entered the mountain cave; and entering saw those
8 dvijas standing on a ledge of the rock. Looking at them as
they were reading, their faces free from blemish, he then
addressed them all, with *mingled* sorrow and joy.

9 "Hail to you, O bráhmans! Know that I am Jaimini, a
disciple of Vyása, who am come to you, being eager for learn-
10 ing. Verily be ye not angry; whereas ye, being cursed by
your father, who was exceedingly wrathful, have been turned
11 into birds, that was indeed altogether fate. In a family of
immense wealth some intelligent members, it is said, were born;
when their wealth was lost, they were well comforted,
12 O bráhmans, by S'abara. Men after giving *to others* become
beggars *themselves;* and others, after killing *men*, have been
killed *themselves;* and *others*, after having overthrown *men*, have
been *themselves* overthrown;—those very men, through the decay
13 of austerities. Thus I have very often seen opposites of this
kind: the world is constantly distressed by the destruction of
14 existence and non-existence. At such thoughts as these in
your minds, ye should not give way to sorrow: so much is
invulnerability to sorrow and joy the fruit of knowledge."

15 Then they all did Jaimini honour, by giving *him* water for
his feet, and the arghya offering; and they bowed to him, and
16 questioned him with deep respect. Then all the birds address-
ed him, the disciple of Vyása, rich in austerities, as he sat at
ease, resting himself, with his fatigue mitigated by the breeze
from their wings.

The birds spoke.

17 "To-day has our birth become fruitful, and our lives have been
well-lived, inasmuch as we see thy lotus-feet which are worthy
18 to be praised by the gods. The blazing fire of our father's
anger, which continues in our bodies, has been quenched to-
19 day by the water of the sight of thee, O bráhman. We trust
that all is well in thy hermitage among the deer and birds,
among the trees too, and the *various* kinds of creepers, shrubs,
20 reeds, and grasses. Or perhaps we *though* respectful have
not spoken this fittingly? Whence can evil befall those who

21 have met with thee? And here, shew us favour, tell us the
cause of thy visit; union with thee, as with the gods, is great
prosperity; by whom, powerful for our good fortune, hast thou
been brought to our view?"

Jaimini spoke.

22 "Let the reason be heard, O bráhmans, why I have come here
to the Vindhya mountain's delightful cave, which is sprinkled
23 with drops of water from the river Narmadá. At first I
questioned the great Muni Márkaṇḍeya, a scion of Bhṛigu's
race, since I found difficulties in connexion with the Mahá-
24 bhárata. And he, when asked by me, replied, 'Droṇa's high-
souled sons are living on the mighty Vindhya mountain;
25 they will declare the full meaning to thee.' And I, impelled
by his speech, have come to this great mountain: therefore
hear *me* fully; having heard, deign to give an explanation."

The birds spoke.

26 "The matter being one specially known to us, we will declare
it; listen then, free from distrust; why should we not tell
27 thee that of which our intellects are cognizant? For even in
the four Vedas, for in the Dharma-śastras also, and in all
the Angas and whatever else is conformable to the Vedas—
28 in these does our intellect range, O best of bráhmans; but
29 nevertheless we are not able to give a promise. Therefore
declare fearlessly what is doubtful in the Mahábhárata; we
will declare it to thee, O thou who art wise in the law; if not
there will be bewilderment."

Jaimini spoke.

30 "Hear, O ye pure ones! the matters in connexion with the
Mahábhárata, which are doubtful to me here; having heard,
31 deign to explain them. Why is Janárdana Vásudeva, who is
the support of everything and the cause of all causes, al-
32 though devoid of qualities, endued with humanity? And why
was Drupada's daughter Kṛishṇá the common wife of the five
sons of Páṇḍu? On this point *there is* very great perplexity.
33 Why did the mighty Baladeva Haláyudha expiate his brah-
34 manicide by engaging in a pilgrimage? And how was it that

the unmarried heroic high-souled sons of Draupadí, whose
protector was Páṇḍu, were slain, as if they had no protector?
35 Let all these doubtful points in connexion with the Mahá-
bhárata be explained to me; that I having attained my object,
may return to my hermitage in comfort."

The birds spoke.

36 "Having paid adoration to Vishṇu, the lord of the gods, the
pre-eminent, the universal soul, the immeasurable, the eternal,
37 and the changeless; to him who subsists in four forms, possessed
of the three qualities, and devoid of qualities, the most choice,
38 the most venerable, the most excellent, and the immortal; *to*
him than whom there is nothing more minute, than whom there
is nothing more immense, by whom—the unborn one, the begin-
39 ning of the worlds—this universe is permeated,—this *universe*
which, characterized by appearance and disappearance, by visi-
bility and invisibility, has, men say, been created and also been
40 destroyed in the end: and having paid adoration with
profound meditation to Brahmá, the creator, who purifies the
three worlds with his mouths as he utters the Ṛic' and Sáma
41 hymns: also having prostrated ourselves before the lord,
conquered by one of whose arrows the bands of the Asuras do
42 not interrupt the sacrifices of the sacrificers: we will declare
the whole doctrine of Vyása, who was wonderful in his actions,
by whom, in delivering the Mahábhárata, justice and the other
virtues were made manifest.

43 "The waters were called Nára by Munis conversant with
truth; they were originally his place of movement*; hence he
44 is called Náráyaṇa. The adorable god, the lord Náráyaṇa, per-
vading all things, lives, O brahman, in a quadruple form: he
45 is possessed as well as devoid of attributes. His first form is
inscrutable; the wise behold it bright; it is covered with gar-
46 lands of flame; it is the acme of perfection to devotees; it is
both far and it is near; it is to be understood as transcending
attributes; when called Vásudeva, it is seen devoid of egoism;
47 its shape, colour, etc., are not real but imaginary; it is indeed
48 always pure; it is the sole form of pre-eminence. His second

* Ayana.

form, called Sesha, supports the earth below with its head;
it is described as being characterized by the quality of darkness;
49 it belongs to the brute creation. His third form is active, and
devoted to the preservation of creatures; it is to be considered
as consisting chiefly of the quality of goodness; it is the
50 fashioner of virtue. His fourth form abides in water; it lies
on a serpent as its bed; its attribute is passion; and it is always
indeed active.

51 "The third form of Vishṇu, which is assiduously intent on the
preservation of creatures, always maintains righteousness on the
52 earth. It destroys the haughty Asuras, the exterminators of
righteousness; it protects the gods, and holy men, who are
53 devoted to the preservation of righteousness. Whensoever,
O Jaimini, the wane of righteousness occurs and the rise of
54 iniquity, then it creates itself. Having formerly become exis-
tent, as a wild boar it repelled the water with its snout, and
55 lifted out the earth like a lotus with one of its tushes. Having
taken the form of the man-lion, it slew Hiraṇya-kaśipu, and
56 destroyed Viprac'itti and other Dánavas. I cannot now enu-
merate its other incarnations, those of the dwarf, etc.: his
57 recent incarnation here was this one in Mathurá. Thus that
form, which is characterized by goodness, becomes incarnate;
and it is designated Pradyumna; it is occupied in the work of
58 preservation. And ever by Vásudeva's will, it exists in divine
form, human form, and brute form, and partakes of their several
natures.

59 "Thus this has been declared to thee, how that the lord
Vishṇu, though all-successful, assumed human form. Hear
again the sequel thereof."

Canto V.

Indra's Transformations.

The Birds explain the second question—Draupadí was the wife of the five Páṇḍavas, because they were partial incarnations of Indra, and she was the incarnation of his wife.

The birds spoke.

1 "Of old, O brahman! when the son of Tvashṭṛi was slain,

Indra's splendour, oppressed by the brahmanicide, suffered a
2 grievous decline. Then because of his wrong conduct Indra's
splendour entered Dharma; and, his righteousness and splendour
being gone, Indra became splendourless.

3 "Then hearing that his son was slain, the prajápati Tvashṭṛi
enraged, tearing out a single matted lock of hair, uttered this
4 speech. 'Let the three worlds and the gods thereof see my
might this day, and let Indra the perverse brahmanicide see,
5 by whom my son when engaged in his own business was destroyed.'
Thus having spoken, he, his eyes red with anger,
sacrificed that lock of hair in the fire.

6 "Then uprose Vṛitra, the mighty Asura, encircled with flame,
huge in body, with great teeth, resembling a mass of broken
7 collyrium. He, the enemy of Indra, of immeasurable soul,
surpassing the might of Tvashṭṛi, mighty in valour, increas-
8 ed daily a bow-shot *in stature.* And Indra, having seen the
mighty Asura Vṛitra *eager* for his slaughter, unnerved by
9 fear, sent seven Ṛishis, desiring peace. Then the affectionate-
minded Ṛishis, who delighted in benevolence towards all crea-
tures, brought about friendship and treaties between him and
10 Vṛitra. When Indra violating the rules of the treaty slew
Vṛitra, then his might overwhelmed by the *sin of the* slaughter
11 waned; and that might which quitted Indra's body entered the
wind, which pervades everything, is imperceptible, and is the
supreme deity of power.

12 "And when Indra, assuming the form of Gautama, violated
13 Ahalyá, then the lord of the gods lost his form. Thereupon his
beauty of limb and feature, which was exceedingly captivat-
ing, forsook the wicked lord of the gods and went to the
Aśvins.

14 "Perceiving the lord of the gods to have lost his uprightness
and glory, to be powerless and formless, the Daityas endeavour-
15 ed to conquer him. Daityas of exceeding might, desirous to
conquer the lord of the gods, were born in the families of kings
16 of surpassing valour, O great Muni. Then the Earth, afflicted
with their weight, once went to the summit of Meru, where is
17 the abode of the heaven-dwelling gods. Afflicted with their

excessive weight, she declared that the cause of her distress
18 arose from the Dánavas and Daityas. 'These Asuras, widely
resplendent, have been slain by you; they have all been born in
19 the world of men in the families of kings; their armies are
numerous indeed: oppressed by their weight, I am sinking
downward; do ye, O ye thirty gods, devise how tranquillity
may be attained for me.'

The birds spoke.

20 "Then the gods descended with portions of their glory from
heaven to earth, to benefit the creatures and to alleviate the
21 burden of the Earth. Dharma himself relinquished the
glory which is innate in the body of Indra, then was born
22 of Kuntí the resplendent raja Yudhishṭhira; Váyu relin-
quished his might, then was born Bhíma; and from the half
of Indra's power was born Dhanañjaya, the son of Pṛithá;
23 Yama's two sons, resembling Indra in form, of glorious dignity,
were born of Mádrí. Thus the adorable Indra became incar-
24 nate in five forms. His auspicious wife was born as Kṛishṇá
25 from Agni: she, Kṛishṇá, is the wife of Indra alone, and of no
one else. The lords of ascetics can even multiply their bodies.
26 "Thus the fact of her being one wife to five men has been
explained to thee; be it heard how Baladeva went to the
Sarasvatí."

Canto VI.

Baladeva's brahmanicide.

The Birds explain the third question—Baladeva, in order to avoid siding with the Páṇḍavas and Kauravas, went to the Raivata forest—Overcome by intoxication, love, and the influences of the place, he killed Súta for not saluting him—To expiate that sin he undertook the pilgrimage.

The birds spoke.

1 The plough-armed Ráma, knowing the perfect affection of
Kṛishṇa for Arjuna, deliberated much—"Can what has been
2 done be better done? Without Kṛishṇa, assuredly, I will not
go near Duryodhana; or how, siding with the Páṇḍavas, shall

3 I slay king Duryodhana, my royal son-in-law and disciple?
Therefore I will go neither to Árjuna nor to king Duryodhana.
4 I will myself bathe myself at holy bathing places, so long as
it conduces to the ending of the Kurus and Páṇḍavas."
5 Having thus taken leave of Kṛishṇa, Arjuna and Duryodhana,
the descendant of S'úra, surrounded by his army, went to Dvá-
6 raká. Arriving at Dváravatí, which was thronged with glad
and well-fed citizens, Ráma Haláyudha drank a draught at the
7 holy bathing places, which are to be visited in future. Having
drank his draught, he then marched to the flourishing park of
Raivata,* taking with him the intoxicated Apsaras-like Revatí.
8 Encircled by a bevy of maidens, the hero went on, intoxicated,
stumbling in his walk. And he saw a forest, fascinating, beyond
9 compare, loaded with the fruits and flowers of every season,
thronged with troops of monkeys, sacred, dotted with clumps of
10 lotus-flowers, a great forest abounding in pools. Listening to the
copious, pleasure-inspiring, love-soft, beautiful, ear-delighting,
melodious songs poured forth from the mouths of the birds, he
11 saw the trees there, loaded with the weight of the fruits of
every season, bright with the blossoms of every season, ren-
12 dered resonant by the birds;—mango trees, hog-plums,†
kámarangas,‡ cocoanuts, and tindaka trees,§ and little bel

* A mountain near Dváraká in Gujarat. The woodland scene described seems to be a fanciful one, compounded from the author's observations everywhere.

† Amrataka, the Hog-plum, *Spondias mangifera;* the modern *amra.* It is both wild and cultivated. I give the botanical names, from Hooker's Flora of British India, of all except the most common, as many of the trees have no English names, and are better known by those names: but there can be no doubt that the various *species* in a *genus* are not always distinguished, and that the Sanskrit names are sometimes as much generic as specific. The descriptions are taken from Roxburgh's Flora Indica, Edn. Clarke, 1874, from Oliver's Indian Botany, 1869, and from Firminger's Manual of Gardening for India.

‡ Bhavya, *Averrhoa carambola,* the modern *kámranga.* A garden tree.

§ I do not find *tindaka* in Prof. Monier-Williams' Dictionary: *tinduka* occurs in verse 14. The late Rev. Dr. Banerjea, in a translation he began, translates it Ebony, which is *Diospyros melanoxylon,* the modern *tindu.* It is a large tree, growing in most woody mountainous parts of India.

13 trees,* cumin,† pomegranates,‡ citrons,§ jack trees,|| mon-
key-jack trees,¶ plantain trees, and very charming ka-
dam trees,** and párávata trees,†† kankola trees,‡‡ nalina
14 trees,§§ docks,|||| marking-nut trees,¶¶ emblic myroba-

* A'bilvaka. I do not find this in the Dictionary. Bilva, the Bel or Bengal Quince, *Ægle marmelos;* the modern *bel-phul* and *s'rí-phal.* Both wild and cultivated. It bears panicles of large white flowers, which are used in worship.

† Jíra, Cumin, *Cuminum cyminum;* the modern *jíra;* this is a slender cultivated annual. Jíra also means *Panicum miliaceum,* Roxb., the modern *cheena,* which is a cultivated cereal from 2 to 4 feet high. (Roxb., p. 104.) Neither seems appropriate.

‡ Dáḍima, the Pomegranate, *Punica granatum;* the modern *dáṛim* or *dálim.* A cultivated tree in India.

§ Víja-púraka, Citron, *Citrus medica,* the modern *nebu.* A cultivated tree in India.

|| Panasa, the Jack or Jack-fruit tree, *Artocarpus integrifolia;* the modern *kánṭhál.* A cultivated tree. (Roxb., p. 633: Oliver, p. 272: not in Hooker).

¶ Lakuc'a, the Monkey-jack, *Artocarpus lacucha;* the modern *dephul.* A garden tree. (Roxb., p. 634; Firminger, p. 188; not in Hooker).

** Nípa, *Anthocephalus cadamba* (*Nauclea cadamba,* Roxb.); also kadamba, the modern *kadam.* A garden tree, highly ornamental with its large, globular, beautiful, orange-coloured heads of flowers, and very useful from its extensive close shade (see Roxb., p. 172).

†† Párávata: the Dictionary says this is *Diospyros embryopteris* (*glutinosa,* Roxb.), which is the modern *gáb:* but this tree is also tinduka, which occurs in the next verse, and tindaka has occurred in verse 12. Párávata means also a dove or pigeon, and has been corrupted into the Bengali páyrá; might not párávata, the tree, be corrupted into the Bengali peyárá, which means the Guava, *Psidium guyava?*

‡‡ Kan'kola. I do not find this in the Dictionary. Read *kan'kellán* for *kan'kolán?* Kan'kella is given as the Asok, *Saraca indica* (*Jonesia asoka,* Roxb.), but this occurs in verse 15.

§§ Nalina. Dr. Banerjea translates this as the Indigo plant, but Prof. Monier-Williams says nalina, *neut.,* is the Indigo shrub, *Indigofera tinctoria;* while nalina, *masc.* as here, is the Carissa carandas; but the latter occurs in the next verse.

|||| Amla-vetasa, the Dock or Sorrel, as Prof. Monier-Williams gives it. The Dock is *Rumex vesicarius,* Roxb. The Sorrel is *Oxalis corniculata,* Hooker (see Oliver, pp. 181 and 269).

¶¶ Bhallátaka, the Marking-nut tree, *Semecarpus anacardium,* the Bengali

lans,* and gáb trees† bearing large fruits, almond trees,‡
karamcha trees,§ yellow myrobalans,|| beleric myrobalans.¶
15 He, Yadu's descendant, saw these and other trees, and also aśo-
16 kas,** punnágas,†† screw-pines,‡‡ and vakulas,§§ c'ampakas,||||

bhela. A tree, growing in all the mountainous parts of India, with large panicles of small greenish yellow flowers. (Roxb., p. 268.)

* A'malaka, the Emblic Myrobalan, *Phyllanthus emblica*, the modern *ámla* (Roxb., p. 684 and Oliver, p. 279). I do not find it in Hooker. *Emblica officinalis* is an earlier name.

† Tinduka, *Diospyros embryopteris* (*glutinosa*, Roxb.), the modern *gáb*. It is a tree common in Bengal, and among the mountains in the Circars. Its fruit is as large as a medium-sized apple.

‡ In'guda, the Almond tree, *Terminalia catappa*, the modern *badám*. A beautiful large tree, growing everywhere.

§ Karamarda, *Carissa carandas*, the modern *karamcha*. A common small tree, with beautiful, white, jasmine-like flowers.

|| Harítaka, the Yellow or Chebulic Myrobalan, *Terminalia chebula*; a large forest tree.

¶ Vibhítaka, the Beleric Myrobalan, *Terminalia belerica*, the modern *bahera*; a large forest tree.

** A'soka, the Asok, *Saraca indica* (*Jonesia asoka*, Roxb.). A middling-sized, very handsome, garden tree, with large, globular bunches of rather large flowers. The flowers are of a beautiful orange colour when they first expand, and gradually change to red, forming a variety of beautiful shades: they are fragrant during the night. (Roxb., p. 312).

†† Punnága, *Rottlera tinctoria*, (Roxb. and Oliver): it is still called *punnág*. I do not find it in Hooker. A tree, a native of Coromandel.

‡‡ Ketakí, the Screw-Pine, *Pandanus odoratissimus*, (Roxb. and Oliver), the modern *keorá*. A large shrub, with panicles of large white, sheath-like leaves, enclosing bundles of closely-packed minute flowers. "It is the tender white leaves of the flowers, chiefly those of the male, that yield that most delightful fragrance, for which they are so universally and deservedly esteemed; for of all the perfumes in the world it must be the richest and most powerful." (Roxb., p. 707.)

§§ Vakula, *Mimusops elenghi*, the modern *bakul*. A tree, commonly cultivated, with flowers middle-sized drooping, white and fragant; but Firminger says they are small, pale-green. (Roxb., p. 318; Hooker, p. 458; Firm., p. 490).

|||| C'ampaka, *Michelia champaca*, the modern *champak* or *chámpá*. A garden tree with large yellow delightful fragrant flowers.

saptaparṇas,* karṇikáras,† and Spanish jasmines,‡
párijáta trees,§ kovidáras,|| mandáras,¶ and jujube
17 trees,** delightsome Bignonia trees†† in blossom, and
devdár trees,‡‡ sál trees,§§ palmyra palms,|||| and ta-

* Sapta-parṇa, *Alstonia scholaris.* An ever-green tree growing in the drier forests of India.

† Karṇikára, *Pterospermum acerifolium,* the Bengali *kanak-champa.* A Himalayan tree, but also grown in gardens. It has very large, pure white, fragrant flowers.

‡ Málati, the Catalonian or Spanish Jasmine, *Jasminum grandiflorum,* the Bengali *játí* or *chamelí,* Hindustani *chambelí.* It is a spreading garden shrub with graceful pinnate foliage and middling-sized white fragrant flowers, which retain their odour when dried and are much used for perfume. (Firm., p. 518). Málati also means the Clove-scented Echites, *Aganosma caryophyllata* (*Echites caryophyllata,* Roxb.), now called *málati,* which is a climbing shrub, with bay-like leaves and sprays of middling-sized fragrant white flowers. (Roxb., p. 245; Firm., p. 518.)

§ Párijáta, *Erythrina indica.* A large tree growing all over India, with racemes of numerous large bright scarlet flowers. This tree is generally called *mandár* now.

|| Kovidára, *Bauhinia variegata,* the Bengali *rakta-kanchan.* A garden tree with large reddish-purple flowers.

¶ Mandára. Prof. Monier-Williams says this is *Erythrina fulgens,* but I do not find it in Hooker or Roxburgh. May it be *E. stricta,* which grows in the Western Peninsular and much resembles *E. indica?* In Bengal *E. indica* is now generally called *mandár.*

** Badara, *Zizyphus œnoplia* (*jujuba* or *scandens,* Roxb.), the Bengali *kul,* the Hindustani *ber.* A small tree with fruit of the size of a large cherry.

†† Páṭala, *Bignonia suaveolens,* Roxb., the modern *párul.* I do not find it in Hooker. A tree, with large, exquisitely fragrant, dark dull crimson flowers. It blossoms during the hot season. Prof. Monier-Williams calls it the Trumpet-flower tree, but I do not find this name in any of the Botanical books I have consulted.

‡‡ Deva-dáru, *Pinus devdara,* Roxb., the modern *devdár.* I do not find it in Hooker. A great tree, native of the mountains north of Rohilkhand. No species of pine is native in the Peninsula (Oliver, p. 294); this tree therefore is quite out of place in this Gujarat scene.

§§ Sála, the Sál tree, *Shorea robusta,* the modern *sál.* An immense timber tree.

|||| Tála, the Palmyra Palm, *Borassus flabelliformis,* Roxb., the modern *tál.* Not in Hooker. Fans are made from the large fan-like leaves.

18 málas,* kiṃśukas,† and fine vanjula trees‡:—inhabited by
chakors,§ and woodpeckers, shrikes,|| and parrots, koíls,¶ and
19 sparrows, green pigeons,** and jívajívaka pheasants,†† by priya-

* Tamála. Prof. Monier-Williams says this is *Garcinia xanthochymus* (*Xanthochymus pictorius*, Roxb.); this is a tree, a native of the mountainous districts in India. But Roxburgh says the Tamála is *Diospyros cordifolia*, which Hooker unites with *D. montana;* this is a common tree.

† Kiṃs'uka, *Butea frondosa*, the Bengali *palásh*. Oliver calls this tree the Dhak, (p. 195), but I do not find this name anywhere else. It is a common tree, with handsome, irregular, orange-red flowers in racemes which are covered with a soft greenish-purple down. (Roxb., p. 540.)

‡ Vanjula, *Ougeinia dalbergioides* (*Dalbergia oojeinensis*, Roxb.). A tree with racemes of numerous, rather small, very pale rose-coloured flowers, somewhat fragrant.

§ C'akora, *Caccabis chukor*. The Chakor is said in Prof. Monier-Williams' Dictionary to be the Greek partridge, *Perdix rufa* or *Tetrao rufus*, but the Greek partridge, *Caccabis saxatilis*, is a different species, inhabiting Europe, from the *chakor* the Asiatic species. The chakor is found in the Himalayas and the other northern ranges. It is always a bird of the hills, and does not occur in Gujarat, where this scene is laid (Jerdon's Birds of India, Edn. Godwin-Austen, Vol. II, p. 564; Hume and Marshall's Game Birds of India, Vol. II, p. 33). *Tetrao rufus* is the name Linnæus gave the European bird. *Perdix rufa* seems, from the edition of his works in the Bengal Asiatic Society's Library, to be an earlier name. There are other partridges in the plains of India, *Ortygornis gularis*, &c., but I do not think the reference can be to them, for the writer seems to be mentioning birds inhabiting the Himalayas; see the note on the *Jívajívaka* pheasant, below.

|| Bhṛinga-rája. Prof. Monier-Williams translates this, Malabar shrike, *Lanius malabaricus*. This bird stands in Jerdon as *Edolius malabaricus*, and is, I am informed by Dr. J. Scully, a king-crow. Another bird may be meant, the Malabar Wood-shrike, *Tephrodornis sylvicola*, but, as the writer seems to be referring to birds found near the Himalayas, bhṛinga-rája may mean any kind of shrike, almost every kind of which is common throughout the greater part of India. (Jerdon, Vol. I, p. 400).

¶ Kokila, the Koíl, *Eudynamys orientalis* (Jerdon, Vol. I, p. 342).

** Hárita, the Green Pigeon, probably the Bengal green pigeon, *Crocopus phœnicopterus*, or the Orange-breasted green pigeon, *Osmotreron bicincta*. The Southern green pigeon, *Crocopus chlorigaster*, and the Green imperial pigeon, *Carpophaga sylvatica*, are not found near the Himalayas.

†† Jívajívaka. Prof. Monier-Williams gives the synonyms jíva-jíva and jívanjíva, and explains the word as a kind of bird supposed to be a pheasant,

putras,* and pied-crested cuckoos,† and by various other birds, warbling pleasingly and very melodiously:—and the lakes, beautiful and placid, crowded on all sides with the lotus water-lilies,‡ and lotuses,§ and the brilliant blue water-

or the chakor. As the chakor is mentioned already, it must have the first meaning. Taking it to be a kind of pheasant, I would suggest that it is the Cheer Pheasant, *Phasianus Wallichi.* The Sanskrit name looks like an onomatopœous one, and the cry of this bird is "something like the words *chir a pir, chir a pir, chir chir, chirwa chirwa.*" Cheer is the native name. The bird is found in Garhwal and Kumaon and the neighbouring country, and inhabits the middle slope of the Himalayas (Hume and Marshall, Vol. I, p. 169: Jerdon, Vol. II, p. 527). If this bird be a pheasant, it is clear the writer is mentioning, not the fauna of Gujarat, but of the country near the Himalayas, for it appears from Hume and Marshall, and Jerdon, that no pheasants are found in India except in the Himalayan and Indo-Burmese mountains and forests.

* Priya-putra. I do not know what this bird is. The name affords no indication.

† C'átaka, the Pied-crested Cuckoo. Prof. Monier-Williams says the bird is *Cuculus melanoleucus*, but I find no such name mentioned in Jerdon. It is the *Coccystes melanoleucos* of Jerdon (Vol. I, p. 339), which he says is called chatak. It is found all over India.

‡ Kumud, the Lotus water-lily, *Nymphæa lotus* (Oliver, p. 155). There seems to be some confusion in distinguishing btween the Sanskrit names for the lotus and the water-lilies, and I would attempt a solution in this and the following notes.

Of the water-lilies, *Nymphæa*, large water-herbs with leaves and flowers *floating* on the surface, there are 2 species common in India, *viz.*, *N. lotus*, the Lotus water-lily, and *N. stellata*, the Blue water-lily.

N. lotus has leaves 6—12 inches broad, and flowers 2—10 inches broad, white, rose, or red. This species combines Roxburgh's *N. rubra* and *N. edulis (esculenta).* Its Sanskrit name is *kumud*, and probably *ambu-ja;* the red variety is *raktotpala.* It closes during the day and opens at night.

The latter species, *N. stellata,* has flowers 1—10 inches broad, slightly odorous. It comprises 3 varieties, (1) *cyanea* (*N. cyanea*, Roxb.), flowers medium-sized, blue; (2) *parviflora*, flowers usually smaller, blue; (3) *versicolor* (*N. versicolor*, Roxb.), flowers larger, white, blue, purple, or flesh-coloured. The blue-flowered *N. stellata* is called *indívara, utpala, kuvalaya* and *nílotpala.* (Hooker, Vol. I, p. 114: Roxburgh, p. 427.)

§ Puṇḍaríka, the Lotus or Sacred Lotus, *Nelumbium speciosum.* This is the only species of *Nelumbium* in India. It is a large erect water-herb with its

21 lilies,* with water-lilies,† and lotuses;‡ and thronged with kádamba geese,§ and ruddy shieldrakes|| and water-fowl,¶
22 with káraṇḍava ducks,** pelicans,†† geese,‡‡ tortoises, and

leaves and flowers *raised high* above the water. Its leaves are peltate, cupped, 2—3 feet in diameter. The flowers are 4—10 inches broad, white or rose-red. Its Sanskrit names are *kamala, nalini, padmini, puṇḍaríka, sarasi-ja,* and *sahasra-patra.* The flower is *padma* and *panka-ja.* The red variety is *kokanada* and *támarasa.* Roxburgh says the white variety is called in Sanskrit *sitámbu-ja,* and the red variety *raktotpala;* but these names more properly designate the white and red varieties of the water-lily (*Nymphæa*), and Prof. Monier-Williams translates them so. The Lotus opens during the day and closes at night (Hooker, Vol. I, p. 116; Oliver's Indian Botany, p. 156; Roxburgh, p. 450.)

* Nílotpala, the Blue water-lily, *Nymphæa stellata,* see note ‡ on kumud, *supra* p. 29.

† Kahlára. Prof. Monier-Williams says this is the White esculent water-lily, *Nymphæa lotus,* but Roxburgh assigns it to his *N. cyanea.* Can it mean the rose-coloured variety of the *N. lotus* or *stellata?* See note ‡ on kumud, *supra* p. 29.

‡ Kamala, the Lotus, *Nelumbium speciosum;* see note § on Puṇḍaríka, *supra* p. 29. But there must be some difference between the two.

§ Kádamba, a kind of goose with dark-grey wings (kala-haṉsa), so Prof. Monier-Williams. It seems to be the Grey Lag-Goose, *Anser cinereus,* which is called *kar-háns* in Behar. (Hume and Marshall, Vol. III, p. 55; Jerdon, Vol. II, p. 779.)

|| C'akraváka, the Ruddy Shieldrake or Brahminy Duck, *Casarca rutila. Anas casarca* is the Linnæan name. (Hume and Marshall, Vol. III, p. 125; Jerdon, Vol. II, p. 791.)

¶ Jala-kukkuṭa. This is probably the Water-hen, *Gallinula chloropus,* commonly called the *jal-murghi,* which means the same. (Jerdon, Vol. II, p. 718.)

** Káraṇḍava, a kind of duck; also called karaṇḍa. I would suggest that this is the Common Teal, *Querquedula crecca,* which is now called *kerra* in the N. W. Provinces, and *kardo* in Sindh. (Hume and Marshall, Vol. III, p, 205; Jerdon, Vol. II, p, 806.)

†† Plava. Prof. Monier-Williams translates this as pelican, *Pelicanus fusicollis;* but I do not find any such species in Jerdon. It may be the Grey pelican, *Pelecanus Philippensis,* which is the most abundant species in India. (Jerdon, Vol. II, p. 858.)

‡‡ Haṉsa. This is of course general, and means any kind of goose or duck.

divers;* thronged with these and other birds swimming in the
water all around.
23 So gazing on the delightful forest, S'auri accompanied by the
maidens gradually proceeded onwards to an incomparable
24 bower of creepers. There he saw brahmans, deeply read in
the Vedas and Vedángas, belonging to the families of Kuśika,
25 and Bhṛigu, Bharadvája, and Gotama, and brahmans sprung
from various famalies, *all* eagerly listening to the tales,
26 seated on large outer garments made of the hide of the black
antelope, and on the kuśa grass and on kuśa-grass seats; and
27 Súta (their bard) in the midst, reciting glorious tales of the
olden times, based on the deeds of the first Surarshis. Seeing
28 Ráma, whose eyes were red with drinking, all the brahmans,
perceiving he was intoxicated, rose up in haste, saluting the
29 plough-bearer, except that scion of the bards. Then filled with
rage, the mighty plough-bearer, who caused all the Dánavas
to quake, rolling his eye, smote Súta.
30 When that bard was slain while repeating the words of the
Veda, all those brahmans, clad in black antelope skins, depart-
31 ed from the wood. And the plough-armed *hero*, perceiving
himself disregarded, thought, "This is a very grievous sin
32 that I have committed; for since I have come here to a
brahmans' abode and have slain Súta, these dvijas perceiving
33 me have all departed. And my body has a disgusting odour,
as it were of blood, and I perceive that I am contemned as
34 a brahmanicide. Fie on my rage, and the wine, my arrogance,
my cruelty! Possessed by them, I have committed this most
35 grievous sin. To expiate it I will perform a twelve-year vow,
making the confession of my deed the uttermost penance.
36 This then is the pilgrimage which I have now undertaken; I
37 will go to the Pratilomá Sarasvatí itself." Hence he, Ráma,
went to the Pratilomá Sarasvatí.

Next listen to this reference to the story of the Páṇḍaveyas.

* Madgu, a kind of diving bird. It is probably the Little Grebe, *Podiceps Philippensis*, commonly called *dub-dubi* from its inveterate diving. (Jerdon, Vol. II, p. 822.) But it may be the Bald Coot, *Fulica atra*, which is also a ready diver (*id.*, p. 715.)

CANTO VII.

The Birth of the Sons of Draupadí.

The Birds explain the fourth question—King Hariś-c'andra incurred Viśvámitra's anger, and to appease him gives up to him his kingdom and all his wealth—Viśvámitra ill-treats the queen, and five Viśve Devas censure him for his brutality—He curses them to be born as men, but exempts them from marriage—They were born as the five sons of Draupadí, and died young.

The righteous birds spoke.

1 There lived formerly in the Tretá Age a most exalted Rájar-
shi named Hariś-c'andra, virtuous in soul, a ruler of the earth,
2 brilliant in fame. No famine, nor sickness, nor untimely death
occurred among men, nor did the citizens delight in evil, while
3 he ruled as king; nor, further, did the people become uproari-
ous through wealth, valour, austerities or spirituous liquors;
nor were any females born who failed to reach womanhood.*
4 And he, of mighty arm, when once chasing a deer in the
5 forest, heard women repeatedly crying, "save us"! The king,
giving over the deer, called out "fear not! who is this per-
6 verse being that, under my rule, behaves with injustice?" At
this interval also the Raudra Vighna-ráj, the opponent of every
7 undertaking, who was following that cry, deliberated:—"This
Viśvámitra, full of heroism, undertaking incomparable austeri-
ties, keeping a vow, is mastering the sciences of S'iva and
others, which have not been perfected before. Those *sciences*
8 being mastered by this man, who governs his mind in patience
and silence, are verily lamenting, afflicted with dread. How
9 can I manage this? Glorious is *this* noblest of the Kauśika
family; I am much weaker than he: these terrified *sciences*
are thus bewailing: it appears to me difficult to be accom-
10 plished. Now this king has come in my way, calling out
repeatedly 'fear not!'; into him indeed entering, I will speedily
accomplish my desire."
11 Then the king possessed by that Raudra Vighna-rája, who had
thus taken counsel with himself, uttered this speech in anger:—

* An allusion to infanticide?

12 "Who is this wicked man that binds fire in the corner of his
garment, when I the lord am present, gleaming with the
13 glowing splendour of my power? He to-day, pierced in every
limb by my arrows, which in their flight from my bow illumine
the other regious of the sky, shall enter upon a long sleep."
14 Thereupon Viśvámitra having heard the king's speech was
enraged: and, when that great Ṛishi was enraged, those
15 sciences perished in a moment. The king moreover, seeing
Viśvámitra, rich in austerities, being terrified, suddenly trem-
16 bled exceedingly like the leaf of the peepul tree.* When the
Muni exclaimed, "wretch!" and "stand!"; then the king fall-
17 ing prostrate in reverence addressed him:—"O adorable lord!
this is my duty! I have committed no fault! Deign not O
Muni! to be angry with me, who am engaged in my duty.
18 A king, conversant with his duties, must give gifts, and
must afford protection, and lifting his bow must wage war,
according to the Dharma-śástras."

Viśvámitra spoke.

19 "To whom, O king, must thou give gifts, whom must thou protect, and with whom must thou wage war? Speedily declare this, if thou fearest unrighteousness."

Hariś-c'andra spoke.

20 "I must always give gifts to brahmans principally, and to others who are straitened in their means; I must protect those in fear; I must make war with enemies."

Viśvámitra spoke.

21 "If your highness, a king, duly regards the duties of kings—I am a brahman desirous of a reward, let the desired fee be given me."

* Ficus religiosa. The leaf, which varies from 2½ to 5½ inches in length and almost the same in breadth, is ovate-cordate, and has a long slender apex (acumen) 1 to 2 inches long. It has a round flexible stalk 2 to 3 inches long, which is twisted so as to make the inner surface of the leaf face outwards from the branch. The leaf hangs downwards by the long stalk, with its inner surface, which is slightly concave, facing outwards, and thus catches the lightest breeze.

The birds spoke.

22 The Raja, having heard this speech with gladdened soul,
deemed himself as it were born anew, and addressed the sage
23 of the Kauśika race: "Be it declared, adorable sir! what, free
from doubt, I must give thee; consider it as already given,
24 albeit most difficult to be obtained, whether gold or money,
son, wife, body, life, kingdom, city, good fortune—whatever is
the desire of my own soul."

Viśvámitra spoke.

25 "O king! this present has been accepted, which thou hast
given: first, however, bestow the fee appertaining to the
Rája-súya sacrifice."

The Raja spoke.

26 "O brahman! I will indeed give your honour that fee. Choose,
O chief of the dvijas, whatever present thou desirest."

Viśvámitra spoke.

27 "*Give me* this earth, with its ocean, and with its mountains,
villages and towns; and thy entire kingdom, O warrior, with
28 its multitude of chariots, horses, and elephants; also thy trea-
sury and treasure; and whatever else thou possessest, excepting
29 thy wife, and son and body, O sinless one! and *excepting* thy
virtue, which, O thou that knowest all the virtues, follows its
possessor when he moves. What need for me to say more?
Let all this be granted me."

The birds spoke.

30 With gladdened mind the king, unperturbed in countenance,
having heard the Ṛishi's speech, joining his hands respectfully
replied, "So be it!"

Viśvámitra spoke.

31 "If all thy property is given me, thy kingdom, the earth, thy
army, thy wealth,—whose is the lordship, O Rájarshi! when I
the ascetic am seated in the kingdom?"

Hariś-c'andra spoke.

32 "At what time I have yielded up the earth to thee, O brah-
man! at that time thou, Sir, art the owner; how much more
now the king."

Viśvámitra spoke.

33 "If O king! the whole earth has been given me by thee,
thou must deign to depart from the realm where I hold sway,
34 unfastening all thy ornaments, such as thy waist-band and
every thing else, and clothing thyself with the bark of trees,
together with thy wife and son."

The birds spoke.

35 Having said "So be it!" and having so done, the king started
to go, in company with his wife S'aivyá and his young son.
36 Then he addressed the king, having obstructed the road as
he was moving—"Where wilt thou go, without giving me the
fee appertaining to the Rája-súya sacrifice?"

Hariś-c'andra spoke.

37 "Adorable Sir! this kingdom has been given thee free from
adversaries: these *our* three bodies, O Brahman! are all that
remain to me this day."

Viśvámitra spoke.

38 "Nevertheless thou must assuredly give me the sacrificial fee;
a promise unfulfilled, especially to brahmans, proves injurious.
39 As long as brahmans delight, O king! in the Rája-súya sacri-
fice, so long indeed must the fee for the Rája-súya sacrifice be
40 given. After making a promise, one must bestow the gift;
and one must fight against assailants; so too the afflicted must
be protected; thus hast thou already agreed."

Hariś-c'andra spoke.

41 "Adorable Sir, I have nought at present; I will give thee
the fee after a while: and show me favour, O Brahmarshi!
bearing in mind noble behaviour."

Viśvámitra spoke.

42 "What length of time must I wait for thee, O guardian of
men! Tell me speedily, or the fire of my curse shall con-
sume thee."

Hariś-c'andra spoke.

43 "In a month will I give thee the fee-money, O Brahmarshi! At
present I have no means; deign to grant me *this* permission."

Viśvámitra spoke.

44 "Go, go, O noble king; observe thy duty; and may thy way
be auspicious! May there be no enemies!"

The birds spoke.

45 Permitted to go, the king departed; his queen, who was
46 unused to walk afoot,* followed him. Seeing that most noble
king departing from the city with his wife and son, the citizens
raised a cry and followed the king, *exclaiming*—

47 "Alas, O master! why leavest thou us, who are afflicted
with continual sufferings? Thou, O king, art devoted to
righteousness, and thou art the benefactor of the citizens.
48 Lead us also, O Rájarshi! if thou regardest righteousness.
Stay a moment, O king of monarchs! Our eyes as bees drink†
49 thy lotus-like mouth. When again shall we behold thee, who,
when thou goest forth, art preceded and followed by kings?
50 Here is thy wife, holding her young son in her hand, following
thee, before whom, when thou goest forth, go thy servants seated
51 on elephants! Here goes to-day walking afoot the king
of monarchs, Hariś-c'andra! Alas, O king, what will thy
52 very youthful, beautiful-browed, soft-skinned, fine-nosed face
become, when injured by the dust on the road? Stay, stay,
53 O best of kings, observe thy own duty. Mildness is a very
noble virtue, especially among kshatriyas; what need have we
of wife, what need of children, or of wealth, or of grain,
54 O master? Abandoning all this, we have become mere
shadows of thee. Alas master! alas Mahárájá! alas, O lord!
55 why dost thou abandon us? Where thou art, there indeed
will we be. That is joy, where thou indeed art. That is our
city where thou art. That is Svarga where thou, our king,
art."

56 Having thus heard the citizens' address the king, overwhelmed
with grief, stood then in the road through very compassion for
57 them. Still Viśvámitra, seeing him distressed by the citi-
zens' exclamations, approaching him, with eyes rolling in anger

* Read *padbhyám* for *pradbhyám*.

† Better *pivúma* for *pibámo*, let us drink?

58 and impatience, spoke: "Fie on thee, vile in thy conduct,
false, crooked in thy speech! who also, after giving me thy
59 kingdom, wishest again to withdraw it." The king thus roughly
accosted by him replied thus trembling, "I am going," and de-
60 parted hastily drawing his wife in his hand. Thereupon the
sage of the Kauśika family suddenly belaboured with a wooden
staff the very youthful toil-wearied wife, as *the king was*
61 drawing her along. Seeing her thus beaten, the king Hariś-
c'andra, oppressed with pain, exclaimed "I am going;" nor did
he utter aught else.

62 But then spoke five Viśve Devas full of pity, "This Viśvá-
mitra is very wicked; what worlds will he obtain, who has
63 uprooted this best of sacrificers from his throne? By whose
funeral ceremony further shall the soma juice expressed at
the great sacrifice be purified, by drinking which we shall
reach the exhilaration that is preceded by incantations?"

The birds spoke.

64 Having heard this their remark, the sage of the Kauśika race,
exceedingly enraged, cursed them—"Ye shall all assume human
65 form!" And propitiated by them, the great Muni added, "Al-
66 though in human form, ye shall have no offspring. There
shall be neither marriage of wives for you, nor hostility: freed
67 from love and anger ye shall become gods again." Thereupon
those gods descended to the mansion of the Kurus with their
own portions; they were born of the womb of Draupadí as the
68 five grandchildren of Páṇḍu. Hence the five heroic Páṇḍa-
veyas did not take to themselves wives, through the curse of
that great Muni.

69 All this has been declared to thee with reference to the tale
of the Páṇḍaveyas. Thy four questions have been answered
in song. What else dost thou wish to hear?

Canto VIII.

The Story of Hariś-c'andra (continued).

Viśvamitra not satisfied demands further fees, and Hariś-c'andra in desperation sells his wife and his son to a brahman and himself to a c'aṇḍála, and gives Viśvámitra all the price—Hariś-c'andra earns his livelihood as the c'aṇḍála's servant at a burning-ground in the most abject state for a year—Then he sees a vision of his future transmigrations with a promise of happiness ultimately—His son is bitten by a snake, and the queen brings the corpse to the burning-ground—They recognise each other and bewail their misfortunes—Both resolve to immolate themselves on their son's funeral pile; but the gods interpose and restore his son to life—Dharma explains that he had personated the c'aṇḍála—Indra calls the king to Svarga, but he refuses to go without his faithful people—He, and his queen and people ascend to Svarga in perfect bliss.

Jaimini spoke.

1 Ye have declared this in order according to my questions:
great is my curiosity regarding the story of Hariś-c'andra.
2 Ah! passing great was the woe incurred by that magnanimous
king; I trust he obtained a happiness fully commensurate,
O bráhmans!

The birds spoke.

3 Hearing Viśvámitra's speech, the king moved on slowly, full
of sorrow, followed by his wife S'aivyá with her young boy.
4 The king having reached the divine city* of Benares—the
choice of S'iva *who pronounced* that it was not to be enjoyed
5 by men. Distressed with sorrow, he travelled afoot with his
compliant wife. On entering the city, he saw Viśvámitra
6 present. Seeing he had already arrived, Hariś-c'andra bowed
reverently and, joining his hands respectfully, addressed the
7 great Muni:—"Here is my life, and this is my son, and this is
my wife, O Muni! Take that as the choicest arghya offering
8 with which thou shouldst quickly deal. Whatever else we
should do, deign to excuse that."

* For *parím* read *purím.*

Viśvámitra spoke.

9 "Gone is the month, O Rájarshi!; let my fee be given me, if thy word regarding the Rája-súya sacrifice be remembered."

Hariś-c'andra spoke.

10 "O brahman, rich in fadeless austerities! to-day the month will, in truth, be completed: await this half-day which remains, *but* not long."

Viśvámitra spoke.

11 "Be it so, Mahárájá! I will come again: unless to-day thou shall make the gift, I will pronounce a curse on thee."

The birds spoke.

12 Thus having spoken the bráhman departed: and the Raja
then took thought—"How shall I give him the fee which has
13 been promised? Whence *can I find* powerful friends?
Whence *can I get* wealth at this moment? Blameworthy is
14 my present: how can I escape going downward? How much
more am I abandoning life! To what region shall I, who am
nothing, go, if I perish without having performed my promise?
15 I shall become a robber of bráhmans, a worm, a wicked man,
the vilest of the vile; or I shall become a slave—better indeed
let me sell myself."

The birds spoke.

16 Then his wife in words broken with weeping answered the
king, who was distressed, dejected, anxious, with downcast
17 face—"Leave off care, O Mahárájá; preserve thy truthfulness;
a man destitute of truth should be avoided like a burning-
18 ground. There is no higher righteousness, they say, for a
man than this, namely, maintaining his truthfulness, O noble
19 man! Oblations to consecrated fire, or study, or the whole
circle of *good* deeds, such as liberality, &c., are fruitless in
20 him who speaks at random. Truthfulness is constantly
declared in the Dharma-śástras to tend to the salvation of men
of understanding; and falsehood to the overthrow of men of
21 uneducated minds. A king named Kṛiti, after offering seven
horse-sacrifices and a Rája-súya sacrifice, fell forthwith from
22 Svarga for falsehood. O king, I have given birth to a child—'

Thus having spoken she wept aloud. The king spoke as follows to her whose eyes were bathed in tears.

Hariś-c'andra spoke.

23 "Cease, lady, thy agitation; here stands thy boy; pray, speak
what thou desirest to say, O thou who art graceful in thy
gait!"

The queen spoke.

24 "O king, I have given birth to a child: the wives of good
men bear fruit in their sons. Do thou therefore, being such a
man, give me in exchange for wealth, and pay the brahman
the fee."

The birds spoke.

25 Hearing this proposal, the king lost his senses; and on re-
26 gaining consciousness lamented, sorely grieved:—"Dire is this
grief, O lady, that thou thus mentionest to me: is thy joyous
27 intercourse with me, wretch that I am, forgotten? Ah! alas!
how couldest thou suggest this, O sweet-smiler. Repugnant
28 is this plan: how can I execute it?" Thus having spoken,
the king, repeating the word "Shame! shame!" fell to the
29 ground overwhelmed by faintness. Seeing the king Hariś-
c'andra prostrate on the earth, the queen full of sorrow,
uttered these piteous words:—

The queen spoke.

30 "Alas! Mahárájá! from whom has come this evil thought,
that thou, who art accustomed to coverings made of the hair
31 of the spotted deer, hast fallen on the *bare* ground? Here
sleeps the king, my lord, on the ground,—he, by whom ten
thousands of choice cattle and wealth were dispensed among
32 brahmans. Ah! woe! what has this king done to thee, O
brahman, that he, the equal of Indra and Vishṇu, has been
33 reduced to a state of coma?" Having soliloquised thus, she,
beautiful-hipped, fell swooning, crushed by the intolerable
34 great weight of her husband's misfortunes. The child seeing
his parents lying thus helpless on the ground, being exces-
35 sively hungry and very unhappy, spoke:—"Father, dear
father, give me some food; mother, mother, give me something

to eat. I have become dreadfully hungry, and the tip of my
tongue is growing parched."

The birds spoke.

36 At this interval arrived Viśvámitra great in austerities;
but, seeing Hariś-c'andra lying on the ground in a swoon,
37 he sprinkled the king with water and addressed him thus:—
"Rise up, rise up, O supreme king; give me the fee I desire.
38 A debtor's misery increases from day to day." Then being
39 refreshed with the snow-cold water, the king, recovering con-
sciousness, and perceiving Viśvámitra, again fell into a swoon,
40 and the Muni grew angry. The brahman, making the king
recover, spoke:—"Let my fee be given me, if thou regardest
41 righteousness. By truth the sun sheds warmth; in truth
the earth stands *firm;* truth in speech is the highest righte-
42 ousness: Svarga is based on truth. Also a hundred horse-
sacrifices and truth are placed in the balance—truth verily
43 outweighs the hundred horse-sacrifices. Otherwise what
motive is there for my speaking thus peaceably to *thee,* base
44 one, evil-intentioned, and cruel, false in speech? Since thou
art powerful as king, let this my kindly feeling be heeded. If
45 O king, thou shalt not give me the fee to-day, when the
sun reaches the Western mountain, then I will assuredly curse
thee."

Having spoken thus the bráhman departed; and the king
46 remained, weak with terror, fugitive, vile, indigent, harassed
by the malicious and the rich. His wife again spoke thus—
47 "Let my proposal be complied with, lest consumed by the
fire of his curse thou perish." But the king, thus urged
48 by his wife again and again, replied—"Lady, here without
pity I proceed to sell thee; what even the malicious could not
49 do, that do I, if my voice be able to utter so hard a speech
as this." Thereupon having so spoken to his wife, he went
unnerved to the city and then, his throat and eyes impeded
with tears, uttered this speech;—

The king spoke.

50 "Ho! ho! citizens, listen ye all to my word. Why do ye
ask me, 'ho! who art thou?' I am mischievous, inhuman,

51 either a very cruel Rákshasa, or even more wicked than that.
52 I, who will not yield up my life, am come to sell my wife. If
any of you has need of the desire of my life as a slave-girl,
let him speak quickly while I survive."

The birds spoke.

53 A certain aged bráhman approaching accosted the king—
"Deliver the slave-girl to me; I am a purchaser, paying
54 ready money. I have no little wealth, and my wife is very
young; she cannot perform the household duties; therefore
55 give me *this girl.* This wealth is proportionate to the skill,
age, beauty and disposition of thy wife: take it; deliver me
56 the maiden." When thus addressed by the brahman, king
Hariś-c'andra's mind was lacerated with grief; nor did he
57 make him any reply. Thereupon the brahman binding up
the money in cash in the end of the king's back-cloth dress,
58 dragged off the queen, seizing her by the hair. But the
child Rohitásya, who had a boy's side-locks of hair, and who
was clutching her dress with his hand, wept on seeing his
mother dragged away.

The queen spoke.

59 "Loose, loose me, noble Sir! while I take a look at my boy.
A future view of him, kind Sir! will be difficult to get.
60 See! come my child to me thy mother thus sold into slavery.
Do not touch me, my royal child! I must not be touched by
61 thee now!" Then suddenly the boy seeing his mother dragged
along, ran to her crying "Mother!" with tear-soiled eyes.
62 The bráhman purchaser, seeing the child had approached,
kicked him with his foot; the latter, however, exclaiming
"Mother!" did not leave hold of his mother.

The queen spoke.

63 "Shew me favour, O master! and buy this boy. Although
purchased, I shall not be a diligent servant to thee, Sir,
64 when separated from him. Do thou in this way beam favourably on me unfortunate; unite me with my child, as a
cow with her calf."

The bráhman spoke.

65 "Take thou this wealth and give me the boy: the wages of a man and woman have been fixed by those conversant with the Dharma-śástras at a hundred, a thousand, and a hundred thousand *pieces*, and a price of ten millions by others."

The birds spoke.

66 Accordingly then he bound that money in the king's upper
garment, and taking the boy bound him close together
67 with his mother. Seeing them both, his wife and son, led
away, the king lamented sorely grieved, sighing deeply again
68 and again. "My wife whom neither the wind, nor the sun,
nor the moon, nor the populace formerly gazed on, here she
69 is, fallen into bondage. Here is my boy, who is sprung from
the Solar race, and whose hands and fingers are very young,
70 disposed of by sale. Shame on me, sorry fool that I am! Ah,
my darling! ah, my child, my pet! my imprudent conduct,
base man that I am, has brought me into thraldom to fate;
yet I am not dead, ah shame!"

The birds spoke.

71 While the king was thus lamenting, the bráhman taking
them both disappeared hastily among trees, houses and other
72 high objects. Then Viśvámitra meeting the king, demanded
the wealth; Hariś-c'andra delivered that money to him.
73 Considering those riches, procured by the sale of the wife,
insufficient, Kauśika enraged addressed the sorrow-stricken
74 king. "O kshatriya, if thou deemest this a fitting sacrificial
fee for me; then behold thou quickly my supreme might,
75 *arising* from austerities well performed here, and from stain-
less bráhmanhood, and from my terrible majesty, and from
my perfect study."

Hariś-c'andra spoke.

76 "More will I give thee, adorable one; be pleased to wait some time; at present I have nought; my wife has been sold, and my young son."

Viśvámitra spoke.

77 "This fourth part that now remains of the day, O king, for that I must wait; nought more must I say to thee."

The birds spoke.

78 So, having uttered the harsh pitiless speech to the supreme king, the angry Kauśika took the money and quickly departed.
79 When Viśvámitra had gone, the king, encompassed by a sea of fear and sorrow, after reflecting in every aspect, spoke aloud,
80 with downcast face :—"Whatever man desires me for a slave, bought with money, let him speak quickly, while the sun yet shines."

81 Then advanced hastily *the god* Dharma, wearing the form of a c'aṇḍála, foul-smelling, disfigured, uncouth, bearded,
82 with projecting teeth, compassionate, dark in complexion, his belly pendulous, his eyes tawny and haggard, his pronunciation rude, and carrying a batch of birds, adorned with gar-
83 lands taken from corpses, a skull in his hand, his face long, horrid *to look at*, talking much and often, surrounded by a pack of dogs, dreadful, a staff in his hand, hideous.

The c'aṇḍála spoke.

84 "I am an applicant to thee; tell me quickly thy own hire, at which, whether little or much, thou art to be acquired."

The birds spoke.

85 There gazing at him, such as he was, cruel-eyed, very coarse, muttering, very bad in disposition, the king asked "Who art thou?"

The c'aṇḍála spoke.

86 "I am a c'aṇḍála, known here in this greatest of cities as Pravíra, famed as the slayer of those condemned to death, the gatherer of blankets from corpses."

Hariś-c'andra spoke.

87 "I should not wish to become the despicable slave of a c'aṇḍála; better to be consumed by the fire of the curse rather than to be thrall to a c'aṇḍála."

The birds spoke.

88 While he was so speaking, the great hermit Viśvámitra

arrived, his eyes rolling with anger and wrath, and said this to the king :—

Viśvámitra spoke.

89 "This c'aṇḍála is ready to give thee no little wealth; why is not my full sacrificial fee paid me?"

Hariś-c'andra spoke.

90 "Adorable descendant of Kuśika! I know myself to be sprung from the Solar race; how, though desirous of wealth, shall I go into bondage to a c'aṇḍála?

Viśvámitra spoke.

91 "If thou wilt not give me the c'aṇḍála's wealth, obtained in exchange for thyself, at the fixed time, I will assuredly curse thee."

The birds spoke.

92 Thereupon the king Hariś-c'andra, his life bound up in
his anxiety, overcome with agitation seized the Ṛishi's feet,
93 exclaiming—"Be thou gracious! I am a slave; I am in suffer-
ing; frightened am I; and I am specially thy votary: shew
me favour, O Brahmarshi! Deplorable is association with
94 c'aṇḍálas. Instead of the balance of the money, I would be
subject to thee indeed, O mighty Muni! thy agent in every
matter, thy servant, obedient to thy will."

Viśvámitra spoke.

95 "If your honour is my servant, then, given by me to the c'aṇḍála for a hundred millions of money, thou hast fallen into slavery."

The birds spoke.

96 When he had so spoken, the low out-caste then, glad in
mind, giving that pelf to Viśvámitra, bound the king and
97 led him, bewildered by blows of the staff, his senses utterly
confused, grieved at his separation from his loved kindred,
to his town.

98 Then king Hariś-c'andra, dwelling in the c'aṇḍála's town,

99 at morning, noon and evening sang this:—"My downcast
girl seeing before her my downcast son, filled with grief,
100 remembers me; *hoping* 'the king will free us both, by
giving, when he has amassed wealth, more wealth than this
to the bráhman.' She, fawn-eyed, does not know that I
101 have done more wickedly. Loss of kingdom, abandonment
of friends, sale of wife and son, and this c'aṇḍála-life that
102 I have sunk to:—alas! a succession of misfortunes." Dwell-
ing in this condition, he remembered unceasingly his beloved
son and his soul-engrossing wife; deprived of all his pro-
perty, and abject.

103 Now for some time king Hariś-c'andra, as a servant to that
man, became a gatherer of garments from dead bodies at the
104 burning-ground, and was instructed by the c'aṇḍála, who
gathered garments from dead bodies—"Stay here day and
105 night on the look out for the arrival of corpses. This part
is to be given to the king, and a sixth part is for the corpse,
let three parts be for me, and two parts for thy wages."

106 Thus instructed he went to the mortuary house and to the
southern quarter, where then stood in Benares the burning-
107 ground, a place of horrible cries, frequented by hundreds of
jackals, strewn with the garlands from corpses, foul-smelling,
108 reeking with smoke, thronged by Piśác'as, Bhútas, Vetálas,
Ḍákinís, and Yakshas, crowded with vultures and jackals,
109 encompassed by packs of dogs, thickly strewn with heaps
of bones, full of dreadful odours; pervaded with the cries
of the friends of the various dead persons and with a terrible
110 hubbub—"Ah! son!—friend!—ah! kinsman!—brother!—
my child, dear to me now!—ah! husband!—sister!—mother!
111 —ah! maternal uncle!—paternal grandfather!—maternal
grandfather!—father!—grandson!—where art thou gone!
—come, my kinsman!"; where was heard a great din of
112 persons uttering such cries *as these;—a place* filled with the
113 sputtering of burning flesh, marrow and fat. Black half-
burnt corpses, their rows of teeth just bursting into view,
grinned from amidst the fire, *as if saying*, 'This is the body's
114 *final* state!' Here the fire crackled along rows of bones of

various ages; and there was the sound of the wailing of the
relations, which was caused by the merriment of the puk-
115 kasas.* There is heard a very loud and frightful sound,—
as if at the close of the age,—of Bhútas, Vetálas, Piśác'as,
116 Gaṇas and Rákshasas singing. Crowded with great heaps
of buffaloes' ordure and cows' dung; and surrounded with
high piles of the ashes derived therefrom, mixed with bones;
117 darkened by the confusion of the crows among the many
offerings, garlands and lamps; filled with many sounds, the
118 burning-ground resembles Naraka.† The burning-ground
reverberated with the fire-pregnant, inauspicious yells of the
she-jackals; it was impenetrable by reason of the terrific cries;
very dire‡ with the close contagion of fear; and painful by
reason of the sounds of lamentation.

119 The king arrived there, unhappy, ready to grieve: "Ah
servants, ministers, bráhmans! Where has that my kingdom
120 gone, O Creator? Ah S'aivyá! ah my young son! forsaking
me, luckless one, through Viśvámitra's fault they both, mine
121 own *relatives*, have gone elsewhere." There revolving thus in
his mind over and over again the words of the c'aṇḍála,
dirty, uncouth in every limb, his hair long, mal-odorous, bear-
122 ing a flag, armed with a club, somewhat resembling Death, and
running hither and thither, exclaiming "This price has been
123 obtained for this corpse, and shall I get it? This is mine,
this is for the king, and this for the head c'áṇḍála;"
the king, while running in all directions, and while alive,
124 entered into another birth. Clothed in patched cloth made
of old rags well fastened together; his face, arms, belly and
feet covered with ashes from funeral piles and with dust;
125 his hands and fingers smeared with various kinds of fat,
oil and marrow; sighing; intent on satisfying *himself* by
126 feeding on various corpses and water;§ his head dressed with

* A low caste.

† *Naraka*, the general name for hell or the place of torment; it is distinguished from *Pátála*, the lower regions.

‡ Read *bheyam* for *bhayam*?

§ The text *náná-śavodana-kṛitáhára* seems to be incorrect.

bands of garlands therefrom; he sleeps not either by day
127 or by night, frequently exclaiming "ah! alas!" In this
manner passed twelve months as if a hundred.

One day that noble king wearied, separated from his kind-
128 red, and uncouth in form, being overpowered by slumber, fell
indeed into a dead sleep; and there on his pallet beheld a
129 great wonder:—Through the power of destiny, he had in
another body by diligent occupation at the burning-ground
130 given the guru his fee, and there was immunity from the inflic-
tion of pain for twelve years. Then he saw himself conceived
131 in the womb of a pukkasa woman. Further the king, when
in that condition, considered thus—"Immediately I am
132 born, I will verily practice the duty of liberality." There-
upon he was born. Then as a pukkasa boy he was always
ready to perform the obsequies of the dead bodies in the
133 burning-ground. On his reaching his seventh year, a dead
bráhman was brought to the burning ground by the rela-
tives; then he perceived that the bráhman had been poor and
134 virtuous. But he, asking for his wage, despised the bráhmans;
those bráhmans mentioned there what Viśvámitra had done,—
135 "Do thou a deed most sinful, and vicious, O evil-doer; Hariś-
c'andra the king was formerly turned by Viśvámitra into
136 a pukkasa for breaking the slumber of a bráhman, by
the destruction of his merit." When he did not have patience
137 with them, they then in anger cursed him—"Go forthwith
thou vilest of men to terrible Naraka." Immediately upon
138 these words, the king still in his sleep saw Yama's mes-
sengers, bearing nooses, terror-inspiring. He saw himself
139 then seized by them and led off by force. Sorely afflicted,
exclaiming, "Alas now, O mother! O father!" he fell
140 into Naraka into a tub of oil. And he was torn asunder beneath
by saws and the edges of razors, and suffered pain in dense
141 darkness, feeding on pus and blood. He saw his dead self,
seven years old, in the form of a pukkasa. Day by day in
142 Naraka he is burnt and roasted in one place; he is afflicted
and shaken in another place; he is killed and torn asunder

in another place; in another he is made to melt away and to
143 blaze; in another place he is assailed with cold winds. He
remained in Naraka one day, which was as long as a hun-
dred years; so a hundred years there in Naraka are called by
144 the demons. Thereafter cast upon the earth he was born as
a dog, eating filth and vomited matter, and enduring cold
145 and heat: in a month he died. Next he saw his body *born*
as an ass, an elephant, a monkey, an ox, a goat, a cat, and
a heron, a bull, a sheep, a bird, a worm, a fish, a tortoise, and
146 a wild boar, a porcupine, a cock, a parrot, a maina,* and mo-
tionless living objects, a snake and other corporeal beings.
147 Day by day consumed with grief he saw the birth of one
living being after another; a day was as a hundred years.
148 A full hundred years thus passed *with him* there *born* among
the lower creation. And the king saw himself born once *again*
149 in his own race. While in that state, he lost his kingdom
in dice-playing; and his wife was carried off, and his son *too;*
150 and he sought the forest alone. There he saw a terrible
ravenous lion approaching with open mouth, accompanied by a
151 young elephant†; and again he was devoured, while ready
to bewail his wife, 'Ah S'aivyá! where art thou gone now,
152 forsaking me here in misery?' Again he saw his wife with
her son *imploring him*, 'Rescue us O Hariś-c'andra! What
153 hast thou to do with dice-playing, my lord? Thy son has
fallen to a lamentable condition, and so has thy wife S'aivyá.'
Then he no longer saw them, though running about again and
154 again. And again he saw,—he the king was seated in

* S'árikā, a mainā. There are several kinds of mainas (or mynas). The best known are the Common maina *Acridotheres tristis,* which is a brown bird common throughout India, and the Nepal Hill maina *Eulabes intermedia,* which is a black bird found along the lower ranges of the Himálayas. Both are commonly caged and learn to talk, but the latter attains much higher proficiency. (Jerdon's Birds of India, Edn. Godwin-Austen, Vol. II, pp. 325 and 339). Prof Monier-Williams says S'áriká is *Gracula religiosa* or *Turdus salica*. The former name is an old name of the Southern Hill maina (*E. religiosa*) and of the Nepal Hill maina (*E. intermedia*). (Id., Vol. II, pp. 337, 339). I do not find the second name in Jerdon.

† *Sarabha;* or a fabulous animal with eight legs, stronger than a lion.

Svarga; she poor thing was brought by force, with dishevelled
155 hair, stript of her garments, exclaiming 'Ah! alas! rescue
me!' in repeated cries. Then again he saw there through
156 Yama's ordainment—the dwellers in the sky are calling out,
'Come hither O king! Yama has been addressed by Viśvá-
157 mitra, O king, regarding thee.' *Yama's servants*, who bore
nooses of serpents, having thus spoken, lead away the prince
158 by force. Yama related Viśvámitra's deed. At that point, how-
ever, his change which resulted from iniquity came to an end.
These were all his states of being which were revealed in sleep;
159 they were all experienced by him during twelve years. When
the twelve years were spent, being brought forcibly by the
160 demons, he saw Yama in bodily shape. Yama addressed the
king, 'This anger of the high-souled Viśvámitra is difficult
161 to be resisted. Kauśika will inflict even death on thy son.
Go thou to the world of men, and undergo the remainder of
thy suffering. When thou art gone there, O supreme king!
162 thou shalt obtain happiness.' And when the twelve years
expired, the king, at the end of his misery, fell from the sky,
being thrust away by Yama's messengers.

163 And when fallen from Yama's world, he awoke through the
agitation of fear, *exclaiming*, "Alas! woe is me!" thinking
of the working of the corrosive substance in his wounds.
164 "In my sleep I have seen grievous woe, the end of which I
do not perceive: but have twelve years, as I have seen in
165 my sleep, gone with me?" he inquired with agitation of the
pukkasas standing there. "No" replied certain of the by-
standers; and others said exactly the same.

166 Then the king grieved at hearing this, sought the gods
for refuge, *ejaculating*, "May the gods bestow blessings on me,
167 on S'aivyá and on my child. Adoration to great Dharma!
Adoration to Kṛishṇa the creator, all-comprising, pure,
168 ancient, and immutable! Adoration to thee, O Vṛihaspati!
and adoration to thee, Indra!"

169 Having uttered this *prayer*, the king employed himself in
the pukkasas' occupation, in fixing the price of corpses, as
if again dead in memory. Filthy, matted-haired, black,

170 armed with a club, despondent was the king. No son had
he, nor wife indeed, in the track of his memory; ruined in
energy was he through the loss of his kingdom; dwelling
then in the burning-ground.

171 To that place came his queen, bewailing, bringing her son
172 dead, for the boy had been bitten by a snake. "Ah my
darling! ah my son, my child!" thus she was oft exclaim-
ing; emaciated, pallid, insane, her hair covered with dust.

The queen spoke.

173 "Alas O king! dost thou not see to-day on earth this
thy child, whom thou didst formerly see playing about, now
bitten by a huge snake and dead?"

174 The king, listening to that her lamentation, hurried *thither*
175 *thinking* "here will be a dead man's blanket." But the king
did not recognise as his wife her, who was weeping sorely,
who worn with his long absence was like a woman in another
176 birth. The princess too seeing him, who formerly had
beautiful locks, *now* with matted curls did not recognise the
177 king, who was like a withered tree. The king seeing the
snake-bitten child, who was characterized with the kingly
178 marks, on the black cloth, fell into a reverie:—"Ah! alas!
to what a state has this child born in the family of some king
179 been brought by malignant Death! For, since I have seen
my child thus lying in his mother's lap, my child Rohitásya
180 with his lotus-like eyes recurs to my memory. Such in-
deed would be my child, *and* of about this age, if dreadful
Death has not made him his thrall."

The queen spoke.

181 "Ah my child! through disregard of some sin this great
and terrible evil has befallen us, the end of which we do not
182 perceive. Ah, my lord king! how dost thou remain placidly
in some place without consoling me who am miserable?
183 Loss of kingdom, forsaking of friends, sale of wife and
child—what has thou not done to the Rájarshi Hariś-c'andra,
O creator?"

184 Hearing this her lament the fallen king, recognising his

185 loved wife and his dead son, exclaimed "Alas! this is indeed my very S'aivyá, this is my child!" and wept consumed
186 with sorrow, and fell into a swoon. She too recognising him fallen into that state, fainted with affliction and sank motion-
187 less to the ground. The king and queen both regaining consciousness together, wailed in deep suffering, oppressed with the load of anguish.

The king spoke.

188 "Alas my child! when I look on thy very young face, with its beautiful eyes, brows, nose and curls, is not my afflicted
189 heart torn asunder? To whom, as he comes to me of himself sweetly babbling, 'Father, dear father,' shall I affectionately exclaim with an embrace, 'My child, my child'?
190 By whose knees shall the yellow dust be brought that shall
191 soil my upper garment, my lap and body? Born of my body and limbs, thou wast the delight of mind and heart to me, who, bad father that I am, sold thee, O my child, like a chattel.
192 After snatching away my large kingdom entire, with its resources and wealth, Fate as a noxious serpent then bit my
193 child. Just gazing on the lotus-face of my son, who has been bitten by the serpent Fate, even I am now blinded
194 by the dire poison." Having thus spoken, incoherent through tears, he took the boy, and embracing him, fell motionless in a swoon.

The queen spoke.

195 "This tiger-like man is known truly by his voice; he has the moon-like mind of a wise man; it is Hariś-c'andra with-
196 out doubt. And his nose is prominent in front and goes downwards; and like opening buds are the teeth of him,
197 the renowned, the high-souled. Wherefore has this king come to the burning-ground to-day?"

Ceasing her grief for her son, she looked at the prostrate
198 king. Agitated, surprised, afflicted, sorely oppressed on account of her husband and son, gazing earnestly, she then saw her husband's abominable staff fit for a low outcaste.

199 Thereupon the long-eyed lady fainted, and gradually regain-
ing consciousness, spoke falteringly :—
200 "Fie on thee, O Fate! most doleful, unruly, abominated, who
hast reduced this god-like king to the position of a low out-
201 caste. Though thou didst make him undergo loss of kingdom,
forsaking of friends and the sale of wife and son, *yet* hast
thou turned the king, after he was parted from us, into this
202 c'aṇḍála. Ah! O king! why dost thou not now raise me,
who am thus afflicted, from the ground and tell me to mount
203 to thy couch? I do not see this day thy regal umbrella, nor
yet thy golden vase, thy chowrie or fan; what is this revolu-
204 tion? He, before whom formerly, when he moved, kings in
the guise of servants freed the earth from dust with their
205 own upper garments,—such having been, he the supreme
king now walks oppressed with grief in the burning-ground,
which is thickly strewn with jars and pots, with skulls fast
fixed therein; where the hair of corpses is concealed by the
206 remains of sacrificial ceremonies and strings; where the
cavities of the dry ground are bedecked with oily exudations;
which is dreadful by reason of the mixing of the marrow and
half-burnt bones with the ashes and charcoal; where the
207 small birds have been scared away by the cries of the
vultures and jackals; which has spread gloom over the
regions of the sky with the colour of the trails of smoke from
208 the funeral piles; where the night-roaming demons are
joyful through the delight of tasting carrion."
209 Thus having spoken the princess embraced the king's neck
and, bearing hundreds of woes and griefs, lamented with sor-
rowful voice,—

The queen spoke.

210 "O king, is it sleep or *waking* truth? Tell me Sir, this
that thou art thinking of: my mind is bewildered indeed.
211 If this be so, O thou conversant with righteousness, there is
no help in righteousness, nor in worship of bráhmans, gods
212 and others, *nor* in protecting the world; there is no *such thing*
as righteousness. Whence are there truth, and candour, and

meekness, in that thou, the devotee of righteousness, hast been
ousted from thy kingdom?"
213 Hearing this her speech, sighing deeply he related in
faltering accents to the slender-limbed lady, how he had
214 become a low outcaste. She also the timid *lady* wept very
long, and sighing deeply, full of grief, told him how her son
had met his death.

The king spoke.

215 "My darling, I choose not to undergo affliction for a long
time, nor is my soul docile, O slender-limbed *lady*. Behold
216 my ill-fortune. If I shall enter the fire, with the permis-
sion of the c'aṇḍála, I shall in another birth go again into
217 bondage to c'aṇḍálas. I shall fall into Naraka, as a worm-
eating insect; into Vaitariṇí* which is slimy with much pus,
218 fat, blood, and sinews. Reaching the Asi-patra wood, I
shall be frightfully cut to pieces; or reaching Mahá-raurava
219 and Raurava I shall be burnt. Surrender of life is the shore
for one sunk in the ocean of grief. I had just one son, who
220 was this boy, to continue my family. He too has sunk
through the violence of the waters of my Fate, which are
very strong. How *shall* I resign my life? I am dependent
221 on others, *and* in a strait. Or, does not a man afflicted with
pain regard evil? There is no such suffering in the brute
222 creation, nor in the Asi-patra forest. Whence is there such
suffering in Vaitariṇí as in the bereavement of a son? I will
223 fall then with my son's body into the blazing fire, O
slender-limbed! Thou must pardon my ill-deeds; and do thou
who hast my permission go to the bráhman's house, O bright
224 smiler! And hearken, O slender-limbed! to my word with
respectful mind. If one makes gifts, if one offers sacrifices,
225 if the gurus are satisfied, there may be union *for me* in an-
other world with my son and with thee. But whence in this
226 world will there be this aim for me? In company with thee
I shall speed happily on in the search for our son, which I
shall make laughingly or somewhat secretly, O bright-smiler.

* The river of Naraka.

227 Thou must pardon at my request all that I have spoken ill;
despise not that bráhman through pride that thou art a
queen; thou must please him with thy utmost efforts, as if
he were thy lord and god, O beautiful *lady!*"

The queen spoke.

228 "I also, O Rájarshi, unable to endure the burden of grief
will assuredly enter the blazing fire with thee here this day."

The birds spoke.

229 Thereupon the king heaping up the funeral pile, placed
his son *thereon;* and then associated with his wife he joined his
230 hands reverently, thinking of the Supreme Soul, S'iva,
Náráyaṇa Hari Vásudeva, the ruler of the gods, who sits in
the cave-like recesses of the heart, *of* Bráhman who is without
beginning or end; of Kṛishṇa, yellow-clad, beautiful.
231 While he was thinking, Indra and all the gods, making
232 Dharma their leader, assembled in haste. Approaching spake
they all—"Ho! O king! hearken, O lord! This is Bráh-
233 man, visible to open sight, and the adorable Dharma himself;
and *here are* all the Sádhyas,* the Maruts,† the Lokapálas,‡
with their vehicles, the Nágas,§ the Siddhas|| and the Gand-
234 harvas,¶ and the Rudras** and the two Aśvins,—these and
and others, many in number, and also Viśvámitra, whom the
235 three worlds could not formerly make a friend. But Viśvá-
mitra desires to proffer thee friendship and good."

He mounted, thereon he met Dharma, and Indra and Viśvámitra.

Dharma spoke.

236 "Be not rash, O king! I Dharma have visited thee, gratified
with thy patience, self-command, truth and other virtues."

* Class of inferior deities.

† Wind-gods.

‡ Guardian-gods of the world.

§ Human-faced serpents of Pátála.

|| Class of demi-gods.

¶ Demi-gods, Indra's celestial musicians.

** Eleven demi-gods (personified roaring of the wind).

Indra spoke.

237 "O virtuous Hariś-c'andra! I Indra have approached nigh
thee; the eternal worlds are won by thee and thy wife and
238 son! Accompanied by thy wife and son, ascend, O king! to
the *third* heaven, which to others is very difficult of attain-
ment, *but* which has been won by thine own deeds."

The birds spoke.

239 Then Indra, the lord, going to the funeral pile, poured
down from the sky a shower of nectar that prevents sudden
240 death, and a very copious shower of flowers, accompanied
with the sound of the heavenly drums, here and there on
241 that closely-gathered assemblage of gods. Then the high-
souled king's son arose, very youthful in body, in per-
242 fect health, placid in his organs and mind. And king
Hariś-c'andra immediately embraced his son; and in pos-
sessing his wife regained his own Fortune. He was decked
243 with heavenly garlands; and was happy, completely satisfied
in heart, and filled with supreme joy.

244 Indra at once re-addressed him. "Accompanied by thy wife
and son, thou shalt gain supreme felicity. Ascend, O vir-
tuous *king*, by the results of thy own actions!"

Hariś-c'andra spoke.

245 "O king of the gods! while unpermitted by my master the
low outcaste, I will not, without having recompensed* him,
ascend to the abode of the gods."

Dharma spoke.

246 "Perceiving this thy affliction that was to be, I myself de-
scended as the low outcaste through an illusion of myself;
and I displayed that inconsiderate conduct."

Indra spoke.

247 Ascend, O Hariś-c'andra, to the supreme abode which is
desired by all mankind on the earth, the abode of men holy in
deed."

Hariś-c'andra spoke.

248 "O king of the gods, adoration to thee! hearken also to this

* For *a-gatvá* read *a-dattvá*?

my speech, that, filled with affection, I speak to thee whose
249 countenance is beautified through benignity. My subjects in
the city of Kośalá* remain with minds sunk in my grief;
how disregarding them shall I now ascend to heaven?
250 The murder of a bráhman, the killing of a guru, the slaughter of cattle, and the slaying of women—equal to these has
been pronounced the great sin *incurred* in the abandonment
251 of one's adherents. Neither in this world nor in the other
do I see happiness for one who abandons an obsequious
252 and innocent adherent, who ought not to be abandoned. If
they go to Svarga in company with me, O lord of the gods!
then I too will go; or *I will go* even to Naraka with them."

Indra spoke.

253 "Many are their merits and sins, various and diverse.
How wilt thou again attain to Svarga which will be enjoyed
by multitudes?"

Hariś-c'andra spoke.

254 "O Indra, by the influence of the householders a king enjoys
his kingdom, and sacrifices with great sacrifices, and works
255 meritorious deeds; and therefore by their influence have I
performed everything; I will not forsake those benefactors
256 in the desire to gain Svarga. Therefore whatever, O lord of
the gods, I have done well, whatever I have given in alms,
whatever sacrifices or prayers I have made, let that be com-
257 mon to them and us. For whatever fruit of my action must
be eaten through long time, let that be *for me* and them together just a single day through thy favour!"

The birds spoke.

258 "So shall it be!" thus having spoken Indra, lord of the
three worlds, and Dharma, and Viśvámitra, Gádhi's son,
259 became propitious in their minds. Indra went from Svarga
to the earth, with a company of ten million heavenly
chariots and addressed the people of Ayodhyá thus, "Ascend
260 ye to heaven." And having heard with affection that
speech of Indra and the king's speech, and having brought

* *I. e.* Ayodhyá.

261 Rohitásya, Viśvámitra himself, great in austerities, with the gods also, the Munis, and the Siddhas, enthroned the king's son in the charming city of Ayodhyá, after enthroning the king.
262 Then all the people, his glad and prosperous friends, with their children servants and wives, ascended to heaven with the king.
263 Those people moved step by step from one heavenly chariot to another. Then king Hariś-c'andra also grew in gladness.
264 The king, attaining unparalleled dignity with the heavenly chariots, sat on the figure of a city which was surrounded with ramparts and walls.

265 Then beholding his prosperity, Uśanas, the eminent spiritual guide of the Daityas, conversant with the meaning and the truth of all the S'ástras, sang a verse there.

S'ukra (Uśanas) spoke.

266 "Like unto Hariś-c'andra there has been no king, nor shall there be. Whoever, when afflicted with his own sufferings
267 listens *to those of others*, may he obtain great happiness! May he who longs for Svarga gain Svarga; may he who longs for a son gain a son; may he who longs for a wife gain a wife; may
268 he who longs for a kingdom gain a kingdom! Ah, the majesty of patience! ah, the great fruit of liberality! since Hariś-c'andra has reached his city and has gained his sovereignty."

The birds spoke.

269 This whole *story of the* deeds of Hariś-c'andra has been declared to thee: hear the remainder of the discourse next,
270 O best of Munis! the outcome of the Rája-súya sacrifice, *which was* the cause of the decay of the earth, and the cause of that outcome, *viz.* the great battle of the Mainá* and Heron.†

* Áḍi, also called S'aráli. The dictionaries all say this bird is *Turdus ginginianus*, which is the old name. It is Jerdon's Bank Maina, *Acridotheres ginginianus*, which is common throughout Upper India, and burrows in the river banks (vol. II, p. 326). Jerdon gives *salik* (śáriká) as the general Bengali name for mainas; but I do not trace either of these two words in his book.

† Vaka. Prof. Monier-Williams called this bird *Ardea nivida*, but I do not find this name in Jerdon. *Bak, bag*, (Bengali) and *baglá* (Hindi) are the general modern names for various kinds of common herons, egrets and

Canto IX.

The Battle of the Mainá and the Heron.

Vaśishṭha, enraged with Viśvámitra for his cruelty to Hariś-c'andra, cursed him to become a heron, and Viśvámitra cursed Vaśishṭha to become a mainá—Both Munis as gigantic birds have a terrible fight, and are at length pacified by Brahmá.

The birds spoke.

1 When Hariś-c'andra had left his kingdom and had gone to
the abode of the thirty gods, there came out from his resi-
2 dence in the water the glorious family priest, Vaśishṭha,
the Muni, who dwelt at the Ganges, at the end of twelve
years; and he heard the whole of the deeds of Viśvámitra,
3 and also the downfall of the noble-dealing king Hariś-
c'andra, and his association with the c'aṇḍála, and his sale
4 of his wife and son. That most illustrious *Muni* having
heard *the story*, being full of affection for the king, grew
wrathful in his dignity against the Ṛishi Viśvámitra.

Vaśishṭha spoke.

5 "It was Viśvámitra who destroyed my hundred sons; yet on
6 that *occasion* I was not so wroth as I am this day, on hear-
ing that this king, who was high-souled, eminent, worshipful
towards the gods and bráhmans, had been ousted from his
7 kingdom. Since that king, truthful, tranquil, devoid of envy
even towards an enemy, faultless also, upright in soul, vigilant,
8 a relier on me, has been reduced to the last extremity together
with his wife dependants and son, has been expelled from
his kingdom by Viśvámitra, and has been greatly worsted,
9 therefore that impious bráhman-hater, uprooted from among

bitterns. The Large Egret (*Herodias alba*, Jerdon), the Smaller Egret (*H. egrettoides*), and the Little Egret (*H. garzetta*) are all white; the Cattle Egret (*Buphus coromandus*) and the Pond Heron, generally known as the Paddy-bird, (*Ardeola leucoptera*), which are most commonly called *bag* and *baglá*, have white bodies (Jerdon, vol. II, pp. 744-751).

the wise, blasted by my curse, the fool, shall be turned into a heron."*

The birds spoke.

10 Hearing the curse, the glorious Viśvámitra likewise,
Kuśika's descendant, inflicted the counter-curse, "Do thou also
11 become a mainá."† Both those most illustrious *sages* were
transformed into birds through their mutual curses, the
glorious Vaśishṭha and Viśvámitra, Kuśika's descendant.
12 Both of them, boundless in might, allying themselves with
other classes *of beings*, fought together, exceedingly exasperat-
13 ed, great in strength and prowess. The Mainá increased in
size to two thousand yojanas; as the Heron, O bráhman,
14 increased to three thousand and ninety. And then those
two, of wide heroism, assailing each other with blows of
15 their wings, created sore fear among the creatures. The
Heron, his eyes swollen with blood, lifting his wings beat
the Mainá; and he also, stretching out his neck, struck the
16 Heron with his feet. Overthrown by the wind from their
wings, mountains fell down on the earth; and struck by the
17 downfall of the mountains the earth quaked; and the earth,
as it quaked, caused the waters of the seas to swell up, and
reeled over on one side, turning towards the descent to Pátála.
18 Living beings perished, some by the fall of the mountains,
others by the waters of the seas, others through the quaking
19 of the earth. Thus everything being terrified was turned
into lamentation, bereft of consciousness; the world was
greatly agitated, and its countries were thrown into confusion,
20 *people exclaiming* "Ah, my child! ah my beloved child! come,
here I am fixed"—"ah my darling *wife!*"—"my beloved
husband!"—"this rock is falling, escape quickly."
21 Then, when the world was thus distressed *and* averted in
terror, surrounded by all the gods, advanced the fore-father,
22 the lord of the universe, and replied to both those *combatants*
who were violently enraged—"Let this your strife cease, and

* See note †, p. 58.

† See note *, p. 58.

let the worlds recover their stability!" Although they heard
23 the words of Brahmá, whose birth is inscrutable, yet both
of them, filled with anger and fury *still* fought, and did not
desist.

24 Thereupon the fore-father, the god, seeing the destruction
of the worlds, and desiring the welfare of both of them, dis-
25 sipated their brute-nature; and the god, the lord of creation,
addressed them both, clothed in their former bodies, Vaśishṭha
and the noble descendant of Kuśika, the state of darkness
having been dispelled:—

26 "Stay thou, my beloved Vaśishṭha, and thou, most virtuous
Kauśika, this contest that, while involved in the state of
27 darkness, ye desire to carry on. This outcome of the Rája-
súya sacrifice of king Hariś-c'andra, and this war between
28 you two, are causing the earth to waste away. Nor moreover
does that best of the Kauśikas offend against that king, *for*
since he has caused him to attain to Svarga, O bráhman! he
29 occupies the position of a benefactor. Do ye both, the
creators of obstacles to *your* austerities, who have fallen into
subjection to lust and anger, cease; for worthy *are your*
prayers, *and* ample *is your* power."

30 Thus admonished by him, both then grew ashamed, and
31 embracing lovingly forgave each other. Thereupon, hymned
by the gods, Brahmá departed to his own world, and Vaśishṭha
to his own place, and Kauśika also to his own hermitage.

32 Those mortals, who shall fittingly relate and who shall fit-
tingly hear this battle of the Mainá and the Heron, and the
33 story of Hariś-c'andra, what they hear shall verily dispel
their sins; nor shall they ever encounter antagonistic
duties.

Canto X.

Conversation between a father and son.

Jaimini asks the Birds for instruction how living beings come into existence and die, and how the fœtus lives and develops—The Birds repeat the explanation that a wise young brahman Sumati, who was nick-named Jaḍa because of his apparent stupidity, but who remembered his former existences, gave his father—He explains how death occurs, and describes the after-existences through which a living being passes according as it has lived well or ill—He describes incidentally the hell Raurava.*

Jaimini spoke.

1 Declare my doubt, when I enquire, O powerful bráhmans,
wherein the appearance and disappearance of living beings
2 consist. How is an animal produced? How too does it
develop? How, again, is it placed when contained within the
3 womb, pressed upon by the limbs? How, again, when it has
issued from the womb, does it grow? And how at the moment
4 of departure is it deprived of the sentient state? Every dead
person also experiences *the results of* both his good and his bad
deeds, and how then do those *deeds* bring about† their results to
5 him? Why does the fœtus not become digested there in the
stomach, as if it were converted into a morsel of food? In the
female's belly, where the various foods consumed are digested
although highly indigestible, how is it that the little animal
6 is not digested there? Declare all this to me, free from
doubtful terms; this very matter is a transcendant mystery,
where men do err.

The birds spoke.

7 Unparalleled is this burdensome question that thou hast
propounded to us; it is difficult to be imagined, touching *as
it does* the existence and death of all living beings. Listen to
8 it, Sir! as a son, most thoroughly righteous, named Sumati,‡
once declared it to his father.

* See Canto XIV.

† For *sampádayanti* read *sampádayatí* (neuter, dual, present participle)?

‡ For *Samatir* read *Sumatir*.

9 A certain highly intelligent bráhman of Bhṛigu's line ad-
dressed his son Sumati who had undergone his initiation, and
10 who was tranquil, and in appearance stupid. "Study the
Vedas, O Sumati, in order from the beginning, be zealous in
obedience to thy guru, make thy food of victuals collected by
11 begging. After that taking upon thee the duties of a house-
holder, and performing the chiefest sacrifices, beget the
12 desired offspring. Next resort to the forest, and then living
in the forest, my son, be a wandering ascetic,* free from
family ties. Thus shalt thou attain that highest object of
religious knowledge, *the Supreme Being*, reaching which thou
shalt not grieve."

The birds spoke.

13 Thus frequently counselled, he through his stupidity never
replied: still the father again and again repeatedly admonish-
14 ed him affectionately. He thus frequently exhorted by his
father, through paternal love, alluringly and in pleasant
terms, spoke thns at length with a laugh:—

15 "Father! I have repeatedly studied this that thou enjoinest
me to-day, the other S'ástras also, and the various mechanical
16 arts. Ten thousand births and more have passed into my
memory; disgusts and gratifications have sported in the
17 decay and the rise of my mind. I have seen partings and
meetings among enemies, friends and wives; I have seen
mothers of various kinds, and fathers of various kinds also.
18 I have tasted joys and sorrows thousands of times. Many
19 kinsmen have I gained, and fathers of divers kinds. I have
also dwelt in women's wombs, slimy with ordure and urine;
and thousands of times have the pains of sicknesses also taken
20 grievous hold of me. Many sufferings have I endured in
my stomach in childhood, and youth and old age: all those do
21 I remember. *I have been begotten* of bráhmans, kshatriyas
and vaiśyas, and even śúdras; and again of cattle and insects,
22 of deer and birds. I have been born moreover in the houses
of kings' dependants, and of kings resplendent in battle, and

* For *parivráṭa* read *parivráṇ*.

23 in thy dwelling also. I have been a servant and a slave
frequently to men. I have been a master and a lord, and a
24 poor man as well. I have given blows, and I have received
blows from others, and my own blows have procured me
blows in return. Others have given me gifts, and I have given
25 gifts to others many a time. I have been gratified also by
the deeds of father, mother, friend, brother, wife and other
relatives. And often have I fallen into misery with my face
26 washed with tears. Whilst thus wandering, O father, in
the crowded circle of mundane existence, I have gained this
knowledge, which procures final emancipation from existence.
27 That being known, all this body of religious rites, called
Ṛic' Yajus and Sáman, is worthless, *and* does not appear fit-
28 tingly to me. Of what use consequently are the Vedas to
me, who am mature in wisdom, satiated with the knowledge
29 of the gurus, void of desires, virtuous in soul? I will gain,
O bráhman! the highest seat, that Supreme Soul, which is
exempt from the qualities of the sixfold actions, pain, pleasure,
30 joy, and love. Hence, O father, I will abandon this well-known
series of pains which is tainted by love, joy, fear, inquietude,
anger, resentment and old age, and which is hampered with
31 hundreds of nooses in close contact ensnaring one's own self as
game, and I will depart. Does not the duty enjoined by
the three Vedas, which abounds in unrighteousness,* resemble
the result of sin?"

The birds spoke.

32 Hearing that his declaration, which was interrupted by joy
and surprise, the eminent father with gladsome mind address-
ed his son.

The father spoke.

33 "What is this thou sayest, my son? Whence arose thy
wisdom? How came thy stupidity before, and thy awakening
34 now? Is this a curse-wrought change inflicted on thee by a
Muni or god, since thy wisdom which was obscured has
become manifest?"

* A pun on *dharma* and *a-dharma*. Prof. Monier-Williams gives *trayí-dharma* as masc. only.

The son spoke.

35 "Listen, father, how this happened to me, entailing pleasure
and pain *on me*, and who I was in another birth, and what
is beyond myself.
36 I was formerly a bráhman, my soul *fixed* on the Supreme
Being; I attained the highest perfection in the considera-
tion of the knowledge of the Supreme Being. While con-
37 tinually occupied in devotion, through constant application
to study, through association with the good, through my
own natural disposition, through deliberation, behaviour and
38 purification, while occupying myself in this indeed I ex-
perienced the sublimest joy at all times, and I gained the
position of a spiritual guide, the most successful remover of
39 the doubts of disciples. A long while afterwards I attained
absolute perfection; and my good disposition warped by
40 ignorance fell into calamity through carelessness. Begin-
ning from the time of my departure I had no failure of
memory, until a year had passed and had returned to my
41 recollection of my births. Being such, I, keeping my organs
under control, will strive indeed, O father, by means of that
my former study, so to act that I may not have another
42 existence. For this is the result of learning and liberality
that I remember *former* existences; this indeed is not obtained,
O father, by men who apply themselves to the duty enjoined
43 by the three Vedas. Being such I, from my former hermitage
indeed, recurring to the duty of perfection, will attain to
devotion to one object and will strive for the final emancipa-
44 tion of my soul. Declare thou then, Sir! what is perplexing
in thy heart: and to this extent let me, bringing the joy,
discharge my debt."

The birds spoke.

45 Thereupon the father spoke to his son that speech of a man of faith, which relates to the perfection of mundane existence, and which *we* have been asked by thee, Sir.

The son spoke.

46 "Listen, O father, how I have often perceived the truth; the circle of mundane existence is ever young, the duration of

47 which is not known. I then tell thee the whole, with thy
permission, O father, commencing from the period of depar-
ture, as no one else will tell thee.

48 "Hot moisture is excited in the body; it is set in motion by
a strong vital air; blazing without fuel it pierces the sites of
49 the vital organs. And then the vital air, called Udána, passes
upwards, impeding the downward course of the water and
food consumed.

50 "Hence he, who has offered presents of water and has given
51 food and drink, obtains joy therefrom in adversity. He also,
who has bestowed food with a mind purified by faith, is then
52 satisfied even without food. He, who has not spoken un-
truth, nor caused a breach of amity, a faithful believer,
53 meets a happy death. Men who have been intent on the
worship of the gods and bráhmans, and who are unspiteful,*
54 fair, charitable, shamefast, die happily. He who would not
forsake righteousness through lust, or anger or hatred, who
acts up to his words and is gentle, meets a happy death.
55 Men who do not give away water, nor give away food, endure
then, on the approach of death, burning thirst and hunger.
56 Those who give away fuel overcome cold; those who give
away sandal *overcome* heat; and those who do not inflict dis-
57 tress *overcome* the woeful life-ending pang. Those who cause
error and ignorance suffer grievous terror; base men are op-
58 pressed with intense pains. A false witness, a liar, and he
who teaches evil, they all and also blasphemers of the
Vedas die in delusion.

59 "Then Yama's officers, terrific, foul-smelling, carrying
hammers and maces, hard-hearted, approach the false man.
60 When they meet his eyesight, trembling seizes him, and he
bewails without ceasing his brother, mother, and children.
61 His voice seems thick, O father! *and* monotonous; and his
sight wanders through terror; and his mouth grows dry with
62 his breathing; his breathing grows loud; his sight fails; next
63 he is pervaded with pains; then he quits the body. Preceded
by the vital airs he assumes another body, similar to the

* For *anusúyavah* read *an-asúyavah*

former, produced by the actions of the former, intended for
chastisement, born of no mother and father, like the previous
one, with the periods of life and death conformable thereto.
64 "Thereupon Yama's messenger speedily binds him with
cruel fetters; drags him, bewildered as he is with the blows
65 of his staff, to the southern region. And so, to some place
which is rough with kuśa grass, thorns, ant-hills, stakes,
and stones, where a fire is raging, which abounds in hundreds
66 of holes, and which is heated by the blazing sun, which is
scorched by his rays, he is haled by Yama's emissaries, terrible
67 through their ghastly cries. Being dragged about by those
fearful *servants*, being eaten by hundreds of she-jackals, he,
the evil-doer, proceeds by an awful road to Yama's abode.
68 Men who give umbrellas and shoes, and who bestow garments,
those men pass along that road in ease; and so also do those
69 who give away food. Thus encountering afflictions, the man
oppressed with sin is led in twelve days to the city of king
Yama.

70 "While the body is being burnt, he experiences a great
burning; also while it is being beaten, and while it is being
71 divided into pieces, terrible agony. While *the body* is being
wetted a living being endures a very long pain, even while
it is inhabiting another body, through the consequences of
72 its own acts. There the deceased feeds on the water that his
relatives offer together with the sesamum seed and the cake
73 that they offer. The anointing with oil by relations, and the
kneading of the limbs that *they perform*,—a living being is
74 nourished thereby, and by what his relations* eat. A living
being does not encounter excessive affliction on the earth
through his deceased relatives; and so when dead he is
nourished by his relatives who make gifts.

75 "Being led off he sees his own abode for twelve days and he
enjoys the water, cake &c. that are offered on the earth.
76 After twelve days, the man who is being carried off, next sees
Yama's city, awful, made of iron, terrible in appearance.
77 Immediately he has gone *there* he beholds Yama, with fiery

* For *sa bándhaváḥ* read *sva-bándhaváḥ* ?

red eyes, like to a mass of broken collyrium; in the midst of
78 Death, the destroyer Time and others; his mouth gaping with
projecting teeth, his countenance dreadful with frowns; a lord,
surrounded by hundreds of deformed, horrible and crooked
79 diseases; busy in *awarding* punishment, with long arms, a
noose in his hand, very formidable. Then the living being
80 takes the happy or miserable course decreed by him. But
the false witness goes to Raurava, and the man who is untruthful. Listen while I describe the nature of that Raurava.

81 "Raurava* is in truth two thousand yojanas in size. Then
there is a chasm, just knee-deep, very difficult to pass over:
82 in it charcoal is heaped up and made level with the ground.
It burns vehemently with its glowing surface of kindled
83 charcoal. In its midst Yama's servitors cast the evil-doer.
84 He runs *about* there, being burnt by the violent flame; and
at each step, his foot is wasted and consumed again *and again;*
day and night he continues on the move.

85 "When he has thus passed over a thousand yojanas he is
released, and then enters another similar *hell* Niraya,† to
86 purge away his sins. Afterwards when he has passed
through all *the hells*, the sinner enters the brute creation,
among worms, insects and birds; among carnivorous animals;
87 among mosquitoes and such like. After having been born
among elephants, trees and such like, among cattle, and
among horses also; and among other evil and noxious crea-
88 tures; he attains humanity, and is born a man, contemptible
as a hunch-back or a dwarf; among c'aṇḍálas, pukkasas and
89 such-like castes; and then accompanied by the remainder of
his sin and merit, he *enters* the castes in ascending order,
90 such as súdras, vaiśyas, kings and so on; also the position
of bráhmans, the gods and Indra. Sometimes in descending
order, and thus evil-doers fall headlong into the hells.

91 "What happens to righteous-doers, listen while I declare
that. They take the holy course decreed by Yama. Bands
92 of Gandharvas singing, bevies of Apsarases dancing, brilliant

* Terrible.

† Devoid of happiness.

with various celestial garlands, bedecked with strings of pearls
93 and anklets and *gay with* music,* and heavenly chariots
beyond compare go forth quickly *to them.* And when
they descend therefrom, they are born in the family of
94 kings and other high-souled men: there observing upright
conduct, they experience vigorous† pleasures, and afterwards
95 they go upwards; and otherwise, when they take the down-
ward *path*, they become men as before.

"This has all been declared to thee, how a living being perishes. Next listen, O Brahmarshi, how the fœtus begins."

Canto XI.

Conversation between the father and son (continued).

Sumati (Jaḍa) explains how living beings are conceived and born, and mentions the evils of all existence.

The son spoke.

1 "Now human impregnation‡ of women is a seed sown in
darkness; immediately it is discharged it sets out from
2 Naraka or Svarga. Dominated thereby the two seeds attain
firmness, O father! and next the character of a speck—of a
3 globule—of a ball of flesh. As there may be a minute seed in
the ball of flesh, so it is called a germ. So the five limbs up-
4 grow according to their parts; and the minor limbs also, the
fingers, the eyes, the nose, the mouth, and the ears, grow out of
the limbs; similarly the nails and other *features grow* out of
5 them. In the skin is developed the hair of the body, and
afterwards the hair of the head. The womb verily increases
6 in size equally with it. Just as the cocoa-nut enlarges together
with its shell, so it grows in size. The womb is situated with
7 its mouth downwards. But at the bottom *of the womb the fœtus*
develops, placing its hands on either side of the knees: and
its thumbs are placed upon the knees, and its finger in
8 front of them; behind the knees are the eyes, and between

* For *-śobhitáni* read *-śobhitá?*

† *Ugra;* or noble.

‡ For *mishekam mánavam* read *nisheko mánavaḥ?*

the knees is the nose; and the buttocks rest on the heels; the arms and legs lie outside.

9 "In this way gradually grows the human being, when
contained in a woman's womb: in the womb of other crea-
10 tures, the position of the fœtus corresponds to its form. The
gastric fluid* renders it firm. It lives on the food and drink
taken by its mother. Thus the gestation of a living creature is
11 meritorious, and constitutes a means of *obtaining* merit. Also
the cord, which is called Ápyáyaní, is fixed in its navel, and it
12 becomes fixed in the belly of women. As women's food and
drink penetrate into their womb, the fœtus increases in size,
its body being nourished thereby.

13 "Numerous matters of its transmigrations occur to its
memory; hence distressed on this side and on that it becomes
14 dispirited, *thinking*, 'Never again will I thus act, when once
I am delivered from this womb; assuredly I will so strive
15 that I do not *again* undergo conception.' Thus it meditates,
recollecting the hundreds of pains attending existence, which
have been experienced aforetime, and which spring from
destiny.

16 "Afterwards in the course of time the fœtus turns round
with its face downwards, since it is born in the ninth or tenth
17 month. While it is being expelled, it is pained by the wind
of the prajápatis, and it is expelled wailing, being pained at
18 heart by its sufferings. And when expelled from the belly, it
falls into an intolerable swoon; and it gains consciousness
19 when it comes into contact with the air. Thereupon Vishnu's
magical power, which effaces consciousness, assails it; its
soul being stupefied thereby, it loses its knowledge.

20 "Thereafter the human being, bereft of knowledge, enters
on childhood; and afterwards on boyhood, youth and mature
21 age; and again the human being undergoes death, and so
birth. Hence he revolves in this round of mundane existence,
like the jar and rope at a well.

22 "Sometimes a man reaches Svarga, sometimes Niraya; and
23 sometimes the dead man goes to Naraka and Svarga. Some-

* *Agni;* or, the digestive faculty.

times indeed re-born here, he obtains *the consequences of* his
own actions; and sometimes the man who has consumed *the*
consequences of his actions, passes at death with a very small
24 *remainder*. And hence he is sometimes born here with a
scanty stock of good and evil, having almost consumed them
25 in heaven* and in hell,† O bráhman! In the hells there is
this very great suffering that the dwellers in Svarga are
visible *thence*, O father; and the denizens of hell rejoice,‡
as they are hurled down. Even in Svarga there is an
26 unparalleled pain in that from the very time of ascension
there this *thought* revolves in one's mind, 'I shall fall *from*
27 *hence*': and from viewing the hells great suffering is felt;
day and night one is cheerless, *thinking* 'I shall go this
28 course.' One who is being born has great suffering in re-
maining in the womb; and after birth one has suffering in
childhood and old age. The connexion also between desire
29 envy and anger is grievous to bear in youth; and old age is
almost all suffering; the heaviest suffering lies in death.
30 Both for him who is borne off by Yama's messengers, and
for him who is hurled down to the hells, there *are* again
destined both conception, and birth, death and hell.
31 "So in this round of mundane existence creatures revolve
about, like the jar and rope at the well; and having been
bound with the fetters of nature, they are bound repeatedly.
32 No pleasure is there a whit, O father, in this world crowded
with hundreds of pains; why then should I in striving for
emancipation from existence observe the three branches of
religion?"

CANTO XII.

Jaḍa describes the Hells Mahá-raurava, Tamas, Nikṛintana, Apratishṭha, Asi-patra-vana, and Tapta-kumbha to his father.

The father spoke.

1 "Good, my son! thou hast declared the deepest obscurity of
mundane existence, relying on the great fruit that grows
2 from the bestowal of knowledge. Therein thou hast verily

* Svar-loka. † Naraka. ‡ For *modante* read *sídante*?

described the Rauravas as well as all the Narakas; tell me of them at length, O mighty in intellect!"

The son spoke.

3 "I have described to thee first the hell Raurava, now listen
to *the description of* the hell named Mahá-raurava,* O father!
4 There for seven times five thousand yojanas all around the
5 earth is made of copper; beneath it† is fire. Heated by the heat
thereof the whole region shines with a light equal to that of
the rising moon, most intensely severe to sight touch and the
6 other *sensations.* There the evil-doer is deposited, bound hand
and foot, by Yama's servants; he moves rolling about in the
7 midst. Preyed upon by crows, herons, wolves, and owls,
scorpions, and mosquitoes, and vultures he is speedily drag-
8 ged out into the road. Burnt and confounded, he exclaims
repeatedly, "Father! Mother! Brother! Dear one!" Full of
9 fear he can get no repose. In this manner therefore emanci-
pation from existence is attained to by violent men, who evil-
minded have committed sin, in ten thousand times ten
thousand years.

10 "Moreover *there is* another *hell* named Tamas;‡ it is bitterly
cold naturally; it is as long as Mahá-raurava, and is enveloped
11 in darkness. There the men, afflicted with the cold, running
about in the awful darkness, encounter *one another* and seek
12 refuge clasping one another. And their teeth adhere together,
chattering with pain through the cold; there are also other
13 plagues the strongest of which are hunger and thirst. A cut-
ting wind, laden with particles of snow, pierces their bones;
pressed with hunger, they feed on the marrow and blood that
14 trickle down therefrom. Constantly licking, they whirl about
in mutual contact. So there in Tamas very great affliction is
15 indeed *endured* by human beings, until, O most worthy
bráhman! their sins are completely consumed.

"Next there is another notable hell, known as Nikṛintana.§
16 In it potter's wheels revolve incessantly, O father! Human

* Very terrible.

† For *tasya* read *tasyá?*

‡ Darkness.

§ Cutting off.

beings are mounted thereon and are cut by the string of Fate
17 which is borne on the fingers of Yama's servant, from the
sole of the foot to the head; and these men do not lose their life
18 *thereby*, most virtuous bráhman! and their portions severed
in hundreds reunite. In this way sinners are cut in sunder
19 during thousands of years, until indeed the whole of their
sins are consumed.

20 "Listen also while I speak of the hell A-pratishṭha, the
occupants of which hell undergo intolerable pain. Those
wheels are there indeed, and jar and well-ropes on the other
21 side, which have been constituted causes of pain to men who
engage in sin. Some human beings mounted on the wheels
22 whirl around there; for thousands of years no other condi-
tion is theirs; and *then* another man is bound to the jar and
23 well-rope, as the jar in the water. Human beings whirl
around, continually spitting out blood, with blood pouring
24 from their faces, *and* with eyes streaming with tears. They
are visited with pains that are beyond endurance by living
creatures.

25 "Hear also of another hell called Asi-patra-vana;* which
has the ground covered with blazing fire for a thousand
yojanas, where they are grievously scorched by the very
26 fierce vehement beams of the sun. The living beings that
inhabit the hell are ever falling down there. In the midst
27 thereof appears a charming forest with moist leaves. The
leaves there are sword-blades, O most virtuous bráhman!
28 Myriads† of powerful black dogs also bark there, with long
29 muzzles, with large teeth, formidable as tigers. Then gazing
at that forest before them, with its cool shades, the living
beings hasten thither, oppressed with raging thirst, crying 'Ah
30 mother! ah dear one!' in deepest woe; their feet burnt by the
fire lambent on the ground. When they wend there, a wind
31 blows, that hurls down the sword-leaves, and so casts the
swords down upon them. Thereat they fall to the earth into
32 a mass of blazing fire, which has pervaded the entire surface

* Sword-leaf-forest.

† For *ayuta-śobhitáḥ* read *ayutáśo 'sitáḥ*?

of the ground, and is constantly licking in other directions.
33 Thereupon the terrific dogs quickly rend many limbs from
the bodies of those wailing ones. I have described this
Asi-patra-vana to thee, dear father!
34 "Next learn of me about the very dreadful Tapta-kumbha.*
On all sides heated pitchers are surrounded with the flames
35 of fire, *and* are filled with oil iron and powder which boil over
on to the heaps of blazing fire. Into them the workers of
36 iniquity are cast head-long by Yama's servants.† They are
boiled, *and* foul the water with the marrow that oozes from
their bursting limbs. Terrible vultures pulling them out
37 fracture the eye-bones of their bursting skulls; again they are
dropped into the same *pitchers* by the impetuous *birds*; again
38 they become united with the liquefied heads, limbs, sinews,
flesh, skin and bones, by means of the oil in the seething vessel.
Then being quickly and vigorously stirred up by Yama's ser-
39 vants with a spoon, the sinners are churned up in the whirling
pool of copious oil. Such is the Tapta-kumbha that I have
fully described to thee, O father!"

CANTO XIII.

Conversation between the father and son (continued).

Sumati relates an incident in one of the periods he spent in hell—King Vipaś-c'it comes there and asks why, in spite of a righteous life, he was condemned there.

The son spoke.

1 Now I was born in a Vaiśya's family in the seventh life
that preceded my present one. Once upon a time I obstructed
2 the cattle at their drinking. In consequence of that act I
was consigned to a very terrible hell, fearful with flames of
3 fire, infested with birds with iron beaks, muddy by reason of
the streams of blood *that flowed* from limbs crushed by
machines, pervaded with the sound of *blood* pouring down
from sinners who are being cut asunder. When cast down

* Burning-pitcher. † For *yámyaḥ* read *yámyaiḥ*.

4 there I spent a hundred years and more, scorched by the
intense heat, and burning with thirst.
5 On a sudden a wind blew on me there, bringing gladness, de-
liciously cool, issuing from out of a pitcher of meal and sand.*
6 Through contact with it all the men were relieved of their
torments, and I too gained a bliss supreme, such as the celes-
7 tial beings enjoy in Svarga. And with eyes fixed in a wide
gaze of joy, *in wonder at* what this was, we saw at hand a
8 peerless perfect man; and Yama's dire servant, staff in hand,
like Indra's thunderbolt, *was* showing the path in front, and
9 a voice *came* saying "come hither!" Then that man seeing
the hell filled with hundreds of tortures, moved with com-
passion, addressed that servant of Yama.

The man spoke.

10 "Ho! servant of Yama! say, what sin have I committed,
for which I have incurred this deepest hell, frightful for its
11 torments? Known as Vipaś-c'it, I was born in the family of
the Janakas, in the country of Videha, in very truth a guar-
12 dian of men. I sacrificed with many sacrifices; I protected
the earth with uprightness; nor did I let fighting rage; no
13 guest departed with averted countenance; nor did I offend
the pitṛis, the gods, the ṛishis or my servants; nor did I covet
other men's wives, or wealth, or aught else belonging to them.
14 At the moon's changes the pitṛis, on *other* lunar days the
15 gods, volnntarily approached mankind† as cows a pool. The
two religious duties, both sacrifice and meritorious work,
perish inasmuch as the performers of domestic sacrifices depart
16 sighing with averted faces. The merit amassed in seven lives
is dissipated by the sighing of the pitṛis; the sighing assuredly
destroys the destiny that springs from three lives. Hence
17 I was ever indeed kindly disposed to what concerned the gods
and the pitṛis; being such, how have I incurred this very
terrible hell?"

* Or, camphor. † Purusha.

CANTO XIV.

Jaḍa's narrative (continued)—The conversation with Yama's officer.*

Yama's officer tells king Vipaś-c'it why he was condemned to hell—He explains to him the nature and results of good and evil deeds generally, and mentions at great length the punishments awarded to various special sins.

The son spoke.

1 Thus interrogated then by that high-souled *king* in our hearing, Yama's officer, though dreadful, with modest speech replied.

Yama's officer spoke.

2 "Mahárájá! it is even as thou hast said, undoubtedly.
Nevertheless thou didst commit, Sir! a very trifling misdeed;
3 I will recall it to thy mind. The wife whom thou hadst, a
princess of Vidarbha, named Pívarí,—her season of aptitude
for sexual intercourse was formerly rendered barren by thee,
4 who wast enamoured of the resplendent Kaikeyí; hence for
the transgression in the matter of her season thou hast incur-
5 red, Sir! a deadful hell such as this. As the Fire expects
the fall of the liquid butter at the time of the Homa oblation,
even so does Brahmá expect the deposit of seed at the
6 approved season. A righteous man who disregarding that
season, may become absorbed in objects of desire, would still
incur sin by reason of the debt due to his ancestors and
7 would fall into hell. Such indeed was thy sin; naught
else is found; come then! go, O king, to the enjoyment of thy
meritorious acts."

The king spoke.

8 "I will go, O servant of the god, where thou shalt lead me.
Something I ask, deign to declare it to me aright. These
9 crows with adamant beaks are tearing out men's eyes; and
these *men* are having their eyes renewed again and again.
10 And what deed have they done? Explain this abominable
thing. Likewise they are tearing out the tongue from these

* The 'Stupid one,' Sumati's nickname.

11 *other men* as it is being reproduced anew. Why are these
grievously afflicted men. torn with a saw? *Why* are these
other men, immersed in oil, boiled among meal and sand?
12 And these *other men* are dragged about by iron-beaked
birds; say, of what kind are they, screaming with loud
cries through the pain caused by the loosened bodily bands.
13 Pained by the wounds in every limb, why are these men, who
have wrought iniquity, struck by the onslaught of the iron
14 beaks day and night. Tell me without reservation, through
what maturing of their acts are these and other torments
seen among sinners."

Yama's officer spoke.

15 "Since thou askest me, O king, concerning the rise of the
fruits of sinful actions, I will tell thee that succinctly *and*
16 correctly. A man verily attains merit and demerit in regular
order; and his sin or his merit diminishes as he consumes it.
17 But no human action, whether virtuous or sinful, quickly
cleanses except by consumption. Diminution arises through
18 consumption. And he abandons merit and demerit through
consuming it; hearken to me! From famine indeed to famine,
19 from affliction to affliction, from fear to fear go needy sin-
ners, more dead than the dead. A manifold course do
20 creatures take through the fetters of their actions. From
festival to festival, from Svarga to Svarga, from happiness to
happiness go the faithful, and the peaceful, the rich, *and* the
21 doers of good. But sinners, when slain by sin, encounter
perils from beasts of prey and elephants, terrors from snakes
22 and thieves; what surpasses this? *Decked* with fragrant
garlands, *clad* in fine apparel, *enjoying* beautiful carriages
dwellings and food, those who are praised ever go to sacred
groves with their meritorious deeds.

23 "Thus men's merit and demerit are amassed in the sum of
many hundreds of thousands of lives: they spring from the
24 germs of pleasure and pain. For as the seed, O king, awaits
the water, so do merit and demerit await him who acts
25 otherwise than at the right time and place. A trifling sin
committed by a man, when it reaches the place and time,

inflicts the pain produced by a thorn, when the foot is planted
26 down *heedlessly*. Then it inflicts the acuter severe pain that
is caused by pins and wedges, and likewise scarcely endurable
27 headaches and other *pains*. It causes *the pains engendered*
by eating unwholesome *things*, by cold, heat, fatigue, inflamma-
tion and such like. Moreover sins have regard to one another
28 amid the confluence of their results. In this way heinous
sins *have regard to* the deteriorated state of protracted
illness, &c ; and *they* verily *tend* to the consequences produced
by weapons, fire, calamity, pain, imprisonment, and so forth.
29 A trifling good deed confers at once a pleasing fragrance, or
30 touch, or sound, taste, or shape ; more marked likewise after
a long time, and great when arising at the proper period.
And in this way pleasures and pains spring indeed out of good
31 and bad actions. *A man* stays here consuming the produc-
tions of numerous mundane existences. And the results of
knowledge or ignorance are checked by race and country,
32 and remain there united merely by outward sign to the soul.
"Never and nowhere doth the man exist who doeth not a
33 wicked or holy act in body, mind, *or* speech. Whatever a man
receives, whether pain or pleasure, whether great or insig-
34 nificant, it produces a changed condition of the mind; by so
much either his virtue, or on the other hand his sin, *gradually*
35 diminishes by consumption, just like food that is being eaten.
In this way these men, dwelling within hell, diminish *their*
36 awful heinous sins by torments day and night. Likewise, O
king, they consume their virtues in the company of the im-
37 mortals in Svarga with the songs and other *joys* of the
Gandharvas, Siddhas and Apsarases. In the condition of a
god, and a human being, and a brute creature, one con-
38 sumes good or evil, arising from virtue or sin, *and* characterized
by pleasure or pain.

"What thou enquirest about of me, O king! namely 'Of what particular sins are the tortures of wicked-doers the consequences?' that I will declare to thee in full detail.

39 "*When* vile covetous men have gazed on others' wives and
40 on others' goods with evil eye and evil mind, these birds

with adamant beaks tear out their eyes; and they have their
41 eyes reproduced continually. Moreover during as many twink-
lings of the eyes as these men have committed the sin, so many
thousands of years they undergo the eye-torture.

42 "Those men who have given instruction in wicked S'ástras,
and those who have advised *such instruction*, for the purpose of
43 completely destroying the sight even of their enemies; those
who have repeated the S'ástra improperly; those who have
given utterance to an evil word; those who have blasphemed
the Veda, the gods, the dvijas and their guru; for so
44 many years these very terrible *birds* with adamant beaks
tear out those men's very tongues as they are continually
reproduced.

45 "Also base men, who have caused dissension among friends,
or dissension between a father and his son and relations,
between a sacrificer and a spiritual preceptor, between
46 a mother and her son who is her companion, and between
wife and husband,—see! these *men* who are such are torn with
a saw, O king!

47 "Also those who cause pain to others; and those who forbid
joyousness; and *those* who deprive *others* of fans, breezy places,
48 sandal, and uśír grass;* and base men who have inflicted
suffering on innocent men at life's end,—these participators
in sin, who are such, are placed within meal and sand.

49 "Moreover the man who eats another's s'ráddha, when
invited by the other to a ceremony either to the gods or to the
pitṛis, he is rent in twain by birds.

50 "But whoever lacerates the vitals of good men with wicked
words, these birds unchecked continually strike him.

51 "And whoever indulges in backbiting, dissembling in
speech, dissembling in mind, his tongue is assuredly torn in
twain thus by sharp razors.

* *Andropogon muricatus*, Roxburgh; the modern *khas-khas*. The roots, when dry, and then gently moistened, emit a pleasant fragrance; they are employed to make large fans; and also screens, which are placed before doors and windows, and which being kept moist during the hot winds render the air that passes through them cool and fragrant (Roxb. p. 89).

52 "Whoever, puffed up, show contempt towards their parents and gurus—these *men*, who are such, are plunged head foremost into a pit *reeking* with pus, ordure and urine.

53 "Those who eat, while the gods, guests and living beings, dependants and visitors, and also the pitṛis, the fire and birds
54 are left unfed; those evil men feed on carrion and exudations, and they become Súc'i-mukha birds,* as large as mountains. Behold! these are men of that kind.

55 "But those who feed a bráhman or a man of another caste in one company disagreeably on earth,—those men, like these persons, feed on ordure.

56 "Whoever eat their own food neglecting a man, who has gone forth in company with them, and who being destitute seeks wealth,—these *men*, who are such, feed on phlegm.

57 "Those men who, without washing their hands and mouth after meals, O king! have touched cattle, bráhmans and the fire,—these hands of theirs placed in fire-pots are licked repeatedly.

58 "But those men who, without washing their hands and mouth after meals, have gazed longingly at the sun, moon and stars,—in their eyes Yama's servants place fire and augment it.

59 "Moreover whatever men have touched cattle, fire, their mother, a bráhman, their eldest brother, father, sister,
60 daughter-in-law, their gurus and the aged with their feet, they stand mid piles of charcoal, with their feet bound with red-hot iron fetters, enduring burning up to the knees.

61 "Whoever have eaten in an unhallowed manner milk, khichree, goat's flesh, and things offered as food to the gods,—
62 the eyes of those sinners, as they *lie* hurled to the ground gazing with starting eyes, are torn out, see! from their faces by Yama's servants with pincers.

* The dictionaries do not say what bird this is. I would suggest from the meaning of the word, that it means a Honey-Sucker (the commonest species of which is the Purple Honey-Sucker, *Arachnechthra asiatica*), or it may be the Hoopoe, *Upupa epops*, which also has a long slender beak (Jerdon, vol. I, pp. 370 & 390.)

63 "And base men who have hearkened to blasphemy against gurus, the gods, and dvijas, and against the Vedas,—these
64 servants of Yama continually drive iron wedges, red as fire, into the ears, of such wicked men who rejoice *in such things* though they bewail *the while.*

65 "Whoever, led by anger and covetousness, have broken up and destroyed beautiful rest-houses,* the abodes of gods and bráhmans, and assemblages in the temples of the gods,—
66 Yama's exceedingly cruel servants continually flay the skins of those men from their body by means of these sharp instruments.

67 "Whatever men have made water in the path of cattle, bráhmans, and the sun, these entrails of theirs are drawn out through the anus by crows.

68 "Where *a man* after having given his daughter to some one, gives her to a second *person*, truly that *man* is thus divided into many portions, and swept along in a stream of burning corrosive.

69 "Whatever man, moreover, engrossed in his own nourishment abandons his destitute children, dependants, wife and
70 other relatives in a famine or in a disturbance, he indeed in his hunger thus gets portions of his own flesh, which Yama's servants cut off and put into his mouth.

71 "Whoever through avarice abandons those who have sought protection and who are dependent *on him* for their livelihood, he indeed is thus tortured by Yama's servants with tortures by means of machines.

72 "Men who check good deeds all their lives long are ground with the grinding of rocks, as *are* these evil-doers.

73 "Men who carry off pledges are bound with bands on all their limbs, and are devoured day and night by insects, scorpions, and ravens.

74 "Wicked men who indulge in sexual intercourse by day, and men who defile others' wives, are worn away by hunger, have their tongues dropping from their palates by reason of thirst, *and* are racked with pangs.

* *Prapá*, road-side sheds for accommodating travellers with water.

75 "Moreover, see the "seemul tree"* with its long iron thorns; mounted *thereon* the bodies *of sinners* are pierced, *and* they are foul with the streams of blood that pour forth.

76 "See also, O tiger-like man! these defilers of others' wives, who are being destroyed by Yama's servants in the "mouse."†

77 "Whatever man, deposing his spiritual preceptor, stubbornly pursues his learning or art,—he verily, bearing thus a
78 rock on his head, undergoes affliction in the public way, suffering exceeding pain, emaciated with hunger day and night, his head quivering through the pain of his burden.

79 "Those who have discharged urine, phlegm or ordure in water,—they, *such as* these *persons*, have come to a hell stinking with phlegm ordure and urine.

80 "Pressed with hunger these men are devouring one another's flesh—these *men* formerly did not eat according to the rules of hospitality mutually.

81 "Those also who have discarded the Vedas and the fires, *themselves* kindling their own fires,—they, *such as* these *persons*, are repeatedly hurled down from the loftiest summit of a mountain.

82 "Those men who have married virgin widows and have grown old to the full extent of life,—these turned into worms are consumed by ants.

83 "By receiving favours from an outcaste,‡ by performing sacrifices *for an outcaste*, by constant attendance *on an outcaste*, a man ever reaches the condition of an insect *that lives* among stones.

84 "The man, who eats sweetmeats all by himself, while his relatives or his friends or a guest look on, eats a pile of burning charcoal.

85 "This man's back is continually devoured by fearful wolves, because, O king! he was a backbiter of people.

* Śálmali, the Cotton or Silk-cotton tree, *Bombax malabaricum* (*heptaphylla*, Roxb.), the Bengali *simul*, the Hindustani *semal*. It is a large tree, common almost everywhere, with stout hard conical prickles (Hooker, vol. I, p. 349; Roxb., p. 514). Here it means a kind of instrument of torture.

† A kind of instrument of torture.

‡ See Canto XV. verse 1.

86 "Blind, moreover, deaf, dumb, this man roams about, sick
with hunger—he, base man, was ungrateful to men who occupy themselves in conferring benefits.

87 "This man, who returns evil for good, working injury to
his friends, very evil-minded, drops into Tapta-kumbha;
88 thereafter he will suffer grinding; then *he will go* to Karam-
bha-báluká;* next *he will undergo* mechanical tortures; then
Asi-patra-vana; and rending with saw-like leaves. After ex-
89 periencing, too, division by the thread of Fate and manifold
torments, how he will obtain expiation herefrom I know not.

90 "Corrupt Bráhmans, for having assailed one another when
assembled at S'ráddhas, drink verily the moisture that exudes
from every limb.

91 "A gold-stealer, a bráhman-slayer, a drinker of spirituous
liquors, a defiler of his guru's bed, remain, being burnt in
92 blazing fire beneath, above, around, for very many thousands
of years; thereafter they are re-born as men afflicted with
93 leprosy, consumption, sickness and other *diseases*. And when
again dead, they enter hell; and when again born, they under-
go a similar malady until the end of the kalpa, O king!

94 "A cow-slayer also goes to hell for a rather less *period*,
namely, during three lives.

"There is likewise a fixed ordinance regarding all minor sins.

95 "To what various grades of creatures, for what several
definite sins, men go, when released from hell—listen to me
while I recount that."

Canto XV.

Conversation between the father and son—(Continued).

The exposition of sins and their punishments is continued, and Jaḍa concludes his story of king Vipaś-c'it—The king by his merit delivers all the inhabitants of hell and ascends to heaven.

Yama's officer spoke.

"For accepting anything of value from an outcaste,† let a dvija be born an ass: but let him who sacrifices for the outcaste become a worm, on his release from hell.

* See Canto XIII, verse 5. † See Canto XIV, verse 83.

2 "But the dvija who has misbehaved towards his spiritual preceptor,* by coveting the latter's wife and the latter's property in his mind, undoubtedly becomes a dog.

3 "The man also who scorns his parents is born an ass; for
reviling his mother and father he is born a mainá;† and he
4 who scorns his brother's wife becomes a pigeon; but for
injuring her he becomes a tortoise.

5 "He who, while eating his brother's piṇḍa, does not pursue his *brother's* welfare, being overwhelmed with folly is indeed born after death a monkey.

6 "He who carries away a deposit is born a worm on his
release from hell. And the detracter when released from hell
7 becomes a Rákshasa. And the man who destroys trust is
born a fish.

"For carrying off through folly paddy, barley, sesa-
8 mum‡ seed, másh beans,§ kulattha beans,|| mustard-seed,¶
chickpeas,** beans,†† áman rice,‡‡ mudga beans,§§ wheat

* Upádhyáya. † S'áriká; see note * p. 49.

‡ Tila, Sesamum, *Sesamum orientale*, Roxb. (*indicum*, Linnæus); the modern *til* (Roxb., p. 491). Not in Hooker.

§ Másha, a kind of bean, *Phaseolus mungo*, variety *radiatus*, the Bengali *másh-kaláy*. It is esteemed the best of all the leguminous plants, and the meal is made into bread for many religious ceremonies. (Hooker, vol. II, p. 203; Roxb., p. 557.)

|| Kulattha, a kind of bean, *Dolichos biflorus*, the Bengali *kulattha* (Hooker, vol. II, p. 210; Roxb., p. 563.)

¶ Sarshapa, Mustard, *Sinapis campestris;* which combines Roxburgh's *S. dichotoma*, (the Beng. *śádá rái* or *sarishá*, Hind. *sarsoṇ*), and *S. glauca* (the Beng. *sveta rái*). From both varieties an oil is expressed which is used in diet, and for various other purposes. (Hooker, vol. I, p. 156; Roxb., p. 497.)

** C'aṇa, Chick pea or Gram, *Cicer arietinum*, the Beng. *buṭ*, *chaná* and *chholá;* it is the same as *vartula*. (Hooker, vol. II, p. 176; Roxb., p. 567; Oliver, p. 196.)

†† Kaláya. This is the general name for most of the commonly cultivated kinds of beans, *Phaseolus*.

‡‡ Kalama, the *áman* (*hemanta*) or later rice, which is sown in May and June and is reaped in December and January. The *áus* (*áśu*) or early rice is sown about April and reaped about August.

§§ Mudga, Green gram, *Phaseolus mungo*, the Beng. *mug* or *mug-kaláy*.

9 and flax, or other crops, a man void of understanding is
born a large-mouthed rat resembling an ichneumon.
"Moreover for improperly touching another's wife he is
10 born a horrible wolf. And the foolish sinner who violates his
brother's wife *becomes* a dog, a jackal, a heron, a vulture, a
11 snake, and a bird of prey,* by degrees. And the sinner, who
has violated his friend's wife, his guru's wife, and the king's
12 wife, becomes a cock-cuckoo when released from hell. The
man of lustful soul is born a hog.

"Let him who hinders sacrifice liberality and marriage become a worm.

13 "And he who gives his daughter away twice is verily born
a worm.
"He who obtains food, without giving some to the gods
14 the pitṛis and bráhmans, is indeed born a crow when released
from hell.
"He who scorns his eldest brother, or a brother who is like
15 a father to him, is indeed born a curlew when dismissed
from hell.
"And the śúdra for approaching a bráhman-woman is born
16 a worm; for begetting offspring of her, let him become an
insect living within wood. And a c'andála *for the same sin*
is born a hog, a small worm, a diver.†
17 "A man ungrateful, base among men, who returns evil for
good, when released from hell is born a small worm, an in-
18 sect, a bird, a scorpion also, and a fish, a crow, a tortoise,
then a pukkasa.
19 "For slaying an unarmed man, a man is born an ass. The
murderer of a woman also and a child-slayer are born worms.
"But for stealing victuals a man is born a fly.
20 "There is moreover a difference among victuals, listen
thereto. For taking rice-food, he is born a cat, when quit

Másha (see note § above) is a variety of this. (Hooker, vol. II, p. 203; Roxb., p. 556).

* Kan-ka. This must mean a bird of prey. Vaka which is a synonym has just been mentioned.

† Madgu; see note * p. 31.

21 from hell; but for taking rice-food mixed with sesamum and
oil-cake *he is born* a rat; and for taking clarified butter
22 an ichneumon; *for taking* goat's flesh, a crow, a diver.* He
who carries away fish-meat *becomes* a crow; he who carries
away venison a hawk; but when salt is taken away, *the offender becomes* a water-crow:† when curdled milk *is taken away*,
23 a worm; and for stealing milk he is born a hen-heron;‡
24 but he who steals oil is born a cockroach; for taking honey
a man is born a gad-fly; for taking a cake, an ant;§ but for
25 stealing pulse|| a small house-lizard;

"For stealing distilled spirits let the sinner become a
francolin partridge;¶ and for taking iron be born a crow.
26 When brass is carried off, *he is born* a green pigeon;**
when a silver vessel *is carried off*, a pigeon; but for taking
27 a golden vessel, he is born a worm; and for stealing
a garment of woven silk he becomes a partridge;†† and
when a silk garment is taken away he is born a silk-

* See note † p. 85.

† Víc'í-káka. I do not find this in Prof. Monier-Williams' Dictionary. I would suggest that it is a Tern, most probably the Black-bellied Tern, *Sterna javanica*, which has a black and grey plumage and is found in every river in India. The Terns are commonly called *gangá-chil* or *gáng-chil*, *i. e.*, the river-kite. (Jerdon, vol. II, pp. 834 and 840.)

‡ Baláká. Baláka is the Pond Heron or Paddy-bird, *Ardeola leucoptera*, the Beng. *konch-bak*. (Jerdon, vol. II, p. 751.)

§ Pipílika; the modern pipṛá or pipṛá denotes the larger species of ants.

|| Nishpáva; this appears to be a general name for most kinds of pulse.

¶ Tittiri, the Francolin or Meadow partridge, of which there are two species in India, (1) the Black partridge, *Francolinus vulgaris* (the modern *titir* or *kala-titar*) which is found throughout the whole of Northern India, and (2) the Painted partridge, *F. pictus* (also called *kala-titar*) which is found in Central and part of Southern India. (Jerdon, vol. II, pp. 558 and 561). The former is probably the bird meant here.

** Hárita; see note ** p. 28.

†† Krakara. Prof. Monier-Williams says this is *Perdix sylvatica*, but I do not find any such name in Jerdon. It is probably either the Grey partridge, *Ortygornis ponticeriana*, which is common throughout the greater part of India, or the Kyah partridge, *O. gularis*, which is found throughout Behar and Bengal. (Jerdon, vol. II, pp. 569, and 572.)

28 worm; when very fine cloth, an instrument of horn* and
fine cloth are carried off, the sinner is born a parrot; and so too
for taking a garment of goat's-hair or sheep's wool, and a linen
29 one; when a cotton thing is taken away he is born a curlew;
and the stealer of a barken thing *is born* a pond-heron; for
30 taking paint and potherbs *he is born* a peacock. The man who
carries off a red garment becomes a jívaṉjíva pheasant;† for
taking splendid perfumes let him become a musk-rat; and *for*
31 *taking* clothes a hare; for theft of fruit a man *becomes* a eu-
nuch; *for theft* of wood, a wood-insect;‡ and a flower-stealer
32 *becomes* a poor man; a carriage-stealer lame; and one who
takes vegetables *becomes* a green pigeon;§ and one who takes
water a pied-crested cuckoo.|| One who takes away land,
after going to Raurava and the other very terrible hells,
33 becomes grass, a bush, a creeper, a climbing shrub, a reed
and a tree by degrees; and the man afterwards, when his sins
34 have been diminished to insignificance, becomes a worm, an in-
sect, and a grasshopper, a bird, an aquatic animal, a deer; and
having attained the condition of kine, *and* despicable *castes*
35 such as c'aṇḍála and pukkaśa, *he becomes* lame and blind, deaf,
leprous, and afflicted with pulmonary consumption; he is seized
with diseases affecting the mouth and the eyes and the
36 anus; and he becomes epileptic; he attains also the condi-
tion of a śúdra. This truly is known to be the course of
stealers of cattle and gold.

37 "And fierce men who steal learning, who fall short in their
rewards to the guru; the man who makes another's wife his
38 own wife,—he becomes a eunuch, the foolish man, when
escaped from the torments *of hell*.

"He who makes the Homa oblation in unkindled fire is
39 born afflicted with the pains of indigestion, and dyspeptic.

"Abuse of others, the returning evil for good, hurting

* S'árngika. I do not find this word in the dictionary.

† Jívaṉ-jíva or jíva-jívaka. See note †† p. 28.

‡ Ghuṇa-kíṭaka: or, an armadillo.

§ Háríta: see note ** p. 28.

|| C'átaka: see note † p. 29.

40 the vitals of others, coarseness, and cruelty, paying court to
other men's wives, perfidy in taking other people's property,
41 and contempt of the gods, dishonesty, fraud towards men,
and avarice, manslaughter, and the continued performance
42 also of whatever things are forbidden;—one should know
these to be the after-characteristics of those who are released
from hell.

"Compassion towards *all* creatures, concord, aid to other
43 people, truth, speech directed towards the welfare of *all*
creatures, inculcation of the authority of the Veda, veneration
of gurus devarshis Siddhas and ṛishis, association with the
44 good, hospitality, study, friendship,—let the wise man under-
stand these and whatever other things constitute the deeds
45 of truth and righteousness, *to be* the marks of sinless men
who have quitted Svarga.

46 "This I have declared explicitly to thee, O king! concerning men, holy and wicked, who eat the fruits of their own actions. Come then, we go elsewhere. Thou hast now seen everything, for thou hast seen hell. Come then, let us go elsewhere."

The son spoke.

47 Thereupon the king prepared to follow him; and then a
cry went up from all the men that abode in torment, 'Be
48 gracious, O king! stay but a moment, for the air that clings
49 to thy body gladdens our mind, and entirely dispels the
burning and the sufferings and pains from *our* bodies, O
tiger-like man! Be gracious, O king!'

50 On hearing this their entreaty, the king asked that servant
51 of Yama—"How do I afford gladness to these men? Have
I done such a mighty deed of merit in the world of mortals,
wherefrom *falls* this gladdening shower? Declare *me* that."

Yama's officer spoke.

52 "Inasmuch as thy body was nourished with the food that
remained, after the pitṛis the gods guests and servants *were*
53 *satisfied*, and since thy mind was attached to them, hence
the air that clings to thy body brings gladness; the torment, O

54 king! does not hurt the evil-doers. Whereas thou didst offer
the horse-sacrifice and other sacrifices according to precept,
hence from seeing thee Yama's engines weapons fires and
55 crows, *which* cause intense suffering, such as crushing cutting
burning and so forth, grow mild, O king! when counteracted
by thy majesty."

The king spoke.

56 "Neither in Svarga nor in Brahma-loka do men experience
such joy, methinks, as arises from conferring bliss on suffering
57 creatures. If, while I am present, torment does not hurt
these men, here then, fair Sir, I will remain firm as a mountain."

Yama's officer spoke.

58 "Come, O king; we proceed. Enjoy the delights won by thine own merit, casting aside here the torments of evil-doers."

The king spoke.

59 "For that reason* I will not go as long as these are in sore
suffering. From my near-presence the denizens of hell grow
60 happy. Fie on the sickly protection-begging† life of that man,
who shews no favour to one distressed, even though he be a
61 resolute foe! Sacrifices, gifts, austerities do not work for the
welfare of him, who has no thought for the succour of the
62 distressed. Whoever bears a cruel mind towards children,
the sick and such like, and towards the aged also, I do not
63 hold him human; he is truly a Rákshasa. But if these men
have pain originating in hell, whether produced by the heat
from fire, or produced by overpowering smells, and *if they*
64 *have* the intense pain arising from hunger and thirst that
causes faintness, yet the grant of deliverance to them excels,
65 I consider, the joy of Svarga. If many sufferers shall obtain
happiness, while I undergo pain, should I not in truth
embrace it? Go thou not therefore long."

* For *tasmát* read *asmát*, (from hence)?

† For *śaraṇárthinam* read *śaraṇárthanam* (from *arthaná*), since *jívanam* is neuter?

Yama's officer spoke.

66 "Here have both Dharma and Indra arrived to lead thee away. Thou must certainly depart from us: go therefore, O king!"

Dharma spoke.

67 "Fittingly worshipped by thee, I lead thee to Svarga; mount this heavenly chariot and linger not; let us go."

The king spoke.

68 "Men in thousands, O Dharma! suffer pain here in hell; and being in affliction they cry to me to save them; hence I depart not."

Indra spoke.

69 "These evil-doers have come to hell in consequence of *their own* deeds; thou also, O king, must go to Svarga in consequence of thy meritorious deed."

The king spoke.

70 "If thou dost know, thou, O Dharma, or thou, O Indra, S'ac'i's lord, how great indeed is my authority, then deign* to speak aright."

Dharma spoke.

71 "Just as drops of water in the sea, or as stars in the sky,
72 or as showers of rain, as the sands in the Ganges—just as
these drops of water and other things are innumerable, O
Mahá-rájá! even so thy merit is in truth beyond reckoning.
73 In thy evincing now this compassion here in the hells, the
reckoning of that *merit* of thine has verily amounted to a
hundred thousand. Then go, O king! enjoy then the abode
74 of the immortals; let these also consume away in hell the
sin arising from their own actions!"

The king spoke.

75 "How shall men attain their desire in things connected
with me, if in my presence these *people* gain no prosperity.
76 Hence, whatever good deeds I possess, O lord of the thirty
gods! by means thereof let the sinners who are undergoing
torment be delivered from hell!"

* For *arhathaḥ* read *arhatha?*

Indra spoke.

77 "Thus hast thou, O king! gained a more exalted station: see too these sinners delivered from hell!"

The son spoke.

78 Then fell there a shower of flowers upon that king, and
Hari making him mount the heavenly chariot led him to the
79 heaven-world. Both I and the others, who *were* there, were
released from the torments; thereafter we entered the other
earthly existences, as determined by the results of our own
actions.

80 Thus these hells have been reckoned up, O bráhman! And
for what particular sin to what particular kind of creature a
81 man descends, it has all been recounted to thee in detail,
as I saw it of yore, having gained the accurate knowledge that
springs from previous experience. What else do I tell thee
next, noble sir?

Canto XVI.

Anasúyá's gain of a boon.

The father asks Jaḍa for instruction on yoga or religious devotion—Jaḍa begins a long exposition, which starts with a story of Anasúyá—A certain brahman was cursed by Máṇḍavya at night that he should die at sunrise, and his devoted wife restrained the sun from rising—All activity ceased, and the gods in alarm besought Atri's wife Anasúyá—At her exhortation the wife relents, the sun rises, and the bráhman dies, but is restored to life by Anasúyá—Anasúyá obtains from the gods the boon that Brahmá, Vishṇu and S'iva should be born her sons, and that she should attain yoga.

The father spoke.

1 Thou hast declared to me, O son, the established nature of
mundane existence which should be shunned exceedingly, *a
nature* which is immutable like the rope and bucket at a well.
2 I have thus then learnt it in its entirety such as it is. Say,
what must I do in this thus-ordained *mundane existence?*

The son spoke.

3 If, O father, thou dost believe my word implicitly, then
abandoning thy condition as a house-holder become a dis-
4 tinguished hermit. Following that *vocation* according to
precept, forsaking thy fire and possessions, directing thy soul
towards the Supreme Soul, indifferent in regard to the various
5 opposites,* relinquishing thy property, become a mendicant,
eating only every other meal, subdued in soul, unwearied,
grown intent on religious devotion,† withdrawn from contact
6 with external things. Thereafter thou shalt attain to that
religious devotion,—which is the cure for connexion with
pain, the cause of final emancipation from existence, incom-
parable, unutterable, devoid of *worldly* attachments; through
connexion with that *devotion* thou wilt never again have union
with living beings.

The father spoke.

7 My son, tell me next of yoga, or religious devotion, the
cause of final emancipation from existence; by which I may
escape such suffering as this, when *I am* again born among
8 living beings. Since I am intent on attachments, and my soul
does not by reason of the bonds of mundane existence attain
to religious devotion, being itself even devoid of religious
9 devotion,‡ speak now of that religious devotion. Sprin-
kle with the water of thy words, which are cool with the
water of the knowledge of Brahma, me whose body and
mind are disordered with pain through the heat of the sun of
10 mundane existence. Re-vivify with the draught of the nectar
of thy words me, *who am* bitten by the black serpent of igno-
11 rance, who am in anguish from its venom, *and* dead. Hasting
with the keys of the knowledge of approved goodness, liberate
me, *who am* galled by the chains of selfishness in the matter
of son, wife, home and land.

* Pleasure and pain, &c.

† Yoga.

‡ Or "devoid of means;" there seems to be a pun on the word yoga.

The son spoke.

12 Listen, dear father! how of yore the wise Dattátreya, when
duly questioned, expounded *the system of* religious devotion
at length to Alarka.*

The father spoke.

13 Whose son was Dattátreya? Again, how did he discourse
about religious meditation? And who was the distinguished
Alarka, who enquired concerning religious meditation?

The son spoke.

14 There was a certain Kauśika bráhman in the town Prati-
shṭhána; he by reason of sins committed in other births was
15 diseased with leprosy. His wife used to honour him her hus-
band, thus diseased, as a god, by anointing his feet, knead-
16 ing his limbs, bathing, clothing, and feeding him, and by
cleansing the flow of mucus, blood etcetera, and with atten-
17 dance in private, and with affectionate conversation. Though
always exceedingly venerated by that modest lady, he being
harsh continually menaced her by reason of his excessively
18 fiery temper. Nevertheless his wife, bowing *before him*, used
to esteem him a divinity;† nevertheless she used to esteem
him, who was extremely loathful, as superior to all.

19 Being also of a constantly roaming disposition, the bráhman
ordered his wife—"Do thou bring me to her dwelling. Pro-
20 cure for me that courtezan whom I saw living in her house
in the high-way, O religious one; she indeed dwells in my
21 heart. I saw the maiden at sunrise, and here is night
come upon us. She does not depart from my heart, ever
22 since I saw her. If she, lovely in every limb, with large
hips and swelling breasts and slender body, does not embrace
23 *me*, then thou wilt indeed behold me die. Beautiful is love
among mankind; and she is courted by many; and I am
unable to go; it appears perplexing to me."

24 Then having heard that speech of her husband who was
sick with love, she his consort, sprung of a high family, very

* For *Anarkáya* read *Alarkáya*, see Canto XXXVI.

† For *davatam* read *daivatam*.

25 virtuous, faithful to her husband, gathered a compact retinue,
and took abundance of money, and bearing her husband on
26 her shoulder, moved on, slow in her gait, along the high
road, in the cloud-covered night, while the sky was revealed
by the fitful lightning; for the bráhman lady was desirous
of doing her husband pleasure.

27 And on the road, the bráhman, while borne on his wife's
shoulder, through fear of thieves in the darkness pushed
28 away Máṇḍavya, who was no thief and who was afflicted with
grievous pain, being impaled on a stake. Enraged at the
29 brush with a foot, Máṇḍavya addressed him—"He, who
has with his foot pushed me away who am thus exceedingly
afflicted, he sinful in soul, base among men, has gotten a
30 miserable condition. At sunrise, helpless, he shall be bereft
of life assuredly: at the sight of the sun indeed he shall
31 perish." Thereupon his wife hearing that most cruel curse,
exclaimed distressed—"The sun verily shall not arise!"

32 Then the sun failed to rise, and there was continual night
for many lengths of day. Thereupon the gods grew afraid,
33 *fearing* "How indeed should not all this *universe* pass into
dissolution, when the Vedas are not uttered, and when it is
deprived of oblations with fire and of the Svadhá and Sváhá?
34 Without the ordinance of day and night, there is an end of
months and seasons: and again from the cessation of these
south and north are not known in the sun's half yearly course.
35 And without knowledge of the half yearly course where would
be time, *such as* the year? Without the year no other know-
36 ledge of time exists. By reason of the utterance of that
devoted wife, the sun rises not: without the sun's rising,
bathing giving of gifts and the other actions *can* not indeed
37 *exist*; nor indeed does the fire spread, and sacrifices are seen
to cease; nor indeed do we get satisfaction without the homa
38 sacrifice. Mortals satisfy us with the appropriate shares of
the sacrifices: we favour mortals with rain for the perfect-
39 ing of their grain and other *crops*. When plants have
ripened, mortals sacrifice to us with sacrifices; worshipped in
40 their sacrifices &c., we bestow on them their desires. For

we pour rain downwards, and mortals make their rain
ascend; for we rain with showers of water, men with showers
41 of clarified butter. And evil-minded men, who do not give
us the periodical sacrifices,* *being* greedy eat themselves our
42 share of the sacrifice. We defile the water, the sun, fire and
the winds, and the earth for the destruction of those mis-
43 chievous sinners. Through partaking of bad water &c., very
dire portents work towards the death of those doers of evil
44 deeds. But to those high-souled men, who after delighting
us consume the remainder themselves, let us allot the blissful
45 worlds. Therefore all this *universe* of a truth does not exist,
unless these things increase and endure. How indeed may
the days be liberated?"—*so* conversed the gods with one
another.

46 Having heard the speech of these assembled gods who were
fearful of the destruction of the sacrifices, the god Brahmá
47 spoke, "Majesty is subdued by majesty indeed, and austeri-
ties also by austerities, O ye immortals! Hearken therefore
48 to my advice. Through the might of the faithful wife the
sun does not rise, and from his not rising loss befalls mortals
49 and you. Hence do ye, through desire that the sun should
rise, propitiate Atri's faithful wife Anasúyá who is rich in
austerities."

The son spoke.

50 She, propitiated by them when they resorted *to her*, said
"Let your wish be asked for." The gods petitioned for day,
saying "Let it be as before!"

Anasúyá spoke.

51 "The might of a faithful wife may not be lost in any wise.
Hence while honouring that good *lady*, I will liberate the day,
52 O ye gods! that day and night may again exist, and that
that good *lady's* own husband shall not perish."

The son spoke.

53 Thus having addressed the gods, she the beautiful went to

* Nitya-naimittikí; see Canto XXX.

her temple, and being asked by that lady regarding the welfare and righteousness of her husband, spoke.

Anasúyá spoke.

54 "Perchance thou rejoicest, O blessed *lady*, at the sight of
thy husband's countenance! Perchance too thou esteemest thy
55 husband far above all the gods! Through obedience indeed
to my husband I have gained a great reward; through the
obtainment of the results of every wish obstacles have been
56 removed. Five debts a man must ever discharge, O virtuous
lady. Thus, he must amass wealth according to the duties
57 of his own caste: and he must next apply the wealth gained
to a fitting object according to the precepts: he should always
live full of compassion, observing truth, candour, austerities
58 and liberality: and he must daily perform the ceremonies
prescribed by the S'ástras and free from anger and enmity,
59 with faith preceding, according to his ability. A man with
great pain gradually obtains the worlds specially allotted to
his own caste, such as that of the Prajá-patis and other worlds,
60 O virtuous *lady*. So women by obedience to their husbands
obtain half of the entire merit painfully earned by their
61 husbands. There is no separate sacrifice for women, nor
śráddha, nor fasting: for by obedience to their husbands
62 indeed they reach these desired worlds. Therefore, O virtuous and exalted *lady*, let thy mind ever be turned towards
obedience to thy husband, since a husband is *a wife's* supreme
63 bliss. Whatever worship the husband may offer by right
ceremonies to the gods, and whatever to the pitṛis and guests,
even one half of that does the wife, whose mind is centred on
him alone, enjoy by very obedience to her husband."

The son spoke.

64 Having heard that her speech, the lady saluted Atri's
wife Anasúyá respectfully in return, and replied thus to her—
65 "Happy am I, favoured am I, and regarded by the gods am
I, since thou, O *lady* blessed by nature, again increasest my
66 faith. I know this—none among women has a condition
equal with her husband, and love for him *tends* to her benefit

67 in this world and the next; through her husband's favour
both here and after death, O illustrious *lady*, a woman gains
68 happiness; for a husband is a woman's deity. Do thou,
being such *a woman*, O exalted *lady*, tell me who have reached
thy temple, what I, a noble* *woman*, must do, or what my
noble *husband* must do, O beauteous one!"

Anasúyá spoke.

69 "Indra and these gods in distress have approached me;
they are searching for the day and night, the virtuous acts
prescribed for which have been discarded in consequence of
70 thy speech. They beg for the natural uninterrupted con-
tinuance of day and night: I am come for that object, and
71 do thou listen to this my speech. Through the absence of
day *there is* the absence of all sacrificial ceremonies; through
the absence of these the gods do not get their nourishment,
72 O ascetic *lady*. Through the destruction of day also all
work is cut short; from the destruction thereof the world
73 will perish through drought. Therefore if thou desirest to
deliver this world from calamity, be gracious, O virtuous
lady, to the worlds; let the sun run his course as before."

The bráhman lady spoke.

74 "Máṇḍavya exceedingly furious, O illustrious lady, has
cursed my lord, saying 'at sunrise thou shalt meet thy
doom!'"

Anasúyá spoke.

75 "If, however, it pleases thee, O lady, then at thy word I
will make thee even a new husband, in form the same as before.
76 For I must in every way propitiate the majesty of faithful
wives, O high-born *lady*—thus I do thee honour."

The son spoke.

77 On her saying 'be it so!' the ascetic *lady* Anasúyá then
summoned the sun, raising up the arghya oblation, at mid-
78 night on the tenth night. Then the adorable sun, in ap-
pearance ruddy as the full-blown lotus flower, with wide
79 disc, rose aloft above the mighty mountain. Forthwith indeed

* For *áryáyá* read *áryayá*?

her husband was bereft of life and fell on the ground; and she caught him as he fell.

Anasúyá spoke.

80 "Be not dejected, O lady; behold my power. Thou
hast succeeded through thy obedience to thy husband.
81 What further need hast thou of austerities? Since I have
nowhere seen another man equal to thy husband, in form,
in disposition, in intellect, with sweetness of speech and
82 other adornments, in very truth let this bráhman, freed
from sickness, young again, obtain life in company with his
83 wife for a hundred autumns. Since I see no other deity the
equal of thy husband, in very truth let this bráhman regain
84 his life in sound health. Since thy* effort is constantly
directed to propitiate thy husband by deed mind and word,
let this dvija then come to life."

The son spoke.

85 Then the bráhman arose, free from illness, young again,
with his own lustre illuminating the dwelling, as it were an
86 ever-youthful god. Then there fell a shower of flowers, ac-
companied with the strains of heavenly instruments and
other musical instruments. And the gods were delighted and
said to Anasúyá.

The gods spoke.

87 "Choose a boon, O blessed *lady*. Inasmuch as thou hast accomplished a great matter for the gods, therefore the gods *will* grant thee a boon, O ascetic *lady*."

Anasúyá spoke.

88 "If ye gods headed by Brahmá, *being* favourable, *will* grant
89 me a boon, and if ye deem me worthy of a boon, then let
Brahmá, Vishṇu, and S'iva become sons to me, and let me
in company with my husband attain religious devotion, to
the end that I may be delivered from affliction."

90 "Be it so," exclaimed Brahmá, Vishṇu, S'iva and the other gods to her; and they departed, duly honouring the ascetic *lady*.

* For *mama* read *tava*?

CANTO XVII.

The Birth of Dattátreya.

The Prajá-pati Atri begot three sons by his wife Anasúyá, namely, Soma, Dattátreya, and Durvásas, who were incarnations of portions of Brahmá, Vishṇu and Śiva respectively—Their offices are described—Dattatreya, assembling young Munis about himself, tested their loyalty, by living immersed in a lake and by revelling in sensual pleasures.

The son spoke.

1 Then after many days' time the adorable Atri, the second
2 son of Brahmá, looked upon his wife Anasúyá. Her, bathed
after menstruation, very lovely in body, seductive and perfect
in form, free from blame, the love-possessed Muni enjoyed
mentally.
3 But while he contemplated her, a powerful wind through
and above brought the change that was produced *in her.*
4 The ten regions of the sky seized the white-lustred form of
Brahmá, as it fell all around, in the form of Soma, charac-
5 terized by passion. That mental Soma was begotten in her
as the son of the prajá-pati Atri, the life and possessor of
6 every excellence. Magnanimous Vishṇu being pleased begot
of her Dattátreya, the bráhman, in whom goodness predomi-
7 nated, by production from his own body. Dattátreya was he
called; he sucked Anasúyá's breast: he was Vishṇu indeed
8 incarnate; he was Atri's second son. He issued from his
mother's womb seven days afterwards; being enraged on
seeing that the haughty king of the Haihayas was near and
9 was offending Atri, being angry he at once desired to burn
up the Haihaya. Filled with indignation at the long pains
and toil of his residence in the womb, a portion of Śiva
10 was born as Durvásas, in whom darkness predominated.
Thus three sons were born of her, being portions of Brahmá,
Śiva and Vishṇu.
11 Brahmá became Soma, Vishṇu was born as Dattátreya,
Śiva was born as Durvásas, through the boon granted by the
12 gods. The prajá-pati Soma, ever causing creepers and medi-

cinal plants and mankind to grow with his cool rays, abides
13 in Svarga. Dattátreya protects offspring from destruction
by the malignant Daityas: and Vishṇu's portion must also be
14 known as the benefactor of the docile. Durvásas, the ador-
able birthless *god*, destroys the scorner; assuming a formidable
15 body, he is haughty in look mind and speech. The adorable
prajá-pati, the son of Atri again created the Soma plant.*
Dattátreya also, *being* Vishṇu, enjoyed objects of sense while
16 engaged in profound meditation. Durvásas, deeming his
father and mother to be the chiefest object of devotion,
assuming *the form* known as 'frantic,' roamed about the earth.
17 Surrounded by the sons of Munis, the lordly yogi Dattátreya
also, desirous of obtaining exemption from *all* attachments,
18 long immersed himself in a lake. Nevertheless those youths,
resorting to the bank of the lake, did not forsake him, who
19 was magnanimous and exceedingly benign. When after a
hundred heavenly years were ended, all those youthful Munis,
through affection for him, still forsook not the bank of the
20 lake, the Muni, taking his noble wife clothed in heavenly
raiment, beautiful and plump in form, arose from the water,
21 thinking, "If these sons of Munis shall forsake me because
of the presence of a woman, then I will remain free from *all*
22 attachments." When nevertheless the sons of the Munis *did*
not forsake him, he next drank intoxicating liquors in com-
23 pany with his wife. Thereupon they did not forsake him,
though he was engrossed in drinking spirituous liquor in
company with his wife, and though he was rendered impure
by addiction to singing, musical instruments and such like,
24 and also by intercourse with his wife; deeming that the high-
souled *Muni when* with her was detached from religious rites.
The lord of yogís, although drinking spirituous liquor, incurred
25 no fault. Dwelling like Mátariśvan within the abodes of
c'aṇḍálas, drinking strong drink he, skilled in yoga, the lord

* The text appears to be corrupt. Another reading has been suggested by Babu Hari Mohan Vidyábhushan, the pandit of the Bengal Asiatic Society, from a MS., *atreḥ putraś* for *atriḥ punaś*; this is preferable and I have adopted it.

of yogís, attended by his wife, performed austerities, being meditated on by yogís who longed for deliverance from mundane existence.

Canto XVIII.

Garga's speech.

Arjuna the son of Kṛita-vírya, on succeeding to his kingdom, resolves to rule worthily—His minister Garga advises him to propitiate the Muni Dattátreya—And narrates how, when the Daityas and Dánavas had conquered the gods, the gods by Vṛihaspati's counsel propitiated Dattátreya, who, being an incarnation of Vishṇu, was enjoying himself with Lakshmí; and how, when the demons penetrated to Dattátreya's hermitage and seized Lakshmí, they were destroyed by Dattátreya.

The son spoke.

1 Once upon a time Arjuna, the son of Kṛita-vírya, when
Kṛita-vírya had departed to heaven, being invited by the
2 ministers and family priest and by the citizens to be in-
augurated as king, spoke thus—
"It is not I will wield regal sway, which surpasses hell, O
3 ministers, if I leave that foolishly unaccomplished, for the sake
of which taxes are levied. Merchants, giving the twelfth part
4 of their wares to the king, travel on the road protected from
robbers by the watchmen. And the herdsmen and husbandmen
giving the sixth part of the ghee, buttermilk and other *pro-*
5 *duce*, enjoy the rest. If the merchants gave a larger portion
than that out of all their wares and other *property*, then
6 that *would tend* to the destruction of the sacrifices and pious
works of the extortionate king who took it. If people who
follow that and other livelihoods are protected by others,
7 hell is surely *the lot* of a king who takes the sixth part as his
revenue. This has been decreed by men of old as the perma-
8 nent income of a king. *When a king* fails to afford protection
from thieves, that *is the same as* theft; and it would be sin in
a king. Therefore if, by performing austerities, he has gained

9 the coveted position of a yogí, he is the only king who possesses
power to protect the earth. Therefore I indeed will be a
weapon-bearer in the earth, worthy of honour, endowed with
prosperity ; I will not make myself a participator in sin."

The son spoke.

10 Understanding that his resolve, standing among the minis-
ters spoke the leading Muni, Garga by name, mighty in
intellect, advanced in age.
11 "If thus thou desirest to act, rightly to govern the king-
dom, then hearken to my speech and act, O royal scion!
12 Propitiate, O king, Dattátreya, the illustrious, who made
his abode once in a bucket, who protects the three worlds,
13 who is busied in religious devotion, who is illustrious, who
looks impartially everywhere, who is a portion of Vishṇu, the
14 upholder of the world, incarnate on earth. By propitiating
him the thousand-eyed Indra gained his abode, which had been
seized by the evil-minded Daityas, and slew the sons of Diti."

Arjuna spoke.

15 "How did the gods propitiate majestic Dattátreya? And
how did Indra regain his godhead, of which he had been
deprived by the Daityas?"

Garga spoke.

16 "There was a very fierce contest between the gods and
Dánavas. The lord of the Daityas was Jambha, and *the leader*
17 of the gods was S'ac'í's spouse. And while they fought a
heavenly year elapsed. Then the gods were worsted, the
18 Daityas were victorious. The gods led by Vipra-c'itti were
vanquished by the Dánavas: they strove to flee, being dis-
19 pirited at the victory of their enemies. Desirous of compass-
ing the slaughter of the army of Daityas, accompanied by the
Bálikhilyas* and Ṛishis, they approached Vṛihaspati and
20 took counsel. Vṛihaspati said, 'Deign to gratify with your
faith Dattátreya, Atri's high-souled son, the ascetic, who is
21 occupied in improper practices. He the boon-giver will grant

* Read 'Bala-khilyas'? These are divine personages of the size of the thumb.

you a boon for the destruction of the Daityas; then, O gods, shall ye and your friends slay the Daityas and Dánavas.'

22 "Thus exhorted the gods then went to Dattátreya's hermitage, and they beheld the high-souled Muni, attended by
23 Lakshmi, hymned by Gandharvas, and engrossed in quaffing spirituous liquor. Approaching they expressed in words their salutations to him, which were the means of accomplishing
24 their objects. And the heaven-dwellers lauded him; they offered him food, viands, garlands and other *presents;* when he stood, they stood near; when he moved, they moved; when
25 he reposed on his seat, they worshipped him with heads down-bent. Dattátreya addressed the prostrate gods, 'What desire ye of me, that ye do me this obeisance?'

"The gods spoke.

26 'The Dánavas, headed by Jambha, have attacked and seized upon the earth the atmosphere and the third world, O tiger-
27 like Muni, and our shares of the sacrifices entirely. Employ thou thy wit to their destruction and our deliverance, O sinless one! Through thy favour do we desire to regain the three worlds which *they now* possess.'

"Dattátreya spoke.

28 'I am drinking strong drink, I have remnants of food in my mouth, nor have I subdued my senses. How is it, O gods, ye seek for victory over your enemies even from me?'

"The gods spoke.

29 'Thou art sinless, O lord of the world; no stain hast thou, into whose heart, purified by the ablution of learning, has entered the light of knowledge.'

"Dattátreya spoke.

30 'True is this, O gods! all learning have I, who am impartial in view: but by reason of association with this woman I
31 am now impure after eating. For commerce with women when continually pursued tends to depravity.'

"Thus addressed, the gods then spoke again.

"The gods spoke.

32 'This woman, O sinless bráhman! is the mother of the
world; she is not depraved, even like the sun's halo of rays,
which touches the dvija and the c'aṇḍála alike.'

Garga spoke.

33 "Thus accosted by the gods, Dattátreya then with a smile
spoke thus to all the thirty *gods*;—'If this be your opinion,
34 then summon all the Asuras to battle, O most virtuous gods,
35 and bring them here before my view—delay ye not—in order
that the glory of their strength may be consumed by the fire
of my glance, and that they may all perish from my sight.'

36 "The valiant Daityas, summoned to battle by the gods in
compliance with that his advice, advanced with fury against
37 the troops of the gods. The gods being slaughtered by the
Daityas were quickly demoralised by fear; they fled in a
38 body, seeking protection, to Dattátreya's hermitage. Even
there the Daityas penetrated, driving forward the heaven-
dwellers, and saw the high-souled mighty Dattátreya; and
39 seated at his left side his wife, Lakshmi, loved by all the
worlds, beauteous, her shape most graceful, her countenance
40 like the moon, her eyes lustrous as the blue water-lily,* her
hips large and breasts full, uttering melodious speech, adorned
41 with every womanly virtue. Seeing her before them, the
Daityas, seized with longing, could not bear the intense love
42 with fortitude; and pined in mind to carry her off. Desisting
from the gods, but desirous of seizing the lady, they were
shattered in vigour, being bewitched by that sin. Then com-
43 pact together they spoke—'If only this jewel of womankind
in the three worlds might be our prize, successful then *should*
44 *we* all *be*—this is our engrossing thought. We are resolved
therefore, let us all, foes of the gods, raise her up, place her
in the palki, and bear her to our abode.'

45 "Thereupon possessed with longing and thus mutually ex-
horted, afflicted by love, the united Daityas and Dánavas
46 raised up his virtuous wife, mounted her in the palki, and

* Nílotpala, the blue water-lily, see note ‡ page 29.

placing the palki on their heads set off for their own homes.
47 Thereon Dattátreya smiling spoke thus to the gods—'Bravo!
ye prosper! Here is Lakshmi borne on the heads of the
Daityas. She has passed beyond the seven stations, she will
reach another, a new one.'

"The gods spoke.

48 'Say, O lord of the world, in what stations has she her
abode; and what result of a man's does she bestow or destroy?'

"Dattátreya spoke.

49 'When stationed on the foot of men, Lakshmi bestows a
habitation; and when stationed on the thigh, clothing and
50 manifold wealth; and when taking her position in the
pudenda, a wife; when resting in the bosom, she grants
offspring; when stationed in the heart, she fulfils the thoughts
51 of men. Lakshmi, is the best *fortune* of fortunate men.
When resting on the neck, she adorns the neck with loved
relatives and wives, and close contact with those who are
52 absent. When abiding in the countenance, the sea-born *god-*
dess bestows beauty fashioned according to her word, real
53 command also, and poetic fire. When mounted on the head,
she forsakes *the man* and thence resorts to another abode. And
here, mounted on their head, she will now desert these *Dai-*
54 *tyas.* Therefore seize your arms and slay these foes of the
gods; nor fear them greatly; I have rendered them impotent;
and through touching another's wife their merit is consumed,
their might is broken.

Garga spoke.

55 "Thereupon those enemies of the gods, being slain by divers
weapons and their heads being assailed by Lakshmi, perished—
56 thus have we heard. And Lakshmi, flying up, reached the
great Muni Dattátreya, being hymned by all the gods who
57 were filled with joy at the slaughter of the Daityas. There-
upon the gods, prostrating themselves before the wise Dattá-
treya, gained as before the uppermost heaven, being freed from
58 affliction. Likewise do thou also, O king! if thou wishest to
obtain matchless sovereignty according to thy desire, straight-
way propitiate him."

CANTO XIX.

The Episode of Dattátreya.

King Arjuna, taking Garga's advice, propitiates Dattátreya, who grants him the boon that he should reign righteously, prosperously and gloriously—Arjuna is then installed in his kingdom, and his reign is described—The blessedness of worshipping Vishṇu, who is Dattátreya, expounded—The story of Alarka is then begun.

The son spoke.

1 Having heard the Ṛishi speak thus, king *Arjuna*, Kṛita-
víryа's son, proceeded to Dattátreya's hermitage and wor-
2 shipped him with faith; by kneading his feet and other
services, and by offering honey and other *delicacies*, and by bring-
ing garlands, sandal, and other perfumes, water, fruit &c.;
3 also with preparations of rice, and by removing the Ṛishi's
fragments of food. Pleased *therewith* the Muni addressed the
4 king in the very same way, as he had formerly addressed the
gods.

"Ever indeed am I an object of reproach for my enjoy-
ment of spirituous liquor and other *bodily pleasures*, and an
object of reproach for this enjoyment in that I have my
5 wife here by my side.* Deign thou not thus to obstruct me
who am unable to benefit *thee;* O conciliate one who is able."
6 Thus the Muni addressed him; and Arjuna Kártavírya, re-
calling that speech of Garga's, replied then, bowing before him.

Arjuna spoke.

7 "Why dost thou beguile me, my lord, resorting to thy illusory devices. Sinless thou art, and this bráhman lady is the path of all existence."

8 Thus invoked, the benign bráhman answered him, the illustrious Kártavírya, the subduer of the earth.

9 "Choose thou a boon; since thou hast declared my secret,
I have felt thereby intense gratification in thee to-day, O
10 king. And the men who shall worship me with perfumes,
garlands and such like, with offerings also of meat and strong

* The text appears obscure.

drink, and with sweetmeats accompanied with clarified butter,
11 —*and who shall worship* me and Lakshmi with songs also and
the worship of bráhmans, and with lute, flute, conchs and other
12 gladsome musical instruments;—to them I will give supreme
gratification, children, wives, wealth and other *blessings*, and I
13 will ward off the violent blows of scorners. Do thou then
choose the choice boon that thy mind desires: my face is very
gracious to thee through thy declaration of my secret name."

Kártavírya spoke.

14 "If my lord thou art gracious, then grant me supreme pros-
perity, whereby I may protect my people and may not incur
15 iniquity. I desire to have knowledge in the customs of others,
irresistibility in fight, and the dexterity of a thousand arms.
16 May my paths be unimpeded on hill, in air, in water, and on
land, and in all the hells! And may my death come from a
17 superior man! And let me have moreover a guide to the
right path when I stray from the path: and may my guests*
be worthy of praise in the imperishable bestowal of wealth!
18 And let there be freedom from impoverishment in my country
with repeated recollection of me! May my faith in thee be
ever in truth unwavering!"

Dattátreya spoke.

19 "Thou shalt receive all those boons in the matters that thou
hast specified; and through my favour thou shalt become a
universal monarch."

Jaḍa spoke.

20 Thereon Arjuna prostrated himself before Dattátreya. And
having convened his *subjects*, he duly received his inaugura-
21 tion. Then he the Haihaya, established in his kingdom,
having received supreme prosperity from Dattátreya, owning
22 exceeding power, made proclamation;—'Henceforth whoever
besides me shall lay hold of a weapon, I shall put him to death
23 as a robber or as one bent on injuring others.' After this
order had been issued, there was no man that bore arms in

* For '*tithayaḥ* read *tithayaḥ*, days?

24 that country, except that valiant tiger-warrior. He it was
who was the guardian of the villages, and he the guar-
dian of the cattle. He it was who was the guardian of the
25 fields and the protector of the dvijas. He also was the
guardian of ascetics, and the guardian of caravans; *the guar-
dian* of those who were sinking amid the fears of robbers,
26 rogues, fire, arms and so forth, *as* in the sea, and of those who
were involved in other calamities; he was the destroyer of
hostile warriors. He it was who was ever remembered as
27 the upholder of mankind. And there was exemption from im-
poverishment, while he ruled as king. He offered many
28 sacrifices, complete with gifts and fees. He also practised
austerities. He performed exploits in battles.

Having seen his prosperity and exceeding honour, the Muni Angiras spoke.

29 "Assuredly kings will not follow in Kártavírya's steps,
either with sacrifices, alms-giving, or austerities, or with high
exploits in battle."

30 On the very day when the king received prosperity from
31 Dattátreya, he performed sacrifice to Dattátreya. And there
all his subjects having seen the king's supreme prosperity
that day offered up sacrifices with devout attention.

32 Such is this magnanimity of the wise Dattátreya, *who
is* Vishṇu, the guru of all things movable and immov-
33 able, endless, high-souled. In the Puráṇas are narrated the
manifestations of the bearer of the bow S'árnga, who is endless,
34 inscrutable, the bearer of the conch discus and club. What-
ever man ponders on his highest form, happy is he, and he
35 may soon pass over mundane existence. 'Ho! I am ever in
truth easy of reach by faith even to Vaishṇavas,'—how is it
that a man should not have recourse to him, whose are these
36 very words? For the destruction of unrighteousness, and for
the practice of righteousness, the god, who is without beginning
and without end, preserves the stability *of nature*.

37 Moreover I tell thee of Alarka* also, the famous birth.

* Read *Alarkam* for *Anarkam*.

And thus has been related the union between the high-souled Rájarshi Alarka, who was faithful to his father, and Dattátreya.

CANTO XX.

The Story of Kuvalayáśva.

King S'atru-jit's son Ṛita-dhvaja receives into intimate friendship two Nága princes in the guise of bráhmans—They live with him by day, and spend the nights in Rasátala —They extol him to their father, and relate his story as follows—Ṛita-dhvaja sets out to succour the bráhman Gálava against a Daitya Pátála-ketu, with the aid of a wondrous horse named Kuvalaya.

Jaḍa spoke.

1 There was formerly a valorous king named S'atru-jit, in whose sacrifices Indra was pleased by receiving the soma
2 juice. His son was a valiant destroyer of his foes; the peer of Vṛihaspati, Indra and the Aśvins in intellect, prowess and
3 beauty. The king's son was continually surrounded by young princes, who were his equals in age, intellect, virtue, prowess
4 and behaviour. He was sometimes resolved on investigating the whole S'ástra literature; at other times engrossed* with
5 poetry, dialogue, singing and the drama. Moreover *he enjoyed himself* both with gambling pastimes, and in the discipline of all kinds of weapons: he was intent on the study of elephants,
6 horses, and chariots suitable for war.† The king's son enjoyed himself in company with the young princes, being
7 absorbed in pleasure by day and night alike. But while they sported there, numbers of young bráhmans, young princes and young vaiśyas of the same age came to enjoy themselves affectionately.

8 Now after a time two young Nágas, the sons of Aśvatara,‡

* For *-sambhavaiḥ* read *-sambhavaḥ?*

† The text appears corrupt; for *yogyáni yuddha-* read *yuddha-niyogya-?*

‡ A Nága prince.

9 visited the surface of the earth from the Nága-world. Dis-
guised in form as bráhmans, youthful, handsome, those two,
in company with the young princes and the other dvijas,
10 remained there linked in friendship, *occupied* with various
amusements. And all those young princes and the young
11 bráhmans and vaiśyas, and those two young Nága princes
engaged in bathing, kneading the limbs &c., adorned them-
selves with garments and perfumes, and occupied themselves
12 with the business of kings.* As day after day went by, the
two young Nágas enjoyed themselves, being bound by affection
13 for the king's son. And the king's son received the highest
pleasure from those two, by various amusements, and by jests,
14 conversation, &c. Apart from those two he neither ate, nor
bathed, nor drank sweet drinks; he did not disport himself,
nor take up his weapons to improve his accomplishments.
15 And those two, spending the night in Rasátala,† mainly oc-
cupied in sighing in the absence of that high-souled *prince*,
visited him day after day.

16 "With whom do ye both, my sons, find supreme affection
in the mortal-world?" thus inquired their father of both
17 those young Nágas. "Whilst I have seen you both many days
here in Pátála, I *ever* behold you both with kindly counte-
nances by day and night."

Jaḍa spoke.

18 Thus questioned by their father himself, the two illustri-
ous sons of the Nága king falling prostrate, with hands reve-
rently joined, replied.

The sons spoke.

19 "*It is* the son of S'atru-jit, dear father, famed by name as
Ṛita-dhvaja, shapely, upright in conduct, a hero, proud, kind
20 of speech, no sneaking tale-bearer,‡ eloquent, learned,
friendly, a mine of excellencies, an honourer of the honour-
21 worthy, intelligent, modest, adorned with courtesy. *Our* mind,

* The text seems incorrect. For *-samyuktáṃś* read *-samyuktáś?*

† The lower world.

‡ Fer *anápṛishṭa-katho* read *anápṛishṭha-katho*.

being ravished by attendance on him, affection for him and
pleasure with him, finds no delight in the Nága-world or the
22 air-world.* By separation from him chill Pátála *does* not
tend to warm us, dear father; through union with him the sun
by day *tends* to gladden us."

The father spoke.

23 "He is the happy son of a holy *father*, whose excellencies
such accomplished persons as ye are thus celebrate even in his
24 absence. There are evil-dispositioned men learned in the
Śástras; there are good-dispositioned men who are fools:
but I esteem him, my sons, the happier who equally possesses
25 *knowledge of* Śástras and a *good* disposition. A father has
indeed a son in that *son*, whose friends always declare his
friendly qualities, and whose enemies his valour, among the
26 good. Perchance ye have preferred a request to him as a
benefactor: he has done something to satisfy your mind, my
27 children. Happy is he! The life of each high-born one has
been *well* lived, when petitioners to him turn not away, and the
28 petition of his friends is not powerless. In my house whatever gold and other *metals*, jewels, animals for riding, and seats
there are, and whatever else imparts delight; that should be
29 given him without hesitation. Fie on the life of that man,
who, while failing to make a return to beneficent friends,
30 believes that he *really* lives! The wise man who, cloud-like,
showers benefits on his circle of friends and injury on his
foes,—*men* wish him prosperity."

The sons spoke.

31 "What might any one do for that successful man, whose
petitioners are all always honoured in his house with *the grant*
32 *of* all their desires. The jewels that are in his house, whence
can we have them in Pátála? *And whence his* animals for
33 riding, his seats, and carriages, ornaments and clothing? The
knowledge that he has, is found nowhere else. Even for the
34 wise he is, dear father, the ablest remover of all doubts. One
thing he has done, and that in our opinion was impossible of

* For *bhuvo loke* read *bhuvarloke*?

accomplishment, cxcept by Brahmá, Vishṇu,* S'iva, and the
other lords."†

The father spoke.

35 "Nevertheless I wish to hear what was his highest deed,
whether it be impossible or possible of accomplishment. Is
36 anything impossible to the wise? Men who have determi-
nation attain to the position of the gods, lordship over the
immortals, and the position of being worshipped by them, or
37 any other coveted arduous thing. There is nothing unknown,
or inaccessible, or unobtainable, either in heaven or here,
to strenuous men who have brought their mind, organs
38 and soul under control. An ant by walking travels thousands
of yojanas; even Garuḍa, if he does not move, does not move
39 a single foot. Where is the surface of the earth, and where
is the site of the polar star? Yet Dhruva the son of king
40 Uttána-páda, a denizen of the earth, reached it. Relate *then*
how the good young prince did his feat, that ye may discharge
your indebtednees, my sons!"

The sons spoke.

41 "The high-souled *prince* has told us this feat he did before,
dear father; that he spent his youth, being noted for his good
conduct.

42 "But formerly, dear father, a certain bráhman, the wise
Gálava, bringing a magnificent steed, approached S'atru-jit;
43 and replied to the king—'A certain vile Daitya, an evil-doer,
O king, springing up, is destroying my hermitage without
44 cause day and night, assuming the several forms of a lion, an
elephant, and forest-roving *beasts*, and of other small-bodied
45 animals. When I am absorbed in profound meditation and
deep contemplation, and intent on vows of silence, he raises
46 obstacles so that my mind wavers. Thou art able instantly
to burn him with the fire of thy anger, but not we. Do I
desire that austerities arduously acquired should be squan-

* Govinda.

† The text seems incorrect. For *tasyásti kartavyam* read *tasya kṛitaṃ káryam*? And for *íśvarád* read *íśvarán*?

47 dered, O king? But one day O king, having perceived the
demon, I heaved a sigh, being distressed by him, and exced-
48 ingly depressed in mind. Thereupon this horse fell forth-
with from the sky itself, and a voice from no corporeal being
49 exclaimed—hearken to it, O lord of men!—"Unwearied the
noble steed can traverse the whole circle of the earth with
50 the sun. He has been produced for thee. Nor is his
course stayed in Pátála, in the sky or in water; nor does he
succumb when moving in every direction, or even among the
51 mountains. Since he will traverse the whole circle of the
earth unwearied, he will become famed in the world under the
52 name Kuvalaya. And the base sinful Dánava, who day and
night torments thee, him shall slay, O bráhman, the king named
53 S'atru-jit mounted on this *horse;* and his son Ṛita-dhvaja get-
ting this jewel of a steed shall attain to fame by means of him."
54 I now have met with thee: do thou, O king, ward off that
obstructer of *my* austerities, for a king is interested *therein.*
55 Therefore I have told thee, O king, of this gem of a horse: do
thou command thy son, so that righteousness may not perish.'
56 "At his word the king, righteous in soul, mounting his son
Ṛita-dhvaja, who had performed a solemn ceremony, on that
57 gem of a horse, sent him away then with Gálava. And the
Muni, taking him, departed to his own hermitage-home."

CANTO XXI.

Kuvalayáśva's marriage with Madálasá.

Ṛita-dhvaja, called also Kuvalayáśva, wounds and pursues the Ḍaitya Pátála-ketu.—In the pursuit he falls through a chasm into Pátála and reaches the city Purandara-pura—There he meets Madálasá, (daughter of the Gandharva king Visvávasu,) whom Pátála-ketu had carried off—He marries her with the help of her companion Kuṇḍalá, who then admonishes them on the blessings of marriage—He kills the Daityas who oppose him, and brings her home to his father, who praises and blesses him.

The father spoke.

1 "Relate my sons what the king's son did after he departed
in company with Gálava; your story is a surprising one."

The sons spoke.

2 "The king's son, residing in Gálava's pleasant hermitage,
subdued every obstacle to the reciters of the Veda.
3 "The base Dánava, infected with frenzy and arrogance, did
not know the prince Kuvalayáśva who was dwelling in Gála-
4 va's hermitage. Then assuming the form of a hog, he ap-
proached to outrage the bráhman Gálava, who was busied in
5 the evening service. On an out-cry by the Muni's disciples,
the king's son hastily mounting the horse pursued the boar,
6 shooting arrows *at him;* and drawing his mighty bow, that
was decorated with pretty designs, he struck *the boar* with an
7 arrow shaped like the half-moon. Wounded by the iron
arrow, the wild beast, intent on its own speedy escape, set off
8 for the large forest dense with mountain trees. The horse
followed him impetuously, swift as thought, being urged on
by the king's son who was obeying his father's command.
9 After traversing thousands of yojanas with speed the quick-
10 paced *boar* fell into an open chasm in the earth. Immediately
after him, the king's son also, on his horse, fell into the great
11 chasm, which was enveloped in crass darkness. Then the
beast was lost to the sight of the king's son therein; and he
saw Pátála clearly there, but not that *animal.*

12 "Next he saw the city called Purandara-pura filled with
hundreds of golden palaces, embellished with ramparts.
13 Entering it, he beheld no man there in the city, and as he
wandered about he next saw there a woman hastening along.
14 He questioned her, the slender-limbed, 'Why or on whose
account are you proceeding?' The noble lady replied not a
15 word and ascended into the palace. And the king's son
fastening up his horse on one side followed her indeed, being
wide-eyed with amazement *but* fearless.

16 "Then he saw reclining on a very spacious couch, all made
17 of gold, a solitary maiden, full of love, as it were Rati;—her
face like the clear moon, her eye-brows beautiful, large-hipped
and full-breasted, scarlet-lipped,* slender-bodied, her eyes

* Vimba-lipped. The Vimba, *Cephalandra indica* (*Momordica monadel-*

18 like the blue water-lily, her nails red-tipped, black-complexion-
ed, soft-*skinned*, her hands and feet copper-coloured, her
thighs round and tapering, her teeth beautiful, her locks
dark-blue fine and strong.
19 "On seeing her, lovely in every limb, as it were a creeper on
the body of the god of Love, the king's son thought her the
20 deity of Rasátala. And the beauteous maiden immediately
she saw him, with his dark blue wavy hair, and well-developed
thighs shoulders and arms, deemed him the god of Love.
21 And she rose up, the noble lady, feeling an agitation in her
mind. The slender one was overcome at once by bashfulness,
22 astonishment and dejection. 'Who is this that has come?
Is he a god, or a Yaksha, or a Gandharva, or a Nága, or a
Vidyádhara, *or* a man accomplished in virtuous deeds and
23 love?' Thinking thus, and sighing often, she seated herself
on the ground and then the fascinating-eyed lady swooned
24 away. The king's son, being also smitten by the arrow of
25 Love, revived her, saying 'Do not fear.' And then that
maiden, whom the high-souled *prince* saw before, being dis-
26 tressed took a fan and fanned her. After reviving her, the
maiden, on being questioned by him, somewhat bashfully made
27 known the cause of her friend's fainting. And the noble lady
related to the king's son in detail all the cause of the fainting,
which occurred at the sight of him; and also her story as the
other lady had told it.

"The lady spoke.

28 'The king of the Gandharvas is named Visvávasu, and this
29 is his beautiful-browed daughter called Madálasá. The son
of Vajra-ketu, a fierce Dánava, the cleaver of his foes, was
30 named Pátála-ketu, a dweller within Pátála. He, raising an
illusion of darkness, carried off this maiden when she was in
her garden, unattended by me, and brought her *here*, the
31 villain. On the coming thirteenth day *of the lunar fortnight*,
it was foretold, an Asura shall carry her off; but he does not

pha, Roxb.) bears a bright scarlet berry, 2 inches long, and 1 in diameter. It is a climber, common everywhere (Hooker, vol. II, p. 621; Roxb. p. 696).

deserve the lovely-limbed *maiden*, any more than a śúdra
32 deserves to hear the Veda. And when the day was over,
Surabhi said to the maiden who was ready to kill herself,
33 "This base Dánava shall not get thee. He who shall pierce
him, when he* reaches the world of mortals, with arrows,
34 that one, O noble lady, shall shortly be thy husband." And
I am her prudent companion, Kuṇḍalá by name, the daughter
of Vindhyaván, and the wife of Pushkara-málin, O warrior.
35 My husband having been killed by S'umbha, I am wandering,
in fulfilment of a vow, from one place of pilgrimage to another
36 by a divine course, ready for another world. Pátála-ketu,
evil-souled, when he had assumed a wild boar's form was
pierced by some one with an arrow, to secure the deliverance
37 of the Munis. And I having really followed him, have
returned in haste: *it is* indeed true, the base Dánava has
been smitten by some one.

38 'And this *lady* fell into a swoon: hear what is the cause.
The maiden is full of affection for thee even at *first* sight, O
39 pride-inspirer! who resemblest the sons of the Devas, distin-
guished for gracious speech and other virtues. And she is
allotted as wife to the other, who has wounded the Dánava.
40 For this reason she fell into the deep swoon, and all her life
the slender-limbed maiden will indeed experience suffering.
41 On thee *is fixed* her heart, O enamoured *hero;* and she will
have no other† husband all her life long. Hence is her suffer-
42 ing. Even so was Surabhi's prophecy. But I have come here,
my lord, through affection for her, experiencing grief; for
there is in truth no difference between one's friend's body and
43 one's own. If this lovely lady gets an approved hero for her
husband, then assuredly may I engage in austerities with a
44 mind at ease. But who art thou? and wherefore hast thou
come here, O high-minded *hero? Art thou* a Deva, or Daitya,
45 Gandharva, Nága, or Kinnara? For not here can men come,
nor is human body such *as thine*. Declare thou that, even as
I have spoken truthfully.'

* The Dánava. † For *c'ányo* read *nányo*.

" Kuvalayáśva spoke.

46 'What thou askest me, O *lady* skilled in holy law, who I
am and why I have come, hear that, O *lady* bright of under-
47 standing! I tell it thee from the beginning. Son of king
S'atru-jit, I was despatched by my father, O beauteous one!
I reached Gálava's hermitage for the purpose of protecting
48 the Muni. And while I was affording protection to the Munis
who observe the holy law, there came one, disguised in hog-
49 like form, to hamper them. Pierced by me with an arrow,
shaped like the half-moon, he rushed away with great speed:
50 mounted on horseback I pursued him. Suddenly I fell as in
play into a chasm, and my horse also. Thus mounted on
51 horseback, wandering alone in darkness, I met with light,
and saw thee lady; and when questioned, thou gavest me no
52 answer whatever. And following thee I entered this splen-
did palace. Thus I have related this truly. No Deva am I,
53 or Dánava, nor Nága, nor Gandharva or Kinnara, O sweet-
smiling one! The Devas and the rest are all objects of venera-
tion to me, O Kuṇḍalá. I am a man; thou must not be afraid
of this at any time.'

The sons spoke.

54 "Gladdened thereby, the noble maiden, gazing dully through
bashfulness on the noble countenance of her friend, uttered
55 no word. And again the friend, being gladdened, answered
him, *after saying to her*, 'Truly has he related it, O maiden
obedient to Surabhi's word!'

" Kuṇḍalá spoke.

56 'O hero, unvarnished truth is the word thou hast spoken;
and her heart, perceiving it no otherwise, will gain com-
57 posure. Surpassing beauty indeed clothes the moon, and
light clothes the sun: prosperity attends the happy man,
fortitude the resolute man, and patience the great man.
58 Thou indeed hast assuredly slain that wicked base Dánava:
how shall Surabhi, the mother of cattle, speak falsely?
59 Therefore happy verily is this *maiden* and blessed with good

fortune, in gaining union with thee. Perform, O hero, the needful ceremony, celebrated according to rule.'

The sons spoke.

60 "'I am ready to comply,' thus spoke the king's son to her,
O father. And she thought of him, the large-thighed* *hero*,
61 the chief of his race. And he taking fuel and kúsa grass,
accepted her immediately, through affection for Madálasá and
62 through respect for Kuṇḍalá. Kindling fire, he sacrificed,
being conversant with the mantras, and caused the blessed
maiden to take part in the marriage ceremony. And as he
63 had come, he departed then, being a wise man, to his own
hermitage-abode for the purpose of practising austerities.
"And the companion† said to the maiden 'My wishes are
64 fulfilled, O lovely-faced one. Now that I have seen thee, re-
splendent in beauty, wedded to this *husband*, I will perform
65 matchless austerities, with a mind at ease; and, having my
sins washed away in the waters of the sacred pilgrimage-
places, I shall not *again* become such as I am *now*."

"And then bending courteously she addressed the king's son, being desirous to go, *yet* shaken in her speech through love for her friend.

"Kuṇḍalá spoke.

66 'No counsel should be given even by men to such as thou
art, O man of boundless understanding! and much less there-
67 fore by women; hence I offer thee no counsel. But yet thou
hast caused me also to confide *in thee* with a mind drawn by
love towards this slender-waisted one: I will remind *thee*, O
68 foe-queller. Verily a husband must ever cherish and protect
his wife. A wife is her husband's help-meet unto the com-

* For *tumbúrum* read *tumborum*, "whose thighs are like the tumba," a kind of long gourd, *Lagenaria vulgaris* (*Cucurbita lagenaria*, Roxb.) It appears to be a wild variety. The common plant is the Sanskrit alávu, the modern *kadu* or *láu*. It bears a large, thick, membranous or almost woody fruit, often 1½ foot long, usually bottle- or dumb-bell-shaped (Hooker, vol. II, p. 613; Roxb., p. 700).

† For *sakhím* read *sakhí?*

69 plete attainment of religion, wealth and love. When both
wife and husband are controlled by each other, then all the
70 three combine, religion, wealth and love. How without a wife
does a man attain to religion or wealth or love, my lord? In
71 her the three are set. So also without a husband a wife is
powerless to fulfil religion and the other *duties*. This three-
72 fold group resides in wedded life. Men cannot perform the
worship of the gods, pitṛis and dependants and of guests, with-
73 out a wife, O prince! And riches, although acquired by men,
although brought to their own home, waste away without a
74 wife, or even where a worthless wife dwells. But there is
indeed no love for him *without a wife*,—this is clearly evident.
By community of the wedded pair in their duties he may
75 attain to the three duties. A man satisfies the pitṛis with
children; and guests with preparations of food; likewise the
immortal *gods* with worship; as a man he satisfies a virtuous
76 wife. Moreover for a woman there is no religion, love,
wealth or offspring without a husband. Hence this three-
77 fold group rests upon wedded life. This have I spoken to
you both; and I go as I have wished. Prosper thou with her
in riches, children, happiness and long life.'

The sons spoke.

78 "Having spoken thus, she embraced her friend and bowed
to the prince; and she departed by a divine course according
to her own purpose.

79 "And S'atru-jit's son, being desirous to depart from Pátála,
mounted her on the horse but was perceived by Danu's off-
80 spring. Thereon they suddenly shouted out, 'She is being
carried off, she is being carried far away, the pearl among
81 maidens, whom Pátála-ketu brought from heaven. Besides
he has won the might of the Dánavas, the iron-staff, the sword,
the club, the spear, the bow, together with Pátála-ketu.'
82 'Stand, stand!' thus exclaiming, the Dánava chiefs then
83 rained* a shower of arrows and spears on the king's son. And
S'atru-jit's son, excelling in valour, split their weapons with

* For *vavarshur* read *vavṛishur*?

84 a multitude of arrows, laughing as if in sport. In a moment
the surface of Pátála was covered with the swords, lances,
spears and arrows, which were split by the multitudes of
85 Ṛita-dhvaja's arrows. Then taking up Tvashṭṛi's weapon
he hurled it against the Dánavas; thereby all those Dánavas
86 together with Pátála-ketu were turned into heaps of bones
bursting with the excessive heat from blazing rings of fire,
just as the oceans were burnt up when the fire of Kapila fell
on them.

87 "Then the prince, seated on horseback, after slaying the
chiefs of the Asuras, came to his father's city with that pearl
88 of women; and prostrating himself he recounted every-
thing to his father, both the visit to Pátála, and the meeting
89 with Kuṇḍalá, and the meeting with Madálasá, and the con-
flict with the Dánavas, and their slaughter with the weapon,
and the return.

90 "His father, having thus heard the exploits of *his* graceful-
minded *son*, was both filled with affection and embracing his
91 son spoke thus—'I have been delivered by thee, O son,
worthy, magnanimous, who hast saved from their fears the
92 Munis who follow true religion. The fame handed down
by my ancestors has been further augmented by me: thou, O
93 son, mighty in valour, hast multiplied it. Now he, who does
not diminish the glory, wealth or heroism which his father
94 has acquired, is known as an ordinary man. But whoever
strikes out by his own might fresh *heroism* still, exceeding his
95 father's heroism, the wise call him great among men. Who-
ever lessens the wealth and heroism and glory acquired by
96 his father, the wise call him base among men. I then had
accomplished even as thou hast the bráhman's deliverance.
And the visit to Pátála that *thou madest*, and the destruction
97 of the Asuras that *thou didst effect*, even this, my child, is
in excess, hence thou art great among men. Therefore thou
98 art fortunate, my boy. I indeed in getting thee, such a son
as this, excelling in virtues, am to be praised even by
righteous men. That man does not, I hold, gain the affec-
99 tion of adopted sons, who does not surpass his son in wis-

dom, liberality and valour. Fie on the birth of him who
100 is known in the world through his father! He who attains
fame through a son, his birth *is the birth* of a nobly born *man.*
The fortunate man is known by reason of himself; the
101 ordinary man by reason of his father and grandfather; the
base man attains distinction through his mother's relations and
his mother. Therefore, my son, prosper thou in riches and
102 heroism and in happiness. And never let this daughter of
the Gandharva be parted from thee.'

"Thus he was addressed by his father kindly again and
103 again in various sort; and after an embrace he was permitted
to depart with his wife to his own residence. He lived there
104 joyfully in the society of his wife in his father's city, and also
elsewhere in gardens, woods, and mountain-tops. And she,
the lovely, the beautiful-waisted, having prostrated herself
before the feet of her parents-in-law, thereafter morning by
morning enjoyed herself in companionship with him."

CANTO XXII.

The story of Kuvalayáśva (continued): Madálasá's death.

Pátála-ketu's brother Tála-ketu, in the guise of a Muni dwelling on the bank of the Yamuná, induces Kuvalayáśva to guard his hermitage, on the pretext that he had certain ceremonies to perform in the water—Disappearing within the water he goes to the palace and reports that Kuvalayáśva had died in battle with the Daityas—Madálasá dies through grief, and the king and queen utter their lamentations, and perform the prince's obsequies—Tála-ketu then returns to the hermitage and releases the prince.

The sons spoke.

1 "Many days afterwards the king again addressed his son,
'Mounting this horse go quickly to rescue the bráhmans,
2 and patrol the earth, morning by morning, day by day,
for the bráhmans' freedom from molestation must always be
3 sought after. There are evil-behaved Dánavas in hundreds,
born in wickedness; do thou so act that the Munis may ex-

4 perience no obstacle from them.' Then the king's son did as
he was directed by his father. After traversing the whole
5 earth, the king's son did obeisance to his father's feet in
the forenoon, as each day came round; and then during the
rest of the day he enjoyed himself with her, the slender-
waisted one.

6 "One day, however, while moving about, he saw Pátála-
ketu's younger brother Tála-ketu, who had fixed his hermitage
7 on the bank of the Yamuná. The wily Dánava had assumed a
Muni's shape. Bearing the previous enmity in mind, he
8 accosted the king's son—'O royal prince! I accost thee, do
thou then accomplish *my request* if thou art willing: nor must
thou refuse my petition, thou that art true to thy promise!
9 I will offer a sacrifice to Dharma, and the oblations also
must be made. The funeral piles must be put up there, since
10 they have not *yet* ascended into the air. Hence give me,
O hero! this thy own ornament that is about thy neck
11 for gold, and guard thou my hermitage, until I praise
within the water the god Varuna, the lord of marine animals,
with the mantras prescribed by the Vedas for Varuna's
12 worship, which cause creatures to thrive, and in haste
return.' To him as he spoke thus the prince did obeisance
13 and then gave his neck-ornament, and replied to him, 'Go
sir! with a mind at ease; I will stay in this very spot near
thy hermitage according to thy command, Sir! until thy
14 coming again. No man shall cause thee molestation here
while I stay. And do thou in *perfect* confidence, without
hurry, O bráhman, accomplish thy purpose.'

15 "Being thus addressed by him, he then plunged into the
water in the river, while the prince guarded the other's magic-
16 raised hermitage. And Tála-ketu went from that river to
the prince's town, and spoke thus in the presence of Madálasá
and other *persons*.

"Tála-ketu spoke.

17 'The hero, Kuvalayáśva, while guarding the ascetics close
to my hermitage, fighting with a certain wicked Daitya

18 and striking down the bráhmans' foes in the conflict with all
his might, was pierced in the breast with a spear by the
19 wicked *Daitya* who resorted to magic. While dying he
gave me this neck-ornament; and śúdra ascetics gave him
20 to the fire in the wood. And the frightened horse which
uttered distressed neighings, with tearful eyes, was led off
21 by that cruel Dánava. This beheld I, malicious, evil-doer.
Whatever should forthwith be done in this *matter*, let it be
22 done without delay. And take this neck-ornament as a consolation to your hearts, for we ascetics may not have anything to do with gold.'

The sons spoke.

23 "Having so spoken, he left it on the ground and departed
as he had come. And those people afflicted with grief, fell
24 down, ill with fainting. Immediately recovering consciousness all those royal handmaids, and the queens and the king
25 lamented sorely distressed. But Madálasá seeing that his
neck-ornament, and hearing that her husband was slain,
quickly yielded up her dear life.

26 "Thereon a great cry arose in the houses of the citizens,
27 even as there was in the king's own house. And the king
beholding Madálasá bereft of her husband and dead, made
answer to all the people, having recovered his composure
28 after due reflection. 'Ye should not weep, nor I, I perceive,
when one considers the fleetingness of even all relations.
29 Why do I bewail my son? Why do I bewail my daughter-in-law? I think after due reflection, that neither should be
30 bewailed, since events happen as they are fated. Why
should my son, who in obedience to me has met death when
engaged in guarding the dvijas according to my command,
31 be bewailed by the intelligent? Assuredly if my son has
quitted *his body* on account of those dvijas, will not that body,
32 to which he resorts, cause him to rise higher? And how is it
possible that this high-born *lady*, thus faithful to her husband,
should be bewailed? For women have no deity besides a hus-
33 band. For she would have to be thus bewailed by us, and her
relatives, and other compassionate persons, if she were

34 separated from her husband. But this noble *lady*, who on
hearing of the death of her husband has immediately follow-
ed her husband, should not for this reason be bewailed by
35 the wise. Those women should be bewailed, who are sepa-
rated *from their husbands;* those should not be bewailed who
have died with them: but this grateful *wife* has not expe-
36 rienced separation from her husband. Verily what woman
in both the worlds would think her husband human, who
gives *her* all happinesses both in this world and the next?
37 Neither should he be bewailed, nor yet this *lady*, nor I, nor
his mother. We were all rescued by him who resigns his life
38 for the sake of the bráhmans. For my high-souled son, by
relinquishing his body which was half consumed, has freed
himself from his debt to the bráhmans, to me, to religion.
39 Though losing his life in war, he did not surrender his
mother's honour, the spotless fame of my family, or his own
heroism.'

40 "Then Kuvalayáśva's mother, having heard of her son's death, looked upon her husband and, immediately after her husband, spoke similarly.

" The mother spoke.

41 'Not such gratification did my mother or my sister get,
O king! as I have felt in hearing that my son has been slain
42 while protecting the Muni. Those who die, sighing, in
great distress, afflicted with illness, while their relatives
lament,—their mother has brought forth children in vain.
43 Those who, while fearlessly fighting in battle to guard cattle
and dvijas, perish crushed with arrows, they indeed are
44 *really* men in the world. He who turns not his back on sup-
pliants, friends, and enemies, in him his father has a *real*
45 son, and *in him* his mother has given birth to a hero. A
woman's pain of conception reaches, I think, its success at
the time when her son either vanquishes his foes or is slain
in battle.'

The sons spoke.

46 "Then the king bestowed the funeral obsequies on his son

and daughter: and having gone forth bathed and offered the water to his son.

47 "And Tála-ketu also, having issued from the Yamuná's
water, spoke this honied speech respectfully to the king's
48 son. 'Depart, O prince; thou hast caused me to be success-
ful. While thou hast remained stationary here, the long
49 wished-for business, and the sacrificial acts to Varuṇa the
high-souled lord of the ocean, all that I have completed, as
I had desired.'

50 "The king's son did him reverence and departed to his
father's city, mounting on that steed which sped along like
Garuḍa and the wind."

Canto XXIII.

Kuvalayáśva's visit to Pátála.

Kuvalayáśva, returning home, learnt what had happened—He mourns his loss, and shunning women lives a cheerful life—The Nága king Aśvatara, hearing this story, engages in austerities and extols Sarasvatí—Sarasvatí, propitiated by him, restores him his companion Kambala, and gives them both perfect skill in poetry and music—Both propitiate S'iva, who at their request gives Aśvatara Madálasá as his daughter, restored to life as before—At Aśvatara's suggestion, his sons invite Kuvalayáśva to their palace in Pátála and introduce him to their father—Aśvatara asks Kuvalayáśva to relate his story.

The sons spoke.

1 The king's son reaching then his own city in haste, desirous
to salute his parents' feet respectfully, and eager to see Madá-
2 lasá, beheld some people of the city downcast, with joyless
countenances, and then again astonished with joyful faces:
3 and other people with wide-open eyes, exclaiming "Hurrah!
hurrah!" embracing one another, filled with the utmost
4 curious interest. "Long mayest thou live, O most fortunate
prince! Thy adversaries are slain; gladden thy parents' mind
and ours also, which is relieved of anxiety.

5 Surrounded before and behind by the citizens who were
crying out thus, his joy forthwith aroused, he entered his

6 father's palace. And his father and mother and other relations embraced him, and then invoked on him auspicious bless-
7 ings, saying "Long mayest thou live!" Thereupon having done obeisance, surprised at what this *might mean*, he questioned his father; and he duly explained it to him.

8 On hearing that his wife Madálasá, the darling of his heart, was dead, and seeing his parents before *him*, he fell into the
9 midst of a sea of shame and grief. He thought, "The maiden, on hearing I was dead, gave up life, the virtuous one: fie on
10 me harsh-minded *that I am!* Malignant am I, worthless am I, that I live most pitiless, when deprived of that deer-eyed
11 one who encountered death for my sake!" Again he thought, having firmly composed his mind, banishing hastily the rising distraction, and breathing hard outwards and inwards, feeling undone.

12 "If I abandon life because she has died on my account, what benefit shall I confer on her? Yet this would be praise-
13 worthy in women's opinion. Or if being downcast I weep, repeatedly exclaiming 'ah! my beloved,' still this would not
14 be praiseworthy in us; for we are men assuredly. Frigid with grief, downcast, ungarlanded, uncleansed, I shall then become
15 an object of contumely to my adversaries. I must cut off my enemies, and obey the king, my father. And how then can I
16 resign my life which is dependant on him? But here, I consider, I must renounce pleasure with woman, and yet that *renunciation* does not tend to benefit the slender-limbed one.
17 Nevertheless in every way I must practise harmlessness, which works neither benefit nor injury. This is little for me *to do* on her account who resigned her life on mine."

The sons spoke.

18 Having thus resolved, Ṛita-dhvaja then performed the ceremony of offering water, and immediately afterwards performed the obsequies; and he spoke again.

Ṛita-dhvaja spoke.

19 "If she, Madálasá, the slender-limbed, were not my wife, I
20 would not have another companion in this life. Besides that fawn-eyed daughter of the Gandharva, I will not love

21 any woman—so have I spoken in truth. Having given up
that wife, who observed true religion, whose gait was like the
elephant's, I will not assent to any *woman*—this have I declared
in truth."

The sons spoke.

22 And having renounced, dear father, all the delights of
woman, bereft of her, he continued to sport in company with
his peers, his equals in age, in the perfection of his good dis-
23 position. This was his supreme deed, dear father. Who is
able to do that which is exceedingly difficult of accomplishment
by the gods, how much more so by others ?

Jaḍa spoke.

24 Having heard their speech, *their* father became dissatified;
and after reflecting the Nága king addressed his two sons, as
if in ridicule.

The Nága king Aśvatara spoke.

25 "If men, deeming a thing impossible, will put forth no effort
26 in the deed, from the loss of exertion there ensues loss. Let
a man undertake a deed, without squandering his own man-
hood; the accomplishment of a deed depends on fate and on
27 manhood. Therefore I will so strive, my sons, hence-
forth—let me so practise austerities diligently,—that this
may in time be accomplished."

Jaḍa spoke.

28 Having spoken thus, the Nága king went to Plakshávata-
raṇa,* the place of pilgrimage on the Himavat mountain, and
29 practised most arduous austerities. And then he praised the
goddess Sarasvatí there with his invocations, fixing his mind
on her, restricting his food, performing the three prescribed
ablutions.†

Aśvatara spoke.

30 "Desirous of propitiating the resplendent goddess Jagad-
dhátrí Sarasvatí, who is sprung from Brahmá, I will praise
31 her, bowing my head before her. Good and bad, O goddess,

* Where the R. Sarasvatí takes its rise.

† At morning, noon, and evening.

whatever *there be*, the cause that confers alike final enancipation and riches,—all that, conjoint and separate, resides in
32 thee, O goddess. Thou, O goddess, art the imperishable and the supreme, wherein everything is comprised; *thou art* the imperishable and the supreme, which are established like the
33 Atom. The imperishable and the supreme is Brahma, and this universe is perishable by nature. Fire resides in wood,
34 and the atoms are of earth. So in thee resides Brahma, and this world in its entirety; in thee is the abode of the sound Om, and whatever is immoveable and moveable, O goddess.
35 In thee *reside* the three prosodial times,* O goddess, all that exists and does not exist, the three worlds,† the three Vedas,
36 the three sciences,‡ the three fires,§ the three lights,|| and the three colours,¶ and the law-book; the three qualities, the three sounds,** the three Vedas, and the *three* áśramas,††
37 the three times, and the *three* states of life, the pitṛis, day, night and the rest. This trinity of standards is thy form, O
38 goddess Sarasvatí! The seven soma-saṃsthá *sacrifices*, and the seven haviḥ-saṃsthá *sacrifices*, and the seven páka-saṃsthá‡‡ *sacrifices*, which are *deemed* the earliest by those

* Mátrá; short, long, and prolated.

† Loka; earth, atmosphere and the sky.

‡ Vidyá; metaphysics (with logic), the art of government, and the practical arts (?)

§ Pávaka; gárhapatya, áhavaníya, and dakshiṇa.

|| Jyotis; fire on the earth, ether in the atmosphere, and the sun in the sky.

¶ Varṇa; or, the three castes.

** Śabda.

†† Áśrama; those of the gṛiha-stha, vana-prastha, and bhikshu.

‡‡ The names of these sacrifices are thus given me by the Pandit of the Bengal Asiatic Society. The Soma-samsthá are (1) agni-shṭoma, (2) atyaugishṭoma, (3) ukthya, (4) shoḍaśin, (5) atirátra, (6) vájaheya, and (7) áptoryáma. The haviḥ-saṃsthá are (1) agnyádheya, (2) agni-hotra, (3) darśa-púrnamásan, (4) c'áturmásyani, (5) paśu-bandha, (6) sautra-maṇi, and (7) agrajaṇeshṭi. The páka-saṃsthá are given differently by different authors. According to Ápastamba they are (1) anpásana-homa, (2) vaiśva-deva, (3) párvaṇa, (4) ashṭaká, (5) śráddha, (6) sarpa-bali, (7) isána-bali. According to Baudháyaṇa, (1) huta, (2) prahuta, (3) áhuta, (4) śúlagava, (5) bali-

who think differently, and which are as eternal as Brahma,*
39 are performed by those, who assert that all things are Brahma,
with the utterance of thy *name*, O goddess. Undefinable,
40 composed of half a measure, supreme, unchanging, imperishable, celestial, devoid of alteration is this thy other supreme
41 form which I cannot express. And even the mouth does not declare it, nor the tongue, the copper-coloured lip, or other *organs*. Even Indra, the Vasus, Brahmá, the Moon and
42 Sun, and Light *cannot declare thy form*, whose dwelling is the universe, which has the form of the universe; which is the ruler of the universe, the Supreme Ruler; which is mentioned in the discussions of the Sánkhya and Vedánta philosophies, and firmly established in many S'ákhás; which is
43 without beginning middle or end; which is good, bad, and neutral; which is but one, is many, and yet is not one; which assumes *various* kinds of existence; which is without name,
44 and yet is named after the six guṇas, is named after the classes, and resides in the three guṇas; which is one among many powerful, possesses the majesty of the S'aktis, and is supreme.
45 Happiness and unhappiness, having the form of great happiness, appear in thee. Thus, O goddess, that which has parts is pervaded by thee, and so also that which has no parts; that which resides in non-duality, and that which resides in duality
46 (O bráhman). Things that are permanent, and others that perish; those again that are gross, or those that are subtler than the subtle; those again that are on the earth, or those that are in the atmosphere or elsewhere;—they all derive their
47 perceptibility from thee indeed. Everything—both that which is destitute of visible shape, and that which has visible shape; or whatever is severally single in the elements; that which is

haraṇa, (6) pratyavarohaṇa, and (7) ashṭaká-homa. According to Gautama, (1) ashṭaká, (2) parvaṇa, (3) śráddha, (4) śravaṇi, (5) ágraháyani, (6) c'aitrí, and (7) áśvayuji.

* A MS. in the Sanskrit College reads *ádye* for *ádyá*, and *sanátane* for *sanátanáḥ*; with this reading the first line of the verse would qualify *devi sarasvati*, if *sanátane* be taken as an *ársha* form of *sanátani*. But these verses seem obscure.

in heaven, on the surface of the earth, in the sky or elsewhere;—is connected with thee by thy vowels and by thy consonants!"

Jaḍa spoke.

48 Thereupon, being praised thus, the goddess Sarasvatí, who is Vishnu's tongue, answered the high-souled Nága Aśvatara.

Sarasvatí spoke.

49 "I grant thee a boon, O Nága king, brother of Kambala; speak therefore: I will give thee what is revolving in thy mind."

Aśvatara spoke.

50 "Give thou me, O goddess, Kambala indeed my former companion, and bestow on us both a conversance with all sounds."

Sarasvatí spoke.

51 "The seven musical notes,* the seven modes in the musical scale,† O most noble Nága! the seven songs also,‡ and the

* Svara, a "musical note." There are 7 *svaras*, viz., *shaḍja*, *ṛishabha*, *gándhára*, *madhyama*, *pañc'ama*, *dhaivata*, and *nisháda*; and they are designated by their initial sounds, *sa*, *ri*, *ga*, *ma*, *pa*, *dha*, and *ni*: but the arrangement varies, and Prof. Monier-Williams in his dictionary places *nisháda* first, *shaḍja* fourth, and *pañc'ama* seventh. Those 7 svaras compose the "musical scale," *gráma* (Beng. *saptak*). The interval between each consecutive pair of notes is divided into several 'lesser notes' called *śruti*; thus there are 4 between *sa* and *ri*, 3 between *ri* and *ga*, 2 between *ga* and *ma*, 4 between *ma* and *pa*, 4 between *pa* and *dha*, 3 between *dha* and *ni*, and 2 betweeen *ni* and *sa* in the higher octave—that is 22 *s'rutis* in all. The *svaras* correspond to the 'natural notes,' and the *s'rutis* to the 'sharps and flats' in European music. (Raja Sourindro Mohun Tagore's *Sangíta-sára-sangraha*, pp. 22—24, where the names of the *s'rutis* are given; and his Victoria-gíti-málá in Bengali, Introduction.)

† Gráma-rága. I do not find this in the dictionary. Does it mean the "series of musical scales" that can be formed by taking each of the notes (*svara*) as the 'key' note? Thus there would be 7 scales, as there are 7 notes. But Raja S. M. Tagore calls this *svara-grám* (Beng.), and he says that only 3 such scales were common in early times, *viz.*, those with *shaḍja*, *gándhára* and *madhyama* as key notes (Victoria-gíti-málá, Introduction, p. 2).

‡ Gítaka. I do not know what the seven songs are.

52 same number of modulations,* so also the forty-nine musical
times,† and the three octaves‡—all these thou and also Kam-
53 bala shalt sing, O sinless one! Thou shalt know more yet
through my favour, O Nága king. I have given thee the four
kinds of quater-verse,§ the three sorts of musical tunes,|| the
54 three kinds of musical movoment,¶ also the three pauses in

* Múrc'haná. This seems to be "running up or down the scale;" it is defined thus—

Kramát svaráṇáṃ saptánám árohaś c'ávarohaṇam
Múrc'hanetyuc'yate gráma-traye táḥ sapta sapta c'a.

As there are 7 scales obtained by taking any of the 7 notes as the key note, there would be 7 *múrc'hanás;* and this applies to the 3 octaves (*gráma-traya*), so that there are 21 *múrc'hanás* altogether (*Sangita-sára-sangraha*, p. 30, where their names are given). But in his Bengali Treatise Raja S. M. Tagore explains *múrc'haná* to be the "passing *uninterruptedly* from one note (*svara*) to another, and in the process sounding all the intermediate notes and lesser notes (*s'ruti*)." This corresponds to 'slurring.' With this meaning the number of possible *múrc'hanás* is almost indefinite.

† Tála, the "division of time in music." It consists of three things, *kála*, the duration of time, *kriyá*, the clapping of the hands (accentuation), and *mána*, the interval between the clappings. It seems to correspond to the 'bar' and the 'kinds of time' in European music. European music has only 3 kinds of time, Common, Triple and Compound, each with a few subdivisions; but in Hindu music there is the utmost variety. I do not know what the 49 tálas here meant are; but Raja S. M. Tagore gives two lists of *des'í-tálas*, one enumerating 120, and the other 72.

‡ Gráma, the "octave." Hindu music uses only three octaves, which are called *nimna* (Beng. *udárá*), *madhya* (*mudárá*) and *uc'c'a* (*tárá*).

§ Pada.

|| Tála. This seems to refer to the classification of the *tálas*, viz., *śuddha*, *sálan.ga* (or *sálan.ka* or *sálaga*, v. r.) and *san-kírṇa*, (Raja S. M. Tagore's Sangíta-sára-sangraha, p. 201); but this classification is also applied to the *rágas* (see his Victoria-gíti-málá, Introduction, p. 9.). The *śuddha* are explained to be the famous kinds complete in themselves; the *sálanga* are those produced by a mixture of two simple ones; and the *sankírṇa* those produced by a mixture of many simple ones.

¶ Laya, "musical speed." The 3 kinds are *druta*, quick, *madhya*, mean, and *vilambita*, slow; the *druta* being twice as fast as the *madhya*, and the *madhya* twice as fast as the *vilambita*. Laya does not take account of prosodial time. This corresponds to "the movement" in European music.

music,* and the four-fold todya.† This thou *shalt know* through
55 my favour O Nága king, and what lies further. What is
contained within this *and* dependant *thereon*, measured in
vowels and consonants—all that I have given to thee and
56 Kambala. *I have* not so *given* it to any other on the
earth or in Pátála, O Nága: and ye shall be the teachers
of all this in Pátála and in heaven and on earth also, ye
two Nágas !"

Jaḍa spoke.

57 Having spoken thus, the lotus-eyed goddess Sarasvatí, the
tongue of all, then disappeared at once from the Nága's view.
58 And then, as it all happened to those two *Nágas*, there was
begotten in both the fullest knowledge in versification,
musical time, musical notes, &c.
59 Then the two Nágas, observing musical time on the lute-
strings, being desirous of propitiating with seven songs the
60 lord who dwells on the peaks of Kailása and Himálaya,
the god S'iva, who destroyed Káma's body, both exerted
61 themselves to the utmost, with voice and tone combined, being
assiduous morning, night, noon and the two twilights. The
bull-bannered god, being long praised by them both, was
62 gratified with their song, and said to both, "Choose ye a
boon." Thereon Aśvatara with his brother doing reverence
63 made request to S'iva, the blue-throated, Umá's lord,—
"If thou, O adorable three-eyed god of the gods, art pleased
64 with us, then grant us this boon according to our desire;

* Yati, "a break in the *laya*" (*laya-pravṛitti-niyama*), 'a rest' in music. The 3 kinds are *samá*, *sroto-gatá*, and *go-puc'c'há*. The *samá* may occur at the beginning, in the middle, or at the end of the *laya*, and in each of the 3 kinds of *laya*. The *sroto-gatá* occurs apparently when the time quickens (*accelerando*) after the rest, that is when the *laya* changes from *vilambita* to *madhya*, or from *madhya* to *druta*, or from *vilambita* or *madhya* to *druta*. The *go-puc'c'há* occurs apparently when the time becomes slower (*rallentando*, *ritardando*) after the rest, that is when the *laya* changes from *druta* to *madhya*, or from *madhya* to *vilambita*.

† Todya. I do not find this word in the dictionary. Does it mean 'drum-music?'

let Kuvalayáśva's deceased wife, Madálasá, O god, at once
65 become my daughter of the same age *as when she died*, remembering her life as before, endowed with the selfsame beauty, as a devotee, and the mother of Yoga; let her be born in my house, O S'iva."

S'iva spoke.

66 "As thou hast spoken, most noble Nága, it shall all happen
through my favour, in very truth. Hearken also to this, O
67 Nága. But when the śráddha is reached, thou shouldst eat
the middle piṇḍa by thyself, most noble Nága, being pure, and
68 having thy mind subdued; and then, when that is eaten,
the happy *lady* shall rise out of thy middle hood, the same in
69 form as when she died. And having pondered on this thy
desire, do thou perform the libation to the pitṛis; immediate-
70 ly she, the fine-browed, the auspicious, shall rise out of thy
breathing middle hood, the same in form as when she died."
71 Having heard this, both then adored S'iva, and returned,
full of contentment, to Rasátala. And so the Nága, Kam-
72 bala's younger brother, performed the śráddha, and also
duly ate the middle piṇḍa; and, while he pondered on that
73 his desire, the slender-waisted *lady* was produced* at once,
in the selfsame form, out of his breathing middle hood.
74 And the Nága told that to no one: he kept her, the lovely-
teethed one, concealed by his women in the inner apartments.
75 And the two sons of the Nága king pursuing pleasure day
by day, played† with Ṛita-dhvaja like the immortals. But
76 one day the Nága king, being intoxicated, spoke to his sons,
"Why indeed do ye not do as I told you before? The king's
77 son is your benefactor in my opinion; why do ye not confer
a benefit on him, the pride-inspirer? Thereupon they both,
being thus admonished by their kindly-affectioned father,
78 went to their friend's city, and enjoyed themselves with
the wise *prince*. Then both, after having held some other
79 talk with Kuvalayáśva, invited him respectfully to come to
their house. The king's son said to them, "Is not this your

* For *yajṇe* read *jajṇe*. † Read *cikriḍáte* for *ciktiḍáte*.

80 house? Whatever is mine, riches, carriages, garments, &c., that
is indeed yours. But whatever ye desire should be given you,
81 riches or jewels, let that be given you, O young dvijas, if ye have
friendly regard for me. Am I cheated by such a cruel fate as
82 this, that ye do not evince any sense of ownership in my
house? If ye must do me kindness, if I am to receive favour
83 from you, then consider my wealth and home as your own.
84 Whatever is yours is mine, mine is your own. Believe ye
this in truth. My life has gone out *into you*. Never again
must ye speak of separate property, O virtuous dvijas:
85 since ye are devoted to my favour, I have adjured you by my
heart affectionately."

Thereupon both the young Nágas, their faces beaming with
86 affection, replied to the king's son, somewhat feigning anger.
"Ṛita-dhvaja, without doubt, we must not think in our mind
87 in this matter otherwise than thou hast now spoken. But
our high-souled father has himself repeatedly said this—'I
88 wish to see that Kuvalayáśva.'" Thereon Kuvalayáśva
rising from his seat of honour, prostrated himself on the
ground, saying, "Be it as your dear father says."

Kuvalayáśva spoke.

89 "Happy am I! Most rich in merit am I! Who else is there
like me, that your father shews an earnest mind to see me?
90 Rise ye therefore, let us go: not even for a moment do I wish
to transgress his command here. I swear by his feet!"

Jaḍa spoke.

91 Having spoken thus the king's son went with them both,
and issuing from the city reached the holy river Gomatí.
92 They passed through it, the Nága princes and the king's son:
and the king's son thought their home *lay* on the other side
93 of the *river*. And drawing *him* thence, they led the prince
to Pátála; and in Pátála he beheld them both as young
94 Nágas, lustrous* with the gems in their hoods, displaying
the svastika marks. Gazing with eyes wide open with
amazement at them both, who were most handsomely formed,

* Read *kṛitoddyotau* for *kṛitodyotau*.

95 and smiling he spoke kindly—"Bravo! most noble dvijas!"
96 And they told him of their father, the Nága king, Aśvatara
by name, peaceful, worthy of honour by the heaven-dwellers.
97 Then the king's son saw charming Pátála; which was
adorned with Nágas, young adult and old, and also with
98 Nága maidens, who were playing here and there, and who wore
beautiful ear-rings and necklaces, as the sky *is decked* with
stars; and elsewhere *resounding with* drums, small drums,
99 and musical instruments, *mingled* with the strains of singing,
which kept time with the sounds of lutes and pipes; filled
100 with hundreds of charming houses. Gazing about on Pátála
S'atru-jit's son the foe-queller, walked *about* accompanied by
those two Nágas his friends.

101 Then they all entered the Nága king's residence, and they
saw the high-souled Nága king seated, clad in heavenly
garlands and raiment, adorned with gems and ear-rings, re-
102 splendent with superb pearl-necklaces, *decorated* with armlets,
blessed with good fortune, on a throne all of gold, the frame of
103 which was overlaid with a multitude of gems coral and lapis
lazuli.

They showed the king to him saying "That is our father;"
104 and they introduced him to their father, saying "This is the
hero Kuvalayáśva." Then Ṛita-dhvaja bowed at the feet of
105 the Nága king. Raising him up by force, the Nága king
embraced him warmly, and kissing him on the head he
106 said "Long mayest thou live, and destroying all thy foes, be
submissive to thy father. My son thy virtues have been
107 mentioned even in thy absence, happy *that thou art*; thy
rare *virtues* have been reported to me by my two sons.
108 Mayest thou indeed prosper thereby in mind, speech, body
and behaviour: the life of a virtuous man is praise-worthy;
a worthless man although alive is dead. A virtuous man,
while accomplishing his own good, brings complete satisfac-
109 tion to his parents, anguish into the hearts of his enemies,
and confidence among the populace. The gods, the pitṛis,
110 bráhmans, friends, suppliants, the maimed and others, and
his relatives also desire a long life for the virtuous man.

The life of virtuous men, who eschew abuse, who are compassionate towards those in trouble, who are the refuge of those in calamity, abounds in *good* fruit."

Jaḍa spoke.

111 Having spoken thus to that hero, the Nága next addressed
his two sons thus, being desirous to do honour to Kuva-
112 layáśva. "When we have finished our ablutions and all the
other proceedings in due order, *when we have* drunk wine and
enjoyed other pleasures, *when we have* feasted up to our
113 desire, we shall then with joyful minds spend a short
time with Kuvalayáśva in *hearing* the story of the success of
114 his heart's festival." And atru-jit's son assented in silence
to that speech. Accordingly the lofty-minded king of the
Nágas did *as he had proposed.*

115 The great king of the Nágas, true to his word, assembling with his own sons and the king's son, filled with joy, feasted on foods and wines, up to fitting bounds, self-possessed and enjoying pleasure.

Canto XXIV.

The story of Kuvalayáśva (continued).

The Recovery of Madálasá.

The Nága king Aśvatara asks Kuvalayáśva what gift he can confer on him—Kuvalayáśva replies he needs nothing, and is sufficiently gratified by the king's favour—The king urges him and at his sons' suggestion the prince asks to see Madálasá even in illusion—The king brings her in as an illusion, and afterwards restores her to Kuvalayáśva.

Jaḍa spoke.

1 His two sons and the king's son respectfully attended the
2 high souled king of the Nágas, after he had banquetted. The
high-souled Nága manifested kindly regard towards his sons'
3 friend with suitable conversation, and said, "Declare, Sir,
what pleasure I must do thee who hast entered my house:

cast away hesitation towards me as a son *would* towards his
4 father. Whether silver or gold, raiment, carriages, or seats,
or whatever thou dost highly appreciate that is hard to be
got—ask that of me."

Kuvalayáśva spoke.

5 "Through thy favour, illustrious Sir! gold and other *wealth*
are in my father's house; I have no need of any such thing
6 at all now. While my father rules this earth for thousands
of years and thou also *rulest* Pátála, my mind is not expectant
7 in solicitation. They are both possessed of Svarga and are
very rich in merit, who from their youth possess, in their
father's lifetime, a mere particle* of wealth amidst his
8 krores of wealth, friends equally-educated, and a body
free from sickness. My father† holds the wealth; have I
9 not youth? When wealth is wanting, men's minds become
prone to petitions. When I have it in full measure, how shall
10 my tongue make petition? Those who need not think
whether they have any riches at home or not, happy are they,
sheltered in the shadow of the tree of their father's arm.
11 But those, who even from childhood losing their father
have had the care of a family, they have in my opinion,
through the ruin of their taste for happiness, been tricked by
12 the Creator. We therefore through thy favour always give
willingly to supplicants the hoards of money, gems and other
13 *wealth* left by our fathers. I have everything then here,
since I have touched thy feet with my crest-jewel, since I have
touched thy body."

Jaḍa spoke.

14 Being answered thus in a modest speech, the noble Nága
replied kindly to the young prince, the benefactor of his sons.

The Nága spoke.

15 "If it be not thy mind to receive of me gems, gold or other
gift; whatever else may please thy mind, mention thou it. I
will give *it thee*."

* Wealth as small as the point of a blade of grass.

† Read *janitrá* for *janitá*.

Kuvalayáśva spoke.

16 "My lord, through thy favour, I whom thou dost ask have
everything at home: it has been gained especially through
17 sight of thee. And herein I am successful, and my life has
been rewarded, that I a mortal have embraced thy body who
18 art divine; that the dust of thy feet has found a seat on
my head. What indeed have I not gained thereby, O Nága
19 king? But if thou needs must give me the boon that I
desire, then let not the faculty of working righteousness
20 depart from my heart. Gold, gems, jewels and such like,
carriages, houses, seats, women, food and drink, and children,
21 and tasteful garlands and ointments,—both these various
objects of desire, and also vocal and instrumental music and
whatever other *music there be*—all this I hold to be the fruit
22 of the tree of good works. Therefore a man must start
from the root thereof; he must exert himself, while ruling
his spirit; nothing in the world is hard of attainment to those
who adhere to good works."

Aśvatara spoke.

23 "So shall thy mind be, O wise man, relying on righteous-
ness; and truly all this is the fruit of righteousness as thou
24 hast said. Nevertheless thou must certainly take, now that
thou hast entered my house, what thou thinkest hard to be
gained in the human world."

Jaḍa spoke.

25 Having heard this his speech, the young prince then
26 looked at the faces of the Nága king's sons. Thereupon both
those heroes prostrating themselves told their father clearly
all the young prince's thoughts.

The sons spoke.

27 "When this *prince's* beloved wife heard that he was slain,
she forsook her dear life, being deceived by a certain cruel,
28 bad-minded Dánava, who shewed his enmity. *She was* the
29 daughter of the Gandharva king; she was named Madálasá.
Then he, mindful of the past, made this vow, dear father,
30 'No other shall be my wife save Madálasá.' This hero Ṛita-

dhvaja longs, dear father, to behold her, lovely-limbed: if this may be done, let it be done."

Aśvatara spoke.

31 "Such magical power as that belongs to one who is exempt from such gross elements. How can this be except as a dream or as an illusion proceeding from S'ambara?"*

Jaḍa spoke.

32 Then S'atru-jit's son prostrated himself before the high-souled Nága king and replied, being touched with affection
33 and modesty. "If thou show† me now, dear father, Madálasá even in illusion, I hold that thou hast done me the greatest favour."

Aśvatara spoke.

34 "Look thou here then, my son, if thou wouldest see the illusion. I must show thee favour; a visitor at one's house, though a child, is master."

Jaḍa spoke.

35 The Nága king led in Madálasá who was concealed in the house, and next he uttered some gibberish distinctly in order
36 to bewilder them. And then he showed the young prince the beauteous lady, saying, "Is she or is she not, O prince, thy wife Mádalasá?"

Jaḍa spoke.

37 Then, seeing the slender one, he lost his reticence that very moment; he moved towards her, uttering the word "Beloved!" And the Nága Aśvatara hasting held him off.

Aśvatara spoke.

38 "It is illusion, my son! touch her not! I told thee so at first. The illusion quickly vanishes when touched or otherwise *meddled with*."

39 Thereupon he fell to the ground, overwhelmed by a faint; and exclaiming "Ah Beloved!" he thought of his noble
40 wife. "Alas for the love of this king towards my steadfast mind, whereby I have been thus overthrown without the

* A Daitya.

† Read *darśayase* for *darśaya te*?

41 weapons of foes. She was shown as an illusion, though it was
clearly no illusion at all by reason of the action of air, water
and fire, earth and ether."

Jaḍa spoke.

42 Then the Nága reviving Kuvalayáśva, related to him the
whole story of her recovery from death and *all* else *that had*
43 *happened.* Thereat rejoicing he took again his loved one, and
after doing obeisance to the Nága departed in great splendour,
mounted on the horse, to his own city, having attained* the
object of his thoughts.

CANTO XXV.

The story of Kuvalayáśva and Madálasá (continued).

Kuvalayáśva, returning home, lives in perfect happiness with Madálasá—He succeeds his father S'atru-jit—A son is born to them, Vi-kránta—Madálasá prattles to the infant.

Jaḍa spoke.

1 Reaching then his city he narrated the whole story fully to
his parents, how he had regained his slender-limbed one who
2 had died. And the beautiful, slender-limbed *lady* bowed at
the feet of her father and mother-in-law, and did honour as
3 before to her kindred with obeisance, embraces and such
4 *greetings*, according to propriety, and their ages. Then the
citizens held a great festival there in the city.

And Ṛita-dhvaja long enjoyed himself with his beautiful-
5 waisted *wife*, both among mountain torrents, and on river
sand-banks, and amid pleasant woods, and in groves. She
also, longing to consume her merit by the delights of love,
6 enjoyed herself with him, her greatly-beloved, in pleasant
places.

7 A long time afterwards the king S'atru-jit, having ruled the
earth worthily, underwent the law of Death. Then the citi-

* Read *abhyupetaḥ* for *abhyupetam* ?

8 zens inaugurated as king his high-souled son Ṛita-dhvaja,
noble in conduct and action.

While he duly protected his subjects as if they were his
9 own sons, Madálasá gave birth to her first-born son. The
10 father gave that clever *child* the name Vi-kránta. The re-
tainers were pleased thereat and Madálasá laughed. Madá-
lasá spoke to her infant boy in the way of prattle,* as he lay
on his back crying not unmelodiously.

11 "Perfect art thou, darling, nor has thy name been given
thee now in mere fancy. This very body of thine is composed
of the five elements, not indeed for this reason dost thou cry
12 —wherefore then? Nor indeed does your highness (this title
is thy birth-right) cry because thou art a king's son. Doubt-
ful are the various good and bad qualities, that are connected
13 with the elements, in all thy organs. Since in a man here the
elements, extremely weak, increase by the means of the ele-
ments, namely, by means of the food and water and other
nutriments given, of what hast thou no gain, of what hast
14 thou no loss? Do not grow infatuated at this thy bodice
which is already decaying, and in that thy body; thy body
is given thee by good and bad deeds; the bodice is fastened
on thee by persons infatuated with pride and other *pas-*
15 *sions*. Do thou greatly esteem *each* aggregate of elements—
some *one aggregate* as a dear father, some *other* as a child,
some *other* as a mother, some *other* as a loved wife, some *other*
16 as thy own *property*, some *other* as not thy own. A man
beguiled in mind thinks that evils tend to assuage evils, that
enjoyments tend to happiness. Again the unwise man, great-
ly beguiled in mind, thinks that these very evils are plea-
17 sures. Laughter, gazing at the bones,† a pair of excessively
bright mocking eyes, firm plump flesh in the breasts and
elsewhere, in a woman—that is Love's abode; is not woman

* Ullápana: not in the dictionary. Ullápa is said to mean "calling out in a loud voice," "change of voice in grief, sickness, &c.;" but no such meaning is admissible here.

† Asthi-sandarśana; this seems meaningless. Akshi-sandarśana seems superfluous.

18 hell? The carriage *rests* on the earth; and the body is
seated in the carriage; and even in the body there is another
seated, the soul. There is not the same perception of owner-
ship in one's body, as there is this excessive infatuation *with
it.*"

Canto XXVI.

The story of Kuvalayáśva (continued).
The Education of his Sons.

Two other sons are born, Subáhu and Śatru-mardana—A fourth son is born whom Madálasá names Alarka—She criticizes these names—The king objects to her way of educating them, and wishes them to be brought up as kshatriyas—She prattles to Alarka.

Jaḍa spoke.

1 Now the queen trained up that son, as he grew day by day,
2 to unselfish thought by talking and other *means.* As he
regularly gained strength, as he gained his father's intelli-
gence, even so he acquired knowledge of himself through his
3 mother's talk. So the youth, instructed by her from his
birth, having understanding and being unselfish, did not
turn his mind towards family life.

4 A second son was born to her. His father named him.
5 When he said "This is Su-báhu," Madálasá laughed. Him
also when a child she spoke to with prattle and other *talk*
the same as before, and thus he, having a good intellect, ac-
quired knowledge from his childhood.

6 When the king named the third-born son Śatru-mardana,
she the beautiful-browed laughed again very long thereat.
7 The slender-limbed mother similarly instructed him also from
childhood. Devoid of desire he performed ceremonies, *but*
not anything beneficial.

8 Now the king, when desirous of naming the fourth son, saw
Madálasá, well-behaved as she was, laughing slightly: the

king, somewhat eagerly curious, spoke to her as she was laughing.

The king spoke.

9 "Tell me the cause of your laughter, at the very time when the name is being given. Vi-kránta, Su-báhu and the other
10 S'atru-mardana,—the names given by me are I think fine, suited to the kshatriya kindred, and indicative of heroism
11 and majesty. If these are not good, lady,—if you think *this* in your mind,—then do thou give a name to this my fourth son."

Madálasá spoke.

12 "I must obey thy command, Mahá-rájá, as thou tellest me;
13 so I will give a name to thy fourth son. 'Alarka'! Learned in religion he shall acquire fame in the world, and this thy youngest son shall have understanding."

14 On hearing that name given the son by the mother, the king, laughing at 'Alarka' as inappropriate, said—

The king spoke.

15 "This name that thou hast given to my son, beauteous lady,—why hast thou given such an inappropriate one? What is its meaning, O Madálasá?"

Madálasá spoke.

16 "This is my fancy, Mahá-rájá; I have given it as being practical. So do thou listen, O king, to the meaninglessness
17 of the names given by thee. Since wise men speak of a pervading soul; and 'kránti' is described as the course which *passes*
18 from one place to another place; since the soul is *all*-pervading in that it is ubiquitous and does not move about; therefore this appellation Vi-kránta, 'passed beyond,' appears
19 to me meaningless. The appellation Su-báhu, 'fine-armed,' given to they second son, that too is meaningless because the
20 soul is incorporeal, O king. The name that thou hast given the third son, Ari-mardana, 'foe-crusher,' I think that too is
21 inappropriate; and listen to the reason as regards it. Since there is only one soul in all bodies, who then, O king, is regarded as its enemy in this world, or who as its friend?

22 Creatures are crushed by creatures; how can the incorpo-
real be crushed? This fancy is meaningless because of the
23 separate existence of anger and the other *passions.* If a
bad name is fixed upon because of mutual dealing, why dost
thou think there is no meaning in the name Alarka?"*

Jaḍa spoke.

24 Being thus excellently addressed by the queen, the king,
having great understanding, assented to his loved wife who
25 spoke correctly. And the fine-browed lady spoke to that son,
just as to the elder sons, what would arouse the intellect.
26 The king said to her. "Why dost thou deal thus, O foolish
one, with the temperament of my child, by giving him a mis-
27 chievous education as *thou didst* before to my *other* sons. If
thou shouldest do what pleases me, if my word should be ac-
28 cepted, then restrain this son within the path of activity. So
the path of action will not lead to utter destruction, O lady;
and so the piṇḍa offering to the pitṛis will not cease, O virtuous
29 one. The pitṛis dwell in the Deva-loka, they are also born as
brutes, they become men likewise, and they reside within the
30 class of elements. By offering the piṇḍa and water a man,
busied in the ceremonies, ever nourishes them, O fine-browed
31 one, both the righteous and the unrighteous, those worn out
with hunger, those harassed by thirst; *he nourishes* the gods
likewise and guests. The gods, mankind, the pitṛis, departed
32 spirits, goblins, and guhyakas, birds, worms and insects live
upon man indeed. Therefore, O slender-limbed, cause my son
33 to acquire thoroughly the whole duty of kshatriyas, as re-
gards this life and life in the next world."

The queen Madálasá, being thus admonished by her hus-
34 band, spoke to her son Alarka, with prattling words.
"Thrive my son! rejoice my husband's mind with *thy* deeds,
35 in order to benefit friends and destroy enemies. Happy art
thou, my son, who alone, with never an enemy, wilt long pro-
tect the earth: from protecting it mayest thou have full
enjoyment of happiness, and from righteousness thou shalt

* Alárka, a furious dog, or a fabulous hog with eight legs.

36 obtain the fruit, immortality. Mayest thou delight the
bráhmans at the holy festivals! Mayest thou fulfil the longing
among thy kinsmen! Mayest thou think kindly in thy heart
for another! Mayest thou restrain thy mind from the wives
37 of others! Please continually the gods with numerous sa-
crifices, and the dvijas who resort *to thee* with wealth. And
thou shalt long satisfy women with unparalleled affections, and
38 thy foes with battles, O hero! As a child gladden the mind
of thy kinsmen; and as a boy *the mind* of thy teacher by
observance of his commands; as a young man *gladden the mind*
of women who are the ornament of high families; as an old
39 man *the mind* of the hermits in the forest. Exercising thy
sovereignty mayest thou gladden thy friends! Guarding the
good, mayest thou offer up sacrifices, darling! Destroying
the wicked and thy enemies in battle, mayest thou meet thy
death, my child, on behalf of cattle and bráhmans!"

Canto XXVII.

The Education of the Sons (continued).

Madálasá instructs Alarka in a king's duties—Enforcing especially the necessity for self-control, prudence and maintenance of the laws.

Jaḍa spoke.

1 Now being talked to in this way by his mother every day,
2 the child Alarka grew in age and intelligence. Then this son
of Ṛita-dhvaja, on reaching boyhood, received investiture
with the sacred thread, and being intelligent did obeisance to
3 his mother and said, "What I ought to do now for happiness
in this world and the next world, tell all that to me who am
bowing respectfully *before thee*?"

Madálasá spoke.

4 "My child, a king inaugurated in his kingdom must in the
first place conciliate his subjects, without obstructing his own
5 duty. Eschewing the seven vices, which are radically injuri-
ous, he must guard himself from his adversaries without de-

6 parting from good counsel. Just as a man meets destruc-
tion in eight ways from a fine-wheeled chariot, so undoubtedly
does even a king without departing from good counsel.
7 And let him recognise the bad and good ministers through
his enemies' faults; and he must strenuously trace out his
8 enemy's spies by spies. But a king must not confide in
friends, acquaintances, or relatives; let a king trust even in
9 an unfriendly person, if so obliged by his affairs. A king
must himself be conversant with the stationary, prosperous
and deteriorating conditions *of state policy*, be familiar with
the merits of the six measures *of military policy*,* *and* not
be enslaved by desire.

10 "A king must first subdue himself, and his ministers, then
his dependants, and afterwards his citizens; then let him,
11 fight against his enemies. But he who, without having
indeed conquered these, desires to conquer his adversaries, he,
with his own self unsubdued and with unsubdued ministers,†
12 is killed by his enemies' party. A king must therefore, my
son, first conquer desire and the other *passions;* for when
they are conquered, victory *is his* assuredly; vanquished by
13 them, a king perishes. Desire, and anger, and covetousness,
intoxication and pride, joy also, and enemies—these in truth
14 *tend* to destroy kings. Let him restrain *himself*, recollect-
ing how Páṇḍu himself was killed when engrossed in love:
15 and how Anuhráda‡ killed his own son through anger; and
how Aila§ was killed through covetousness; how Vena|| was
killed by dvijas through intoxication: how Anáyus'¶ son Bali
16 *was killed* through pride; Puranjaya through joy. Recol-
lecting how, when these were conquered, high-souled Marutta
vanquished all, let a king cast out these his own faults.

* *Viz.*, *sandhi*, peace; *vigraha*, war; *yána*, marching; *ásana*, encamping; *dvaidhí-bháva*, dividing his forces; and *saṃśraya*, alliance.

† For *'jitátmá jitámátyaḥ* read *'jitátmájitámátyaḥ?*

‡ Son of Hiraṇya-kaśipu.

§ Purúravas.

|| A son of Anga.

¶ She was his mother.

17 "A king should learn the ways of the crow, cuckoo and
bee, of the deer, serpent and peacock, of the goose, cock and
18 the red goat. A king should act like an insect against an
opponent; and a king should carry out the ways of the ants at
19 a fitting time. A king, who possesses the natural character
of the moon and the sun, ought to know for the sake of good
policy the behaviour of sparks of fire and of the seeds of the
20 seemul tree.* And a king ought to gather wisdom from
a courtezan, the lotus flower,† and a grasshopper, a doe-hare,
and the breast of pregnant women, and also from a woman of
the cow-herd caste.

21 "A king should assume the five forms of Indra, the Sun,
Yama and the Moon, and also of the Wind in the work of
22 government. Just as Indra *nourishes* the people on the earth
with showers of water for four months, so should a king
23 nourish *them* with largesses. Just as the Sun draws up the
water with his rays for eight months, so *should* a king *collect*
24 the tolls and other *dues* by truly subtle means. Just as Yama
restrains friend and foe when the time arrives, so a king
should be impartial towards friend and foe, towards the
25 vicious and the virtuous. Just as by gazing on the full
Moon, a man grows affectionate, so, where the people are all
peaceful, that is the practice *he should adopt* from the moon.
26 Just as the Wind moves mysterious among all creatures, so
should a king move among the citizens, ministers and others,
and among his relatives by *the agency of* spies.

27 "The king, my child, goes to Svarga, whose mind is at-
tracted neither by covetousness, nor by love, nor by riches, as
28 by other *motives.* The king goes to Svarga, who keeps
within their duty erring foolish men, who are swerving from
29 their duty. He, in whose kingdom the duties of the *four*
classes and the *four* periods of a bráhman's life do not fall
into desuetude, has, my child, eternal happiness after death
30 and in a future state. A king's highest duty, and that which

* S'álmali; see note * p. 82. The pods contain a quantity of silky cotton which is blown about, when the pods burst.

† *Nelumbium speciosum;* see note § p. 29.

brings supreme felicity for him, is the maintenance among men of their own laws,* since it is disturbed by evil-minded
31 men. By protecting creatures indeed a king reaches success; he who duly protects gains by his efforts a portion of righteousness."

Canto XXVIII.

The Education of the Sons (continued).
Madálasá's Exhortation.

Madálasá enunciates to Alarka the special duties of the four castes—and of the four periods of a bráhman's life—and the duties common to those four castes and periods, which must be strenuously maintained.

Jaḍa spoke.

1 Having listened to that his mother's exhortation, Alarka also further questioned his mother both about the duties of the *four* classes, and about the duties appertaining to the *four* periods of a bráhman's life.

Alarka spoke.

2 "Thou hast expounded, gracious lady, this *the duty* relating to the system of kingly government. I wish to hear that duty which concerns the *four* classes and the *four* periods of a bráhman's life."

Madálasá spoke.

3 "A bráhman's *duty* is held to be threefold—liberality, study, sacrifice. There is no other fourth duty. His duty is regard-
4 less of his position. Irreproachable sacrificial and educational occupations, and the acceptance of gifts from the purified —this is fitly proclaimed his threefold means of livelihood.
5 Liberality, study, sacrifice—this is declared *to be* the threefold duty of a kshatriya also: protection of the earth, and subsistence by weapons are his means of livelihood. Liberality, study, sacrifice,—that indeed is the threefold *duty* of a vaiśya

* Dharma.

also: merchandise, and the tending of cattle, and agriculture
7 are his means of livelihood. Liberality, and sacrifice, obe-
dience to dvijas, I have declared to be the threefold duty of
the śúdra also; and his means of livelihood are a handicraft,
8 obedience likewise to dvijas, nourishing them, buying and
selling. These are said to be the duties of the *four* classes.

"Hear also the connexions among the *four* periods of a bráh-
9 man's life. A man who has not erred from the duty of his
own class gains perfect felicity: he goes to hell after death,
10 if he has served what is forbidden. And as long indeed as
a dvija is not invested with the sacred thread, so long, my
son, he acts, speaks and eats unrestrainedly.

11 "When duly invested with the sacred thread, *he becomes* a
brahma-c'árin in his guru's house, and he should dwell there.
12 I relate his duty; hear it of me. Private study, atten-
dance on fire, bathing, and wandering about for alms, and
always *eating* that food after informing his guru and obtain-
13 ing permission from him. *He should be* diligent in the guru's
business; there should be thorough evoking of his affection;
and when summoned by him, he should read intently, his mind
14 withdrawn from everything else. After acquiring one, two or
all the Vedas from his guru's mouth, he is authorized *to give* the
15 guru his fee with words of eulogy. But let him enter on the
gṛiha-stha period when desirous of the period of family life;
or, by his own wish, on the vána-prastha period and on the
16 fourth *period*. Or let the dvija await his decease there in
the guru's house, *obedient* to the guru's son if the guru be
17 dead, or to the guru's disciple, if there be no son. Obedient,
free from self-conceit, let him pass through the period of a
brahma-c'árin.

"Next when he has desisted therefrom, through desire for
18 a gṛiha-stha's status, let him then rightly marry a wife,
sprung from the family of a different* Ṛishi, his equal, free
from sickness, not deformed, for the sake of a gṛiha-stha's
19 status. And having gained money by his own toil, let him duly

* *A-samána.* His family and hers should not be descended from the same Ṛishi. This indicates exogamy.

please the pitṛis, gods and guests by faith; and also nourish
20 those who resort *to him*, his dependants and children, and
his female relatives, and the afflicted, the blind, and the out-
cast, the birds and the cattle,* to the utmost of his power
21 with gifts of food. This is the duty of a gṛiha-stha; sexual
intercourse also at the proper season: but he should not, to
the utmost of his power, neglect the performance of the five
22 sacrifices. And let the man himself, being zealous to the best
of his power, together with his dependants, eat the remains
of the food consumed by the pitṛis, the gods, the guests and
paternal kinsmen.

23 "Now I have declared this gṛiha-stha period distinctly. I
describe to thee the duty of the vána-prastha: be it heard.
24 Having seen the succession of his offspring, and the stoop of
his body, let the wise man enter upon the vána-prastha period,
25 for the purpose of purifying his soul. In it *there is* the
enjoyment of the forest, and attraction by penances, sleep-
ing on the ground, sacred study, ceremonies for the pitṛis
26 gods and guests, the homa oblation, the three daily ablu-
tions,† the wearing matted hair and a bark dress, and dili-
gence in meditation unceasingly, the use of forest unguents.
27 This is the vána-prastha period, for the purification of sin,
and beneficial to the soul. But after that *comes* another, the
last, *period* of the bhikshu.

28 "But hear from me the nature of the fourth period, which
with its peculiar duties has been described, my darling, by
29 high-souled *men* conversant with its duties.‡ Renunciation
of every association, sacred study, abstinence from anger,
control over the senses, no long dwelling in one habitation,
30 abstaining from undertakings, and eating food obtained by
begging once *a day*, also desire for the awakening of know-
31 ledge of the soul, and gazing at the soul. Now I have
acquainted thee with this duty in the fourth period.

"Hear from me the common *duty* of the other classes and of

* For *paśavas* read *c'a paśúṃs?*

† At dawn, noon, and sunset.

‡ For *yaḥ sva-dharmo 'sya* read *sva-dharmo yasya?*

32 the periods of life. Truthfulness, purity and harmlessness,
freedom from envy, and patience, mercy, generosity,* and con-
tentment *is* the eighth virtue.
33 "These duties have been succinctly described to thee con-
cerning the classes and the periods of life: and *a man* should
34 stand wholly within these his own peculiar duties. And
the man, who, overstepping his own duty named according to
his own class or period of life, should behave otherwise,
35 should be punished by the king. And the king who over-
looks men, who after forsaking their own duties commit sin,
36 loses his pious acts. Therefore a king must vigorously
punish all the classes that behave contrary to their special
duties, and he must keep them within their own occupations."

CANTO XXIX.

Madálasá's Exhortation (continued).

Madálasá explains to Alarka the position of a gṛiha-stha—and personifies as a cow, the Vedas, pious acts, the words of the good and the words sváhá, svadhá, vashaṭ and hanta—She describes the bali offering, and utsarga oblation—the duties of a gṛiha-stha to guests—the śráddha—and further duties to guests—She pronounces a blessing on the gṛiha-stha state—and quotes a song by Atri on it.

Alarka spoke.

1 "And what men must do who are engaged in the gṛiha-stha
period; and what becomes confined in the absence of action,
2 and what increases by action; and what is beneficial to men;
and what a good man should avoid at home; and how things
are done—declare that accurately to me who ask."

Madálasá spoke.

3 "My child, a man on assuming the gṛiha-stha status, thereby
nourishes all this earth and conquers the worlds he longs for.
4 The pitṛis, the Munis, the gods, living things, and mankind,

* For *akárpyanyam* read *akárpaṇyam* ?

and worms, insects, and flying creatures, birds, cattle, and
5 Asuras subsist upon the gṛiha-stha, and derive satisfaction
from him; and gaze indeed at his countenance, *wondering*,
'Will he give us *anything?*'
6 "The support of everything is this cow, my child, which consists of the three *Vedas*, in which the universe is established,
7 and which is believed to be the cause of the universe. Her
back is the Ṛig-Veda; her loins the Yajur-Veda; her face
and neck the Sáma-Veda; and her horns are pious acts; her
8 hair the excellent words of the good; her ordure and urine
are tranquillity and prosperity; she is supported on feet which
are the *four* classes; she is the sustenance of the worlds; being
9 imperishable she does not wane. The word sváhá,* and the
word svadhá,† and the word vashaṭ, my son, and the other
10 word hanta are her‡ four teats. The gods *drink* of the
teat which is the word sváhá; and the pitṛis of that consisting of svadhá; and the Munis of that which is the word
11 vashaṭ; the gods, living things and Asuras, and mankind
drink constantly of the teat which is the word hanta.
Thus this cow consisting of the three *Vedas*, my child, fattens
12 them. And the man, who grievously sinning causes their
destruction, sinks into the hell Tamas,§ the hell Andha-
13 támisra‖ and the hell Támisra.¶ And the man, who gives
this cow drink with his own children and with the immortals
and other *objects of worship* at the proper time, attains Svarga.
14 "Therefore, my son, a man must nourish the gods, ṛishis,
and pitṛis and men and living things daily, even as his own
15 body. Therefore having bathed and become clean he should,
composed in mind, delight the gods, ṛishis and pitṛis, and the
16 prajá-pati also with water at the *proper* time. And a man**
having worshipped the gods with the fragrant flowers of the
great-flowered jasmine, should next delight Agni; and the
17 bali offering should also be made. Let him cast the bali

* The oblation to the gods.

† The oblation to the pitṛis.

‡ Read *tasyáḥ* for *tasyá*.

§ Darkness.

‖ Complete darkness.

¶ Deep gloom.

** Read *mánavaḥ* for *mánaváḥ*.

offering to Brahmá and the Viśva-devas inside the house, and
18 to Dhanvantari to the north-east; let him offer the bali
eastward to Indra, southwards to Yama, and the bali west-
19 wards to Varuṇa, and northwards to Soma. And let him also
give the bali to Dhátṛi and Vidhátṛi at the house-door, and
let him give it to Aryaman outside and all around the houses.
20 Let him offer the bali to night-walking goblins in the air, and
let him scatter it to the pitṛis, standing with his face south-
21 ward. Then the gṛiha-stha, being intent *and* having his mind
well composed, should take the water and cast it, as a wise
22 man, into those places for those several deities, that they may
rinse out their mouths.

"Having thus performed in his house the family-bali, the
23 pure gṛiha-stha should perform the utsarga oblation respect-
fully for the nourishment of living things. And let him
scatter it on the ground both for the dogs, and low-caste men
24 and the birds; for certainly this *offering* to the Viśva-devas
is declared *to be one for* evening and morning.

"And then he, as a wise man, having rinsed out his mouth,
25 should look towards the door the eighth part of a muhúrta,
whether a guest is to be seen. He should honour the guest,
who has arrived there, with rice and other *food* and with
26 water and with fragrant flowers and other *presents*, according
to his power. He should not treat as a guest a friend, nor a
27 fellow-villager, nor one who bears the name of an unknown
family, nor one who has arrived at that time. Men call
28 a bráhman who has arrived, hungry, wearied, supplicat-
ing, indigent, a guest; he should be honoured by the wise
according to their power. A learned man should not inquire
29 his lineage or conduct, nor his private study; he should esteem
him, whether handsome or unhandsome in appearance, as a
prajá-pati. For since he stays but a transitory time, he is
30 therefore called an a-tithi, 'a guest.' When he is satisfied, the
gṛiha-stha is released from the debt which arises from hospita-
lity. The guilty man, who without giving to the guest him-
31 self eats, he incurs only sin and feeds on ordure in another life.
The guest transferring his misdeeds to that *man*, from whose

32 house he turns back with broken hopes, and taking *that man's*
merit, goes off. Moreover a man should honour a guest re-
33 spectfully according to his power with gifts of water and
vegetables, or with just what he is himself eating.

"And he should daily perform the śráddha with rice and
34 other *food* and with water with regard to the pitṛis and bráh-
mans; or he should feed a bráhman. Taking up an agra* of
35 the rice, he should present it to a bráhman: and he should
give an alms to wandering bráhmans who ask. The alms
should be the size of a mouthful, the agra four mouthfuls.
36 Bráhmans call the agra four times a hanta-kára.† But
without giving food, or a hantakára, an agra or an alms,
37 according to his substance, he must not himself eat. And
he should eat, after he has done reverence to guests, friends,
38 paternal kinsmen, relatives, and petitioners, the maimed, and
children and old men and the sick.

"If a man consumed with hunger, or another who is destitute
39 wants food, he should be fed by a householder who has ade-
quate‡ substance. Whatever kinsman is dispirited when he
40 reaches a prosperous kinsman, the latter gets the sin that has
been done by the dispirited man. And the precept must be
observed at evening, and he should do reverence to the guest
41 who has arrived there after sunset, accordingly to his ability,
with a bed, a seat and food.

"Thus a weight is placed on the shoulder of one who
42 undertakes family life. Vidhátṛi, and the gods, and the
pitṛis, the great Ṛishis, all shower bliss *on him*, and so also
43 do guests and relatives: and the herds of cattle and the flocks
of birds, and the minute insects that *exist* besides, are satisfied.
44 And Atri himself used to sing songs on this *subject*, noble one!
Hear those, O noble one! that appertain to the gṛiha-stha
period—'Having done reverence to the gods, and the pitṛis
45 and guests, relatives likewise, and female relations, and,
gurus also, the gṛiha-stha who has substance should scatter

* A measure.

† A formula of salutation, or an offering to a guest.

‡ Read *samarthe* for *samartho*?

the fragments on the ground for both dogs and low caste men
46 and birds: for he should certainly perform this *offering* to the
Viśva-devas evening and day. And he should not himself eat flesh, rice and vegetables and whatever may have been prepared in the house, which he may not scatter according to the precept.' "

Canto XXX.

Madálasá's Exhortation (continued).

Madálasá explains to Alarka the ceremonies to be performed by a gṛiha-stha, which are of three kinds, continual, occasional and periodical—She explains the occasional śráddha, which is celebrated for men and women.

Madálasá spoke.

1 "Now what the gṛiha-stha's ceremonies are, the continual, and the occasional, and the periodical, listen thereto, my son.
2 "The continual are comprised in the five sacrifices,* these that I have described to thee: and the occasional are the others, such as the ceremony on the birth of a son, and so
3 forth. The periodical† are recognisable by the learned as the sacrifices at the moon's changes, the śráddha and others.
"Here‡ I will tell thee of the occasional śráddha celebration,
4 of the birth-ceremony that should be performed similarly by men on the birth of a son; and everything duly related in order that should be done at marriages and on other *occasions*.
5 And in this the Nándí-mukha pitṛis§ must be worshipped;
and he should give the piṇḍas mixed with curds and contain-
6 ing barley, facing northward or eastward, with composed
mind making the oblation. Some men like it with the offer-

* Brahma (*i. e.* Veda)-yajna, deva-yajna, pitṛi-yajna, manushya-yajna, and bhúta-yajna (all created beings.)

† Read *nitya-naimittikam* for *nitya-naimittika*.

‡ Read *atra* for *tatra?*

§ Nine pitṛis, *viz.*, the six parents, grandparents and great-grandparents on the paternal side, and the grandfather, great-grandfather and great-great-grandfather on the maternal side.

7 ing to the Viśva-devas omitted. And in this *ceremony* the
dvijas must be arranged in pairs, and must be worshipped in
dextral circumambulation. This is the occasional *ceremony*
during growth, and the other is the funeral obsequies.

8 "And the śráddha for a single deceased person should be
performed on the day of the death; listen to that. And it
should be performed omitting the offering to the gods, and
9 with a single vessel. And the oblations-with-fire* should not
be made in the fire without the ceremonies. And he should
10 give one piṇḍa to the deceased person near the fragments of
food, and sesamum-seed and water on the right, accompanying
them with the recollection of that person's name. 'May he
11 be exempt from decay,' let *the celebrant* say, and 'may enjoyment
be his,' let *the others* delighted say, at the place where
the bráhmans are dismissed. Men must do this every month
12 for a year. Now at the expiration of the year, or whenever
the ceremony is performed by men, the śráddha for deceased
sapiṇḍas must be performed for him also: *so* the rule is
13 stated; and that *must be* without the offering to the gods,
and accompanied with a single argha offering in a single
vessel. And that ceremony *must* not *be performed* there in
14 the fire without offering the oblations-with-fire: and on the
right there, he should feed the single dvijas.

"And there is another distinction, consisting in an extra
15 ceremony every month; do thou listen attentive to me, as I
tell *thee* of it, while it is being described. He should fill
four vessels there with sesamum-seed, perfume and water,
16 three for the pitṛis, one for the deceased person, my son.
And he should scatter the arghya-oblation in the three vessels,
and in the deceased's vessel,† uttering the words 'Ye
17 samáná' *&c.*, he should perform the rest as before.

"This śráddha for a single deceased person is ordained
18 precisely the same for women also. The śráddha for deceased
sapiṇḍas does not exist for them, if they have no son. The
śráddha for a single deceased person must be performed

* Ávâhana.

† Read *preta-pátre* for *preta-pátram*?

19 every year for a woman by the men, duly on the day of her
death, as has been here mentioned for men.

"But if there are no sons, the sapiṇḍas; if they are want-
20 ing, the sahodakas,* and those who may be the mother's
sapiṇḍas and those who may be the mother's sahodakas,
should duly perform this ceremony for *a man* who has no
21 son, *and for one* who has begotten *only* a daughter. The
daughters and *their* children should in this way perform *the
ceremony* for the maternal grandfather. But those who are
designated as the sons of two such persons should worship
22 their maternal and paternal grandfathers fittingly with the
occasional śráddhas.

"When all *these relatives* are wanting, the women should
perform *the ceremony* without the mantras for their husbands;
23 when they too are wanting, the king should cause *the cere-
mony* to be performed by a member of his own family, and
the cremation and all the other ceremonies *to be performed*
24 properly by men of that caste; for the king indeed is kins-
man to all the classes.

"Thus these continual and occasional *ceremonies* have been
25 described to thee, my child. Hear the other periodical cere-
mony appertaining to the śráddha. The new moon is
just the cause there, and the time is the moon's waning: the
fixed time indicates the constancy of that *ceremony*."

CANTO XXXI.

Description of the Párvaṇa S'ráddha.

Madálasá mentions the seven sapiṇḍa ancestors, and the lepa-bhujas, and the remoter ancestors—She explains how the celebrant of the śráddha nourishes them all—She enumerates the times for the śráddha, and the persons who should and who should not be invited to it—She describes how the śráddha should be performed.

Madálasá spoke.

1 "After the performance of the śráddha to deceased sapiṇḍas,
he who is the father's great-grandfather passes to *the class of*

* The samánodakas.

those who feed on the lepa,* having lost *his share* in the piṇḍa
2 offered to the pitṛis. He, who is the fourth there-above
among those who feed on the lepa bestowed by the *deceased's*
son, ceases to eat *thereof* and obtains the satisfaction that is
freed from the relationship.

3 "The father, and grandfather, and also the great-grand-
father—these truly must be known as the three males who
4 are related by the piṇḍa.† And those who are related by
the lepa are said to be the three others reckoning upwards
from the grandfather's grandfather: and the celebrant is
5 the seventh among them. Such have Munis declared this
seven-ancestral relationship to be, reckoning from the celebrant
upwards. And there-above are those beyond participation in
the lepa.

6 "Next *are classed* all the other ancestors, both those who
dwell in Naraka, and those who have become animals, and
those who reside within living creatures and other things.

7 "By what several means the celebrant, while performing
the śráddha rightly, nourishes all those *ancestors*, hear that,
my child.

8 "Now truly *those ancestors* who have become piśac'as obtain
satisfaction from the food that men scatter on the ground.
9 Those *ancestors*, my son, who have become trees, receive satis-
faction from the water that drips from the bathing garment
10 on the ground. But the drops of water, that fall from the
limbs on the ground, *minister* nourishment to those *ancestors* in
11 the family who have attained divinity. And when the
piṇḍas are taken up, the particles of food that *fall* on the
earth,—*those ancestors* in the family who have become animals
12 gain nourishment therefrom. The children moreover in
the family who, being capable of performing religious cere-
monies but not having undergone the purificatory rites, are
burnt *on their death*, they in their distress subsist on the
13 scattering of the food and the water *used* in scouring. And

* The wipings of the hands after offering the funeral oblations to the three sapiṇḍas.

† Sapiṇḍas.

the water, both *that* which *is used* by bráhmans for rinsing out
the mouth after meals, and *that* which *is used by them* for
sprinkling the feet,—the other *ancestors* likewise gain satisfac-
14 tion indeed therefrom. So whatever water and food is
scattered by the celebrant and by those dvijas, *whether it be*
15 unsullied or fragmentary, that, my child, in the family of
those who duly perform the śráddhas, nourishes the other
ancestors who have been born among the several crea-
16 tions. With the śráddhas, which men perform with ill-got-
ten wealth, are satisfied *those ancestors wha have been* born as
c'aṇḍálas, pukkaśas and other *men of degraded castes.*

17 "Thus many here derive nourishment, my child, through
their relations who perform the śráddhas, by means of the
18 casting away of food and drops of water. Therefore a man
should perform the śráddha in faith according to rule even
with vegetables: no one perishes in the family of one who
performs the śráddha.

19 "I will mention the periodic times for it; and learn of
me by what rule men perform it.

20 "The śráddha must necessarily be performed on the night
of the new moon, at the moon's waning every month, and on
the eighth days* also.

21 "Learn of me the voluntary seasons. On the arrival of a
distinguished bráhman, on an eclipse of the sun or moon, at
the solstice, at the equinox, at the sun's passage from one sign
22 into another, and on the occasion of a portent,† my son, on
acquiring property worthy of a śráddha, and on seeing a bad
dream, and at occultations of the constellation or planet
under which one is born, one should perform the śráddha
according to one's inclination.

23 "A distinguished bráhman learned in the Veda, a yogí,
one who knows the Veda, one who has mastered the Jyesh-
ṭha-sáman, one who has thrice kindled the fire Nác'iketa, one
who knows the three verses which begun with 'madhu,'‡ one

* Of three months.

† For *vyatipáte* read *vyatípáte*. This word has several other meanings, which are admissible.

‡ Rig-V. I. 90. 6—8.

who knows the 'tri-suparṇa' hymns, one who knows the six
24 Vedángas, a daughter's son, a Ṛitvij priest, a daughter's husband, and a sister's son, and a father-in law also, and one who is skilled in the business of the five sacred fires, and one who
25 is eminent in austerities, a maternal uncle, and one who is anterior to one's parents, a disciple, a relative by marriage, and a kinsman—these bráhmans are all worthy of invitation to a śráddha.

26 "A religious student who has been incontinent, and a sick man, and one who has a limb superfluous or deficient, the son of a widow remarried, and a one-eyed man, an adulterine son,
27 and a widow's bastard, my son, a traitor to his friends, one who has bad nails, an impotent man, a man with brown teeth, a bráhman negligent of his duties, a man cursed by his father,
28 a slanderer, a vendor of soma juice, one who has deflowered his daughter, a medical man, and one who has discarded his guru and father, a hired teacher, a friend,* and
29 the husband of a previously-married woman, one who discards the Vedas, and one who abandons the sacred fire, a man who has been corrupted by the husband of a low caste woman,† and others who habitually practise improper acts, —*all these persons* are verily to be shunned in ceremonies to the pitṛis, (O bráhmans.)

30 "The celebrant should invite the above-mentioned bráhmans on the day before, to the function performed in honour of the gods and pitṛis, and should fetch them also.

31 "And both he, who shall perform a śráddha that ought to be performed by those self-controlling men, and he, who indulges in sexual intercourse after having offered the śráddha and eaten the food,—the ancestors of these two men verily
32 lie down in that semen a month. Moreover he who eats at a śraddha and he who goes *to a śráddha* after intercourse with
33 a woman,—the ancestors of those two men feed on semen and urine for that month. Therefore a wise man must first issue

* Bhṛitakádhyápako mitraḥ. This seems strange.

† For *vṛishalí-pati-dúshitaḥ* read *vṛishalí-dúshitá-patiḥ*, one who has married a low-caste woman or a deflowered girl?

34 an invitation; and men who have intercourse with women
before the day arrives must be shunned.

"With his mind controlled he should feast those who
35 have come seeking for alms, or ascetics who control themselves at the proper times, after first propitiating them
with prostrations and other *reverential acts.* Just as the time
36 of the waning moon is dearer to the pitṛis than that of the
waxing moon, so the afternoon pleases the pitṛis more than
the forenoon. One should do reverence to these dvijas, who
37 have arrived at his house, with a welcome; and with the
pavitra in hand he should seat those, who have rinsed out
their mouths, on seats. In the case of the pitṛis the number
of bráhmans should be uneven, and in the case of the Gods*
38 even; or, according to the circumstances of the *celebrant*, there
should be one bráhman for the pitṛis and one for the Gods.
In like manner for the maternal ancestors *the number of bráhmans should be uneven or only one.* The bráhmans intended
39 for the Viśva-devas may be identical *on the side of the pitṛis
and maternal ancestors;* but some other men desire that they
should be distinct. He should place the bráhmans intended
for the Gods with their faces toward the east, and those for
40 the pitṛis toward the north.† The ceremony due to the
maternal ancestors has been similarly expounded by the wise.

Let the intelligent man giving kuśa grass for a seat, and
41 worshipping with the arghya and other offerings, giving
things pure and such like, and obtaining permission from
them,—let the wise dvija perform the invocation to the gods
42 according to the mantras. And having also given the arghya
offering to all the deities with barley and water, and having
duly given perfume, garlands, water and incense accompanied
43 with a lamp, let him both perform the whole of the dextral
circumambulation for the pitṛis; and having given a double
quantity of darbha grass, and having obtained permission

* For *devai* read *daive.*

† The text is very obscure, and seems corrupt. For this translation I am indebted to Babu Harimohan Vidyábhushan, the Pandit of the Bengal Asiatic Society.

21

44 from them, let the intelligent man perform the invocation to
the pitṛis, prefacing it with the mantras. And let him also
perform the dextral circumambulation and give the arghya
45 offering and barley and money and sesamum seed, intent
on pleasing the pitṛis. Then permitted by the dvijas who
46 say, 'Perform the ceremonies in the fire!' let him offer rice
unmixed with condiments or salt according to rule. The first
rite consists in uttering 'Sváhá!' to fire, the bearer of
47 oblations to the pitṛis; and let the next be 'Sváhá!' to
Soma who is esteemed by the pitṛis; and the third offering is
48 'Sváhá!' to Yama, the lord of the departed. And let him
put the remains of the offering into the vessels of the dvijas;
and taking hold of the vessels let him give the rice according
49 to rule. He should say affably "Ho, do ye enjoy yourselves
happily!"* and then they also should eat happily, with their
50 minds attentive thereon and observing silence. And a man
should leisurely give them whatever food they like best, dis-
51 playing no wrath and alluring them appropriately. And let
him utter the mantras which vanquish the Rákshasas, and let
him strew the ground with sesamum seed and with white
mustard: for the śráddha possesses abundant devices for
52 protection. And let the man, permitted by the *dvijas* who say
"Ye are satisfied and we are satisfied by those who are
nourished and satisfied," scatter food everywhere on the
53 ground. Similarly then having obtained permission, let him,
with voice body and mind controlled, give *the dvijas* severally
54 water† to rinse out their mouths. Then, my son, let him
with his left hand put the piṇḍas with rice and sesamum-seed
on the darbha grass, near the remains of the food, for the
55 pitṛis. Let him composedly also give them water with the
part of the hand‡ sacred to the pitṛis, since O prince! he
56 celebrates the sacrifice with faith for the pitṛis. Similarly
he should, after giving the piṇḍas on behalf of the maternal
grandfathers according to rule, then give water for rinsing

* For *yathá sukham* read *yathá-sukham?*

† For *ápaḥ* read *apaḥ*.

‡ Pitṛi-tírtha, the part between the forefinger and thumb.

out the mouth together with scent, garlands &c.; and having
57 given the bráhmans' fee according to his ability, address
them "May Svadhá be fortunate!" and let him cause them,
who being satisfied say "Be it so!" to pronounce the Vaiśva-
58 devika *mantras*. Let him say "May they be pleased!" "Hail
to you, O Viśve devas." And on those bráhmans, saying, "Be it
59 so!" he should request their benedictions. He should dismiss
them, addressing them pleasantly and prostrating himself in
faith; and he should attend them as far as the door, and he
60 should return, a gladdened man. Then he should perform
the continual ceremony, and should also feed guests. And
some very good men wish for a continual ceremony to the
61 pitṛis, and others *do* not *wish it* for the pitṛis. He should
perform the remainder as the first part: some think 'not
with a separate cooking vessel,' some *prefer it* repeated exactly
62 in the same order.* Then the celebrant should eat that rice
in company with his servants and others.

Thus should the man skilled in religious law perform com-
63 posedly the śráddha to the pitṛis, or so as satisfaction accrues
to the bráhmans. There are three pure things in a śráddha,
64 sesamum-seed,† sacrificial grass, and the sesamum-plant;‡
and they say these, (O princely bráhman,) are to be avoided,
65 anger, journeying, haste. A silver vessel is also commended
at śráddhas, my son. Now silver is for use, for looking at and
for giving away; for when the offering to the pitṛis is milked
out in a silver *vessel*, the pitṛis give ear to the earth;§ hence
the pitṛis desire silver, which increases their affection.

---

* The text seems obscure.

† Dauhitram, see note ‡, p. 84.

‡ Tila.

§ The text seems incorrect.

CANTO XXXII.

The ordinance of the S'ráddha.

Madálasá explains what kinds of food please the pitṛis at śráddhas and for what periods—what kinds are to be avoided—what sites should be avoided for the ceremony—what men and animals should be excluded—and what defilements must be avoided—Yogís must have priority at the s'ráddha—ancient songs are to be sung—and what benefits accrue from the performance.

Madálasá spoke.

1 Next hear, my son, with faith this* that I say,—what is to
be avoided in order to please the pitṛis, or what conduces to
their pleasure.
2 The pitṛis are satisfied with clarified butter and riçe for a
month. The paternal grandfathers receive satisfaction with
3 fish-meat for two months. Venison should be known to satis-
fy the pitṛis for three months; and the flesh of hares
4 nourishes the pitṛis for four months; birds' flesh *satisfies them*
for five months; hog's flesh for six months; goat's flesh for
5 seven months; and flesh of the black antelope† for eight
months; flesh of the ruru deer gives them satisfaction for
nine months, without doubt; flesh of the gayal‡ gives them
6 satisfaction for ten months. Moreover sheep's flesh§ satisfies
the pitṛis for eleven months; and milk of kine or anything
7 made of milk *satisfies them* a year. Flesh of the rhinoceros,
flesh of the red-goat, the dark tulsi plant,|| and honey, and
8 flesh of the rhinoceros¶ and whatever else is *given* by members

* For *imam* read *idam*.

† For *aineyam* read *aiṇeyam*.

‡ For *gavasyámisham* read *gavayámisham ?*

§ For *úrabhram* read *aurabhram*.

|| Kála-śáka: *Ocymum sanctum*, Roxb. I do not find it in Hooker.

¶ Dauhitra; but the rhinoceros is already mentioned.

of their own family, and turmeric and soma juice, and a śrád-
dha performed at Gayá without doubt yield the pitṛis end-
9 less satisfaction. S'yámáka* grain and rája-śyámáka† grain,
and likewise small-grained rice,‡ wild rice,§ and paushkala
grain, *these* among grain tend to satisfy the pitṛis.
10 Barley, vríhi rice||, and sesamum-seed, and wheat, green
gram,¶ and mustard, priyangu** seed, kovidára†† seed, and
11 the finest pulse,‡‡ markaṭaka§§ seed, rája-másha|||| pulse, and
aṇu¶¶ grain should be eschewed at a śráddha. Vipráshika***
12 seed and lentils††† are forbidden in a śráddha. Garlic‡‡‡ and
red garlic,§§§ onions,|||||| carrots,¶¶¶ asparagus,**** and
13 whatever other *vegetables* are shunned on account of their taste

* This according to Roxburgh is *Panicum frumentaceum*, the Beng. *śyámá*; but he says the Beng. *syámá* also denotes *P. colonum*.

† Perhaps this may be *Panicum hispidulum*, which Roxburgh says is called Beng. *bara-śyámá*.

‡ Prasátika.

§ Nívára.

|| The *áus*, or rainy season crop?

¶ Mudga; see note §§, p. 84.

** Priyangu, *Panicum italicum*, (Roxb. p. 101.)

†† Kovidára, *Bauhinia variegata*; see note ||, p. 27.

‡‡ Nishpáva; see note ||, p. 86.

§§ Markaṭaka; this does not seem to be known.

|||| Rája-másha. Prof. Monier-Williams says this is *Vigna catiang* (*Dolichos catjang*, Linn. and Roxb.). (Hooker, vol. II, p. 205).

¶¶ *Panicum maliaceum*, Roxb., the modern *chíná*.

*** Vipráshika; not given in the Dictionary.

††† Masúra. Prof. Monier-Williams says this is either *Ervum hirsutum* or *Cicer lens* (Roxb. p. 567). The former is the modern *masúr chaná*, and the latter *masúr*. Hooker appears to combine both in *Vicia hirsuta*, which seems to be the common Lentil (Hooker, vol II, pp. 177 and 179).

‡‡‡ Laśuna.

§§§ Gṛiñjana.

|||||| Paláṇḍu.

¶¶¶ Piṇḍa-múlaka.

**** Karambha, *neut*. Prof. Monier-Williams does not give the *neut*, but says karambhá, *fem*., is *Asparagus racemosus*, which is also called śata-múlí. (Roxb. p. 291; not in Hooker).

and colour; gándháriká* and kadus,† salts and salted things,
14 and reddish juices,‡ and things that are manifestly salt—these
should be indeed avoided in a śráddha. And whatever has been obtained by talk or through bribes or other *improper means* is not commended, nor what has been acquired from an outcaste;
15 and wealth that has been obtained unlawfully as the purchase-price of a bride is forbidden in this *ceremony*. And water that is bad-smelling and frothy, and very scanty, and
16 water that cattle would disdain, and what has been taken by night, and what has been left after every one has cooked, and what is unfit for drinking in a tank—that water should
17 be avoided always in the ceremony to the pitṛis. All milk from deer, sheep, camels, and from animals that have uncloven hoofs, from buffaloes, and from the yak, and cow's
18 milk that is not more than ten days old,§ and what has been brought to a person who has asked for it on account of
19 the pitṛis,—such milk must be always avoided by the good in the śráddha ceremony.

And in this ceremony ground must be avoided that is swarming with insects, that is rough, and that has been
20 scorched by fire, and that is hot with the words of enemies and wicked men, and that is foul-smelling.

Men who disgrace their family or who injure their family by
21 separating themselves from the śráddha, naked men and criminals may destroy the ceremony to the pitṛis with their glance; a eunuch, and a man repudiated *by his relations*, a cock, and
22 the village hog, and a dog, *each* ruins śráddhas by his look, and so also do Rákshasas.

Hence let a man offer *the ceremony* being well secluded, and

* Gándháriká; not in the Dictionary. Professor Monier-Williams says gándhárí denotes *Hedysarum alhagi* (Roxb., p. 574), and the Prickly Nightshade (which appears to be *Solanum Jacquini*, Roxb., p. 191); but neither seems appropriate. The text as it stands seems corrupt. For *gándhárikám* read *gandholikam*, which might mean "dry ginger"?

† Alábu; see note * page 118.

‡ Niryása; or 'gums.'

§ A-nirdaśa. This seems strange.

23 scattering the ground with sesamum seed. Thus may safety
be secured in the śráddha even for both, my child.

What has been touched by a corpse or by a recently-
24 delivered woman,* and by those who have been long ill, by
outcastes, and by filthy persons, does not nourish the pitṛis.

And the celebrant must moreover avoid the sight of a
25 woman who is in her courses; and he must shun sitting together with bald-pated men and drunken men at a śráddha, out of respect.

And whatever is infested with hair-lice, and whatever has
26 been gazed at by dogs, and whatever is putrid and stale, and
the brinjal,† and ferments,‡ and whatever has been fanned by the wind from clothing, are indeed to be avoided at a śráddha.

27 Whatever, in the shape of articles of food possessed by
thee, is given with supreme faith to the pitṛis according to
28 their name and family, that becomes food for them. Hence
a man of faith, who desires the pitṛis' satisfaction, must place the best that he has in the vessel and according to rule at a ceremony to the pitṛis.

29 And the yogís must always be fed by a wise man at a
śráddha; for the pitṛis are patrons of religious devotion;
30 hence one should ever worship them. Now if a yogí is fed
first, he can save the person for whom the sacrifice is offered and those who feast, just as a boat saves in water, better than thousands of bráhmans.

31 At this *ceremony* also songs in honour of the pitṛis are sung
by those who recite the Veda, *songs* which were§ formerly sung
32 by the pitṛis to king Purúravas. "When will any one of us have
a son, the chief among his race, who, eating the remains of
33 food left by the yogís, will offer the piṇḍa on earth? Or *will
offer* the piṇḍa, buffalo-beef, the clarified butter, or the vegeta-

* For *śava-sútaka-saṃspṛishṭam* read *sútaká-śava-saṃspṛishṭam?*

† Vártáki, the brinjal, *Solanum melongena*, Roxb., the modern *begun*. Prof. Monier-Williams calls it the egg-plant. It is a well-known and favourite vegetable. I do not find it in Hooker.

‡ For *abhishaváṃs* read *abhishavás?*

§ For *ásín* read *ásan*.

ble kála* mixed with sesamum-seed, or khichree at Gayá for
34 our monthly satisfaction? May we obtain† the offering to
the Viśva-devas and the soma juice, buffalo-beef, and the
finest clarified butter, and the divine *food*‡ by getting a young§
rhinoceros!"

35 Let him duly offer the śráddha on the thirteenth day and when the moon is in the asterism Maghá, *and* milk mixed with honey and clarified butter during the winter half of the year.

36 Let a man therefore, my son, worship his own pitṛis in faith,
hoping to gain all his wishes and his own deliverance from
37 evil. Men's pitṛis, when delighted with śráddhas, please the
Vasus, the Rudras and the Ádityas, the constellations, the
38 planets and the stars. The pitṛis, when delighted with
śráddhas, bestow long life, wisdom, wealth, knowledge,
Svarga, final emancipation from existence, and joys and
sovereignty.

39 I have declared to thee, my son, the śráddha ceremony as it has been expounded: hear, my child, the praise of the Voluntary S'ráddhas according to the *various* days *on which they are performed.*

Canto XXXIII.

The benefits to be obtained from the Voluntary S'ráddhas.||

Madálasá explains the benefits to be obtained from performing the śráddha voluntarily with a view to the benefits—on the various days of the lunar fortnight—and when the moon is in the different asterisms.

Madálasá spoke.

1 The first day of the lunar fortnight, *if the śráddha be performed on it, is auspicious* for the acquisition of wealth; the

* There are many plants of this name.

† For *aśnuvámahe* read *aśnuvámahai?*

‡ *Ásúryam* in the text, but it seems incorrect. Read *ásuryam* or *ásuram* from *asura?* *Ásura* is in the dictionary, but not *ásurya.*

§ *Vishána-varjya,* hornless.

|| Kámya S'ráddha.

second bestows men; and the third seeks for boons; the
2 fourth destroys enemies; in the fifth a man acquires for-
tune; in the sixth he may become worthy of worship: in the
seventh he acquires chieftainship; in the eighth the highest
3 prosperity; in the ninth he gains women; in the tenth
perfect gratification of his wishes. So let him, assiduous in
4 the ceremonies, gain all the Vedas in the eleventh. And in
the twelfth the worshipper of the pitṛis gains continual vic-
tories, offspring, mental vigour, cattle, prosperity, indepen-
5 dence and perfect nourishment. The man of intense faith,
who performs the śráddha on the thirteenth day, gains length
6 of life and sovereignty undoubtedly. Since one is successful in
śráddhas by means of choice food, he, whose ancestors died or
7 were slain with weapons in their youth, should, if he wishes
for their pleasure, perform the ceremony on the fourteenth
day. The pure man, who performs the śráddha diligently on
8 the night of the new moon, obtains all his wishes and attains
Svarga everlastingly.

By worshipping the pitṛis *when the moon* is in the asterism
9 Kṛittiká, a man obtains Svarga. A man who wishes for
offspring may obtain it *when the moon is* in the asterism
Rohiṇí; and he may gain vigour *when she is* in the Saumya
signs of the Zodiac;* and he may obtain valour *when she is*
in the asterism Árdrá; and lands and other *possessions when*
10 *she is* in Punar-vasu; and nourishment by always worshipping
when she is in Pushya; and noble sons *when she is* in A-śleshá;
and pre-eminence among his relations *when she is* in Maghá;
11 and good fortune *when she is* in Phalguní.† And the man of
liberal disposition obtains offspring *when she is* in Uttará
Phalguní. A man who offers śráddhas *when she is* in Hasta
12 verily attains excellence. And so a man of goodly form may
obtain offspring *when she is* in C'itrá. Sváti bestows success
13 in trade; Viśákhá gives philoprogenitiveness. Men who per-
form *the śráddha when the moon is* in Anurádhá attain imperial
rule; and *when she is* in Jyeshṭhá lordship; and *when she is*

* They are Taurus, Cancer, Virgo, Scorpio, and Capricornus.

† For *phalguṇí* read *phalguní*.

14 Múla perfect health. Acquisition of fame *comes from performing the śráddha when she is* in Áshádhá; and freedom from grief in Uttará Áshádhá. And one gains bright worlds by *performing it when she is* in S'ravaṇa; and immense wealth
15 *when she is* in Dhanishṭhá. One may acquire intimate knowledge of the Vedas *when she is* in Abhi-jit; and success in medicine *when she is* in S'ata-bhishaj; goats and sheep *by performing the ceremony* in Bhádra; and amorous dalliance
16 in the latter part of Bhádra. And one who performs the śráddha *when she is* in Revatí acquires the baser metals; and *when she is* in Aśviní horses; and *when she is* in Bharaṇí full length of life.

Hence a man who is skilled in true knowledge should perform the voluntary *śráddhas* at these seasons.

Canto XXXIV.

*Alarka's Education—The exposition of Virtuous Custom.**

Madálásá mentions the benefits of the observance of Virtuous Custom—which consists in the pursuit of righteousness, wealth and love—She mentions a large number of general rules regarding religious worship, eating, social behaviour, private actions, and marriage—She gives general rules regarding the sacrifices, and describes the portions of the hand to be used therein—and mentions how one's residence should be chosen.

Madálasá spoke.

1 "Thus, my son, should the gods and pitṛis be worshipped by a householder with the oblations to the gods and the oblations to the pitṛis; and with food *should* guests and kinsmen,
2 living creatures, all dependants, cattle, birds and ants, beggars and other petitioners *be worshipped* by the dweller in a
3 house, who observes the good customs and performs the domestic sacrifices, my child. He incurs sin if he neglects the periodic ceremonies."

* Sad-áo'ára.

Alarka spoke.

4 "Thou hast declared to me, mother, the threefold ceremonies
to be observed by men, the perpetual, the occasional, and the
5 periodic.* I wish to hear, O lady who gladdenest thy family,
about Virtuous Custom by practising which a man gains happi-
ness in the next world and in this."

Madálasá spoke.

6 "A householder must ever maintain Virtuous Custom tho-
roughly: for one who has lost Virtuous custom has no happi-
7 ness here or in the next world. Sacrifice, alms-giving and
austerities do not tend to the welfare of a man here, who
8 habitually transgresses Virtuous custom. For a man who
follows bad custom does not find long life here. One must
earnestly follow Virtuous custom; Virtuous custom destroys
what is inauspicious.

9 "I will expound to thee my son, the nature of that virtuous
custom. Hear it from me with single mind, and even so
maintain it.

10 "A householder who performs the domestic sacrifices must
strive to accomplish the three-fold objects of life:† in full suc-
cess therein lies the householder's own success here and in the
11 next world. With a quarter of his Wealth let him, master of
himself, lay up a store for the next world; and with half let
him support himself and perform the periodic śráddhas;
12 and treating a quarter as his capital, he should increase it,
by exerting himself on his own account. Thus, my son, Wealth
13 ought to be fruitful according to Virtuous custom. Similarly
a wise man must practise Righteousness in order to withstand
sin; and so also the third, Love, yields fruit here indeed on ac-
14 count of the next world. And the third, Love, is not impeded
through fear of diminution. Love also is said to be two-fold
15 from its not being opposed by this three-fold class. Let a man
consider all these successive correlations.

"Hear from me those opposite correlations, such as Right-
16 eousness, &c. Righteousness aims at a succession of right-

* Nitya, naimittika, and nitya-naimittika.

† Dharma, káma and artha.

eousness.* Righteousness is not destructive to one's own Wealth. And Love is diverse from both; and those two again are diverse from it.

17 "At the Bráhma moment a man should think of and ponder over Righteousness and Wealth, after rising up and rinsing out his mouth, standing towards the east, self-restrained,
18 pure: let him worship the twilight with the constellations in the east, the twilight with the sun in the west, as is right: he should not neglect it even when free from adversity.

19 "He should eschew conversation with the wicked, falsehood, and harsh speech, evil books, evil words and the homage of evil, my son.

20 "Evening and morning, with soul restrained he should offer the homa oblation.

"He should not gaze up at the orb of the sun at sunrise or at sunset.

21 "He should look in a mirror in order to dress his hair; he should wash his teeth; and delight the gods in the very foremoon.

22 "He should not defecate or void urine in a path leading to the villages, to temples, to places of pilgrimage or to the fields, nor on cultivated ground, nor in a cattle-pen.

23 "He should not gaze at another's wife naked. He should not look at his own ordure. He should avoid seeing, touching and talking with a woman in-her-courses.

24 "He should not void urine, or defecate, or engage in sexual intercourse in water.

25 "He should not step on ordure, urine, hair, ashes or potsherds: and a wise man should not step on husks, charcoal, bones or decayed things, or on rope, clothing, &c., whether on a road, or on the earth.

26 "Moreover a householder should do reverence to the pitṛis, gods and mankind, and to living creatures, according to his
27 capability, and afterwards eat himself. And a man should always eat his food, facing the east or the north, with his

* *Or*, brings wealth as a consequence of righteousness.

mouth well rinsed out, restraining his speech, pure, with his mind intent on his food and *with his face* between his knees.

28 "An intelligent man should not divulge another's fault except in the event of injury.

"Food should be avoided in which salt is visible, and which is very hot.

29 "A man of self-control should not defecate nor void urine while walking or standing.

"And he should not eat anything at all while rinsing out
30 his mouth. While he has remains of food in his mouth, he should not carry on any conversation and he should cease his reading, and he should not touch a cow, a bráhman, fire, or his own head:

31 "Nor should he look at the sun or the moon or the constellations with passionate desire.*

"And he should avoid a broken seat and bed and cup.

32 "He should offer a seat to gurus, accompanying *the offer*
with rising up and other respectful acts; and he should salute
33 them respectfully and converse *with them* agreeably; and
he should follow them. He should not speak about them adversely.

"And when clad in a single garment he should not eat nor engage in the worship of the gods.

34 "An intelligent man should not carry dvijas, nor should he void urine in fire, nor should he ever bathe or sleep naked.

35 "And he should not scratch his head with both hands; nor
36 should men wash their heads frequently without cause. And
when his head is washed he should not touch his body with oil at all.

"And he should cease his own reading, when every one is abstaining from reading.

37 "He should never void urine against a bráhman, the wind,
cattle or the sun; facing north by day, and facing south by
38 night, he should do his voidance of urine and fæces during
illness† whenever he desires.

* Kámatás.

† For *ábádháshu* read *ábádhásu*.

"He should not talk of his guru's evil-doing, and he should
39 appease him when angry. He should not listen to abuse
when others utter it.

"And he should yield the path to bráhmans, to the king, and
40 to one who is ill with pain, to his superior in learning, to a
pregnant woman, to a man labouring under a burden, to a
younger man, to the dumb, blind and deaf, to a drunken man,
41 and to a mad man, to a prostitute, to an enemy, to a child and
to an outcaste.

"An intelligent man should respectfully circumambulate a
42 temple, and a fig-tree standing on a sacred spot, and a place
where four roads meet, his superior in learning, a guru and
a god.

"He should not carry shoes, clothes, garlands &c. that
others are carrying.

43 "He should avoid the sacred thread, an ornament, and the
water-pot on the fourteenth, eighth and fifteenth days of the
44 moon and at its four changes. He should also eschew rub-
bing his body with oil, and sexual intercourse with his wife,
on those days.

"And a wise man should never stand with his foot or his leg
45 extended: nor should he throw out both his feet; nor should
be press one foot on the other.

46 "He should eschew deadly attacks, abuse and calumny. A
clever man should not display deceit, self-conceit, or sharp-
ness. He should not disgrace with ridicule fools, insane per-
47 sons, or those in calamity, the deformed, or magicians, or those
who have limbs deficient or superfluous.

"He should not inflict punishment on another in order to in-
struct a son or disciple.

48 "Likewise the wise man should not draw his seat towards
him and sit down.

"He should not prepare a cake, khichree or flesh for himself.
49 He must have his food evening and morning, after doing re-
verence to his guests.

"Facing eastwards or northwards, restraining his voice, he
50 should always wash his teeth, my child.

"He should eschew the prohibited vegetables.
51 "A man should certainly not sleep with his head to the
north, nor with his head to the west; he should sleep, plac-
ing his head to the north east or east.
"He should not bathe in perfumed water, nor at night; bath-
52 ing except by day is declared to be most potent for calamity;
nor when he has not bathed, should he wipe his limbs with a
53 cloth or with his hands. Nor should he shake his hair, nor
should be shake his clothes.* Nor should an intelligent man,
when he has not bathed, ever apply unguents..
54 "Nor should he wear red clothing, nor even variegated or
black clothing: nor should he make a complete change of his
55 clothing or in his ornaments. And transparent† raiment
should be avoided, and also whatever is very much damaged,
and *whatever* is infested with lice, or has been trampled on,
56 or has been looked at by dogs, and has been licked or thrown
down, or has been befouled by the extraction of pus.
"He should never eat flesh from the back, or flesh unfit for
57 the gods and pitṛis, or prohibited flesh, my son, or things
which are visibly salt. Food that is long stale or that is not
58 fresh must be avoided, my royal son, because of the changes
that occur in flour, vegetables, sugarcane and milk; and meat
long stale must be avoided, because of the change‡ that
occurs in it.
59 "He should avoid lying down at sunrise and sunset.
"Not when unbathed, nor when reposing, nor while thinking
60 of other things, nor when sitting on his bed or on the earth,
nor when making a sound,§ nor when clad in a single garment,
61 nor when speaking, nor without giving to spectators, but
when bathed a man should eat evening and morning accord-
ing to rule.
62 "A wise man should not resort to other men's wives. Adul-
tery destroys the religious acts and the life of man. Nothing

* For *vásasí* read *vásámsi ?*

† For *vidaśam* read *viśadam ?* I do not find *vidaśa* in the dictionary.

‡ For *vikárámśc'a* read *vikárác'c'a ?*

§ For *śabdavat* read *śabdayan ?*

63 indeed is so short-lived in the world, as a man's intercourse
with another's wife here.

"Let him perform the worship of the gods, and the cere
64 monies to fire, and the respectful salutation to his guru, and
also the ceremony of eating his food, after duly rinsing out his
65 mouth. Facing eastwards or northwards he should reverent-
ly rinse out his mouth, my son, with frothless, inodorous, pure
66 and holy water. He should avoid the five earths from be-
neath water, from a habitation, from an ant-hill, from ground
infested with mice, and where purificatory actions &c. have
been carried on. After washing his hands and feet and sprink-
ling water on them he should, *with his face* between his knees,
67 and composed mind, rinse out his mouth. He should drink
water three or four times after twice wiping the sides of his
68 mouth, the apertures of the body, and his head. After duly
rinsing out his mouth with water, being pure, he should per-
form the ceremony to the gods, the ṛishis, and the pitṛis di-
69 ligently. A man should always perform *the ceremonies*, pre-
serving a composed mind. A wise man should rinse out his
mouth, after he has sneezed, or spitten out, or donned his
70 raiment. After a sneeze, and licking, and a vomit, and spitting
&c., he should rinse out his mouth, touch a cow's back, and
71 look at the sun; and he should hold up his right ear, since
this is in his power; in the absence of the former, he should
72 do the latter; if the former be wanting, it is desirable to do
the latter.

"He should not gnash his teeth, nor beat his own body.

73 "He should also avoid sleep, reading and food at both twilights; and sexual intercourse and setting out on a journey at the evening twilight.

74 "In the fore noon, dear son, he should in faith perform his
worship to the gods, and at noon to men, and in the afternoon
75 to the pitṛis. And with head bathed, he should perform the
ceremonies to the gods or the pitṛis. And he should trim his
beard facing eastwards or northwards.

76 "He should eschew a maiden although well-born, if she is deformed, or sickly, or disfigured, or tawny-coloured, or talkative,

77 or contaminated by everybody. And one who is free from
deformity, who has a beautiful nose, and is marked with
all the auspicious marks—such a maiden as that should a man
78 always marry who desires welfare. He should marry one
who is in the seventh or fifth degree distant from his parents:
he should guard his wife, and he should shun jealousy, by day,
in sleep and in sexual intercourse.

79 "He should avoid a deed that causes pain* to others, and
the infliction of pain on living creatures.

"A woman, during menstruation, should be avoided by all
80 the castes for four nights. He should avoid just the fifth night
of the moon in order to avoid the birth of females: then let
him approach *his wife* on the sixth night, *that night* is the
81 best among the even *nights*, my son. Sons are begotten on
the even nights, daughters on the odd nights: therefore a
wise man who wishes for a son should always cohabit *with his*
82 *wife* on the even nights. Lawless men *cohabit with their wives*
in the morning, and eunuchs at evening.

"After shaving, and vomiting and sexual intercourse, my
83 son, the wise man should resort to the place where bodies
are burnt† and should bathe, keeping his clothes on.

"One should not revile or ridicule the gods, the Vedas,
84 or dvijas, good, truthful or magnanimous men, a guru, or
devoted and virtuous wives, or persons who are sacrificing or
85 performing austerities, my son. One should never listen to
those unmannerly persons who do such things.

"One should not mount on a high bed or seat, nor on a low
one.

86 "One should neither dress unbecomingly, nor speak unbecomingly. *One should be* clad in pure white raiment, and
adorned with white flowers.

87 "Neither with the haughty, nor with the insane, nor with
fools, nor yet with the unmannerly should a wise man form
friendship; nor yet with those of bad disposition, nor yet with
88 those who are corrupted with thieving and other vices, nor yet

* Upa-tápaka; not in the dictionary.

† Kaṭa-bhúmi.

with spend-thrifts, nor with the covetous, nor yet with enemies,
nor with prostitutes, nor with inferiors, nor with the husbands
89 of prostitutes. He should never make *friendship* with the
mighty, nor with inferiors, nor with reprobates, nor with the
90 ever-timid, nor yet with fatalists. He should contract friend-
ship with good men, with those who always observe Virtuous
custom, with the wise, with the honest, with the powerful,
with those who are resolute in action.

91 "In company with one's friends, the initiated, the king,
Snátaka brahmans, and one's father-in-law, one should do re-
verence to the Ṛitvij priest, and the five other venerable per-
92 sons and to guests. One should do reverence, my son, to
dvijas, who have dwelt for a year, with an offering of honey
and milk according to one's ability and with alacrity at fitting
93 times. And the brahman who desires bliss should observe
their governance, and if intelligent he should not contradict
them even though always scolded by them.

94 "Having performed the household worship properly in the
fitting place and in due order, he should next worship the fire
95 and offer it the oblations in due order. He should make the
first offering to Brahmá, and then to to the prajá-pati, and the
96 third to the Guhyas, and the next to Kaśyapa. Then having
offered to Anumati* he should next offer the household bali
and the constant oblations, that I have already explained to
97 thee, according to the ritual. Next he shonld make the offer-
ing to the Viśva-devas, then the offerings to all creatures, and
separately to the gods according to place and apportionment.
98 And he should make the three oblations to Parjanya, the
Dharitrís, and to Máṇaka,† and to Váyu in every direction,
99 to the east and other regions of the sky in due order; and to
Brahmá, to the Air and to the Sun in order, and to the Viśva-
100 devas and to all beings; and then he should offer to the
Dawn, and to S'iva northwards; and southwards to the pitṛis,
101 exclaiming 'Svadhá, reverence!' Having done it on the

* The fifteenth day of the moon's age, personified.

† This is said to *Arum Indicum*, the Beng. *mán-kachu*, the stems and tubers of which are generally eaten (Roxb., p. 625).

right and to the north west, saying, 'O Yakshma,* this is for
thee!' he should, if he wishes, offer the remains of the food
102 and the water from the vessel according to the rule. Then
taking up the first part of the food, he should offer it with the
benediction Hanta to the brahman according to the rule and
justice.

103 "He should perform the ceremonies to the gods and other
objects of worship, with each one's special portion of the hand according to rule; and he should perform the ceremony of rinsing
out the month with the portion of the hand sacred to Brahmá.
104 This is called the portion of the hand sacred to Brahmá for
the purpose of rinsing out the mouth, *viz.*, a line drawn to the
105 left of the thumb of the right hand. The pitṛis' portion of
the hand is said to be the part between the forefinger and
the thumb; by that he should offer the water and other obla-
106 tions to the pitṛis, except in the nándí-mukha śráddha. And
the gods' portion of the hand is at the tips of the fingers; the
ritual of ceremonies to the gods should be performed there-
with. The prajá-pati's portion of the hand is at the root of
the little finger, his ceremony must be performed† therewith.
107 Thus always with these portions of the hand sacred to the
gods and pitṛis, he should always perform the ceremonies,
108 never with any other portion of the hand. It is proper al-
ways to rinse out the mouth with the *portion of the hand*
sacred to Brahmá; and *to offer* the oblation to the pitṛis with
the *portion of the hand* sacred to the pitṛis; and that to the
gods with the portion of the hand sacred to the gods; and
the offering to the prajá-pati with his own *portion of the hand.*
109 A wise man should perform the cake-and-water ceremony to
the nándí-mukha ancestors, and whatever *is offered* to the
prajá-pati, with the *portion of the hand* sacred to the prajá-
pati.

110 "A sensible man should not carry water and fire at the same
time; nor should he thrust out both his feet towards guru
and the gods.

* Pulmonary disease.

† Read káryam for káyam?

111 "He should not look at a heifer sucking.
"He should not drink water with the hands joined together.
"At all periods of personal purification whether important
112 or unimportant, he should not delay for the sake of purification.

"He should not blow the fire with his mouth.

"One ought not to take up one's abode, my son, where
113 four things do not exist, *viz.*, a person who pays debts, and a
physician, a bráhman learned in the Vedas, and a river full
of water. Where there is a king who has vanquished his
114 foes, who is powerful, and who is devoted to righteousness,
there should a wise man always dwell: whence *can come*
happiness, when the king is worthless? Where the king is
115 unassailable, where the earth is prolific, where the citizens
are well governed and always practise justice, where folk are
116 charitable, there does residence bestow happiness. In a
country where the husbandmen are not generally gluttonous,
and where all medicinal herbs *are procurable*, there should a
117 sensible man dwell. One ought not, my son, to dwell there,
where these three things are constant, a person desirous of
conquering, and a former enemy, and folk who are always
118 holding festival. A wise man should always dwell among
good-tempered neighbours.

"Thus, my son, have I, thy well-wisher, expounded this to thee."

CANTO XXXV.

The education of Alarka (continued).

An exposition of things permitted and forbidden.

Madálasá describes what food may be eaten and what not—how various things are to be cleansed when impure, and what things are always pure—how one who has contracted impurity should purify himself—what actions and conduct one should avoid—

She insists on the necessity of maintining the daily sacrifice—She mentions what holidoys are allowed the various castes—She describes certain post-funeral ceremonies—and purification after deaths and births.

Madálasá spoke.

1 Next do thou hearken to the remedial measures for things
forbidden and permitted. Rice should be eaten that has been
2 kept awhile, mixed with oil, and long stored; and wheat,
barley, and butter-milk and preparations thereof unmixed
with oil. The hare, the tortoise, the go-sámp,* the porcupine,
3 and the rhinoceros, my son,—these indeed may be eaten; and
the domestic pig and fowl should be eschewed. The remains
of food at a śráddha after the pitṛis and gods and other *reci-*
pients have been satisfied may be eaten at the desire of the
4 bráhmans. A man who eats flesh that has been killed for the
purpose of medicine is not defiled.
5 Shells, stones, gold, and silver, ropes, and garments, and
vegetables, roots and fruits, and wicker-work vessels and lea-
6 ther, and gems, diamonds, and coral, and pearls, and men's
bodies are best cleansed with water; just as iron things with
7 water, and stone by scrubbing. Oily vessels are cleansed with
warm water, and winnowing baskets, grain and antelope-skins,
8 and the pestle and mortar for husking rice, and thick cloths,
and a store by sprinkling; and all kinds of bark-made things
9 are best cleansed with water and earth. Grass, wood and
medicinal herbs are best cleansed by sprinkling; and all
10 woollen things and hair have ceremonial purity. White mus-
tard is cleansed with oily sediment or the sediment from
sesamum seed. Things that are injured are always cleansed
11 with water, my son. So also cotton things are cleaned with
water and ashes. Timber, ivory, bone and horn are best
12 cleaned by scraping. Earthen pots are purified ceremo-
nially by re-burning.

Pure are alms, a workman's hand, wares for sale, and a

* Godhá, the Go-sámp a very large kind of lizard found in jungle.

13 woman's face, whatever passes along the high-road, what is
unknown, what is brought by slaves and other *menials*, what is
admirable for its sound, what is long past, what is screened by
14 many, what is light, what is extremely abundant, what is
young, and what is done by the old and the sickly, kitchens
when the business in them is ended, women who are suckling
15 children. Pure also are running water, and odourless bubbles.
The ground is cleansed through time, by the rubbing of
16 bodies, and the passage of cattle, by smearing, by digging,
by watering, by houses, by sweeping and by worship.

Things infested with hair-lice, or sniffed at by cattle, or
17 infested with flies should be sprinkled with earth water and
ashes to be cleansed, my son; things made of udumbara
18 wood* with vinegar; tin and lead with salt. Brass things
are cleaned with ashes and water; and the over-flows of fluids
are pure. A thing soiled by ordure *is cleaned* with earth and
19 water and by removing the smell; and other such-like things
by removing the colour and smell.

Water is pure that has satisfied cattle, that is in its natural
20 state, that is lying on the earth; and likewise flesh that has
been slain by C'aṇḍálas, Kravyádas and others. And clothes
and other things lying on the high-road are said *to be made*
21 pure by the wind. Dust. fire, a horse, a cow, the shade, the
rays *of the sun and moon*, the wind, the earth, drops of water,
and mosquitoes and other *insects* inflict no contamination
though they may have been in contact with what is corrupt.
22 A goat and a horse are pure as regards their face; but the face
of a cow or calf is not pure when the mother is in milk; a hawk
23 is pure when it knocks fruit down. A seat, a bed, a carriage,
boats, and grass on the road—they are purified by the rays of
the moon and sun and by the wind, in the same way as articles
of trade.

24 After walking along the high road, and after matters of
bathing, hunger, drinking, and weariness, one should change

* Udumbara, *Ficus glomerata*, Roxb.; a large tree, common about villages (Roxb. p. 646.)

25 one's clothes and duly rinse out one's mouth. Bad roads,* mud,
and water, when one comes into contact with them, are cleaned
by leaving them alone; and things made of mud or brick†
are cleansed by contact with the wind.

26 On taking up a morsel of rice-food that has been damaged
through over-maturity, he should discard it, and should rinse
out his mouth with water and earth, and should sprinkle the
27 remainder with water. One who has eaten bad food whether
wittingly or unwittingly, should fast for three nights in order
to assuage‡ that fault.

28 After touching a menstruous woman, a horse, a jackal, and
other *animals*, or a woman recently delivered of a child, or
people of low caste, one should bathe for the sake of purifica-
29 tion; and so should those who have carried a corpse. After
touching an oily human bone a man becomes clean when he
has bathed; *after touching* a dry *human bone* he becomes clean
by rinsing out his mouth, or by touching a cow, or by gazing
30 at the sun. Moreover one should not disregard blood, spittle,
aud unguents for the body.

A wise man should never stand in gardens and other
31 places in the afternoons. Nor should one hold converse with
a woman hated by the populace or with a widow.

One should cast remnants of food, ordure, urine and the water used for washing the feet, outside the house.

32 Without taking up five piṇḍas one should not bathe in another man's water; one should bathe in holy ponds, and in the Ganges, in lakes and rivers.

33 After touching or holding converse with blasphemers of the
gods, pitris, and holy śástras, sacrifices, prayers and other
sacred objects, one should purify one's self by gazing at the
34 sun. And after looking at a menstruous woman, a śúdra, an
outcaste, or a dead body, the unrighteous, a woman recently
delivered of a child, a eunuch, a naked person, and persons
35 of low caste, and on those who give away children, and

* Vi-rathyá; not in the dictionary.

† Ishṭa, brick?

‡ For *upaśamenu* read *upaśamáya*?

on the paramours of other men's wives, the wise must in-
36 deed perform this purification of themselves. One conver-
sant with righteousness, after touching forbidden food, a wo-
man recently delivered, a eunuch, a cat, a rat, a dog, or a
cock, and an outcaste, what is cast away, a C'aṇḍála, and
37 those who carry away corpses, is purified by bathing; and so
also *one who has touched* a woman in her courses, and the
domestic hog, and even two men who have been contaminated
by the impurity of a newly-delivered woman.

38 The base man, both he who daily neglects the continual
ceremony, and he who is abandoned by bráhmans, is polluted.
39 One should never allow the continual ceremony to cease; but
if it is neglected, there is a stoppage to the re-birth of his
deceased *relatives*.

40 A bráhman should spend ten days, exempt from alms-giving,
the Homa sacrifice and other *pious acts:* and a kshatriya
41 should spend twelve days: and a vaisya half a month; but a
śúdra should remain a month, exempt from his peculiar occu-
pation: thereafter all should pursue their own occupation, as
already expounded.

42 Water ought to be presented to a departed person, after his
body has been burnt outside by his relatives,* on the first,
43 and fourth, seventh and ninth days *of the moon*. His relatives
should gather together the ashes and bones on the fourth day;
it is prescribed that after gathering them together, they
44 should touch their limbs with them. But the sahodakas
should perform all the ceremonies, after the gathering to-
gether of the remains. If the sapiṇḍas are touched by them,
then both the sapiṇḍas and the sahodakas lose their purity.†

45 If a person dies directly of his own free will, by the sword,
by water, by hanging, or by fire, by poison, by a fall, or
in any other *unnatural way*, or by religious fasting to death,
or by fasting to death from vindictive motives;‡ or if he

* Gotrika.

† For *mṛitáhani* read *mṛijá-hánis*.

‡ For verse 45 of the text read—

Anvaksham ic'c'hayá śastra-toyodbandhana-vahnishu
Visha-prapátádi-mṛite práyonaśanayor api.

46 dies as a child, or as a sojourner in a foreign country, or as a
religious mendicant, purification will be effected at once; and
others say the period of impurity* is declared to be three days
47 for the sapiṇḍas; but if, after the other person is dead, the
sapiṇḍa also dies, in this case the ceremonies must be perform-
ed during the days called the period of the first impurity.
48 This same ordinance is applied also to the impurity caused
by the birth of sapiṇḍas, among sapiṇḍas and properly among
49 sahodakas also. When a son is born, the father must bathe
with his clothes on. And if, after one *child* has been born
50 there, another should be born, the purification in that case
also is prescribed according to the days of the elder-born *child*.

When ten or twelve months or half a month have elapsed,
51 all the castes should duly perform their respective rites and
ceremonies. Next the ekoddishṭa *śráddha* should be performed
52 for the departed person. And men of understanding must
give gifts to the bráhmans; whatever is most desired in the
world, and whatever is prized at home, those very things
53 therefore must one who hopes for immortality give to a *bráh-
man* endowed with good qualities: but at the end of the days,
after they have touched water, a chariot, a weapon, a goad
54 and a rod, and after they have performed the ceremonies,
they should make the oblation† ordained by the laws of their
55 respective castes, and *perform* all pure acts that confer bliss in
the next world and in this.

A wise man must study the three *Vedas*, and must be con-
56 tinually occupied therein; he must amass riches righteously,
and strenuously perform sacrifices; and he must fearlessly do
57 whatever does not entail censure on the soul of him who does it,
my son, and whatever ought not to be concealed in public. The
good man that so does, my child, brings splendour to his home
by acquiring righteousness wealth and love.

The text appears to be corrupt. This amended reading is taken from a private MS. consulted by the pandit of the Bengal Asiatic Society for me, but *práyánas'anayor* seems preferable.

* *A-śauc'akam*; not in the dictionary.

† For *upádánam* read *upadánam?*

CANTO XXXVI.

The Story of Madálasá (concluded).

Ṛita-dhvaja Kuvalayáśva on reaching old age resigns his kingdom to his son Alarka, and Madálasá gives him a token-ring—Both depart to the forest to practise austerities.

Jaḍa spoke.

1 Being thus instructed by his mother, Ṛita-dhvaja's son at-
2 tained his youth and duly married a wife, and begat sons,
and as a lord offered sacrifices, and always closely observed
3 his father's commands. Then after a long time Ṛita-dhvaja,
on reaching extreme old age, anointed his son in the sovereign-
4 ty, and with righteous soul desirous to depart to the forest to
practise austerities in company with his wife descended *from
his throne*, a mighty protector, an illustrious king.

5 And Madálasá delivered this her last discourse to her son,
in order that her son might abandon attachment to sensual
pleasures.

Madálasá spoke.

6 "When intolerable pain, arising from separation from thy
dear kinsmen, or caused by the opposition of thy enemies, or
springing from the destruction of thy wealth or from thy own
7 self, may befall thee as thou rulest thy kingdom, observing the
laws of a householder—for the householder who depends on
8 selfishness makes unhappiness his abode—then, my son, draw
forth and read from this ring that I have given thee the
writing that is inlaid in delicate letters on the plate."

Jaḍa spoke.

9 So saying, she gave him a golden ring, and the blessings
10 appropriate for a man who lives the family life. Then
Kuvalayáśva and his queen Madálasá, bestowing on their son
the kingdom, departed to the forest to practise austerities.

CANTO XXXVII.

The conversation between the Father and Son (continued).
The discrimination of the Soul.

Alarka ruled righteously and prosperously, but was greatly addicted to pleasure—His brother Subáhu, wishing to correct him, formed an alliance with the king of Káśi—Both attacked Alarka to wrest the kingdom from him, and reduced him to great straits—In his distress he looks at Madálasá's token-ring and seeks relief from Dattátreya—He explains to Dattátreya wherein lies his suffering, and launches into a metaphysical disquisition on the soul, the mind, the body, and pleasure and pain.

Jaḍa spoke.

1 And Alarka also, righteous in soul, protected justly and
like children his glad people who practised each his own
2 business. Inflicting punishment on the wicked, and worthily
affording protection to the peaceable, he experienced intense
delight; and he offered great sacrifices.

3 And there were born to him sons, mighty and valiant,
righteous in soul, magnanimous, who were adversaries to evil
4 conduct. And he amassed wealth by means of righteousness,
and righteousness again by means of wealth; and since those
two things are not antagonistic, he enjoyed even the pleasures
5 of sense. Thus many years passed away as if but a single day,
while he ruled the earth, devoted to righteousness, wealth
6 and *the gratification of his* desires. No feelings of indifference
occurred while he enjoyed his loved objects of sense; nor
again did he grow satiated in amassing righteousness and
wealth.

7 His brother Subáhu, who roamed the forests, heard that he
was thus besotted in his attachment to pleasure, and uncon-
8 trolled in his senses. The prince, being desirous of admo-
nishing him, pondered long and concluded that an alliance on
his part with the king's enemies would be beneficial to the

9 king. Then he cleverly made repeated visits to the king of
Káśí, who had numerous armies and chariots, as his protector,
in order to regain his kingdom.

10 That king collected together his army against Alarka, and
despatched a messenger *to demand that* the kingdom should be
11 gived up to Subáhu. Alarka refused, cognizant of his own
justice, to give up the kingdom then in obedience to that command, and returned answer to the messenger of the king of
12 Káśí;—"Let my elder brother come to me with affection and
ask for the kingdom for himself. I will not yield up the
13 smallest bit of territory through fear on an attack." Even
wise Subáhu made no request then. Supplication is not the
duty of kshatriyas, for he was mighty in valour.

14 Then the king of Káśí accompanied by all his army
15 marched to attack the country of king Alarka. And forthwith
forming a close union with the coutiguous *kings* he attacked
with some of their many vassals, and reduced him to
16 subjection. And without harassing Alarka's neighbouring
kings by molesting their realms, he thus subjugated both the
17 governors of the fortresses and the forest tribes. He reduced into submission some kings by bribes, and some by
creating dissension, and others who were well-affected towards
Alarka by conciliation.

18 Then the king with his small army, harassed by the adversary's host, found his treasury depleted extremely by the foe
19 that blockaded his city. And being thus straitened and with
his treasury diminishing daily, he fell into intense dejection
20 and perplexity of mind. After suffering the keenest pain, he
then bethought him of the ring, about which his mother Ma-
21 dálasá had formerly spoken to him. Then bathing and purifying himself, he addressed the bráhmans, and drawing out
22 *the ring* saw the motto thereof in clear characters. The king
pronounced what his mother had written thereon, while the
hair of his body was visibly standing erect, and his eyes were
23 expanded with joy:—'Association must be shunned by every
soul; if to shun it be impossible, it should be formed with the
24 good, for association with the good is a panacea. Love must

be shunned by every soul; if to eschew it be impossible, it should be displayed towards the desire for final emancipation from existence, for that desire is a cure therefor.'

25 Now having exclaimed repeatedly, 'How can men really
attain bliss?', and having decided that it was through the desire for final emancipation since that desire is appropriate*
26 thereto, the king next pondering upon association with the
good, and suffering the most poignant grief, visited illus-
27 trious Dattátreya. On meeting him, magnanimous, stainless
and devoid of attachments, he prostrated himself and wor-
28 shipped him and addressed him with propriety; "O bráh-
man! show me favour, thou who art the refuge of refuge-seekers! Remove affliction from me, who am in affliction, and over-addicted to desires."

Dattátreya spoke.

29 "At once indeed do I remove thy affliction, O king. Tell
me truly, wherefore hast thou that affliction, O king?"

Jaḍa spoke.

30 Being thus addressed by that wise *Muni*, the king pondered
31 over the seat and the nature of his three-fold affliction. The
king, being noble in intellect, held long and repeated deliberation with his soul, being steadfast the while, and then laughing spoke thus:—

32 "It is not myself, nor the earth, nor the sea, nor the stars,
nor the wind, nor the air; but I wish for happiness in bodily
33 *concerns*. Pleasure and pain pass to deficiency or excess in
this body composed of five elements; what welfare should
34 I not get, if such I might have, in another body wherein I
should possess a constant and perfect good-disposition and should be raised and depressed through inequalities? Moreover a man of self-denial is perceived by his difference
35 *from others*. And so does bodily pleasure or pain generate a
good disposition in one who looks upon the subtle third por-
36 tion which exists merely a moment? Since pain dwells in
the mind,† and pleasure again is a mental thing; therefore

* For *tatsangato* read *tatsangatá?* † Manas.

neither pain nor pleasure belong to the Ego; for the Mind is
37 not the Ego. Inasmuch as neither Self-consciousness,* nor
Mind, nor Intellect† is the Ego, why then does the in-born
38 pain in something else affect me? Since the Ego is not the
Body, nor the Mind, the Ego is distinct from the Body and
the Mind. Therefore let pleasures and pains dwell in the
39 Mind or in the Body; how is the Ego concerned hereat? If
my elder brother covets the sovereignty over this body, it is
an aggregate of five elements. How then is my Self concerned
with the action of the qualities therein? He when seated
40 therein and I are distinct as regards the Body. He who alto-
gether lacks hands and other organs, flesh, bones and head,
what connexion, even a slight one, has that man here with
41 elephants, horses, chariots and other treasures? Hence my
Self has no foe, it has no pain, it has no pleasure, nor city, nor
treasury, nor army composed of horses, elephants, &c., neither
has he, nor a third person, nor any one, nor have I *any of*
42 *these things*. For as the air that occupies the orb‡ of a small
water-jar and a pitcher, though one, is perceived in many
ways, so Subáhu and the king of Káśí and I, methinks, are
perceived among bodies by bodily differences."

CANTO XXXVIII.

The conversation between the Father and Son (continued).
A series of questions.

Dattátraya moralizes on the consciousness of Self and its results, under the parable of a tree, and asserts the non-materiality of the Soul. Alarka asks for instruction about Yoga *or religious devotion.*

Jaḍa spoke.

1 Then the king prostrating himself before the magnanimous

* Ahankára. † Buddhi. ‡ For *maṇḍalu* read *maṇḍala*.

bráhman Dattátreya, renewed his speech, bending respectfully before him.
2 "No whit of affliction have I, O bráhman, when I look *on*
things in a proper frame of mind: those who look on things
3 amiss are always sunk in a sea of unhappiness. In whatever
thing a man's intellect becomes self-engrossed, he receives
4 woes therefrom and pays them back. There is not so much
pain when a cat eats an unselfish sparrow or mouse, as when
5 it eats a domestic fowl. I then feel neither pain nor pleasure,
since I am beyond the material world.* Whoever is subject
to created things by means of created things, is indeed sensitive to pleasure and pain."

Dattátreya spoke.

6 "It is even so, O tiger-hero! as thou hast just declared.
The thought 'it is mine' is the root of pain; and the thought
7 'it is naught of mine' is the root of calmness. From my
question indeed has this sublime knowledge sprung up in
thee, who hast cast off the conviction 'It is mine', as if it
were the cotton of the seemul tree."†
8 "With the thought 'it is I' the germ has sprung up; with
the thought 'it is mine,' the germ has grown shoulder-high:
and home and lands are its topmost boughs; children and
9 wife and other relations are its young shoots; wealth and
corn are its great leaves; it has developed not once only; and
merit and demerit are its outmost flowers; pleasure and pain
10 are its full-grown fruit. There it fills the path of final
emancipation; it oozes out at the commingling of fools; it is
rich with festoons of bees which are the desire to be doing;
11 knowledge of what ought to be done is the full-grown tree.
Those who, wearied with the road of worldly existence, betake
themselves to its shade are dominated by error, knowledge
12 and happiness; where is their superiority? But those, who

* Prakṛiti.

† The capsules when ripe burst, and the silky cotton inside is scattered over the ground for many yards around.

hew down the tree of selfishness with the axe of learning,
which is sharpened on the whet-stone of association with the
13 good, travel along that path. Reaching the cool, dustless,
thornless grove of religious knowledge, the wise, ceasing from
action, attain supreme emancipation from existence.
14 "Neither art thou, O king, nor am I a gross object consist-
ing of the elements and of organs: neither must I declare *we
are* an elementary rudiment, nor that we both have a soul as
15 an eternal organ. Or, whom O king do I see the chief of us two,
since the conscious soul* is sublime, and the *personal* aggre-
16 gate consists of qualities. Just as mosquitoes, the dumbur
trees,† reeds, munja grass,‡ fish and water have separate
existences though they dwell together, so is it with the body
and the soul, O king."

Alarka spoke.

17 "Adorable Sir! through thy favour has sublime knowledge
of this kind been revealed to me, which causes one to discern
18 the power of the Supreme Intellect; but no stability remains
here in my mind which is assailed by objects of sense; nor
moreover do I see how I may be delivered from the bonds of
19 Nature, or how I may cease to exist again, or how I may
attain in perpetuity to this state of being devoid of qualities and
20 to one-ness with Brahma. Therefore, O bráhman, mighty in
knowledge! expound religious devotion§ properly to me, who
thus beseech thee, prostrate before thee, for association with
the good is beneficial to men."

* Kshetrajna.

† Udumbara, *Ficus glomerata,* Roxb, the modern *dumbur,* (p. 646) not in Hooker.

‡ *Saccharum munja,* Roxb. (p. 82).

§ Yoga.

Canto XXXIX.

Yoga, or Religious Devotion.

Dattatreya continues his exhortation—Final emancipation from existence is attained through yoga or religious devotion,—and the means are restraint of the breath, mental abstraction, restraint of the senses, and deep meditation. These means are analyzed and explained at length. What circumstances are inimical to yoga. The improper performance of yoga entails bodily ailments. How such bodily ailments may be cured. The signs of the proper performace of yoga.

Dattátreya spoke.

1 A yogí's removal of ignorance by the attainment of know-
ledge is 'mukti'; *this is* union with Brahma, and separation
2 from the *three* qualities of Nature. 'Mukti,' or final emancipa-
tion from existence, *comes* from religious devotion; and reli-
gious devotion *comes* rightly from knowledge, O king; know-
ledge comes through suffering; suffering *is the lot* of those
3 whose minds are engrossed with self. Hence the man who
desires final emancipation should strenuously discard *every*
association; when associations drop, the designation 'it is
4 mine' disappears. Freedom from selfishness tends indeed to
happiness; the perception of faults *comes* from passionlessness;
and passionlessness *comes* indeed from knowledge; knowledge
5 is preceded by passionlessness. That is one's house, where
one resides; that is food, by which one lives; that which tends
to final emancipation is described as knowledge or ignorance.
6 By consuming merits and demerits, O king, and through not
7 doing voluntarily constant acts that ought to be done, through
not amassing subsequent *acts*, and through diminishing *acts*
that have been previously amassed, the body never again falls
into the bonds of action.

8 This I have declared to thee, O king! Listen also to this
religious devotion from me, by adopting which the religious
devotee may attain to an eternal identity with Brahma.

9 First indeed the soul must be conquered by soul; it is
indeed a hard victory for religious devotees. He should put
10 forth effort in that victory. Hear from me the means thereto.
He should burn up his faults by restraining his breath,* and
his stains by steady mental abstraction,† his sensual enjoy-
ments by restraining his senses,‡ and his unbridled qualities by
11 deep meditation.§ Just as impurities are burnt out of metals
when they are melted, so the faults wrought by the organs of
12 sense are burnt out by restraining the breath. The religious
devotee should first accomplish the regulation of his breath.
Now stopping the inhalation|| is designated práṇáyáma,
13 'restraining the breath.' Práṇáyáma is of three kinds, which
are named the 'slight,' the 'medium' and the 'intense.'¶
14 I will describe its measure; hear it of me, O Alarka! The
'slight' extends during twelve mátrás or prosodial instants,
and the 'medium' is double that, and the 'intense' is well-
15 known as containing thrice that number of instants. The
time of a mátrá is that of the winking and opening the eye-
lids once. The measure of twelve mátrás is fixed for the
16 reckoning of the práṇáyáma. With the first he should overcome
perspiration, and with the second agitation, and with the third
17 dejection; he should gradually overcome his faults. Now as
lions, tigers and elephants, when kindly treated become mild,
so the breath falls within the control of the religious devotee.
18 As an elephant-driver brings a rutting elephant under control
according to his wish, even so a religious devotee who has the
19 wish brings his breath to perfect control. For as the proud
lion when tamed does not attack deer, so the obstructed wind
20 destroys men's guilt but not their body. Therefore the reli-
gious devotee while engaged in devotion should pay good heed
to the restraining of his breath.

Hear its four conditions that bestow the result of final
21 emancipation. *They are* cessation** *of the consequences of action*,

* Práṇáyáma.

† Dháraṇá.

‡ Pratyáhára.

§ Dhyána.

|| A'-pána, a meaning not in the dictionary.

¶ Uttaríya, a meaning not in the dictionary.

** Dhvasti.

and the power of obtaining everything,* harmony† and
serenity,‡ O king! Hear also their nature as I describe it in
22 order. Where the fruits of good and bad actions die away,
and the mind attains pellucidity,§ that is called 'dhvasti.'
23 When the religious devotee himself always continuously resists
the desires of this world and of the next world, such as covet-
24 ousness and infatuation, that is 'prápti' everlasting. When
the religious devotee possessed of equal power perceives, by
25 the advantage of his knowledge, the past and future remotely
concealed meanings of the moon, sun, stars and planets, and
gains success, then occurs the condition of práṇáyáma called
26 'saṃvid.' *The state* by which his mind, and his five vital airs,
his organs of sense and the objects of those organs become
serene, is called 'prasáda.'

27 Hear also, O king, the characteristics of práṇáyáma, and
what kind of seat is enjoined for one who always practises
yoga.

28 Adopting the padma half seat, and the svastika sitting
posture, he should utter the syllable Om! in his heart and
29 practise his religious devotion. Sitting evenly on an even
seat, drawing in both his feet, and firmly fixing his thighs
30 rightly in front, he should cover his mouth; he should sit
without touching his private parts with his heels, with
his senses under control; he should raise his head slightly;
31 he should not close his teeth together. Gazing at the tip of
his own nose and not looking around, the religious devotee
should conceal the activity of darkness with passion, and that
32 of passion with goodness, and taking his stand in unsullied
goodness should practise devotion. He should hold in his
organs of sense from their objects of sense, and his breath and
33 other faculties and his mind, he should advance to abstrac-
tion with a steadfast cohesion. But he who should draw in
34 his desires, as a tortoise draws in all its limbs, always
delighting in soul and self-collected, sees soul in soul. The
35 wise man after purifying himself externally and internally,

* Prápti.

† Saṃvid.

‡ Prasáda.

§ Apa-kasháya-tva; not in the dictionary.

and filling out his body from the navel to the neck, should
advance to abstraction. A 'dháraṇá,' or steady mental
36 abstraction, is called twelve práṇáyámas. Two kinds of
dháraṇá are known in religious devotion by devotees who are
conversant with the truth. Moreover when a religious
37 devotee is steeped in devotion and controls his soul, all his
faults perish, and he becomes whole; and he sees supreme
38 Brahma and the qualities of Nature separately, the sky and
the primordial atoms and the unsullied soul.

Thus a religious devotee, who restricts his food and who is
39 intent on restraining his breath, should occupy ground, which
has been thoroughly and gradually reclaimed, as it were his
house. Unreclaimed ground when it is taken possession of
40 increases faults, diseases and foolishness, therefore he should
not occupy unreclaimed ground.

'Práṇáyáma' or restraining the breath is so called from the
41 restriction* placed on the breath; and this is called 'dháraṇá'
or mental abstraction, by which the mind is abstracted; since
42 the organs, which are occupied with words and other *actions*,
are restrained by religious devotees by means of devotion, that
is called 'pratyáhára,' or restraining the senses.

And the means for this is declared by paramarshis who
43 were religious devotees, so that diseases and other faults may
not spring up in a religious devotee. Just as the thirsty may
44 drink water gradually by vessels, pipes and other *means*, so a
religious devotee who has overcome his distress may drink air.
First in the navel, and next in the heart, and thirdly in the
45 breast, then in the neck, the mouth, the tip of the nose, in the
eye, eye-brows, and the middle of the head, and in what is
46 there-beyond, is known the highest mental abstraction. By
attaining to these ten mental abstractions he reaches equality
with the imperishable. Not puffed up, nor hungry, nor
47 wearied, and undisturbed in mind, the yogí should practice
his yoga respectfully in order to attain final occupation, O
king!

* Upa-saṃ-rodha; not in the dictionary.

When it is neither very cold nor warm, when there is no
48 strife, when it is not windy, at these times the *ascetic* who is
deep in meditation should not* practice yoga. In a place
where there is a noise, or fire, or water, or where study is going
49 on, in a decayed cow-shed, at a place where four roads meet,
amid a collection of dry leaves, in a river, in a burning-ground,
in a place infested by snakes, in a place of fear, or on the edge
50 of a well, amid a number of funeral piles or ant-hills—in these
places a learned man should avoid practising yoga. And if
there is no appearance of goodness, he should avoid the place
51 and time. *There should be* no sight of evil during the practice
of yoga; hence he should avoid that. Whoever disregards
these places and in his infatuation practises yoga, verily his
52 faults tend to his hindrance. Hearken to me in this. Deafness,
stupidity, failure of memory, dumbness, blindness and fever—
53 those several *evils* straightway befall him who practises yoga in
ignorance.

If a yogí should have these faults through inadvertence,
54 yogís should attend to their cure in order to destroy them.
Hearken to me in this. He should engage in mental abstraction, after eating rice-gruel, mingled with oil and very warm.
55 In the diseases of rheumatism, flatulence, and enlargement of
the abdomen, circulation of the internal or obstructed wind of
56 the body should be regulated by a diet of rice-gruel.† In
tremor‡ a yogi should fix his mind on a mountain as it is
steady, in dumbness on the faculty of speech, and in deafness
57 on the ear; just as one whose tongue is parched with thirst
should meditate on a mango fruit. In whatever respect the
body is disordered, in that very respect he should think
58 steadily of whatever thought may remedy the disorder, *such
as*, a cooling thought amidst heat, and a heating thought
amidst cold. He should place a stake on his head and beat
wood with wood.

* For *na yogam* read *sa yogam*, he should practice yoga?

† This is the translation of the Pandit of the Bengal Asiatic Society: the text seems obscure.

‡ For *kalpe* read *kampe;* so a MS. in the Sanskrit College.

59 In that way memory immediately recurs to a yogí who has
lost his memory. He should think steadily of the wind and
60 fire which indeed pervade the heaven and the earth. These
injuries are cured through what is non-human or what springs
61 from goodness. If goodness that is non-human should enter
within a yogí, he should utterly burn out the sin that dwells
in his body by steady thought of the wind and fire.

Thus must every soul that is wise in yoga compass its
62 preservation, O king, since the body is the means of attain-
ing righteousness, wealth, love and final emancipation from
existence. The yogí's knowledge perishes through perplexity
at the narration of the marks of the activities, therefore the
63 activities must be hidden. Tranquillity,* perfect health,
gentleness, a pleasant odour, scanty excretions, a fine com-
plexion, benignity, and softness of voice, are indeed the first
64 indications of the activity of yoga. A loving person proclaims
one's virtues in one's absence. That creatures do not fear him
is the chiefest sign of complete perfection. He who is not
injured by excessive cold, heat, or other *natural agents*, and does
not fear other persons, has attained complete perfection.

CANTO XL.

The Yogí's bliss.

Dattátreya explains to Alarka the ailments that beset a yogí's soul and mentions their five varieties. He describes the yogí's duties, the stages by which final emancipation is attained, the eight premonitory marks of final emancipation, and the results of union with the Supreme Spirit.

Dattátreya spoke.

1 I will succinctly declare to thee the ailments† that prevail
in the soul of a yogí when it is viewed: hearken to me.

2 He longs for rites performed with a view to future fruition,
and the objects of human desire, for women, the fruits of

* A-lolya; not in the dictionary.

† Upa-sarga.

alms-giving, for science, for supernatural power, for the baser
3 metals and riches, for heaven, god-head, and supreme god-
head, for actions that yield copious supplies of elixir vitæ,*
for flying on the storm-winds, for sacrifice, and the power of
4 inhabiting water and fire, for the fruits of śráddhas that con-
tain every gift, and religious mortifications. Thus he longs
5 when mentally ailing by reason of fasting, meritorious acts,
and worship of the gods, and by reason of those several
actions.

A yogí should strenuously restrain his mind when beset
6 with such thoughts. By making his mind cling to Brahma he
is liberated from ailments. When these ailments are overcome
7 other ailments still beset a yogí, arising out of goodness, pas-
sion and ignorance.

Ailments arising from illusive vision,† from hearing, and.
from the deity,‡ and mental aberration,§ and enthusiasm||—
8 these five are roots of bitterness which tend to embarass the
religious meditations of yogis. The ailment arising from
9 illusive vision is such to a yogi because in it appear Vedic
matters, poetic matters, science and the mechanical arts with-
out end. The ailment connected with hearing is so-called
10 because he perceives the meanings of sounds in all their com-
pleteness, and he receives sound from thousands of yojanas.
11 The wise call that ailment one from the deity, as in the case of
a madman, when like a god he sees all around and in the eight
12 directions. When the yogí's mind wanders without support
through his own fault by reason of his fall from all the rules of
13 good custom¶—that is well known as mental aberration. When
the seething whirl-pool** of knowledge like a whirl-pool of

* Read *rasáyana-c'ayáḥ* for *rasáyana-c'ayaḥ ?*

† Prátibha. Prof. Monier-Williams gives the meaning "relating to divination," but in this place it seems to relate to vision, as the context shows.

‡ Daiva.

§ Bhrama.

|| Ávarta. Deliberation, revolving (in the mind), so Prof. Monier-Williams; but it seems a much stronger word.

¶ Ác'ára.

** Ávarta.

water engulphs the mind—that ailment is called enthusiasm.
14 All beings of divine origin, when their religious meditation
is destroyed by these great and terrible ailments, revolve
again and again.

15 Therefore the yogí, having clad himself with a mental white
blanket, should cast his mind prone on supreme Brahma, and
meditate on him. A yogí should always be intent on
religious meditation, he should eat sparingly, he should subdue
16 his senses. The yogí should contemplate in his head the
subtle conditions of the seven objects, *viz.*, earth &c.; he
should contemplate the subtle earth, until he comprehends its
17 subtlety.* He deems the earth to be his soul, and he quits
its bonds. Moreover he quits the subtle taste in water,* and
18 also the form in the fire; and he likewise quits touch in the
wind, as he bears the subtle form in mind; and he quits the
19 subtle activity of the sky, and likewise its sound. When he
enters with his mind into the mind of all created things, his
mind bearing a mental subtle condition of them becomes
20 subtle also. Likewise the man, conversant with religious
devotion, on attaining to the intellect of all creatures, gains
and relinquishes the most perfect subtlety of intellect. For
21 the man conversant with religious devotion, who relinquishes
these seven subtle things after having thoroughly compre-
22 hended them, there is no retrogression, O Alarka! The soul-
cognisant man, after fully seeing the subtlety of these subtle
conditions of the seven objects, then utterly abandoning it
23 may proceed to supreme bliss. And towards whatever created
thing he evinces feeling, O king! to that very thing he be-
24 comes attached, and he perishes. Therefore the corporeal being,
who after perceiving the mutually-associated subtle things
25 abandons them, may gain supreme bliss. Having conjoined
these very seven subtle things, O king! passionlessness
towards created and other things tends to the final emanci-
pation from existence of the man cognisant of the entities.†

* For *tat-saukhyam* read *tat-saukshmam*; so a MS. in the Sanskrit College.

† For *atsu* read *apsu*?

‡ Sad-bháva.

26 When he becomes attached to perfumes and other *delights*, he
perishes; he again reverts to human nature apart from
27 Brahma. Whatever subtle created thing the yogí desires,
after transcending the subtle conditions of these seven objects,
28 in that very thing he meets his extinction, O king! He
meets his extinction in the bodies of gods or Asuras, or of
Gandarvas, Nágas, or Rákshasas; nowhere does he gain any
attachment.

29 Where minuteness, and lightness,* greatness and the power
of obtaining every thing, freedom of will,† and lordship, and
30 magical domination and again self-mortification are—one finds
these eight sovereign-like qualities fully indicate union with
31 the Supreme Spirit,‡ O king. The quality of minuteness is far
subtler than the subtle; lightness *means* swiftness; greatness
consists in being universally reverenced; the power of obtain-
32 ing everything, inasmuch as nothing is impossible of obtain-
ment by him; freedom of will *consists* in his power of pervading
all things; and lordship inasmuch as he is lord; magical
33 domination indeed, the yogí's seventh quality *consists* in his
subjugating *things;* where the wishes are said to remain
stationary,§ there|| is self-mortification. By these causes of
34 sovereignty I have declared O king! in eight points the
indicatory marks¶ of the yogí's final emancipation from
existence, and of his sublime union with the Supreme Spirit.

Thenceforth for him there is no birth, nor growth, nor
35 death; he neither decays nor does he alter; neither from
Bhúr and the other worlds, nor from the family of created
beings, does he experience severance, or moisture, or burning
36 or dryness; nor is he captivated by sounds or other *sensual
impressions;* nor do sounds and other *impressions* exist for

* Laghimá.

† Prákámya.

‡ Nir-váṇa.

§ But better, for *apyuktam* read *santyaktam?* "Where the objects of the wishes are renounced."

|| For *yatra* read *tatra?*

¶ Saṃsúc'aka: a word not in the dictionary.

him; one who experiences them is not united with them.
37 For as an impure lump of gold, when its impurities are purg-
ed away by fire, unites with another lump into one, and
38 undergoes no difference; even so the ascetic, when his faults
are burnt out by the fire of religious devotion, unites with
39 Brahma. As fire when thrown into fire may attain sameness;
and, bearing the same name and having the same substance
40 may not be perceived by any distinction; even so the yogí,
when his stains are burnt away, attains to union with supreme
Brahma, and never acquires a separate existence, O king!
41 As water when thrown into water unites, so the yogi's soul
attains to sameness in the Supreme Soul.

Canto XLI.

The Yogí's religious course.

Dattátreya expounds to Alarka how a yogí should live;—from whom he should gather his alms;—what his alms should be;—how he should eat after worshipping the five vital airs;—what his religious obligations are;—and how he attains to final emancipation from existence.

Alarka spoke.

1 Adorable Sir! I desire to hear thoroughly about a yogí's religious course, since the yogí while pursuing the way to Brahma does not sink into despondency.

Dattátreya spoke.

2 Respect and disrespect, which two things cause men plea-
sure and distress, these are opposites and effect the yogí's final
3 bliss. Respect and disrespect, these two things men indeed
describe as poison and ambrosia; of them disrespect is am-
brosia, but respect is a dire poison.

4 He should plant his foot after it is purified by his eye; he should drink water that has been purified through cloth; he

should use speech that is purified with truth; and he should
meditate on what is purified by the intellect.
5 The yogí should nowhere become a guest, nor attend
śráddhas, or sacrifices, pilgrimages to the gods, or festivals,
6 nor visit the banker for the sake of any advantage. The yogí
should roam about for alms among what is flung away, among
what is smokeless, where the charcoal is extinguished, among
all people who have eaten, but not constantly among all the
7 three. The yogí should not move about occupied in religious
meditation and spoiling the path of the good, so as that folk
8 should despise him or treat him with disrespect. He should
seek his alms among house-holders, and at the houses of
vagrant mendicants:* his livelihood is declared to be the best
9 and first one. Also the ascetic should ever resort to modest,
faithful, tranquil and high-souled brahman householders who
10 are learned in the Vedas; above and after them, to uncorrupt
and non-outcasted men. The practice of seeking alms among
men of no caste is the last livelihood he should wish for.
11 Alms consists of rice-gruel,† or dilute butter-milk,‡ milk or
barley-gruel,§ fruit, roots, or panic seed,‖ grain, oil-cake, and
12 meal. And these are fine articles of food, and cause a yogí
to obtain felicity. A muni should employ them with faith
and with the most perfect meditation.
13 Having first taken one sip of water, let him remain silent
with mind composed; and then is prescribed the first oblation
to the vital air called Práṇa,¶ and the second should be to the
14 vital air Apána;** and the next to that called Sam-ána;††

* Yáyávara.

† For *yavágúm* read *yavágús?* The dictionary gives this word as fem., and *yavágúm* seems an impossible neuter.

‡ Takram.

§ Yávaka.

‖ Priyangu, *Panicum italicum*, (Roxb. p. 101.)

¶ Práṇa; this has its seat in the lungs, and expresses pre-eminently life and vitality.

** Apána; the vital air that goes downwards, and out at the anus.

†† Sam-ána; the vital air that circulates about the navel, and is essential to digestion.

the fourth to that called Ud-ána ;* and the fifth to that called
15 Vy-ána.† Having performed *these oblations* separately, while
restraining his breath, he should at length eat according to
his inclination. He should drink water once again, and after
rinsing out his mouth, he should touch his heart.

16 Honesty and sanctity, self-sacrifice, and uncovetousness,
and harmlessness are the five principal religious obligations
17 of mendicants. Freedom from anger, reverence towards gurus,
purity, abstemiousness in food, and constant study of the
18 Vedas—these are the five well-known observances. He should
devote himself to essential knowledge, which can effect his
objects ; for the multiplicity of knowledge that exists here is
19 a hindrance to religious meditation. He who acts with the
thirst, that he ought to know this and he ought to know that,
may perhaps never gain that knowledge in thousands of ages.
20 Discarding associations, subduing anger, eating sparingly,
and controlling his organs, he should regulate the gates *of
his body* by the intellect, and apply the understanding to
21 profound contemplation. The yogí who is constantly occupied
with religious meditation should always have due recourse
to profound contemplation, in empty places and in
22 caves and in forests. Control over the speech, control over
the actions, and control over the mind, are the three *controls :*
he who invariably possesses these controls is a great 'three-
23 control' ascetic. Who, O king, is agreeable, and who is disagreeable
to him to whom all this universe, both real and
unreal, and composed of good qualities and bad qualities, is
composed of the Supreme Soul ?

24 When he whose intellect is purified, to whom clods and
gold are alike, and whose mind is thus composed towards all
created things, comprehends the supreme eternal and immutable
to be the supreme condition he ceases to be born
25 again. The Vedas and all sacrifices and ceremonies are very
good ; prayer is better than sacrifice ; and the path of know-

* Ud-ána ; the vital air that rises up the throat and passes into the head.

† Vy-ána ; the vital air that circulates or is diffused through the body.

ledge than prayer; and profound contemplation cut off from associations and feelings *is better* than knowledge; when that
26 is attained, the eternal is gained. He who is composed in mind, who is intent on Brahma, who is attentive, and pure, whose delight is concentrated on one object, and who controls his organs—that high-souled man may compass this yoga or religious meditation; thereupon he gains final emancipation from existence through his own religious meditation.

Canto XLII.

Exposition of the word " Om " with regard to the Law of Religious Devotion.

Dattátreya expounds the composition, meaning and efficacy of the sacred word "Om"—It designates the Supreme Soul Brahma; and thorough comprehension of it and meditation on it bring final absorption into Brahma.

Dattátreya spoke.

1 The yogí who lives thus, rightly busied in religious devotion, cannot be turned away even by hundreds of other lives.
2 And when he has beheld the Supreme Soul, visible, existing
in all forms, whose feet and head and neck the universe
3 composes, the lord and creator of the universe, let him in
order to attain thereto utter the one mighty and holy syllable
Om! Let it be his study as he listens to its true form.
4 A and U and M are its three letters; these are its three
instants; they are characterized by goodness, passion and
5 ignorance. And another, a half instant,* which has its seat
on the top *of the syllable*, is without quality and can be
understood by yogís only. It is called gándhárí,† as it is to
6 be uttered in the gándhára note.‡ Being pronounced it

* Annsvára, into which the M may be converted?

† A meaning not in the dictionary.

‡ See note * page 130.

reaches the head, and it conveys the feeling of ants moving *over the body.*

7 As the syllable Om being pronounced reaches the head, the yogí who is lost in meditation of Om should become united with Brahma, the Supreme Soul. Life is his bow, the soul is
8 his arrow, Brahma is the target sublime. It is to be pierced by the heedful man; he should be united with Brahma, as the arrow *becomes embedded in the target.*

The syllable Om, consisting of three and a half instants,
9 should be known in its true sense as the three Vedas—the Ṛic', Sáma and Yajus—the three worlds, the three fires, and
10 *the three deities* Vishṇu, Brahmá and S'iva. And the yogí, who is absorbed in religious meditation thereon, may obtain extinction therein.

Moreover the letter A is designated the bhúr-loka, or terrestrial world; and the letter U the bhuvar-loka, or atmospheric
11 world; and the letter M with its nasal mark is decided to be the svar-loka, or celestial world. Now the first instant is called the discrete,* and the second the indiscrete, and the
12 third instant is the intellectual faculty;† the half instant is the highest abode.‡ In this very order must these stages of
13 religious meditation be known. By uttering the word Om, everything both existent and non-existent may be grasped. Now the first instant is short, the second is long, and the
14 third is prolated, and the half instant is not cognisant to speech.

Such is this word. Brahma is designated the Supreme
15 "Om." The man who truly understands it and further meditates on it, escaping the circle of mundane existence
16 casts off the three-fold bonds, and gains sublime extinction in Brahma, the Supreme Soul. And he who is bound with the unconsumed *results of* his actions, after experiencing death
17 through ill omens,§ and recollecting it at the time of his

* Vyaktá.

† C'ic'-c'hakti.

‡ Final emancipation from existence.

§ Arishṭatas.

departure, attains to a yogí's condition again. Hence by means of imperfect religious devotion, or again by perfected religious devotion, are always to be known the ill omens, so that he does not sink into despondency at the time of his departure.

Canto XLIII.

An account of Ill Omens.

Dattátreya mentions the signs of approaching and impending death, which are partly natural phenomena and partly dreams—also the appropriate seasons for religious devotion—and by various similes and apophthegms indicates how final emancipation from existence is to be attained—Alarka thanks Dattátreya for all the instruction and, going to the king of Káśí and Subáhu, relinquishes his kingdom in their favour.

Dattátreya spoke.

1 "Listen Mahárájá; I will declare those ill omens to thee,
by considering which the yogí knows his own death.
2 "The man who does not see the path of the gods,* the pole-
star, the planet Venus, the moon's shadow and the morning
3 star,† may not live more than a year. The man, who sees the
sun's orb devoid of rays and fire encircled with rays, does
4 not live more than eleven months. He, who in his dreams
clearly perceives gold and silver in his vomit and in his urine
5 and fæces, may live ten months. He who sees departed
persons, Pis'ác'as and other *demons* and the cities of the
Gandharvas and golden-coloured bulls, lives nine months.
6 He who when stout becomes thin, and when thin becomes
stout quite unaccountably, and loses his natural functions,
7 lives for eight months. He, whose foot becomes cracked at
the heel or at the toe in dust and in mud, lives seven months.

* Deva-márga; said to mean the penis or anus.

† Arundhatí.

8 If a vulture, a pigeon, a raven, or a crow, or a hawk, or a
blue bird alights on one's head, that indicates a life of six
9 months. When a man is assailed by flocks of crows or a
shower of dust, or when he sees his shadow unnatural, he
10 lives four or five months. When he sees lightning flashing
in the south in a cloudless sky, or sees a rainbow at night,
11 his life will last two or three months. He who cannot see his
own body in clarified butter, in oil, in a mirror, or in water,
or who sees it head-less, does not live more than a month.
12 When the smell from a yogí's body resembles that of a goat
or the smell from a corpse, know O king that his life will be
13 half a month. When one's breast and foot dry np imme-
diately after he has bathed, and when water does not
14 quench his thirst as he drinks, he lives ten days.
"When the wind as it strikes one cuts one's vitals, and
when one feels no delight from the touch of drops of water,
15 his death has arrived. Whoever sits on a bear, a monkey or
a carriage, and goes singing towards the south in his sleep,
16 for him death brooks no delay. He whom a woman clad in
red or black raiment, and singing and langhing, carries off to
17 the south in his sleep, he will live no longer. He who sees
a single powerful naked mendicant laughing and leaping in
18 his sleep may find death impending. The man, who sees him-
self sunk to the crown of his head in a sea of mud in his
19 sleep, dies at once. And he, who sees charcoal amidst the
hair of the head, or ashes or a waterless river issuing from a
serpent, in his sleep, will after ten days die on the eleventh
20 day. He, who in his sleep is beaten with stones by formi-
dable and hideous black men who raise their weapons aloft,
21 may die at once. He, in front of whom a she-jackal runs
howling at sun-rise, whether meeting him or passing him,
22 dies at once. He, whose heart is possessed with hunger
immediately after he has eaten, and whose teeth chatter, has
23 without doubt* reached the end of his life. He who does not
perceive the smell of a lamp, and who is terrified in the day

* For *saṃśayam* read *saṃśayaḥ* ?

as well as at night, and who does not see himself reflected in
24 another's eyes, lives no longer. He, who has seen both a rain-
bow at midnight and all the planets in the day-time, should
25 as a sensible man deem his life consumed away. He, whose
nose becomes crooked, and whose ears bend down or stick up,
26 and whose left eye waters, has lost his life. When his face
becomes reddish, or his tongue black, a wise man should
27 know that his death is impending. And one should know
that he, who in his sleep journeys to the south on a camel, or
28 an ass, or a carriage, will die outright. He, who cannot
hear his own murmuring when he shuts his ears, and who
cannot see the light with his eyes, lives indeed no longer.
29 He over whom a door is closed after he has fallen into a pit,
and who cannot rise up from the hole, in his sleep, his life
30 ends thereat. Sight directed upwards and unsteady,* and
blood-shot and rolling around, and warmth in the mouth, and
31 dryness at the navel prognosticate a new body for men. He
who in his sleep may enter the fire, and not come out there-
from, or if he *similarly* enters water, his life ends thereat.
32 The man who is attacked by evil spirits at night or by day,
without doubt meets death at the end of the seventh night.
33 One should pronounce that death is impending over the
man who sees his own clean white clothing red or black.

34 "A revolution in men's natural disposition and a reversal
in their nature proclaim always that Yama and Death are at
35 hand; as when a man despises and reviles those very persons
to whom he has always been well-behaved, and whom he has
36 considered most deserving of his reverence; when he does
not worship the gods; when he abuses the aged, the gurus
and brahmans; and when he shows no kind treatment to his
37 mother, father, or sons-in-law, or to yogís skilled in learning
or to other high-souled men. But when the time arrives,
wise men† must understand that.

38 "And yogís must always diligently understand at the close

* Sampratishṭha; not in the dictionary.

† For *purushas* read *purushais*?

of the year that ill omens produce their results day and night,
39 O king. And the obvious very formidable series of results
therefrom must be considered; and having ascertained them,
40 he should fix that time in his mind, O king. And having
ascertained that time accurately, the yogí should resort to a
safe place and apply himself to religious devotion, so that
41 that time may not be fruitless to him. And the yogí having
beheld the ill omen and abandoning the fear of death, and
having regarded then its nature, as it has come after a long
42 time, should apply himself to religious devotion as an
adept therein in just that part of the day, both in the fore-
43 noon, and in the after-noon and at mid-day on that day. Or
where he has seen that ill omen during a part of the night,
there he should engage in religious devotion until that
44 day arrives. Then abandoning all fear, and mastering that
time self-controlled, he should stay in that habitation or
45 wherever he feels his soul firm, and engage in religious medita-
tion on the Supreme Soul after overcoming the three qualities:
and when his soul grows composed of the Supreme Soul, he
46 should cease even from the use of his mind. Thereupon he
attains to that sublime absorption into the Supreme Soul,
which is beyond the senses, which transcends the intellect
and which is unspeakable.

47 "All this I have declared to thee, Alarka, in its real meaning.
Hearken to me briefly how thou mayest attain to that
Brahma.

48 "The moon-stone does not emit water, if untouched by the
rays of the moon; that is a well known simile for a yogí.
49 That the sun-stone as long as it remains untouched by the
rays of the sun does not emit fire, is also a simile for a yogí.
50 Ants, rats, ichneumons, house-lizards, and sparrows inhabit a
house like the owner of it, and when it is broken down they
51 go elsewhere; but since they feel no such pain at the destruc-
tion of that house as the owner *feels*, O king; that simile
52 points to the yogí's perfect bliss. *An ant*, though it is compos-
ed of earth and has but a small body, constructs a heavy heap
of earth with the still minuter point of its mouth: that is a

53 lesson for a yogí. When yogís see a tree, clothed with leaves
flowers and fruit, being destroyed by cattle, birds, men and
54 other *creatures*, they become perfected. When a yogí sees the
tender horns of the young ruru deer, which look merely like
the forehead-mark, growing together with him, he may attain
55 final beatitude. When a yogí takes a vessel full of liquid
from a mound on the earth, and when he sees the human
56 body towering up high, what has he not learnt? When a
yogí has truly understood the effort that a man makes, when
all his wealth sufficient for his living has been dug up, he
57 has attained success. That is one's house where one dwells;
that is food on which one lives; and that is wealth by
which one prospers; that is happiness *when one thinks* 'what
58 self-interest have I in this matter.' Just as a man, although
he is importuned by his organs, accomplishes his object by
their means, so a yogí may accomplish his highest *aim* by
means of the intellect and other *faculties* of other persons."

Jaḍa spoke.

59 Then king Alarka prostrated himself before Atri's son, and bowing courteously and filled with intense joy, spoke thus:—

Alarka spoke.

60 "O joy! that this most sore dread, which has sprung from
my defeat by my foes, and which has rendered me anxious
about my life, has been caused by the gods, O bráhman!
61 O joy, that the victorious attack from the immense hosts of
the king of Káśí (routed by which I have come here) has
62 brought about for me this meeting with thee! O joy, that
my army was weak! O joy, that my dependants were slain!
63 O joy, that my treasury became exhausted! O joy that I
grew terrified! O joy, that thy feet came to my recollection! O joy, that all thy words have found an abode in my
64 mind! O joy, that I have both gained knowledge from
meeting with thee, Sir! O joy, that thou hast also shown
compassion to me, O bráhman!

65 "Although destitute a man attains success at the auspicious rise of the Soul, just as this calamity tends to my benefit

66 through my meeting with thee. Subáhu is my benefactor,
and so also is Káśí's lord, through both of whom I have come
67 to thy presence, O noble lord of the yogís. Now I have had
the stains of ignorance burnt out by the fire of thy favour.
I will so strive that I may not become such a vessel of misery.
68 I will quit my position as a householder, which is a forest of
trees of pain, on receiving permission from thee, my high-souled instructer in wisdom."

Dattátreya spoke.

69 "Depart O king! fare thee well! As I have declared unto thee, so do thou practise, free from egotism, free from pride, in order to attain to final emancipation from existence."

Jaḍa spoke.

70 Thus addressed he prostrated himself before that *Muni*,
and hastened to where the king of Káśí and his elder brother
71 Subáhu were. Alarka hastening near smilingly addressed
the king of Káśí, that valiant hero, in the presence of
72 Subáhu:—"O king of Káśí, who desirest my kingdom, enjoy
thou the mighty kingdom even as it pleases thee, or give it to Subáhu!"

The king of Káśí spoke.

73 "Why, O Alarka! hast thou relinquished the kingdom
without a contest? This is not right for a kshatriya; and
74 thou, Sir, knowest the law of the kshatriyas. When his
counsellors are vanquished, a king should abandon the fear
of death, and fix his arrow aiming at his enemy as his target.
75 Having conquered him, a king should certainly enjoy the
choice delights of his desire, and should sacrifice with large sacrifices in order to gain final bliss."

Alarka spoke.

76 "Even of this very nature was my mind before, O hero!
77 Now my object is changed, and do thou hear the cause. As
this *body* is an aggregate formed of the elements, so is the
heart of men, and so are all the qualities likewise even among
78 all animals. Since this intellectual faculty is single indeed,
and there is no other, how then does knowledge create the

79 condition of friend and enemy, of lord and servant? I fell
into that dire misery which was produced by fear of thee,
and I have gained knowledge from Dattátreya's favour, O
80 king. When one subdues all the senses, and abandons utterly
every association, and fixes one's mind on Brahma, in that
81 victory is the sublimest victory. And since there is nothing
else to be accomplished in order to attain that final beatitude,
82 therefore restraining his senses he attains final beatitude. I
then am not thy foe; nor art thou my enemy; Subáhu here
is not my injurer. I have seen all this as my own soul; seek
then another adversary, O king!"

83 Thus he addressed the king. Then uprose Subáhu delighted, and saluting his brother with the word 'O joy!' spoke thus to the king of Káśí.

Canto XLIV.

Jaḍa's exposition in his conversation with his father (*concluded*).

Subáhu explains to the king of Káśí that it was to reclaim his brother Alarka to a proper frame of mind, that he had induced the king to conquer Alarka—Subáhu expounds to the king the conditions of attaining final emancipation from existence, and both depart—Alarka resigns his kingdom to his son, and betaking himself to the forest attains final bliss.

Here ends Jaḍa's exposition to his father.

The Birds then conclude by saying that Jaḍa and his father attained final bliss.

Subáhu spoke.

1 "In that I have resorted to thee for refuge, O tiger-king, I have secured every *object*. I will depart. Rest thou happy!"

The king of Káśí spoke.

2 "What object hast thou secured, Sir? And what aim
hast thou attained? Declare that to me, O Subáhu, for I
3 feel a keen curiosity. Thou didst stir me up, saying 'Conquer

and give me the great kingdom, that belonged to my great-
4 grandfather and is dominated by Alarka.' Thereupon I
attacked the kingdom of this thy younger brother, and
brought this army for thee. Therefore enjoy it as befits thy
race."*

Subáhu spoke.

5 "O king of Káśí, hearken, why I made this endeavour, and
6 stirred thee up, Sir, to an unwonted endeavour. This my
brother, who understands truth is addicted† to unrefined
7 pleasures. My two elder brothers are wise and unbeguiled,
because our mother dropped admonition into the ears of both
of them and into mine, just as she dropped milk in their
8 mouths and mine during our infancy, O king. Our mother
taught those subjects, that men consider should be known,
to both of them and to me, but not to him, *Alarka*,
9 who wished to be illustrious, O king. As merchants, who are
travelling for gain, feel a common grief, if one of them
10 perishes, so is it with us, O king. Since he, *Alarka*, has
caught the infatuation of domestic life, and is perishing, O
king; since he is related to this *my* body, and bears the idea
11 of a brother; hence I, concluding that he would obtain the
perception of passionlessness through suffering, resorted to thee,
12 Sir, to carry out the undertaking. Therefore he has been
brought through distress to passionlessness through instruc-
tion, O king; the work has been accomplished; mayest thou
13 fare well. I depart. 'Having dwelt in Madálasá's womb, and
having drank of her breast, may he not follow the path that
14 is travelled by the sons of other women, O king!' So I
deliberated and I did it all by resorting to thee; and it has
been accomplished. I will again depart to seek final beati-
tude.

15 "I do not approve of those, O king! who neglect their
own family, a kinsman, or a friend, when these are in difficul-
ties; for, though possessed of organs, they are maimed indeed.

* For *bhunkshvasva kuloc'itam* read *bhunkshva svakuloc'itam ?*

† For *s'akto* read *sakto ?*

16 He who falls into difficulties when he has an able friend, or
member of his own family, or kinsman, they should be denied
righteousness, wealth, love and final emancipation, but he
17 *should* not *be denied* them. Through association with thee,
O king, I have accomplished this great undertaking. Well
mayest thou fare! I will depart. Mayest thou participate
in knowledge, most noble *king!*"

The king of Káśí spoke.

18 "Thou hast done a great benefit to good Alarka; how is it
19 thou dost not turn thy mind to benefit me? Since association of good men with good men yields fruit and is not barren, therefore I have attained the prosperity that is bound up with thy patronage."

Subáhu spoke.

20 "The four-fold aims of men are known as righteousness,
wealth, pleasure, and final emancipation from existence.
There thou hast righteousness, wealth and pleasure, all of
21 them,—the last is wanting. I will succinctly expound it to
thee; listen now with singleness of mind thereto; and having heard and rightly deliberated strive after bliss, O king!
22 Thou must have no dealings, O king, with the notion "Mine,"
nor the notion "I"; for when one considers rightly, righteousness has no correlation in the absence of righteousness.
23 When thou hast thought in thy soul, 'I must comprehend of
what I am'; when thou hast thought in after nights 'I must
24 consider the external and the internal'; thou must discern
him whose beginning, attributes and ending are imperceptible, who is changeless, devoid of intelligence, both perceptible and imperceptible; and thou shalt discern 'Who am I?'
25 When this indeed is discerned thou hast discerned everything.
To discern the soul in what is not soul, and one's own pro-
26 perty in what is not one's own—this is folly. I as such have
passed everywhere, O king, according to the intercourse of
the world. I have declared all this that thou hast asked:
now I depart."

27 Having spoken thus to the king of Káśí, the wise Subáhu

departed. And the king of Káśí having done obeisance to Alarka departed to his own city.

28 Alarka, also, enthroned his eldest son as king, and abandoning every tie resorted to the forest, for his own perfection.
29 After a long time becoming purged of the contrary qualities and free from all worldly possessions, he attained an unparalleled pitch of religious devotion and gained supreme and final
30 bliss. Perceiving all this universe with its gods, demons and human beings perpetually bound and being bound in the
31 meshes woven of the qualities; being drawn by the causes brought into existence by sons and other *children*, by nephews and other *relations*, and by one's own and other people's pro-
32 perty, and so forth; oppressed with woe, wearing diverse appearances, wholly enclosed within the mud of ignorance, possessing no deliverer; and *perceiving* himself wholly passed
33 beyond, the large-minded *king* sang this song—"Alas, woe is it that I occupied the kingdom formerly! So have I since learnt. There is no happiness superior to religious devotion."

Jaḍa spoke.

34 Dear father, do thou practise this sublime religious devotion to attain final emancipation from existence; whereby thou shalt attain to that Supreme Soul, in reaching which
35 thou shalt not grieve. Then I also will go. What need have I of sacrifices? what need of prayers? Action in one who has attained success works towards re-absorption into the
36 Supreme Soul. Obtaining permission from thee, I also, free from the contrary qualities, free from worldly possessions, will so strive after final emancipation that I may attain to supreme bliss.

The birds spoke.

37 Having thus addressed his father, and having obtained permission from him, the wise *Jaḍa*, abandoning all worldly
38 possessions, departed, O bráhman. His father also, who was most large-minded, in like course after becoming a vána-
39 prastha entered on the fourth stage of life. There having met with his son, and having forsaken the bonds formed of

the qualities &c., he attained supreme perfection, being wise and having acquired self-knowledge at the same time.

40 All this has been declared to thee, O bráhman, which thou, Sir, did ask of us—at full length and with truth. What else dost thou desire to hear?

Canto XLV.

The Birth of Brahmá.

Jaimini thanks the Birds for all the information they have given him, and asks about creation, the world, mankind &c.,—In reply they relate what Márkaṇḍeya had taught Kraushṭuki regarding all those matters, as follows.

Márkaṇḍeya extols this Puraṇa as having emanated from Brahmá and having been handed down by eminent ṛishis—Adoration is paid to Brahmá.

The identity of Pradhána and Prakṛiti is asserted—Brahmá alone existed at first—From him emanated Pradhána, which is called the Imperceptible—Out of it issued Mahat (the Intellectual priciple)—And out of Mahat issued Ahankára (the principle of Individuality) with its three characters, the Evolving, the Modifying, and the Energizing—The Evolving Ahankára created sound, touch, form, taste and smell, and their corresponding elements, ether, air, light, water and earth—The Modifying Ahankára produced the eleven human organs—The characters of the elements are expounded.

Mahat and the other principles produced an egg, the composition of which is described—It was animated by Brahmá as the Soul, and it contained the universe, the gods, demons and mankind.

Jaimini spoke.

1 Ye have well related this to me, O noble bráhmans, both activity and inactivity, the two-fold deeds enjoined by the
2 Veda. Ah, through your father's favour, ye have such knowledge as this, by which ye have overcome folly although
3 ye have descended to this animal state. Happy are ye in

that your mind, steadfast in your pristine state towards *the*
attainment of final emancipation, is not swayed by the be-
4 wilderments that spring from objects of sense. O joy that
the wise lord Márkaṇḍeya made you known to me as the dis-
5 sipators of every doubt! For men who wander in this closely-
thronged mundane existence there is available association
6 with such as your honours; not for ascetics. If I after gain-
ing association with you who have perspicacity in knowledge
should not succeed in my object, then assuredly* there can
7 be no success for me elsewhere. Both in activity and in
inactivity, in knowledge and deed, no one else has, I think,
a mind so unsullied as your honours have.

8 If then your mind, O noble bráhmans, is favourable to-
9 wards me, then deign to expound this completely;—How did
this universe, both moveable and immoveable, come into
existence? And how will it fall into dissolution at the pro-
10 per time, most excellent *bráhmans?* And how came the
families† that sprang from the gods, the ṛishis, the pitṛis,
created things &c.? And how did the Manvantaras occur?
11 And what was the history of the families *of old;* and whatever
creations and whatever dissolutions *of the universe have oc-*
curred; and how the ages have been divided; and what the
12 duration of the Manvantaras *has been;* and how the earth
remains stable; and what is the size of the world; and *what*
are the oceans, mountains and rivers and forests according to
13 their situation; *what is* the number of the worlds, the bhúr-
loka, svar-loka &c., including the lower regions; and *what is*
the course of the sun, moon, and other planets, of the stars and
14 heavenly bodies also. I wish to hear of all this which is
destined to subversion;‡ and what will be the end when this
universe is dissolved.

The Birds spoke.

15 Unparalleled is this load of questions which thou hast

* For *pyúnam* read *núnam*.

† For *vaṃśád* read *vaṃśá ?*

‡ Áhúta-samplava.

asked, O bráhman: we will declare it to thee; listen to it
16 here, O Jaimini, as Márkaṇḍeya expounded it formerly to the
calm and wise Kraushṭuki, a young bráhman, who had com-
17 pleted his term of studentship. Kraushṭuki asked the high-
souled Márkaṇḍeya, whom the bráhmans were waiting upon,
18 what you have asked, my lord; and we will tell thee what
19 the Muni, Bhṛigu's son, told him with affection; listen, O
bráhman, after having paid adoration to the Forefather Brah-
má, the lord of the universe, the origin of the universe, who
presided over creation, who in the form of Vishṇu *presides*
over its maintenance, and who in the form of the terrible
S'iva destroys it at the dissolution.

Márkaṇḍeya spoke.

20 Formerly as soon as Brahmá, whose origin is inscrutable,
came into being, this Puráṇa and the Vedas issued* from his
21 mouths; and many paramarshis composed the collections of
the Puráṇas; and the Vedas were divided by them in a
22 thousand ways. Righteousness and knowledge, passionless-
ness, and sovereignty—these four indeed were not perfected
23 without instruction from him, the high-souled. His seven
mind-born† ṛishis took the Vedas from him, and his mind-born
24 ancient munis took the Puráṇa. C'yavana took it from
Bhṛigu, and he declared it to the bráhmans; and this *puráṇa*
25 was repeated by the high-souled ṛishis to Daksha; and then
Daksha repeated it to me. I will now tell it to thee: it de-
26 stroys strife and sin. Hear all this from me with composure,
illustrious Muni, as I formerly heard it when Daksha related
it.

27 Having paid adoration to the origin of the universe, un-
born, changeless, the asylum, the upholder of the moveable
28 and immoveable universe, the supreme object, Brahmá, the
first male,—the cause which, itself unbegotten,‡ *works* in pro-

* Anuvinihsṛita, not in the dictionary.

† Mánasa.

‡ Anaurasya; not in the dictionary.

duction, maintenance and dissolution, wherein everything is
29 established—having paid adoration to him, Hiraṇya-garbha,
the framework of the world, the wise, I will duly tell of the
30 multitude of created things, matchless, great, primeval, formed
for special ends, various in shape, possessing characteristics, as-
certainable by the five standards of measure, possessing the
31 five streams of life, governed by the soul, existent as if per-
petual and temporary—listen thereto with sublime composure,
illustrious Sir!

32 Pradhána is the cause, which is designated the Imperceptible,
and which the great ṛishis call the subtle, permanent Prakṛiti,
33 composed of good and evil. Brahmá at first existed certain,
imperishable, undecaying, immeasurable, self-dependent, des-
34 titute of odour, form, and taste, devoid of sound and touch,
without beginning or end, the origin of the universe, un-
changed* by the power of the three qualities, not modern,†
35 unknowable. Subsequent to the dissolution, all this *universe*
was pervaded by him completely.

Then from him, in whom the *three* qualities existed in
equipoise, and in whom the Soul‡ became prevalent, O Muni;
36 and next from the coming into existence of the qualities
which were being created, at the time of creation the first
37 principle Pradhána came into existence. It enveloped
Mahat;§ as the seed is enveloped by its rind, even so Mahat
was enveloped by the Imperceptible. It is three-fold, that
characterized by goodness, that by passion, and that by
38 ignorance. Then from it was evolved Ahankára,|| which is
three-fold, the Modifying,¶ the Energizing,** and the Evol-
39 ving†† which is characterized by darkness. And it was en-
veloped by Mahat, just as Mahat was by the Imperceptible.

Now the Evolving *Ahankára*, modifying itself, created the
40 subtle element‡‡ of sound§§ next. From the subtle element

* For *-prabhavápyayam* read *-prabhavávyayam?*

† A-sámprata.

‡ Kshetra-jna.

§ The great Intellectual principle.

|| The principle of Individuality.

¶ Vaikárika.

** Taijasa.

†† Bhútádi.

‡‡ Tan-mátra.

§§ For *śabdas tanmátrakam* read *śabda-tanmátrakam?*

of sound *came* the Ether, which has the property of sound; now ether is the sound-element, and the evolving *Ahankára*
41 enveloped it then. The subtle element of touch is indeed born next without doubt; the mighty Air is born, its pro-
42 perty of touch is well known. And the air, modifying itself, created the *subtle* element of form; Light was produced from
43 the air; it is said to have the property of form; the air which is the element of touch enveloped the element of form. And light, modifying itself created the *subtle* element of taste;
44 therefrom indeed water also was produced; it has the property of taste; now the element of form enveloped the water*
45 which is the element of taste. And the water, modifying itself, created the *subtle* element of smell; therefrom Solid
46 Matter† is produced; smell is well known to be its property. Now in each *element* resides its *peculiar* subtle element; thereby its possession of that subtle element is a well-established fact. And hence those *elements* are uniform, inasmuch as no
47 difference can be predicated. They are all neither calm, nor terrible, nor crass.‡ This is the creation of the elements and the subtle elements from Ahankára when it is characterized by darkness.

48 From Ahankára in its Modifying character, which is distinguished by goodness and possesses goodness in excess, the modificatory creation began at once.

49 The five organs of the intellect,§ and the five organs of action, men call *these* the energetic|| organs; they are the ten
50 Vaikárika deities. The mind¶ is the eleventh *organ* among them. *Such* are the Vaikárika deities known to be. The
51 ear, the skin, the pair of eyes, the tongue, and fifthly the nose; men say** *these* are *the organs* connected with the intellect for the purpose of perceiving sound and the other *impressions*. The pair of feet, the anus, the organ of generation, the pair of hands, and the voice may rank as fifth *with*

* For *ápo* read *apo;* for the water was enveloped by the light which preceded it; but the change spoils the metre.

† Sangháta. ‡ Múḍha. § Buddhi.

|| Taijasa. ¶ Manas. ** For *vakshyate* read *c'akshate?*

52 *them;* walking, evacuation, *sexual* delight, manual work and
speech—that is the work *for each of these organs respectively.*

Ether has the element* of sound only. When the element
53 of touch accrued, Air comes into existence with two proper-
ties†; touch is known *to be its peculiar* property. Moreover,
when to form accrued both the properties, sound and touch,
54 then Fire also *came into existence* with its three‡ properties;
it has sound and touch and form. Sound, and touch and
55 form,—when the element of taste accrued *to them*, then Water
with its four properties *came into existence;* it is to be known
as being characterized by taste. Sound and touch and form
56 *and* taste, *when* smell accrued, they consolidated with the
element of smell enclosed this Earth; hence earth has five
properties; it is seen to be the gross one among created
things.

57 Calm and terrible and crass§ are their distinguishing
marks; thereby they are known: they contain one another
58 through their mutual interpenetration. Within the earth
is contained all this|| visible and invisible world firmly en-
closed. And those distinguishing marks are perceptible by
59 the organs of sense, and are recollected by reason of their
permanency. They take each successive one the property of
its preceding one. These seven *principles* when un-combin-
60 ed are distinct and have various energies: they could not have
created mankind, unless they had united. And meeting in
61 mutual combination, they become mutually dependent; and
when they all unite into one, they have the marks of a single
complex body.

By reason of their being governed by the Soul¶ and also
62 through the favour of the Imperceptible, Mahat and the other
principles, which have different limits, cause an egg to come
into existence. There like a bubble on water, the egg gra-
63 dually increased by means of the things that existed, O *Sage*
most intelligent! In its enlarged state it lay on the water.

* Mátra.

† Guṇa.

‡ For *dvi-guṇas* read *tri-guṇas?*

§ Múḍha.

|| For *imam* read *idam?*

¶ Purusha.

The Soul,* having increased inside the egg sprung from Pra-
64 kṛiti, took the name Brahmá; it indeed was the first cor-
poreal being, it indeed is called Purusha. And Brahmá
65 existed first, the original maker of created beings. That egg
enclosed all these three worlds with all that they contain
moveable and immoveable. Meru was born from it, and as
66 the after-birth *were born* the mountains; the oceans were the
fluid contained within that egg which held the great Soul.
Within that egg was all this world, with the gods and de-
67 mons and mankind, and the continents and other lands, the
mountains and oceans, *and* the throng of luminous worlds.

Then the egg was enveloped by water, air, fire and ether
68 and by the evolving Ahankára externally, ten times over by
each of them. It was then surrounded† by Mahat which I
69 have mentioned, which had the same magnitude. Mahat
together with them all was enveloped by the Imperceptible.
With these seven coverings formed from Prakṛiti was the
70 egg enveloped. Enveloping one another the eight Prakṛitis
existed. This very Prakṛiti is permanent; and that Purusha
is limited by it.

71 Hear thou, moreover, briefly of him who is spoken of by
the name Brahmá. Just as one sunk in water, on emerging
from it, seems to be born from water‡ and flings the water
72 away, so Brahmá is *both* Prakṛiti and the Soul.§ The Im-
perceptible is declared to be his sphere of action;|| *hence*
73 Brahmá is called Kshetra-jna, the Soul. A man should
know all these characteristics of the Soul and its sphere of
action.

Such was this creation from Prakṛiti; and it is governed by the Soul; the first *stage of creation* was preceded by non-intelligence, it became manifest like the lightning.

---

* Kshetra-jna.

† For *veshṭitaḥ* read *veshṭitam ?*

‡ For *jala-sambhavam* read *jala-sambhavaḥ ?*

§ Vibhu.

|| Kshotra.

Canto XLVI.

The computation of Brahmá's life.

Márkaṇḍeya moralizes on Brahmá and Prakṛiti—and describes Vishṇu and S'iva as special forms of Brahmá—He explains how human and divine years are reckoned, the duration of the four ages, the Kṛita, the Tretá, the Dvápara and the Kali, and of a Manvantara, and the length of Brahmá's day and life.

Kraushṭuki spoke.

1 Adorable Sir! thou hast related to me correctly the genesis
of the egg, and thou hast told me of the birth of the mighty
2 Soul Brahmá within the egg of Brahmá. I wish to hear this
from thee, O scion of Bhṛigu's race, when things are not
created, and nothing exists, everything having been destroyed
by Time at the end of the dissolution *of the Universe.*

Márkaṇḍeya spoke.

3 When all this universe becomes dissolved in Nature,* this
4 dissolution is designated 'natural'† by the wise. When the
Imperceptible subsists within itself, and when all modification is suspended, Nature and the Soul‡ subsist with same-
5 ness of character. Then both darkness and goodness subsist
in equipoise, neither being in excess or in deficiency, and
6 permeated by each other. Just as oil exists in sesamum
seeds, or as ghee in milk, so passion also exists permeant
within darkness and goodness.

7 The day of the Supreme Lord§ lasts from the birth of
Brahmá, as long as the two half paras which compose his
life ;|| and his night during the dissolution is of the same
8 duration.¶ Now at the dawn of day he awakes, he who is

* Prakṛiti. † Prákṛita. ‡ Purusha. § Pareśa.

|| The text seems incorrect; a better reading obtained from a MS. belonging to Babu Nagendra Chandra Basu of Calcutta is *utpatter* for *utpattir*, and *áyur vai* for *áyusho*. See verse 42.

¶ The same MS. reads *tat-samaḥ samayo* instead of *tat-samá saṃyame*; with practically the same meaning.

the origin of the universe, who is without beginning, who is the cause of all things, whose soul transcends thought; every one else works in an inferior way.

9 The Supreme God, quickly enters into Nature and the Soul,
as the lord of the universe, and agitates them with his intense
10 supernatural power. Just as love, or a breeze of Spring,
entering into young women tends to produce agitation, so
does he, who is the embodiment of supernatural power.
11 When Pradhána is agitated, the god Brahmá is born and is
contained within the cavity of the egg, as I have *already*
12 told thee. At first he is the agitator; as the husband of
Nature, he is *the thing* to be agitated; and he exists with
13 contraction and expansion even in the state of Pradhána. He
is born, *though* he is the birth-place of the universe; though
devoid of qualities, he possesses the quality of passion; when
he assumes the character of Brahmá, he engages in creation.
14 In the character of Brahmá he creates mankind; then
possessing an excess of goodness, he becomes Vishṇu and
15 protects them righteously; then, with darkness preponderating in him, he as Rudra dissolves the whole universe with
its three worlds, and sleeps. He possesses the three qualities,
16 *and yet* he is destitute of qualities. Just as he is at first the
pervading Soul, *then* the preserver, and *lastly* the destroyer,*
so he takes appellations which designate him as Brahmá,
17 Vishṇu or S'iva. As Brahmá he creates the world; and as
Rudra he destroys them; and as Vishṇu he holds a neutral
position. These are the three conditions of the Self-existent.
18 Passion *and* Brahmá; darkness *and* Rudra; goodness *and*
Vishṇu the lord of the world: these indeed are the three
19 deities; these indeed are the three qualities. These verily
are mutually paired, and are mutually dependant: they are
not separated for a moment; they do not forsake one another.
20 Thus Brahmá, the four-faced god of gods, is anterior to
the universe: assuming the quality of passion, he engages in
creation.

* *Lávaka* (from *lú*), one who cuts to pieces, one who destroys. Would not *láyaka* (from *lí*) be better, one who brings on the dissolution?

21 Brahmá who is adored as Hiraṇya-garbha, the first of the
gods, and without beginning, who sits in the middle of the
22 lotus-like earth, was born in the beginning. One hundred
years is the full length of life for him, the high-souled, according to the true Bráhmya computation. Hear from me how it is reckoned.

23 A káshṭhá is said *to be composed* of fifteen winks of the
eyelids; and thirty káshṭhás *make* a kalá; and thirty such
24 kalás *make* a muhúrta. A day and night among men contain,
it has been settled, thirty muhúrtas; and with thirty days
25 are reckoned the two lunar fortnights and the month; of
six months consists the sun's half-yearly course; the two half-yearly courses on the south and north *of the equator compose* the year. Such a year is a day and night of the gods;* the day thereof is the sun's northern half-yearly course.

26 Now of twelve thousand divine years consist the four ages named the Kṛita, the Tretá, &c. Hear from me how they are divided.

27 Now the Kṛita age is said *to have contained* four thousand
years; its commencing twilight was four hundred years, and
28 the closing twilight was of the same *duration*. The Tretá
age was three thousand divine years; and three hundred *years* was its commencing twilight, which was indeed of that duration, and its closing twilight was of the same *duration*.
29 The Dvápara age was two thousand years; and its commen-
cing twilight is declared to have been two hundred *years*, and
30 its closing twilight was two hundred years. The Kali age
is a thousand divine years, O brahman; two hundreds of years are called its commencing and closing twilights.

31 This period of twelve thousand *divine years* is called a yuga; it has been laid down by the poets; a thousand times this *period* are called one of Brahmá's days.

32 In one of Brahmá's days, O brahman, there may be four-
teen Manus. They live according to their portions; that
33 thousand is divided among them. The gods, the seven

* Thus one divine year = 360 human years.

ṛishis, and Indra, Manu, and the kings his sons, are created
with Manu and pass to dissolution with him in regular order.
34 Seventy-one repetitions of the four ages, with a fraction in excess, *constitute* a manvantara; hear from me its computation in
35 human years. Thirty full crores reckoned duly, O brahman,
36 and sixty-seven lakhs more by reckoning, and twenty thousands—this is the period *of seventy-one times the four ages* without the excess fraction; this is called a manvantara.
37 Hear it from me in divine years; eight hundred thousands of years by divine reckoning,* and fifty-two thousands of
38 years more in addition. A day of Brahmá is declared to be this period multiplied fourteen times.† At its termination the dissolution is declared by the wise to be the necessary *result*, O brahman.

39 The Bhúr-loka, the Bhuvar-loka and the Svar-loka are perishable and pass‡ to dissolution; and the Mahar-loka
40 stands, yet the dwellers therein by reason of the heat go to the Jana-loka. And Brahmá sleeps indeed during the night in the three worlds which have been dissolved into one ocean.
41 That night is of exactly the same duration. At its termina-

* This line as it stands in the text seems incorrect. The four ages contain 12,000 divine years or 4,320,000 human years, and 71 times this period contain 8,52,000 divine years, or 306,720,000 human years. This latter period agrees with the enumeration in verse 36 (*viz.*, 30,67,20,000 years), but instead of the former the text gives 8,000 + 52,000, *i. e*, 60,000 divine years, unless we read *śata-sahasráṇi* for *varsha-sahasráṇi*. *Yutam*, however, seems wrong as regards both grammar and meaning.

† This does not agree with verse 31, if we take the words "this period" to refer to verses 35, 36 and 37. In verse 31 one of Brahmá's days is said to be 12,000,000 divine years or 4,320,000,000 human years, but 14 times the period mentioned in the latter verses contain 11,928,000 divine years, or 4,294,080,000 human years. We must bring in here the excess fraction referred to in verse 34, which by calculation is found to be $\frac{3}{7}$; thus $71\frac{3}{7}$ times the yuga of 12,000 divine years = $857,142\frac{6}{7}$ divine years of the manvantara and 14 times this last period exactly = 12,000,000 divine years of Brahmá's day. Similarly with regard to human years.

‡ For *áyáti* read *áyánti?*

tion creation begins again. And so *passes* one of Brahmá's
42 years, and a hundred years is the whole. For a hundred of
his years is denominated a Para; and a Parárdha or half a
43 Para is well-known to be composed of fifty years. So then a
Parárdha of his *life* has elapsed, O brahman; at the close of
which occurred the Mahá-kalpa, *which* is famed as the Pádma.
44 Of the second Parárdha which is now passing, O brahman,
the first kalpa (or cycle) ordained is this one called the
Váráha.

CANTO XLVII.

*The Creation from Prakṛiti and the Vikáras.**

Márkaṇḍeya continues—After the Pádma Mahá-kalpa Brahmá awoke, and as Náráyaṇa raised the earth out of the sea of dissolution and fashioned it in its present shape—Then he created, first, the vegetable world—secondly, the animal world—thirdly, the gods—fourthly, mankind—fifthly, Anugraha—and sixthly, the bhútas—Markaṇḍeya summarizes the nine creations, viz., these six, and the three described in Canto XLV.

Kraushṭuki spoke.

1 Tell me fully how Brahmá, the adorable, the creator, the lord of all creatures, the master, the divine, created *all* creatures.

Márkaṇḍeya spoke.

2 Here I tell thee, O brahman, how the adorable eternal framer of the worlds created all the universe moveable and immoveable.

3 At the dissolution which followed the Pádma† *Mahá-kalpa*, the lord Brahmá awoke after having slept through the night.

* The products evolved from Prakṛiti.

† For *padmávasáne* read *pádmávasáne?*

Then with goodness predominating in him he gazed on the
4 empty world. And here men utter this verse to Náráyaṇa,
who has Brahmá's own form, god of the universe, changeless
5 in might. "Nárá *means* water and bodies"*—we have thus
heard it is a name for water; and in it he lies, hence he is
called Náráyaṇa.

6 On awaking he knew that the earth had disappeared with-
in that water, and then *became* desirous through reflection to
7 deliver† the earth therefrom. He assumed as of old in the
kalpas and other *times*, other bodies such as those of a fish, a
tortoise and other *animals*, and likewise he took the body of
8 a boar. The lord who is composed of the Vedas and sacri-
fices assumed a heavenly form composed of the Vedas and
sacrifices, and entered the water; he reached everywhere and
9 existed everywhere. And the lord of the world raised the
earth out of the lower regions, and set it free in the water,
while the Siddhas who abode in Jana-loka bent their thoughts
10 on him. The earth floated like an immense boat on that
ocean, but does not sink by reason of the amplitude of its size.
11 Then he made the earth level and created the mountains on
the earth. Formerly when creation was burnt up by the
12 then world-destroying fire, those mountains on the earth were
totally consumed by that fire. The rocks were engulphed in
that one ocean, and the water was driven together by the
13 wind; wherever they adhered and remained, there the moun-
tains grew into being. Then he divided the earth, adorned
14 with seven dvípas; and he fashioned the four worlds, the
Bhur-loka and the others, as before.

While he pondered on creation, as of old in the kalpas and
15 other *times*, he next became manifested as devoid of intelli-
gence, as enveloped in darkness. Darkness, folly, infatuation,
16 gloominess, and blind consciousness—ignorance,‡ composed of
these five, became manifested out of the Supreme Soul.
Creation irrational became established in five ways while he
17 was meditating. Externally and internally it was destitute of

* Tanavaḥ. † Sam-ud-dhára; not in the dictionary. ‡ A-vidyá.

light,* its soul was concealed, it consisted of vegetation;†
and since vegetation is declared to be "primary,"‡ hence
this is indeed the Mukhya creation.
18 He considered that creation incapable of causation,§ and
thought of *creating* another yet. While he was meditating
on its creation, the animal world, in which the stream of life‖
19 is horizontal,¶ came next into existence. Since its activities
are *displayed* horizontally, hence it** is known as the "tiryak-
srotas." Cattle and other *quadrupeds* are well-known as being
of that kind; they are indeed characterized chiefly by igno-
20 rance and are unintelligent; and they stray in wrong courses,
and in their ignorance are subservient to knowledge; they
are self-swayed, and devoted to self; they comprise twenty-
21 eight classes. They all possess light* internally, but they
are mutually circumscribed.††

He thought even that *creation* was incapable of causation,
22 and while he meditated, another came into existence; now
this, the third, was the group of beings in which the stream
of life passed upwards;‡‡ it was characterized chiefly by good-
ness. Those beings abound in pleasure and affection; they
23 are uncircumscribed outwardly and inwardly; and possess
light* externally and internally; they originated from an up-
ward stream of life. Now that third *creation* of the *Supreme
Being who was* satisfied in soul *thereat* is known as the crea-
24 tion of the gods. When that creation came into being,
Brahmá was pleased.

* Prakáśa. This is defined by S'rí-dhara Svámí to mean "clear knowledge" (prakṛishṭaṃ jṉánam). It had no clear external perception of sound &c., or clear internal feeling of happiness, &c.

† Naga. ‡ Mukhya.

§ For *dṛishṭvá sádhakam* read *dṛishṭvásádhakam*; see the second line of verse 21.

‖ Srotas; or the current of nutriment. ¶ Tiryak.

** For *sá* read *saḥ?*

†† A'-vṛita. S'rí-dhara explains this as, "mutually ignorant of their birth, nature, &c."

‡‡ U'rdhva-srotas.

Then he meditated further on another creation *which should*
25 *be* capable of causation and be the highest. While he medita-
ted so, and meditated on truth, the group of beings in which
the stream of life passes downwards,* and which is capable
of causation,† next became manifest out of the Impercepti-
26 ble. Since *the streams of life in them* moved downwards,
hence they‡ are "arvák-srotas;" and they possess light§
copiously; they are characterized chiefly by ignorance and pas-
27 sion. Hence they have abundance of suffering, and are con-
tinuously engaged in action; and they possess light externally
and internally. They are mankind and are capable of causation.
28 Anugraha‖ was the fifth creation; it is disposed in four
ways, by contrariety,¶ and by perfection,** bytranquillity,††
29 and by satisfaction‡‡ likewise. The objects of this creation
moreover have knowledge of the past and of the present.
30 The creation of the origins of the gross elements§§ and the
gross elements‖‖ is called the sixth; they all possess com-
prehensiveness,¶¶ and are prone to mutual division;*** and
the origins of the gross elements are to be known as both
impulsive and devoid of propensities.
31 Now the creation of "mahat" is to be known as the first
by Brahmá; and the second of the "tan-mátras" is called
32 the creation of the "bhútas;" and the third creation is that
of the "vikáras,"††† and it is perceptible by the senses. So was
produced the creation from Prakṛiti wherein Intelligence pre-

* Arvák-srotas.

† For *sádhakaḥ* read *sádhakam?*

‡ For *ta* read *te?*

§ Prakáśa, see note * p. 230.

‖ This is the Pratyaya-sarga or intellectual creation of the Sánkhya philosophy. But S'rí-dhara explains it as an inferior creation of gods (deva-sarga), who are characterized by both goodness and ignorance. It is characterized by ignorance because it is nourished by the ignorance among immoveable objects and the animal creation; it is characterized by goodness, because it harmonizes with and thrives upon the perfection and satisfaction among mankind and the gods; and it is called Anugraha, because it favours (anugrahaka) the several natural dispositions of those objects.

¶ Viparyaya. ** Siddhi. †† S'ánti. ‡‡ Tushṭi.

§§ Bhútádika. ‖‖ Bhúta. ¶¶ Pari-graha. *** Saṃ-vi-bhága.

††† The products evolved from Prakṛiti.

33 ceded. The "mukhya" creation was the fourth, the mukhya things are known as immoveable. The fifth was that called
34 "tiryak-srotas"* and "tairyag-yonya." Next was the sixth *creation*, that of the "úrdhva-srotas";† it is known as the creation of the gods. Then the creation of the "arvák-srotas"
35 is the seventh; it is that of mankind. The eighth creation is "anugraha"; it is characterized by goodness and ignorance. These *last* five creations are known as those which were evolved from the Vikáras,‡ and the *first* three as those
36 evolved from Prakṛiti.§ The ninth creation was Prákṛita and also Vaikṛita; it is known as "Kaumára."|| Thus these nine creations of the Prajá-pati have been declared.

CANTO XLVIII.

The Course of Creation.

Márkaṇḍeya relates how Brahmá created the Asuras, the gods, the pitṛis and mankind, and the night and day and the two twilights—He mentions the times when those beings are powerful —He relates the creation of the Rákshasas, Yakshas, Serpents, Piśác'as, and Gandharvas—Next of all beasts, birds and other animals—Then of various sacred hymns and metres—Then of the lightning, thunder, and other phenomena—And lastly Brahmá assigned all things their shapes, pursuits and names.

Kraushṭuki spoke.

1 O adorable Sir, right well hast thou related the creation briefly to me; tell me, O bráhman, fully of the origin of the gods.

* For *tiryak-srotas* read *tiryak-srotás ?*

† For *tato 'rddha-srotasáṃ* read *tathorddhva-srotasáṃ ?*

‡ Vaikṛita. § Prákṛita.

|| This is the creation of Níla-lohita Rudra (see Canto LII) and of Sanat-kumára and the other mind-born sons of Brahmá, the Kumáras. This creation is called prákṛita because Rudra sprang into existence by himself, as mentioned in that canto, verse 3. It is also called vaikṛita, because the Kumáras were created by Brahmá in the form he assumed of a vikára (vikṛiti-bhúta).

Márkaṇḍeya spoke.

2 *Creation* is impregnated with the good and bad* actions of
previous existence, O bráhman; and because of this well-
known law†, created beings, though they are destroyed in the
dissolution, are not delivered, *from the consequences of their
actions.*

3 The gods and other *divine beings*, and stationary things, and
the four classes of mankind, O bráhman, were produced in
his mind when Bráhmá was engaged in creation.

4 Then being desirous of creating the four classes of beings,
namely, the gods, the Asuras and the pitṛis, and mankind, he
5 infused‡ himself in the waters. The particle of darkness
grew up in excess as the Prajá-pati was rapt in medita-
tion. First then out of his buttocks, as he was desirous
6 of creating, were produced the Asuras. And then he cast
aside that body which was composed of the particle of dark-
ness; that body cast aside by him forthwith became Night.

7 Being desirous of creating, he assumed another body and
experienced delight; then were produced from his mouth the
8 Gods in whom goodness predominates. And the mighty lord
of created beings abandoned that body also, and when cast
aside it became Day wherein goodness predominates.

9 Then he took another body which was indeed characterized
by the particle of goodness; the Pitṛis were produced from
10 him while he deemed himself to be a pitṛi. The lord, after
creating the pitṛis, abandoned that body also, and when
abandoned it became the Twilight that intervenes between
11 day and night. Next the lord assumed another body charac-
terized by the particle of passion, and then were produced
12 Mankind who spring from the particle of passion. After
creating mankind, the lord abandoned that body, and it be-
came the Twilight that ends the night and begins the day.

13 Thus these bodies of the wise God of gods have become
famed as the night and day, and the evening twilight and

* For *kuśalá kuśalair* read *kuśalákuśalair*.

† For *khyátá* read *khyátyá ?*

‡ Or, united himself with.

14 the morning twilight, O bráhman. Three are characterized
by the particle of goodness, namely, the morning twilight, the
evening twilight and the day; the night is characterized by
15 the particle of darkness, hence it *is called* Tri-yámiká.* Hence
the gods are powerful by day, but the Asuras by night, and
mankind at the coming of the morning twilight, and the pitṛis
16 at the evening twilight. *At these times these classes of beings* are
undoubtedly powerful and unassailable by their foes; and
when they light upon the adverse times they lose their power.
17 The morning twilight, the night, the day, and the evening
twilight, these four are indeed the bodies of the lord Brahmá,
and they are invested with the three qualities.

18 Now after creating these four, the Prajá-pati, feeling hunger
and thirst, took another body composed of passion and dark-
19 ness during the night; during its darkness the adorable
unborn *god* created bearded monsters wasted with hunger;
20 and they endeavoured to eat up that body. Some of those
monsters, who said "let us preserve† it from them," were
called Rákshasas *in consequence;* and those who said "let us
devour‡ it" were *called* Yakshas, from yakshaṇa, 'eating,'§
O bráhman.

21 When the creator Brahmá saw them, the hair of his head
through his displeasure grew withered|| and lost its erectibi-
22 lity.¶ Through its downward gliding** it became the Ser-
pents,†† and from its loss‡‡ *of erectibility* they are known as
the Ahis or Snakes. Thereupon in anger at having seen the
23 Serpents, he fashioned beings possessed with anger;§§ they
were born as the flesh-eating *demons,* tawny-hued and fierce.

* That is, "having its course with the three others," from *tri* and *yáma* (from root *yá*); or, "keeping the three others in check," from *tri* and *yáma* (from root *yam*). The meaning "having three watches" from *tri* and *yáma* (from root *yá*) is discarded here.

† Rakshâma. ‡ Khádáma.

§ Yakshaṇa seems a mistake for jakshaṇa.

|| For *s'íryanta* read *śírṇās tu?*

¶ Samárohaṇa-hína. ** Sarpaṇa. †† Sarpa. ‡‡ Hínatva.

§§ For *krodhátmáno* read *krodhátmano?*

Next while he meditated on the earth,* the Gandharvas
24 were born as his offspring. They were born from him as he
drank speech in,† hence they are known as the Gandharvas.
When these eight classes of divine beings were created, the
25 lord next created other things, birds and cattle.‡ He created
goats§ from his mouth; and he created sheep from his
26 breast; and Brahmá fashioned kine|| from his belly and from
his loins; and from his feet swift¶ horses and asses, and hares
27 and deer, camels and mules and other *animals of* various
kinds; plants and fruit-trees were produced from the hair of
28 his body. When he had thus created the cattle and plants,
the lord performed a sacrifice.

From him at the beginning of the kalpa, at the commence-
29 ment of the Tretá Age issued the cow, the goat, mankind, the
sheep, the horse, the mule, and the ass (these animals men
call domestic cattle), and *others* (*which they call* wild animals,
30 hearken to me), *namely* the beast of prey, the cloven-hoofed
beast, the elephant, monkeys, fifthly birds, sixthly aquatic
beasts, and seventhly creeping animals.

31 And for the sacrifices he fashioned from his front mouth
the gáyatrí, and the ṛic'a strophe, the tri-vṛit hymn of praise,**
32 the rathantara sámans, and the agni-shṭoma verses. And he
created from his right mouth the yajur hymns, the tri-shṭubh
metre, sacred hymns,†† and the fifteen hymns of praise,‡‡ and
33 the bṛihat-sáman and the uktha verses.§§ He fashioned from
his hindmost mouth the sáman hymns, the metre jagatí, and

* Dhyáyato gám. † Pivato vác'am; the derivation is not apparent.

‡ *Paśavo;* by ancient use for *paśún.*

§ *Ajáḥ* for *aján,* by ancient use; so also *avayo* for *avín* 'sheep.'

|| *Gávas* for *gás,* by ancient use. But the MS. in the Sanskrit College Library, Calcutta, reads instead—

Tataḥ svac'c'handato 'nyáni vayáṃsi vayaso 'sṛijat.

"Then he created other winged animals from his bodily energy according to his wish."

¶ Samátanga; not in the dictionary: from the root *sam-á-tang?*

** The eleventh hymn of the ninth Maṇḍala of the Ṛig-Veda sung in a special way. †† C'handas. ‡‡ Stoma.

§§ *For uktaṃ read ukthaṃ.*

the fifteen hymns of praise,* the vairúpa sáman, and the ati-
34 rátra verse.† He created from his left mouth the twenty-
first Atharva hymn, and the aptor-yáman sacrificial verse,†
the anu-shṭubh metre and the viráj metre.
35 The mighty adorable *god* created at the beginning of the
kalpa the lightning, the thunderbolts and the clouds, and
36 the ruddy rainbows, and the periods of life.‡ And crea-
ted things great and small were produced from his limbs.
Having created the first four classes of beings, the gods,
37 the Asuras, the pitṛis and mankind, he next created the
things that exist both immoveable and moveable, the Yakshas,
the Piśác'as, the Gandharvas and the bevies of Apsarases,
38 men and Kinnaras and Rákshasas, birds, cattle, wild animals
and snakes, and whatever is changeless and changeful,
stationary and moveable.
39 Whatever actions they were severally endowed with ori-
ginally at their creation, those very *actions* they are endowed
40 with when they are created again and again. Noxiousness
and harmlessness, gentleness and cruelty, righteousness and
unrighteousness, truth and falsehood,—animated thereby they
have their being; therefore they severally take delight in
41 those *characteristics*. The lord, the creator, himself ordained
diversity and specialization§ among created things in their
42 organs and pursuits and bodies. And he assigned the names
and shapes of created things, and propounded the duties of
the gods and other *beings*, even by the words of the Veda at the
43 beginning. He gives names to the Ṛishis, and to the *several*
created classes|| among the gods, and to the other things that
44 were brought forth at the close of the night.¶ As the signs
of the seasons appear at *their appropriate* season,** and various
forms appear amid alteration, so those very *signs and forms*
appear as actual facts†† in the ages and other *periods*.

* Stoma; but another reading is *seventeen*.

† A part of the seven soma-saṃstha sacrifices.

‡ Vayáṃsi; or, birds.

§ Viniyoga.

|| Sṛishṭi.

¶ For *sarvaryyante* read *s'arvaryante ?*

** For *yathárttau* read *yatharttau ?*

†† Bháva.

45 Such then* *were* the creations of Brahmá whose origin
is undiscernible; they occur from kalpa to kalpa as he awakes
at the close of his night.†

Canto XLIX.

The Course of Creation.

Márkaṇḍeya describes the creation of the primeval human race, and their simple condition and happy life—When they ultimately died out, modern men fell from the sky, and lived in kalpa trees—Passionate affection sprung up among them—and covetousness next, which destroyed the trees, and drove them to form communities—Their measures of length are explained—and fortresses, towns, villages and houses described—The Tretá Age began—with the existing rivers and vegetation—and the people lived on the vegetation—They then took private possession of property according to might, and the vegetation perished—Then they supplicated Brahmá, and he created all existing cereals and plants—The seventeen cereals and the fourteen sacrificial plants are specified—Brahmá ordained their means of livelihood, which could be gained only through labour, and their laws, castes, &c. —The spheres assigned to various classes after death are mentioned.

Kraushṭuki spoke.

1 Thou hast told me, Sir, of the group of beings in which
the stream of life‡ passes downwards; tell me fully, O
2 bráhman, how Brahmá created the human creation, and how
he created the classes of men, and how their qualities, O
wise Sir; and tell me what business has been assigned to
the bráhmans and those other classes severally.

Márkaṇḍeya spoke.

3 While Brahmá was first creating and was meditating on
truth, he created a thousand pairs *of human beings* from his
4 mouth, O Muni; when born, they come into being, charac-
terized chiefly by goodness, and self-glorious. He created

* For *ta* read *tu?*

† For *sarvaryyante* read *s'arvaryante?*

‡ Or, current of nutriment.

5 another thousand pairs from his breast; they were all
characterized chiefly by passion, and were fiery and impa-
tient. And he created again another thousand miserable
6 pairs from his thighs;* they were known as characterized
chiefly by passion and ignorance, and as enviously disposed.
7 And he created another thousand pairs from his feet; they
were all characterized chiefly by ignorance, and were un-
fortunate and little of understanding.

Then those living beings, produced in pairs, were rejoicing
8 together; urged by their mutual distress they hastened to
sexual intercourse. Thenceforward pairing originated in
8 this kalpa. Women did not have their courses month by
month; hence they did not then bring forth offspring, although
10 they engaged in sexual intercourse. They bring forth just
pairs of children once at the close of life. Thenceforward
11 pairing originated in this kalpa. By meditation and thought
those human beings give birth *to offspring* once. Sound and
the other objects of sense were pure severally in their five
marks.

12 This was this creation of the human race which the Prajá-
pati formerly *produced*. Sprung of his lineage they worship-
13 ped this world, and they pay homage to rivers, lakes, and
seas and the mountains also. During that age those *human*
14 *beings* lived indeed feeling little cold or heat. They received
delight according to their natural dispositions from the objects
of sense, O wise *Sir;* no opposition, nor enmity, nor envy
15 existed among them. They paid homage to the mountains
and the seas; they lived wholly without habitations; their
actions were unswayed by love; their minds were always
16 joyful. Neither Piśác'as, nor Nágas, nor Rákshasas, nor en-
vious men, nor cattle, nor birds, nor crocodiles, nor fish, nor
17 creeping insects, nor egg-born animals hindered *them*, (for
those *animals* are the offspring of iniquity,) nor roots, nor
18 fruits, nor flowers, nor the seasons, nor the years. Time was
always happy; there was neither heat nor cold in excess; as
19 time passed by, they attained wonderful perfection. More-

* For *marutaḥ* read *úrutaḥ*.

over they enjoyed satisfaction in the fore-noon and at noon;
and again satisfaction came without exertion to those who
20 wished for it, and exertion also sprang up in the mind of
those who wished for it. The water was exquisite. Perfec-
21 tion was merry with many a delight for them;* and another
was produced that conferred every wish. And with bodies
22 uncared for, those human beings had lasting youth. Without
resolve they produce offspring in pairs; alike is their birth
23 and form, and together also they die. Devoid of desire and
hatred they lived to each other. All were equal in form and
24 length of life, without inferiority or superiority. They live
their measure of life, four thousand human years; nor have
25 they misfortunes through affliction. Everywhere moreover
the earth was entirely blessed with good fortune.

26 As the people died in the course of time, so their prosperity
gradually perished everywhere; and when it had altogether
27 perished, men fell down from the sky. Those kalpa trees
were commonly produced which are called houses; and they
28 brought forth every kind of enjoyment to those *people.* At the
beginning of the Tretá age the *people* got their subsistence
from those *trees.* Afterwards in the course of time passionate
29 affection† sprung up suddenly among them. By reason of
the occurrence of passionate affection menstruation occurred
month by month, and conception frequently took place.
30 Then those trees were called houses‡ by them. But branches
certainly fall from other trees, O bráhman; and they yield
31 clothing and ornaments out of their fruits. In the separate
cavities of the same *fruit* of those *trees* was produced very
strong honey, which excelled in smell, colour and taste, and
32 which no bee had made; on that they subsisted at the begin-
ning of the Tretá age.

Afterwards in course of time those *people* grew covetous
33 besides; their minds being filled with selfishness they fenced

* The text *siddhir námnávayo na sá* seems incorrect; instead of it, another MS. reads *siddhir nánárasollasá*, which I have adopted.

† Rága.

‡ Does this mean the trees were called houses (*griha*) from the offspring (*garbha*) begotten there?

the trees* round; and those trees perished by reason of that
34 wrong conduct on their part. Strife sprang up in conse-
quence; their faces felt cold and heat and hunger. Then
for the sake of combination and resistance they made towns
35 at first; and they resort to fortresses in inaccessible deserts
and wastes, in mountains and caves; also they industriously
36 constructed with their own fingers an artificial fort on trees,
on mountains and in water, and they first made measures
intended for measurement.

37 A minute atom, a para súkshma, the mote in a sunbeam,†
the dust of the earth, and the point of a hair, and a young
louse,‡ and a louse,§ and the body of a barley-corn;|| men
38 say each of those *things* is eight times the size of the preced-
ing thing.¶ Eight barley-corns *equal* an angula or finger-
39 breadth;** six finger-breadths are a pada,†† and twice that
is known as a span;‡‡ and two spans make a cubit measured
with the fingers closed in at the root of the thumb;§§ four
cubits *make* a bow, a pole,|||| and equal two náḍikás; two
40 thousand bows make a gavyúti;¶¶ and four times that are
declared by the wise to be a yojana;*** this is the utmost
measure for purposes of calculation.

41 Now of the four *kinds of* fortresses three occur naturally;
the fourth *kind of* fortress is artificial. Now those men
42 constructed it laboriously;††† and *they* also *constructed*, O

* For *vṛikshás* read *vṛikshámṣ?* † For *trasha-reṇur* read *trasa-reṇur.*

‡ For *nishkám* read *likshá.* § For *yúkám* read *yúká.* || Yavodara.

¶ For *ekádaśa-guṇaṃ teshám* another MS. reads *kramád ashṭa-guṇányáhur,* which is much better.

** For *yava-madhyam* another MS. reads *yaványashṭau.*

†† A foot's breadth? ‡‡ For *vitasti-dviguṇam* read *vitastir dviguṇam?*

§§ For *-veshṭanam* read *-veshṭanaḥ?* This relation indicates a long arm, or small hands and feet. An average cubit so measured would be equal to about 15 inches. |||| Daṇḍa.

¶¶ A stretch of pasture-ground. Taking the cubit at 15 inches, this length would be 10,000 feet, or about $1\frac{9}{10}$ mile.

*** Taking the cubit at 15 inches, the yojana equals 40,000 feet, or about $7\frac{1}{2}$ miles.

††† The text *tac' c'a kuryát satastu te* appears corrupt. A better reading is *tac' c'akrur yatnatas tu te* from a MS. in the Sanskrit College Library.

bráhman,* the pura,† and the kheṭaka, the droṇí-mukha‡
likewise,§ and śákhá-nagarakas and the three kinds of kar-
43 vaṭakas,|| and the grámas together with the arrangement of
the ghoshas,¶ and the separate habitations therein; and *they*
44 *built* lofty ramparts surrounded on all sides with fosses. *They*
made the pura, or town, extend for a quarter of a yojana in
every direction, and slope down to water on the east; *they*
made it auspicious and *peopled it* with colonies from noble
families.** And with a half of it they laid out the kheṭa,††
and with a quarter of it the karvaṭa;‡‡ and then the inferior
portion *which is made* with the remaining quarter is called the
46 droṇí-mukha.§§ A town destitute of ramparts and fosses|||| is

* For *dvijaḥ* read *dvija?* The vocative seems preferable as Márkaṇḍeya is relating what happened in a previous age, and the work described would not fall to a bráhman's duty. If *dvijaḥ* be retained, the word *kuryát* must be understood.

† This is explained in verse 44.

‡ These two words are explained in verse 45.

§ For *tadva* read *tadvad.*

|| These two words are not in the dictionary; they are explained in verses 45 and 46. For *karvaṭakam trayí* read *karvaṭaka-trayím?*

¶ Sanghosha is not in the dictionary. For *gramá-sanghosha-vinyásaṃ* read *grámaṃ sa-ghosha-vinyásaṃ?* Gráma is explained in verse 47, and ghosha in verse 50.

** S'uddha-vaṃśa-vahirgamam.

†† Prof. Sir M. Monier-Williams explains kheṭa, "a village, the residence of peasants and farmers; a small town, half a pura"; but here it apparently means a particular portion of the pura; does it mean the "inhabited or residential area"?

‡‡ This word is said to mean "a village, market-town, the capital of a district," but here it denotes a particular portion of the pura; does it mean the bazár or the "area occupied with the market and shops"?

§§ This word said to mean "the capital of a district, the chief of 400 villages," but here it evidently refers to the lowest part of the pura; does it mean the "area inhabited by the labouring population or the lowest classes"?

|||| For *prákáraṃ parikhá-hínam* read *prákára-parikhá-hínam?* Or, is the verse intended to say that a town surrounded with a rampart but without a fosse is a *varma-vat?* This would agree better with the meaning of *varma-vat.* Prof. Sir M. Monier-Williams explains it as "an unfortified (?) town."

called a varma-vat ; and a śákhá-nagaraka* is another kind *of*
47 *town* which possesses ministers and feudatory princes. Moreover, a dwelling place† which abounds with śúdras and water,‡ where the cultivators are independently prosperous,§ and which is situated on land that can be used for fields, is called
48 a gráma.|| The dwelling-place, which men make, different from cities and other abodes, for the sake of their business,
49 is to be known as a vasati by modern men.¶ The gráma which springs up on the land of another *gráma*, and thrives, which has no fields of its own, which is for the most part vicious, and which is the resort of a king's favourites, is
50 called an ákrimí.** And a collection of cattle and herdsmen, who have brought their utensils *there* on carts, where there is no barter, is called a ghosha ;†† its situation on the land may be wherever they please.

51 Those *people* thus made towns and other *abodes* for themselves to dwell in ; they made houses for the *several* couples

* This word is said to mean, " a ' branch-town,' a suburb," but here is seems to mean a ' town with branches,' a " capital town " or " metropolis."

† Vasati ; see verse 48.

‡ For *śúdra-jala-práyáḥ* read *śúdra-jala-práyá ?*

§ For *-kṛshíbaláḥ* read *-krishíbalá ?*

|| The village. The word thus denotes a local area, and includes both the dwellings and the fields. It seems to designate specially the large and prosperous villages.

¶ The word is explained in the dictionary as " a dwelling-place, dwelling-house, abode, residence," but here it is explained to be a " mart," apparently either permanent or temporary. It corresponds to the modern (Persian) word *ganj*, or the vernacular word *hâṭ* (Sanskrit haṭṭa), in Bengal. The word *vasati* appears as *basti* in the modern vernaculars, and means in Bengal " the populated part of a village," and " the part of a town occupied by the common bamboo-built houses." The verse seems to indicate that the word *vasati* was either newly-coined, or had recently acquired (or the author wished it to acquire) a special meaning. The complete change from this meaning to that of the modern *basti*, which rather excludes any notion of trade, is note-worthy.

** Or *akrimí*. These words are not in the dictionary. If we might read *á-kramí* instead, the word would be rather appropriate.

†† This word is said to mean " a station of herdsmen." It appears to denote a temporary dwelling only, resorted to for purposes of pasturage.

52 to dwell in. As trees were their first kind of houses, so, with
a remembrance of all that, those people built their houses.
53 As *some* branches of a tree go in one direction, and others go
in another direction, and *some* rise upwards and some bend
downwards, even so they fashioned the branches *in their*
54 *houses.* Those branches, which were the branches of the
kalpa trees at first, O bráhman, became rooms in the houses
in consequence among those *people.*

55 Those *people* ruined *the trees* by their strife, and afterwards
pondered* on their means of livelihood. When the kalpa
56 trees had utterly perished along with the honey, those people
were distressed by their afflictions, and suffered from thirst
and hunger. Then became manifest their perfection at the
57 beginning of the Tretá age. For their other business was
spontaneously accomplished;† they had rain according to
their desire. The waters of their rain are the rivers‡ which
58 *flow* here. By the obstruction of the rain§ the rivers, which‖
existed on the earth scanty of water before that, became¶
deep flowing channels.

59 And then by their union with the earth plants came into
existence, of fourteen kinds, both those which grow on uncultivated soil, and those which grow unsown, both culti-
60 vated and wild. And trees and shrubs bearing flowers and
fruit in their seasons were produced. This manifestation of
61 vegetation appeared first in the Tretá age. On that vegeta-
tion the people subsist in the Tretá age, O Muni. And then
62 lapsing into novel passion and covetousness those people next
took possession of rivers and fields, mountains, and trees,
shrubs and plants in their own right even according to might.

* For *ac'intayat* read *ac'intayan ?*

† For *várttá-sva-sádhitá* read *várttá sva-sádhitá ?*

‡ Nimna-gata *neut* = nimna-gá ? This meaning is not in the diotionary.

§ For *vṛishṭyávaruddhair* read *vṛishṭyavarodhair ?*

‖ Nimnagáḥ ye. If this is correct, we must tako nimna-ga *masc.* as "a river," a meaning not given in the dictionary; if we read nimna-gáḥ *fem* as usual, we must read *yáḥ* for *ye.*

¶ For *abhavat* read *abhavan ?*

63 Through that *their* sin those plants perished before their very
eyes, and the earth then devoured those plants at once, O
64 most wise bráhman.* Moreover when that *vegetation* had
perished, those people fell into still further confusion.

Suffering from hunger, they resorted to Brahmá, the most
65 high, as their preserver. And he, the mighty lord, knowing
full well then that the earth had swallowed it up,† milked
66 her treating mount Meru as her calf.‡ This earth-cow was
then milked by him, the cereals came into existence on the
67 face of the earth, the seeds, the cultivated and wild plants
besides, which are annuals,§ known *as comprising* seventeen
classes according to tradition. The various kinds of both
68 rice and barley, wheat, aṇu grain,‖ sesamum, priyangu,¶
udára,** koradúsha,†† and c'ínaka,‡‡ másha,§§ green gram,‖‖
69 and masúra,¶¶ the finest pulse,*** and kulatthaka,††† áḍhaka

* For *dvijaḥ* read *dvija?*

† Grasta. The context seems to require this word to be taken in an active sense.

‡ The calf is tied near the cow, while she is being milked, as otherwise, it is said, she will not let her milk flow.

§ Phala-pákánta.

‖ *Panicum miliaceum*, the modern *chiná*, Roxb. p. 104. It is a cultivated cereal, grown on an elevated, light, rich soil, immediately after the rains.

¶ See note ** p. 165.

** The Dictionary says this is a kind of grain with long stalks, but I cannot trace it out in Roxburgh.

†† *Paspalum scrobiculatum*, the modern *kodo*, Roxb. p. 93. He says "The seed is an article of diet with the Hindoos, particularly with those who inhabit the mountains and most barren parts of the country, for it is in such countries only where it is cultivated, it being an unprofitable crop, and not sown where others more beneficial will thrive. I have eaten of the boiled grain, and think it as palatable as rice."

‡‡ This is said to be *Panicum miliaceum* which is already mentioned; the word means fennel also, but that is inappropriate. I do not find any other grain of this name.

§§ See note § p. 84.

‖‖ *Mudga*; See note §§ p. 84.

¶¶ See note ††† p. 165.

*** Nishpáva; see note ‖ p. 86.

††† See note ‖ p. 84.

pulse,* and chick-pea† and hemp‡ are known as the seven
teen *classes.* These are the olden kinds of cultivated plants.
70 And there are fourteen kinds of plants for use in sacrifices,
both cultivated and wild, *viz.*, the various kinds of both rice
71 and barley, wheat, aṇu grain, sesamum, and seventh§ among
them priyangu, and eighth kulatthaka, and śyámáka|| grain,
72 wild rice, wild sesamum,¶ and gavedhuka** grass, kuruvinda††
grass, markaṭaka,‡‡ and veṇu-gradha ;§§ and these indeed are
traditionally known as the fourteen cultivated and wild plants
73 *for use in sacrifices.* When *these* plants are abandoned,|||| they
do not spring forth again.

Thereupon the adorable self-existent Brahmá devised
74 means of livelihood for the advancement of those *people,* and
the perfection of the hands which results from work. Thence-
forward plants were produced, which must ripen after plough-
75 ing. But when their livelihood was thoroughly ordained, the

* The dictionary does not give áḍhaka, *masc.* or *fem.*, as the name of any plant; but áḍhakí, *fem.*, is said to mean a kind of pulse, *Cajanus indicus*, Spreng. I do not find it in Roxb., but Oliver calls the Pigeon Pea *Cajanus.*

† For *c'anakáś* read *c'aṇakáś.* See note ** p. 84.

‡ S'aṇa. For *gaṇáḥ* read *śaṇáḥ*, as in several MSS.

§ The reckoning seems wrong; priyangu is the sixth and kulatthaka the seventh.

|| See note * p. 165.

¶ Yattila is not in the dictionary. For *yattilá* read *jartiláḥ.*

** *Coix barbata,* Roxb. p. 649; it is a coarse grass, and cattle do not eat it. It is also said to mean *Hedysarum lagopodioides,* which is mentioned by Roxburgh (p. 573), but of which I find no description in his work.

†† *Cyperus rotundus,* Roxb. p. 66; a common grass, the roots of which dried and powdered are used as a perfume.

‡‡ This has been mentioned in Canto XXXII, verse II, and is described in the dictionary as "a kind of wild panic; a species of grain." I find that *Carpopogon pruriens* is assigned by Roxburgh to the Sanskrit word *markati* (p. 553). That is a common legume, but he says no use seems to be made of it, except that the hairs of the legumes are used as a vermifuge and are believed to be poisonous.

§§ This is not in the dictionary, and I do not know what it is.

|||| Prasṛishṭá. Does this mean that these plants grow only in a cultivated state?

lord himself next established bounds for them according to
76 justice and according to their qualities; also the laws of
the castes and of the four periods of a bráhman's life, and
of the worlds* with all their castes which duly maintain
righteousness and wealth, O most righteous *Muni*.
77 Prájápatya† is traditionally declared to be the sphere
assigned after death to bráhmans who perform the ceremonies.
Aindra‡ is the sphere of kshatriyas who flee not in battle.
78 Máruta§ is the sphere of vaiśyas who observe their own
proper laws. Gándharva‖ is *the sphere* of the various claases
79 of śúdras who perform *menial* service. The sphere of those
eighty-eight thousand ṛishis who live in perpetual chastity
has been traditionally declared to be that of the inhabitants
80 of Jupiter. The sphere of the Seven Ṛishis¶ has been tradi-
tionally declared to be that of hermits. Prájápatya** is the
sphere of householders; the abode of Brahmá is for those
men who have abandoned all worldly concerns; the world
of immortality is for yogís—such is the ordinance of the
various spheres *assigned after death.*

CANTO L.

The mandate to the Yaksha Duḥsaha.

Brahmá next created the nine Sages, Bhṛigu, Pulastya, Pulaha, Kratu, Angiras, Maríc'i, Daksha, Atri and Vasishṭha—and also Rudra, Sankalpa and Dharma—All these were all-wise and devoid of passions—Brahmá in anger created a being half male, half female, who at his order divided himself into many male and female beings.

* Loka.

† The heaven of the pitṛis ?

‡ The 18th lunar mansion ?

§ The constellation Sváti.

‖ Gándharva is the name of one of the nine portions of Bhárata-varsha; but this seems inappropriate.

¶ The constellation Ursa Major.

** See verse 77.

Brahmá then created the Manu Sváyambhuva and his wife S'ata-rúpá—They had two sons Priya-vrata and Uttána-páda, and also two daughters. Ruc'i married one daughter Ṛiddhi and begat Yajṉa and Dakshiṇá.

Daksha married the other daughter Prasúti and begot 24 daughters, whose names are mentioned, and who became Dharma's wives, and also 11 other daughters whose names are mentioned, and who became the wives of the other sages and of Agni and the Pitṛis—The children of these daughters are mentioned.

A-dharma and his offspring are mentioned, Naraka, Bhaya, Mṛityu &c.—The actions of Mṛityu's sons are explained—Chief among them is Duḥsaha—to him Brahmá assigned a dwelling and raiment, a long catalogue of bad deeds as nourishment, and certain places and times for his success, but excluded a list of other persons and places from his influence.

Márkaṇḍeya spoke.

1 Then while he was meditating, mankind were begotten
in his mind, together with their occupations, and implements
2 which were produced from his body. Spirits in bodily form*
were produced from the limbs of him, the wise *god*. All
those whom I have already mentioned came into existence.
3 All created beings from the gods down to those whose
condition is stationary are known to be subject to the three
qualities:† such was the constitution of created things,
immoveable and moveable.

4 When all that offspring of him, the wise one, did not in-
crease, he created other mind-born sons like unto himself, *viz.*,
5 Bhṛigu, Pulastya, Pulaha, Kratu, and Angiras, Marîc'i, Dak-
sha, and Atri, and the mind-born Vasishṭha ‡—these were the
6 nine *sons* of Brahmá, they are positively mentioned in the
Puráṇas.

Next Brahmá further created Rudra, whose birth was from
7 his soul when it was angry, and Sankalpa, and Dharma who
was begotten before all the preceding sons.

* Kshetra-jṉa.

† Goodness, passion, and ignorance.

‡ For *Vaśishṭham* read *Vasishṭham*.

And those who with their sons and other *relatives* were first
8 created by the Self-existent, felt no attachment for the worlds,
but showed disregard and were composed in mind. They
all knew the future, they were free from passion, free from
envy.
9 When they thus showed disregard at the creation of the
worlds, the high-souled Brahmá grew very wrathful; *then*
10 was produced there a male* like to the sun, possessed of an
immense body, the body being half man's and half woman's.
11 "Divide thyself" said the god, and then disappeared. And
he being thus accosted separated the female and male
natures; and he divided the male nature into eleven parts.
12 Then the divine lord divided the male and female natures
into many parts with men, gentle and cruel, calm, black and
white.
13 Next the lord Brahmá *became* the guardian of his off-
spring by creating the first Manu Sváyambhuva,† begotten
14 from and like unto himself, O bráhman,‡ and the woman
S'ata-rúpá, who was cleansed from blemishes through austeri-
ties. The divine and mighty Manu Sváyambhuva took her
15 for his wife. And through him her husband S'ata-rúpá
brought forth two sons, Priya-vrata and Uttána-páda, famed
16 through their own actions, and two daughters also, Ṛiddhi
and Prasúti. Then their father gave Prasúti *in marriage* to
17 Daksha and Ṛiddhi to Ruc'i§ of yore. The Prajá-pati *Rúc'i*
took *his wife*, and from them both a son Yajṉa was born and
a daughter Dakshiṇá,‖ O illustrious Sir; *these two* then
18 *became* husband and wife, and Yajṉa begat of Dakshiṇá
twelve sons; the glorious sons of Yajṉa and Dakshiṇá were
19 the gods well known as the Yámas in the epoch of *Manu*
Sváyambhuva.

* Purusha.

† The son of Svayam-bhú (the Self-existent *Brahmá*).

‡ For *dvijaḥ* read *dvija?*

§ He is one of the Prajá-patis.

‖ This verse must refer to Ruc'i, as Daksha's progeny is mentioned in verse 19.

And Daksha moreover begat twenty and four daughters of
20 Prasúti; hear also from me their names in order—S'raddhá
(Faith), Lakshmí (Good Fortune), Dhṛiti (Constancy), Tushṭi
(Satisfaction), Pushṭi (Nourishment), Medhá (Mental Vigour),
21 and Kriyá (Action), Buddhi (Intelligence), Lajjá (Modesty),
Vapus (Bodily Beauty), S'ánti (Tranquillity), Siddhi (Perfection), and Kírti (Fame) the thirteenth. The lord Dharma
took these daughters of Daksha for his wives.
22 Besides them and younger were the eleven lovely-eyed
daughters—Khyáti (Celebrity), and Satí (Truth), Sambhúti
(Fitness), Smṛiti (Memory), Príti (Affection), and Kshamá
23 (Patience), and Sannati (Humility),* and Anasúyá (Sincerity), U'rjá (Strength), Sváhá (the oblation to the gods),
and Svadhá (the oblation to the pitṛis). The Ṛishis Bhṛigu,
24 Bhava† and Marîci, and the Muni Angiras also, Pulastya
and Pulaha, and Kratu,‡ Vasishṭha, and Atri, Vahni and the
25 Pitṛis in order—*these* Munis, the most illustrious among Munis,
took *these* daughters, Khyáti and the others, *in marriage*.§

S'raddhá gave birth to Káma (Love); and S'rí‖ to Darpa
26 (Pride); Dhṛiti to Niyama (Restraint) her son; and Tushṭi
also to Santosha (Contentment); Pushṭi to Lobha (Covetousness); Medhá to S'ruta (Revelation); Kriyá to Daṇḍa
(Punishment), Naya (Prudence), and Vinaya (Decorum);
27 Buddhi gave birth to Bodha (Wisdom); and Lajjá to Vinaya
(Decorum); Vapus to Vyavasáya (Industry) her son; and
28 S'ánti gave birth to Kshema (Ease); Siddhi to Sukha
(Happiness); Kírti to Yaśas (Renown). These were the offspring of Dharma.

She¶ bare by Káma a grandson to Dharma, *namely*, Harsha (Joy) who brims over with joyousness.

* For *Santatiś* in the text read *Sannatiś* see Canto LII, v. 24.

† That is, S'iva; and he married Satí. She put an end to herself in consequence of her father Daksha's curse, and was re-born as the daughter of Himavat, when Siva married her again. See Canto LII, vv. 12-14.

‡ For *Krituś* read *Kratuś*.

§ See Canto LII, vv. 14, &c.

‖ *I. e.* Lakshmí.

¶ This seems obscure.

29 Now Hiṃsá (Injury) was the wife of A-dharma (Unright-
eousness); and Anṛita (Falsehood) was born of her, and a
daughter Nirṛiti (Destruction) *was born* of her, and two sons
30 Naraka (Hell) and Bhaya (Fear), and Máyá (Illusion) and
Vedaná (Pain). And with these two *females the two sons
formed* two married pairs; and of those two, Máyá gave birth
to Mṛityu (Death) who carries created beings away, and
31 Vedaná gave birth by Raurava* to her son Duḥkha (Misery).
And Vyádhi (Sickness), Jará (Old Age), S'oka (Grief),
Tṛishṇá (Thirst) and Krodha (Anger) were begotten by
32 Mṛityu; or all these, who have the characteristics of A-dhar-
ma, are traditionally declared to have sprung from Duḥkha.
No wife have they, nor son; they all live in perpetual chas-
tity.

33 Nirṛiti also was the *wife of Mṛityu*, and Mṛityu had another
wife called A-lakshmí (Ill Fortune); and by the latter Mṛityu
34 had fourteen sons. These are his sons by A-lakshmí;
they carry out Mṛityu's commands; they visit men at the
35 times of dissolution; hear about them. They dwell in the ten
organs of sense and in the mind; for they influence man or
36 woman each towards his own object of sense; and assailing
the organs of sense they influence men by means of passion,
anger and other *feelings*, so that men suffer injury through
unrighteousness and other *evil ways*, O bráhman.

37 And one of them takes possession of self-consciousness,
and another resides in the intellect; *hence* bewildered by
folly, men strive to destroy women.

38 And another† famed by his name Duḥsaha‡ *resides* in men's
houses; he is wasted with hunger, his face is downwards
bent; he is naked, clothed in rags, and his voice is as hoarse
39 as a crow's. He was created by Brahmá to eat all *beings*.
Him, exceedingly terrific by reason of his long teeth, open-
mouthed, very terrible, and ravenous in mind, him thus ad-

* Raurava is the name of a particular hell, but here it seems to be equivalent to Naraka.

† For *anye* read *anyo* ?

‡ The "Unendurable," "Intolerable."

40 dressed Brahmá, the store-house of austerities,* the fore-
father of the worlds, he who is entirely consubstantial with
Brahma, the pure, the cause of the universe, the changeless.

Brahmá spoke.

41 "Thou must not devour this universe; quit thy anger,
keep thee calm; cast off the atom of passion and forsake this
career of ignorance."

Duḥsaha spoke.

42 "I am wasted with hunger, O ruler of the world, I am
thirsty also and my strength is gone. How may I be satisfied,
O master? How may I grow strong? And tell me, who
will be my refuge where I may abide tranquil?"

Brahmá spoke.

43 "Thy refuge *shall be* men's houses, and unrighteous men
shall be thy strength. Thou shalt be satisfied, my child, with
44 their neglect to perform the constant sacrifices. And spon-
taneous boils *shall be* thy raiment; and for food† I give to
thee whatever is injured, and what is infested with vermin,
45 and what has been gazed into by dogs, likewise what is con-
tained in broken pots, what has been made still by the breath
from *a man's* mouth, the fragments that remain from a meal,
what is unripe, that on which perspiration has fallen,‡ what
46 has been licked, what has not been cooked properly, what
has been eaten of by people sitting on broken seats, and *food*
that has fallen on the seat,§ and what turns away from the
sky|| at the two twilights, what is distinguished by the
47 sound of dancing and musical instruments, what a woman in
her courses has polluted, what such a woman has eaten of
and has gazed at, and whatever food or drink has been
48 damaged¶ at all—these *shall be* for thy nourishment, and
whatever else I give to thee; whatever persons, who have

* Or, for *tapaso nidhiḥ* read *tapaso nidhe*, vocative?

† For *áharaṃ* read *áhâraṃ*?

‡ For *a-svinnam* read *á-svinnam*?

§ For *ásannágatam* another reading is *ásandí-gatam* which is preferable.

|| Vi-din-mukha; not in the dictionary.

¶ Upa-gháta-vat; not in the dictionary.

not performed their ablutions, have sacrificed or given in
49 alms, without faith or in contempt; what has been cast away
without the previous use of water, and what has been rendered valueless, and what has been exhibited in order to be discarded, and what has been given away through utter amaze-
50 ment; what is corrupt, and what has been given away by a
person in anger or in pain, that O goblin,* thou shalt obtain†
as thy reward; and whatever the son of a re-married widow
51 does as an undertaking for the next world, and whatever
the daughter of a re-married widow *so does;* that, O goblin,
shall be for thy satisfaction. The wealth-procuring ceremonies *in which* a maiden engages along with her lover for
52 the sake of the obligation of dower, and the ceremonies also
which are performed according to wicked books, *shall be* for
thy nourishment, O goblin; and whatever has been studied
53 for the sake of enjoying wealth‡ and whatever has not been
read truly—all that I give thee, and *these* periods also for thy
perfection. Thou shalt ever have conquering power, O
54 Duḥsaha, among men, if they approach a pregnant woman
carnally, or if they transgress the evening rites and the
constant ceremonies, and among men who have been corrupted
by wicked books, deeds or conversation.

55 "Thy business lies in creating social dissensions, in rendering cookery useless, and in interrupting cookery; and thy
56 dwelling shall perpetually be in household wrangling. And
men shall dread thee§ in what pines away,|| and in bullock-carts and other *conveyances* which are shut up, in rooms which
57 are not sprinkled at twilight, and at death. On the occasions
of eclipses of the stars¶ and planets, and at the appearance

* Yaksha.

† *Tad-bhági* in the text seems incorrect. Another reading is *tad-gámi;* but *tvad-bhági* and *tvad-gámi* seem preferable. Another reading is *prápsyasi,* and this I have adopted.

‡ For *arthaṃ nirvṛitam* another and better reading is *artha-nirvṛitau* which I have adopted. A third reading is *áśu vikṛitam.*

§ For *tvattvo* read *tvatto ?*

|| A-poshyamáṇe.

¶ Nakshatra.

of the three kinds of portents, thou shalt, O goblin, over-
58 come men who disregard propitiatory ceremonies. Men who
fast vainly, who always delight in gambling and women, who
confer benefits according to thy word, and who are religious
hypocrites, *shall be thy prey.*

59 "Study by one who is not a brahma-c'ári, and sacrifice
performed by an unlearned man; austerities practised in a
forest* by men who indulge in worldly pleasures† and by
60 men of unsubdued soul; the action which is done according
to their respective occupations by bráhmans, kshatriyas,
vaiśyas and śúdras, who have fallen *from their castes,* and who
61 desire to gain the objects of the next world, and whatever
the results of that *action*—all that shall be thine, O goblin.
And more yet I give thee for thy nourishment; hearken
62 thereto. *Men* shall give thee a plenteous bali offering at the
close of the Vaiśvadeva ceremony, first uttering thy name
and then saying "this is for thee."

63 "Abandon the house of him, who eats only properly cooked
food according to rule, who is pure within and without, who
64 is free from covetousness, who governs his wife.‡ Abandon
that house, O goblin, *where* the gods and the pitṛis are wor-
shipped with their respective oblations, and where the female
65 relatives and guests are honoured. And abandon that house
also, where concord§ dwells at home among the children, the
aged, the women and men, and among the various classes of
66 kinsmen. Abandon that house, O goblin, where the women-
folk are delighted, are not eager to go outside, and are always
67 modest. Abandon that house, O goblin, at my command,
where the bedding and viands are suited to the ages and rela-
68 tions *of the inmates.* Abandon that house, O goblin, where
the inmates are always kind, and busied in good deeds, and
69 possess the common household utensils. And thou must also
ever abandon that house, O goblin, where *the inmates* do not

* For *tapo-vane* read *tapo vane?*

Grámya-bbuj.

‡ For *'jita-strîkas* read *jita-strîkas?*

§ For *maitrí-gṛihe* read *maitrí gṛihe?*

keep their seats while the religious preceptors, the aged, and
70 dvijas are standing and where they do not stand. That will
not be an excellent abode for thee, where the house-door is
not penetrated by trees, shrubs or other *vegetation*, nor by a
71 man who pierces one's vitals. Abandon the house of the
man who supports the gods, the pitṛis, mankind and guests
72 with the remnants of his food. Abandon, O goblin, such
men as these, the true in word, the forbearing in disposition,
the harmless, and those free from remorse, and also the un-
73 envious. Abandon the woman, who is devoted to her husband's
service, who keeps aloof from associating with bad women, and
who feeds on the food which has been left by her family and
74 husband. Abandon the *bráhman* dvija always, whose mind is
engrossed with sacrifice, study, discipline and alms-giving, and
who has made his livelihood by means of the performance of
75 sacrifices, teaching, and receiving alms.* And abandon, O Duḥ-
saha, the kshatriya who is always energetic in alms-giving,
study, and sacrifice, and who earns his livelihood from good
76 taxes and by the occupation of arms. Abandon the stainless
vaiśya, who is endowed with the three previous virtues,† and
who gains his livelihood from the keeping of cattle and trade
77 and cultivation. Abandon also the śúdra, who is diligent in
alms-giving, sacrifice and the service of dvijas, and who sup-
ports himself by menial service under bráhmans and other
dvijas, O goblin.

78 "In whatever house the master of the house earns his
livelihood without contravening śruti and smṛiti, and where
79 his wife is obedient to him from her very soul, and where the
son shows reverence to his spiritual preceptor and the gods
and his father, and where the wife shows reverence to her
husband—whence should there be fear of misfortune in that
80 *house?* When a house is smeared over in the evenings, and
thoroughly sprinkled with water, and the bali of flowers is
81 made in it, thou canst not gaze thereat, O goblin. The
houses where the sun sees not the beds, and where fire and

* K-dána.

† Guṇa, *viz.*, alms-giving, study and sacrifice.

water are constantly kept, and where the lamps behold the
82 sun, are places patronized by Lakshmí. That house is not
a resort for thee, where *are kept* a bull, sandal-wood perfume,
a lute, a mirror, honey and ghee, and where copper vessels
are used both for poisons and for the clarified butter of holy
oblations.

83 "That *house* is thy temple, O goblin, where thorny trees
grow, and where leguminous plants creep about, *and where* the
84 wife is a re-married widow, and ant-hills are found. That
house is thy dwelling, wherein live five men, and three
women, and as many cows, and where the fire from the fuel
85 is mere darkness. Thou shalt quickly, O goblin, parch up
the house, which contains one goat, two asses, three cattle,
86 five buffaloes,* six horses, and seven elephants. Wherever a
spade, a dá,† a basket, and also a caldron and other utensils are
87 scattered about, they may give thee shelter. Sitting by
women on the wooden pestle and mortar, and also upon
udumbara wood,‡ and the utterance of sacred verses at the
88 privy, this shall be advantageous for thee, O goblin. Roam,
O Duḥsaha, to thy heart's content, in that house where *all*
kinds of corn whether cooked or uncooked, and where the
89 scriptures also are disdained. Endless misfortunes take up
their abode in that house, where fire *lies* upon the lid of the
90 caldron or is offered with the point of a spoon. Thou, O
goblin, and other Rákshasas also shall have a dwelling in the
house, where human bones lie and where a corpse remains a
91 whole day and night. Resort at once to those men who feed
on a kinsman's piṇḍa and water, without giving any to the
sapiṇḍas and sahodakas.

92 "Abandon the house where the lotus and the white lotus
are found, *where* a maiden *dwells* who feeds on sweetmeats,§

* Máhisha (m ?); in this sense, not in the dictionary.

† Dátra, a large heavy knife with a curved-in point, used for all purposes of cutting, chopping and splitting.

‡ This is forbidden because the tree is holy.

§ Modakáśiní; aśin, from aś, to eat, not in the dictionary.

93 and where a bull and a fine elephant* are kept.† Abandon
the habitation where the unarmed, the deities, and those who
bear arms without engaging in battle, are esteemed worthy
94 of honour by men. Roam not in that house, where are cele-
brated as of yore the great urban and rural festivals which
95 were famous of old. Visit those unlucky men who fan them-
selves with winnowing fans,‡ and who bathe with the water
poured from jars§ or with the drops of water from cloths,
96 and with water *splashed up* by the tips of their nails. Join not
thyself with the man who establishes the country customs, the conventional ordinances, the laws regarding kinsmen, who performs the victorious homa oblation and the auspicious sacrifice to the gods, who maintains perfect personal purification according to the precepts, and who fashions the public talk."

Márkaṇḍeya spoke.

97 Having spoken thus to Duḥsaha, Brahmá disappeared from sight there, and the other followed the command of the lotus-born god.

---

* For *vṛishabhairávato* read *vṛishabhairávatau ?*

† For *kalpyate* read *kalpyete* or *kalpyante ?*

‡ This seems to be the best meaning; but if so *śúrpa-vátán* would be more intelligible.

§ *Ye kurvanti* must be understood.

Canto LI.

The Offspring of Duḥsaha.

Duḥsaha had eight sons and eight daughters—their names are mentioned—The evil functions of the several sons and daughters are described, and the remedies against them—Their offspring are mentioned, and their evil actions described.

These beings are almost all personifications of physical injuries, moral vices and social offences.

Márkaṇḍeya spoke.

1 Duḥsaha had a wife named Nirmáshṭi*; now she was begotten in Kali's wife when she saw a c'aṇḍála at the time of
2 her menstruation. They had sixteen children, who pervade the world, eight sons and eight daughters, *all* very terrible.
3 Dantákṛishṭi and Ukti, and Parivarta the next, Anga-dhṛish
4 and S'akuni and Gaṇḍa-pránta-rati, Garbha-han and the last Sasya-han were their male children. And they had eight
5 daughters besides; hear their names from me. The first was Niyojiká, and the second Virodhiní, and Svayaṃ-hára-karí,
6 Bhrámaṇí, Ṛitu-háriká, and two other very terrible daughters Smṛiti-hará and Víja-hará; and the eighth daughter was named Vidveshaṇí who causes terror to mankind.
7 I will describe what the *several* functions of the eight sons *are*, and what are the remedies against the evils *which they work*; hearken *to me*, O bráhman.
8 Dantákṛishṭi† taking his station in the teeth of newly born children produces intense wind,‡ with the desire of effecting

* Prof. Sir M. Monier-Williams gives the name as Nir-márshṭi (Uncleaned) which seems preferable.

† Teeth-attracter, Lock-jaw ?

‡ Saṃ-harsha; or bristling of the hair of the body.

9 an attack from Duḥsaha. The remedy against him is to be
applied by men by means of white mustard cast upon the bed
10 and upon the teeth of the sleeping *child;* and by bathing it
with medicinal herbs of great splendour, by reciting good
scriptures,* and by supporting† it on a camel, a thorn, a
sword, a bone, or a linen cloth.

11 Now the second son assigns good and bad fortune to men,
while he says repeatedly, "let it be so!"; hence *he is called*
12 Ukti,‡ and that is his precise function. Hence wise men
must always say, "May fate be auspicious!" And when any-
13 thing bad is heard or spoken, let praise be offered to S'iva,
and to Brahmá, the spiritual preceptor of all that exists both
moveable and immoveable, *and* to each person's own parti-
cular family-deity.

14 *The son* who finds delight in always interchanging the
fœtus between one womb and another, and in interchanging
the words *in the mouth* of a speaker, is called Parivartaka§;
15 a wise man should preserve himself against him by means of
white mustard and the prayers and spells that destroy
Rákshasas.

16 And another *son*‖ like the wind announces good and bad
fortune as indicated by throbbings in men's bodies; and *the
remedy* against him is to strike the side of the body with kúsa
grass.

17 Another son S'akuni¶ stationed on a crow or some other
bird, announces weal or woe by means of food or birds.**
With regard thereto, however, the Prajá-pati has said, "In
18 an evil matter delay and the abandonment of the undertaking
are best; in a good matter one should act very speedily."

* For *sac'c'hvdstra* read *sac'c'hástra.*

† Vidháraṇa; not in the dictionary.

‡ The Word of Fate.

§ The Interchanger.

‖ Anga-dhṛish, the Assailer of the body.

¶ S'akuni, a Bird (in general). The word *kus'alaiḥ* in the text is not supported by the MSS. and seems wrong. They read *S'akuniḥ* (which I have adopted) or *śakunam,* "an omen."

** *Khaga-tas,* this seems the best meaning; but it might also be read *kha-gatas* as an adjective to *S'akuniḥ.*

Another son* stationed in the borders of the cheeks for
19 half a muhúrta, O bráhman, consumes every undertaking, and
eulogium, and sincerity. By addresses to bráhmans, by
20 praiṣe to the gods, and by extracting roots, O bráhman, by
ablutions with cows' urine and mustard seed, so also by
worship paid to the constellations and planets, and also by
the observance of righteousness and the Upanishads, by
21 repeatedly looking at weapons, and by contempt for birth
Gaṇḍa-piánta-rati succumbs.

Another most terrible son,† moreover, destroys the fruit
22 of pregnant women. *Women* should always secure protection
against him by constant personal purification, by writing out
famous spells, by wearing auspicious garlands and other
23 *decorations*, by dwelling in well-cleaned houses, and by abstaining from over-exertion, O bráhman.

The other son Sasya-han‡ moreover is he who destroys the
24 growth of the crops. Against him indeed one should secure
protection by wearing worn-out shoes, and by walking on the
25 left *side*, and by causing a c'aṇḍála to enter *the field*, and by
offering the bali outside, and by eulogizing the soma juice.

And Niyojiká§ is the daughter who incites some men to
26 seize and otherwise *molest* other men's wives and other men's
goods. Immunity from her comes by reciting purifying
prayers, by refraining from anger, covetousness and other
27 *passions*, and by resistance *with the thought* 'She is inciting me
to these *acts*.' When one is railed against or beaten by
28 another, one should wisely think 'she is inciting him,' and
should not fall into subjection to her. In *this* mundane existence, where there are other men's wives and other *alluring*
29 *objects*, the wise man should consider, 'She is inciting my
mind and my soul here.'

And the next daughter who causes opposition between a
30 loving married couple, among relatives and friends, between
parents and children, and among fellow-caste-people||—

* Gaṇḍa-piánta-rati, the Reveller in the borders of the cheeks.

† Garbha-han, the Fœtus-destroyer. ‡ The Crop-destroyer.

§ The Inciter. || Sávarṇika; in this sense not in the dictionary

she is Virodhiní.* One should secure protection from her
31 by offering the bali, by enduring outrageous language, and
by observing the śástras and Virtuous Custom.

Another daughter destroys grain from granaries and houses,
32 the milk from cows, and ghee, and the produce from prolific
things. She is called Svayaṃ-hárikᆠ; she is ever addicted
33 to concealment. She consumes the half-cooked food out of
the kitchen, and whatever is kept in the store-house ; and she
always consumes whatever food is being served up‡, along
34 with the person who eats it. She takes the remains of food
from men and also their food. She is hard to be restrained.§
She takes the success which men have accomplished from
35 their business offices and from their abodes, O bráhman. She
is constantly taking the fluid and the milk out of cows' udders and women's breasts, the ghee out of curdled milk, the
oil out of sesamum seed, and the spirituous liquor out of the
36 liquor-stores, the colour out of saffron‖ and other *coloured
objects*, and the thread out of cotton *clothes*. She is rightly
named Svayaṃ-háriká, *for* she is perpetually taking *things*
37 away, O bráhman. For the sake of protection *against her* one
should make a pair of peacocks and an artificial woman ;
and prophylactic marks¶ should be drawn** on the house,
and allowing *the house* to be littered with fragments of food††
38 should be avoided, and vessels in which milk and other *things
have been kept* should certainly be cleaned with the ashes of
the incense *offered* to the gods in the sacrificial fire. *All* that
is well-known to be a preservative.

39 Now the other daughter, who produces perturbation in a

* The Strife-maker. † The Voluntary thief.

‡ For *pari-vis'yamáṇaṃ* read *pari-vishyamáṇaṃ*. This half-line has nine syllables by poetic license.

§ The MSS. read *dur-dhará* instead of the text *dur-hará*. I have adopted the former; the latter might mean "a confirmed thief."

‖ For *kusambhuka* read *kusumbhaka ?* This would be the same as *kusumbha*, but is not in the dictionary.

¶ Rakshás. ** For *lakhyá* read *lekhyá*.

†† For *c'a soshmatá* another reading is *c'oc'c'hishṭatá* which I have adopted as preferable.

40 man who dwells in one place, is called Bhrámaṇí.* Now a
man should secure protection *against her* by scattering white
mustard seed on his seat, on his bed, and on the ground
41 where he sits; and a man should reflect, 'This wicked,
evil-minded *creature* causes me to go astray'; he should
mutter the 'Bhuvas' hymn repeatedly, with composed mind.
42 Another daughter robs women of their monthly courses,
when they have begun and before they have begun†; she is
43 known as Ṛitu-háriká,‡ the daughter of Duḥsaha. One
should cause *one's women-folk* to bathe at places of pilgrimage,
at temples, beside sacred public objects,§ on mountain tops,
at the confluence of rivers, and in excavated places in order
44 to subdue her. And one who knows the spells and knows
the principles of action *should cause them to bathe* at the four
changes of the moon and at dawn,|| O bráhman; and a
physician¶ who is skilled in medicine *should cause them to
bathe* with choice herbs combined together.
45 And Smṛiti-háriká** is another *daughter* who deprives
women of their memory. And she may be overcome by
observing places distinguished separately.
46 And Víjápaháriṇí†† is another *daughter* very terrible,
who robs man and woman *of their seed.* And she may be
overcome by eating clean food and by bathing.
47 And the eighth daughter named Dveshaṇi,‡‡ who causes
terror among mankind, is she who renders a man, or even
48 a woman, newly hated. Now in order to vanquish her,
one should offer an oblation§§ of sesamum seed moistened
with honey, milk and ghee; and one should also perform
a sacrifice which will procure friends in order to vanquish her.

* The Bewilderer.

† For *atha pravṛittaṃ* another reading is *tathápravṛittaṃ* which I have adopted as preferable. A third reading is *athápavṛittiḥ*.

‡ The Stealer of the Menses.

§ C'aitya; the primary meaning, "a funeral pile," seems inappropriate here.

|| For *parvamúshasi* read *parvasúshasi*.

¶ For *vedyaḥ* read *vaidyaḥ*.

** The Stealer of the Memory.

†† The Stealer of seed.

‡‡ The Hater.

§§ Homayet; verb from homa? Not in the dictionary.

49 Now these sons and daughters have thirty-eight children,
O bráhman; hear from me their names.
50 Vijalpá (Chatterer) was Dantákṛishṭi's daughter, and Kala-
há (Quarreller) also. Vijalpá indulges in contemptuous,
51 false and corrupt talk. In order to vanquish her, let the wise
house-holder ponder on her and preserve his self-control.
52 Kalahá is always creating disturbances in men's houses; she
is the cause why families perish. Hearken how she may be
subdued. One should throw blades of durbá grass smeared
53 with honey, ghee, and milk in the bali ceremony, and offer a
sacrifice to fire, and extol one's friends, for the performance
of a propitiatory rite to avert evil from all living beings, and
boys along with their mothers, and the sciences, and pe-
54 nances,* religious vows and the great moral duties.† In the
cultivation of land and in the profits of trade let *men* always
55 pacify me. And let the Kushmáṇḍas and the Yátu-dhánas‡
and whatever other *beings* are named according to their
classes, let *these*, when duly adored, always become pacified.
56 By the favour of Maha-deva,§ and by the counsel of Maheś-
vara|| let all these soon become satisfied with regard to men.
57 When pleased let them cast aside every evil deed and evil
work, and every result that springs from the great sins, and
58 whatever else causes obstacles. By their favour indeed let
obstacles wholly perish. And in all marriages and in cere-
59 monies performed for increase *of prosperity*, in meritorious
undertakings and in religious devotion, and in the worship of
spiritual teachers and the gods, in the rites of prayer and
60 sacrifice, and in the fourteen pilgrimages, in the pleasures
enjoyable in bodily health, and in happiness, liberality and
wealth, and among the aged, children and the sick, let them
always pacify me.

61 Ukti *had sons* Soma-pá, Aṃbu-pá, and Ambho-dhi, and
Savitṛi, Anila and Anala¶; and he had also a son Kála-

* For *tapasás'* read *tapasáṃ*? † *Saṃyamasya yamasya c'a.*

‡ Two classes of evil-spirits. § S'iva. || S'iva.

¶ That is, Soma-drinker, Water-drinker, Ocean, Sun, Wind and Fire. This line, however, seems incongruous.

62 jihva* who resides in the palms.† He torments those bad
men in whose mothers he abides.

Now Parivarta had two sons, Virúpa‡ and Vikṛiti,§ O
63 bráhman; and they both inhabit the tops of trees, ditches,
ramparts and the sea. They both interchange the fœtus
64 from one pregnant woman to another, if she walks about
among trees and the other *places which they frequent*, O
Kraushṭuki. In truth, a pregnant woman should not ap-
65 proach a tree, nor a mountain, nor a rampart, nor the sea,
nor a ditch.

66 Anga-dhṛish begat a son, by name Pis'una. If he enters
the marrow inside men's bones, he consumes the energy of
even invincible men.

S'akuni begat five sons, S'yena (Hawk), Káka (Crow), and
67 Kapota (Pigeon) Gṛidhra (Vulture) and Ulúka (Owl).‖ The
gods and the demons took them. And Mṛityu (Death) took
68 S'yena; Kála (Destiny) took Káka; and Nirṛiti (Destruction)
took Ulúka who causes great terror; Vyádhi (Sickness) *took*
Gṛidhra *and was* his lord; and Yama himself took Kapota.
69 And the evil beings which sprang from them are indeed said to
produce sin. Hence he, on whose head a hawk and the
70 other birds should alight, should take effectual pacificatory
measures for his safety, O bráhman. *If* they are born inside
71 a house *or if* likewise water should settle in a house, a man
should abandon that house *and also a house* on the top of
which pigeons alight. *When* a hawk, a pigeon, and a vul-
ture, a crow, and an owl have entered a house, O bráhman,
72 one shonld prophesy the end of the residents in that dwelling.
A wise man should abandon such a house and should employ
73 pacificatory measures. Even in sleep indeed it is unlucky to
see a pigeon.

And the offspring of Gaṇḍa-pránta-rati are said to be six
74 *in number*. They dwell in women's menses. Hear from me

* Black-tongue.

† For *tála-niketanaḥ* read *tálu-niketanaḥ*, who resides in the palate?

‡ Deformed. § Ill-health.

‖ For *gṛidhrolúkais'* read *gṛidhrolúkáu*?

also their peculiar periods. Of his offspring one *takes possession of* the first four days *after menstruation* and the thirteenth
75 day; and another is powerful on the eleventh day; another at dawn; and two others on occasions of śráddhas and alms-
76 giving; and another at festivals; hence these *days* should be shunned by the wise *in sexual intercourse.*

Garbha-hantṛi had a son Nighna* and a daughter Mohaní.†
77 The former enters within and eats the fœtus; and after he has eaten it, the latter beguiles‡ it. Through her beguiling,
78 the *offspring* are born *as* snakes, frogs, tortoises, and reptiles also, or yet again as ordure. The son may enter into the six-months pregnant woman who in waywardness eats flesh§; or
79 into the woman, who seeks the shade of a tree by night or at a place where three or four roads meet, who stands in a burning-ground or any place pervaded by strong smells, who
80 leaves off her upper garment, or who weeps at midnight.

And Sasya-hantṛi *had* one *son* named Kshudraka (Puny).
81 He is constantly injuring the growth of the crops, when he has gained a weak place. Listen thereto. And he, who sows
82 highly pleased at the beginning of an inauspicious day, provides an entrance behind *him for this sprite* into the fields which touch other fields along their boundaries.‖ Hence it is the proper practice that a man should worship the moon,
83 and then carry out his undertaking and sow his seed in gladness and contentment, with a companion.

84 Niyojiká, who was Duḥsaha's daughter as I have said, gave birth to four daughters who bear the names Prac'odiká (Instigator), Mattá (Intoxicated), Unmattá (Frantic) and Pra-
85 mattá (Wanton). Now they are always entering into young women in order to destroy them, *and* incite them here vehemently towards unrighteousness with the appearance of righteousness, and to love which bears no appearance of love,
86 and to that which is not wealth with the appearance of

* Nighna means "dependant"; but here it rather seems to mean "slayer."

† Beguiler. ‡ Mohayate.

§ For *gurviṇí-máṃsam* read *gurviním máṃsam.*

‖ Antopasangishu. Upa-sangin, a word not in the dictionary.

wealth, and to a final emancipation from existence which bears no appearance of final emancipation. Evilly disposed without purity they lead *young women* to gaze at strange men;
87 those angry sprites* cause strange men to wander *near women*
for the sake of philandering. Those female *sprites* enter into a house and into clothing when they are reddened by sunset,†
88 and wherever the bali is not offered to Dhátṛi and Vidhátṛi
at the proper time. They make a sudden‡ attack upon men
89 and women§ among those people who eat or drink with drops
of water clinging to them.

Virodhiní *had* three sons, C'odaka (Instigator)‖ and Grá-
90 haka (Seizer) and the other Tamaḥ-prac'c'hádaka (Gloom-
enveloper). Hear their characters from me. Where the pestle and mortar, and where a woman's shoes and her *upper*
91 *and lower* garments are befouled by contact with burning oil,
and are disdained; and where *people use* a seat, after first drawing it *to them* with a winnowing basket or a hatchet or
92 other *implement* or with their foot; and where pastime is held
in a house without respecting the *place* which has been smeared *and cleaned*; where fire is taken up and carried elsewhere in
93 the bowl of a spoon—there Virodhiní's sons are impelled and
display their activity. One dwells in men's and women's
94 tongues and utters falsehood as truth; he is called C'odaka;
he works calumny in the house. And another who acts with
95 care dwells in the ears and is exceedingly evil-minded; he
takes hold of people's words; so he *is called* Gráhaka. The third is he who, with evil mind, attacks men's minds and
96 enveloping them with darkness arouses anger; so he *is called*
Tamaḥ-prac'c'hádaka.

Now Svayaṃ-hárí gave birth to three *sons* by C'aurya
97 (Theft), Sarva-hárí,¶ Arddha-hárí,** and also Vírya-hárí.††

* For *tábhir ashṭábhiḥ* read *tábhí rushṭábhiḥ*.

† The text violates sandhi and seems obscure. I have adopted a different reading, *sandhyá-rakte hy-athámbare* instead of *sandhyarksheshu udumbare*.

‡ For *ásv* read *ás'v*?

§ For *nava-nárīshu* read *nara-nárīshu*.

‖ For *C'odaka-gráhakas* read *c'odako gráhakas*?

¶ He who steals the whole.

** He who steals half.

†† He who steals one's vigour.

In the houses of those who do not riuse their mouths out after meals, and in the houses of those who observe bad customs,
98 and among those who enter the kitchen with unwashed feet, and in granaries and cattle-pens *and* houses where perfidy
99 prevails—in such *places* all these *sprites* fittingly sport and have their pleasure.

Now Bhrámaṇí *had* one son; he is known as Káka-jangha
100 (Crow-leg). No one possessed by him can get pleasure in the town. He enters into the man, who while eating sings to a friend, and who sings and laughs *at the same time*, and
101 who indulges in sexual intercourse during the twilight, O bráhman.

The daughter Ṛitu-háriṇí gave birth to three daughters;
102 the first daughter was Kuc'a-hará,* the next Vyaṇjana-hári-
103 ká,† and the third daughter was called Játa-háriṇí.‡ The first robs of both breasts the maiden, all whose marriage rites are not performed duly, or are performed after the prescribed
104 time. And *the second* robs of her signs of puberty the married maiden, who has been married without duly offering the śráddha, and without paying due reverence to her mother.
105 When the lying-in chamber is destitute of fire and water, and is devoid of incense, when it has no lamp or weapon or pestle,
106 when it is destitute of ashes§ and mustard-seeed, the *third* daughter enters in, and bringing about immediate delivery snatches away the new-born child, and castes the child away
107 in that very place, O bráhman; she is called Játa-háriṇí; very terrible is she, she feeds on flesh. Hence one should strenuously guard *against her* in the lying-in chamber.

108 And she, *who* destroys the memory of men destitute of self-control through inhabiting empty abodes, *had* a son, by name
109 Pra-c'aṇḍa (Impetuous). From his son's sons were born the Líkas|| in hundreds and thousands and eight tribes of C'aṇ-
110 ḍálas, very terrible with staves and nooses. Then the Líkas and those tribes of C'aṇḍálas were possessed by hunger, and ran at

* She who steals the breasts.

† She who steals the signs of puberty.

‡ She who steals new-born children.

§ Bhúti.

|| A class of evil spirits.

111 one another, desirous of eating one another. But Pra-c'aṇḍa
restrained the several tribes of C'aṇḍálas, and established
them with such and such ordinances: hear what those are.
112 Hearafter from to-day whoever shall give a dwelling to the
Líkas, I will assuredly cause an unparalleled punishment to
113 fall on him. The female Líka who shall give birth to offspring in the dwelling of a C'aṇḍála,* her child shall die first
and she also shall perish at once.

114 Now Víja-háriní, who robs man and woman of their seed,
gives birth to two daughters, Váta-rúpá† and A-rúpá.‡ *I*
115 *will tell* thee of her method of attack. The man or the wife,
to whom Váta-rúpá casts a son at the end of the impregnation,
suffers from the seminal secretion becoming dried up through
116 disorder of the wind within the body.§ Similarly both the
man who eats without first bathing, and *the man* who eats
flesh,‖ are deprived of their seed at once by A-rúpá. A man
or a woman, if *he or* she neglects personal cleanliness, lapses
into sterility.¶

117 Now the daughter called Vi-dveshaṇí has a countenance
rugged with frowns. She had two sons, Apa-kára** and Pra-
118 káśaka.†† These two sons come to a man, who delights
in calumny, who is inconstant, and who uses impure water,
119 and who hates mankind, and stay *with him permanently.*
Hated by mother, by brother, by beloved friends, by kinsmen,
120 by strangers, a man perishes from righteousness or wealth.
Now one *son*, working sin, divulges‡‡ *men's* peculiar qualities
121 in the world; and the second plucks away§§ one's good
qualities and the friendship that exists among people.

* *C'aṇḍála-yonyo 'vasathe* seem wrong; read *c'aṇḍála-yony-avasathe* instead?

† She who has the form of wind. ‡ Form-less.

§ Váta-śukra-tvam; such is said to be the meaning of this word.

‖ *Viyoginaḥ* in the text seems wrong. I have adopted another reading, *yo vai tathaiva piśitáśanaḥ* for *yo 'sau tathá c'ápi viyoginaḥ*.

¶ This sentence is made the first line of verse 118 in the text, and is clearly out of place there. I have placed it after verse 116 which is the natural context.

** Apa-karsha, which must be the real name of the son (see verse 121) is preferable to Apa-kára, for neither son has anything to do with *injuries*; but all the MSS. read *apakára*, and I have not ventured to alter it.

†† That is, Divulger. ‡‡ Pra-káśayati. §§ Apa-karshati.

All these are the offspring of Duḥsaha, in the pedigree of *that* goblin*; they are notorious as observers of wicked customs; *it is they* who have overspread the whole world.

Canto LII.

The Creation and Appellations of the Rudras.

Márkaṇḍya narrates the creation of Rudra in his eight personalities—and mentions their names, stations, wives and sons—He mentions briefly the wives and offspring of the ṛishis, Bhṛigu (from whom he himself was descended), Maríći, Angiras, Atri, Pulastya, Pulaha, Vasishṭha, and Agni, and also of the Pitṛis.

Márkaṇḍeya spoke.

1 Such was the creation, which Brahmá of inscrutable origin
made, characterized by darkness. I will tell thee of the
creation of the Rudras. Hearken to me while I narrate it.
2 Now they were eight sons indeed *of Brahmá*, and *they had*
wives and children.
At the beginning of the kalpa, while the Lord was medi-
3 tating about a son who should be his equal, there appeared
in his lap a youth blue and red in *colour;* and running about
4 he cried with a sweet voice, O bráhman. "Why criest
thou?" answered Brahmá to him as he cried. "Give me a
5 name," then replied he to the lord of the world. "Thou art
named 'Rudra,'† O divine one; cry not, assume some forti-
6 tude," thus was he addressed. Then he cried seven times more,
and the Lord gave him seven other names, and stations for
7 these eight *personalities*, and wives and sons, O bráhman. The
Lord, the forefather, called him Bhava, Sarva, and I'sána,
8 and Pasu-pati, Bhíma, Ugra, *and* Mahá-deva. He gave these
names, and assigned stations for these—the sun, water, the
9 earth, fire, the wind, and the ether, an initiated bráhman,

* For *yakshaṇaḥ* read *yakshasya*?

† By a pun on the root *rud*, to cry, to weep; *rudra* would thus mean "crier," "weeper."

and the moon. These were the wives* in order,—Su-varc'a-
ná, and Umá, and Vi-keśí, and the next Svadhá, Sváhá, the
10 Diśas† and Díkshá, and Rohiṇí in due order—of the sun and
the other *stations*, O bráhman, together with Rudra and the
11 other names. And there were born *to him* gradually C'ara,
and S'ukra, Lohitánga, Mano-java, Skanda, and Sarga, San-
tána and Budha successively.

12 Such was Rudra himself. He found Satí for his wife‡;
and through Daksha's curse Satí quitted her body. She
13 was the daughter of Himavat by Mená, O bráhmaṇ; her
brother was Mainákа, the chiefest friend of Ambho-dhi (the
14 Ocean.) And the lord Bhava married her again as his only
wife.

Khyáti *the wife* of Bhṛigu§ gave birth to the two gods
15 Dhátṛi and Vidhátṛi, and to S'rí who was the wife of the
supreme god Náráyaṇa. Áyati and Niyati were the two
16 daughters of high-souled Meru; they *became* the wives of
Dhátṛi and Vidhátṛi. A son was born from each of them,
both Práṇa and Mṛikaṇḍa.

17 *The latter* was my illustrious father. I am his *son* by
Manasviní; Veda-śiras is my son, he was born of Dhúṃravatí.
18 Hear also from me of *the offspring* of Práṇa. Dyutimán
was the son begotten by Práṇa, and A-jaras was his son
also; from them both issued many sons and grandsons.

19 Sambhúti was the wife of Maríc'i‖; she brought forth
Paurna-mása; he high-souled *man* had two sons Vi-rajas and
20 Parvata; but I will defer *mentioning* their sons till I detail
the genealogies, O bráhman.

And Smṛiti was the wife of Angiras,¶ and daughters were
21 born *of her*, S'iníbalí, and Kuhu, Ráká and Bhánumatí.

Moreover, An-asúyá gave birth by Atri** to sons without
22 blemish, Soma, and Durvásas and the yogí Dattátreya.

Dattoli was born the son of Pulastya†† by his wife Príti:

* Tanavaḥ.

† The eight regions of the sky.

‡ See Canto L, verses 22-25.

§ See Canto L, versas 22-25.

‖ See Canto L, verses 22-25.

¶ See Canto L, verses 22-25.

** For *anusúyá* read *anasúyá*; see canto L, verses 23-25.

†† See Canto L, verses 22-25.

23 he was known as Agastya in a previous life during the
Sváyambhuva Manv-antara.

Now Kshamá, the wife of the Prajá-pati Pulaha* brought
24 forth three sons, *who were* Kardama, and Arva-víra and
Sahishṇu.

Now Sannati was the wife of Kratu†; she gave birth to
25 the Bálikhilyas, the sixty thousands, which they are, of ṛishis
who live in perpetual chastity.‡

26 Now seven sons were born of Urjá by Vasishṭha,§ Rajas,
Gátra and Urdhva-báhu, and Sa-bala, and An-agha, Su-tapas,
S'ukta; all these are well-known as seven Ṛishis.

27 Agni, who is arrogant, was the eldest son of Brahmá; by
him Sváhá‖ begat three sons of exalted vigour, O bráhman,
Pávaka, and Pavamána, and S'uc'i who pervades¶ water;
29 but in descent from them were forty and five others. These
and the father and his three sons are often spoken of as the
invincible and illustrious forty and nine.

30 Brahmá created the Pitṛis** whom I have mentioned to
thee, who are the Agni-shváttas,†† the Barhi-shads,‡‡ those
who *did* not maintain the sacred fire *on earth* and those who
31 *did* maintain the fire.§§ By them Svadhá‖‖ gave birth to
two daughters, Mená and Dháriṇí; they both were teachers
of the Veda, and they both were female yogís.

---

* See canto L, verses 22-25. † See canto L, verses 22-25.

‡ For *úrddha-ratasám* read *úrddhva-retasám*.

§ See canto L, verses 23-25.

‖ For *kháhá* read *sváhá*; see canto L, verses 23-25.

¶ Jaláśinam.

** This account differs from what Manu says (III, 193-199).

†† The Manes, especially of those who on earth neglected the sacrificial fire. ‡‡ A particular class of the Pitṛis.

§§ *An-agnayas* and *ságnayas*; these appear to be the same as Manu's *Agni-dagdhas* and *An-agni-dagdhas*, (III. 109).

‖‖ See canto L, 23-25.

Canto LIII.

The Story of the Sváyambhuva Manv-antara.

Márkaṇḍeya states the duration of the Manv-antaras, and mentions the names of the Manus past, present and future—He mentions the descendants of Manu Sváyambhuva and his son Priya-vrata, and explains how the whole world with its seven continents was peopled by them and divided among them—Jambu-dvípa was assigned to Priya-vrata's son Agnídhra, and was portioned out among Agnídhra's sons—His eldest son Nábhi begot Ṛishabha, and Ṛishabha begot Bharata, to whom India was assigned.

Kraushṭuki spoke.

1 Adorable Sir! I wish to hear fully of this Sváyambhuva
Manv-antara also which thou hast mentioned. Tell me of it,
2 and also of the duration of this Manv-antara, and *its* gods and
ṛishis, and the kings who *ruled during it*, and also who was
the lord of the gods *during it*, adorable Sir!

Márkaṇḍeya spoke.

3 *The duration* of the Manv-antaras has been declared to be
the four yugas multiplied by seventy-one and a fraction.*
Hear the duration of a Manv-antara from me in human
4 reckoning. Thirty times ten millions are announced, and
twenty thousands, and sixty-seven lakhs† more by computa-
5 tion—this is the length of the Manv-antara *in human years*,
omitting the fraction: it is known to be eight hundreds of
6 thousands and fifty two thousands more besides *of years* by
the divine reckoning.

At first was the Manu Sváyambhuva, then the Manu
7 Svároc'isha, Auttama,‡ and Támasa, Raivata, and C'ákshusha;
these six Manus have passed, and Vaivasvata *is the Manu* now.
8 These are to come, the five Sávarṇas and Rauc'ya, and
Bhautya.§ Of these I will tell thee fully afterwards in con-

* See Canto XLVI, verses 34—38.

† Niyuta. Verses 4, 5 and 6 agree with Canto XLVI, verses 35—37.

‡ For *auttamas* read *auttamis*.

§ The text appears to be wrong. For *Sávarṇiḥ panc'a rauc'yáś'a bhautyáś* read *Sávarṇáḥ panc'a rauc'yaś'a bhautyaś*. The five Sávarṇa or Sávarṇi Manus

9 nexion with *their respective* Manv-antaras, and of their gods
and ṛishis, *and* the lords of the Yakshas and the Pitṛis who
lived during each, of their commencement and end, O bráhman.
10 Hear who were his offspring, and who were the wives of
those their high-souled sons.
11 Now Manu Sváyambhuva had ten sons equal to himself,
by whom all this tributary earth with its seven continents,
with its mountains, and with its oceans was peopled accord-
12 ing to its countries. It was first *peopled* in the Sváyam-
bhuva period in the Kṛita and Tretá ages by the sons of
Priya-vrata and the grandsons of Sváyambhuva.
13 A daughter was begotten of Prajá-vatí by the hero Priya-
vrata. Now that illustrious daughter *gave birth* through the
14 Prajá-pati Kardama to two daughters and ten* sons; those
two *daughters* were Saṃráj† and Kukshi; their ten brothers
15 were warriors equal to the Prajá-pati *their father*. Agnídhra,
and Medhá-tithi, and Vapush-mat‡ the next, Jyotish-mat,
Dyuti-mat. Bhavya, Savana, they were seven *of them* indeed.
16 Priya-vrata anointed those seven as kings over the seven
continents. According to that his statute, hear *their* conti-
nents also from me.
17 Their father made Agnídhra thus king over Jambu-dvípa;
18 and he made Medhá-tithi lord over Plaksha-dvípa; and he
made Vapush-mat lord of S'álmali, Jyotish-mat lord over
Kuśa-dvípa, Dyuti-mat lord over Krauñc'a-dvípa, Bhavya
19 lord over S'aka-dvípa, and his son Savana ruler over Push-
kara-dvípa.

Mahá-víta and Dhátaki were the two sons of *Savana*, the
20 ruler over Pushkara-dvípa; he divided the Pushkara§ land
into two parts, and assigned to them *one part each.*

are n°. 8 Sávarṇi, n°. 9 Dakhsha-sávarṇi, n°. 10 Brahma-sávarṇi, n°. 11 Dharma-sávarṇi and n°. 12 Rudra-sávarṇi.

* Only seven are mentioned in verse 15.

† This name as a feminine is not in the Dictionary.

‡ Vapushyat in the text seems incorrect. Vapush-mat is given correctly in verses 18 and 26.

§ For *pushkaraḥ* read *pushkaraṃ?*

Bhavya had seven sons, hear them by name from me;
21 both Jala-da, and Kumára, Su-kumára, Manívaka, and Kuśot-
22 tara, Medhávin, and Mahá-druma the seventh. He portioned
out *for them* countries in S'áka-dvípa, which were named after them.

Moreover Dyuti-mat had seven sons; hear them also from
23 me; Kuśala, and Manu-ga, Ushṇa, and Prákara, Artha-káraka,
and Muni, and Dundubhi who was famed as the seventh.
24 And they had *countries* in Krauṉc'a-dvípa, which were named
after them.

In Kuśa-dvípa itself also there were seven countries called
25 by the names of the sons of Jyotish-mat; hear their names
from me—Ud-bhida, and Vaiṇava, Su-ratha, and Lambana,
26 Dhṛitimat, and Prákara, and Kápila the seventh.

And Vapush-mat the lord of S'álmali had seven sons, both
27 S'veta, and Harita, Jímúta, and Rohita, Vaidyuta, and Mána-
28 sa, and Ketu-mat the seventh. And they had seven *countries*
in S'álmali, which bore the same names.

29 Medhá-tithi, the lord of Plaksha-dvípa had seven sons, and
Plaksha-dvípa *was divided* into seven *parts* by the countries
which were named after them, first the S'áka-bhava country,
30 then S'iśira, Sukhodaya, and Ánanda, and S'iva, and Kshe-
maka, and Dhruva.

In the five *continents*, which begin with Plaksha-dvípa and
31 end with S'áka-dvípa, righteousness also must be known as
arising from the divisions of the castes and the *several* stages
of a bráhman's life. *The righteousness* which is settled,* and
springs from one's natural disposition, and is exempt from
32 the rules of harmlessness is well-known to be universal in
these five continents.

His father *Priya-vrata* gave Jambu-dvípa to Agnídhra at
33 the first, O bráhman. He had nine sons indeed, who were
equal to the Prajá-pati *Priya-vrata*. The eldest was named
34 Nábhi; his younger brother was Kim-purusha; the third *son*
was Havir-varsha; the fourth was Ilávṛita; and the fifth
35 son was Vaśya; the sixth was called Hiraṇya; the seventh

* Nitya.

of them was Kuru; the eighth was known as Bhadráśva; and
the ninth was Ketu-mála. *Designated* by their names was
the arrangement of *their* countries.
36 Perfection *exists* naturally in Kim-purusha, and the other
continents,* with the exception of that named from the
mountain Himat†; and *the perfection* is almost complete hap-
37 piness *which comes* without exertion. There is no adversity
there, nor old age, death or fear; neither righteousness nor
unrighteousness existed there, nor *had the people differences of*
38 *position, such as* high, low or middling; nor have the four
ages existed *there*, nor periodic times, nor the seasons of the
year.

Now Agnídhra's son Nábhi had a son Ṛishabha, O bráhman.
39 Ṛishabha begot Bharata, a hero, the best among his hundred
sons. Ṛishabha having anointed his son *in his stead* betook
himself to the strictest life of a wandering religious mendi-
40 cant, and devoted himself to austerities, an illustrious *hermit*,
dwelling in Pulaha's hermitage. His father gave Bharata
the southern country named after the mountain Hima‡;
41 hence the country is called Bhárata after the name of that
high-souled *king*. Bharata also had a righteous son called
42 Su-mati; and Bharata transferred the kingdom to him and
departed to the forest.

Now during the Sváyambhuva period Priya-vrata's sons,
43 and their sons and grandsons enjoyed§ the earth with its
seven continents. This was the Sváyambhuva creation; I
44 have narrated it to thee, O bráhman. What else shall I
fully tell thee of in the first Manv-antara?

---

* For *kimpurushákhyáni* read *kimpurushádyáni*?

† Himáhvaya. See also verses 40 and 41 where this is said to be a name for India. This meaning is not in the dictionary.

‡ Himáhva; this meaning, 'India," is not in the dictionary.

§ For *bhuktvá* read *bhuktá*.

CANTO LIV.

The description of Jambu-dvípa.

Márkaṇḍeya tells Kraushṭuki further the size of the earth, and the order and dimensions of the seven continents and their oceans—He describes Jambu-dvípa, the countries in it, and Meru and the other mountains; and mentions various local facts.

Kraustuki spoke.

1 How many are the continents, and *how many* the oceans,
and how many are the mountains, O bráhman? And how
many are the countries, and what are their rivers, O Muni?
2 And the size of the great objects *of nature*,* and the Loká-
loka mountain-range; the circumference, and the size and
3 the course of the moon and the sun also—tell me all this at
length, O great Muni.

Márkaṇḍeya spoke.

4 The earth is fifty times ten million *yojanas*† broad in
every direction,‡ O bráhman. I tell thee of its entire consti-
5 tution, hearken thereto. The dvípas which I have mentioned
to thee, began with Jambu-dvípa and ended with Pushkara-
dvípa, O illustrious bráhman; listen further to their dimen-
6 sions. Now *each* dvípa is twice the size of the dvípa *which
precedes it in this order*, Jambu, and Plaksha, S'álmala, Kuśa,
7 Kraunc'a and S'áka, and the Pushkara-dvípa. They are
completely surrounded by oceans of salt *water*, sugar-cane
juice, wine, ghee, curdled milk, and milk, which increase
double and double, *compared with each preceding one.*

8 I will tell thee of the constitution of Jambu-dvípa; hearken
to me. It is a hundred thousand yojanas in breadth and length,
9 it being of a circular shape.§ Himavat, and Hema-kúṭa,
Nishadha,|| and Meru, Níla, S'veta and S'ṛingin are the seven

* Mahá-bhúta. † This word must obviously be supplied; see verse 8.

‡ Taking the yojana as 40,000 feet (see Canto xlix, 40), this diameter of the earth equals 3,787,878,788 miles.

§ Vṛittau. This distance cannot apply to the circumference (vṛitti) as well, for the circumference, length and breadth cannot all be the same.

|| The text reads Ṛishabha, which disagrees with other Puráṇas and verses 22 and 23.

10 great mountain-systems* in it. Two of these great mountain-ranges† are a hundred thousand yojanas in extent, *and are situated* in the middle *of Jambu-dvípa ; there are* two *more* mountain-ranges which are south of those two, and two *more*
11 which are north. They are severally less by ten and ten thousand *yojanas* in length‡; they are all two thousand *yojanas*
12 in height, and they have the same breadth. And six of the mountain-ranges in it extend into the sea. The earth is low on the south and north, it is highly elevated in the middle.

13 On the southern half of the elevated ground§ are three countries, and on the north are three. Ilávṛita is situated between those halves, *and* is shaped like the half-moon.
14 East of it is Bhadráśva, and west is Ketu-mála.||

Now in the middle of Ilávṛita is Meru, the mountain of
15 gold. The height of that immense mountain is eighty-four¶ thousand *yojanas ;* it penetrates downwards sixteen *thousand*
16 *yojanas,* and it is just sixteen *thousand yojanas* broad ; and since it is fashioned like a cup,** it is thirty-two *thousand yojanas* broad at the summit. It is white, yellow, black and
17 red on the east and other *sides* consecutively ; and a bráhman, a vaiśya, a śúdra, and a kshatriya *are stationed there* according to the castes. Moreover, upon it on the east and the *seven*
18 other *directions of the sky* consecutively†† are *the Courts* of Indra

* Varsha-parvata.

† Nishadha on the south of Meru, and Níla on the north, according to the Vishṇu-Puráṇa, Bk. II, ch. ii.

‡ The text of the first line of verse 11 seems wrong : read instead, as in the MS.—*Daśabhir daśabhir nyúnáḥ sahasrais te parasparam.* Hema-kúṭa (south of Nishadha) and S'veta (north of Níla) are 90,000 yojanas long. Himavat (south of Hema-kúṭa) and S'ṛingin (north of S'veta) are 80,000 yojanas long. The decrease is due to their position in the circle of the earth. See Vishṇu-Puráṇa, Bk. II., ch. ii.

§ Vedi.

|| These are the nine countries mentioned in canto liii, verses 32-35.

¶ For *c'atur-asíti* read *c'atur-aśíti ?*

** S'aráva ; other authorities compare it to the inverted seed vessel of a lotus, which is somewhat like an inverted cone.

†† The MS. reads *puryo dikshu* for *púrvádishu,* with practically the same meaning.

and the other Loka-pálas; and in the centre is Brahmá's
Court, which is fourteen thousand yojanas high.
19 Moreover below it are the subjacent hills* with a height
of ten thousand *yojanas*. On the east and other sides con-
20 secutively are *the mountains* Mandara, Gandha-mádana, and
Vipula, and Su-párśva†; they are decorated with trees as
standards. The kadam tree‡ is the standard on Mandara,
21 the jambu tree§ on Gandha-mádana, and the aśvattha tree|| on
Vipula, and the great banyan¶ on Su-párśva. These mountains
22 are eleven hundred yojanas in extent. Jaṭhara and Deva-
kúṭa are two mountains on the east side; they stretch up to
Níla and Nishadha without any space intervening between
23 them. Nishadha** and Páripátra are on the west side of Meru;
these two mountains, like the two former, extend to Níla
24 and Nishadha. Kailása and Himavat are two great *mountains*
on the south; they stretch east and west; they extend into
25 the ocean. S'ṛingávat and Járudhi, moreover, are two moun-
tains on the north; they, like *the two* on the south, extend
26 into the ocean.†† These eight are called the boundary moun-
tains, O bráhman. Hima-vat, Hema-kúṭa and the other
27 mountains *comprise*, one with another, nine thousand yojanas,
eastward, westward, southward and northward. Similarly
Meru stretches to the four quarters in the middle in Ilávṛita.
28 The fruits which the jambu‡‡ tree *produces* on the mountain

* Vishkambha-parvata.

† Mandara is on the East; Gandhá-mádana on the South; Vipula on the West; and Su-párśva on the North. See Canto lvi, verses 7, 13 and 16.

‡ See note **, page 25.

§ Eugenia Jambolana, Hooker, vol. II, p. 499; Roxb. p. 398. A large tree, common everywhere, with a rather crooked trunk, shining leaves, and edible fruit. The bark yields brown dyes.

|| Called also *pippala*; *Ficus religiosa* (Oliver, p. 272; Roxb. p. 642); the modern *peepul*; a large spreading tree with a grateful shade, common everywhere. See also note *, p. 33.

¶ Vaṭa, *Ficus benghalensis* (Oliver, p. 272; *F. indica*, Roxb. p. 639), the large, common, well-known tree.

** Read *Ṛishabha*?

†† For *antarvántar* read *arṇavántar*?

‡‡ For *jambá* read *jambvá*?

Gandha-mádana, are as large as an elephant's body; they
29 fall on the top of the mountain. From their juice springs
the famous Jambú river, in which is found the gold called
30 Jámbú-nada. That river passes around Meru and then
enters Jambú-múla, O bráhman; and those people drink of it.
31 In Bhadráśva Vishṇu *is figured* with a horse's head; in
Bhárata* he has the shape of a tortoise; and he is *like* a
boar in Ketu-mála; and he has a fish's form in the north.
32 In all those four *countries*, worldly affairs are governed
by the arrangement of the constellations, O bráhman; *the
people there* study the influence of the planets.

CANTO LV.

The Geography of Jambu-dvípa.

Márkaṇḍeya mentions the forests and lakes and mountains around Meru—All the heavenly beings dwell in that region where there is the most charming scenery—Bhárata alone is the land of action, which entails merit and sin.

Márkaṇḍeya spoke.

1 Hear from me of the four forests and lakes which exist on
2 Mandara and the three other mountains,† O bráhman. On
the east is *the forest* named C'aitra-ratha, on the southern
mountain the forest Nandana, on the western mountain *the
forest* Vaibhrája, and on the northern mountain *the forest*
3 Sávitra. On the east is the lake Aruṇoda,‡ and on the south
Mánasa, on the west of Meru is S'ítoda, and Mahá-bhadra on
the north.
4 On the east of Mandara are the mountains S'ítártta,§ and
C'akra-muṇja, and Kulíra, Su-kanka-vat, and Maṇi-śaila,
5 Vṛisha-vat, Mahí-níla, Bhavác'ala, Sa-bindu, Mandara, Veṇu,
Támasa, and Nishadha, and Deva-śaila.

* For *bhárite* read *bhárate* ?

† For *śailashu* read *śaileshu*.

‡ Or Varuṇoda, see Canto lvi, verse 6.

§ *S'ítárttaś* read *S'ítántaś* ? See verse 17, and Canto lvi, verse 6.

6 The mountain S'ikhara with its three peaks,* and Kalinga,
Patangaka, Ruc'aka, and the mountain Sánu-mat, and Tám-
7 raka, Viśákha-vat, S'vetodara, and Sa-múla, and Vasu-dhára,
Ratna-vat, Eka-śṛinga, Mahá-śaila, Rája-śaila, Pipáṭhaka, and
8 Paṉc'a-śaila, Kailása, and Hima-vat the loftiest of mountains;
these mountains are said to lie on the south side of Meru.
9 Su-raksha,† and S'iśiraksha, Vaidurya, and Kapila,‡ and
10 Piṉjara, Mahá-bhadra, Su-rasa, Kapila, Madhu, Aṉjana,
Kukkuṭa, Kṛishṇa, and Páṇḍura the loftiest of mountains,
and the mountain Sahasra-śikhara, Páripátra, and S'ṛinga-
11 vat; these mountains are well-known as lying on the west of
Meru beyond the subjacent hills§ which are on the west side.
12 Hear yet the other *mountains* on the north. S'ankha-kúṭa,
Vṛishabha, and the mountain Haṃsa-nábha, and the moun-
13 tain Kapilendra, Sánu-mat, and Níla, Svarṇa-śṛingin, S'áta-
śṛingin, Pushpaka, Megha-parvata, Virajáksha, Varáhádri,
14 Mayúra, and Járudhi; these are said to be the mountains on
the north of Meru, O bráhman.
The valleys among these mountains are exceedingly charm-
15 ing; they are decorated with forests *and* lakes of the clearest
water. In them men are born who practise meritorious deeds,
16 O bráhman. These are terrestrial Svargas, O bráhman; they
surpass Svarga with their excellences. In them no fresh
17 merit or sin accrues. Even the gods are said to enjoy merit
in them. And on these mountains, S'ítánta‖ and the rest, O
18 bráhman, are the great and resplendent abodes of the Vidyá-
dharas, the Yakshas, the Kin-naras, the Nágas, and the
19 Rákshasas, and the gods, and the Gandharvas, which possess
great merit and are studded with charming groves which the
gods *frequent*. And the lakes are charming; the breeze is

* See Canto lvi, verse 9. S'ikhara must be first mountain on the south, and *tri-kúṭa* must be an adjective qualifying it.

† See Canto lvi, verse 14.

‡ The text "Kapila" seems erroneous, as it mentions Kapila again in the next line. Another reading is Pingala.

§ For *viskambhát* read *vishkambhát*; see Canto liv, verse 19.

‖ See verse 4.

20 pleasant at every season. Nor anywhere on these mountains
do men have any kind of mental agitation.
21 Thus have I told thee of that four-leaved lotus-flower
which is the earth; its leaves are Bhadráśva, Bhárata and
the other countries on the four sides. The country named
22 Bhárata, which I have told thee of on the south, is the land
of action; nowhere else is merit and sin acquired; this must
be known to be the chief *country*, wherein everything is
23 fixedly established.* And from it a man gains Svarga and
final emancipation from existence, or the human world and
hell, or yet again the brute-condition, O bráhman.

Canto LVI.

The Descent of the Ganges.

Márkaṇḍeya describes the course of the River Ganges from the moon on to mount Meru, then in four streams flowing east, south, west and north, of which the southern stream was allowed by S'iva to flow through India at the entreaties of King Bhagíratha.

He describes briefly the happy condition of all the other countries (except India) in Jambu-dvípa.

Márkaṇḍeya spoke.

1 The foot of Náráyaṇa, moreover, who is the origin of the
universe,† supports the earth. The divine river Ganges
2 which issued thence flows in three courses. She enters the
moon, which is the womb of the nectar and the receptacle of
the waters, and thence, having purified with her contact the
rays of the sun‡ which is indissolubly connected *with the moon*,
3 she fell on the summit of Meru, and then divided into four
streams. As she fell from the summit and the sides and the
outer bounds of Meru, she turned around, and finding no
4 support fell scattering her waters widely. Dividing her
waters equally at the foot of Mandara and the three other
5 *mountains*, she fell, piling high the rocks broken off from their
bases by her waters.

* Prati-shṭhita.

† *Jagad-yonim* in the text seems impossible. Read *jagad-yoneḥ* ?

‡ Or, being purified by contact with the rays of the sun.

The eastern stream, which is celebrated by its name Sítá,*
6 flowed to the forest C'aitra-ratha,† and overflowing it, passed
on to the lake Varuṇoda,‡ and thence to the mountain
S'itánta,§ and thence to the other mountains *on the east* in
7 order. Descending to the earth in her course, she flowed
from Bhadráśva into the ocean.

Moreover the *second stream* called Alaka-nandá flowed
8 south towards Gandha-mádana into the *forest* Nandana that
delights the gods and that lies at the foot of Meru, and over-
9 flowed the lake Mánasa with great force, and reached the de-
lightful kingly mountain S'ikhara,‖ and thence overflowed all
10 the mountains which I have mentioned in order on the south,
and reached the lofty mountain Hima-vat. There the bull-
11 bannered S'iva held her and would not let her go. The
lord was propitiated by *king* Bhagíratha with fastings and
hymns, and S'iva released her there. She entered the south-
12 ern ocean in seven *streams, and* in three *streams* on the east;
inundating as a great river the south with the overflow from
her stream, behind Bhagíratha's chariot.

13 Moreover the great river famed as Sva-rakshu fell on
Mount Vipula on the west side, and went towards the forest¶
14 Vaibhrája; and thence the great river overflowing the lake
S'ítoda reached the mountain Sva-rakshu,** and thence she
15 went to the mountain Tri-śikha;†† and thence falling on the

* The text appears incorrect. For *púrváśite 'tivikhyátá* read *púrvá síteti vikhyátá?*

† See canto lv, verse 2.

‡ Or Aruṇoda, see canto lv, verse 3.

§ See canto lv, verse 4.

‖ See canto lv, verse 6.

¶ For *sác'alam* read *sá vanam?* See canto lv, verse 2.

** There seems to be a confusion in the text between the names of the river and the mountain, which latter is called *Su-raksha* in canto lv, verse 9; for *Sva-rakshuḥ* then read *Su-raksham?*

†† This name seems erroneous. See canto lv, verse 9, where S'iśiráksha is mentioned as the second mountain. No mountain of the name Tri-śikha is mentioned in that and the following verses among the western mountains. The two should agree; compare Vṛishabha in verse 18, and canto lv, verse 12.

summits of the other mountains *on the west* in order, she
reached Ketumála and entered the salt ocean.

16 Now she flowed on to mount Su-párśva also, which is at
the foot of Meru; there she is famed as Somá. She flowed
17 to the wood of Savitṛi.* Overflowing† it, she reached lake
Mahá-bhadra;‡ and thence she passed as a great river to
18 mount S'ankha-kúṭa;§ and thence reaching in succession
Vṛishabha and the other mountains *on the north*, and over-
flowing the Northern Kurus she entered the great ocean.

19 Thus I have appropriately described to thee, O bráhman,
this *river*, the Ganges, and the countries according to their
20 arrangement in Jambu-dvípa. In Kim-purusha and all the
other *countries* dwell people, who have almost unalloyed
happiness, who are free from sickness, and who are exempt
21 from low and high diversities of condition. In each of the
nine countries in it are seven mountain ranges. And then
in each country there are rivers flowing down from the
22 mountains. In Kim-purusha and the seven other countries,
O bráhman, waters bubble up *from the ground;* here in Bhá-
23 rata *we have* rain. And in these eight countries‖ men enjoy
a perfection which comes from the trees, from their own
natural dispositions, from the localities, from the water, from
24 their mental condition and from their actions.¶ The tree-
bestowed perfection is obtained from the trees that grant
them every wish; the natural is well-known as that which
springs from the natural disposition; and the local delight
25 is that which is connected with the land itself; and the
water-given** *perfection comes* from the delicacy of the water;
and the mental is derived from meditation; and the *perfec-
tion which comes* from reverential service and the performance
of other duties is denominated righteousness-produced.††

* Sávitra; see canto lv, verse 2.

† For *pávayantí* read *plávayantí*.

‡ See canto lv, verse 3.

§ See canto lv, verse 12.

‖ For *vashershv* read *varsheshv*.

¶ *Karma-já*, this seems preferable to *dharma-já* in verse 25.

** For *toyátthá* read *toyotthá*.

†† Dharma-já; verse 23 reads *karma-já* instead, which seems preferable.

26 And in these countries the ages do not exist, nor bodily nor mental sicknesses; nor is there any undertaking involving merit or demerit there, O bráhman.

CANTO LVII.

Márkaṇḍeya mentions the nine divisions of Bhárata, one of which is India—He mentions the seven mountain ranges in India (exclusive of the Himálaya Mountains) and names twenty-two separate hills—He mentions the chief rivers in India, grouping them according to the mountain ranges out of which they rise—He mentions the chief peoples in India and on its borders, arranging them according to the main natural divisions of the country—and he concludes with general descriptive remarks and an encomium on India as the sole land of action.

Kraushṭuki spoke.

1 Adorable Sir! thou hast fully described this Jambu-dvípa.
Just as thou hast declared it, merit-producing action *exists*
2 nowhere else, nor *action that tends* to sin, except in Bhárata,
O illustrious Sir! And from this *land* both Svarga is at-
tained, and final emancipation from existence, and the me-
3 dium end also. Verily nowhere else on earth is action
ordained for mortals. Therefore tell me, O bráhman, about
4 this Bhárata in detail, and what are its divisions, and how
many they are, and *what is its* constitution accurately; it is
the country,* and what are the provinces and the mountains
in it, O bráhman?

Márkaṇḍeya spoke.

5 Hear from me the nine divisions of this country Bhárata;
6 they must be known as extending to the ocean, but as being
mutually inaccessible. *They*† *are* Indra-dvípa, Kaśerúmat,‡

* Varsha.

† This and the three following verses agree closely with the Kúrma Puráṇa canto xlvii, verses 22—25.

‡ The dictionary gives the word as *kaśeru-mat;* the Kúrma Puráṇa as *kaseruk-mat* (canto xlvii, verse 22), in preference. Another form is said to be *Kasetu.*

7 Támra-varṇa,* Gabhasti-mat, and Nága-dvípa, Saumya,
Gándharva,† and Váruṇa; and this is the ninth dvípa
among them, and it is surrounded by the sea.‡ This dvípa
8 is a thousand yojanas from south to north.§ At its east end
are the Kirátas,|| and at the west the Yavanas.¶ Within
it dwell bráhmans, kshatriyas, vaiśyas and śúdras, O bráh-
9 man. They accomplish their purification with the occupa-
tions of sacrifice, meditation, trade, &c.; and they seek their
10 mutual business through these occupations, and they gain
Svarga or final emancipation from existence, merit and sin
then.

The seven mountain ranges** in it are Mahendra,††

* The Kúrma Puráṇa gives the word as *támra-parṇa* in preference (canto xlvii, verse 22). It is Ceylon.

† Or, *gandharva*, Kúrma Puráṇa, canto xlvii, verse 23.

‡ This is understood to mean India, as the following verses show; see Wilson's Vishṇu Puráṇa, Edn. FitzEdward Hall, Book II, chap. iii, note on the similar passage. But this Puráṇa states clearly enough (see verse 59 below) that India is not surrounded by the sea, but bounded by it only on the east, south, and west, and only partially so on the east and west, for verse 8 places the Kirátas and Yavanas there respectively.

§ The yojana is defined in canto xlix, verse 40, to be about 40,000 feet; this length therefore is 7,576 miles.

|| The Kirátas are the uncivilized tribes of the forests and mountains; here the word appears to denote all the races with the Burmese type of features along the eastern limits of India.

¶ The Greeks originally, and afterwards the Mohammedans.

** For the notes in this Canto I have consulted, Wilson's Vishṇu Puráṇa (Edn. FitzEdward Hall), General Cunningham's Ancient Geography of India (1871), his Archæological Survey of India Reports, besides other works and maps.

†† "Mahendra is the chain of hills that extends from Orissa and the northern Circars to Gondwana, part of which near Ganjam is still called Mahindra Malei or hills of Mahindra." Wilson's Vishṇu Puráṇa, Book II, chap. iii, note. The rivers which flow from these hills are named in verses 28 and 29, but only a few of them have been identified. This range then appears to be the portion of the Eastern Ghats between the Godaveri and Mahánadi rivers, and the hills in the south of Berar. See, however, note on the S'ukti-mat range on the next page.

11 Malaya,* Sahya,† S'ukti-mat,‡ the Ṛiksha moun-

* This is the southern portion of the Western Ghats. Only four rivers are mentioned in verses 27 and 28 as rising in these hills, and none of them appear to have been identified; but as the River Kaveri is said in verses 26 and 27 to rise in the Sahya mountains, the Malaya mountains can be only the portion of the Western Ghats from the Nil-giris to Cape Comorin.

† The Sahya mountains are the Northern portion of the Western Ghats, and, as appears from the rivers which rise in them (see verses 26 and 27), extend from the River Tapti down to the Nil-giris.

‡ This range is not definitely identified, nor the rivers which are said in verses 29 and 30 to rise in it.

General Cunningham says the R Suktimati "derived its name from the Suktimál (sic) mountains, in which it had its source"; asserts that the river must be the same as the Mahánadí; and infers that the S'ukti-mat mountains must "correspond with the high range of mountains to the south of Sehoa and Kánker, which gives rise to the Mahanadi, the Pairi and the Seonath rivers, and which forms the boundary between Chattisgarh and the feudatory state of Bastar." (Arch. Survey Reports, vol. XVII, pp. 24 and 69; and map at end.) His premises seem to me unsafe; and his conclusion confounds the S'ukti-mat range with the Mahendra range, and must be incorrect, for the latter range appears to be identified beyond doubt.

Mr. Beglar proposes to identify the R. S'ukti-matí with the Sakri (which is a tributary of the Ganges, and flows northwards about 35 miles east of Gaya), to connect the river with the S'ukti-mat range, and apparently to identify the range with the hills in the north of the Hazaribagh district. He proposes to strengthen this position by identifying the rivers Kiyul (another tributary of the Ganges, east of the Sakri) and Kaorhari (which I do not find, but which seems to be another small tributary) with the Ṛishi-kulyá and Kumárí, which rise in the S'ukti-mat mountains; see verses 29 and 30. (Arch. Survey Reports, vol. VIII, pp. 124 and 125). But the S'ukti-mat range and S'ukti-matí river do not seem necessarily connected; neither this nor the Váyu Puráṇa makes the river rise in the S'ukti-mat range, (see verse 23); Sakri does not appear the natural equivalent for S'ukti-matí, (there is besides another river Sakri, a tributary of the Seonath,) nor Kiyul and Kaorhari of Ṛishi-kulyá and Kumárí; Sakri corresponds better with S'akulí (see verse 23); and the hills in the north of the Hazaribagh district are not remarkable, and are rather the termination of the Vindhya range than a separate mountain system.

The only mountains, which have not been appropriated to the Sanskrit names, are the Aravalli mountains and the southern portion of the Eastern Ghats, so that this range might be one of these two; and if the former are rightly included in the Páripátra Range, (see note ‡, next page) the S'ukti-mat range might be the southern portion of the Eastern Ghats and

tains,* and Vindhya,† and Páripátra.‡ And there are other hills besides them in thousands, which are situated
12 near them. Their summits are broad and lofty, and are delightful and spacious;—Koláhala,§ and Vaibhrája,||

the hills of Mysore. If, however, the S'ukti-mat range must be placed in Berar, the Mahendra range will be restricted to the Eastern Ghats.

* These are said to be the mountains of Gondwana, see Wilson's Vishṇu-Puráṇa, Book II, chap. iii, note. Judging from the rivers which are said in verses 21 to 25 to rise in the Vindhya and Ṛiksha Ranges, it appears this range consists of the hills which form the water-shed between the Narbudda, Sone and Mahanadi on one side, and the Tapti and northern tributaries of the Godavari on the other side; that is, it comprises the Satpura Hills, and the hills extending through the middle of Berar and the south of Chutia Nagpur nearly into West Bengal.

† For *vindhaś* read *vindhyaś*. This does not denote the whole of the modern Vindhya Range, but only the portion of it east of Bhopal, and also the water-shed hills which extend from it into Behar, as will appear from a comparison of the rivers which rise in it according to verses 21—23.

‡ Called also Páriyátra. This is the western portion of the modern Vindhya Range, west of Bhopal, as appears from the rivers which rise in it according to verses 19 and 20. Prof. Wilson says (Vishṇu Puráṇa, Book II, chap. iii, note) "the name, indeed, is still given to a range of mountains in Guzerat (see Colonel Tod's Map of Rajasthan)," and that may be considered an offshoot of the main range. If the Váyu Puráṇa is right in reading Varṇáśá instead of Veṇvá in verse 19, this range would also probably include the Aravalli mountains in Rajputana. If this be so, the configuration of this range, a curve around the west and south of Malwa, would suggest a derivation for both the names, *viz.*, Páripátra, from *pari* + *pátra*, "the mountains shaped like an enclosing receptacle", or "the mountains which form a protection around;" or Páriyátra, from *pari* + *yá*, "the mountains which curve around." The name may thus still survive in the Pathar range, which lies between the rivers Chambal and Banás. (Arch. Survey Reports, vol. VI, p. 1 and map; and vol. XIV, p. 151).

§ Mr. Beglar proposes to identify this hill with the Kawa Kol range, which is east of the R. Sakri (a tributary of the Ganges about 35 miles east of Gaya); but there does not appear to be anything about the range agreeing with the description in the text. (Arch. Survey Reports, vol. VIII, pp. 123 to 125, and map at end).

|| This as a mountain is not mentioned in the dictionary, and I do not find any such mountain. The Váyu Puráṇa reads *Vaihára* instead (xlv. 90), which is a synonym for a famous hill called *Vaibhára* or *Baibhára*, near Raja-griha,

13 Mandara,* the hill Durdura,† Váta-svana,‡
and Vaidyuta, § Mainâka, || and

and about 28 miles north-east of Gaya. (Cunningham's Anc. Geog. of India, vol. I, p. 452, map, and p. 463; Arch. Survey Reports, vol. 1, p. 21 and plates III. and XIV.; vol. III., p. 140).

* Mandara, the famous mountain, is situated about 35 miles south of Bhágalpúr, in Behar (Arch. Survey Reports, vol. VIII., p. 130). There was another mountain of this name in the neighbourhood of S'veta-giri and Kailása; see Mahá-Bhárata, Sabhá-P. li. 1858; Vana-P. cxxxix. 10820-30; and Anuśás-P. xix. 1434. This Mandara seems to have been the famons mountain originally.

† This form is not in the dictionary, but it occurs in the Rámáyaṇa Sundara-K. xcv. 25, and is the same as Dardura, which is the usual form, and Dardara, which is mentioned in the dictionary. It was a mountain or group of mountains, in the extreme Sonth of India. It is mentioned in the Mahá-Bhárata, Sabhá-P. li. 1891–3, where the context suggests that it was on the borders of the C'ola and Páṇḍya kingdoms; and it appears to be intended in the Annśás-P. clxv. 7658, by the name Dururduda, which violates the metre. Malaya and Dardura are mentioned as the two highest mountains in the extreme Sonth in the Raghu-V. (iv. 51.) In a paper on the Geography of Ráma's Exile, in the *Journal*, R. A. S., April 1894, p. 262, I have proposed to identify this mountain with the Nilgiris.

‡ This as a mountain is not mentioned in the dictionary. The Váyu Puráṇa reads Pátandhama instead (xlv. 91). I do not find either. But Mr. Beglar found a hill Bathan or Bathani in south Behar, and mentions a hill called Banthawa or Pandhawa in Buddhist records. These names might be easy corruptions of Pátandhama. (Arch. Survey Reports, vol VIII., p. 46).

§ This as a mountain is not mentioned in the dictionary, and I do not find it. Is it to be connected with Baijnath or Vaidya-nath, the famous place of pilgrimage, near the R. Karma-náśá, sonth of Ghazipúr? There does not seem, however, to be any prominent hill there. (Arch. Survey Reports, vol. VIII, p. 137; and vol. XIX, p. 27). Or, shonld the reading be *Vaidúrya?* This seems preferable. The Vaidúrya Mts. are the Satpura Range; compare Mahá-Bhárata, Vana-P. lxxxviii. 8343; lxxxix. 8354–61; and cxxi; and *Journal*, R. A. S., April 1894, p. 245.

|| There were three mountains of this name. One is the famous Mountain in the north; it is called a son of Hima-vat by the apsaras Mená, and was a part of the great Hima-vat Range. It was near Kailása, Gandha-mádana and S'veta-giri (see M-Bh., Sabhá-P. iii. 58-60; Vana-P. cxxxv. 10694-5; cxxxix. 10820; and clviii. 11540; and Bhíshma-P. vi. 237): and from Vana-P. cxlv. 11054-64; and Hari-Vaṁśa cxxxiii. 7598–7605, it appears to have

Svarasa,* Tunga-prastha,† Nága-giri,‡ Roc'ana,§ the
14 hill Páṇḍara,|| the hill Pushpa,¶ Dur-jayanta,**

been situated near the eastern sources of the Ganges; hence this Mainâka probably denoted the group of hills in the north of the Almora district; but these passages are not quite consistent. The Rámáyaṇa in Kishk. K. xliv. 35–37 places lake Mánasa on Mt. Krauñc'a, (which is called Mainâka's son, in Hari-V., xviii. 941–2,) and Mainâka beyond Krauñc'a; but those geographical cantos, xl to xliv, seem to be a late interpolation.

Another Mainâka is the fabulous mountain situated in the sea, midway between the southern point of the Indian Peninsula and Ceylon; see Rámáyaṇa, Sund. K. vii; and in this connexion see canto lii., verse 13.

And the third Mainâka is in Western India, apparently in Khandesh as it seems to be connected with C'yavana; see M.-Bh., Vana-P. lxxxix. 8364–5. In Gen. Cunningham's Arch. Surv. Reports (vol. VIII, p. 124) the R. Sone is said to be called Mainâka-prabha, from the mountain in which it rises, but Mainâka is probably a mistake for Mekala.

* This as a mountain is not mentioned in the dictionary; and I do not find it. The Váyu Puráṇa reads Sasurasa, or Su-sarasa instead (xlv. 90); I do not find any such hill. Surasa is one of the mountains mentioned in canto lv. verse 9.

† I do not find this. The Váyu Puráṇa reads Gantu-prastha instead (xlv. 91) which seems a mistake.

‡ I do not find this. In a list of mountains in Hari-Vaṁśa, clxviii., 9499–9505 are mentioned Nága and Nága-ráṭ. Perhaps these mountains may be placed in the Nága country, near Nágpúr in the Central Provinces.

§ I do not find this.

|| The Váyu Puráṇa reads Páṇḍura (xlv. 90); neither is mentioned in the dictionary as a mountain. Should we read Páṇḍava instead? There are two hills now which are called Páṇḍua Hill or the Páṇḍus' Hill, one found by Mr. Carlleyle, north-west of Bairát (or Vairáṭa) in Alwar (Arch. Survey Reports, vol. VI, pp. 95–101); and the other by Mr. Beglar, north of Hatta and near the R. Ken in Bandelkhand, where pilgrimages are still made (*id.* vol. VII., p. 56).

¶ I do not find this. Pushpaka is one of the mountains mentioned in canto lv. verse 13. A river called Pushpa-já is said to rise in the Malaya Mts. (see verse 27, below).

** I do not find this. The Váyu Puráṇa reads Uj-jayanta instead (xlv. 92), which Gen. Cunningham identifies with Girnar hill, which is situated on the east side of Juna-gaḍh in the peninsula of Gujarat (Anct. Geog., vol. I. p. 325). It was in Su-ráshṭra (M.-Bh., Vana-P. lxxxviii. 8347–9). There are also the Ajanta Hills, north-east of Aurangabad (Arch. Survey Reports, vol. IX.,

Raivata,* and Arbuda,† Ṛishyamúka,‡ and Gomanta,§

p. 121) which seem to be the same as the Ajayanti Hill (Anc. Geog. of India. vol. I. p. 555).

* Raivata, or Raivataka, was near Dváraká or Kuśa-sthalí, which was near the extreme western promontory, and was the capital of the country Ánarta, in the peninsula of Gujarat; for in the M.-Bh., a festival on this mountain is described, in which the citizens of Dváraká went out there with their families, in thousands, on foot or in carriages (Ádi-P. ccxix. 7906–17); and it is called the ornament of the gate of that city in the Hari-V. (cxiii. 6361–70; and cxiv. 6410–15.). The Girnar hill mentioned in the last preceding note is sometimes identified with this hill, but Mt Girnar is about 110 miles from Dváraká, and this distance is incompatible with either of the passages quoted. There does not appear to be any mountain close to that city, but the Baradá group of hills is not far from it, and they are the only hills that comply with the conditions (see Arch. Surv. of W. India, by J. Burgess, Káṭhiáwáḍ, pp. 12, 15, 84 and 154). Raivata is not necessarily a single mountain, for the Hima-vat, Vindhya and other ranges are often spoken of in the singular. I would therefore propose to identify Raivata with the Baradá Hills in Hálár, the western corner of the peninsula.

† The modern Mount Abu, at the south end of the Aravalli range. Vasishṭha is said to have had his hermitage there (M.-Bh., Vana-P. lxxxii. 4097–8). The country around Arbuda was noted for its breed of horses (*id.* Sabhá-P. l. 1851.)

‡ Ṛishyamúka is in the Dekhan. It was the scene of Ráma's meeting with Sugríva and Hanúmán. I have proposed to identify it with the range of hills which stretches from Ahmadnagar to beyond Naldrug and Kalyani, dividing the Manjira and Bhima rivers (*Journal*, R. A. S., April, 1894, p. 253).

§ There are two hills of this name. One is mentioned in the Hari-Vaṁśa as situated in a gap or opening (*vivara*) of the Sahya Mts. (xcvi. 5331–40). It was three or four days' journey by swift chariot from Karavíra-pura (xcvi. 5325–40; and c. 5650–52), *i.e.*, probably 100 or 120 miles in a hilly country: and that city, which was the capital of the country Padmávata, was on the Sahya Mts. on (and therefore near the source of) the R. Veṇvá, and presumably near S'úrpáraka (xcv. 5212, 5228–31; and xcvi. 5283–5322). This R. Veṇvá would therefore appear to be the river Purna (or one of the other small rivers south of Surat), flowing into the Gulf of Cambay, south of the R. Tapti; Karavíra-pura would have been near its source on the Western Ghats, and Gomanta would probably be the hills S. or S.-E. of Nasik. The other Gomanta is the hill of Gwalior. Gen. Cunningham says it was originally called *Gopác'ala* and *Gopa-giri*, *Gopáhvaya*, and later, *Go-manta*

15 Kúṭa-śaila,* Kṛita-smara,† and S'rí-parvata,‡ and Kora,§ and other mountains in hundreds. By them the people, both Mleććhas and Áryas, are mingled together according to their divisions.

16 The chief rivers of which those *people* drink, hear them from me duly. Gangá, Saras-vatí,|| Sin-

(Arch. Survey Reports, vol. II. pp. 372, 373). The Váyu Puráṇa mentions *Go-dhana* instead (xlv. 91); but I have met with no hill of this name elsewhere; it suggests *Go-vardhana*, but *Go-vardhana* does not suit the metre.

* I do not find this.

† I do not find this. Is this to be connected with the Káramár hill, in Gándhára? (Arch. Survey Reports, vol. II. pp. 92 and 106, and map at p. 87; vol. XIX. p. 126).

‡ S'rí-parvata, or S'rí-śaila, is the name of a lofty rock which over-hangs the R. Kṛishṇá in the Kurnool District; it is the site of a famous temple called Mallikárjuna, one of the twelve great Linga shrines (Arch. Surv. of S. India, by R. Sewell, Vol. I. 90; Arch. Surv. of W. India, by J. Burgess, p. 223). The Agni Puráṇa places S'rí-parvata on the R. Káverí, and says it was dedicated to the goddess S'rí by Vishṇu, because she had once performed some austerities (cxiii. 3, 4). But Mr. Beglar, in a list of tírthas where portions of Párvatí's body are fabled to have fallen when she was destroyed at Daksha's sacrifice, mentions "Sri Parvat, near the Karatoya River." This may perhaps be the river mentioned in verse 25, for I do not think there is any such hill near the other Karatoyá in North-East Bengal.

§ The Váyu Puráṇa reads *Káru*, or *Ketu* (xlv. 92) and a mountain *Koṇva* is mentioned in the Bhágavata-P. (V. xix. 16); none are mentioned as mountains in the dictionary. There is a hill called Kolla in Mewat (Arch. Survey Reports, vol. XX. p. 133).

|| The modern Sursooty, between the Jumna and Sutlej. For a clear description, see Arch. Survey Reports, vol. II. 214, &c; and XIV. pp. 87-90 and Plate XXVI. There can be little doubt that in ancient times it was a very much larger river than it is now; see an interesting paper in the *Journal*, Beng. Asiat. Socy. 1886, Part II. p. 340; but in later times it perished, as it does now, in the sands of the desert, and *Vinaśana* was the name of the place where it disappeared (M.-Bh., Vana-P. lxxxii. 5052–5; and S'alya-P. xxxviii. 2119-20.). South and East of it was the *Dṛishadvatí*, and between them lay the sacred region called *Brahmávarta* (Manu II. 17, 18) and Tri-pishṭapa (M.-Bh. Vana-P. lxxxiii. 5074 and 7075) and also apparently *Brahma-kshetra* (*ibid.*, 5076). The name *Saras-vatí*, however, was given to the seven rivers *Su-prabhá*, *Káñc'anákshí*, *Viśálá*, *Manoramá*, *Ogha-vatí*, *Su-reṇu* and *Vimalodaká* (*id.*, S'alya-P. xxxix. 2188–2216.)

17 dhu,* and C'andra-bhágá † also, ‡ and
Yamuná, and S'ata-dru, § Vitastá, || Irávatí, ¶
Kuhu,** Go-matí, †† and Dhúta-pápá, ‡‡ Báhudá, §§

* The Indus. As to its ancient course through Sindh, see *Journal*, Beng. Asiat. Socy., 1886, Part II. p. 323.

† The R. Chenab, in the Punjab. It was also called the *Asikní*, the Greek Akesines.

‡ Or, "and another *C'andra-bhágá*." There were two rivers of this name (M.-Bh., Bhíshma-P. ix. 322 and 327), but I have found no data to identify the second.

§ The R. Sutlej; the Greek Hyphasis. In ancient times this river probably did not join the Beas, as it does now, but pursued an independent course to the confines of Sindh. It flowed South-West from where it issues from the Himalayas, into the channel called the Naiwal and then along the dry bed called the Hakra or Ghaggar, at a distance of 30 to 50 miles south of, and more or less parallel to, its present conrse. See *Journal*, Beng. Asiat. Socy., 1886, Part II. p. 332.

|| The modern R. Jhelam, in the Panjab; the Greek Hydaspes.

¶ The modern R. Ravi, in the Panjab; the Greek Hydraotes.

** This does not appear to be known, though it is also mentioned by the Váyu (xlv. 95) and Kúrma Puráṇas (xlvii. 27), both of which read *Kuhú*. As it is mentioned in conjunction with rivers in the Panjab, is it to be identified with the *Kubhá* (Ṛig-V. x., 75. 6.), the Greek *Kōphēn*, the modern Kabul river? (Cunningham, Anc. Geog. of India, I. 37).

†† The modern Goomti, which joins the Ganges on the left bank below Benares. There was, however, another and older Go-matí (Ṛig-V. x. 75. 6), which is probably the modern R. Gomal, a western tribntary of the Indus (Mnir, Sansk. Texts, II. 357).

‡‡ Gen. Sir A. Cnnningham says this is a name of the Go-matí (Arch. Surv. Repts, I. 315). The text is *Go-matí Dhúta-pápá c'a*; and the Váyu (xlv 95), Kúrma (xlvii. 27), Varáha (lxxxv.) and Vishṇu Puráṇas all read the same. The two words are also linked together in the Mahá-Bhárata (Bhíshma-P. ix. 325), bnt not, I believe, in the Rámáyaṇa, where the Go-matí is generally called "crowded with cattle." *Dhúta-pápá* then either means the Go-matí, and the translation would be, "and the sin-cleansing Go-matí;" or it denotes some tributary of that river.

§§ There were two rivers of this name, this one (see M-Bh., Bhíshma-P. ix. 337), and another in the Dekhan (*ibid.*, 322; Anuśás.-P. clxv. 7653: and Rámáyaṇa, Kishk. K. xli. 13). This river is mentioned in various passages (M-Bh., Vana-P. lxxxiv. 8045-6; lxxxvii. 8323; xcv. 8513; S'ánti-P. xxiii. 668, &c.; Anuśás-P. xix. 1408–11; and Hari-Vaṁśa xii. 710), and from these

18 and Dṛiśad-vatí,* Vi-pásá,† Deviká,‡ Rankshu,§
Niśćírá,|| and Gaṇḍakí,¶ and Kauśiká** are the rivers††

it appears to have been a considerable river between the Go-matí and Ganges, in or near the territory of Ayodhyá, and having its source well up in the Himálayas. The only river which satisfies these conditions is the modern Ramgangá, which joins the Ganges on the left, near Kanauj; and this river therefore is probably the Báhudá.

* Or, better, *Drishad-vatí*; the famous river between the Saras-vatí and Jumna. It was the southern and eastern boundary of Brahmávarta (Manu ii. 17). For a full description, see Cunningham, Arch. Surv. Repts., II. 214, &c.; and XIV. 87-90, and plate xxvi. See also note under *Saras-vatí* in verse 16.

† Read *Vi-páśá*, for *Vi-pásá*. It is the modern R. Bias, in the Panjab, the Greek Hyphasis. It is now a tributary of the Sutlej, but was probably altogether separate in olden times, for the Sutlej then had an independent course considerably to the sonth-east.

‡ There are two Devikás, one in the Dekhan (Rámáy. Kishk. K. xli. 13), and this river (M-Bh., Bhíshma-P. ix. 324; Anuśás-P. xxv. 1696-7; and Vana-P. ccxxi. 14229). From the second of these passages it appears that the northern Deviká was near Kashmir, and it may probably be identified with the modern river *Deeg*, a tributary of the Ravi on its right bank. The *Deviká*, which is mentioned in Vana-P. lxxxii. 5044–9, seems to be a lake, and may be the same as *Deviká Sundariká hrada* in Anuśás.-P. xxv. 1707–8.

§ I do not find any river of this name mentioned elsewhere. The Váyu Puráṇa reads *Ikshu* (xlv. 96), and this occurs in the M-Bh. (Bhíshma-P. ix. 324); but I have found no data to identify it. Probably, however, we should read *Vakshu* or *Vankshu*, which is the Oxus.

|| This is not in the dictionary. The Váyu Puráṇa gives the same name (xlv. 96), and the Varáha reads *Nisvírá* (lxxxv); while other readings are *Niśc'itá*, *Nirvírá*, and *Mic'itá*. The *Niśc'itá* and two other rivers, the *Nic'itá* and *Nívárá*, are mentioned in the Bhíshma-Parva list (ix. 326, 328), and the *Nirvírá* in M-Bh., Vana-P. lxxxiv. 8116–9, but there appears to be nothing to identify them beyond that the Nirvírá is connected with the Kauśikí (see note ** below) in the last passage and its context.

¶ The R. Gandak, which flows into the Ganges on its north bank near Patna. It has shifted its course considerably; and formerly it flowed east of its present course, through the middle of the districts of Champaran, Muzaffarpur and Darbhanga.

** Or, generally, *Kauśikí*; the modern R. Kosi, which flows into the Ganges on its north bank, through the district of Purnea. It has shifted its course very remarkably. Formerly it flowed east of its present position.

†† Or, as the text may be read, "*and* the Apagá flow," &c. There is a river

which flow from the slopes of Hima-vat, O bráhman.

19 The Veda-smṛiti, * Veda-vatí, †
Vritra-ghní, ‡ and Sindhu, §

called the *Apagá* in Kuru-kshetra (M-Bh. Vana-P. lxxxiii, 6038–40; Cunningham's Arch. Surv. Repts., XIV. 88, and plate xxvi). The Kúrma Puráṇa reads *Lohiní c'eti* instead (xlvii. 28); and the Váyu (xlv. 96) and Varáha Puráṇas lxxxv) mention the *Lohita*. The *Lohita* is the Brahma-putra, which till last centnry flowed round the south side of the Garo Hills, and then southward through the districts of Maimansingh and Dacca. *Lohiní*, though fem., no doubt means the same. The Váyu Puráṇa reads *Kauśikí c'a tritíyá tu* instead (xlv. 96), which may mean the "third *Kauśikí*," for there seem to be three rivers of this name (see M-Bh., Vana-P. ccxxi. 14231); or may refer to a river *Tritíyá* which is mentioned in the M-Bh. (Sabhá-P. ix. 373); bnt I would suggest as preferable, *Kauśikí Karatoyá tu*, or *Kouśikí c'a tri-srotás tu*. The *Karatoyá* is the modern Kuratee in the Bogra District in North Bengal; and *Tri-srotas* or *Triḥ-srotasí* (see M-Bh., Sabhá—P., ix. 375) is, I believe, the ancient name of the modern Teesta, which is east of that; both now flow into the Brahmaputra; but the first formerly flowed into the delta, before the Ganges and Brahmaputra shifted their courses. (Cunningham, Arch. Surv. Repts., XV. 127 and 131, and plates i. and xxxiii. The Varáha Puráṇa adds the *C'akshush-matí* (lxxxv), an unknown name.

* Or *Veda-smṛitá*. Both names are mentioned in the M-Bh., the former in Annśás-P. clxv. 7651, and the latter in Bhíshma-P. ix. 324; and the *Veda-smṛiti* is also mentioned in the Bhágavata-P. (V. xix. 17); but I have found nothing to identify it.

† Or *Vedasiní*, or *Vetasiní*. I have not met with these two names elsewhere; the *Veda-vatí* is mentioned in the M-Bh., (Bhíshma-P. ix. 324; Annśás.-P. clxv. 7651), bnt there appears to be nothing to identify it.

‡ Or *Vrata-ghní*, as the Kúrma Puráṇa reads (xlvii. 28). I have not met with either name elsewhere, and the river is not known apparently.

§ This is most probably the modern *Kali Sindh*, a tributary of the R. Chambal, thongh it may also be the *Sindh*, which is a tribntary of the Jumna, between the Chambal and Betwa. The former is the more probable, because it is a large river and rises well np in the Páripátra range, and suits the following incident better. This Sindhn was a river of mnch note, and on it was a great tírtha, where Agastya met Lopá-mndrá, daughter of the King of Vidarbha, and she chose him for her husband (M-Bh., Vana-P. xcvi, xcvii; and cxxx. 10541). The name of this tírtha may have been *Sindhúttama*, (*id.* lxxxii, 4082–4095; and Annśás-P. clxv. 7650); but if so, it must be distinguished from the great tírtha *Sindhúttama*, which was on the Indus (Vana-P. lxxxii. 5021).

Veṇvá,* and Ánandiní † also, Sadá-nírá, ‡ and Mahí, §

* This name is not in the dictionary, but it occurs several times, and is a variation of *Veṇá*. There is a river of this name in the Dekhan (see verse 24, note to *Veṇyá*), and one in Western India (see verse 26, note to *Veṇyá*), but I have not met with any river of this name in North India. Both the Váyu (xlv. 97), and the Kúrma (xlvii. 29) Puráṇas read *Varṇáśá* instead; the Varáha reads *Parṇá* instead (lxxxv), and the Kúrma offers *Parṇá* and *Parṇáśá* in a note, (*loc. cit.*) The Varṇáśá or Parṇáśá is the modern *Banás*, and there are two rivers of this name; one a tributary of the Chambal, rising near Udaypur (Cunningham, Arch. Surv. Repts., VI., plate i.), and the other, a stream rising near Mt. Ábu and flowing into the Rann of Kachh; the former is the larger, and is probably the river meant in the text. Cunningham writes the name *Parṇáśá* (*id.* VI. 157) and *Parṇa-náśá* (*id.* XV. 132), but the latter form seems doubtful. Devávṛidha is said to have married one of these rivers (Hari V. xxxviii. 1999, and 2004–10), probably the second.

† Or, *Sánandiní*. The Váyu (xlv. 97) and Kúrma (xlvii. 29) Puráṇas read *C'andaná* instead, and the latter proposes *Bandhaná* and *Sábandhaná* in a note. The Varáha reads *C'andanábhá náśadác'árá* (lxxxv.) for this and the next river, but not very intelligibly. None of these names appear to be identified.

‡ The river "that is always filled with water." The inclusion of this name among the rivers that rise in the Páripátra Mountains is strange yet the Kúrma Puráṇa places it in the same group (xlvii. 29, note). I have met with no river Sadá-nírá except that in North India. A river Sadá-nírá-mayá is mentioned in Bhíshma-P ix. 340, but there is nothing to identify it. The Váyu Puráṇa reads *Satírá* and *Sadátírá* instead (xlv. 97), but I have not found these names elsewhere.

A few remarks may be offered about the *Sadá-nírá* in North India. Sáyana says it is the Karatoyá, the modern Kurattee (see verse 18, note††), but it is stated in the Sata-patha Bráhmaṇa (I. iv. 1), that the Sadá-nírá was the boundary between Kosala and Videha. It is therefore identified with the R. Gandak by Dr. Eggeling (*loc. cit.*, note) and Muir (Sansk. Texts, II. 419–422). But the old stream of the Gandak flowed through the districts of Champaran, Muzaffarpur and Darbhanga, *i. e.*, through the middle of the Videha country; and the Gaṇḍakí and Sadá-nírá are mentioned as distinct rivers in M–Bh., Sabhá-P xix., 794. The Sadá-nírá can hardly, therefore, be the same as the Gandak, and is more probably the modern *Rapti*, a tributary of the Sarayú, and the midway position of the Rapti eminently satisfies the position of a boundary.

§ The R. Mahí, which rises in Malwa and falls into the Bay of Cambay. The Váyu Puráṇa has a variant, *Mahatí* (xlv. 97), and the Varáha reads *Rohí*

20 Párá,* C'arman-vatí,† Núpí,‡ Vidiśá,§ and Vetra-vatí,‖ S'iprá,¶ and Avarṇí ** also are known †† as those connected with the Páripátra mountains.

21 The S'oṇa,‡‡ and Mahá-nada,§§

(lxxxv.); both seem incorrect. The *Mahitá* mentioned in M-Bh., Bhíshma-P. ix. 328, appears to be this river.

* Or Pará, according to the Váyu Puráṇa (xlv. 98). This is said to be the modern R. Parbatí, which rises in Bhopal and falls into the Chambal (Cunningham, Arch. Surv. Repts., II 308 and Rennell's Atlas of 1781).

† For *C'arman-vatí*, read *C'armaṇ-vatí.* The R. Chambal, the largest tributary of the Jumna.

‡ This is not in the dictionary. The Kúrma Puráṇa mentions the *Surá* and the *Súryá* (xlvii. 29), but I have found no other mention of them, and they do not appear to be known.

§ This must, no doubt, be connected with the town Vidiśá, which was on the R. Vetra-vatí (Megha D. i. 25) the modern R. Betwa (see next note). Vidiśá appears to be the modern town Bhilsa. The R. Vidiśá therefore was probably the small tributary which joins the Betwa on its left bank at Bhilsa.

‖ The modern R. Betwa, which rises near Bhopal and flows into the Jumna. There was another river of this name in Western India (Hari-V. clxviii, 9514–6). The Varáha Puráṇa reads *Veda-trayí* wrongly (lxxxv).

¶ This is the river on which *Ujjayiní*, the modern Ujjain, stands (Megha D. i. 31, 32). Another S'iprá is mentioned in verse 24.

** This is not in the dictionary, and I have not found it elsewhere. The Váyu Puráṇa reads *Avantí* instead (xlv. 98), which is preferable, and would be the river of the Avanti country (see notes to verses 52 and 55, below). The R. Avantí therefore is probably the river which rises near Mhow and flows into the Chambal. The Varáha Puráṇa reads *Vapantí* (lxxxv.) erroneously.

†† For *smatáḥ*, read *smṛitáḥ*.

‡‡ The R. Sone which rises near the source of the Narbada and flows into the Ganges above Patna. It was also called *Hiraṇya-báhu* and *Hiraṇya-váha;* the Greek Erannoboas. For changes in its course, see Cunning. Arch. Surv. Repts., VIII. 4–24.

§§ Or, *Mahá-nadí.* It flows through Orissa into the Bay of Bengal. The main stream is now considered to be the river which rises near Kanker, but that cannot be the source meant in the text, for it would belong to quite a different water-shed. The Mahá-nada here must designate the branch now called the Hasdu or Hestho, which rises near the source of the Sone. (Cunning., Arch. Surv. Repts., XVII. plate i.). The Varáha Puráṇa omits the Mahá-nadí altogether, and reads *Jyotí-rathá* instead (lxxxv). This river, which is also

Narmadá, * Su-rathá, † Adri-já, ‡ Mandákiní, §
and Daśárṇá, || and C'itra-kúṭá ¶ also,
22 C'itrotpalá, ** and Tamasá, †† Karamodá, ‡‡

called *Jyoti-rathyá* (M-Bh., Vana-P. lxxxv. 8150) and *Jyoti-rathá* (Hari-V. clxviii 9510–12) is said to be a tributary of the S'oṇa in the former passage, and is placed in the Dekhan in the latter. It is, therefore, probably the modern *Johila*, the southern of the two sources of the R. Sone.

* The modern Narbada or Nerbudda, which rises near the Sone and flows into the Gulf of Cambay.

† This is not in the dictionary, and I have not met the name elsewhere; it is a synonym of *Jyotí-rathá?* (See last page, note §§). The Kúrma Puráṇa mentions the *Su-rasá* (xlvii. 30), and so also the Varáha (lxxxv); instead of this and the next river the Váyu Puráṇa reads *Su-mahá-drumá* or, *Surahádrumá* (xlv. 99); but I have not met with any of these names elsewhere, except Su-rasá in the Bhágavata-P. (V. xix. 17)

‡ This is not in the dictionary, but is mentioned in M-Bh., Anuśás-P. clxv. 7648. I have found nothing to identify it.

§ The R. Mandakin, which flows near Mt. Chitrakut into the R. Paisuni, a tributary of the Jumna between the Ken and the Tons (Cunning., Arch. Surv. Repts., XXI. 11). Mr. Beglar's proposal to identify it with the R. Reur, a southern tributary of the Sone (*Ibid.* XIII. 42–54) depends upon his identification of Mt. C'itra-kúṭa with Ramgarh hill in Chhattisgarh, and is untenable (see Journal, R. A. S., April, 1894, page 240). The river Reur, or Rer, is also called Araud, and all these forms appear to point to *Eraṇḍá* as the original name.

|| The river of the country Daśárṇa, the modern R. Dasán, between the Betwa and the Ken.

¶ This is not in the dictionary. It is no doubt to be connected with Mt. C'itra-kúṭa, the modern Chitrakut (see Journal, R. A. S. April, 1894, page 239), and is probably the stream which flows round the south and east of the modern Mt. Chitrakut, past Karwi into the Jumna.

** This is not in the dictionary, but a *C'itropalá* is mentioned in M-Bh, Bhíshma-P. ix. 341. Cunningham says C'itrotpalá is the name of the modern main-stream of the Mahá-nadí below its junction with the Pairi (Arch. Surv. Repts., VII. 155, and XVII. 70); but that river as mentioned already (page 295, note §§) would belong to a different water-shed.

†† Or *Támasí*, as the Kúrma Puráṇa reads (xlvii. 30). It is the R. Tons which flows into the Ganges on the right bank below Allahabad.

‡‡ This is not in the dictionary, and I have not found the name elsewhere. The Váyu Puráṇa (xlv. 100) and the Varáha (lxxxv.) read *Karatoyá* instead. Should we read *Karma-nodá*, as a synonym of *Karma-náśá?* The river

Píśác'iká, * and Pippali-śroṇí † also, Vi-páśá, ‡
23 the river Vañjulá, § Sumerujá, || S'ukti-matí, ¶

meant is no doubt the modern Karamnasa, which flows into the Ganges on the right bank just above the Sone.

* I have not met with this river elsewhere. Piśác'a was a name given to various races, chiefly barbarous hill tribes (Muir, Sansk. Texts, II. 59). In this place it would, no doubt, mean the tribes inhabiting Rewah and Chuta Nagpore, and the Piśác'iká is probably one of the southern tributaries of the Sone, such as the Rer (see page 296, note §), or Kanhar.

† Or *Pipyalá śroṇí*, as the Váyu Puráṇa reads (xlv. 100); or *Pippalá*, as the Varáha reads (lxxxv). I have not found any data to identify it, but have seen the name assigned to the modern river *Paisuni* or *Parsaroni*, a tributary of the Jumna between the Ken and the Tons (Arch. Surv. Repts., XXI. 11), and these words may well be corruptions of *Pippali-śroṇí*.

‡ This appears to be the river mentioned in M.-Bh., Anuśás-P. xxv. 1733 and perhaps 1710-11 also. It is probably the modern Bias which flows past Saugor and joins the R. Ken, a tributary on the right bank of the Jumna. (Cunning., Arch. Surv. Repts., XXI. 157, and plate xxxiv). The Ken or Kiyán, an important stream, does not appear to be mentioned; it is said to be a corruption of *Karṇa-vatí* (*Ibid.* 156; and II. 446), though Lassen gives *Káyana* as its ancient form (Ind. Alt., Map). Was *Vi-páśá* the ancient name of this whole river? The Vi-páśá in the Panjab is mentioned in verse 18. The Varáha Puráṇa reads *Viśálá* (lxxxv), and the Kúrma mentions this name as a variant (xlvii. 31). There are several rivers of this name, and the river here meant is no doubt the *Saras-vatí Viśálá* at Gaya (M.-Bh., S'alya-P. xxxix. 2188–9, and 2205–6), probably the modern Lilajan which flows past Bodh Gaya.

§ I have not found this name elsewhere. The Varáha Puráṇa reads *Vañjuká* (lxxxv), the Kúrma *Mañjulá* (xlvii. 31), and the Váyu *Jambulá* (xlv. 100). Of these names I have met only with Mañjulá elsewhere (M.-Bh., Bhíshma-P. ix. 341), but with no data to identify it. The river meant is probably that on which Gaya stands; its eastern source is called the *Mohana*, its middle portion the *Phalgu*, and the eastern branch, into which it divides, the *Jumna*.

|| The Váyu Puráṇa reads *Siterajá* (xlv. 101), and the Varáha *Vírajá* (lxxxv). I have not met with any of these names elsewhere, but the M.-Bh. mentions three rivers *Vírá* (Bhíshma-P., ix. 329), *Víra-vatí* (*ibid.*, 332) and *Vírankará* (*ibid.*, 333), which are all distinct. The Matsya Puráṇa reads two names instead, the *S'uní* and *Lajjá* (cxiii. 26), probably erroneous.

¶ This river has been much written about but does not seem to be identified safely yet. See p. 285, note ‡; and also Cunning., Arch. Surv. Repts.,

S'akulí,* Tridivá in regular order,† Vega-váhiní ‡ also § flow from the slopes of the Vindhya || Mountains.

IX. 55. It is mentioned in the Hari-Vaṁśa (clxviii. 9509–13) and is said there to be in the Dekhan; it seems to be meant by the name *Mukti-matí* in M.-Bh., Bhíshma-P. ix. 342; and perhaps it is referred to in Hari-V. xxxvii. 1980–7. These passages, however, may allude to two rivers of this name. It was the river on which stood S'ukti-matí, the capital of C'edi; see note to C'edi in canto lviii, verse 16.

* The Váyu Puráṇa reads *Makruṇá* or *Makshaṇá* (xlv. 101), and the Varáha *Pankiní* (lxxxv), but I have not met with any of these names elsewhere. The S'akulí, however, may probably be identified with the R. Sakri, which flows into the Ganges on the south, about half-way between Patna and Monghyr (Cunning., Arch. Surv. Repts., VIII. plate i; and XV. plate iv). There is also another Sakri which is a tributary of the R. Seonath, a tributary of the Mahánadí (*id.* XVII. plate i), but that rises rather in the Ṛiksha Mts. The Bhíshma-P. list mentions a river called *Makarí* (ix. 331); and the Matsya Puráṇa reads *Mukuṭá* instead (cxiii. 26).

† The text *Tridivá-kramu* seems wrong, and I have adopted the reading of the Váyu Puráṇa *Tridivá kramát*, which is preferable. The word *kramát*, if right, would indicate that the rivers are mentioned in regular order from west to east. The Tridivá is also mentioned in the M.-Bh., (Bhíshma-P. ix. 324; and Anuśás.-P. clxv. 7654), but no data are given to identify it. It may be noticed there is a river called the *Krumu* (Ṛig.-V., X. 75.6), which is probably the modern R. Kuram, a tributary of the Indus, south of the Kabul R. (Muir's Sanskr. Texts, II. 357); but it cannot be intended here. Another Tridivá is mentioned in verse 28.

‡ This is not in the dictionary, but it occurs in M.-Bh., Sabhá-P. ix. 371. The Váyu (xlv. 100) and Varáha (lxxxv) and Kúrma Puráṇas (xlvii. 31) read *Bálu-váhiní* instead, and the last gives *Ratna-váhiní* as a variant. I have not met with either of these names elsewhere.

§ The Varáha Puráṇa adds another river *Rátrí* (lxxxv), but I have not met with it elsewhere.

|| The text reads *Skandha*, which is clearly wrong. The Váyu (xlv. 101) Kúrma (xlvii. 31) and Varáha Puráṇas (lxxxv) read *Ṛiksha*. There is certainly some confusion in this group of rivers, for the Mandákiní, Daśárṇá, and Tamasá rise in the Vindhya watershed, while the S'oṇa, Mahá-nada, and Narmadá rise rather in the Ṛiksha Mts; but the rivers mentioned in verse 24 rise in the Ṛiksha Mts, so that the proper reading here should no doubt be *Vindhya*. The Agni Puráṇa says the Narmadá rises in the Vindhya Mts. (cxviii. 7); so that perhaps this river and also the Sone and the Hasdu branch of the Mahánadi, which all rise close together near Amara-kaṇṭaka,

24 The S'iprá,* Payoshṇí,† Nir-bindhyá,‡ Tápí,§ and

may have been considered to belong to the Vindhya watershed. There seems to have been some vagueness in this matter, for the Utkalas and (Dakshiṇa) Kosalas are classed among the races who inhabited the Vindhya Mts. in verses 53 and 54.

* One S'iprá has been mentioned already in verse 20, and the Hari-Vaṁśa says there is a S'iprá in the southern region (clxviii. 9509). The Váyu Puráṇa reads *Madrá* instead (xlv. 102); and the Kúrma (xlvii. 32) and Varáha (lxxxv) *S'ighrodá*. I have not found either of these names elsewhere, but a river *S'ighrá* is mentioned (M.-Bh., Bhíshma-P. ix. 336) and another called *S'ivá* (*ibid.*, 332). The Matsya Puráṇa reads *Kshiprá* (cxiii. 27).

† The Payoshṇí was in the southern region (M.-Bh., Vana-P. lxxxviii. 8329–35); it was the river of Vidarbha (*ibid.* cxx. 10289-90), and was separated from the Narmadá by the Vaidúrya Mts. (*ibid.* cxxi. 10306-7). It was the modern river Purna (the tributary of the Tapti) together with the lower part of the Tapti into which the Purna continues. A careful consideration of King Nala's remarks (*ibid.* lxi. 2317–9) with a map will show that the view described could only have been obtained from a position on the Satpura Mts. about longitude 75°; hence the Payoshṇí visible from there could be only the lower part of the Tapti. Such was considered the main stream in old times, and it was a famous and sacred river. Gen. Cunningham's proposal to identify the Payoshṇí with the Pahoj, a tributary of the Jumna between the Sindh and Betwa, (Arch. Surv. Reports, VII. plate xxii.) is untenable as regards this famous river; but there were two rivers of this name (M.-Bh., Bhíshma-P. ix. 324 and 327), and the Pahoj may be the other Payoshṇí. The Varáha Puráṇa reads *Payollí* (lxxxv), which seems a mistake.

‡ Or *Nir-vindhyá*; or according to the Váyu Puráṇa, *Nir-bandhyá* (xlv. 102). One river Nir-vindhyá is mentioned in the Megha-D. (I. 28 and 29, commentary) as lying between the R. Vetra-vatí (or Betwa) and Ujjayiní (Ujjain), and (if the Párá is rightly identified with the modern Parbati, see note to verse 20) must be the modern Parwan which is west of the Parbati; but that river rises in the Vindhya Range according to the Megha-Dúta, and belongs to the Páripátra watershed according to verses 19 and 20 above; on either view it is out of place here. There was, however, another large river of this name in the Dekhan, for it is mentioned along with the Payoshṇí, the Tápí and the Godávarí and its tributaries in the Bhágavata-Puráṇa (V. xix. 17), and judged by its position there, it may be the Pen-ganga a tributary of the Warda.

§ See note to Payoshṇí above. This is the upper part of the modern Tapti before it joins the Purna. This branch was hardly known in early times; it does not appear to be named in the Mahá-Bhárata or Rámáyaṇa, nor

Nishadhá-vatí,* Veṇyá,† and Vaitaraṇí,‡ Siníbálí, § Kumud-

is it mentioned in the copious list in the Bhíshma-P. (ix). The reason was, no doubt, it was hidden amid hills and forests.

* Or *Nishadhá*, as the Váyu Puráṇa reads (xlv. 102). I have not met with this name elsewhere, but it naturally suggests a connexion with Nishadha, the realm of Nala. As regards Nishadha, see the note to verse 54 below. This river then may be one of the small tributaries of the Narmadá or Tapti, which rise in the middle part of the Satpura Range. The Kúrma Puráṇa reads *Mahánadí* instead (xlvii. 32), which may mean the Mahánadí in Chhattisgarh and Orissa, but is unsatisfactory, as it has mentioned that river before (*ibid.*, 30). The Matsya Puráṇa reads *Ṛishabhá* instead (cxiii. 27), which I have not met elsewhere.

† This form is not in the dictionary. The Váyu Puráṇa reads *Veṇvá* (xlv. 102); the Kúrma reads *Vinná* and gives *Veṇyá* and *C'intá* as variants (xlvii. 32). *C'intá* is no doubt an error. The other names are merely different forms of the same word. The river is called *Veṇvá* in the Hari-V. (clxviii. 9509–10) and also in the M.-Bh. (Sabhá-P. xxx. 1118), but in the latter poem it is generally called *Veṇá*, and this seems the proper term (Bhíshma-P. ix. 335; Anuśás-P. clxv. 7648; Vana-P. lxxxviii. 8328, clxxxix. 12909, and lxxxv. 8176–7; whether the same river is also meant in line 8175 is not clear). From the passage last cited it appears the *Veṇá* is the river which joins the Godávarí and Varadá (the modern Warda), that is, the modern Wain-ganga and its continuation the Pranhita. The Varáha Puráṇa reads *Veshṇápáśá* (lxxxv) which seems a mistake. This river appears to be also called *Su-veṇá* (M.-Bh., Vana-P. clxxxix. 12909) in contra-distinction to the *Kṛishṇa-veṇá* (*ibid.*; and also *id.* Vana-P. lxxxv. 8180-1; Bhíshma-P. ix. 335, and Anuśás.-P. clxv. 7648; and Hari-V. clxviii. 9509–11) which appears from the second passage to be a tributary of the Veṇá, and which I have proposed to identify with the western tributary rising near Deoghar and Seoni (Journal, R. A. S., 1894, p. 244). Another river of this name is mentioned in verse 26, and a *Veṇvá* in verse 19.

‡ This is no doubt the modern Bytarni, which flows through the north of Orissa; and if it is rightly classed here, the Ṛiksha Range must include the hills which stretch along the south of Chuta Nagpore.

§ The Váyu Puráṇa reads *S'itibáhu* (xlv. 102), the Kúrma *Baláká* (xlvii. 32) and the Varáha *Vedipálá* (lxxxv). None of these rivers are mentioned in the dictionary, but the name *S'inibáhu* is given. I have not found any of these names elsewhere, except *Baláká* in M.-Bh., Anuśás.-P. xxv. 1706–7, which may be a river, but appears from the context to be in Northern India. Perhaps the reading should be *S'ilávatí* or *S'ilāvatí*, which seems to have been the ancient name of the modern river Selye; this after uniting with the Rúp-

25 vatí,* Karatoyá,† Mahá-gaurí,‡ and Durgá,§ and Antaḥ-śirá ; ||

narain is the river on which Tamluk, the ancient *Támra-liptaka* (see verse 44 below), is situated; and which may well find mention here. Perhaps the name *Balákà* may be connected with the modern river Barákar, a tributary of the Damudá; these two combined form the largest river in Western Bengal, and flow close to Tamlnk. Tamluk was a famous port, and it would be strange if the rivers near it were overlooked. The M.-Bh. mentions a river *Śata-balá* (Bhíshma-P. ix. 328). The Matsya Puráṇa reads *Viśva-málá* instead (cxiii. 37). I have not met either name elsewhere.

* I have not met with this name elsewhere. It may be the Subarna-rekha or one of the small rivers in the north of Orissa; or may we conjecture *Damud-vatí*, and identify it with the R. *Damudá* in West Bengal? See the last note.

† One river of this name in North Bengal has been mentioned in verse 18 note††; and there was another of the same name in the north of India (M.-Bh, Anuśás.-P. xxv. 1699); neither can be meant here. I have not found any *Karatoyá* elsewhere, which rises in the Ṛiksha range. The Váyu Puraṇá reads *Toyá* instead (xlv. 103), and so also the Varáha (lxxxv); but I have not found this name elsewhere. Perhaps the reading should be *Karabhác'a. Karabhá* or *Kapiśá* is the name of a river on the confines of Utkala and Kalinga (Raghu-V. iv. 38, commentary), but no details are given to identify it. The name *Kapiśá* suggests identification with the modern Cossye or *Kansai* (the chief river in the Midnapur district) which is said to be modified from *Kaṁsavatí*, but may well be a corruption of *Kapiśá-vatí.*

‡ This is also mentioned in M.-Bh., Bhíshma-P. ix. 341. It is no doubt a synonym of *Brahmáṇí* and *Bráhmaṇí*, all being names of Durgá; it would then be the modern R. Brahmaṇi in Orissa.

§ There are two rivers of this name mentioned in the Bhíshma-P. list (ix. 337 and 341) in the M.-Bh., and the second is that intended here, as it is placed with the *Mahá-gaurí;* but I have not met with the name elsewhere. It may be a synonym of the small river Bráhmaṇi which flows through the Moorshedabad district into the right bank of the Bhágírathí branch of the Ganges.

|| This is not in the dictionary. The Váyu (xlv. 103) and Kúrma (xlvii. 33) Puráṇas read *Antaḥ-śilá.* The Varáha reads *Antyágirá* (lxxxv), which is no doubt an intended synonym. I have not met with any of these names elsewhere, but *Antra-śilá* is mentioned (M.-Bh., Bhíshma-P. ix. 337). *Antaḥ-śilá* seems to be the correct form; and if the name is descriptive, the river is probably one of the northern tributaries of the Mahánadi; all of which are encompassed with hills. See however a people called *Antar-giryas* in verse 24 below.

those rivers* flow from the slopes of the Ṛiksha† Mountains, have holy waters and are bright.

26 The Godávarí,‡ Bhíma-rathá,§ Kṛishṇá,|| and another¶

* The Varáha Puráṇa mentions also *Maṇijálá S'ubhá* (lxxxv); I have not found the former name elsewhere; but the *S'ubhá* is mentioned in the Hari-Vaṁśa (clxviii. 9509–10), and a river *Maningá* is mentioned in the Bhíshma-P. list (ix. 342). There are no data to identify them, except that the passage in the Hari-Vaṁśa places the S'ubhá in the Dekhan.

† The text reads *Bindhya* or *Vindhya*, and yet makes the next group of rivers also rise in the same range. The Váyu (xlv. 103) and Kúrma (xlvii 33) and Varáha (lxxxv) Puráṇas read the same; but the proper reading must be *Ṛiksha* as the Vishṇu Puráṇa says (Bk. II. Chap. iii), for the Tápí, Veṇyá and Vaitaraṇí certainly do not rise in the former mountains but in the latter. The Agni Puráṇa wrongly groups the Tápí and Payoshṇí with the Godavari and other rivers as rising in the Sahya Mts.

‡ The modern Godaverí. This river was famous from the earliest times. Jana-sthána, the scene of Ráma's first conflict with the Rákshasas was the country on both its banks between its tributaries the Manjira and Pranhita (see Journal, R A. S , 1894, p. 247).

§ Or *Bhíma-rathí* as the Váyu (xlv. 104) and Varáha (lxxxv) Puráṇas read: *Bhíma-rakshí* which the Kúrma gives (xlvii. 34) seems incorrect. The former is the name as given in the M.-Bh. (Vana-P. lxxxviii. 8328; Bhíshma-P. ix. 327; and Anuśás.-P. clxv. 7653). This is the modern Bhima, the tributary of the Krishṇá, rising near Poona. The Varáha Puráṇa adds immediately *Marathí* (lxxxv); is it a mistaken repetition of the last three syllables of the preceding river? I have found no such river.

|| The modern Kistna. This river received very little notice in ancient times, and was almost unknown compared with the Godávarí and Káverí. Besides its inclusion in the Bhíshma-P. list (ix. 340), it is doubtful if it is so mentioned in the M.-Bh., or Rámáyaṇa. It is omitted from the lengthy account of Sahadeva's conquests in the south (Sabhá-P. xxx), and the detailed pilgrimage itineraries (Vana-P., Tírtha-yátrá-P.) and other geographical discourses. It does not occur in the story of Raghu's conquests even in the late poem, the Raghu-Vaṁśa. The reason seems to be that the country through which it flows was nearly all forest in ancient times.

¶ For *tathápará* of the text the Váyu Puráṇa reads *c'a vañjulá* (xlv. 104) and the Kúrma *c'a vaśyatá* or *c'a vatsarí* (xlvii. 34). I have not found these names elsewhere. Perhaps we should read some name like *Mañjirá*, as the large southern tributary of the Godávarí is now called, though its earliest name was apparently *Mandákiní* (Rámáy., Yuddha K. cx. 38, 39; Journal, R. A. S., 1894, p. 250).

Veṇyá,* Tunga-bhadrá,† Suprayogá,‡ Váhyá,§ and the
27 river Káverí; || these noble rivers¶ issue from the slopes
of the Sahya** Mountains.

The Kṛita-málá,†† Támra-parṇí,‡‡ Pushpa-

* This form is not in the dictionary. The Varáha Puráṇa reads *Veṇá* lxxxv); the Kúrma *Veṇá* or *Varṇá* (xlvii. 34); and the Váyu *Vaiṇí* (xlv. 104)—all mere variations, the proper name no doubt being *Veṇá*. This is the third river of this name mentioned here, see verses 19 and 24. It is probably the same as the *Víṇá* in the Bhíshma-P. list (ix. 328), and the *Veṇṇá* in the Bhágavata Puráṇa (V. xix. 17). Is it to be identified with the R. Penner which is between the Kistna and Kaveri; though the Sanskrit name of the Penner is said to be Pinákí (Arch. Surv. of S. India, by R. Sewell, I. 123 and 129)?

† The modern Tumbhudra, the large southern tributary of the Kistna, consisting of the combined streams of the Tunga and Bhadra.

‡ This is not in the dictionary, but it is also mentioned in the Bhíshma-P. list (ix. 328) and in the Vana-P. (ccxxi. 14232), and was a large and known river. Though not apparently identified, it is probably one of the large western tributaries of the Kistna.

§ This is not in the dictionary, but the Varáha Purána agrees (lxxxv) and the Matsya (cxiii. 29). I have not found the name elsewhere and it does not appear to be identified. The Agni P. reads *Váradá* (cix. 22), the large southern tributary of the Kistna called Varada or Vedavati.

|| The modern Cavery or Coleroon in south India. It was better known than the Kistna in ancient times. It is mentioned in the M.-Bh., (Vana-P. lxxxv. 8164–5; clxxxix. 12910; and Bhíshma-P. ix. 328) and Rámáy. (Kishk. K. xli. 21 and 25). King Jahnu is said in the Hari-Vaṁśa to have married this river, and made the Ganges his daughter (xxvii. 1416–22; and xxxii. 1757–61).

¶ The Matsya (cxiii. 29) and Varáha (lxxxv) Puráṇas add the *Vañjulá*; as to which see verse 26 note ¶.

** The text reads *Bindhya* or *Vindhya* here, after having read it already in verse 25; and offers *Sahya* a as variant in a note. The latter is manifestly the proper reading, and agrees with the Kúrma (xlvii. 34) and Váyu (xlv. 104) Puráṇas.

†† This is not in the dictionary. The Agni Puráṇa agrees with it (cxviii. 8); the Kúrma reads *Ṛitu-málá* (xlvii. 35), the Varáha *S'ata-málá* (lxxxv), and the Bhágavata *Kata-málá* (V. xix. 17). Is it to be identified with the Vedamali which flows out north of Cochin? The people of *Kac'c'ha* or Cochin are mentioned in canto lviii. verse 28.

‡‡ This is mentioned as a place of pilgrimage in the M.-Bh. (Vana-P.

28 já,* Sútpalá-vatí;† these are rivers‡ which rise in the Malaya Mountains, and have cool water.

And the Pitṛi-somá, § and Ṛishi-kulyá, || Ikshuká, ¶ and

lxxxviii. 8340), and the Raghu-V. says (iv. 49 and 50), that the vanquished Páṇḍya kings gave Raghu the choicest pearls from the sea at the month of the R. Támra-parṇí, where (the commentator adds, it is well-known) pearls were produced. This river then was in the Páṇḍya country and flowed into the G. of Manaar. It is the modern *Chittar*, the river of Tinnevelly (Arch. Surv. of S. India, by R. Sewell, I. 303).

* The Váyu Puráṇa reads *Pushpa-játi* (xlv. 105), the Kúrma *Pushpa-vatí* (xlvii. 35), and the Varáha *Pushpá-vatí* (lxxxv). I do not find any of these names elsewhere. A tírtha *Pushpa-vatí* is mentioned (M.-Bh., Vana-P. lxxxv. 8154–5), but it was situated between Dakshiṇa Kosala (Chhattisgaṛh) and C'ampá (Bhagalpur). A river *Pushpa-veṇí* is mentioned (*id.*, Bhíshma-P. ix. 342), which is joined with a river *Utpalá-vatí* and therefore is probably the same as the river in the text. A *Pushpa-váhiní* is mentioned as situated in the south in the Hari-Vaṁśa (clxviii. 9510–2).

† This is the same as the *Utpalá-vatí* mentioned in the last note (M.-Bh. Bhíshma-P. ix. 342) and the *Utpalá* (Hari-V., clxviii. 9510-2); and the Váyu (xlv. 105) and Kúrma (xlvii. 35), Matsya (cxiii. 30) and Varáha (lxxxv) Puráṇas read *Utpalá-vatí.*

‡ There are only six noteworthy rivers rising in the Malaya Mts., *viz.*, the Vaigai, Vaippar and Chittar on the east, the Amaravati (a tributary of the Kaveri) on the north, and the Ponani and Peri or Veda-mali on the west. The Chittar is the Támra-parṇí, hence the three others named in the text must be found among the five remaining modern rivers.

§ Not in the dictionary. The Váyu Puráṇa reads *Tri-sámá* (xlv. 106), and the Agni P. also (cxviii. 8); while the Varáha reads *Tri-yámá* (lxxxv). I have met only with the Tri-sámá elsewhere (Bhágavata Puráṇa, V. xix. 17). It is probably one of the small rivers on the Eastern coast, for the interior behind these mountains was not well known. The Matsya Puráṇa reads *Tri-bhágá* (cxiii. 31) which I have not met elsewhere.

|| This is the river on which Ganjam stands, and it bears the same name still. It is mentioned in the Bhíshma-P. list (ix. 343). The Váyu Puráṇa reads *Ṛitu-kulyá* (xlv. 106), by mistake. Another *Ṛishi-kulyá* is mentioned in verse 29.

¶ This is not in the dictionary. The Váyu (xlv. 106) and Varáha Puráṇas (lxxxv) read *Ikshulá*; and *Ikshudá* which the Matsya Puráṇa reads (cxiii. 31) is a variant. I have not found any of these names elsewhere, but the R. *Ikshu* is mentioned (M.-Bh., Bhíshma-P. ix. 324). It is probably one of the small streams on the Eastern coast.

29 Tridivá,* Lángúliní,† and Vaṁśa-kará‡ are known to spring from the Mahendra § Mountains.

The Ṛishi-kulyá,|| and Kumárí,¶ Manda-gá,** Manda-

* This is the second *Tridivá*, see verse 23; but I have not found two rivers of this name mentioned anywhere else. Instead of *Tridivá c'a yá* as in the text, the Matsya Puráṇa reads *Tridivác'alá* (cxiii. 31).

† This is the modern *Languliya*, on which Chicacole stands, between Vizianagram and Calingapatam. The Varáha Puráṇa reads *Múliní* or *Lámúliní* (lxxxv) and the Matsya *Múlí* (cxiii. 31); I have not found these names elsewhere and they seem incorrect. The *Lángalí* mentioned in the M.-Bh. (Sabhá-P. ix 374), is probably this river.

‡ The Varáha Puráṇa reads *Vaṁśa-vará* (lxxxv), and the Váyu *Vaṁśa-dhará* (xlv. 106); the latter is the correct name. It is the modern *Bans-dhará*, the river on which Calingapatam stands.

§ The Kúrma Puráṇa omits this group of rivers altogether, and puts three of them *Tri-sámá*, *Ṛishíká* and *Vaṁśa-dháriṇí* into the next group (xlvii. 36). The Matsya Puráṇa mentions three more rivers, the *Támra-parṇí*, *S'aravá* and *Vimalá* (cxiii. 31), but all these seem doubtful. A Támrá-parṇí has been mentioned in verse 28. A *S'arávatí* is named in the Bhíshma-P. list (ix. 327), and a *Vimalá* or *Vimalodá* in various passages (*e. g.* S'alya-P. xxxix. 2214–5; Hari-V., clxviii. 9517–8); but they are in Northern and Western India.

In note †† on page 284, the Mahendra mountains are said to be "the portion of the Eastern Ghats between the Godavari and Mahanadi rivers and the hills in the south of Berar," but this proposition must be modified on a full consideration of all the foregoing identifications. Gondwana as used by Wilson was applied to a very wide tract in Central India. The Mahendra Mts. cannot extend as far west as Berar nor beyond the Wain-ganga; and must be limited to the hills between the Mahanadi, Godavari and Wain-ganga, and may perhaps comprise only the portion of the Eastern Ghats north of the Godavari. It is in this last tract only that the name has survived. See Raghu Vaṁśa, iv. 43.

|| This is the second Ṛishi-kulyá, see verse 28. The Váyu Puráṇa reads *Ṛishíká* (xlv. 107), and the Varáha *Ṛishiká* (lxxxv), and the Matsya *Káśiká* (cxiii. 32). I have not met with these names elsewhere.

¶ The Váyu Puráṇa reads *Su-kumárí* (xlv. 107), and the Varáha *Lúsatí* I have not found these names elsewhere, but the Kumárí is mentioned in the Bhíshma-P list (ix. 343).

** This is mentioned in the Bhíshma-P. list (ix. 340). The Varáha Puráṇa reads *Manda-gáminí* (lxxxv); and for this and the next river the Kúrma reads *Gandha-mádana-gáminí* (xlvii. 36), which is probably erroneous.

30 váhiní,* Kṛipá,† and Paláśiní ‡ are known to spring in the
S'ukti-mat § Mountains.

All the rivers || possess holy merit; all are rivers flowing
31 into the ocean; all are mothers of the world; ¶ they are
well-known to cleanse from all sin.

* This is mentioned in the Bhíshma-P. list (ix. 340), but hardly in the same connexion.

† The Váyu Puráṇa reads *Kúpá* (xlv. 107), and the Kúrma *Kshiprá* or *Rúpá* (xlvii. 36). I do not find any of these names elsewhere. A river *Kṛityá* is mentioned in the Bhíshma-P. list (ix. 326), but that appears from its context to be in north India.

‡ This is mentioned in the Bhíshma-P. list (ix. 330), but in so different a connexion that the references appear to be to two separate rivers. The Matsya Puráṇa reads *Páśiní* (cxiii. 32), which however I have not met elsewhere.

§ These Mts. are but very rarely mentioned, and in page 285 note ‡ I have noticed what has been written about them. They were in the Eastern region, for Bhíma in his conquests in that quarter marched from Hima-vat towards Bhalláṭa and conquered the S'ukti-mat Mountain (M-Bh., Sabhá-P. xxix. 1079). Though Bhalláṭa does not appear to have been identified, the only noteworthy hills in the east which have not been assigned to the other great ranges are the Garo, Khási and Tipperah Hills which bound Bengal in that direction. Can these be the S'ukti-mat Mts.? There seems to be no improbability in this, for the river Lohita or Brahma-putra and the country Káma-rúpa, which is in the Assam Valley, were known. If this identification is satisfactory, the R. *Kumárí* may be the modern *Someśwarí* which flows southward between the Garo and Khasi Hills (both being names of Durgá); and the *Kṛipá* may perhaps be the *Kapili* which flows into the Brahma-putra a little above Gauhaṭi, the ancient Káma-rúpa; the other streams are not recognizable.

|| Saras-vatyaḥ. Or should this mean only the rivers called *Saras-vatí*? There were seven rivers specially distinguished by this name (M.-Bh, S'alya-P. xxxix. 2188-9), namely, 1. the *Su-prabhá* among the Pushkaras (*ibid.* 2198-2200), that is, near Ajmir; 2. the *Káñc'anákshí* in Naimisha forest (*ibid.* 2201-4), which was on the Go-matí; 3. the *Viśálá* at Gaya (*ibid.* 2205-6); 4. the *Mano-ramá*, the swift stream flowing from Himavat in the north part of Kosala (*ibid.* 2207-10); 5. the *Ogha-vatí*, which seems to be in Kuru-kshetra (*ibid.* 2212-3); 6. the *Su-reṇu*, which seems to be in Kuru-kshetra or near Gangá-dvára (*ibid.* 2211-4); and 7. the *Vimalodá* or *Vimalodaká* at Haimanta-giri (*ibid* 2214-5).

¶ Viśvasya mátaraḥ; compare M-Bh., Bhíshma-P. ix. 344.

And others, small streams, are mentioned in thousands,
32 O bráhman, those which flow only during the rainy season, and
those which flow at all seasons.

The Matsyas,* and Aśvakúṭas,† and Kulyas,‡

* The people and their country both went by the name *Matsya*. This country was part of the region called Brahmarshi (Manu ii. 19). It was south or south-west of Indra-prastha, the modern Delhi (M-Bh., Sabhá P., xxx. 1105-6; the mention in *ibid.* xxix. 1083 may be a mistake; but the Matsyas are named twice in the Bhíshma-P. list, ix. 347 and 348, unless one name be a mistake for Vatsa); and it was west of S'úrasena, which was the country round Mathurá, the modern Muttra (Viraṭa-P., v. 141-5; see note in canto lviii. verse 7): hence Matsya comprised the modern Alwar State and the land around that. It appears to have extended up to Kuru-kshetra, because no other country which could intervene is mentioned in Manu ii. 19. Its capital was Upaplavya or Upaplava (S'alya-P., xxxvi. 1973-6) which was 1½ or 2 days' journey by chariot from Hástinapura (Udyoga-P., lxxxiii. 3010-17; lxxxv. 3040; and lxxxviii. 3101). Cunningham says *Matsya* was the country west of Agra and north of the R. Chambal, *i. e.*, the whole of Alwar with portions of Jaypur and Bharatpur; and its capital was Vairáṭa, the modern Bairat (Arch. Surv. Repts., II. 242; and XX. 2, and plate i).

The Váyu Puráṇa reads *Vatsas* instead (xlv. 110). *Vatsa* or *Vátsya* was in the region east of Delhi (Sabhá-P., xxix. 1084), and king Vatsa who is said to have given his name to the country was grandson of Divodása, king of Benares (Hari-V., xxix. 1587, 1597; and xxxii. 1753). *Kauśámbí* was the capital, and it has been identified by Cunningham with the modern Kosam which is on the north bank of the Jumna about 31 miles above Allahabad. Hence the country was also called *Kauśámba* (Arch. Surv. Repts., I. 301-310). Vatsa or Kauśámba therefore comprised the lower part of the Ganges and Jumna Doab and also probably the tract south of that, on the other side of the Jumna.

† The Váyu Puráṇa reads *Kisashṇas*, *Kisashṭas* or *Kisadyas* instead (xlv. 110); but none of these names are in the dictionary. The Matsya reads *Kirátas* (cxiii. 35) but they are out of place here. The text reads *Matsyáśvakúṭáḥ kulyáśc'a*, but I would suggest instead *Matsyáś c'a Kanyákubjáś c'a*, thus reading *Kanyá-kubjas* or *Kánya-kubjas* instead of *Aśvakútas and Kulyas.* Kanyá-kubja or Kánya-kubja is the modern Kanauj, on the Ganges about 50 miles above Cawnpore; it was a famous city all through Indian history. People called *Sukuṭyas* are mentioned (Bhíshma-P. ix. 347), *Aśvakas* (*ibid.* 351), and *Aśvátakas* (*ibid.* li. 2105).

‡ This is not in the dictionary as a people; the word occurs in Vana-P., (cxxv. 10408), but does not appear to mean a people there. See the last note.

33 the Kuntalas,* the people of Káśi,† and the Kośalas,‡
and the Atharvas, and Arka-lingas,§ and the Maḷakas,‖

* This country is said by Muir to be one of the Piśác'a countries (Sansk. Texts, II. 59), but there were three people of this name, one in the Dekhan (Bhíshma-P., ix. 367), who are mentioned in verse 48 below; and two others elsewhere (*ibid.* 347 and 359). Those mentioned in verse 347 are the people meant here, for they are grouped with the people of Káśi and Kosala; and they probably occupied the country near Chunár (south of Benares), which Cunningham calls Kuntila (Arch. Surv. Repts., XI. 123). The third people were probably in the West.

† Benares, the ancient *Váráṇasí.* It was the capital of an ancient and famous kingdom. According to the Rámáyaṇa Káśi was a kingdom (Ádi-K., xii. 20) while Prayága and the country all around it was still forest (Journal, R. A. S., 1894, pp. 237-239). Its sacred character dates from comparatively late times, for it was one of the exploits for which Kṛishṇa was extolled that he burnt it for a succession of years and devastated it (Udyoga-P., xlvii. 1883; and Hari-V., clxi. 9142-3). For some vicissitudes in its early history, see Hari-V., xxix. and xxxii.

‡ Kośala, Kosala or Uttara Kosala, with its capital Ayodhyá, is the modern Oudh. Gen. Cunningham says it meant more particularly the country north and east of the R. Rapti (Arch. Surv. Repts., I. 327; and XVII. 68); but it seems rather to have denoted the country stretching from the Rapti on the east (see page 294 note ‡) to the confines of the Kuru and Páñc'ála kingdoms on the west. Northward it was bounded by the tribes that inhabited the slopes of the Himalayas, and southward by the kingdom of Benares. It was distinguished from another Kosala, which was called Dakshiṇa or Mahá Kosala and which is mentioned in verse 54.

§ These two names are not in the dictionary, and I have not found them elsewhere; they seem to be mistakes. The Váyu Puráṇa reads instead of them *atha párśve tilangáś c'a* (xlv. 111); but this is doubtful and unsatisfactory, for the Tilangas are mentioned as a southern people in canto lviii. verse 28. The Matsya reads *and Ávantas and Kalingas* (cxiii. 36), but these are hardly satisfactory; the former are mentioned in verses 52 and 55, and the latter in verses 37 and 46 below. Perhaps Arka-lingas may be meant as a synonym of Súrya-vaṁśas, the Solar Race, yet this again is hardly satisfactory, for that race reigned in Kosala, which has just been mentioned separately. There is a low group of Bráhmans in Behar called Atharvas (Risley's Tribes and Castes of Bengal, I. 26).

‖ This is not in the dictionary and seems erroneous. The Váyu Puraṇa reads *Magadhas* instead (xlv. 111), the people of Magadha or South Behar, but this is unsatisfactory for the Magadhas are mentioned in verse 44. The

and Vṛikas *; these † are well known generally as the peoples who inhabit the Central Region.‡

Matsya reads *Múkas* (cxiii. 36), which I have not met elsewhere. The reading should be *Malajas* probably. They are mentioned in the M-Bh. (Bhíshma-P. ix. 357), aud Rámáyaṇa (A'di-K. xxvii. 16–23), and from the course described in the latter poem as taken by Viśvá-mitra and Ráma it appears they were neighbours of the Karúshas, (see note to verse 53), and occupied the district of Sháhábád, west of the Sone, for Viśvá-mitra and Ráma crossing from the Sarayú to the south of the Ganges entered that district, which had been inhabited by the Malajas (*ibid.*, 8-16.)

* The Vṛikas are named in Bhíshma-P., li. 2106, and a king Vṛika is alluded to in the Hari-Vaṁśa (xiii. 760-61); but there is nothing to identify them. The Matsya Puráṇa reads *Andhakas* (cxiii. 36). The Andhakas were a subordinate family of the Yádava race, and are often mentioned in the M.-Bh. (*e.g.* Udyoga-P. lxxxv. 304), and Hari-Vaṁśa (xxxv. 1907-8; and xxxix. 2041; and xciv. 5190-5204), but they dwelt in Su-ráshṭra in the West and appear to be out of place here. The most probable reading seems to be the *Vrajas*, the people of *Vraja* (or *Vṛiji*, as it was also called), the modern Braj, the country north-west of Mathurá or Muttra.

† This is a short list. Besides these the Váyu Puráṇa has two lines at the beginning of this group, *viz.*, "the Kurus, the Páñcálas, and the S'álvas, and the Jángalas, the S'úrasenas, the Bhadrakáras, the Bodhas and the lords of S'ata-patha" (xlv. 109 and 110); much like a passage in the M.-Bh. (Bhíshma-P., ix. 346-7). The Matsya has the same lines, but gives the last two names as *Báhyas* and *Paṭac'c'aras* (cxiii. 35, 36). For the Kurus, see canto lviii. verse 9; for the Páñcálas, canto lviii. verse 8; for the S'álvas, canto lviii. verse 6; the Jángalas are no doubt the people of Kuru-jángala, see note to Kuru, canto lviii. verse 9; for the S'úrasenas, see canto lviii. verse 7. The Bhadrakáras are mentioned in the M.-Bh. (Sabhá-P., xiii. 590) and may perhaps be the same as the Bhadras mentioned in Vana-P. ccliii. 15256; they appear from these passages to have been situated on the west bank of the Jumna, somewhere between Delhi and Muttra. The Bodhas are mentioned in the M.-Bh. (Sabhá-P., xiii. 590; Bhíshma-P., ix. 347) and are probably the same as the Bodhis (Rámáy., Ayodh-K. lxx 15), who appear to have been situated on the eastern confines of the Panjab. I have not met Báhyas elsewhere; it seems erroneous. S'ata-patha seems to be erroneous, and Paṭac'c'ara is much better. The Paṭac'c'aras are mentioned in the M-Bh. (Sabhá-P. xiii. 590–1; xxx. 1108; Viráṭa-P., i 11-12; &c.,) and appear from the second of these passages to have occupied the tract south of the Apara-matsyas, that is, probably the country south-west of Gwalior.

‡ Madhya-deśa, the whole of the Ganges basin from the Panjab as far

34 Now along the northern half of the Sahya mountains * that region, in which the river Godávarí *flows*, is a delightful
35 one compared even with the whole earth; Go-vardhana is the charming city of the high-souled Bhárgava race. †

east as the confines of Behar; but Manu restricts it and defines its limits thus (ii. 21)—north, the Himalayas; south, the Vindhya Range; west, Vinaśana which is where the R. Saras-vatí perishes in the desert (M-Bh., S'alya-P. xxxviii. 2119-20); and east, Prayága or Allahabad.

* The text *Sahyasya c'ottare yás tu* seems incorrect; these words cannot well go with the preceding verse, for no people north of the Sahya Mts. and south of the Páripátra Mts. could be within Madhya-deśa; and they do not agree with the following words. The Váyu Puráṇa reads *sahyasya c'ottarárddhe tu*, which I have adopted. That Purána agrees and is a little fuller—"Now along the northern half of the Sahya Mts., where the river Godávarí *flows*, that region is a delightful one within the whole of this earth. This paradise named Go-vardhana was built there by Sura-rája for the sake of Ráma's spouse; the trees and herbs there were brought down from above by the Muni Bharadvája for the sake of Ráma's spouse. He made a delightful wooded tract the private part of the palace (antaḥ-pura)" (xlv. 112–114). The Matsya Puráṇa reads *Sahyasyánantare c'aite* and is similar, but varies at the second sentence, thus—"Where for the sake of Ráma's spouse *the hill* named Go-vardhana, Mandara, Gandha-mádana, trees from Svarga and heavenly plants *(oshadhíḥ*, acc.) were brought down by the Muni Bharadvája for the sake of the spouse; hence that region excels in flowers, therefore it has become delightful." (cxiii. 37–39). The Ráma alluded to here must be Ramá Jámadagnya or Paraśu-Ráma, who dwelt in this region; see the next note.

† These people are here placed on the east side of the Sahya Mts. among the sources of the Godávarí. This region and the country west of it on the other side of these mountains and the tract northwards to the Narmadá are connected in many a story with Bhṛigu, his son C'yavana and his descendants Ṛic'íka, Jamadagni and Paraśu-Ráma (*e. g.* M-Bh., Adi-P. clxxviii. 6802–10; Vana-P. cxxi and cxxii with S'ata-patha Bráhmaṇa IV. i. 5; Vana-P. lxxxix. 8364-5; cxv. 10150-2; S'ánti-P. xlix. 1778–82; Vana-P. xcix. 8681–2 with S'ánti-P. ii). The Bhárgavas were however a numerous race and spread into other regions; they are also mentioned as one of the eastern peoples in verse 43 below. They held a high position and appear to have been numerous in king Kṛita-vírya's kingdom at Máhish-matí, and after his death their wealth, it is said, brought down on them the hostility of the Kshattriyas (Ádi-P. clxxviii. 6802-15). Go-vardhana (*masc.*) as a city is not in the dictionary. I have not found it alluded to elsewhere.

The North-western peoples are these—The Váhlíkas *

* *Váhlíka* or *Báhlika* or *Bálhika* is said in the dictionary to be the modern Balkh, and in Lassen's map to be the ancient Bactriane; but there was another country, if not two tribes of this name, in the Panjab. The name is written *Váhlíka* or *Váhlika* and there may have been a distinction between the two words, for both are mentioned in the Bhíshma-P. list (ix. 354 and 361). These were not uncommon names, and there were two princes called Váhlíka between Paríkshit and Bhíshma in the Lunar Dynasty, and the later prince is styled a king (M -Bh., A'di-P , xciv. 3745, and 3750-51; and xcv. 3798-3800). The Váhlíkas are mentioned twice in the Rámáyaṇa and are placed in the western region (Kishk. K. xliii. 5), and also in the northern region (*ibid.*, xliv. 13). A distinction as between two people of this name is also indicated by the mention of two independent kings of the Váhlíkas reigning contemporaneously in the M.-Bh. (A'di-P. clxxxvi. 6992; Sabhá-P. xxxiii. 1266 and 1272; Udyoga-P. iii. 74 and 77). One of these two peoples was closely connected with the Madras, for S'alya, king of Madra, is also called lord of the Váhlíkas (A'di-P. cxiii. 4425-40; and lxvii. 2642), and his sister Mádrí is called Váhlíkí also (*ibid.*, cxxv. 4886); and an ancient eponymous king Váhlíka is placed in the same *Krodha-vaśa gaṇa* with the eponymous kings Madraka and Suvíra (*ibid.*, lxvii. 2695-6). The other people of this name appear to have been closely connected with the Daradas who were a mountain-tribe in the north of the Panjab (see note to verse 38), and are the modern Dards of Dardistan; for an ancient king Darada the Váhlíka is mentioned who did not belong to the Krodha-vása group (A'di-P. lxvii. 2694), and the Váhlíkas are linked with the Daradas (Bhíshma-P. cxviii. 5484) and are mentioned with the Kámbojas and Yavanas and other ultra-Panjab tribes (Droṇa-P. cxxi. 4818; see also Sabhá-P. xxvi. 1031-2). If these inferences may be trusted, one Váhlíka or Váhlika was situated in the plains of the Panjab alongside Madra-deśa and very possibly south of it (see Rámáy., Ayodh-K. lxx. 16-19, with note to Madrakas in verse 36, and note to Kaikeyas in verse 37) *i. e.*, between the rivers Chenab and Sutlej; and the other among the lower slopes of the Himalayas, very possibly between the Chenab and Bias. The name Váhlíka appears to have been altered in later times to *Báhíka* seemingly by a punning resemblance to *vahis*, "outside," because they were shut out by the Saras-vatí, Kuru-kshetra and other natural features from the central country which remained true to Brahmanism. The people of the Panjab were then collectively called *A'raṭṭas* or *Báhíkas*, and they and all the tribes beyond were stigmatized as impure and contemptible by the arrogant and intolerant brahmans of Madhya-deśa (Muir's Sansk. Texts. II. 482, and M-Bh., Karṇa-P. xliv. 2026 &c.; see also Cunningham's Arch. Surv. Repts., II. 6, 14,17, 195, &c).

and the Váṭadhánas,* *and* the A'bhíras,† the Kála-

* This people is mentioned in several passages in the M-Bh. (Sabhá-P. l. 1826; Udyoga-P. iii. 86; Bhíshma-P. ix. 354; and Droṇa-P. xi. 398), and their name appears to be derived from an eponymous king *Váṭadhána*, who was of the same *Krodha-vaśa* group as the eponymous kings of the Váhlíkas, Madras and Sauvíras (Adi-P. lxvii. 2695-9). No doubt therefore they dwelt alongside those tribes. Their country Váṭadhána was part of the territory stretching from Pañc'a-nada to the Ganges, over which the hosts assembled on the Kauravas' side spread at the beginning of the great war (Udyoga-P. xviii. 596-601), and it was in the western region (Sabhá-P. xxxi. 1190-1). From these data it may be inferred that the Váṭadhánas inhabited the country on the east side of the Sutlej, southward from Ferozpur. Manu declares a Váṭadhána to be the offspring of an outcaste brahman and a brahman woman (x. 21), but that is no doubt an expression of the same arrogance which in later times stigmatized all the Panjab races as outcastes (as mentioned in the last note), for Váṭadhána *dvijas* were among the people whom Nakula conquered (Sabhá-P. xxxi. 1190-1). The Váyu Puráṇa reads Váḍhadhánas (xlv. 115) erroneously.

† They were an aboriginal tribe and are called mlec'c'has and dasyus. (M-Bh.,Vana-P. clxxxviii. 12838-40; and Mausala-P. vii. 222, &c.) They were scattered over various tracts and gained their livelihood in various ways. Three divisions of them are mentioned in the M-Bh. (Sabhá-P. xxxi. 1192), those who dwelt along the river Saras-vatí, those who lived by fishing, and those who inhabited the mountains. The first group occupied the north portion of the desert as far east as Vinaśana on that river, for it is said the river perished there because of her hatred of them (S'alya-P. xxxviii. 2119-20), and as far west as Pañc'a-nada (Mausala-P. vii. 220–242; and viii. 270; where Pañc'a-jana is probably a mistake for Pañc'a-nada); this group is probably the tribe of A'bhíras mentioned in Bhíshma-P. ix. 354, and Rámáy., Kishk. K. xliii. 19. The second group must no doubt mean those who lived by the sea and not simply on rivers, hence it would have inhabited the coast along the Rann of Kachh and the delta of the Indus; and it is no doubt the tribe of A'bhíras mentioned in Kishk. K. xliii. 5. The context indicates that the third group were the mountaineers of the Aravalli Range and the hills of Malwa; but there was another section of this group which appears to have occupied the hilly tracts in the north or west of the Panjab, for it is classed with the Daradas and Káśmíras (Bhíshma-P. ix. 375; and see note to verse 38), and with the Páradas (Sabhá-P. l. 1832; and see note to verse 37). The A'bhíras were closely connected with the S'údras in these three groupings (Sabhá-P. xxxi. 1192; and see note to next verse). The descendants of all these A'bhíras are the modern Ahirs who are scattered widely over Hindustan

36 toyakas,* and the Aparántas,† and the S'údras,‡ the

proper. Another body of A'bhíras was found in the Dekhan (see verse 47). The A'bhíras are said in the Hari-Vaṁśa to have been dominated by the Daityas and Dánavas in ancient times, and to have been the chief inhabitants of the country from the Jumna to the peninsula of Gujarat (xciv. 5142-80).

* So also in the Matsya Puráṇa (cxiii. 40). This word is written *Kálajashaka* in the M.-Bh. (Bhíshma-P., ix. 354), but I have not found either name elsewhere. Possible readings might be *Bála-jartikáḥ* or *Bála-káthikáḥ*. The former, however, seems inappropriate; the *Jartikas* are the same as the Báhíkas (Karṇa-P. xliv. 2033; Arch. Surv. Repts., II. 13 and 195) who are noticed in the note to "Váhlíkas" (page 311). The "*Bálas* and *Káthis*" would be a preferable reading. The Bálas, according to Cunningham, occupied the northern portion of Sindh and were ousted from there about the middle of the seventh century A D. and moved south-east. The Káthis (the *Kathæi* of the Greek writers), according to the same authority occupied the Rechna Doab between the Chenab and Ravi rivers and also probably the northern portion of Sindh; they have retained the former territory, but those who held the latter were driven from it about the middle of the seventh century A.D. and settled in the peninsula of Gujarat where they have given the name Káthiáwāṛ to a district (Arch. Surv. Repts., II. 33–37).

† *Aparánta* means "living at the western border." A people of this name is mentioned in the M.-Bh. (Bhíshma-P., ix. 355), and allusion is often made to *Aparánta* and the *Aparántas* (*e.g.*, Vana-P., ccxvii. 7885-6; and S'ánti-P., xlix. 1780–2); but the word, though it no doubt designates a people living in the extreme west, yet seems to have a general meaning in most passages (see verse 52 below), and those passages which use it in a restricted sense do not agree—thus *Aparánta* is stated to be a country in the middle of the sea (Raghu-V., iv. 58, commentary), yet the *Aparántikas* in canto lviii., verse 34 are placed in the tortoise's tail, that is, north of Sindhu and Sauvira which are placed by verse 30 in the right hind foot. Cunningham, judging from the spots where coins have been found, was inclined to locate them in Northern Sindh and parts of West Rajputana (Arch. Surv. Repts., XIV. 136, 137) which will satisfy canto lviii., verse 34. The Váyu Puráṇa reads *Aparítas* instead (xlv. 115) which seems erroneous. The Rámáyaṇa mentions simply the *Aparas* (Kishk.-K., xliii. 23). The Matsya Puráṇa reads *Purandhras* (cxiii. 40) erroneously.

‡ The *S'údras* are often linked together with the *A'bhíras* (M.-Bh., Sabhá-P., xxxi. 1192; Bhíshma-P., ix. 375; Droṇa-P., xx. 798; S'alya-P., xxxviii. 2119-20). They appear to have been considered dasyus (S'ánti-P., clxxi. 6372, and clxxiii. 6446) and mlec'c'has (Vana-P., clxxxviii. 12838–40 where *S'úra* seems a mistake for *S'údra*); yet their women are alluded to in rather favourable terms (Sabhá-P., l. 1829). They were divided into the same

Pallavas,* C'arma-khaṇḍikas,† Gándháras,‡ and Gabalas,§

three groups as the Ábhíras, *viz.*, men of the plains, men of the sea-coast, and men of the hills (Sabhá-P., xxxi. 1192), inhabiting much the same regions (see note to Ábhíras in verse 35; for *S'úras* in Rámáy., Kishk.-K., xliii. 19 read probably *S'údras*), hence it would seem these two people were considerably intermixed and were probably closely connected aboriginal races. One group of the S'údras was known to the Greeks as *Sudrakæ*, and is placed by Cunningham in the middle of the triangle of the Panjab (Anc. Geog., I. 214–218; and Arch. Surv. Repts., II.).

* This is no doubt a mistake for *Pahlavas*, which the Váyu Puráṇa reads (xlv. 115) and which occurs in canto lviii., verse 30; though *Pallavas* are mentioned in the M.-Bh. (Vana-P., li. 1990). The Pahlavas are understood to be the *Pehlavi* or ancient *Persians*. Two people of this name are mentioned in the Bhíshma-P. list (ix. 355 and 375), but there appear to be no data to make a distinction as the allusions to the Pahlavas are generally vague, unless it be supposed there was a Pahlava colony in the Panjab; and this supposition would suit this verse, for the Persians were altogether outside India. The Hari-Vaṁśa says King Sagara defeated a great confederation of Pahlavas and other people, abrogated their laws, degraded them and made them wear beards (xiii. 763–4; and xiv. 775–783); but this seems a late fable, on a par with their being called dasyus (*id.*, cxv. 6440–3). The Rámáyaṇa has an absurd fable about the creation of the Pahlavas and other foreign races by Vasishṭha (Ádi-K., lv. 18–20; and lvi. 2–3); when contending with Viśvá-mitra he made his cow create Pahlavas. S'akas, Yavanas, &c., and Viśvá-mitra destroyed them all in succession.

† Or *C'arma-maṇḍalas* as in the Bhíshma-P. list (ix. 355) which this Puráṇa has followed closely in enumerating this group of races. The Váyu, however, reads the same as in the text (xlv. 115). I have not found any of these names elsewhere; but the name suggests identification with *Samarkand.* The Matsya Puráṇa reads *Átta-khaṇḍikas* or *C'átta-khaṇḍikas* (cxiii. 40) which appear to be erroneous.

‡ *Gándhára* was the whole of the lower basin of the Kabul river, (Arch. Surv. Repts., II. 15, and map to p. 87). It was a famous country in ancient times, its kings ranked with the highest Indian Sovereigns, and its princesses married into the noblest royal families. The passages in which the Gándháras are pronounced bad and impure (*e.g.*, S'ánti-P., lxv. 2429–31; and ccvii. 7560–1; and Karṇa-P. xliv. 2070) betray the interpolated sentiments of a later age (Muir's Sansk. Texts, II. 482).

§ This is not in the dictionary. The Váyu Puráṇa reads *Yavanas* instead (xlv. 116), and so also the Matsya (cxiii. 41); this word is supposed to have denoted the Greeks originally, but the Yavanas appear to have been known

37 the Sindhus,* Sauvíras,† and Madrakas,‡ and the

in India long before Alexander's time. The Bhíshma-P. list mentions the *Giri-gahvaras* in this region (ix. 375).

* Primarily *Sindhu* meant the country along the Indus, but it has generally denoted the lower portion of that country, that is, the modern *Sindh* more or less closely. It is placed by canto lviii., verse 30 in the Tortoise's right hind foot, and it stretched down to the peninsula of Káthiáwár which is called the territory of Sindhu-Rája in the Hari-Vaṁśa (cxiv. 6407–12) The Sindhus are mentioned frequently in the M.-Bh., and are named twice in the Bhíshma-P. list, first in connexion with the Pulindas (ix. 348), and again in conjunction with the Sauvíras (ix. 361), but there do not appear to be any other passages which tend to shew a division. Sindhu had a well-known breed of horses (Droṇa-P., xxiii. 973).

† The Sauvíras claimed descent from an eponymous king *Suvíra* of the same Krodha-vaśa group as the Madras and Váhlíkas (M.-Bh., Ádi-P., lxvii. 2695–6); but the genealogy of Suvíra in the Hari-Vaṁśa (xxxi. 1679) is fanciful. Sauvíra was closely connected with Sindhu, for the two are often coupled together, and Jayad-ratha king of Sindhu was also lord of Sauvíra and the Sauvíras, and is styled Saindhava and Suvíra indifferently (Vana-P., cclxiii. 15576–81; cclxvi. 15618 and 15635–7; and cclxvii. 15639–51). Cunningham identifies Sauvíra with the country between the Indus and Jhelam, that is, the Sindh-Sagar Doab (Arch. Surv. Repts., II. 4–6, 14 and 23); that hardly agrees with the position assigned to it in the Tortoise's right hind foot, but the collocation of races in that region is rather confused. May we suppose that Sauvíra was rather the name of the *people* while Sindhu more properly denoted the *territory?* The Sauvíras might then have inhabited the northern part of Sindhu, and Sauvíra would have been that portion only of the larger area. This theory seems to satisfy the conditions generally.

Along with the Sauvíras and Saindhavas the Kúrma Puráṇa mentions (xlvii. 40) "the Húṇas (or Kúṇas), the Mályas (or S'álvas), the inhabitants of Bályá (or Kalpa)." For the *Húṇas*, see note to canto lviii., verse 45; *Kúṇa* seems erroneous; for the *S'álvas*, see canto lviii. verse 6; *Málya* seems erroneous; *Bályá* and *Kalpa* seem unidentifiable.

‡ The *Madras* or *Mádras* claimed descent from an eponymous king Madraka of the same Krodha-vaśa group as the Sauvíras and Váhlíkas (M.-Bh., Ádi-P., lxvii. 2695–6; and see note on page 311); but his genealogy in the Hari-Vaṁśa (xxxi. 1679) seems fanciful. Cunningham places Madra between the Jhelam and Ravi rivers, that is, in the Chej and Rechna Doabs (Arch. Surv. Repts., II. 4, 8, 14 and 39), yet he also says it is the country between the Jhelam and Bias, or between the Chenab and Bias (*ibid.*, 196);

people who dwell along the S'atadru,* the Kalingas,†

but it could hardly have comprised much of the Chej Doab for the Kaikeyas occupied the greater part of that (see note to next verse). The capital of Madra was *S'ákala* (Sabhá-P., xxxi. 1197) which Cunningham has identified with the modern Sangala, on the R. Apagá which is the modern Ayak (Arch-Surv. Repts., II. 195–6 and Karṇa-P., xliv. 2033). The R. Irávatí flowed through Madra-deśa, but near the eastern border (*ibid.*, 2038-41; and Matsya Puráṇa cxiv. 7 and 15-18.) Madra then was the country around Sangala, with the tracts on either side watered by the Chenab and Ravi. It was a famous kingdom. The weird story told about king Vyushitáśva's queen (A'di-P., cxxi. 4695–4714) no doubt means her sons became Madras and did not originate the Madras. In later times the brahmans of Hindustan pronounced the Madras, like the Gándháras, base and impure (S'ánti-P., ccvii. 7559–61; and Hari-V., xiv. 784); see especially Karṇa-P., xliv. 2033-53, where the Madras are abused in good set terms. The Váyu Puráṇa reads *Bhadrakas* erroneously (xlv. 116).

* That is, the Sutlej, *S'atadru-ja.* But this seems mistaken, for the Váyu Puráṇa reads *S'akas* and *Hradas* (xlv. 116); and the Matsya *S'akas* and *Druhyas* (cxiii. 41). The S'akas, therefore, are no doubt one of the people meant (see note to canto lviii., verse 6). Hrada seems erroneous. The Druhyas may be connected with Yayáti's son Druhyu who was king of the West, (Hari-V. xxx. 1604 and 1618), but I have not met with them elsewhere.

† This seems erroneous. These people are mentioned in verse 46, and there seems to be no ground for thinking any Kalingas lived in North India; yet Kalingas are mentioned in such a connexion (Bhíshma-P., ix. 376; and lxxi. 3132; and see note to Arkalingas in verse 33), and a town *Kalinga-nagara* is mentioned in the Rámáy. on the west of the Go-matí and not far from it (Ayodh. K., lxxiii. 14, 15). A tribe called *Kulingas* is alluded to (Droṇa-P., cxxi. 4819). The Váyu Puráṇa reads *Kulindas* instead (xlv. 116), which is no doubt right. Cunningham says the Kulindas or Kunindas are the modern Kunets who occupy Kullu and the Simla hills and the slopes below, along both sides of the Sutlej (Arch. Surv. Repts., XIV. 116 and 125–130). The Kuliṅdas extended further east along the southern slopes of the Himalayas as far as Nepal, for they were the first nation which Arjuna conquered in his Northward march from Indra-prastha (Sabhá-P., xxv. 996), and they also occupied the hills north of Mandara, that is, the Almora hills (*id.*, li. 1858–9; and note* to page 287 above); indeed the name appears to have comprised a considerable body of hill tribes, for "all the countries of Kulinda" are spoken of (Vana-P., clxxvii. 12350).

The Matsya Puráṇa reads *Pulindas* (cxiii. 41). The Pulindas were a rude tribe inhabiting the Himalayas and intermixed with Kirátas and Tanganas the Páradas,* the Hára-bhúshikas,† the Máṭharas,‡ and the Bahu-bhadras,§ the Kaikeyas,|| the Daśa-máli-

(Vana-P., cxl. 10863-5; and Droṇa-P, cxxi. 4846–7; and see notes to verses 40 and 41); they were considered mlec'c'has (Vana-P., clxxxviii. 12838–40), and are declared to have become degraded because of the extinction of sacred rites, &c. (Annśás.-P., lvii. 2103, &c.). There was another body of Pulindas in Central India (Sabhá-P., xxviii. 1068; and xxx. 1120; and S'ánti-P., ccvii. 7559).

* The Páradas are generally mentioned with hill tribes (Sabhá-P., l. 1832; li. 1869; and Droṇa-P., cxxi. 4819). They appear to have been a hill tribe like the Kulindas and Tanganas (see note to verse 41 below) and to have dwelt in the western portion of the Himalayas (Sabhá-P., li. 1858–9), though they are placed in the tortoise's right hind foot by canto lviii., verse 31; the races placed there, however, are strangely confused. Manu says they were Kshattriyas and became degraded because of the extinction of sacred rites, &c. (x. 43–44); and the Hari-Vaṁśa says king Sagara degraded them and ordered them to wear long hair (xiii. 763–4; and xiv. 775–83), and they were mlec'c'has and dasyus (*id.*, cxv. 6440–42). The Váyu Puráṇa reads *Paritas* instead (xlv. 116).

† This is not in the dictionary. The Váyu Puráṇa reads *Hára-púrikas* instead (xlv. 116), and the Matsya *Hára-múrtikas* (cxiii. 41); but I have not found any of these names elsewhere. Should the reading be *Hára-húṇakas?* The Hára-húṇas are mentioned in the M.-Bh., as a people outside India on the west (Sabhá-P., xxxi. 1194; l. 1844; and Vana-P., li. 1991).

‡ The Váyu Puráṇa reads *Ramaṭas* instead (xlv. 117), and the Matsya *Rámaṭhas* (cxiii. 42), and the Kúrma mentions a people called *Rámas* (xlvii. 41). The reading should, no doubt, be *Ramaṭas, Ramaṭhas* or *Rámaṭhas;* they were a western people mentioned in the M.-Bh. (Sabhá-P., xxxi. 1195; Vana-P., li. 1991; and S'ánti.-P., lxv. 2430). The *Ramaṇas* (Bhíshma-P., ix. 374) may be the same people. There are, however, no sufficient data to identify any of them.

§ The Váyu Puráṇa reads *Raddha-kaṭakas* instead (xlv. 117); the M.-Bh. mentions the *Báhu-bádhas* (Bhíshma-P., ix. 362) and the *Bálabhadras* (Karṇa-P. vi. 153); and the Matsya Puráṇa reads *Kaṇṭakáras* (cxiii. 42); but none of these seems satisfactory and I have not met any of them elsewhere.

|| These people were called *Kekayas, Kaikayas* and *Kaikeyas.* An eponymous ancestor Kaikeya is assigned to them by the Hari-Vaṁśa (xxxi. 1679), but his genealogy seems fanciful. They were a powerful and famous nation, and were noted bowmen (Sabhá-P., iv. 126; and Vana-P., cclxvii. 15654). They inhabited the Panjab and appear to have joined the Madras, for the two are sometimes coupled together (Sabhá-P., li. 1870; and Droṇa-P., xx. 799); and

38 kas,* and the settlements† of Kshattriyas, and the families of Vaiśyas and S'údras.‡

The Kámbojas,§ and the Daradas,|| and the

canto lviii. places them both in the tortoise's left side (verses 42 and 45). Their capital was *Rája-griha* (Rámáy., Ádi-K., lxxix. 35–44) or *Giri-vraja* (*id.*, Áyodh. K., lxxi. 1; and lxxii. 1). Lassen places the Kaikeyas between the Ravi and Bias rivers. Cunningham, however, dissents and places them on the line of the Jhelam, west of the Báhíkas, and proposes to identify Giri-vraja with Girják, which was the ancient name of Jalalpur on that river (Arch. Surv. Repts., II. 14); and this agrees with the Rámáy. (Ayodh. K., lxx. 16–19).

* These people are mentioned in the M.-Bh. (Bhíshma-P., ix. 374). The Váyu Puráṇa reads *Daśa-mánikas* (xlv. 117). Does the word mean "the ten tribes of Málikas"? The *Málikas* may perhaps be identified with the *Malli* (Arch. Surv. Repts., II. 37). The Matsya Puráṇa reads *Daśa-námakas* (cxiii. 42), which seems mistaken.

† *Upa-ni-veśa*, a word not in the dictionary. It seems to be synonymous with *ni-veśa* which appears to be the word meant in the corresponding passage in the Bhíshma-P. list (ix. 374, *kshattriyá yoniveśáś c'a*; but *kshattriyopaniveśáś c'a* would be preferable). Ni-ves'a is used elsewhere in the M.-Bh. (*e.g.*, Sabhá-P., xiii. 615; and xix. 798), and in the Rámáy. (Kishk.-K, xliii. 24), and appears to denote a military colony or settlement in a foreign country.

‡ That is, S'údras as a caste, and not as a race; as a race they have been mentioned in verse 36.

§ The Kámbojas were in the extreme north of the Panjab beyond the Indus, and were classed with the Daradas (Sabhá-P., xxvi. 1031), with Yavanas and S'akas (Udyoga-P., xviii. 590), and with C'inas (Bhíshma-P., ix. 373). Their country was famous for its large and fleet breed of horses which are often mentioned (Sabhá-P., l. 1824; Bhíshma-P., lxxi. 3131; Droṇa-P., xxiii. 972; cxxi. 4831-2;—also Rámáy., Ádi-K., vi. 24; and Sundar.-K., xii. 36;—and Raghu-V., iv. 70). Lassen places Kámboja doubtfully south of Kashgar and east of the modern Kafiristan (Ind. Alt., map). They were Áryans by language (Muir's Sansk. Texts, II. 368–9). Manu says (x. 43–44) they were Kshattriyas and became degraded through the extinction of sacred rites, &c.; they are called mlec'c'has (Vana-P., clxxxviii. 12838–40) and said to have evil customs (S'ánti-P., ccvii. 7560–61). The Hari-Vaṁśa says they were degraded by King Sagara and ordered to shave the whole of the head like the Yavanas (xiii. 763–4; and xiv. 775–83). The Rámáy. has an absurd fable about their origin (Ádi K. lvi. 2; see page 314 note *).

|| Darada is the modern Dardistan, the country north of Gándhára and north-west of Káśmír. This region satisfies all the allusions to the Daradas. They were a hill people (Droṇa-P., cxxi. 4835–7 and 4846–7; neighbours

39 Varvaras,* the Harshavardhanas,† and the C'ínas,‡ the

of the Káśmíras (*id.*, lxx. 2435), of the Kámbojas (Sabhá-P., xxvi. 1031), and of the C'ínas and Tusháras (Vana-P., clxxvii. 12350); they fought largely with stones and were skilled in slinging stones (Droṇa-P., cxxi. 4835-47). Manu says they were Kshattriyas and became degraded because of the extinction of sacred rites, &c. (x. 43 and 44); and like the Páradas and others they were considered mlec'c'has and dasyus (Hari-V., cxv. 6440–6442).

* This word is also written *Barvara* and *Barbara*, and often means any barbarous race. The Varvaras are generally mentioned in conjunction with the S'akas or Yavanas (Sabhá-P., xxxi. 1199; Vana-P., ccliii. 15254; S'ánti-P., ccvii. 7560-61; &c); and from these allusions it appears they were mainly a western or north-western race; but Varvaras were also to be found in the east or north-east of India (Sabhá-P., xxix. 1088), and seemingly also in the south (Vana-P., li. 1989) like the S'avaras (S'ánti-P., lxv. 2429). The name no doubt represents the rolling of the letter *r* or rough and unknown speech; hence it would be applied to various rude tribes.

† This is not in the dictionary. The Váyu Puráṇa reads *Priya-laukikas* instead (xlv. 118), but I have not found either word elsewhere. Canto lviii mentions certain *Bhoga-prasthas* (verse 42) in the north. All these names seem suggestive, and may perhaps be equivalents of *Utsava-sanketa* (people who have no marriage and practise promiscuous intercourse, *utsava* meaning affection, and *sanketa*, a gesture of invitation) a people mentioned in the M.-Bh. in the north among the hills (Sabhá-P., xxvi. 1025) and west (*id.*, xxxi. 1191); though also in the south (Bhíshma-P., ix. 363); and the Raghu-V., places them in the Himalayas (iv. 78). This derivation of Utsava-sanketa is given in a note to the commentary on Raghu-V., iv. 77.

‡ The Chinese; but *C'ína* comprised the country of Thibet along the whole range of the Himalayas, for the C'ínas are linked with the Kámbojas in the north-west (Bhishma-P., ix. 373), they are frequently mentioned among the retinue of Bhaga-datta king of Prág-jyotisha, in the east (*e.g.*, Udyoga-P., xviii. 584-5; see note to verse 44 below), and they were near the sources of the Ganges in the country midway between those regions (Vana-P., clxxvii. 12350; S'ánti-P., cccxxvii. 12226–9). The country had a valuable breed of horses (Udyoga-P., lxxxv. 3049). In the M.-Bh. the C'ínas are always spoken of with respect and even admiration (Udyoga-P., xviii. 584–5), and one of their kings called Dhautamúlaka is classed among eighteen famous ancient kings who extirpated their kinsmen (*id.*, lxxiii. 2730); hence Manu's remark that the C'ínas were Kshattriyas and became degraded because of the extinction of sacred rites, &c. (x. 43 and 44) betrays the sentiments of a later age. The Váyu Puráṇa reads *Pínas* (xlv. 118) erroneously. The Rámáy. mentions also *Apara-c'ínas* (Kishk.-K., xliv. 15), "the further C'ínas."

Tukháras* are the populous† *races of* men outside.‡
And the Átreyas,§ the Bharadvájas,|| and Pushkalas,¶ the

* For *tu khárás* read *tukhárás*. The Tukháras are mentioned in the M.-Bh. (Sabhá-P., l. 1850) and Rámáy. (Kishk.-K., xliv. 15). The Váyu Puráṇa reads *Tusháras* (xlv. 118), and they are mentioned in the M.-Bh. (Vana-P., li. 1991; S'ánti-P., lxv. 2429; &c.). The two names seem to mean the same people. They were an outside northern race bordering on the Himalayas (Vana-P., clxxvii. 12350). In the Hari-Vaṁśa they are classed along with S'akas, Daradas, Pahlavas, &c., and considered to be mlec'c'has and dasyus (cxv. 6440–42), they are ranked with wild hill-tribes as originating from king Vena's sins (v. 310–11), and are said to have been repressed by king Sagara (xiv. 784). Lassen identifies them with the *Tochari*, and places them on the north side of the Hindu Kush (Ind. Alt., map). The Rámáy. has an absurd fable about their origin (Ádi.-K., lvi. 3; see page 314, note *).

† *Bahulá*. The Váyu Puráṇa reads *Pahlavas* or *Ratna-dháras* instead (xlv. 118), probably erroneously; the former have been mentioned in verse 36. I have not met with the latter word elsewhere, but it may be noticed that great quantities of precious stones were found among the Tukháras and other northern nations (Sabhá-P., l. 1849–50).

‡ *Váhyato-naráḥ*. The Váyu Puráṇa reads *Váhyatodaráḥ* or *kshatodaráḥ* instead (xlv. 118) erroneously.

§ This tribe is mentioned in the Bhíshma-P. list (ix. 376). The Hari-V. says that king Raudráśva's ten daughters all married the ṛishi Prabhá-kara of Atri's race and gave rise to the Átreyas (xxxi. 1660–68); and Átreyas are mentioned as a family of brahmans dwelling in Dvaita-vana (M.-Bh., Vana-P., xxvi. 971) which was a forest and lake near the Saras-vatí (*ibid.*, clxxvii. 12354–62). The Matsya Puráṇa reads "the *Atris*" (cxiii. 43), which is the same. Are they to be identified with the Átreya gotra of brahmans (Risley's Tribes and Castes of Bengal, I. 27) formerly living perhaps in Sirmour or Garhwal; or to be connected with R. Átreyí (Sabhá-P., ix. 374) the modern Atrai in North Bengal? The former seems more probable.

|| Or Bháradvájas; they are named in the Bhíshma-P. list (ix. 376). Bharadvája is often mentioned in the M.-Bh. in connexion with the upper part of the Ganges near the hills (*e.g.*, Ádi-P., cxxx. 5102–6; clxvi. 6328–32; Vana-P., cxxxv. 10700–728; and S'alya-P., xlix. 2762–2824). These were no doubt his descendants, living in Garhwál or Kumaon. The name Bharadvája is given to various caste divisions (Risley's Tribes and Castes of Bengal, I. 96.)

¶ The Váyu (xlv. 119) and Matsya (cxiii. 43) Puráṇas read *Prasthalas* and they are no doubt the same as the *Proshakas* (Bhíshma-P., ix. 376)

40 Kuśerukas,* the Lampákas,† the S'úlakáras,‡ the

all being placed in the same connexion. If Cunningham is right in identifying Lampáka with Lamghan (see second note below), Pushkala suggests *Pushkalávatí* or *Pushkarávatí* (Rámáy., Kishk.-K., xliii. 23), the ancient capital of Gándhára (Anc. Geog., I. 49), but the Gándháras have been mentioned in their proper place in verse 36 above. I have not met the name Proshakas any where else.

Prasthala was a country closely connected with Trigarta, for Su-śarman king of Trigarta is also called lord of Prasthala (Viráṭa-P., xxx. 971; Bhíshma-P., lxxv. 3296; lxxxviii. 3856; and Droṇa-P., xvii. 691), and Trigarta comprised the territory from Amballa and Pattiala to the R. Bias (see note to verse 57). Prasthala was also near the Panjab (Droṇa-P., xvii. 691; and Karṇa-P., xliv. 2063-70), and in the second of these passages its people are classed along with the Panjab nations, and all according to the ideas of a later age were pronounced degraded (Muir, Sansk. Texts. II. 482). From these data it seems Prasthala must have been the district between Ferozpur, Pattiala and Sirsa. If this position be right, the Prasthalas do not fall into the group of northern peoples named in the text, and the correct reading cannot be *Prasthalas.*

* The Váyu Puráṇa reads *Kaserukas* (xlv. 119); and the Matsya *Daserakas* (cxiii. 43). I have not met the first form of name elsewhere; but the Daśerakas, or Dáśerakas, or Dáserakas are mentioned as joining in the great war in the M.-Bh. (*e.g.*, Bhíshma-P., l. 2080; cxviii. 5483; Droṇa-P., xi. 397; and xx. 798); and they appear to have comprised several bands, as the word *gaṇa* is nearly always added to the name; but there are no data to identify them.

† This name occurs in the M.-Bh. (Droṇa-P., cxxi. 4846–7) and there the Lampákas are described as a monutain tribe, like the Daradas and Pulindas, who fought largely with stones and were skilled in slinging stones; but otherwise there are very few references to them in the M.-Bh. Lassen identifies Lampáka with the Lambagæ and places them south of the Hindu-Kush, in modern Kafiristan. Cunningham says Lampáka is the modern Lamghan, north-east of Kabul (Anc. Geog., I. 17 and 27), which agrees with Lassen. The Matsya Puráṇa reads *Lampakas* (cxiii. 43), no doubt by a mistake.

‡ The Váyu Puráṇa reads *Stanapas* or *Tunapas* (xlv. 119). I have not met any of these names elsewhere, but the latter words resemble the *Stana-yoshikas* (Bhíshma-P., ix. 376), and also *Tanayas* (*ibid.*, 371), whose grouping however is different. The Matsya Puráṇa reads *Talagánas* (cxiii. 43), which seems erroneous. Perhaps the S'úlakáras may be identified with the Sunuwárs, a cultivating tribe of Nepal, forming part of the highest class (Risley's Castes and Tribes of Bengal, II. 281).

41

C'ulikas,* and the Jágudas,† and the Aupadhas,‡ and the Animadras,§ and the races of Kirátas,|| the

* The Váyu Puráṇa reads *Píḍikas* instead (xlv. 119). Canto lviii. verse 37 places the C'úlikas in the Tortoise's tail at the westernmost part of India. I have not met with either name elsewhere. The Matsya Puráṇa reads *Sainikas* (cxiii. 43), "Soldiers."

† Or *Juguḍas* according to the Váyu Puráṇa (xlv. 119). The Jáguḍas are mentioned in the M.-Bh. (Vana-P., li. 1991). The Matsya Puráṇa reads *Jángalas* (cxiii. 43), which is of no help, for it cannot refer to Kuru-jángala (see note to Kurus, canto lviii, verse 9), and I have not met with any other Jángala; but the same Puráṇa mentions the Jaguḍas as a people through whose country the Indus flows, so that they appear to be north or east of Kashmir (cxx. 46–48).

‡ The Váyu Puráṇa reads *Apagas* instead (xlv. 120). I have not met with either name elsewhere. Should the reading be *Ápavas*, the descendants of Vasishṭha? Átreyas and Bharadvájas have been mentioned, and Gálavas are named in verse 57.

§ Or *Ánimadras* or *C'ánimadras*. The Váyu Puráṇa reads *C'álimadráś c'a* (xlv. 120). None of these names are in the dictionary, and I have not met any of them elsewhere.

|| The word *Kiráta* is no doubt the same as the modern names *Kiráti* and *Kiránti*, which mean "a native of the Kiránt-des or mountainous country lying between the Dud-Kosi and the Karki rivers in Nepal. The term includes the Khambu, Limbu and Yákhá tribes; and the Dannár, Hayu and Thámi also claim to be Kiránti," but their claim is disputed by the first three tribes which are superior (Risley's Castes and Tribes of Bengal, I. 490). But formerly they had a much larger range and were spread along the greater part of the southern side of the Himalayas, for Arjuna encountered them in his northern expedition (Sabhá-P., xxv. 1002), Bhíma in his eastern (*id.*, xxix. 1089), and Nakula in his western expedition (*id.*, xxxi. 1199). They formed a group of closely allied yet distinct tribes or clans, for two separate Kiráta kings are named (Sabhá-P., iv. 119 and 120), seven kings are alluded to (*id.*, xxix. 1089), "all the Kirátas" are spoken of (Vana-P., li. 1990), and they are mentioned thrice in the Bhíshma-P. list (ix. 358, 364 and 376). Their chief territory was among the mountains Kailása, Mandara (see page 287 note *) and Haima (Anuśás.-P., xix. 1434), that is, the region around Lake Mánasa. They were allied to the Tanganas (see next verse) and Pulindas (see page 316 note †) for the three people inhabited one large kingdom ruled by Su-báhu, who was king of the Pulindas (Vana-P., cxl. 10863–6) and is also styled a Kiráta (*id.*, clxxvii. 12349). The tribes differed much in material condition, for some were civilized and

41 Támasas,* and the Haṁsa-márgas,† the Káśmíras,‡ and the Tunganas,§ the S'úlikas,|| and the

open to friendly intercourse (Vana-P., cxl. 10865-6; and Udyoga-P., lxiii. 2470), and others were clad in skins, lived on fruit and roots and were cruel (Sabhá-P., li. 1865). Their women were used as slaves (*ibid.*, 1867). The Rámáy. describes them as wearing thick top-knots (Kishk.-K., xl. 30). Manu's remark that the Kirátas were kshattriyas and became degraded because of the extinction of sacred rites, &c. (x. 43 and 44) reflects the opinions of a later age.

* The same people are mentioned again in verse 57, but I have not found the name elsewhere, and it is not in the dictionary. The Váyu Puráṇa reads *Tomaras* (xlv. 120), and the Bhíshma-P. agrees (ix. 377). The Matsya Puráṇa mentions the Tomaras and the Haṁsa-márgas as two tribes through whose countries flows the R. Pávaní, one of the three large rivers which rise in the middle of the Himalaya mountain-system and flow eastward (cxx. 57–59). The river is doubtful, but the passage places the Tomaras and the Haṁsa-márgas in the east of Thibet.

† "The duck-fowlers." They are mentioned again in verse 56, and also in the Bhíshma-P. list (ix. 377); and seem to be the same as the *Haṁsa-padas* (Droṇa-P., xx. 798) and perhaps *Haṁsa-káyanas* (Sabhá-P., li. 1870); but there appear to be no data to identify them, except that they were a people in eastern Thibet as explained in the last note.

‡ The people of Kashmir. They are named twice in the Bhíshma-P. list (ix. 361 and 375).

§ Or better, as the Váyu Puráṇa reads, *Tangaṇas* (xlv. 120); the Rámáy. calls them Ṭankaṇas (Kishk.-K., xliv. 20). They were a mountain tribe and are mentioned rather often in the M.-Bh., where two sections are spoken of, the *Tangaṇas* and *Para-tangaṇas* (Sabhá-P., li. 1859; Bhíshma-P., ix. 372; and l. 2083), that is, "the nearer" and "the further" Tangaṇas. They were intermixed with the Kirátas and Pulindas (or Kulindas), for they all inhabited a large kingdom ruled over by Su-báhu, which was in the middle portion of the Himalayas (Vana-P., cxl. 10863–5; Sabhá-P., li. 1858-9); and they are also linked with the Ambashṭhas (Droṇa-P., cxxi. 4819). They are said to have occupied the upper part of the valley of the R. Sarayú (dict.). Like other hill tribes they fought largely with stones and were skilled in slinging stones (Droṇa-P., cxxi. 4835–47).

|| This resembles S'úlakáras in the last verse. The Váyu Puráṇa reads *C'úlikas* (xlv. 121), which has also been mentioned in that verse. The S'úlikas are mentioned in the Matsya Puráṇa as a people through whose country flows the R. C'akshu, one of the three large rivers which rise in the middle of the Himalaya mountain-system and flow westward (cxx. 45, 46).

42 Kuhakas,* the Urṇas,† and Darvas;‡ these *are the peoples of* the Northern countries.

Hear from me *the peoples who inhabit* the Eastern countries. The Adhrárakas,§ the Mudakaras,|| the Antar-

C'akshn may perhaps be meant for Vakshu, which is the Oxus; if so, the S'úlikas would be a people on the Oxus in Turkestan.

* *Kuhaka* means a juggler. The Váyu Puráṇa reads *C'áhukas* or *Ahukas* or *A'hukas* (xlv. 121); A'huka was the name of a family of the Andhakas (*e.g.*, M.-Bh., Udyoga-P., lxxxv. 3041; and Hari-V., xxxviii. 2017-24), hnt they were in the west aud cannot be meant here. I have not met with any of these words elsewhere as the name of a people in the north. The proper reading may be *Kuhukas*. Kuhuka wonld be the same as Kuhu, and the Kuhus are mentioned in the Matsya Puráṇa as a people on the line of the Indus (cxx. 46-48).

† These people are mentioned again in verse 57. A country *Urṇa-deśa* is placed by Lassen on the Sutlej north of Garhwal (Ind. Alt., map). The whole of the upper Sutlej valley is now called Nari-khorsum or Hun-des. The Váyn Puráṇa reads *Púrṇas* here (xlv. 121), which seems erroneons.

‡ These appear to be the same as the *Dárvas* in verse 57. They were a northern people and are generally associated with the Trigartas and Daradas (Sabhá-P., xxvi. 1026; and li. 1869) and other tribes in the north of the Panjab (Bhíshma-P., ix. 362) A river or town called Darví is mentioned (*ibid.*), and a tírtha Darví-sankramaṇa is placed hetween the sources of the Jumna and Indus (Vana-P., lxxxiv. 8022-4); and this tract perhaps was their territory. But Lassen places the Dárvas between the Indns and Jhelam in the north-west of Kashmir (Ind. Alt., map).

§ This seems incorrect. The Váyu Puráṇa reads *Andhravákas* (xlv. 122), which is hardly acceptable, the *Andhras* being properly in the South, rather than in the East, and being presumably intended in verse 48 (see note to *Andhas*). The Matsya Puráṇa reads *Angá vangá* instead (cxiii. 44), which is preferahle, but these nations are mentioned below (see page 325 note ‡ and page 326 note *).

|| The Matsya Puráṇa reads *Madgurakas* (cxiii. 44), and the Váyu *Sujarakas* (xlv. 122). I have not found any of these names elsewhere, except that *Madguras*, "divers," are mentioned in a totally different connexion in the Hari-Vaṁśa (xcv. 5233-9). Seemingly the word should he connected with *Modá-giri* in the Eastern region where a kingdom once existed (M.-Bh., Sabhá-P., xxix. 1095); is it to be identified with the modern Mungir (commonly Monghyr) on the Ganges in Behar, where there is a small outcrop of hills. Cunningham says *Mudgala-puri*, *Mudgaláśrama* (to which the Matsya Puráṇa reading approximates) and *Mudga-giri* were the old names of

43 giryas,* the Vahir-giras,† and the Pravangas‡ also,

Mungir; and an earlier name was *Kashṭa-haraṇa-parvata* (XV. 15 and 18), but this last is open to the objection that no name can well be older than that preserved in the M.-Bh. The *Mudgalas* are mentioned in Droṇa-P., xi. 397.

* Or *Antar-giri*. as the Matsya Puráṇa reads (cxiii. 44). They are mentioned in the Bhíshma-P. list (ix. 357). The name, no doubt, means "those who dwell amid the hills," and as the people are placed in all these passages in proximity to the Angas, it seems reasonable to identify Antar-giri with the Rajmahall hills (in the modern district of the Santhal Parganas) which form a marked natural division between Anga and Vanga. In the only other passage where I have found this name (Sabhá-P., xxvi. 1012) *Antar-giri, Vahir-giri* (see next note) and *Upa-giri* are mentioned in obvious contradistinction and are placed in the Northern region; it is doubtful, therefore, whether they denote the tracts mentioned here; and they may perhaps refer to some portion of the slopes of the Himalayas.

† Or *Vahir-giri* as the Matsya Puráṇa reads (cxiii. 44). The name, no doubt, means "those who dwell outside the hills," and these people are mentioned along with the Angas and Malajas in the Bhíshma-P. list (ix. 357). If we may identify Antar-giri with the Rajmahall hills (see the last note), Vahir-giri might well designate the outskirts of those hills bordering on Anga, that is, the southern portions of the Bhagalpur and Monghyr districts and the lands bordering thereon to the south in the Santhál Parganas and Hazaribagh.

‡ I have not met this name elsewhere, though it is stated in the dictionary to be the name of a people and analysed thus, *Pravaṃ-ga* = *Plavaṃ-ga*; I would suggest, however, that it should be read here as *Pra-vangas*, "those who are in front of the Vangas," *i. e.*, the *Angas*. The Matsya Puráṇa reads *Angas* and *Vangas* (cxiii. 44). The Angas are clearly meant. Anga was a distinct and settled country in early times, and its princes were allied with Aryan royal families (M.-Bh., A'di-P., xcv. 3772 and 3777; and Rámáy., A'di-K., x. 1–10). This people are said to have been so called after an eponymous king Anga; he, Vanga, Kalinga, Puṇḍra and Suhma are described with considerable circumstantial detail as the five sons of king Bali's queen (Bali being king of the Eastern region) by the ṛishi Dírgha-tamas (M.-Bh., A'di-P., civ. 4217–21; and Hari-V., xxxi. 1684–93). Anga comprised the modern districts of Bhagalpur and Monghyr, excluding the extreme north and south portions. The ancient name Anga dropped out of use and *Bihar* (of Buddhist origin) has usurped its place; is the word Pra-vanga here significant of the change? The capital was first called *Málini*, and that name is said to have been superseded by the name *C'ampá* in honour of a king C'ampa, Loma-páda's great grandson (Hari-V., xxxi. 1699 and 1700; and M.-Bh., 'Sánti-P., v. 134-5), but the

the Rangeyas,* the Mánadas,† the Mána-vartikas,‡

Rámáy. makes a punning connexion between this name and the groves of c'ampaka trees around the town (Ádi-K., xvii. 23); it is the modern Bhagalpur on the south bank of the Ganges (Vana-P., lxxxv. 8156). The tract near C'ampá was called *Súta-vishaya* (Vana-P, cccvii. 17150-51), that is, "the land of bards or charioteers." The Angas are mentioned twice in the Bhíshma-P. list (ix. 353 and 357); it does not appear why.

* This is, no doubt, a mistake for *Vangeyas* which the Váyu Puráṇa reads (xlv. 122), and *Vangas* which the Matsya mentions (cxiii. 44). The Vangas or Vangeyas were the people of *Vanga* or Banga, the original of the modern Bengal. Vanga was a distinct country in early times and is frequently mentioned, though the references to it very rarely convey any definite information. It lay beyond Anga, to the south-east; and was connected with Kalinga, for the Angas, Vangas and Kalingas are constantly linked together as people closely allied by race and position, (*e. g.*, Droṇa-P., lxx. 2436). And the Vangas are said to have been so called after an eponymous king Vanga who was Anga's and Kalinga's brother (see last note). Vanga comprised the northern portion of Western and Central Bengal, *i. e.*, the modern districts of Birbhum, Moorshedabad, Bardwan and Nuddea. Its capital in early times does not appear to be mentioned. In later times the name was extended over the whole of Central Bengal, for the Raghu Vaṁśa describes the Vangas as dwelling in the islands of the Ganges delta, warring chiefly in boats, and transplanting their rice seedlings into the fields just as at the present day (iv. 36, 37). In those early times the upper part of the delta consisted of numerous islands separated by large rivers, and the southern part could not have been formed.

† The Váyu Puráṇa reads *Máladas* (xlv. 122) which appears preferable, and this may mean the people of the modern district of Maldah, in which the old cities of Gauṛ and Paṇḍua are situated, while the town Maldah itself is old (Cunningham, Arch. Surv. Repts., XV. 77). The *Maladas* are mentioned as an eastern people in the M.-Bh. (Sabhá-P., xxix. 1081-2; and also Droṇa-P., vii. 183), but without data enough to say where they were.

‡ The Váyu Puráṇa reads *Mála-vartinaḥ* (xlv. 122). The M.-Bh. mentions the *Mána-varjakas* (Bhíshma-P., ix. 357) and they appear from the context to be the people meant here. The name seems intended to carry a meaning, either "people who live decorously" according to the text, or "people who are devoid of decorum" according to the last word. Does it refer to a wild tribe in a state of nature? Or does Mána-vartika (Mána-vartin) mean Mán-bhúm (Mána-bhúmi) a district in West Bengal? The *Málavánakas* mentioned in the Bhíshma-P. list (ix. 367) belong to a different group altogether.

the Brahmottaras,* the Pravijayas,† the Bhárgavas,‡

* The Matsya Puráṇa reads *Suhmottaras* (cxiii. 44), which is preferable. This means the "people north of Suhma." Suhma was a well-known country. It was generally classed with Puṇḍra (*e. g.*, M.-Bh., Ádi-P., cxiii. 4453) and both of them are declared to be closely allied to Anga, Vanga and Kalinga by being derived from five eponymous kings of those names who were brothers (M.-Bh., Ádi-P., civ. 4217–21; Hari-Vaṁśa, xxxi. 1684–93). Suhma was near the sea (Sabhá-P, xxix. 1099; and Raghu-V., iv. 34 and 35), and Dáma-lipta (Támra-lipta, the modern Tamluk, see next verse) is said to be within its borders in the Daśa-kumára-c'arita (Story of Mitra-gupta). *Suhma* therefore corresponded with the modern districts of Midnapur and Bankura and perhaps also Purulia and Manbhum in West Bengal. *Suhmottara* would be the tract north of that, and was probably the same as *Pra-suhma* (Sabhá-P., xxix. 1090). The *Mahyuttaras* of the Bhishma-P. list (ix. 358) seem to be the same people under an error in the spelling.

The reading *Suhmottaráḥ*, however, is hardly satisfactory in omitting the Suhmas and referring indefinitely to the people north of them, and I would suggest that the proper reading should be *Suhmotkaláḥ*, "the Suhmas and Utkalas." The *Utkalas* were well-known (though not I believe mentioned often in the M.-Bh.), and were a rude tribe of very early origin, for they do not appear to have had any close affinities with the races around them, and the Hari-Vaṁśa throws their origin back to the fabulous time of Ilá (x. 631-2). Their territory reached on the east the R. Kapiśá (Raghu-V., iv. 38), which Lassen identifies with the modern Subarṇa-rekhá near the northern boundary of Orissa (Ind. Alt., Map), but which I propose to identify with the R. Cossye in Midnapore (see page 301 note †); and on the west they touched the Mekalas, for the two people are coupled together in the M.-Bh. (Bhíshma-P., ix. 348; see also Droṇa-P., iv. 122, and Karṇa-P., xxii. 882) and Rámáy. (Kishk.-K., xli. 14), and the Mekalas were the inhabitants of the Mekala hills, *i. e.*, the hills bounding Chhattisgaṛh on the west and north. Northward dwelt the Puṇḍras and southward the Kalingas. Hence Utkala comprised the southern portion of Chuta Nagpur, the northern Tributary States of Orissa and the Balasore district. Various derivations have been suggested of the name Utkala, but I would only draw attention to some of the above passages where Utkala and Mekala are placed together as if their names possessed something in common. See also in verse 53.

† The Matsya Puráṇa reads the same (cxiii. 44), but I have not found them mentioned elsewhere They appear from the context to be the same as the *Právṛisheyas* of the Bhíshma-P. list (ix. 358).

‡ These are mentioned in the Bhíshma-P. list (ix. 358), and were perhaps an off-lying branch of the Bhárgava race in the East; see note to verse 35.

44 the Jñeya-mallakas, * and the Prág-jyotishas, † and

The Hari-Vaṁśa mentions a prince called *Bhárga* or *Bhárgava*, who founded Bhṛigu-bhúmi or Bhárga-bhúmi; and as he was a grandson of Divodása king of Benares, his country may perhaps have been in the Eastern region (xxix. 1587 and 1597; and xxxii. 1753). The Bhíshma-P. list names also *Bhárgas* here (*loc. cit.*).

* The Váyu Puráṇa reads *Geyamarthakas* (xlv. 123), and the Matsya *Geyamálavas* (cxiii. 44), and the Bhíshma-P. list omits the corresponding name (see ix. 358). None of these names are in the dictionary, and I have not met any of them elsewhere.

† Prág-jyotisha was a famous kingdom in early times and is often mentioned in the M.-Bh. The references to it, however, are rather perplexing, for in some passages it is called a Mlec'c'ha kingdom ruled over by king Bhagadatta, who is always spoken of in respectful and even eulogistic terms (*e. g.*, Sabhá-P., xxv. 1000-1; and l. 1834; Udyoga-P., clxvi. 5804; and Karṇa-P., v. 104-5), and in other passages it is called a Dánava or Asura kingdom ruled over by the demons Naraka and Muru (Vana-P., xii. 488; Udyoga-P., xlvii. 1887–92; Hari-V., cxxi. 6791–9; cxxii. 6873, etc.; and clxxiv. 9790; and Annotations to Kishk.-K., xliii. in Gorresio's Rámáyaṇa); while in some other passages the allusions seem mixed (*e. g.*, Sabhá-P., xiii. 578–80, which seems to call Bhagadatta a Yavana; and as to this, see *id.* l. 1834–6). The second class of passages occur, I believe, only in descriptions of Kṛishṇa's exploits; they are spoilt by hyperbolical laudation and are probably later than the first class. Prág-jyotisha was placed in the North region (Sabhá-P., xxv. 1000; and Vana-P., ccliii. 15240–2), but was also considered to be in the East as in the text here. North of it seemingly lay tracts called Antar-giri, Vahir-giri and Upa-giri (Sabhá-P., xxv. 1000—xxvi 1012) which appear to be the lower slopes of the Himalayas and the Terai; and it was close to the mountains for Bhagadatta is called S'ailálaya (Strí-P., xxiii. 644). It bordered on the Kirátas and C'ínas for they formed his retinue (Sabhá-P., xxv. 1002; Udyoga-P., xviii. 584-5). He also drew his troops from among the people who dwelt in the marshy regions near the sea, *Ságaránúpa* (Sabhá-P., xxv. 1002; xxxiii. 1268-9; and Karṇa-P., v. 104-5), and it is even said he dwelt at the Eastern Ocean (Udyoga-P., iii. 74); these marshy regions can only be the alluvial tracts and islands near the mouths of the Ganges and Brahma-putra as they existed anciently. These data indicate that Prág-jyotisha comprised the whole of North Bengal proper. The Raghu Vaṁśa places it seemingly beyond the Brahma-putra (iv. 81); but Kálidása was a little uncertain in distant geography. Its capital was called Prág-jyotisha also. Although the people were mlec'c'has, the Rámáyaṇa ascribes the founding of this kingdom to Amúrta-rajas, one of the four sons of a great king Kuśa (A'di-K.,

the Madras, * *and* the Videhas, † *and* the Támra-

xxxv. 1–6). Amúrta-rayas, as the name is generally written in the M.-Bh., is mentioned there simply as father of the famous king Gaya (*e. g.*, Vana-P., xcv. 8528–39; and Droṇa-P., lxvi. 2334, &c).

* This seems an impossible name here (see verse 36). The Váyu Purána reads *Muṇḍas* instead (xlv. 123) which is permissible. The Muṇḍas are a large Dráviḍian tribe in Chuta Nagpur (Risley's Tribes and Castes of Bengal, II. 101), and are named in the M.-Bh. (Bhíshma-P., lvi. 2410).

The Matsya Puráṇa however reads *Puṇḍras* instead (cxiii. 45) and the Bhíshma-P. list also mentions them in this region (ix. 358). This is the best reading, for the Puṇḍras were held to be closely allied to the Angas, Vangas and Suhmas (see page 325 note ‡, page 326 note * and page 327 note *), and should rightly be placed here along with those races, rather than in the South according to verse 45. The name occurs in various forms, *Puṇḍraka* (Sabhá-P., iv. 119), *Pauṇḍra*, (Ádi-P., clxxxvii. 7020), *Pauṇḍraka* (Ádi-P., clxxxvi. 6992; Sabhá-P., xxxiii. 1270) and *Pauṇḍrika* (Sabhá-P., li. 1872). They appear to be used often as if equivalent (*e. g.*, Sabhá-P., xiii. 584), and yet a distinction seems to be made between Puṇḍras and Pauṇḍras for they are separately mentioned in the Bhíshma-P. list (ix. 358 and 365); and Puṇḍras, Puṇḍrakas and Pauṇḍrikas are all mentioned in one passage (Sabhá-P., li. 1872–4). All, however, appear to have composed one people, and they were not a barbarous nation. From the arrangements of names and descriptions given in various passages (Ádi-P., cxiii. 4453; Sabhá-P., xiii. 584; xxix. 1091–7; Vana-P., li. 1988; Ásvamedh.-P., lxxxii. 2464-5) it appears the Puṇḍras had the Káśis on their north, the Angas, Vangas and Suhmas on their north-east and east; and the Oḍras on their south-east; hence their territory corresponded to the modern Chuta Nagpur with the exception of its southern portions. Their bounds on the south were no doubt the land of the Utkalas (see page 327 note *). In one passage (Ádi-P., lxvii. 2679) it is stated an ancient king Balína reigned over both Pauṇḍra and Matsya; this suggests that their territory extended to near the R. Chumbal anciently (see page 307 note *), and tends to part them from the Angas, Vangas, &c.

† Videha was a famous country in early times. Cunningham says it appears to have comprised the northern portion of North Behar from the R. Gaṇḍak to the R. Kauśikí or Kosi (Arch. Surv. Repts., XVI. 34 and map); but its western boundary was the Sadá-níra (see page 294 note ‡), and it seems Videha extended from the Rapti to the Kosi. Northwards it extended close to the Himalayas, and on the south it was bounded by a kingdom, the capital of which was Vaiśálí (Rámáy., Ádi-K., xlvi. 10–11; and xlviii. 21–25), or the modern Besarh which is about 27 miles north of Patna (Arch. Surv. Repts., I. 55; and XVI. 6 and 34). The capital was *Mithilá* (Rámáy., Ádi-K.,

42

liptakas,* the Mallas,† the Magadhas,‡ the Go-

xlix. 9–16; and M.-Bh., S'ánti-P., cccxxvii. 12233–8), and this name often designated the country itself, especially in the Rámáyaṇa. The people were called Videhas (or Videgha, as the earlier form was, see S'ata-P. Bráh. I. iv. 14), and also Mithilas (Vana-P., ccliii. 15243). Its kings, who were often highly educated (S'ánti-P., cccxxvii. 12215–25), are generally called Janaka, which seems to have been the ordinary royal title (Vana-P., cxxxiii. 10637). Cunningham says the capital was Janakpur, which is now a small town just within the Nepal border, north of where the Mozufferpur and Darbhanga districts meet (Arch. Surv. Repts., XVI. 34 and map), but I have not met this name in Sanskrit works.

* Or *Támra-liptas.* The country and people are often mentioned in the M.-Bh., and both forms of the name are used (A'di-P., clxxxvi. 6993; Sabhá-P., xxix. 1098; and Droṇa-P., lxx. 2436). The name was modified into Táma-liptaka which the Váyu Puráṇa reads (xlv. 123), and Táma-lipta (which occurs in canto lviii. verse 14), and Dáma-lipta (see Story of Mitra-gupta in the Daśa-kumára-c'arita), and corrupted into the modern *Tamluk.* The town Tamluk is in the Midnapur district near the mouth of the Rupnarayan River. It used to be a famous port during the middle ages of Indian history. The country Támra-liptaka corresponded therefore to the eastern part of the present district of Midnapur.

† The Váyu Puráṇa reads *Málas* (xlv. 123). This people appear to be the Málés (properly Máls) and Mál Pahániyas, two Dráviḍian tribes which now inhabit the Rájmahall and Rámgarh hills in Western Bengal (Risley's Tribes and Castes of Bengal, II. 51 and 66). The Matsya Puráṇa reads S'álvas (cxiii. 45) erroneously.

‡ Or Mágadhas. Magadha comprised the present districts of Gaya and Patna. It was a famous kingdom from the earliest times. The Rámáyaṇa says it was founded by Vasu one of the four sons of a great king Kuśa (A'di-K., xxxv. 1–9); and the M.-Bh. says it was established by Vṛihad-ratha, who was son of Vasu king of C'edi (Adi-P., lxiii. 2361–5; and Hari-V., xxxii. 1805), but who is also called an Auga (S'ánti-P., xxix. 921–31.) One appears to be an eastern account and the other a western account, but there may be truth in both accounts, for there was an interval of eight or twelve generations between the two periods spoken of. Both agree that Giri-vraja was made the capital by the founder of the kingdom, the former says by Vasu (*loc. cit.*), and the latter says by Vṛihad-ratha (Hari-V., cxvii. 6598; Sabhá-P., xx. 798–800). Cunningham has identified Giri-vraja with the modern Giryek on the Panchana river about 36 miles north-east of Gaya (Arch. Surv. Repts., I. 16 and plate iii). Rája-gṛiha appears to have been another name of the capital (A'di-P., cxiii. 4451-2; and A'śvamedh-P., lxxxii. 2435–63), but Cun-

mantas,* are known as the peoples in the East.†
45 Now the other peoples who dwell in the Southern Region‡
are the Puṇḍras,§ and Kevalas,|| and Go-lángulas¶ also,

ningham identifies it with the modern Raj-gir about 6 miles west of Giryek (Arch. Surv. Repts., I. 20 and plate iii). The oldest name of this country is said to have been *Kikaṭa*, which occurs in Ṛig-Veda III. 53.14 (Muir's Sansk. Texts, II. 362, 363).

* The Váyu Puráṇa reads *Govindas* (xlv. 123); and the Matsya *Gonarddhas* (cxiii. 45); and the latter people are mentioned in canto lviii. verse 23, but are placed in the South. I have not met with an Eastern people of any of these names elsewhere.

† The Kúrma Puráṇa adds *Káma-rúpa* (xlvii. 38), the modern Kamrup or Gauhaṭi in Assam. It is mentioned in the Raghu-Vaṁśa (iv. 84), but not, I believe, in the Rámáyaṇa nor Mahá-Bhárata.

‡ Dakshiṇápatha; this generally means South India below the Vindhya Range, and a line from Amara-kaṇṭaka to the north of Orissa.

§ This seems to be erroneous, for the Puṇḍras were not properly in the South, and they have been noticed in their appropriate place in the East (see page 329 note *). The Váyu Puráṇa reads *Páṇḍyas* instead (xlv. 124) and so also the Matsya (cxiii. 46), and this is, no doubt, the proper reading, for otherwise this nation, which was the most famous and best known in the South, would be omitted from this list. Páṇḍya is often mentioned in the M.-Bh.; but not in the Rámáy., except in the geographical canto (Kishk. K., xli. 15 and 25) which is probably an addition to the original poem. It comprised the modern districts of Madura and Tinnevelly. The capital was Mathurá, the modern Madura. The Páṇḍyas belong to the Dráviḍian family, but the Hari-Vaṁśa makes them, or more probably the royal house, descendants of the Paurava race; it says Páṇḍya, Kerala, Kola and C'ola were four brothers and gave origin to the four peoples of those names (xxxii. 1832–6).

|| This is; no doubt, a mistake for *Keralas*, which the Váyu (xlv. 124) and Matsya (cxiii. 46) Puráṇas read; and the Bhíshma-P. list twice (ix. 352 and 365; though the first mention is probably a mistake). They were a forest-tribe (Sabhá-P., xxx. 1174–5) and are placed on the west side by the Raghu-Vaṁśa (iv. 53–54). They are said to be descended from an eponymous king Kerala, and to be closely allied to the Páṇḍyas, C'olas, &c. in the Hari-Vaṁśa (xxxii. 1836). They appear to have occupied the whole of the west coast from Calicut to Cape Comorin.

¶ "The Cow-tails;" a pure fancy, stories of tailed races being common all over the world. It may correspond to Gonarddhas in canto lviii, verse 23; but the Matsya Puráṇa reads *C'olas and Kulyas* (cxiii. 46), and the Váyu

46 the S'ailúshas,* and Múshikas,† the Kusumas,‡ the

C'aulyas and *Kulyas* (xlv. 124); and the proper reading should, no doubt, be *C'olas* and *Kolas*. The Hari-Vaṁśa makes these two tribes closely allied to the Páṇḍyas and Keralas (see the last two notes).

C'ola was a kingdom in early times (Sabhá-P., li. 1891–3) and is often mentioned in the M.-Bh. (*e. g.*, Vana-P., li. 1988; and Sabhá-P., xxx. 1174, where C'oḍra is, no doubt, a mistake for C'ola; also Bhíshma-P., ix. 367; and Droṇa-P. xi. 398). The Hari-Vaṁśa says king Sagara degraded them (xiv. 784). C'ola comprised the modern districts of Tanjore, Trichinopoly, Pudukota and South Arcot.

The *Kolas* are scarcely ever mentioned; yet they appear to be referred to in Sabhá-P., xxx. 1171, and Áśvamedh.-P., lxxxiii. 2476–7. Their position is uncertain. Are they to be identified with the *Koravas* or *Kurrus*, who are a vagrant tribe in Madras (Madras Census of 1891, Report, p. 304).

* Canto lviii, verse 20 mentions the *S'ailikas*; and the Váyu Puráṇa (xlv. 125) and Matsya (cxiii. 47) read *Setukas*. I have not found any of these names elsewhere, but *S'aila* occurs in Vana-P., ccliii. 15250, perhaps as the name of a country near Páṇḍya in the extreme south, so that S'ailikas might mean its people. Does Setuka refer to Ráma's *setu* or Adam's bridge and mean the people who live close to it?

† The Bhíshma-P. list mentions these people in the same connexion (ix. 366), and another Southern people called *Múshakas* twice (ix. 366 and 371). Canto lviii mentions instead of them the *Ṛishikas* in the South (verse 27), and the *Mṛishikas* in the South-east (verse 16). I have not found the latter name elsewhere, but the Ṛishikas appear to have been well-known, there being one people of that name in the North (Sabhá-P., xxvi. 1033–6; Rámáy., Kishk-K., xliv. 13; and Matsya Puráṇa cxx. 53) and another in the South (Kishk-K., xli. 16; and Hari-V., cxix. 6724–6). The Matsya Puráṇa reads *Sútikas* (cxiii. 47) which appears to be erroneous.

‡ Canto lviii omits this people and names *Kumuda* hill (verse 26). The Váyu Puráṇa reads *Kumanas* (xlv. 125), and the Matsya *Kupathas* (cxiii. 47). I have not found any of these names elsewhere. Probably the reading should be *Kurumbas* or *Kurubas*. The ancient Kurumbas or Pallavas occupied a territory which comprised the modern districts of Madras, Chinglepnt, North and South Arcot, Salem and the south-east portion of Mysore, with Káñc'í, the modern Conjeveram, for their capital, and their power attained its zenith about the 7th cent. A. D., or perhaps a century or two later After their overthrow they were scattered far and wide and are numerous now in most of the districts south of the R. Kistna in the middle and eastern parts of the Madras Presidency and in Mysore (Madras Census of 1891, Report, pp. 259 and 289).

Náma-vásakas,* the Mahá-ráshṭras,† Máhishakas‡ and Ka-

* This is, no doubt, the same as the *Vana-vásakas* of the Bhíshma-P. list (ix. 366), with which the Váyu Puráṇa agrees in reading *Vana-vásikas* (xlv. 125). As this name simply means "Forest-dwellers," it may include several races, who inhabited the great Southern forests; or it may denote the people of the kingdom called Vana-vásin, which was founded by Sárasa in the Dekhan (Hari-V., xcv. 5213 and 5231–3). Perhaps they may be identified with the Banjáris or Lambádis, who are the great travelling traders of South India; and who are supposed to be descendants of Bálin and Sugríva the Vánara kings in the Rámáyaṇa (Madras Census of 1891, Report, pp. 186 and 279). The Matsya Puráṇa reads *Váji-vásikas* (cxiii. 47), which seems erroneous.

† The people of Mahá-ráshṭra, the modern Mahraṭṭas, whom canto lviii also considers to be in the South (verse 23). The name is a late one as I have not found it in the Mahá-Bhárata or Rámáyaṇa. It was a large kingdom in Hiuen Thsang's time in the 7th cent. A. D., and Cunningham makes it comprise nearly the western half of the Dekhan between the 16th and 20th parallels of latitude, with its capital at Kalyáni (Anc. Geog. of India, I. 553).

The Matsya Puráṇa reads *Nava-ráshṭras* (cxiii. 47), but not well, for this country and people are mentioned in the M-Bh. as one of the kingdoms near the Kurus, and as situated in the south-west of Madhya-deśa or on the borders of Rajputana (Sabhá-P., xxx. 1110; and Viráṭa-P., i. 11–12); and the Hari-Vaṁśa derives them from an eponymous king Nava, making him and the progenitors of the Yaudheyas, Ambashṭhas and S'ivis (which were tribes in or near the Panjab) all sons of king Uśínara (xxxi. 1674–8). Nava-ráshṭra is therefore out of place here.

‡ So also in the Bhíshma-P. list (ix. 366), or *Máhishikas* as the Matsya Puráṇa reads (cxiii. 47). These people are, no doubt, the same as the *Máhishmakas* (Aśvamedh.-P., lxxxiii. 2475–7), that is, the people of *Máhish-matí.* Máhish-matí was an ancient and famous city (Sabhá-P., xxx. 1125–63) and was situated on the R. Narmadá, at a place where the Vindhyas and the Ṛiksha Mts. (the Satpura range) contract the valley (Hari-V., xcv. 5218, &c). Muc'ukunda was its founder according to that passage, and Mahish-mat according to another (*id.*, xxxiii. 1846–7). Their descendant was the great Arjuna Kártavírya (*ibid.*, 1850–xxxiv. 1890). Máhish-matí is identified with the modern Maheswar on the Narmadá in the Imp. Gaz. of India (Vol. X, p. 329), but this hardly agrees with the notices in Sanskrit writings; for Maheswar must have lain within the ancient Avanti (see verse 52), and Avanti was held to be sometimes in the South and sometimes in the West, whereas Máhish-matí is never, I believe, placed anywhere but in the South.

47 lingas* on all sides,† A'bhíras,‡ and Vaiśikyas,§ A'ḍhakyas,||

A more easterly position, such as Mandhátá or near there, seems better. At the time of the great war its king was Níla and his people were called Líláyudhas (Udyoga-P., xviii. 592–3) or Níláyndhas (Bhíshma-P., lvi. 2414). Its people were afterwards declared to have become degraded because of the extinction of sacred rites, &c. (Anuśás.-P., xxxiii. 2103–4; Muir's Sanskrit Texts, I. 177). A *Máhishikí*, which seems to be a river, is mentioned in the Rámáy. in this region (Kishk.-K., xli. 16.)

* Or *Kálingas*. Kalinga was an ancient kingdom, its kings were famous (A'di-P., lxvii. 2701), and its princesses married into the Aryan royal families (*e. g.*, A'di-P., xcv. 3774–5, & 3780; and S'ánti-P., iv). Its people were closely allied to the Angas and Vangas, and the three nations are often linked together (*e. g.*, A'di-P., ccxv. 7820; and Droṇa-P., lxx. 2436), and this connexion is emphasized by the allegation that these three and also the Suhmas and Puṇḍras were descended from five eponymous brothers (see page 325 note ‡). Kalinga comprised all the Eastern coast between the Utkalas on the north (Raghu-V., iv. 38) and the Telingas or Telugus on the south. The R. Vaitaraṇi (the modern Byturni) flowed through it, and the Mahendra Mts. (the Eastern Ghats) were within its southern limits (A'di-P., ccxv. 7820–24; and Raghu-V., iv. 38–43). Kalinga therefore comprised the modern province of Orissa and the district of Ganjam and probably also that of Vizagapatam. The Matsya Puráṇa makes Kalinga extend as far west as the Amara-kaṇṭaka hills (clxxxv. 12), but Kalinga there is, no doubt, an error for Kosala. Certain Kalingas have been mentioned in verse 37 above.

† *Sarvaśaḥ*. This seems to be rather a stereotyped phrase. The Matsya Puráṇa also reads the same (cxiii. 47). *Púrvaśaḥ* would be a preferable reading, for the Kalingas occupied a large part of the Eastern coast and do not appear to have inhabited any other part of the Dekhan.

‡ These may have been an off-lying branch of this aboriginal race (see note to verse 35). The Váyu Puráṇa reads *Abhíras* here (xlv. 126). The Matsya Puráṇa reads *Kárúshas* (cxiii. 48); they are the same as the *Karúshas* mentioned in verse 53; they come in their proper position there and are out of place here.

§ This is not in the dictionary. For *saha vaiśikyá* read either one word or *saha vaiśikyair*. The Váyu (xlv. 126) and Matsya (cxiii. 48) Puráṇas read *Eshíkas* or *Aishíkas*; but I have not found any of these names elsewhere.

|| I have not met this name elsewhere and it is not in the dictionary. The Váyu Puráṇa (xlv. 126) and the Matsya (cxiii. 48) read *A'ṭavyas*, and this may mean either "forest-dwellers," or more probably "the people of *Aṭaví*," which is mentioned as a city in the Dekhan, but without any data to identify it (Sabhá-P., xxx. 1176).

and the S'avaras,* the Pulindas,† the Vindhya-mauleyas,‡ the people of Vidarbha§ and the Daṇḍa-

* The S'avaras are an aboriginal tribe, according to some Drávidian, and according to others Kolarian. They are mentioned rarely in the M.-Bh. (S'ánti-P., lxv. 2429; clxviii. 6294–6303; clxxiii. 6415; and ccvii. 7559–61) and Rámáy. (A'di-K., i. 59; Araṇya-K., lxxvii. 6–32; &c). They are represented in these passages as dwelling in Central India and the Dekhan, as being wicked Dasyus, and as practising evil customs. They are still found scattered about in those parts and also towards Orissa, under the names Sabar, Saur, Suir, &c. In the Madras Presidency they are found chiefly in the Ganjam and Vizagapatam districts (Madras Census of 1891, Report, p. 254.) "The Savars believe their original condition to have been that of a wandering tribe, roaming through the hills of Orissa and Chota Nagpur, living on the fruits of the forest and acknowledging the rule of no recognized chief." (Risley's Castes and Tribes of Bengal, II. 241–246); and this belief agrees, if we extend their range, with the earliest notices of them. See also Cunningham, Arch. Surv. Repts., XVII and XX.

† These people are mentioned again in verse 50 as being also in the West, and there appears to have been a Northern branch of them in the Himalayas (see page 316 note †). This Southern branch seems from the M.-Bh. to have occupied the middle portion of the Dekhan (Sabhá-P., xxx. 1120; and Bhíshma-P., ix. 369; and Rámáy., Kishk.-K., xli.17), and extended eastward where they had a great city (Sabhá-P., xxviii. 1068). They were an aboriginal tribe, for they were mlec'c'has (Vana-P., clxxxviii. 12838–40); they became out-castes from not seeing bráhmans (Anuśás.-P., xxxiii. 2104–5); they are called wicked and are said to have practised evil customs (S'ánti-P., ccvii. 7559–61). The Váyu Puráṇa reads *Pulindras* (xlv. 126) erroneously.

‡ The Váyu Puráṇa reads *Vindhya-múlíkas* (xlv. 126), which is synonymous, "those who dwell at the foot of the Vindhya mountains," or "the aborigines of the Vindhya mountains." I have not met this name as describing any particular people, and taken in its general meaning it would include the races mentioned in verses 53–55 below: but perhaps it may be read as an adjective to "Pulindas." The Matsya Puráṇa reads *Vindhya-pushikas* (cxiii. 48), which seems erroneous.

§ Vidarbha was one of the most ancient and renowned kingdoms in the Dekhan (Vana-P., xcvi. and xcvii). It comprised the valley of the Payoshṇi, the modern Purna and the middle portion of the Tapti (see page 299 note † and Vana-P., cxx. 10289–90), and corresponded to the western part of the modern *Berar* and the valley-country west of that. It is said to have been founded by a king Vidarbha who built a city called Vidarbhá (Hari-V., cxvii. 6588 and 6605–8; and Vana-P., lxxii), which seems to have been the same

48 kas,* the Paurikas,† and the Maulikas,‡ the Aśmakas,§

as Kuṇḍina the capital (Vana-P. lxxii: and Hari-V., civ. 5800–7; cxviii. 6661–2). Its most famous king was Bhíshmaka, who held the title "king of the Dekhan" (*id.*, cxvii. 6590–1). The people were *Bhojas* (Udyoga-P., xlvii. 1881) or perhaps only the royal family was so called (*id.*, clvii. 5350–1; Sabhá-P., xiii. 585–8), and so also in the Raghu-Vaṁśa with reference to a period many generations anterior (vi. 59 and 69; and vii). The name Bhoja seems to have more than one application, for the Bhojas together with the Andhakas and Vṛishṇis belonged to the Yádava race (Hari-V., xciv. 5181–5204), and the name appears to have been applied also in a much wider sense to Kshattriyas descended from Yayáti (Sabhá-P., xiii. 566–71).

* The Daṇḍakas are mentioned in the M.-Bh. (Sabhá-P., xxx. 1169) and were the inhabitants of the forest region called *Daṇḍakáraṇya*. Daṇḍaka originally was the name of the immense forest, where Ráma went in banishment, and which is described in the Rámáy. as covering the whole of Central India from Bundelkhand on the north to southward of the Godaveri (*Journal, R. A. S.*, 1894, p. 241); but as this forest was gradually cleared away by the spread of the Aryan colonies, its limits diminished till at last Daṇḍaka denoted only the country around the sources of the Godaveri and lower part of the Tapti (M.-Bh., Sabhá-P., xxx. 1169; Vana-P., lxxxv. 8183–4). It could only have been at this stage that its inhabitants could well have been described by the name Daṇḍakas, and it is no doubt the people of that moderate area who are meant here. To account for the name the Hari-Vaṁśa has provided an eponymous king Daṇḍaka who made Daṇḍakáraṇya (x. 637–9).

† The people of Puriká. This may be either the famous town *Puri* in Orissa, or the town *Puriká* which Muc'ukunda is said to have built on the northern slope of the Ṛiksha Mts. in the kingdom of Máhish-matí (Hari-V., xcv. 5220–8); but the latter seems more probable, judging from the context. For Máhish-matí, see page 333 note ‡. The Váyu Puráṇa reads *Paunikas*, (xlv. 127); is this to be connected with Poonah, south-east of Bombay? I have not met it elsewhere.

‡ The Váyu Puráṇa reads *Maunikas* (xlv. 127); and *Mauleyas* are mentioned in Sabhá-P., li. 1871; but I have not found any of these names elsewhere.

§ This as a people is not in the dictionary. The Váyu Puráṇa reads *Asmakas* (xlv. 127), but Aśmaka seems to be the proper form. These people are mentioned in the Rámáy. (Kishk.-K., xli. 17) and M.-Bh. (Droṇa-P., xxxvii. 1605–8); and are placed in the middle of India by canto lviii. verse 7. They may have been the descendants of Aśmaka, who was the son of king Kalmásha-páda Saudása's queen Madayantí by Vasishṭha (Ádi-P., cxxii.

Bhoga-vardhanas,* Naishikas,† Kuntalas,‡ Andhas,§ Udbhi-
49 das,|| Vana-dárakas¶; these ** *are the peoples of* the countries
of the Southern region.††

4736–7; and clxxvii. 6777–91), and who founded the town Paudanya (*ibid.*, 6791). A queen Aśmakí is mentioned in the Lunar line (*id.*, xcv. 3766).

* I have not found this name elsewhere. Perhaps it may be connected with the Southern Utsava-sanketas (Bhíshma-P., ix. 368; and see page 319 note †).

† This is not in the dictionary. It much resembles the *Násikyas* of canto lviii. verse 24, who are, no doubt, the people of Nasik, north-east of Bombay; but they seem to be intended by *Násikyávas* in verse 51. Naishadhas can hardly be meant, for they are named in verse 54 and were not in South India. The Váyu Puráṇa reads *Nairṇikas* (xlv. 127) which somewhat resembles the *Nairṛitas* of the Bhíshma-P. list (ix. 359).

‡ A people of this name have been mentioned in verse 32, as dwelling in Madhya-deśa. The Kuntalas here were in the Dekhan and are the same as those mentioned in Bhíshma-P., ix. 367, and Karṇa-P., xx. 779. It appears Kuntala lay in the region between Belgaum and Bellary (Arch. Surv. of W. India, No. 5 by J. F. Fleet, p. 6; and No. 10 by J. Burgess, p. 72 note).

§ The Váyu Puráṇa reads *Andhras* (xlv. 127), which is, no doubt, right. Andhas are mentioned in the M.-Bh. (Udyoga-P., xviii. 586; and Bhíshma-P. x. 357), but mistakenly for Andhakas and Andhras respectively. The Andhras or Ándhras were a rude race in early times (Sabhá-P., iv. 119; xxx. 1175; xxxiii. 1270; and Vana-P., li. 1988); but they established a kingdom during the third and second centuries B. C. Andhra was a kingdom also in Hiuen Thsang's time in the 7th century A.D., and comprised the eastern portion of the Nizam's territories, with its capital at Warangal, according to Cunningham (Anc. Geog. of India). Another capital was Dhenukákaṭa, which is Dharaṇikoṭa near Amarávatí on the Kistna (Arch. Surv. of W. India, No. 10 by J. Burgess, p. 32). Andhra is said to be probably the same as Telinga (*ibid.*, p. 72 note; and dictionary), and is taken to be the Sanskrit name for Telugu in the Madras Census Report. Telugu is the speech of the region extending from a parallel of latitude a little north of Madras northward as far as Ichapur in Ganjam; it does not penetrate into Mysore nor the western limits of Anantapur and Bellary, but is spoken by many of the inhabitants of the Nizam's Dominions and the Central Provinces (Report, p. 188).

|| This is not in the dictionary and I have not met with it elsewhere.

¶ "Wood-splitters." The Váyu Puráṇa reads *Nalakálikas* (xlv. 127), other forms of which are *Nalakánanas* and *Nabhakánanas* (dict.).

** The Kúrma Puráṇa adds *Magadhas* (xlvii. 38) mistakenly; they are mentioned in their proper place in verse 44.

†† For *Dakshiṇátyás* read *Dakshiṇáyás*? The Matsya Puráṇa keeps pace

Hear from me *the names of* the Western peoples. The Súryárakas,* the Kálibalas,† and the Durgas,‡ and the
50 Aníkaṭas,§ and the Pulindas,|| and the Sumínas,¶ the

with the text as far as the "Daṇḍakas" and then jumps at once, without any intimation, to the Western peoples beginning with the "Kulíyas" who correspond to the "Pulindas" of verse 50.

* This is obviously a mistake for *Súrpárakas*, which the Váyu Puráṇa reads (xlv. 128). Súrpáraka or S'úrpáraka (both forms seem correct, though the dictionary gives only the latter) was the country in the West where Ráma Jámadagnya dwelt (Vana-P., lxxxv. 8185); though it is also placed in the South (Sabhá-P., xxx. 1169; and Vana-P., lxxxviii. 8337), because it was near the Southern sea in the Western region (S'ánti-P., xlix. 1778–82). It bordered on the sea near Prabhása (Vana-P., cxviii. 10221–7), which is the modern Somnath in the peninsula of Káthiáwár; it included the country around the mouth of the Narmadá (Anuśás.-P., xxv. 1736), and the mouth of that river was so specially connected with Ráma that it was called Jámadagnya (Matsya Puráṇa, cxciii. 33–34). He built the city Súrpáraka there (Hari-V., xcvi. 5300), and Dr. Burgess has identified it with the small modern town Supara near Bassein, north of Bombay. The country Súrpáraka therefore comprised the littoral tract from about Bassein to about the R. Narmadá. (Arch. Surv. of W. India, No. 10 p. 31). The proper reading in Rámáy. Kishk.-K., xliii. 5, should, no doubt, be "the Súrpárakas also" instead of "the extensive towns" (Gorresio's Edition, Annotations).

† This is not in the dictionary. The Váyu Puráṇa reads *Kolavanas* (xlv. 128), but I have not found either name elsewhere. Perhaps this is to be connected with *Kalwan*, a town about 37 miles north of Nasik (which is mentioned in page 339, note ||).

‡ This is not in the dictionary and I have not found the name elsewhere; but the *Durgalas* are mentioned in the Bhíshma-P. list (ix. 359). Perhaps this is to be connected with *Dúngar-pur*, a town and state about 90 miles north-east of Ahmedabad.

§ Or Aníkaṭas, or C'áníkaṭas; neither is in the dictionary. The Váyu Puráṇa reads *Kálítakas* (xlv. 128); but I have not found these words elsewhere. These names suggest *Calicut*, but that is too far south to be admissible here in the Western region.

|| See note to verse 47 above. This branch would be among the hills south-west of Malwa or the southern portion of the Aravalli hills probably The Váyu Puráṇa reads *Puleyas* (xlv. 129), and the Matsya *Kulíyas* (cxiii. 49); but I have not met with either name elsewhere.

¶ This is not in the dictionary. The Váyu Puráṇa reads *Surálos* (xlv. 129), and the Matsya *Sirálas* (cxiii. 49); but I have not found any of these words

Rúpapas,* and the Svápadas,† and the Kurumins,‡ and
51 all the Kaṭháksharas,§ and the others *who are called* Násikyávas,|| and the others *who live* on the north bank of the Narmadá,¶ the Bhíru-kaććhas,** and the Máheyas,†† and

elsewhere. Are these two names to be identified with *Israel?* There was an ancient Jewish colony, the modern Beni-Israel, on the Bombay coast before the 2nd cent. A. D. (Hunter's Indian Empire, p. 234).

* The Váyu (xlv. 129), and the Matsya (cxiii. 49) Purāṇas read *Rúpasas.* I have not met either name elsewhere. The Bhíshma-P. list mentions *Rúpaváhikas* (ix. 351).

† This as the name of a people is not in the dictionary; but *S'va-pac'a* "dog-cooking," (=*S'va-páka,* which would not suit the metre) occurs, as the name of a degraded tribe (Manu, x. 19 and 51). Tri-śanku is said to have associated with the S'va-pákas, when discarded by his father (Hari-V., xii. 721–3). The Váyu Puráṇa (xlv. 129) and the Matsya (cxiii. 49) read *Tápasas,* which resembles the *Tápasáśramas* placed in the south region by canto lviii. verse 27, which might mean the descendants of ascetics.

‡ This is not in the dictionary. The Váyu Puráṇa reads *Turasitas* (xlv. 129), but I have not met either name elsewhere. The Matsya reads *Taittirikas* (cxiii. 49), which resembles the *Tittiras* mentioned in Bhíshma-P., l. 2084 but there are no data to identify them.

§ This is not in the dictionary. The Váyu Puráṇa reads *Paraksharas* (xlv. 129), and the Matsya *Káraskaras* (cxiii. 49). The *Páraśavas* of canto lviii verse 31 appear to be the same people. I have not met with any of these names elsewhere, except Káraskaras in Sabhá-P., xlix. 1804, but the Páraśavas might mean a tribe which claimed descent from Paraśu-Ráma.

|| This is not in the dictionary. The Váyu Puráṇa reads "Násikyas and others" (xlv. 130); this agrees with the *Násikyas* of canto lviii, verse 24 except that the latter are placed in the South. The Násikyas are, no doubt, the people of Nasik, which is an ancient and sacred city north-east of Bombay. The Matsya Puráṇa reads "and others who *are called* Vásikas" (cxiii. 50), but I have not met this name elsewhere.

¶ The Váyu Puráṇa (xlv. 130) and the Matsya (cxiii. 50) say "within the Narmadá."

** Or *Bháru-kac'c'has* as the Matsya Puráṇa reads (cxiii. 50). These are, no doubt, the same as the *Bhṛigu-kac'c'has* of canto lviii. verse 21. The word is the Greek Barugaza and survives in the modern Bharuch or Broach, a large town near the mouth of the Narmadá (Anc. Geog. of India). The Váyu Puráṇa reads *Bhánu-kac'c'hras* (xlv. 130) erroneously. None of these names occur I believe in the Rámáyana or Mahá-Bhárata.

†† These are, no doubt, the people who dwelt along the R. Mahi (see page

52 the Sárasvatas* also, and the Káśmíras,† and the Su-ráshṭras,‡ and the Avantyas,§ and the Arbudas‖ also. These are the Western peoples.

53 Hear the inhabitants of the Vindhya Mountains.¶ The

294, note §) north of Baroda. The *Máhikas* of the Bhishma-P. list (ix. 354) are no doubt the same.

* So also the Matsya Puráṇa (cxiii. 50). "The people who dwell along the R. Saras-vatí," which is, no doubt, the small river of that name that flows into the sea at Prabhása, the modern Somnath, in the peninsula of Káthiáwár (Vana-P., lxxxii. 5002–4; and S'alya-P., xxxvi. 2048–51). They are not the same as the Śárasvatas of canto lviii. verse 7, who were in Madhya-deśa. The Váyu Puráṇa reads instead "Sahasas and S'áśvatas" (xlv. 130); I have not found either name elsewhere, but the *S'áśikas* of the Bhíshma-P. list (ix. 354) are, no doubt, the same as the second of these.

† This name is altogether out of place here, and the Káśmíras have been mentioned in their proper position in verse 41. The Váyu Puráṇa reads *Kac'c'hvíyas* instead (xlv. 131) and the Matsya *Kac'c'hikas* (cxiii. 51), which indicate the correct reading. They are the people of *Kac'c'ha* (see canto lviii. verse 28) the modern Kachh or Kutch.

‡ Su-ráshṭra is a country frequently mentioned in the M.-Bh., but the references seldom convey any definite information. It included the peninsula of Káthiáwár and the country around the G. of Cambay—that is, not quite all the modern territory called Gujarat (Vana-P., lxxxviii. 8344–9). It is very rarely alluded to in the Rámáy. (see once in A'di-K., xii. 23). The old name survives in the town Surat near the mouth of the Tapti.

§ This form is not given in the dictionary; read *A'vantyáś* for *Avantyáś?* They are the people of Avanti; see note to verse 55 where the Avantis are mentioned again, and more appropriately, for canto lviii. verse 22 places them in the Tortoise's right side, *i.e.*, the South: but they were considered to be in both regions.

The Váyu Puráṇa (xlv. 131) and the Matsya (cxiii. 51) read *A'nartas*, which is perhaps better, as they are placed by canto lviii. verse 30 in the Tortoise's right hind-foot. A'narta was the country which had for its capital Dváraká or Dvára-vatí or Kuśa-sthalí, the modern Dwarka on the sea-shore at the extreme west of the peninsula of Kathiáwar (S'ánti-P., cccxli. 12955; Hari-V., cxiii. 6265–6). It was Kṛishṇa's special kingdom, but it was founded long before (Hari-V., x. 642–9; and xciv. 5163–9).

‖ The people of Arbuda, the modern Mt. Abu near the south end of the Aravalli hills.

¶ For *Vindha-nivásinaḥ* read *Vindhya-nivásinaḥ*; see verse 55. Vindhya is used here in its general and wider meaning, as denoting the whole mountain-

Sarajas,* and Karúshas,† and the Keralas,‡ and Utkalas,§

chain from Gujarat eastwards, and not in the precise sense given it in verses 21–23, because the Naishadhas, Avantis and other western people are included in this group.

* I have not met with this name elsewhere, and it is not in the dictionary. The Váyu Puráṇa (xlv. 132) and the Matsya (cxiii. 52) read *Málavas*, which is no doubt correct. Málava is the modern Málwa; and the people are generally mentioned in the M.-Bh. as a tribe rather than as a settled nation (*e.g.*, Sabhá-P., xxxiii. 1270; li. 1871; and Vana-P, ccliii. 15256). Málava does not appear to have been so extensive however as Málwa and, as this passage indicates, denoted rather the upper portion of that region bordering on the Vindhyas, west of Avanti.

† The name is also written *Kárusha*, *Kárúsha* and *Kárushaka*. This people constituted a powerful nation under king Danta-vakra in the Páṇḍavas' time (Sabhá-P., xiii. 575–7; and Hari-V., xci. 4963); but they seem to have consisted of several tribes (Udyoga-P., iii. 81) and were not looked upon as closely allied to the races around them, for their origin is carried directly back to an eponymous ancestor Karúsha, a son of Manu Vaivasvata, in the Hari-Vaṁśa (x. 614; and xi. 658). The position of Karúsha is indicated by the following allusions. It is linked with C'edi and with Káśi (Ádi-P., cxxiii. 4796; Bhíshma-P., ix. 348; liv. 2242; lvi. 2415; cxvii. 5446; and Karṇa-P., xxx. 1231), and with the Vátsyas or Vatsas (Droṇa-P., xi. 396; see page 307, note*); it was not a very accessible country (Sabhá-P., li. 1864); and here it is said to rest on the Vindhyas. Moreover Danta-vakra acknowledged Jarásandha, king of Magadha (see page 330 note ‡) as his suzerain (Sabhá-P., xiii. 575–7; and Hari-V., xci. 4963). Karúsha therefore was a hilly country, south of Káśi and Vatsa, between C'edi and Magadha; that is, it comprised the hilly country of which Rewa is the centre, from about the R. Ken on the west as far as the confines of Behar on the east. I have discussed Karúsha in a paper on "Ancient Cēdi, Matsya and Karūṣa" in the Bengal Asiatic Society's *Journal*, 1895, Part I. p. 249.

‡ This must be incorrect, for the Keralas were a well-known people in the South; see note to *Kevalas* in verse 45. The Váyu Puráṇa (xlv. 132) and Matsya (cxiii. 52) read *Mekalas*, which is no doubt right. They are mentioned in the M.-Bh. (Bhíshma-P., ix. 348; and li. 2103) and occupied the Mekala hills and the hilly country around. The Mekala hills are the hills in which the R. Sone rises (Rámáy., Kishk.-K., xl. 20), and which bound Chhattisgarh on the west and north. These people are often coupled, as here, with the Utkalas.

§ See page 327, note *. Utkala had a wide extension and falls within this group as well as within the Eastern group.

the Uttamarṇas,* and the Daśárṇas,† the Bhojyas,‡ and
54 the Kiskindhakas,§ the Tośalas,|| and the Kośalas,¶

* The *Uttamas* are mentioned in the Bhíshma-P. list (ix. 348) and are no doubt the same people. The Matsya Puráṇa reads *Auṇḍrámáshas* (cxiii. 52). A people called *Urddhva-karṇas* are mentioned in canto lviii. verse 16. I have not, however, found any of these names elsewhere.

† This people formed a well-known kingdom in early times (Ádi-P., cxiii. 4449; Vana-P., lxix. 2707-8; and Udyoga-P., cxc.–cxciii), and inhabited the country watered by the R. Daśárṇá, the modern Dasan, a tributary of the Jumna. They are named thrice in the Bhíshma-P. list (ix. 348, 350 and 363), which seems inexplicable. They are mentioned both in the Eastern and in the Western regions in the accounts of Bhíma's and Nakula's campaigns (Sabhá-P., xxviii. 1063–5; and xxxi. 1189); the former of these allusions is correct, but the latter seems to be an error. The capital was Vidiśá, see page 343, note †.

‡ Or better, *Bhojas*, as the Váyu (xlv. 132) and Matsya (cxiii. 52) Puráṇas read. This name, as mentioned in page 335, note §, seems to have had more than one application. Bhojas as a Yádava tribe dwelt in Kṛishṇa's kingdom in Su-ráshṭra; and Bhojas inhabited Mṛittikávatí, which seems from the various references to it to have been situated somewhere on the north-eastern limits of the modern Gujarat (Vana-P., xiv. 629; xx. 791; cxvi. 10172–6; ccliii. 15245; Mausala-P., vii. 244–5; and Hari-V., xxxvii. 1980–7; and xxxviii. 2014). These may be the Bhojas mentioned in the text, inhabiting the extreme western end of the Vindhya range.

§ Or better, *Kishkindhakas*, as the Matsya Puráṇa reads (cxiii. 52). They are no doubt the same as the *Kaiskindhyas* of canto lviii. verse 18; but they cannot have any reference to Kishkindhyá in the Rámáy., for that country lay far to the south of the Godavari (see *Journal*, R. A. S., 1894, pp. 255, &c.), and is referred to in M.-Bh., Sabhá-P., xxx. 1122. The Kishkindhakas mentioned in the Hari-Vaṁśa (xiv. 784) may be the people intended here, but there appear to be no data to identify them.

|| The Matsya Puráṇa reads *Stośalas* (cxiii. 53). They are not in the dictionary, but *Toshala* and *Tosala* are given doubtfully. I have not however found any of these names elsewhere.

¶ These are the people of Dakshiṇa Kosala or Mahá-Kosala, the modern Chhattisgaṛh. In the *Journal*, R. A. S., 1894, p. 246, some reasons have been given for placing the Pañc'ápsaras lake, where Ráma spent ten years of his exile, in this region. May one hazard the conjecture that it was in consequence of his long residence here, that a colony from North Kosala invaded this region, established a kingdom here and gave their name to this country? The connexion was ancient (Áśvamedh.-P., lxxxii. 2464–5).

the Traipuras,* and the Vaidiśas,† the Tumburas,‡ and the Tumbulas,§ the Paṭus,|| and the Naishadhas,¶

* The people of Tripurá, the modern Tewar, on the R. Narmadá. It was a famous city (Sabhá-P., xxx. 1164; Vana-P., ccliii. 15246) deriving its name from a legend that the demons had a triple city *Tri-pura* here, made of gold, silver and iron, and S'iva destroyed it at the intercession of the gods; this is a favourite subject with the poets (Karṇa-P., xxxiii and xxxiv; and see Aitareya-Brahm., I. iv. 23 and 24, for the story in an older form); see also Cunningham's Arch. Surv. Repts., VIII. 124; IX. 54–55; and, XXI. 23; but his connexion of Tripurá with C'edi in early times is mistaken, see paper on "Ancient Cēdi, Matsya and Karūṣa" in *Journal*, Bengal Asiatic Society, 1895, Part I. p. 249.

† For *Vaidiśas* read *Vaidiśás*. These are the people of *Vidiśá*. It was a famous town, the capital of the country Daśárṇa, and situated on the R. Vetra-vatí, the modern Betwa, a little way east of Ujjain (Megha-D., i. 24, 25 and 28). It is probably to be identified with the modern Bhilsa, or rather with Bes-nagar the ancient capital which is close to Bhilsa (Cunningham's Stupa of Bharhut, 132, &c). The Váyu Puráṇa reads *Vaidikas* (xlv. 133), which seems erroneous, though the Vaidiśas are really included among the Daśárṇas in the last verse.

‡ These are mentioned as a wild aboriginal tribe who inhabited the slopes of the Vindhya Mountains in the Hari-Vaṁśa (v. 310–11). The Matsya Puráṇa reads *Tumuras* (cxiii. 53), and the *Tumbumas* (Bhíshma-P., l. 2084) may be the same.

§ The Váyu Puráṇa reads *Tumuras* (xlv. 133); see the last note. The Matsya reads *Tumbaras* (cxiii. 53). This is no doubt a tribe closely allied to the last.

|| This people seems to be the same as the *Paṭac'c'aras*, who are mentioned several times in the M.-Bh.; see page 309, note *. The Váyu Puráṇa reads *Shaṭsuras* (xlv. 133), and the Matsya *Padgamas* (cxiii. 53); but I have not met either of these names elsewhere.

¶ The people of Nishadha; the *Nishadhas*, as the Váyu Puráṇa reads (xlv. 133). This country is chiefly known from the story of its king Nala (Vana-P., liii.–lxxix); otherwise it is rarely mentioned. The chief data for fixing its position are Nala's remarks to his wife when he is banished from his kingdom (*id.*, lxi. 2317–9); and, as stated in note † to page 299, it seems to me the view which he describes could only be obtained completely from a position on the Satpura Mountains about longitude 75° E. The text says also Nishadha rested on the Vindhya Mountains. Hence it may be inferred that Nishadha comprised the country south of the Vindhyas between long. 74° and 75°, with Avanti to the north-east and Vidarbha to the south-east. Its

55 Annajas,* and the Tushṭi-káras,† the Vírahotras,‡ and the Avantis.§ All these peoples dwell on the slopes of the Vindhya Mountains.

capital was probably in the Tapti valley; Damayantí in wandering from it found her way north-eastward to C'edi (see note to C'edi in canto lviii. verse 16).

* I have not met this name elsewhere and it is not in the dictionary. The Matsya Puráṇa reads *Arúpas* (cxiii. 54) which seems erroneous. The Váyu Puráṇa reads *Anúpas* (xlv. 134) which is no doubt correct. Anúpa means "a country situated near water," or "a marshy country." It was applied to various tracts near the sea, generally in the combination *ságaránúpa*, *e.g.*, in Bengal (Sabhá-P., xxv. 1002; xxix. 1101; and xxxiii. 1268–9); in or near the Páṇḍya kingdom in the South (Udyoga-P., xviii. 578); in the north and west of the peninsula of Kathiawar (Hari-V., cxiii. 6361–9; and cxiv. 6410–11); and on the western coast generally (Udyoga-P., iii. 81); but the name was more specially applied to a tract on the west coast which constituted a kingdom in the Páṇḍavas' time (Sabhá-P., iv. 123). The only country which rests on the Vindhyas and borders on the sea is the tract on the east of the G. of Cambay, north of the Narmadá, and this no doubt was Anúpa. It is also indicated that Su-ráshṭra, Anúpa and Ánarta were contiguous countries, and that Anúpa lay beyond and south of Su-ráshṭra (Hari-V., xciv. 5142–80). When the kings of Máhish-matí (see page 333, note ‡) were powerful, the valley of the lower Narmadá and Anúpa would naturally fall under their sway, and this no doubt explains why Kártavírya is called "lord of Anúpa" (Vana-P., cxvi. 10189–90), and king Níla also (Bhíshma-P., xcv. 4210).

† I have not found this name elsewhere, and it is not in the dictionary. The reading should no doubt be *Tuṇḍikeras* as the Váyu Puráṇa reads (xlv. 134). A Tuṇḍikera king is mentioned in the M.-Bh. (Droṇa-P., xvii. 691), and the Tuṇḍikeras (Karṇa-P., v. 138); and the Tuṇḍikeras are said in the Hari-Vaṁśa to be a branch of the Haihaya race (xxxiv. 1895). There is a town called Tendukhera a little north of the Narmadá at nearly long. 79° E.; and as this site suits the text, it may be presumed these people occupied that position in the Narmadá valley. The Matsya Puráṇa reads *S'auṇḍikeras* (cxiii. 54), not quite correctly.

‡ The Váyu Puráṇa (xlv. 134) and the Matsya (cxiii. 54) read *Vítihotras* which is no doubt correct. Vítihotra was a famous Haihaya king, and the Vítihotras were a branch of that race (Hari-V., xxxiv. 1895). They are called *Vítahotras* in the M.-Bh. (Droṇa-P., lxx. 2436). Being Haihayas, they probably occupied a part of the upper Narmadá valley.

§ They have been mentioned already in verse 52. Avanti had the Narmadá flowing through it (Sabhá-P., xxx. 1114; and Vana-P., lxxxix. 8354–8)

56 Next I will tell thee also *the names of* the countries which rest against the Mountains.* The Níháras,† and the Haṁsa-márgas,‡ the Kurus,§ the Gurgaṇas,||

and was on the lower portion of that river, for it is placed in the South in the first of these passages, and in the West in the second passage and in verse 52. It appears to have been bounded by the Ṛiksha Mountains (Satpura range) on the south (Vana-P., lxi. 2317), but its limits on the north are not clear. Its capital, though not mentioned in the M.-Bh., was Ujjayiní or Viśálá, the modern Ujjain, in later times (Megha-D., i. 31). Avanti therefore comprised the region of the sources of the Chambal and the country south-westward as far as the Satpura range. Two brothers Vinda and Anuvinda are often named as the kings of Avanti in the M.-Bh. (Udyoga-P., clxv. 5753; Droṇa-P., xcix. 3682–92; and Karṇa-P., xiii. 498–9), but they were also Kaikeyas and led Kaikeya troops (*ibid.*, 492–524). May it be inferred a branch of the Kaikeyas had invaded and conquered Avanti?

* *Parvatáśrayin.* These mountains are it seems only the Himalaya range. This group repeats many of the tribes mentioned in verses 40–42.

† I have not met this name elsewhere. Are these the modern Newárs, who inhabit the great valley of Nepal and its vicinity, and who were the owners of the country prior to the Gurkhá invasion (*Journal*, Beng. As. Socy., Vol. LXIII, Part I, 213, 214 and 217). The Váyu Puráṇa reads *Nigarharas* (xlv. 135), but I have not found it elsewhere. The Matsya reads *Niráháras* (cxiii. 55) which seems erroneous.

‡ See page 323 note †. The Matsya Puráṇa reads *Sarvagas* (cxiii. 55) which seems erroneous.

§ These are probably the Uttara or Northern Kurus, for the Kurus of Madhya-deśa could not properly be described as dwelling among mountains. They seem to have been the stock from which the Kurus of Madhya-deśa separated off, for the period when Dhṛita-ráshṭra and Páṇḍu were born is described as a golden age, in which both branches of the Kurus engaged in happy rivalry (Ádi-P., cix. 4337–46); but the wistful recollections of their ancient home idealized it afterwards into a blissful land, where fancy gave itself free scope (Rámáy., Kishk.-K., xliv. 82–115). They seem to have occupied the uppermost valleys of the Indus near its sources, with Kailása lying beyond (Vana-P., cxlv. 11025–35); and fervid imagination also placed them close to Mount Meru on its north side (Bhíshma-P., vi. 207–8; and vii. 254), or in the region Hari-varsha, and declared men could not enter their sacred land (Sabhá-P., xxvii. 1054–8). They are described as living in primitive happiness, and women had the utmost freedom there (cxxii. 4719–23; and Rámáy., *loc. cit.*).

|| This is not in the dictionary and I have not met it elsewhere. Are these

57 the Khasas,* and the Kunta-právaraṇas,† the
Urṇas,‡ the Dárvas,§ the Sakṛitrakas,|| the Tri-

people the modern Gurungs, an important tribe of Tatar race, who dwell now throughout Nepal, but whose territory was formerly the country about Lamzung, Ghandrung and Siklis, west of the great valley of Nepal (*Journal*, Bengal Asiatic Society, Vol. LXIII. Part I. 213, 217 and 223–229; Risley's Castes and Tribes of Bengal, I. 304)? The Váyu Puráṇa reads *Tanganas* here (xlv. 135), after having named them previously (*ibid.*, 120); see verse 41. The Matsya reads *A-pathas* (cxiii. 55), which seems erroneous.

* The Khasas or Khaśas are generally mentioned as a half-civilized tribe outside India, along with S'akas, Daradas, &c. (Sabhá-P., li. 1859; Droṇa-P., xi. 399; and cxxi. 4846–7). They are said to have been defeated and degraded by Sagara (Hari-V., xiv. 784), and were considered mlec'c'has (*id.*, xcv. 6440–1; see also Muir's Sansk. Texts, II. 482). The Khasas in the text, however, may perhaps be identified with the Khas, who were formerly a small clan but have developed into the predominant military order of the kingdom of Nepal through intermarriages with bráhmans (*Journal*, Bengal Asiatic Society, Vol. LXIII. Part I. 217–223). See canto lviii. verse 6.

† I have not found this name elsewhere. The Váyu Puráṇa reads *Kuśa* instead of Kunta (xlv. 136), which does not seem satisfactory. The proper reading should no doubt be *Karṇa-právaraṇas*, "those who cover themselves with their ears," a people mentioned several times in the M.-Bh. (Sabhá-P., li. 1875; and Bhíshma-P., li. 2103). They are placed in the South in the story of Sahadeva's conquests (Sabhá-P., xxx. 1170) and among the Kirátas in the Eastern region in the Rámáy. (Kishk.-K. xl. 29); but it seems permissible to identify them with the *Ulúkas*, for a story is told about an Ulúka named *Právára-karṇa* (Vana-P., cxcviii. 13334). The Ulúkas dwelt in the Himalayas (*ibid.*), and formed a kingdom in the Páṇḍavas' time (Udyoga-P., clix. and clx), but it seems impossible to fix their position more definitely than somewhere in Nepal (Sabhá-P., xxvi. 1014–20). The word Karṇa-právaraṇa is also used as an adjective, for Hanúmán saw female Rákshasas in Lanká "three-eared and pin-eared, long-eared, ear-less, and one-eyed and one-eared, and having their ears as a covering" (Rámáy., Sund.-K., xvii. 24); and it was an ancient belief that there were people with immense ears which covered their bodies (Plin., iv. 13; and vii. 2; Mandeville's Travels, chap. xix). The Matsya P. mentions *Kutha-právaraṇas* and *Karṇa-právaraṇas* (cxx. 56 and 58).

‡ This people have been already mentioned in verse 42.

§ These appear to be the same as the *Darvas* mentioned in verse 42; see Cunningham's Arch. Surv. Repts., II. 15; and XIV. 145.

|| This is not in the dictionary; but it seems to be the same as *S'akṛid-gráhas* or *Sakṛid-gráhas*, who are said to be a terrible mlec'c'ha tribe in the North

gartas,* and the Gálavas,† the Kirátas,‡ and the Támasas.§
58 And in this *Bhárata is established* the law of the four ages,
the Kṛita, Tretá and the two others. Such is this country
59 Bhárata, constituted with a four-fold conformation.|| On its
south and west and east is the great ocean; the Himavat
range *stretches along* on its north, like the string of a bow.¶
60 Then this country Bhárata *is filled* with every kind of seed,
O bráhman. *It has* the supremacy of Brahmá, the lordship
of the Ruler of the Immortals, the divinity of the gods, and

(Bhíshma-P., ix. 373). There appear to be no data to fix their position unless they may be connected with the *Sakṛin-nandá*, which seems to be a river in the east of Nepal (Vana-P., lxxxiv. 8137). The text might also be read "and the Kṛitrakas," but I have found no such name elsewhere.

* Or Traigartas. Trigarta was considered to be in the Northern region (Sabhá-P., xxvi. 1026) and also in the Western (*id.*, xxxi. 1189). It is generally mentioned in connexion with the Sindhus, Madras and other Panjab nations (*id.*, li. 1870; Vana-P., cclxiv. 15593–9; cclxx. 15743; Bhíshma-P., xviii. 688; cxviii. 5485; cxx. 5649; Droṇa-P., vii. 183; and also Hari-V., xci. 4965–70). It was near the Kurus, for the Páṇḍavas when burnt out of Váraṇávata visited the Trigartas and other contiguous nations (Ádi-P., clvi. 6084–7); and also near Matsya and S'álva, for these two kingdoms had often raided into Trigarta (Viráṭa-P., xxx). From these indications it appears that Trigarta must have touched the Panjab on the west, and the Kurus on the south-east, and been close to Matsya (see page 307 note *) and S'álva (see note to canto lviii. verse 6) on the south; hence it must have comprised the country from Amballa and Pattiala to the R. Bias, *i.e.*, the Jalandhar doab and the country south-east of that. Cunningham includes Kangra also (Arch. Surv. Repts., II. 16; and XIV. 116 and 117; and Buddh. Cave Temples, p. 93). At the time of the great war Prasthala belonged to Trigarta (see note on page 321), and so brought the Trigarta territories close to Matsya and S'álva.

† These people, no doubt, claimed to be the descendants of the ṛishi Gálava (Hari-V., xxvii. 1463–7; and xxxii. 1767–76), who was a famous son of Viśvámitra (Anuśás.-P., iv. 249–259; Udyoga-P., cv–cxviii; and see cantos XX and XXI above), or took their name from him; see similarly the Átreyas and Bharadvájas of verse 39.

‡ See note to verse 40.

§ These have been already mentioned in verse 41.

|| *C'atuḥ-saṁsthána-saṁsthitam.*

¶ This implies that the Himavat range included also the Sulaiman Mountains along the west of the Panjab. The simile must refer to a drawn bow, with the string angular in the middle.

61 the mortal nature of men.* *It has various* kinds of wild
animals, cattle and aquatic animals; † and all creeping things
likewise. And from it are produced ‡ all immovable things,
62 together with things good or bad. No other land of action
exists among the worlds, O bráhman. Even among the gods,
63 O saintly bráhman, this is ever in truth § the wish—"Oh,
that we shall become men on the earth, when we fall from
our divine condition! A man indeed does actions that the
64 gods and demons cannot do!" Those who are involved in the
fetters of such action, who are eager to proclaim their own
actions, || and who are possessed of a small portion of happiness perform no action at all.

Canto LVIII.

Márkaṇḍeya continuing represents India as resting upon Vishṇu in the form of a tortoise looking eastward, and distributes the various countries and peoples accordingly over the several parts of his body, together with the corresponding lunar constellations. He gives an astrological application to this arrangement and enjoins the performance of religious rites to avoid calamity. He also distributes the constellations of the Zodiac over the Tortoise's body.

Kraushṭuki ¶ spoke

1 Adorable Sir! Thou hast duly declared Bhárata to me, its
2 rivers, mountains, countries, and *the people* who inhabit it.

* *Marutas tathá* seems incorrect. Read instead *martyatá tathá?*

† *Mṛiga-paśv-apsara-yonis.* The meaning of "aquatic animal" is given to *ap-sara* but not to *ap-saras* in the dictionary.

‡ For *pra-yáti* read *pra-játiḥ?*

§ For *sadá esha* read *sadaivaisha?*

|| This seems rather meaningless. For *sva-karma-khyápanotsukaiḥ* the MS. reads *sva-karma-kshapanonmukhaiḥ*, "who are averse to diminishing the stock of their actions;" but *kshapanotsukaiḥ* seems preferable, "who are eager to diminish the stock of their actions."

¶ For *Kroshṭukir* read *Kraushṭukir.*

But thou didst previously make mention of the Tortoise, *who is* the adorable Vishṇu, in Bhárata; I desire to hear fully about his position.

3 What position does he, the god Janárdana, occupy in his form of the Tortoise? And how are weal and woe indicated thereby to mankind according to *the position of* his face and of his feet? Expound all that about him.

Márkaṇḍeya spoke

4 With his face looking eastwards the adorable Tortoise-formed
god takes his position, when he approaches this nine-portioned
5 country Bhárata, O bráhman. The constellations are arrang-
ed all about him in nine divisions, and the countries * also,
O bráhman. Hear duly from me which they are.
6 The Veda-mantras,† the Vimáṇḍavyas,‡ the S'álvas,§

* The arrangement of the countries is very far from correct; and this canto cannot be compared with the last canto for accuracy. To make the shape of India conform to that of a Tortoise lying outspread and facing eastwards is an absurd fancy and a difficult problem.

† This is not in the dictionary and I have not found the name elsewhere. Does it mean "those who observe the Vedas and the Mantras especially" or has it any reference to Brahmávarta?

‡ I have not found this elsewhere and it is not in the dictionary. *Máṇḍavyas* are mentioned in verse 38.

§ Or *S'álveyas* as they were also called (Vana-P. cclxiii. 15576–82). The S'álvas are often mentioned in the M.-Bh. They were near the Kurus (Viráṭa-P. i. 11–12) and the Trigartas (*id.*, xxx); and in the beautiful story of Satya-vat and Sávitrí, he was a S'álva prince and she a Madra princess (Vana-P. ccxcii, &c.). Other indications of S'álva are given in the allusions to Kṛishṇa's conquest of it, but the story is marred because the people are called Daityas and Dánavas, and *Saubha* which seems to have been the capital is described as a city and as situated in the air, and also as able to move about freely (Vana-P. xiv–xxii; Udyoga-P. xlvii. 1886; and Droṇa-P. xi. 395). The S'álva king attacked Dvára-vatí, and Kṛishṇa in retaliation killed him and destroyed Saubha at the gulf of the sea (*ibid.*), which can be none other than the Raun of Kachh. From these indications it appears S'álva was the country along the western side of the Aravalli hills. Saubha is incapable of being determined. S'álva seems to have contained another city called *Márttikávata* (or *Mṛittiká-vatí?*), which is probably the same as the Mṛittiká-vatí mentioned in page 342, note ‡ (Vana-P. xiv. 629; and

and the Nípas,* and the S'akas,† and the Ujji-

xx. 791). The Hari-Vaṁśa says king Sagara degraded the S'álvas (xiv. 784), but this is a late fable for the S'álva king was one of the leading monarchs in Krishṇa's time (*id*, cviii. 6029), and was brother of S'iśu-pála king of C'edi (Vana-P. xiv. 620–7); and other allusions shew that S'álva was a famous kingdom before that (Udyoga-P. clxxiii and clxxiv; and Anuśás.-P. cxxxvii. 6267); besides which, Satya-vat and Sávitrí rank with the noblest characters in ancient Indian story. The weird legend of Vyushitáśva's queen no doubt means her sons became S'álvas and did not originate the race (A'di-P. cxxi. 4695-4714), as in the case of the Madras (page 315, note ‡).

* The Nípas began with king Nípa of the Paurava race, who established his dynasty in Kámpilya, the capital of Southern Páñc'ála, about 12 or 15 generations anterior to the Páṇḍavas; the dynasty flourished in king Brahma-datta who was contemporary with their fifth ancestor Pratípa, and it was destroyed in Bhíshma's time (Hari-V., xx. 1060–73; M-Bh., A'di-P. cxxxviii. 5512–3; and Matsya-P. xlix. 52 and 53) in the person of Janamejaya, nicknamed Durbuddhi, who after exterminating his kinsmen was himself killed by Ugráyudha (Udyoga-P. lxxiii. 2729; Hari-V., xx. 1071–2; and Matsya-P. xlix. 59). Kámpilya is the modern Kampil on the old Ganges between Budaon and Farokhabad (Cunningham, Arch. Surv. Repts., I. 255). Pṛishata, who is said to have been the last king's grandson but was a Páñc'ála with a different ancestry, obtained the kingdom and handed down a new dynasty to his son Drupada (Hari-V., xx. 1082–1115; and xxxii. 1778–93). The Nípas who survived are mentioned in the M.–Bh. as an inferior people (Sabhá-P. xlix. 1804; and l. 1844).

† The S'akas were originally an outside race and are mentioned often in the M-Bh. They were considered to be mlec'c'has (Vana-P. clxxxviii. 12838–9), and were classed generally with Yavanas, but also with Kámbojas, Pahlavas, Tukháras and Khaśas (Sabhá-P. xxxi. 1199; l. 1850; Udyoga-P. iii. 78; xviii. 590; Droṇa-P. xi. 399; xx. 798; cxxi. 4818; S'ánti-P. lxv. 2429; and Vana-P. li. 1990; and also Rámáy., Kishk. K. xliv. 13). Their home therefore lay to the north-west, and they are generally identified with the Scythians (Lat. Sacæ). They penetrated into India by invasions, and a branch is mentioned in the M-Bh. as in the Eastern region, apparently in Behar (Sabhá-P. xxix. 1088; and li. 1872; see also Rámáy., Kishk. K. xl. 21). Buddha S'ákya-muni is considered to have been of S'aka race. Their inroads continued through many centuries, and were resisted by various kings; and they are mentioned in the text as having established themselves in Madhya-deśa. The Hari-Vaṁśa makes them the descendants of Narishya one of Manu Vaivasvata's sons (x. 614 and 641); another account says they were Kshattriyas and became degraded from having no brahmans (M-Bh., Anuśás.-

hánas,* my child,† the Ghosha-sankhyas,‡ and the
7 Khaśas,§ the Sárasvatas,|| the Matsyas,¶ the S'úrasenas,**

P. xxxiii. 2103; and Manu x. 43-44). The Rámáy. has an absurd fable about their creation (A'di-K. lvi. 3; see page 314 note *).

* Ujjihána is given in the dictionary as the name of a region, but have not met it anywhere. Perhaps it is to be identified with the town *Urjihánd*, which was situated south-east of Várana-sthala, which is the same as Hástinapura, or near it (Rámáy., Ayodh. K. lxxiii. 8-10); and in that direction there is now a town called *Ujhani* about 11 miles south-west of Budaon.

† *Vatṣa;* but it would be better to read *Vatsá*, "the Vatsas;" see page 307, note.*

‡ This is not in the dictionary and I have not found the name elsewhere. It may mean "those who are reckoned among Ghoshas or herdsmen," and be an adjective to Khaśas.

§ Or *Khasas*. They were an outside people on the north, as mentioned in page 346 note.* In one passage they are placed between Meru and Mandara near the R. S'ailodá (Sabhá-P. li. 1858-9), that is somewhere in Western Thibet; according to the Matsya Puráṇa the R. S'ailodaká rises at Mt. Aruṇa which is west of Kailáśa and flows into the Western Sea (cxx. 19-23). Khaśa has been connected with Kashgar. The Khaśas also made inroads into India, for they are classed among the Panjab nations in a passage in the M-Bh., which shews its later age by its tone (Karṇa-P. xliv. 2070), and they are mentioned in the text here as settled in Madhya-deśa. Manu says they were Kshattriyas and became degraded by the loss of sacred rites and the absence of brahmans (x. 43-44).

|| "Those who live along the Saras-vatí," that is, the sacred river north of Kuru-kshetra. They are not the same as the people named in canto lvii, verse 51.

¶ See page 307 note *.

** S'úrasena lay immediately south of Indra-prastha or Delhi (Sabhá-P., xxx. 1105-6), and comprised the country around Mathurá, the modern Muttra (Hari-V., lv. 3093-3102; and xci. 4973) to the east of Matsya (Viráṭa-P., v. 144-5); and it extended apparently from the Chambal to about 50 miles north of Muttra (see Cunningham, Arch. Surv. Repts., XX. 2). The S'úrasenas belonged to the Yádava and Haihaya race, for Mathurá the capital is specially called the capital of the Yádavas, and the kings who reigned there belonged to that race (Hari-V., lvii. 3180-83; lxxix. 4124-34; xc. 4904; cxiv. 6387; and xxxviii. 2024 and 2027). A king named S'úrasena, a son of Arjuna Kártavírya, is mentioned (*id.*, xxxiv. 1892), who is, no doubt, intended as the eponymous ancestor of this people, for Arjuna who vanquished Rávana was slightly anterior to Ráma, and the Hari-Vaṁśa says S'úrasena occupied this

and the people of Mathurá,* the Dharmáraṇyas,† the
Jyotishikas,‡ the Gaura-grívas,§ the Guḍas ‖ and
8 the Aśmakas,¶ the Vaidehakas,** and the Pañ-

country after S'atru-ghna's time (*id.*, lv. 3102); see next note. The S'úrasenas constituted a powerful kingdom shortly before the Páṇḍavas' time, and Kṛishṇa killed Kaṁsa, who was one of the chief monarchs of that age, broke up the sovereignty and betook himself to A'narta. In later times S'úrasena presumably regained importance, for it gave its name to S'auraseni one of the chief Prákṛits.

* Mathurá was the capital of S'úrasena as mentioned in the last note, and is the modern Muttra on the R. Jumna (Hari-V., lv. 3060–61). The Hari-Vaṁśa says that Madhu, king of the Daityas and Dánavas, and his son Lavaṇa reigned at Madhu-pura and Madhu-vana (lv. 3061–3); and during Ráma's reign S'atru-ghna killed Lavaṇa, cut down Madhu-vana and built Mathurá on its site (lv. 3083–96; and xcv. 5243–7); and after the death of Ráma and his brothers Bhíma of the Yádava race according to one passage (*id.*, xcv. 5243–7) took the city and established it in his own family; and S'úrasena (see the last note) according to another passage occupied the country around (*id.*, lv. 3102). It is said Bhíma's son Andhaka was reigning in Mathurá while Kuśa and Lava reigned in Ayodhyá (*id.*, xcv. 5247–8). These passages seem to make a marked distinction between the population in the country and the dynasty in the city.

† Dharmáraṇya was the name of a wood near Gayá (Vana-P. lxxxiv. 8063–4; Anuśás.-P. xxv. 1744; and clxv. 7655; with Vana-P. lxxxvii. 8304–8).

‡ This is not in the dictionary and I have not found the name elsewhere; but Buchanan Hamilton says there was a class of brahmans in Behar, called *Jausi*, the vulgar pronunciation of Jyotish (Vol. I. p. 156).

§ These are stated in the dictionary as in the text to be a people in Madhya-deśa; but I have not met the name elsewhere. The word may however be an adjective, "yellow-necked," and qualify Guḍas and Aśmakas which are joined together in a compound.

‖ These are stated in the dictionary as in the text to be a people in Madhya-deśa, but I have not found the name elsewhere. Probably it is to be connected with the country Gauḍa which Cunningham says was formerly the southern part of North Kosala, *i.e.* the southern portion of the tract between the Ghogra and Rapti rivers (Arch. Surv. Repts. I. 327). The town Gauṛ in the Maldah district in Behar, which was once the capital of the Bengal kingdom, is too far east to be admissible here.

¶ See page 336, note §.

** The people of Videha, see page 329, note †.

c'álas,* the Sanketas,† the Kankas‡ and Márutas,§ the

* Pañc'ála or Páñc'ála was a large country, comprising the territory on both banks of the Ganges, and bounded on the north by Sub-Himalayan tribes, on the east by the same tribes and Kosala, on the south by S'úrasena, the junction of the Jumna and Chambal, and Kánya-kubja (A'di-P., cxxxviii. 5512–3 and Viráṭa-P., v. 144), and on the west by the Kurus and S'úrasenas (Sabhá-P., xxviii. 1061; and Bhíshma-P., ix. 346). The Páñc'álas originated in the descendants of Ajamíḍha by his wife Nílí, though the M.-Bh. (A'di-P., xciv. 3722–3) and Hari-Vaṁśa (xxxii. 1776–80, with which agrees the Matsya Puráṇa, xlix. 43–4 and l. 1–4) differ in the number and names of the descendants. These passages from the Hari-Vaṁśa and Matsya Puráṇa date their rise about eight or nine generations prior to the Páṇḍavas, and the passage from the M.-Bh. seems to point to a much earlier kingdom. The country being large was divided into two kingdoms, the Ganges being the dividing line (A'di-P., cxxxviii. 5509–16); to the north was North Pañc'ála or Ahi-c'c'hatra, with its capital at Ahi-c'c'hatrá, the modern Ahichhatr, 18 miles west of Bareilly and 7 north of Aonla (Cunningham, Arch. Surv. Repts., I. 255–7); and to the south was South Pañc'ála, with its capital at Kámpilya, the modern Kampil, on the old Ganges between Budaon and Fa‹khabad (*ibid.* 255). The Sṛiñjayas, or descendants of Sṛiñjaya, who are often mentioned in the M.-Bh. (*e.g.*, A'di-P., cxxxviii. 5476; and Droṇa-P., xxi. 883, 895 and 915) appear to have reigned in North Pañc'ála, and the Nípas in South Pañc'ála see page 350 note *); on the destruction of the latter, Pṛishata of the former dynasty united the two kingdoms, but Droṇa conquered his son Drupada and re-established the two kingdoms, keeping North Pañc'ála himself, and restoring the South to Drupada who then reigned in Kámpilya and Mákandí (A'di-P. cxxxviii; Hari-V., xx. 1060–1115).

† Putting aside the Utsava-sanketas (see page 319 note †), the only instance where I have met this name is in the M.-Bh. (S'ánti-P., clxxiv. 6514) where it is introduced apparently as the name of a town; but there is nothing to indicate where it was, and it is not so given in the dictionary. Probably however the reading here and there should be *Sáketa*, that is, Ayodhyá and its people. Otherwise they are not mentioned in this group where they should be, and they can hardly be intended by the Kośalas in verse 14.

‡ These are mentioned in the M.-Bh. only as an outside race, along with the Tukháras, S'akas, Pahlavas, &c. (Sabhá-P., l. 1850; and S'ánti-P., lxv. 2429) Their being mentioned here in the middle of India suggests that they must have invaded and settled there. It may be noticed also that Yudhishṭhira took the name Kanka during his disguised residence at Viráṭa's Court (Viráṭa-P. vii. 224).

§ I have met no people of this name elsewhere. Perhaps the reading

Kála-koṭisas,* and Páshaṇḍas,† and the inhabitants of
9 the Páripátra mountains,‡ the Kápingalas,§ Kururváhyas,‖

should be *Málavas*, the people of Malwa (see page 341 note *); they are mentioned in verse 45 below, but their more appropriate position is here.

* I have not met this name elsewhere, but it may mean the people of *Kála-koṭí*, which is mentioned in the M.-Bh. as a place of pilgrimage (Vana-P., xcv. 8513), and which appears from the context to be between the Ganges and the Báhudá (the Ram-ganga or perhaps the Gurra east of it; see page 291 note § §). *Koṭi-tírtha* mentioned in the Matsya Puráṇa (cv. 44) seems to be the same. Moreover Kála-koṭí may be the same as *Kála-kúṭa*, which is alluded to occasionally (Sabhá-P., xxv. 997; Udyoga-P., xviii. 596–601; and perhaps A'di-P., cxix. 4637), and for which the second passage indicates a similar position.

† "Heretics;" applied to Jains and Buddhists. I have met with no people of this name.

‡ See page 286 note ‡.

§ I have not met this name elsewhere. A river called *Kapiñjalá* is mentioned in the Bhíshma-P. list (ix. 334), but without any data to identify it. Two other readings may be suggested *Kálingakas, i.e.*, Kalingas (see page 316, note †); or better perhaps *Kálañjaras*, the inhabitants of Kalinjar, an ancient and celebrated hill and fort 33 miles south of Banda in Bundelkhand; it is mentioned only as a *tírtha* in the M.-Bh. (Vana-P., lxxxv. 8198–8200; lxxxvii. 8317; and Anuśás.-P., xxv. 1721-2).

‖ This reading appears to be wrong, but it is not easy to suggest another entirely satisfactory. It is clear, however, that the *Kurus* are one of the races meant. *Váhyas* are said to be a people in the dictionary.

The Kurus occupied the country from the S'ivis and Sub-Himalayan tribes on the north to Matsya, S'úrasena and South Pañc'ála on the south, and between North Pañc'ála on the east and Maru-bhúmi (the Rajputana desert) on the west. Their territory appears to have been divided into three parts, Kuru-kshetra, the Kurus and Kuru-jángala (A'di-P., cix. 4337–40). Kuru-kshetra, 'the cultivated land of the Kurus,' comprised the whole tract on the west of the Jumna and included the sacred region between the Saras-vatí and Dṛishad-vatí (Vana-P., lxxxiii. 5071–8 and 7073–6; Rámáy., Ayodh.-K., lxx. 12; and Megha-D., i. 49-50); it is said to have obtained this name because it was raised to honour, *pra-kṛishṭa*, by Kuru (S'alya-P., liv. 3009); the Hari-V., in xxxii. 1800, inverts the course of history, and this explanation was afterwards confused and altered into that of his *ploughing* it (*e.g.*, Matsya-P., l. 20–22). Kuru-jángala, 'the waste land of the Kurus,' was the eastern part of their territory and appears to have comprised the tract between the Ganges and North Pañc'ála (Rámáy., Ayodh.-K., lxx. 11; and M.-Bh., Sabhá-P., xix. 793-4). The

and the Uḍumbara people,* and the Gajáhvayas†—these are in the middle‡ of the Tortoise as he lies within the water.

10 To these *people*, who dwell in his middle, the three constellations, Kṛittiká, Rohiṇí and Saumyá,§ reveal|| weal and woe, O bráhman.

middle region between the Ganges and Jumna seems to have been called simply the Kurus' country. The capital was Hástinapura (see note† below), and Kháṇḍava-prastha or Indra-prastha, the modern Delhi, was a second capital founded by the Páṇḍavas (A'di-P., ccvii. 7568–94). Kuru was the eleventh ancestor of the Páṇḍavas (*id.*, xciv. 3738–51; and xcv. 3791–3820; and Hari-V., xxxii. 1799–1800).

* Uḍumbara is Kac'hh or Kutch according to Lassen (Ind. Alt., Map) and Cunningham (Arch. Surv. Repts, XIV. 115 and 135), and their identification may apply to the *Audumbaras* mentioned in Sabhá-P., li. 1869; but the Uḍumbaras here are placed in Madhya-deśa. I have not met with the name elsewhere and it is not in the dictionary. Certain descendants of Viśvá-mitra were called *Audumbaras* (Hari-V., xxvii. 1466); and there was a river *Uḍumbará-vatí* in the South (*id.*, clxviii. 9511).

† The people of Hástina-pura or Hastiná-pura, the capital of the Kurus (see page 354 note ||), which is situated on the old bed of the Ganges, 22 miles north-east of Meerut; lat. 29° 9′ N., long. 78° 3′ E. It is said to have been founded by king Hastin who was the fourth ancestor of Kuru (A'di-P., xcv. 3787–92; and Hari-V., xx. 1053–4); but he is omitted from the genealogy in A'di-P., xciv. 3714–39 and Hari-V., xxxii. 1754–6 and 1795–9. By a play on the meaning of the word *hastin*, 'elephant,' the city was also called Hastina-pura (A'śrama-vás.-P., xvii. 508 and xxxvi. 1010), Gaja-pura (dict.), Gajáhvaya (Udyoga-P., clxxvi. 6071), Gaja-sáhvaya (A'di-P., cxiii. 4441 and 4460), Nága-pura (*ibid.*, 4461–2), Nágáhva (dict.), Nága-sáhvaya (A'di-P., cxxxi. 5146) Váraṇáhvaya (A'śrama-vás.-P., xxxix. 1098), and Váraṇa-sáhvaya (dict.). It seems probable, however, that the derivation from 'elephant' is the real one, because of the numerous freely-coined synonyms with that meaning, and because there was another town Váraṇávata among the Kurus not far from Hástina-pura (A'di-P., cxlii, with the description of the Páṇḍavas' subsequent movements, cxlix.-cli., and clvi. 6084–7), and also a place called Váraṇa-sthala among the Kurus or North Páñc'álas (Rámáy., Ayodh.-K., lxxiii. 8) which was perhaps the same as Hástina-pura (see page 351, note *).

‡ *Madhye* in verse 7.

§ This does not appear to be the name of any nakshatra, but seems to mean Mṛiga-śiras or A'grahâyaṇí, which follows Rohiṇí and precedes A'rdrá (verse 15 and note).

|| *Vi-páṭaka*; not in the dictionary.

11 *The hills** Vṛisha-dhvaja,† and Añjana,‡ Jambv-
ákhya,§ and Mánavác'ala,|| Súrpa-karṇa,¶ Vyághra-mukha,**
12 Kharmaka,†† *and* Karvaṭáśana; ‡‡ *these* hills, §§ the
people of Mithilá,|||| the S'ubhras,¶¶ and the Vadana-

* *Girayo* in verse 12; see note §§ below.

† I have not met with this name anywhere else, and it is not in the dictionary as the name of a hill. Is it to be identified with Baidyanath, near Deogarh in the Santal Parganas, where there is said to be one of the twelve oldest lingas of S'iva (Imp. Gaz. of India, Art. Deogaṛh)?

‡ This may be the mountain from which Sugríva summoned his vassal monkeys (Rámáy., Kishk.-K., xxxvii. 5), and also the mountain called *Añjanábha*, mentioned in the M.-Bh. (Anuśás.-P., clxv. 7658); but there are no data to identify it.

§ *Jambu-mat* is given in the dictionary as the name of a mountain, but I have not met with either name elsewhere.

|| This is mentioned in the dictionary, but I have not found it anywhere else.

¶ Or, no doubt, *S'úrpa-karṇa*, but I have not met with either as the name of a mountain, nor is it given in the dictionary.

** I have not met with this as the name of a mountain elsewhere, nor is it in the dictionary. On hill Udaya-giri near Bhubaneswar, about 20 miles south of Cuttack, are a number of rock-cut caves, and one is sculptured in the form of a tiger's open mouth, and is known by the name *Vyághra-mukha*; can this be the hill intended here? It would be somewhat out of place here, but the grouping in this canto is far from perfect.

†† I have not found this name elsewhere, nor is it in the dictionary. Is it to be connected with the *Kharak-pur* hills in the south of the Monghyr District in Behar? A people called *Karbukas* are mentioned in the East in the Rámáy. (Kishk. K. xl. 29).

‡‡ This is not in the dictionary, and I have not met with it elsewhere; but it is no doubt to be connected with the country or town *Karvaṭá*, which is mentioned in conjunction with Támra-lipta and Suhma in the west of Bengal (M.-Bh., Sabhá-P., xxix. 1098-9). See *Karbukas* in the last note.

§§ The two lines of verse 12 must, it seems, be inverted, so as to bring the word *girayo* next to the mountains named in verse 11: otherwise the word is meaningless.

|||| For Mithilá, see page 329 note †; but the people of Videha have been mentioned already in verse 8 as situated in Madhya-deśa.

¶¶ I have not met this name elsewhere, nor is it in the dictionary as the name of a people. Probably the reading should be *Suhmas*; see p. 327 note *. The Sumbhas (Rámáy., Kishk.-K., xl. 25) are no doubt the same.

danturas,* and the C'andreśvaras † also, and the Khaśas, ‡
13 and the Magadhas, § the Prág-jyotishas, || and the Lauhityas, ¶
the cannibals who dwell on the sea-coast;** *the hills* Púrṇotkaṭa,†† Bhadra-gaura,‡‡ and Udaya-giri;§§
14 and the Kaśáyas,|||| the Mekhalámushṭas,¶¶ the Táma-

* This is in the dictionary as the name of a people, but I have not met with it elsewhere. It may mean "showing their long teeth when speaking;" but here it is no doubt the name of a people as stated in the dictionary.

† I have not found this elsewhere nor is it in the dictionary as the name of a people. A people called *C'andra-vatsas* are mentioned in the M.-Bh. (Udyoga-P., lxxiii. 2732).

§ See page 346 note * and page 351 note §. Here a branch of these people is placed in the East of India.

‡ See page 330 note ‡.

|| See page 328 note †.

¶ The people of *Lauhitya* (M.-Bh., Sabhá-P., xxix. 1100; and li. 1864) which was the country on the banks of the R. Lohita, or Lauhitya (Sabhá-P., ix. 374; Rámáy., Kishk.-K., xl. 26; and Raghu-V., iv. 81) or Lohityá (Bhíshma-P., ix. 343), and probably also Lohita-gangă (Hari-V., cxxii. 6873–6), the modern Brahma-putra. The mention of Lohita in Sabhá-P., xxvi. 1025 and Lauhitya in Anuśás.-P., xxv. 1732 appears to have a different application; and a place Lohitya is mentioned in Rámáy, Ayodh.-K., lxxiii. 13, as situated between the Ganges and Go-matí. Viśvá-mitra had certain descendants called Lohitas (Hari-V., xxvii. 1465) or Lauhitas (*id.*, xxxii. 1771) who may have been the children of his grandson Lauhi (*id.*, xxvii. 1474).

** *Sámudráḥ purushádakáḥ*; that is, on the coast of the Bay of Bengal which was the Eastern Ocean. They are mentioned in the Rámáy. (Kishk.-K., xl. 30).

†† This is mentioned in the dictionary, but I have not found it elsewhere.

‡‡ This is in the dictionary, but I have not found it elsewhere.

§§ There are several hills of this name; that intended here is no doubt the hill near Rája-gṛiha, or Rajgir. Its ancient name Cunningham says was Ṛishi-giri (Arch. Surv. Repts., I. 21 and plate iii), which is mentioned in the M.-Bh. (Sabhá-P., xx. 798–800).

|||| This is not in the dictionary and I have not found it elsewhere. The proper reading is probably *Káśayo*, "the Káśis," the people of Benares (see page 308 note †). They are a little out of place here, and should fall within the former group (verses 6–9), but are not mentioned there, and therefore come in here probably, for the grouping in this canto is far from perfect.

¶¶ This is not in the dictionary, and I have not found it elsewhere. The first part of the word is no doubt a mistake for *Mekala* or *Mekalá*, for the

liptas,* the Eka-pádapas,† the Vardhamánas,‡ and the Kośalas§ are situated in the Tortoise's face.

15 The three constellations Raudra,|| Punar-vasu, and Pushya are situated in its face.

Now *these are* the countries which are *situated* in
16 the *Tortoise's* right *fore* foot: listen while I mention them,
O Kraushṭuki.¶ The Kalingas,** the Bangas,†† and the

Mekalas and Mekala hills are not mentioned in any other groop in this canto and may be intended here, though considerably out of their proper position (see page 341 note ‡). There was also a town or river called *Mekalá*, which (if a river) was distinct from the Narmadá; but it appears to have been more on the western side (Hari-V., xxxvii. 1983) and therefore less admissible in this passage. I would suggest that the second part of the word should be *Puṇḍrás*, "the Puṇḍras" (see page 329 note *). The text *Mekhalá-mushṭás* however might mean "those who have been robbed of the triple zone" worn by the first three classes (see Manu, ii. 42) and might then be an adjective qualifying Kaśáyas.

* Or *Támra-liptakas*; see page 330 note *.

† "People who have only one tree;" but perhaps the reading should be *Eka-pádakás*, "people who have only one foot"? It was a common belief that such people existed, see M.-Bh., Sabhá-P, l. 1838 (where they are placed in the South) and Pliny, vii. 2; and it lasted down to modern times, see Mandeville's Travels, chap. XIV. See *Eka-pádas* in verse 51.

‡ The people of Vardhamána, the modern Bardhwan (commonly Burdwan) in West Bengal. It is not mentioned in the Rámáy., nor M.-Bh., but is a comparatively old town.

§ This can hardly refer to Kosala, or Oudh (see page 308 note ‡) for, if so, this people would have been placed along with the people of Mithilá and Magadha in verse 12; whereas here the Kosalas are separated off from those nations by the insertion of three hills in verse 13, and are grouped with the Mekhalámushṭas, Támra-liptas and Vardhamánas. Kosala here must therefore mean Dakshiṇa Kosala which is mentioned in canto lvii, verse 54, as lying on the slope of the Vindhya mountains (see page 342 note ¶), and especially the north and east portions of it, for the southern part is placed appropriately in the right fore foot in verse 16.

|| This appears incorrect. Read *Raudrí (fem.)*, a name for the constellation Árdrá.

¶ For *Kroshṭuke* read *Kraushṭuke.*

** See page 334 note*.

†† See page 326 note*.

Jaṭharas,* the Kośalas,† and the Mṛishikas,‡ and the C'edis,§

* They are mentioned in the Bhíshma-P. list (ix. 350) but with no data to identify their territory. Here they are joined in one compound with Kalingas and Bangas.

† The people of Dakshiṇa or Southern Kosala; see page 342 note ¶; the south portion is especially meant, see verse 14.

‡ See page 332 note †.

§ There is no mention of a people called C'edis in the Eastern region in the older poems; but Cunningham repeatedly places a C'edi race in Chhattisgarh (Arch. Surv. Repts., IX. 54–57; and XVII. 24), yet in ancient times it was not so. C'edi was then one of the countries near the Kurus (M.-Bh., Viráṭa-P., i. 11-12; Udyoga-P., lxxi. 2594-5). It is placed in the Eastern region in the account of Bhíma's conquests there (Sabhá-P., xxviii. 1069–74) and also in the South region in the description of Arjuna's following the sacrificial horse (Áśva-medh.-P., lxxxiii. 2466–9); and it is also mentioned along with the Daśárṇas (see page 342 note †) and Pulindas (see page 335 note †) in the former passage. C'edi bordered on the Jumna, for king Vasu when hunting in a forest sent a message home to his queen across that river, and the forest could not have been far from his territory (Ádi-P., lxiii. 2373–87). C'edi, moreover, is often linked with Matsya and Karúsha (*e.g.*, Bhíshma-P., ix. 348; liv. 2242; and Karṇa-P., xxx. 1231; see page 307 note * and page 341 note †), and with Káśi and Karúsha (*e.g.*, Ádi-P., cxxiii. 4796; and Bhíshma-P., cxvii. 5446). It was closely associated with Matsya and must have touched it, for an ancient king Sahaja reigned over both (Udyoga-P, lxxiii. 2732); and it seems probable that king Vasu's son Matsya became king of Matsya (Ádi-P., lxiii. 2371–93; and Hari-V., xxxii. 1804–6). From these indications it appears C'edi comprised the country south of the Jumna, from the R. Chambal on the north-west to near C'itrakúta on the south-east; and on the south it was bounded by the plateau of Malwa and the hills of Bundelkhand.

Its capital was *S'ukti-matí* or *S'ukti-sáhvayá*, (Vana-P., xxii. 898; and Áśva-medh.-P., lxxxiii. 2466-7) and was situated on the R. *S'ukti-matí*, which is said to break through the Koláhala hills (Ádi-P., lxiii. 2367–70; see page 286 note §). This river rises in the Vindhya Range, and must be east of the R. Daśárṇá, which is the most westerly river that rises in that range (compare notes † and ‡ on page 286); it is probably the modern R. Ken, for which I have found no Sanskrit name. Hence the Koláhala hills were probably those between Panna and Bijawar in Bundelkhand, and the capital S'ukti-matí was probably near the modern town Banda. The kingdom of C'edi seems to have been founded as an offshoot by the Yádavas of Vidarbha (Matsya-Purána, xliii. 4-7; and xliv. 14 and 28–38); and after it had lasted through some 20 or 25 reigns, Vasu Upari-

and the Urdhva-karṇas,* the Matsyas† and others who
17 dwell on the Vindhya mountains,‡ the Vidarbhas,§ and the Nárikelas||, the Dharma-dvípas¶, and the Elikas,** the Vyághra-grívas,†† the Mahá-grívas,‡‡ the bearded
18 Traipuras,§§ the Kaiskindhyas,|||| and the Haima-kúṭas¶¶, the Nishadhas,*** the Kaṭaka-sthalas†††, the Daśárṇas,‡‡‡ the naked Hárikas,§§§ the Nishádas,|||||| the Kákulá-

c'ara, who was a Kaurava of the Paurava race, invaded it from the north some nine generations anterior to the Paṇḍavas, and conquering it established his own dynasty in it (*id*, l. 20–50), which lasted till after their time. For a full discussion see *Journal*, Bengal As. Socy., 1895, Part I., p. 249.

* "Those who have erect ears;" but I have not met this name elsewhere, and it is not, probably, the name of any people.

† This seems wholly out of place here: see page 307 note*.

‡ These mountains are also out of place here; they die away in Behar, that is, in the region occupied by the Tortoise's head.

§ These are absolutely out of place here; see page 335 note §.

|| Nárikela is given in the dictionary as the name of an island, but I have not met with any people of any such name elsewhere.

¶ I have not met with this name any where else.

** Or Ailikas. Neither name is in the dictionary, and I have not found them elsewhere. A river *Elá* is mentioned as situated in the Dekhan (Hari-V., clxviii. 9512), but without data to identify it.

†† "Having necks like tigers"; perhaps an epithet to Traipuras.

‡‡ "Large-necked"; perhaps also an epithet to Traipuras.

§§ The people of Tripura, see page 343 note*; but they are quite out of place here.

|||| These seem to be the same as the Kiskindhakas; see page 342 note §.

¶¶ The people of Hema-kúṭa. I have found mention of only one Hema-kuṭa: it was a mountain or group of mountains in the Himalayas in the western part of Nepal (M.-Bh., Vana.-P., cx. 9968–87); but that does not seem appropriate here.

*** See page 343 note ¶. These people are altogether out of place here.

††† The people of Kaṭaka, the modern Cuttack in Orissa. This is a modern name and is mentioned in the Daśa-kumára-c'arita (Story of Soma-datta). The name given to it by the Brahmans was *Váráṇasí* in emulation with Benares.

‡‡‡ See page 342 note†. These people are altogether out place here.

§§§ This name is not in the dictionary and I have not found it elsewhere.

|||||| The Nishádas were an aboriginal race and are described as very black, dwarfish and short-limbed, with large mouth, jaws and ears, with pendent

19 lakas,* and the Parṇa-śavaras,†—these all are in the right
fore foot.
The three constellations A-śleshá, and Paitrya‡
20 and the First Phálguṇís have their station in the
right fore foot.

nose, red eyes and copper coloured hair, and with a protuberant belly. Their name is fancifully derived from the command *nishída*, "sit down," given to the first of them who was created. (Hari-V., v. 306–10; and Muir's Sansk. Texts, II. 428.) They were specially a forest people, and were scattered all over Northern and Central India. The earliest references shew, they occupied the forest tracts throughout North India. In Ráma's time they held the country all around Prayága and apparently southwards also (*Journal*, R. A. S., 1895, page 237); but in the Páṇḍavas' time they occupied the high lands of Málwa and Central India (M.-Bh., Sabhá-P., xxix. 1085; xxx. 1109 and 1170; and A'śvamedh.-P., lxxxiii. 2472-5) and still formed a kingdom (Udyoga-P., iii. 84; and xlvii. 1884). It would seem that, as the Aryans extended their conquests, the Nishádas were partly driven back into the hills and forests of Central India, and were partly subjugated and absorbed among the lowest classes of the population as appears from casual allusions (Rámáy., A'di-K., ii. 12; and M.-Bh., A'di-P., cxlviii; and Vana-P., cxxx. 10538-9). They are also mentioned as being pearl-divers and seamen in an island which seems to be on the west coast (Hari-V., xcv. 5214 and 5233–9). They were looked upon as very degraded in later times, but at first their position was not despicable, for Ráma and Guha king of the Nishádas met as friends on equal terms (Ayodh.-K., xlvi. 20; xlvii. 9-12; and xcii. 3); and it seems Kṛishṇa's aunt S'ruta-devá married the king of the Nishádas (Hari-V., xxxv. 1930 and 1937-8).

* I have not found this name elsewhere, nor is it in the dictionary. Perhaps it is to be connected with S'rí-kákula, the modern Sreewacolum, a town 19 miles west of Masulipatam. It was founded by king Sumati of the S'áta-váhanas or Andhras, and was their first capital (Arch. Surv. of S. India by R. Sewell, I. 55; and Report on Amarávati, pp. 3 and 4).

† These were a tribe of S'avaras (see page 335 note*) who lived upon leaves; hence their name according to the dictionary; but a forest tribe would hardly live solely on leaves. Might it not more properly mean "the S'avaras who wear leaves"? A girdle of leaves was the ordinary clothing of most of the aboriginal tribes; see Dalton's Ethnology, *passim*. They appear to be the modern *Páṇs*, a very low aboriginal caste, common in Orissa and the Eastern Circars.

‡ This must mean *Maghá*, which comes between A-śleshá and Púrva-Phalguṇí—a meaning not in the dictionary.

Lanká,* and the Kálájinas,† the S'ailikas‡, and the
21 Nikaṭas,§ and those who inhabit the Mahendra|| and
Malaya¶ Mountains and *the hill* Durdura,** and those
who dwell in the Karkoṭaka forest,†† the Bhṛigu-
22 kac'c'has,‡‡ and the Konkanas,§§ and the Sarvas,|||| and the
A'bhíras¶¶ who dwell on the banks of the river Veṇí,***

* Rávaṇa's capital in Ceylon.

† This is given in the dictionary as the name of a people and analysed thus—*kála-ajina*, "those who wear black antelope skins;" but I have not found the name elsewhere.

‡ Perhaps the same as the *S'ailúshas* in canto lvii, verse 46.

§ This name is not in the dictionary, and I have not met it elsewhere.

|| See page 284, note †† and page 305, note §; yet these may be the mountains at C. Comorin, see *Journal*, R. A. S. 1894, p. 261.

¶ See page 285 note*.

** See page 287 note†.

†† Karkoṭaka was the name of the Nága king whom Nala saved from a forest fire (M.-Bh., Vana-P., lxvi); where that happened is not clear, but probably it was somewhere in the middle or eastern part of the Satpura range (see page 343 note ¶); can that region be intended here? Karkoṭaka is also stated in the dictionary to be the name of a barbarous tribe of low origin, but I have not met with them elsewhere. Perhaps this word, however, may be connected with the modern Karáḍ, a town in the Satara District, near which are many Buddhist caves. Its ancient name was *Karahákaḍa* or *Karahákaṭa* according to inscriptions (Arch. Surv. of W. India by J. Burgess, Memo. No. 10, page 16, and Cunningham's Stupa of Bharhut pp. 131, 135 and 136), and it seems to be the same as *Karaháṭaka* mentioned in the M.-Bh. (Sabhá-P., xxx. 1173) and spoken of there as heretical, *páshaṇḍa*, no doubt because it was a Buddhist sanctuary as evidenced by its caves. See also Matsya P. xliii. 29 about Karkoṭaka.

‡‡ See page 339 note**.

§§ Or, more correctly, *Konkaṇas*. They are the inhabitants of the modern Konkan, the Maráṭhi-speaking lowland strip between the Western Ghats and the sea, from about Bombay southward to Goa. The Hari-Vaṁśa says king Sagara degraded these people (xiv. 784).

|||| These people are not mentioned in the dictionary and I have not met with them elsewhere. Perhaps the reading should be the *Sarpas*, i.e., "the Nágas," or the *S'aravas* who are named in M.-Bh. (Bhíshma-P., l. 2084, unless this be a mistake for S'avaras.)

¶¶ See page 312 note†.

*** This is no doubt the same as *Veṇyá*, the name of two rivers in the

the Avantis,* the Dása-puras,† and the Akaṇin‡ people,
23 the Mahá-ráshṭras§, and Karṇáṭas ||, the Gonarddhas¶,
C'itra-kúṭakas**, the C'olas††, and the Kolagiras‡‡,

Dekhan; see canto lvii, verses 24 and 26. Either river is admissible in this passage, but the Wain-ganga is meant more probably, because it flows through territory occupied by aboriginal tribes.

* See page 340 note § and page 344 note §.

† Or, better, *Dáśa-puras*, the people of Daśa-pura. This was the capital of king Ranti-deva (Megha-D., I. 46–48), and seems from the context there to have been situated on or near the R. Chambal in its lower portion. But the two accounts of Ranti-deva (M.-Bh., Droṇa-P., lxvii; and S'ánti-P., xxix. 1013–22) describe him as exercising boundless hospitality chiefly with animal food, and fancifully explain the origin of the river, C'armaṇ-vatí, as the juices from the piles of the hides of the slaughtered animals; this suggests that he reigned along the upper portion of the river.

‡ Or *A'kaṇin*. Neither is in the dictionary, and I have not found them elsewhere.

§ See page 333 note †.

|| The Canarese. Karṇáṭa properly comprises the south-west portion of the Nizam's Dominions, and all the country west of that as far as the Western Ghats, and south of that as far as the Nilgiris. It did not include any part of the country below the Ghats, but its application has been greatly distorted by the Mohammedans and English. The name is probably derived from two Dravidian words meaning "black country," because of the "black cotton-soil" of the plateau of the Southern Dekhan (Caldwell, Grammar of the Dravidian Languages, 34 and 35; and Hunter's Imp. Gaz. of India, Art. Karnátik). The Karṇáṭakas are mentioned in the Bhíshma-P. list (ix. 366).

¶ *Go-narda* is given in the dictionary as the name of a people in the Dekhan, but I have not found either form elsewhere. Goa is said to have had a large number of names in ancient times; but this does not appear to have been one of them (Imp. Gaz. of India, Art. Goa).

** The people of C'itra-kúṭa; it appears to have been the range of hills (comprising the modern mount Chitrakut) extending from south of Allahabad to about Panna near the R. Ken (see *Journal*, R. A. S., 1894, p. 239); but these people are very much out of place here.

†† See page 331 note ¶.

‡‡ This name does not seem to be connected with the Kolas who are mentioned in verse 25. The Kolagiras are no doubt the same as the *Kolvagireyas*, who are placed in South India in the description of Arjuna's following the sacrificial horse (As'va-medh.-P., lxxxiii. 2475–7); and they would presum-

the people who wear matted hair* in Krauñc'a-dvípa,†
24 the people who dwell by the Káverí and on *mount*

ably be the inhabitants of *Kolagiri*, which is placed in Sonth India in the account of Sahadeva's conquests there, and which appears to have been an extensive region for the *whole* of it is spoken of (Sabhá-P., xxx. 1171). Kolagiri may mean "the hills belonging to the Kols," but the Kols seem to be intended by the Kolas in verse 25. Kolagira may be compared with *Kodagu*, the ancient name of Coorg, which means 'steep mountains' (Imp. Gaz. of India, Art. Coorg), and might therefore have led to the modification of the final part of the name to agree with the Sanskrit *giri*; but see page 366 note ‡. The name Kolagira somewhat resembles the *Golángulas* of canto lvii, verse 45; and Golángula might be a corruption of *Kodungalúr*, which is the modern town Cranganore, 18 miles north of Cochin. It had a good harbour in early times, and was a capital town in the 4th century A.D. Syrian Christians were established there before the 9th century, and the Jews had a settlement there which was probably still earlier. It is considered of great sanctity by both Christians and Hindus (Imp. Gaz. of India, Art. Kodungalúr).

* *Jaṭá-dhara*; the dictionary gives it as a proper name. Jaṭá also means "long tresses of hair twisted or braided together, and coiled in a knot over the head so as to project like a horn from the forehead, or at other times allowed to fall carelessly over the back and shoulders."

† This was no doubt the county of which *Krauñc'a-pura* was the capital, for *dvípa* appears to have had the meaning of "land enclosed between two rivers," the modern *doab*; cf. *S'ákala-dvípa*, the doab in which S'ákala (see page 315 note ‡) was situated, and the *Seven dvípas* all in North India (Sabhá-P., xxv. 998-9). The Hari-Vaṁśa says Sárasa, one of Yadu's sons, founded Krauñc'a-pura in the South region in a district where the soil was copper-coloured and champaka and aśoka trees abounded, and his country was known as Vana-vási or Vana-vásin (xcv. 5213 and 5231–3); and also that that town was near the Sahya Mts., and was situated apparently south of a river Khaṭvángí and north of Gomanta hill (xcvi. 5325–40). If Gomanta was the modern Goa, these indications agree fairly well with the Krauñc'álaya forest mentioned in the Rámáy. (Araṇ.-K., lxxiv. 7), which appears to have been situated between the Godavari and Bhima rivers (*Journal*, R. A. S., 1894, page 250). But the town Bana-vási or Banawási, which was a city of note in early times, is in the North Kanara district, on the R. Warda (tributary of the Tungabhadra), 14 miles from Sirsí, in lat. 14° 33′ N., long. 75° 5′ E. (Imp. Gaz. of India, Art. Banavasi; Arch. Surv. of W. India, No. 10, pp. 60 note and 100); and this is south of Goa. This was the country of the Vana-vásakas (see page 333 note *).

Ṛishyamúka,* and those who *are called* Násikyas,† and
those who wander by the borders of the S'ankha and
Sukti‡ and other *hills* and of the Vaidúrya mountains,§
25 and the Váric'aras,|| the Kolas,¶ those who inhabit
C'armapaṭṭa,** the Gaṇa-váhyas,†† the Paras,‡‡ those who
26 have their dwellings in Kṛishṇá-dvípa,§§ and the peoples
who live by the Súrya hill|||| and the Kumuda hill,¶¶

* See page 289 note ‡.

† These are, no doubt, the people of Nasik; see page 339 note ||.

‡ The text is *S'ankha-sukty-ádi-vaidúrya-śaila*, which may be so rendered as to make S'ankha and Sukti two of the hills which compose the Vaidúrya chain. I have not met with them elsewhere, and neither is in the dictionary as the name of a hill. Sukti can hardly be an error for the S'ukti-mat range (see page 306 note §).

§ This is the Satpura range, for the Páṇḍavas in their pilgrimage went from Vidarbha and the R. Payoshṇí (the Purna and Tapti, see page 299 note †), across these mountains, to the R. Narmadá (Vana-P., cxx. and cxxi). This range was placed in the Southern region (*ibid.*, lxxxviii. 8343), and also apparently, as *Vaidúrya-śikhara*, in the Western region (*ibid.*, lxxxix. 8359–61); and in the former of these two passages it is called *maṇi-maya*.

|| I have not found this name elsewhere, nor is it in the dictionary.

¶ See page 331 note ¶, but the passages cited there with reference to this people appear to refer to the Kolagiras; see page 363 note ‡‡. The Kols are a collection of aboriginal tribes, who are said to have dwelt in Behar in ancient times, but who now inhabit the mountainous districts and plateaux of Chutia Nagpur and are to be found to a smaller extent in the Tributary States of Orissa and in some districts of the Central Provinces (Imp. Gaz. of India, Art. Kol).

** This is not in the dictionary and I have not met it elsewhere. Is it to be identified with Salem in Madras?

†† I have not met this elsewhere. Does it refer to the Ganapati dynasty which flourished on the eastern coast during the 13th cent. A.D.?

‡‡ This is not in the dictionary and I have not found it elsewhere.

§§ I have not met this name elsewhere, but it obviously refers to the R. Kṛishṇá or Kistna, and probably means one of the doabs (see page 364 note †) beside that river, either between the Kistna and Bhíma or between the Kistna and Tungabhadra.

|||| I have not met this name elsewhere.

¶¶ I have not found this name elsewhere. Comparing the various readings,

the Aukhávanas,* and the Piśikas,† and those who *are called*
27 Karma-náyakas,‡ and those who *are called* the Southern Kaurushas,§ the Ṛishikas,|| the Tápasáśramas,¶ the Ṛishabhas,** and the Siṁhalas,†† and those who inhabit

it seems to have some connexion with the *Kusumas* of canto lvii verse 46; see page 332 note ‡.

* This is not in the dictionary, and I have not found it elsewhere. Perhaps it is to be connected with the *Okhalakiyas* mentioned in Arch. Surv. of W. India, no. 10, pp. 34-35.

† Or as the text may be read, *Sapiśikas.* Piśika is in the dictionary, but I have not met with either name elsewhere.

‡ I have not found this name elsewhere and it is not in the dictionary. Perhaps the reading should be *Kambu-náyakas* or *Kombu-náyakas*, and mean the people of Coorg. "According to tradition, Coorg was at this period (16th century A.D. ?) divided into 12 *kombus* or districts, each ruled by an independent chieftain, called a *náyak*" (Imp. Gaz. of India, Art. Coorg). The similarity of the names is very remarkable.

§ This name is not in the dictionary and I have not met with it elsewhere Perhaps it should be *Kárushas* (see page 341 note †), and the people intended are a southern branch of that nation.

|| These are the people mentioned in the Rámáy. (Kishk -K., xli. 16) and M.-Bh. (Karṇa-P., viii. 237) and Hari-Vaṁśa (cxix. 6724–6). There was also a river called the *Ṛishiká* (M.-Bh., Vana-P., xii. 493) which may be connected with the same people. I have found no further data for fixing their position. See page 332 note †; the *Múshikas* mentioned there may perhaps be the people dwelling on the R. *Musi*, the tributary of the Kistna on which Haidarabad stands (Imp. Gaz. of India, Art. Kistna).

¶ I have not met this name elsewhere nor is it in the dictionary. Perhaps it refers to the descendants of ascetics, see page 339 note †.

** These are, no doubt, the inhabitants of *Ṛishabha-parvata* mentioned in the M.-Bh. (Vana-P., lxxxv. 8163-4) and placed there between S'rí-parvata and the Káverí. S'rí-parvata is on the Kistna in the Karnul district (see page 290, note ‡). The Ṛishabha hills are therefore probably the southern portion of the Eastern Ghats, but none of the ranges there appears to have any name resembling this.

†† The people of Ceylon. They are named in the M.-Bh.; it is said the Siṁbala king attended Yudhishṭhira's Rája-súya sacrifice (Sabhá-P., xxxiii. 1271; and Vana-P., li. 1989); and the Siṁhalas brought to him presents of lapis lazuli, which is the essence of the sea (*samudra-sára*), and abundance of pearls and elephants' housings (Sabhá-P., li. 1893-4). They are also named as fighting on the Kauravas' side in the great war (Droṇa-P., xx. 798).

28 Káñc'í*, the Tilangas,† and the peoples who dwell in Kuñjara-darí ‡ and Kac'c'ha, § and Támra-parṇí, ‖—such is the Tortoise's right flank.

29 And the constellations, the Last Phálguṇís, Hastá and C'itrá are in the Tortoise's right flank.

This name is not I believe given to Ceylon in the Rámáy., but the name *Simhiká* is given to a terrible female Rákshasa who dwelt in the middle of the sea between India and Ceylon, and whom Hanúmán killed as he leapt across to the island (Kishk.-K , xli. 38; and Sund.-K., viii. 5–13).

* This is *Káñc'í-puram* or *Káñc'í-varam*, the modern Conjevaram, about 37 miles south-west of Madras. It is not, I believe, mentioned in the Rámáy. or M.-Bh., unless the *Káñc'yas* who are named as fighting in the great war (Karṇa-P., xii. 459) are the people of this town, but the proper reading there should probably be *Káśyas*, the people of Káśi or Benares. Conjevaram, nevertheless, is a place of special·sanctity, and is one of the seven holy cities of India. Hwen Thsang speaks of it in the 7th century A.D. as the capital of Dráviḍa. It was then a great Buddhist centre, but about the 8th century began a Jain epoch, and that was succeeded by a period of Hindu predominance (Imp. Gaz. of India, Art. Conjevaram).

† This form is not in the dictionary; but it is no doubt the same as *Tailanga* or *Tri-linga*, that is Telinga, the modern Telugu country. It coincided more or less with the ancient kingdom of Andhra (see page 337 note §). I have not found this name in any shape in the Rámáy. or M.-Bh.; Andhra is the name which occurs in those books.

‡ This probably means "the valleys of the Kuñjara hills," and the reference may be to mount Kuñjara, which is mentioned in the Rámáy. as situated in the South, but not in a clear manner (Kishk.-K., xli. 50). I have not met the name elsewhere, but as this place is joined with Kac'c'ha in one compound (see next note) it may mean part of the Travancore hills. Kuñjara-darí is given in the dictionary as the name of a place.

§ This is *Kochchi*, the modern Cochin, in Travancore. It is not I believe mentioned in the Rámáy. or M.-Bh., except once in the latter book in the account of Sahadeva's conquests in the South (Sabhá-P., xxx. 1176). Both Christians and Jews are said to have settled here early in the Christian era, and they were firmly established here by the 8th century.

‖ This is the name of the modern river Chittar in the extreme South (see page 303, note ‡‡), and also of the district near it. It appears, moreover, to be the name of a hill in the extreme South (Bhíshma-P., vi. 252). It is also the name of a town in Ceylon, after which the name was extended to the whole island (dictionary). The island seems to be meant by the words *Támráhvaya dvípa* in the M.-Bh. (Sabhá-P., xxx. 1172).

30 And next is the outer foot.* The Kámbojas,† and Pah-
lavas,‡ and the Baḍavá-mukhas,§ and the Sindhus || and Sau-
31 víras,¶ the Ánartas,** the Vanitá-mukhas,†† the Drávaṇas,‡‡
the Sárgigas,§§ the S'údras,|||| the Karṇa-prádheyas ¶¶

* *Váhya-pádas;* the right hind foot is meant as is stated expressly in verse 33, but (because perhaps this word is vague) the names that follow are sadly confused and belong to all regions in the west and north-west.

† See page 318, note §; they are out of place here.

‡ See page 314, note *; these also are out of place.

§ This should perhaps be connected with *Baḍavá*, a tírtha apparently in Kashmir (M.-Bh., Vana-P., lxxxii. 5034–42). A river of the same name is mentioned (*id.*, ccxxi. 14232), but that seems from its context to be rather in South India. Badavá-mukha (which means 'submarine fire') may also mean "having faces like mares"; and a people called *Aśva-mukhas* are mentioned in Matsya Puráṇa, cxx. 58, as dwelling north of the Himalayas: see also verse 43 below.

|| See page 315, note *; they are hardly in place here.

¶ See page 315, note †; these are out of place here.

** See page 340 note §. The name is derived from an eponymous king Ánarta, who was the son of S'aryáti one of the sons of Manu Vaivasvata (Hari-V., x. 613 and 642–9).

†† "Those who have faces like women." I have not met this name elsewhere. It seems, however, to be a proper name and not an adjective.

‡‡ This as a name is not in the dictionary, and I have not found it elsewhere.

§§ Or "and the Argigas or Árgigas," as the text may be read. These names are not in the dictionary and I have not met with them elsewhere. Perhaps the correct reading should be *S'áryátas*. They were a tribe, so-called from their chief S'aryáta the Mánava, who settled down near where the ṛishi C'yavana dwelt, and gave his daughter Su-kanyá to the ṛishi to appease his wrath (S'ata-P. Bráh., IV. i. 5). He is called S'aryáti in the M.-Bh. (Vana-P., cxxi. 10312; and cxxii.) where the same story is told rather differently; and also in the Hari-Vaṁśa, where he is said to be a son of Manu and progenitor of Ánarta and the kings of Ánarta (x. 613, and 642–9). From all these passages it appears the S'áryátas were in the West, in Gujarat; and C'yavana as a Bhárgava is always placed in the West, near the mouths of the Narbada and Tapti. But perhaps the most probable reading is *Bhárgavas;* they were in the West (see page 310, note †).

|||| See page 313 note ‡.

¶¶ This name is not in the dictionary and I have not found it elsewhere. It can have nothing to do with *Karṇa* one of the heroes of the M.-Bh., for he

and Varvaras,* the Kirátas,† the Páradas,‡ the
32 Páṇḍyas§ and the Páraśavas,|| the Kalas,¶ the
Dhúrtakas,** the Haimagirikas,†† the Sindhu-kálaka-

reigned in Anga in the East. *Prádheya* means a descendant of Prádhá, one of Daksha's daughters, and that also is inadmissible. It suggests *Rádheya*, which was a metronymic of Karṇa, but that is equally unsuitable. It seems therefore the words must be taken as a whole forming one name, and then it suggests comparison with *Karṇa-právára* which would be the same as Karṇa-právaraṇa (see page 346, note †).

* See page 319, note *. This word is compounded with the preceding name; it hardly seems to be in place here.

† See page 322, note ||; they seem to be out of place here, unless any Kirátas inhabited the southern part of the Aravalli hills or the extreme western part of the Vindhya mountains, and that seems improbable. See also *Adhama-kairátas* in verse 44 below, and *Kirátas* are mentioned again in verse 50.

‡ See page 317, note *; they seem to be out of place here.

§ These people are out of place here; see page 331, note §; they should be properly in the right flank.

|| I have not met this name elsewhere; but, no doubt, it denotes some people, who claimed descent from Paraśu-Ráma and who would therefore be somewhere on the western coast between Bombay and the Narmadá; see page 310, note †. It is said there was a dynasty of Páraśava kings after the great Paurava line came to an end (Matsya Puráṇa, l. 73–76) but it does not appear where.

¶ This is not in the dictionary, and I have not met it elsewhere. It suggests a connexion with the *Kálibalas* of canto lvii, verse 49; but *Kala* also means, "emitting a low or inarticulate sound," and it was an old fable that a people existed, who could not speak articulately, but hissed like serpents, see Mandeville's Travels, chap. xviii. and xix. *Kala* occurs again in verse 36.

** I have not found this elsewhere as the name of a people. The word however means "a rogue" and may be an adjective to Haima-girikas.

†† The people of *Hema-giri*. This is not given as the name of a place in the dictionary, but it may be a synonym for *Hema-kúṭa* or *Hema-śṛinga*. It is said in the M.-Bh. the latter is the portion of Himavat from which the Ganges issued formerly (Ádi-P., clxx. 6454-5), and *Hiraṇya-śṛinga* is probably the same (Bhíshma-P., vi. 237). Hema-kúṭa was near the rivers Nandá and Apara-nandá and between the sources of the Ganges and Kauśikí (Vana-P., cx. 9968–87); and it is alluded to in other passages but they are not clear (*e.g.*, *id.*, clxxxix. 12917; Bhíshma-P., vi. 198, 202, 236 and 246). The last of

vairatas,* the Sauráshṭras,† and the Daradas,‡ and the
33 Drávidas, § the Mahárṇavas ‖ —these peoples are situated in
the right hind foot.

And the Svátís,¶ Viśákhá and Maitra** are the three *corresponding* constellations.

34 *The hills* Maṇi-megha,†† and Kshurádri,‡‡ and Khañjana,§§

these passages says the Guhyakas dwell on Hema-kúṭa. The Matsya Puráṇa says Hema-śṛinga is south-east of Kailása, and the R. Lauhitya, or Brahmaputra, rises at its foot (cxx. 10–12); and that two rivers rise in Hema-kúṭa which flow into the eastern and western seas (*ibid.*, 64-5).

* This seems to be erroneous, yet it is not easy to suggest an amendment. The first part, no doubt, refers to the R. Sindhu and the Sindhu people but the latter part appears unintelligible. Perhaps the reading should be *Sindhu-kúla-suvírakáḥ* or *Sindhavás c'a suvírakáḥ* meaning the Sindhus and the Suvíras (see page 315, notes * and †); but these two people have been mentioned already in verse 30.

† The people of Suráshṭra; see page 340, note ‡.

‡ See page 318, note ‖. They are quite out of place here.

§ The Drávidas are often alluded to in the M.-Bh. (*e.g.*, Sabhá-P., xxxiii. 1271; Vana-P., li. 1988; Karṇa-P., xii. 454; &c.), but are not mentioned in the Rámáy., I believe, except in the geographical canto (xli. 18). They are sometimes closely connected with the Páṇḍyas (Sabhá-P., xxx. 1174), but the name was applied in a general way to denote the southern branches of the races now classed as Dravidian, and it is the same as *Tamil* (Caldwell's Grammar of the Dravidian Languages, pp. 12–15). Their territory included the sea coast in early times (Vana-P., cxviii. 10217). It is also said they were kshattriyas and became degraded from the absence of brahmans and the extinction of sacred rites (Anuśás.-P., xxxiii. 2104-5; Manu, x. 43-44).

‖ I have not met this name elsewhere. It means "dwelling by the ocean," and is probably an epithet of Drávidas, for they bordered on the sea as mentioned in the last note.

¶ The plural seems peculiar.

** Or Anu-rádhá.

†† I have not met this elsewhere. It may be the same as Mt. *Maṇi-mat* (Droṇa-P., lxxx. 2843); which appears to be also intended in Vana-P., lxxxii. 5043, and if so would denote the range of hills enclosing Kashmir on the south, according to the context. It may also be the same as the "jewelled mountain *Su-megha*" mentioned in the Rámáy. (Kishk.-K., xliii. 40).

‡‡ This is not in the dictionary, and I have not found it elsewhere.

§§ This is not in dictionary as the name of a mountain, and I have not found it elsewhere.

and Asta-giri; * the Aparántika people, † and Haihayas, ‡

* This does not appear to be the name of any particular mountains, but rather denoted in a vague way mountains in the west behind which the sun sets. It is mentioned in the Rámáy. as Asta-giri (Kishk.-K., xxxvii. 22), and as Asta-parvata (*id.*, xliii. 54).

† See note to Aparántas, page 313, note †. This half line *Aparántiká Haihayáśc'a* is a syllable too long; it would be better to read either *Aparántá* or omit the *c'a*.

‡ The Haihayas were a famous race, the descendants of an eponymous king Haihaya, who is said to have been a grandson or great-grandson of Yadu, the eldest son of Yayáti (Hari-V., xxxiii. 1843-4; and Matsya Puráṇa, xliii. 4–8. Yadu is said to have been king of the north-east region (Hari-V., xxx. 1604, 1618), but the references to the earliest movements of the Haihayas are hardly consistent. Mahish-mat, who was fourth in descent from Haihaya, is said to have founded the city Máhish-matí on the Narmadá (see page 333, note ‡; and *id.*, xxxiii. 1846-7), and his son Bhadra-śreṇya is said to have reigned in Káśi or Benares, which the Vítahavya branch of the Haihayas had previously conquered from its king Haryaśva, but Haryaśva's grandson Divodása defeated them and regained his capital (M.-Bh., Anuśás.-P., xxx. 1949–62; Hari-V., xxix. 1541-6; and xxxii. 1736-40). The great king Arjuna Kártavírya, who was ninth in descent (Hari-V., xxxiii. 1850–90; and Matsya P., xliii. 13–45), reigned in Anúpa and on the Narmadá and had the great conflict with Ráma Jámadagnya, which ended in the overthrow of the Haihayas (M.-Bh., Vana-P., cxvi. 10189—cxvii. 10204; and S'ánti-P., xlix. 1750–70; and pages 338 note *, and 344 note *). The Haihayas and Tálajanghas in alliance with S'akas, Yavanas, Kámbojas and Pahlavas are said to have driven Báhu king of Ayodhyá out of his realm, but his son Sagara drove them out and recovered the kingdom (Vana-P., cvi. 8831-2; and Hari-V, xiii 760 —xiv. 783).

The Haihaya race comprised the following tribes, Vitihotras (or Vítahavyas?), S'áryátas, Bhojas, Avantis, Tauṇḍikeras (or Kuṇḍikeras), and Tálajaṅghas; the Bharatas, Sujátyas and Yádavas are added, and the S'úrasenas, Ánartas and C'edis also appear to have sprang from them (Hari-V., xxxiv. 1892–6; and Matsya-P., xliii. 46–49). Comparing the territories occupied by these tribes, it appears the Haihaya race dominated nearly all the region south of the Jumna and Aravalli hills as far as the valley of the Tapti inclusive of Gujarat in ancient times (see pages 333 note ‡, 335 note §, 340 note §, 342 note ‡, 344 all the notes, 351 note **, 352 note *, and 368 note §§); and Cunningham says that two great Haihaya States in later times had their capitals at Manipur in Mahá Kosala (or Chhattisgarh) and at Tripura (or Tewar) on the Narbada (Arch. Surv. Repts., IX. 54–57).

35 the S'ántikas,* Viprasastakas,† the Kokankaṇas,‡ Pañc'a-
dakas,§ the Vamanas,|| and the Avaras,¶ the Tárakshuras,**

* I have not met this elsewhere, and it is not in the dictionary as the name of a people. It may be the same as the *S'áśikas* (M.-Bh., Bhíshma-P., ix. 354; perhaps the *S'aśakas* in Vana-P., cclìii. 15257 are the same); or the reading may be *S'ákalas*, the people of S'ákala, the capital of Madra (see page 315, note, ‡).

† This is not in the dictionary and I have not met it elsewhere. It appears to be a proper name and not an adjective.

‡ This is not in the dictionary and I have not found it elsewhere. Perhaps the reading should be *Kokanadas*, a people in the north-west classed with the Trigartas and Dárvas (M.-Bh, Sabhá-P., xxvi. 1026), or *Kokarakas* who seem to be the same (Bhíshma-P., ix. 369).

§ This is given in the dictionary as the name of a people, but I have not met it elsewhere. Perhaps a better reading would be *Pañc'adakas* or *Pañc'a-nadas*, "the people living beside the R. Pañc'anada," which appears to be the single stream formed by the confluence of the five rivers of the Panjab (M.-Bh., Vana-P., lxxxii. 5025; Bhíshma-P., lvi. 2406; and dictionary); but this name seems to be also applied to the five rivers collectively (Vana-P., ccxxi. 14229), and to the country watered by those five rivers (Sabhá-P., xxxi. 1193; Udyoga-P., iii 82; and xviii. 596–601; Karṇa-P., xlv. 2100 and 2110; &c.; Hari-V., xcii. 5018; and Rámáy., Kishk.-K., xliii. 21), and to the inhabitants of it (Bhíshma-P., lvi. 2406; and Karṇa-P., xlv. 2086): see also Lassen's map (Ind. Alt.).

|| This is given in the dictionary as the name of a people, but I have not found it elsewhere. Perhaps a better reading would be *Vánavas*, who are mentioned in the M.-Bh. (Vana-P., ix. 362), or *Vanáyavas*. There was a district called *Vanáyu* or *Vánáyu*, which appears to have been situated in the north-west, and which was famous for its breed of horses (M.-Bh., Bhíshma-P., xci. 3974; Droṇa-P., cxxi 4831; Karṇa-P. vii 200; and Rámáy., A'di-K., vi 24). It appears to be the modern Bunnu in the north-west of the Panjab.

¶ This is not given as the name of a people, and the word means, "low," and "western." This name may be compared with *Aparas*, a people mentioned in the Rámáy. (Kishk.-K., xliii 23); and see page 313, note † and Aparántikas in verse 34. But a better reading for the text *hy-avarás* is perhaps *Varvarás*; see page 319, note * and page 369, note *.

** This is not in the dictionary, and I have not met with it elsewhere; but *Tárakshati* and *Tárakshiti* are given as the name of a district to the west of Madhya-deśa. There was also a kingdom called *Turushka* in later times (Arch. Surv. of W. India, Memo. No. 10, p. 7). The Turushkas are the Turks, and their country Turkestan. A people called *Tárkshyas* are mentioned in M.-Bh., Sabhá-P., li. 1871.

the Angatakas,* the S'arkaras,† the S'álma-veśmakas,‡
36 the Guru-svaras,§ the Phalguṇakas,|| and the people who
dwell by the *river* Veṇu-matí,¶ and the Phalgu-
lukas,** the Ghoras,†† and the Guruhas,‡‡ and the

* I have not found this elsewhere, and it is not in the dictionary. A place called *Anga-loka* is assigned to the west in the Rámáy. (Kishk.-K., xliii. 8), and *Angas* and *Anga-lokyas* are mentioned to the north of India in the Matsya Puráṇa (cxx. 44 and 45).

† This is not in the dictionary, and I have not found it elsewhere. A river *Sárkarávartá* is mentioned (Bhágavata Puráṇa-V., xix. 17), but appears to be in the south. A great house-holder and theologian Jana S'árkarákshya is alluded to (C'hándogya-Up.-V., xi. 1). Perhaps the reading may be *S'ákalas*, the people of S'ákala the capital of Madra (see page 315, note ‡).

‡ This is not in the dictionary, and I have not fonnd it elsewhere. It suggests *śála-veśmakas*, "those who live in honses with spacions rooms," and it may be an adjective to S'arkaras. Perhaps we should read *S'álvas* as the first part of the word (see page 349, note §) but, if so, the latter part seems unrecognizable.

§ I have not met with this elsewhere, and it is not in the dictionary. It may be an adjective, "deep-voiced," describing the Phalguṇakas. Perhaps the reading shonld be *Gurjaras* They appear to have been settled in the Panjab or Upper Sindh, and to have been driven out by the Bálas about 500 A.D., and pushed gradually southward, till at length they occupied the country around the peninsula of Kathiawar, thence called Gujarat after them (Cnnningham, Arch. Surv. Repts., II 64–72). Or perhaps the reading might be *Gurusthala*; a river *Guru-nadí* is mentioned in the west region, but without data to identify it (Hari-V., clxviii. 9516–8).

|| Or better, *Phalgunakas*. I have not met with it elsewhere. A similar name P*halgulukas* occurs jnst below.

¶ This is not in the dictionary, and I have not met with it elsewhere. It occnrs again in verse 39. A people called *Veṇikas* are mentioned in the M.-Bh. (Bhíshma-P., li. 2097).

** This resembles Phalguṇakas above. I have not found it elsewhere. A mountain called *Phena-giri* or *Phala-giri* is mentioned in the Rámáy. as situated in the west near the month of the Indus (Kishk.-K., xliii. 13–17, and Annotations).

†† These are no doubt the same as the *Ghorakas* mentioned in the M.-Bh., Sabhá-P., li. 1870; but I have not found any data to fix their position.

‡‡ I have not met this elsewhere, but it is stated in the dictionary to be the name of a people in Madhya-deśa, and the word is also written *Guḍuha*, *Gulaha* and *Guluha*.

Kalas,* the Ekekshaṇas,† the Váji-keśas,‡ the Dírgha-
37 grívas,§ and the C'úlikas,|| and the Aśva-keśas,¶ *these* peoples are situated in the Tortoise's tail.

38 And *so situated* also are the three constellations Aindra,** Múla, and Púrvá Ashádhá.

The Máṇḍavyas,†† and C'aṇḍakháras,‡‡ and Aśvakálanatas,§§

* This has occurred before in verse 31.

† "The one-eyed." It was an old belief that such people existed. "Men with only one eye in their forehead" are mentioned in the M.-Bh. (Sabhá-P., l. 1837); the Cyclopes are famous in Greek and Latin literature; and a one-eyed race is spoken of as dwelling somewhere in the Indian Ocean by Mandeville (Travels, Chap XIX).

‡ "Those who have hair or manes, like horses." I have met no such name elsewhere, except that the synonymous name *Aśva-keśas* occurs in the next line of this verse. Neither is it in the dictionary.

§ "The long-necks." I have met no such name elsewhere.

|| This name is the same as the *C'ulikas* mentioned in canto lvii. verse 40, but the position does not quite agree; these are in the west and the others in the north. A people *Vindha-c'ulakas* are named in the Bhishma-P. list (ix. 369) and appear to be in the north A dynasty of kings called C'úlikas is said to have reigned after the great Paurava line came to an end (Matsya Puráṇa, l. 73–76).

¶ "Those who have hair, or manes, like horses." It is the same as *Váji-keśas* mentioned above.

** For *Aindra-múlam* read *Aindram múlam.* Aindra is the same as Jyeshṭhá.

†† They are mentioned again in verse 46. They may be a tribe which claimed descent from the ṛishi *Máṇḍavya*, to whom Janaka king of Videha is said to have sung a song (M.-Bh., S'ánti-P., cclxxvii), and whose hermitage is alluded to, as situated somewhere perhaps between Oudh and North Behar (Udyoga-P., clxxxvii. 7355); but Máṇḍavya-pura is said in the dictionary to be situated on the R. Godavari. A people called *Maṇḍikas* are mentioned in the M.-Bh. (Vana-P., ccliii. 15243). The Vimáṇḍavyas are named in verse 6 above.

‡‡ I have not met this name elsewhere, nor is it in the dictionary; but it suggests *Kandahar*, and the position agrees. A people *C'arma-khaṇḍikas* are mentioned in canto lvii. verse 36.

§§ This seems a compound. The first part appears to be the *Aśvakas;* they are mentioned in the M.-Bh. (Bhíshma-P., ix. 351), and are placed in the north-west and identified with the Aspasii and Assakani by Lassen (Ind. Alt., Map). The latter part however is very doubtful. A people *Lalitthas* are mentioned in the M.-Bh. (Droṇa-P., xvii. 692) and appear from the context to have been a north-western race.

39 and the Kunyatálaḍahas,* the Strí-váhyas,† and the Bá-
likas,‡ and the Nṛi-simhas§ *who dwell* on the Veṇu-
40 matí‖, and the other *people* who dwell in Valáva¶, and the
Dharma-baddhas,** the Alúkas,†† the people who occupy

* This appears to mean the same people as the *Kanyakáguṇas* of the Bhíshma-P. list (ix. 360). It seems to be a compound, but the component names are very uncertain. The latter part may be *Laḍakas*; they are mentioned in the M.-Bh. (Bhíshma-P., l. 2083), though there are no data to identify them; but *Laḍaha* is given in the dictionary as the name of a people. As regards the first part *Kuṇapa* and *Kunaha* are given in the dictionary as the name of a people; and *Kulatthas* are mentioned in the M.-Bh. (Bhíshma-P., ix. 373) and Matsya Puráṇa (cxx. 44) as a people to the north of India. A country *Kolúka* is placed in the west in the Rámáy., and Kolúta seems to be another name for it (Kishk.-K., xliii. 8, and Annotations). A country *Kulúta* is also mentioned in the M.-Bh. (Karna-P., xii. 475 and 485).

† I have not met this elsewhere, and it is not in the dictionary. It may perhaps mean "those who live apart from women;" but the reading is more probably *Strí-rájya*. This was the name of a country and people, mentioned in the M.-Bh. and situated apparently north of the Himalayas, near the Húṇas and Tanganas (Vana-P., li. 1991; and S'ánti-P., iv. 114). *Strí-loka* is mentioned apparently as a place north-west of India in an alternative reading to Rámáy., Kishk.-K., xliii. 20 (Gorresio's Edition, Annotations).

‡ This is not in the dictionary, and I have not found it elsewhere. The reading should probably be *Báhlikas* or Váhlikas, see page 311, note *.

§ "The men-lions." I have not met this elsewhere, and it is not in the dictionary as the name of a people.

‖ This is not in the dictionary and I have not found any river of this name in the north-west. It has been mentioned in verse 36 above.

¶ *Valáva-stha;* this might also be read as *Vala + avasthá*. I have not met either word elsewhere. A town or river *Baláká* is mentioned in the M.-Bh. as situated in North India (Anuśás.-P., xxv. 1706).

** "Those who are firmly attached to the Law"; or perhaps *Dharma-buddha*, "those who are enlightened in the law." It seems to be an adjective rather than a proper name, and may qualify Alúkas. I have not met with it elsewhere as a proper name, and the nearest resemblance to it is *Báhu-bádha* of the Bhíshma-P. list (ix. 362); see page 317, note §. The *Madhumattas* of the same list (ix. 360) are probably the same people.

†† This is not in the dictionary, and I have not found it elsewhere. The people intended are no doubt the *Ulúkas*, and the text should read *tatholúká* instead of *tathálúká*. For the Ulúkas see page 346, note †.

Uru-karma *—*these* peoples are in the Tortoise's left hind † foot. ‡

41 Where also Áshádhá and S'ravaṇá *and* Dhanishṭhá are situated.

The mountains Kailása, § and Hima-vat, Dhanush-mat, ‖ and
42 Vasu-mat, ¶ the Krauñćas, ** and the Kurus †† and Vakas, ‡‡

* I have not met this elsewhere and it is not in the dictionary. It is perhaps to be connected with the *Urṇas;* see page 324, note †. A people called *Urdamarus* are placed in the north in the Matsya Puráṇa (cxx. 48).

† For *párśve* read *paśc'e?*

‡ This verse closes with the word *bhágure;* it is not in the dictionary and seems to be erroneous. Should the reading be *bhásure,* "brilliant," an epithet to Áshádhá and S'ravaṇá?

§ This mountain is of course constantly mentioned throughout Sanskrit literature, and the references indicate that it was on the north of the middle portion of the Himalaya range. The name is given in modern maps to the range of mountains which is situated immediately north of the Mánasa lakes, and in which the Indus rises.

‖ This is given in the dictionary, but I have not met with it elsewhere. It may perhaps refer to Himavat; see canto lvii verse 59, where the range is compared to a bow in shape.

¶ I have not found this elsewhere and it is not in the dictionary as the name of a hill. It may perhaps mean "abounding in wealth" and qualify Himavat.

** These are no doubt the people who dwelt near the Krauñc'a group of mountains. This group is called the son of Maináka, which is called the son of Himavat, and therefore appears to have been a portion of the Maináka mountains in the great Himavat mountain system (Hari-V., xviii. 941-2). It is mentioned in the Rámáy. as having lake Mánasa on its summit with Maináka lying beyond (Kishk.-K., xliv. 32-37); but in the Megha-Dúta Krauñc'a is placed south of that lake, and there is said to be a pass through it leading to the lake (I. 58 and 59 with commentary). The pass must apparently be the valley of the source of the Sarju or Ghogra, and the Krauñc'a mountains would therefore be the portion of the Himalaya chain bounding Nepal at the extreme north-west.

†† These must be the Uttara Kurus, see page 345, note §. The Kurus in Madhya-deśa have been mentioned in verse 9 above.

‡‡ These are mentioned in the dictionary, but I have not found them elsewhere. A people called *Varvas* are alluded to in the Matsya Puráṇa (cxx. 47).

and the people who *are called* Kshudra-víṇas,* the Rasálayas,† and the Kaikeyas, ‡ the Bhoga-prasthas, § and the Yámunas, ||

* "Those who have small lutes." This is not in the dictionary and I have not met with it elsewhere. A people called *Kshudrakas* are mentioned in the M.-Bh. (Karṇa-P., v. 137); they lived in north India and are generally named in conjunction with the Málavas (Sabhá-P., li. 1871; Bhíshma-P., li. 2106; lxxxviii. 3853; Droṇa-P, lxx. 2435), and are said to be the Greek *Oxydraci.*

† I have not found this elsewhere. It may mean "those who dwell near the river Rasá" which is mentioned in the Ṛig-V. (x. 75, 6). I have met with no other allusion to it, but Dr. Muir thinks it is probably are affluent of the Indus (Sansk. Texts, II. 356 and 357).

‡ See page 317 note ||.

§ I have not met with this word elsewhere, though it is given in the dictionary as the name of a people. Perhaps the reading should be *Bhoja-prastha,* as a synonym of *Bhoja-nagara,* which is mentioned in the M.-Bh. as the capital of king U'śínara or Ushínara, father of king S'ivi (Udyoga-P., cxvii), both of whom were famous monarchs and are often alluded to in the M.-Bh. (*e.g.,* Vana-P., cxxxi. 10582–94; cxcvi. 13274; Droṇa-P., lviii; and S'ánti-P., xxix. 932–7). According to the genealogies given (Hari-V., xxxi. 1674–9; and Matsya Puráṇa, xlviii. 15–21) various Panjab races claimed descent from Uśínara, but the name Uśínaras was especially appropriated to the descendants of S'ivi (Vana-P., cxxxi. 10582). The Uśínaras are alluded to occasionally (*e.g.,* Karṇa-P., v. 137; Aitar. Bráh., viii. 3, 14; and Kaushít.-Up., iv. 1), but S'ivi or S'ibi is the name which is generally used in the M.-Bh. From these passages and others (*e.g.,* Sabhá-P., xxxi. 1189; li. 1870; Vana-P., cxciv. 13249–55; cclxv; cclxx. 15718 and 15743; Bhíshma-P., xviii. 688–90; and li. 2104) it appears the S'ivis were grouped with the Trigartas, Madras, and other Panjab nations on one side and with the Kurus, S'úrasenas and Matsyas on the other side, that is, with all the nations which surrounded Brahmávarta; and that their territory was near the Jumna and close to Tri-vishṭapa or Tri-pishṭapa which was part of Brahmávarta (Vana-P., cxxx. 10556 – cxxxi. 10595; with lxxxiii. 6054-5 and 7073–8; and page 290, note ||). The S'ivis or Uśínaras therefore appear to have possessed the country at the upper part of the Sarasvatí, Dṛishad-vatí and Jumna, from Saharanpur to Pattiala; with the Ambashṭhas to the north-west (see page 379 note ‡). In later times they shared the degradation which the brahmans pronounced on the nations of the north-west because of the absence of brahmans among them (Anuśás.-P., xxxiii. 2103).

|| These are mentioned in the Bhíshma-P. list (ix. 358) and were the people who inhabited the Yámuna hills. The Páṇḍavas in returning from their visit beyond the Himalayas came to the Yámuna hills, and then to

43 the Antar-dvípas,* and the Trigartas,† the Agníjyas,‡ the Sárdana peoples,§ the Aśva-mukhas‖ also, the Práptas,¶
44 the long-haired C'iviḍas,** the Dáserakas,†† the Váṭa-dhánas,‡‡ and the S'ava-dhánas,§§ the Pushkalas,‖‖

the Sarasvati (Vana-P., clxxvii. 12346–62). The hosts collected on the Kauravas' side before the great war overspread all the country from Pañc'a-nada (the Panjab) to Ahic'c'hatra (see page 353, note *) including the Yámuna hills (Udyoga-P., xviii. 596–601). Hence it appears these hills were the portion of the Himalayas, in which the Jumna has its sources, and which separate it from the Sutlej.

* Dvípa in this connexion cannot mean any island, and must mean a *doáb* (see page 364, note †). The Antar-dvípas then would mean "those who dwell within the doabs." I have not met with this word elsewhere, and here it is probably an adjective to the Trigartas, to whom it is very appropriate.

† See page 374, note *.

‡ I have not found this elsewhere, and it is not in the dictionary. The proper reading should no doubt be *A'gneyas.* They are mentioned in the M.-Bh. (Vana-P., ccliii. 15256). A ṛishi or man called A'gneya Su-darśana is spoken of who dwelt in Kuru-kshetra (Anuśás.-P., ii. 102–172); and the A'gneya S'alya-kírtana is alluded to in the same region (Rámáy., Ayodh.-K., lxxiii. 3). It seems probable therefore that the A'gneyas were a small tribe inhabiting the northern part of Kuru-kshetra.

§ Or perhaps "and the Ardana peoples." I have not met with either name elsewhere, nor are they in the dictionary.

‖ These are mentioned in the Matsya Puráṇa (cxx. 58). The synonymous name *Baḍavá-mukhas* occurs in verse 30 above. It may be noted here that it was an old belief there were people who had heads like dogs, Cynocephali (Pliny, vi. 30; Mandeville's Travels, chap. xviii).

¶ I have not found this elsewhere. It may perhaps mean the people called *Vadhras* or *Badhnas* in the Bhíshma-P. list (ix. 363).

** This is not in the dictionary, but *C'ivuka* or *C'ibuka* is given. I have not however met any of these names elsewhere. The word *c'ipiṭa* means "flat-nosed."

†† See page 321, note *.

‡‡ See page 312, note *.

§§ This is not in the dictionary, and I have not found it elsewhere. It seems to be formed on the same plan as *Váṭa-dhána* and *Yátu-dhána.* It may perhaps mean "those who place their dead in receptacles," yet it seems rather to be a name.

‖‖ See page 320, note ¶.

and Adhama Kairátas,* and those who are settled
45 in Taksha-śilá,† the Ambálas,‡ the Málavas,§ the
Madras,|| the Veṇukas,¶ and the Vadantikas,** the
46 Piṅgalas,†† the Mána-kalahas,‡‡ the Húṇas,§§ and the

* The basest or rudest races of Kirátas; see page 322, note ||.

† The Greek Taxila. It is mentioned in the M.-Bh. The name is generally connected with Takshaka king of the Nágas; it is said he killed Arjuna's grandson king Parikshit according to a curse; and that king's son Janamejaya invaded Taksha-śilá and conquered it (Adi-P., iii. 682–3 and 832–4; xl-xliv; and xlix. 1954; l. 1991). It appears however to have been named from the Takkas, whose capital it was, and Cunningham has identified it near the modern Shah-dheri or Dheri Shahan in the Panjab. It was a large and famous city and the Takkas held all the country around (Arch. Surv. Repts., II. 6, 111, 112; XIV. 8). It appears to have contained a great Buddhist university also.

‡ These would be the people of Ambála. This name is a late one. It may probably be derived from the old *Ambashṭha*, the name of a people often mentioned in the M.-Bh. They are said to have been descendants of king Uśínara and to have been closely related to the S'ivis; see page 377, note § (Hari-V., xxxi. 1674–9; Matsya Puráṇa, xlviii. 15–21). They were in the north-west and are generally mentioned along with north-western nations especially the S'ivis and Trigartas (M.-Bh., Sabhá-P., xxxi. 1189; Bhíshma-P., xviii. 688–90; cxviii. 5486; cxx. 5649; and Droṇa-P., vii. 183). It seems, very probable therefore that they occupied the country between Ambála, and the Sutlej with the S'ivis on their east and south and the Trigartas on their north-west.

§ See page 341, note *; but they are quite out of place here.

|| See page 329, note *.

¶ This is not in the dictionary, and I have not found it elsewhere. A people called *Veṇikas* are mentioned in M.-Bh., Bhíshma-P., li. 2097.

** I have not met with this elsewhere.

†† These people are mentioned in the Rámáy., as situated in the West (Kishk.-K., xliii. 23, alternative reading; Gorresio's Edition, Annotations). A river *Piñjalá* is included in the Bhíshma-P. list (ix. 335). But perhaps Pingala is an adjective here, "light brown," and qualifies Húṇas; for the Huns appear to have been a light-complexioned people; see note §§ below.

‡‡ I have not met this as a name elsewhere. It may be an adjective, "quarrelsome through pride," and qualify the Húṇas.

§§ The Huns. They are mentioned as an outside people to the north along with C'ínas, &c., (Vana-P., li. 1991; Bhíshma-P., ix. 373; and S'ánti-P., cccxxvii. 12229), but are not often alluded to at first. In the Raghu-Vaṁśa

Kohalakas,* the Máṇḍavyas,† the Bhúti-yuvakás,‡ the S'átakas,§ the Hema-tárakas,|| the Yaśo-matyas,¶ and the
47 Gándháras,** the Khara-ságara-ráśis,†† the Yaudheyas,‡‡ and the Dásameyas,§§ the Rájanyas,|||| and the S'yámakas,¶¶

they are placed on the northernmost part of the Indus, and the commentator calls them *Mujjanapadákhyáḥ kshattriyáḥ* (iv. 67-68). They appear to have been of a light complexion, for their women are pictured as having made their cheeks pale red (*páṭala*) by beating them in grief (*ibid.*). For the Ephthalitee or White Huns, see Cunningham's Arch. Surv. Repts., II. 75–79. All the valley of the Upper Sutlej is called Hundes. A people called *Hára-húṇas* are also alluded to in the M.-Bh. as an outside people to the north-west (Sabhá-P., xxxi. 1194; and l. 1814).

* I have not found this elsewhere, but it seems to be the same as the *Kokarakas* (Bhíshma-P., ix. 369) and *Kokanadas* (Sabhá-P., xxvi. 1026), both of whom appear to have been a tribe to the north of the Panjab.

† See page 374, note ††.

‡ I have not met this elsewhere. Perhaps it should be connected with *Bhúti-laya*, which was a place in the north of the Panjab (Karṇa-P., xliv. 2062-3).

§ I have not found this elsewhere.

|| This is not in the dictionary and I have not met with it elsewhere.

¶ I have not found this elsewhere; it seems to mean a people who live on a river Yaśo-matí.

** See page 314, note ‡.

†† I have not met this elsewhere and it is not in the dictionary. Certain *Khara-patha* countries are alluded to in the Matsya Puráṇa (cxx. 56); but the name in the text should probably be split up into two names.

‡‡ These people are generally mentioned along with the Trigartas, Madras and other Panjab nations (Sabhá-P., li. 1870; and Karṇa-P., v. 137), and the epithet *adri-ja*, "mountaineer," seems to be applied to them (Droṇa-P., clxi. 7208). They are said to have been descended from king Uśínara, like the S'ivis and Ambashṭhas (Hari-V., xxxi. 1674–8). I have not found any thing more to indicate their position, but judging from the portions of the Panjab occupied by other nations the Yaudheyas may perhaps be placed north of the Madras near Lahore.

§§ Or *Dásamíyas*, as they were also called (Sabhá-P., l. 1825). They were a people in the Panjab; they are called out-castes and are denounced in the Karṇa-P. of the M.-Bh. like the other Panjab nations (xliv. 2054–6, and 2069; and xlv. 2090), but I have found no data to fix their position.

|||| *Rájanya* means a "kshattriya" or "noble," but here it seems to be the name of a people. I have not found it as such elsewhere.

¶¶ I have not met with this elsewhere and it is not in the dictionary.

and the Kshema-dhúrtas* have taken up their position in the Tortoise's left flank.

48 And there *is* the constellation Váruṇa,† there the two *constellations* of Praushṭha-padá‡.

And the kingdom of the Yenas§ and Kinnaras,|| *the country* Praśupála,¶ and *the country* Kíc'aka,**

* I have not found this elsewhere. A king of Kulúta named *Kshema-dhúrti* is mentioned in the M.-Bh. (Karṇa-P., xii. 475, &c.).

† Or S'ata-bhishaj.

‡ They are Púrva-bhádra-padá and Uttara-bhádra-padá.

§ The word *Yena* must be a mistake, and the name meant should, no doubt, be joined with *Kinnara-rájyam*. The proper reading may be either *Yauna-kinnara-rájyam*, or better perhaps, *C'ína-kinnara rájyam*. For C'ínas, see page 319, note ‡. Yauna appears to be an abbreviated form of Yavana and is rarely met with (see M.-Bh., S'ánti-P., ccvii. 7560); the Yavanas were in the north-west; see page 314, note §, yet they are mentioned again in verse 52.

|| The Kinnaras are said in the dictionary to be mythical beings with a human figure and the head of a horse; such creatures have been already alluded to, see Baḍavá-mukhas in verse 30, and Aśva-mukhas in verse 43. They were placed on Mount Gandha-mádana (Vana-P., cxliii. 10964–8), on Mount Mandara (Droṇa-P., lxxx. 2848–52), and generally in the central region of the Himalayas (Raghu-V., iv. 78); and they are probably meant by the *Kiṅkaras* in Rámáy., Kishk.-K., xliv. 13. The Kinnaras were to some extent identified with the *Kimpurushas*, though both are mentioned separately in the Matsya-Purana, cxx. 48-49. It is stated in the dictionary that this occurred in later times, but the chief of the Kimpurushas is said in the M.-Bh. to have dwelt at Gandha-mádana (Udyoga-P., clvii. 5352) which was the Kinnaras' territory. The Kimpurushas are described as forming a kingdom in the Páṇḍavas' time and owning the country beyond S'veta-parvata (Sabhá-P., xxvii. 1038-9; Hari-V., xcii. 5013–5; and xcix. 5493–5). They are alluded to as being men of an inferior type (Aitar. Brah., II. i. 8), and as being forest-men (S'ánti-P., clxix), and also as skilled in the use of the bow (Udyoga-P., clvii. 5352).

¶ This is, no doubt, a mistake for *Paśu-pála* which is stated to be the name of a country and people to the north-east of Madhya-deśa (dict.). They are mentioned along with Kirátas and Tangaṇas and are placed among the lower Himalayan ranges in the Rámáy. (Kishk.-K., xliv. 20). Another reading in that passage is *Páṁśapálas* (see Annotations).

** The text is *sa-kíc'akam*. This seems to be the region of the reeds or bamboos called *kíc'akas*; they are said to line the banks of the R. S'ailodá in the North (Rámáy., Kishk.-K., xliv. 76–79; M.-Bh., Sabhá-P., li. 1858-9;

49 and the country of Káśmíra,* and the people of Abhisára,† the Davadas,‡ and the Tvaṅganas,§ the Kulaṭas,||
50 the Vana-ráshṭrakas,¶ the Sairishṭhas,** the Brahma-

and Raghu-V., iv. 73). It is not clear where this country was. The R. S'ailodá is placed between Meru and Mandara in the passage from the M.-Bh., and the Khasas, Páradas and Tanganas dwelt near it. The R. S'ailodaká is said to rise at the foot of Mount Aruṇa, west of Kailása, in the Matsya Puráṇa (cxx. 22-23).

A people called *Kíc'akas* are mentioned in the M.-Bh., as being near the Matsyas, Trigartas and Páñc'álas, *i.e.*, in Madhya-deśa (A'di-P., clvi. 6084–7), and Kíc'aka was the name of the general of Viráṭa king of Matsya (Viráṭa-P., xiv. 376-7). The dictionary states that they were a tribe of the Kekayas (see page 317, note ||) and that Eka-c'akrá was one of their towns; but Eka-c'akrá seems rather to have been in Madhya-deśa (A'di-P., clvii. 6104–9; clx. 6207; clxiv. 6306; and Vana-P., xi 388–415), and Arrah in Behar claims to be that town. Perhaps there may be some confusion with Kíkaṭa, the old name of Behar, in this.

* *Káśmírakaṁ ráshṭram*; it is called *Káśmíraka-mandala* (M.-Bh., Vana-P., cxxx. 10545-6; and Anuśás.-P., xxv. 1695); see page 323, note ‡. It is quite out of place here.

† This was a country in the north of the Panjab and its capital was *Abhisárí* (M.-Bh., Sabhá-P., xxvi. 1027; and Bhíshma-P., ix. 361). It is not often mentioned (Karṇa-P., xiv. 540-1; and see also perhaps Droṇa-P., xciii. 3379-80), unless the *Abhishádhas* or *Abhisháhas* are the same people (Bhíshma-P., xviii. 688; cxviii. 5485; Droṇa-P., clxi. 7207). But Abhisára is quite out of place here in the north-eastern region.

‡ This is not in the dictionary. I have met with it elsewhere only in Hari-Vaṁśa, xcix. 5503-4, but there it is a mistake for *Darada;* compare xcii. 5022-3, and xci. 4966–70. The Daradas are out of place here; see page 318, note, ||. They are mentioned in verse 32 also.

§ No doubt a mistake for Tanganas, see page 323, note §.

|| This is not in the dictionary, but a people called *Kulati* are mentioned there. I have not found it elsewhere. The word resembles *Kulúta* (Karṇa-P, xii. 475 and 485) and *Kolúta* and *Kolúka* (Rámáy., Kishk.-K., xliii. 8, and Annotations) which seem to be the modern Kulu near the source of the R. Bias, but it is out of place here. A similar name *Kuruṭas* is mentioned in verse 51.

¶ This is mentioned in the dictionary, but I have not found it elsewhere. Vana-ráshṭra as "the country of forests" would apply well to the densely wooded tracts of Assam.

** I have not met with this elsewhere and it is not in the dictionary. A

purakas,* and the Vana-váhyakas,† the Kirátas‡ and
Kauśikas§ and A'nandas,|| the Pahlava¶ and Lolana** peo-
51 ples, the Dárvádas,†† and the Marakas,‡‡ and the Kuruṭas,§§
the Anna-dárakas,|||| the Eka-pádas,¶¶ the Khaśas,***
the Ghoshas,††† the Svarga-bhaumánavadyakas,‡‡‡

place called *Sairíshaka* is mentioned, but it was west of Delhi (M.-Bh., Sabhá-P., xxxi. 1187-8).

* This is mentioned in the dictionary, and Brahma-pura is said to be the name of a peak in the Himálayas, but I have not met either name elsewhere.

† This is in the dictionary but I have not found it elsewhere.

‡ See page 322, note ||; and canto lvii, verse 8.

§ These would be the people dwelling on the banks of the R. Kauśikí or Kosi (see page 292, note **).

|| This is not in the dictionary and I have not found it elsewhere. The text should no doubt read *Nandá* separate from *Kiráta-kauśiká*, and the people are the *Nandas*, those who live on the banks of the rivers Nandá and Apara-nandá, which are often mentioned as situated in the North between the Ganges and Kauśikí or Kosi, and near the R. Báhudá and Mt. Hemakúṭa (M.-Bh, Adi-P., ccxv. 7818-9; Vana-P., lxxxvii. 8323; cx. 9968-87; and Droṇa-P, liv. 2092).

¶ See page 314, note *. They are altogether out of place here.

** This is given in the dictionary, but I have not met with it elsewhere.

†† This seems to be a mistake; it seems the reading should be either *Dárvádyá*, "the Dárvas and others," or *Dárvá dámarakáś*. For the Dárvás see page 324, note ‡.

‡‡ Or perhaps *Dámarakas* as suggested in the last note. Maraka is given in the dictionary but I have not found it elsewhere. It suggests *Muru* and *Naraka*, the names of two Dánava or Asura chiefs in Prág-jyotisha whom Kṛishṇa conquered (M.-Bh., Sabhá-P., xiii. 578; Vana-P., xii. 488; Udyoga-P., xlvii. 1887-92; cxxix. 4408-9; clvii. 5353-8; S'ánti-P., cccxli. 12954-6; and Hari-V., cxxi. 6791—cxxiii. 6921). Prág-jyotisha was the North of Bengal, see page 328, note †.

§§ This is not in the dictionary and I have not found it elsewhere. Is it to be connected with the R. Karatoyá, the modern Kuratee (see page 292, note ††)?

|||| This is not in the dictionary and I have not found it elsewhere.

¶¶ "The men with only one foot," see page 358, note †.

*** They are mentioned above in verse 6; see also page 346 note *.

††† I have not met with these elsewhere. The *Ghosha-saṅkhyas* are mentioned in verse 6 above.

‡‡‡ This seems to be a compound name, but it is not in the dictionary and

52 and the Hingas,* and the Yavanas,† and *those* who *are called* C'ira-právaraṇas,‡ the Tri-netras,§ and the Pauravas,‖
53 and the Gandharvas,¶ O bráhman. These people are situated in the Tortoise's north-east foot.

And the three constellations, the Revatís,** Aśvi-daivatya††
54 and Yámya,‡‡ are declared *to be situated* in that foot *and tend* to the complete development of actions,§§ O best of munis.

And these very constellations *are situated* in these places,‖‖

I have not found any thing like it elsewhere. As an adjective it might mean, "faultless as Svarga and the planet Mars," but that seems inappropriate.

* I have not met with this elsewhere and it is not in the dictionary.

† The Yavanas were in the North-west, see page 314, note §, and also canto lvii, verse 8; but they seem to have spread widely and here they are mentioned in the North-east.

‡ "Those who wear bark clothing." I have not met with it elsewhere as the name of a people.

§ "The three-eyed people." It was believed there were such people, see M.-Bh., Sabhá-P., l. 1837.

‖ The Paurava race was descended from Púru, one of Yayáti's sons (M.-Bh., A'di-P., lxxxv. 3533-4; and xcv. 3762–4) who is said to have got Madhya-deśa (Hari-V., xxx. 1604 and 1619); and the Pauravas spread in various directions. A Paurava kingdom is placed in the North region, in the account of Arjuna's conquests there (Sabhá-P., xxvi. 1022-5) and that may be the nation intended here. There were also Pauravas elsewhere (*e g.*, S'ánti-P., xlix. 1790–2; and A'di-P., clxxxvi. 6995; but Sabhá-P., xxx. 1164 is probably a mistake).

¶ The Gandharvas were fabled to be heavenly musicians, but they are also spoken of as a people dwelling beyond lake Mánasa, and it is said Arjuna conquered them and brought back a tribute of fine roan horses (*tittiri-kalmásha*) from their country (Sabhá-P., xxvii. 1041–3). It is said the Gandharvas are more powerful by night (A'di-P., clxx. 6504). It is also fabled that the gods obtained Soma from them because they lust after women (Aitar. Brah., I. v. 27); and they were said to possess or inspire people (*id.*, V. v. 29; and Bṛih. A'raṇ. Up., III. iii. 1 and vii. 1).

** For *Revatyáś* read *Revatyaś*; the plural is sometimes used.

†† Or Aśviní.

‡‡ Or Bharaṇí.

§§ *Pákáya.*

‖‖ There do not appear to be any particular reasons why the lunar constellations are assigned to the respective portions of the Tortoise's body.

55 O bráhman. These places, which have been mentioned in
order, undergo calamity* when these *their constellations* are
occulted,† and gain ascendancy,‡ O bráhman,§ along with
56 the planets which are favourably situated. Of whichever con-
stellation whichever planet is lord, both *the constellation and
the corresponding country* are dominated by it; || at its ascend-
ancy ¶ good fortune accrues to that country, O best of munis.
57 Singly *all* countries are alike; fear or prosperity** comes
to people according as *either* arises out of the *particular*
58 constellation and planet, O bráhman. *The thought*, that man-
kind are in a common predicament with their own particular
constellations when these are unfavourable, inspires fear.
Along with the *particular* planets there arises from *their*
occultations an unfavourable *influence* which discourages exer-
59 tion. Likewise the development of the conditions *may be*
favourable; and so when the planets are badly situated *it tends*
to produce slight benefit to men and to themselves with the
60 wise who are learned in geography.†† When the *particular*
planet is badly situated,‡‡ men *even* of sacred merit have fear
for their goods or cattle-pen, their dependants, friends or
61 children or wife. Now men of little merit feel fear in their
souls, very sinful men feel it everywhere indeed, but the
62 sinless never in a single place. Man experiences good or evil,
which may arise from community of region, place and people,
or which may arise from having a common king, *or* which
may arise peculiarly from himself,§§ *or* which may arise
63 from community of constellation and planet. And mutual
preservation is produced by the non-malignity |||| of the pla-

* *Píḍyante.*

† *Píḍá.*

‡ *Abhy-udaya.*

§ For *vipram* read *vipra.*

|| The text is *tad-bhávito bhayam*; but it seems better to take the whole as one word.

¶ *Utkarsha.*

** *S'obhana*, "brightening up."

†† These verses seem rather obscure.

‡‡ For *du-sthe* read *duḥ-sthe.*

§§ For *átsajam* read *átma-jam.*

|||| For *grahádausthyena* read *grahádauḥsthyena.*

nets; and loss of good *is produced* by the evil *results which spring* from these very *planets*, O lordly bráhman.
64 I have described to thee what is the position of the Tortoise among the constellations. But this community of countries
65 is inauspicious and also auspicious. Therefore a wise man, knowing the constellation of *his particular* country and the occultation of the planets, should perform a propitiatory rite for himself and observe the popular rumours, O best *of men*.
66 Bad impulses* both of the gods and of the Daityas and other *demons* descend from the sky upon the earth; they have been called by sacred writings "popular rumours"† in the world.
67 So a wise man should perform that *propitiatory rite;* he should not discard the popular rumours. By reason of them
68 the decay of corrupt traditional doctrine‡ befits men. Those *rumours* may effect the rise of good and the casting off of sins, *also* the forsaking of wisdom,§ O bráhman; they cause *the*
69 *loss* of goods and other *property*. Therefore a wise man, being devoted to propitiatory rites and taking an interest in the popular rumours, should have the popular rumours *proclaimed*
70 and the propitiatory rites performed at the occultations of planets; and *he should practise* fastings devoid of malice, the praise-worthy laudation of funeral monuments and other *objects of veneration*, prayer, the homa oblation, and liberality
71 and ablution; *he should* eschew anger and other *passions*. And a learned man should be devoid of malice and shew benevolence towards all created things; he should discard evil
72 speech and also outrageous words. And a man should perform the worship of the planets at all occultations. Thus all terrible things which result from the planets and constellations
73 are without exception pacified with regard to self-subdued men.

This Tortoise described by me in India is in truth the
74 adorable lord Náráyaṇa, whose soul is inconceivable, *and* in whom everything is established. In it all the gods have their

* *Daurhṛidáḥ;* the dictionary gives this word only as neuter.

† Loka-váda. ‡ Dushtágama. § Prajñá-háni.

75 station, each resorting to his own constellation. Thus, in its
middle are Agni, the Earth, and the Moon, O bráhman. In
its middle are Aries and the next two constellations;* in its
76 mouth are Gemini and the next constellation; and in the
south-east foot Cancer and Leo are situated; and in its
side are placed the three signs of the zodiac, Leo, Virgo
77 and Libra: and both Libra and Scorpio are in its south-
west foot; and at its hinder part† is stationed Sagittarius
78 along with Scorpio; and in its north-west foot are the
three *signs* Sagittarius and the next *two;* and Aquarius and
79 Pisces have resorted to its northern side; Pisces and Aries
are placed in its north-east foot, O bráhman.

The countries are placed in the Tortoise, and the constella-
80 tions in these countries, O bráhman, and the signs of the zodiac
in the constellations, the planets in the signs of the zodiac.‡
Therefore one should indicate calamity to a country when
81 *its particular* planets and constellations are occulted. In that
event one should bathe and give alms and perform the homa
oblation and the rest of the ritual.

This very foot of Vishṇu, which is in the midst of the planets, is Brahmá.

Canto LIX.

Description of the Earth continued.

Márkandeya tells of the continents Bhadráśva and Ketumála, and the country of the Northern Kurus, and describes their mountains, rivers and people.

Márkaṇḍeya spoke

1 Thus then have I declared this continent Bhárata accurately,
O muni, and the Kṛita, Tretá, and Dvápara, and Kali *ages*
2 which are the four ages.§ And now indeed there is a fourfold

* Taurus and Gemini; the signs of the Zodiac overlap in the different stations.

† *Pṛishṭhe;* but *puc'c'he* would be better.

‡ For *graha-ráśishu* read *grahá ráśishu?*

§ For *tathá-tishya-c'atushṭhayam* read *tathá tishya-c'atushṭayam.*

classification* in these ages, O bráhman. Four, three and
3 two *hundreds* and one hundred of autumns men live here in
the Kṛita, Tretá and two other ages respectively, O bráhman.
Hear from me of the continent Bhadráśva, which is situated
4 east of the magnificent eastern mountain Deva-kúṭa.
Both S'veta-parṇa, and Níla, and the lofty mountain S'aivála,
5 Kaurañja, Parṇa-śálágra—these indeed are the five mountain
ranges. There are many small mountains besides, which are
6 offshoots of those *ranges;* the countries *there* are distinguished
by them, they are of various shapes *and occur* in thousands.
Moreover they are like white water-lilies and are auspicious
7 with their pure summits. Such-like and diverse also are
other *hills* by hundreds and thousands. The S'ítá, the
8 S'aṅkhávatí, the Bhadrá, and the C'akrávartá and many other
rivers spread abroad there, bearing down volumes of cold
water. In this country mankind are lustrous as shells and
9 like pure gold;† they associate with the celestials; they are
holy; their lives last a thousand years; neither inferior nor
10 superior exists among them; they are all of equal appearance;
they are endowed naturally with patience and the
seven other good qualities.
And there the god Janárdana has a horse's head and four
11 arms; with head, chest, penis, feet and forearms *resembling a
horse's*, and he has three eyes. And thus the objects of sense
are perceptible by him, the lord of the world.
12 Now hear from me about the continent Ketumála which
is on the west.
13 Viśála, Kambala, Kṛishṇa, Jayanta, Hari-parvata, Viśoka,
and Vardhamána—these seven are the mountain ranges.
There are other hills by thousands, among which a multitude
14 of people dwell. Those people dwell *there* in hundreds, the
Maulis‡ huge in stature, the S'ákas, Potas and Karambhakas,§

* *C'atur-varṇyo*, a masc. abstract noun.

† *S'aṅkha-śuddha-hema-sama-prabháḥ.*

‡ This and the following words seem to be the names of people; mountains and rivers in these continents are named, and it seems most natural and reasonable to take these words as names.

§ *S'ákapotakarambhakáḥ;* or perhaps "S'ákas, Potakas and Rambhakas."

15 and those who are distinguished by their thumbs,* who drink
of the great rivers, the Vaṅkshu, the S'yámá, the Svakambalá,
the Amoghá, the Kámini, the S'yámá, and of others in
16 thousands. And here life is equal to the above-mentioned
lives in Bhadrás'va. And here the adorable Hari wears a
boar's shape and *resembles a boar* in feet, face, chest, back and
17 flanks. And the lunar constellations are beautiful in *that*
country which enjoys three constellations *only*. Such is this
continent of Ketumála, which I have described to thee, O best
of munis.

18 Next I will tell *thee* of the Northern Kurus; hearken to
me now.

There the trees yield sweet fruit, they bear blossoms and
19 fruit in constant succession; and they produce garments and
ornaments inside their fruits; verily they bestow all one's
20 desire; they yield fruit according to all one's desire. The
ground abounds with precious stones; the air is fragrant and
always delightful. Mankind are born there, when they quit
21 the world of the gods. They are born in pairs; *the pairs* abide
an equal time, and are as fond of each other as c'akravákas.
22 Their stay there is fourteen and a half thousands *of years*
indeed. And C'andra-kánta is the chief of the mountains,
23 and Súrya-kánta is the next; they are the two mountain
ranges in that continent. And in the midst thereof the great
river Bhadra-somá flows through the earth with a volume of
24 sacred and pure water. And there are other rivers by thou-
sands in that northern continent; and some flow with milk
25 and others flow with ghee. And there are lakes of curdled
milk there, and others lie among the various hills. And fruits
26 of various kinds, which taste rather like amṛita, *are produced*
by hundreds and thousands in the woods in those continents.
And there the adorable Vishṇu has his head turned to the
27 east and wears a fish's shape. And the lunar constellations
are divided† into nine parts, three and three, and the regions
of the sky are divided into nine parts, O best of munis.

* *Aṅgula-pramukhás.*

† For *vibhakto* read *vibhaktir?*

28 And in the ocean are *the islands* C'andra-dvípa, and next
Bhadra-dvípa; and there also within the ocean is the famous
island Puṇya, O great muni.

29 Thus I have described this northern continent of Kuru,
O bráhman. Hearken while I tell *thee* of Kim-purusha and
the other continents.

CANTO LX.

The description of the Earth concluded.

Márkaṇḍeya briefly describes the continents, Kim-purusha Hari-varsha, Ilávṛita, Ramyaka and Hiraṇ-maya, and their inhabitants.

Márkaṇḍeya spoke:

1 I will tell *thee*, O bráhman, what the continent Kim-
purusha is; where men with *real* bodies live ten thousand
2 *years;* where men and women are indeed free from sickness
and free from sorrow, and there the fig-tree* is called shaṇḍa;
3 it grows very high, it is like a grove.† Those men are always
drinking the juice of its fruit; and the women are born with
lasting youthfulness and are fragrant as the lotus.‡

4 Next to Kim-purusha is mentioned Hari-varsha. There
5 mankind are born of the appearance of gold; they all de-
scend there from the world of the gods, and are shaped like
the gods in all respects. In Hari-varsha all the men quaff
6 fine sugar-cane juice; neither old age afflicts them there, nor
do they suffer from decay at all; and they live in truth for
the whole of their time free from sickness.

7 I have mentioned Ilávṛita, which is in the middle, the
continent of Meru. The sun does not burn there, nor do men
8 suffer from decay; and they do not grasp at selfish gains.§

* *Plaksha.* † *Nandanopamaḥ.*

‡ *Utpala-gandhikáḥ;* this word, *neuter*, also means a species of sandal of the colour of brass and very fragrant.

§ *Labhante nátma-lábhañ c'a;* it seems impossible to take these words with *raśmayaś c'andra-súryayoḥ.*

The rays of the moon and the sun, of the constellations and
9 planets there are the sublime lustre of Meru. Mankind are
born there bright as the lotus flower, fragrant as the lotus
flower; they feed on the juice of the jambu fruit; and
10 their eyes are as wide as the lotus leaf. And their life
there lasts for thirteen thousand years. There is a saucer-
11 shaped expanse in the middle of Meru* in Ilávṛita; therein
is the great mountain Meru; thus is made known Ilávṛita.

Next I will tell of the continent Ramyaka; hearken thereto.
12 And there the green-leaved Indian fig-tree† is the lofty tree.
And the people there pass their time drinking the juice of its
13 fruit. There the men who eat its fruit live for ten thousand
years; they are pre-eminent for sexual pleasures and are
pure; they are free from old age and ill odours.

14 And north of that is the continent famed by name as
Hiraṇ-maya; where the river Hiraṇ-vatí gleams with abun-
15 dant lotuses. Mankind there are born with great strength,
full of vigour, with large bodies, eminently good, wealthy and
benign of look.

Canto LXI.

The Story of the Bráhman in the Svároc'isha Manvantara.

Márkaṇḍeya begins the relation of the Svároc'isha Manvantara—A young bráhman, by virtue of a magic ointment applied to his feet, visits the Himálaya mountains in half a day—The scenery there described—He wishes to return home, but the magic ointment has been dissolved by the snow, and he loses his way—The Apsaras Varúthiní meets him, and falling in love with him begs him for his love—He refuses all her entreaties, and at length appeals to the gárhapatya fire to help him homeward.

Kraushṭuki spoke :

1 Thou hast duly related what thou wast asked, O great muni,

* For *meru-madhye* read *meru-madhya.*

† *Nyag-rodha*, Ficus indica.

namely, the constitution of the earth, ocean, &c., their dimen-
2 sions, also the planets and their dimensions, and the constitu-
tion of the constellations, and the bhúr-loka and the other
3 worlds, and all the Lower Regions. And thou hast declared
the Sváyambhuva Manvantara to me, O muni. Next I wish
to hear about the Manvantaras which succeeded that, the
deities who ruled over the Manvantaras, the ṛishis, and the
kings who were their sons.

Márkaṇḍeya spoke:

4 I have made known to thee the Manvantara which is
called Sváyambhuva. Now next to that hear about another
which is named after Sváročisha.*
5 There lived a certain bráhman eminent among the dvijas
in the town Aruṇáspada on the bank of the Varuṇá; and he
6 surpassed the Asvins † in beauty of form. He was gentle
in disposition, upright in conduct, he had studied all the
Vedas and Vedáṅgas; always gracious to guests, he was
7 the refuge of all persons who arrived at night. Now he
had this intention, "I *will* see the earth which has most
charming forests and gardens, and is embellished with many a
town."
8 Now a certain guest once arrived at his abode, who was
acquainted with the powers of various medicinal herbs, and
9 skilled in the magic art. Now being requested by the former,
whose mind was purified by faith, he described to him both
10 countries and charming towns, forests, rivers,‡ and moun-
tains, and holy sanctuaries. Then the former filled with
11 astonishment said to that best of bráhmans, "In that thou
hast seen many countries thou art not worn with excessive
toil, thou art not very old in life, nor hast thou long passed
thy youth; how dost thou roam the earth in a short time,
O bráhman?"

* For *svaroc'isháklyam* read *sváróc'isháklyam?*

† *Aty-aśvinau*, "one who surpasses the two Aśvins;" see Prof. Sir M. Monier-Williams' Grammar, rule 126 *i*.

‡ For *nadyaḥ* read *nadíḥ*.

The bráhman spoke:

12 By the power of spells and medicinal herbs my course is rendered free, O bráhman; verily I travel a thousand yojanas in half a day.

Márkaṇḍeya spoke:

13 Then the bráhman made him this answer in return with due
14 respect, believing * the word of that wise bráhman, "Adorable Sir, give me the favour that comes from the power of
15 spells; I have an intense desire to see this earth." And that bráhman of exalted intellect gave him an ointment for the feet; and offered careful counsel † regarding the region which the other mentioned.
16 Now the bráhman, with his feet anointed by the other, went to see the Hima-vat range, where many a cascade
17 pours down, O best of dvijas, for he thought, "Since I can indeed travel a thousand yojanas in half a day,‡ I will cer-
18 tainly return in the other half of it." He reached the top of Hima-vat, not much fatigued in body, O bráhman. Then he roamed about there over the surface of the snowy moun-
19 tain. Now the ointment on his feet, which was extracted from the choicest medicinal herbs, became washed off by the
20 melting snow which accumulated on his feet. Thereupon he grew slack in his walk, as he wandered about hither and thither. He saw the peaks of the snowy range which most
21 fascinate the mind. Gazing at *those peaks* which are loved of the Siddhas and Gandharvas, and where the Kin-naras disport themselves, which are delightful here and there for
22 play and pastime among the gods and other *heavenly beings, and* which were thronged with hundreds of bevies of heavenly Apsarases, the bráhman, whose hair stood erect with delight,
23 was not satiated, O muni. Filled with rapture he gazed at the mighty mountain range Hima-vat, which in one place captivated him with the fall of the broken water from a

* For *śrad-dhadháno* read *śrad-dadháno.*

† *Abhi-mantrayámása;* this meaning is not given to the verb in the dictionary.

‡ For *dináddhana* read *dinárddhena.*

torrent, and which in another place was made resonant with
24 the cries of peacocks as they danced, and which was thronged
here and there with pied-crested cuckoos,* lapwings and
other pretty birds, and with cock-koils and humming bees,
25 which captivated the ear, and which was fanned by breezes
perfumed with scents from trees that were in full blossom.

26 And after viewing the mighty mountain Hima-vat as it
thus was, the young bráhman resolved to go homewards,
27 intending to see it *again* the next day. Now he had lost the
ointment from his feet, his step was slow by reason of his
28 long *walking*, he pondered "What is this? I have acted
unwisely, if the ointment is destroyed, having dissolved off
me by the melted snow; and this mountain is very difficult
29 of access, and it is a long distance that I have come here. I
shall suffer loss in my rites. How shall I kindle a fire and do
my dutiful homage and all else *that is needful?* I have fallen
30 into a terrible strait. 'This is charming! that is charming!'—
with my sight so engrossed on this fine mountain, I shall not
31 be satiated even in hundreds of years. The melodious talk of
the Kin-naras ravishes my ears all around, and my nose eagerly
32 seeks the scents from the trees that are in full blossom, and
the breeze is delightful to the touch, and the fruits are full of
juice, and the charming lakes forcibly captivate the mind.
33 In these circumstances then if I may chance to see some
ascetic, he may point out the road for me to go homeward."

Márkaṇḍeya spoke:

34 The bráhman, reflecting so, wandered yet on the snowy
mountain; having lost the efficacy of the medicinal herbs
35 from his feet, he sank into intense fatigue. And Varúthiní
saw him, that goodly muni, as he was wandering; she a
choice Apsaras, of high station, the daughter of Múli,† and
36 beauteous in shape. As soon as she saw him Varúthiní

* *C'dtaka;* see page 29 note †.

† *Mauleyá.* The dictionary gives *Mauleya* as the name of a people, but that meaning seems inappropriate here. As a patronymic *Mauleyí* would appear more correct. See verse 46 below.

felt her heart drawn towards that noble bráhman by love,
37 in truth she was immediately filled with affection. She
thought, "Who then is this, of most fascinating appearance?
38 My birth may reach its reward if he do not despise me. How
handsome his shape! How graceful his gait! How deep his
39 gaze! Where is there his equal on the earth? I have seen
the gods and the Daityas, the Siddhas, the Gandharvas and
the Nágas; how is it there is not even one who rivals this
40 high-souled man in figure? If he should fall in love with
me as I *have fallen in love* with him, the store of merit
41 which he has acquired may be attainable by me here. If he
should cast a really loving glance on me to-day, then there
would be no other woman in the three worlds, who has
gained more merit than I."

Márkaṇḍeya spoke:

42 So reflecting the heavenly maiden, who was sick for love,
43 showed herself in very lovely form. Now on seeing her,
gracefully-formed Varúthiní, the young bráhman approached
44 with deference and spoke this word—"Who art thou, O
maiden bright as the lotus-cup? Or on whom dost thou
attend? I am a bráhman, I have come here from the city
45 Aruṇáspada. The ointment on my feet, by the power of
which I came here, has perished being dissolved by the
melting snow here, O maiden of fascinating glance!"

Varúthiní spoke:

46 I am the daughter of Múli, of high station; I am well-
known by name as Varúthiní. I roam here at all times
47 indeed on this charming mountain. Being such I am com-
pelled by the sight of thee, O bráhman, to declare my love.
Do thou enjoin me what I must do, I am now submissive
to thee."

The bráhman spoke:

48 O benign sweet-smiler, tell me the means whereby I may
go to my own home. Loss *is befalling* us in all our actions,
49 and grievous loss befalls a bráhman in the perpetual and

occasional *ceremonies.* Therefore, O lady, do thou deliver me
50 from the Himálaya mountains. Absence from home is never
commended in bráhmans. I have not sinned, O timid one;
51 *it was my* curiosity to see *other* countries. All actions and
the perpetual and occasional *ceremonies* are accomplished by
a bráhman when he stays at home; so they are lost if he
52 dwells away from home. Such as thou art, why should
I say much. Do then, O illustrious *lady*, so that I may see
my own abode ere the sun sets.

Varúthiní spoke:

53 Speak not so, illustrious Sir; let not that day come for me,
in which abandoning me thou shalt resort to thy own abode!
54 Ah! since heaven is not more charming, O young bráhman,
55 then abandoning the gods' abode we *will* stay here. Sport-
ing with me on this beloved snowy mountain, thou thyself,
56 O my beloved, wilt not remember thy mortal kinsmen. Seized
and rendered submissive by love, I too will give thee here
garlands, garments, ornaments, loving joys,* and dainty food
57 and unguents. Charming is the song of the Kin-naras,
accompanied with the strains of the lute and flute; the
58 breeze brings gladness to the body; there is warm food, the
water is pure. Longed for by the mind is the bed, fragrant is
the ointment. While thou remainest here, illustrious Sir,
59 what more wilt thou have in thine own house? While thou
remainest here, never will old age light on thee. This is the
60 land of the thirty *gods;* it gives fullness to youth!" Having
spoken thus, the lotus-eyed *maiden*, full of affection, exclaim-
ing sweetly "Be thou gracious!" suddenly embraced him
in the eagerness of her mind.

The bráhman spoke:

61 Touch me not; go to some other *man* who is like thyself,
O worthless one! I have been wooed in one way, thou indeed
62 approachest me in a very different way. The oblation to
the gods, offered evening and morning, sustains the eternal

* *Bhoksha*, not in the dictionary; read *bhoga*

worlds; the whole of these three worlds is established on the oblation to the gods, O foolish one!

Varúthiní spoke:

63 Am I not dear to thee, O bráhman? Is not the mountain charming? Leaving aside the Gandharvas, the Kin-
64 naras and the others, whom dost thou desire? Surely, Sir, thou shalt go away from here to thy own abode without doubt; enjoy with me for a very little while the delights that are hard to be won.

The bráhman spoke:

65 I continually desire the gárhapatya and the two other fires; the fire-place is charming to me; my dear wife is the goddess who diffuses *herself about me.**

Varúthiní spoke:

66 Compassion, O bráhman, is the foremost of the eight good qualities of the soul; why dost thou not display it towards
67 me, O cherisher of truth and righteousness? Forsaken by thee, I do not live; and I am full of affection for thee; I say not this falsely; be gracious, O gladdener of thy family!

The bráhman spoke:

68 If thou art in truth full of affection, and dost not speak to me out of mere politeness, then tell me the means by which I may go to my own home.

Varúthiní spoke:

69 Surely, Sir, thou shalt go away from here to thy own abode without doubt; enjoy with me for a very little while the delights that are hard to be won!

The bráhman spoke:

70 *Striving* after delights is not at all commended in bráhmans, O Varúthiní; † *such* striving in bráhmans tends to weariness in this world, and yields no fruit after death.

* *Vistaraṇí*, not in the dictionary. † For *Varúthiní* read *Varúthini.*

Varúthiní spoke:

71 If thou savest me who am at the point of death, thou wilt
have the fruit of merit itself in the next world, and delights
72 in another life; and thus the two things will procure thee
prosperity in this world; if thou dost refuse, I shall die and
thou wilt incur sin.

The bráhman spoke:

73 My spiritual preceptors have told me that one should not
covet another's wife; therefore I long not for thee; bewail
thy love or be thou withered!

Márkaṇḍeya spoke:

74 Having spoken thus, the illustrious *bráhman*, self-controlled
and pure, touched water and prostrating himself addressed
75 the gárhapatya fire with this muttered prayer,—"O adorable
Gárhapatya fire! thou art the source of all rites; from thee
and thee alone come the áhavaníya fire and the dakshiṇa
76 fire! By the nourishment given by thee the gods subsist
who cause the rain, the crops and other *benefits*; by the crops,
77 and them alone, the whole world subsists. Thus this world
subsists through thee—by this truth *I adjure thee* that I may
78 see my home to-day, ere sets the sun! By this truth *I adjure
thee* that I may behold the sun to-day while I sit in my
house, so that I may not neglect the Vedic rites at the proper
79 time! And that, as the thought of and the longing for
another's goods and another's wife have never occurred to
me, so this *virtue* may be perfected in me!"

Canto LXII.

About the Svároc'isha Manvantara.

The young bráhman is succoured by Agni and returns home—A Gandharva Kali sees Varúthiní disconsolate and in the guise of the bráhman gains her love.

Márkaṇḍeya spoke:

1 Now as the young bráhman thus spoke, the Gárhapatya
2 Fire in sooth appeared at hand upon his body; and with it

surmounting him, he stood amid a circle of light, and illu-
3 mined that place as if he were Agni in bodily form. Now
vehement love seized upon the heavenly maiden as she beheld
4 the bráhman, who *stood* there in so *glorious a* form. Then
the young bráhman,* surmounted by that Fire, immediately
5 started to go as before; and he departed in haste while the
slender-shaped heavenly *maiden* gazed after him as far as
6 her eye could reach, her throat quivering with sighs. Then
in one moment from that time the bráhman reached his own
abode and performed all the rites as he had mentioned.
7 Now she, the beauteous in every limb, *remained* with soul
and mind clinging fast to him, and passed the remainder of the
8 day and also the night in almost ceaseless sighing. And
the faultlessly-shaped maiden sighing *and* crying "Ah! Ah!"
continually, reproached herself, "O luckless one *that I am!*"
9 *though* her eyes were fascinating. Neither in sport, nor in
food, nor yet on delightsome forest, nor on the charming
10 glens did she then fix her joy. She turned her desire to-
wards a pair of billing ćakravákas. Forsaken by him the
finely-shaped maiden reproached her own youthful woman-
11 hood, "How happened it † that I came to this mountain,
forcibly attracted by evil fate? And how happened it that
12 he, such a man as that, crossed the range of my eye? If
that grand *man* shall not come to me to-day, verily the intoler-
13 able fire of *my* love for him will consume me away. The song
of the cock-koil which was so delightful, this self same *song*
when disunited ‡ from him is burning enough, as it were,
to me to-day."

Márkaṇḍeya spoke:

14 Thus she poured forth her words, O bráhman, § absorbed in
love, and her passion for him grew every moment then.

* For *dija-naṇdanaḥ* read *dvija-nandanaḥ*. † Kva.

‡ Read in preference *hínáṁ* for *hínaṁ*, to agree with *mám?*

§ The text reads, *Jagáma muni-sattamam;* but these words seem meaning-less from the context. *Jagáda muni-sattama* seem preferable, and I have ventured to adopt them in the translation.

15 Now a Gandharva named Kali was enamoured of her, and
16 had been rejected by her before. He beheld her in that
condition. Then he pondered, "Why now is this Varúthiní,
who moves as gracefully as an elephant, faded by the *hot*
17 blast of sighing on this mountain? Has she been wounded
by some muni's curse, or has any one treated her with dis-
honour, since she keeps on bedewing her face copiously with
18 tears?" Then Kali through curiosity meditated on that
matter full long, and perceived the truth by the power of
19 concentrated thought. Comprehending that *matter* of the
muni,* Kali pondered again, "I have well accomplished this,
20 by reason of fortunate actions done before. Though often
entreated by me who love her, she, this very *maiden*, rejected
21 *me*; to-day I shall gain *her*. She is in love with a human
being; by virtue of that *fact* she shall all-unsuspectingly
bestow her love on me while I assume his shape. Why
then do I delay?"

Márkaṇḍeya spoke:

22 Thereupon he assumed that bráhman's shape by his inherent
power, and moved to where sits Varúthiní disconsolate.
23 Seeing him, a little wide grew the eyes of the finely-shaped
maiden. In her slender form she approached him and ex-
24 claimed "Be kind!" again and again; "Bereft of thee I
shall assuredly abandon my life; thereby *thou wilt incur*
very sore unrighteousness, and thy sacred ceremonies will
25 come to ruin. Joining with me in this charming glen
among the great glens, thou wilt certainly acquire right-
26 eousness by saving me. Life verily has some remnant † for
me, O wise *bráhman!* Surely thou hast returned for that
reason, and bringest gladness to my heart."

Kali spoke:

27 What am I doing? My ceremonies suffer harm while I
linger here. Dost thou tell me such a tale as this, O slender-

* Or better perhaps, for *Muneḥ* read *Mune*, "O Muni."

† For *sávaśesham* read *c'ávaśesham?* Ava-śesha may apparently be neuter sometimes.

28 waisted maiden? Therefore I am fallen into a strait. Thou must do * what I say, and not otherwise, if there is to be union between me and thee, lady, to-day.

Varúthiní spoke:

29 Be kind! What thou sayest, that I *will* do for thee without falsehood—I say this without fear—whatever I must do now for thy sake.

Kali spoke:

30 Thou must not gaze on me while we meet in union in the wood to-day; thou must close thine eyes, O lady with beautiful brows, the while thou dost unite with me.

Varúthiní spoke:

31 So be it as 't is good to thee! As thou wishest, so let it be! Truly I must remain submissive to thee now in every way.

CANTO LXIII.

About the Svároc'isha Manvantara.

The Apsaras Varúthiní had by the Gandharva Kali a son who was named Sva-roc'is—He delivered a maiden Mano-ramá and her father the Vidyá-dhara Indívara from a curse—and married her.

Márkaṇḍeya spoke:

1 Then with her he sported on mountain tops, which charmed the heart with their blossoming forests, and midst
2 charming lakes, and in pleasant glens, and on sand-banks in the rivers, and in other delightsome places, with merry
3 heart, O bráhman. With eyes closed fast during their embraces, she thought by reason of his ardour that his form was
4 that of the *young bráhman* surmounted with fire. Then after a time she conceived a child, O best of munis; *it took* its form from the Gandharva's energy and *her* dwelling in thought on

* For *karoshi* read *kurushva*?

5 the bráhman. Then he having soothed Varúthiní in her
pregnant condition departed, *still* assuming the bráhman's
shape; she gave him a loving dismissal.

6 The *child* was born a boy, with a splendour like the blazing
orb of light, illuminating all the regions of the sky with his
7 own lustre like the sun. Because he shines with his own
lustre,* like the sun, the boy became therefore famed by the
8 appropriate name Sva-roćis. And the noble boy grew day
by day in age and with a multitude of good qualities, just
9 as the new moon increases with its daily increments; he
acquired skill in archery, and learnt the Vedas in due order
and the sciences; then the noble *boy* entered on the period
of early manhood.

10 Once upon a time, while he who was fascinating in his
ways was roaming on Mount Mandara, he saw a lonely
11 maiden helpless with fear on the mountain's slope. Seeing
him, at once she uttered the words "Save me!" "Fear not!"
he exclaimed to her whose eyes were flooded with fear;
12 "Why is this?" said the high-souled *youth* in heroic speech.
Thereupon she gave *him this* account, in words broken by
her palpitating breath.

The maiden spoke:

13 I am indeed the daughter of the Vidyá-dhara Indívara,
Mano-ramá by name; I was born of Maru-dhanvan's daughter.
14 Vibhá-varí daughter of the Vidyá-dhara Mandára was my
friend, and Kalá-vatí, the muni Pára's daughter, was my other
15 *friend*. With them I went to Kailása's lofty † slope. There
I saw a certain muni; exceedingly thin was his face through
16 his austerities, wasted was his neck through hunger, vigour-
less was he, deep sunk were the pupils of his eyes. I laughed
17 *at him*, and then he grew enraged and cursed me, in a very
infirm voice and with his shoot-like lower lip somewhat
quivering‡—"Since thou hast laughed *at me*, O ignoble and
18 bad ascetic maiden, a Rákshasa shall therefore overcome thee

* *Sva-roc'ibhir.* † For *attamam* read *uttamam.*

‡ For *kiñc'it-kalpitádhara-pallavaḥ* read *kiñc'it-kampitádhara-pallavaḥ ?*

in no long time indeed." But when the curse was pro-
19 nounced, my two friends upbraided the muni—" Fie!
through thy want of forbearance, done is thy bráhman-hood,
done all thine austerities! Thou art violated through thy
wrathfulness, thou art not greatly worn out * through aus-
20 terities. The dwelling-place of forbearance is verily bráh-
man-hood; the controlling of wrath is the performance of
austerities." Hearing this the *sage* of measureless glory
21 cursed both of them also,—" Leprosy in the limbs shall light
on one of you, and consumption on the other." Exactly as
he said, it befell them both immediately.

22 So on my track also a mightly Rákshasa is approaching.
Dost thou not hear his loud roar, as he thunders forth, even
23 close at hand? To-day is the third day that he quits not my
back. Now out of all the multitude of weapons I give thee
24 the *weapon* which strikes to the heart; save me from this
Rákshasa, O high-minded *youth!* Rudra, who wields the
bow Pináka, himself gave it to Sváyambhuva originally;
25 Sváyambhuva gave it to Vaśishṭha the chief of the Siddhas;
he moreover gave it to C'itráyudha, my mother's father;
26 he again, as father-in-law, himself gave it to my father as
a wedding gift. I, though a maiden, learnt, O hero! from my
27 father *how to use this* Heart of all weapons, which destroys
every foe. This is it, take it quickly, the essence of all
28 weapons, then slay this vile-souled *Rákshasa* who has come
into conflict with sacred spell.†

Márkaṇḍeya spoke:

29 "Yea!" then quoth he, and she sprinkling water on it
gave *him* the Heart of weapons together with the spell for
stopping its secret virtue.

30 In this interval *appeared* that Rákshasa. Then with apall-
ing aspect, and roaring with a loud roar, he came hastily on.
31 He looked at that *demon* who was exclaiming—" Overpowered
by me, to what dost thou resort for deliverance? Come

* *Ati-karshitaḥ*; or, " thou art not greatly attracted by austerities."

† *Brahma-samágatam.*

speedily to me! What *good is it* to delay thy being devoured?"
32 Seeing him at hand, Sva-roćis thought, "Let him seize *her*,
so *will* the great muni's word *become* true with regard to her."
33 The Rákshasa approaching with haste seized the maiden of
beauteous waist, as she was piteously bewailing, "Save me,
34 Save me!" Then Sva-roćis enraged looked at the active and
most terrible weapon, and plunging it into that Rákshasa
35 looked on it with unwinking eyes. Vanquished thereby * the
night-stalking *demon* then quitted her and said—"Be gracious!
36 let the weapon be kept in peace, and hearken! I have been
delivered by thee, O most glorious *hero!* from a very grievous
curse, which was inflicted by wise and exceedingly fierce
37 Brahma-mitra. *It is* a benefit (none other greater can I
receive from thee, O illustrious *hero!*), whereby I have been
delivered from a great and most sore curse."

Sva-roćis spoke:

38 Why wert thou cursed formerly by the high-souled muni
Brahma-mitra, and what kind of curse was imprecated *on thee?*

The Rákshasa spoke:

39 The bráhman Brahma-mitra had mastered the thirteen
sections of the Atharva Veda, and had just studied the Áyur-
40 veda which is divided into eight parts. And I was well
known by the name Indívara; I was the father of this *maiden.*
I was the son of the swordsman Nala-nábha king of the
41 Vidyá-dharas. And at first I besought the muni Brahma-
mitra, "Deign, adorable Sir! † to communicate to me the
42 whole of the Áyur-veda." But though entreated often by me
who remained bent with respect, he did not bestow on me the
43 science of the Áyur-veda, O hero: then indeed I gained the
science of the Áyur-veda, as he was communicating it to his
disciples, by rendering myself invisible ‡, O sinless man. §
44 Now when the science was gained after a space of eight

* For *tadábhibhútaḥ* read *tadabhibhútaḥ?*

† For *bhagaván* read *bhagavan?* Or, for *arhasi* read *arhati?*

‡ For *antardháya-gena* read *antardhána-gena?*

§ For *anadha* read *anagha.*

months, I gave way to excessive and repeated fits of laughter
45 out of my great delight. Recognizing me by the laughter,
the muni, enraged and with quivering neck spoke thus to
46 me in harsh words—"Since thou in invisible *form*, like a
Rákshasa, * hast snatched the science from me, O evil-minded
47 one, and despising me hast indulged in laughter; therefore
thou shalt be assuredly cast out as a terrible Rákshasa by
48 my curse, O wicked one, after seven nights." On his utter-
ing this, I propitiated him by prostrating myself before him
and by other acts of deference; the bráhman with his mind
49 immediately softened, said to me again—"What I have
uttered will assuredly come to pass, O Gandharva; *it can* not
happen otherwise; but after becoming a Rákshasa, thou
50 shalt regain thy own form, when with memory dead and in
anger thou shalt wish to devour thy own child. Thou shalt
be turned into a night-stalking demon; when smarting with
51 the fire of thy child's weapon, thou shalt again obtain thy
own consciousness, and recover thy own body, and likewise thy
52 own station in the Gandharva world." Since such I am and
since I have been delivered by thee, O illustrious hero, from
this most fearful demon-condition, therefore perform my re-
53 quest. This maiden give I thee as wife, accept her; and
take, O high-minded man, the whole of the Áyur-veda with
its eight parts, which I acquired from beside that muni.

Márkaṇḍeya spoke :

54 Having so spoken he, gleaming in heavenly raiment, be-
decked with garlands and ornaments, and bearing his pris-
55 tine heavenly body, bestowed the science. After bestowing
the science, he next proceeded to give his daughter. Then
the maiden spoke to her father who had regained his own form,
56 "Although love † has sprung up exceedingly with me, even at
first sight, for this high-souled man, who is especially my
57 benefactor, O father; yet this *maiden* is my friend and that one al-
so, they are afflicted with pain for my sake; hence I do not desire

* For *rákshasenaiva* read *rákshaseneva* ? He was a Gandharva then.

† For *anarágo* read *anurágo* ?

58 to gratify myself in delights with this man. Such baseness
cannot be displayed even by men; how shall a woman like me
59 behave so with things pleasing to her disposition. Since such
I am and since those two maidens are afflicted with pain for
my sake, O father, I will likewise remain in their pain, burnt
with the fire of their grief."

Sva-roćis spoke:

60 By the favour of the Ayur-veda I will make thy two friends fresh again, removing thy great grief, O maiden with beautiful waist.

Márkaṇḍeya spoke:

61 Then Sva-roćis married that beauteous-eyed maiden, whom
her father himself gave, according to the rites on that moun-
62 tain. And having comforted * the proud maiden then given
away, the Gandharva departed then to his own city by a
heavenly course.

63 And then *Sva-roc'is* also, accompanied by the slender maiden,
went to that garden, where the pair of maidens *dwelt* speech-
64 less and diseased † through that curse. Then unconquered
Sva-roćis, knowing their condition accurately, brought them
both back to a healthy body by means of medicines and po-
65 tions which cure disease. Then the two maidens, most re-
splendent, freed from disease, beautiful, rendered that moun-
tain more luminous ‡ than the regions of the sky by their own
beauty.

Canto LXIV.

About the Svároc'isha Manvantara.

Vibhá-varí and Kalá-vatí then tell Sva-roc'is their story,—and he marries them both.

* For *abhi-śántya* read *abhi-śántvya?*

† *Agadáturam;* a compound adjective from *a-gada* and *átura.*

‡ *Uj-jyoti;* not in the dictionary.

Márkaṇḍeya spoke:

1 Now the maiden, being thus freed from her disease and
filled with joy, spoke thus * to Sva-roćis—"Hear my word,
2 O lord. I am the daughter of the Vidyá-dhara Mandára,
famed by name as Vibhá-varí.† O my benefactor, I offer *thee*
3 my very self, do thou accept me. And I will give thee
knowledge, by which the utterances of all created things shall
become manifest to thee. Be thou favourably inclined!"

Márkaṇḍeya spoke:

4 "So be it!" said Sva-roćis, wise in righteousness. And then
the second maiden spoke these words—
5 "A youthful brahma-ćárin was my father, by name Pára,
a brahmarshi, exceedingly illustrious, thoroughly learned in
6 the Vedas and Vedáṅgas. Formerly in a spring-time, which
was charming by reason of the songs of the male koils,
an Apsaras known as Puñjiká-staná approached near him.
7 Then the noble muni was moved so that he could not but
speak of love. By their union I was born of her on this great
8 mountain. My mother abandoned me, a girl, all alone, in this
desolate forest on the earth's surface, which swarms with
9 snakes and wild beasts, and went away. Since then being
nourished daily by the moon's increasing phases, which cause
10 wane to wax again‡, I have grown up, O best *of men*. Hence
Kalá-vatí § is the name which my high-souled father gave me
11 when he took me. My high-souled *father*, when solicited by a
Gandharva, did not give me who am beautiful of face || *in marriage to him* then, hence he was cursed ¶ by Áli ** the foe of

* For *uvác'eda* read *uvác'edaṁ* ?

† "The resplendent."

‡ *Kalábhir varddhantíbhir ava-kshayam.* The allusion appears to be to the waxing of the moon after its waning.

§ "Possessing the digits of the moon."

|| For *subhánaná* read *śubhánaná* ?

¶ For *saptas* read *śaptas.*

** Or, *Ali*, as the text may be read. This name is not in the dictionary, and I have not met with it elsewhere. *Áli* may however be taken as an

12 the gods and perished*. I was about to destroy myself then
from excessive despair. S'ambhu's wife Satí who is true to
13 her promises prevented me, *by saying*, 'Grieve not, beauteous-browed maiden; thou shalt have an illustrious husband by
14 name Sva-roćis, and *thy* son by him shall be a Manu. And
all the Nidhis† shall submissively obey thy command, and
shall give thee wealth according to thy desire, O beauteous
15 one! Take, my child, the knowledge by the power of which
thou shalt succeed; this knowledge is called Padminí, it is
16 greatly worshipped by Mahá-padma.' So spake to me
Daksha's daughter Satí, who is devoted to truth. Thou art
17 Sva-roćis in sooth—the goddess will not speak amiss. I now
offer that knowledge and myself in my true form to *thee* who
hast given me life; do thou receive them with favour
beaming from thy face on me."

Márkaṇḍeya spoke:

18 "So be it!" said he to the maiden Kalá-vatí. The loving
glances of Vibhá-varí and Kalá-vatí urged him on to joy;
19 and he, lustrous as the immortals, then took the hands of both
in marriage, while heavenly musical instruments sounded
out and the Apsarases danced.

CANTO LXV.

About the Svároc'isha Manvantara.

Sva-roc'is lived in pleasure with his wives till aroused by a conversation between two birds, and by a deer's remarks.

Márkaṇḍeya spoke:

1 Then he, lustrous as the immortals, accompanied by his
wives, lived in pleasure on that high mountain where were

adjective meaning "idle, worthless", and the text rendered "by a worthless foe of the gods", but this cannot refer to the Gandharva.

* This passage seems erroneous. *Gandharveṇa* cannot be taken with *pitrá* (see verse 5) nor with *devárіṇá*.

† See canto lxviii.

2 charming woods and cascades. The Nidhis,* being subject
through *the knowledge* Padminí, brought gems for every kind
3 of enjoyment, sweets and melodies, garlands, raiment,
ornaments, richly scented unguent, most brilliant golden
4 seats according to his desire, golden things (illustrious Sir!),
pots and vessels, and also beds of divers kinds arrayed with
5 heavenly coverings. Thus accompanied by them, he lived in
pleasure at his own liking on that fine mountain, perfumed
with heavenly odours and other *fragrance*, and illuminated
6 with *his* lustre. And they enjoyed supreme delight, for that
they were with him, sporting on that high mountain even as
in Svarga.

7 A grey lag-goose† said to a hen-ćakra-váka who was in
some water, being moved to desire at the dalliance and union
8 between him and those two *wives*—"Happy is this *man*,
exceeding merit has he, who in the heyday of youth enjoys
9 eagerly-desired delights with these darling wives. Young
men are worthy of praise, their wives are not of exceeding
beauty; few are the wives and husbands of exceeding beauty
10 in the world! A man dearly longs for the women he loves;
a woman desires to obtain a lover; most rare is it to find a
11 wedded pair rich in mutual affection. Happy is this *man*
whom his darlings long for; these *women* are indeed very
dear to him; verily, it is among the happy that mutual
12 affection exists!" Hearing this speech uttered by the grey
lag-goose, the hen-ćakra-váka scarcely surprised in mind
13 spoke to her— "This *man* is not happy, because modesty
springs not from proximity with other women; he is enjoy-
ing one or other of the women, his mind does not *dwell* on
14 all *of them*. Since the heart's affection has only one basis,
my friend, how then will this man be affectionate to *several*
15 wives? These *women* are not beloved by their husband, nor
is *this* husband beloved by them; these *women* are only just
16 an amusement as any other attendant *might be*. And if he
is desired by these *women*, why then does he not quit his

* See canto lxviii. † *Kala-haṁsí*; see page 30 note §.

life? He embraces some loved woman, the while he is in the
17 thoughts of some other loving woman. He is bartered at
the price of the bestowal of knowledge, as if he were a servant. Because of the excitements,* affection verily exists not
18 equally towards many women. O grey lag-goose! my husband is happy, and I indeed am happy; he, for his mind is fixed steadfastly on me alone, and I, for mine is on him alone."

Márkaṇḍeya spoke:

19 Sva-roćis the unconquered, understanding the speech of all living creatures, on hearing *this* was ashamed and pondered, "it is indeed true, without any falsehood."

20 After a hundred years had passed from that time, while sporting on the great mountain, while sporting with *his wives*
21 around him, he saw a buck in front of him, with very glossy and plump limbs, playing among a herd of does, and surrounded with does shaped like he was, which were in the rutting time.†
22 The buck then said to the does who were sniffing with outstretched nostrils, "O ye charming *does*, one should behave with-
23 out bashfulness; *but* I am not Sva-roćis, nor am I like him in disposition, O pretty-eyed does! Many have no modesty; do
24 ye, who are such, go to him. Now as one female who follows after many males is a laughing-stock among mankind, just so is one male, who is gazed on by many females with lustful
25 glances. He suffers loss from day to day in his deeds of righteousness; and he is always attached to some other wife,
26 and addicted to other loves. Do ye love some other, who is like that, who has that disposition, who turns away from the future world; *it will be* well for you; I am not a rival of Sva-roćis."

* *Pravartato.*

† *Vásitábhiḥ*; this appears to refer to the rutting season.

Canto LXVI.

About the Svároc'isha Manvantara.

Sva-roc'is had three sons whom he settled in separate kingdoms, Vijaya in a city Vijaya in Káma-rúpa, Meru-nanda in Nanda-vatí in the North, and Prabháva in Tála in the South.—One day he met the goddess of a forest, and had by her a son Dyuti-mat Svároc'isha, who became a Manu.—Sva-roc'is, being again admonished by a conversation between two ducks, gives himself up to a religious life and dies.

Márkaṇḍeya spoke:

1 Thus were those does discarded by the buck. Sva-roćis,
2 hearing it, thought how he must have fallen; and he set
his mind on quitting those *his wives*, O best of munis, spoken
of as he had been by the hen-ćakra-váka and the buck, and
3 despised as he was for his animal behaviour.* Yet on again
meeting with them, his love increased. Casting aside those
4 disparaging speeches he sported for six hundred years. But
while performing the works of righteousness without hindrance to righteousness, wise Sva-roćis continues to enjoy
the pleasures of sense with those *wives*.

5 And then three sons were born to Sva-roćis, Vijaya, and
6 Meru-nanda, and mighty Prabháva; and Indívara's daughter
Mano-ramá gave birth to Vijaya, Vibhá-varí to Meru-nanda,
7 and Kalá-vatí to Prabháva. And by the power of the
knowledge named Padminí,† which accomplishes all pleasures,
8 he their father built three cities for them. Now he gave a
noble city named Vijaya on a hill in Káma-rúpa‡ in the
9 Eastern region to his son Vijaya at first; and he made
Meru-nanda's city the famous one in the north, called Nanda-

* *Mṛiga-c'aryá.*

† See canto lxviii.

‡ The western portion of Assam. A town on a hill there can only be in the Himalayas in the North, or in the Garo and Khasia hills on the South; neither seems a likely situation for an ancient *Hindu* capital.

10 vatí,* which is begirt with lofty ramparts and walls; and he
made Kalá-vatí's son Prabháva to dwell in the famous city
Tála† which is situated in the Southern region. Having
11 thus settled his sons in their cities, he, the manly hero, sported
with those his wives in charming highlands.

12 Now once upon a time he went to the forest for sport with
bow in hand. Seeing a boar a long distance off, he drew
13 his bow; and then a certain doe approached him and said,
"At me let the arrow be shot; show *me this* favour," again
14 and again; "What need hast thou to slay him now? lay me
low quickly; an arrow discharged by thee will free me from
suffering."

Sva-roćis spoke:

15 I do not perceive thy body to be diseased. What then is the reason that thou wouldest quit thy life?

The doe spoke:

16 Without him on whom, though his heart is devoted to other females, my mind has fixed her seat, I *must* die; what other remedy is there in this life?

Sva-roćis spoke:

17 Who would not love thee, timid one? Or with whom art thou in love, that failing to gain him thou resolvest to quit thy life?

The doe spoke:

18 It is thee I desire; be welfare thine! Thou hast captivated my heart. Hence I choose death, let the arrow be discharged at me.

Sva-roćis spoke:

19 Thou art a doe with eyes always in motion; I bear a

* This is not in the dictionary and I have not found it elsewhere. Perhaps it may be connected with the river *Nandá*, and the people *Nandas*, see page 383 note ||.

† Or Purantála; neither seems to be in the dictionary, nor have I found any reference to them elsewhere.

human form; how shall there be union between such as me and thee?

The doe spoke:

20 If thy mind has any regard for me, do thou embrace me;
or if thou dost think good, I will do as thou desirest. I
shall be supremely honoured by thee, Sir, such as thou art.

Márkaṇḍeya spoke:

21 Sva-rocis then embraced the doe; and as soon as he em-
22 braced her, she assumed a heavenly body. Then filled with
astonishment said he, "Who art thou?" And she told him
this story in words rendered slow by love and modesty.—
23 "I have been besought by the gods, *I* the goddess of this
forest, *with the demand that* 'Verily a Manu must be begotten
24 of me by thee.' O magnanimous man! Beget that son, who
shall guard the terrestrial world, of me who am full of
love. I speak to thee according to the gods'* behest!"

Márkaṇḍeya spoke:

25 Forthwith he begat in her a son marked with every aus-
26 picious mark, full of energy like unto himself. And as soon
as he was born, heavenly instruments of music sounded forth,
the Gandharva princes sang, and bands of Apsarases danced;
27 the *celestial* elephants bedewed him with drops *of water,*
and the ṛishis rich in austerities and the gods scattered also
28 a shower of flowers around. Beholding his splendour his father
himself bestowed on him the name Dyuti-mat, since the
29 regions of the sky were illuminated by his splendour. The
boy named Dyuti-mat possessed great strength and valour;
since he was son of Sva-rocis, he became *known as* Svárocisha.
30 Sva-rocis also once, while roaming by a charming mountain
31 cascade, saw a duck attended by his mate. He said then to
his mate, who was full of continuous longings, — "Restrain
32 thyself, I have played with thee full long. What dost thou need
with pleasures at all times? Old age has fallen *on us,* the

* For *davánáṁ* read *devánáṁ*.

time to relinquish them has come to me and thee also, O water-roamer!"

The female duck replied:

33 What time is unfit for pleasures? The world is all composed
of pleasures. Bráhmans with souls subdued perform sacri-
34 fices in order to get pleasures. Moreover people of discri-
mination, being eager for pleasures experienced and not yet
experienced, both give alms and perform the full round of
35 righteous acts. Why then dost thou not wish for pleasures?
Pleasure is the reward of effort among men who have dis-
crimination and among brute animals, how much more among
those who have subdued their souls?

The duck spoke:

36 The mind of those who are not attached to pleasures is
with the Supreme Soul. And when will it be so among those
37 who have contracted attachments towards relatives? Crea-
tures perish when attached to son, friend and wife, just as
38 aged wild elephants when sunk in lake or mire or sea. Or
dost thou not see, lady, how Sva-roćis, in whom attachments
have grown up and who has been devoted to his lusts
from his boyhood, has sunk in the watery mire of affection?
39 Sva-roćis' mind was exceedingly sunk in his wives in his
youth, now in his sons and grandsons; whence will it obtain
40 deliverance? I am not the equal of Sva-roćis, nor am I one
to be distressed by females, O water-roamer! I possess also
discrimination in pleasures, and I have desisted *therefrom* now.

Márkaṇḍeya spoke:

41 Sva-roćis hearing this speech from a bird felt disturbed in
mind; taking his wives he departed to another grove to prac-
42 tise austerities. After performing severe austerities there
with his wives, he, lofty in mind, reached the pure worlds
with every stain removed.

CANTO LXVII.

The Story of Svároc'isha concluded.

Márkaṇḍeya mentions the gods, ṛishis and kings in the Svároc'isha Manvantara.

Márkaṇḍeya spoke :

1 Then the adorable god made the Prajápati named Sváro-
ćisha Dyuti-mat a Manu. Listen to his Manv-antara; who
2 were the gods during that period, who were the munis and
their sons, who were the princes, listen while I tell *of them*,
O Kraushṭuki.

3 The gods in that period were the Párávatas and also the
Tushitas. O bráhman; and in Sváróćisha's period the
4 Indra was famed as Vipaś-ćit. Ūrja, Tamba and Práṇa,
Dattoli and Ṛishabha, Niśćara and C'árva-vírat were the seven
5 ṛishis in that *period*. And seven sons had that high souled
Manu, C'aitra, Kim-purusha, &c., very valiant, guardians of
6 the earth. So long as his Manv-antara lasted, all this earth
was enjoyed among the outspreadings of his family. That
was the second *Manv*-antara.

7 Now the man who hears of Sva-roćis' deeds and Sváro-
ćisha's birth, and believes them, is delivered from his sins.

CANTO LXVIII.

*A description of the Nidhis.**

Márkaṇḍeya tells of the knowledge called Padminí, of the eight Nidhis connected with it, and of the influences which they exercise over men.

Kraushṭuki spoke :

1 Adorable Sir! thou hast related it all fully to me, both Sva-roćis' deeds and Sváróćisha's birth. Now tell me at

*These are demi-gods who preside over and influence men's propensities, pursuits, pleasures, tastes, &c.

2 length about the knowledge named Padminí which compasses
all pleasures, and about the Nidhis who are allied thereto,
3 and about the nature of the eight Nidhis who *exist*, and the
composition of their wealth. I desire to hear it expounded
by thee thoroughly, O guru!

Márkaṇḍeya spoke :

4 The knowledge which is named Padminí has Lakshmí for
its deity, and the Nidhis for its supporters. Listen while I
5 tell thee of it. *The Nidhis* therein are Padma and Mahá-
padma, and Makara, and Kaććhapa, Mukunda and Nandaka,
Níla, *and* S'aṅkha is the eighth Niḍhi. These live in real
6 good-fortune*; verily perfection springs from them. These
eight Nidhis indeed have been proclaimed to thee, O Kraush-
7 ṭuki†. By means of the gods' favour and by attendance on
good men a man's wealth is always watched over by them,
8 O muni. Listen while I tell thee what their nature is like.

First, the Nidhi named Padma belongs, O bráhman, to
9 Maya,‡ to his son, and to the sons and grandsons of his *son*
perpetually. And a man dominated thereby may become the
10 perfection of politeness, since this Nidhi is supported by good-
ness, yields great enjoyment *and* is sincere. And he amasses
11 immense quantities of gold, silver, copper and other metals,
and buys and sells them ; he also makes sacrifices, and be-
12 stows the sacred fee ; and he causes a palace to be built and
temples for the gods, applying his mind thereto.

And another Nidhi who is supported by goodness is
13 known as Mahá-padma. He has goodness for his chief quality.
And a man dominated thereby amasses rubies and other gems,
14 pearls *and* coral, and buys and sells them ; and he gives to
those whose disposition is towards religious devotion, and
15 has dwellings constructed for them ; and he himself develops
into that disposition. And from him are born *others* of simi-

* Or, prosperity ; *satyám ṛiddhau.*

† *Tava kroshṭuke* ; this violates the metre ; read instead *kraushṭuke tava ?*

‡ Maya was an Asura, the great artificer of the Dánavas, and constructed a magnificent Court for the Páṇḍavas ; see Mahá-Bhárata, Sabhá-P., i and iii.

16 lar disposition in the descent of sons and grandsons. *This Nidhi comes* only from prior good-fortune *, and does not depart for seven generations.

The Nidhi who is composed of darkness † is named
17 Makara. And a man on whom he looks ‡ is indeed born characterized chiefly by ignorance, though good in disposi-
18 tion. He gathers together arrows, swords, spears and bows, and shields and rope, and attains to friendship with kings; and he gives to kings who occupy themselves with heroic
19 deeds, and to those whom they esteem; and he finds pleasure in buying and selling weapons and in nothing else. This *Nidhi* belongs to a man singly, and does not descend to
20 his progeny. Such *a man* may meet§ death for the sake of wealth at the hands of robbers and also in battle.

And the man on whom the Nidhi, who *is called* Kaććhapa,
21 casts his eye is dominated by ignorance, because that Nidhi is characterized by darkness; and he performs all the rules
22 of life‖ along with men who have acquired merit, and *makes* all *those rules* consist in *mere* acts; he confides in no one.
23 Just as a tortoise draws all its limbs in, so *drawing in* all his thoughts while unharmed he remains with diffuse mind.¶ He gives not nor does he enjoy, being afraid of destruction
24 thereby; he makes his resting-place on the earth. That Nidhi also is limited to men singly.

And another Nidhi, who is named Mukunda, is composed
25 of the quality of passion.** The man on whom he looks becomes of the same quality, O bráhman. He gathers together lutes, flutes and drums, and *any* musical instrument of per-
26 cussion; he bestows wealth on singers and dancers, and on minstrels, bards, sycophants *and* those who are skilled in

* For *púrvárddha-mátraḥ* the Bombay Edition reads *púrvarddhi-mátraḥ*, which I have adopted.

† Or ignorance; *támasa*.

‡ *Ava-lokita*; frequently used in this canto.

§ For *savraje* read *sa vrajet ?*

‖ *Vyavahára*.

¶ *Áyata-mánasaḥ*; or better *áyatta-mánasaḥ* "with submissive mind"?

** *Rajas*.

27 drama; he bestows pleasures *on them* day and night, and
enjoys *life* along with those *companions*, O bráhman; and he
finds no delight in women of loose character, nor with other
28 folk of that kind. He forms a single union, the man to whom
this Nidhi resorts.

And composed of passion and darkness is another great
29 Nidhi called Nanda. The man on whom he looks attains to
eminent firmness.* He gathers together all *kinds of* miner-
30 als and precious stones and trade-wares,† grain and other
articles, and also buys and sells *the same*; he is the support
31 of his own family and of *each* visitor and guest; he does not
brook disrespectful language although it be very slight,
O great muni! and when praised he entertains strong affec-
32 tion *and* proffers *it;* and whatever object of desire he wants,
he has recourse to tenderness *to obtain it.* He has many
33 wives, who are prolific *and* very beautiful to *his* delight. And
the Nidhi Nanda passes down to seven generations, and when
strongly developed *passes on* to the *next* descendant with an
34 eighth portion, O best *of men!* and he bestows length of
life on all men. Nanda verily provides support to kinsmen
35 indeed, and to those *guests* who have arrived from afar; and
he is not held in honour in the next world; affection does
not belong to him, *but* is born among those who dwell together;
36 he causes laxity among those who were former friends, and
affection with others.

Moreover the great Nidhi who contains goodness and
37 passion is termed Líla.‡ A man united with him may become
of that disposition. He leads a man to collect clothing, cotton
38 cloth, grain and other fruit and flowers, also pearls, coral,
and shells, and small shells and other *similar things*, timber
and other *materials* and whatever else is produced in water,
39 O muni; he leads him to buy and sell other things. In
nothing else does his mind delight; and he constructs ponds

* Or solidity: *stambha.*

† For *puṇya-dhányádikasya* read *paṇya-dhányádikasya?*

‡ For *sa-líla-sañjñas* read *sa líla-sañjñas?* He is also called *Níla* in verse 5 above and verse 41 below.

40 and tanks and places for pleasure; and *such* a man makes
embankments across rivers and plants trees; and after
enjoying unguents, flowers and other objects of delight he is
41 born again. And this Nidhi named Níla persists for three
generations.

And composed of passion and darkness is another Nidhi
42 who is named S'aṅkha. And the *man who is* lord of this
Nidhi is led by him to possess the same qualities, O bráhman.
He exists in *a man* singly, and does not pass on to another
43 generation. Listen, O Kraushṭuki, to the character of a man
who possesses the Nidhi S'aṅkha. *It is when* quite alone *that*
he enjoys food and clothing such as he himself has made;
44 his family eat wretched food and wear no bright clothing;
he makes no gift to friend, wife, brother, son, daughter-in-
45 law and other *relatives*. Always intent on his own nourish-
ment is the man who possesses S'aṅkha.

Thus these Nidhis have been described, the deities of wealth
46 among men. When their looks are blended, the blended
Nidhis produce results according to their natures, just as *each*
nature described above springs indeed from the aspect *of a
particular Nidhi.* And in sovereignty over them all *sits*
Lakshmí, *who is* this *knowledge called* Padminí of the dvijas.

Canto LXIX.

About the Auttána Manv-antara.*

King Uttama banished his queen to a forest because of her persistent unloving behaviour.—A bráhman whose wife had been carried off invokes the king's help to recover her.—The king in searching for her reaches a muni's hermitage, and is censured by the muni for his conduct to the queen.

Kraushṭuki spoke:

1. O bráhman, thou hast described to me the Svároćisha

* This should be *Auttoma;* see canto liii, verse 7, and lxxii, verse 39. It seems to be a mistake caused by the fact that Uttama was son of *Uttána-páda*, see verse 3. It occurs in the next canto, but is corrected in canto lxxi.

2 manv-antara at length and also the eight Nidhis, whom I
asked about. Thou didst tell me of the Sváyambhuva manv-
antara before that. Tell me of the third manv-antara which
is named after Uttama.*

Márkaṇḍeya spoke:

3 There was a son of Uttána-páda named Uttama, son of
4 Su-rući,† famous, great in strength and valour, and righteous
of soul, and magnanimous, a monarch rich in valour. Excell-
5 ing all created beings he shone in valour like the sun. He
was the same both to foe and friend, to his city and to his
son, being one who understood righteousness; and he was like
Yama to the wicked, and like Soma to the good, O great muni!
6 A knower of righteousness, Uttána-páda's son Uttama
married a maiden of Babhru's race named Bahulá, as supreme
7 Indra *married* famous S'aći. His mind was always exceedingly
affectionate *to her*, O noble bráhman,‡ just as is the moon's
8 *mind* which has fixed its abode in Rohiṇí. Verily his mind
felt no attachment to any other object; in sleep also that
king's mind rested on her. And the king at the very sight
9 of her, who was most beautiful in every limb, was continually
touching her body, and at the touch of her body he became
10 one with her.§ The king's words, although kindly, caused
annoyance to her ears, and she deemed his special respect as
11 humiliation from him. She contemned a garland when given
by him, and *his* beautiful ornaments; and she arose as if
pained in body when he drank the choice nectar *of her lips*;
12 and only a moment did the king hold her by the hand when
he enjoyed her. She ate very little food, O bráhman, and
13 that with no great delight. Thus she was not favourable to
the magnanimous *king* who was favourable to her; *yet* more
abundant and excessive love did the king show.

14 Now once the king, when engaged in drinking, respectfully

* *Auttama* would be preferable, as he was the Manu, see canto lxxii, verse 39; read then *kathayauttama-sañjñitam* for *kathayottama-sañjñitam*?

† Or *Su-ruc'i*, a feminine name.

‡ For *dvija-varyá* read *dvija-varya*?

§ *Tan-maya.*

caused that wilful *queen* to hold a drinking cup which
15 had been cleansed with wine, he being *then* surrounded with
accomplished attendants* who were melodious in their singing,
and who were assiduously singing and chanting while kings
16 looked on; but she does not wish to take that cup, turning
her face away from it, in the sight of the kings. Thereat
17 the king was enraged. Breathing hard like a serpent, when
set at nought by his dear queen, *as if* a husband not dear
18 *to her*, he called the door-keeper and said,—"O door-keeper!
Take this lady of evil heart to a desolate forest and abandon
her forthwith! Deliberate thou not on this my command!"

Márkaṇḍeya spoke:

19 Thereupon the door-keeper, deeming the king's word was
not to be questioned, mounted the beautiful-browed lady in a
20 chariot and left her in a forest. And she, when abandoned
thus by the king in the forest and being away from his sight,
21 held he had done her the greatest favour. And king Auttá-
na-pádi, with soul and mind burning with the anguish of love
22 for her, took no other wife. He remembered her who was
beauteous in every limb, day and night bereft of ease, and
ruled his kingdom, governing his people righteously.

23 While he ruled his people, as a father his own children,
a certain bráhman suffering in mind arrived and spoke
thus—

The bráhman spoke:

24 O Mahá-rája! in grievous suffering am I; hearken while I
speak. Men's deliverance from pain comes from no where
25 but the king! Some one carried off my wife by night while
I slept, without unlocking the house door. Deign to bring
her back to me.

The king spoke:

26 Knowest thou not, O bráhman, who carried her off or
where has she been taken? With whom *shall* I strive in
fight? or whence *shall* I bring her back?

* *Vára-mukhyaiḥ*; the dictionary gives only the *fem.*, *vára-mukhyá*, "a royal courtezan."

The bráhman spoke :

27 While I slept just as I was, with the door fastened, O king,
why and by whom my wife was carried off—this thou, Sir,
28 knowest. Thou art our guardian, O king, whose due is the
levy of a sixth part *of our wealth.** Therefore men sleep
at night, freed from anxiety about justice.

The king spoke :

29 I have not seen thy wife. Tell me what is she like in
body, and *what is her* age; and of what disposition is the
bráhman lady ?

The bráhman spoke :

30 Sharp-eyed is she, very tall, short-armed, thin-faced,
ungainly in form, O king. I defame her not by this *description*;
31 very harsh in speech, and ungentle is she in disposition,
O king—thus I have described my wife; she is a do-nothing,
32 unpleasant in look, and she has slightly passed early woman-
hood, O king. Such is my wife in form; true is this I have
spoken.

The king spoke :

33 Enough hast thou had of her, O bráhman. I *will* give
thee another wife. An excellent wife tends to one's happiness,
34 such a one as that is verily a source of pain. Bodily beauty
consists in healthfulness,† O bráhman, its cause is a noble
disposition. She who has neither beauty nor good disposition
should be abandoned for that very reason.

The bráhman spoke :

35 "A wife must be guarded," O king—such is our highest
divine teaching. When a wife is guarded, the offspring is guar-
36 ded. For the Soul ‡ is born in her, hence she must be guarded,
O king. When the offspring is guarded, the Soul is guarded.
37 When she is not guarded, there will arise confusion among
the castes; that will hurl one's forefathers down from
38 Svarga, O king. And I may have loss of righteousness from

* For *shaḍágádána* read *shaḍ-bhágádána?* See verse 39.

† There is a play on words here, *kalyáṇí*, "an excellent (wife)," and *kalye*, "in healthfulness."

‡ Or, one's self; *átmá*.

day to-day, while I remain wifeless; and that, through the
destruction of the perpetual ceremonies, *will tend* to my down-
39 fall. And in her will be my offspring, O king. She will
give thee the sixth part; she will be a cause of righteousness.
40 For that reason I have declared this to thee. Bring back my
wife who has been carried off, my lord, since your honour is
placed supreme for our protection.

Márkaṇḍeya spoke:

41 The king, on hearing him so speak, took thought, and
mounted his great chariot which was furnished with every
42 useful requisite. Hither and thither he wandered over the
earth with that *bráhman*, and saw a fine hermitage of ascetics
43 in a large forest; and alighting there he entered and saw a
muni, seated on a silken cushion, and blazing as it were with
44 splendour. Seeing the king arrived, he rose in haste, and
welcoming him with full respect commanded his disciple to
45 bring the arghya offering. His disciple said to him quietly
—"Why should the arghya be given to him, O muni? Think
well of it and command me, for I carry out thy command."
46 Then the bráhman being acquainted with the king's history,
with self-possession did him respect in conversation and by
giving him a seat.

The ṛishi spoke:

47 Why hast thou come here, Sir; and what dost thou wish
to do? I know thee, O king, to be Uttána-páda's son Uttama.

The king spoke:

48 A bráhman's wife was carried off from his house by some
one whose person is unknown, O muni: to seek her I have
49 come here. Deign, adorable Sir, in compassion to tell me, who
have reached thy house and am prostrate *before thee,* what
I ask thee!

The ṛishi spoke:

50 Ask me, O king, without fear what thou must ask. I will
tell thee truthfully if I ought to tell it thee.

The king spoke:

51 Why is the arghya offering kept back, which thou wast pre-

pared to give me on first seeing me on my arrival at thy house, O muni?

The ṛishi spoke:

52 When through agitation at the sight of thee, O king, I commanded this disciple *to give it,* then I was cautioned by him.
53 Through my favour he knows the future in this world, as
54 I know both the past and the present thoroughly. When he said, "Consider and give thy order," then I also knew it; hence I did not give thee the arghya according to precept.
55 Truly O king, thou art worthy of the arghya and *thou belongest* to the race of Sváyambhuva; nevertheless we deem thee Uttama not fit for the arghya.

The king spoke:

56 What then have I done, O bráhman, whether wittingly or unwittingly, that arriving after a long time I am not worthy of the arghya from thee?

The ṛishi spoke:

57 Hast thou forgotten, both that thou didst abandon thy wife in the forest, and that along with her thou didst abandon
58 all thy righteousness, O king. Through neglect of religious acts a man becomes unfit to be touched by his adherents, like one on whom ordure and urine have been showered;* thou
59 hast neglected an act of permanent observance. Just as a complaisant wife must bear with her husband though he be of bad disposition, so a wife although of bad dispo-
60 sition must be cherished *by her husband,* O king. Ungracious indeed was that bráhman's wife who was carried off; nevertheless he, being a lover of righteousness, very much excels †
61 thee, O king. Thou establishest other men in their proper ways of righteousness when they swerve *therefrom,* O king. What other person will establish thee when thou swervest from thy righteousness?

* *Várshikí,* a noun, not given in the dictionary; it must apparently mean "a shower."

† *Ud-yáti-taráṁ.* The only meanings assigned to *ud-yá* in the dictionary are, "to go up or out, to rise, originate."

Márkaṇḍeya spoke:

62 A gazing-stock was the king when thus addressed by the wise *ṛishi*; and saying "So be it!" he enquired about the
63 bráhman's wife who had been carried off—"Adorable Sir, who has taken away the bráhman's wife, or where is she? Thou Sir knowest unerringly the past and the future in this world."

The ṛishi spoke:

64 A Rákshasa named Valáka, son of Adri, has captured her, and thou shall see her now in Utpalávataka forest, O king.
65 Go, unite the bráhman with his wife quickly. Let him not become a seat of sin as thou art day after day.

Canto LXX.

About the Auttána Manv-antara.*

King Uttama finds the bráhman's wife in the forest and is courteously received by the Rákshasa, who says he carried her off in order to impair the bráhman's religious merit.—At the king's request the Rákshasa consumes her evil disposition and restores her to her husband.

Márkaṇḍeya spoke:

1 Then *the king* prostrated himself before the great muni, and mounted his chariot, and went to the forest Utpalávata
2 mentioned by him. And the king saw † the bráhman's wife, in appearance such as her husband described her, eating the
3 fruit of the bel tree; ‡ and asked—"How didst thou come to

* This should be *Auttama*, see page 419, note *.

† For *dadárśa* read *dadarśa*.

‡ *Śrí-phala*, the fruit of the *bilva* or *vilva* tree, *Ægle marmelos*, and also the tree itself. It is a pretty large tree, a native of the mountainous parts of the East coast, and also found in the low lands; its fruit is considered "nutritious, warm, cathartic; in taste delicious; in fragrance exquisite"—Roxburgh's Flora Indica, vol II. 579-80. See page 25 note *; but I have made an error there in assigning the name *bel-phul* to this tree. *Bel-phúl* is the name of the double Arabian jasmine, *Jasminum Zambac*, Roxb. (I. 88) or *J. Sambac*, Oliver. This jasmine is a shrub with delightfully fragrant white

this forest, lady? tell me plainly; art thou the wife of Su-śarman Vaiśáli? *

The bráhman woman spoke:

4 I am daughter of the bráhman Ati-rátra, who dwells in the
forest, *and* wife of Viśála's son whose name thou hast uttered.
5 Being such, I was carried off by the evil-minded Rákshasa
Valáka, while asleep at the extremity of my house, *and* parted
6 from my brothers and mother. May that Rákshasa become
ashes, by whom I have been parted thus from my mother,
brothers and other *relatives*! Here I remain in great affliction.
7 Bringing me to this very dense forest he has cast me off.
I know not what is the reason he neither has intercourse with
me nor devours me.

The king spoke:

8 Perchance thou knowest, where has the Rákshasa gone after leaving thee? I have been sent here by thy husband indeed, O bráhman lady.

The bráhman woman spoke:

9 The night-stalking *demon* stands at the edge of this very forest. Enter and see him, Sir, if thou dost not fear him.

Márkaṇḍeya spoke:

10 Then he entered by the path that she showed, and saw the
11 Rákshasa attended by his retinue. Then the Rákshasa hurry-
ing, the moment he saw him, touching the earth with his
head from afar indeed, approached his feet.

The Rákshasa spoke:

12 Thou hast done me great favour in that thou hast come
to my abode here. Give me thy command. What *shall* I do,
13 such as I am here? I dwell within thy country. Accept thou
this arghya offering, and let this seat be placed *for thee*. We
are servants, thou, Sir, art master; command me firmly.

flowers, and is in common cultivation. Its Sanskrit name is *malliká*, and also *saptalá*; and *bel-phúl* is the common modern name both for the flower and for the plant itself. It has numerous other vernacular names, and Roxburgh says *bela* is one of them, but this seems doubtful.

* Son of Viśála; see next verse.

The king spoke:

14 Thou hast done everything, even every rite due to a guest.*
Why hast thou brought the bráhman's wife *here*, O night-
15 stalker? She is not comely; there are others *comely*, if thou
didst carry her off for a wife: if to devour her, why hast thou
not eaten her? Tell me this.

The Rákshasa spoke:

16 We do not feed on men; such are other Rákshasas. But we
eat the fruit that springs from a good deed, O king; and we
17 consume the natural disposition of men and women, being
treated with disrespect, and *yet* honoured; we are not eaters
18 of living creatures. When we have eaten the patience of
men, they become enraged; and when we have eaten their
19 evil nature, they also become virtuous. We have Rákshasís
who are fascinating, rivalling the Apsarases in beauty, O
king; while they are *with us*, how should we delight in
the females of mankind?

The king spoke:

20 If she is not for sensual enjoyment nor for food, O night-roamer, why then didst thou enter the bráhman's house and carry her off?

The Rákshasa spoke:

21 That excellent bráhman, learned in spells, keeps on expelling
me, when I go to sacrifice after sacrifice, by uttering spells that
22 destroy Rákshasas, O king. By reason of his spells and ex-
pulsive rites we were a-hungered; where *shall* we go? that
23 bráhman† is the priest at every sacrifice. Therefore we
inflicted this damage‡ on him; without a wife a man becomes
unfit to perform sacrifices.

Márkaṇḍeya spoke:

24 At his announcement of the high-minded bráhman's im-

* There appears to be a mistake in this line, read *kṛitaván eva tvam* instead of *kṛitam eva tvayá*? or else *sarvá evátithi-kriyáḥ* for *sarvám evátithi-kriyám*? unless *kṛita-ván* is nnderstood in the second half of the line.

† *Dvijaḥ* seems preferable to *dvija*.

‡ *Vaikalyam*, "impaired or mutilated condition."

paired condition the king became exceedingly dejected then,
25 *thinking* "While he speaks of the bráhman's impaired condi-
tion, *it is* me indeed he censures. That best of munis also
26 said I was unworthy of the argha offering. As the Rákshasa
also has spoken to me of that bráhman's impaired condition, I
being in like *plight* am placed in a great strait, because I
am wifeless."

Márkaṇḍeya spoke :

27 While he thus thought, O muni, the Rákshasa spoke again
to the king, bowing in obeisance and placing his hands to-
28 gether respectfully—"O king, favour with thy command
me, thy servant, prostrate before thee*, a dweller within thy
realm."

The king spoke :

29 Since thou hast said, O night-roamer—"We feed on a *per-
son's* disposition," hear then from me what deed we solicit.
30 Do thou consume this bráhman woman's evil disposition this
day; since she will have her evil disposition eaten by thee,
31 she may then become good in behaviour. Take her to his
house whose wife she is, O night-roamer. When this is done,
thou hast done all for me who am come *as a guest* to thy
house.

Márkaṇḍeya spoke :

32 Thereupon the Rákshasa, entering within her though his
own faculty of illusion, devoured her evil disposition by his
33 own power at the king's command. Being rid entirely of
that very violent evil disposition that bráhman's wife said
34 to the king—"By the maturing of the fruit of my own
actions I was separated from that magnanimous *man*, *my*
husband; this night-roaming *demon* was the cause thereof.
35 He is not in fault, nor that magnanimous *man*, my husband;
mine in truth was the fault, no one else's. A good deed is
36 verily enjoyed. In some *former* life I separated myself from
some *husband;* that same *separation*† has been encountered

* For *tvaṁ* read *tváṁ* ?

† Or perhaps *dosha*, "fault," should be understood.

again even by me.* What fault *is there* in this magnanimous *man?*"

The Rákshasa spoke:

37 I *will* cause her to reach her husband's house at thy command, my lord. Enjoin me whatever else should be done for thee, O king!

The king spoke:

38 When this is done, thou hast done all for me, O night-roamer. And thou must come, O hero, at the time of action when I recall thee to mind.†

Márkaṇḍeya spoke:

39 "So be it!" then quoth the Rákshasa, and taking the bráhman woman conveyed her, purified then by the removal of her evil disposition, to her husband's house.

Canto LXXI.

About the Auttama Manv-antara.

King Uttama visits the ṛishi, learns his queen has been taken to Pátála by a Nága king, who then curses his daughter for hiding the queen from him—and he is also told his unhappy married life was caused by adverse planetary influence.

Márkaṇḍeya spoke:

1 Now the king, after despatching the woman to her husband's
house, sighed and thought, "What good deed may there be
2 in this? The high-minded *muni* declared I was wretched
because of my unfitness for the arghya offering; and this
night-roaming *demon* spoke of 'impaired condition' with
3 reference to the bráhman. Being such, what shall I do,
for I abandoned her, my wife? Or *shall* I enquire of that
best of munis who has the eye of knowledge?"
4 Thus pondered the king, and mounting the chariot went
where *dwelt* the great muni, righteous in soul, who knew the
5 three periods of time. And descending from the chariot he

* Or perhaps for *mayápy-upagataḥ* we should read *mayy-apy-upagataḥ*?

† For *c'a te* read *tvayá*, in order to make a pronoun agreeing with *smṛitena*? See canto lxxii, verses 15 and 16.

approached and prostrated himself before that *muni*, and
related how happened his meeting with the Rákshasa, and
6 his interview with the bráhman woman, and the removal of
her evil disposition,* and her despatch to her husband's
house, and what was his business in coming *back*.

The ṛishi spoke :

7 I knew this before, which thou hast done, O king, and
8 the whole of thy business in coming *back* to me. Ask me
here "what must I do?" with anxious mind; and since
9 thou art come, O king, hear what thou must do. A wife
is a potent cause of righteousness, wealth and love among
men; and in particular one who forsakes her has in sooth
10 abandoned righteousness. A wifeless man, O king, is not
fit for his own works, *be he* bráhman or kshatriya, vaiśya or
11 even śúdra, O king. No brilliant deed didst thou do, Sir,
when thou didst abandon thy wife; for as women must not
forsake a husband, so men *must not forsake* a wife.

The king spoke :

12 Adorable Sir, what *shall* I do, such as I am? *It was* the
maturing of my actions, that I abandoned *her* because she
was not favourably disposed *to me* while I was favourable
13 *to her*. Whatever one does, that one endures with one's
mind burning, *even* that with one's inmost soul terrified at
14 the pain of separation thereby, adorable Sir. But now I know
not where she when abandoned in the forest has gone, or
whether she has been devoured by lions, tigers and night-
roaming *beasts* in the forest.

The ṛishi spoke :

15 She has not been devoured by lions or tigers or night-
roaming *beasts*, O king, but she is now in Rasátala with un-
blemished character.

The king spoke :

16 Who conveyed her to Pátála? How dwells she there
uncorrupted? Most wonderful is this, O bráhman; deign to
tell me *of it* as it happened.

* For *doḥ-śílyápagamaṁ* read *dauḥ-śílyápagamaṁ* ?

The ṛishi spoke:

17 In Pátála is a Nága king and he is famed as Kapotaka.
He saw her when abandoned by thee she was wandering
18 in the great forest. Enamoured of her then he declared his
object and carried the beautiful young *queen* to Pátála, O
19 king. Now that wise Nága king has a beautiful-browed
20 daughter named Nandá, O king, and a charming wife. That
daughter saw thy beautiful *queen, and* thinking, "this bright
lady will become a rival wife to *my* mother," brought her to
her own house and concealed her in the women's apartments.
21 But Nandá, when entreated, *continually* refuses to answer the
king; then the father cursed her his daughter that she should
22 become dumb. Thus did he curse his daughter; and she,
thy wife, remains there, O king, carried off by that Nága king,
detained by his daughter, *and still* chaste.

Márkaṇḍeya spoke:

23 Rejoicing greatly thereat, the king asked the eminent
bráhman * *what was* the reason of his ill-fortune with regard
to his darling wife.

The king spoke:

24 Adorable Sir! I meet with the utmost affection from all
the world, what then is the reason, why my own wife is not
25 very tender? On the one hand I dearly long for her even
beyond my own life, O great muni, and on the other she
is ill-disposed towards me. Say, what is the reason, O
bráhman.

The ṛishi spoke:

26 When thou didst take her hand in marriage, the Sun and
Mars and Saturn *looked on* thee, and Venus and Jupiter
27 looked on thy wife. At that moment the moon was *favourable to thee*, and Mercury to her. Those two *groups of
planets* are mutually hostile; hence *they have been* exceedingly *adverse* to thee, O king. Go then; attended by thy

* The text reads *dvija-varjyam*. But *dvija-varyam*, which the Bombay edition reads, is much better and I have adopted it; see *rája-varyya* in canto lxxii, verse 2. The translation of the text would be "putting aside bráhmans."

wife, rule the earth in thy righteousness, and perform every rite that pertains to righteousness!

Márkaṇḍeya spoke:

29 At this exhortation king Uttama prostrated himself before the *muni*, and then mounting his chariot went to his own city.

Canto LXXII.

About the Auttama Manv-antara.

The bráhman performs a sacrifice which turns the queen's heart to the king, and the Rákshasa brings her back from Pátála—The bráhman frees the Nága princess from the curse, and she coming to thank the king promises him a son who shall be a Manu—Accordingly a son is born who was the Manu Auttama.

Márkaṇḍeya spoke:

1 Then arriving at his city, the king saw the joyful bráhman accompanied by his wife also who was sweet-dispositioned.

The bráhman spoke:

2 O noble king, successful am I inasmuch as righteousness has been preserved by thee, who art wise in righteousness here and who bringest *back* my wife.

The king spoke:

3 Successful art thou, O bráhman, because thou observest thy own laws of righteousness. I am in a strait, who have no wife at home, O bráhman.

The bráhman spoke:

4 O king, if she, *thy queen*, has indeed been devoured by wild beasts in the forest, away with her! Why dost thou not take another's hand in marriage? Falling under the dominion of anger thou didst not preserve righteousness.

The king spoke:

5 My darling wife is not devoured by wild beasts; indeed she is alive, with character unblemished. How *shall* I act in this *matter*?

The bráhman spoke:

6 If thy wife lives and has not gone astray, why then dost thou commit a sin which will render thee wifeless in another birth?

The king spoke:

7 In sooth, although she were brought back, she is ever opposed to me, O bráhman, *she would tend* to unhappiness, not to happiness; enough! her friendship is not at all towards me. Do thou so strive for me that she may become submissive *unto me.*

The bráhman spoke:

8 The Vara sacrifice* is beneficial for mutual affection
between thee and her. I *will* perform the Mitra-vindá †
9 sacrifice which those perform who wish for friends; for it
produces affection between two persons who love not each
other; it creates ‡ the warmest § *affection* between wife and
husband, O king. I *will* perform that sacrifice for thee.
10 Fetch thy beautiful-browed wife from wherever she is now,
O king; she shall feel the warmest love for thee!

Márkaṇḍeya spoke:

11 Thus admonished, the king then collected all the materials
12 requisite, and the bráhman performed that sacrifice. Seven
times then the bráhman performed the sacrifice in repetition
13 in order to procure for the king his wife. When the great
muni deemed that he had aroused friendliness within her towards her husband, then he, the bráhman, addressed the
14 king—"Fetch her, O king, who is dear to thee, close to thy
soul; enjoy *all* enjoyments with her, and offer sacrifices,
being *duly* respected."

Márkaṇḍeya spoke:

15 Thus exhorted by the bráhman the king a-wondering then recalled to mind the very valiant, truthful, night-roaming

* *Vareshṭi.* † "Friend-finding."

‡ *Sañ-jananí*: not in the dictionary. *Sañ-janana* is given only as a neuter noun.

§ *Param*: *anu-rágam* or some similar non-feminine noun must be understood; unless we read *parám* to agree with *príti* as in the next verse.

16 *Rákshasa.** And he, *the Rákshasa*, being remembered by him,
approached the king at once then, and prostrating himself
before the great muni exclaimed, "What *shall* I do?"
17 Thereupon, after the king had declared *the matter* fully, he
18 went to Pátála and brought the queen back. And she, when
brought back, gazed on her husband then with exceeding love
and said "Be gracious!" again and again, while filled with
19 joy. Thereat the king embraced the stately lady impetuously
and said—"Darling, I am indeed well pleased! why dost thou
keep on repeating that?"

The queen spoke:

20 If thy mind is inclined with favour to me, O king, then I make thee this request; do thou do it as an honour to me.

The king spoke:

21 Speak out fearlessly whatever thou desirest from me, lady. Thou shalt certainly obtain it, timid one! I am all docile towards thee and not otherwise.

The queen spoke:

22 On my account the Nága cursed his daughter *who is* my
friend; he said "Thou shalt become dumb," and she became
23 dumb. If thou, Sir, canst for love of me *devise* a remedy for
her to cure her deprivation of speech, then what *wilt* thou
not have done for me?

Márkaṇḍeya spoke:

24 Then said the king to the bráhman—"What kind† of ceremony *is there* for this, in order to dispel her dumbness?" And he replied to the king:—

The bráhman spoke:

25 O king, I *will* perform a sacrifice to Saras-vatí at thy word. Let this thy wife discharge her debt *of gratitude* by stimulating the power of speech in that *friend*.

Márkaṇḍeya spoke:

26 The bráhman performed the sacrifice to Saras-vatí on her

* See canto lxx, verse 38.

† For *kidṛiśí* read *kídṛiśí*?

behalf, and uttered the hymns addressed to Saras-vatí, with composed mind.

27 Thereupon Garga* spoke to the maiden, who had recovered her speech, in Rasátala—"This most difficult benefit has been effected by thy friend's husband."

28 Having gained this information Nandá sped in haste to the
city. Then the Nága's daughter, embracing her friend the
29 queen and praising the king with auspicious words again and
again, spoke sweetly, *she*, the Nága maiden placing herself
upon a seat,—

30 "By this benefit, that thou, O noble hero, hast done me
now,† my heart is drawn out. Listen to what I tell thee.
31 Thou shalt have a son great in valour, O king; he shall
32 wield the discus unresisted on this earth. He shall be skilled
in the principles of all the useful sciences,‡ devoted to the
practice of righteousness, in truth a Manu, the wise lord of
a manv-antara."

Márkaṇḍeya spoke:

33 Having thus bestowed a boon on him, the Nága king's daughter then closely embraced her friend and departed to Pátála, O muni.

34 While the king lived in pleasure there along with her and
35 ruled his subjects, a very long time passed by. Then the son
was born of her to the high-souled king, like the lovely full-
36 orbed moon at the period of full-moon. At the birth of that
high-souled *child* all the people rejoiced, heavenly drums
sounded forth, and a shower of flowers fell.

37 Seeing that his body would be lovely and his disposition
also, and *reflecting* that he was the son of Uttama,§ the assem-
38 bled munis gave him a name *saying*, "He is born in an ex-
cellent‖ family and at an excellent time in it; he has excel-
lent limbs; hence he shall be Auttama."

* See canto lxxv, verse 13. Garga was the mame of an old ṛishi, a descen dant of Bharad-vája and Aṅgiras (see M.-Bh., S'alya-P. liii); and also o various other persons.

† For *mamághuná* read *mamádhuná?*

‡ The Artha-śástras.

§ *Auttama.*

‖ *Uttama.*

Márkaṇḍeya spoke:

39 So he was Uttama's son and was famed as Anttama by
name. He was a Manu, possessing the majesty of such;
hearken to me, O Bh// Bhaguri.
40 He who listens constantly to the entire story of Uttama
and also the birth of Uttama,† never experiences enmity;
41 nor shall the man who listens to it or reads it ever incur
42 separation from his loved wife or sons or kinsmen. Hearken
while I tell thee, O bráhman, about his manv-antara,
and hear who was the Indra in it and who were the gods
and ṛishis.

Canto LXXIII.

End of the Auttama Manv-antara.

Márkaṇḍeya names the gods of the Auttama Manv-antara and their lord, and mentions the kings and ṛishis.

Márkaṇḍeya spoke:

1 Listen while I speak of the gods, the Indra, the ṛishis, the
kings in this third manv-antara of the Prajá-pati Auttama.
2 Thus the *first group of* gods was the Sva-dhámans,‡ who
acted according to their name; and another also, the second
3 group of the thirty *gods*, was the Satyákhyas. § Now the
gods in the third group were the S'ivákhyas, || O best of
munis: now they were auspicious by nature; they are de-
4 clared to have destroyed sin. And the fourth group of the
gods therein was the Pratardanákhyas, ¶ O best of munis,
5 in the period of Anttama Manu. And the gods in the fifth
group therein were the Vaśa-vartins,** O bráhman; now

* *Bhágure*; see canto lviii, verse 40, note ‡. It is said to be a patronymic of Kraushṭuki.

† But *Auttama* seems preferable: read *c'aivauttamasya* for *c'aivottamasya?*

‡ "Deities who reside in their own dwellings."

§ "Named after truth," or "named as true."

|| "Named as auspicious."

¶ "Named Pratardanas."

** "Those who are obedient to *another's* will." This half line has a syllable too much.

all of them indeed had natures corresponding to their
6 names, O great muni. And these five groups of gods are
reported to have fed of the sacrifices. All the groups were
twelve in the manv-antara which appertained to that best
7 of Manus. Their lord* *was* illustrious; may he become the
spiritual preceptor in the three worlds! Having offered a
8 hundred sacrifices, he was verily named Su-śánti.† Now
a song, which is embellished with the words composing
his name in order to avert portents *emanating* from him, is
9 sung by men on the earth even to this day,— "Sweetly serene
is the kindly ruler of the gods, he bestows sweet serenity." He
is attended by the S'ivas and Satyas ‡ and other *groups* of
10 gods and also by the Vaśa-vartins. § Without birth || *was
he*, absolutely pure, supernatural.

Very powerful and valiant were that Manu's sons, renowned,
11 like unto the thirty gods. The descendants of his sons ruled
over the earth as kings during the manv-antara of that
12 Manu of supreme splendour. Of his four ages were reckoned
in truth seventy-one and a half, *of the ages* called Ḳrita,
Tretá and so on, which I have declared in the *account of
13 the* Age. By the innate splendour of the austerities of *that*
most excellent high-souled *Manu his* seven sons became the
seven ṛishis in that period.

14 This third manv-antara I have declared to thee. Now the
15 fourth is called the period of Manu Támasa, who born of an
animal's womb illuminated the world with his fame; hearken
16 to the birth of that Manu, as I tell thee, O bráhman. And
the exploits of all those¶ *Manus* transcend the cognizance
of the senses; and the birth of the high-souled *Manus* is to be
known *as such*, and *their* majesty *also*.

* *Indro.*

† "Sweetly serene."

‡ See verses 2 and 3 above.

§ For *vaśa-vartinaḥ* read *vaśa-vartinaiḥ?*

|| *Aja*; or "a leader."

¶ For *amúnáṁ* read *amśháṁ?*

Canto LXXIV.

About the Támasa Manv-antara.

King Sva-ráshṭra being driven from his kingdom by enemies became an ascetic, and met his deceased queen in the shape of a doe during a great flood.—He begot a son by her who became the Manu Támasa.—The gods, ṛishis and kings of that manv-antara are named.

Márkaṇḍeya spoke:

1 There lived on the earth a famous king, by name Sva-
ráshṭra, valiant, an offerer of many sacrifices, wise, invincible
2 in battles. The sun being invoked by his ministers gave
him a very long life; and he had a hundred happy wives,
3 O bráhman. The wives of that long-lived *king* were not
very long-lived, O muni; and in time his servants, ministers
4 and people came to their end. And he, being bereft * of his
wives and his servants who were his equals in age, was
dejected in mind and dwindled in vigour day and night.
5 A neighbouring king named Vi-marda ousted him then from
his kingdom, failing *as he was* in vigour, deprived of his
6 devoted adherents, greatly afflicted. And being ousted †
from his kingdom, he went to a forest, despairing in mind,
and taking up his abode on a sandbank in the Vitastá,
7 illustrious *as he was*, he practised austerities. Undergoing
the five fires in the hot season,‡ exposing himself *naked* to
the showers § in the rainy season, and lying in water in
the cold season, he *lived* abstaining from food, strict in his
devout rites.

8 Afterwards *there occurred*, while he practised his austerities,
a great flood day after day in the rainy season, with the
9 clouds pouring down rain incessantly. The east could not be

* For *yukto* read *tyakto* (see verse 5)? The Bombay edition reads *mukto*.

† For *c'yutaṁ* read *c'yutaḥ*?

‡ Four fires around and the sun over-head; see Manu vi. 23.

§ For *abhraṅkashádikaḥ* read *abhrávakáśikaḥ*, which is the word in Manu vi. 23.

distinguished, nor the south, nor the west, nor the north;
10 everything looked as if besmeared with darkness. The king,
forced then in the excessive flood to seek the river bank,
could not reach it although seeking it, being carried away
11 by the exceedingly furious current. Now the king, after
being carried a long way by the swollen water, chanced upon
12 a Rauha doe in the water and seized her by her tail. Borne
along by that flood he passed over the surface of the land
hither and thither in the darkness; at length he reached a
13 bank. Crossing an expanse of mud, which was extremely
hard to be crossed, the king being drawn along by her still,
14 gained another charming forest. The Rauha doe dragged
the illustrious king along in the darkness there, while he
clung to her tail, enfeebled throughout his nervous system.
15 And he experienced an intense pleasure which arose from
touching her, as he wandered continually in the darkness,
16 with his mind drawn out in love *to her*. Perceiving that
the king was enamoured of her, *and was* engrossed in touching her back, the doe verily spoke to him within that
forest:—

17 "Why dost thou touch my back with trembling hand?
18 Quite otherwise has this affair turned out, O king. To no
unsuitable object has thy mind gone *forth*; not unapproachable am I to thee, O king; but this Lola creates an obstacle
to my union with thee."

Márkaṇḍeya spoke:

19 And the king, on hearing the doe say thus, was aroused to
curiosity and spoke thus to the Rauha doe.

20 "Tell *me*, who art thou? How dost thou, a doe, speak
language* like human beings? And who is this Lola who
creates an obstacle to my union with thee?"

The doe spoke:

21 I was formerly thy darling Utpalávatí, O king, thy
wife, thy queen above a hundred *others*, Dṛiḍha-dhanvaṇ's
daughter.

* *Mṛigí-vákyam* seems preferable as two words and not a compound.

The king spoke:

22 What deed then didst thou do,* that thou hast reached this *animal* condition? And true to thy husband, devoted to righteousness, such *as thou wert*, how hast thou thus become like this?

The doe spoke:

23 While a girl in my father's home I went with my com-
panions to a wood to play, *and* saw a deer united with a
24 doe. Then approaching close I struck the doe. Frightened
by me she fled away, *and* then the deer enraged said to me,
25 "Silly girl! why art thou so insane? Fie on this thy evil
disposition, by which thou hast rendered this period of
26 impregnation fruitless for me!" Frightened then at hearing
him speaking language as of a human being, I said to him—
"Who art thou who hast reached this *animal* condition?"
27 Thereupon he replied—"I am son of the ṛishi Nirvṛiti-ćakshus,
by name Su-tapas, but being enamoured of *this* doe I became
28 a deer, and followed her in love, and she longed for me in
this wood. Thou hast parted *us*, O naughty girl, therefore
29 I inflict a curse on thee." And I said—"Knowing thee not,
I have sinned, O muni; be gracious! deign not Sir to cast a
30 curse on me." And so addressed the muni gave me this
reply, O king,—"I do not inflict a curse on thee, if I *may*
31 give myself to thee." And I said—"I am not a doe, nor
of deer-like form; in *this* wood thou wilt find another doe;
32 meanwhile let thy feeling towards me be repressed." When
thus addressed he exclaimed, his eyes red with anger, and
his lower lip quivering—"'No doe am I' saidst thou!
33 thou shalt become a doe, O silly girl." Then exceedingly
agitated I fell prostrate before the highly-enraged muni,
who had resumed his own form, and exclaimed "Be
34 gracious!" again and again; "a girl is unskilled in words,
hence I spoke as *I did*; assuredly women who have no
35 father choose a husband themselves; and since I have a
father, how can I choose, O best of munis, or do wrong?

* For *kintu yávat kṛitaṃ* read *kiṁ tvayá vai kṛitaṃ?*

36 at thy feet I bow, be gracious, my lord!" While thus I lay
prostrate, exclaiming repeatedly, "Be gracious! be gracious,"
O high-minded *king*, that lordly muni spoke—"My uttered
37 word never goes amiss. After thy death thou shalt become a
doe in this very wood in *thy next* birth; and in the doe-
38 condition thou shalt conceive within thee the muni Siddha-
vírya's mighty-armed son named Lola, O proud lady; and
39 when the embryo is conceived within thee, thou shalt re-
member thy former life; regaining thy memory, thou
40 shalt also utter human language. After his birth thou shalt
be freed from the doe-condition *and* be honoured by thy
husband; thou shalt attain to the worlds which * are un-
41 attainable by those who commit sin. And he, Lola, mighty
in valour, shall indeed strike down his father's foes, and
conquer the whole earth and then become a Manu."

42 Incurring this curse I died and reached this brute con-
dition,† and through thy touch that embryo has come into
43 being in my womb. Hence I say—To no unsuitable object
has thy mind gone forth *in coming* to me, nor am I unap-
proachable; ‡ *but* this Lola who is conceived within me
creates an obstacle.

Márkaṇḍeya spoke:

44 Being thus addressed the king also experienced intense
joy then, thinking, "My son will conquer my enemies and be-
come a Manu on the earth."

45 Afterwards the doe brought forth that son marked with
the auspicious marks; and at his birth all created things
46 rejoiced, and especially the king. At the birth of that
mighty son the doe was freed from the curse and attained
47 to the sublime worlds. Then all the ṛishis assembled, O
best of munis, and perceiving the future prosperity of that
48 high-souled *child* gave him a name—"He was born of his
mother while she existed as an ignorant animal,§ and the

* For *ya* read *ye*.

† For *tíryaktvam* read *tiryaktvam*.

‡ For *agamyo* read *agamyá?* see verse 18.

§ *Támasíṁ bhajamánáyáṁ yoniṁ.*

56

world was enveloped in darkness,* *hence* he shall be Támasa."
49 Then Támasa was brought up by the father in the forest.
When he reached *the age of* intelligence he spoke thus to his
50 father, O best of munis,—"Who art thou, dear father?
and how am I thy son? and who was my mother? and why
hast thou come *here*? Tell me this truly."

Márkaṇḍeya spoke:

51 Thereupon his father, the large-armed king, narrated to
his son how he was ousted from his kingdom and *all* other
52 *events*. And on hearing all that, he invoked the sun and
obtained celestial weapons together with the spells that
53 controlled them in their completeness. Having mastered
the use of the weapons he vanquished those enemies, and
bringing them near his father released them, when they were
permitted by the *father* to depart, observing *thus* his own
54 righteousness. And his father, after seeing his son's face
happy, quitted his body and attained to the worlds, which he
had won for his own by austerities and sacrifices.

55 He having conquered the whole earth as king by the name
Támasa, became a Manu by name Támasa. Hear about his
56 manv-antara: who were the gods, who was the ruler,† and who
was the lord of the gods, and who were the ṛishis, and who
were that Manu's sons, the guardians of the world.

57 The Satyas and next the Su-dhís, the Su-rúpas, and the
Haris, these were the classes of gods therein, seven and
58 twenty *in number*, O muni. And S'ikhi Indra, mighty, great
in valour, distinguished by a hundred sacrifices, became the
59 lord of those gods. Jyotir-dhúman, Pṛithu, Kávya, C'aitra,
Agni, and Valaka, and also Pívara, *these* seven, were the
60 seven ṛishis, O bráhman. And Nara, Kshánti, and S'ánta,
Dánta, Jánu, Jaṅgha and others were Támasa's sons, very
mighty kings.

* *Tamasá.*

† For *yat-patir* read *tat-patir*, according to the Bombay edition.

Canto LXXV.

Raivata's Manv-antara.

The ṛishi Ṛita-vác' had a son who was bad because born under the constellation Revatí, and the ṛishi made the constellation fall with his curse.—A daughter was born therefrom whom the ṛishi Pramuc'a adopted and named Revatí.—King Durgama visited Pramuc'a and married Revatí, and the constellation was restored to its place at the marriage.—They had a son, the Manu Raivata.—The gods, ṛishis and kings in his period are named.

Márkaṇḍeya spoke:

1 Moreover the fifth Manu was the famous one named Raivata. Listen! I tell thee fully about his birth.

2 There was an illustrious and famous ṛishi named Ṛita-vác'.
To that high-souled *ṛishi* who had no son a son was born at
3 the termination of the constellation Revatí. He performed
the birth ceremony and all other rites for that *son* according
to the ordinances, and also the investiture with the sacred
4 thread and other *ceremonies*. And he was of bad disposition,
O muni. And even from his *son's* very birth the ṛishi, that
lordly muni, became afflicted with a lingering disease; his
5 mother suffered extreme pain, being attacked with leprosy
and other *diseases*. And his father in his affliction pondered—
6 "Why is this?" And that his son also, being exceedingly
wicked in mind, took another muni's son's wife whom he met.
7 Then dejected in mind Ṛita-vác' spoke thus—"Better is it
8 for men to have no son than a bad son! A bad son is always
causing trouble to his father's and mother's heart; and casts
9 downwards his ancestors who dwell in Svarga. He benefits
not his friends, he satisfies not his ancestors, he causes suf-
fering to his parents—fie on the birth of that *son* who
10 commits evil deeds! Happy are they whose sons are com-
mended by all the world, who benefit others, who are peaceful,
11 who are devoted to good work! Uneasy and dull, averse to
the next world, tending towards hell *and* not towards beatitude
12 is our life which depends on our son. A bad son brings

misery on his friends and joy to his adversaries, and he assuredly brings untimely old age on his parents."

Márkaṇḍeya spoke:

13 With his thoughts thus burning through the conduct of his exceedingly perverse son, the muni questioned Garga * as to what had happened.

Ṛita-váć spoke:

14 Keeping my religious vows strictly I learned the Vedas
formerly according to precept; after acquiring the Vedas
15 I married a wife according to precept. Along with my wife,
the rites to be performed, those enjoined by revealed religion,
those enjoined by tradition, the oblations made in fire with
the *exclamation* vashaṭ, I have never failed to perform to the full
16 unto this day, O great muni. Following the ordinances
prescribed concerning conception, without gratifying † my lust
and in order to have a son, I begot this *son*, I who fear *the*
17 *hell* named Put, O muni. Is it through his own fault or
through my fault, that this *son* has been born, bringing
suffering on us *and* causing grief to his kinsmen by his
bad disposition, O muni?

Garga spoke:

18 O best of munis, this thy son was born at the termination
of *the constellation* Revatí; therefore *he causes* thee suffering
19 since he was born at an evil time. This is no transgression
by thee nor yet by his mother, nor by thy family; but
the termination of Revatí befell *as* the cause of his bad
disposition.

Ṛita-váć spoke:

20 Because this my only son's bad disposition sprang from the termination of Revatí, let that Revatí therefore fall quickly!

Márkaṇḍeya spoke:

21 When he uttered this curse, the constellation Revatí verily fell, while all the world beheld with minds pervaded with as-

* See canto lxxii, verse 27.

† For *anurundhyatá* read *anurudhyatá*.

22 tonishment. And the constellation Revatí, falling on and
around the mountain Kumuda, suddenly illuminated* its
23 woods, ravines and cascades. And the mountain Kumuda,
by reason of her down-fall, became famous as Raivataka,†
a mountain exceedingly charming through the whole earth.
24 But the beauty of that constellation became the lake Paṅka-
jiní;‡ therefrom a maiden was born then exceedingly
25 brilliant in form. The muni Pramuća saw her who was
born from Revatí's beauty, and so gave her a name, the name
26 Revatí, O Bháguri. And illustrious Pramuća nourished her,
who had been born near his hermitage, in that same land.
27 Now seeing the maiden *grown* to the bloom of youth, *and*
beautifully formed, the muni bethought—"Who may be
28 her husband?" While he thus pondered a long time passed
by, O muni; nor did the great muni light upon a bridegroom
29 equal to her. At length the muni Pramuća entered his room
where the sacred fire burned, to ask Agni about a bridegroom
30 for her. Agni replied to the questioner,—"Great in strength,
great in valour, kind of speech, fond of righteousness, the
king named Durgama shall assuredly be her husband."

Márkaṇḍeya spoke:

31 And immediately there reached his hermitage, O muni, in
32 the course of hunting that wise king Durgama, who was
sprung from Priya-vrata's lineage, great in strength and
prowess, Vikrama-śíla's son, born of Kálindí's womb. The
33 king entered the hermitage and, not seeing the ṛishi, hailed
the slender maiden *with the word* "Dear!" and asked:—

The king spoke:

34 Whither has he gone from this hermitage, the adorable
lordly muni? I wish to pay him my affection here. Tell him
so, O bright maiden!

Márkaṇḍeya spoke:

35 The bráhman, who was in the room where the sacred fire

* For *bháshayámása* read *bhásayámása*.

† See page 289 note *

‡ Or, "a lake of lotuses."

burned, heard that his speech and the hailing her as "Dear!"
36 and came out in haste. The muni saw high-souled king Durgama, bearing the royal insignia, bowing respectfully before him.
37 Now on seeing him he spoke at once to his disciple Gautama —"Gautama! bring quickly the argha offering for this king.
38 At length he has come alone after a long time, this king and in particular my son-in-law; I deem him worthy of the argha."

Márkaṇḍeya spoke:

39 Thereat the king pondered on the reason for *his using the term* son-in-law and understood it not; therefore keeping
40 silence the king accepted the argha. When the king had taken a seat and accepted the argha, the bráhman, the great
41 muni, addressed him a welcome—"I trust thou farest well in thy home, in thy treasury, and army, in thy friends, in thy servants and ministers, and in thy own self whereon
42 rests every thing, O king of mighty arm! And thy wife fares well; since she is indeed at hand, I ask not therefore about her, *but I hope* thy other wives fare well!"

The king spoke:

43 Through thy favour I have no ill-fortune any where, O strict observer of vows; and my curiosity is aroused, what wife have I here, O muni?

The ṛishi spoke:

44 Most noble Revatí, beautiful even through the three worlds, is thy wife of exquisite figure; dost thou not know her, O king?

The king spoke:

45 My lord! Su-bhadrá, S'ánta's daughter, Káverí's daughter, and Su-játá born in Su-ráshṭra, and Varútha's daughter
46 Kadambá, Vipáṭhá, and Nandiní—*these* I know as my wives, O bráhman; they remain at my home. I know not Revatí, adorable Sir; who then is she?

The ṛishi spoke:

47 *She is* this *maiden* of beautiful complexion, whom thou didst address just now as "Dear!" Hast thou forgotten, O king? Worthy of praise is this lady of thy house!

The king spoke:

48 In truth I said so, but no improper feeling had I, O muni. Deign not to be angry with me for this, I beseech thee, Sir!

The ṛishi spoke:

49 Thou speakest truly, O king; no improper feeling hadst
thou. Thou didst utter this *word*, being impelled by Agni,
50 O king. I asked Agni, "Who *shall be* her husband?" O
king; and he replied that thou thyself, Sir, shouldst verily
51 be her bridegroom this day. Take her then; I give thee
the maiden, O king, and thou didst hail her as "Dear!"
How dost thou decide?

Márkaṇḍeya spoke:

52 At his address the king then kept silence; and the ṛishi
53 prepared to perform her wedding ceremony. The maiden
spoke a little thing to her father who was prepared for the
marriage, her countenance bent downward with respect—
54 "If thou lovest me, dear father, deign to give me a favour;
perform then my marriage in the constellation Revatí, since
I have won thy favour."

The ṛishi spoke:

55 Fair maiden! the constellation Revatí is not declared to be one that unites with the moon. The constellations appropriate to thy marriage are others, O beautiful-browed!

The maiden spoke:

56 Dear father! without that *constellation* the time appears to me unprofitable. How may the marriage of such as me take place at an unprofitable time?

The ṛishi spoke:

57 The famous ascetic named Ṛita-váć was enraged against
Revatí; in his anger he caused the constellation to fall down.
58 And I have promised thee as wife to this *king*, O maiden
with intoxicating eyes; and if thou desirest not the marriage,
we have fallen into a strait!

The maiden spoke :

59 Dear father ! Why did that muni Ṛita-váć perform austerities in that fashion ? Have I nought *to do* with thee as father ? Am I the daughter of an unworthy bráhman ?

The ṛishi spoke :

60 Thou art not the daughter of an unworthy bráhman, nor of an ascetic, O maiden. Thou art daughter to me who am striving to make other gods.*

The maiden spoke :

61 If my father is a practiser of austerities, why then does he not raise this constellation to the sky and perform my wedding under the constellation ?

The ṛishi spoke :

62 Be it so ! prosperity be thine, fair maiden ; be thou affectionate ! I raise the constellation Revatí to the moon's pathway for thy sake.

Márkaṇḍeya spoke :

63 Then by the power of his austerities the great muni placed
the constellation Revatí as before in conjunction with the
64 moon, O bráhman. And full of affection he celebrated his
daughter's marriage accompanied with sacred texts according
65 to rule, and said to his son-in-law again, "Tell me, O king,
what *shall* I give thee as a wedding gift ? I will give even
that which is hard to be obtained, *for* irresistible are my
austerities."

The king spoke:

66 Of Manu Sváyambhuva's lineage † I am sprung, O muni. I choose as gift a son who shall reign over a manv-antara through thy favour.

The ṛishi spoke :

67 This thy wish shall be fulfilled. As a Manu thy son shall enjoy the whole earth, and shall be wise in righteousness, O king.

* *Deván* ; this seems erroneous, but the Bombay edition reads the same.

† For *santato* read *santatau ?*

Márkaṇḍeya spoke :

68 Then taking her the king went to his own city. From him
69 was born of Revatí a son, the Manu Raivata, possessed of
all righteousness, unconquered by mankind, who understood
the meaning of every sacred book, who knew the Vedas, the
sciences and the books of practical arts.

70 Hear most composedly, O bráhman, about the gods, the
munis, the lord of the gods and the kings in his manv-antara,
71 as I mention them. The gods therein were the Su-medhases.
And the kings were Vaikuṇṭha and Amitábha, fourteen *and*
72 fourteen, O bráhman. And now the lord of those very four
classes of gods was named Vibhu, who was the regarder of
73 a hundred sacrifices, O king. Hiraṇya-loman, Veda-śrí, and
also U'rddhva-báhu, Veda-báhu, and Su-dháman and the
74 great muni Parjanya, and illustrious Vaśishṭha who was
thoroughly versed in the Vedas and Vedánta—these were
75 the seven ṛishis also in Manu Raivata's period. Bala-bandhu
mighty in valour, and also Su-yashṭavya, and Satyaka and
others were Manu Raivata's sons.

76 Now *these* are the Manus down to Raivata, whom I have
told thee about; they were indeed connected with Sváyam-
bhuva, except* Manu Svárocisha.†

Canto LXXVI.

The Sixth Manv-antara.

C'ákshusha when an infant was taken by a hag from his parents and changed for the son of king Vi-kránta, and was brought up as a prince.—On reaching boyhood he revealed the fraud, and abandoning his princely state became an ascetic.—Brahmá made him the sixth Manu.—The deities, ṛishis and kings of his period are mentioned.

* For *ṛiter* read *ṛite* with the Bombay edition.

† The Bombay edition adds a verse within brackets. "He who may hear or read the sublime story of these *Manus* continually, is delivered from all sins *and* attains to the world that is earnestly desired."

Márkaṇḍeya spoke:

1 Thus I have narrated these five manv-antaras to thee.*
Hear about this sixth period, *that* of the Manu C'ákshusha.
2 In another birth he was born from the eye† of the supreme
deity, hence in this birth also he retained the condition‡ of
3 C'ákshusha, O bráhman.§ His mother repeatedly makes him
prattle|| as he lies in her lap after his birth, and embraces
4 him lovingly and then again makes him prattle.¶ Being
indeed born with a recollection of his previous existences, he
5 laughed as he lay on his mother's lap. His mother said to
him angrily then—"I am frightened; what is this, my child,
that there is laughter in thy mouth? Thou art born with
premature intelligence. Perhaps thou seest something
bright!"

The son spoke:

6 Dost thou not see, a cat in front wishes to devour me?
And another, *the hag* who seizes newly-born children,** has
7 vanished. And since thou, lady, looking on me lovingly in
thy affection for thy son, dost keep on making me prattle and
8 dost embrace me much, while thy hair rises up and thine
eyes are suffused with tears springing from love, therefore
9 I chanced to laugh. Hear also the reason of it. The cat
intent on its own object looks on me who am attached *to
thee;* and the other also, *the hag* who seizes newly-born
10 children, has vanished. Just as these two, with hearts solici-
tous for their own self-interest,†† were busy over me, even

* For *tava* read *tathá?* The Bombay edition reads *mayá.*

† *C'akshushaḥ.* ‡ Or "appellation."

§ The Bombay edition inserts an explanatory verse here—"Bhadrá, wife of the high-souled royal ṛishi An-amitra, gave birth to a son, *who was* very wise, pure, who remembered his former lives, a *very* sovereign." See verse 27.

|| *Ul-lápya.* *Ul-lap* is not given as a verb in the dictionary; *ul-lápa* is given as a noun meaning "calling out in a loud voice; change of voice in grief, sickness, &c.;" but those meanings seem inadmissible here. See *ul-lápana* in canto xxv, verse 10.

¶ *Ul-lápayati.* ** *Játa-háriṇí;* see canto li, verse 102.

†† For *snigdha-hṛidayá* read *snigdha-hṛidaye* to agree with *ete pra-vṛitte,* as the Bombay edition reads.

so thou appearest to me to be engaged in thy own self-in-
11 terest. But the cat *and the hag* who seizes newly-born
children *aimed* at enjoying me; thou on the other hand de-
sirest to obtain good results from me which shall be enjoyed
12 gradually. Thou dost not know me who I am, nor the benefit
that I have conferred. Our meeting is for no very long time,
13 a period of five and seven days. Nevertheless thou lovest
and embracest me excessively with tears *in thine eyes*;
sincerely thou callest me "dear child" and "lovely darling."

The mother spoke:

14 "It is not for the sake of a benefit that I embrace thee
lovingly, my darling, nor shall I be deprived of thee, if this
15 shall be for thy pleasure.* I have *now* relinquished *any*
self-interest which shall accrue to me from thee."†

16 So saying she left him and went out of the lying-in house.
The hag Játa-hárinı́ then seized him when left, his body and
external organs of sense being apathetic, his heart and soul
17 pure. Having seized the boy she placed him then as a new-
born *child* on the bed of king Vi-kránta's wife, and took his
18 new-born son and carried him‡ to another house, and tak-
ing a son from that *house* she, Játa-hárinı́, in regular course
19 devoured *this* third *child*. Now carrying *children* off in succes-
sion she devours the third *child*, totally devoid of pity; but
she makes a substitution thus with the other two day after day.

20 And then king Vi-kránta performed the purificatory rites,
21 which appertain to a prince, for that very son; and as father
king Vi-kránta gave him the name Ánanda according to rule,
22 being *himself* filled with intense joy. Now when as a youth
he had donned the sacred thread, his spiritual guide ordered
him—"Approach before thy mother respectfully and salute
23 her!" Hearing that his guru's speech, he smiled and spoke
thus—"Which of my mothers shall I praise, her who gave
me birth or her who has nourished me?"

* This seems a little involved, but both editions read alike.

† For *tatto* read *tvatto*.

‡ For *tvam* read *tam?* but both editions read *tvam*.

The guru spoke:

24 Not the latter, indeed! Thy mother who bore thee, noble *youth*, is Rutha's daughter, Vi-kránta's chief queen, Haimini by name.

Ánanda spoke:

25 She is the mother of C'aitra, who dwells in the village Viśála, as son of the leading bráhman Bodha, and who was born of her. I *come* from elsewhere.

The guru spoke:

26 Whence art thou? tell me, O Ánanda. What C'aitra again dost thou mention? It appears to be a great difficulty. Where wast thou born? What dost thou say of this?

Ánanda spoke:

27 I was born in a kshatriya king's house of his wife Giri-
bhadrá, O bráhman. The *hag* that steals new-born children
28 took me; she left me here, and taking Haiminí's son also
carried him further to the house of the leading bráhman
29 Bodha, and devoured the bráhman Bodha's son. Haiminí's son
has been consecrated with the sanctifying rites of a bráhman
30 there. I have been consecrated here by thee as guru, illus-
trious Sir. I must obey thy command: which *mother shall*
I approach, O guru?

The guru spoke:

31 Extremely intricate, my child, is this great difficulty that has befallen. I understand it not at all, for my wits are wandering as it were through enchantment.

Ánanda spoke:

32 What case of enchantment is there here, while the world
is thus constituted? Who is whose son, O bráhman ṛishi?
33 Or who is not whose kinsman? Beginning from his birth,
whatever man enters into connexions, the others who are
connected *with him* are made to pass away by death, O
34 bráhman. Moreover when he is born here, whatever con-
nexion he has with kinsmen, that also ceases with the end-
35 ing of his body. This is the entire process. Hence I say,
"Who is not a kinsman to one who dwells in this worldly

existence? Or who is a kinsman for ever?" Is thy mind
36 bewildered? I have had two fathers indeed in this very
birth, and two mothers; is it wonderful that *it should be*
37 otherwise in the *recurring* birth of the body? Being such, I
will practise austerities. Do thou bring here C'aitra, who is
indeed the son of this king, from the village Viśála.

Márkaṇḍeya spoke:

38 Thereupon the king was astonished with his wives and
kinsmen; withdrawing his feeling of ownership from that
39 boy, he permitted him *to depart* to the forest. Fetching his
son C'aitra he made him worthy of the kingdom, after
honouring the bráhman who brought him up in the belief
that he was his son.

40 And he, Ánanda, a mere boy, practised austerities in the
great forest, in order to consume away his actions *which*
41 *were* adversaries in the path to final emancipation. And
to him then as he practised austerities spoke the divine
Prajá-pati—"Why art thou performing severe austerities
my child? tell me that."

Ánanda spoke:

42 Desirous of purity of soul I perform austerities, adorable
lord! setting my face towards consuming the actions which
tend to fetter me.

Brahmá spoke:

43 He who is lord over consumed actions is fit for final emanci-
pation, not he who engages in action. Hence Sir! thou shalt
obtain final emancipation, when thou hast the lordship of
44 goodness. Thou must be the sixth Manu; go; do accor-
dingly! Enough of austerities for thee! When thou hast
done that, thou shalt obtain final emancipation.

Márkaṇḍeya spoke:

45 Being thus exhorted by Brahmá, he then the high-minded
replied, "So be it!" and went directing himself to that
46 pursuit. He ceased indeed from austerities. Turning him
away from austerities Brahmá addressed him as C'ákshusha;

formerly he was *known* by *that* name; he became famous as
Manu C'ákshusha.

47 He married Vidarbhá, daughter of king Ugra, and begot
by her sons celebrated for valour.

48 Hear, O bráhman, who were the gods of the period, while
he reigned over the manv-antara; and who were the ṛishis,
49 and *who was* the Indra, and who were his sons. The gods
therein were named A'ryas; they formed one group of eight
persons; it *was composed* of those who had done famous
deeds, who partook of the oblations at the sacrifice, O bráh-
50 man, of those who were famous for strength and valour,
who were hardly to be gazed at because of their halo of
splendour. And the second class of gods was called Prasú-
51 tas, consisting of eight persons. There was another class
of gods also called Bhavyas, consisting of just eight persons;
and a fourth class therein was called Yútha-gas, which also
52 consisted of eight persons. There were, moreover, other
gods called Lekha in a fifth class also in that manv-antara,
53 O bráhman; those so named fed indeed on amṛita. And
the Indra was Mano-java, who offered a hundred sacrifices
and became their lord; *he was* reckoned the eater of a por-
54 tion of the sacrifices. And Su-medhas, and Vi-rajas, Havish-
mat, Un-nata, Madhu, Ati-náman, and Sahishṇu were the
55 seven ṛishis. Manu C'ákshusha's sons, chief of whom were
Urú,* Puru, and S'ata-dyumna, very great in strength, were
the kings of the earth.

56 Thus I have narrated to thee the sixth manv-antara, O
bráhman, both the birth and the exploits of high-souled
57 C'ákshusha. He who subsists at the present time is named
Manu Vaivasvata; hear from me about the gods and other
chief personages in his, the seventh, period.

---

* For *Urú* read *Uru*.

Canto LXXVII.

The Vaivasvata Manv-antara.

The Sun married Tvashṭṛi's daughter Sañjñá, and their children were Manu Vaivasvata and Yama—Márkaṇḍeya narrates, how the Sun's splendour was pared down by Tvashṭri because she could not endure it.

Márkaṇḍeya spoke:

1 The Sun Mártaṇḍa's wife was Viśva-karman's illustrious
2 daughter, by name Sañjñá. The Sun begot of her *a son*, a
Manu, of celebrated fame, learned in many sciences; since
he was Vivasvat's son, he was called Vaivasvata in sooth.
3 And Sañjñá used to shut her eyes when the Sun gazed on
her, and the Sun in anger thereat spoke sharply to Sañjñá—
4 "Because thou dost always imprison thine eyes when thou
seest me, O silly one, thou shalt therefore give birth to Yama,
the imprisoner * of mankind."

Márkaṇḍeya spoke:

5 Thereupon the goddess, unnerved by fear, became wild-
eyed, and the Sun seeing her agitated glances addressed her
6 again—"Since thine eye-sight has become agitated,† now
that thou hast seen me, thou shalt therefore give birth to a
daughter, the river Vi-lolá." ‡

Márkaṇḍeya spoke:

7 Hence through that her husband's curse Yama verily was
born of her, and also Yamuná this famous and very great
8 river. And *it was* with pain *that* Sañjñá, the noble lady,
endured the Sun's splendour; and then unable to bear the
9 splendour she fell into thought—"What am I to do? Where
am I to go? Where shall I go that I may find ease? And
10 how shall the Sun, my husband, control his wrath?" So
pondering in many ways, the Prajá-pati's illustrious daughter

* A play on the words *saṁ-yama, yama* and *saṁ-yamana.*

† *Vi-lolita.*

‡ This means the Yamnuá, see the next verse. This name is not given in the dictionary and I have not met with it elsewhere.

then thought much of actually taking refuge with her father.
11 Thereupon the famous lady having resolved to go to her
father's house fashioned her body, that the Sun loved, in
12 shadow-form, and addressed her *shadow-self*—"*Remain* thou
here in the Sun's house even as I; and behave thou becom-
13 ingly to the children even as to the Sun. And though ques-
tioned say nothing of this my going away; say always this,
'I am she indeed, Sañjñá by name.'"

The Shadow-Sañjñá spoke:

14 "O lady, I will obey thy order *and* will *so* declare, as far
as *suffering* my hair to be seized and as far as *undergoing*
curses; it is performed indeed as far as drawing curses down
upon myself."

15 The goddess*, receiving this *assurance*, then went to her
father's abode. She saw Tvashṭṛi there cleansed from stain
16 by means of austerities. And being honoured by him, Viśva-
karman, with much respect, she remained in her father's
17 house some time, unreproached. Then her father spoke to
the beautiful lady, his daughter, when she had dwelt there
not very long, after praising her and prefacing *his speech*
with love and much respect—

18 "Now while I have been seeing thee my child, the days
though very many may be *reckoned as* equal to half a mo-
19 ment; nevertheless righteousness suffers loss. Dwelling a
long time among kinsmen brings no good repute to women;
kinsmen hold a woman's *proper* residence is in her husband's
20 house. Such art thou, and thou art mated to a husband, the
Sun, the lord of the three worlds; deign not my daughter
21 to dwell a long time in thy father's house. Being such, go
thou to thy husband's home. I am pleased; thou hast been
honoured by me. Thou must come again to see me, my
beautiful one."

Márkaṇḍeya spoke:

22 Thus was she admonished by her father then, and she
agreeing saluted her father respectfully and went to the

* For *daví* read *deví*.

23 Northern Kurus, O muni, disliking the Sun's heat, afraid of
his splendour; and there she practised austerities, changed
into a mare's shape.
24 The lord of day thinking *the shadow-form* was Sañjñá, begot
25 of that other two sons and a charming daughter. Now the
Shadow-Sañjñá was very affectionate to the *other* children
just as to her own; Sañjñá did not use to show special atten-
26 tion to her daughter and two sons daily by caresses * and
other marks of pleasure. Manu accepted that *affection* from
27 her; Yama did not bear it patiently from her, and indeed he
lifted his foot in anger to kick her, but, again moved with
forbearance towards her, did not strike it against her body.
28 Thereupon, O bráhman, the Shadow-Sañjñá in anger cursed
Yama, her upper lip quivering slightly, and her delicate
29 hand shaking—"Because thou spurnest me, thy father's
wife, disrespectfully with thy foot, this thy foot shall there-
fore fall this very day to the earth."

Márkaṇḍeya spoke:

30 Yama, terrified on hearing the curse that his mother had
pronounced on him, went to his father and falling prostrate
before him spoke:—

Yama spoke:

31 O father, this great marvel was never seen by any one,
that a mother casting love away imprecates a curse on her
32 son. She is not mother to me in the same way as Manu calls
her his *mother*; no mother would abandon her good qualities
even towards sons devoid of good qualities.

Márkaṇḍeya spoke:

33 Hearing this speech from Yama, the adorable Dispeller of
darkness called the Shadow-Sañjñá and asked her—"Where
34 has she gone?" And she answered—"I am Tvashṭṛi's daughter
Sañjñá, O god of fire, thy wife; through thee these children
35 were begotten of me." Now when, as Vivasvat was thus
questioning her repeatedly, she did not speak *further*, the Sun
36 enraged thereat prepared to curse her. Thereupon she told

* For *nalinádi* read *lálanádi*, with the Bombay edition.

the Sun what had happened, and the god knowing the truth
went to Tvashṭṛi's abode.
37 He then paid honour to the Sun, the *god* honoured by the
three worlds, who had visited his house, with sublime faith.
38 Viśva-kṛit on being asked about Sañjñá, then told him—
"She came indeed here to my house, saying she had been
39 verily sent by thee." And the Sun, collecting his mind in
meditation, perceived her in mare's shape practising austeri-
40 ties among the Northern Kurus, and the Sun understood the
purpose of her austerities, namely, 'May my husband become
41 mild in body, beautiful in form.' "Pare down my splendour
now" quoth the Sun also to Sañjñá's father Viśva-karman,
42 O bráhman. And Viśva-karman thereupon pared down the
splendour of the year-revolving Sun, and obtains the praises
of the gods.

Canto LXXVIII.

*The Birth of Vaivasvata in the Sávarṇika Manv-antara.**

Márkaṇḍeya relates how the gods praised the Sun, what became of the splendour pared off from the Sun, and how the Sun regained his wife—He mentions the positions assigned to the Sun's children.

Márkaṇḍeya spoke:

Then the gods and the devarshis assembling praised in words the Sun, who is worthy of being praised by the entire three worlds.

The gods spoke:

2 "Adoration to thee who hast the nature of the Ṛic'!
adoration to thee who hast the nature of the Sáman! adoration
to *thee* whose form has the nature of the Yajus! *to thee* who
3 hast the glory of the Sámans! Adoration to *thee* who hast
become the sole domain of knowledge, to the cleanser of
darkness! to thee who hast the nature of pure light! to the

* This title is a mistake as the canto shews. It should be the Vaivasvata manv-antara.

4 purified, to the stainless Soul! Adoration to the most excel-
lent, to the desirable one! to the utmost one, to the supreme
Soul! Adoration to *thee* whose nature pervades the entire
5 universe, to the embodiment of Soul!" (This fine delight-
some eulogy must be heard by men with faith. Having become
a disciple and having given also the guru his fee *one may hear*
6 *it* rapt in meditation. It must not be heard by those who
have become empty-handed. Now may this become fruitful!)
"*Adoration* to the being who is the universal cause, to
7 the goal* of men of wise intellect! Adoration to *thee*
who hast the nature of the sun, who hast the nature of
the brilliant Soul! Adoration to thee, the illuminator, and
8 adoration to the maker of day! And adoration to the causer
of night, to the maker of twilight and moon-light! Thou
art this universe, *thou art* the adorable! With thee, as thou
9 revolvest above the world, the entire egg of Brahmá, devoid
of intelligence,† with *everything* moveable and immoveable,
turns round! This universe when touched by thy rays
10 comes to life, pure! Water and other *objects* are cleansed
by contact with thy rays! Oblations, alms-giving and the
other deeds which compose righteousness tend to no benefit
11 so long as this world has no contact with thy rays! All
these Ṛic'es verily are thine; these Yajushes on the other *hand*
12 *are thine* also; and all the Sámans drop from thy body! Since
thou are composed of the Ṛic', O lord of the world, and thou
13 indeed art composed of the Yajus, and composed also of
the Sáman, therefore, O lord, thou art composed of the
three! Thou verily art Brahmá's form; *thou art* the
14 highest and the lowest also! Moreover *thou art* material and
non-material; *thou art* minute and *yet thou* dost exist in
massive shape! Thou hast the form of Time, composed of
moments, káshṭhas and other *divisions of time, yet* subject
to decay! Be gracious! Of thine own will mitigate the
innate splendour of thy form!"

* *Nishṭháyai.*

† Or, illusory; *á-viddha.*

Márkaṇḍeya spoke :

15 Being extolled thus by the gods and devarshis, the im-
perishable globe of splendour shed his splendour then.
16 That *portion of* the Sun's splendour which was composed of
the Ṛic' became the earth, and of *that portion* composed of
17 the Yajus *was made* the sky, *and that portion* composed of
the Sáman *became* heaven.* Of the fifteen shreds of his
splendour which were pared off by Tvashṭṛi, the high-souled
18 Tvashṭṛi verily made Sarva's † trident, the discus of Vishṇu
and the Vasus, the very terrible *weapon* of S'aṅkara, and
19 Agni's spear and Kuvera's palki ; and all the fierce weapons
of the others who are the gods' foes, and of the Yakshas and
20 Vidyádharas—those Viśva-kṛit made. And therefore the
adorable lord bears *only* a sixteenth part. His splendour
was pared off by Viśva-karman into fifteen parts.
21 Then assuming a horse's form the Sun went to the Northern
22 Kurus, and saw Sañjñá there disguised in mare's shape. And
she, seeing him approaching and afraid of a strange male,
went towards him face to face, intent on guarding her rear.
23 And thereupon as the two met there and joined their noses,
two sons issued from the mare's mouth, Násatya and Dasra ;
24 and at the termination of the flow of semen Revanta was
born, bearing sword, shield and armour, mounted on horse-
25 back, furnished with arrows and quiver. Then the Sun dis-
played his own peerless form, and she gazing upon his true
26 form felt a keen joy ; and the Sun, the robber of the waters,
brought home this his loving wife Sañjñá restored to her
own shape.
27 Her eldest son then became Vaivasvata Manu ; and her
second son Yama became the righteous-eyed *judge* because
28 of the curse. His father himself made an end of the curse
by saying—" Insects taking flesh ‡ from his foot shall fall to
29 the earth." And because he is righteous of eye, impartial

* Svarga.

† Siva's.

‡ For *tritíyo mám samáddya,* which is erroneous, the Bombay edition reads *kṛimayo máṁsam ádáya* which is intelligible ; but *patishyatíti* which both editions read in the next line must then be changed to *patishyantíti.*

to friend and foe, therefore the Dispeller of darkness ap-
30 pointed him over the southern region.* And Yamuná be-
came the river which flows from the recesses of mount
Kalinda. The Aśvins were made the gods' physicians by
31 their high-souled father. And Revanta also was appointed
king of the Guhyakas. Hear also from me the places assign-
32 ed to the Shadow-Sañjñá's sons. The eldest son of the
Shadow-Sañjñá was equal to Manu the eldest-born; hence
33 *this* son of the Sun obtained the title Sávarṇika. He also
shall be a Manu when Bali *shall become* Indra. He was
appointed by his father as the planet Saturn among the
34 planets. The third of them, the daughter named Tapatí,
had a son Kuru, king of men, by king Sambaraṇa.†
35 *Thus* I describe the seventh period, that of Manu Vaivas-
vata, his sons, the kings, the ṛishis, the gods *and* the king of
the gods.

Canto LXXIX.

The praise of Vaivasvata in the Sávarṇika Manv-antara.‡

Márkaṇḍeya names the deities, munis and kings of the Vaivasvata Manv-antara.

Márkaṇḍeya spoke :

1 The Ádityas, the Vasus, the Rudras, the Sádhyas, the
Viśve-devas, the Maruts, the Bhṛigus, and the Aṅgirases are
the eight whereof the classes of gods are traditionally held
2 *to be composed.* The Ádityas, the Vasus, the Rudras are to
be known as Kaśyapa's sons; and the Sádhyas, the Vasus,§

* *Yámye.*

† She married the Paurava king Sambaraṇa and was the twelfth ancestress of the Páṇḍavas; see Mahá-Bhárata, Ádi-P. xciv. 3738-9; xcv. 3791; and clxxi. 6521–clxxiii. 6616.

‡ This is a mistaken title as the canto shews.

§ This seems a mistake for Maruts; for *vasavo* read *maruto?* But both editions read alike.

3 the Viśve-devas are the three groups of Dharma's sons. Now
the Bhṛigu class of gods are the sons of Bhṛigu, and *the Aṅgirases* are the sons of Aṅgiras. And it is the present
creation. Máríc'a is to be known as the lord at present.
4 And the Indra is named Úrjjasvin, high-souled, the con-
sumer of a share of the sacrifices. Now all those lords of
5 the thirty gods, who have passed away, and who have
not *yet* come, and who reign now, are to be known as having
equal characteristics—all indeed are thousand-eyed, wielders
6 of the thunder-bolt, smiters asunder of cities; all are
bestowers of gifts, pre-eminent, bearers of crests, walking
like elephants; they are all receivers of a hundred sacrifices,
7 dominating created things with their splendour, possessing
the good qualities of sovereignty with righteousness and
other pure actions, masters of the past, the future and the
present.
8 Hear also about this triple *world*, O bráhman. Bhúr-loka
is traditionally held to be this earth; antariksha is held to
be the sky,* and svarga is called heaven†—*such* is spoken
of as the triple-world.
9 And Atri and Vaśishtha and the great ṛishi Káśyapa, and
10 Gautama, Bharadvája and Viśvá-mitra Kauśika, and also
the adorable son of the high-souled Ṛic'íka, namely Jamad-
agni—these seven are thus the munis in the present period.
11 Ikshváku,‡ and Nábhaga,§ and Dhṛishṭa-śarmáti,‖ and

* *Divaḥ*; read *divaṁ*, neuter?

† *Divya.*

‡ Ikshváku was the eldest son of Manu Vaivasvata. He got Madhya-deśa and was the ancestor of several dynasties, the chief of which was the Solar dynasty that reigned in Ayodhyá (Hari-Vaṁśa, x. 634, and xi. 661–8; M.-Bh., Sabhá-P. xiii. 568–9; Rámáy., A'di-K. lxxii. and Ayodh.-K. cxix).

§ Or Nábhága. He was father or ancestor of famous king Ambarísha (Hari-V., x. 613 and 641; M.-Bh., Droṇa-P. lxiv; Sánti-P. xxix. 993–7, and ccxxxiv. 8597; and Anuśás.-P. cxxxvii. 6252).

‖ This is given as a single name, but should be two; thus for *Dhṛishṭa-śarmátir* read *Dhṛishṭaḥ S'aryátir*, "Dhṛishṭa and S'aryáti" according to the Bombay edition. Dhṛishṭa or Dhṛishṇu was ancestor of the Dhárshṇaka kshattriyas (Hari-V., x. 613 and 642). S'armáti should be S'aryáti or

12 famous Narishyanta,* Nábhaga† and Dishṭa,‡ and Karúsha,§
and Prushadhru,|| world renowned Vasu-mat¶—these are
the nine celebrated sons of Manu Vaivasvata.

13 I have declared this Vaivasvata period to thee, O bráhman.
When he hears and reads this, a man forthwith is freed from
all sins and gains great merit, O best *of munis.*

CANTO LXXX.

The Sávarṇaka Manv-antara.

Márkaṇḍeya names the ṛishis, gods and kings of that period.

Kraushṭuki** spoke:

1 Thou hast told me†† about these seven Manus, Sváyambhuva
and the rest, the gods, the kings and munis which *ruled* in
2 their periods. Tell me, O great muni, of the seven other
Manus which shall follow in this kalpa, and the gods and

S'aryáta; he dwelt in the country around the Gulf of Cambay, and founded a dynasty which reigned in Ánarta (Hari-V., x. 613 and 642-9; M.-Bh., Vana-P. cxxi. 10312, and cxxii; Anuśás.-P. xxx. 1945; S'ata-p. Bráh. iv. 1. 5; and page 368 note §§).

* Or Narishya; he is said to have been the progenitor of the S'akas (Hari-V., x. 614 and 641).

† This and the next name should apparently be read as one, *viz.*, for *Nábhago dishṭa* read *Nábhagádishṭa*, or better, *Nábhágárishṭa*. He is said to have had two sons, who were vaiśyas and became bráhmans (Hari-V., x. 614, and xi. 658).

‡ See the preceding note.

§ This should be Karúsha as the Bombay edition reads. He was the progenitor of the Karúshas, who were reckoned as kshattriyas (Hari-V., x. 614, and xi. 658); they occupied the country of which Rewa is the centre, see page 341 note †.

|| Or better, Pṛishadhra as the Bombay edition reads; it is said he was cursed by his guru and became a śúdra (Hari-V., x. 614, and xi. 659).

¶ He must be the same as Práṁśu (Hari-V., x. 614), but I have found no clear allusions to him elsewhere.

** For *Kroshṭukir* read *Kraushṭukir.*

†† *Tvayá* would be better than *mayá*; the Bombay reading *mama* is preferable.

other *rulers*, whoever they may be, *who shall characterize their periods.*

Márkaṇḍeya spoke :

3 I have told thee about Sávarṇi also who was the son of the Shadow-Saññá; equal to his eldest *brother* Manu, he shall
4 be the eighth Manu. Ráma,* Vyása and Gálava,† Dípti-mat,‡ and Kṛipa,§ Ṛishyaśṛiṅga,|| and Droṇi¶ were** the seven ṛishis†† of that *period.*
5 And the Suta-pas and Amitábhas and Mukhyas shall be the gods in three *divisions*; and *each* group of these three is said‡‡ to be composed of twenty, *and* to have the three
6 good qualities. Tapa and Tapas,§§ and S'akra, Dyuti, Jyotis, Prabhá-kara, Prabhása, Dayita, Gharma, Tejas, Raśmi,|||
7 Vakratu, and so forth are the Suta-pas, the twenty-fold

* Jámadagnya.

† The name of a son of Viśvá-mitra, and a famous ṛishi; see M.-Bh., Anuśás.-P. iv. 249-59; Hari-V. xxvii. 1460-63, xxxii. 1767-76, and xii. 724-9. A story of him is told in cantos xx and xxi *ante*; and a long story in M.-Bh., Udyoga-P. cv. and cxiii-cxviii. He is also referred to in S'ánti-P. cclxxxix; but the Gálava mentioned in Hari-V. xx. 1047-50 belonged to a later period and was probably a descendant.

‡ I have not met with this name elsewhere as the name of a ṛishi, nor is it as such in the dictionary.

§ The name of one of Dhṛita-ráshṭra's councillors, a well-known figure in the Mahá-Bhárata. He was son or descendant of S'arad-vat.

|| The name of a famous ṛishi, who was brought up in seclusion in a forest; he put an end to a long drought in Aṅga during king Loma-páda's reign, and by sacrifice obtained four sons for king Daśa-ratha of Ayodhyá; see Rámáy., A'di-K. viii. 7—ix. 69; x-xiv and xvii and xviii; M.-Bh., Vana-P. cx. 9991—cxiii. 10094; S'ánti-P. ccxxxiv. 8609; and Anuśás.-P. cxxxvii. 6269.

¶ This is not the name of any ṛishi, and the name should apparently be *Droṇa* or his son *Drauṇi* Aśvatthámaṇ. Both are leading figures in the Mahá-Bhárata.

** *Abhavan*; the past for the future.

†† All these names are the names of past ṛishis, and this manv-antara, the Sávarṇika, is still future; see canto liii. verses 7 and 8.

‡‡ For *kathitáś* read *kathitaś*?

§§ *Tapas tapaś c'a*; the two words must be different, it seems; and tapas, *neuter*, is supported by the following jyotis, *neuter.*

||| Or *Tejo-raśmi*, as one name.

group of gods. Prabhu, Vibhu, Vibhása and others are like-
8 wise another group of twenty. Hear also from me the third
group of Amita gods ; Dama, Dánta, Ṛita, Soma, and Vinta
9 and the rest are the group of twenty. And these *shall be*
celebrated as Mukhya* gods, rulers of the manv-antara—
they are verily the sons of Máríc'a *and* of the Prajá-pati
10 Káśyapa, and they shall be in the future during Sávarṇa
Manu's period. Now the lord of them, O muni, shall be Bali
11 Vairoc'ani, the Daitya who dwells in Pátála at present, bound
by a compact.†

And Virajas, and Arvavíra, Nirmoha, Satya-vác', Kṛiti, Vishṇu and others, the sons of Sávarṇa Manu, *shall be* kings.

Canto LXXXI.

Commencement of the Deví-Máhátmya.

The slaughter of Madhu and Kaiṭabha in the account of the Sávarṇika Manv-antara.

King Su-ratha being defeated and driven from his kingdom took refuge in the forest with a muni—He met a vaiśya who had been driven from his home by his relatives, and both asked the muni about the selfish feelings which still possessed them.—He ascribes those feelings to the goddess Mahá-máyá or Great Illusion, and relates how Brahmá lauded the goddess at the end of a former kalpa in order to seek deliverance from the demons Madhu and Kaiṭabha, and how Vishṇu awaking slew the demons.

Om ! Reverence to C'aṇḍiká.

Márkaṇḍeya spoke :

Súrya's son Sávarṇi *is he* who is called the eighth Manu.
2 Hear about his birth, as I tell it at full length, how by
reason of the authority of the Great Illusion‡ that illustrious

* "Principal," "chief." † *Samaya-bandhanaḥ*; or "bound for a season."
‡ *Mahá-máyá.*

son of the Sun, Sávarṇi, became the king of the *eighth*
manv-antara.
3 In times ago in the Svároc'isha period, a king named Su-
ratha, sprung of the race of C'aitra, reigned over the whole
4 earth. And while he guarded his subjects duly as if *they*
were his own children, there arose hostile kings, who did
5 not destroy the Kolas.* He the bearer of a very powerful
sceptre had war with them, and was defeated in war by
them, inferior though they were, *those* non-destroyers of the
6 Kolas. Then coming to his own city he reigned as king over
his own country. That illustrious *king* was attacked then by
7 those powerful enemies. His powerful and corrupt ministers,
who were evil-disposed to a weak person, thereupon robbed
8 him of treasury and army even there in his own city. Hence
the king deprived of his sovereignty departed alone on horse-
9 back to a dense forest under the pretence of hunting. There
he saw the hermitage of the noble dvija Medhas, inhabited
by wild animals which were peaceful, graced by the muni's
10 disciples; and he dwelt there some time, honoured by the
muni. And roaming hither and thither in that fine hermi-
11 tage of the muni, he fell into thought there then, his mind
being distraught by selfishness, egotistical—"Lost indeed
is the city *which* I guarded formerly. Whether it is guarded
righteously or not by those my servants of wicked conduct,
12 I know not. My chief war-elephant, always ardent, has passed
into the power of my foes; what pleasures will he obtain?
13 They who were my constant followers now assuredly pay
14 court to other kings with favour, riches and food. The
treasure which I amassed with great difficulty will go to
waste through those men, addicted to unbecoming expendi-
15 ture, who are squandering it continually." These and other
matters the king thought of continually.

* *Kolávidhvaṁsinaḥ.* This is an adjective in the nom. plural, agreeing with *bhúpáḥ*, and not a gen. case; and it is also a single compound, as appears from the next verse. Besides various fanciful explanations, the commentator renders *kola* as *śúkara*, and the whole word as "Yavanas." It seems plain that the Kolas mean aboriginal races, the Kols, and the whole word denotes some enemies who were in alliance with the Kolas.

Near the bráhman's hermitage there he saw a solitary
16 vaiśya, and asked him, "Ho! who art thou? and what is the
reason of thy coming here? Why appearest thou as if full
17 of sorrow, as if afflicted in mind?" Hearing this speech of
the king, which was uttered in friendly mood, the vaiśya,
18 bowing respectfully, replied to the king, "I am a vaiśya,
Samádhi by name, born in a family of wealthy *folk*, and have
been cast out by my sons and wife, who are wicked through
19 greed for wealth. And bereft of riches, wife and sons, taking
my wealth I have come to the forest, unhappy and cast out
20 by my trusted kinsmen. In this state I know not what is
the behaviour of my sons as regards prosperity or adversity,
21 nor of my family nor of my wife. Here I dwell. Is welfare
theirs at home now or ill-luck? How are they? Are my
sons living good or evil lives?"

The king spoke:

22 Why dost thou, Sir, fix thy mental affection on those
covetous *folk*, thy sons, wife and others, who have cast thee
out from thy wealth?

The vaiśya spoke:

23 This very thought has occurred to me, just as thou hast
uttered it, Sir. What *can* I do? My mind does not enter-
24 tain implacability; and my mind, which bears affection as of a
master to his family, is affectionate to those very persons,
who have abandoned affection for a father and driven me
25 out in their greed for riches. I do not comprehend, although
I know it, O high-minded Sir, how it is that the mind is prone
26 to love even towards worthless kinsmen. On their account
my sighs *flow* and distress of mind arises. What *can* I do
since my mind is not relentless to those unloving *relatives*?

Márkaṇḍeya spoke:

27 Thereupon they both, the vaiśya named Samádhi and the
28 noble king approached the muni, O bráhman, and having
both observed the etiquette worthy of him, as was proper,
they sat down *and* held various discourse, the vaiśya and the
king.

The king spoke:

29 Adorable Sir! I desire to ask thee one thing; tell me that;
since it tends to afflict my mind without *producing* submis-
30 siveness of my intellect. I have a selfish feeling for my
kingdom, even with regard to all the requisites of regal
administration, although I know *what it is, yet* like one who
31 is ignorant; how is this, O est of munis? And this *man*
has been set at nought and cast off by his children, wife and
servants; and when forsaken by his family he is nevertheless
32 exceedingly full of affection *towards them.* Thus he and I
also are both excessively unhappy; our minds are drawn by
selfish thoughts to *this* matter, even though we perceive the
33 faults in it. How *happens* this then, illustrious Sir, that we
are deluded although aware *of it, and that* this state of delu-
sion besets me and him, who are each blind in respect of
discrimination?

The ṛishi spoke:

34 Every animal has *this* knowledge in objects cognizable by
the senses and an object of sense reaches it thus in divers ways,
35 illustrious Sir! Some living beings are blind by day, and
others are blind at night; some living beings can see equally
36 well by day and at night. Mankind know what is true, but
not they alone indeed, because cattle, birds, wild animals
37 and other *creatures* all certainly know it; and men have * the
same knowledge which those wild animals and birds have,
and equally both *wild animals and birds* have the other *know-*
38 *ledge* which those men have. Though *they* have such know-
ledge, look at these birds, which, though distressed by hunger
themselves, are *yet* because of *that same* delusion assiduous in
39 dropping grains into the beaks of their young ones. Human
beings are full of longings towards their children, O hero; do
they not *pass* from greed *for self* unto mutual benefaction; †

* The Bombay edition reads *na* instead of *c'a*, "men have not the same knowledge, &c."

† This is very noteworthy. The altruistic virtues are here said to have been evolved out of the parental virtues.

40 dost thou not perceive this? Nevertheless they are hurled
into the whirlpool of selfishness *which is* the pit of delusion;
through the power of the Great Illusion * they make worldly
41 existence permanent.† Marvel not then at this. This is the
contemplation-sleep of the lord of the world, and the Great
Illusion *that comes* from Hari; by it the world is completely
42 deluded. Verily she, the adorable goddess, Great Illusion,
forcibly drawing the minds even of those who know, presents
43 them to delusion. By her is created this whole universel
both moveable and immoveable; she it is who when propitious
bestows boons on men with a view to their final emancipation,
44 She is Knowledge supreme; she is the eternal cause of final
emancipation, and the cause of the bondage of worldly
existence; she indeed is the queen over all lords.

The king spoke:

45 Adorable Sir! Who then is that goddess whom thou stylest
Mahá-máyá? How was she born, and what is her *sphere of*
46 action, O bráhman? And what is her disposition, and what
is her nature, and whence did she originate, the goddess—all
that I wish to hear from thee, O thou most learned in sacred
knowledge!

The ṛishi spoke:

47 She exists eternally, embodied as the world. By her this
universe was stretched forth. Nevertheless her origin is in
48 many ways; hear it from me. When she reveals herself
in order to accomplish the purposes of the gods, *it is* then
said in the world that she is born; she is also named the
49 Eternal One.‡ While the adorable lord Vishṇu, stretching
Sesha out, wooed the sleep of contemplation at the end of
the kalpa, when the universe was converted into absolute
50 ocean, then two terrible Asuras named Madhu and Kaiṭabha,§

* Mahá-máyá.

† For *Saṁsára-sthiti-káriṇaḥ* the Bombay edition reads *Saṁsára-sthiti-káriṇá*, "they are hurled, &c., through the power of the Great Illusion which makes worldly existence permanent."

‡ *Nityá.*

§ See Hari-Vaṁśa, ccii. 13562-81.

springing from the root of Vishṇu's ear, sought to slay
51 Brahmá. Brahmá the Prajá-pati stood on the lotus *that grew*
from Vishṇu's navel; and seeing those two fierce Asuras
52 and sleeping Janárdana, *and* standing with heart solely thereon
intent, in order to awaken Hari, extolled that Sleep of con-
53 templation which had made its dwelling in Hari's eyes— the
lord of splendour *extolled* Vishṇu's Sleep, which is Queen of the
universe, the supporter of the world, the cause of permanence
and dissolution, full of reverence, incomparable.*

Brahmá spoke:

54 Thou art Sváhá, thou art Svadhá; thou indeed art Vashaṭ-
kára, *thou* hast sound for thy soul; † thou art the nectar
of the gods, the two eternal letters,‡ *thou* existest having
55 the three-fold mátrás for thy soul; § *thou* existest half a
mátrá in duration *yet* eternal; thou indeed canst not be
uttered specifically; thou art || the Sávitrí, ¶ *thou art* the
56 divine mother** sublime. By thee indeed everything is main-
tained, by thee this world is created, by thee†† it is pro-
tected, O goddess! and thou dost always consume it at the
57 end. At its emanation thou didst take the form of creation,
and in protecting it thou hast the form of permanence, and
at the end of this world *thou* wilt have the form of con-
58 traction, O thou who containest the world! Thou art the

* The Bombay edition introduces *staumi* and some changes in the second line, and reads this verse as the beginning of Brahmá's invocation.

† Or, "thou hast heaven for thy soul," *svarátmiká*. The meaning "sound" seems preferable, as it agrees with the rest of the verse.

‡ *Om?* The commentary overlooks this expression, *akshare nitye*.

§ "The three prosodial measures." The expression *tridhámátrátmiká*, is also divided by the commentator into *tri-dhámá trátmiká*, "*thou* hast the three mansions, (*i.e.*, the three worlds, the three Vedas, the three chief deities, &c.), *thou* hast the preserver (Vishṇu) for thy soul."

|| For *sá tvam* the Bombay edition reads *sanḍhyá*, "the twilight."

¶ The Gáyatrí verse.

** For *deví jananí* the Bombay edition reads *Veda-jananí*, "the mother of the Veda."

†† For *tvayetat* read *tvayaitat*.

Great Knowledge, the Great Illusion, the Great Vigour, the
Great Memory, and the Great Delusion,* the Lady, the Great
59 Goddess, the Great Demon.† And thou art the original
source ‡ of the universe, the exciting cause of the three
qualities; thou art the Night of the world's destruction, the
60 Great Night, and the Night of delusion, terrible! Thou art
Good Fortune, thou art Queen, thou art Modesty; thou art
Intelligence characterized by perception; thou art Shame,
Nourishment, and Contentment, Tranquillity and Patience
61 also. Thou art terrible, armed with sword, with spear, with
club, and with discus, with conch, with bow, and having as
62 weapons arrows, slings § and an iron mace. Thou art gentle,
yea more than gentle, exceedingly beautiful to those who are
wholly gentle; thou art indeed beyond the highest and the
63 lowest, Queen supreme! And whatever or wherever a thing
is, whether good or bad, thou art the energy which all that
possesses, O thou who art the soul of everything. *Can* I
54 extol thee *more than this?* || By thee, who art such, he
indeed, who created the world, who protects the world,¶ who
consumes the world, is brought under the dominion of sleep.
65 Who is able here to extol thee? Since Vishṇu, I and S'iva
have been made by thee to assume bodies, who then may be
66 powerful *enough* to extol thee? Being such, do thou, O
goddess, lauded thus, bewitch these two unassailable Asuras,
67 Madhu and Kaiṭabha, with thy exalted powers, and let the
imperishable master of the world be lightly brought back to
consciousness, and let him rouse up his intelligence to slay
these two great Asuras!

* Or rather, "thou hast the great delusion," *Mahá-mohá*.

† *Mahásurí*. The Bombay edition reads *Maheśvarí*, "the Great Queen."

‡ *Prakṛiti*.

§ *Bhuśuṇḍi*. After explaining this word as a contraction of *bhuja-śatru-muṇḍí*, "she who cuts off enemies with her arms," the commentator says it =*go-phaṇiká*, "a sling." The dictionary says it is "a kind of weapon (perhaps a kind of fire-arms)."

|| *Mayá* as in the Bombay edition is preferable to *tadá*.

¶ For *gajatpátátti* read *jagat páty atti* according to the Bombay edition; see verse 56.

The ṛishi spoke:

68 Then the goddess of darkness, extolled thus by the Creator
there in order to awaken Vishṇu to slay Madhu and Kaiṭabha,
69 issued forth from his eyes, mouth, nose, arms and heart and
breast, and stood in the sight of Brahmá whose birth is
70 inscrutable; and Janárdana, master of the world, being
quitted by her, rose up from his couch in the universal ocean;
71 and he saw those two then, Madhu and Kaiṭabha, evil of soul,
excelling in heroism and prowess, red-eyed through anger,
72 fully prepared to devour Brahmá. Thereupon the adorable
lord Hari rose up and fought with those two, striking them
73 with his arms, for five thousands of years. And they, exceedingly frenzied with their power, deluded by the Great Illusion, exclaimed to Keśava, "Choose a boon from us!"

The god spoke:

74 Be ye both now content with me; ye must both be slain by me! What need is there of any other boon here? Thus much indeed is my choice.

The ṛishi spoke:

75 Gazing then at the entire world which was nothing but water, those two, who had been thus tricked, spoke to the adorable lotus-eyed *god*,—"Slay us where the earth is not overwhelmed with water." *

The ṛishi spoke:

76 "Be it so" said the adorable wielder of the conch, discus and club, and cutting † them with his discus clove them both asunder, heads and buttocks.

77 Thus was she born when praised by Brahmá himself. Now listen again, I tell thee of this goddess' majesty.

* The Bombay edition makes this sentence the second line of a new verse and reads as the first line of it—*Prítau svas tava yuddhena ślághyas tvaṁ mṛityur ávayoḥ,* "We are pleased at the battle with thee; thou art worthy of praise as Death to us!"

† For *kṛitvá* read *kṛittvá?*

CANTO LXXXII.

The Deví-máhátmya.

Slaughter of the army of the Asura Mahisha.

The gods were defeated in a great battle formerly by the Asuras and driven from heaven, and the Asura Mahisha became supreme.—All the gods gave forth their special energies, which combined and formed the goddess C'aṇḍiká.—They gave her their weapons, and she fought with and destroyed the Asuras.

The ṛishi spoke:

Of yore there was a fight for a full hundred years between
the gods * and Asuras, when Mahisha was lord of the Asuras
2 and Indra *lord* of the gods; in it the army of the gods was
vanquished by the Asuras who excelled in valour, and the
Asura Mahisha after conquering all the gods became the
3 Indra. Then the vanquished gods, placing the Prajá-pati
Brahmá at their head, went where *abode* S'iva and Vishṇu.
4 The thirty *gods* described to them accurately what had
happened, the full story of the gods' discomfiture which
5 had been wrought by the Asura Mahisha,—"He, *Mahisha*, in
his own person domineers over the jurisdictions of the
Sun, Indra, Agni, Váyu and the Moon, of Yama and Varuṇa
6 and of the other *gods*. Cast out by that evil-souled Mahisha
from Svarga all the hosts of the gods wander on the earth
7 like mortals. It has *now* been related to you both, all that
has been wrought by the foe of the Immortals, and we have
sought *you both* as a refuge; let his destruction be devised!"
8 Having thus heard the words of the gods, Vishṇu was
wroth and S'iva *also*; both their faces became furrowed with
9 frowns. Then issued forth great energy † from the mouth
of Vishṇu who was full of intense anger, *and from the*
10 *mouths* of Brahmá and S'iva; and from the bodies of Indra,

* For *Davásuram* read *Devásuram*.

† *Tejas.*

and the other gods went forth a very great energy; and it
11 *all* amalgamated. The gods beheld the mass of intense
energy there like a burning mountain, pervading the other
12 regions of the sky with its blaze; and that unparalleled
energy born of the bodies of all the gods, which pervaded
the three worlds with its light, gathering into one became
13 a female. By what was S'iva's energy her face was developed, and by Yama's *energy* grew her hair, and her arms
14 by Vishṇu's energy, by the Moon's her twin breasts; and
her waist came into being by Indra's *energy*, and by Varuṇa's
15 her legs and thighs, by the Earth's energy her hips, by
Brahmá's energy her feet, her toes by the Sun's energy, and
by the Vasus' *energy* her hands and fingers, and by Kuvera's
16 her nose; and her teeth grew by the Prajá-pati's energy,
17 and three eyes were developed by Agni's energy; and her
eyebrows *were* the energy of the two twilights, and her ears
Váyu's *energy;* and the coming into being of the energies of
the other gods *became* the auspicious *goddess.*

18 Then gazing at her, who had sprung from the combined
energies of all the gods, the Immortals who were afflicted by
19 Mahisha felt a keen joy.* The bearer of *the bow* Pináka
drawing a trident forth from *his own* trident gave it to her;
and Kṛishṇa gave a discus pulling it out of his own discus;
20 and Varuṇa gave her a conch, Agni a spear, Máruta gave a
21 bow and a quiver filled with arrows.† Indra lord of the
Immortals *gave* a thunder-bolt pulling it out of *his own*
thunder-bolt; the Thousand-eyed gave her a bell from his
22 elephant Airávata. Yama gave a rod from his own rod of
Fate, and the lord of the waters a noose; and the Prajá-pati
gave her a necklace of beads, Brahmá an earthen water-pot;
23 the Sun bestowed his own rays on all the pores of her skin,
and Destiny ‡ gave her a sword and a spotless shield;

* The Bombay edition inserts a verse here. "Then the gods gave her also their own several weapons; wishing for victory they shouted aloud to the victorious *goddess* 'Conquer! conquer!'"

† For *váṇa-púrṇe* read *váṇa-púrṇá?*

‡ Or Time, *Kála.*

24 and the Ocean of milk a spotless necklace of pearls and also
a pair of undecaying garments. And a celestial crest-jewel, a
25 pair of ear-rings, and bracelets, and a brilliant half-moon
ornament, and armlets over all her arms, and also a pair of
26 bright anclets, a necklet of the finest *make*, and rings and
gems on all her fingers—*these* Viśva-karman gave to her, and
27 *also* a brightly polished axe, weapons of many shapes and also
armour that could not be pierced. And Ocean gave her a
28 garland of fadeless lotus-flowers for her head and another for
her breast, and a very brilliant lotus-flower *besides*. Himavat
29 *gave* her a lion to ride on and gems of various kinds. Kuvera
gave a drinking cup full of wine. And S'esha, the lord of all
30 the serpents, who supports this earth, gave her a serpent-
necklace adorned with large gems. Honoured by other gods
31 also with *gifts of* ornaments* and weapons, the goddess
uttered a loud roar blended with a horse-laugh again and
again. The whole welkin was filled with her terrible roar.
32 By that penetrating and exceedingly great *roar* a great echo
33 arose, all the worlds shook and the seas trembled, the earth
quaked and all the mountains moved. And "Conquer thou!"
exclaimed the gods with joy to her who rode on the lion
34 and the munis extolled her as they bowed their bodies in
faith.

Seeing all the three worlds greatly agitated, the foes of the
35 Immortals uniting all their armies rose up together, with up-
lifted weapons. "Ha! what is this?" exclaimed the Asura
36 Mahisha in wrath, and rushed surrounded by all the Asuras
towards that roar. Then he saw the goddess, pervading the
37 three worlds † with her light, causing the earth to bow at the
touch of her feet, grazing the firmament with her crest,
shaking the whole of Pátála with the twang of her bow-string,
38 standing pervading the sky all around with her thousand
arms. Then began a battle between the goddess and the

* For *bhashaṇair* read *bhúshaṇair*.

† For *vyápta-loka-trayam* read *vyápta-loka-trayám*, with the Bombay edition; otherwise this word, read as a neuter noun, separates *devím* from the feminine adjectives which follow.

39 enemies of the gods, in which every region of the sky was
illumined with the weapons and arms hurled in abundance.
And the Asura Mahisha's general, the great Asura named
40 C'ikshura, *fought with her;* and *the Asura* C'ámara attended by
his cavalry fought along with others. The great Asura
41 named Udagra with six myriads of chariots *fought;* and
Mahá-hanu with a thousand myriads gave battle; and the
42 great Asura Asi-loman with fifty millions; with six hundred
myriads Váskala fought in the battle; Ugra-darśana * with
43 many troops of thousands of elephants and horses, and sur-
rounded with ten million chariots fought in that battle; and
44 the Asura named Viḍála fought in the battle there, surround-
ed with fifty myriads of myriads of chariots. And other
45 great Asuras in myriads, surrounded with chariots, elephants
and horses, fought with the goddess in that battle there. Now
46 the Asura Mahisha was surrounded with thousands of ten
million times ten millions of chariots and elephants and horses
in the battle there. With iron maces and javelins, with spears
47 and clubs, with swords, with axes and halberds they fought
in the battle against the goddess. And some hurled spears,
48 and others nooses, but they assailed the goddess with blows
from their swords in order to slay her.

And then the goddess C'aṇḍiká clove, as it were in merest
49 play, those weapons and arms by raining forth her own
weapons and arms. The goddess betrayed no exertion in her
50 countenance, while the gods and ṛishis were praising her. The
queenly goddess hurled her weapons and arms at the Asuras'
bodies. The lion also that bore the goddess, enraged *and*
51 with ruffled mane, stalked among the armies of Asuras, like
fire through the forests. And the deep breaths, which
52 Ambiká fighting in the battle breathed forth, came into real
being at once as troops by hundreds and thousands. These
fought with axes, with javelins, and swords and halberds,
53 destroying the Asura bands, being invigorated by the god-

* Instead of *pari-váritaḥ* I take the reading of the Bombay edition *Ugra-darśanaḥ* as a proper name. The Calcutta text contains no name as a nominative in this line or the next.

dess' energy. And *of* these bands *some* raised a din with
54 large drums, and others with conchs, and others besides with
drums, in that great battle-festival. Then the goddess with
55 her trident, her club, with showers of spears, and with her
sword and other weapons slaughtered the great Asuras in
56 hundreds, and laid others low who were bewitched with the
ringing of her bell; and binding other Asuras with her noose
dragged them on the ground. And others again, cloven in
57 twain by sharp slashes of her sword *and* crushed * by blows
with her mace, lie on the ground; and some grievously
58 battered by her club vomited forth blood. Some were felled
to the ground, pierced in the breast by her trident. Some
being closely massed together were cut in pieces † by the
59 torrent of her arrows in the battle-field. Following the manner
of an army,‡ the afflicters of the thirty *gods* gave up the
ghost; some with their arms cut off, and others with severed
60 necks; their heads fell from others, others were torn asunder
in the middle; and other great Asuras fell to the earth with
61 legs clean cut off; some were cloven by the goddess into two
parts, with a single arm and eye and foot *to each part*; and
others fell and rose again, although with head cut off.
62 Headless corpses, *still* grasping the finest weapons, fought
with the goddess; and others danced there in the battle,
keeping time to the strains of the musical instruments.
63 Corpses, with heads severed, *still* held swords and spears and
lances § in their hands; and other great Asuras *were* shouting
64 to the goddess, "Stand! stand!" || With the prostrate chariots,
elephants and horses and Asuras the earth became impassable

* *Vi-pothita; vi-puth* is not in the dictionary.

† For *kṛitáḥ* read *kṛittáḥ?*

‡ *Senánukáriṇaḥ;* but the commentator translates it, "fighting in the rear of the army." The Bombay edition reads *śailánukáriṇaḥ*, "who resembled mountains."

§ For *ushṭi* read *ṛishṭi*.

|| The Bombay edition adds a line to this verse, "while from their mangled limbs *flowed* streams of blood *(rudhiraugha-viluptáṅgáḥ)* in that appalling battle."

65 where that great battle took place. And large rivers formed
of torrents of blood straightway flowed along there amidst
the armies of Asuras, and among the elephants, Asuras and
horses.
66 Thus Ambiká brought that great army of the Asuras to
utter destruction in a moment, even as fire *utterly consumes*
67 a huge pile of grass and timber. And the lion, with quivering
mane, *stalked on* roaring aloud.* While he prowled † as it
were for lives out of the bodies of the foes of the Immortals,
68 the battle was fought there between those troops of the
goddess and the Asuras, so that the gods in heaven sending
down showers of flowers gratified ‡ her.§

Canto LXXXIII.

The Deví-máhátmya.

The slaying of the Asura Mahisha.

The description of the battle is continued—The goddess slew the Asura chiefs in single combat and finally the Asura Mahisha.

The ṛishi spoke:

1 Now the great Asura, the general C'ikshura, seeing that
army being slaughtered, advanced in wrath to fight with
2 Ambiká. The Asura rained a shower of arrows on the god-
dess in the battle, as a cloud *deluges* mount Meru's summit
3 with a shower of rain. The goddess, cutting asunder the
masses of his arrows then as it were in play, smote his horses
4 with her arrows and their charioteer; and split his bow forth-
with and his banner raised high aloft; and with swift

* The Bombay edition repeats here the second line of verse 50.

† *Vi-c'invati*, the loc. case, with *siṁhe* understood.

‡ Or "lauded," according to another reading.

§ For *eshāṁ* read *enāṁ*.

missiles pierced his limbs as he *stood* with shattered bow.
5 His bow shattered, his chariot useless, his horses killed, his
charioteer slain, the Asura armed with sword and shield
6 rushed at the goddess. With the utmost celerity he smote
the lion on the head with his sharp-edged sword, and struck
7 the goddess also on her left arm. His sword shivered to
pieces as it touched her arm (O prince). Thereon red-eyed
8 with anger, he grasped his pike, and he, the great Asura,
flung it at Bhadra-kálí, as it were the Sun's orb blazing
9 brightly with its splendour from out the sky. Seeing that
pike falling on her, the goddess hurled her pike, *and* it
shattered that pike into a hundred fragments and the great
Asura also.

10 When he, Mahisha's very valiant general, was slain,
C'ámara, the afflicter of the thirty *gods*, advanced mounted
11 on an elephant; and he also hurled his spear at the goddess.
Down to the ground Ambiká quickly struck it, assailed with
12 a contemptuous hoot and rendered lustre-less. Seeing his
spear broken *and* fallen, C'ámara filled with rage flung a pike;
13 and that she split with her arrows. Then the lion leaping
up fastened on to the hollow of the elephant's forehead, and
fought in close combat aloft with that foe of the thirty *gods*;
14 but both then fell, as they were fighting, from the elephant
to the ground. They fought closely locked together with
15 most terrible blows. Then quickly springing up to the sky,
and descending, the lion severed C'ámara's head with a blow
from his paw.

16 And Udagra was slain in battle by the goddess with stones,
trees and other *things*, and Karála also was stricken down
17 by her teeth and fists and feet.* And the goddess enraged
ground Ud-dhata to powder with blows from her club; and
killed Váskala with a dart, Támra and Andhaka with arrows.
18 And the supreme three-eyed goddess slew Ugrásya and Ugra-
19 vírya and Mahá-hanu also with her trident. With her sword
she struck Viḍála's head clean down from his body. She

* *Danta-mushṭi-talaiś;* or, according to the commentator, "with the lower parts of her ivory sword-hilt."

despatched both Dur-dhara and Dur-mukha to Yama's abode
with her arrows.*

20 Now, as his army was being thus destroyed utterly, the
Asura Mahisha in his own buffalo-shape terrified *her* troops.
21 Some *he laid low* by a blow from his muzzle, and others by
stamping with his hooves, and others *because they were* lashed
22 with his tail and gashed with his horns, and others again by
his impetuous rush, his bellowing and his wheeling career,
and others by the blast of his breath—*thus* he laid *them* low
23 on the face of the earth. Having laid low the van of her
army, the Asura rushed to attack the great goddess' lion.
24 Thereat Ambiká displayed her wrath. And he, great in
valour, pounding the surface of the earth with his hooves in
his rage, tossed the mountains aloft † with his horns and
25 bellowed. Crushed by his impetuous wheelings the earth
crumbled to pieces; and the sea lashed by his tail overflowed
26 in every direction; and the clouds pierced by his swaying
horns were rent to fragments; mountains fell in hundreds
from the sky, being cast down by the blast of his breath.

27 C'aṇḍiká looked on the great Asura, as swollen with rage he
rushed on, and gave a way to her wrath then in order to slay
28 him. She flung her noose full over him, and bound the great
Asura fast. And he quitted his buffalo shape when held
29 bound in the great battle, *and* then became a lion suddenly.
While Ambiká is cutting off his head he took the appearance
30 of a man with scymitar in hand. Straightway the goddess
with her arrows swiftly pierced the man together with his
scymitar and shield. Then he became a huge elephant, and
31 tugged at *her* great lion with his trunk and roared, but the
goddess cut off his trunk with her sword as he made his tugs.

* The Bombay edition inserts four lines here. "And she, who is the Night of Fate, laid Kála low with her rod of Fate. She belaboured Ugra-darśana with very fierce blows from her scymitar. She clove Asi-loman indeed with her sword in the battle-festival. Her troops, her lion and the goddess *herself* raised aloud the battle-cry of victory along with *those battle*-festivals."

† *Uc'c'aiḥ*, which the Bombay edition reads, is preferable to *uc'c'án*, "high *mountains*."

32 Next the great Asura assumed his buffalo shape again, and
so shook the three worlds with all that is moveable and im-
33 moveable therein. Enraged thereat C'aṇḍiká, the mother of
the world, quaffed a sublime beverage again and again,* *and*
34 laughed as her eyes *gleamed* ruddy. And the Asura roared
out, puffed up with his strength and valour and frenzy, and
35 hurled mountains against C'aṇḍiká with his horns. And she,
shivering to atoms with showers of arrows those *mountains*
that he hurled, spoke to him in confused words, while her
mouth was rendered ruddier by the mead *that she had drunk.*

The goddess spoke:

36 Roar, roar on *thy* brief moment, O fool, the while I quaff
this mead! The gods shall soon roar, when I shall slay thee
even here.

37 Exclaiming thus she leaped upwards and sat herself on that
great Asura, and kicked him on the neck with her foot and
38 struck him with her spear. And thereupon he, being assailed
by her foot, half issued forth † from his own mouth in sooth,
39 being completely encompassed by the goddess' valour. That
great Asura being thus attacked half issued forth indeed.
The goddess struck off his head with her great sword and
laid him low. ‡

40 Then perished all that Daitya army with great lamentation.
And all the hosts of the gods rose to the highest exultation.
41 The gods and the great heavenly ṛishis poured forth praises
to the goddess, the Gandharva chiefs burst into song and the
bevies of Apsarases into dances.

* See canto lxxxii, verse 29.

† For *eváti* the Bombay edition reads *evásíd.*

‡ The Bombay edition inserts two verses here. "Thus the *Asura* named Mahisha was destroyed by the goddess along with his army and his bands of friends, after he had bewitched the three worlds. When Mahisha was slain, all created things in the three worlds then uttered *the shout* 'Conquer thou!' along with gods and Asuras and men."

Canto LXXXIV.

The Deví-máhátmya.

The Slaying of the Asura Mahisha concluded.

The gods poured forth their praises to C'aṇḍiká on her victory—And she gave them the boon that she would always befriend them, if they recalled her to mind in calamities.

The ṛishi spoke:*

1 When that most valiant evil-souled army of the gods' foes was vanquished by the goddess, Sakra and the hosts of other gods poured forth their praises to her with their voices, reverently bending down their necks† and shoulders, while their bodies looked handsome because their hair stood erect with exultation.

2 The goddess, who stretched out this world by her power,
Whose body comprises the entire powers of all the hosts of gods,
Her, Ambiká, worthy of worship by all gods and great ṛishis,
We bow before‡ in faith; may she ordain blessings for us!

3 May she, whose peerless majesty and power Ananta
Adorable, Brahmá and Hara cannot in sooth declare,
May she, C'aṇḍiká, to protect the entire world
And to destroy the fear of evil turn her mind!

4 *Her, who is* Good-Fortune herself in the dwellings of men of good deeds, Ill-Fortune

* The Bombay edition inserts a preliminary verse here—"Then all the hosts of gods with Indra at their head began to sing the praise of the goddess, when the Asura Mahisha was slain." This is tautological and superfluous.

† For *-śiro-'dharáṃsá* read *-śirodharáṃsá* as in the Bombay edition.

‡ *Natáḥ sma;* so again in verse 4. This seems a peculiar use of the particle *sma*. Similarly *pra-ṇatáḥ sma* in canto lxxxv, verse 7.

In those of men of sinful souls; *who is* Intelligence in the hearts of the prudent,
Who is Faith *in those* of the good, *and* Modesty *in that* of the high-born man;*
Her, *even* thee, we bow before; protect the universe, O goddess!

5 Can we describe† this thy thought-transcending form?
Or thy abundant surpassing valour that destroyed the Asuras?
Or thy surpassing‡ feats which *were displayed* in battles
Among all the hosts of Asuras, gods and others, O goddess?

6 *Thou art* the cause of all the worlds! Though characterized by the three qualities, by faults§
Thou art not known! Even by Hari, Hara and the other *gods thou art* incomprehensible!
Thou art the resort of all; *thou art* this entire world which is composed of parts!
Thou verily *art* sublime original Nature|| untransformed!

7 Thou, whose complete divinity by means of utterance
Finds satisfaction in all sacrifices, O goddess,¶
Art verily Sváhá, and givest satisfaction to the Pitṛi-hosts!
Hence thou art in truth declared by men to be Svadhá also.

8 Thou *art she*, who effects final emancipation, and performs great thought-transcending penances!
Thou studiest** with thy organs, which are the essence of strength,†† well-restrained!

* For *kula-jana-prabhasya* read *kula-jana-prabhavasya*, with the Bombay edition.

† *Kiṁ varṇayáma.*

‡ For *taváti yáni* the Bombay edition reads *tavádbhutáni*, which is equivalent.

§ For *doshair* the Bombay edition reads *devair*, which is inferior.

|| *Prakṛiti.*

¶ The Bombay edition reads plurals.

** *Abhy-asyase*; átmane-pada, which seems rare.

†† *Sattva-sáraiḥ* of the Bombay edition is preferable to *tattva-sáraiḥ*.

With munis, who seek final emancipation and who have shed all their faults,
Thou art The Knowledge, adorable, sublime in sooth, O goddess!

9 Sound is thy soul! *thou art* the repository of the most spotless ṛić and yajus hymns,
And of the sámans, which have the charming-worded texts of the Ud-gítha!
Thou as goddess *art* the triple *Veda*, the adorable, and for the existence and production
Of all the worlds art active; *thou art* the supreme destroyer of their pains!*

10 Thou art Mental Vigour,† O goddess! thou hast comprehended the essence of all the Scriptures!
Thou art Durgá; the boat *to cross* the difficult ocean of existence; devoid of attachments!
Thou art S'rí, who has planted her dominion alone in the heart of Kaiṭabha's foe!
Thou indeed art Gaurí, who has fixed her dweling in the moon-crested *god!*

11 Slightly-smiling, spotless, resembling the full moon's
Orb, beautiful as the choicest gold, *and* lovely *was thy face!*
Yet 't was very marvellous that, being swayed by anger,
The Asura Mahisha suddenly smote thy face when he saw it.

12 But after seeing thy wrathful *face*, O goddess, terrible with its frowns,
And sheeny in hue like the rising moon, that Mahisha
Did not forthwith yield up his life, 't was passing wonderful!

* This half verse admits of more than one translation. I have adopted from the commentary what seems the most natural meaning. *Várttá* seems obscure; the commentary explains it as *vṛittánta-rúpá*, "having the form of events" or "having the form of history;" or as *kṛishi-go-rakshádi-vṛittir*, "following the occupations of cultivation, cattle-rearing and such like."

† *Medhá*.

For who can live after beholding the King of Death enraged?

13 Be gracious, O goddess, as supreme lady, to life!
When enraged thou dost forthwith destroy *whole* families!
Known at this very moment is this, that here is brought to its end
The Asura Mahisha's most extensive might!

14 Esteemed are they among the nations, theirs are riches,
Theirs are glories, and their sum of righteousness* perishes not,
Happy are they indeed, *and* they possess devoted children, servants and wives,
On whom thou, well-pleased, dost always bestow prosperity, O lady!

15 All righteous actions ever indeed, O goddess,
With utmost respect the man of good deeds daily performs,
And gains heaven thereafter by thy favour, O lady.
Dost thou not by him† bestow rewards even on the three worlds, O goddess?

16 Thou, O Durgá, when called to mind, dost remove terror from every creature!
Thou, when called to mind by those in health, dost bestow a mind extremely bright!
What *goddess* but thou, O dispeller of poverty, pain and fear,
Has ever benevolent thoughts in order to work benefits to all?

17 By these slain *foes* the world attains‡ to happiness; thus let these
Forsooth practise sin *so as to descend* to hell for long!§

* Or *bandhu-vargah*, "whole body of kinsfolk," according to the Bombay edition.

† *Tena*, or "therefore."

‡ Or *upaitu*, "may it attain," according to the Bombay edition.

§ This appears to be one meaning given in the commentary; another, which seems to be preferred, is to read *náma narakáya* as *na áma-narakáya*, "let these not practice sin *so as to descend* to the Hell of Disease for long!"

'Meeting death in battle let them proceed to heaven'—
Thinking thus, thou dost assuredly destroy the enemies, O goddess!

18 Having indeed seen them, why dost thou not, O lady, reduce to ashes
All the Asuras, since thou directest thy weapons against the foes?
'Let even enemies, purified by dying in arms, attain in sooth to the *bright* worlds'—
Such is thy most kindly intention towards even them.

19 And though, neither by the sharp flashes* of abundant light from thy scymitar,
Nor by the copious lustre of thy spear-point, the eyes of the Asuras
Were destroyed; yet, as they gazed upon thy countenance
Which bore a portion of the radiant moon, this very thing *happened.*

20 Thy disposition, O goddess, subdues the conduct of men of evil conduct;
And this *thy* form surpasses thought and rivalry by others;
And thy valour vanquishes those who have robbed the gods of their prowess;
Thou hast as it were† manifested pity thus even on enemies!

21 To what my this thy prowess be compared?
And whereto thy form most charming, which strikes fear among foes?
Compassion in mind and relentlessness in battle are seen
In thee, O goddess, who bestowest boons even on the three worlds!

22 Through the destruction of the foes, these three worlds entire
Have been saved by thee. Having slain them in the battle-front

* *Visphuraṇa*; not in the dictionary.

† Or *prakaṭitaiva*, "thou hast indeed manifested," as in the Bombay edition.

Thou hast led even those hosts of foes to heaven, and dispelled the fear
Which beset us from the frenzied foes of the gods. Reverence to thee!

23 With thy spear protect us, O goddess!
Protect us with thy sword also, O Ambiká!
By the clanging of thy bell protect us,
And by the twanging of the thong of thy bow!

24 In the east guard us, and in the west;
O C'aṇḍiká, guard us in the south
By the brandishing of thy spear,
And also in the north, O goddess!

25 Whatever gentle forms of thee wander about in the three worlds,
And whatever exceedingly terrible *forms wander*, by means of them guard us and the earth!

26 Thy sword and spear and club, and whatever other weapons, O Ambiká,
Rest in thy pliant hand, with them guard us on every side!

The ṛishi spoke:

27 Thus was she, the Upholder of the worlds, hymned by the
gods, and they paid honour to her with celestial flowers that
blossomed in Nandana, and with perfumes and unguents.
28 Moreover all the thirty *gods* in faith censed her with heavenly
incenses. Benignly sweet in countenance she spoke to all
the prostrate gods.

The goddess spoke:

29 Choose, ye thirty all! whatever ye desire of me, for I grant
it with pleasure, being highly honoured by these hymns.*

The gods spoke:

30 Thou, O adorable lady, hast accomplished all, nought
remains *undone*, in that this Asura Mahisha, our foe has

* The Bombay edition inserts another verse here—"'And whatever else must be done, I do not deem it difficult.' Hearing this speech from the goddess, those heaven-dwellers made answer."

31 been slain. Yet if thou must grant us a boon, O goddess
great! whenever we call thee, call thee to mind, do thou
32 away with our direst calamities! And whatever mortal
shall praise thee with these hymns, O lady of spotless countenance, to prosper him in wealth and wife and other blessings by means of riches, success and power do thou incline always, O Ambiká, who art propitious to us!

The ṛishi spoke:

33 Being thus propitiated by the gods for the good of the world and on their own *behalf*, " Be it so!" said she, Bhadrakálí; and vanished from their sight, O king.

34 Thus I have narrated this, O king, how the goddess came into
being of yore from out of the gods' bodies, she who desires the
35 good of all the three worlds. And again she came into existence
having the body of Gaurí, just as she did before, in order
36 to slay the wicked Daityas and S'umbha and Niśumbha, and
to preserve the worlds, as benefactress of the gods. Hearken then to what I have declared to thee. I have truly told it thee.

Canto LXXXV.

The Deví-máhátmya.

The goddess' conversation with the Asura's messenger.

The Asuras Sumbha and Niśumbha conquered the gods and drove them from heaven.—The gods invoked C'aṇḍiká at Himavat in a hymn, appealing to her by all her attributes to help them.—Párvatí came there and C'aṇḍiká sprang forth from her body.—The servants of Sumbha and Niśumbha saw her and extolled her perfect beauty to Sumbha.—He sent a messenger to invite her to marry him.—She explained that by a vow she could marry no one who did not conquer her in fight.

The ṛishi spoke:

Of yore the Asuras S'umbha and Niśumbha, trusting in

their pride and strength, robbed S'aći's lord of the three
2 worlds* and of his portions of the sacrifices; they both
usurped likewise the sun's dignity and the moon's dominion,
3 and Kuvera's and Yama's and Varuṇa's; and they both
exercised Váyu's authority and Agni's *sphere of* action.†
Thereby the gods were scattered, deprived of their sover-
4 eignties *and* put to rout. The thirty gods, bereft of their
dominion *and* set at nought by those two great Asuras, all
5 recall to mind that never-vanquished goddess,—"Thou didst
grant us the boon,‡ 'As *ye when* in calamities *shall* call *me* to
mind,§ that very moment will I put an end to all your direst
6 calamities.'" Making this resolve the gods went to Hima-
vat, lord among mountains, and there raised their hymn to
the goddess, who is Vishṇu's illusive power.||

The gods spoke:

7 Reverence to the goddess, to the great goddess!
To her who is auspicious reverence perpetually!
Reverence to Prakṛiti the good!
Submissive we fall prostrate before her! ¶
8 Reverence to her who is terrible, to her who is constant!
To Gaurí, to Dhátrí reverence, *yea* reverence!
And to the Moon-light,** to her who has the moon's form,
To her who is happy, reverence continually!

* For *traikokyam* read *trailokyam*.

† The Bombay edition inserts a line here—

anyeshám c'ádhikárán saḥ svayam evádhitishṭhati

and reads the first three words with the preceding words, but does not explain the last four in its commentary. I would suggest that the line should run thus—

anyeshám adhikárámś c'a svayam evádhitashṭhatuḥ

"and they themselves dominated the lordships of the other gods."

‡ See canto lxxxiv, verse 31.

§ *Smṛitákhiláḥ*, i.e., *smṛitá*, and *akhiláḥ* agreeing with *paramápadaḥ*.

|| *Vishṇu-máyá*.

¶ *Praṇatáḥ sma tám*; *sma* is used here with a past participle.

** *Jyotsnáyai*.

9 Falling prostrate, to her who is propitious, to Prosperity,*
To Perfection let us pay † reverence, *yea* reverence!
To Nirṛiti,‡ to the goddess of Good-Fortune of kings,
To thee, S'arváṇí, reverence, *yea* reverence!
10 To Durgá, to her who is a further shore difficult to be reached,§
To her who is essential, to her who works all things,||
And to Fame also, to her who is blue-black,¶
To her who is smoke-dark reverence continually!
11 Before her who is *at once* most gentle and most harsh
We fall prostrate; to her reverence, *yea* reverence!
Reverence to her who is the foundation of the world!
To the goddess *who is* Action reverence, *yea* reverence!
12 To the goddess who among all created things
Is called Vishṇu's illusive power,
Reverence to her, *yea* reverence to her!
Reverence to her, reverence, *yea* reverence!
13 To the goddess who among all created beings
Bears the name Consciousness,**
Reverence to her, *yea* reverence to her!
Reverence to her, reverence, *yea* reverence!
14 To the goddess who among all created beings
Stands firm †† with the form of Intellect,‡‡
Reverence to her, *yea* reverence to her!
Reverence to her, reverence, *yea* reverence!

* For *Vṛidvyai* read *Vṛiddhyai*. But the Bombay edition reads *mṛidvyai*, "to her who is gentle."

† *Kurmo;* the Bombay edition reads *Kúrmyai*, "to the female Tortoise."

‡ "Dissolution."

§ *Durga-páráyai.*

|| *Sarva-káriṇyai;* this violates the metre. The Bombay edition reads better, *sarva-káriṇi*, "O thou who workest all things!"

¶ *Kṛishṇáyai.*

** *C'etaná.*

†† *Saṃsthitá;* or "abides." The commentary explains it as *samyak sthitá.*

‡‡ *Buddhi-rúpeṇa.*

15 To the goddess who among all created beings
Stands firm with the form of Sleep,
Reverence to her, *yea* reverence to her!
Reverence to her, reverence, *yea* reverence!

16 To the goddess who among all created beings
Stands firm with the form of Hunger,
Reverence to her, *yea* reverence to her!
Reverence to her, reverence, *yea* reverence,

17 To the goddess who among all created beings
Stands firm with the form of Shadow,
Reverence to her, *yea* reverence to her!
Reverence to her, reverence, *yea* reverence!

18 To the goddess who among all created beings
Stands firm with the form of Energy,*
Reverence to her, *yea* reverence to her!
Reverence to her, reverence, *yea* reverence!

19 To the goddess who among all created beings
Stands firm with the form of Thirst,
Reverence to her, *yea* reverence to her!
Reverence to her, reverence, *yea* reverence!

20 To the goddess who among all created beings
Stands firm with the form of Patience,
Reverence to her, *yea* reverence to her!
Reverence to her, reverence, *yea* reverence!

21 To the goddess who among all created beings
Stands firm with the form of Speciality,†
Reverence to her, *yea* reverence to her!
Reverence to her, reverence, *yea* reverence!

22 To the goddess who among all created beings
Stands firm with the form of Modesty,
Reverence to her, *yea* reverence to her!
Reverence to her, reverence, *yea* reverence!

23 To the goddess who among all created beings

* *S'akti-rúpeṇa.*

† *Játi.* The commentary explains it as *nityaikánugata-pratyaya-hetur aneka-samaváyiní.*

Stands firm with the form of Peaceableness,
Reverence to her, *yea* reverence to her!
Reverence to her, reverence, *yea* reverence!
24 To the goddess who among all created beings
Stands firm with the form of Faith,
Reverence to her, *yea*, reverence to her!
Reverence to her, reverence, *yea* reverence!
25 To the goddess who among all created beings
Stands firm with the form of Loveliness,
Reverence to her, *yea* reverence to her!
Reverence to her, reverence, *yea* reverence!
26 To the goddess who among all created beings
Stands firm with the form of Good-Fortnne,
Reverence to her, *yea* reverence to her!
Reverence to her, reverence, *yea* reverence! *
27 To the goddess who among all created beings
Stands firm with the form of Activity,
Reverence to her, *yea* reverence to her!
Reverence to her, reverence, *yea* reverence!
28 To the goddess who among all created beings
Stands firm with the form of Memory,
Reverence to her, *yea* reverence to her!
Reverence to her, reverence, *yea* reverence!
29 To the goddess who among all created beings
Stands firm with the form of Mercy,
Reverence to her, *yea* reverence to her!
Reverence to her, reverence, *yea* reverence! †
30 To the goddess who among all created beings
Stands firm with the form of Contentment,
Reverence to her, *yea* reverence to her!
Reverence to her, reverence, *yea* reverence!
31 To the goddess who among all created beings

* The Bombay edition inserts here a similar verse, invoking the goddess in the form of Steadfastness (*dhṛiti*).

† After this verse and after verse 30 the Bombay edition inserts two similar verses, invoking the goddess in the form of Good Policy (*níti*) and Nourishment (*pushṭi*) respectively.

Stands firm with the form of Mother,
Reverence to her, *yea* reverence to her!
Reverence to her, reverence, *yea* reverence!

32 To the goddess who among all created beings
Stands firm with the form of Error,
Reverence to her, *yea* reverence to her!
Reverence to her, reverence, *yea* reverence!

33 To her who both governs the organs of sense
Of created beings, and *rules* among all
Created beings perpetually,—to her
The goddess of Pervasiveness reverence, *yea* reverence!

34 To her who exists pervading this entire
World with the form of Thinking Mind,
Reverence to her, *yea* reverence to her!
Reverence to her, reverence, *yea* reverence!

35 Praised by the gods afore-time because of eagerly-desired protection,
And waited upon by the lord of the gods *many* days,
May she, the goddess, the origin of brightness, accomplish for us
Bright things, *yea* good things, and ward off calamities!

36 And she, who is both reverenced as queen by us gods,
Who are tormented now by the arrogant Daityas,
And whom we called to mind as we bow our bodies in faith,*
She this very moment destroys † all our calamities!

The ṛishi spoke:

37 While the gods were thus engaged in *offering* hymns and
other *reverential* acts, Párvatí came there to bathe in the water
38 of the Ganges, O prince. She, the beautiful-browed, said to
those gods,—"Whom do ye, lords, hymn here?" And spring-

* *Bhakti-vinamra-múrttibhiḥ* must be taken with *asmábhir*, though it is ill-placed as the verse stands. It would be better to read the second half of the verse thus—

Yá c'a smṛitá bhakti-vinamra-múṛttibhiḥ
Sarvápadas tat-kshaṇam eva hanti naḥ.

† *Hantu*, "may she destroy," would be better than *hanti*.

ing forth from the treasure-house of her body the auspicious
39 goddess spoke—"For me this hymn is uttered by the assembled gods, who have been set at nought by the Daitya
40 S'umbha and routed in battle by Niśumbha." Because Ambiká issued forth from the treasure-house* of Párvatí's body, she is therefore named in song as Kaushikí†
41 among all the worlds. Now after she had issued forth, the other also, *even* Párvatí, became Kṛishṇá; she is celebrated as Káliká; she fixed her abode on Mount Hima-vat.

42 Thereafter C'aṇḍa, and Muṇḍa, the two servants of S'umbha and Niśumbha, saw Ambiká displaying her sublime and most
43 captivating form; and both spake out unto S'umbha;—

"What woman then, most surpassingly captivating, dwells
44 here, illuminating Mount Hima-vat, O great king? Such sublime beauty was never in sooth seen by anyone anywhere; let it be ascertained if she is any goddess, and let her be taken
45 possession of, O lord of the Asuras. A gem among women, surpassingly beautiful in body, illuminating the regions of the sky with her lustre, *there* she is then, O lord of the
46 Daityas; deign, Sir, to look at her. Moreover, whatever gems, precious stones, elephants, horses and other *valuable things* indeed exist in the three worlds, O lord, all those display their splendour at this present time in thy house.
47 Airávata, gem among elephants, has been captured from Purandara; and this Párijáta tree and also the horse Uććaiḥ-
48 śravas. Here stands the heavenly chariot yoked with swans in thy court-yard; it has been brought here, the wonderful *chariot* composed of gems, which belonged to Brahmá.
49 Here is the Nidhi Mahá-padma,‡ captured from the Lord of wealth. And the Ocean gave a garland made of filaments
50 and of undying lotus flowers. In thy house stands Varuṇa's umbrella, which streams with gold. And here is the choice
51 chariot that belonged to Prajá-pati formerly. Thou, O lord,

* *Kosha*; but *kośa* is better.

† *Kauśikí* is better. The derivation is of course absurd.

‡ See canto lxviii, verse 12.

hast carried off Death's power which is named Utkránti-dá.*
The noose of the Ocean-king is in thy brother's possession.
52 And Niśumbha has every kind of gem which is produced
in the sea. Agni also gave thee two garments which are
53 purified by fire. Thus, O lord of the Daityas, all gems
have been captured by thee; why dost thou not seize this
auspicious lady, *this* gem of womankind?"

The ṛishi spoke:

54 S'umbha, on hearing this speech then from C'aṇḍa and
Muṇḍa, sent the great Asura Su-gríva as messenger to the
55 goddess, *saying*—"Go and address her thus and thus
according to my words, and lightly conduct *the matter* so that
she may come *to me* of her own good pleasure." He went to
56 where the goddess sat on a very bright spot in the mountain
and spoke gently with mellifluous voice.

The messenger spoke:

57 O goddess! S'umbha, lord of the Daityas, is supreme lord,
over the three worlds. A messenger am I, sent by him; to
58 thy presence here I have come. Hearken to what he has
said, whose command is never resisted among all beings of
divine origin, *and* who has vanquished every foe of the
59 Daityas—"Mine are all the three worlds; obedient to my
authority are the gods, I eat every portion of the sacrifices
60 separately. The choicest gems in the three worlds are alto-
gether under my power; and so are the finest elephants and
the chariot of the lord of the gods, since I have captured
61 *them*. That gem among horses, named Uććaiḥ-śravasa, which
came forth at the churning of the sea of milk, was presented
to me by the immortals who prostrated themselves *before me*.
62 And whatever other created things in the shape of gems
existed among the gods, Gandharvas and Nágas, they *were
presented* even to me, O brilliant lady. I esteem thee
63 O goddess, to be the gem of womankind in the world; do

* "Giving an exit," "granting departure."

thou, *who art* such, approach unto me, since I am an enjoyer
64 of gems. Either to me, or to my younger brother Niśumbha
of wide-reaching prowess, approach thou, O lady of quick
65 side-glances, since thou art in truth a gem. Supreme
dominion beyond compare thou shalt gain by wedding me.
Understand and consider this, and come unto wedlock with
me!"

The ṛishi spoke:

66 Thus accosted the goddess, smiling deeply within *herself*,
she, Durgá the adorable *and* good, who supports this world,
sang *this reply* then.

The goddess spoke:

67 Truly hast thou spoken; nought hast thou uttered falsely
herein. Sovereign of the three worlds is S'umbha, and like
68 unto him is Niśumbha also! But how can that which has
been promised concerning this *myself* be fulfilled falsely?
Hearken, what vow I made formerly by reason of my small
69 understanding *at that time*,—'He who vanquishes me in fight,
who forces my pride from me, *and* who is my match in
70 strength in the world, he shall be my husband.' Let S'umbha
come here then, or Niśumbha the great Asura; let him
vanquish me—what need of delay here? and let him lightly
take my hand *in marriage!*

The messenger spoke:

71 Proud art thou! Talk not so before me, O goddess!
What male in the three worlds may stand front to front with
72 S'umbha and Niśumbha? All the gods verily stand not face
to face with even the other Daityas in battle, O goddess;
how much less *canst* thou *so stand*, a woman single-handed!
73 With S'umbha and those other *Daityas*, against whom Indra
and all the other gods stood not in battle, how shalt thou,
74 a woman, venture face to face? Do thou, *being* such, to
whom I have in sooth delivered my message, go near unto
S'umbha and Niśumbha; *let it not be that* thou shalt go with

thy dignity shattered in that thou wilt be dragged *thither* by thy hair!

The goddess spoke:

75 So strong as this is S'umbha! and so exceedingly heroic is
Niśumbha! What *can* I do, since *there stands* my ill-con-
76 sidered promise of long ago? Go thou thyself; make known
respectfully to the lord of the Asuras all this that I have said
to thee, and let him do whatever is fitting.

Canto LXXXVI.

The Deví-máhátmya:

The slaying of Sumbha and Niśumbha's general Dhúmra-loc'ana.

Sumbha despatched his general Dhúmra-loc'ana and an army to capture the goddess and she destroyed them.—He then despatched C'aṇḍa and Muṇḍa with another army.

The ṛishi spoke:

1 The messenger, on hearing this speech from the goddess,
was filled with indignation, and approaching related it fully
2 to the Daitya king. The Asura monarch then, after hearing
that report from his messenger, was wroth and commanded
Dhúmra-loćana, a chieftain of the Daityas;—
3 "Ho! Dhúmra-loćana, haste thee together with thy army;
fetch by force that shrew, *who will be* unnerved when dragged
4 along by her hair. Or if any man besides stands up to offer
her deliverance, let him be slain, be he an Immortal, a Yaksha
or a Gandharva forsooth."

The ṛishi spoke:

5 Thereupon at his command the Daitya Dhúmra-loćana went
6 forthwith quickly, accompanied by sixty thousand Asuras. On
seeing the goddess stationed on the snowy mountain, he cried
aloud to her there—"Come forward to the presence of S'umbha
7 and Niśumbha; if thou wilt not, lady, approach my lord with

affection now, I *will* here take thee by force, *who wilt be* unnerved since thou shalt be dragged along by thy hair!"

The goddess spoke:

8 Sent by the king of the Daityas, mighty *thyself*, and accompanied by an army, thou dost thus take me by force—then what *can* I do unto thee?

The ṛishi spoke:

9 At this reply the Asura Dhúmra-loćana rushed towards her.
10 Then Ambiká with a mere roar reduced him to ashes. And
the great army of Asuras enraged poured on Ambiká a shower
11 both of sharp arrows and of javelins and axes. The lion that
carried* the goddess, shaking his mane in anger and uttering a
12 most terrific roar, fell on the army of Asuras; he slaughtered
some Asuras with a blow from his fore-paw, and others
with his mouth, *and* others, very great Asuras, by striking
13 them with his hind foot.† The lion with his claws tore out
the entrails of some, and struck their heads off with a cuff-like
14 blow. And he severed arms and heads from others, and
shaking his mane drank the blood *that flowed* from the entrails‡
15 of others. In a moment all that army was brought to destruction by the high-spirited lion, who bore the goddess *and* who was enraged exceedingly.
16 When he heard that that Asura Dhúmra-loćana was slain
by the goddess, and all his army besides was destroyed by the
17 goddess' lion, S'umbha, the lord of the Daityas, fell into a
rage and his lip quivered greatly, and he commanded the two
18 mighty Asuras C'aṇḍa and Muṇḍa,—"Ho, C'aṇḍa! Ho, Muṇḍa!
take with you a multitude of troops and go there; and going
19 there bring her here speedily, dragging her by her hair or
binding her; if ye have a doubt of that, then let her be slain
outright in fight by all the Asuras brandishing all their
20 weapons. When that shrew is slain and her lion striken down,
seize her, Ambiká, bind her and bring her quickly!"

* *Tu váhanaḥ* in the Bombay edition is better than *sva-váhanaḥ*.

† *C'araṇena* of the Bombay edition is better than *c'ádhareṇa*.

‡ For *kaushṭhád* read *koshṭhád*.

Canto LXXXVII.

The Deví-máhátmya.

The slaying of C'aṇḍa and Muṇḍa.

The goddess Kálí destroyed the second Asura army and also the generals C'aṇḍa and Muṇḍa—C'aṇḍiká gave Kálí as a reward the name C'ámuṇḍá.

The ṛishi spoke:

1 Then at his command the Daityas, led by C'aṇḍa and
Muṇḍa, *and* arrayed in the four-fold order of an army, march-
2 ed with weapons uplifted. Soon they saw the goddess, slightly
smiling, seated upon the lion, on a huge golden peak of the
3 majestic mountain. On seeing her some of them made a
strenuous effort to capture her, and others approached her
holding their bows bent and their swords drawn.

4 Thereat Ambiká uttered her wrath aloud against those foes,
5 and her countenance then grew dark as ink in her wrath. Out
from the surface of her forehead, which was rugged with
frowns, issued suddenly Kálí of the terrible countenance,
6 armed with a sword and noose, bearing a many-coloured
skull-topped staff,* decorated with a garland of skulls, clad in
a tiger's skin, very appalling because of her emaciated flesh,
7 exceedingly wide of mouth, lolling out her tongue terribly,
having deep-sunk reddish eyes, *and* filling the regions of the
8 sky with her roars. She fell upon the great Asuras impetuous-
ly, dealing slaughter among the host, and devoured that army
9 of the gods' foes there. Taking up the elephants with one
hand she flung them into her mouth, together with their rear-
10 men and drivers and their warrior-riders and bells. Flinging
likewise warrior with his horses, *and* chariot with its driver
into her mouth, she ground them most frightfully with her
11 teeth. She seized one by the hair, and another by the neck;
and she kicked another with her foot, and crushed another
12 against her breast. And she seized with her mouth the

* For *khaṭṭáṅga* read *khaṭváṅga* here and again in verse 14.

weapons and the great arms which those Asuras abandoned,
13 and crunched them up with her teeth in her fury. She
crushed all that host of mighty and high-spirited Asuras;
14 and devoured some and battered others; some were slain with
her sword, some were struck with her skull-topped staff, and
other Asuras met their death being wounded with the edge of
her teeth.

15 Seeing all that host of Asuras laid low in a moment,
C'aṇḍa rushed against her, Kálí, who was exceedingly appal-
16 ling. Muṇḍa the great Asura covered her, the terrible-eyed
goddess, with very terrible showers of arrows and with dis-
17 cuses hurled in thousands. Those discuses seemed to be
penetrating her countenance in multitudes, like as very many
solar orbs *might penetrate* the body of a thunder-cloud.
18 Thereat Kálí, who was roaring frightfully, laughed terribly
with excessive fury, showing the gleam of her unsightly teeth
19 within her dreadful mouth. And the goddess, mounting upon
her great lion, rushed at C'aṇḍa, and seizing him by his hair
20 struck off his head with her sword. And Muṇḍa also rushed
at her when he saw C'aṇḍa laid low; him also she felled to the
21 ground, stricken with her scymitar in her fury. Then the army,
so much as escaped unslain, seeing C'aṇḍa laid low and most
valiant Muṇḍa also, seized with panic fled in all directions.

22 And Kálí, holding C'aṇḍa's head and Muṇḍa also, approached
C'aṇḍiká and said, her voice mingled with passionate loud
23 laughter—"Here I have brought thee C'aṇḍa and Muṇḍa, two
great beasts; thou thyself shalt slay S'umbha and Niśumbha
in the battle-sacrifice."

The ṛishi spoke:

24 Thereon, seeing those two great Asuras C'aṇḍa and Muṇḍa
brought *to her*, auspicious C'aṇḍiká spoke to Kálí *this* witty
25 speech,* "Because thou hast seized both C'aṇḍa and Muṇḍa
and brought *them*, thou, O goddess, shalt therefore be famed
in the world by the name C'ámuṇḍá!"

* *Lalitam vac'aḥ*; *a bon mot.*

Canto LXXXVIII.

The Deví-máhátmya.

The slaying of Rakta-víja.

Sumbha sent forth all his armies against C'aṇḍiká—To help her the Energies (Saktis) of the gods took bodily shape—C'aṇḍiká despatched Siva to offer terms of peace to Sumbha, but the Asura hosts attacked her and the battle began—C'aṇḍiká's fight with the great Asura Rakta-víja is described—He was killed.

The ṛishi spoke:

1 After both the Daitya C'aṇḍa was slain and Muṇḍa was laid
low, and many soldiers were destroyed, the lord of the Asuras,
2 majestic S'umbha, with mind overcome by wrath, gave com-
3 mand then to array all the Daitya hosts,—"Now let the
eighty-six Daityas, upraising their weapons, *march forth* with
all their forces; let the eighty-four Kambús* march forth
4 surrounded by their own forces; let the fifty Asura families
who excel in valour *go forth*; let the hundred families of
5 Dhaumras† go forth at my command. Let the Kálakas,‡ the
Daurhṛitas,§ the Mauryas,|| and the Kálakeyas,¶—let these
Asuras, hastening at my command, march forth ready for
battle."

6 After issuing these commands S'umbha, the lord of the
Asuras, who ruled with fear, went forth, attended by many

* *Kambú* means a thief or plunderer. The commentary says *Kambús* are a class of Daityas.

† "The descendants of Dhúmra." *Dhúmras* is the reading in the Bombay edition. They are a class of Daityas.

‡ A group of Dánavas.

§ The Bombay edition reads *Daurhṛidas*, "the descendants of Durhṛid."

|| "The descendants of Mura." Mura or Muru is referred to generally in connexion with Prágjyotisha; *e.g.*, Mahá-Bhárata, Sabha-P., xiii. 578; Vana-P., xii. 488; and Udyoga-P., xlvii. 1887-92: Hari-V., cxxi. 6791-6801.

¶ A group of Dánavas. They are mentioned in the Mahá-Bhárata, Sabhá-P., iv. 118; Udyoga-P., clvii. 5379: and Vana-P., c. 8691.

7 thousands of great soldiers. C'aṇḍiká, seeing that most
terrible army at hand, filled the space between the earth and
8 the firmament with the twanging of her bow-string. Thereon
her lion roared exceedingly loud, O king; and Ambiká
9 augmented* those roars with the clanging of her bell. Kálí,
filling the regions of the sky with the noise from her bow-string, from her lion and from her bell, *and* expanding her
mouth wide with her terrific roars, had the predominance.†
10 On hearing that roar which filled the four regions of the sky,
the Daitya armies enraged‡ surrounded the goddess' lion and
Kálí.

11 At this moment, O king, in order to destroy the gods' foes,
and for the well-being of the lion-like Immortals, there issued
12 forth endowed with excessive vigour and strength the
Energies§ from the bodies of Brahmá, S'iva, Guha and Vishṇu
and of Indra also, and went in the forms of those *gods* to
13 C'aṇḍiká. Whatever was the form of each god, and whatever his ornaments and vehicle, in that very *appearance* his
14 Energy advanced to fight with the Asuras. In the front of a
heavenly car drawn by swans advanced Brahmá's Energy, bearing a rosary of seeds and an earthen water-pot; she is called
15 Brahmáṇí. Maheśvara's *Energy*, seated on a bull, grasping a
fine trident, and wearing a girdle of large snakes, arrived,
16 adorned with a digit of the moon. And Kumára's *Energy*,
Ambiká, with spear in hand and riding on a choice peacock,
17 advanced in Guha's shape to attack the Daityas. Likewise
Vishṇu's Energy, seated upon Garuḍa, advanced with conch,
18 discus, club, bow and scymitar in hand. The Energy of Hari,
who assumes the peerless form of a sacrificial boar, she also

* For *c'opavṛiṁhayat* read *c'ápy avṛiṁhayat* as in the Bombay edition.

† *Jigye*; *ji* is here used by itself in the Átmane-pada. The commentary gives "vanquished *the enemies*" as an alternative translation. It mentions *jajñe* as an alternative reading, which means then "expanded her mouth wide with her terrific roars."

‡ For *sa-roshair* the Bombay edition reads *śaraughair* "with multitudes of arrows."

§ *S'aktayaḥ.*

19 advanced assuming a hog-like form. Nṛi-siṁha's *Energy*
assuming a body like Nṛi-siṁha's arrived there, *adorned* with
a cluster of constellations hurled down by the tossing of his
20 mane. Likewise Indra's *Energy*, with thunder-bolt in hand,
seated upon the lord of elephants and having a thousand eyes,
21 arrived; as *is* S'akra, such indeed was she. Then those
Energies of the gods surrounded S'iva. He said to C'aṇḍiká,
"Let the Asuras be slain forthwith through my good-will."
22 Thereupon from the goddess' body there came forth
C'aṇḍiká's Energy, most terrific, exceedingly fierce, howling
23 like a hundred jackals. And she the unconquered said to
S'iva, who was smoke-coloured and had matted locks, "Be
thou, my lord, a messenger to the presence of S'umbha and
24 Niśumbha. Say unto the two overweening Dánavas, S'umbha
and Niśumbha, and to whatever other Dánavas are assembled
25 there to do battle—'Let Indra obtain the three worlds,
let the gods be the enjoyers of the oblations; go ye to Pátála
26 if ye wish to live. Yet if through pride in your strength ye
are longing for battle, come ye on then! let my jackals be
27 glutted with your flesh.'" Because the goddess appointed
S'iva himself to be ambassador,* she has hence attained fame
as S'iva-dútí in this world.
28 Those great Asuras however, on hearing the goddess' speech
fully announced, were filled with indignation and went where†
29 Kátyáyaní‡ stood. Then, at the very first, the arrogant and
indignant foes of the Immortals in front poured on the god-
30 dess showers of arrows, javelins and spears. And gracefully
she clove those arrows, darts, discuses and axes, which were
hurled,§ with large arrows shot from her resounding bow.||
31 And in front of her stalked Kálí then, tearing the foes asunder

* For *daityena* read *dútyena* as in the Bombay edition, or perhaps *dautyena*. "with the rank of ambassador."

† *Yatra* as in the Bombay edition is better than *yataḥ*.

‡ A name of C'aṇḍiká.

§ For *pratihán* read *prahitán*.

|| *Dhmáta-dhanur-muktair*; the commentary explains *dhmáta* as *maurví-ṭaṁ-káreṇa śabditam*, "resonant with the twanging of the bow string."

with the onset of her darts and crushing them with her skull-
32 topped staff.* And Brahmáṇí caused the foes to lose their
courage by casting water *on them* from her earthen pot, *and*
33 weakened their vigour, by whatever *way* she ran. Maheś-
wara's *Energy* slew Daityas with her trident, and Vishṇu's
Energy with her discus, and Kumára's *Energy*, very wrathful,
34 slew them with her javelin. Torn to pieces by the down-
rush of the thunder-bolt *hurled* by Indra's *Energy*, Daityas and
Dánavas fell on the earth in hundreds, pouring out streams
35 of blood. Shattered by the hog-embodied *Energy* with blows
from her snout, wounded in their breasts by the points of her
36 tushes, and torn by her discus, *demons* fell down. And Nṛi-
siṁha's *Energy* roamed about in the battle, devouring other
great Asuras who were torn by her claws, as she filled the
37 intermediate region of the sky with her roaring.† Asuras,
demoralized by S'iva-dúti with her violent loud laughs, fell
down on the earth; she then devoured those fallen ones.
38 Seeing the enraged band of Mothers‡ crushing the great
Asuras thus by various means, the troops of the gods' foes
perished.

39 Rakta-víja, a great Asura, seeing the Daityas, who were
hard-pressed by the band of Mothers, intent on fleeing, strode
40 forward to fight in wrath. When from his body there falls
to the ground a drop of blood, at that moment starts up from
41 the earth an Asura of his stature. He, a great Asura, with
club in hand fought with Indra's Energy, and Indra's *Energy*
42 then struck Rakta-víja with her thunder-bolt; blood flowed
quickly from him when wounded by the thunder-bolt. There-
upon stood up together *fresh* combatants, like him in body,
43 like him in valour; *for* as many blood-drops fell from his
body, so many men came into being, like him in courage,
44 strength and valour. And those men also who sprang from
his blood fought there with the Mothers *in a combat*, dreadful
45 because of the sweep of their very sharp weapons. And again

* For *khaṭṭáṅga* read *khaṭváṅga*.

† *Nádápúrṇa-dig-antará*. The reading of the Calcutta edition *nádápúrṇa-dig-ambará* is hardly satisfactory.

‡ *Mátṛi-gaṇa*; *i.e.*, the Energies.

when his head was wounded by the fall of her thunder-bolt,
his blood poured forth; therefrom were born men by thou-
46 sands. And Vishṇu's *Energy* struck at this *foe* with her discus
in the battle. Indra's *Energy* beat that lord of the Asuras
47 with her club. The world was filled by the thousands of
great Asuras, who were his equals, *and* who sprang from the
blood that flowed from him when cloven by the discus of
48 Vishṇu's *Energy*. Kumára's *Energy* struck the great Asura
Rakta-víja with her spear, and Varáha's *Energy* also *struck*
him with her sword, *and* Maheśvara's *Energy* with her trident.
49 And the Daitya Rakta-víja, *that* great Asura, filled full of
wrath, struck every one of the Mothers in turn with his club.
50 By the stream of blood, which fell on the earth from him
when he received many wounds from the spears, darts and
other *weapons*, Asuras came verily* into being in hundreds.
51 And those Asuras who sprang from *that* Asura's blood pervaded
the whole world; thereat the gods fell into the utmost terror.
52 Seeing the gods dejected, C'aṇḍika spoke with haste; she said
53 to Kálí, "O C'ámuṇḍá! stretch out thy mouth wide; with this
mouth do thou quickly take in the great Asuras, which are
the drops of blood, that have come into being out of Rakta-
54 víja† at the descent of my weapon *on him*. Roam about in
the battle, devouring the great Asuras who sprang from him;
so shall this Daitya with his blood ebbing away meet destruc-
55 tion. *These* fierce *demons* are being devoured by thee and at
the same time no others will be produced."

Having enjoined her thus, the goddess next smote him with
56 her dart. Kálí swallowed Rakta-víja's blood with her mouth.
57 Then he struck C'aṇḍiká with his club there; and the blow of
his club caused her no pain, even the slightest, but from his
58 stricken body blood flowed copiously, *and* from whatever
direction it came, C'ámuṇḍá takes it then with her mouth. The
great Asuras, who sprang up from the flow of blood in her
59 mouth, C'ámuṇḍá both devoured them and quaffed his blood.
The goddess smote Rakta-víja with her dart, her thunder-bolt,

* For *yodhai* read *yo vai* as in the Bombay edition.

† For *Rakta-vindoḥ* read *Rakta-víját*, as in the Bombay edition.

60 arrows, swords and spears, when C'ámuṇḍá drank up his blood.
Stricken with *that* multitude of weapons, he fell on the earth's
61 surface, and the great Asura Rakta-víja became blood-less,
O king. Thereat the thirty gods gained joy unparalleled,
O king. The band of Mothers which sprang from them
broke into a dance, being intoxicated with blood.

Canto LXXXIX.

The Deví-máhátmya.

The slaying of Niśumbha.

Niśumbha attacked the goddess C'aṇḍiká and was worsted in single combat.—Sumbha came to his help, but the goddess foiled him, and slew Niśumbha—Numbers of the Asuras were destroyed.

The king spoke:

1 Wonderful is this that thou, Sir, hast related to me,
the majesty of the goddess' exploits in connexion with
2 the slaying of Rakta-víja; and I wish to hear further what
deed did S'umbha do after Rakta-víja was killed, and *what*
the very irascible Niśumbha *did*.

The ṛishi spoke:

3 After Rakta-víja was slain and other *demons* were killed
in the fight, the Asura S'umbha gave way to unbounded wrath,
4 and Niśumbha also. Pouring out his indignation at behold-
ing his great army being slaughtered, Niśumbha then rushed
5 forward with the flower of the Asura army. In front of him
and behind and on both sides great Asuras, biting their lips
6 and enraged, advanced to slay the goddess. S'umbha also went
forward, mighty in valour, surrounded with his own troops,
to slay C'aṇḍiká in his rage, after engaging in battle with
7 the Mothers. Then occurred a desperate combat between
the goddess and S'umbha and Niśumbha, who both, like two

thunder-clouds, rained a most tempestuous shower of arrows
8 on her. C'aṇḍiká with multitudes of arrows quickly split
the arrows shot by them, and smote the two Asura lords on
their limbs with her numerous weapons.

9 Niśumbha grasping a sharp scymitar and glittering shield
struck the lion, the noble *beast* that bore the goddess, on the
10 head. When her animal was struck, the *goddess* quickly
clove Niśumbha's superb sword with a horse-shoe-shaped
arrow, and also his shield on which eight moons were pour-
11 trayed. When his shield was cloven and his sword too, the
Asura hurled his spear; and that his *missile* also, as it came
12 towards her, she split in two with her discus. Then Niśum-
bha, the Dánava, puffed up with wrath, seized a dart; and
that also, when it came, the goddess shattered with a blow of
13 her fist. And then aiming* his club he flung it against
C'aṇḍiká, yet that was shivered by the goddess' trident and
14 became ashes. As that lordly Daitya then advanced with
battle-axe in hand, the goddess struck him with a multi-
tude of arrows and laid him low on the ground.

15 When his brother Niśumbha, who was terrible in prowess,
fell to the ground, *S'umbha* in utmost fury strode forward to
16 slay Ambiká. And he, standing in his chariot, appeared to
fill the entire sky with his eight arms, which were *lifted* far
on high grasping his superb weapons.

17 Beholding him approaching, the goddess sounded her
conch, and made her bow also give forth from its string a
18 note which was exceedingly hard to endure. And she filled
all regions with the clanging of her bell, which caused
19 the vigour of all the Daitya hosts to die away. Then her
lion filled the heaven, the earth and the ten regions of the
sky with loud roars, which checked the copious flow of
20 the exudation from the *demons'* rutting elephants. Kálí
springing upward then struck the heaven and the earth with
21 both her hands; the boom thereof drowned those previous
sounds. S'iva-dútí† uttered a loud inauspicious laugh. At

* *Ávidhya.* The Bombay edition reads *ádáya,* "taking."

† *I. e.,* C'aṇḍiká; see canto lxxxviii, verse 27.

those sounds the Asuras trembled; * S'umbha gave way
22 to utmost rage. When Ambiká cried out "Stand, O evil-
souled! stand!" the gods who had taken their stations in the
air then called *to her*, "Be thou victorious!"

23 The spear flaming most terribly, which S'umbha approaching
hurled, that, gleaming like a mass of fire as it came along, was
24 driven aside by a great fire-brand. The vault between the
three worlds reverberated with S'umbha's lion-like roaring, *but*
the dreadful sound of the slaughter *among his soldiers* sur-
25 passed that, O king. The goddess split the arrows shot by
S'umbha, and S'umbha the arrows that she discharged, *each*
with *her and his* sharp arrows in hundreds and thousands.
26 C'aṇḍiká enraged thereat smote him with a dart. Wounded
therewith he fell in a faint to the ground.

27 Thereupon Niśumbha, regaining consciousness, seized his bow
again and struck the goddess, *and* Kálí and the lion with
28 arrows. And the Dánava lord, *that* son of Diti, putting forth
a myriad arms, again covered C'aṇḍiká with a myriad discuses.†
29 The goddess then enraged, *she*, Durgá who destroys the afflic-
tions of adversity, split those discuses and those arrows with
30 her own arrows. Then Niśumbha seizing his club rushed
impetuously at C'aṇḍiká to slay her outright, with the Daitya
31 host surrounding him. As he was just falling upon *her*,
C'aṇḍiká swiftly clove his club with her sharp-edged scymi-
32 tar. And he took hold of a dart. C'aṇḍiká with a dart
hurled swiftly pierced Niśumbha, the afflicter of the Immor-
tals, in the heart, as he approached with dart in hand.
33 When he was pierced by the dart, out of his heart issued
another man of great strength and great valour, exclaiming
34 "Stand!" When he stepped forth, the goddess laughing aloud
then struck off his head with her scymitar; thereupon he
fell to the ground.

35 The lion then devoured those Asuras whose necks he had
crushed with his savage teeth, and Kálí and S'iva-dútí *de-*
36 *voured* the others. Some great Asuras perished, being

* For *Asurástreshu* read *Asurás tresuḥ* as in the Bombay edition.

† For *c'akráyudhena* read *c'akráyutena* as in the Bombay edition.

pierced through by the spear *held* by Kumára's *Energy;*
others were driven back by the water purified by the spell
37 *uttered* by Brahmá's *Energy*; and others fell, pierced by the
trident *wielded* by S'iva's *Energy;* some were pounded to
dust on the ground by blows from the snout of Varáha's
38 *Energy;* some Dánavas were cut to pieces by the discus
hurled by Vishṇu's *Energy;* and others again by the thunder-
39 bolt discharged from the fingers of Indra's *Energy.* Some
Asuras perished outright, some perished by reason of the
great battle, and others were devoured by Kálí, S'iva-dútí
and the lion.

Canto XC.

The Deví-máhátmya.

The slaying of Sumbha.

Ambiká absorbed all the other goddesses, and fighting with Sumbha in single combat, killed him.—The universe was then filled with joy.

The ṛishi spoke:

1 Seeing his brother Niśumbha slain, who was dear to him
as his life, and his army being slaughtered, S'umbha in
2 wrath spoke thus—"O Durgá, who art tainted with the
arrogance of strength, bring not thy pride *here*, thou who,
trusting in the strength of the other *goddesses*, dost fight in
exceeding haughtiness!"

The goddess spoke:

3 Alone verily am I in the world here; what other *goddess* is there besides me? See, vile one! that these *goddesses*, who have their divine power from me, are entering into me indeed.

4 Then all those goddesses, Brahmáṇí and the others, became absorbed into the goddess' breasts; Ambiká then remained alone indeed.

The goddess spoke:

5 Whereas I existed* with my divine power in many forms here—that has been drawn in by me, truly alone I stand *now.* Be thou steadfast in combat!

The ṛishi spoke:

6 Thereupon commenced a battle between them both, the
goddess and S'umbha, while all the gods and the Asuras
7 looked on—*a battle* without quarter. With showers of arrows,
with sharp weapons and also with pitiless missiles both
engaged anew in a combat which set all the world in fear.
8 And the lord of the Daityas broke the heavenly missiles,
which Ambiká discharged in hundreds, with *weapons* that
9 parried them. And the supreme goddess in merest play
broke the heavenly missiles that he discharged, with fierce
10 shouts, ejaculations and other *sounds.* Then the Asura
covered the goddess with hundreds of arrows, and the god-
dess enraged thereat split his bow also with her arrows.
11 And when his bow was split the lord of the Daityas took
up his spear. The goddess split it, as he held it in his
12 hand, with a discus. Next the supreme monarch of the
Daityas, seizing his scymitar and sun-like *shield,* on which
a hundred moons were pourtrayed, rushed at the goddess†
13 at that monent. Just as he was falling upon her, C'aṇḍiká
hastily split his scymitar with sharp arrows shot from her
bow, and his shield *also* which was spotless as the sun's rays.
14 With his steeds wounded, with his bow split, without a
charioteer, the Daitya then‡ grasped his terrible mace, being
15 ready to slay Ambiká. As he was falling upon her, she clove
his mace with sharp arrows; nevertheless raising his fist
16 he rushed swiftly at her. The lordly Daitya brought his
fist down on the goddess' heart, and the goddess also smote
17 him on his breast with her palm. Wounded by the blow of

* For *yadá sthitá* read *yad ásthitá* as in the Bombay edition.

† For *deví* read *devím.* The Bombay edition reads *taṁ hantum.*

‡ For *sadá read tadá.*

her palm the Daitya king fell suddenly on the earth; and
18 again indeed he rose up, and springing upward he seized
the goddess and mounted on high into the sky. There also
19 C'aṇḍiká, being without any support, fought with him. The
Daitya and C'aṇḍiká then fought at first with each other in
the sky in a close combat, which wrought dismay among the
20 Siddhas and munis; after carrying on the close combat for a
very long time with him, Ambiká lifted him up then and
21 whirled him around *and* flung him on the earth. When flung
thus he touched the earth, he raised his fist hastily and
rushed, evil of soul *as he was*, with the wish to kill C'aṇḍiká.
22 Seeing him, the lord of all the Daitya folk, approaching,
the goddess then pierced him in the breast with a dart and
23 felled him down on the earth. Shattered by the point
of the goddess' dart he fell lifeless on the ground, shaking
the whole earth and its seas, islands and mountains.
24 When that evil-souled *demon* was slain, the universe
became placid, the earth regained perfect well-being, and the
25 sky grew pure. Portent-clouds, which were full of flame
before, became tranquil, and the rivers kept within their
26 channels, when he was stricken down there. All the bands
of gods then grew exceedingly joyful in mind, when he was
27 slain; the Gandharvas sang out sweetly, and others *of*
them sounded their instruments, and the bevies of Apsarases
danced; and favourable breezes blew, very brilliant grew the
sun, and the tranquil sacred fires blazed *freely*, and tranquil
became the *strange* sounds that had occurred in the regions
of the sky.

CANTO XCI.

The Deví-máhátmya.

The Eulogy of the Goddess.

The gods offered a hymn of praise to the goddess.—She granted them the boon that she will always become incarnate and deliver the world whenever it is oppressed by demons.

The ṛishi spoke:

1 When the great lord of the Asuras was slain there by the goddess, Indra and the other gods led by Agni offered praise to her, Kátyáyaní, because they had gained their desire;* and their faces shone forth, and their hopes became manifest.†

2 "O goddess, who removest the sufferings of thy suppliants, be gracious!
Be gracious, O mother of the whole world!
Be gracious, O queen of the universe! safeguard the universe!
Thou, O goddess, art queen of *all* that is moveable and immoveable!

3 Thou alone hast become the support of the world,
Because thou dost subsist in the form of the earth!
By thee, who existest in the form of water, all
This *universe* is filled, O thou inviolable in thy valour!

4 Thou art Vishṇu's energy, boundless in thy valour;
Thou art the germ of the universe, *thou art* Illusion sublime!
All this *world* has been bewitched, O goddess;
Thou indeed when attained‡ art the cause of final emancipation from existence on the earth!

5 All sciences are portions of thee, O goddess;
So are all females without exception in the worlds§!
By thee alone, as mother, this world has been filled!
What praise *can there be* for thee? *Thou art* beyond praise, the sublimest expression‖!

* For *ishṭa-lambhád* read *ishṭa-lábhád* with the Bombay edition.

† The Bombay edition reads *vikáśi-vaktrábja-vikáśitáśáḥ*, which means much the same.

‡ *Prapanná*; but *prasanná*, "well-pleased," in the Bombay edition is better.

§ The Bombay edition reads—

striyaḥ samastáḥ sakalaṁ jagac' c'a.

"*So are* all females, and *so is* the whole world."

‖ *Paroktiḥ*; or "the expression of the sublime."

6 When *as being* the goddess, who constitutes every created thing,
And who bestows Svarga and final emancipation from existence,
Thou are praised—for thy praise again
What sublime words can be sufficient?

7 O thou, who abidest under the form of Intelligence
In the heart of every living creature;
O goddess, who bestowest Svarga and final emancipation from existence,
O Náráyaṇí, reverence be to thee!

8 Thou in the form of minutes, moments and other *portions of time*,
Dost bring resnlts to pass;
O thou who art mighty in the death of the universe,
O Náráyaṇí, reverence be to thee!

9 O thou who art beneficent with every happiness,
O *lady* auspicious, who accomplishest every petition,
O giver of refuge, O Tryambaká, O brilliant one,
O Náráyaṇí, reverence be to thee!

10 O eternal goddess, who constitutest the energy
Of creation, permanence and destruction,
O *thou* abode of good qualities, who consistest of good qualities,
O Náráyaṇí, reverence be to thee! *

11 O thou who ridest in a heavenly car yoked with swans,
Who assumest the form of Brahmáṇí,†
O goddess who sprinklest kuśa-grass-steeped water,‡
O Náráyaṇí, reverence be to thee!

12 O thou who holdest a trident, the moon and a serpent,

* The Bombay edition inserts a verse here—

O thou who art the Supreme Way for the salvation
Of those that seek refuge, of the woe-begone and of the afflicted,
O goddess who takest suffering away from every one,
O Náráyaṇí, reverence be to thee!

† The Energy (*śakti, fem.*) of Brahmá. The swan is his vehicle.

‡ The Commentary translates *ksharikâ* as *kshepaṇa-káriṇí* or *á-sektrí*.

Who art borne on a huge bull,
With the natural character of Máheśvarí,*
O Náráyaṇí, reverence be to thee!

13 O thou who art attended by the peacock and cock,
Who bearest a great spear, O sinless one;
O thou who takest thy station in Kaumárí's† form,
O Náráyaṇí, reverence be to thee!

14 O thou who holdest as thy finest weapons
A conch, discus, club, and the bow S'árṅga,
Be gracious, O thou who hast Vaishṇaví's‡ form;
O Náráyaṇí, reverence be to thee!

15 O thou who graspest a huge formidable discus,
Who hast uplifted the earth with thy tushes,
O auspicious one, who hast a hog-like form,§
O Náráyaṇí, reverence be to thee!

16 O thou who in the fierce man-lion|| form
Didst put forth thy efforts to slay the Daityas,
O thou who art connected¶ with the deliverance of the three worlds,
O Náráyaṇí, reverence be to thee!

17 O thou who hast a diadem and a great thunderbolt,
Who art dazzling with a thousand eyes,
And who tookest away Vṛitra's life-breath, O Aindrí;**
O Náráyaṇí, reverence be to thee!

18 O thou who with the nature of S'iva-dútí††

* The Energy (*śakti*) of Maheśvara or S'iva. The trident, moon and serpent are his emblems and ornaments, and the bull is his vehicle.

† The Energy of Kumára or Kárttikeya. The peacock is his vehicle, and the cock is an attendant of his parents, S'iva and Párvatí.

‡ The Energy of Vishṇu. The conch, discus, club and bow are his weapons.

§ The Energy of Vishṇu in his incarnation as a boar.

|| The Energy of Vishṇu in his incarnation as a lion-headed man.

¶ Another reading is *Trailokya-tráṇa-mahite,* "O thou who art honoured with the deliverance of the three worlds."

** The Energy (*śakti*) of Indra, the slayer of Vṛitra. The diadem is his ornament, the thunder-bolt his weapon, and he has a thousand eyes.

†† See canto lxxxvii, verse 25.

Slewest the mighty hosts of the Daityas,
O thou of terrible form, of loud shrieks,
O Náráyaṇí, reverence be to thee!
19 O thou who hast a face formidable with tushes,
Who art decorated with a garland of heads,
O C'ámuṇḍá, who grindest shaven heads,
O Náráyaṇí, reverence be to thee!
20 O Lakshmí, Modesty, Wide-Knowledge!
O Faith, Nourishment, Svadhá, Immoveable!
O Great-Night, Great-Illusion!*
O Náráyaṇí, reverence be to thee!
21 O Mental-Vígour, Sarasvatí, Choice One!
O Welfare, Wife of Babhru,† Dark One!
O Self-controlled Queen, be thou gracious!
O Náráyaṇí, reverence be to thee!‡
22 O thou who hast the nature of all, Queen of all!
O thou who possessest the might of all!
From terrors save us, O goddess!
O goddess Durgá, reverence be to thee!
23 Kindly is this thy countenance,
Which is adorned with three eyes;
May it guard us from all created things!
O Kátyáyaní, reverence be to thee!
24 Formidable with flames, exceedingly sharp,
Destroying the Asuras without quarter,
May thy trident guard us from fear!
O Bhadra-kálí, reverence be to thee!
25 Thy *bell*, that fills the world with its ringing
And destroys the glories of the Daityas,
May thy bell guard us, O goddess,

* The Calcutta edition reads "Wide-knowledge" again here.

† *I.e.*, S'iva.

‡ The Bombay edition inserts a verse here—

O thou, the limit of whose hands and feet is everywhere,
Whose eyes and head and mouth are everywhere,
Whose ears and nose are everywhere;
O Náráyaṇí, reverence be to thee!

Even us like children from sins!
26 Besmirched with the blood and fat of the Asuras
As with mire, gleaming with rays,
May thy scymitar be for our welfare!
O C'aṇḍiká, to thee we bow!
27 Thou destroyst all sicknesses, when gratified;
But when wrathful *destroyest* all longed-for desires.
No calamity *befalls* men who have sought unto thee!
They who have sought unto thee become verily a refuge *themselves!*
28 This slaughter that thou hast now wrought
On the great Asuras who hate righteousness, O goddess,
By multiplying thy body in many forms,—
O Ambiká, what other *goddess* achieves that?
29 In the sciences, in the scriptures, which need the lamp of discrimination,
And in the ancient sayings, who but thou
Within the pit of selfishness, wherein is exceeding great darkness,
Causes this universe to whirl about most grievously?
30 Wherever *dwell* Rákshasas and virulently-poisonous Nágas,
Wherever foes *exist*, wherever the powers of the Dasyus,
And where flaming fire *appears* amid the ocean,
There abiding thou dost safeguard the universe!
31 O queen of the universe, thou safeguardest the universe!
Thou hast the nature of the universe, for thou upholdest the universe.
Thou art the lady worthy to be praised by the lord of the universe. They are
The refuge of the universe, who bow in faith before thee!
32 O goddess, be gracious! Protect us wholly from fear of our foes
Perpetually, as *thou hast* at this very time *saved us* promptly by the slaughter of the Asuras!*
And bring thou quickly to rest the sins of all the worlds

* For *yathá sura-badhád* read *yathásura-badhád.*

And the great calamities which have sprung from the maturing of portents!

33 To *us* who are prostrate be thou gracious,
O goddess, who takest away affliction from the universe!
O thou worthy of praise from the dwellers in the three worlds,
Bestow thou boons on the worlds!"

The goddess spoke:

34 I *am ready to* bestow a boon. O ye hosts of gods, choose whatever boon ye desire in your mind; I grant it as a thing that benefits the worlds.

The gods spoke:

35 O queen of all, complete thou* thus indeed the pacification of every trouble of the three worlds, and the destruction of our enemies.

The goddess spoke:

36 When the twenty-eighth age has arrived, in the Vaivasvata
Manv-antara, two other great Asuras shall be born, S'umbha
37 and Niśumbha. Then born as the offspring of Yaśodá's womb
in the cowherd Nanda's house, *and* dwelling on the Vindhya
38 mountains, I will destroy them both. And again becoming
incarnate in a very terrible form on the face of the earth, I
39 will slay the Vaiprac'itta† Dánavas; and when I devour those
fierce and great Vaiprac'itta Asuras, my teeth shall become
40 red like the flowers of the pomegranate. Hence the gods
in Svarga and men in the world of mortals praising me shall
always talk of me as "Red-toothed."‡
41 And again after a period of a hundred years during which
rain and water shall fail, praised by the munis I shall be
42 born, but not womb-begotten, on the earth. Then because
I shall behold the munis with a hundred eyes, mankind shall
therefore celebrate me as "Hundred-eyed."§

* For *tvathá* read *tvayá*.

† The descendants of Viprac'itti.

‡ *Rakta-dantiká.*

§ *S'atákshí.*

43 Next, O ye gods, I shall support* the whole world with the
life-sustaining vegetables, which shall grow out of my own
44 body, during a period of heavy rain. I shall gain fame on
the earth then as S'ákambharí; † and in that very period I
shall slay the great Asura named Durgama.

45 And again when taking a terrible form on mount Himavat I
shall destroy Rákshasas for the sake of delivering the munis,
46 all the munis bowing their bodies reverently shall laud me
then; hence my name "The terrible goddess"‡ shall become
celebrated.

47 When Aruṇáksha§ shall work great trouble in the three
worlds, I shall take a bee-like form, *the form* of innumerable
48 bees, and shall slay the great Asura for the welfare of the
three worlds, and folk shall then extol me everyone as
Bhrámarí.||

49 Thus whenever trouble shall arise caused by the Dánavas,
at each such time I shall become incarnate and accomplish
the foes' destruction.

Canto XCII.

The Deví-máhátmya.

The slaying of Sumbha and Niśumbha concluded.

The goddess descants on the merits of this poem and the beneficent results of reading and listening to it.—The gods regained their rights and the Daityas departed to Pátála.—Her attributes and beneficence are extolled.

* *I.e.*, nourish.

† "Herb-bearing" or "Herb-nourishing."

‡ *Bhímá Deví.*

§ Or *Aruṇákhya* in the Bombay edition; "When the *Asura* named Aruṇa shall work, &c."

|| "The bee-like *goddess*."

The goddess spoke:

1 And whoever with mind composed shall praise me constant-
ly with these hymns, I will quiet down every trouble for him
2 assuredly. And those who shall celebrate the destruction of
Madhu and Kaiṭabha, the slaughter of the Asura Mahisha,
3 and the slaying of S'umbha and Niśumbha likewise; and
those also who shall listen* in faith to *this poem of* my
sublime majesty on the eighth day *of the lunar fortnight,* on
4 the fourteenth and on the ninth, with intent mind, to them
shall happen no wrong-doing whatever, nor calamities that
arise from wrong-doing, nor poverty, nor indeed deprivation of
5 their desires.† Never shall he experience fear from enemies,
from robbers, nor from kings, nor from weapon or fire or
6 water-flood. Hence this *poem of* my majesty must be read
by men of composed minds and listened to by them always
7 with faith, for it is the supreme course of blessings. Now
may *this poem of* my majesty quell all kinds of calamities,
which arise from grievous pestilence,‡ and the three-fold
8 portent. Where this *poem* is duly read constantly at my
sanctuary, I will never forsake that *place, and* there my
9 presence is fixed. At the offering of the bali, *and* during
worship, in the ceremonies with fire, *and* at a great festival,
all this story of my exploits must verily be proclaimed and
10 listened to. I will accept with kindliness both the bali
worship that is paid, and the oblation by fire that is offered, by
11 him who understands or him who understands not. And at
the great annual worship that is performed in autumn time,
the man, who listens filled with faith to this *poem of* my
12 majesty, shall assuredly through my favour be delivered from
every tronble, *and* be blessed with riches, grain and children.
13 From listening to this *poem of* my majesty moreover *come*
splendid issues and prowess in battles, *and* a man becomes

* The Bombay edition reads *stoshyanti,* "shall celebrate in song."

† *Ishṭa-viyojana*; or "separation from loved ones." *Viyojana* is not in the dictionary.

‡ *Mahá-márí*; or "cholera."

14 fearless.* When men listen to *this poem of* my majesty,
enemies pass to destruction, and prosperity accrues and their
15 family rejoices. Let *a man* listen to *this poem of* my majesty
everywhere, at a ceremony for securing tranquillity, and after
seeing an ill-dream and when planets are greatly eclipsed.
16 *Thereby* portents turn into calm, and *also* dreadful eclipses of
the planets, and *also* an ill-dream which men have seen; and
17 a sweet dream appears. It produces peacefulness in children
who have been possessed by the demon that seizes children,† and
it is the best promoter of friendship among men when union
18 is dissolved; it is the most potent diminisher of the power
of all men of ill livelihood; verily through reading it, *comes*
19 the destruction of Rákshasas, goblins and Piśáćas. All this
poem of my majesty brings *a man* near unto me. And by
means of cattle, flowers, arghya offerings and incenses, and
20 by the finest perfumes and lamps, by feasts *given* to bráhmans,
by oblations, by sprinkled water day and night, and by
various other objects of enjoyment, by gifts yearly—*the*
21 *favour* which *comes by such means*, such favour is won from me
when this story of my noble exploits is once heard. When
22 heard it takes away sins and confers perfect health. *This*
celebration of me preserves created beings from *future* births,
even this story of my exploits in battles, the annihilation of
23 the wicked Daityas. When it is heard, no fear, that is
caused by enmity, springs up among men. And the hymns
which ye have composed, and those composed by bráhman
24 ṛishis, and those composed by Brahmá bestow a splendid
mind.‡ He who is surrounded by a raging fire in a forest

* The text as it stands is incorrect, for *parákrama* is masc., and *parákramam*, acc., has no verb. I have read therefore *parákramaś ća* for *parákramaṁ ća*. The Bombay edition reads *tathotpattíḥ pṛithak śubháḥ parákramáṁś ća*, and the commentary translates the verse thus—"From listening to this *poem of* my majesty, and to my splendid diverse appearances *in the forms of the Energies*, and to my feats of prowess in battles, a man becomes fearless."

† *Bála-graha*; see canto li.

‡ Or *gatim*, "course" or "issue."

25 or on a lonesome road, or who is encompassed by robbers in
a desolate spot, or who is captured by enemies, or who is
prowled after by a lion or tiger or by wild elephants in a
26 forest, or who is under the command of an enraged king,
or who is sentenced to death, or who has fallen into bonds,
or who is whirled around by the wind, *or* who stands in a
27 ship in the wide sea, or, *who is* in the most dreadful battle
with weapons falling *upon him*, or who is afflicted with pain
28 amidst all *kinds of* terrible troubles—*such* a man on calling
to mind this story of my exploits is delivered from his strait.
Through my power lions and other *dangerous beasts*, robbers
and enemies, from a distance indeed, flee from him who calls
to mind this story of my exploits.

The ṛishi spoke:

29 Having spoken thus the adorable C'aṇḍiká, who is fierce in
prowess, vanished there, while the gods were gazing indeed
30 *on her*. The gods also relieved from fear, their foes being
slain, all resumed their own dominions as before, participating
in their shares of sacrifices.

31 And the Daityas—when S'umbha, that most fierce foe of
the gods, who brought ruin on the world *and* who was peerless
32 in prowess, had been slain by the goddess in fight, and
Niśumbha also great in valour *was slain*—all came to Pátála.

Thus that adorable goddess, although everlasting, *yet*
33 taking birth again and again, accomplishes the safeguarding
of the world, O king. By her this universe is bewitched; she
34 verily gives birth to the universe. And when besought, she
bestows knowledge; when gratified, she bestows prosperity.
35 All this egg of Brahmá, O king, is pervaded by her, *who is*
Mahákálí at Máhákála,* *and* who has the nature of the Great
Destroying Goddess.† She indeed is Mahá-márí at the fated
36 time; she indeed is creation, the Unborn; she indeed the Eternal
gives stability to created beings at their fated time. She indeed

* A shrine sacred to S'iva at Ujjain; see Raghu-Vaṁśa, vi. 32–34; and Megha-Dúta i. 34.

† *Mahá-márí*; see verse 7 above.

is Lakshmí, bestowing prosperity on the houses of men while
37 she abides with *them*; and she indeed when she is absent
becomes the goddess of Ill Fortune* unto their destruction.
When hymned *and* worshipped with flowers, and with incense,
perfumes and other *offerings*, she bestows wealth and sons, and
a mind brilliant in righteousness.

Canto XCIII.

The Deví-máhátmya (concluded).

After hearing this poem, king Su-ratha and the vaiśya practised austerities and worshipped the goddess.—C'aṇḍiká appeared to them and gave the king the boon that he should be Manu Sávarṇi in a future life, and bestowed knowledge on the vaiśya.

The ṛishi spoke:

1 I have now related to thee, O king, this sublime *poem* the
Deví-máhátmya. Such majestic power has the goddess, by
2 whom this world is upheld. Moreover knowledge is conferred
by her who is the adorable Vishṇu's Illusive power. By her
thou and this vaiśya and other men of discrimination, and
3 celebrated men are bewitched; and others shall become
bewitched. Go unto her, the supreme queen, as to a place of
refuge, O great king. She indeed, when propitiated by men,
bestows enjoyment, Svarga and final emancipation from
existence.

Márkaṇḍeya spoke:

4 Having heard this his speech, king Su-ratha fell prostrate
before the illustrious ṛishi who performed severe penances,
5 and being down-cast by his excessive regard for self and
by the deprivation of his kingdom, went forthwith to per-
6 form austerities; and the vaiśya, O great muni, in order to
get a vision of Ambá, took up his station on a sand-bank

* *A-lakshmí.*

7 in a river; and the vaiśya practised austerities, muttering the
sublime hymn to the goddess. They both made an earthen
image of the goddess on that sand-bank, and paid worship
8 to it with flowers, incense, fire and libations of water. Ab-
staining from food, restricting their food, concentrating their
minds on her, keeping their thoughts composed, they both
9 offered the bali offering also sprinkled with blood drawn
from their own limbs. When they continued with subdued
souls to propitiate her thus for three years, C'aṇḍiká, who
upholds the world, well-pleased spoke in visible shape.

The goddess spoke:

10 What thou dost solicit, O king, and thou O rejoicer of thy
family, receive ye all that from me; well-pleased I bestow it.

Márkaṇḍeya spoke:

11 Then the king chose a kingdom that should not perish in
another life, and in this *life* his own kingdom wherein the
12 power of his enemies should be destroyed by force. Then
the vaiśya also, whose mind was down-cast, chose know-
ledge,—*to be* wise, knowing '*what is* mine,' *and* '*what* I
am,'—*knowledge* that causes the downfall of worldly attach-
ments.

The goddess spoke:

13 O king, thou shalt obtain thine own kingdom in a very few
days, after slaying thine enemies; it shall be steadfast for
14 thee there; and when dead thou shalt gain another life from
the god Vivasvat, and shalt be a Manu on earth, by name
15 Sávarṇika. And O excellent vaiśya, I bestow on thee the
boon which thou hast besought of me; knowledge shall be
thine unto full perfection.

Márkaṇḍeya spoke:

16 Having thus given them both the boon that each desired,
the goddess vanished forthwith, while extolled by them
both in faith.

17 Having thus gained the boon from the goddess, Su-ratha
the noble kshattriya shall obtain a new birth through the
Sun, and shall be the Manu Sávarṇi.

CANTO XCIV.

The Rauc'ya and future Manv-antaras.

Márkaṇḍeya mentions briefly the succeeding Manus, the ninth to the thirteenth, and declares what shall be the names of the gods, ṛishis and kings in their several periods.

Márkaṇḍeya spoke:

1 I have duly declared unto thee this *account of the* Sávarṇika
Manv-antara, and also the Deví-máhátmya which tells of the
2 slaughter of the Asura Mahisha. And the origins of the
Mothers also which were from the goddess in the great battle,
3 and the origin as well as the life of the goddess C'ámuṇḍá, and
the majesty of S'iva-dútí, the slaying of S'umbha and Niśum-
bha, and the killing of Rakta-víja—all this has been narrated
to thee.

4 Now hear O noble muni, of the next *Manu* Sávarṇika. And
Daksha's son shall be Sávarṇa, who *will be* the ninth Manu.
5 I tell thee about that Manu, *and* who *shall be* the gods, the
munis *and* the kings *in his period*. The Páras and the Maríćis
6 and the Bhargas and the Su-dharmans *shall be* the gods; these
shall be in threes; they shall be twelve groups in all; now
7 their lord* shall be Sahasráksha, great in power. He, who is
at present Agni's six-faced son Kárttikeya, shall be the Indra,
8 by name Adbhuta, in that Manu's period. Medhátithi, Vasu,
Satya, Jyotish-mat and Dyuti-mat, Sabala another, and Havya-
9 váhana another—*these shall be* the seven ṛishis. Dhṛishṭa-ketu,
Varha-ketu, Pańća-hasta, Nir-ámaya, Pṛithu-śravas, and
10 Arćish-mat, Bhúri-dyumna, Vṛihad-bhaya—these *shall be* the
royal sons of that son of Daksha, yea the kings.

Now hear, O bráhman, about the next Manv-antara, *that* of the
11 tenth Manu. And in the tenth Manv-antara of the wise son of
Brahmá, the Sukhásínas and the Niruddhas *shall be* the gods,
12 with three classes *each*, according to tradition; they indeed

* Indra.

shall be the gods, a hundred in number, *in the period* of *that* future Manu. As there *shall be* a hundred sons* *of his*,
13 so *shall there be* a hundred gods then. And S'ánti shall be the Indra, endowed with all Indra's good qualities. Hear thou
14 who shall indeed be the seven ṛishis then; Ápo-múrtti and Havish-mat, Su-kṛitin and Satya, Nábhága and A-pratima,
15 and Váśishṭha the seventh. And Su-kshetra and Uttamaujas and valiant Bhúmi-sena, and S'atáníka, Vṛishabha and An-
16 amitra, Jayad-ratha, Bhúri-dyumna, and Su-parvan—these shall be that Manu's sons.

17 Hear about the period of Dharma's son Sávarṇa. The Vihaṅ-gamas, and the Káma-gas and the Nirmáṇa-ratis shall be *the gods* of three kinds; each shall be a group of thirty.
18 Now the Nirmáṇa-ratis shall be those who preside over the months, seasons and days; and the Vihaṅ-gamas *shall be those who preside over* the nights;† the groups of Káma-gas
19 *shall be* those who preside over the moments.‡ Their Indra shall be named Vṛisha, celebrated for valour. And Havish-
20 mat, and Varishṭha, and another ṛishi§ Aruṇi, and Niś-ćara and An-agha, and another great muni Vishṭi, *and* Agni-deva the seventh,—these *shall be* the seven ṛishis in that period.
21 Sarvatra-ga and Su-śarman, Deváníka, Purúdvaha, Hema-dhanvan, and Dṛiḍháyu shall be the sons of that *Manu*, *yea* the kings.

22 When the twelfth Manv-antara of Rudra's son, the Manu named Sávarṇa, shall have arrived, who *shall be* the gods
23 and munis,—hear about them. The Su-dharmans, the Su-manases, the Haritas and the Rohitas and the Su-varṇas

* For *práṇinám* read *putráṇám* as in the Bombay edition.

† Both the Calcutta and Bombay editions read *rátrayo 'tha*, which is the plural of *rátri*; but this word should apparently be analogous to *mauhúrtta* in formation, and be an adjective derived from *rátri*. Perhaps the reading should be *rátrakás tu* instead.

‡ This seems to be the meaning intended by the word *mauhúrttáḥ*; but the only meaning given in the dictionary is "astrologer."

§ Both editions read *ṛishṭir*, but it can hardly be right, for it would be a proper name, and the number would then exceed seven. It seems to be a mistake for *ṛishir*.

shall be the gods therein; these five *shall be* ten-fold groups.
24 Now their Indra shall be known as Ṛita-dháman, great in
power, endowed with all Indra's good qualities. Hear from
25 me the seven ṛishis also—Dyuti, Tapas-vin, Su-tapas, Tapo-
múrtti, Tapo-nidhi, and Tapo-rati another, and Tapo-dhṛiti
26 the seventh. Deva-vat, and Upa-deva, Deva-śreshṭha, Vidú-
ratha, Mitra-vat, and Mitra-vinda, shall be the sons of that
Manu, *yea* the kings.

27 Listen while I tell thee of the *Manu's* sons and of the
seven ṛishis and of the kings in the turn of the thirteenth
28 Manu named Raućya. The gods therein *shall be* the Su-
dharmans, the Su-karmans, and the Su-śarmans the others;
29 all these verily *shall be* the gods, O best of munis. Their
Indra *shall be* Divas-pati, great in power, great in valour.
30 Now hear while I tell thee of the seven ṛishis who shall be
then—Dhṛiti-mat, and A-vyaya, Tattva-darśin, Nir-utsuka,
Nir-moha, and Su-tapas another, and Nish-prakampa the
31 seventh. C'itra-sena and Vi-ćitra, Nayati, Nir-bhaya, Dṛiḍha,
Su-netra, and Kshatra-buddhi, and Su-vrata *shall be* the sons
of that *Manu*.

Canto XCV.

The Story of Ruc'i.

A Prajá-pati named Ruc'i formerly lived in solitary discomfort—His forefathers appeared to him and urged him to marry—He demurred and they insisted on the importance of marriage.

Márkaṇḍeya spoke:

1 A Prajá-pati Rući, who was devoid of self, free from pride,
fearless and moderate in sleeping, formerly roamed this earth.
2 Seeing that he was destitute of fire, had no habitation, that
he ate but once a day, had no hermitage, *and* was cut off from
all attachments, his ancestors spoke to him, the muni.

The Pitṛis spoke:

3 Dear son, wherefore hast thou not done the sacred *deed of*
taking a wife, since that is the cause of gaining Svarga and

final emancipation from existence? without that there is
4 bondage perpetually. A house-holder by paying worship to
all the gods and the Pitṛis likewise, to ṛishis and guests, gains
5 the *heavenly* worlds. He apportions the gods *their share* by
uttering 'sváhá' aloud, the Pitṛis by uttering 'svadhá' aloud,
6 created beings and other guests by the giving of food. Being
such *a negligent one*, thou dost incur bondage by reason of
the debt due to the gods, bondage by reason of the debt due
to us also, *bondage* unto men and created beings day by day,
7 by not begetting sons, by not satisfying the gods and Pitṛis.
And how, by not fulfilling *these duties* through folly, dost thou
8 hope to go the good way? We think affliction, one *affliction*
after another, may be for thee in this world, O son; hell
likewise when thou art dead, *and* affliction in sooth in another
birth.

Rući spoke:

9 Wedlock tends to excessive suffering, and is a downward
10 course toward sin; hence I took no wife hitherto. Control which
is gained over one's self, this is effected by firm suppression;* it
is the cause of final emancipation from existence; that *emanci-*
11 *pation* verily comes not from wedlock. That the soul, though
besmirched with the mire of selfishness, be washed clean day
by day by those who have no family ties with the waters of
12 thought—better verily is this! The soul, which is marked
with the mire of actions that have developed during many
existences, must be washed clean with the waters of good
perceptions by wise men who keep their bodily organs under
control.

The Pitṛis spoke:

13 Fitting it is that those who have their organs under control
should cleanse their soul; but does this path, wherein thou
wendest, O son, tend to final emancipation from existence?†

* *Ni-yantraṇa*; a word not in the dictionary.

† I take *kintu* as *kiṃ tu* interrogatively; but the Bombay edition reads *lepáya* for *mokshâya* and *kintu* then would mean simply "but"—"but this path, wherein, &c., tends to defilement."

14 Moreover evil is driven away by means of disinterested* gifts,
and by results and enjoyments which are good or ill according
15 to former actions. Thus no bondage befalls him who acts
with a tender heart, and such action being disinterested tends
16 not to bondage. Thus a former action done, which consists of
merit and demerit, is diminished day and night by enjoyments
which consist of pleasure and pain, O son, among mankind.
17 Thus wise men cleanse their soul and guard it from bonds;
thus, on the other hand, indiscrimination, which is the mire
of sin, does not lay hold of it.

Ruci spoke:

18 It is declared in the Veda, ignorance is the path of action,
O my forefathers. How then do ye, sirs, despatch me on the
path of action?

The Pitṛis spoke:

19 Ignorance in very truth is this† action *thou mentionest*—this
maxim is not erroneous; nevertheless action is the cause un-
20 doubtedly of full acquisition of knowledge. On that *view* the
restraint, which bad men observe because they do not perform
what is enjoined, *should tend* ultimately to final emancipation
from existence;‡ on the contrary it produces a downward
21 course. But thou thinkest, O son, 'I will cleanse my soul'; yet
thou art burnt up by sins which arise from not performing what
22 is enjoined. Even Ignorance exists for the benefit of men,
just as poison does; although it is different, it *does* not in truth
tend to bondage§ by reason of the means which are put into
23 practice. Therefore, O son, do thou take a wife according to
precept; let not thy birth be unprofitable by thy not observ-
ing the business of ordinary life fully.

* *An-abhisandhita*: *abhi-sandhita* is not in the dictionary.

† For *evait* read *evaitat.*

‡ The Bombay edition reads *násau* instead of *so 'nte,* and the meaning is "*does* not *tend* to final emancipation."

§ The Bombay edition reads *bandháyányá yato hi sá,* "because it is different, it *tends* in truth to bondage." Or if *anyá yato* be read as one word *a-nyáyato,* it would mean "because of iniquity it *tends* in truth to bondage."

Ruci spoke:

24 I am now aged; who will bestow a wife on me, O my forefathers? Moreover it is hard for a poor man to take a wife.

The Pitris spoke:

25 Our downfall will assuredly come to pass, O son, and so also will thy downward course; thou dost not welcome our speech.

Márkaṇḍeya spoke:

26 Having spoken thus, the Pitris suddenly vanished from sight while he beheld them, O best of munis, just as lights when blown by the wind.

Canto XCVI.

The story of Ruc'i (continued).

Perturbed by his forefathers' admonition Ruc'i offered worship to Brahmá, and Brahmá promised he should gain his desire with the Pitṛis' help—Ruc'i poured forth therefore a long hymn and prayer to the Pitṛis.

Márkaṇḍeya spoke:

1 The bráhman ṛishi *Ruc'i*, being greatly agitated in mind at
that his forefathers' counsel, wandered about the earth, desir-
2 ous *to find* a maiden. Failing to obtain a maiden he, illu-
minated by the fire of his forefathers' counsel, fell into deep
3 thought, while his mind was exceedingly agitated—"What
can I do? Where am I going? How am I to take a wife?
May that come to pass quickly, which will effect my fore-
4 fathers' advancement!" While the high-souled *muni* pon-
dered thus, a thought occurred *to him*—"I *will* propitiate
5 lotus-born Brahmá with austerities." Thereupon he per-
formed austerities to Brahmá for a hundred celestial years,
and for the purpose of propitiating him engaged then in the
6 utmost self-mortification. Brahmá the forefather of the
worlds thereupon showed himself *and* said to him—"I am

7 well-pleased, declare thy earnest wish." He fell prostrate
then before Brahmá, *who is* the origin of the world, and declared
what he wished earnestly *to do* according to the counsel of his
forefathers. And Brahmá hearing his earnest wish spoke
to the bráhman Rući.

Brahmá spoke:

8 Thou shalt be a Prajá-pati; thou shalt create human folk.
After creating human folk, O bráhman, *and* begetting sons
9 and performing ceremonies, thou shalt then, after thy dominion
shall be taken away, attain perfect felicity. Being such,
10 do thou take a wife as enjoined by thy forefathers; and after
reflecting on this desire, perform worship to the Pitṛis;
those Pitṛis indeed being gratified shall bestow on thee
the wife and sons desired. When satisfied what may thy
ancestors not bestow?

Márkaṇḍeya spoke:

11 The ṛishi* on hearing this speech from Brahmá, whose
birth is inscrutable, performed worship to the Pitṛis on
12 a distant sand-bank in a river, and also gratified the
Pitṛis, O bráhman, with these praises, respectfully, with
single mind, subduing his body, and bending his neck in
faith.

Ruc'i spoke:

13 I pay reverence unto the Pitṛis who dwell as presiding
deities in the śráddha; and whom even the gods verily delight
with *invocations* concluding with *the word* svadhá at the
14 śráddha. I pay reverence unto the Pitṛis, whom maharshis,
who desire to obtain enjoyment and final emancipation from
existence, delight with mental śráddhas *and* with faith in
15 Svarga. I pay reverence unto the Pitṛis, whom the Siddhas
delight with all *kinds of* incomparable heavenly offerings at the
16 śráddhas in Svarga. I pay reverence unto the Pitṛis, whom the
Guhyakas also, who earnestly desire boundless sublime pros-

* For *ṛisher* read *ṛishir*?

perity because they are absorbed therein,* honour with faith.
17 I pay reverence unto the Pitṛis, who are always honoured by
mortals on the earth, *and* who grant *unto men* to attain unto
18 the desired worlds by means of faith at the śráddhas. I pay
reverence unto the Pitṛis, who are always honoured by
bráhmans on the earth, *and* who grant generative power for
19 the obtaining of what they earnestly desire and long for. I pay
reverence unto the Pitṛis, whom indeed forest-dwelling *ascetics*,
who are restrained in their diet *and* whose stains have been
washed away by austerities, delight with śráddhas performed
20 in the forests. I pay reverence unto the Pitṛis, whom
bráhmans, who practise the vow of perpetual celibate student-
ship *and* who have subdued their souls, delight with intense
21 meditation continually. I pay reverence unto the Pitṛis,
whom as being bestowers of benefits in the three worlds princes
delight with śráddhas and all *kinds of* food-oblations accord-
22 ing to precept. I pay reverence unto the Pitṛis, whom
vaiśyas, who take pleasure in their own occupations, honour
with flowers, incense, food and water continually on the earth.
23 I pay reverence unto the Pitṛis, whom as famed by the name
Su-kálin† śúdras also in faith always delight with śráddhas in
24 this world. I pay reverence unto the Pitṛis, whom as feeding
on the svadhá great Asuras, who have forsaken deceit and
25 arrogance, always delight with śráddhas in Pátála. I pay
reverence unto the Pitṛis, whom Nágas, who wish to obtain
their desires, honour with śráddhas *and* all *kinds of* enjoy-
26 ments according to precept in Rasátala. I pay reverence
unto the Pitṛis, whom the Serpents,‡ who possess spells,
enjoyments and good fortune, always delight there indeed
27 with śráddhas according to precept. I pay reverence unto
the Pitṛis, who dwell visibly both in the world of the gods
and in the atmosphere, and who are worthy of worship by
gods and other *beings* on the face of the earth. May they

* *Tan-maya-tvena*; referring to wealth, because they are the attendants of Kuvera the god of wealth, and guardians of his treasures?

† A class of Pitṛis regarded as the especial Pitṛis of Śúdras.

‡ *Sarpaiḥ*.

28 receive my offering. I pay reverence unto the Pitṛis, who
have become *united* with the Supreme Soul, *who yet* in bodily
form dwell verily in a heavenly car, and to whom as effecting
deliverance from affliction the noblest yogins offer sacrifice
29 with minds cleansed from defilement. I pay reverence unto
the Pitṛis, who also in bodily form in heaven feed on the
svadhá for the purpose of *bestowing* desirable benefits, *and*
who are powerful to bestow all desired *objects and* who grant
30 deliverance to those who have no engrossing interests. May
all the Pitṛis be delighted herein, who signify desires to those
who wish *for them, namely*, godhead, Indra's status, or what
is more than this, *and also* sons, cattle, might *and* houses of
31 their very own! May the Pitṛis, who always dwell in the
moon's rays, in the sun's orb and in a white heavenly car, be
delighted herein with food and water, with perfumes and
32 other *odours;* may they obtain nourishment herefrom! And
may the Pitṛis, who have satisfaction from the clarified butter
in the oblation to Agni, who dwelling in the bodies of bráh-
mans feed on *the same, and* who reach intense delight by the
offering of the piṇḍa, be *satisfied* herein with food and water!
33 May they, who have been greatly pleased by the chief
máharshis with rhinoceros-flesh and with dark sesamum seeds,
which attract the minds of celestial beings *and* are much
desired by the gods, and with the herb Ocimum sanctum,
34 reach intense delight herein! And may all poems which are
exceedingly coveted be for them, who are honoured by the
Immortals! May they then be present here at the flowers,
35 perfumes, food and enjoyments which I have procured! May
they, my forefathers,* who receive honour day by day, who
should be worshipped on earth at the end of the month *and*
on the eighth day, and who should be worshipped at the
end of the year and at its beginning,† obtain satisfaction
36 herein! *May they*, who as being luminous as the full moon‡
are worthy of worship from bráhmans, and who as having

* Or, "The Pitṛis."

† *Abhyudaye;* or "the rising *of the sun*"?

‡ *Kumudendu-bháso.*

the hue of the rising sun *are worthy of worship* from
kshattriyas, and who as bestowers of gold *are worthy of*
worship from vaiśyas, and who as resembling the indigo plant*
37 *are worthy of worship* from śúdra folk, may they all reach
delight with my offering of flowers, perfumes, incense, food,
water and other *gifts* and with the fire-oblation also! Before
38 them, the Pitṛis, I am ever prostrate. May they, who eat
of the food-oblations, *those* splendid sacrifices, which have
been previously *offered* to the gods for the sake of exceeding
delight, and who when delighted become creators of welfare
for us, be delighted herein! I am prostrate before them.
39 May they, who expel† Rákshasas, goblins and fierce Asuras,
yea, what is unpropitious to people, *and* who are the most
ancient of gods, *and* who are worthy of worship by the lord
of the Immortals, be delighted herein! I am prostrate before
40 them. May the Agni-shvátta‡ *Pitṛis*, the Barhi-shad§ *Pitṛis*,
the A'jya-pa|| *Pitṛis* and the Soma-pá¶ *Pitṛis* attain delight
41 in this śráddha! I have delighted the Pitṛis. May the bands
of Agni-shvátta Pitṛis protect the eastern region for me!
And may the Pitṛis who are known as Barhi-shads protect
42 the southern *region!* May the A'jya-pa *Pitṛis* likewise *protect*
the western *region*, and the Soma-pá *Pitṛis* the northern
region from Rákshasas, goblins and Piśáćas, and indeed from
43 harm *inflicted* by Asuras! And may their ruler Yama safe-
guard me everywhere! The Viśva, Viśva-bhuj, A'rádhya,
44 Dharma, Dhanya, S'ubhánana, Bhúti-da, Bhúti-kṛit *and* Bhúti
are nine classes which *exist* among the Pitṛis. The Kalyáṇa,
45 Kalyatá-kartṛi, Kalya, Kalyataráśraya, Kalyatá-hetu *and* Án-
agha—these six, they are known as classes *of Pitṛis* also.

* *Nílí-nibháḥ.* This is obscure.

† *Nir-náśayantas.* As a verb this is not given in the dictionary.

‡ The spirits of those who on earth neglected the sacrificial fire. See Manu III. 195 and 199.

§ See Manu III. 196 and 199.

|| Those who were the sons of Pulastya and the ancestors of the vaiśya order. See Manu III. 198.

¶ Those especially who were the progenitors of the bráhmans. See Manu III. 197 and 198.

46 The Vara, Vareṇya, Vara-da, Pushṭi-da and Tushṭi-da, Viśva-
pátṛi and Dhátṛi—these seven indeed are also classes. The
47 Mahat, Mahátman, Mahita, Mahimá-vat *and* Mahá-bala—these
five moreover are classes of Pitṛis, being destroyers of sin.
Sukha-da, and Dhana-da also, Dharma-da and Bhúti-da*
48 besides—such also is likewise called a four-fold class of Pitṛis.
There are thus thirty-one classes of Pitṛis, who pervade the
entire world. Delighted with me, may they be satisfied and
ever grant me what is beneficial.

Canto XCVII.

The bestowal of a boon by the Pitṛis in the Rauc'ya Manv-antara.

A body of light appeared in the sky, and Ruc'i offered a hymn to all the deities and Pitṛis—The Pitṛis appeared, and to enable him to be a Prajá-pati granted him the boon of a wife—They commend the hymn offered to them and declare its manifold efficacy.

Márkaṇḍeya spoke:

1 Now while he offered praises thus, a lofty pile of light
2 appeared suddenly, suffusing the sky. When he saw that
very great light, which remained stationary encompassing the
world, Ruc'i sank to the earth on his knees and sang this
hymn.

Ruc'i spoke:

3 I pay reverence† ever to those Pitṛis, who are honoured,
incorporeal,‡ luminously splendid, who are rapt in meditation,

* This word occurs twice, in verses 44 and 47. The Bombay edition reads the same. It seems to follow the Calcutta edition rather closely after the Deví-máhátmya.

† *Namasyámi.* It is used with the object in the genitive here and in verse 6; in the accusative in verses 4, 5, 7, 10 and 11; and in the dative in verses 8 and 9. The construction with the accusative is the only one mentioned in the dictionary.

‡ The Bombay edition reads *A-múrttánáṁ c'a múrttánám,* "who are incorporeal and who are corporeal."

4 and who possess supernatural sight. And I pay reverence to
those granters of *men's* desires, *who are* the leaders of Indra
and the other *gods,* and of Daksha and Máric'a, of the seven
5 ṛishis and of other *sages.* I pay reverence to all the Pitṛis of
Manu and the other chief munis, and of the sun and moon,
6 among the waters and in the sea. With conjoint hands I
pay reverence likewise to the constellations and planets, to
7 wind and fire and the sky, and to heaven and earth. And with
conjoint hands I pay reverence to the devarshis' progenitors,
unto whom reverence is paid by all the worlds, *who are* always
8 givers of what is imperishable. With conjoint hands I pay
reverence always to the Prajá-pati* Kaśyapa, to Soma† and to
9 Varuṇa, and to the princes of religious devotion. Reverence
to the seven classes *of Pitṛis* moreover in the seven worlds!‡
I pay reverence to self-existent Brahmá who is contemplation-
10 eyed. I pay reverenee to the Somádhára and Yoga-múrtti-
dhara classes of Pitṛis, and to Soma the father of the worlds.
11 I pay reverence moreover to the other Pitṛis who have the
form of fire,§ because this universe is entirely composed of
12 Agni and Soma. Now these who *dwell* in *this* light, and who
have the bodies of the moon, sun and fire,|| and whose true na-
ture is the world, and whose true nature is Brahmá¶—to all
13 those Pitṛis, practisers of religious devotion, *I pay* reverence
with subdued mind, reverence, *yea* reverence. May they, the
consumers of the svadhá, be gracious unto me!

Márkaṇḍeya syoke:

14 Being thus praised by him, O best of munis, those Pitṛis
issued forth with their splendour, illuminating the ten regions
15 of the sky; and he beheld them standing in front then,

* For *Prajá-pateḥ* read *Prajá-pate?*

† Or, "the moon." 'Soma' seems to be played upon in its various meanings in these verses.

‡ Or, "Reverence to the seven classes *of Pitṛis* and to the seven worlds!"

§ 'Agni' is also played upon in its different meanings.

|| "Soma, Súrya and Agni."

¶ Or, "Brahman."

adorned with the flowers, perfumes and unguents which he
16 had presented *unto them.* Falling prostrate again in faith,
again indeed joining his hands, full of respect he exclaimed,
separately *to each of them,* "Reverence to thee!" "Reverence
17 to thee!" Well-pleased the Pitṛis thereupon said to him, the
best of munis, "Choose thou a boon." To them he spoke,
bending his neck respectfully.

Ruc'i spoke:

18 Brahmá has commanded me now to be the maker of a *new* creation. In such capacity I desire to obtain a wife, *who shall be* happy, of heavenly kind, prolific.

The Pitṛis spoke:

19 Here verily for thee let a wife be produced forthwith who
shall be most fascinating, and by her thou shalt have a son,
20 a Manu supreme, the ruler of a Manv-antara, wise, charac-
terized by thy very own name, being called Raućya *from*
21 *thee,* O Rući; he shall attain fame in the three worlds. He
shall also have many sons, great in strength and prowess,
22 great of soul, guardians of the earth. And thou, becoming
a Prajá-pati, shalt create people of the four classes; and
when thy dominion shall come to an end and *thou shalt be*
wise in righteousness, thou shalt thereafter attain perfect
felicity.
23 And whatever man shall gratify us with this hymn
in faith, we being gratified *will give* him enjoyments and
24 sublime spiritual knowledge, perfect bodily health, and wealth,
and sons, grandsons and other *descendants* :* because verily
those who desire *blessings* must constantly praise us with this
25 hymn. And he who shall recite this hymn, which causes us
pleasure, with faith at a śráddha, standing the while in front

* The Bombay edition inserts a verse and a half here—"We will give [the foregoing blessings] assuredly and whatever else is earnestly desired. Therefore men who continually desire sacred recompenses in the world and the imperishable gratification of the Pitṛis—*such* men must praise us with a hymn."

26 of the bráhmans as they feast, that śráddha, shall un-
doubtedly become ours imperishably, because of our pleasure
in hearing the hymn when *a man* makes close approach *unto us.*
27 Although a śráddha be performed without a bráhman learned
in the Veda, although it may be vitiated by means of wealth
28 which has been gained unjustly, or although it be performed
in any other *defective* manner, or although moreover it be
performed with blemished offerings unfit for a śráddha, or
be performed also at a wrong time *or* in a wrong place, or
29 yet be unaccompanied by the *proper* ordinances, or *if* it is
performed by men without faith or in reliance on deceit—
nevertheless *such a* śráddha shall be to our delight because
30 this hymn is uttered *thereat.* Wherever this hymn which
brings us happiness is recited at a śráddha, there delight
31 accrues unto us, lasting for twelve years. This *hymn recited*
in the winter yields delight for twelve years; and this beauti-
ful hymn *recited* in the dewy season *yields* delight for twice
32 *that number of* years; *when recited* at a śráddha ceremony in
the spring *it tends* to delight *us* for sixteen years; and this
hymn recited in the hot season causes delight for sixteen *years*
33 indeed. When a śráddha although performed imperfectly is
consummated with this hymn in the rainy season, imperish-
34 able delight accrues unto us, O Rući. When recited at the
time of a śráddha even in the autumn season, it yields us
35 delight with men which lasts for fifteen years. And in whose-
soever house this *hymn* remains constantly in written form,
there shall we be present when a śráddha is performed.
36 Therefore *standing* at a śráddha in front of the feasting
bráhmans, O illustrious Sir! thou must hear this *hymn* which
supplies nourishment unto us.*

* The Bombay edition adds—"Having spoken thus, his ancestors (Pitṛis) departed to heaven, O best of munis."

CANTO XCVIII.

The marriage of Máliní and the conclusion of the Raućya Manv-antara.

Rući married an Apsaras named Máliní, and had by her a son, the Manu Raućya, who will be the ruler of a manv-antara.

Márkaṇḍeya spoke :

1 Thereupon from the midst of that river uprose an exqui-
site Apsaras, charming, slender-shaped, named Pramloćá.
2 And she spoke to high-souled Rući in very sweet accents,
bowing courteously *towards him, she,* beautiful-browed Pram-
loćá, verily a choice Apsaras.
3 "A maiden of exceeding bodily beauty is my daughter, O
best of ascetics; she was begotten by Varuṇa's high-souled
4 son Pushkara. Take her when I give her, *a maiden* of exqui-
site complexion, to be thy wife; a Manu of great intellect
shall be born of her as son to thee!"

Márkaṇḍeya spoke :

5 When he replied, "So be it," to her, she fetched up from
6 out that water then a shapely maiden named Máliní; and on
that sand-bank in the river Rući, best of munis, after sum-
moning the great munis together, took her hand *in marriage*
7 according to the ordinances. Of her was born to him a son,
great in valour, great in intellect; he was *named* Raućya
8 after his father's name; he was famous on this earth. And
in his manv-antara who will be the gods and the seven ṛishis
and his sons and the kings, they have been duly told to thee.
9 Increase of righteousness, and perfect health, and the growth
of riches, grain and children—*this* without doubt is for men
in this manv-antara, which *thou hast* heard about.
10 After hearing of both the praise of the Pitṛis and the
classes of the Pitṛis also, a man obtains all his desires
through their favour, O great muni.

CANTO XCIX.

Eulogy of Agni and fire.

There was formerly a very irascible muni named Bhúti, to whom everything was subservient—He left his hermitage once and put his disciple Śánti in charge—The sacred fire went out, and Śánti in consternation offered up a long prayer and eulogy to Agni.

Márkaṇḍeya spoke:

1 Hear next thereafter about the birth of Bhautya, and about the gods, the ṛishis, his sons and the kings of the earth *in his period.*

2 There was a disciple of Aṅgiras, by name Bhúti, very
irascible, a muni who used to invoke bitter curses for a small
matter, *and* who spoke harshly on *the occasion of* a trans-
3 gression. At his hermitage Mátariśvan blew not very
fiercely, the sun caused no excessive heat, nor Parjanya
4 excessive mud, nor did the moon even when full cause
excessive cold with its rays, through fear verily of that
5 irascible *and* very glorious *muni.* And the seasons, aban-
doning their course, produced flowers and fruit at all times
on the trees that grew in his hermitage according to his
6 command. And the waters that flowed near his hermitage
glided on according to his pleasure, and when taken into
7 his water-pot were frightened at that high-souled *muni.* He
was impatient of excessive trouble and was exceedingly
irascible, O bráhman.

And that illustrious *muni* having no son set his mind on
8 austerities. Desiring a son, restricting his food, exposing
himself to cold, wind and fire, he fixed his mind on austeri-
ties indeed with the resolve, "I *will* practice austerities."
9 The moon did not tend to make him very cold, nor the sun
to make him very hot, nor did Mátariśvan blow on him
10 severely, O great muni. And Bhúti, best of munis, being

greatly pained by the couples of opposite causes* did not obtain that desire and so ceased from his austerities.

11 His brother was Su-varćas. Being invited by him to a
sacrifice *and* being desirous of going, *Bhúti* said to his high-
12 minded disciple named S'ánti, who was calm, who had the
measure of religious knowledge,† who was well-behaved,
always zealous in the guru's business, observant of good
customs, noble, an excellent muni.

Bhúti spoke:

13 I shall go to the sacrifice of my brother Su-varćas, O
S'ánti, being summoned by him, and do thou listen to what
14 thou must do here. Thou must keep watch over the fire in
my hermitage thus *and* thus diligently, so that the fire may
not become extinguished.

Márkaṇḍeya spoke:

15 Having given this command and receiving the answer
"Yea" from his disciple S'ánti, the guru went to that his bro-
ther's sacrifice, being summoned *thereto* by his younger *brother.*
16 And while S'ánti is fetching fuel, flowers, fruit and other *things*
from the forest for that high-souled guru's maintenance, and is
17 performing other business, being faithfully obedient to his
guru, the fire which was the root of his welfare‡ died out
18 during that *interval.* Seeing the fire had died out, S'ánti,
sorely distressed and afraid of Bhúti, fell, *though* of great
intellect, into manifold anxiety, *thinking*—
19 "What am I to do? or how will the guru's return be?
I must accomplish something now; what, when done, would
20 be a good thing done? If my guru sees this extinguished
fire occupying the hearth, he will assuredly devote me at
21 once because of it to some grievous calamity. If I kindle
another fire here in the fire-place, then he who sees everything
22 visibly§ will of a surety turn me into ashes. As such I am
sinful on account of the wrath and curse of that guru. I do

* Heat and cold; and so on.

† *Akṣha-pratima*; a difficult word.

‡ *Bhúti-parigrahaḥ*; a pun on the words.

§ Agni.

not grieve so much for myself as for the sin committed against
23 the guru. The guru on seeing the fire extinguished will
certainly curse me, or Agni *will be* angry. That brahman is
24 truly of such *immense* power! With what fitness will not he,
under whose command the gods live in terror of his majestic
power, assail me who have committed sin!"

Márkaṇḍeya spoke:

25 After pondering thus in many ways, being always afraid of
that guru he, best of intelligent *munis*, sought refuge with
26 Agni. Controlling his mind then he offered a hymn to the
seven fires; and with thoughts intent on them he joined his
hands and knelt down on the ground.

S'ánti spoke:

27 Om! Reverence to the high-souled perfecter of all created
things, to him who has one, two and five side-altars at the
28 rája-súya *sacrifice*, to the six-souled *god*! Reverence to the very
brilliant one, who gives *their* functions* to all the gods, to
him who has S'ukra's form! Thou bestowest permanence
29 on all the worlds. Thou art the mouth of all the gods! The
oblation that is taken by thee, O adorable one,† cheers all the
30 gods! All the gods have their life-breath in thee! The obla-
tion sacrificed in thee turns into a fiery‡ cloud; and after-
wards the modification which it undergoes in the form of
31 water, by that comes the growth of all herbs, O wind-chario-
32 teered *god*. Upon all the herbs animals live in happiness. Men
perform sacrifices among the herbs also which thou hast crea-
ted. With sacrifices also gods and Daityas and Rákshasas like-
33 wise are fattened, O Purifier; those sacrifices have thee for their
support, O Fire. Hence thou art the origin of everything; and
34 thou, O Fire, art composed of everything. The gods, Dánavas,
Yakshas, Daityas, Gandharvas and Rákshasas, men, cattle,

* Or "means of subsistence."

† Instead of *tvayáttum bhagaván haviḥ*, the Bombay edition reads *tvayát-tam bhagavan haviḥ*, which I have adopted.

‡ *Anala-megha* in the Bombay edition is preferable to *amala-megha* "a pure cloud."

35 trees, deer, birds and reptiles are all fattened and nourished
up by thee, O Fire. From thee indeed they take their birth,
and in thee likewise they meet their dissolution at the end.
36 Thou, O god, createst the waters, thou again indeed consumest them, and by thee they are rendered wholesome *to be*
37 the source of nourishment for breathing beings. Thou abidest
among the gods under the form of glowing light* among
the Siddhas with loveliness, among Nágas under the
form of poison, among birds under the form of wind:
38 Among mankind thou art anger; among birds, deer and
other *animals thou art* silliness;† thou art stability among
trees; thou art hardness with reference to the earth;
39 thou art fluidity in water, O adorable *god;* and thou
hast the form of swiftness in the wind; thou moreover,
O Fire, with thy faculty of permeation abidest as soul in the
40 sky.‡ Thou, O Fire, *who art* the end of all created beings,
movest about safe-guarding them. Wise men style thee one;
41 again they style thee three-fold.§ Having fashioned thee in
eight ways, they fashioned the original sacrifice‖. Supreme
42 ṛishis say this universe was created by thee. Without thee
verily the whole world would perish at once, O Fire. A twice-born man proceeds on the course which is ordained by his own
43 actions, when he has paid worship to thee with oblations to
the gods, oblations to deceased ancestors and other offerings
after uttering *the words* svadhá and sváhá. Living beings
have in truth the innate power of modification,¶ O thou who

* *Tejo-rúpeṇa.*

† *Mohaḥ.*

‡ The Bombay edition reads *nabhasi tvaṁ vyavasthitaḥ* instead, "thou abidest in the sky," omitting "as soul."

§ The three kinds of sacrificial fire, gárhapatya, áhavaníya and dakshiṇa.

‖ The Bombay edition reads instead *yajña-váham akalpayan*, "having fashioned thee in eight ways they fashioned (or esteemed) *thee to be* him who conveys the sacrifice *to the gods*."

¶ *Pariṇámátma-víryá.* The Bombay edition reads *-víryáṇi*, a plural neuter instead of a singular feminine noun; but it means the same. If *pariṇáma*, "alteration," "modification," means "adaptation," this passage is a remarkable anticipation of modern scientific generalization.

44 art honoured by the Immortals. Flames issuing *from thee,*
moreover,* burn up all created things. O most brilliant
Játa-vedas,† thine verily is this creation of the universe!
45 Thine are the Vedic ceremonial *and* the world which consists
of all created things. Reverence to thee, O yellow-eyed
46 Fire! Reverence be to thee, O consumer of oblations! O
Purifier, reverence be to thee now; reverence to thee, O
bearer of oblations *to the gods.*‡ Thou verily art the maturer
of the universe by reason of *thy* maturing§ things that are
47 eaten and drunk. Thou art the maturer of the crops; and
thou art the nourisher of the world. Thou verily art cloud,
48 thou art wind, thou art seed that produces the crops. Thou
indeed hast been, and shalt be, and art for the nourishing of
all created things. Thou art light among all created things;
49 thou art the illuminating Sun. Thou art day, thou also art
night; and thou art both the twilights. Thou hast golden
semen, O Fire; thou art the cause of the production of
50 gold; and thou hast gold within thy bosom;|| thou hast
lustre like unto gold! Thou art a muhúrtta, and thou a
51 kshaṇa; thou art a truṭi and thou a lava; ¶ thou existest
in the form of kalás, káshṭhás, nimeshas and other *periods of*
time, O lord of the world. Thou art all this *universe.* Thou
art Destiny, which consists in continuous change.

52 Thy tongue which is *called* Kálí brings about the conclusion
at the fated time, O lord; *by it*** preserve us from fear, from
53 sins and from the great terror of this world! Thy tongue,
which is named Karálí†† is the cause of the great dissolution
of the world; by it preserve us from sins and from the great
54 terror of this world! And thy tongue which is called Mano-

* *Tvatto,* "from thee," would seem preferable to *tato,* "moreover."

† A name of Agni.

‡ The Bombay edition inserts a line here—"Thou indeed art the purifier of the universe because of *thy* purification of all existing things."

§ *Pác'aka* and *pác'ana;* the metaphor is from "cooking" with fire.

|| *Hiraṇya-garbhas.*

¶ Various measures of time.

** Instead of *bhayát,* "from fear," the Bombay edition reads *tayá,* "by it."

†† "Formidable."

javá* is characterized by the quality of lightness; by it pre-
55 serve us from sins and from the great terror of this world! Thy
tongue which is *called* Su-lohitá† accomplishes their desire
for created beings, by it preserve us from sins and from the
56 great terror of this world! Thy tongue which is *called*
Sa-dhúmra-varṇá‡ causes sickness among breathing beings,
by it preserve us from sins and from the great terror
57 of this world! And thy tongue which is *called* Sphuliñ-
giní,§ because it is altogether shapely, by it preserve us
58 from sins and from the great terror of this world! And
thy tongue which is called Viśvása-dá|| bestows blessings
on breathing beings; by it preserve us from sins and from
59 the great terror of this world! O yellow-eyed, red-necked,
black-pathed¶ consumer of oblations, save me from all faults;
60 deliver me here from worldly existence! Be gracious, O
seven-flamed Fire, O Kṛiśánu, O bearer of the oblations *to*
the gods! Thou art proclaimed by the eight names of Agni,
61 Pávaka, S'ukra and the rest. O Agni, O thou who didst
spring up before all created beings, O Vibhá-vasu, be gra-
cious, O thou who art called the Carrier of the oblations *to the*
gods, O changeless one whom I extol!
62 Thou art Fire imperishable, thou hast inconceivable beauty,
thou prosperest greatly, *thou art* hard to be endured,** ex-
ceedingly ardent: or thy surpassing valour, which is changeless
and terrible, vanquishes him who injures all the worlds.††

* "Swift as thought."

† "Very red."

‡ "Smoky-coloured."

§ "Having sparks of fire."

|| For *viśvá sadá* read *viśvása-dá*; "bestowing confidence"; the Bombay edition reads *viśva-sṛijá*, "creating the universe."

¶ *Kṛishṇa-vartman* "black-pathed" of the Bombay edition is better than *kṛishṇa-varṇa* "black-hued" of the Calcutta edition.

** For *dush-prahaso* read *dush-prasaho* as in the Bombay edition.

†† This passage appears to be corrupt. It runs thus in the Calcutta edition;—

Tvam a-vyayam bhímam a-śesha-lokaṁ
Samúrtako hanty athavâti-víryam.

63 Thou art the sublime principle of being,* that dwells in the
lotus-heart of every being,† unending, worthy of praise.
By thee was stretched out this universe which comprises what
is moveable and immoveable. O consumer of oblations, thou
64 art one in many forms here! Thou are undecaying; thou
art the earth with its mountains and forests; *thou art* the
sky that holds the moon and the sun; thou art everything
that exists daily;‡ and thou art the submarine fire that
is held within the bosom of the great ocean; thou standest with
65 superhuman power in thy hand.§ Thou art always,
worshipped as the 'Consumer of oblations' at the great
sacrifice by great ṛishis who are devoted to self-restraint; and
when extolled thou drinkest the soma at the sacrifice, and
eatest the oblations also, that are offered in fire with *the ex-*
66 *clamation* vashaṭ, for thy well-being. Thou art longed for||
continually by bráhmans here for the sake of recompense;
and thou art sung of in all the Vedáṅgas. For thy sake
bráhmans, who are zealously devoted to sacrificing, study the
67 Vedáṅgas at all times. Thou art Brahmá who is devoted to
sacrificing, and also Vishṇu, goblin-ruling *S'iva*, *Indra* lord of
the gods, Aryaman, *and* water-dwelling *Varuṇa*. Both the

which seems unintelligible. The Bombay edition reads;—

Tavá-vyayam bhímam a-śesha-loka-
Savardhakaṁ hanty athaváti-víryam.

and I have followed it except as regards the word *sa-vardhakam* which seems incorrect. By comparing the two versions it may be conjectured that the proper reading should be *sam-mardakam*, or *sam-indhakam* or some such word, and I have ventured to translate it by the general phrase, "who injures."

* Or "goodness," *sattva*. The Bombay edition reads *tattva*, "essential truth."

† For *-puṇḍaríkas tvam* the Bombay edition reads *-puṇḍaríka-stham*, which seems preferable.

‡ *Ahar-diváklilam.*

§ Or, "in thy ray of light," *kare*. The Bombay edition has a wholly different reading here;—

Bhaván vibhuḥ pivati payáṁsi pávaka.

"Thou as lord drinkest the waters, O Fire!"

|| *Ihyase;* but the reading in the Bombay edition *ijyase*, "thou art sacrificed unto," is better.

sun and moon and all the gods and Asuras gratifying *thee*
68 with oblations obtain *from thee* much-prized rewards. Every-
thing, though corrupted with grave malady to the utmost
degree, becomes pure when touched by thy flames. Of ablu-
tions the most excellent by far is that which is *performed* with
ashes; therefore munis wait upon thee pre-eminently at even-
69 ing.* Be gracious, O Fire, who art named the Pure! Be
gracious, O Air, who art unsullied *and* exceedingly brilliant!
Be gracious unto me now, O purifying *Fire* who comest from
lightning!† Be gracious, O Consumer of oblations! Protect
70 thou me! With the auspicious form that is thine, O Fire, and
with the seven flames that are thine—when praised *by us* protect
us therewith, O god, even as a father *protects* the son whom he
has begotten!

CANTO C.

The Fourteen Manv-antaras concluded.

Agni pleased with the hymn granted Śánti two boons; namely, the fire was re-kindled; and Bhúti obtained a son who will be the Manu Bhautya, and became gentle to all.—Agni also blessed the hymn.—The gods, ṛishis and kings in the Bhautya manv-antara are named.—The merits obtained by hearing about the manv-antaras are proclaimed.

Márkaṇḍeya spoke:

1 Being thus hymned by him the adorable Fire thereupon
appeared before him there, encircled with a halo of flame,
2 O muni. And the god who abounds in light, pleased‡ indeed

* The Bombay edition inserts a short verse here:—"After doing that, people, who have easy self-control, by means of real faith gain heaven which is sung of by multitudes."

† For *vaidyutádya* the Bombay edition reads *vaidyutábha*, "who hast a lightning-like splendour."

‡ For *príta-stotreṇa* read *prítaḥ stotreṇa*?

with that hymn, O bráhman, spoke with a voice as deep as a thunder-cloud's to S'ánti who fell prostrate *before him.*

Agni spoke:

3 Well pleased am I with thee, O bráhman, for the praise which thou hast offered in faith. I grant thee a boon; choose what thou desirest.

S'ánti spoke:

4 O adorable god, I have accomplished my object inasmuch
as I see thee in bodily shape; nevertheless deign to hear me
5 who bow *to thee* in faith. My guru has gone from the
hermitage to his brother's sacrifice, O god, and when he shall
return to the hermitage may he see the sacrificial altar*
6 with thee for its master. The sacrificial altar that has been
forsaken by thee through my transgression, O Fire, may the
7 bráhman see that now presided over by thee as before! And
if thou shewest me grace in any other way, O god, then let
8 my guru who is sonless obtain a distinguished son. And as
my guru will display friendliness to his son, so may his mind
9 become gentle towards to all beings. And whoever shall
praise thee† with *this* hymn, whereby thou art pleased with
me, O changeless *god*, mayest thou whom I have propitiated
bestow a boon on him!

Márkaṇḍeya spoke:

10 On hearing this his speech, Agni, being highly conciliated with the hymn and with his devotion to his guru, spoke to that best of bráhmans.

Agni spoke:

11 Inasmuch as thou hast asked, O bráhman, for two boons
on thy guru's behalf *and* not for thyself, therefore I am
12 exceedingly pleased with thee, O great muni. All this shall

* For *dhishṭyam* read *dhishṇyam* as in the Bombay edition, here and in the next verse and verse 21. In the next verse *dhishṇya* is treated as a neuter noun, but the dictionary gives *dhishṇya,* masc. only, this meaning.

† For *paśyatám* read *yaś c'a tvám* with the Bombay edition.

happen to thy guru which thou hast prayed for—he shall be
13 friendly to all beings and shall have a son. The son shall
be the lord of a manv-antara, by name Bhautya, great in
strength, great in valour, great in knowledge, O thou who
praisest thy guru.*
14 And whoever with composed mind shall praise me with
this hymn, all his desire shall come to pass and he shall
15 have merit. At sacrifices, on festival days, at places of
pilgrimage, at sacrifices, at oblations to the gods, and at
ceremonies let *a man* read this sublime *hymn*, which yields
16 nourishment to me, *to attain* unto righteousness. This
sublime *hymn*, which yields pleasure to me, when heard once,
O bráhman, shall without doubt destroy sin committed by
17 day and night. This *hymn* when heard shall at once quell
the faults and other *defects* that attend improper oblations
and times, and the faults which *are committed* by unworthy
18 men also who have made such *mistakes*. This hymn of praise
to me, when heard by mortals at full-moon, at new-moon *and*
on other sacred festivals, shall destroy sin.

Márkaṇḍeya spoke:

19 Having spoken thus, adorable Agni became invisible forth-
with, while he indeed looked on, O muni, just as *the flame*
20 upon a lamp expires. And when Agni had departed, S'ánti,
with mind fully satisfied *and* with the hair of his body stand-
ing erect with gladness, entered the guru's hermitage.
21 There he saw the fire blazing brightly on the guru's sacrificial
altar as before; thereat he felt an intense joy.
22 At this moment the *guru* also of that high-souled *disciple*
returned from his younger brother's sacrifice to his own
23 hermitage; and before him the disciple paid respectful
salutation to his feet. And the guru, after accepting the seat
24 and worship *offered*, said to him then—"My son, I feel
exceeding loving-kindness to thee and to other creatures also.
I know not what this is; if thou *knowest*, my son, tell this
25 quickly unto me." Thereupon the bráhman S'ánti declares

* *Guru-stava.* This is better than reading it *gurus tava*.

all that, *namely*, the extinction of the fire and the other
26 *incidents*, to his teacher truly, O great muni. On hearing it
the guru with eyes moist through affection embraced him,
and gave the disciple the Vedas and Aṅgas and Upáṅgas,
O great muni.

27 A son was born to Bhúti, the Manu named Bhautya. Hear
from me of the gods, ṛishis and kings in his manv-antara,
28 namely, those who shall belong to *that* future *Manu*, while
I declare them at length; and who shall be the lord of the
29 gods *in the time* of that *Manu* famous for his deeds. Both
the C'ákshushas and the Kanishṭhas, the Pavitras and the
Bhrájiras, and the Dhárávṛikas—these *shall* be the five
30 classes of gods according to tradition. S'ući shall be the
Indra of those gods then, great in strength, great in valour,
31 endowed with all an Indra's qualities. And Agnídhra, and
Agni-báhu, S'ući and Mukta, Mádhava, S'ukra and Ajita—
these seven *shall* be the ṛishis then according to tradition.
32 Guru, Gabhíra, and Bradhna, Bharata and Anugraha, and
33 Strímánin * and Pratíra, Vishṇu and Saṅktandana,† Tejas-
vin and Subala—these *shall be* the Manu Bhautya's sons. I
have declared this fourteenth manv-antara to thee.

34 After hearing of the manv-antaras thus in order, O best of
munis, a man obtains merit, and a diminished succession.‡
35 By listening to the first manv-antara a man obtains
righteousness. By listening to S'váróćisha's *period* he
36 gains all his desires. He obtains wealth from *listening to*
Auttami's *story*, and acquires knowledge in *hearing the story*
of Támasa; and when Raivata is heard about, he finds
37 intelligence *and* a handsome wife. Perfect health accrues
to men when C'ákshusha is heard of, and strength when
Vaivasvata *is heard of*, and virtuous sons and grandsons
38 when the Sun's *son* Sávarṇika is heard of. A man obtains
greatness of soul when Brahma-Sávarṇa *is heard of*, a bright
intellect when Dharma-Sávarṇika *is heard of*, victory when

* S'rímánin in the Bombay edition is better.

† San-krandana in the Bombay edition.

‡ Of future births?

39 Rudra-Sávarṇika *is heard of.* A man *becomes* the chief of his
kindred *and* is endowed with good qualities, when Daksha-
Sávarṇika is heard of; he makes his enemies' power small *
40 after hearing of Raućya, O best of men. He acquires the
favour of the gods when the Bhautya manv-antara is heard
of, and *also* obtains the sacred fire and sons endowed with
41 good qualities. And whoever listens to all the manv-antaras
in regular order, O best of munis, hearken to his supreme
42 reward also. After hearing of the gods, ṛishis, Indras, Manus,
their sons the kings, and their genealogies therein, he is
43 delivered from all his sins. And the other gods, ṛishis,
Indras and kings who rule over those manv-antaras are
pleased *with him*, and when pleased they bestow a bright
44 intellect. Having obtained then a bright intellect and having
performed a splendid deed, he attains a splendid course as long
45 as the fourteen Indras *continue.*† May all the seasons be
salubrious; may all the planets be benign! Assuredly they
are so, when he has listened to the ordinance of the manv-
antaras in their order.

CANTO CI.

The Announcement of the Genealogies.

Márkaṇḍeya alludes to the famous races of kings and begins an account of the creation.—Brahmá created Daksha, and Daksha's daughter Aditi bore to Kaśyapa a son Mártaṇḍa, who was the Sun incarnate.—Márkaṇḍeya tells of the Mundane Egg and Brahmá's birth from it,—and expounds the word "Om."

Kraushṭuki‡ spoke:

1 Adorable Sir, thou hast duly expounded the ordinance of
the manv-antaras, and I have ascertained it from thee

* *Ni-śátayati*; not in dictionary.

† For *c'atur-daśaḥ* read *c'atur-daśa* with the Bombay edition.

‡ The discourse goes back to Canto lxxx, and Kraushṭuki, who has disappeared during the Deví-máhátmya and the concluding account of the Manv-antaras, re-appears here with the genealogical portion of the Puráṇa.

2 gradually *and* at length. As I wish to hear of the complete
genealogy of the kings of the earth, beginning from Brahmá
and the other *progenitors*, O best of dvijas, do thou declare
it to me duly, adorable Sir.

Márkaṇḍeya spoke:

3 Listen, my son, to the origin of all the kings and their
exploits, taking for the commencement the Prajá-pati who is
4 the source of *this present* world, for this *his* progeny is
adorned with kings, who celebrated many sacrifices, who
were victorious in battle, who were wise in righteousness,
5 who were numbered by hundreds. And by hearing of the
exploits of these high-souled kings and their manifestations*
6 a man is delivered from all sins. The race, in which *arose*
Manu and Ikshváku, An-araṇya,† Bhagíratha and other
kings in hundreds, who *all* protected their territories well,
7 were wise in righteousness, performed sacrifices, were heroic
and understood thoroughly the sublimest *matters*—when one
hears about that race, a man is delivered from a multitude
8 of sins. Hear then about this race wherefrom thousands
of *subordinate* lines of kings were separated off like *subsidiary*
stems from a banyan tree.

9 The Prajá-pati Brahmá, being desirous of yore of creating
various peoples, created Daksha from his right thumb,‡ O
10 best of dvijas; and the adorable lord Brahmá who causes
the birth of the worlds, *and* who is the supreme maker of
the worlds, created a wife for him from his left thumb.
11 Resplendent Aditi was born as a daughter to that Daksha,
12 and of her Kaśyapa begot divine Mártaṇḍa,§ who has the
nature of Brahmá,|| who bestows boons on all the worlds,

* *Utpattayaś c'a*; the Bombay edition reads the same. This is the nomin., and is inadmissible; read instead *utpattíś c'aiva*?

† This is the reading of the Bombay edition and is right. The Calcutta edition reads *Raṇavanya*; this name is given in the dictionary, but I have not met with it elsewhere.

‡ *Aṅgushṭhád dakshiṇád daksham*; a play on the word. § *I.e.*, the Sun.

|| The Bombay edition also reads *Brahmá sva-rúpam*; but read *Brahma-svarúpam* instead?

and who constitutes the beginning, the middle and the end
in the operations of the creation, continuance and termination
13 *of the world*; from whom *proceeded* this universe and in whom
everything subsists, O dvija; and whose nature this world
14 with its gods, Asuras and men possesses; who constitutes
everything, *who is* the soul of all, the Supreme Soul, eternal.
The Sun took birth in Aditi, after she had first propitiated
him.

Kraushṭuki spoke:

15 Adorable Sir, I desire to hear what is the Sun's nature and
what is the cause *why* he, the earliest god, became Kaśyapa's
16 son; and how he was propitiated by divine Aditi and Kaśyapa;
and what he, the divine Sun, said when propitiated by her;
17 and what truly was his majestic power when he became
incarnate, O best of munis. I wish to hear it in its fulness
duly related, Sir, by thee.

Márkaṇḍeya spoke:

18 Clear sublime Knowledge, Light, Luminosity eternal *and*
free, Perfect Isolation,* Understanding, Visible Manifesta-
19 tion,† Freedom of will, and Comprehension,‡ and Intelli-
gence, and Perception, Memory and Discernment—these are
20 the forms of that luminous Form here. Hearken also,
illustrious sir, while I tell thee at length what thou hast
asked, how the Sun became manifest.

21 In this *world*, destitute of light, obscure, which was
enveloped with darkness all around, a single huge egg came
22 into existence, an imperishable most potent cause.§ It split
open; within it stood the adorable fore-father, lotus-born
Brahmá himself, who is the creator of the worlds, the lord.
23 Out of his mouth issued the great word "Om," O great muni;
and then the Bhúr, after that the Bhuvas,|| and imme-

* *Kaivalyam.*

† *Ávir-bhúḥ*; a word not in the dictionary.

‡ *Saṁ-vid.*

§ See Manu I. 5, &c.

|| These and the following words appear to mean both the utterances themselves and also the worlds that go by the same names, the Bhúr-loka

24 diately thereafter the Svar.* These three mystic words
therefore *express* the essential property of the Sun. Now
from this essential property *indicated by* "Om" comes the
25 subtle sublime form of the Sun. Next there *issued* the gross
Mahar-*loka*, then the grosser Jana-*loka*, then the Tapo-*loka*,
then the Satya-*loka*;—these are the seven-fold substantial
26 *forms*. His permanent forms exist and do not exist, inasmuch
as they assuredly come into existence in innate disposition
and in feeling.†
27 The *word* "Om" which I have uttered, O bráhman, which
has a beginning and an end, *which is* sublime, subtle, formless,
most sublime, permanent—that is the Supreme Spirit,
yea his body.

Canto CII.

The Majesty of the Sun.

Márkaṇḍeya says that from Brahmá's mouths issued the four Vedas and explains their peculiar qualities and transcendent merits—The gods and the Vedas are but manifestations of the Sun.

Márkaṇḍeya spoke:

1 Now when that egg split open, out of the anterior mouth
of Brahmá whose origin is inscrutable, O muni, came forth
2 first the Ṛić hymns, at once resplendent as the flowers of
the China rose,‡ glorious in form, but disconnected,§ and
divided into separate portions, *and* therefore bearing the

and the Bhuvar-loka; and the meaning seems to be that, as he uttered each mystic word, the corresponding world came into existence.

* The *Svar-loka*.

† *Svabháva-bhávayor bhávaṁ yato gac'c'hanti saṁśayam*. The Bombay edition reads the same, but it seems obscure. I have ventured to read *gac'c'hyanty a-saṁśayam* instead.

‡ Javá; *Hibiscus rosa Sinensis*. The flowers are very large and of a brilliant crimson-scarlet colour, very conspicuous.

§ Not in the order in which they are now arranged. For *tejo-rúpánta-saṁhatáḥ* the Bombay edition reads *tejo-rúpá hy a-saṁhatáḥ*, which I have adopted.

3 form of passion.* Out of his right mouth *issued* the Yajus
hymns, unimpeded, coloured like the colour of gold, and
4 disconnected. Out of the posterior mouth of the lord
Brahmá, who is the highest *of all*, were revealed the Sáman
5 hymns, and the C'handas hymns. And the entire Atharvan†
then, resplendent as a mass of black pigment or a cluster
of bees,—that which has a nature as terrible as possible,‡
which contains the magical rites and the rites for removing
6 calamities,—became manifest out of the Creator's left mouth;
it is composed chiefly of pleasure, goodness and darkness,§
and has the essential properties of gentleness and harshness.
7 The Ṛić hymns have the quality of passion; and goodness
is the quality|| of the Yajus hymns, O muni; the Sáman
hymns have the quality of darkness; darkness and goodness
8 *exist* in the Atharvan hymns. These *emanations*, blazing
indeed with unrivalled glory, obtained each a separate station
almost at first.¶

9 That then was the original glory which is declared** by
uttering *the word* "Om." The glory which comes from the
essential nature thereof—that, having encompassed it com-
10 pletely, remains fixed. As is the glory which consists of the
Yajus, such is that of the Sámans, O great muni; they have
11 grown into one in resorting to a supreme glory. Rites for
the removal of calamities, and rites for promoting growth
and magical rites also—these three things gained union††
with the three *Vedas*, the Ṛić and the *two* others, O bráhman.

* *Rajo-rúpa-vahás.*

† *Atharváṇam*, neut. nomin. The meaning given in the dictionary is "the work, *i.e.*, ritual of the Atharva-Veda," but here it must mean the Atharva-Veda itself. This Veda receives marked praise here.

‡ *Yávad-ghora-svarúpaṁ tad.*

§ *Sukha-sattva-tamaḥ-práyam*; *sukha* is peculiar in this connexion.

|| For *guṇá* read *guṇo*? It is remarkable that a higher quality is given to the Yajur-Veda here than to the Ṛig-Veda.

¶ *Púrvam iva.*

** *Abhi-śabdyate*; *abhi-śabd* as a verb is not in the dictionary.

†† *Layam agamat.* The reference seems to be to the Atharva-Veda; see verse 5 where these rites are said to be part of that Veda. This passage then

12 This universe became most stainless then through the sudden
destruction of darkness, and was to be developed horizontally,
13 upwards and downwards, O bráhman ṛishi. That excellent
glory of the C'handas became then an orb, and grew into
14 oneness with the supreme glory, O bráhman. Since it
obtained the name of A'ditya at the very beginning, it became
also the essentially unchanging cause of this universe, O
illustrious Sir.

15 The triple *Veda*, which is named the Ṛić, Yajus and Sáman,
gives warmth in the morning and at mid-day and in the
16 afternoon also. The Ṛić hymns give warmth in the forenoon,
and the Yajus hymns truly at mid-day, and the Sáman
hymns give warmth truly in the afternoon, O best of munis.
17 Rites for the removal of calamities are deposited* in the
Ṛić hymns in the forenoon, rites for promoting internal
growth in the Yajus hymns *at mid-day, and* magical rites
18 lastly in the Sáman at evening. Magical rites moreover
should be performed at mid-day and in the afternoon equally,
but the particular *ceremonies* for the Piṭris should be performed with the Sáman in the afternoon.

19 In the creation *of the world is manifested* Brahmá, who is
composed of the Ṛić hymns; in its permanence† Vishṇu
who is composed of the Yajus hymns; and S'iva, who is
composed of the Sáman, at the dissolution; therefore its
20 sound is impure.‡ Thus the adorable Sun, whose self is
the Veda, who abides in the Veda and whose self is Vedic
21 knowledge, is called the Supreme Soul.§ And he, the
eternal, who is the cause of creation,|| permanence and
dissolution, on taking recourse to passion, goodness and the

refers to the changes by which that work gained rank as a Veda. But these words may also mean "became blended with the three *Vedas;*" see verse 17 below.

* *Vinyastaṁ.*

† For *sthito* read *sthitau* as in the Bombay edition.

‡ Manu says the sound of the Sáma-Veda is in a measure impure because it is sacred to the Piṭris (IV. 124).

§ *Paraḥ purushaḥ.*

|| For *svarga-* read *sarga-* as in the Bombay edition.

other qualities, acquires the names of Brahmá, Vishṇu and the other gods.

22 Now ever to be praised by the gods is he whose body is the Veda,
Yet who has no body, who was in the beginning, who is embodied in all mortals;
Who is the Light that is the refuge of the universe, who has righteousness that passes knowledge,
Who is to be attained unto in the Vedánta, supreme beyond *things that are* sublime!

Canto CIII.

Hymn to the Sun.

Brahmá, finding the Sun's glory too great for creation, offered a hymn to the Sun.—The Sun contracted his glory, and Brahmá accomplished the creation.

Márkaṇḍeya spoke:

1 Now when *the egg* was being heated by his glory above
and beneath, the lotus-born Forefather, being desirous of
2 creating, pondered—"My creation although accomplished
will assuredly pass to destruction through the intense glory*
of the Sun, who is the cause of creation, dissolution and per-
3 manence, great of soul. Breathing beings *will* all *be* bereft
of breath, the waters will dry up through his glory, and
4 without water there will be no creation of this universe."
Pondering thus the adorable Brahmá, Forefather of the
world, becoming intent thereon, composed a hymn to the
adorable Sun.

Brahmá spoke:

5 I pay reverence *to thee* of whom everything consists
Here, and who consistest of everything;
Whose body is the universe, *who art* the sublime Light
Whereon religious devotees meditate;

* *Abhi-tejasaḥ*; a word not in the dictionary.

6 Who art composed of the Ṛić hymns, who art the repository of the Yajus hymns,
And who art the origin of the Sáman hymns; whose power passes thought;
Who consistest of the three *Vedas*;* *who art* half a short syllable as touching grossness,†
Whose nature is sublime, who art worthy of the fullness of good qualities.‡

7 To thee,§ the cause of all, who art to be known as supremely worthy of praise,‖
The supreme Light *that was* at the beginning, not in the form of fire;¶
And *who art* gross by reason that thy spirit is in the gods —*to thee* I pay reverence,
The shining one, who wast in the beginning, the sublimest beyond the sublime!

8 Thine is the primeval power, in that urged on thereby
I achieve *this* creation, which is in the forms of water, earth, wind and fire,
Which has those *elements*, the gods and other *beings* for its objects, *and* which is complete with the word "Om" and other *sounds*—
Not at my own wish; and *that I effect* its continuance and dissolution in the self-same manner.

* For *trayí-mayí* read *trayí-mayo* as in the Bombay edition.

† *Sthúlataydrdha-mátrá*; this seems obscure.

‡ *Guṇa-pára-yogyaḥ*. This may be taken in several ways; "who art adapted to the fullest measure of *a suppliant's* good qualities," or "who art worthy of religious devotion by reason of the fullness of *thy* good qualities," or "who art worthy of religious devotion with the fullness of *a suppliant's* good qualities."

§ For *taṁ* read *tváṁ* as in the Bombay edition.

‖ The Bombay edition reads, but not so well, *paramaṁ ća veḍyam*, "and who art to be known as the sublimest one."

¶ The Bombay edition reads instead, *ádyam paraṁ jyotir a-vedya-rúpam*, "the supreme Light that was in the beginning, whose form passes knowledge."

9 Thou verily art fire. By reasou of thy drying up of the water thou achievest*
The creation of the earth and the primeval completion of the worlds.
Thou indeed, O lord, pervadest the very form of the sky.
Thou in five ways protectest all this world.
10 They who know the Supreme Soul sacrifice with sacrifices to thee,
Who hast the nature of Vishṇu, who consistest of all sacrifices, O Sun!
And self-subdued *ascetics*, who curb their souls and thoughts, meditate
On *thee*, the lord of all, the supremest, while they desire final emancipation from existence for themselves.
11 Reverence to thee, whose form is divine;
To thee, whose form is sacrifice, be reverence;
Yea to thee who in thy very nature art the Supreme Spirit,
Who art meditated upon by religious devotees!
12 Contract thy glory, since the abundance of thy glory
Tends to obstruct creation, O lord, and I am ready to begin creation!

Márkaṇḍeya spoke:

13 Being praised thus by the Creator Brahmá, the Sun
contracted his supreme glory *and* retained but very little.
14 And the lotus-born god accomplished the creation of the
world. Thus in those intervals of the former kalpas
15 illustrious Brahmá created indeed, as before, the gods,
Asuras and other *beings*, and mortals, cattle and other
animals, trees and shrubs and the hells, O great muni.

CANTO CIV.

Praise of the Sun.

Brahmá finished the creation—He had a son Maríc'i, who had a son

* For *karomi*, "I achieve," the Bombay edition reads *karoshi*, which I have adopted as preferable.

Kaśyapa—Kaśyapa married Daksha's thirteen daughters, and begot by them the gods, demons, mankind, animals, birds, &c.—The gods were subdued by the demons, and Aditi offered a hymn to the Sun, imploring his help.

Márkaṇḍeya spoke:

1 Having created this world, Brahmá then separated off the
castes, the bráhman's four periods of life, the seas, the
2 mountains, and the islands even as before. The adorable
lotus-born *god* fixed the forms and abodes of the gods,
Daityas, Nágas and other *beings*, as before, according to the
Vedas* indeed.
3 Brahmá had a son, who was famed as Maríći; his son was
4 Kaśyapa, namely Káśyapa by name.† Daksha's thirteen
daughters were his wives, O bráhman; and they had many
children *who were* the gods, Daityas, Nágas and the rest.
5 Aditi gave birth to the gods who rule over the three worlds,
Diti to the Daityas, and Danu to the fierce Dánavas whose
6 prowess is wide-reaching. And Vinatá *bore* Garuḍa and
Aruṇa; Khasá the Yakshas and Rákshasas indeed; and
7 Kadru bore the Nágas; Muni bore the Gandharvas; from
Krodhá were born the Kulyas; and from Rishṭá the bevies
of Apsarases; and Irá bore Airávata and other elephants, O
8 dvija; and Támrá bore daughters of whom S'yení was the
chief, O dvija, from *all of* whom were born the hawks,
9 vultures, parrots and other birds; from Ilá were born the
trees; from Pradhá the various kinds of aquatic animals.‡
This is the progeny which was begotten of Aditi by Kaśyapa.§
10 And by her sons and daughters' sons, by her sons' sons and

* For *devebhyas* the Bombay edition reads *Vedebhyas*, which is preferable.

† *Káśyapo náma námataḥ*; the Bombay edition agrees, but this can hardly be right. Káśyapa would be name of Kaśyapa's descendants.

‡ For *Pradháyáspatasáṁ gaṇáḥ* read *Pradháyá yádasáṁ gaṇáḥ* as in the Bombay edition.

§ Kaśyapa's wives and children are given differently in other authorities, *e.g.*, Mahá-Bhárata, Ádi-p., xvi, lxv. and lxvi; Kúrma Puráṇa xviii; Agni Puráṇa xix.

daughters' grandsons* and other *descendants* this world was overspread, yea by the offspring of those *males* and those *females*, O muni.

11 The chief of those sons of Kaśyapa are the hosts of gods. Now these hosts are characterized by goodness, by passion
12 and by ignorance, O muni. Brahmá, the chief of those learned in sacred lore, the highest *of all*, the Prajá-pati, made the gods participators in the sacrifices, and rulers over the
13 three worlds. The hostile Daityas and Dánavas and Rákshasas combining harassed them, and a very terrible war occurred
14 between them. Now the deities were vanquished for a thousand divine years, and the powerful Daityas and Dánavas
15 were victorious, O bráhman. Then Aditi, seeing her sons cast out and robbed of the three worlds by the Daityas and
16 Dánavas, O best of munis, and deprived of their shares of sacrifices, was exceedingly afflicted with grief, and made the
17 utmost efforts to propitiate the Sun. Concentrating her mind *thereon*, restricting her food, observing the utmost self-repression, she hymned the Sun, the ball of light that dwells in the sky.

Aditi spoke:

18 Reverence to thee who hast a sublime subtle golden body, O splendour of those who have splendour, O lord, O reposi-
19 tory of splendours, O eternal one! And the ardent form which thou hast who drawest up the waters for the benefit of the worlds, O lord of the *heavenly* cattle, to that I bow
20 reverently! The most ardent form which thou hast, who bearest the nectar that composes the moon to take it back during the space of eight months, to that I bow reverently!
21 The well-fattened† form which thou *hast*, who verily dischargest all that same nectar to *produce* rain, to that thy
22 cloud-*form* be reverence, O Sun! And that light-giving form of thine, which tends to mature the whole kingdom of plants that are produced through the pouring forth of

* *Dauhitrika*, a word not in the dictionary.

† *Á-pyáyaka*; a word not in the dictionary.

23 water, to that* I bow reverently! And that form of thine
which, when there is excessive cold by reason of the pouring
forth of snow and other *causes*, tends to nourish the crops
of that *winter* season—to the passing over of that thy *form*
24 be reverence! And that form of thine, which is not very
ardent and which is not very cold, *and* is mild in the season
of spring, to that be reverence, O divine Sun, *yea* reverence!
25 And *thy* other *form*, which fattens both all the gods and the
pitṛis, to that which causes the ripening of the crops be
26 revenence! That one form of thine which, being composed
of nectar for the vivification of plants, is quaffed by the
gods and pitṛis, to that, which is the soul of the moon, be
27 reverence! That form of thine which, consisting of the
universe, is combined with Agni and Soma these two forms
of the Sun,† to that, the soul of which is the good quali-
28 ties,‡ be reverence! That form of thine which, named the
three-fold *Veda* by reason of the unity of the Ṛić, Yajus and
Sáma *Vedas*, gives heat to this universe, to that be reverence,
29 O luminous one! That thy form moreover, which transcends
that *former one*, which is enunciated by uttering the word
"Om," *and* which is subtle, endless *and* stainless, reverence
be to that, the soul of which is Truth!

Márkaṇḍeya spoke:

30 In this manner the goddess, self-restrained, abstaining from food, offered praise day and night, desirous of propitiating the Sun, O muni.

31 A long time thereafter the adorable Sun rendered himself
visible to her, Daksha's daughter, in the sky, O best of
32 dvijas. She beheld a huge mass of glory, dwelling in the
sky and stationed on the earth, full of light, most difficult
33 to be gazed at because of its halo of flame. Seeing him then,
the goddess became bold to the utmost and spoke—

* For *tam̃* read *tan*?

† The Bombay edition reads *ápyáya-dáha-rúpábhyám*, "two forms of fatness and conflagration."

‡ *Guṇátmane* in the Bombay edition is better than *gaṇátmane*.

"Be gracious to me! I *can* not gaze on thee, O lord of the
34 *heavenly* cattle. Since I while fasting have beheld thee, at
first standing in the sky *and* most difficult to be gazed upon,
35 *and* afterwards as brilliant and burning, even so I behold
thee here on earth a globe of glory. Be gracious; may I see
thy form, O maker of day! O thou lord, who hast compassion on thy believers, I believe; protect my sons!

36 Thou, the Creator, createst this universe;
Exerting thyself thou protectest it to make it permanent;
In thee everything passes to its dissolution at the end. Thou art it.
Besides thee verily there is no other way *of existence* in all the world!

37 Thou art Brahmá *and* Hari! thou bearest the name Aja!* Thou art Indra,
The lord of wealth *Kuvera*, the lord of the pitṛis *Yama*, the lord of the waters† *Varuṇa*, the wind *Vayu*!
Thou art the Moon, Agni, the lord of the sky, the supporter of the earth,‡ the Ocean!
What praise must be given to thee who art the splendour of all souls and forms?

38 O lord of sacrifice, bráhmans devoted to their own ceremonies, day by day,
Praising thee with manifold words, offer sacrifice to thee.
Meditating on thee with firmly restrained minds
And absorbed in religious devotion mortals§ attain unto the sublimest condition.

39 Thou warmest, thou maturest the universe; thou protectest it, thou turnest it to ashes.

* Either "the unborn one," or "the driver, mover, instigator."

† *Ambu-patiḥ* violates the metre; read *ap-patiḥ* as in the Bombay edition.

‡ *Gagana-patiḥ mahí-dharo*; this is the reading of the Bombay edition. The Calcutta reading *gagana-mahí-dharo* makes the verse two syllables short.

§ *Martyáḥ*, the reading of the Bombay edition. The Calcutta edition reads instead *yoga-múrtyá*, "by means of the body which belongs to religious devotion;" but this violates the metre.

Thou makest it manifest, thou makest it sound forth* with thy rays which are pregnant with water.
Thou createst it again also in unerring manifestations.
Thou art reverenced by mortal *beings* that move, but art unapproachable by workers of iniquity.†

Canto CV.

The Birth of Márttaṇḍa.

The Sun revealed himself to Aditi and became her son as Márttaṇḍa—This name is explained—Márttaṇḍa destroyed the demons and restored the gods to their sovereign positions.

Márkaṇḍeya spoke:

1 Thereupon from out of that his own glory the Sun re-
vealed‡ himself; the lord, the Sun, appeared then, like unto
2 glowing copper. And the luminous one spoke, O muni, unto
the goddess, who fell prostrate when she beheld him—
3 "Choose from me the coveted boon that thou desirest." And
she, lying prostrate with her head *on the ground and* pressing
the earth with her knees, answered the Sun who present in
his very person offered her a boon:—
4 "O god! be gracious; the three worlds have been snatched§
from my sons, and the shares in sacrifices *also*, by both the
5 Daityas and the Dánavas who excel them in strength. Do
thou, O lord of the *heavenly* cattle, bestow on me favour for

* *Hrádayasi* in both editions. The meaning is no doubt "to shout for joy;" see the Bible, Psalm lxv. 9-13.

† The Bombay edition reads the second half of this verse very differently—"Thou the lotus-born *god* createst it; thou who art named the Unwavering one protectest it, and thou destroyest it at the end of the age. Thou alone art awful in form!"

‡ For *ádir bhúto* read *ávir-bhúto*, as in the Bombay edition.

§ For *kritaṁ* read *hṛitaṁ*.

that purpose; with a portion *of thyself* enter thou into brother-
6 hood with them and destroy their enemies. In order that my
sons may again partake of the shares of the sacrifices, O lord,
7 and may become rulers of the three worlds, O Sun, do thou
then most graciously show compassion* on my sons, O Sun,
who removest the afflictions of suppliants; thou art called the
Author of permanence."

Márkaṇḍeya spoke:

8 Thereupon the adorable lord, the Sun, the robber of the
waters, spoke unto prostrate Aditi, O bráhman, while his
9 countenance was benign with favour†—"Taking birth in thy
womb with all my thousand portions, I *will* speedily destroy
the foes of thy sons, O Aditi, in security."‡
10 Having spoken thus the adorable Sun vanished *from her
sight*; and she ceased from her austerities, having gained all
11 her desire. Thereupon the Sun's ray called Sausumna§ from
out of his thousand rays|| became incarnate in the womb of
12 the mother of the gods, O bráhman. And she, with her
mind composed, performed the arduous ćándráyaṇa penance¶
and other austerities. Being pure she conceived him, knowing
13 that the embryo was a heavenly one, O bráhman. Then
spoke Kaśyapa to her with words somewhat confused through
14 anger,—"Why dost thou destroy the egg in thy womb by
continual fasting?" And she said to him,—"Seest thou
this egg within my womb, O wrathful man? It has
not been destroyed; it shall be for the death of our
adversaries."

* For *anukampá* read *anukampám*.

† For *prasádaṁ sumukho* read *prasáda-sumukho*.

‡ For *nir-vṛitáḥ* read *nir-vṛitaḥ*.

§ This is the reading of both the editions, but it is not in the dictionary. *Su-shumṇa* is the name of one of the Sun's seven principal rays, that which is supposed to supply heat to the moon. The reading here should therefore presumably be *Su-shumṇa* or *Saushumṇa*.

|| For *raśmi-sahasraṁ* read *raśmi-sahasrát* as in the Bombay edition.

¶ See Manu vi. 20.

Márkaṇḍeya spoke:

15 Having spoken so she, who is the path of the gods,*
in anger at her husband's words, gave birth to the child then
16 which blazed brilliantly with glory. Kaśyapa, on seeing the
child which shone like the rising sun, fell prostrate and
17 praised it respectfully with ancient Ṛić hymns. Being
so praised, he revealed himself from out the fœtal egg, having
a lustre like unto the petal of a lotus-flower, pervading the
18 regions of the sky with his glory. Moreover a voice deep
as a thunder-cloud's, addressing† Kaśyapa, best of munis,
from the air, spoke, issuing from no corporeal being—
19 "Whereas thou, O muni, hast spoken of this egg as des-
troyed‡ to thee, therefore, O muni, this thy son shall be
20 called Márttaṇḍa. And he as lord shall exercise the Sun's
sway on the earth; and he shall slay the Asuras, the foes
who have carried off the shares of the sacrifices."
21 The gods hearing this speech from heaven assembled
together, *and* experienced unparalleled joy; and the Dánavas
22 were bereft of their vigour. Thereupon Indra challenged
the Daityas to battle; and the Dánavas filled with joy
23 encountered the gods. Terrible was the battle of the gods
with the Asuras, wherein all the regions between the worlds
were rendered brilliant with the light from the arms and
24 weapons. In that battle the adorable Márttaṇḍa looked at
those great Asuras, and being burnt up by his splendour they
25 were reduced to ashes. Thereupon all the dwellers in
heaven experienced unparalleled joy, and praised Márttaṇḍa
26 the source of splendour and also Aditi; moreover they re-
gained their own spheres of dominion and their shares of the
sacrifices as before; and the adorable Márttaṇḍa also exer-
27 cised his own dominion. Like unto a rounded ball of fire
with rays *shooting out* both downward and upward like a
globular flower-head of the kadamba, the Sun assumed a
body that did not flash over-poweringly.

* This is the Bombay reading, *suráraṇiḥ*. The Calcutta reading *surávaniḥ* seems incorrect.

† For *ábhásya* read *ábháshya?* ‡ *Máritam aṇḍam.*

Canto CVI.

The paring down of the Sun's body.

The Sun married Viśva-karman's daughter Sañjñá and had three children by her, Manu Vaivasvata, Yama and Yamuná—Sañjñá could not endure the Sun's glory and leaving her shadow C'háyá departed—C'háyá-Sañjñá took her place and had three children by the Sun—She cursed Yama for unfilial conduct, but the Sun minimised the curse and perceived the deception.—The Sun visited Viśva-karman and the latter placing the Sun on his wheel pared down his glory—The world was thrown into chaos as the Sun was whirled around—The gods and celestial beings hymned the Sun.

Márkaṇḍeya spoke:

1 Now the Prajá-pati Viśva-karman, after falling prostrate
and propitiating him, gave his daughter named Sañjñá to
2 *the Sun*, Vivasvat.* Manu Vaivasvata was begotten by
Vivasvat of her then, and his nature has been already indeed
3 declared particularly.† He, *Vivasvat*, lord of the *heavenly*
cattle, begot three children of her, two most illustrious sons
4 and a daughter Yamuná, O muni. Manu Vaivasvata was the
eldest, the god who presides over śráddhas, the Prajá-pati;
5 then were born Yama and Yamí as twins. With the exceed-
ing splendour that Márttaṇḍa Vivasvat possessed, he scorched
the three worlds and the moveable and immoveable things
6 therein very grievously. But Sañjñá saw Vivasvat's globe-like
form and, being impatient of his great splendour, gazed at
her own shadow *C'háyá* and spoke:—

Sañjñá spoke:

7 Fare thee well! I will go to my father's very own abode.
Yet thou must stay here without change at my command, O

* See Canto lxxvii. The same story is repeated here.

† See Canto lxxviii, verse 27, and Canto lxxix.

8 fair one; and thou must show honour to these two boys for
me and to *this* daughter who is of noble rank; and thou must
not declare this at all to the god.

C'háyá *the Shadow* spoke:

9 "Unto *enduring* the seizing of my hair, unto undergoing
curses, O goddess, I will never declare thy intention; go where
thou wishest."

10 Being addressed thus by C'háyá, Sañjñá went to her
father's dwelling; and there she, the beautiful of eyes,
11 abode some time in her father's house. Her father told her
again and again to go to her husband. Then turning herself
into a mare she departed to the Northern Kurus, O bráhman.
12 There, *like* a chaste wife, she practised austerities, fasting,
O great muni.

When Sañjñá had gone to her father, C'háyá, assiduous to
13 *Sañjñá's* command, and assuming her form, waited on the
Sun; and the adorable Sun begat of her, *he* thinking *it was*
14 of Sañjñá, two sons in addition and a daughter. The first-
born of the two sons was equal to the eldest *son* Manu,
15 hence he was *called* Sávarṇi, O best of dvijas. And the
other, who was the second *son*, became the planet Saturn.
16 And the daughter who was Tapatí, her king Samvaraṇa
chose in marriage.*

Now as queen Sañjñá used to behave to those her own sons,
17 *C'háyá* did not behave to those eldest born *sons* with such
affection. Manu suffered that *conduct* in her, and Yama did
18 not suffer it in her. Now being sorely distressed when his
father's wife used to beseech him frequently, he Yama, by
reason of both anger and childishness and indeed by the
19 force of predestination, threatened C'háyá-Sañjñá with his
foot, O muni, and thereupon *the Shadow*-Sañjñá,† full of
resentment, cursed Yama severely.

* See Mahá-Bhárata, Âdi-p. xciv. 3738, xcv. 3791; and clxxi-clxxiii where it is described how Sambaraṇa while hunting met her, fell in love with her and gained her at length after propitiating the Sun. Her son was Kuru, the progenitor of the Kauravas.

† This must be *C'háyá-Sañjñá*; but both editions read *Sañjñá*.

C'háyá spoke :

20 "Since thou threatenest thy father's wife, a venerable *lady*, with thy foot, thy very foot shall therefore assuredly drop down."

21 Now Yama was deeply afflicted in mind at that curse, and he, righteous of soul, along with Manu made it all known to his father.

Yama spoke :

22 O lord, our mother behaves not with equal affection towards
us *all*; leaving us aside who are the elder, she wishes to foster
23 the two younger. I lifted my foot against her, but did not let
it fall on her body; whether *it was* through childishness or
24 through foolishness, do thou, Sir, deign to pardon it. I have
been cursed, dear father, by my mother in *her* anger. Since
I am her son, verily therefore I revere her, my mother, (O best
25 of ascetics). Even towards unworthy sons a mother is not
wanting in good feelings, O father; how shall *a mother* say
26 this out—"May thy foot drop down, O son!" Think, O
adorable* lord of the *heavenly* cattle, *of some way* so that
through thy favour this my foot may not drop down now by
reason of my mother's curse.

The Sun spoke :

27 Without doubt, my son, this curse must take effect here,
since anger entered into thee, who art wise in righteousness
28 *and* who speakest truth. For all curses indeed a remedy
assuredly exists; yet nowhere is there that which can turn a
29 curse away from those who are cursed by a mother. This
thy mother's word then cannot be made false; I will *however*
devise something as a favour for thee, because of my love for
30 *thee my* son. Insects taking *some* flesh *from thy foot* shall go
forth to the earth;† her word *is thus* made true, and thou
shalt be saved.

* For *bhagaván* read *bhagavan* as in the Bombay edition.

† See Canto lxxviii, verse 28.

Márkaṇḍeya spoke:

31 Now the Sun said to C'háyá,—"Why among thy sons,
who are quite equal, dost thou show more affection to one?
32 Assuredly thou art not Sañjñá the mother of these; thou art
some one *else* come *in her stead; for* how could a mother curse
one son even among worthless children?"

Márkaṇḍeya spoke:

33 And she avoiding that *question* gave no answer to the Sun.
And he concentrating his soul fell into abstract thought* and
34 perceived the truth. C'háyá-Sañjñá saw the lord of heaven
was ready to curse her, and trembling with fear declared *to*
35 *him* what had happened, O bráhman. Now the Sun, enraged at
hearing that, went then to his father-in-law. And he paid
honour fittingly to the Maker of day, and being strictly
religious he pacified him who wished to burn him up in his
wrath.

Viśva-karman spoke:

36 Permeated with surpassing glory is this thy form which
is so hardly endurable; hence Sañjñá, unable to endure it,
37 practises austerities in the forest in sooth. Thou shalt now
see her, Sir, thy own wife, beautiful in her behaviour, prac-
tising most arduous austerities in the forest on account of
38 thy *too glorious* form. I remember Brahmá's word: if it
please thee, my lord, I *will* restrain thy beloved form, O lord
of heaven.

Márkaṇḍeya spoke:

39 Inasmuch as the Sun's form was formerly spherical, so the
40 adorable Sun said to Tvashṭṛi, "Be it so!" And Viśva-
karman, being permitted by the Sun in S'áka-dvípa, mounted
the Sun on his wheel and set to work to pare down his glory.
41 While the Sun, which was the centre of all the worlds, was
whirling round, the earth with its oceans, mountains and
42 forests mounted up to the sky, and the whole heavens with
the moon, planets and stars went downward, *and* were tossed

* For *muktas* read *yuktas* as in the Bombay edition.

43 together *and* confused, O illustrious bráhman. And all
creatures also were scattered about with the waters out of
the ocean;* lofty hills were shattered to pieces, their sum-
44 mits and roots were torn asunder. The supports of the pole,
all the asterisms,† O best of munis, with their bands and
45 foundations splitting, went downwards in thousands. Hurled
away by the wind caused by the swift whirling, great
clouds wandering about with terrible thunder crumbled to
46 pieces all around. The earth, the air and the nether regions,
rolled about by the Sun's whirling, uttered their voices;
47 there was exceeding chaos then, O best of munis. While all
the worlds were whirling round, O bráhman, the divine
ṛishis and the gods with Brahmá sang praises to the Sun:—
48 "Thou art the most ancient god among the gods; this is
known from thy nature. At the periods of creation, conti-
nuance and dissolution thou existest with a triple division.
49 Hail to thee, O lord of the world, thou producer of warmth,
rain and snow! Have pleasure in the peace of the worlds,
O god of gods, O Maker of the day!"
50 And Indra approaching the god, as he was being pared
down, praised him,—"Be victorious, O god who pervadest
51 the world! Be victorious, O lord of all the worlds!" And
the seven ṛishis next, with Vasishṭha and Atri at their head,
praised *the Sun* with various hymns, exclaiming "Hail!
52 hail!" And the Bálikhilyas then, filled with joy, praised the
Sun with the noblest and most ancient Ṛić hymns enunciated
53 in the Veda, as he was being pared down—"Thou, O master,
art final emancipation from existence to those who strive
after emancipation; thou art worthy to be contemplated as
the supreme *one* by those who engage in contemplation!
Thou art the way for all created beings, even for those who
54 are occupied with ritual.‡ May there be a blessing for the

* This is the reading of the Bombay edition which is preferable, *abdhitaḥ*, instead of *arc'ishaḥ*.

† For *dhishṭyáni* read *dhishṇyáni*.

‡ *Karma-káṇḍe*; the department of the Veda which relates to ceremonial acts and sacrificial rites.

people, O lord of the gods! May there be a blessing for us,
O lord of the worlds! May there ever be a blessing for us in
what is two-footed! And may there be a blessing for us in
what is four-footed!"

55 Then the bands of Vidyádharas and the Yakshas, Rákshasas
and Nágas joining their hands reverently all fell prostrate
56 with their heads before the Sun, and uttered words such as
these, giving joy to his mind and ears,—"May thy glory become
endurable to created beings, O thou who causest created
57 beings to exist!" Next Háhá and Huhu, Nárada and Tumburu,
who were skilful in music, and who were accomplished in the
58 three musical scales based on the shaḍja, madhyama and
gándhára notes,* began to sing in joy-giving *accents* to the
Sun both with modulations † and *various* divisions of time,‡
59 with combinations.§ And Viśvác'í and Ghṛitáćí, Urvaśí and
Tilottamá, Menaká and Saha-janyá and Rambhá,|| the choicest
60 among the Apsarases, danced whilst the Sun, the lord of the
worlds, was being pared down, the while they displayed ¶
many dramaṭic actions replete with amorous and coquettish
61 gestures and dalliance. Then were caused to give forth their
music there flutes and lutes, and other musical pipes, drums
62 and kettle-drums, tabours, large drums and double drums, the
drums of the gods *and* conchs in hundreds and thousands.
And every *place* was rendered loudly resonant by the
63 Gandharvas who were singing, and the bevies of Apsarases
who were dancing, and with the sounds of trumpets and
musical instruments.

Then all the gods, joining their hands reverently, and
64 bowing their bodies in faith, prostrated themselves before
the Thousand-rayed *god* as he was being pared down. In

* See page 130, note †.

† *Múrc'haná*; see page 131, note *.

‡ *Tála*; see page 131, notes † and ||. But the Bombay edition reads *tánais'*, "with protracted tones."

§ *Sa-prayogaiḥ*; or *samprayogaiḥ* as in the Bombay edition.

|| For *Rambhás'c'a* read *Rambhá c'a*.

¶ Both editions read *kurvanto*, but read *kurvatyo* instead?

that resounding noise, where all the gods were gathered together, Viśva-karman then gradually diminished his glory.

65 After hearing thus of the paring down of the body of the Sun, who is the cause of the cold, rainy and hot seasons, *and* who is praised by Vishṇu on the lotus seat of S'iva, one goes* to the Sun's world at the close of life.

Canto CVII.

Hymn to the Sun.

Viśva-karman praises the Sun, while he is reducing the Sun's splendour.

Márkaṇḍeya spoke:

1 While the Sun was being pared down, the Prajá-pati Viśva-karman then uttered this hymn, wherewith his hair stood erect with joy,† to the Sun.

2 "To the Sun, who is compassionate for the welfare of those
who fall prostrate *before him,* who is great of soul, who has
seven equally swift horses, who has great glory, who awakens
the beds of lotuses, who splits asunder‡ the covering of the
3 veil of darkness, be reverence! To him who works merit
through the superabundance of fire, who gives many objects
of desire, who reclines amid beams of radiant fire, who brings
4 welfare to all the world, be reverence! To the Sun, who is
without birth§, the cause of the three worlds, the soul of
created beings, the lord of the *heavenly* cattle, the bull,
highest among those who are greatly compassionate, the home
5 whence the eye originated,|| be reverence! To the Sun, who

* For *vajati* read *vrajati.*

† *Udbhúta-pulaka-stotram;* both editions read the same, but *udbhúta-pulakaḥ stotram* would seem preferable.

‡ *Ava-páṭine;* a word not in the dictionary.

§ *Ajáya;* or "*who is* the driver, the instigator."

|| *C'akshuḥ-prabhaválayáya;* or "the pre-eminent abode of the eye."

is maintained by knowledge, *who is* the inmost soul,* the foundation of the world, desirer of the world's welfare, the self-existent, the eye of all the worlds, highest among the
6 gods, boundless in glory, be reverence! *Thou*, for a monent the crest jewel of the day-spring mountain†, the honoured messenger‡ of the hosts of gods to the world, thou, whose body consists of a thousand wide-spreading rays of light,
7 shinest on the world, driving away the darknesses. By reason of *thy* intoxication from drinking up like spirituous liquor the darkness of the world, thy body has acquired a deep red *hue*,§ O Sun, so that thou shinest exceedingly with
8 masses of light that calls the three worlds into life. Mounting thy equally proportioned chariot that sways about gracefully and is widely pleasing||, with horses that are ever unwearied¶, O adorable *god*, thou coursest the broad world
9 for *our* good.** O Sun, thou purifier of the three worlds, protect me, who am devoted to thy parrot-hued steeds, *and who am* most pure†† through the dust of thy feet, *and who am*

* For *jñána-bhútántarátmane* (the third syllable of which violates the metre, the *Vaṁśa-sthavila*) the Bombay edition reads *jñána-bhṛite 'ntarátmaṅe*, which I have adopted.

† For *udayác'ala-mauli-mâline* (the last word of which violates the metre, the *Sumukhí*) the Bombay edition reads *udayác'ala-mauli-maṇiḥ*, which I have adopted.

‡ *Sura-gaṇa-mahita-hito;* both editions read the same, but the word *mahita* violates the metre; it should consist of a long and a short syllable. Perhaps the word should be *mánya*.

§ For *vilohita-vigrahát* (which violates the metre in the last word) the Bombay edition reads *vilóhita-vigrahatá*, which is correct.

|| *C'áru-vikampitam uru-ruc'iram;* both editions read the same, but it violates the metre, the *Sumukhí*. I would suggest as an amendment *Ruc'ira-vikampitam úrdhva-c'aram*, "that sways about pleasingly, moving on high."

¶ For *akhila-hayair*, which violates the metre, read *akhinna-hayair* with the Bombay edition.

** *C'arasi jagad-dhitáya vitatam;* both editions read the same, but it violates the metre, the *Sumukhí*. The metre is satisfied by altering the words, *c'arasi hitáya jagad vitatam*.

†† Instead of *-pavitra-talam* I take the Bombay reading *-pavitra-tamam*.

prostrate *before thee*, O thou who art kind to folk that bow
10 *to thee*! Thus to the Sun, who exists as the procreator of all
the worlds, *who is* the sole cause of the glory that calls the
three worlds into life,* who exists as the lamp of all the
worlds—to thee, O choicest of the thirty *gods*, I ever prostrate
myself!"†

CANTO CVIII.

The Majesty of the Sun.

From the glory pared off from the Sun, Viśva-karman made the gods' weapons.—The Sun found his wife among the Northern Kurus and begat of her the Aśvins and Revanta.—The stations allotted to the Sun's offspring are declared.

Márkaṇḍeya spoke:

1 While he was thus hymning the Sun Viśva-karman kept
intact in spherical shape the sixteenth part of the glory of
2 the lord of heaven; and when fifteen parts of his glory
had been pared away, the Sun's body was exceedingly beauti-
3 ful and charming then. And with the splendour that was
pared away from him was fashioned Vishṇu's discus; and
4 S'iva's trident, and Kuvera's palki, the rod of the lord of
the dead, and the spear of the gods' general. And Viśva-
5 karman made the brilliant weapons of the other gods with
the Sun's splendour for the quelling of their foes. He
whose splendour had been thus pared down shone with no
6 excessive splendour. Márttaṇḍa retained a body resplendent
in every limb.

* Instead of *Tri-bhuvana-pávana-dháma-bhútam*, which violates the metre, the *Pushpitágrá*, I have taken the Bombay reading *Tri-bhuvana-bhávana-dháma-hetum ekam*.

† The Calcutta reading *Devam praṇato 'smi Viśva-karmáṇam* violates the metre, and is incorrect because it is Viśva-karman who is speaking. I have followed the Bombay reading *Tridaśa-vara praṇato 'smi sarvadá tvám*. Instead of these last two words *Viśva-karmá* might well be read.

Concentrating his thoughts he beheld his wife in the form
7 of a mare, unassailable by all created beings by reason of her
austerities and self-repression. And going to the Northern
8 Kurus, the Sun became a horse and approached her. And
she, beholding him approaching, because of her fear of a
strange male, went face to face with him, being intent on
9 guarding her rear. And thereupon they joined their noses,
when they both met there, and his glory *passed* from the
10 Sun's two nostrils* into the mare. Two gods were begotten
there, the two Aśvins, who are the two best physicians,
namely Násatya and Dasra, the sons who issued forth from
11 the mare's† mouth; these two are indeed the sons of Márt-
taṇḍa while he bore a horse's form. And at the termination
of the flow of his semen was born Revanta, holding a sword
12 and bow, clad in armour, riding on horseback, *and* carrying
arrows and a quiver.

Then the Sun revealed his own unsullied form. She
13 perceiving his form was mild felt a joy; and the Sun, the
robber of the waters, led to his own home this his wife
14 Saňjñá, changed *again* into her own form and full of love.

After that he who was her first-born son became Manu
Vaivasvata.

15 And the second was "Yama"‡ because of the curse, and
he was "The Righteous-eyed" because of *his father's* favour.
Now *he was called* Yama as having been greatly afflicted in
16 mind by that curse; *and* since righteousness delights him,
he is known therefore as the "King of righteousness."
17 'Worms taking flesh from thy foot shall fall to the earth'—
so saying his father himself put§ an end to this curse. And
because he is righteous-eyed, he is impartial to the good and
18 the evil. Therefore the Dispeller of darkness appointed him
to the southern region; his adorable father gave to him the

* *Násikábhyám.* *Násiká* here has its original meaning.

† The Calcutta edition reads *aśva-vaktrád* and the Bombay *aśvi-vaktrád*; read however *aśvá-vaktrád?*

‡ "Restraint, check."

§ For *c'akte* read *c'akre.*

19 duty of protecting the world, O bráhman, and the lordship
over the pitṛis.

And the Sun, being well-satisfied, made Yamuná the river
which flows from the recesses of *mount* Kalinda.

20 The two Aśvins were made the gods' physicians by their
high-souled father.

And Revanta was appointed to the lordship over the
21 Guhyakas; and even thus spoke the adorable *god* then who
is acknowledged by the world,—"Thou shalt indeed be
22 worthy of worship by the entire world, my child; and
mortals, who shall call thee to mind amid the terrors of
forests and other *lonely places*, of great conflagrations, of
enemies and robbers, shall be delivered out of great calamity.
23 Comfort, intelligence, happiness, kingship, perfect health,
fame, exalted position—*these*, when worshipped *and* well-
satisfied, thou shalt bestow on men."

24 And C'háyá-Saññjñá's son Sávarṇa was of very great fame;
he will be the eighth Manu, *by name* Sávarṇaka, in a future
25 time. At present, indeed, *this* lord performs terrible austeri-
ties on Meru's summit. His brother became the planet Saturn
26 according to the Sun's command.* Now the Sun's daughter,
who was younger than they, O bráhman, became that
best of rivers, the Yamuná, which cleanses the world.†

27 Now I will speak fully of Manu Vaivasvata, who was the
illustrious eldest *son*, and to whom belongs this present
28 creation. He, who may either hear or read of this, the
origin of the gods who are the offspring of Vivasvạt, and
29 of the Sun's majesty, may obtain deliverance when he falls
into calamity and may gain great fame. This *story of the*
majesty of the primeval god, the high-souled Márttaṇḍa,
when listened to, quells the sin that has been committed
by day or night.

* See Canto cvi, verse 15. In Canto lxxviii, verse 33 he and his elder brother are not distinguished clearly.

† This is a mistake, see verse 19 above. She was Tapatí, see Canto lxxviii, verse 34, and Canto cvi, verse 16.

CANTO CIX.

Praise of the Sun.

Márkaṇḍeya tells the story of king Rájya-vardhana.—After the king had reigned many years, his queen sorrowed over finding a grey hair in his head—He comforted her and resolved to depart to the forest—His vassals and subjects tried to dissuade him and in vain—They performed many austerities in order to propitiate the Sun and went to Káma-rúpa and continued their worship—At length the Sun appeared to them in bodily shape.

Kraushṭuki spoke:

1 Adorable Sir! thou hast well declared the birth of the Sun's offspring, the majesty of the primeval god and his nature
2 at very full length. Nevertheless I desire, O best of munis, to hear more about the Sun's majesty comprehensively; deign therefore with favour to tell me of it.

Márkaṇḍeya spoke:

3 Be it heard *then!* I tell thee of the majesty of the primeval god, Vivasvat, what he did formerly when worshipped by mankind.

4 There was a famous king, Dama's son, *named* Rájya-vardhana;* he, lord of the earth, kept the earth well protected.
5 Now the realm, being protected by that high-souled *monarch* in righteousness, increased day by day in people and wealth, O
6 bráhman. And joyous and thriving exceedingly were all the subordinate kings on the earth without exception, while he *was* king; *and so also were his* people, both town and country
7 folk. No portent *visited them*, nor sickness, nor the fear that comes from serpents, nor was there fear of drought there,
8 while Dama's son was king. And he offered up great sacrifices, and gave gifts to those who asked; he enjoyed even the

* He is mentioned in the Vishṇu Pur. IV. i. Dama was son of Narishyanta and grandson of the great Marutta. The story of these three kings is told in cantos cxxix to cxxxvi below, and the Puráṇa ends abruptly with Dama. Rájya-vardhana is called Ráshṭra-vardhana in the Váyu Puráṇa,

pleasures of sense without hindrance to true righteousness.
9 While he ruled the kingdom thus *and* protected his people
duly, seven thousand years passed away as if a single day.
10 Now the daughter of Vidúratha, king of the South, was his
11 queen, Mánini by name *and* high-spirited* *indeed.* One day
she, the fine-browed noble *lady*, shed tears when his head had
not been dressed with ointment, in the sight of the king's
12 folk. When her tear-drops *fell* on the king's body, he saw
Mánini was of tearful countenance then and questioned her.
13 In sooth beholding her weeping and shedding tears silently,
14 Rájya-vardhana asked Mánini, "Why is this?" But she,
being prudent, when questioned by her husband, replied then,
15 "It is nothing." The king questioned her again.† And after
the king *had* questioned her often, she, the slender-waisted
lady, showed him a grey hair growing among his abundant
16 locks. "Look at this, O king; is this a cause of vexation to
me, most luckless that I am?" And the king laughed thereat.
17 With a smile quoth he to his wife—while listened all the
kings and citizens, *and* the kings who were assembled there—
18 "Away with grief, O wide-eyed *lady!* thou must not weep,
pretty one! Birth, growth, decline of life and other changes
19 *befall* all living beings. I have studied all the Vedas; I have
offered sacrifices by thousands; I have given *alms* to bráh-
mans; and I have begotten sons, O *lady* of finest countenance;
20 I have enjoyed along with thee pleasures which are very
hardly attainable by mortals; and I have protected the earth
21 well; I have borne myself ably in battles; I have laughed
with my beloved friends; and I have sported in the heart
of the woods. What else is there which I have not done,
22 that thou art frightened at grey hairs, O lady? Let my hair
become grey; let wrinkles come to me, O beauteous one; let
my body pass into weakness; *for* I have been successful, O
23 Mánini! Because thou hast shown me a grey hair on my
head, O lady, here then I take medical treatment therefor
24 through resorting to the forest. First in childhood *there is*

* *Mánini.*

† For *bhúpaḥ* read *bhúyaḥ*.

childhood's action; similarly *there is* action which *is natural*
in youth; and also such as is fitting in early manhood; in old
25 age there is resort to the forest. Since those who lived before
me did so, lady, and also those who lived before them,
I see no reason whatever then for thee to shed tears. Away
26 with thy vexation! Does not the sight of this grey hair
cause me elevation? Weep not; it is futile."

Márkaṇḍeya spoke:

27 Then the kings and citizens who were in his presence did
him reverence, and the kings addressed Rájya-vardhana with
conciliatory words, O great ṛishi:—

28 "It is not for thee to weep with this thy wife, O king; it is
29 we *who* must weep here, or rather all living beings. Since
thou, O master, speakest the word indicating that thou wilt
dwell in the forest, life falls therefore from us who have been
30 tenderly cherished by thee, O king. We will all go, O king,
if thou goest to the forest. All the inhabitants of the earth
31 will thereby suffer loss in all their ceremonies without doubt,
when thou, O master, shalt take up thy abode in the forest;
and if that *loss* tends to injure righteousness, let that *course*
32 be discarded. Seven thousand years this earth has been
guarded by thee; have regard, O king, to the great merit that
33 has accrued therefrom! The austerities, which thou, O great
king, wilt perform while dwelling in the forest, are not worth*
the sixteenth part of this thy guardianship over the earth!"

The king spoke:

34 "Seven thousand years I have protected this earth; now
35 this my time has come to dwell in the forest. I have begotten
children. Now that I have seen my children and their de-
scendants, Death truly will not allow me a very few days.
36 Understand, O citizens, that this grey hair on my head has
become a messenger from ignoble Death, who is very sharp
37 in his actions. Being such, I will place my son in my kingdom,
and abandon worldly pleasures, and will, as a dweller in the
forest, perform austerities until Yama's troops arrive *for me*."

* For *nárhanti* read *nárhati*?

Márkaṇḍeya spoke:

38 Being desirous of departing to the forest the king then en-
quired of the astrologers about the *best* days and moments for
39 anointing his son in the kingdom. And on hearing the king's
speech they became confused in mind; they who were skilled
in the scriptures knew not the day nor moment nor the hours.*
40 And the astrologers spoke to the king *with voices* inarticulate
with tears;—"Our various knowledge has perished after that
we have heard this thy speech, O king."
41 Then *people* came in a multitude both from other cities and
also from dependent countries, and next from that city.
42 Springing up, O muni, the most eminent bráhmans, their heads
quivering *with emotion*, addressed the king who desired to
43 depart to the forest;—"Be gracious! Protect us, O king,
as we have been protected a long time past. The whole world
will sink down, when thou, O king, hast betaken thyself to
44 the forest. Do thou then so act, O king, that the world sink
not. And while we, such *as we are*, live *our* very short time, O
hero, we desire not to see the regal throne deprived of thee, O
lord."

Márkaṇḍeya spoke:

45 Thus both they and other dvijas heading the citizens, and
kings, dependants and ministers appealed *to him*, and appealed
46 again and again; *but* when he does not withdraw his deter-
mination to *take up his* abode in the forest, and returns them
47 the answer, "Death will not suffer it," both his ministers and
dependants, and the citizens, and the aged men and the dvijas,
assembled together and took counsel, "What must be done
48 here?" While they took counsel, O bráhman, this reso-
lution developed there among those who were devotedly attached
49 to that most righteous king—'Giving ourselves over absolutely
to deep meditation, we *will* with composed minds propitiate
the Sun with austerities and beseech him for this king's life.'
50 Being all resolved alike there on *that* object, some *of them* paid
adoration to the Sun with *their own* bodies, by presenting to

* *Horá* (the Greek word); or "the rising of the zodiacal signs."

him the argha offering and presents and other oblations in due
51 course; others gratified the Sun by maintaining silence, and
52 others by repeating the Ṛić, Yajus and Sáman hymns; and
other dvijas abstaining from food and lying down on river sand-
banks, wearied with austerities, made propitiation of the Sun;
53 and others, applying themselves to the oblation to Fire, day
and night repeated hymns composed to the Sun; others cast-
54 ing their eyes on the Sun remained standing there. Even
thus, applying themselves to those several rites, did they work
in manifold ways with exceeding determination in order to
propitiate the Sun.

55 Now while they were striving thus to propitiate the Sun, a
56 Gandharva named Su-dáman came near and spoke thus—"If
ye desire, O dvijas, to propitiate the Sun, let this then be done,
57 whereby the Sun will become well-pleased. Therefore—there
is a forest named Guru-viśála, frequented by the Siddhas, in
very mountainous Káma-rúpa—go there verily in haste.
58 There perform your propitiation of the Sun with minds com-
pletely composed; the Siddhas' friendly region is there; there
ye shall obtain all your desires."

Márkaṇḍeya spoke:

59 On hearing this his speech, those dvijas went to that forest
and beheld the sacred and beautiful shrine of the Sun there.
60 Those bráhmans and *men of* other castes, diminishing their food,
and being indefatigable, O bráhman, offered worship there en-
61 riched with incense, flowers and oblations; and with composed
minds, celebrating his worship with flowers, ungnents and
other *gifts*, with incense, perfumes and other *fragrance* also,
with prayers, sacrificial oblations, food, lamps and other *offer-
ings*, those dvijas gratified the Sun, O bráhman.

The bráhmans spoke:

62 Let us approach the Sun as our refuge, the god who in splen-
dour surpasses gods, Dánavas and Yakshas, the planets, and
63 the heavenly bodies; the lord of gods, who dwelling also
in the sky makes *everything* around brilliant, and penetrates
64 the earth and the atmosphere with his rays; *even him who has*

the names Áditya, Bháskara, Bhánu, Savitṛi, Divákara, Púshan
65 and Aryaman, Svar-bhánu ;* him who has flaming rays, who is
the fire which shall destroy *the universe* at the end of the four
ages, difficult to be gazed at, who persists to the end of the
final dissolution ; the lord of yogins, and the never-ending *one ;*
66 *who is* red, yellow, white and black ; him who dwells in the
oblation made to Fire by ṛishis, and among the gods of sacri-
fice ; imperishable, sublime, secret, who is the supreme gate to
67 final emancipation from existence ; and who traverses the sky
with hymns in the form of horses which are yoked together at
his rising and setting ; who is always intent on circumambulating
68 Meru reverently. And we have sought unto the light-giver,
who is not true and yet true, *who is* a sacred multiform place
of pilgrimage, *who is* the permanence of the universe, and is be-
69 yond thought; *him* who is Brahmá, who is S'iva, who is Vishṇu,
who is Prajá-pati ; *who is* the wind,† the atmosphere and water,
70 the earth and its mountains and oceans ; *who is* the planets, the
constellations, the moon and other *heavenly bodies*, trees bear-
ing blossom and fruit, *other* trees and herbs ; who sets in mo-
tion righteousness and unrighteousness, among created
beings, *those* which are manifest and *those* which are
71 not manifest. Brahmá's *body*, and S'iva's, and Vishṇu's
is the body, of thee, the Sun, whose special nature is three-fold
72 indeed. May the Sun be gracious! *May* the Sun, of whom, *as*
lord without beginning, all this world composes the body, and
who is the the life of the worlds—may he be gracious to us!
73 *May* the Sun, whose first‡ form is luminous *and* can hardly be
gazed upon because of its circle of splendour, *and whose* second
74 *form* is the gentle lunar *orb*—may he be gracious to us! And
may the Sun, from those two forms of whom this universe has
been fashioned consisting of Agni and Soma—may he, the god,
be gracious to us!

* As a name of the Sun, not in the dictionary.

† Váyu.

‡ For *eka-bhásvaraṃ* read *ekam bhásvaraṃ ?* The Bombay edition reads *ekam aksharam* "whose first form is imperishable."

Márkaṇḍeya spoke:

75 While they are thus entirely worshipping him with praise
and faith, the adorable Sun became pleased after three months,
76 O bráhman. Thereupon issuing from his orb, with the same
splendour as his disk *possesses*, the Sun, who is hardly to be
77 gazed at, descended and displayed himself to them. Those
bráhman folk bowing in faith then prostrated themselves
before the Sun, who is without beginning, *as he* manifested
himself in bodily shape, while they quivered with thrills of
78 awe; *exclaiming* "Reverence, reverence be to thee, the thousand-
rayed one! Thou art the cause of everything—brilliant every
whit. Thou art to be invoked against harmful assault, being
the site of all sacrifices; and to be meditated upon by those
skilled in religious devotion. Be thou gracious!"

CANTO CX.

The Majesty of the Sun, concluded.

King Rájya-vardhana's subjects besought of the Sun that the king might reign ten thousand years more, and the Sun granted it—But the king, distressed that the boon did not include all his family and subjects, went and propitiated the Sun, and at length gained his desire—This story is commented on and its merits are extolled.

Márkaṇḍeya spoke:

1 Well-pleased then, the adorable Sun said to all the populace
—"Choose, O ye dvijas and other *people*, what ye have wished
to obtain from me!"

2 Thereupon those bráhmans and other people gazing in fear
on the fiery-rayed *Sun*, as he stood before *them*, prostrated
themselves and said, O bráhman:—

The people spoke:

3 Prostrating themselves they said then to the lord of the
world who proffered them a boon—"O adorable Dispeller of
4 darkness, if *thou art* pleased with our faith, then let our king

live* ten thousand years, free from sickness, victorious over his enemies, rich in his treasury, *and* with firmly-enduring youth! May Rájya-vardhana live ten thousand years!"

Márkaṇḍeya spoke:

5 "So be it!" said the Sun to the populace, and became too dazzling for sight, O great muni. And they, having gained
6 the boon *and* joyous *thereat*, assembled about the king. And having gained the boon completely from the thousand-rayed *god*, O bráhman, they made known to the king how it had happened.

7 On hearing that, his queen Máninî rejoiced, O bráhman; and the king pondered a long while and said nothing to the people.
8 Thereupon she Máninî, whose mind was filled with joy, exclaimed to the king her husband—"How fortunate! Prosper,
9 O king, with long life!" Thus did Máninî courteously salute her husband in *her* delight, *but* the king said nothing, his mind
10 being numbed with thought, O bráhman. She addressed her husband again, as he was rapt in thought with countenance bent downwards,—"Why dost thou not give way to joy in
11 *this* supreme *moment of* exaltation, O king? Thou shalt live free from sickness, with firmly-enduring youth, ten thousand years from to-day. Why nevertheless dost thou not rejoice?
12 But declare thou the reason, why thou hast thy mind drawn away by thought, even when a supreme *moment of* exaltation has been reached, O king?"

The king spoke:

13 How *has a moment of* exaltation come, O lady, and why dost thou courteously salute me? When thousands of afflictions
14 are incurred, is courteous salutation wished for?† I shall live alone ten thousand years, *but* not thou; when calamity
15 befalls thee, shall I not have affliction? When I see sons, grandsons, and great-grandsons and other beloved relatives
16 dead, will *my* affliction indeed be small? And when *my* most faithful servants *are dead*, and when *my* circle of friends is

* *Jîvatám*; átmane-pada; and again in this verse.

† For *sabhájanayishyate* read *sabhájanam ishyate* as in the Bombay edition.

dead, there will then be boundless affliction for me continual-
17 ly, O lady. They who with emaciated *bodies*, constantly
attached to * righteousness, have performed austerities for my
sake, they shall die, *and* I who enjoy *the benefit* shall live—this
18 is censurable! † This, such *as it is*, *is* a calamity *that* has be-
fallen me, O *lady* of beautiful hips; *it is* not *a moment of* exalt-
ation. How again *is it* thou dost not think in that thou dost
courteously salute me now?

Máninî spoke:

19 O great king, as thou hast said, so indeed *it is*; herein there
is no doubt. I and the citizens in our affection for thee did
20 not perceive this mistake. Since it has gone so, consider what
should be done in this *matter*, O lord of men. What the ador-
able Sun has said in his graciousness shall not be otherwise.

The king spoke:

21 *It is* a benefit that *my* citizens and servants have done to
me out of affection; how shall I taste enjoyments, without
22 discharging my obligation to them? I *then* in this position
will go with subdued mind to the mountain from to-day‡ and
will practise austerities, abstaining from food, resolved to pro-
23 pitiate the Sun. Since I shall live in firmly-enduring youth
free from sickness ten thousand years through that god's favour
24 therefore, if the adorable Sun grants us this favour, that all
my people, *my* servants, and thou and my children, sons,
25 grandsons and great-grandsons, and *my* friends *shall also* live,
O lovely-faced one—then I shall continue in the kingdom and
26 shall taste enjoyments with delight. If the Sun does not do
this, then, O Máninî, I will practise austerities on the moun-
tain there, abstaining from food until my life perish.

Márkaṇḍeya spoke:

27 Being thus addressed by him, she said to the king then, "Be
it so!" And she also went with him to that mountain. The
28 king going with his queen to the sanctuary there engaged in

* *Ni-san-tata*, not in the dictionary.

† *Dhik-kara*, not in the dictionary.

‡ The Bombay edition inserts two lines here doubtfully.

worshipping the Sun, being assiduous in his service, O bráhman,
29 *and* becoming emaciated through want of food ; and she, just
as that king *did*, practised severe austerities likewise, endur-
30 ing cold, wind and the sun's heat. While he was worshipping
the Sun and practising great austerities, when a year and
part *of the next year* had passed, the Maker of the day was
31 pleased then and granted him, O dvija, a boon according to
his desire for the sake of all his dependants, citizens and other
subjects, and his sons, O excellent bráhman.

32 On gaining the boon, the king going to his city ruled his
33 kingdom in joyousness, protecting his people righteously ; and
he offered many sacrifices, gave away gifts day and night, and
in company with Mániní indulged in enjoyments, being wise in
34 righteousness. He rejoiced* with his sons, grandsons and other
descendants, with his dependants and citizens† for ten thousand
years ; he remained continuously youthful.

35 A Bhárgava named Pramati, after seeing that his exploit, sang
this song while his heart was drawn out with astonishment,—
36 "Lo, the power of faith in the Sun, in that king Rájya-var-
dhana has been born for the increase of life of his own people
as well as of himself!"

37 Thus I have related to thee, O bráhman, what thou didst
ask me, *namely*, the majesty of the lord‡ Áditya Vivasvat, the
38 god who was in the beginning. The man who, after
hearing the whole of that *story of* the Sun's sublime majesty
with the bráhmans, reads it also during the space of seven
39 nights, is delivered from his sins.§ And the intelligent
man, who may hold this fast, becomes free from sickness,
possessed of riches *and* opulent; and is born *again* a man of
40 great understanding in a great family of wise men.|| And

* For *samuditaḥ* read *sa muditaḥ*.

† *Pauttraiḥ* in the text; but read probably *pauraiḥ*, which I have adopted.

‡ *Vibho;* but *vibhoḥ* seems preferable and I have adopted it. The Bombay edition reads *áditaḥ*, "what thou didst ask me from the first."

§ Or "reads it also, is delivered from the sins which he has committed during seven nights" as the Bombay edition reads.

|| The Bombay edition inserts here, though doubtfully—"And he truly

miserable are they who are smitten herein by the Sun, O best
of munis.* The repetition of each of these *verses* during three
41 twilights destroys sin. And in whatever sanctuary of the Sun
all this *poem of his* majesty is recited, there the adorable *Sun*
42 withdraws not his presence. Therefore thou, O bráhman, who
desirest to gain great merit, must retain this *poem of* the Sun's
43 sublime majesty in thy mind and must mutter it over. Verily
he who makes a gift of a milch cow with gilded horns and
most handsome body, and the man *who* self-possessed listens
to this *poem* for three days—equal are the merit and reward
of them both, O bráhman !†

Canto CXI.

The guide to the genealogies.

Manu had seven sons, whose names are mentioned—and also a child, who was born as a daughter named Ilá, and afterwards became a man by name Su-dyumna—This child as Ilá had a son Purúravas, who reigned at Pratishṭhána, and as Su-dyumna had three sons.

Márkaṇḍeya spoke :

1 Such power has the adorable Sun, who is without beginning
and without end, concerning whose majesty thou, O Kraush-
2 ṭuki, dost ask me in faith. He is the Supreme Soul among
religious devotees who meditate deeply on the dissolution of
their intellects ; ‡ *he is* the Conscious Soul among those who

who after hearing of this exploit sacrifices with great sacrifices replete with boons and fees, gains honour as his reward."

* The Bombay edition reads differently—"And the verses which were herein addressed [read *abhihitá* for *abhihatá?*] to the Sun, O best of munis, the repetition of each of these *verses* during three twilights destroys sin."

† For *dvijágryam* read *dvijágrya.*

‡ This is the best meaning that I can get out of the text—*Paramátmá sa yogínáṁ yuñjatáṁ ćetasáṁ layam*, which is the reading in the Calcutta, Bombay, and Poona editions, though the last in its corrigenda alters it to *yogánáṁ*,

apply the Sáṅkhya doctrine to the knowledge of spirit; and
he is the Lord of sacrifice among those who are sacrificers: *
3 while Vishṇu, S'iva and B'rahmá *each* supports the Sun's
supremacy.

Manu was his son, a solver of doubts in all matters, the ruler
4 of a manv-antara, whose is the seventh period, O bráhman.

Ikshváku, Nábhaga *and* Rishṭa—who were great in strength
5 and prowess—and Narishyanta, Nábhága, Púshadhra and
Dhṛishṭa;† these were that Manu's sons, *each* the guardian of
6 a separate kingdom. All were celebrated in fame, all had the
utmost skill in arms and weapons.

Seeking yet again for a son *who should be* more distinguished,
7 Manu, best of the skilful ones, offered a sacrifice to Mitra
and Varuṇa; in which *sacrifice* moreover when the offering was
perversely made through the improper conduct‡ of the priest,

and then *sa yogánám* must be read as one word *sa-yogánám*. But the text is no doubt corrupt; *yogínám* should be *yoginám*, and *yuñjatám* should perhaps be *yuñjánánám*, though both Parasmai-pada and Átmane-pada have the meaning "to meditate deeply." Mahámahopádhyáya Hara Prasád S'ástrí suggests also that *layaḥ* would be better than *layam* and would translate thus, "He is the Supreme Soul to those who are successful in meditation [*i.e.*, the Vedántists]; he is that in which the minds of those who are engaged in meditation, *but who are not yet successful*, are absorbed" [*i.e.*, the Saguṇa Brahman of the Vedántists].

* *Yajñeśo yajvinám api*; but *yajvanám* must be read for *yajvinám*, and Mahámahopádhyáya Hara Prasád S'ástrí gives it the meaning "to those who consider sacrifices to be the means leading to beatitude" [*i.e.*, the Mímáṁsists].

† Only seven sons are mentioned here. The number is generally given as ten. There is much diversity regarding the names of all of them except Ikshváku, Nariṡhyanta, and Dhṛishṭa. Other names omitted are S'aryáti, Karúsha, Vena, and Práṁśu. See Wilson's Vishṇu Puráṇa, book IV, chapter i, notes. The second and third names Nábhaga and Rishṭa are sometimes given as a single name, Nábhágadishṭa in the Veda and Nábhánedishṭha in the Aitareya Bráhmaṇa; and the last-named book says—he was given to sacred study, his brothers deprived him of his share in the paternal property, and referred him to their father, and by his father's advice he helped the Aṅgirasas in their sacrificial session and obtained great wealth (V. ii. 14).

‡ For *ćápahṛite* read *ćápahute*, as in the Poona edition. The verb *apa-hu* is

8 O great muni, a daughter was born to Manu named Ilá, slender of waist. On seeing that daughter born there, Manu
9 offered praise to Mitra and Varuṇa then and spoke this word,
—"When I made made the sacrifice *with the prayer*, 'Through
10 your favour may I obtain a distinguished son,' a daughter was born to me who am wise. If ye being gracious grant me a
11 boon, then let this my daughter, through the favour of you both, become a son endowed with surpassing virtues!" And when these two gods in sooth said, "Be it so!" that same
12 daughter Ilá became forthwith *a son* famed by the name Su-dyumna.

And afterwards that wise son of Manu, while roving the
13 forest a-hunting, was turned into a woman through the wrath of the god;* in which *condition* Soma's son Budha begat of
14 her a son named Pururavas,† who was a mighty universal monarch. When that son was born, Su-dyumna again per-
15 formed a great horse-sacrifice and regained a man's nature *and* became a king.

Su-dyumna during his manhood had three sons, Utkala,‡
16 Vinaya§ *and* Gaya,|| *who were* most valiant, given to sacrificing, great in bodily strength. Now those three sons, who
17 were born to him during his manhood, enjoyed this earth ¶ while governing their minds in righteousness.

not in the dictionary. The Poona commentary explains *apahute apaćárát* by *viparíta-havane vyatyayát.*

* The Hari-V. narrates only one change, namely, from womanhood (after she had given birth to Purúravas) to manhood (x. 615-37).

† Properly *Purúravas*, as in verse 17.

‡ From whom were descended the Utkalas, see note * on canto lvii, verse 43, and also verse 53, pp. 327 and 341 *ante*; all the authorities agree about this.

§ He is also called Vinata, Vinatáśva, and Haritásva by different authorities. He was king of the East according to the Matsya Pur., and king of the West according to the Hari-V. (x. 631–2) and Váyu Pur.

|| He gave his name to the city Gayá, as all the authorities agree; and he was king of the East as the Hari-V. says (x. 631–2).

¶ The Bhágavata Pur. says wrongly all three sons were rulers of the South, *Dakshiṇápatha.*

But Purúravas, who was born of that monarch *Su-dyumna*
18 during his womanhood, got no share of the earth, because he
was Budha's son. Thereupon at Vasishṭha's word Pratish-
ṭhána,* an excellent city, was given to him; he became king
in that exceedingly charming *city*.

CANTO CXII.

The Story of Púshadhra.

Manu's son Púshadhra while hunting accidentally killed a bráhman's cow—The bráhman's son fell into a rage and cursed him—The bráhman reproved his son for his passionate conduct, but the curse could not be altered and Púshadhra became a śúdra.

Márkaṇḍeya spoke:

1 Manu's son who was named Púshadhra † went a-hunting to
a forest. While walking about in that dense lonely forest he
2 lighted upon no deer at all, he was scorched by the sun's rays,
and his body was seized with hunger, thirst and heat as he
3 walked hither and thither. Then he saw there a beautiful
cow which yielded milk for sacrifice, belonging to a bráhman
who maintained the sacrificial fire, half the body of which was
4 hidden among creepers. ‡ Thinking she was a gayál, he shot
her with an arrow, and she fell to the earth, pierced to the heart
5 with the arrow. Thereupon the sacrificial priest's son Tapo-
rati,§ who was a religious student, on seeing his father's sacri-
6 ficial cow stricken down cursed him; and sent forward his son

* Manu gave this city to Su-dyumna who was excluded from the paternal dominions because he had been a female, and Su-dyumna gave it to Purúravas. It was situated on the north bank of the Ganges at its junction with the Yamuná (Hari-V., xxvi. 1371 and 1411-2).

† This name is generally written *Prishadhra*, which is the correct form.

‡ This is the reading of the Poona edition, *latántar-deha-ćhannárdhám*; the text of the Calcutta edition is erroneous. The Bombay edition reads less properly *latántar-deha-ćhinnárdhám*.

§ I have not found this name elsewhere.

named Vábhravya* who tended the cow. Then, O muni, his
7 mental feelings were overcome by wrath and resentment; *and* he
fell into a rage, while his eyes rolled and were blurred with drops
of perspiration that trickled down. The king Púshadhra seeing
8 that muni's son enraged said,—"Be gracious, wherefore dost
thou give way to anger like a śúdra. No kshatriya, no
vaiśya † in truth indulges so in wrath as thou dost like a
śúdra, *thou* who art born in the noble family of a bráhman."

Márkaṇḍeya spoke :

9 When that son of a pre-eminent *bráhman*‡ was upbraided
thus by the king, he cursed the evil-souled *king, saying :* "Thou
10 shalt become § a śúdra indeed! Whatever sacred lore thou
hast learnt from thy guru's mouth shall waste away, because
thou hast hurt this my guru's sacrificial cow."
11 When cursed thus the king became angry, *yet* he was tor-
mented greatly by that curse. He took water up in his hand,
12 intent on cursing *the other* in retaliation, O bráhman. That
bráhman also gave way to wrath in order to destroy the king.
His father approached him hastily and forbad him in sooth,
saying—
13 "My son, enough, more than enough, of wrath which
does not counteract hostility! || Verily calmness is beneficial
to the twice-born in things of this world and of the next
14 world. Anger destroys austerities; and the angry man falls
away from long life; the angry man's knowledge melts away,

* This is a patronymic from Vabhru or Babhru Viśvámitra had a son Vabhru from whom was descended the family of the Vabhrus (Mahá-Bh., Anuśás.-p., iv. 249–259; Hari-V., xxvii. 1463–67; but see Aitar. Bráh. VII. iii. 18); and S'annaka had a pupil named Vabhru (Wilson's Vishṇu-P.—edit. F. Hall—III. vi.); but the name Vábhravya soon after Manu's time seems out of place.

† The Poona edition gives the right reading, *na kshatriyo na vá vaiśya ;* the Calcutta edition wrongly puts the accusatives.

‡ *Maulinaḥ ; =śreshṭhasya* according to the commentator. This meaning is not in the dictionary.

§ For *bhavishyati* read *bhavishyasi.*

|| For *kopenáyáti-vairiṇá* read *kopenápratívairiṇá* as in the Poona edition.

15 and the angry man fails of his object also. There is no right-
eousness in the man of angry disposition; and the passionate
man obtains not his object; nor among those whose minds are
possessed by wrath is the obtaining of their wishes enough for
16 happiness. If the king has killed this cow with his full know-
ledge, it is right for one, who perceives what is for his own
17 benefit, to extend pardon here. Or *if* he has slain this my
cow in ignorance, how then is he worthy of a curse, since his
18 mind was not evil? Whatever man, while seeking his own
good, harasses another—merciful men should shew pardon to
19 that *man* in the knowledge that he is benighted.* If wise
men inflict punishment for what is done by a man in ignorance,
I esteem him more than the wise men; better are the men
20 who are ignorant. † Invoke thou no curse now on this king,
my son; by her own action indeed this cow has fallen in a
painful death."

Márkaṇḍeya spoke:

21 Púshadhra also, prostrating himself with bowed neck be-
fore the muni's son, exclaimed aloud, "Be gracious!" and "She
22 was slain by me in ignorance, for I thought she was a gayál;
a cow must not be killed; through ignorance, O muni, I slew
thy sacrificial cow. Be thou also gracious to me, O muni!"

The ṛishi's son spoke:

23 Since my birth, O king, I have uttered nothing in vain,
and my anger this day can never be altered, illustrious sir.
24 Therefore I cannot make this curse otherwise, O king; *but*
the second curse which was prepared for thee is averted.
25 The father then took the son who had spoken thus and went
to his own hermitage. And Púshadhra in sooth became a
śúdra.

* Or, "to that man whose understanding is foolish."

† *Tam* appears to be the right reading; but read *tad* instead of *tam*? "then better than the wise are, in my opinion, the men who are ignorant."

Canto CXIII.

Nábhága's exploits.

Karusha's descendants were the Kárushas—Dishṭa's son was Nábhága; Nábhága wanted to marry a vaiśya maiden—Her father referred the matter to the king Dishṭa, and the king consulted the ṛishis—They declared the prince might marry her, provided he first married a kshatriya maiden—He spurned that and took her—The king tried to vanquish him by force, but was caused by a bráhman to desist, on the ground that the prince had degenerated into a vaiśya.

Márkaṇḍeya spoke:

1 Karusha's sons were the Kárushas,* *who were* kshatriyas
and warriors. Now they were seven hundred valiant men;
and from them *descended* others in thousands.
2 Now Dishṭa's† son was Nábhága; ‡ he continued in the
bloom of youthfulness. He saw a most surpassingly charm-
3 ing vaiśya maiden. As soon as he beheld her, the prince was
stricken in mind with love; he became absorbed in sighs and
4 reproaches. He went to her father and asked for the vaiśya
maiden in marriage; and then to the prince, whose mental
5 feelings were under the dominion of the god of love, spoke
her father—to the king's son *spoke* he, joining his hands respect-
fully, being afraid of the *prince's* father, this speech as he
6 bowed with deference, O bráhman—"Nobles of thy class are
the enjoyers of the earth; dependants are we, paying tax to

* *See* note † to canto lvii, verse 53, p. 341 *ante*.

† This Dishṭa must be the Rishṭa mentioned in canto cxii, verse 4. The name is given variously as Nedishṭha, Dishṭa, and Arishṭa. The Hari-Vaṁśa says two of his sons though vaiśyas became bráhmans (xi. 658); and the Bhágavata Pur. says two of his sons, though kshatriyas obtained bráhmanhood (IX. ii. 17).

‡ Nábhága and his descendants are named in Vishṇu Pur. IV. i. The Puráṇas agree generally that he was degraded to be a vaiśya. His descendants and their exploits form the remainder of this Puráṇa. There were other kings afterwards of the same name.

you. Why dost thou earnestly desire connexion with us who are not thy equals ?"

The prince spoke :

7 Equality of the human body is wrought by love, folly and other *feelings*. So indeed the human body is endowed with
8 those very *feelings* at the *appropriate* time,* and thus in truth those *feelings* also come into existence for its benefit. And different *feelings*, different *persons* exist when folk exist of
9 separate castes. Moreover, other *feelings* also† that are inappropriate become proper according to season, and *likewise* appropriate *feelings* become inappropriate; for propriety de-
10 pends upon season. As the body is fattened by food and other *things* that are longed for, so that same *body* when used‡ with
11 due regard to season is well regulated.§ Do thou accordingly bestow this *thy* highly esteemed daughter on me; otherwise calamity will be beheld in my body.

The vaiśya spoke :

12 We are under another's authority, and thou art under another's authority, *namely* the king's. When he thy father permits thee, take thou *her*; I *will* give her.

The prince spoke :

13 Those who treat gurus|| with respect should consult their gurus¶ in all things that must be done; but not in such things as this, things which are not to be done, ** do the words of

* *Or*, "season."

† For *anyán api* read *anyány api*, as in the Poona edition.

‡ *Bhuktam*. The Poona edition reads *bhútam*; and the meaning would be "that same *body* when so constituted with due regard to season is well regulated."

§ *Pariśishyate*. I take this as the passive of *pari-śás*; but *pari-śás* is not in the dictionary.

|| Venerable persons, parents or spiritual preceptors.

¶ For *guruvo* read *guravo* here and in the next verse.

** For the text *ídṛiśeshv a-káryeshu* it seems *ídṛiśeshu káryeshu* would be better—"but not in such businesses as this do the words of gurus have scope."

14 gurus have scope. What has Love's conversation to do with
listening to gurus? This is incompatible. In other things
men should consult their gurus.

The vaiśya spoke:

15 Such, *even* this, is Love's talk! I, I here, *will* ask the guru,
thine, the suitor's. My talk is not based on the speech of
love.

Márkaṇḍeya spoke:

16 When addressed thus the prince became silent. And he,
the vaiśya, related to that *prince's* father all that the prince
17 thought. Thereupon his father summoned, before him the
chief dvijas, Ṛićíka* and the other bráhmans, and the prince;
and he made known *the matter* as it had been announced *to*
18 *him*; and after making it known he, being so situated *in the*
matter, said to the munis,—"The best of dvijas deign † to
declare what ought to be done."

The ṛishis spoke:

19 O prince, if thou hast love for this vaiśya's child, then let
this ordinance of righteousness‡ verily be *observed*, but *let it*
20 *be observed* in the order *enjoined* by law. Marriage was *enjoined*
for princes in the first place with the daughter of one who had
been *royally* anointed. Be it *so now first in thy case*; and immediately afterwards this *maiden also* shall become thy wife.

* A famous ṛishi, son of Bhṛigu and father by Satya-vatí of Jamadagni; see Mahá-Bh., S'ánti-p. xlix. 1716-21; Hari.-V., xxvii. 1423-63, and xxxii. 1761-76; and Vishṇu Pur. IV. vii. He married Satya-vatí, daughter of Gádhi king of Kánya-kubja, by giving a present of a thousand horses for her (Mahá-Bh., Vana-p. cxv. 10144-153, and Udyoga-p. cxviii. 4005-7). Though Satya-vatí is connected with the R. Kauśikí (the R. Kosi, see canto lvii, verse 18, note **) in the passages cited above from the Hari V. and Vishṇu Pur., yet Ṛićíka is generally connected with the west coast around the Gulf of Cambay (see Mahá-Bh., Vana-p. cxviii. 10221-27 and the two other passages last cited above), and Dyuti-mat king of S'álva (see canto lviii, verse 6, note §) gave his kingdom to Ṛićíka (Mahá-Bh., S'ánti-p. ccxxxiv. 8607, and Anuśás-p. cxxxvii. 6267).

† For *arhanti* read *arhantu?* "Let the best of dvijas deign, &c."

‡ *I.e.*, marriage.

21 In this way no wickedness will attach* *to thee* when *thou* enjoyest her thus; otherwise it does accrue: thy *high* rank *comes* from marriage with exalted maidens.†

Márkaṇḍeya spoke:

22 When admonished thus, he flung aside altogether that
speech of those high-souled *munis;* and going outside he
23 seized her, and raising his sword aloft exclaimed,—"I have
carried off the vaiśya's daughter by the Rákshasa form of
marriage; let him who has power here rescue her!"

24 Then the vaiśya seeing his daughter seized, O bráhman,
hastened to that *prince's* father for help, exclaiming "Save
25 her!" His father enraged thereat gave command to his great
army—"Let him be slain; let wicked Nábhága who violates
26 righteousness be slain!" Thereon that army fought indeed
with the king's son; it was laid low then in great numbers by
27 him, who was skilled in weapons, with his weapon. The king,
on hearing that the army was slain by the prince, went forth
28 himself indeed to fight, surrounded by his army. In the
battle then which took place between the king and his son, the
father excelled the prince in weapons and arms.

29 Thereupon a wandering Muni suddenly approached from out the air and spoke back to the king;—

30 "Cease from combat. O illustrious sir, thy high-souled son
is in the right here; moreover fighting between thee and a
31 vaiśya‡ is not according to righteousness, O king. A bráhman who marries wives among all the castes, provided that
he marries first a bráhman woman, incurs no injury in his
32 bráhman-hood. Likewise a kshatriya who marries first a
kshatriya's daughter, *incurs no harm if he marries wives from
lower castes;* and therefore, O king, these other *wives*§ fall not

* *Bhavitá* in the Poona edition is better than *bhavati.*

† The Calcutta edition reads *utkṛishṭábálikáṁ haran;* the Poona reading is *utkṛishṭábála sarvadá,* and the Bombay reading *utkṛishṭábálaká-nayát.* From these readings it would seem the correct reading should be *utkṛishṭa-bálikâ-nayát,* and I have adopted this.

‡ Explained in verses 35 and 36 below.

§ *I.e.,* daughters of vaiśyas and śúdras, as the commentator explains.

33 from their own righteousness. Thus a vaiśya, *who marries* first
a vaiśya woman and afterwards a girl born from a śúdra
family, is not excluded from the vaiśya family. The law is
34 *thus* declared in order. Bráhmans, kshatriyas, vaiśyas, who
do not *first* marry women of the same caste,* fall by marrying
35 women of other castes, O king. Whatever excluded woman
a man marries after neglecting union in *his own* caste, of that
36 *woman's* caste let him indeed† become a participator. This
thy son, who is such, has fallen to vaiśya-hood; he is of
wretched understanding. He has no right to combat with
37 thee a kshatriya. We do not acknowledge this to be a reason
for combat, O royal scion; and since this shall be *so*, desist
thou from the business of battle!"

Canto CXIV.

Nábhága's exploits.

Nábhága married the vaiśya maiden and became a vaiśya—He had a son Bhanandana, who with the help of the ṛishi Nípa conquered the earth and offered the sovereignty to his father Nábhága—Nábhága declined it as he was a vaiśya, and his wife Su-prabhá then explained to him, that she was not really of vaiśya descent, but the daughter of king Su-deva who became a vaiśya under the ṛishi Pramati's curse, because he would not rescue Pramati's wife from his own friend Nala.

Márkaṇḍeya spoke:

1 The king thereupon desisted from battle with his son; and
2 he indeed, that *king's* son, married that vaiśya maiden. He
became a vaiśya thereby. Starting up he spoke to the king,—
"O king, let it be declared to me what I must do."

* For *sa-varṇá-* read *sva-varṇá-*? but the meaning would be the same.

† For *no 'pi tad-vastu-bhág* read *so 'pi tad-varṇa-bhág* as in the Poona edition.

The king spoke:

3 Let Bábhravya* and the other ascetics, who are engaged in the superintendence of righteousness, declare what is the occupation for this *man* for *the end of* righteousness—do thou act accordingly.

Márkaṇḍeya spoke:

4 Then those munis seated in the council announced that for
him the tending of cattle and cultivation and trade *should be*
5 the highest righteousness. And the king's son complied with
what was declared by those expounders of righteousness to be righteousness for him who had fallen from his own *sphere of* righteousness.

6 A son was born to him afterwards, who was famed by the
name Bhanandana.† Being sent by his mother *who said*, "Be
7 a keeper of cattle, my son," he went forth; and when enjoined
thus by his mother, he prostrated himself before his mother and went to the royal ṛishi Nípa‡ who had resorted to mount
8 Himavat; and approaching him Bhanandana held his feet
according to rule, and prostrating himself before this royal ṛishi spoke:

9 "Adorable sir, verily I have been commanded by my mother
thus, 'Be thou a keeper of cattle'§; and *yet* I must protect
10 the earth; how *can there be* assent to her? Verily I must
protect the earth,‖ when it may be appropriated¶ *by men*.
11 This my earth is assailed by powerful heirs. Shew me how
I may gain the earth through thy favour, O lord; I will carry out thy command; I am prostrate before thee."

* See note * page 591.

† Or *Bhalandana* according to the Vishṇu Pur. IV. i.

‡ This was apparently Nípa of the Paurava race, who was king of Kámpilya. He had a hundred sons who were all styled Nípas. His dynasty lasted till Ugráyudha killed all the Nípas just before the Páṇḍavas' time; see Hari-V., xx. 1040, 1060-73, 1082-86; Matsya Pur. xlix. 52-59.

§ *Go-pála.*

‖ *Gauḥ pálaníyá.* There a double pun here with *go*, "cattle" and "the earth," and the verb *pál*, "to tend" and to protect."

¶ There is also a play on the words *sví-karaṇa*, "assent," in verse 9 and *sví-kṛita*, "appropriated," here.

Márkaṇḍeya spoke :

12 The royal ṛishi Nípa then gave to high-souled Bhananda
13 a complete set of weapons, O bráhman. After acquiring skill
in the weapons he went to his paternal uncle's sons, Vasuráta
and the other sons, O dvija; he was *so* commanded by that
14 high-souled *ṛishi*. He demanded half of the kingdom as be-
fitted his father and paternal grandfather; and they said,—"A
15 vaiśya's son thou art; how shalt thou enjoy the earth?" A
battle then occurred between Bhananda who was skilled in
weapons and those his kinsmen Vasuráta and the rest, who were
16 angry and showered weapons *on him*; but vanquishing them
all when their troops had been shattered with his weapons,
he, wise in righteousness, took the earth away from them by
17 righteous combat. After vanquishing his foes, he next pre-
sented all the earth and the sovereignty to his father; and his
father did not accept it, and in front of his wife made an-
swer to the son then.

Nábhága spoke :

18 O Bhananda, this kingdom is thine; let it which was ruled
by thy ancestors be ruled by thee.

The king spoke :*

19 I did not rule the kingdom; I was not devoid of the capacity
for it † formerly; but preferring a vaiśya's condition I obeyed
20 my father's command to that effect. Because I showed want
of affection for my father in that I wedded a vaiśya maiden, I
did not *become* a king, who enjoys the sacred worlds until the
21 subversion *of the world* has arrived. ‡ If disregarding his
command again I rule over the earth, there is verily no final
emancipation from existence for me thereafter even during
22 hundreds of kalpas. Nor indeed is it fit that I, who have my

* This heading is superfluous; it is still Nábhága who speaks.

† *Násámarthya-yutaḥ*. The commentator explains it by *ati-sámarthya-yuto 'pi*, "I did not rule the kingdom, although I possessed exceptional capacity formerly."

‡ For *yávad-áhúta-samplavaḥ* the Bombay and Poona editions read *yávad-ábhúta-samplavam*. An *avyayí-bháva* compound is preferable.

own pride, should enjoy the kingdom which thou hast won by
thy arm, when I have no desire for it, like any weakling.*
23 Rule thou the kingdom thyself the while, or relinquish it to
thy heirs. For me it is good to keep my father's command
and not to rule the earth.

Márkaṇḍeya spoke:

24 Laughing thereat his wife, the lady Su-prabhá by name,
made answer to her husband, "O king, take the mighty king-
25 dom. Thou art no vaiśya, nor indeed was I born of a vaiśya
family, O king; thou art a kshatriya and I also was born of a
26 family of kshatriyas. Formerly there was a famous king Su-
deva † by name, and his friend was king Dhúmráśva's son
27 Nala.‡ Accompanied by his friend he went to the wood Ámra-
vana, § he to sport with his wives in the month of spring, O
28 king. Accompanied by those wives and attended by that friend
29 he enjoyed many *kinds of* drinks and food then. Afterwards
he saw the extremely fascinating and royally born wife of
30 Ćyavana's son Pramati || on the bank of a tank. His friend
Nala, who was intoxicated and not in his right mind, laid hold
of her, the while she cried out "Save *me*, Save *me*!" even as
31 the king looked on. Her husband Pramati, on hearing her
32 cry, at once came up hastily exclaiming "What is it?" Then

* For *durbalasyeha* read *durbalasyeva*, as in the Poona edition.

† The most famous king of this name appears to have been Su-deva of the Káśis who had a great contest with the Vítahavyas, and was father of Divodása (Mahá-Bh., Anuśás.-p. xxx. 1950-54); but this story pays no regard to chronology.

‡ There were many kings of this name, but none of them (as far as I have found) son of Dhúmráśva. One of the kings of Vaiśálí was Dhúmráśva (Vishṇu Pur. IV. i.)

§ I have not found any wood of this name in western India where this story is laid; but Ámra-vana may mean simply "a grove of mangoes."

|| Ćyavana was a famous ṛishi, son of Bhṛigu. He married Sukanyá daughter of Manu's son Śaryáti, and by her had a son Pramati. Pramati married Ghṛitáćí; see Mahá-Bh., Ádi-p. v. 870 and 871, and viii. 939, 940; and Vana-p. cxxii: also Śata-patha Bráh. IV. 5; Aitar.-Bráh. VIII. iv. 21). Ćyavana's region was in the west near the mouth of the R. Narmadá, see Mahá-Bh., Vana-p. lxxxix. 8354, 8364 and 8365; cii. 8737–40 and cxxi. 10312.

he saw king Su-deva standing there, and his wife in the
33 grasp of Nala, who was very much out of his senses. Pramati
spoke to the king then,—

"Make this man quiet! And thou art the ruler; thou, Sir, art the king; and this Nala is a bad man, O king."

Márkaṇḍeya spoke:

34 On hearing that distressed ṛishi's appeal, Su-deva *deterred*
by reason of Nala's high position replied,—"I am a vaiśya;
35 seek someone else, a kshatriya, in order to rescue her." Then
Pramati enraged, burning forth as it were with splendour,
made answer to the king who said "I am a vaiśya."

Pramati spoke:

36 Be it so! thou, Sir, art a vaiśya.* A kshatriya *is so named* because he guards one from injury.† Kshatriyas hold the weapon in order that there may be no cry of distress. Thou being such art no kshatriya; verily thou shalt be a vaiśya of base family.

Canto CXV.

Su-prabhá continues her story to Nábhága—That Pramati reduced Nala to ashes, and, on Su-deva's imploring pardon, mitigated the curse on Su-deva, with the promise that he should regain his kshatriya-hood—Also that she had been the daughter of the royal ṛishi Su-ratha, and had been cursed by Agastya to be born a vaiśya woman temporarily.

Márkaṇḍeya spoke:

1 After imprecating the curse on him then, Pramati, the
descendant of Bhṛigu, enraged *and* burning up, as it were, the
three worlds by reason of his wrath, spoke to Nala, O dvija;—
2 "Inasmuch as thou, Sir, intoxicated with lust, forcibly seizest
my wife here in my hermitage, become thou therefor ashes

* For *vaiśya* read *vaiśyaḥ* as in the Poona edition.

† *Kshatriyaḥ kshata-rakshaṇát.* For a different derivation; see canto cxxii. 24.

3 forthwith." And then immediately as he uttered that speech,
Nala, *consumed* by the fire that sprang from *the* *ṛishi's* body,
became forthwith a heap of ashes.

4 On seeing that *ṛishi's* power then Su-deva sobered thereat,
bending himself in reverence, said thus—"Grant pardon!
5 grant pardon! Let that which I have spoken,* adorable sir,
a thing disordered by reason of intoxication through drinking
spirituous liquor, be pardoned; be thou gracious; let this
6 curse be turned aside!" Being thus propitiated by him, Pra-
mati, the descendant of Bhṛigu, whose anger had passed off
when Nala was burnt up, replied with mind devoid of strong
7 feeling;—"The word which I have uttered shall not be otherwise;
nevertheless being gracious I will do thee a supreme favour.
8 Thou, sir, shalt be a vaiśya by race—of this there *can* be no
doubt; *thou*, a kshatriya, shalt be a vaiśya soon in the *very*
9 *next* birth. When a kshatriya's son shall seize thy daughter
by force, thou being seized by one of thy own race shalt then
10 become † a kshatriya *again*, O vaiśya." Thus that Su-deva
as a vaiśya became my father, O king.

11 Hear also, illustrious sir, all the *story* ‡ who I am. There
was of yore a royal ṛishi named Su-ratha on *mount* Gandha-
mádana, who practised austerities, restricted his food, aban-
12 doned *worldly* associations, *and* abode in the forest. On his
seeing then a mainá § fallen from a hawk's beak to the
ground, compassion sprang up within that high-souled *ṛishi*,
13 and he swooned therewith; then when the swoon passed off, I
was produced from his body, and seeing me he took me with
14 a loving mind. "Because she has been born from me, while I
was overcome with compassion, she shall therefore be *known* by
15 the name Kṛipá-vatí" ||—so said he, *my* lord. Thereafter
growing up in his hermitage, I *used to* wander day and night

* For *yad uktavám̐s tvam*, read *yad uktavám̐s tvám* as in the Poona edition, and the commentator says *aham* must be understood.

† For *bhavishyati* read *bhavishyasi*.

‡ For *tvat-sarvam̐* read *tat sarvam̐*.

§ *Śáriká*, a bird.

|| "Full of compassion."

through the woods also with my girl-companions of the same
16 *age.* Then the muni Agastya's brother, who was known as
Ágastya,* while seeking for forest-products in the forest,
17 was angered by my girl-companions and cursed *me; and I said*
—"No offence have I committed against thee, O best of dvijas;
why because of an offence by other girls hast thou cursed *me?*"

The ṛishi spoke:

18 "By reason of contact with the bad even that which is not
bad becomes bad, just as a jar containing the five substances
obtained from cows † *becomes spoilt* if a drop of spirituous
19 liquor falls *into it.* Since thou hast fallen prostrate and propitiated me *by declaring* 'I am not bad,' hear therefore what‡
20 favour I *will* do to thee, O maiden. When, being born in a
vaiśya family, thou shalt admonish thy husband § to *undertake* kingly rule, thou shalt then fully recover the remembrance
21 of *this* existence; and thou shalt resume thy kshatriya caste
along with thy husband and shalt obtain heavenly pleasures.
Go *now*, let fear depart from thee!"

22 Thus was I cursed formerly by that great ṛishi, O king of
kings; and my father was thus cursed by Pramati formerly.
23 So thou art not a vaiśya, O king; nor was my father a vaiśya;
nor indeed am I; || how dost thou, who art not degraded,
become degraded in *marrying* me who am not degraded?

* Or Agastya.

† Milk, cheese, butter, urine and dung.

‡ For *śriṇuyát* read *śriṇu yat*, as in the Poona edition.

§ *Tvam putram*, "thou shalt admonish thy son, &c.," is the reading in the Calcutta and Poona editions, but the latter in its Corrigenda alters it to *svapatim*, and I have followed this.

|| *Na tvaṁ hi* is the reading in the editions, but is incorrect. I venture to amend it to *na tv-aham*, and have translated it accordingly. Another emendation is to read *sa* for *na*, and then the meaning of these and the following words would be—"How indeed dost thou, who art such *and* who art undegraded, become degraded in *marrying* me who am undegraded?"

Canto CXVI.

The Exploits of Bhananda and Vatsa-prí.

Nábhága declined the kingdom and Bhanandana became king—He had a son Vatsa-prí—A Daitya king Kujṛimbha, who had a magic club called Sunanda, opened a great hole near king Vidúratha's city and carried the princess Mudávatí down to Pátála—Her brothers failed to rescue her and were made captive—Vatsa-prí killed the Daitya, after she destroyed the club's magic power, and rescued her and her brothers—She was named Sunandá after the club, and Vatsa-prí married her.

Márkaṇḍeya spoke :

1 On hearing this herspeech and his son's, the king, wise in
2 righteousness, addressed his wife and son again,—" Inasmuch
as I relinquished the kingdom at my father's command, I will
not take it again ; why dost thou, *O wife*, draw out my soul
3 with vain words ? Standing *fast* in my duties as vaiśya I will
pay thee taxes, *my son*. Enjoy thou the whole kingdom, or
relinquish it if thou wishest."

4 Being addressed thus by his father, prince Bhanandana *
then governed the kingdom in righteousness and in like wise
5 married a wife. Unrepulsed was his discus in the earth, O
bráhman, and his mind *was* not *set* upon unrighteousness. All
6 kings were in subjection to him. He performed a sacrifice according to precept ; he rules the earth well. He in sooth was
the only lord ; his commands pervaded the earth.

7 A son was born to him, namely Vatsa-prí by name, who, a
high-souled *king*, surpassed his father with the multitude of
8 his good qualities. And his wife was Saunandá, daughter of
Vidúratha, who was devoted to her husband, an illustrious
woman. He gained her by his valour in slaying the Daitya
king Kujṛimbha,† the enemy of Indra.

* Or *Bhalandana* according to Vishṇu Pur. IV. i. where his descendants are given.

† The Calcutta text reads *Kujumbha* here and in verse 9, incorrectly ; see verse 16.

Kraushṭuki spoke :

9 Adorable sir, how did he gain her through the destruction of Kujṛimbha? Tell me this story with benignant mind.

Márkaṇḍeya spoke :

10 There was a king named Vidúratha * whose fame was cele-
brated in the earth. Two sons were born to him, Su-níti and
11 Su-mati. Now Vidúratha went to the forest once upon a time
to hunt. He beheld a very great pit, as it were the earth's
12 mouth thrust up. On seeing it he pondered, "What is this
dreadful thing? I trow *it is* a hole *down* to Pátála: it has
13 not belonged to the earth a long while." While thinking thus,
he saw in a lonely wood there an ascetic brahman named Su-
14 vrata approaching, and the king being astonished asked him,
—"What is this? *It is* very deep *and* displays the earth's
belly which is situated within."

The ṛishi spoke :

15 "Knowest thou it not, O king? for thou art deemed by me
to have spies as thine eyes. † A king ought to know everything
16 that passes on the face of the earth. A very valiant fierce
Dánava dwells in Rasátala; because he makes the earth to
17 yawn, ‡ he is therefore called Ku-jṛimbha. Whatever has been
produced, whether produced on the earth or in heaven, is
wrought by him, O king; how is it then that thou dost not
18 know him, Sir? That wicked-souled *demon* carried off the
club named Su-nanda, which Tvashṭri fashioned of yore; there-
19 with he slays his enemies in battle. Hidden within Pátála *that*
Asura cleaves this earth with it, and makes doors *of exit* for
20 all the Asuras; with that weapon, the club Su-nanda, the
earth has been pierced in this *spot*. How shalt thou, Sir, enjoy

* The story shows that this king's capital was near the river Nirvindhyá which was apparently in the Málwa region (see verses 27 and 33). There were several kings of this name, but I have found none who had two sons of the names mentioned.

† For *vág-arthas*, which the Calcutta and Bombay editions have, read *ćárák-shas* as in the Poona edition.

‡ *Jṛimbhayati.*

21 this earth unless thou conquerest him? That fierce, mighty
adversary of the gods, armed with the club, destroys sacrifices
22 *and* fattens up the Daityas. If thou slayest this foe, whose
sphere is in Pátála, thou *shalt* thereby *become* lord of all the
23 earth, the supreme monarch. That mighty *demon's* club is
called Saunanda by men-folk; and the wise moreover speak of
24 it* as partly strong and partly weak; yet when touched by a
woman it loses its power on that day,† O king; on the following
25 day it issues forth with its power *regained.* That *demon* of
evil ways does not know then the majestic power of the club,
nor the defect which comes at the touch of a woman's fingers,
that is, the collapse of its power.

26 "Thus I have declared to thee, O king, the might of that
evil-souled Dánava and of his club. As I have spoken, so do
27 thou comport thyself. This hole which he has made in the
earth is near thy city, O king; why art thou foolishly ‡ unconcerned
about it, Sir?"

28 Now when that *rishi* had spoken thus and departed, the
king went to his city and took counsel with his ministers who
29 were skilled in counsel within his city. He made known to
the ministers all that *story* as he had heard it, both the majestic
30 power of the club and also the waning of its power. Now his
daughter Mudá-vatí, who was by his side, heard that counsel
which the king was taking with his ministers.

31 But some days afterwards, the Daitya Kujṛimbha carried off
that maiden, who was possessed of energy, from a grove, while
32 she was accompanied by her maiden-friends. On hearing
that, the king's eyes were distraught with anger, and he said
to his two sons, "Hasten quickly ye two who are well acquainted
33 ed with the forests: there is a hole on the bank of the Nir-vindhá;
§ go ye *down* thereby to Rasátala and slay him who with
most evil mind has carried Mudá-vatí off."

* For *tam* read *tad* as in the Poona edition.

† On the day on which it is touched, *sparśa-dine* (comment.)

‡ For *yathá* read *vṛithá* as in the Poona edition.

§ Or *Nirvindhyá*, as in the Poona edition, which is the preferable form; see canto lvii, verse 24, note ‡.

Márkaṇḍeya spoke:

34 Thereupon those two sons of his, following on the steps of that
demon, reached that hole and in excessive wrath fought with
35 Kujṛimbha with *the aid of* their own army. Then occurred a
very terrible combat between them with maces, swords, spears,
36 javelins, and axes and arrows without intermission. After it
that Daitya, who possessed the might of illusive power, bound
those two princes in battle after slaying all their soldiers.
37 On hearing of that, the king spoke thus to all his soldiers,
"*I* have fallen into utter misery, now that my sons are in
38 bonds, (O best of munis); whoever shall slay that Daitya
and shall set my daughter there free, I will bestow even her,
39 the large-eyed maiden, on him." Even thus the desperate
king made a proclamation in his city then in order to obtain
the deliverance of his sons and daughter from bondage, O
muni.
40 Bhanandana's son Vatsa-prí then heard of that *promise* in
sooth, which was proclaimed abroad—he, possessed of strength,
41 skilled in weapons, endowed with heroism. And arriving *there*
he saluted this noblest of kings, and bowing with deference
42 spoke to him who was *his own* father's peerless friend;—"Command me in sooth speedily; I *will* deliver thy two sons and
also thy daughter, after slaying that Daitya through thy very
glory."

Márkaṇḍeya spoke:

43 Embracing him joyfully, *who was* his dear friend's son, the
king said:
44 "Go thou to full success,* my dear son. My dear son shall
stand in *my* place, if he performs the precept thus. Do this
quickly, my dear son, if thy mind is resolute."

Márkaṇḍeya spoke:

45 Then armed with scymitar and bow, having a leathern bow-guard and finger-protector bound *on him,* the heroic *prince*
46 went in haste to Pátála by that hole. The prince made
his bow-string twang with an exceedingly vehement sound

* For *saṁsiddhai* read *saṁsiddhyai*, as corrected in the Poona edition.

then, wherewith the whole of Pátála was filled throughout.
47 Hearing the sound of the bow-string, the Dánava king, Kujrimbha came forward then in excessive wrath, attended by his
48 army. Then occurred a battle between him and the king's son, one with his army against the *other* with his army, mighty
49 against mighty. When the Dánava had fought with him for three days, he was filled with rage in his soul and rushed
50 to *get* his club. Worshipped with perfumes, garlands and incense, it stands in the private apartments, O illustrious sir; *for*
51 *it had been* fashioned by the Prajá-pati.* Mudá-vati, who knew well the *secret of the* club's majestic power, bowing her
52 neck very low, touched the noble club then. Until the great demon grasps the club again, till then the beautiful maiden touched it many times under pretence of paying reverence
53 to it. Going *back* then the king of the demons fought with the club. Vainly fell the blows of the club on those
54 enemies. But inasmuch as the supreme weapon, the club Saunanda, had lost its power, O muni, the Daitya fought with his weapons and arms against his foe in the battle.
55 With his arms and weapons the demon was not the prince's equal, and that, his might with the club, had been
56 dissipated by the maiden.† Conquering then the Dánava's weapons and arms, the king's son forthwith forced him from his chariot; and then *the demon* grasping his shield and scy-
57 mitar rushed at him again. The prince felled that enemy of the lord of the thirty *gods*, as he rushed forwards violently incited and displaying his rage,—*felled him* to the earth with his weapon of fire which gleamed like the Fire that burns up the
58 world *finally*. That foe of the thirty *gods* was wounded grievously in the heart by the fiery weapon and quitted his body. And forthwith there was high festival among the huge snakes within the confines of Rasátala.

59 Then fell a shower of flowers upon the king's son; the Gandharva lords sang forth, the gods' instruments of music
60 sounded out. And the prince, after slaying that *demon*, set free

* See verse 18.

† For *buddhyá* read *tanvyá* as in the Poona edition.

the king's two sons and the slender-shaped maiden Mudá-vatí.
61 And the king of the serpents, Ananta who is named S'esha,
62 took that club, when that Kujṛimbha was slain; and he, S'esha
lord of all the serpents, was satisfied with her; he rich in austerities had meditated with glee upon the course of Mudá-
63 vatí's mind. Because the most beautiful *maiden* had repeatedly touched the club Sunanda, knowing the power of the
64 touch of a woman's palm* *on it*, therefore the serpent
king in his joy gave Mudá-vatí then the name Su-nandá, derived from the quality of *the club* Saunanda, O dvija.
65 And the prince brought her in company with her two brothers to their father's presence quickly, and bowing down
66 spoke to him thus—"*Here* are brought *thy* two sons, dear
father, and here *is brought* Mudá-vatí according to thy command; what else I must do, declare thou that."

Márkaṇḍeya spoke:

67 Thereat the king's heart was filled with gladness, and he
exclaimed aloud, "Well done! well done!" *and* "Splendid!
68 my dear son, my dear son! I am honoured by the thirty *gods*,
my dear son, for three reasons—in that I have both gained thee
69 for my son-in-law, and that the foe has been stricken down, and
that my children have come unharmed to me here again; there-
70 fore take her hand now on *this* auspicious day—I have said it;
make my word true—*that* thou, O prince, be joined in joy with my daughter Mudá-vatí, a maiden of lovely form."

The prince spoke:

71 I must obey thy command, dear father; what thou sayest I *will* do. Thou verily knowest, dear father, *that* in this *matter* we are in truth unchanged.

Márkaṇḍeya spoke:

72 Then the great king performed the series of marriage *rites* for them both, for his daughter Mudá-vatí and Bhanandana's

* Read *yoshit* as part of the compound *yoshit-karatala-sparśa-* &c., and not separately as in the Calcutta edition.

73 son. Thereafter Vatsa-prí in his early manhood sported with
her in charming regions and in palaces and on hill-tops.
74 As time passed on, his father Bhanandana grew old *and*
75 departed to the forest; Vatsa-prí himself became king. He
offered up sacrifices continually, while protecting his people
with righteousness. Now the people, being protected by that
high-souled *monarch* as if *they were his* children, prospered;
76 and in his realm there was no confusion among the castes;
and no one felt any fear of robbers, rogues or villains, nor any
fear of calamities, while he ruled as king.

Canto CXVII.*

Khanitra's exploits.

Vatsa-prí was succeeded by his son Práṁśu, and Práṁśu by his son Prajáti.—Prajáti had five sons, of whom Khanitra succeeded him—Khanitra's special prayer is given—He made his four brothers subordinate kings—The minister of one of them subdued the other brothers and tried to gain the supreme power for his master through magic performed by the family priests of all four brothers—The magic produced a female deity which destroyed the four priests and the minister.

Márkaṇḍeya spoke:

1 To him, *Vatsa-prí*, were born of Su-nandá twelve sons,
2 Práṁśu, Praćíra and S'úra, Su-ćakra, Vikrama, Krama, Balin,
Baláka, and Ćaṇḍa and Praćaṇḍa, Su-vikrama and Sva-rúpa—
all *princes* of great parts, most victorious in battle.
3 The eldest of them, Práṁśu, who was great in valour, was
king; these others were subordinate to his authority like de-
4 pendants. At his sacrifice the earth† justified her name by
reason of the many multitudes of things, which she gave away

* The Calcutta edition makes a mistake in the numbering. It omits cxvii, calls this Canto cxviii, and continues the mistaken numbering to the end.

† *Vasun-dhará*, "container of wealth."

to the twice-born and which she parted with to the inferior
5 castes. While he duly protected his people as if his own be-
gotten children, the sacrifices then, which he performed with
6 the accumulation of wealth that lay in his treasury, were hun-
dreds of thousands; their number is not reckoned by ten
thousand or such a *figure*, *nor* by ten millions, nor by a thousand
billion or such a *figure*, O muni.

7 Pra-játi* was his son; at whose sacrifice Indra, gaining
unparalled gratification along with the gods who partake of
8 shares of sacrifices, the chiefest of the mighty,† smote nine
nineties‡ of valiant Dánavas and Bala and Jambha noblest of
9 Asuras, and smote other very valiant foes of the gods.

Prajáti had five sons, of whom Khanitra was chief, O muni.
10 Of them Khanitra became king; he was celebrated for his
personal feats of prowess. He was a pacific, truth-speaking
11 hero; he delighted in *doing* good to all living creatures; he
took delight in his own *sphere of* righteousness constantly; he
waited upon the aged, he was well versed in the Vedas, he
was eloquent, endowed with modesty, yet skilled in weapons
12 and no boaster. He was the beloved of all people continually;
he uttered this *prayer* day and night;—

'Let all created things rejoice, let them be affectionate
13 even in solitary *places!* May there be welfare for all created
things, and may they be free from affliction! May created
things experience no bodily sickness nor any mental diseases!
14 May all created things cherish friendliness to every living
being! May there be bliss for all the twice-born; may they have
15 mutual lovingkindness! May all castes have full prosperity,
and may *all* deeds attain perfect accomplishment! May the
worlds *be propitious* to all created things! May your mind
16 always be propitious! Desire ye at all times what is good for your
son even as for yourselves! Similarly be ye benevolent in mind

* He is called Prajáni in the Vishnu Pur. (IV. i.) and Pramati in the Bhágavata Pur. He seems to be the same as Prasandhi in the genealogy in Mahá-Bh., Áśvam.-p. iii. 65.

† That is, Indra.

‡ *Daśádhikáshṭaśatím*, comment.

17 to all created things! This is unbounded good for you. Moreover who sins against whom, that he causes any harm to any
18 one besotted in mind? To him assuredly * comes that resnlt, *that* which accrues to the doer *thereof*. So thinking, ho! let the
19 people be informed of their duties † to all, ‡ lest *ye* wise people shall undergo secular sin. § May there ever be bliss on the
20 earth for him, who loves me now; and may even he, who hates me, see good things in this world!'
21 Such was that king's son Khanitra in disposition; he was endowed with every good quality; he possessed good fortune, his eyes were like a lotus-leaf. He appointed those his *four*
22 brothers to separate kingdoms out of affection, and he himself enjoyed this earth bounded by the seas; *thus* he placed S'auri over
23 the east *region*, Mudávasu ‖ over the south, Sunaya over the western region, *and* Mahá-ratha over the northern. They and
24 that king had separate families *of bráhmans* as purohitas, and also munis, who descended in a regular lineage of ministers. S'auri's *purohita was* a bráhman ¶ Su-hotra by name who sprang
25 from the family of Atri; Udávasu's was Kusávartta, who was born of the lineage of Gautama; a Káśyapa by name Pra-mati
26 was Sunaya's purohita; Vásishṭha was purohita to king Mahá-ratha. Those four kings indeed enjoyed their own kingdoms,
27 and Khanitra was their over-lord, being over-lord of all the earth. King Khanitra was always kindly to those *his* four
28 brothers and to all his people as to his own sons.
One day S'auri was addressed by his minister Viśva-vedin—
29 "O king, we have somewhat to say unto thee in private. He, who possesses all this earth, to whom *all* kings are in subjec-
30 tion, is the king, and *so will be* his son and his grandsons and thereafter his descendants. These others, his brothers, are

* For *nyúnaṁ* read *núnaṁ* as in the Poona edition.

† The Poona edition reads *hita-buddhayaḥ*, and the meaning would then be "be friendly-minded."

‡ Or, 'in all things.'

§ *Laukikam pápam.*

‖ Or better *Udávasu*, as in the Poona edition and in verse 25.

¶ Family priest. For *dvijáḥ* read *dvijaḥ* as in the Poona edition.

31 kings of very small * territories; and his son is smaller than
he;† and his grandsons *will be* of smaller make. Degenerat-
32 ing in time from individual to individual, his descendants *will*
become dependant on agriculture for their living, O king. *Thy*
brother, bestowing affection and power on his brothers, *yet* makes
33 no division of the patrimony.‡ What affection *will he have,*
O king, for the two more distant, *his* brothers' sons§? His
mind *will be* more distant with regard to their two sons, O
34 king. By what thing that is to be done will his son be endowed
with affection? Or *if* a king is satisfied by anything whatsoever,
35 yet to what end then do kings entertain ministers?|| The
whole kingdom is enjoyed by me while I remain thy minister.
36 Dost thou retain that to no purpose,¶ if it gives** satisfaction?
Sovereignty accomplishes what should be done; an instru-
37 ment is desired by one who operates. And the acquirement
of sovereignty†† is what thou must accomplish; thou art the
worker, we are the instrument. Do thou, being such, rule
the kingdom that belonged to thy father and grandfather by
means of us, the instruments. We shall not bestow benefits
on thee in another world.

The king spoke:

38 Inasmuch as the eldest *brother* is king (O monarch), *and*
we are his younger brothers, he therefore enjoys the earth
39 and we *enjoy* small *portions of the* earth. Now we are five

* For *kalpa-vishayádhipáḥ* read *svalpa-vishayádhipáḥ* as in the Poona edition.

† *Tat-putraś cálpakas tasmát*, referring to each of the brothers; but a plural reading would be preferable, "their sons are smaller than they."

‡ *Uddháram*. The Poona edition reads *bhrátuḥ sneha-balárpiṇaḥ*, and the meaning would then be, "Thy brother makes no division of the patrimony for a brother who bestows affection and power:" though *arpa* and *arpin* are not in the dictionary.

§ For *snehakaḥ* the Poona edition reads better *snehaḥ kaḥ*.

|| For *mantra-parigrahaḥ* the Poona edition reads better *mantri-parigrahaḥ*.

¶ For *sukhádhárayase* read *mudhá dhárayase* as in the Poona edition.

** For *kurute* the Poona edition reads *kurushe*.

†† For *rájya-lubdhaś* read *rájya-lambhaś* as in the Poona edition.

brothers, and *there is but* one earth, O high-minded *sir*, hence how can there be entire sovereignty over it separately *for us?*

Viśva-vedin spoke:

40 Be this so here!* If *there is but* one earth, O king, do thou
thyself take possession of it; do thou Sir, as eldest *brother*,
41 rule the earth. Be thou the absolute ruler, exercising entire
sovereignty, unto all. And the ministers *whom they have* entertained strive for them† as I *strive* for thee.

The king spoke:

42 Since the eldest, the king, esteems us affectionately like sons, how shall I display against him a selfishness that relates to the world?

Viśva-vedin spoke:

43 When seated in the kingdom, thou mayest do worship as the eldest with new kingly honours. What is this position of youngest and eldest? Sovereignty is for men who want it.

Márkaṇḍeya spoke:

44 And on the king's assenting, "So be it," O best *of men*,
Viśva-vedin the minister brought his brothers into subjection
45 *to him* then, and *brought* their purohitas *into subjection* to him-
self in ceremonies performed for the removal of obstacles and
other *rites*. Next he employed *them* in spells directed against
46 Khanitra, and severed his faithful *adherents* by conciliation,
gifts and other *means;* and he exerted the utmost efforts in
47 repelling punishment from his own *folk*. And while the four
purohitas were performing an exceedingly arduous magical
incantation day by day, there was produced a four-fold female
48 deity‡ *which was* very formidable, had a large mouth, was ex-
ceedingly terrible to behold, held a large pike raised aloft, was
49 lofty and was exceedingly pitiless. It came to the place then
where king Khanitra was, and it was cast out by that un-
50 blemished *king's* store of merit. The four-fold female deity

* For *bhaváṁs tatra* read *bhavatv atra* as in the Bombay edition.

† *Tesháṁ;* the commentator explains thus, *bhrátṛíṇáṁ kárya-vishaye.*

‡ *Kṛityá-ćatushṭaya.*

fell on those evil-souled purohitas of *his brother* kings, and on
51 Viśva-vedin indeed. Then were burnt up by that female
deity, who assailed them, those purohitas and Viśva-vedin the
minister who gave evil counsel to S'auri.

Canto CXVIII.*

Khanitra's exploits concluded.

Khanitra, on hearing of the destruction of the family priests, lamented and took the blame on himself—He resigned the kingdom to his son Kshupa, departed to the forest, and died there in sanctity.

1 Thereupon there was great dismay in all the world, in-
asmuch as those *purohitas* dwelling in separate cities perished
2 at the same time. *Khanitra* heard then that his brothers' puro-
hitas had reached their death, and that his brother's minister
3 Viśva-vedin also had been burnt up. Khanitra the great king
was extremely surprised, *wondering* "What is this?" O best
4 of munis; and knew not the cause. Then the king asked
Vasishṭha who had come to his palace, what the reason was
why those, the minister and purohitas of his brothers, had
5 perished. When questioned by him the great muni related
then how it had happened, what S'auri's minister had said
6 and what S'auri had replied to him, and what he, that evil
minister, had performed as a means of producing dissension
7 among the brothers and what the purohitas had done; for what
reason they, the purohitas who were absolutely compassionate
even to an enemy, had perished, while injuring that sinless
8 king. On hearing that, the king reproached himself exceed-
ingly then, exclaiming, "Alas! I am *sore* stricken!" in Vasish-
ṭha's presence, O dvija.

The king spoke:

9 "Fie on me, who am of unholy composition, of scanty good-

* Canto cxix in the Calcutta edition.

fortune, destitute of splendour! Sin which is utterly contemn-
ed by all the worlds has been committed *by me* through the
10 fault of fate. That is the reason why those four bráhmans
have perished: what other man besides me will there be more
11 sinful on the earth? If I were not a man here on the earth,
they, my brothers' purohitas, would not have perished then.
12 Fie on the kingdom! fie too on my birth in the family of great
kings—I who have become the cause of the destruction of the
13 bráhmans! They, my brothers' sacrificing priests, met their
end while working at their masters' object; no wicked
men were they; I am wicked in causing their destruction.
14 What am I to do? Where am I to go? No one verily is a
sinner on the earth but I who have become the cause of the
bráhmans' destruction."

15 Thus grieving in heart, king Khanitra being desirous of
16 departing to the forest anointed his son *to the throne*. After
anointing his son who was named Kshupa to the kingdom,
the king departed to the forest, along with his three wives, to
17 *perform* austerities. Going there he, best of kings, being well-
versed in the ordinances concerning vána-prasthas, performed
18 austerities three hundred and fifty years. Now, when his
body had become emaciated through austerities, the noble
king, having restrained all the organs of sense, quitted his life
19 while dwelling in the forest, O chief of bráhmans. He went
then to the sacred worlds which yield every desire *and* are
undecaying, which are to be gained by kings by means of
20 horse-sacrifices and other sacrifices. And those his three wives
quitted their life at the very same time with him, *and* gained
the same world* along with him indeed, their most high-
souled *lord*.

21 This is *the story of* Khanitra's exploits; when heard, it
destroys stains; and *it destroys the stains* of those who read it,
illustrious sir. Hear next about Kshupa.

* For *vápuḥ samálokyaṁ* read *avápuḥ sálokyam* as in the Poona edition.

Canto CXIX.*

Vivimśa's exploits.

Kshupa emulated a more ancient king of the same name and enriched the bráhmans—He was succeeded by his son Víra; and Víra by his son Vivimśa whose was a prosperous reign.

Márkaṇḍeya spoke:

1 Now Khanitra's son Kshupa on receiving the kingdom protected his people, while delighting them in righteousness, even
2 as his father *had done.* That king was by disposition liberal of gifts, and a sacrificer of sacrifices; he was just alike both to foe and friend in the path of the administration of justice and so forth.

3 One day the king, while at his own residence, O muni, was addressed by his bards,—"As *was* king Kshupa of yore, so art
4 thou, sir."† Of yore there was a king Kshupa,‡ Brahmá's son; as had been the exploits of this *king*, such that one indeed endeavoured *to achieve.*

The king spoke:

5 I wish to hear of the exploits of the most high-souled Kshupa. If such can be accomplished by me, I will perform them.

The bards spoke:

6 That king made cattle-*keeping* bráhmans § multitudes of yore, O king; and with the *tribute of the* sixth portion that high-souled *king* performed a sacrifice on the earth.

* Canto cxx in the Calcutta edition.

† For *tathábhavat* read *tathá bhaván* as in the Poona edition.

‡ It must apparently be this Kshupa to whom reference is made in the Mahá-Bh. (Śánti-p. clxvi. 6164-65 and 6192-93) where it is said that after the sword was fashioned Manu gave it to Kshupa for the protection of the people, and Ikshváku got it from Kshupa.

§ *Go-bráhmaṇán.* The compound occurs again in verses 10 and 12. It does not seem to mean "cattle and bráhmans," for this meaning hardly suits the verb used, and the compound occurs twice in the singular in verse 12. In that verse the Poona edition varies in reading *go-bráhmaṇáh*, plural, but both editions agree in reading *go-bráhmaṇáya*, singular.

The king spoke :

7 Who like me will follow those high-souled kings ? Never-
theless, may he be strenuous after the exploits of *those kings*
8 of exalted exploits ! Hear then the promise which I now
9 make—I will imitate the great king Kshupa's exploits. I
will perform sacrifices three and three on the present and
future* gathering of the harvests on the earth which has four
10 streams—this promise I have made. And the tribute which
cattle-*keeping* bráhmans gave to *that* king of yore, the very
same I will restore to the bráhmans and the cattle.

Márkaṇḍeya spoke :

11 Having thus pledged his word, Kshupa performed it accord-
ingly. He, best of sacrificers, offered three sacrifices on the
12 appearance of the crops. And the very tribute which a cattle-
keeping bráhman gave to kings before, of that same quantity
gave he other wealth to the cattle-*keeping* bráhman.
13 He had a son, Víra,† of *his wife* Pramathá, a blameless
prince, by whose majesty and valour kings were brought into
14 subjection. And his dear wife was a Vidarbha princess named
Nandiní ; he, the lord, begat a son Viviṁśa‡ of her.
15 While Viviṁśa was ruling the earth, as a king of great vi-
16 gour, the earth became densely populated with men. Par-
janya rained in *due* season, and the earth abounded with
17 harvests, and the harvests were most fruitful, and the fruits
were full of juice, and the juices gave nourishment, *yet* the
nourishment caused no outrageous behaviour ; nor did the
stores of riches become causes of debauchery among men.
18 His enemies were cowed by his energy, O great muni. The
people, who were *all* a band of friends, *desire* good health ; the
19 citizens desire mirth. After performing very many sacrifices,

* *Sasyápáte gatágate ; = śasya-práptau játáyám ajátáyáṁ vá* (comment.)

† This king is called Viṁśa in the Vishṇu Pur. (IV. i). Between Kshupa and Viṁśa a king Ikshváku is inserted in the genealogy given in Mahá-Bh. Áśvam.-p. iii. 65-68.

‡ The Vishṇu Pur. calls him Viviṁśa or Viviṁśati (IV. i).

after protecting the earth well, he met his death in battle and departed hence to the world of Indra.*

CANTO CXX.†

Khanínetra's exploits.

Viviṁśa was succeeded by his son Khanínetra, who was a great sacrificer—Being son-less he went hunting to kill a deer for a sacrifice, and two deer came, one having no offspring and the other many—Each pressed his claim to be killed, but the king refused to kill either.

Márkaṇḍeya spoke:

1 His son was Khanínetra, great in strength and prowess, at
whose sacrifices sang the Gandharvas, filled with astonishment,
2 *thus*—"Like unto Khanínetra there will be no other sacrificer
on earth." After completing ten thousand sacrifices, he gave
3 the earth with its seas away. And *he it was* who, after giving
away all the earth to high-souled bráhmans, acquired wealth
through austerities fully performed, and lavished *that also*;‡
4 and after obtaining unparalleled increase of riches from that
most noble giver, bráhmans accepted no donation from any
5 other king, O bráhman:—*he it was* who sacrificed sixty-seven
thousand and sixty-seven hundred and sixty-seven sacrifices
with abundance of largesse.

6 That monarch being son-less engaged in a hunt with the
desire of *obtaining* flesh for a sacrifice to the pitṛis in order to
7 obtain a son, O great muni. He rode on his horse, away from
his troops, absolutely alone in a great forest, having his
leathern bow-guard and finger-protector bound on him, and
8 carrying arrows, sword and bow. A deer issuing out of a dense

* For *śatru-lokam* read *śakra-lokam*, as in the Poona edition.

† Canto cxxi in the Calcutta edition.

‡ The Poona edition reads *ásádyámoćayat sádhikena* for *ásádya moćayet sádhitena*, "acquired wealth through austerities and lavished that together with more besides" (*kośa-stha-dravyeṇa saha*).

forest from another side said to the horse that carried him—"Accomplish thy object by killing me."

The king spoke:

9 Other deer on seeing me flee in great terror; how *is it that* thou wishest to yield thyself as a gift to death?

The deer spoke:

10 I have no son, O great king; vain is the purpose of my existence; while wandering about I do not perceive the *use of* maintaining my life here.

Márkaṇḍeya spoke:

11 Now another deer approached the king and said in the
presence of that *first* deer—"Enough of this, O king; slay me,
12 perform thy rite with my flesh. As thou mayest *thus*
succeed in thy object, so *will* that also *be* beneficial to me.
13 Thou, O great king, desirest to sacrifice to thy pitṛis in order
to *obtain* a son; how wilt thou gain thy earnest wish by means
14 of the flesh of this *other* son-less *deer?* As is the rite that is to
be performed, such *is* the thing one should offer. Knowledge
of the odours of sweetly-odorous things is not ascertained by
means of ill-odorous things.

The king spoke:

15 This *other deer* has declared to me that the reason of his indifference to worldly desires is his son-lessness: tell thou me what is the reason of thy indifference to worldly desires in thy abandonment of life.

The deer spoke:

16 Many are my sons, O king; many are my daughters also;
in the miseries of my anxieties for whom I dwell as amid the
17 flames of a raging conflagration. O king, this most weakly
deer-tribe is to be mastered by every one, and I have excessive
self-interest in those my children—therefore I am distressed.
18 I am in fear of men, lions, tigers, wolves, and other *ravenous*
beasts, but not of a feeble *animal, nor* of all good creatures, *nor*
19 even of a dog or jackal, my lord. Being such, I desire most

earnestly for the sake of my kindred, that all this earth may
be free for once from the fear of men, lions, and other *beasts.*
20 Some *animals,* cows, goats, sheep, horses and such like, feed
on grass; for their thriving I wish those *beasts* sent to de-
21 struction. After those *beasts* then have departed *and* my off-
spring *remain* separate, anxious thoughts occur by hundreds
22 to *me* whose mind is enveloped by self-interest, *such as*—'Has
a son of mine while browsing in the forest encountered a
crafty trap, or a thunderbolt, or a noose? or has he fallen
into the power of a man, or lion or other *dangerous creature?*
23 *What condition* has this one reached? what condition have
those *sons* of mine reached, who while actually grazing
24 have now gone to the very great forest?' On seeing
that those my sons have reached my presence,* O king,
I, panting somewhat, wish for night however as security
25 At dawn I desire day earnestly as security, *and* when
the sun has set *I desire* again the night *earnestly*: when
26 will there be safety at every time? This I have declared
to thee, O king, is the cause of my anxiety. Be gracious
to me therefore—let this *thy* arrow be discharged at me!
27 That is the cause why pierced by hundreds of sufferings I
thus forsake even my life; hearken thou as I speak, O king!
28 Named 'The Sun-less' are the worlds, to which those who kill
themselves go; *but* cattle that are suitable for sacrifice attain
29 *thus* to exalted stations,† O lord. Agni was a domestic animal‡
formerly; the lord of the waters was a domestic animal; and
so was the Sun, who gained exalted stations *and* reached his
30 culmination in sacrifice.§ Shew me this pity then, and conduct
me to an exalted position; and thou shalt obtain the earnestly
desired wish of thy soul by gaining a son.

* This is the reading of the Bombay edition *práptán mamábhyáśam;* instead of the Calcutta reading *prápta-samábhyásam,* which seems incorrect; *samábhyása* is not in the dictionary.

† *Uttama-lokán* (comment.)

‡ *Paśu.*

§ Or "and the Sun gained exalted stations *and* reached his culmination in sacrifice.'

The first deer spoke:

31 O supreme king, this deer must not be killed; he is happy
as a kind doer, who has many sons; I must be killed who have
no progeny.

The second deer spoke:

32 Happy in truth art thou, sir *deer*, being such a one for whom
suffering exists in a single body! He who has many bodies has
33 manifold sufferings. But formerly when I was single, the suf-
fering that arises from the body *consisted* then in my regard
for myself; that become doubled when there was a wife.
34 When children were born, then as many as they were, so many
35 sites in my body did my sufferings find in sooth. Hast not
thou, sir, been successful, for whom existence has not tended
to excessive suffering? My offspring are for suffering in this
36 world, and *will be* of opposite qualities in the next world. Since
I do that for the preservation and nourishment of my children,
and am anxious *about that*, my birth *will* therefore certainly *be*
in hell.*

The king spoke:

37 I know not, O deer, whether he who has offspring is happy
in this *world*, or he who has no son; and this undertaking of
38 mine in order to obtain a son makes my mind vacillate. Off-
spring verily tend then to cause suffering both in this *world*
and in the other *world*; nevertheless, debts come upon those
39 who have no son—so have I heard. I being such will strive
to obtain a son, without the slaughter of breathing beings, O
deer, even with very arduous austerities, as did a king of yore.

Canto CXXI.†

Karandhama's exploits.

Khanínetra propitiated Indra and obtained the gift of a son, Ba-

* The Poona edition reads instead *ćintayámi ća sambhútiṁ tena me narako dhruvam*, "and am anxious about my offspring (*sambhúti = santati*, comment.) therefore hell is certainly *destined* for me."

† Canto cxxii in the Calcutta edition.

lááva—King Baláśva was besieged by his rebellious vassal kings and was delivered by an army which issued from his hands that shook with distress—Hence he was named Karandhama.

Márkaṇḍeya spoke :

1 Thereupon the king went to the sin-destroying *river* Go-
matí,* and, practising self-restraint, gratified the god Puran-
2 dara there. And assiduously practising severe austerities,
subduing his voice, body and mind, *and* controlling himself,
3 the king gratified Indra in order to obtain a son. The ad-
orable Indra, lord of the gods, was gratified with his praise,
4 austerities and faith, and said to him, O great muni,—"By
reason of these austerities, faith and praise uttered *by thee*,
I am well satisfied with thee, O king ; choose a boon, sir!"

The king spoke:

5 May I who am son-less obtain a son, *who shall be* chief among all who bear arms, and always unrepulsed in his sovereignty,† a doer of righteousness, a knower of righteousness, *and* skilful.

Márkaṇḍeya spoke:

6 And when Indra said to him, "Be it so!" the king gained
his desire. The king returned to his own city to protect his
7 people. As he was performing sacrifice there, as he was duly
protecting his people, a son was born *to him* then through
8 Indra's favour, O bráhman. The king, his father, gave him
the name Baláśva,‡ and caused the son to acquire *skill in* every
9 kind of weapon. When his father died, O bráhman, he stood

* See p. 291, note ††.

† For *ćábhyáhataiśvaryo* read *ćávyáhataiśvaryo* as in the Poona edition.

‡ He was also called Suvarćas (Mahá-Bh., Áśvam.-p. iii. 72-79) and Balakáśva or Subaláśva; but his most famous name was Karandhama which is fancifully explained in verse 21, and in the above-mentioned passage of the Mahá-Bhárata. A king Vibhúti or Ati-vibhúti is sometimes inserted between Khanínetra and this king. This famous Karandhama must be distinguished from another king of the same name, who was fourth in descent from Yayáti's son Turvasu (Hari-V., xxxii. 1829-31; and Matsya Pur. xlviii. 1, 2.)

as king in the supreme sovereignty.* Baláśva brought all
10 kings on tbe earth into subjection; and the king after first
taking away their choicest property,† made all the kings pay
him tribute; and he protected his people.
11 Now all those kings as claimants were furious against him; and
at all times they neither rose up *before him* nor paid him tribute.
12 They stood up‡ then in their own countries; disregarding con-
tentment as the chief *good*, those kings seized that king's terri-
13 tory. That king held fast his own kingdom by force,§ O muni,
and made his stand in his own city. Many kings besieged him.
14 Kings, very great in valour, possessing military apparatus and
riches, assembled then and besieged that king in that city.
15 Now the king was enraged at that siege of his city, *but*, having
very little treasure and a small army, fell into the utmost
16 distress. Beholding no succour *though* possessing an army,
O best of dvijas, he put his hands before his face and sighed
17 in mental suffering. Then compacted together|| by the breath
from his mouth, *which issued* through the interstice between
his hands, tbere went forth¶ in hundreds warriors accom-
18 panied by chariots, elephants and horses. Thereby in a
moment all that city of that king was pervaded by a host of
forces, choice by reason of their extreme strength, O muni.
19 Surrounded then by that exceeding great host of forces, the
king sallied forth from that city and conquered those *foes*.
20 And after vanquishing them the king, having great good for-
tune, brought them into subjection and made them pay tri-
21 bute again as before, illustrious *sir*. Because from his agi-

* The Mahá-Bh. says Kbanínetra was deposed by his subjects (*Áśvam.-p.* iii. 70-72.)

† *Sára-grahaṇa-púrvakam; sára = śreshṭha-vastu* (comment.)

‡ *Vyutthitáḥ.* The root *vy-ut-thá* is given only in the causal form in the dictionary.

§ For *pṛithiviśe balán* the Poona edition reads *pṛithiviśo 'balán; pṛithiviśo balán* appears therefore to be the correct reading.

|| *Samáhatáḥ* appears to be the reading, but hardly yields a suitable meaning; *samáhitáh*, "put into order," "arrayed" would be preferable.

¶ For *hasta-viraván* read *hasta-vivarán*, and for *ni-jagmuḥ* read *nir-jagmuḥ* as in the Poona edition.

tated hands was produced an army which burnt up his
22 foes, Baláśva is thence called Karandhama.* He was righteous of soul and great of soul; he was benevolent to all living creatures. King Karandhama was celebrated in the three
23 worlds. And Power, which is denounced by Righteousness itself approaching the king, who had undergone intense suffering, granted him the destruction of his enemies.†

Canto CXXII.‡

Avíkshita's exploits.

Karandhama had a son Avíkshita, who was so called because benign planets looked upon his birth—Avíkshita was a great prince; he was chosen by many princesses and he also carried off others at their svayam-varas—He carried off Vaisaliní princess of Vidiśá, and other kings arrayed themselves against him.

Márkaṇḍeya spoke:

1 Vírya-ćandra's§ beautiful-browed daughter was named Vírá;
she was noble in her vows. She chose the great king Karan-
2 dhama *for her husband* at her svayam-vara. That valiant king
of kings begat of her a son named Avíkshita,|| who attained
3 fame on the face of the earth. When that son was born,

* The derivation given here is from *karayor dhutayor*, but this is insufficient; the root *dhmá* would support this fanciful explanation better than *dhu* or *dhú*.

†The verse seems involved. The Poona edition has been followed. It reads *sampráptam paramám ártim* for *sampráptasya parám ártim*, and *nṛipam* for *nṛipaḥ*; and the commentator says *balam* is the subject and *ari-vináśanam* the object.

‡ Canto cxxiii in the Calcutta edition.

§ I have not found this king elsewhere.

|| He is called Avíkshit and Avíkshi in various passages in the following cantos (see canto cxxx, verse 22); see also Mahá-Bh., Áśvam.-p. iii. 80-85, and Vishnu Pur. IV. i. In the former of these passages he is also called Kárandhama, is highly extolled as a great king, and is said to have reigned at the beginning of the Tretá Age with Angiras as his priest.

the king asked *the astrologers* who could read fate—"I trust
my son *is born* under an excellent constellation, at an excellent
4 conjuncture? And I trust that benignant planets have looked
upon my son's birth; I trust it did not pass into the path of
view of evil planets?"
5 When addressed thus by him, the astrologers spake then to
the king—"When the moment, the constellation and the con-
6 juncture have been excellent, thy son has been born *to be* great
in valour, great in his parts, great in strength. O great king, thy
7 son shall be a great king. The *planet Jupiter*, preceptor of the
gods, has looked on him, and Venus which is the seventh;
and the Moon the fourth *planet* has looked upon this thy son;
8 and Soma's son *Mercury* also, which is stationed at the edge,
9 has guarded him. The Sun has not looked on him; nor *has* Mars
or Saturn *looked on* thy son, O great king. Happy is this thy
son! he will be endowed with all good fortune and prosperity."

Márkaṇḍeya spoke:

10 On hearing this the astrologers' speech, the king was filled
with gladness in his mind, *and* going then to his own abode he
said—
11 "The preceptor of the gods has looked on him, *and so has*
Soma's son Mercury. The Sun has not looked on him, nor
12 has the Sun's son* nor Mars. This word 'Has looked upon'†
that ye, sirs, have uttered often,—celebrated by reason of it
his name shall be Avíkshita."

Márkaṇḍeya spoke:

13 His son Avíkshita learnt the whole of the Vedas and Vedáṅ-
gas. He acquired too from Kaṇva's son perfect *skill in* every
14 weapon. The prince surpassed both the Physicians of the
gods in figure, Váćas-pati in intellect, the Moon in loveliness,
15 the Sun in splendour, the Ocean in steadfastness, and the
Earth in endurance, full of valour *as he was*. In heroism no
one was the equal of that high-souled *prince*.

* *Arka-súnu.*

† *Avaikshata* from the root *ava+íksh.*

16 At her svayam-vara Hema-dharma's daughter Vará chose him
for her husband; so also did Sudeva's daughter Gaurí, Balin's
17 daughter Su-bhadrá, Víra's daughter Lílávatí, Víra-bhadra's
daughter Anibhá,* Bhíma's daughter Mánya-vatí, Dambha's
18 daughter Kumud-vatí. And those *maidens* who, awaiting the
precise moment at their svayam-varas, did not approve him,†
19 even them the hero prince took by force. Driving off all the
kings and the fathers and families of those *princesses and* trusting in his own valour, the mighty *prince* was indeed proud of his strength.

20 Now one day he *seized* Vaiśáliní of the beautiful teeth,
daughter of the Vaidiśa‡ king Viśála, as she was waiting for
21 the proper moment at her svayam-vara; after vanquishing
all the kings he seized her by force, because in her own free
fancy she chose him not, O bráhman-ṛishi, just as, proud of
22 his strength, *he had seized* other *princesses*. Then all those
kings, being repeatedly driven off by that haughty prince
and being sorely dejected, spoke to one another, *all* throng-
23 ing together,—

"Fie on the birth of you kings, who being endowed with
strength submit to this defrauding deed § *at the hands* of
24 a single *man, and* who are many, of the same caste! A
kshatriya *is he* who delivers from injury|| *a man*, who is being
killed by ferocious men; that is the name of such a one; for
25 in vain verily do others bear *that name!* Of you, sirs, who,
though born of kshatriya lineage, cannot save even your own
selves from injury at the hands of this scoundrel, what is
26 your resolution like? Let the praise, which is poured forth
to you ¶ by *bards* and minstrels and heralds, be true—let it

* Or *Nibhá*.

† For *ćaivaṁ nábhinandanti* read *ćainaṁ nábhyanandanta* as in the Poona edition.

‡ The adjective of Vidiśá, a town, see p. 343, note †.

§ For *lalanám* read *vañćanám* as in the Bombay edition.

|| *Kshatriyo yaḥ kshata-tráṇaṁ karoti*. This fanciful derivation is also in Raghu-Vaṁsa ii. 53. For a different derivation, see *ante*, canto cxiv, 36.

¶ For *ća* read *vaḥ* with the Bombay edition.

not be in vain—O heroes, by reason of the destruction of your
27 foes! Let not this *story* vainly spread itself about by messen-
gers belonging to other regions,* O kings! *Ye* all rely on your
manhood, *ye are* sprung from exalted families. Who fears
28 not death? Who is immortal without battling? With these
thoughts *ye* whose profession is arms must not abandon your
manhood."

29 On hearing this the kings were filled with openly displayed
wrath; all spoke *at once* to one another and rose up with
30 their weapons. Some mounted chariots, some elephants and
others horses; others overpowered with wrath advanced on
foot against him.

Canto CXXIII.†

Avíkshita's exploits.

The kings had a great battle with Avíkshita and conquered and captured him.—The svayam-vara was re-opened, but the princess would not choose any husband, and the wedding was postponed.

Márkaṇḍeya spoke:

1 Thus were prepared for battle those kings and princes, who
had been beaten off repeatedly and yet were not destroyed‡ at
2 that time. Then began a terrible battle between him and them,
between *the prince* single-*handed* and many kings and noble
3 princes, O muni. In great ferocity they fought, assailing him
with their swords, spears, clubs, arrows, and hands; and he
4 *fought* with them all. The prince mighty and skilled in wea-
pons pierced them with hundreds of fierce arrows; and they

* The Calcutta edition reads *ćaratáṁ sá vṛithaivaisha bhúpaś ćárair dig-antaraiḥ*; the Bombay edition *ćaratáṁ sá tathaivaishá bhúpáś ćárair dig-antare*; and the Poona edition *ćaratám má vṛithaivaisha bhúpa-śabdo dig-antare.* The first is incorrect; the second is sound whether it reads *dig-antare* or *dig-antaraiḥ*, and the third is also good. Comparing these, the best reading appears to be *ćaratám má vṛithaivaishá bhúpáś ćárair dig-antaraiḥ*, and I have taken this.

† Canto cxxiv in the Calcutta edition.

‡ For *a-víkshitáḥ* read *a-vi-kshitáḥ* as in the Bombay edition.

5 pierced him with sharp arrows. He cut off the arm of one, and the neck of another; and pierced another in the heart,
6 and smote another in the breast. He cut off the trunk of an elephant and the head of a horse, and *wounded* the horses of the chariot of these *foes*,* and the driver of the chariot of
7 another. And he split in two with *his own* arrows his enemies' arrows which were falling on him, and in his agility cracked
8 the scymitar of another and the bow of another. One prince perished when his armour was torn away by the *prince*, and another who was on foot being wounded by Avíkshita quitted the battle.

9 When that entire band of kings was thus thrown into confusion, seven hundred warriors stood *forth* resolute unto death,
10 who were nobly born, in the flower of their age, heroic, valiant, and modest, after all the army was defeated *and* was in a panic of
11 flight. Now the king's son coming to close quarters with those kings fought in righteously-conducted determined combat.†
12 Deeply angered by this and that *foe*, he, great in his strength,

* For *tathányeshám* read *rathasyaishám*, which the Bombay edition seems to mean by *rathasyeshám*.

† *Dharma-yuddha*, "battle according to the (kshatriyas') code of Right." It appears to mean a battle according to the fair rules of war, fought out to the end till one or other combatant is completely vanquished or slain. Thus Bhishma said to Karṇa—"If this most terrible enmity cannot be relinquished, I give permission, O Karṇa; fight thou with the desire to gain heaven. Without passion, with impetuosity subdued, do the deed of a king in sooth, to the utmost of thy power, with thy full effort, conducting thyself according to the conduct of good men . ...Thou shalt gain from Dhanañjaya the worlds which are won by the righteousness of kshatriyas (*kshatra-dharma*). Fight without arrogance, relying on thy strength and valour, for there is nought better for a kshatriya than righteously conducted battle" (*dharmya yuddha:* M.-Bh., Bhíshma-p. cxxiv. 5851-4). Again, Soma-datta said to Sátyaki,—"How is it that thou, O Sáttvata, hast forsaken the righteousness of kshatriyas, which was seen of old by the high-souled gods, and delightest in the righteousness of Dasyus? At one who has turned to flee, at one in distress, at one who has laid down his arms, at one who begs for quarter—how indeed did a wise man, who delights in the righteousness of kshatriyas, *ever* strike at *such a one* in battle?" (Droṇa p. clvi. 6730-1). The matter is summed up by Karṇa thus—"This, we

set himself to cleave asunder their harness and armour* also;
13 and enraged thereat, O great muni, those princes forsaking
the code of Right† all together fought with him, who continued
to fight according to the code of Right, while their faces were
14 wet with drops of perspiration. One pierced him with multi-
tudes of arrows, another split his bow, another splitting his
15 banner with arrows, laid it low on the ground. Moreover,
others smote his horses, and others broke his chariot, and others
besides smote‡ his back with blows of their clubs *and* with
16 arrows. When his bow was split, the king's son enraged then
grasped his sword and shield, but that also another struck down.§
17 When his sword and shield were broken, he best of club-wield-
ers grasped his club; and another, like a dexterous man, split
18 it with a sharp curved-headed arrow. The kings, turning
their faces away from righteously conducted combat, surround-
ed him and pierced him, some with a thousand arrows, some
19 with a hundred. He fell exhausted on the earth, one torment-
ed by many; and those illustrious princes then bound him.

20 Having captured that king's son by unrighteousness they
21 all in company with king Viśála entered the Vaidiśa city, glad
and merry, taking the king's son bound. And the maiden,
who was holding her svayam-vara, was placed by that *king* in
22 front of them; and was asked by her father again and again,
and likewise by the family priest,—"Take by the hand *as thy*
23 bridegroom *him* who among *these* kings pleases thee." When
the high-spirited maiden chose not any *of them* as her bridegroom,
O muni, the king enquired of the astrologer then concerning
24 her marriage,—"Tell *me* the most distinguished day for the
wedding; such a battle as this which has occurred to-day im-
poses an obstacle."

have heard, is a kshatriya's chiefest righteousness (*dharma*), that he lie, slain in battle, highly honoured by the good." (Karṇa-p. xl. 1858–9).

* *Viććhinna-yantra-kavaćán* in the Calcutta and Bombay editions; but the Poona edition reads *viććhinna-patra-kavaćán* "their vehicles and armour."

† *Dharmaṁ utsṛijya.*

‡ For *atáḍayat* read *atáḍayan* with the Bombay edition.

§ For *anyena pátayat* read *anyo nv apátayat* as in the Bombay edition.

Márkaṇḍeya spoke :

25 When asked thus by the king, the astrologer reflected there-
on and perceiving the real truth spoke with troubled mind*
26 to the king,—" There will be, O king, other days here, charac-
terized by excellent conjunctures, auspicious, and after no long
27 *delay*. Thou shalt perform the wedding† when they have
arrived, O bestower of honour. Enough of this *day*, wherein a
great obstacle has presented itself, O noble Sir ! "

Canto CXXIV.‡

Avíkshita's exploits.

Avíkshita's mother Vírá roused up his father and allied kings to rescue Avíkshita, and they defeated Viśála and his confederates—Avíkshita was set free, but refused to marry the princess as she had seen him overpowered, although she praised him and his father entreated him—She vowed to marry no one else, and departed to the forest and wore herself away with austerities—The gods in compassion sent a messenger to her and promised that she should have a son who should be a universal monarch—She then regained her health.

Márkaṇḍeya spoke :

1 Karandhama heard then that his son had been captured ; and
2 his wife Vírá and other kings also *heard it*. On hearing that
his son had been captured unrighteously, the king pondered
a long time in company with the neighbouring§ kings, O
3 great muni. Some of the kings said, — " All *those* kings should
be slain, who *banding* themselves all together captured him
4 single-*handed* unrighteously in fight." "Let the army be
made ready ; why sit the others still ? Let wicked Viśála be

* For *dur-maná* read *dur-manáḥ*.

† The Calcutta text is *karishyati viváhártham*, and the Bombay text *karishyasi viváha tvam ;* the proper reading should then be *karishyasi viváhaṁ tvam*.

‡ Canto cxxv in the Calcutta edition.

§ For *samastaiḥ* read *samantaiḥ* with the Bombay edition.

5 slain!" said others who were assembled there. And others
said,—"Righteousness was first discarded in this *affair* by
Avíkshit,* who acting unjustly forcibly seized *the princess* who
6 did not desire him. In all svayam-varas then he has reduced
all the princes to ruin at once; when *they* combined, he was
subdued."

7 On hearing this their speech Vírá, mother of a hero, daugh-
8 ter of a race of heroes, *and* wife of a hero, rejoiced *and* spoke
in view of her husband and of the other kings,—"A noble
9 deed, O kings, has my son who feasts on noble deeds done, in
that vanquishing all the kings he seized the maiden by force.
While fighting for that *object* single-*handed* he was captured†
10 unrighteously. Even that I reckon entails no deterioration
on my son in battle. For this in truth is manliness, that a
11 man under the influence of passion‡ recks not so of good poli-
cy, just as a lion when attacking *recks not*. Many maidens§
12 presented for *their* svayam-vara have been seized by my son
in full sight of exceedingly proud kings. What comparison
is there between birth in a kshatriya family and entreaty
13 which is used by the feeble? By force verily a kshatriya takes
things to himself in the presence of the mighty. On the other
hand do not weaklings, being bound with iron chains, pass
14 into subjection? Do kings imbued with righteousness, who do
daring deeds, pass *thereinto*? Away then with weak-minded-
15 ness! Praiseworthy in sooth is his captivity! *Let there be*
the down-rush of your weapons among bodies and heads!
After ye have actually taken from the kings *their* territory,
16 sons and other wealth, then the objects aimed at by your
valour, *even their* wives,‖ have become *matters of* import-

* For *mahíkshitaiḥ* the Bombay edition reads *ahavíkshitá*; the correct reading seems to be *avíkshitá* and this I have adopted.

† For *yuddha* read *baddha* with the Bombay edition.

‡ *Amarsha-vaśán* in the Bombay edition is better than *adharma-vaśán*.

§ Both editions read *kanyaká*; but the plural *kanyakáḥ* is required by the adject. *bahvyo*.

‖ For *bháryáśárya-nimittáni* read *bháryá vírya-nimittáni* as in the Bombay edition.

ance.* Hasten then quickly to battle; mount ye the chariots;
17 make ready the elephants and horses without delay, and also
the charioteers.† What think ye of battling with many kings?
18 Deeds have occurred, indeed, enough to satisfy a warrior in a
small battle. Who finds not strength *when* amongst petty
19 kings and other *petty men* that inspire no fear? For in sooth,
O muni, the man who, after prevailing so as to slay *my* son's
foes‡ which have all pervaded the world, is self-controlled,
he shines forth§ a hero, just as the sun *after prevailing over*
the darknesses."

Márkaṇḍeya spoke:

20 Thus was king Karandhama aroused to boldness by this *his*
wife. He set his army in array to slay his son's foes, O muni.
21 Then occurred a conflict between him whose son had been cap-
22 tured and all those kings and Viśála, O great muni. Three
days lasted the battle then between king Karandhama and
23 the kings who followed Viśála's lead. When all that confederacy
of kings was almost defeated,‖ Viśála with arghya offering in
24 hand approached Karandhama then. And that king highly
honoured Karandhama with kindly feeling. On his son being
25 set free,¶ he abode there that night in happiness. And when

* Or, "the objects of *your* wives and spiritual guides then attained to importance." The Bombay edition reads differently in verse 15 and the first half of verse 16;—"For you also, who, by accomplishing the slaughter of your foes *and* by taking away in sooth the territory, sons and other wealth of the kings, *stood* foremost, a wife became then of exceeding importance as being the *sum of the* objects of your valour." But neither text seems satisfactory, and the future appears to be intended rather than the past.

† For *sa-sárathim* read *sa-sárathi* as in the Poona edition (corrigenda).

‡ The Bombay edition reads differently, thus,—"Who finds not strength *when* amongst petty kings and other *petty men*, that inspire no fear in one who has really displayed his prowess against foes? For in sooth the man who, after prevailing over all those *men* which have pervaded the world, was self-controlled, shone forth, &c."

§ *Vyaroćata + iti.* The past tense does not seem happy, and the *iti* is wrong. *Viroćate ća* is the reading of the Poona edition (corrigenda), and is preferable.

‖ For *parájaya-práyaṁ* read *parájita-práyaṁ* as in the Poona edition (corrigenda.

¶ For *viyukte* read *vimukte* as in the Poona edition (corrigenda).

Viśála taking the maiden came near, Avíkshit spoke before
his father touching the marriage, O bráhman ṛishi :—
26 "O king, I will not take this *maiden*, nor any other woman,
in whose very sight I have been vanquished by adversaries in
27 fight. Bestow her on some one else, and let her choose some one
else, who is unscathed in fame and valour *and* has not been
28 subjected to indignity by adversaries. Since I have been van-
quished by adversaries just as this weak girl *might be*, what
manhood have I here? there is no difference between her and
29 me. Self-reliance is the quality of men; a girl is always
dependant on others. Of what kind is the manhood of that
30 man who is even dependant on others? How shall I, *who am
such*, show her *again* the face *which she has* often seen, I who
have been worsted to the ground in her presence by adverse
kings?"

31 When he had thus spoken, the king spoke to the maiden,—
"Thou hast heard, dear child, the speech of this high-souled
32 *prince* as he has been speaking. Choose another as thy hus-
band in whom thy mind delights, O beauteous one. We bestow
perfume * on whomsoever thou dost honour.† Adopt one of
these two very courses, O sweet-faced one!"

The maiden spoke:

33 Vanquished he has been by many *together*, *yet* they dealt not
absolutely honourably in the fight which brought loss to his
34 fame and valour, O king. Since he set himself single-*handed*
to battle with many, like a lion with elephants, he has mani-
35 fested thereby the highest heroism. *It is* not only *that* he
stood *fast* in the battle, *but* also *that* they were all defeated.
36 He displayed prowess also abundantly by his efforts.‡ All the
kings have by unrighteousness conquered him, who is endued
with heroism and prowess *and* who observed righteous combat;

* *Vásam*; or "a dwelling," or "clothing."

† For *ádṛitáḥ* read *ádṛitiḥ* with the Bombay edition; *ádṛiti* is not in the dictionary. The Poona edition reads *yasmiṁs te hy ádṛitam manas* with the same sense.

For *yat tena* read *yatnena*, as in the Bombay edition.

37 what fame *is there* herein? And it is certainly not for mere
beauty *that* I have become desirous of him, O father! His
38 heroism, prowess and fortitude captivate my mind. What
need then of much speaking? Do thou make entreaty to this
most excellent king on my behalf; no other shall be my husband.

Viśála spoke:

39 O prince! my daughter has pronounced this splendid declaration, and *there lives* not on the earth a royal youth, who is thus
40 indeed thy peer. Thy heroism cannot be gainsaid, and thy
prowess is surpassing; purify my family, O warrior, by marrying my daughter!

The prince spoke:

41 I will not take her nor any other woman, O king, for in my inmost self my intellect is womanish, O lord of men.

Márkandeya spoke:

42 Then spoke Karandhama,—"O son, take thou this beauteous-browed daughter of Viśála; she is deeply enamoured of thee."

The prince spoke:

43 No infringement of thy command have I ever committed before, O lord; command me in such wise, dear father, as I may obey thy command.

Márkaṇḍeya spoke:

44 Since the prince was so exceedingly determined in his sen-
timents, Viśála also troubled in mind spoke to his daughter,*
45 —"Turn back thy mind, my daughter, even from this object
choose some other as thy husband; there are many princes *here*

The maiden spoke:

46 A boon I choose, dear father! If this *prince* wants me not, no other than *a course of* religious austerities shall be my husband in this life!

Márkaṇḍeya spoke:

47 Then king Karandhama stayed there three days joyously

* For *satám* read *sutám*.

48 with Viśála and returned to his own city. Avíkshita also, after
being soothed by his own father and the other kings *and* by
precepts of ancient times, returned to his city.

49 That maiden also went to the forest, being set free by her
relatives, and practised austerities, abstaining from food *and*
50 adhering to utter passionlessness. Now when abstaining from
food she had dwelt *there* three months, she reached the deepest
distress, being emaciated, in the lowest *condition* and prostrat-
51 ed.* The maiden was weakened in energy, extremely thin in
body, even ready to die. The princess then made up her mind
52 to quit the body. Thereupon the gods, perceiving that she
had made up her mind to abandon herself, assembled and des-
53 patched the gods' messenger to her. Approaching the maiden
he said :—

"I am a messenger, O princess, sent to thee by the thirty
54 *gods*; hearken to what must be done! Thou, O lady, must not
forsake thy body which is exceedingly difficult to be obtained.
Thou, O fortunate one, shalt become the mother of a universal
55 monarch; and along with thy son, who shall have slain his
foes and whose command shall be unresisted, thou, O illustrious
56 *lady*, shalt long enjoy the earth and its seven continents. He
must kill the enemy Taru-jit in the presence of the gods, *and*
Aya and cruel S'aṅku, *and* then establish the people in right-
57 eousness. All the four castes must be fully safeguarded accord-
ing to their respective *rules of* righteousness; he must slay
the robbers, the mleććhas and others who work wickedness.
58 He must sacrifice with manifold sacrifices replete with gifts
and largesse, and with horse-sacrifices and other *sacrifices* six
thousand in number, O noble *lady*."

Márkaṇḍeya spoke:

59 Seeing that messenger of the gods, stationed in the air, *ad-
orned* with heavenly garlands and unguents, the weakened
60 princess then said this,—"Truly thou hast come from Svarga,
a messenger of the gods without doubt; nevertheless how

* *Kṛiśádhama-nisantatá*; *ni-san-tata* om *ni-san-tan*, not in the dictionary.

61 shall I have such a son without a husband? 'No one but
Avíkshita shall be my husband in this life,'—this I vowed
62 in my father's presence. And me he wants not, *though* he
was admonished by my father and *his* sire Karandhama, and
though he was entreated by me also in seemly wise."

The gods' messenger spoke:

63 What need of this further speaking, O illustrious *lady!* A
son shall be born to thee. Abandon not thyself unright-
64 eously! Remain in this very forest and nourish up thy emaci-
ated body. Through the power of austerities all this shall be
well for thee.

Márkaṇḍeya spoke:

65 After speaking thus, the messenger of the gods went *away*
as he had come. And the beautiful-browed *lady* nourished
up her body day by day.

Canto CXXV.*

Avíkshita's exploits.

Avíkshita's mother induced him to engage in the 'What-want-ye?' penance, in which he declared he would bestow on any one who asked whatever he wanted—His father Karandhama, being entreated by his ministers, pressed Avíkshita to forgo his religious continence and beget a son—Avíkshita though very loth was obliged to promise compliance.

Márkaṇḍeya spoke:

1 Now Avíkshita's mother Vírá, mother of a hero, called her
son Avíkshita on a sacred day and said:—

2 "*My* son, permitted by thy high-souled father, I will engage
in a fast; *it is* this difficult *penance*, the 'What-want-ye?'†

* Canto cxxvi, in the Calcutta edition.

† *Kim-iććhakaḥ,* "Whatever one wants *I will give.*" A penance in which one binds one's self to satisfy the wish of any applicant (comment.)

3 And it depends* on thy father, and must be achieved by
thee and by me also. When thou hast consented, *my* son.
4 I *will* then give my endeavours thereto. I will give thee
half the riches from *thy* father's great treasury; thy riches
5 depend on thy father, and I have his permission. To be
achieved through affliction is *the part of the penance* that
depends upon me; it will indeed be a noble thing. If, on
the other hand, any *part of it* may be achievable by thee
6 through strength and prowess, that will indeed be unachievable
by thee otherwise, or will be achievable with difficulty.
If then thou givest me a promise, *my* son, I also will pledge
thee here the very same thing. Tell me what thou thinkest."

Avíkshita spoke:

7 Riches depend on my father; I indeed have no ownership
therein.† I will perform what can be accomplished by my
8 body, as thou hast said, *even* the 'What-want-ye?' penance,
O mother—cease then from anxiety and distress‡—if it
has been approved for me by the king, *my* father, the master
of the riches.

Márkaṇḍeya spoke:

9 Then the queen applied herself wholly to that penance. She
performed the worship of the king of kings§ as directed,
10 with self subdued, and *the worship* of all the Nidhis|| and of
the band of Nidhi-guardians and of Lakshmí, with profound
faith, with voice, body and mind restrained.

11 Now this king Karandhama dwelt in his house in a sequestered
part. As he sat there, his ministers, learned in
the books of Good Policy, addressed him.

The ministers spoke:

12 O king, this thy time of life has reached its decline, while

* *A'yattas.*

† For *mám asi tvaṁ* read *mat-svámitvaṁ* as in the Bombay edition.

‡ Or "cease then, mother, from anxiety and distress with regard to the 'What-want-ye' penance." (comment.)

§ Kuvera (comment.)

|| See canto lxviii.

thou art ruling the earth. Thy only son Avíkshit has for-
13 sworn possession of his wives; and he has no son. When
he shall reach thy condition,* O king, thy territory will
14 assuredly pass to thy enemies then. There will be ruin to
thy family, and ruin to the cakes and water *offered* to the
pitṛis; thou wilt have this great dread of enemies† with
15 loss of sacrifices. Contrive therefore, O king, so that thy
son *shall* again steadfastly apply his mind so as to benefit
the pitṛis!

Márkaṇḍeya spoke:

16 At this moment the king heard the sound of Vírá's family
priest speaking to *some* petitioner;—
17 "'Who wishes for what, that is hard to be achieved?
Who must achieve what?'—this 'What-want-ye?' *penance*
Karandhama's queen is intent upon!"
18 Now prince Avíkshit also heard the priest's speech and
replied to all the petitioners who were assembled at the
19 king's gate;—"Let him speak out, for whom I must ac-
complish *anything* with my body; my illustrious mother
20 is intent upon the 'What-want-ye?' *penance*. Let all peti-
tioners hear me. I have promised then; what want ye?
here I give it, while the 'What-want-ye?' *penance* is being
performed!"

Márkaṇḍeya spoke:

21 Thereupon the king, on hearing this speech that fell from
his son's mouth, springing up said to his son,—"I have a
petition; grant it me!"

Avíkshit spoke:

22 Tell me, dear father, what I must give to your highness;
I must do it for thee, whether *it be* difficult, *or readily* accom-
plishable, or truly hard to be accomplished!

* *I.e.*, the decline of life; *nishṭhám = antam* (comment.)

† *Te 'ri-bhayaṁ*; this is the Bombay reading. The Calcutta edition reads *te viravaṁ*, which is incorrect; *virava* is masc., and a Vedic word. The Poona edition reads *te vivaraṁ*, "thou wilt have this great breach with loss of sacrifices."

The king spoke :

23 If thou art true to thy word, and thou grantest the 'What-want-ye ?' *boon*, show me then the face of a grandson lying upon my lap !

Avíkshit spoke :

24 I am thy only son, and religious continence is my *lot*, O king ; no son have I, how *can* I show *thee* a grandson's face ?

The king spoke :

25 Thy religious continence tends to sin, if thou holdest to this. Therefore deliver thou thy own self and show me a grandson !

Avíkshit spoke :

26 Any other *thing* that may be arduous,* O great king, command me that. Intercourse with women has been eschewed by me, with passionlessness—let it be so *still !*

The king spoke :

27 *Thou* in sooth hast seen victory over enemies who were
fighting *against thee* with numbers ; yet, there if thou hast
28 recourse to passionlessness, then *thou art* unwise. Yet what
need have we of more talking ? Abandon thy religious continence. At thy mother's desire show thou me a grandson's face !

Márkaṇḍeya spoke :

29 When the king, *though* accosted by the son in many *words*,
30 makes no other request, the son then spoke again ;—"By
granting thee the 'What-want-ye ?' *boon*, I am in a strait,
dear father. I will therefore without shame wed a wife
31 again. He, who in a woman's sight has been vanquished
and has fallen to the face of the earth, shall further be that
woman's husband—this is exceedingly hard, dear father.
32 Nevertheless what am I to do here, who have passed under
the power of Truth's fetters ? I will do as thou hast said ;
do thou enjoy thy prevailing *in this matter !*"

* For *visham asmán* read *vishamaṁ syán* as in the Bombay edition.

CANTO CXXVI.*

Avíkshita's exploits.

Avíkshit while hunting found a Daitya had seized a maiden who called herself his (Avíkshit's) wife—He killed the Daitya—The gods appeared and offered him a boon—He asked for a son, and they said he should have a son, who would be a universal monarch, by her.—She then explained to him she was king Viśála's daughter, and told him her history.

Márkaṇḍeya spoke :

1 The prince went hunting in the forest one day, piercing deer
and wild boars and tigers and other beasts *and* elephants.
2 Suddenly he heard the cry, "Save *me!* Save *me!*" from a
woman who was screaming aloud very often *in a voice* in-
3 articulate through terror. The prince exclaiming, "Fear not!
fear not!" urged his horse in haste *thither* whence the sound
4 proceeded. And the maiden then cried out, *for* seized by
Danu's son Dṛiḍha-keśa in the lonely forest *was she*, a high-spirited *lady* :—

5 "I belong to Karandhama's son and I am Avíkshit's wife;
a villain is carrying off into a thicket *me, the wife* of the
6 wise king. I, wife of him, before whom all the kings with
the Gandharvas and Guhyakas could not stand, am carried
7 off! I here, wife of him, Karandhama's son, whose wrath
is like *that* of Death, *whose* prowess is like Indra's, am carried off!"

Márkaṇḍeya spoke :

8 On hearing this, the king's son, bearer of the bow, reflected,—

9 "What is this? Have I a wife here in the forest? She is surely an illusion *produced* by the wicked Rákshasas who inhabit the forest. However† I have certainly come; I will ascertain the whole cause."

* Canto cxxvii in the Calcutta edition.

† *Atha-vá.*

Márkaṇḍeya spoke :

10 Hastening on then he beheld a surpassingly fascinating
maiden alone in the forest, adorned with every *kind of* orna-
11 ment, seized by Danu's son Dṛiḍha-keśa who bore a staff, and
screaming out pitifully "Save *me!* save *me!*" again and
12 again. "Fear not!" said he to her, and exclaiming "Thou
art slain!" to him, *he said*—

"What wicked *man* exercises rule over this earth while
13 Karandhama is king here,* before whose majesty all kings
bow down to the earth?"

Seeing him at hand then, grasping his choice bow, the
14 slender-limbed *maiden* exclaimed more than once—"Save
me!" and—

"Here I am carried off! I am king Karandhama's daughter-in-law and Avíkshit's wife. I am carried off by this wicked *demon* in the forest,—*I* who belong to a master—as if I belong to no master."

Márkaṇḍeya spoke :

15 Thereupon Avíkshit considered the speech so uttered,—
"How in truth is she my wife? or how *is she* my dear father's
16† daughter-in-law? However I *will* set her free, the slender
maiden; I will find that out afterwards. Kshatriyas bear
arms for the sake of delivering the afflicted."

17 Then the angry hero addressed that most evil-minded
Dáṇava,—"Release her and depart while alive; otherwise
18 thou shalt not live!" Quitting her then the Dánava raised
his staff aloft and rushed at him; and he also, *the prince,*
19 poured a shower of arrows on him. The Dánava, filled
with exceeding frenzy, warded them off with a multitude
of arrows, and hurled his staff that was studded with a
20 hundred spikes at the prince. The prince split it then, as it
was rushing onwards, with arrows. And he, *the Dánava*, grasp-
ing aloft a tree that was near, stood firmly in the battle *and*

* Or, "Who is *this* wicked man, while Karandhama rules this earth as king here, &c."

† The Calcutta edition numbers this verse 15 also, and numbers all the following verses incorrectly.

21 then hurled that tree at *the prince* who was discharging clouds
of arrows. And he shattered it into small fragments with
22 crescent-headed arrows shot from his bow.* And the
Dánava next flung a piece of rock at the prince, and it fell
vainly on the ground, *for* he avoided† it by agility.
23 Whatever the enraged Dánava flung at the prince, each
thing the king's son playfully split with multitudes of arrows.
24 Then, his staff being shattered and all his weapons shattered,
he raised his fist in anger and rushed upon the prince.
25 Karandhama's son struck off his head with a two-edged sword,‡
as he was in the act of falling *upon him*, and felled him to the
very ground.

26 When that Dánava, the evil doer, was slain, all the gods
exclaimed to Karandhama's son, "Well done, well done!"
27 The gods said to the prince then, "Choose *thee* a boon!"
and he replied by reason of his desire to benefit his father,
"I choose a son, great in valour."

The gods spoke:

28 Verily thou shalt have a son, *who shall be* a universal monarch
great in valour, by this very maiden in sooth whom thou,
O sinless one, hast delivered!

The prince spoke:

29 Being bound to my father by a bond of truthfulness I wish
for a son, *but* having been vanquished by the kings in fight
30 I have discarded wedlock. And I have abandoned king
Viśála's daughter, who wanted§ me, and she has for my
31 sake abandoned union with *any* man but me. How then
after discarding her, Viśála's daughter, shall I with cruel
soul‖ marry another woman now?

* For *kármukam ujjhitaiḥ* read *kármuka-moćitaiḥ* as in the Bombay edition.

† For *uńćitá* read *ujjhitá* with the Bombay edition.

‡ *Vetasa-patra*, a "reed-leaf" or "cane-leaf." It is not in the dictionary, but appears to denote a weapon shaped like the leaf of a reed or of a cane, and would seem to mean something like a narrow double-edged sword.

§ For *yávati* read *yáćati* as in the Poona edition.

‖ For *nṛiśaṁsánám* read *nṛiśaṁsátmá* as in the Poona edition.

The gods spoke :

32 This very maiden is indeed thy wife, whom thou dost always
extol, *even* Viśála's beautiful-browed daughter, who has
33 devoted herself to austerities for thy sake. Of her shall
be born to thee a son *who shall be* a hero, an embellisher of
the seven continents,* a sacrificer of a thousand sacrifices,
a universal monarch.

Márkaṇḍeya spoke :

34 After announcing this to Karandhama's son the gods
departed, O bráhman ; and he then addressed her *who was*
35 *his* wife—"Say, timid one, what now is this ?" And she
told him *this* story :—

"When thou, sir, didst forsake me, I forsook my kins-
36 folk and came away to the forest in despair. There I wished
to quit *this* body which became almost wasted away with
austerities, O hero, *but* a messenger of the gods came to me
37 and prevented *me, saying*—'Thou shalt also have a son,
a universal monarch great in valour, who shall please the
38 gods and slay the demons.' By this command from the gods
that messenger of the gods prevented me. I did not abandon
39 my body, having my thoughts *fixed* on union with thee. And
the day before yesterday, O illustrious one, I went to Gangá-
hrada† to bathe, and as I went down *into the water*, I was drag-
40 ged away by a certain old Nága. He took me then to Rasátala,
and there in front‡ of me stood Nágas and Nága wives
41 and youths in thousands ; they approached and offered me
praise, and *some* others paid me worship ; and the Nága
42 women besought me respectfully,—'Do thou shew favour
to us all ; thou must turn aside thy son,§ *who will* seek to
43 slay *us* who *shall* have incurred offence. The Nágas will

* Or "islands" or "do-abs," *dvípa*.

† This is also mentioned as a sacred place of pilgrimage in the Mahá-Bh., Vana-p. lxxxiii. 7046-49, and Anuśás.-p. xxv. 1720-21.

‡ For *puram* read *puraḥ*, as in the Poona edition.

§ The son which should be born to her in the future, named Marutta. See canto cxxx, verses 11-14.

commit offence against thy son; for that reason *thou* must
44 turn him aside; let this favour be done!' And when I
said, 'Be it so,' they decorated me with divine ornaments
from Pátála and with choicest flowers odorous and fragrant.
45 And that Nága brought me back to this world, as lovely
46 as *I was* before, as beautiful in form as before. Seeing me
so beautiful and adorned with every *kind of* ornament, this
most evil-minded Dṛiḍha-keśa seized me in the desire to
47 carry me off. By the strength of thy arm, O prince, I
have been rescued; therefore be gracious, O mighty-armed
one; receive me! Equal to thee lives no other prince in
the world; I speak the truth."

CANTO CXXVII.*

Avíkshita's exploits.

Avíkshit agreed to marry the rescued maiden—The Gandharvas appeared then, and one of them explained she was his daughter and had been born as king Viśála's daughter Bhávini because of Agastya's curse—They were married and lived in the Gandharvas' world—She gave birth to a son there—All the celestial beings came to the boy's birth-ceremony, and because of the blessings invoked for him from the Maruts he was called Marutta.

Márkaṇḍeya spoke:

1 On hearing this her speech, he remembered his father's
fine speech which the king had uttered upon the promise re-
2 garding the "What-want-ye" *penance*, and prince Avíkshit re-
plied to the maiden, he with mind full of love to the maiden
who had also abandoned all enjoyments for his sake,—
3 "When I forsook thee, O slender one, I was vanquished
by my enemies. I have *now* met† thee here after conquering
the foes; what *shall* I do?"

* Canto cxxviii in the Calcutta edition.

† For *samprápto* read *samprápta* as in the Poona edition.

The maiden spoke :

4 Take thou my hand *in wedlock* in this charming forest. May the union of a loving *maiden* and a lover be fraught with merit !

The prince spoke :

5 Be it so ; may welfare be thine ! Destiny itself is the cause here. Otherwise how have thou and I met together here ?*

Márkaṇḍeya spoke :

6 At this moment, O muni, the Gandharva Tunaya arrived, accompanied by the fairest Apsarases and surrounded by other Gandharvas.

The Gandharva spoke :

7 O prince, this high-spirited *maiden* is my daughter, by
name Bhámini. By reason of Agastya's curse she became
8 Viśála's daughter. *It was* Agastya who was angered with
her as she was playing in a child's manner, so he cursed
9 her then, *saying*, "Thou shalt become a woman ! "† And we
appeased him by saying, "She is a child and cannot
reflect ; do thou show favour for the offence against thee,
10 O bráhman ṛishi." Being appeased by us the great muni
said this—"I passed a lenient curse on her, because I
considered she is *but* a child ; it cannot indeed be altered."
11 By reason of that curse by Agastya my daughter was born
in Viśála's house as this beautiful fine-browed *maiden*, called
12 by the name Bhávini. Therefore I have come on this
account ; take this princess *who is* my daughter *in marriage* ;
of her thou shalt have a son, a universal monarch.

Márkaṇḍeya spoke :

13 Uttering the words "Be it so ! " the prince then took her‡

* *Anyatra tvam ahaṁ ća samágataḥ* ; the Poona edition reads *atra tvam ahaṁ ćaiva samágataḥ*. These can hardly be correct ; read *atra tvam ahaṁ ćaiva samágatau* ?

† That is, of human race. The Gandharvas were semi-celestial.

‡ For *tathety uktveti tasyátha* read *tathety uktvá tatas tasyáḥ* as in the Poona edition.

hand according to the ordinance, and Tumburu* offered
14 up the sacrifice there. The gods and Gandharvas sang forth,
and bevies of Apsarases danced, the clouds dropped down
15 flowers, and the heavenly instruments sounded forth,† as
the prince united in marriage with her, who became the
instrument for the agent of the deliverance of the whole
world.

16 Then they went everyone with that high-souled *muni* to the
Gandharvas' world, and she and the prince *went also*, O muni.
17 Prince Avíkshit took his joy in company with Bhávini, and she
obtained the riches of enjoyment together with him there.
18 Sometimes he sports with that slender one in a charming grove
19 near the city; sometimes on a low hill;‡ sometimes on a sand-
bank brightened by geese and sárasa cranes in a river; some-
times near the mansion and in the very resplendent palace.
20 In other charming pleasure-grounds he sported in company
with the slender *bride*, and she with that high-souled *prince*.
21 Munis, Gandharvas and Kinnaras offered them both food and
unguents, clothing, *and* the choicest garlands, beverages and
other *gifts* there.

22 And when the hero sported with Bhávini in the hardly
accessible world of the Gandharvas, the bright *bride* gave
23 birth to a son. When he was born, *who would be* great in
valour, a tiger among men, the Gandharvas perceiving what
24 he would accomplish held a great festival; and some *of them*
sang, and others beat drums and kettle-drums and double
drums, and others played on flutes, lutes and other *musical*
25 *instruments*; and many bevies of Apsarases also danced
there; the clouds showered down flowers while they rumbled
26 with gentle sound. Now while that medley of sounds so con-

* A muni, see verse 26. He may be the person mentioned in the Mahá-Bh., whose happy conjugal life with his wife Rambhá was famous (Udyoga-p. cxvi. 3975). There was a Gandharva of this name (Sabhá-p. li. 1881), and in the Vishṇu Pur. as a friend of Nala Ćandanodaka-dundubhí.

† *Ni-sasvanuḥ*; this root as a verb is not in the dictionary.

‡ *Upa-parvate*; not in the dictionary. The Poona edition reads *vara-parvate*, "on a choice hill."

tinued, the muni Tumburu, who was remembered by Tunaya,*
27 approached† and performed the birth-ceremonies. All the
gods assembled, and the pure divine ṛishis ; and from Pátála
28 *came* the Nága lords, S'esha, Vásuki, and Takshaka ; and
there came also the chiefs of the gods and Asuras, of the
Yakshas and Guhyakas, O bráhman, and all the Winds‡
29 also. Then the Gandharvas' great city was thronged with
those who had come, all the ṛishis, gods, Dánavas and Nágas
30 and the munis. Tumburu then performed the birth-ceremony and other rites, and performed the rite, which is preceded by praises, to secure good fortune on behalf of that boy,
saying—

31 "*As* a universal monarch, great in valour, mighty of arm,
great in strength, exercise thou sovereignty over the entire
32 earth a long time. May Indra and all these other world-
guardians and the ṛishis bestow bliss and foe-destroying
33 valour on thee, O hero! May the wind§ tend to what is
auspicious for thee, *even* the east *wind* that blows no dust!
May the south wind which is clean and unflagging tend to
34 gentleness for thee! May the west wind bestow heroism
on thee, the noblest *heroism* on thee! And may the north
wind likewise confer on thee excellent strength also!"

35 At the end of this rite to secure good fortune a voice
spake, issuing from no *earthly* body,—

"Because the preceptor uttered this *phrase* 'Marut-tava'‖
36 repeatedly, hence this *boy* shall be famed on earth as
'Marutta;' and because kings shall pass into subjection to
37 his commands on the earth, this *boy as a* hero shall stand on

* Tumburu had solemnized the parents' wedding, see verse 13. Tunaya is the Gandharva of verse 6. The Poona edition reads instead *praṇayena smṛito*, "who was remembered with affection."

† For *játa-játa-karmákaron* read *'bhetya játa-karmákaron* as in the Poona edition.

‡ *Váyu* in the plural ; they are mentioned here because of the invocation which comes afterwards, in which they are called *Marut*.

§ *Marut*, with *tava* or *te* added here and in the following sentences.

‖ "*May* the wind for thee ;" the words used in the preceding invocations.

the head* of all kings. *As* a universal monarch, great in valour,
38 he shall assail kings and shall unobstructed enjoy the earth
which contains seven continents. He shall be chief among
kings who offer sacrifices. His shall be the supremacy among
kings by reason of valour and heroism."

Márkaṇḍeya spoke :

39 On hearing this speech uttered by some one from among
the dwellers in heaven, all were gratified, the bráhmans and
Gandharvas also and his mother and father.

Canto CXXVIII.†

Marutta's exploits.

Avíkshit returned and presented his son to his father Karandhama, and there was great rejoicing—The boy grew up, learned in sacred lore and skilful with all weapons—Karandhama resigned the kingdom, but Avíkshit refused it because of the shame of his former captivity—Marutta was made king, and Karandhama retired to the forest.

Márkaṇḍeya spoke :

1 Then the prince, taking that beloved son and followed by
his wife‡ and the bráhmans and Gandharvas, went to his
2 city. Reaching his father's palace he extolled his father's feet
with respect; and *so did* his slender-limbed *wife*, the bashful
3 princess. And the prince holding his infant son addressed
king Karandhama, who was seated on the throne of justice in
4 the midst of kings,—"Behold this face of thy grandson who
rests in my lap, as I promised formerly to thee for my mother's
5 sake at the 'What-want-ye?' *vow*." So saying he laid that
son then on his father's lap, and related to him everything as

* Or "at the head."

† Canto cxxix in the Calcutta edition.

‡ For *padbhyáṁ* read *patnyá*, as in the Poona edition.

6 it had occurred. The *king* embracing his grandson, while his
eyes were beclouded with tears of joy, felicitated himself again
7 and again in saying "Fortunate am I!" Then he duly paid
honour to the assembled Gandharvas with the arghya offering
and other *presents*,* forgetting other needs by reason of his
joy.†

8 In the city then there was great rejoicing in the houses of the
citizens, *who exclaimed*—"A son has been born to our master!"
9 O great muni. In that glad and opulent city sportive cour-
tesans of the prettiest forms danced an exquisite dance to the
10 accompaniment of songs and musical instruments. And the
king with glad mind bestowed on the chief bráhmans both
gems and riches, cattle, clothing *and* ornaments.

11 The boy grew thenceforward, as the moon *waxes* in its bright
fortnight. He was the source of pleasure to his parents, and
12 the desire of the people. He acquired the Vedas first from the
religious teachers, O muni, then *skill in* all kinds of weapons,
13 then complete knowledge of archery. When he had completed
his efforts in the use of the sword and bow, he next overcame
toil like a hero in *learning the use of* other weapons also.
14 Then he obtained weapons from Bhárgava,‡ descendant of
Bhṛigu,—bowing modestly *and* intent on pleasing his guru, O
15 bráhman. Accomplished in *the use of* weapons, skilled in
the Veda, thoroughly master of the knowledge of archery,
deeply versed in all sciences—none *such* had there been before
him.

16 Viśála also, on hearing all this story of his daughter and of
the ability of his daughter's son, rejoiced exceedingly in mind.

17 Now the king *Karandhama* had attained his wishes, in that he
had seen his son's son *and* had offered many sacrifices, and had

* For *'rdhyádiná* read *'rghyádiná*, as in the Poona edition.

† The Poona edition amplifies this and, instead of the second line as in the Calcutta edition, reads—"Then he duly paid honour to the assembled Gandharvas with the arghya offering and other *presents* joyfully, *and* dismissed them with propriety. He continues playing with his grandson, forgetful of other needs."

‡ That is Sukra Áćárya (comment.). He was the preceptor of the Asuras.

18 bestowed gifts on those who asked. He had performed all ceremonies; he was united with his fellow-*kings* *; having safe-
guarded the earth righteously, he had conquered his enemies;
19 he was endowed with strength and intelligence. Being desirous
of departing to the forest he addressed his son Avíkshit—
"*My* son, I am old, I am going to the forest, take over the
20 kingdom from me. I have done what ought to be done;
nothing remains but to anoint thee. Do thou who art highly
accomplished in thy opinions take the kingdom which I have
21 transfered to thee." Being addressed thus, Avíkshit the prince,
respectfully bowing down, said to his father who was desirous
of going† to the forest to *perform* austerities,—
22 "I will not, dear father, do the safeguarding of the earth;
shame departs not from my mind; do thou appoint some one
23 else to the kingdom. Since I when captured was delivered by
my dear father and not by my own valour, how much manliness
24 then have I? The earth is protected by *real* men. I who was
not sufficient to protect even myself, how shall I, *being* such,
25 protect the earth? Cast the kingdom on some one else. On
the same level as a woman‡ is the man who is downright
injured§ by another. And my soul *has been delivered* from
delusion by thee, sir,|| who hast delivered me from bondage.
How shall I, *being* such, who am on the same level as a woman,
become king?"

The father spoke:

26 Not distinct ¶ in sooth is the father from the son, nor the

* *Su-varṇair,* = *máṇḍaliká-nṛipaiḥ* (comment.), "with his provincial kings," "with his vassal kings."

† For *yiyásus* read *yiyásum*, as in the Poona edition.

‡ For *mantrí sa-dharmaḥ* read *sa strí-sadharmaḥ*, as in the Poona edition.

§ *Ava-druhyate;* the verb *ava-druh* is not in the dictionary.

|| For *átmá 'moháya bhavato* the Poona edition reads *átmá 'moháć ća bhavatá;* and the comment. says *amohát* = *snehát* (which seems strange). The meaning then would be, "Since I myself have been delivered from bondage by thee, sir, out of affection, how shall I &c." But I have ventured to read *átmá moháć ća bhavatá*.

¶ *Na bhinna;* according to the comment. this means *putra-nirúpita-bheda-viśishṭo na*.

son from the father. Not delivered by any one else *then* wast thou, who wast delivered by thy father.

The son spoke:

27 I cannot direct my heart in any other wise, O king. There is exceeding shame in my heart—I, who was delivered by thee.
28 He who has been rescued by his father consumes the glory acquired by his father; and let not the man, who is known by
29 reason of his father, exist in the family. Let mine be that course, which is the course of those who have themselves amassed riches, who have themselves attained to fame, who have themselves come forth safe out of difficulties!

Márkaṇḍeya spoke:

30 When he, although exhorted* often by his father, spoke thus, O muni, the king then appointed his† son Marutta to
31 the kingdom. Receiving from his grandfather the sovereignty as authorized by his father, he ruled well, inspiring gladness among his friends.

32 And king Karandhama, taking Vírá also, departed to the forest to *practise* austerities with voice, body and mind re-
33 strained. After practising very arduous austerities there a thousand years, the king quitted his body and gained the
34 world‡ of Indra. His wife Vírá then practised austerities a hundred years longer, with her hair matted and *her body*
35 covered with dirt and mud, desirous of gaining the same world as her high-souled lord who had reached Svarga, making fruits and roots her food, dwelling in Bhárgava's hermitage, encircled by wives of twice-born men, *and* sustained by the devoted attendance of the twice-born.

* For *yadápy ukto* read *yadá prokto*, as in the Poona edition. Avíkshit is mentioned in the Mahá-Bh., Áśvam.-p. iv. 80-85, but rarely elsewhere. His name chiefly occurs in the patronymic form *Ávíkshita* applied to Marutta. There was another Avíkshit, a son of Kuru, Ádi-p. xciv. 3740.

† *Tasya*, i.e., Avíkshit's.

‡ For *sa lokatám* read *sa-lokatám*.

CANTO CXXIX*

Marutta's exploits.

Marutta reigned as a universal monarch—Samvarta was his priest—Marutta was a great sacrificer, and a liberal benefactor to bráhmans—Some verses in his honour are quoted—But the Nágas troubled the ṛishis grievously, and his grandmother Vírá sent him a message to administer justice and secure peace.

Kraushṭuki spoke :

1 Adorable sir, thou hast fully narrated all this to me, *namely*, Karandhama's exploits and what were Avíkshit's exploits. I
2 wish to hear of the exploits of the high-souled king Marutta,† Avíkshit's son ; ‡ he is heard of because of his surpassing
3 feats as a universal monarch, of great parts, a warrior, a beloved *king*, high-minded, wise in righteousness and a doer of righteousness, a real protector of the earth.

Márkaṇḍeya spoke :

4 Receiving from his grandfather the kingdom with his father's consent, he protected it righteously, as a father protects

* Canto cxxx in the Calcutta edition.

† He is famed as a universal monarch (Mahá-Bh., Áśvam.-p. iv. 86-91 and Vishṇu Pur. IV. i), and it said he gained his supreme sovereignty through his prosperity (*ṛiddhyá*; Sabhá-p. xiv. 650). He was one of the sixteen greatest and most famous kings of antiquity (Droṇa-p. lv. 2170-83 ; S'ánti-p. xxix. 910-17). He is said to have offered a sacrifice to the bráhman ṛishi Uśíravíja at the Jámbu-nada lake in the Northern region (Udyoga-p. cx. 3842-3), and was praised for his liberality in that he gave his daughter to Aṅgiras (S'ánti-p. ccxxxiv. 8602 ; Anuśás.-p. cxxxvii. 6260), but more probably to Áṅgirasa, that is, Samvarta, see verse 11 note.

There were other less famous kings of the same name, as Marutta, son of Karandhama and fifth in descent from Yayáti's son Turvasu (Hari-V., xxxii. 1829-1834 ; Vishṇu Pur. IV. xvi) ; Marutta, fifth in descent from S'aśa-vindu (Hari-V., xxxvii. 1972-75 ; Matsya Pur. xliv. 24 ; also Váyu and other Puráṇas ; and probably Mahá-Bh., S'ánti-p. xxix. 981) ; and one or two more of the same or similar name.

‡ For *Avikshitasya* read *Ávíkshitasya*. Marutta's father is generally spoken of here as *Avíkshit* and not as *Avíkshita*. The Poona edition reads *Ávaikshatasya*.

5 his own begotten sons. He sacrificed very many sacrifices ap-
propriately, whereat most suitable fees *were given away*, *as* a king
whose mind took pleasure* in the commands of his sacrificing
6 priest and family priest. His discus was unresisted in the
seven continents; and his course uninterrupted† in the sky, in
7 the lower regions, in the waters and elsewhere. He gained
riches thereby, being duly intent on his own rites, O bráh-
man, and sacrificed with great sacrifices to Indra and the
8 other gods;‡ just as these other castes also, unwearied each in
its own business *and* possessing riches amassed thereby, per-
9 formed pious obligations and other rites. The earth while
under high-souled Marutta's protection entered into rivalry
with the dwellers in the dwellings of the thirty gods,§ O best
10 of twice-born men. Not only were all kings of the earth sur-
passed by him, but even the king of the gods *was surpassed* by
him as a sacrificer with declarations|| of a hundred sacrifices.¶
11 Now his sacrificing priest was Aṅgiras' son Samvarta,**
who was Vṛihaspati's brother, high-souled, a treasure-house of

* Or, "was subservient to"; *ramya* = *vaśya* (comment.).

† For *ćápy anaviććhinná* read *ćásya na viććhinná*, as in the Poona edition.

‡ The Vishṇu Pur. says—he offered an unparalleled sacrifice, his utensils were of gold, Indra was intoxicated with his libations *of soma*, and the bráhmans were enriched (IV. i). So also Mahá-Bh., Áśvam.-p. x. 275-92.

§ It is said in the Mahá-Bh., the earth brought forth fruit without ploughing and was garlanded with *ćaityas* in his reign (S'ánti-p. xxix. 910-17).

|| *S'ata-yajñábhisandhibhiḥ*; the Poona edition reads *śata-yajño 'pi śaṅkitaḥ*.

¶ The Mahá-Bh. says he overcame Indra in rivalry and so incurred Vṛihaspati's opposition (S'ánti-p. xxix. 910-14).

** The Mahá-Bh. says Aṅgiras was Avíkshit's priest (Áśvam.-p. iv. 80-85). Aṅgiras had two sons, Vṛihaspati and Samvarta, and there was rivalry between them, but Vṛihaspati the elder got the pre-eminence and became Indra's purohita. Marutta in rivalry overcame Indra, and Vṛihaspati who desired Indra's good repulsed Marutta, and declined to be his family priest. Marutta then by Nárada's advice went to Váráṇasí (Benares) and secured Samvarta as his priest (Droṇa-p. lv. 2170-71; S'ánti-p. xxix. 910-15; and Áśvam.-p. iv. 86 to ix. 274). There was a great quarrel between Vṛihaspati and Samvarta in consequence (*ibid.*, and Váyu Pur.). The Aitareya Bráhmaṇa says Samvarta inaugurated Marutta with the *Mahábhisheka* ceremony, the great inauguration ceremony of Indra (VIII. iv. 21).

12 austerities. The golden mountain Yuñjavat* is frequented by
the gods; he struck down its summit *and* carried it off† for
13 that king. The whole of that *king's*‡ territory, allotment§
and other property and palaces were made brilliant, all golden,
by that *priest* at a sacrifice by means of austerities, O bráh-
14 man. And in this *connexion*, those who are interested in Ma-
rutta's exploits sing songs, while all ṛishis *are* carrying on their
study without intermission, thus—
15 "Equal to Marutta never lived a sacrificer on the face of
the earth—at whose sacrifice *his* dwelling-house was cast and
16 also golden palaces *as largesse*, Indra was made intoxicated
with soma *and* twice-born *bráhmans* with gifts, *and* Indra and
other chiefs of the thirty *gods* became waiters to the bráh-
17 mans. At what king's *sacrifice* was everything of gold aban-
doned, as at Marutta's sacrifice, by the twice-born *bráhmans*,
18 whose houses were stocked with gems?‖ And at his sacrifice
what gold in the shape of palaces and other *things* was cast *as
largesse*, that indeed the three *other* castes received; therefrom
some *of them* gave similar gifts."¶
19 While thus he ruled the kingdom and protected his subjects
well, a certain ascetic came, O best of munis, and said to him
20 —"Thy father's mother, seeing the community of ascetics

* For *Yuñjavat* read *Muñjavat*, as in the Poona edition. It is a mountain on the ridge of Himavat (Mahá-Bh., Áśvam.-p. viii. 180). It seems to have been also called Muñjávaṭa, and the summit Muñja-prishṭha. It was visited by Vasu-homa, king of Aṅga, and Ráma and Mándhátṛi (Śánti-p. cxxii. 4469-75). It was a sacred place of pilgrimage (Kúrma Pur. II. xxxvii. 38). This may be meant by Mujavant in Atharva-Veda I. xxv. 2, 8. There was another place of pilgrimage called Muñja-vaṭa which was apparently in or near Kuru-kshetra (Mahá-Bh., Vana-p. lxxxiii. 5092, and lxxxv. 8210).

† For *hṛitaṁ* the Poona edition reads *kṛite*, "he struck down its summit for that king's sake."

‡ *Yasya*, i.e., Marutta's.

§ *Bhága*.

‖ For *ratná-púrṇa-gṛihe* read *ratná-púrṇa-gṛihair*, as in the Poona edition.

¶ The Poona edition adds a verse here—The well-behaved folk, who had their thoughts satisfied by what was given away, also offered sacrifices therewith in various places separately."

overwhelmed with poison by the Nágas who are raging with frenzy, saith this to thee, O king:—
21 "Thy grandfather, after protecting the earth well, has departed to heaven, and I am able to practise austerities here,
22 dwelling in Aurva's* hermitage. I, being such, perceive disorganization while thou rulest the kingdom, such as was not† while thy grandfather and thy ancestors *reigned*, O
23 king. Assuredly *thou art* heedless or addicted to sensual enjoyments, or thy senses are uncontrolled, in that thou dost not know the wicked and the good because they, *thine organs*, are
24 blind *because thou hast no* spies. Now the Nágas, who have come up from Pátála possessed with frenzy, have bitten seven sons of
25 munis, and have defiled the tanks, and have defiled the clarified butter offered in sacrifice with sweat, urine and ordure. Tribute has long been given to the Nágas, *thus* fully indicating
26 an offence. These munis are able to reduce the Nágas to ashes, but have no authority herein; thou indeed hast the
27 authority herein. Kings' sons have the happiness that comes of sensual enjoyments so long, O king, as the water of *regal* in-
28 auguration is not poured on their head. *But when kings they must think*—'What friends *are there?*' 'Who is an enemy?' 'How great is my enemy's strength?' 'Who am I?' 'Who are in my minister's party?' Or, 'Who are my *vassal* kings?'
29 'Either such a one is ill-disposed, *or he has been* alienated by others; what *is he* like with regard to *my* adversaries also?' 'Who is wholly a *liege*-man to me herein in the city or in the

* Aurva was a famous ṛishi descended from Bhṛigu. The Matsya Pur. says he was son of Bhṛigu's son Ápnuvána and was father of Jamadagni, and that he established the gotras of the Bhárgavas (cxciv. 14-29). It is said king Sagara was brought up in his hermitage (Hari-V., xiii. 762-xiv. 795) and learnt from him the Vedas and the use of arms (Vishṇu Pur. III. viii, and IV. iii). The Mahá-Bh. says he was born when the Bhárgavas were almost exterminated by the princes of Kártavírya's race after Kártavírya's death, because they did not restore at the demand of those princes the riches which they had amassed as Kártavírya's sacrificial priests; and it explains his name by saying he was born from his mother's thigh (Ádi-p. clxxviii. 6802-15 and clxxix. 6827).

† For *tenábhúd* read *te nábhúd*.

30 country?' He who puts his trust *solely* in deeds of right-
eousness is besotted. *A king must take practical notice*—'Who
behaves quite properly?' 'Who must be punished?' 'Who
must be protected?' Or, 'What men must be regarded* by
31 me, who *have to* consider† the person to be subdued, the place
and the time with regard to *my* condition of alliance or
disunion?'‡ Further, a king should ward off unknown
32 spies by other spies. A king should set spies upon all his
ministers and other *servants*. In this and in other ways a
king, whose mind is intent upon business, should constantly
33 spend day and night, but not be engrossed with *sensual* enjoy-
ments. The possession by kings of bodies is not for the sake
34 of *sensual* enjoyment, O king; it excites them to *undertake*
trouble§ in the *work of* protecting the earth and their own
righteousness. For a king who protects the earth and his own
35 righteousness well, there is great trouble in this world *and*
supreme undecaying happiness in heaven. Recognizing this
36 therefore, O king, discard *sensual* enjoyments and deign to
undertake trouble in this *world* for the protection of the earth.
The calamity, which originating from the Nágas has thus be-
37 fallen the rishis, while thou art reigning, O king, thou being
blind *because thou hast no* spies dost not even know it. What
need of saying more in this *matter?* Let punishment be inflicted
38 on him who is wicked; protect thou the well-behaved, O king;
thou shalt gain the sixth part *allowed thee as tribute* by right-
eous law. By witholding protection thou shalt without doubt
39 fully acquire all the sin that is committed by wicked men
through unruliness. Do what thou wishest!

"I have told *thee* all this that thy grandmother saith to thee. Act, when things are so, as pleases thee, O king."

* *Upekshyás*; or "must be disregarded."

† For *avekshatá* read *avekshatám?* "Let *a king* consider, &c."

‡ For *sanga-bheda-tayá dámya-* the Poona edition reads *mantra-bheda-bhayád atra*, "who *have to* consider place and time in this *matter* by reason of fear lest my counsel should be divulged."

§ Or "*it is meant* for *undertaking* great trouble."

Canto CXXX.*

Marutta's exploits.

Marutta visited his grandmother's hermitage and set the Nágas' world on fire—They implored his mother Bháviní's protection according to her old promise—She and Avíkshit accepted their entreaties and went to Marutta.

Márkaṇḍeya spoke:

1 On hearing this speech from the ascetic, the king became
covered with shame. Exclaming, "Fie on me, who am blind
2 *because I have no* spies," he sighed and took his bow. He went
hastily then towards Aurva's hermitage and made obeisance
to his father's mother Vírá with his head, and to the ascetics
3 as was proper; and they lauded him with blessings. And
seeing the seven sons,† the ascetics, bitten by the Nágas on
4 the ground, the king reproached himself repeatedly in front
of them, and said thus,—

5 "What I do now unto the wicked Nágas, who despise my valour and who hate the bráhmans, let all the world with the gods, demons and mankind see that!"

Márkaṇḍeya spoke:

6 So saying the king took his weapon Saṁvartaka‡ in anger,
in order to destroy all the Nágas that roamed in Pátála
7 and on the earth. The Nágas' world burst into flame then
suddenly all around; while it was being burnt by the glowing
8 power of the great weapon§, he hemmed it in. 'Ah! Ah!
dear father'—'Ah! mother!'—'Ah! Ah! dear child'—*such*
cries arose then among the Nágas in that confusion caused by

* Canto cxxxi in the Calcutta edition.

† For *sután* read *mritán*, "the seven dead ascetics"?

‡ *Saṁvartaka*, "the fire that will destroy every thing at the end of the world." The Calcutta edition reads *Sad-vartaka*.

§ For *maháṁs tu tejasá* the Poona edition reads *mahástra-tejasá*, which I have followed.

9 the weapon. Some with the ends of their tails burning, other
Nágas with their hoods *burning*, both seized their children and
and wives, *and* abandoned their ornaments and clothing.
10 Quitting Pátála they went for protection to Marutta's mother
Bhávini, who had formerly given *them a promise* of safety
11 then.* Approaching her all the Nágas, sick with terror,
prostrated themselves and spoke thus in broken *accents*,—
"Let that be remembered *which* was formerly declared *by thee*
12 to us. What we entreated† formerly after prostrating our-
selves in Rasátala, the time for that has here arrived; save us, O
13 mother of the hero! Let thy son be turned aside, O queen;
let us retain‡ our lives. All the world of the Nágas is being
14 burnt by the fire from his weapon. For us, who are being
thus utterly burnt up by thy son, there is no other refuge but
thou; have mercy on us, O renowned lady!"

Márkaṇḍeya spoke:

15 Hearing this their speech and remembering what she had
said at first, the good *lady* spoke this speech to her husband
with agitation,—
16 "I related to thee before indeed, what the Nágas in Pátála
after making petition said to me with reference to my son.
17 They are these who have come in terror; they are being burnt
by his splendour; these *sought* refuge with me before *and* I
18 gave them *a promise of* safety. Those who have come to me
for refuge have approached thee for refuge, *for I do* not observe
a righteousness separate *from thine*. I have come to thee for
19 refuge. Therefore do thou turn aside our son Marutta by thy
word; when besought by me also, he will assuredly proceed§
to quietness."

* The promise was given in canto cxxvi, verses 42-44. For the text *yayá dattaṁ tadábhayam* a better reading would be *yathá dattaṁ tayábhayam*, "since she had formerly given *them a promise of* safety." See verse 17.

† For *abhyarśitam* read *abhyarthitam*, as in the Poona edition.

‡ *Sáyojyam*; a word not in the dictionary. *Sáyujyam* is given there, and this is the reading of the Poona edition.

§ *Abhy-upa-yásyati*; this verb is not in the dictionary.

The king spoke:

20 Marutta has given way to wrath which has become fixed in a great crime. It will be hard, I think, to turn away the wrath of him, thy son.

The Nágas spoke:

21 We have sought thy protection; shew us favour, O king; weapons are borne in order to save from pain him who is wounded.

Márkaṇḍeya spoke:

22 On hearing that speech of the Nágas who had become suppliants for protection, and being entreated by his wife, most famous Avíkshi* spoke,—

23 "I go, lady, and *will* with haste speak to that thy son in order
to deliver the Nágas: those who have come for protection must
24 not be forsaken. If he, the king, does not draw back his
weapon at my word, then I will parry the weapon of that thy son with *my own* weapons."

Márkandeya spoke:

25 Thereupon Avíkshi, noblest of kshatriyas, took up his bow and accompanied by his wife went in haste to Bhárgava's hermitage.

Canto CXXXI.†

Marutta's exploits (concluded).

Avíkshit called on Marutta to spare the Nágas, but Marutta insisting on his duty refused—Avíkshit proposed to fight with him, and Marutta, though deprecating such combat, agreed—The rishis intervened, the Nágas restored the dead rishis to life, and all parted affectionately—Marutta's wives and successor are named.

Márkandeya spoke:

1 Now he, *Avíkshit*, on seeing *his* son there‡ grasping his choice

* Here and in verse 25 the text shortens the name to Avíkshi. So also in canto cxxxi, verses 9, 11, and 17. See canto cxxii, verse 2, note.

† Canto cxxxii in the Calcutta edition

‡ *Tatra* of the Bombay edition is better than *tasyáḥ*.

bow, *and seeing* his *son's* bow and keen weapon filling all the
2 regions *of the sky* with its fiery light, belching forth a great
flame, illuminating all the surface of the earth, penetrating *down*
into Pátála, unendurable, dreadful and terrifying, *and actually*
3 ready *for use*—he, seeing the king whose countenance was
wrinkled with frowns, *said,*—"Be not thou wrathful, O
4 Marutta; let thy weapon be drawn back." More than once
so said he, lofty-minded *Avíkshit,* to him, the *varying* course
of whose colour speedily vanished *in pallor.* Listening to
his father's speech and looking at him again and again, he,
5 *still* grasping his bow, prostrated himself before his parents
with veneration and replied:—

"Most grievously have the Nágas offended me, O father.
6 While I rule this earth, they despising my might advanced to
7 the hermitage and bit seven youthful munis; and the fire-offer-
ings of these ṛishis who dwell in the hermitage have been
defiled by the evil-behaved *Nágas,* while I am reigning, O
8 king. Morever every one of the tanks has in truth been
defiled by them. This then is the reason; thou must say
nothing *in their favour,* O father. I am not to be turned aside
as regards the bráhman-killing Nágas."

Avíkshi* spoke:

9 If these *Nágas* have slain bráhmans, they will go to hell when dead. Let this my word be complied with; desist from using thy weapon.

Marutta spoke:

10 I will not pardon these wicked offenders. I in truth shall go to hell if I strive not to curb these sinners. Turn me not back, O father!

Avíkshi spoke:

11 These Nágas have come to me for refuge. Because of the veneration due to me draw back thy weapon. Enough of thy wrath, O king!

* The text reads *Avíkshi* here and in the following places. See canto cxxii, verse 2, note.

Marutta spoke:

12 I will not pardon these wicked offenders. How shall I,
transgressing my own righteousness, comply with thy word?
13 By inflicting punishment on him who ought to be punished
and by protecting the well-behaved, a king gains the sacred
worlds and disregards the hells.

Márkaṇḍeya spoke:

14 When the son thus repeatedly forbidden by his father
draws not back the weapon, he, *the father*, then spoke again,—
15 "Thou injurest these terrified Nágas who have come to me
for refuge, although *thou art* forbidden; I will therefore
16 employ a means to counteract thee. I also acquired *skill in*
weapons; not thou alone art skilled in weapons on the earth;
and how great *will be* thy manhood in my presence, O most
ill-behaved one?"
17 Avíkshi, the lordly muni, with eyes dusky-red through anger,
18 strung his bow and grasped the weapon of fate. Next he
fitted in his bow the noblest weapon of fate, which was
surrounded with fiery light, which could slaughter hosts of
19 foes, which had great vigour. Then made hot by the weapon
of conflagration,* quaked the whole heaven and earth with the
seas and mountains, O bráhman, when the weapon of fate† was
raised aloft.

Márkaṇḍeya spoke:

20 Marutta also, seeing that weapon of fate made ready by his
father, spoke aloud,—

"This my weapon is raised aloft for the punishment of the
21 wicked—not to kill thee. Why dost thou, sir, discharge the
weapon of fate at me, thy son, who observe true righteous-
22 ness and who have ever indeed obeyed thy command? I
must protect my subjects fully, illustrious *sir;* why dost thou
thus prepare the weapon to kill me?"

Avíkshi spoke:

23 We are determined to accomplish the rescue of him who

* *Saṁvarta;* see canto cxxx, verse 6.

† *Kálástra.*

has come for refuge; thou art his assailant, thou shalt not be
24 let go alive by me. Either slay thou me by the might of
thy weapon and then slay the wicked Nágas here; or I will
25 slay thee with my weapon and save the great Nágas. Fie on
the life of that man that shews no favour to one in pain, who
has come seeking for protection even though certainly belong-
26 ing to an enemy's party! A kshatriya am I; these terrified
Nágas have come to me for protection; thou indeed art their
injurer; why shouldest thou not be killed by me?

Marutta spoke:

27 Whoever tends to be an obstacle to the protection of the
subjects, whether he *be* a friend or even a kinsman or a father
28 or a spiritual preceptor, he must be killed by a king. I, *being*
such *a king*, will fight with thee; be not thou angry, O father.
I must preserve my own righteousness, I have no anger
against thee.

Márkaṇḍeya spoke:

29 Seeing those two determined to kill each other, Bhárgava
and the other munis sprang up then and stood between them,
30 and said,—"Thou must not discharge thy weapon against this
thy father; nor must thou slay this thy son who is renowned
for his deeds."

Marutta spoke:

31 I must as king slay the wicked *and* guard the good; and
these are wicked Nágas. What is my fault in this *matter*, O
ye twice-born?

Avíkshi spoke:

32 I must rescue those who have come *to me* for refuge, and
this my son is an offender,* who kills those that have come
for refuge, O bráhmans.

The ṛishis spoke:

33 These Nágas whose eyes are rolling about in terror say,
'We *will* bring to life again those bráhmans who were bitten
34 by wicked Nágas.' Enough then of combat! Be ye both

* For *aparádhyaḥ* read *aparáḍhí*, as in the Poona edition.

appeased, O noble kings! Ye both indeed, who are faithful to your promises, are well acquainted with righteousness.

Márkaṇḍeya spoke:

35 Now Vírá approaching her son said this,—"At my word
36 this thy son has tried to kill the Nágas. That is finished.
When the bráhmans live *unmolested* and the dead *munis* also
come to life again, *the Nágas may* be set free, since they have
sought thee for protection."

Bhávini spoke:

37 I was formerly entreated by these denizens of Pátála; for that
38 reason I commissioned this my husband in this *matter*. There-
fore *has occurred* this noble outcome, splendid, in both of them,
both in my husband *and my* son, in thy grandson and *thy* son.

Márkaṇḍeya spoke:

39 Those Nágas then restored those bráhmans to life both by
means of various divine herbs and by drawing out the poison.
40 The king then bowed at his parents' feet; and he, *Avíkshit*,
41 embracing Marutta affectionately spoke thus—"Be thou a de-
stroyer of thy enemies' pride; long do thou protect the earth;
be thou also merry with thy sons and grandsons; and may they
not be haters of thee!"
42 Permitted* then by the bráhmans and by Vírá to depart,
the two kings mounted the chariot together; and Bhávini
went to her own city.
43 Vírá also, best of those who maintain righteousness, after
performing very great austerities, gained the same world* as
her husband, she an illustrious wife, devoted to her lord.
44 Marutta also protected the earth fully in righteousness, and
having vanquished the six classes of enemies enjoyed enjoy-
45 ments as king. And his wife was Prabhá-vatí, the illustrious
daughter *of the king* of Vidarbha; and Suvíra's daughter
46 Sauvírí was *also his wife*; Su-keśí, daughter of the Mágadha

* For *ánujñáto* read *anujñátau*, as in the Poona edition.

† For *sá lokatám* read *sa-lokatám*, as in the Poona edition.

king Ketu-vírya was *his wife.* Kekayí also, daughter of
47 Sindhu-vírya king of Madra, and Kekaya's *daughter* Sairan-
dhrí, *and* Vapush-matí, *daughter* of the lord of Sindhu,* *were
also his wives;* and Su-śobhaná, daughter of the king of C'edi,
48 was his wife. And his sons by those *queens* became eighteen
kings, O bráhman. Chief among them and the eldest son was
Narishyanta.
49 Such in valour was Marutta, a great king, great in strength·
His discus was unopposed in the seven continents; equal to
50 whom no other king ever lived or shall live. After hearing of
these exploits of that royal ṛishi, high-souled Marutta, who was
51 endowed with goodness and prowess, *and* who was of boundless
vigour, and of *his* pre-eminent birth, O bráhman, *a man* is
freed from all offences.

CANTO CXXXII.†

Narishyanta's exploits.

Marutta gave the kingdom to his son Narishyanta—Narishyanta resolved to do some great deed and performed a great sacrifice at which he enriched the bráhmans for life—Consequently he could not induce any bráhmans to attend a second sacrifice except after great difficulty—All bráhmans then were themselves offering sacrifices.

Kraushṭuki spoke:

1 Adorable sir, thou hast narrated all Marutta's exploits; the
wish to hear completely about his descendants prevails *in me.*

* These names seem to be confused so as to be in impossible combinations, for Sindhu, Kekaya and Madra were distinct countries, see canto lvii, verses 36 and 37. For *Saurindhrí* read *Sairandhrí* as in the Poona edition. The second line of verse 46 and the first of verse 47 would read better thus, by merely transposing the words,—

Sutá ća Sindhu-víryasya Sindhu-bhartur Vapush-matí,
Madra-rájasya Sairandhrí, Kekayasya ća Kekayí.

"Vapush-matí also daughter of Sindhu-vírya lord of Sindhu, Sairandhri *daughter* of the king of Madra, and Kekayí *daughter of the king* of Kekaya *were also his wives.*"

† Canto cxxxiii in the Calcutta edition.

2 I wish to hear of those among his descendants, as thou describest them, who were lords of the earth, worthy of sovereignty, *and* endowed with valour, O great muni.

Márkaṇḍeya spoke:

3 Marutta's son was famed as Narishyanta*; he was the
4 eldest and indeed the best of the eighteen sons. And for
eighty-five thousands of years the lordly kshatriya Marutta
5 enjoyed the entire earth. After ruling the kingdom according to his own righteousness, after offering peerless sacrifices,
he anointed his eldest son Narishyanta *as king* and departed to
6 the forest. With his mind concentrated on one idea the king practised great austerities there. He ascended to the sky, covering the heaven and earth with his glory, O bráhman.

7 His son Narishyanta, being wise, pondered *thus*, considering how his father had acted and other kings also,—

8 "In my family my ancestors have been high-souled kings.
Offerers of sacrifices, they protected the earth righteously, being
9 powerful; and they were givers of riches; they turned not
back in battle. But who is able to imitate the exploits of
10 those high-souled *kings?* Yet the righteous deed which they†
did with sacrifices and other *offerings*, that I wish to do; and
11 that is not *feasible*; what *can* I do? The earth is protected
according to righteousness; what virtue has the king in this?
If he does not duly protect, a king *is* sinful *and* goes to hell.
12 If he has riches, a king must certainly offer great sacrifices,
and must bestow gifts; what *is there* wonderful herein? A
13 king is the refuge of those who are perishing. High birth
and shame and anger, dependance on hostile folk and one's
own rules of righteousness ensure that there is no fleeing from
14 battle. As all this has been well achieved by my ancestors and
15 by my father Marutta, who *now* can do it so *well?* What
then shall I do, that has not been done by those ancestors, who
16 were sacrificers, choice *men*, gentle, and who turned not back

* He and his descendants are given in Vishṇu Pur. IV. i. He must be distinguished from Narishyanta or Narishya one of the sons of Manu Vaivasvata see page 588.

† For *teṇa* read *tair yat* as in the Bombay edition.

from battle, whose manliness did not fail in great battles and
conflicts* ? With whose deed shall I coming strive unappal-
17 ledly ? Moreover those kings, *my* ancestors, themselves
performed sacrifices unweariedly, but did not have them per-
formed by others ; I *will* do that."

Márkaṇḍeya sp ke :

18 After deliberating thus the king performed a single sacrifice,
the like of which, made splendid by the lavishing of riches, no
19 one else had performed. Now after giving very great wealth
to the twice-born *bráhmans*, enough for life, the king further
20 gave them a hundred times as much food at the sacrifice, *and*
cattle, clothing, ornaments and granaries and other *gifts*.
Thus he intoxicated each one of them who dwelt in the earth.
21 Consequently when the king began a sacrifice again, he got no
twice-born *bráhmans* then to conduct it after the sacrifice had
22 been begun. Whatever bráhmans the king selects for the
business of sacrificial priesthood,† they said everyone to him,—

"We have consecrated ourselves for a sacrifice elsewhere.
23 Choose thou some one else ; the riches which thou didst lavish
among us, there is no end thereof. Yet thou mayest give
wealth *to others* at *thy* sacrifices."

Márkaṇḍeya spoke :

24 And the lord of the whole earth obtained no bráhmans then
as sacrificial priests. He began then to give a gift on the
25 space outside the sacrificial altar. Neverthless they did not
accept it at all, having their houses full of wealth. In order
to give again to a twice-born *bráhman* he spoke thus, being de-
jected,—

26 "Alas ! *it is* very splendid that there is no poor bráhman
anywhere in the earth : and *it is* not splendid that this
27 treasury is useless to one who does not sacrifice. No one

* For *mahat-saṅgráma-saṁsargá visaṁvádita-paurusháḥ* read *mahat-saṅ-gráma-sammardeshv avisaṁvádi-paurusháḥ* as in the Bombay and Poona editions.

† For *árttijya-karmaṇi* read *ártvijya-karmaṇi*.

undertakes sacrificial priesthood* ; all folk among the twice-born are sacrificing, and do not assent when we are giving a gift."

Márkaṇḍeya spoke:

28 Prostrating himself then before some twice-born bráhmans
again and again in faith, he appointed them sacrificial priests
at his own sacrifice. They performed the great sacrifice.
29 And this was very surprising,—when that sacrifice *offered* by
the king took place, all folk of the twice-born on the earth
30 were offering sacrifices at that time; no one was *present* as a
spectator thereat. Some of the twice-born were having sacri-
fices offered, and some of them were themselves offering sacri-
31 fices. Whenever king Narishyanta sacrificed, *people* might
make a sacrifice on the earth entirely with the riches *given* by
32 that giver. Now in the eastern region there were more than
one hundred and eighty million sacrifices; in the west seventy
33 millions† in sooth; in the south fourteen *tens of millions;* and
in the north there were then fifty *tens of millions* of sacrifices
at one time, O bráhman muni, when Narishyanta was sacrificing.
34 Such, O bráhman, was Marutta's son king Narishyanta of
yore, righteous in soul, famed for his strength and manliness.

Canto CXXXIII.‡

Dama's exploits.

Narishyanta was succeeded by his son Dama, an accomplished king—Sumaná daughter of the king of Daśárṇa chose him as her husband at her svayam-vara—Three other princes tried to take her by force, and Dama, after appealing to the assembled kings against their conduct, was left in accordance with marriage rules to assert his right by arms—He defeated those kings and married Sumaná.

Márkaṇḍeya spoke:

1 Narishyanta's son was Dama,§ the tamer of the wicked and

* For *árttijyam* read *ártvijyam.*

† For *koṭyá* read *koṭyo* as in the Poona edition.

‡ Canto cxxxiv in the Calcutta edition.

§ He and his descendants are given in Vishṇu Pur. IV. i.

of enemies; like Indra's was his strength; compassion such
2 as a muni's was his disposition. That very famous *son* was
born to that king of Indra-sená, a princess descended from
Babhru,* after abiding nine years in his mother's womb.
3 Because while abiding in her womb he caused his mother to
acquire self-restraint, and because *it was supposed*, 'this prince
4 also will be self-restrained in disposition,' therefore indeed his
family priest, who knew the three times,† gave Narishyanta's
son the name 'Dama.'‡

5 Now prince Dama learnt the knowledge of the bow entirely
6 from Vṛisha-parvan, king of men;§ and he learnt *the use of* all
kinds of weapons thoroughly from the noble Daitya Dun-
7 dubhi‖ who dwelt in Tapo-vana;¶ and *he learnt* the Vedas
and all the Vedáṅgas from S'akti;** and controlling himself
he learnt the practice of religious devotion from the royal ṛishi
A'rshṭi-sheṇa††.

* This may be Babhru or Vabhru, son of Druhyu, son of Yayáti (Hari-V., xxxii. 1837). There were other kings of the same name later, as Vabhru son of Deváv̥ridha (Hari-V., xxxviii. 2010-13, and Matsya Pur. xliv. 56), Babhru son of Viśva-garbha (Hari-V., xcv. 5252), &c.

† The past, the present and the future.

‡ "Self-control."

§ This would appear to be Vṛisha-parvan, a famous king of the Dánavas (Mahá-Bh., A'di-p. lxxxi. 3367-8, Sabhá-p.iii. 58-60), whose daughter S'armishṭhá married Yayáti (*ibid.*, and A'di-p. xcv. 3760-1, Udyoga-p. cxlviii. 5042-5; Hari V., xxx. 1600-3; and Vishṇu Pur. IV. x). There was a famous hermitage called Vṛisha-parvan's hermitage near Mount Kailása in the Himálayas (Mahá-Bh., Vana-p. clviii. 11541-3, clxxvii. 12340-44), but that Vṛisha-parvan appears to have been contemporary with the Páṇḍavas, according to the first of these last two passages.

‖ I have not found a Daitya of this name elsewhere.

¶ This means a "grove where austerities are practised"; but there appears to have been a place of this name, for Yayáti retired there (Vishṇu Pur. IV. x).

** This appears to be Vasishṭha's son who was called S'akti (Wilson's Vishṇu Pur.—edit. F. Hall—I. p. 8, and III, iii., pp. 35 and 36) and, better, S'aktri (Mahá-Bh., A'di-p .clxxvii. 6757, clxxviii. 6792-4; S'ánti-p. cccli.) He was Paráśara's father (*loc. cit.*), see canto cxxxiv. verse 32.

†† For *A'rshṇi-sheṇa* read *A'rshṭi-sheṇa*, as in the Poona edition. He is mentioned in the Mahá-Bh., as having a famous hermitage near Mount

8 Him, who was naturally high-souled, who was accomplished
in arms and was great in strength, did Sumaná, when placed*
9 at the svayam-vara by her father, choose as her husband, *she*,
daughter of mighty Ćáru-karman† king of Daśárṇa,‡ while
all the kings looked on, who had assembled there for her sake.
10 Now the Madra§ king's son Mahá-náda, who was great in
11 strength and prowess, was also deeply enamoured of her, and
so also *were* the son of Saṅkrandana king of Vidarbha,|| and
prince Vapush-mat, who bore a great bow and was of lofty
12 intellect. Now seeing that Dama, tamer of the wicked and of
enemies, was chosen by her,¶ they took counsel *thus* with one
another there, being infatuated by love,—

13 "We *will* seize this beautifully-formed maiden from him by
force and go home. She shall be his among us, whom she,
14 the *maiden* of beautiful hips, shall take with the intention
that he shall be her husband according to the ordinance of the
svayam-vara—his wife she shall be, delivered over according
15 to righteousness by our wish. Yet *if* that *maiden* of intoxi-
cating eyes does not desire any of us, then she shall be his who
shall slay Dama."

Márkaṇḍeya spoke:

16 Having formed this resolve, those three princes seized that
most beautifully-formed *maiden*, as she attended by Dama's
17 side. Thereupon some kings among them who were of his**
party cried out, and other kings shouted out *on the other side*;

Gandha-mádana in the Himálayas (Vana-p. clviii. 11626-7, S'alya-p. xli, Anuśás.-p. xxv. 1741), and he is there made a contemporary of the Páṇḍavas. That Árshṭishena or another of the same name was son of S'ala (or Laśa), who was son of Su-hotra (Hari-V., xxix. 1518-20; see also the Váyu, Brahma and Bhág. Puráṇas).

* *Kṛitá; svayam-vare kṛite pitrá*, "at the svayam-vara arranged by her father," would seem better.

† I have not found this name elsewhere.

‡ See canto lvii, verse 53.

§ See p. 315, note ‡.

|| See canto lvii, verse 47.

¶ For *te 'tha yátávṛitaṁ* read *te tayá taṁ vṛitaṁ* as in the Poona edition.

** *Tat-pakshá*, i.e., apparently "of Dama's party."

18 some took a neutral position. Then Dama, looking at those
kings all around, made this appeal with full presence of mind,
O great muni.

Dama spoke:

19 "Ho, *ye* kings! Since *men* say a svayam-vara is among the
duties of righteousness, *is it* unrighteousness or righteousness
20 that these have seized her by force? If *it is* unrighteousness,
it is no duty of mine that there shall be another wife *for me;*
or *if it is* righteousness, then enough of the life which is
retained in an outrage by an enemy!"

21 Then king Ćáru-dharman,* king of Daśárṇa, making that
22 assemblage keep silence, spoke, O great muni,—"If this which
Dama has spoken depends on righteousness or unrighteousness,
O kings, declare *it* then, so that mine and his righteousness be
not violated."

Márkaṇḍeya spoke:

23 Then certain kings addressed that king,—"With mutual
affection the Gándharva ceremony *of marriage* is ordained for
24 kshatriyas,† but it is not for vaiśyas, śúdras or twice-born
bráhmans. And it has been effected by this thy daughter in
25 that she has preferred Dama. Thus according to righteous-
ness this thy daughter *belongs* to Dama, O king. He who
behaves otherwise, proceeds through infatuation *as* one licen-
tious in soul."

26 And others, high-souled kings, who belonged to the party of
the *hostile* kings, spoke this speech to the king of Daśárṇa, O
bráhman,—

27 "Why say they through infatuation *that* this Gándharva *form*
is *the rule of* righteousness for him who is kshatriya-born?
But this is certainly not approved. There is another‡
28 form *also*, the Rákshasa,§ for those who live by *bearing*
arms. Now whoever carries off this *maiden* by force after

* Or *Ćáru-karman* in verse 9 above.

† See Manu iii. 26 and 32.

‡ For *na tvasha śástá nányo hi* read *na tv esha eva śásto 'nyo*, as in the Poona edition.

§ See Manu iii. 26 and 33.

slaying those who beset his path, his in truth she is by the
29 Rákshasa marriage, O kings. Of the two *forms of* marriage
this *Rákshasa form* is esteemed the more excellent here among
kshatriyas; hence Mahánanda* and the other *princes* have
acted righteously."

Márkaṇḍeya spoke:

30 Then the kings, who had first addressed the *assembled* kings,
spoke again *this* speech dealing with the righteousness of their
caste *as concerned* with mutual affection ;—
31 "It is true the Rákshasa *form* also is commended as an
excellent ordinance for kshatriyas, but the maiden has approved
him, *Dama*, as her husband under her father's authority.
32 Now *she* who is carried off by force *by a man*, who has killed
her father or kinsman—that is declared to be the Rákshasa
33 ordinance—*provided* she is living in the possession of no one else
as husband.† In this completion of the Gándharva *form*
here—since this *maiden* chose Dama in the sight of all the
34 kings—what Rákshasa marriage *has there been* here? A
maiden when married certainly retains not her maidenhood,
35 and marriage creates a bond‡ on a maiden, O kings. These
particular *princes*, who are prepared to take her by force from
Dama, let them do *so* then, if they are strong *enough*; but
that is not good."

Márkaṇḍeya spoke:

36 Hearing that, Dama with eyes reddened with wrath strung
37 his bow and spoke this speech,—"If my own wife is carried
off by strong men before my eyes—what then *is* the value of
the existence of an impotent man as regards his family or his
38 two arms? § Fie on my weapons! fie on my valour! fie on my
arrows! fie on my bow! fie on my useless birth in the family
39 of high-souled Marutta! If these powerful *princes* in their in-

* Or *Mahánáda*, as in verse 10.

† This is according to the comment., which makes *nánya-bhartṛi-kare sthitá* a clause qualifying the preceding words. The comment. explains *hatvá pitṛi-sambandham* as "severing her tie to her father."

‡ *Sambandhaḥ*; =*svámitvam*, "ownership" (comment.).

§ For *bhujámyám* read *bhujábhyám*, as in the Poona edition.

fatuation take my wife and depart while I live, shame on my useless possession of a bow!"
40 So exclaiming, mighty Dama, the tamer of great enemies, then addressed all those other kings with Mahánanda at their
41 head,—"Here *stands* the surpassingly bright maiden, pretty in form, and with intoxicating eyes; what has he *to do* with life,
42 to whom this high-born *maiden becomes* not wife? Thinking thus, O kings, so strive ye in combat that ye may by vanquishing me proudly make her your wife."
43 Having challenged them thus, he then discharged a shower of arrows there, covering the kings *therewith* as *a storm of rain*
44 *covers* trees with darkness. Those heroic kings also discharged arrows, pikes, spears and maces, and Dama playfully clove the
45 *missiles* used by them. They also *clove* the arrows shot by him, and Narishyanta's son clove the multitudes of arrows
46 *discharged* by those kings, O muni. As the fight went on then between Dama and the princes, Mahánanda penetrated with
47 sword in hand where Dama *was*. Dama, seeing him advancing with sword in hand in the great fight, discharged showers of
48 arrows as Indra *pours out* the rains. Mahánanda immediately then clove those his missiles, which composed meshes of arrows,
49 with his sword *and* avoided others. Mahánanda, great in valour, next mounted on Dama's chariot in fury then and fought
50 with Dama. As Mahánanda was fighting agilely in many ways, Dama shot an arrow gleaming like the fire of fate into
51 his heart. Mahánanda, with himself pierced *as he was*, pulled out the *arrow* that had stuck in his heart, and then hurled
52 his glittering sword against Dama. And Dama dashed *aside* this torch-like sword, which was falling on him, with a pike, and cut Mahánanda's head off with a double-edged sword.*
53 When Mahánanda was killed, the kings in a mass turned backwards, *but* Vapush-mat, king of Kuṇḍina,† stood his
54 ground; and full of strength, pride, and frenzy he fought with Dama. He was son of a king of the Southern country

* *Vetasa-patra.* See canto cxxvi verse 24.

† See p. 335, note §.

55 and was a habitual fighter.* As that *prince* was fighting
fiercely, he, *Dama*, with a scymitar† lightly clove both his
56 charioteer's head and his banner in the battle. His sword
being broken, that *prince* then seized his mace studded with
many spikes, and he, *Dama*, hastily split that also while it
57 was in his very hand. Whilst Vapush-mat is taking up
another choice weapon, during that interval Dama pierced
58 him with an arrow and laid him low on the ground. That
prince was laid low on the ground then, powerless in his limbs
59 and quivering, *and* ceased in his mind from fighting. After
gazing on him as he lay so with no *more* thought of fighting,
Dama restraining himself‡ abandoned him, and taking Sumaná
went forth with happy mind.

60 Then the king of Daśárṇa filled with pleasure performed
the marriage of those two, of Dama and Sumaná, according to
61 the ordinances. Dama wedded to his wife remained a short
time there in the city of the king of Daśárṇa, and departed with
62 his wife to his own abode. And the king of Daśárṇa§ gave
him elephants, horses and chariots, cattle, horses, asses and
63 camels, and many slaves both female and male, clothing, ornaments, bows and other *apparel*, the choicest household utensils
of his own ; and sent him away, replete also with those other
vessels.

CANTO CXXXIV.||

Dama's exploits.

Dama returned home triumphant—Narishyanta transferred the kingdom to him and retired with his queen Indra-sená to the forest—

* *Raṇa-goćaraḥ.*

† For *kara-bálam*, which form is not in the dictionary, read *kara-bálena* or better *kara-pálena ?*

‡ He did not give him the *coup de grace.* Vapush-mat re-appears in the next canto.

§ For *Daśárṇádhipateś ćásau* read *Daśárṇádhiptiś ćásmai*, as in the Poona edition.

|| Canto cxxxv in the Calcutta edition.

The defeated prince Vapush-mat met him there, and in revenge killed him—Indra-sená sent tidings to Dama that he should punish the murderer.

Márkaṇḍeya spoke :

1 Thus the prince gained her, Sumaná, as his wife, O most
great muni, and prostrated himself* at his father's and
2 mother's feet; and she, beautiful-browed Sumaná, bowed then
before her parents-in-law. And they were both welcomed then
3 with blessings by them both. And a great festival was held
in Narishyanta's city itself, since *Dama* had both married a
4 wife *and* arrived from the city of the king of Daśárṇa. On hear-
ing that he was *thus* connected *by marriage* with the lord of
Daśárṇa and that the kings were defeated, king Narishyanta
5 rejoiced with his son. And Dama, son of the great king,
sported with Sumaná amidst choice gardens and woodland
spots, in palaces and on the summits of hills.

6 Now after a long time Sumaná, daughter of the king of
7 Daśárṇa, while sporting with Dama conceived a child. And
king Narishyanta, who had enjoyed enjoyments as lord of the
earth, reached his declining years, and anointing Dama to the
8 kingdom departed to the forest; and his wife Indra-sená also
went as a female ascetic. He dwelt there according to the
ordinance of vána-prasthas.†

9 Saṅkrandana's son Vapush-mat, *king* of the Southern region,
most evil in conduct, went to the forest to kill deer, with a small
10 body of followers. He saw Narishyanta as an ascetic dirty
and mud-covered, and his wife Indra-sená most extremely
11 weakened by austerities, and asked,—"Who art thou, a bráh-
man, or a forest-wandering kshatriya, or a vaiśya who has
12 reached the vána-prastha stage?‡ Tell me!" The king,
being under a rule of silence, gave him no answer at all then;
and Indra-sená told him all that truly.

Márkaṇḍeya spoke :

13 And on knowing that that Narishyanta was his enemy's

* *Praṇamya sa* is the reading, but *praṇanáma* would be better.

† For *váṇaprastha* read *vánaprastha.*

‡ For *váṇaprastham* read *vánaprasthyam?*

father, Vapush-mat exclaiming "I have got him!" both
14 seized him angrily by his matted locks and, while Indra-sená
bewailed "Alas! Alas!" with sobbing voice, drew forth his
sword angrily and spoke this word,—
15 "I will seize the father of that Dama, who defeated me in
battle *and* who carried Sumaná off from me; let Dama protect
16 him! I will kill the father of that evil-minded *man*, who cast
off all the princes that had assembled for the maiden's sake.
17 Let that Dama, who evil-souled naturally domineers in battles,
prevent it; such *as I am* here, I kill that foe's father."

Márkaṇḍeya spoke:

18 So saying that king Vapush-mat, evil in conduct, cut off
19 his head also, while Indra-sená cried out. The muni folk and
other forest-dwellers then said to him, "Shame! Shame!"
And after looking at him he, *Vapush-mat*, went from the
forest to his own city.

20 When that Vapush-mat had gone, she, Indra-sená, sighing deeply despatched a śúdra ascetic to her son's presence, *saying*,—

21 "Go thou quickly *and* tell my son Dama my word. Thou
verily knowest what tidings of my husband are told here;
22 nevertheless thou must tell my son, what I say in my very sore
affliction after having seen such an outrage* as this fallen on
23 the king;—'Thou art king, appointed by my lord—a protector
of the four stages of life. Is it fit that thou dost not safeguard
24 the ascetics?† My lord Narishyanta was engaged in the
austerities of an ascetic; and there is no such lord for *me* who
25 bewail, while thou art such a lord.‡ Vapush-mat dragged
him by the hair with violence and then killed him for no fault;
26 thus thy king has attained to glory. In these circumstances

* *Laṅghaná*; this word in the feminine gender is not in the dictionary. It occurs again in verses 33 and 36.

† For *mad-bharttádhikṛito* read *mad-bhartrádhikṛito*; for *ki yuktaṁ* read *kiṁ yuktaṁ*; and for *yan nirîkshasi* read *yan na rakshasi*, as in the Poona edition.

‡ This is according to the comment., with the Poona reading *náthe* instead of *násti*.

do thou that whereby righteousness may not be violated—so do
27 thou! I must not* say more than this, for I am an ascetic. And
thy father was an aged ascetic unvitiated by any offence. Do
thou determine what should be done to that *man* who killed him.
28 Thou hast heroic ministers who can expound the meaning of all
the scriptures. Consider with them and do what ought to be
29 done in these circumstances. We ascetics have no authority
in this *matter*, O king. "Do thou this"—"*do* thou so"—
30 such is a king's speech.† As Vidúratha's‡ father was slain
by the Yavana, so *has* this *king*, *the father* of thee, *my* son,
31 *been slain*; thereby thy family has been destroyed. The father
of the Asura king Jambha was bitten by Nágas, *and* that
king also destroyed the Nágas who inhabited the whole of
32 Pátála. Paráśara,§ when he heard that his father S'akti‖
had been smitten by a Rákshasa, cast the whole race of
33 Rákshasas into the fire. Moreover a kshatriya cannot verily
endure the outrage which any other *person* makes against
his lineage; how much less *will he endure* the murder of his
34 father? *It is* not this thy father *who* is slain, *it is* not on him
that the weapon has been made to fall; *it is* thou *who* hast been
slain here I deem, *it is* on thee *that* the weapon has been made
35 to fall. Who indeed fears this *foe*, that has laid his weapon

* For *ća naiva* read *ćara na* as in the Poona edition.

† The Poona edition reads *bhúyo 'pi bháshitum* for *bhúpati-bháshitam*, 'We ascetics have no authority here, O king, to say thus "Do thou this," *or* even further "*Do* thou so."'

‡ This may be the Vidúratha mentioned above in canto cxvi, verse 10. There were other kings of the same name, but all later in time, and it does not appear any of them were killed by a Yavana; as Vidúratha son of Kuru, of the Paurava race (Mahá-Bh., Ádi-p. xcv. 3791-5, S'ánti-p. xlix. 1790-97, and Hari-V., xxxii. 1816), Vidúratha son of Bhajamána (Hari-V., xxxix. 2032, and Matsya Pur. xliv. 77), and another later Vidúratha (Hari-V., xcii. 5015-8, and xcix. 5493-5504).

§ Paráśara was a famous ṛishi, son of S'aktri or S'akti, see canto cxxxiii, verse 7. He was father by Satya-vatí of Kṛishṇa Dvaipáyana (Mahá-Bh., Ádi-p. lx. 2209, xcv. 3801-2, and S'ánti-p. cccli). But he is wholly out of time in this story.

‖ For *pitari S'aktau* read *pitaraṁ S'aktiṁ* as in the Poona edition.

on *simple* forest-dwellers; let him not fear thee, my son, as king,
36 or let him fear *thee*.* Since this outrage has been directed
against thee, do thou take thorough measures therefore against
this Vapush-mat with his dependants, kinsmen and friends.'"

Márkaṇḍeya spoke :

37 Dismissing him, Indra-dása, to whom this message had been
communicated, the noble-spirited lady embracing her lord's
body entered the funeral pyre.

CANTO CXXXV.†

Dama's exploits.

Dama bewails his father's death and vows vengeance against the murderer.

Márkaṇḍeya spoke : ‡

1 At *the tidings of* his father's death declared by that ascetic§
Dama blazed out with exceeding wrath, as fire is intensified||
2 with clarified butter. Now that steadfast *king* burning with
the fire of wrath, O great muni, crushed his hands together
and spoke out this speech ;—
3 "Like a master-less *wretch* my dear father has been slaugh-
tered, while I his son actually live, by a very cruel *man* who has
4 overwhelmed my family. Let not people utter the calumny¶
that I, such as *I am*, condone *this* by reason of impotence. I am
in authority to quell the unruly and to protect the well-behaved.
5 My father has been slain even by him—seeing *that*, my enemies

* This is the Poona and Bombay reading, *putrasya má bibhetu* for *viprasya márite tu ;* but both seem corrupt.

† Canto cxxxvi in the Calcutta edition.

‡ The Bombay and Poona editions make the story more precise by inserting a verse here—"That śúdra ascetic as commanded by Indra-sená went and relates to Dama his father's death as *narrated* above."

§ For *samákhyátaṁ badham* read *samákhyáte badhe* as in the Poona edition.

|| For *uddhṛitaḥ* read *uddhataḥ* as in the Poona edition.

¶ For *nyáya-vádo jane tasyápy* read *nápavádo janena syád* as in the Poona edition.

live.* What *is the good* then of this much lamentation?
6 And why again *the cry*, 'Alas! dear father!'? What should
be done by lamentation here, that I, such as *I am*, *will* do
here. When I give no gratification to my sire with the blood
that spurts from that Vapush-mat's body, then I will enter the
7 fire! If no water-oblation *be made* to my dear slain father with
the blood of that *king* in fight,† and *if no* feast *be given* duly
to twice-born *bráhmans* with flesh, then I will enter the fire!
8 If those who are named Asuras, gods, Yakshas, Gandharvas,
Vidyádharas, and Siddhas give him assistance, even them also
I, such as *I am*, possessed with fury *will* reduce to ashes with
9 multitudes of weapons. I will kill in battle that *king* of the
Southern country, who is cruel, very unrighteous‡ *and* un-
worthy of praise, and I will then enjoy the whole earth also;
10 or failing to kill him I will enter the fire. I will forthwith
slay *him*, most evil-minded, who slaughtered an old man
among the ascetics,§ who dwells in the forest, is greatly
agitated at peaceful words,‖ accompanied *as he is* by all his
kinsmen, friends, and army of foot-soldiers, elephants and
11 cavalry. Let all the assembled bands of my gods see the

* The Poona edition reads *Pitaraṁ ćápi nihataṁ drishṭvá jívaty a-sattamaḥ*, "and seeing my father slain, the evil man lives."

† Or read *saṅkhye 'vinipátitasya*, "to my dear father, who was slain not in battle, with that king's blood"? The Bombay and Poona editions omit the second quarter-verse and read as the third quarter-verse *kuryám pitus tasya ća piṇḍa-dánaṁ*, "Let me with his blood make the water-oblation, and with his flesh a fitting feast to bráhmans and the oblation of the funeral cake to that father of mine; if not, then I will enter the fire!" *Tasya* in the first quarter-verse may refer to *pituḥ*, but by position *tasya máṁsena* corresponds to *tać-ćhonitena*; the result is extraordinary, but see verses 34 to 36 on page 683 below.

‡ The Poona edition reads *nishṭhúram* for *niḥ-śúram*; and the comment. explains *á-dhármikam* as *atyantam a-dhármikam*.

§ For *tápasa-vṛiddha-mauninaṁ* the Bombay and Poona editions read *tápasa-vṛiddha-ghátinaṁ*; but both violate the metre. Read *tápasa-vṛiddha-ghátaṁ*?

‖ The Poona edition reads the second quarter-verse thus—*vana-sthagaṁ sádhu-vidhiṁ vidagdham*, "a forest-rogue, observing good ordinances, cunning;" but *sádhu-vidhiṁ* is erroneous. The Bombay reading is similar.

destruction that I, such as *I am*, will verily make, taking my
bow, armed with a sword, and mounted in my chariot,
12 meeting my enemy's might. Whoever shall be his comrade
to-day when he comes to battle with me again, I am prepared,
with my two arms as my soldiers, speedily to destroy his family
13 utterly.* If in this battle the king of the gods with
thunderbolt in hand, and the lord of the pitṛis too raising his
terrible sceptre wrathfully, *and* the lord of wealth, Varuṇa and
the Sun strive to safeguard him, I will nevertheless slaughter
14 *him* with multitudes of choice sharp arrows. May the
vultures be satisfied this day with the flesh and blood of that
man, by whom was killed, while I the son am powerful, my dear
father, whose mind was subdued, who was without fault, who
dwelt in a small spot in the forest,† who ate *only* fruits that
had fallen, who was friendly to all beings!"

CANTO CXXXVI.

Dama's exploits—The slaying of Vapush-mat.‡

Dama consulted his ministers and resolved to kill Vapush-mat—He and Vapush-mat met with their armies, and he killed Vapush-mat in fight—He celebrated his father's obsequies with Vapush-mat's flesh and blood.

Márkandeya spoke:

1 When Narishyanta's son Dama uttered this vow, his eyes
rolled with anger and passion, while he covered his beard with
2 his hand. *Exclaiming* "Alas! I am stricken!" he kept his
father in mind and reproached Fate; and he addressed all
those ministers; he brought the family priest there.

* For *tathaiva* read *tasyáśu* as in the Poona edition, or *tasyaiva* as in the Bombay edition.

† *Kánanákhaṇḍalauko*, or *-ká* as in the Bombay and Poona editions.

‡ This and the next cantos are the ending given in the Bombay and Poona editions. The Calcutta edition gives a short ending, quite different, which is printed at the end. This ending is printed as an Appendix to the latter edition, but the text there is very incorrect; and I have followed the text in the former editions, noting only such variations as appear worthy of notice.

Dama spoke:

3 Tell me what should be done in this *matter*, now that my
dear father has reached the gods' abode. Ye, sirs, have heard
4 what that śúdra ascetic has said. That king was aged, an
ascetic, engaged in the vána-prastha's vow, observing the rule
of silence, unarmed and *dwelling* with my mother Indra-sená.
5 She who was associated with him told the exact account to
Vapush-mat. Thereupon the evil-souled *foe*, drawing his
scymitar and seizing *my father's* matted locks with his left hand,
6 killed the world's master as if he were a masterless *churl*.
And my mother, having actually commissioned me, was utter-
7 ing the word "Shame!" and, *calling me* feeble in lot *and* void
of good fortune, has entered the fire. Embracing him, Narish-
8 yanta, she has departed to the abode of the thirty gods. I
being such will now do what my mother has said. And let
my army composed of elephants, horses, chariots, and infantry
9 be arranged. If I drive not away the enmity against my
father, if I kill not my father's murderer and comply not with
my mother's word, how can I endure to live here?

Márkandeya spoke:

10 The ministers hearing his speech exclaimed "Alas! Alas!"
and did accordingly therefore, while distraught in mind. Ac-
11 companied by his dependants, army, and chariots, and by his
retinue, they, placing king Dama at their head and taking
the blessings of the brahman family priest who knew the
12 three *divisions of* time, went forth. Breathing hard like the
Serpent king, Dama advanced against Vapush-mat, while
slaying the wardens on his boundaries and other neighbouring
princes, and hastening* towards the southern region.

13 Seeing him approaching, Vapush-mat was filled with pa-
tience;† and Saṅkrandana's son Vapush-mat recognized Dama,
who had arrived attended by his retinue, by his ministers, and
14 by his dependants. With unwavering mind he directed his
armies; and issuing from his city he despatched a messenger *to*

* *Tvaran* of the Calcutta Appendix is better than *tvaráḍ*.

† *Marsha-púritaḥ*. This is hardly appropriate, unless it means "was filled with caution."

15 *announce*,—"Come thou on more quickly! Narishyanta with
his wife awaits thee! O thou of kshatriya caste, approach near
16 me! These sharp arrows discharged by my arm, which are
thirsting, shall pierce thy body in battle and drink thy
blood."

17 But Dama, on hearing all that speech from the messenger,
went on hastily, remembering his previously uttered vow,
18 breathing hard like a serpent. And the man who boasted of
his army* was summoned to battle. And then there was an
exceedingly *fierce* combat between Dama and Vapush-mat.
19 And *the armies* fought, both chariot-rider against chariot-rider,
elephant-rider against elephant-rider,† horseman against
horseman, O bráhman ṛishi. That battle was tumultuous,
20 while all the gods, Siddhas, Gandharvas, and Rákshasas looked
on. The earth quaked, O bráhman, as Dama fought in that
21 battle. There was no elephant, no chariot-rider, no horse
which could endure his arrows. Next Vapush-mat's general
22 fought with Dama, and Dama pierced him deeply in the heart
with an arrow at close-quarters. When he fell, his army
verily was seized with a panic to flee.

23 Then spoke Dama, tamer of his foes, to *their* master thus,—
"Where goest thou, wicked one, after having slaughtered my
24 father, who was an ascetic and weapon-less and practising
austerities? Thou art a kshatriya; stay thou!" Then stay-
ing back he, Vapush-mat, attended by his younger brother
25 fought with Dama. Mounted in his chariot he fought in com-
pany with his sons, relations, and kinsmen. With the arrows
discharged from his bow the regions of the sky were then
26 pervaded,‡ and he filled Dama and his chariot with multitudes
of arrows quickly. And thereupon Dama in wrath excited by
27 his father's murder split the arrows discharged by them § and

* *Pumán sená-vikatthanaḥ*; but *Vapushmán sainya-katthanaḥ* is suggested as better, "And Vapush-mat who boasted of his army was summoned to battle."

† *Náginá*; this meaning is not in the Dictionary.

‡ For the first *tataḥ*, *tasya* would be better.

§ *Ćićchedástáṁś ćharáṁs* or *ćićcheda táṁś ćharáṁs*; both readings are admissible.

pierced them also with other *arrows.* In that way he brought
28 down to Yama's abode the seven sons, the relations and kins-
men and friends,* each with a single arrow, O dvija.
29 And Vapush-mat after his sons and kinsmen had been killed,
mounted in a chariot fought wrathfully with him in battle
with serpent-like arrows.† And Dama split those his arrows,
30 O great muni.‡ And those two fought together, being ex-
asperated, wishing to conquer each other, each one's bow being
quickly split by the impetus of the other's arrows. They both,
31 great in strength, grasping their swords, made play. § Dama,
reflecting for a moment on the king his father who had been
32 killed in the forest,|| seized *Vapush-mat* by the hair and attacked
him and felled him to the earth ; and with his foot on his neck,
33 raising his arm he exclaimed,—" Let all the gods, men, Ser-
pents *and* birds see the heart also of Vapush-mat, who is of
34 kshatriya caste, split open ! " And so saying Dama tore open
his heart also, and desirous of drinking ¶ was forbidden by the
gods from *tasting* the blood.
35 Then he offered the water-oblation to his dear father with
the very blood. Having discharged his debt to his father he
36 returned to his own house. And with Vapush-mat's flesh he
offered the cakes *to his father*, he feasted the bráhmans who
were sprung from families of Rákshasas.**
37 Such verily were the kings born of the Solar Race. Others
also were of fine intellect, heroic, sacrificers, learned in right-
38 eousness, deeply versed in the Vedánta. And I am not able to

* *Mitrán ;* the masculine with this meaning is unusual.

† The Calcutta Appendix reads *sa rathí vibudhopamaḥ,* " He, riding in his chariot, resembled a god "—which probably would refer to Dama.

‡ *Ća mahá-mune,* a mere expletive. The Calcutta Appendix reads *pratyuváća ha.*

§ Or " made feints." The Calcutta Appendix reads *gṛihíta-khaḍgam udyamya ćikríḍati Vapushmati,* " While Vapush-mat raising the sword in his grasp was making play," or " making a feint," Dama, &c.

|| The Calcutta Appendix reads *jñátvá pitaraṁ ća sthitaṁ vane.*

¶ The Calcutta Appendix reads *svátta-kámaś* for *pátu-kámaś.*

** An extraordinary statement.

mention them fully.* By listening to their exploits a man is delivered from sins.

Canto CXXXVII.

Conclusion.

The Birds close here the long discourse delivered by Márkaṇḍeya, and Jaimini thanks them and departs.

The Birds spoke:

1 Having spoken thus, O Jaimineya,† the great muni Már-
kaṇḍeya let the muni Kraushṭuki depart, and performed the
2 mid-day ceremony. From him we also have heard what we
have declared to thee, O great muni. For this was perfected
by Him who is without beginning.‡ Spoken formerly by the
3 Self-existent One to the muni Márkaṇḍeya was *this* which we
have uttered to thee. *It is* sacred, pure, *and* grants length of life;
it bestows righteousness, love, wealth and final emancipation
4 from existence; it delivers immediately from all sin those who
read *it*, those who hear *it*.

5 And the very four questions indeed, which thou didst put to
us at the very first—the conversation between the father and son,
and the creation by the Self-existent One, and the administra-
6 tions § of the Manus, and the exploits of the kings, O muni,
this we have declared to thee. What now dost thou wish to
hear? After hearing or reading ‖ all these *matters* in assem-

* Dama's descendants are given in the Vishṇu Pur. IV. i. His son was Rájya-vardhana, who is the subject of cantos cix and cx, above.

† He and the Birds reappear from canto xlv. The text is *Jaimineyam*, "Having spoken thus to Jaimineya;" but the Birds have been relating to Jaimini what Márkaṇḍeya had before told to Kraushṭuki, and this reading is unsuitable unless Jaimineya be taken as Kraushṭuki's patronymic; and that it cannot be, for Kraushṭuki's patronymic is said to have been Bháguri, see pp. 436 and 445. I have ventured therefore to read *Jaimineya* instead.

‡ *Anádi-siddham.* The Calcutta Appendix reads *aṇimá-siddham*, "perfect in minuteness."

§ *Sthiti*; or "positions."

‖ The Calcutta reading *paṭhitvá* appears preferable to *paṭhate*.

7 blies, a man discarding all sins may reach absorption into
Brahman at the end.*

There† are eighteen Puráṇas which the Forefather spoke.
8 Now the seventh of them is to be known as the very famous
Márkaṇḍeya *Puráṇa.*‡ *They are* the Bráhma, the Pádma, and
9 the Vaishṇava, the S'aiva and the Bhágavata, and also the Nára-
díya besides, and the Márkaṇḍeya as seventh, the A'gneya which
was declared the eighth, and the Bhavishya ninth, the Brahma-
10 vaivarta tenth, the Laiṅga known as the eleventh, Váráha de-
11 clared the twelfth, the Skánda next as thirteenth, and the
Vámana fourteenth, and the Kaurma fifteenth, and the Mátsya,
and the Gáruḍa and next the Brahmáṇḍa.

12 He who may read the titles of the eighteen Puráṇas, *who*
repeats § them at the three periods of the day continually,
may obtain the result of a horse-sacrifice.

13 Both creation and secondary creation, genealogy and the
manvantaras and the exploits in the genealogies *constitute* a
Puráṇa with the five characteristics.||

14 This Puráṇa which contains the four questions is indeed of
the highest quality. Now when it is heard, sin committed in
15 hundreds of ten millions of ages perishes. Brahmanicide and
other sins, and other *deeds* that are vile, all those perish *there-*
16 *by*, like grass smitten by the blast. The merit that is gained
by making gifts at Pushkara¶ accrues from hearing this
Puráṇa; and *a man* attains to a benefit superior to all the Vedas
17 by completely acquiring *this*. *A man* should worship him who
may cause it to be heard, as he *worships* the divine Fore-

* The Calcutta Appendix here introduces Jaimini's reply which is at page 688; and puts what follows here regarding the Puráṇas as a separate pronouncement by Brahmá.

† The Calcutta Appendix puts all that follows down to verse 30, and also the concluding two verses, into the mouth of Brahmá, and places it at the very end.

‡ This sentence is omitted from the Calcutta Appendix.

§ For *japato* read *japate*.

|| This verse and the next are not in the Calcutta Appendix.

¶ See p. 306, note ||.

father, *with perfumes and flowers and with *gifts of* clothing
18 and with gratifications to bráhmans. And kings should give
according to their ability villages and other lands and carriages.† After hearing all this Puráṇa, which is augmented
with the objects of the Veda *and* which is the sole abode of
the Dharma-śástras, *a man* may obtain every object.‡ After
19 hearing the entire Puráṇa, let a wise man do full reverence to
Vyása for the sake of the benefits of righteousness, wealth, love
and final emancipation from existence as *therein* declared. Let
20 him give his spiritual preceptor a cow, accompanied with gold,
clothing and ornaments. In order to gain the benefits *that come*
from hearing it let him gratify his spiritual preceptor with gifts.
21 He who, without paying reverence to the man who reads
the Puráṇa out, hears a single verse, acquires no merit; verily
22 he is known as a Scripture-thief. § Not him do the gods
gladden, nor the Pitṛis, with sons; and they desire not || the
śraddha given *by him* nor the benefit *gained* by bathing at
23 sacred places of pilgrimage. He incurs the censure of a Scripture-thief in an assembly of good men. Wise men must not
24 listen to this scripture with contempt; but when *this* noble
scripture is contemned as it is being read by sages,¶ *the offender*
becomes dumb; he is born as a fool in seven births.
25 Now he, who after hearing *this* seventh Puráṇa may
further do reverence to it, being delivered from all sin verily
26 purifies his own family. The purified *man* goes without doubt
to Vishṇu's eternal world; never shall he falling therefrom
27 become a man again.** By the very hearing of *this* Puráṇa
a man may obtain supreme union with the universal soul.

* The Calcutta Appendix reads *śrúyeta pújayeć ćhástram,* "let him hear and reverence *this* śástra."

† The Calcutta Appendix reads instead—"And he should give according to his ability royal carriages and other vehicles."

‡ This verse and the next two are not in the Calcutta Appendix.

§ *Sástra-ćoraḥ.*

|| *Ca neććhanti* of the Calcutta Appendix is better than *tatheććhanti.*

¶ *Sádhubhiḥ.*

** The Calcutta Appendix reads—"Moreover until seven Manus *are gone,*

28 No gift should be made to an atheist, to one fallen from
his caste, to a contemner of the Vedas, to one who contemns
religious preceptors and twice-born men, or moreover to one
who has broken his vows, to one who contemns his parents, to
29 one who contemns the Vedas, S'ástras and other *scriptures*, or
to one who infringes the rules of good breeding, or indeed to
one who is passionate towards his caste-folk. To these *men*
certainly no gift must be made, even when one's life is at its
last gasp.

30 If entirely through covetousness or infatuation or fear one
should read *this Puráṇa* or cause it to be read, he may assuredly go to hell.

Márkaṇḍeya spoke:

31 All this story is characterized by righteousness, and bestows
heaven and final emancipation from existence. Who hears it
32 or may read it, his earnest endeavour is achieved; he is never
affected by the pain of mental or bodily sickness; he is delivered from bráhmanicide and other sins, there is no doubt
33 of this. Good *men* become *his* kindly * friends, affectionate
in mind. No enemies nor robbers will ever arise *against him*.
34 Aspiring to what is good, † and eating savoury food, he
perishes not with famines; *nor* with sins touching others'
wives or others' property, or with injury to others or with
35 such like crimes; and he is continually freed from many pains,
O best of dvijas. Success, affluence, memory, peace, good
fortune, nourishment, and contentment—may *each of these*
36 be his continually, who hears this story, O bráhman! The
man who hears the whole of this Márkaṇḍeya Puráṇa is not
to be lamented; nor is he indeed to be lamented who recites
this poetical work properly, O dvija. Endowed with perfection that is purified by knowledge of religious devotion, ‡
and surrounded even in Svarga and the other worlds by Indra

he may, after enjoying delights according to his wishes, and after enjoying the very earth, attain to supreme union with the universal soul."

* *Su-jana* of the Calcutta Appendix is better than *sva-jana*.

† *Sad-artho;* or perhaps "being in good circumstances"?

‡ Or "possessing pure success in the knowledge of religious devotion."

and other gods and other *heavenly beings*, he is always reverenced
37 in Svarga. And after hearing this Purána, which is replete
with knowledge and intelligence, being mounted in a choice
heavenly car he is magnified in Svarga.

38 And the number of the syllables in the Puráṇa has been
declared by him who is intelligent in exactitude. There are
39 of verses six thousands and eight hundreds also, thereto are
added eighty-nine verses *and* eleven—pronounced of yore by
the wise muni Márkaṇḍeya.

Jaimini spoke:

40 In India there was not *that* which burst asunder my doubts,
O ye twice-born ;* ye, sirs, have accomplished that which no
41 one *else* now will do. Ye have attained long life, are good,†
and are clever in knowledge and intelligence. And thus let
there be unerring intelligence in the application of the
42 Sáṅkhya doctrine *to the knowledge of spirit!* Let evil-mindedness *that springs* from pain wrought by a father's curse depart
from you!"‡ After speaking this much the muni went to
his own hermitage, pondering over the speech uttered by the
Birds, which was sublimely noble.

End of the Márkaṇḍeya Puráṇa.

---

* The Calcutta Appendix reads more bluntly, "In India twice-born *brahmans* have lost the power of bursting asunder perplexities and doubts."

† For *santu* of the Bombay and Poona editions read *santaḥ* with the Calcutta Appendix.

‡ *Vyapaitu vaḥ.* See pages 13–16.

DIFFERENT ENDING

according to the Calcutta Edition.

CANTO CXXXVI.*

Conclusion.

The story of Dama breaks off—A high encomium is passed upon this Puráṇa.

Márkaṇḍeya spoke:

1 When king Dama had spoken thus, his father's enemy fled. "My father was an ascetic; and let *any* other *man* practise great austerities fearlessly." Dama said nothing to them when he saw them intent on flight.

Márkaṇḍeya spoke:†

2 All this story is characterized by righteousness, *and* bestows heaven and final emancipation from existence. Who hears it &c.

* Canto cxxxvii in the Calcutta edition.

† Here the narrative ends abruptly; and what follows is the same as verses 31 to 37 on page 687 above. The Purána ends with them according to the Calcutta edition.

Note to the Index.

The system of transliteration followed in this translation is one that was in use formerly, yet has not been quite uniform. The transliterations of Sanskrit words contained in this Index have been revised and are brought into agreement with the system that is now approved by the Asiatic Society of Bengal and the Royal Asiatic Society. Sanskrit words are printed in the Roman character; all other words are put in italics, whether vernacular or English, Latin or Greek, and the spelling of vernacular words is generally that in common use.

The locality of geographical names is indicated by the letters M (Madhya-deśa), C (Central India), and N., S., E., W., NE., NW., SE., and SW. which explain themselves.

Abbreviations used.

aps. Apsaras.
b. brāhman.
bd. bird.
c. country.
cer. cereal.
cst. constellation, asterism.
d. demon (Daitya, Dānava, Asura, Rākṣasa).
dg. demi-god; celestial being.
dt. district.
dyn. dynasty.
f. family.
f.d. female demon.
for. forest.
g. god.
gb. goblin.
gdh. gandharva.
gr. grass.
gs. goddess.
h. hill.
hb. herb.
isl. island.
k. king.
kst. kṣatriyā.
l. lake.
m. man.
mt. mountain.
mts. mountain-range.
p. people.
pat. patronymic.
pfn. personification.
pl. place.
pr. prince.
prs. princess.
ps. person.
pt. plant.
q. queen.
r. river.
rs. ṛṣi.
sf. sacrifice.
t. town, city.
ti. tīrtha, place of pilgrimage.
tr. tree.
w. woman.

INDEX.

Abhi-jit *cst.* 170.
Ābhīra *p.* NW, M. 312–314.
Ābhīra *p.* S. 334, 362.
Abhiṣaha *p.* NW ? 382.
Abhisāra *c.* NW. 382.
Abhisārī *t.* NW. 382.
Ābilvaka *pt.* 25.
Ābu mt. W. 289, 340.
Ācāra, *see* Custom.
Acridotheres bd. 49, 58.
Āḍhaka, -kī *pt.* 244, 245.
Āḍhakya *p.* S. 334.
Adhama-kairāta *p.* N. 369, 379.
A-dharma *pfn.* 247, 250.
Adhrāraka ? *p.* E. 324.
Āḍi *bd.* 58.
Aditi *gs.* 550–552, 559, 560, 563–565.
Āditya *g.* 168, 461, 555, 582, 586.
Adri *d.* 425.
Adrijā *r.* 296.
Ægle tr., *see* Bilva.
Aganosma pt., *see* Mālatī.
Agastya *rs.* 270, 293, 601–603, 645, 646.
Āgastya *rs.* 603.
Ages, the Four, 32, 218, 224, 226, 347, 387, 437.
Āgneya *p.* N. 378.
Agni *g.* 10, 23, 152, 247, 249, 270, 387, 398, 399, 445, 447, 460, 473, 474, 489, 495, 512, 524, 532, 535, 539–548, 561, 562, 582, 621.
Agni *rs.* 442.
Agnīdhra *k.* 271–274.
Agnījya ? *p.* N. 378.
Agniṣvātta *pitṛs*, 270, 533.
Āgrahāyaṇī *cst.* 355.
Ahalyā *b. w.* 22.
Ahaṅkāra 190, 217, 220–223.
Ahicchatra *c.* M. 353, 378.
Ahicchatrā *t.* M. 353.
Ahīr p., *see* Ābhīra.
Ahmadnagar t. W. 289.
Āhuka *p.* W. 324.
Aila *k.* 146.
Ailika ? *p.* SE. 360.
Aindra *pl.* 246.
Aindra *cst.* 374.
Air 217, 221, 222.
Airāvata *eleph.* 474, 494, 559.
Aiṣīka ? *p.* S. 334.
Aja (=*Sun*) 562, 572.
Ajamīḍha *k.* 353.
Ajanta *h.* W. 288.
Ajaras *rs.* 269.
Ājyapa *pitṛs*, 533.
Akanin *p.* C ? 363.
Akesines r. NW. 291.
Ākrimī, *village*, 242.
Alakanandā *r.* N. 281.
Alarka *k.* 93–109, 142–145, 148, 151, 155, 170, 171, 180, 186–190, 194, 198–202, 207, 210–216.
Alāvu *pt.* 118, 166.
Ali, Āli *dg.* 407.
Alimadra ? *p.* N. 322.
Allahabad t. 310.
Almond tr. 26.
Almora t. N. 288, 316.
Alms 203, 685–687.
Alstonia tr. 27.
Alūka ? *p.* NW. 375.
Alwar dt. M. 288, 307.
Āmalaka *tr.* 25, 26.
Amara-kaṇṭaka *mt.* C. 298, 331, 334.
Amaravati r. S. 304.
Amarāvatī *t.* S. 337.
Ambā, *see* Ambikā.
Ambāla t. and *p.* N. 321 [illegible] 379.
Ambarīṣa *k.* 462.
Ambaṣṭha *p.* NW. 323, 333, 377–380.
Ambhodhi *d.* 262.
Ambikā *gs.* 476–482, 487, 488, 494, 498, 502, 507–511, 516.
Ambuja *pt.* 29.
Ambupā *f.d.* 262.
Amita *gods*, 465.
Amitābha *k.* 449.

Amitābha *gods*, 464.
Amla tr. see Āmalaka.
Amla-vetasa *pt.* 25.
Amoghā *r.* NW. 389.
Amra tr. see Amrataka.
Amrataka *tr.* 23.
Āmra-vana *for.* W.? 600.
Amūrtarajas *k.* 328.
Amūrtarayas *k.* 329.
Anagha *rs.* 270.
Anala *d.* 262.
Anamitra *k.* 450.
Ānanda *k.* and *c.* 273.
Ānanda *k.* 451–453.
Ānanda? *p.* NE. 383.
Ānandinī *r.* 294.
Ananta *g.* 482.
Ananta (=Śeṣa), 609.
An-araṇya *k.* 551.
Ānarta *k.* 368.
Ānarta *c.* and *p.* 289, 340, 344, 352, 368, 371, 463.
Anas bd. 30.
Anasūyā *w.* 91, 95–99, 249, 269.
Anāyus 146.
Andha? *p.* S. 337.
Andhaka *p.* W. 309, 324, 336, 337.
Andhaka *k.* 352.
Andhaka *d.* 479.
Andha-tāmisra *hell,* 152.
Andhra *p.* SE. 324, 337, 361, 367.
Andhravāka *p.* 324.
Andropogon gr. 79.
Aṅga *k.* 325.
Aṅga *p.* and *c.* E. 324–329, 334, 369, 464, 655.
Aṅga *k*? 146.
Aṅga? *p.* N. 373.
Aṅga-dhṛṣ *d.* 257, 258, 263.
Aṅga-loka *pl.* W. 373.
Aṅgataka? *p.* W. 373.
Anger (Krodha), 15, 16, 250.
Aṅgiras *rs.* 108, 246, 249, 269, 435, 462, 539, 625, 653, 654.
Aṅgiras *demi-gods,* 461, 462.
Āṅgirasa *f.* 588, 653.
Anibhā *prs.* 627.
Anīkaṭa *p.* W. 338.
Anila *d.* 262.
Animadra *p.* N. 322.
Añjana *mt.* NW. 279.
Añjana *mt.* E. 356.
Añjanābha *mt.* 356.
Annadāraka? *p.* NE. 383.
Annaja *p.* C. 344.
Anser bd. 30, 409, 410.
Ant, 147, 170, 206, 210.
Antaḥ-śilā, -śirā *r.* E? 301.
Antar-dvīpa *p.* N. 378.
Antar-giri *dt.* N. 325, 328.
Antar-giri *p.* E. 325.
Antargirya *p.* E. 301, 324, 325.
Antelope 31, 164, 181.
Anthocephalus tr. 25.
Antra-śilā *r.* E? 301.
Antyāgirā? *r.* E? 301.
Aṇu *cer.* 165, 244, 245.
Anugraha, 228, 231.
Anuhrāda *pr.* 146.
Anumati *pfn.* 178.
Anūpa *c.* W. 344, 371.
Anurādhā *cst.* 169, 370.
Anuvinda *k.* 345.
Apagā *r.* M. 293.
Apagā *r.* NW. 316.
Apakāra *d.* 267.
Apāna, *vital air,* 203.
Apara *p.* 313, 372.
Apara-cīna *p.* NE. 319.
Apara-matsya *p.* M. 309.
Apara-nandā *r.* N. 369, 383.
Aparānta *p.* W. 313, 371.
Aparāntika *p.* W. 371, 372.
Aparīta *p.* NW. 313.
Apatha *p.* N. 346.
Āpnuvāna *rs.* 656.
Apratiṣṭha *pl.* 71, 73.
Apsaras, 2–8, 24, 68, 78, 236, 391, 393, 413, 427, 481, 511, 538, 559, 571, 646, 647.
Āpyāyanī, 70.
Arachnechthra bd. 80.
Arand r. C. 296.
Āraṭṭa *c.* and *p.* NW. 311.
Aravalli mts. 286, 289, 312, 338, 340, 349, 369.
Arbuda *mt.* W. 289, 340.
Arbuda *p.* W. 340.
Arcot dt. S. 332.
Ardana? *p.* N. 378.
Ardea bd. 58.
Ardeola bd. 59, 86.
Ardha-hārī *f.d.* 265.
Ārdrā *cst.* 169, 358.
Argha, Arghya *offering,* 18, 38,

97, 156, 161, 162, 423–429, 446, [581, 633.
Argiga? p. W? 368.
Ari-mardana pr. 143.
Arişṭa k. see Nābhāgārişṭa.
Arişṭanemi dg. 6.
Arjuna (Kārtavīrya) k. 101, 106–108, 310, 333, 344, 351, 371, 656.
Arjuna (Pāṇḍava) k. 8, 23, 24, 316, 322, 359, 363, 379, 384, 629.
Arka-liṅga p. M. 308.
Arrah t. M. 382.
Ārṣṭiṣena k. and rs. 669, 670.
Artha-kāraka k. and c. 273.
Artocarpus tr. 25.
Arum pt. 178.
Aruṇa g. 559.
Aruṇa mt. N. 351, 382.
Aruṇa d. 518.
Aruṇākṣa d. 518.
Aruṇāspada t. N. 392, 395.
Arundhatī *star*, 207.
Arūpa? p. C? 344.
A-rūpā f.d. 267.
Arvavīra rs. 270.
Ārya *race*, 290.
Ārya, *gods*, 454.
Aryaman g. 153, 545, 582.
Āṣāḍhā cst. 170, 374, 376.
Asiknī r. NW. 291.
Asi-loman d. 476, 480
Asi-patra *for*. 54, 71–74, 83.
Aśleṣā cst. 169, 361.
Aśmaka p. M. 352.
Aśmaka p. S. 336.
Aśmaka k. 336.
Asmaka, p. S. 336.
Aśmakī q. 337.
Aśoka tr. 25, 26, 364.
Asparagus pt. 165.
Aspasii p. NW. 374.
Āśrama 148–151, 246.
Ass, 83–85, 209, 235, 255.
Assakani p. NW. 374.
Assam, 382, 411.
Asta-giri mt. 371.
Asta-parvata mt. 371.
Asterisms, 168–170.
Astrologer, 580, 626, 630, 631.
Asura d. 20–23, 104, 115, 120, 152, 201, 232, 233, 236, 328, 383, 416, 469–484, 494–512, 515–519, 524, 531, 533, 546, 552, 558, 560, 565, 605, 611, 648, 650, 677, 679.
Aśvaka p. NW. 307, 374.
Aśvakālanata p. NW. 374.
Aśva-keśa p. W? 374.
Aśva-kūṭa p. M. 307.
Aśva-mukha p. W. and N. 368, 378, 381.
Aśvātaka p. M. 307.
Aśvatara k. 109, 125, 127, 130, 132, 135–139.
Aśvattha tr. 277.
Aśvatthāman b. 464.
Aśvinī cst. 170, 384.
Aśvins g. 22, 55, 109, 392, 460, 461, 574–576, 626.
Aṭavī t. S. 334.
Āṭavya p. S. 334.
Atharva Veda, 236, 404, 554.
Atharva p. M. 308.
Ati-nāman rs. 454.
Ati-rātra b. 426.
Atithi 153.
Ati-vibhūti k. 623.
Atom 128.
Atrai r. E. 320.
Ātreya p. N. 320, 347.
Ātreyī r. E. 320.
Atri rs. 95, 96, 99, 102, 151, 154, 246, 249, 269, 320, 462, 570, 621.
Atri p., see Ātreya.
Atta-khaṇḍika? p. NW. 314.
Audumbara p. M.? 355.
Aukhāvana p. S.? 366.
Auṇḍrāmāṣa p. M.? 342.
Aupadha p. N. 322.
Aurangābād t. W. 288.
Aurva rs. 656, 658.
Auttama, Manu *and* manvantara, 271, 419, 425, 429, 432, 435–437, 549.
Auttāna, see Auttama.
Auttānapādi k. 421.
Āvāhana *offering*, 156.
Avanta? p. M. 308.
Avanti r. M. 295.
Avanti c. M. 295, 333, 340–345, 363, 371.
Avantya p. M. 340.
Avara p. W. 372.
Avarṇī r. M. 295.
Averrhoa tr. 24.
Avīkṣi / Avīkṣit,-ta { k. 625, 628, 631, 634–642, 645–654, 658–664.

Avīkṣit (*son of* Kuru) *pr.* 652.
Āvīkṣita *pat.* 652, 653.
Aya *d.* 636.
Ayak r. NW. 316.
Āyati *gs.* 269.
Ayodhyā *t.* 57, 58, 308, 352, 353, 371.
Āyur-Veda, 404–406.

Babhru *b.* 591.
Babhru *k.* 669.
Babhru (Śiva) *g.* 515.
Babhru *k.* 420.
Bābhravya *b.* 591.
Bābhravya, *b.* 598.
Bactriane c. N. 311.
Badām tr. 26.
Badara *tr.* 27.
Baḍavā *ti.* NW. 368.
Baḍavā *r.* S. ? 368.
Baḍavā-mukha *p.* N. 368, 378, 381.
Badhna *p.* N. 378.
Bag, *Baglā*, *bd.* 58, 59.
Baheṛa tr. 26.
Bāhīka *p.* NW. 311, 313, 318.
Bāhlika *p.*, *see* Vāhlīka.
Bāhu *k.* 371.
Bāhubādha *p.* NW. 317, 375.
Bahubhadra *p.* NW. 317.
Bāhudā *r.* M. 291, 354, 383.
Bāhudā *r.* S. 291.
Bahulā *q.* 420.
Bāhya *p.* M. ? 309.
Baibhāra h. M. 286.
Baidyanāth h. E. 287, 356.
Baijnāth, *see Baidyanāth*.
Bairāt t. M. 288, 307.
Bak bd. 58.
Bakul tr. see Vakula.
Bala *d.* 4, 611.
Bāla *p.* NW. 313, 373.
Bala-bandhu *k.* 449.
Bālabhadra *p.* NW. 317.
Bala-deva, *see* Bala-Rāma.
Bāla-graha *d.* 520.
Balāka *bd.* 86.
Balāka *pr.* 610.
Balākā *r.* C. ? 300, 301.
Balākā *r.* or *t.* N. 375.
Balakāśva *k.* 623.
Bālakhilya *ṛṣis*, 102, 270, 570.
Bala-Rāma *k.* 3, 19, 23, 24, 31.
Balāśva *k.* 623–625.
Balasor dt. E. 327.
Bālhika *p.*, *see* Vāhlīka.
Bali *offering*, 151–153, 178, 253, 254, 259–261, 265, 519.
Bali *k.* 146 (325).
Bali *dg.* 461, 465.
Bālika *p.* NW. 375.
Balin *k.* 627.
Balin *pr.* 610.
Bālin *k.* 333.
Balīna *k.* 329.
Balkh c. N. 311.
Bālu-vāhinī *r.* M. ? 298.
Bālyā ? *pl.* NW. 315.
Banās r. M. 286, 294.
Banavāsi t. S. 364.
Banda t. M. 359.
Bandelkhand dt. M. 288, 336, 354, 359.
Bandhanā *r.* M. ? 294.
Baṅga *p. see* Vaṅga.
Banjāri p. S. 333.
Bankura dt. E. 327.
Bannu dt. NW. 372.
Bansdharā r. SE. 305.
Banthawa h. E. 287.
Banyan tr. 277, 551.
Baradā hills, W. 289.
Barākar r. E. 301.
Barbara *p.* N. 319.
Bardhwān t. and *dt.* 326, 359.
Barhiṣad *pitṛs*, 270, 533.
Bark clothing, 35, 42, 150, 181.
Barley 84, 155, 161, 162, 165, 181, 203, 240, 244, 245.
Baroda t. W. 340.
Barugaza t. W. 339.
Barvara *p.* N. 319.
Bassein t. W. 338.
Bathan-i h. E. 287.
Bauhinia tr. 27, 165.
Bean pt. 84.
Bear, 208.
Bees, 36, 147.
Begun pt. 167.
Bel tr. 25, 425.
Bela pt. 426.
Belgaum t. S. 337.
Bellary t. S. 337.
Bel-phūl pt., *see* Mallikā.
Benāres t. 38, 46, 307, 308, 360, 367, 371, 654; *see* Kāśī *and* Vārāṇasī.
Bengal, 326, 328, 383.
Beni-Israel p. W. 339.
Ber tr., *see* Jujube.

Berār c. 284, 286, 305, 335.
Besaṛh t. M. 329.
Bes-nagar t. M. 343.
Betwa r. M. 295, 343.
Bhadra p. M. 309.
Bhadra r. S. 303.
Bhadrā r. NE. 388.
Bhadrā q. 450.
Bhadra-dvīpa isl. S.? 390
Bhadra-gaura h. E. 357.
Bhadraka p. NW. 316.
Bhadra-kālī gs. 479, 488, 515.
Bhadra-kāra p. M. 309.
Bhādrapadā cst. 381.
Bhadra-somā r. N. 389.
Bhadra-śreṇya k. 371.
Bhadrāśva k. and c. NE. 274, 276, 278, 280, 281, 387, 388.
Bhagadatta k. 8, 9, 319, 328.
Bhāgalpur t. and dt. E. 325, 326.
Bhagīratha k. 280, 281, 551.
Bhāguri pat. 436, 445, 684.
Bhajamāna k. 677.
Bhallātaka tr. 25.
Bhāminī gdh. 646.
Bhananda-na k. 597–599, 604, 607–610.
Bhānukacchra? p. W. 339.
Bharadvāja rs. 31, 310, 320, 435, 462.
Bharadvāja / Bhāradvāja } p. N. 320, 347.
Bharaṇī cst. 170, 384.
Bharata k. 271, 274.
Bharata p. M.? 371.
Bhārata c. 274, 278, 280, 282, 283, 347–349, 387, 688.
Bhārga k. 328.
Bhārga p. E. 328.
Bhārga-bhūmi dt. E. 328.
Bhārgava f. 310, 327, 368, 586, 650 652, 656, 660, 663.
Bhārgava p. E. 327.
Bhārgava k. 328.
Bharuch t. W. 339.
Bhautya, Manu, 271, 539, 546–550.
Bhava g. 268, 269.
Bhava rs. 249.
Bhavācala mt. N. 278.
Bhāvinī prs. 645, 647, 658, 659, 664,
Bhavya k. 272, 273.
Bhavya tr. 24.
Bhavya gods, 454.
Bhela tr. 25.
Bhilsa t. M. 295, 343.
Bhīma (Pāṇḍava) k. 23, 322, 342, 359.
Bhīma (Yādava) k. 352.
Bhīma k. 627.
Bhīma dg. 268.
Bhima r. S. 289, 302, 364.
Bhīmā gs. 518.
Bhīma-rakṣī r. S. 302.
Bhīmarathā, -thī, r. S. 302.
Bhīrukaccha p. W. 339.
Bhīṣma k. 9, 350, 629.
Bhīṣmaka k. 336.
Bhoga-prastha p. N. 319, 377.
Bhoga-vardhana p. S. 337.
Bhoja f. 336, 342.
Bhoja p. W. 342, 371.
Bhoja-nagara t. NW.? 377.
Bhoja-prastha? t. NW.? 377.
Bhojya p. C.? 342.
Bhopāl dt. C. 286.
Bhrāmaṇī gb. 257, 261, 266.
Bhrāmarī gs. 518.
Bhṛgu rs. 19, 31, 63, 219, 224, 246, 249, 269, 310, 462, 595, 600–602, 650, 656.
Bhṛgu demi-gods, 461, 462.
Bhṛgu-bhūmi dt. E.? 328.
Bhṛgu-kaccha p. W. 339, 362.
Bhṛṅga-rāja bd. 28.
Bhubaneswar t. E. 356.
Bhūr 201, 206, 218, 227, 229, 462, 552.
Bhūta gb. 46, 47.
Bhūti rs. 539, 540, 546, 548.
Bhūtilaya pl. NW. 380.
Bhūti-yuvaka p. N. 380.
Bhuvas 206, 227, 261, 552.
Bias r. NW. 291, 292, 311, 315, 318, 321, 347, 382.
Bias r. M. 297.
Bignonia tr. 27.
Bihār c. 286, 325, 329, 382.
Bilva tr. 25, 425.
Bīrbhūm dt. E. 327.
Birds, The, 1-6, 9-12, 16-21, 32, 34-45, 55-65, 216-218, 684, 688.
Blue water-lily, 29, 30, 104, 115.
Boar, 85, 114, 117, 164, 166, 181, 184, 278, 389, 502-504, 514.
Bodha p. M. 309.
Bodha b. 452.
Bodhi p. M. 309.
Body, 15, 23, 66–70, 190.

Bombax tr. 82.
Borassus tr. 27.
Brahmā *g.* 5, 17, 20, 59, 61, 76, 95, 98, 99, 112, 127, 129, 153, 172, 178, 179, 206, 217–220, 223–238, 244–251, 256, 258, 268, 270, 277, 347, 387, 449, 453, 459, 465, 470–474, 482, 494, 502, 509, 521, 524, 529, 530, 535, 536, 545, 550–562, 570, 582, 588, 685.
Brahma-cārin, 149, 160.
Brahma-datta *k.* 350.
Brahma-kṣetra *dt.* 290.
Brahma-loka 89.
Brahma-mitra *rs.* 404.
Brahman *g.* 55, 92, 128, 129, 192, 193, 196, 199–202, 205, 206, 210, 213, 251, 535, 588, 685; *see* Supreme Soul.
Brāhman-hood, 14, 43, 596.
Brahmāṇī *gs.* 502, 504, 509, 513.
Brahmāṇī *r.* E. 301.
Brāhmanī *r.* E. 301.
Brahmanicide, 3, 19, 22, 23, 31, 57, 83, 616, 661, 685, 687.
Brāhman's duties, 148.
Brahma-pura *mt.* N. 383.
Brahma-puraka *p.* NE. 382, 383.
Brahma-putra r. NE. 293, 328, 357, 370.
Brahmarṣi *dt.* M. 307.
Brahmāvarta *dt.* M. 290, 292, 349 377.
Brahminy Duck, 30.
Brahmottara *p.* E. 327.
Braj dt. M. 309.
Briñjal pt. 167.
Broach t. W. 339.
Buddha, 350.
Buddhi (*Intelligence*), 190, 221, 249.
Buddhist, 354, 362, 367.
Budha *dg.* 269, 589, 590.
Budh Gayā t. M. 297.
Buffalo 47, 166–168, 255.
Bull, 255, 256.
Buphus bd. 59.
Burdwān, *see Bardhwān*.
Burning-ground, 38, 39, 46–48, 51, 53, 177, 197, 264.
Buṭ pt. 84.
Butea tr. 28.
Bytarni r. E. 300, 334.

Caccabis bd. 28, 29.
Cāhuka? *p.* N. 324.
Caitra *k.* 415, 466.
Caitra *rs.* 442.
Caitra *pr.* 452, 453.
Caitraratha *for.* 278, 281.
Cajanus pt. 245.
Cakora *bd.* 28, 29.
Cakra-muñja *mt.* N. 278.
Cakravāka *bd.* 30 389, 399, 409 411.
Cakrāvartā *r.* NE. 388.
Cakṣu *r.* N. 323.
Cākṣuṣa, Manu and manvantara, 271, 449, 450, 453, 454, 549.
Cakṣuṣmatī *r.* N.? 293.
Calicut t. S. 331, 338.
Cālimadra? *p.* N. 322.
Calingapatam t. SE. 305.
Cāmara *d.* 476, 479.
Camel, 166, 209, 235, 258.
Campa *k.* 325.
Campā *t.* E. 325.
Campaka *tr.* 26, 326, 364. [524.
Cāmuṇḍā *gs.* 499, 505, 506, 515,
Caṇa *pt.* 84.
Canarese p. S. 363.
Caṇḍa *d.* 494, 495, 497–501.
Caṇḍa *pr.* 610.
Caṇḍakhāra *p.* NW. 374.
Caṇḍāla *caste*, 38, 44–47, 53, 54, 59, 68, 85, 87, 100, 104, 159, 182, 184, 257, 259, 266, 267.
Candanā *r.* M.? 294.
Caṇḍikā *gs.* 465, 473, 476, 480-482, 487, 488, 499–511, 516, 521–523.
Candrabhāgā *r.* NW. 291.
Candrabhāgā *r.* N.? 291.
Candra-dvīpa *isl.* S.? 390.
Candra-kānta *mts.* N. 389.
Candra-vatsa *p.* E.? 357.
Candrāyaṇa *penance*, 564.
Candreśvara *p.* E. 357.
Cānīkaṭa? *p.* W. 338.
Cānimadra? *p.* N. 322.
Cannibalism 357, 679, 683.
Carissa tr. 25.
Carmakhaṇḍika *p.* N. 314, 374.
Carma-maṇḍala *p.* N. 314.
Carmaṇ-vatī *r.* M. 294, 363.
Carma-paṭṭa *t.* S. 365.
Carpophaga bd. 28.
Carpopogon pt. 245.
Carrot pt. 165.
Cāru-dharman *k.* 671.

Cāru-karman *k.* 670.
Cārvavīrat *rs.* 415.
Casarca bd., see Cakravāka.
Castes, duties of, 148–151, 246, 594–597.
Cat, 49, 85, 184, 191, 450.
Cātaka *bd.* 29, 87, 394.
Cāṭṭakhaṇḍika? *p.* N. 314.
Cattle, 74, 80, 83, 182, 235, 238, 255, 587, 598.
Caulya? *p.* S. 332.
Caurya (*Theft*) *pfn.* 265.
Cavery r. S. 303.
Cedi *c.* and *p.* M. 298, 341–344, 350, 359, 371, 665.
Cephalandra pt. 114.
Cereals, 165, 166, 244.
Ceylon 284, 288, 362, 366, 367.
Chakor bd. 28, 29.
Chambal r. M. 286, 295, 345, 351, 359, 363.
Chambeli, Chameli, see Mālatī.
Champā, Champak, tr., see Campaka.
Chanā pt. 84, 165.
Chandas, 554, 555.
Chatak bd. see Cātaka.
Chāyā-Sañjñā *gs.* 456–461, 464, 566–569, 576.
Cheer pheasant, 29.
Chej doab NW. 315, 316.
Chenab r. NW. 291, 311, 313–316.
Chhattīsgaṛh dt. C. 285, 327, 341, 342, 359, 371.
Chicacole t. SE. 305.
Chick-pea pt. 84, 245.
China, 319.
Chinā cer., see Aṇu.
Chinā pt., see Jīra.
China rose, see Javā.
Chingleput dt. S. 332.
Chitrakūṭ mt. M. 296, 363.
Chittar r. S. 304, 367.
Cholera, 519.
Christian, 364, 367.
Chūtia Nāgpur dt. 286, 297, 327, 329, 335, 365.
Cibuka, *p.* N. 378.
Cicer pt. 84, 165.
Cikṣura *d.* 476, 478.
Cīna *p.* NE. 318, 319, 328, 379, 381.
Cīnaka *cer.* 244.
Cintā? *r.* C.? 300.
Cīra-prāvaraṇa? *p.* NE. 384.
Citrā *cst.* 169, 367.
Citra-kūṭa *mt.* M. 296, 359, 363.
Citra-kūṭā *r.* M. 296.
Citra-kūṭaka *p.* S.? 363.
Citron tr. 25.
Citropalā, Citrotpalā *r.* M.? 296.
Citrus tr. 25.
Civiḍa *p.* N. 378.
Civilization, early, 238–246.
Civuka *p.* N. 378.
Coccystes bd. 29, 87, 394.
Cochin t. and *dt.* SW. 303, 367.
Cock, 147, 166, 184.
Cocoanut tr. 24, 69.
Codaka *gb.* 265.
Coḍra? *p.* S. 332.
Coix gr. 245.
Cola *k.* 331.
Cola *p.* S. 287, 331, 332, 363.
Coleroon r. S. 303.
Combat 124, 629, 630, 673.
Comorin, cape, S. 285, 331.
Conjeveram t. S. 332, 367.
Conjugal life, 118, 119, 422, 424, 430, 433, 456.
Constellations, 168–173, 259, 278, 348, 349, 355, 358, 361, 367, 370, 374, 376, 381, 384–389, 443, 447, 535, 626.
Continents, 272–277.
Coorg dt. 364, 366.
Coot bd. 31.
Corpse, 44–50, 183, 184.
Cossye r. E. 301, 327.
Covetousness, 15, 16.
Cranganore t. S. 364.
Creation, 217–225, 228–248, 268.
Creator, 10, 20, 47, 50, 51, 137.
Crime, see *Sin*.
Crocodile, 238.
Crocopus bd. 28, 86, 87.
Crops, care of, 259, 260, 264, 598.
Crow, 47, 72, 76, 85, 86, 147, 208, 258, 263.
Cuckoo 5, 7, 29, 85, 87, 147, 394.
Cuculus bd. 29.
Cucurbita pt. 118.
Culika, Cūlika *p.* N. 322, 323.
Cūlika *p.* W. 374.
Cūlika *dyn.* 374.
Cumin, Cuminum pt. 25.
Curlew bd. 85, 87.
Custom (Ācāra), 2, 107, 170–185, 199, 251–268.

Cuttack t. E. 360.
Cyavana *rs.* 219, 288, 310, 368, 600.
Cynocephali p. 378.
Cyperus gr. 245.

Dāḍima *tr.* 25.
Daitya *p.* and *d.* 9, 10, 22, 23, 58, 100-105, 109, 112-123, 312, 349, 352, 386, 395, 465, 481, 488, 493-511, 514, 515, 518-521, 541, 559, 560, 563, 565, 604-608, 641, 669.
Ḍākinī *gb.* 46.
Dakṣa *dg.* 219, 246-249, 269, 259, 369, 408, 524, 535, 550, 551, 590, 561.
Dakṣiṇā *pfn.* 247, 248.
Dakṣiṇa Kosala, *see* Kosala, Dakṣiṇa.
Dakṣiṇāpatha *c.* S. 331.
Dalbergia tr. 28.
Dālim tr. 25.
Dama *k.* 577, 668-689.
Dāmalipta t., *see* Tāmraliptaka.
Dāmaraka? *p.* NE. 383.
Damayantī *q.* 344.
Damudā r. E. 301.
Dānava *p.* and *d.* 10, 21, 23, 31, 101-105, 113-123, 138, 312, 328, 349, 352, 383, 416, 501-504, 507-509, 517, 518, 541, 559, 560, 563, 565, 581, 605-608, 611, 642, 643, 648.
Dancing, 3, 4, 251.
Daṇḍa *pfn.* 249.
Daṇḍaka *for.* S. 336.
Daṇḍaka *p.* S. 335, 336.
Daṇḍaka *k.* 336.
Dānta *k.* 442.
Dantākṛṣṭi *d.* 257, 262.
Danta-vakra *k.* 341.
Danu *dgs.* 119, 559, 641, 642.
Danuār p. N. 322.
Darada *p.* NW. 311, 312, 318-321, 324, 346, 370, 382.
Darada *k.* 311.
Darbha *gr.* 161, 162.
Dard p. NW. 311.
Dardistān c. NW. 311, 318.
Dardura *mt.* S. 287.
Dāṛim, *tr.* 25.
Darkness (Tamas), *see* Qualities.
Darva, Dārva *p.* NW. 324, 346, 372, 383.
Ḍārvāda? *p.* NE. 383.
Darvī *t.* or *r.* N. 324.
Darvī-saṅkramaṇa *tī.* N. 324.
Daśamālika *p.* NW. 317.
Daśamānika *p.* NW. 318.
Dāsameya, Dāsamīya *p.* NW. 380.
Dasān r. M. 296, 342.
Daśanāmaka *p.* NW. 318.
Daśa-pura, *t.* M. 363.
Dāśapura *p.* M. 363.
Dāsapura? *p.* M. 363.
Daśa-ratha *k.* 464.
Daśārṇa *c.* and *p.* M. 296, 342, 343, 359, 360, 670, 671, 674, 675.
Daśārṇā *r.* M. 296, 298, 342.
Daseraka, Dāseraka *p.* N. 321, 378.
Dāśeraka *p.* N. 321.
Dasra *g.* 460, 575; *see* Asvins.
Dasyu *p.* 312-314, 317-320, 335, 516, 629.
Dattātreya *rs.* 93, 99-109, 187-193, 198, 202, 205, 207, 212, 213, 269.
Dattoli *rs.* 269.
Dattoli *rs.* 415.
Dauhitra, *animal*, 164.
Daurhṛda, Daurhṛta *demons*, 501.
Davada? *p.* NE. 382.
Day, 224-227.
Death g. 47, 51, 207-210, 250; *see* Mṛtyu.
Deeg r. N. 292.
Delhi t. 307, 351, 355.
Deogaṛh t. E. 356.
Dephul tr. 25.
Destiny, 474, 543, 646; *see* Fate.
Deva-dāru *tr.* 27.
Deva-kūṭa *mts.* N. 277, 388.
Deva-śaila *mt.* N. 278.
Devāvṛdha *k.* 294, 669.
Devdār tr. 27.
Devikā *r.* N. 292.
Devikā *r.* S. 292.
Devikā *l*? 292.
Devī-māhātmya, 465-522, 524.
Dhak tr. 28.
Dhanañjaya *k.*, *see* Arjuna (Pāṇḍava).
Dhaniṣṭhā *cst.* 170, 376.
Dhanuṣ-mat *mt.* N. 376.
Dhanvantari *g.* 153.
Dhāraṇā (*mental abstraction*), 194, 196.
Dhāriṇī *ps.* 270.
Dharaṇi-koṭa t. S. 337.
Ḍharitrī *deities*, 178.

Dharma g. 9, 22, 23, 38, 44, 50, 55–57, 90, 122, 246–249, 462, 525.
Dharma, see *Righteousness*.
Dharma-baddha p. NW. 375.
Dharma-dvīpa p. W. 360.
Dharmāraṇya *for*. and p. M. 352.
Dharma-śāstra, 2, 19, 33, 39, 686.
Dhārṣṇaka f. 462.
Dhātaki k. 272.
Dhātṛ g. 10, 153, 269.
Dhātrī gs. 489.
Dhaumra *demons*, 501.
Dhautamūlaka k. 319.
Dhenukākaṭa t. S. 337.
Dheri Shāhan t. NW. 379.
Dhṛṣṇu k. 462.
Dhṛṣṭa k 462, 588.
Dhṛta-rāṣṭra k. 345.
Dhṛti-mat k. and c. 273.
Dhruva pr. 112.
Dhruva k. and c. 273.
Dhūmra-locana d. 497, 498.
Dhūmrāśva k. 600.
Dhūmravatī w. 269.
Dhūrtaka p. W. 369.
Dhūta-pāpā r. M. 291.
Diospyros, various trees, 24–28.
Dīpti-mat rs. 464.
Dīrgha-grīva p. NW. 374.
Dīrgha-tamas rs. 325.
Dissolution of the universe, 218, 219, 224, 227, 229.
Diṣṭa, see Nābhagādiṣṭa.
Diti gs. 102, 508, 559.
Diver bd. 31.
Divodāsa k. 307, 328, 371, 600.
Doab 364, 378.
Dock pt. 25.
Dog, 44, 46, 49, 73, 74, 84, 85, 153, 155, 166, 167, 175, 184, 251.
Dolichos pt. 84, 165.
Drauni ? rs. 464.
Draupadī q. 3, 20, 21, 32, 37; see Kṛṣṇā.
Drāvaṇa p. NW. ? 368.
Drāviḍa c. and p. S. 367, 370.
Dṛḍha-dhanvan k. 439.
Dṛḍha-keśa d. 641, 642, 645.
Dreams, 207–211, 263.
Droṇa b. 1–8, 17, 19 (464).
Droṇi rs. 464.
Droṇī-mukha pl. 241.
Dṛṣadvatī r. M. 290, 292, 354, 377.
Drupada k. 3, 19, 350, 353.
Druhya p. NW. 316.
Druhyu k. 316, 669.
Dubdubi bd. 31.
Duck, 30.
Dud-Kosi r. E. 322.
Duḥsaha d. 246–268.
Dumbur tr. 192.
Dundubhi k. and c. 273.
Dundubhi d. 669.
Dūṅgarpur t. W. 338.
Durbā gr. 262.
Dur-buddhi k. 350.
Dur-dhara d. 480.
Durdura mt. S. 277, 362.
Durga p. W. 338.
Durgā gs. 484, 485, 490, 496, 508, 509, 515.
Durgā r. E. ? 301.
Durgala p. W. 338.
Durgama k. 445, 446.
Durgama d. 518.
Durjayanta mt. W. 288.
Dur-mukha d. 480.
Dururduda ? mt. S. 287.
Durvāsas rs. 2, 5, 99, 100, 269.
Duryodhana k. 23, 24.
Dvaitavana *for*. M. 320.
Dvāpara *age*, 224, 226, 387, 388.
Dvārakā t. W. 24, 289, 340, 349.
Dvāravatī t., see Dvārakā.
Dveṣanī gb. 261.
Dvīpa, *doab*, 364, 378.
Dwārka t. W. 340.
Dyuti-mat rs. 269.
Dyuti-mat k. 272, 273.
Dyuti-mat, Manu, 411–415.
Dyuti-mat k. 595.

Earth, The, 218, 243–245, 271–280, 462, 474.
Earth (element), 217, 221, 222.
Eating, rules of, 170–180.
Ebony tr. 24.
Echites pt. 27.
Edolius bd. 28.
Egg, Mundane, 217, 222–225, 459, 521, 550–553, 556.
Egg-plant, 167.
Ego, 190, 191, 215.
Egret bd. 58, 59.
Eka-cakrā t. NW. ? 382.
Eka-cakrā t. M. 382.
Ekapāda-ka p. NE. 358, 383.
Ekapādapa ? p. NE. 358.

Eka-śṛṅga *mt.* N. 279.
Ekekṣaṇa *p.* NW. 374.
Ekoddiṣṭa *sf.* 185.
Elā *r.* S. 360.
Elements, 217, 220–222, 231, 557.
Elephant, 77, 235, 255, 256, 413, 414, 466, 474, 494, 559.
Elika *p.* SE. 360.
Emancipation from existence, *see Final emancipation.*
Emblica tr. 25, 26.
Energies, goddesses, see Sakti.
Ephthalites p. N. 380.
Eraṇḍā? *r.* C. 296.
Erannoboas r. M. 295.
Ervum pt. 165.
Erythrina tr. 27, 494.
Eṣīka *p.* S. 334.
Ether, 221, 222.
Eudynamis bd., see Kokila.
Eugenia tr. 277.
Eulabes bd. 49.

Fate, 18, 52–54, 70, 73, 83, 123, 127, 178, 258, 263, 474, 662, 680; *see Destiny.*
Fennel pt. 244.
Ferozpur t. NW. 312, 321.
Ficus, trees, 33, 182, 192, 277, 390, 391.
Fig, see Ficus.
Final emancipation from existence, 2, 64, 71, 72, 92, 128, 168, 189–194, 198–202, 205, 206, 210–216, 265, 280, 283, 284, 453, 469, 512, 513, 527, 528, 570, 599, 687.
Fire (element), 222, 581, 582, 608.
Fires, sacred, 82, 128, 159, 160, 176, 178, 206, 391, 397–399.
Flax pt. 85.
Flesh-food, 164, 167, 168, 174, 175, 181, 182, 264, 267, 679, 683.
Flute, 396, 417, 571, 647.
Fœtus, 62, 69, 70, 258, 259, 263–266.
Food (various), 180, 181.
Form (element), 217, 221, 222.
Forms, Divine; Indra's, 21–23; Viṣṇu's, 1, 20, 21; Brahmā's, 224, 225, 229.
Fortress, 240, 241.
Fowl, domestic, 181, 191.
Francolinus bd. 86.
Fruit, wonderful, 389.
Fulica bd. 31.

Gab tr. 25, 26.
Gabala *p.* NW. 314.
Gabhastimat *c.* 284.
Gādhi *k.* 57, 595.
Gajāhvaya *t.* and *p.* M. 355.
Gaja-pura *t.* M. 355.
Gaja-sāhvaya *t.* M. 355.
Gālava *rs.* 109, 112–114, 117, 347, 464.
Gālava *p.* N. 347.
Gallinula bd. 30.
Gaṇa *dg.* 47.
Gaṇapati *dyn.* 365.
Gaṇa-vāhya *p.* E. 365.
Gandak, see Gaṇḍakī.
Gaṇḍakī *r.* M. 292, 294, 329.
Gandhamādana *mts.* N. 277, 278, 281, 287, 310, 381, 602, 670.
Gandhamādana-gāminī? *r.* 305.
Gaṇḍa-prānta-rati *gb.* 257, 259, 263.
Gāndhāra *c.* and *p.* NW. 314, 316, 318, 321, 380.
Gāndhārī, *sound*, 205.
Gāndhārī *pt.* 166.
Gāndhārikā *pt.* 166.
Gandharva *dg.* 55, 68, 78, 103, 113–117, 121, 126, 138, 201, 207, 232, 235, 236, 279, 393–401, 405–408, 413, 481, 495, 497, 511, 541, 559, 571, 581, 608, 619, 641, 645–650, 679, 682.
Gandharva *p.* N. 384.
Gandharva *c.* 284.
Gāndharva *pl.* 246.
Gāndharva *c.* 284.
Gāndharva *marriage*, 671, 672.
Gandholika *pt.* 166.
Gaṅgā, *see* Ganges.
Gangā-chil, gāng-chil bd. 86.
Gaṅgā-hrada *l.* M.? 644.
Ganges 6, 59, 183, 280–282, 290, 303, 319, 320, 369, 493, 590.
Ganjam t. and *dt.* E. 284, 304, 334–337.
Gantu-prastha? *mt.* 288.
Garbhahan-tṛ *gb.* 257, 259, 264.
Garcinia tr. 28.
Garga *rs.* 101–106, 435, 444.
Garhwāl dt. N. 29, 320.
Garlic, pt. 165.
Garo hills E. 306.
Garuḍa, *bird*, 6, 8, 112, 125, 502, 559.
Gāthā, 235, 261.

Gātra *rs.* 270.
Gauḍa *c.* E. 352.
Gauhāṭi t. NE. 306, 331.
Gaur t. E. 326, 352.
Gaura-grīva *p.* M. 352.
Gaurī *gs.* 484, 488, 489.
Gaurī *prs.* 627.
Gautama *rs.* 22, 462, 612.
Gautama *b.* 446.
Gavedhuka *gr.* 245.
Gaya (*son of* Vaivasvata) *k.* 589.
Gaya (*son of* Amūrtarayas) *k.* 329.
Gayā *t.* M. 165, 168, 297, 306, 330, 352, 589.
Gayāl, bt. 164, 590, 592.
Geography, 271–384, 387–391.
Geyamālava *p.* E. 328.
Geyamarthaka *p.* E. 328.
Ghaggar r. N. 291.
Ghāṭs mts. E. *and* W. 284, 285.
Ghogra r. M. 376.
Ghora-ka *p.* W. 373.
Ghoṣa *p.* NE. 383.
Ghoṣa (*village*), 241, 242.
Ghoṣa-saṅkhya *p.* M. 351, 383.
Ghṛtācī *aps.* 4, 571.
Ghṛtācī *w.* 600.
Ghuṇa-kīṭaka, *insect,* 87.
Ginger, 166.
Giri-bhadrā *q.* 452.
Giri-vraja *t.* NW. 318.
Giri-vraja *t.* E. 330.
Girjak t. NW. 318.
Girnar h. W. 288, 289.
Giryek t. E. 330.
Goa t. SW. 362–364.
Goat, 147, 164, 182, 235, 255.
Goblins, 250–268, 533, 545.
Godāvarī *r.* S. 284, 286, 302, 305, 310, 336.
Godhā, *reptile,* 181.
Godhana *mt.* M.? 290.
Golāṅgula *p.* S. 331, 364.
Gomal r. NW. 291.
Gomanta *mt.* N. 289.
Gomanta *mt.* W. 289, 364.
Gomanta *p.* E. 330, 331.
Gomatī *r.* M. 134, 291, 306, 316, 623.
Gomatī *r.* NW. 291.
Gonarda *p.* S. 363.
Gonarddha *p.* S. 331, 363.
Goṇḍwāna c. C. 284, 286, 305.
Goodness (Sattva), *see Qualities.*
Goomti r. M. 291.
Goose, 30, 147, 409, 410.
Gopācala *mt.* M. 289.
Gopa-giri *mt.* M. 289.
Go-sāṁp, reptile, 181.
Gotama *rs.* 31.
Gourd pt. 118.
Govardhana *mt.* M. 290, 310.
Govardhana *t.* W. 310.
Govinda *g.* 112; *see* Viṣṇu.
Govinda *p.* E. 331.
Gracula bd. 49.
Grāhaka *gb.* 265.
Gram pt. 84, 165, 244.
Grāma (*village*), 241, 242.
Grāma (*music*), 131.
Grāma-rāga (*music*), 130.
Grasshopper, 147.
Grebe bd. 31.
Greek, 284, 314.
Gṛhastha, 149–156, 186.
Gṛñjana *pt.* 165.
Guava tr. 25.
Guḍa *p.* M. 352.
Guḍuha *p.* M. 373.
Guha *g.* 502.
Guha *k.* 361.
Guhya *dg.* 178.
Guhyaka *dg.* 370, 461, 530, 576, 641, 648.
Gujarāt c. W. 24, 28, 29, 286, 313, 338–342, 368, 373.
Gulaha, Guluha *p.* M. 373.
Gurgaṇa *p.* N. 345.
Gurjara *p.* NW. 373.
Gurkha p. N. 345.
Guruha *p.* W. 373.
Guru-nadī *r.* W. 373.
Gurung p. N. 346.
Guru-sthala? *p.* NW. 373.
Guru-svara? *p.* NW. 373.
Guru-viśāla *for.* E. 581.
Gwalior t. M. 289.

Hāhā *dg.* 571.
Haidarābād t. S. 366.
Haihaya *k.* 371.
Haihaya, *p.* M., C. and W. 99, 107, 344, 351, 371.
Haima *mt.* N. 322.
Haimagirika *p.* NW. 369.
Haimakūṭa *p.* SE. 360.
Haimanta-giri *mt.* N.? 306.
Haiminī *q.* 452.

Hakra r. N. 291.
Hālār dt. W. 289.
Halāyudha *k.* 3, 19, 24; *see* Bala-Rāma.
Haṁsa *bd.* 30.
Haṁsakāyana *p.* N. ? 323.
Haṁsa-mārga *p.* N. 323, 345.
Haṁsa-nābha *mt.* N. 279.
Haṁsa-pada *p.* N. ? 323.
Hanta, 151, 152, 179.
Hanū-mat, *monkey*, 289, 346, 367.
Hara *g.* 482, 483.
Hāra-bhūṣika *p.* NW. 317.
Hāra-hūṇa *p.* NW. 317, 380.
Hāra-mūrtika *p.* NW. 317.
Hāra-pūrika *p.* NW. 317.
Hare, 164, 181, 235.
Hari *g.* 55, 91, 389, 469–472, 483, 502, 562.
Hari *gods*, 442.
Hārika *p.* SE. 360.
Hari-parvata *mts.* NW. 388.
Hariścandra *k.* 32–61.
Harita *k.* and *c.* 273.
Hārīta *bd.* 28, 86, 87.
Harītaka *tr.* 26.
Haritāśva *k.* 589.
Hari-varṣa *c.* N. 345, 390.
Harṣa-vardhana *p.* N. 319.
Hary-aśva *k.* 371.
Hasdu r. C. 295, 298.
Hasta *cst.* 169, 367.
Hastin *k.* 355.
Hastinā-pura } *t.* M. 307, 351, 355.
Hāstina-pura }
Haviḥ-saṁsthā *sf.* 128.
Havir-varṣa *k.* and *c.* 273.
Haviṣ-mat *rs.* 454.
Hawk, 182, 208, 263.
Hayu p. N. 322.
Hazāribāgh dt. C. 285.
Hedysarum pt. 166, 245.
Hell, 7, 62, 68, 71–91, 101, 107, 149, 280, 485, 622, 661, 662, 687.
Hema-dharma *k.* 627.
Hema-giri ? *mt.* W. 369.
Hema-kūṭa *mts.* N. 275–277.
Hema-kūṭa *mt.* N. 360, 369, 370, 383.
Hema-kūṭa *mt.* SE. 360.
Hema-śṛṅga *mt.* N. 369, 370.
Hema-tāraka ? *p.* N. 380.
Hemp pt. 245.
Herodias bd. 59.
Heron bd. 49, 58–61, 72, 85, 86.
Hestho r. C. 295.
Hibiscus tr. 553.
Hima *mt.*=Himavat
Himālaya mts., *see* Himavat.
Hima-vat *mts.* 5, 28, 29, 127, 132, 249, 275–283, 287, 293, 345, 347, 369, 376, 391–396, 475, 488, 489, 494, 518, 598, 655, 669, 670.
Hiṁsā *pfn.* 250.
Hiṅga *p.* NE. 384.
Hiraṇ-maya *c.* N. 390, 391.
Hiraṇ-vatī *r.* N. 391.
Hiraṇya *k.* and *c.* 273.
Hiraṇya-bāhu *r.* M. 295.
Hiraṇya-garbha *g.* 220, 226.
Hiraṇya-kaśipu *k.* 146.
Hiraṇya-loman *rs.* 449.
Hiraṇya-śṛṅga *mt.* N. ? 369.
Hiraṇya-vāha *r.* M. 295.
Hire, see Wages.
Hog, see Boar.
Hog-plum tr. 23.
Homa, 87, 94, 150, 172, 184, 256, 386.
Honey-sucker bd. 80.
Hoopoe bd. 80.
Horn article, 87.
Horse, 182, 183, 235, 255, 278, 388, 457, 460, 567, 573, 575.
Horse-sacrifice, 41, 89, 616, 685.
House, ancient, 239–243.
Hrada ? *p.* NW. 316.
Huhu *dg.* 571.
Hun p. 379.
Hūṇa *p.* N. 315, 375, 379.
Hun-des c. NW. 324, 380.
Hydaspes r. NW. 291.
Hydraotes r. NW. 291.
Hymns, see Gāthā.
Hyphasis r. NW. 291, 292.

Ichneumon, 210.
Ikṣu ? *r.* N. 292.
Ikṣu *r.* E. ? 304.
Ikṣudā *r.* E. 304.
Ikṣukā *r.* E. 304.
Ikṣulā *r.* E. 304.
Ikṣvāku *k.* 462, 551, 588, 617.
Ikṣvāku (*son of* Kṣupa) *k.* 618.
Ilā *prs.* 327, 587–589.
Ilā *demi-goddess*, 559.
Ilāvṛta *k.* and *c.* N. 273, 276, 277, 390.

Illusion, see Mahā-māyā.
Impurities, 172–185.
Incarnations, 23; Indra's, 12–14, 23; Viṣṇu's, 21; Daityas' 22, 23.
India, see Bhārata.
Indigo pt. 25.
Indigofera pt. 25.
Indīvara *pt.* 29.
Indīvara *dg.* 401–404, 411.
Indra *g.* 4, 8–15, 21–23, 38, 40, 50, 55–57, 68, 75, 90, 97, 102, 109, 129, 147, 153, 227, 276, 415, 420, 436, 437, 442, 454, 461, 462, 473, 474, 496, 502–505, 509, 512, 514, 524–526, 532, 535, 545, 549, 550, 562, 565, 570, 604, 611, 619, 623, 641, 648, 652–655, 669, 673, 680, 687.
Indra-dāsa *m.* 678.
Indra-dvīpa *c.* 283.
Indra-prastha *t.* M. 307, 316, 351, 355.
Indra-senā *q.* 669, 674–678, 681.
Indus r. 291, 293, 312, 315, 318, 322, 324, 345, 376, 377, 380.
Infanticide, 32.
Iṅguda *tr.* 26.
Intelligence (Buddhi), 15, 16, 221, 231.
Intoxication, 24, 31, 133, 146, 600, 602.
Irā *demi-gs.* 559.
Irāvatī *r.* NW. 291, 316.
Īśāna *dg.* 268.
Israel 339.

Jack tree, 25.
Jackal, 46, 47, 53, 67, 85, 183, 208.
Jaḍa *b.* 62, 69, 71, 76, 83, 91, 107–110, 127, 130–145, 186–190, 211.
Jagad-dhātrī *gs.* 127.
Jāguḍa *p.* N. 322.
Jahnu *k.* 303.
Jaimineya *b.* 684.
Jaimini *rs.* 1–4, 17–21, 38, 62, 217, 219, 684, 685, 688.
Jain, 354, 367.
Jalada *k.* and *c.* 273.
Jala-kukkuṭa *bd.* 30.
Jalālpur t. NW. 318.
Jalandhar doab N. 347.
Jamadagni *rs.* 310, 462, 595, 656.
Jāmadagnya *pat.*, see Paraśu-Rāma.
Jāmadagnya *dt.* W. 338.
Jambha *d.* 102, 103, 611, 677.
Jambu *tr.* 277, 391.
Jambū *r.* N. 278.
Jambu-dvīpa, 271–283.
Jambulā *r.* M.? 297.
Jambu-mat *mt.* 356.
Jambū-mūla *c.* N. 278.
Jāmbunada *l.* 653.
Jāmbūnada *gold*, 278.
Jambv-ākhya *h.* E. 356.
Janaka *k.* 330.
Janaka *f.* 75, 374.
Janakpur t. N. 330.
Jana-loka, 227, 229, 553.
Janamejaya *k.* 350.
Janamejaya *k.* 379.
Janārdana, 2, 5, 19, 349, 388, 470, 472; *see* Kṛṣṇa *and* Viṣṇu.
Janasthāna *dt.* 302.
Jāṅgala *p.* M. 309.
Jāṅgala? *p.* N. 322.
Jaṅgha *k.* 442.
Jānu *k.* 442.
Jar and well-rope, 70–73, 91.
Jarāsandha *k.* 341.
Jaritāri *b.* 8.
Jartika *p.* NW. 313.
Jārudhi *mt.* N. 277, 279.
Jasmine pt. 27, 152.
Jasminum pt. 24–27, 152, 425, 426.
Jaṭādhara? *p.* S. 364.
Jāta-hāriṇī *gb.* 266, 450, 451.
Jaṭhara *mts.* N. 277.
Jātī *pt.* 27, 152.
Jausi *f.* 352.
Javā *tr.* 553.
Jayadratha *k.* 315.
Jayanta *mts.* NW. 388.
Jew, 339, 364, 367.
Jhelam r. NW. 291, 315, 318, 324.
Jīmūta *k.* and *c.* 273.
Jīra *pt.* 25.
Jīvajīva-ka *bd.* 28, 87.
Jīvañjīva *bd.* 28, 87.
Jñeyamallaka *p.* E. 328.
Johila r. C. 296.
Jonesia tr. 25, 26, 364.
Juguḍa *p.* N. 322.
Jujube tr. 27.
Jumna r. M.; *see* Yamunā.
Jumna r. E. 297.
Junāgaḍh t. W. 288.
Jupiter, *planet*, 246, 431, 626.

Jyeṣṭhā *cst.* 169, 374.
Jyeṣṭha-sāman, 159.
Jyotīrathā, -thyā, *r.* C. 295, 296.
Jyotir-dhāman *rs.* 442.
Jyotiṣika *p.* M. 352.
Jyotiṣ-mat *k.* 272, 273.

Kābul r. NW. 291, 314.
Kaccha *dt.* W. 303, 340.
Kaccha *dt.* S. 367.
Kacchapa *dg.* 416, 417.
Kacchika *p.* W. 340.
Kacchvīya *p.* W. 340.
Kachh dt. W. 312, 340, 349, 355.
Kadam tr., *see* Kadamba.
Kadamba *tr.* 25, 277, 565.
Kadambā *q.* 446.
Kādamba *bd.* 30.
Kadru *demi-gs.* 559.
Kadu pt. 118, 166.
Kāfiristān c. NW. 318, 321.
Kahlāra *pt.* 30.
Kaikaya *p.*=Kaikeya.
Kaikeya *k.* 317.
Kaikeya *p.* NW. 316–318, 345, 377, 382, 665.
Kaikeyī *q.* 76.
Kailāsa *mt.* N. 6, 132, 277, 279, 287, 322, 345, 351, 370, 376, 382, 402, 669.
Kairāta *p.* N. 379.
Kaiṣkindhya *p.* C. 342, 360.
Kaiṭabha *d.* 465, 469–472, 484, 519.
Kāka-jaṅgha *gb.* 266.
Kākulālaka *p.* SE. 360, 361.
Kala *p.* W. 369, 374.
Kāla, *see Fate.*
Kāla *pt.* 168.
Kāla *d.* 480.
Kalaha *gb.* 262.
Kala-haṁsa *bd.* 30.
Kāla-jihva *gb.* 262.
Kālājina *p.* C. ? 362.
Kālajoṣaka *p.* NW. 313.
Kālaka *demons*, 501.
Kālakeya *demons*, 501.
Kālakoṭī *ti.* M. 354.
Kālakoṭisa *p.* M. 354.
Kālakūṭa *ti.* M.? 354.
Kalama *pt.* 84.
Kālañjara *p.* M. 354.
Kāla-śāka *pt.* 164.
Kala-titar bd. 86.
Kālatoyaka *p.* NW. 312, 313.
Kalāvatī *w.* 402, 406-408, 411, 412.
Kalāya *pt.* 84.
Kali *d.* 257.
Kali *dg.* 398-401.
Kali *age*, 224, 226, 387, 388.
Kālī *gs.* 499-509.
Kālibala *p.* W. 338, 369.
Kālikā *gs.* 494.
Kalinda *mt.* N. 461, 576.
Kālindī *q.* 445.
Kaliṅga *c.* and *p.* SE. 325–327, 333, 334, 358, 359.
Kaliṅga *k.* 325.
Kaliṅga ? *p.* M. 308, 316, 354.
Kaliṅga ? *p.* NW. 316.
Kaliṅga *mt.* N. 279.
Kāliṅga=Kaliṅga *p.* SE.
Kāliṅgaka *p.* C. 354.
Kaliṅga-nagara *t.* M. 316.
Kaliñjar h. M. 354.
Kali Sindh r. M. 293.
Kālītaka *p.* W. 338.
Kalmāṣapāda *k.* 336.
Kalpa (*Age*), 228, 229, 235–238, 268.
Kalpa (*Tree*), 239, 243.
Kalpa ? *pl.* 315.
Kalwan t. W. 338.
Kalyāni t. S. 289, 333.
Kāma *g.* 115, 132, 249.
Kamala *pt.* 30.
Kāmaraṅga *tr.* 24.
Kāmarūpa *c.* NE. 306, 331, 411, 577, 581.
Kāma-śāstra, 2.
Kambala *k.* 125, 130–133.
Kambala *mts.* NW. 388.
Kāmboja *c.* and *p.* NW. 311, 318, 319, 350, 368, 371.
Kambū *demons*, 501.
Kambunāyaka ? *p.* S. 366.
Kāminī *r.* NW. 389.
Kampil t. M. 350, 353.
Kāmpilya *t.* M. 350, 353, 598.
Kāmrūp dt. NE. 331.
Kaṁsa *k.* 352.
Kaṁsavatī ? *r.* E. 301.
Kanak-champa tr. 27.
Kanara dt. S. 364.
Kanauj t. M. 292, 307.
Kañcanākṣī *r.* M. 290, 306.
Kāñcī *t.* S. 332, 367.
Kāñcipuram t. S. 367.
Kāñcivaram t. S. 367.

Kāñcya? *p.* S. 367.
Kandahar t. NW. 374.
Kandhara *bd.* 6–8.
Kangra dt. NW. 347.
Kanhar r. C. 297.
Kaṅka *p.* M. 353.
Kaṅka *p.* N. 353.
Kaṅka *bd.* 6, 7.
Kaṅkella *tr.* 25.
Kaṅkola *tr.* 25.
Kaṇṭakāra? *p.* NW. 317.
Kāṇṭhāl tr. 25.
Kanyakāguṇa? *p.* NW. 375.
Kānyakubja *t.* M. 307, 353, 595.
Kaorhari r. C. 285.
Kapila *rs.* 120.
Kapila *mt.* N. 279.
Kāpila *k.* and *c.* 273.
Kapilendra *mt.* N. 279.
Kapili r. NE. 306.
Kāpiṅgala *p.* M. 354.
Kapiñjalā *r.* 354.
Kapiśā *r.* E. 301, 327.
Kapotaka, Nāga *k.* 431.
Karabhā *r.* E. 301.
Karāḍ t. S. 362.
Karahākaḍa *t.* S. 362.
Karahākaṭa *t.* S. 362.
Karahāṭaka *t.* S. 362.
Karāla *d.* 479.
Kāramār mt. NW. 290.
Karamarda *tr.* 26.
Karambha *pt.* 165.
Karambha-bālukā *pl.* 83.
Karambhaka? *p.* NW. 388.
Karamcha tr. 26.
Karamnāsa r. M. 297.
Karamodā *r.* M. 296.
Karaṇḍa *bd.* 30.
Kāraṇḍava *bd.* 30.
Karandbama *k.* 622–625, 631–644, 649–653.
Karandhama *k.* 653.
Kārandhama *pat.* 625.
Kāraskara *p.* W. 339.
Karatoyā *r.* NE. 290, 293, 383.
Karatoyā *r.* C. 290, 294.
Karatoyā *r.* E. 301.
Karatoyā? *r.* N. 296.
Karavīra-pura *t.* W. 289.
Karbuka *p.* E. 356.
Kardama *rs.* 270, 272.
Kardo bd. 30.
Kar-hāṁs bd. 30, 409, 410.
Karkaśā *aps.* 4.
Karki r. N. 322.
Karkoṭaka *for.* S. 362.
Karkoṭaka *k.* 362.
Karma, *doctrine of,* 10, 57, 62, 67–71, 77, 78, 87–90, 193–233, 282, 283, 528, 592.
Karma-nāśā *r.* M. 287, 296.
Karma-nāyaka *p.* S. 366.
Karma-nodā? *r.* M. 296.
Karṇa *k.* 368, 369, 629.
Karṇaprādheya *p.* W. 368.
Karṇa-prāvaraṇa *p.* N. 346, 369.
Karṇāṭa *c.* and *p.* S. 363.
Karṇāṭaka *p.* S. 363.
Karṇavatī *r.* M. 297.
Karṇikāra *tr.* 27.
Karnul dt. S. 366.
Kārtavīrya *k., see* Arjuna.
Kārttikeya *g.* 524, 574.
Kāru *mt.* 290.
Karūṣa *k.* 341.
Karūṣa *k.* 463, 588, 593.
Karūṣa } *p.* C. 309, 334, 341, 359,
Kārūṣa } 366, 463, 593.
Kāruṣaka *p.*=Kārūṣa.
Karvaṭa *c.* or *t.* E. 356.
Karvaṭa-ka (*town*), 241.
Karvaṭaśana *h.* E. 356.
Kaśāya? *p.* E. 357.
Kaseruka *p.* N. 321.
Kaserukmat *c.* 283.
Kaśerumat, Kaśerūmat *c.* 283.
Kasetu *c.* 283.
Kashgar c. N. 318.
Kāśī *t.* M. (=*Benares*), 187–190, 207, 211–216, 308, 329, 341, 357, 359, 367, 371, 600.
Kāśi *p.* M. 357, 367.
Kāśikā *r.* 305.
Kāśmīra *c.* and *p.* NW. 312, 318, 319, 322, 323, 340, 370, 382.
Kaṣṭa-haraṇa-parvata? *pl.* E. 325.
Kāśya *p.* M. 367.
Kaśyapa *dg.* 178, 461, 535, 550–552, 559–565.
Kāśyapa *rs.* and *f.* 462, 465, 612.
Kaṭaka t. SE. 360.
Kaṭaka-sthala *p.* SE. 360.
Katamālā *r.* S. 303.
Kathæi p. NW. 313.
Kaṭhākṣara *p.* W. 339.
Kāthi p. NW. 313.
Kāthiāwāṛ dt. W. 313, 338, 340, 344, 373.

Kātyāyanī *gs*. 503, 512, 515.
Kaurañja *mt*. NE. 388.
Kaurava *pat*., *race*, 6–9, 23, 24, 37, 360, 378, 567.
Kauruṣa *p*. S. 366.
Kauśāmba *c*. M. 307.
Kauśāmbi *t*. M. 307.
Kauśika *pat*. 34, 37, 43, 44, 50, 61, 93, 462.
Kauśika *p*. NE. 383.
Kauśikā *r*.=Kauśikī.
Kauśikī *r*. NE. 292, 293, 329, 369, 383, 595.
Kauśikī *gs*. 494.
Kāverī *r*. 285, 290, 303, 364, 366.
Kāverī *q*. 446.
Kāvya *rs*. 442.
Kawa Kol mts. E. 286.
Kāyana? *r*. M. 297.
Kekaya *p*.=Kaikeya.
Kekaya *k*. 665.
Kekayī *q*. 665.
Ken r. M. 288, 297, 341, 359.
Keora, *shrub*, 26.
Kerala *k*. 331.
Kerala *p*. S. 331, 332.
Kerala *p*. C. 341.
Kerra bd. 30.
Keśava *g*. 472; *see* Viṣṇu.
Ketakī *pt*. 7, 26.
Ketu *mt*. 290.
Ketumāla *k*. and *c*. NW. 274–278, 282, 387–389.
Ketumat *k*. and *c*. 273.
Ketu-vīrya *k*. 665.
Kevala? *p*. S. 331.
Khambu p. N. 322.
Khāṇḍava-prastha *t*. M. 355
Khāndesh dt. W. 288.
Khanīnetra *k*. 619–624.
Khanitra *k*. 610–617.
Khañjana *h*. NW. 370.
Kharakpur hills E. 356.
Kharapatha *c*. N. 380.
Kharasāgararāśi? *p*. N. 380.
Kharmaka *h*. E. 356.
Khas p. N. 346.
Khaśa *p*. N. 346, 350, 351, 357, 383.
Khasa *p*. N. 346, 382.
Khasā *demi-gs*. 559.
Khāsi hills E. 306.
Khas-khas gr. 79.
Khaṭvāṅgī *r*. S. 364.
Kheṭaka (*town*), 241.
Khichree, 168, 174.
Khyāti *w*. 249, 269.
Kīcaka *c*. NE. 381.
Kīcaka *p*. M. 382.
Kīcaka *m*. 382.
Kīkaṭa *c*. E. 331, 382.
Kimpuruṣa *k*. and *c*. N. 273, 274, 282, 381, 390.
Kimpuruṣa *k*. 415.
Kiṁśuka *tr*. 28.
King, *his duties*, 144–148, 157, 656, 657, 666.
King-crow bd. 28.
Kiṅkara? *p*. N. 381.
Kinnara *p*. N. *and* E. 116, 117, 236, 279, 381, 393–397, 647.
Kirānti p. N. 322.
Kirāta *p*. and *c*., N. *and* E. 284, 307, 316, 322, 323, 328, 346, 347, 369, 379, 381, 383.
Kirati p. N. 322.
Kisadya *p*. M. 307.
Kisaṣṇa *p*. M. 307.
Kisaṣṭa *p*. M. 307.
Kiskindhaka *p*. C. 342, 360.
Kiṣkindhyā *c*. S. 342.
Kistna r. S. 302, 303, 365.
Kite bd. 86.
Kiyān r. M. 297.
Kiyul r. E. 285.
Kochchi t. S. 367.
Koḍagu dt. S. 364.
Kodo cer. 244.
Koduṅgalūr t. S. 364.
Kohalaka *p*. N. 380.
Koīl bd., *see* Kokila.
Kokanada *p*. NW. 372, 380.
Kokanada *pt*. 30.
Kokaṅkaṇa *p*. NW. 372.
Kokaraka *p*. NW. 372, 380.
Kokila *bd*. 28, 394, 399, 407.
Kol p. C. 364, 365, 466.
Kola *k*. 331.
Kola *p*. C. 331, 332, 363, 365.
Kola *p*. 466.
Kolagira *p*. S. 363, 365.
Kolagiri *dt*. S. 364.
Kolāhala *mt*. C. 286, 359.
Kolavana *p*. W. 338.
Kolla h. M. 290.
Kolūka, Kolūta *c*. N. 375, 382.
Kolvagireya *p*. S. 363.
Kombunāyaka? *p*. S. 366.
Koṅc-baḳ bd. 86.

Konkan dt. S. 362.
Koṅkana *p.* S. 362.
Koṇva *mt.* 290.
Kophēn r. NW. 291.
Kora *mt.* 290.
Koradūṣa *cer.* 244.
Korava, tribe S. 332.
Kosala, Dakṣiṇa or Mahā-, *c.* C. 299, 308, 334, 342, 358, 359, 371.
Kosala, Uttara, *c.* M. 294, 308, 342, 352, 353, 358.
Kosalā *t.* M. 57.
Kosam t. M. 307.
Kosi r. NE. 292, 329, 383, 595.
Kovidāra *tr.* 27, 165.
Krakara *bd.* 86.
Krama *pr.* 610.
Kratu *rs.* 246, 249, 270.
Krauñca *mt.* N. 288, 376.
Krauñca *p.* N. 376.
Krauñca-dvīpa 272–275.
Krauñca-dvīpa *dt.* S. 364.
Krauñcālaya *for.* S. 364.
Krauñca-pura *t.* S. 364.
Krauṣṭuki *b.* 217, *and passim* 224–237, 263–283, 348, 358, 391, 415–419, 436, 463, 550, 552, 587, 653, 665, 684.
Kravyāda, *caste*, 182.
Krodhā *demi-gs.* 559.
Kṛpa *rs.* 464.
Kṛpā *r.* 306.
Kṛpāvatī *prs.* 602.
Kṛṣṇa *k.* and *g.* 23, 24, 50, 55, 308, 328, 340, 342, 349–352, 361, 383, 474.
Kṛṣṇa *mt.* N. 279.
Kṛṣṇa *mts.* NW. 388.
Kṛṣṇa Dvaipāyana *rs.* 677.
Kṛṣṇā *r.* S. 290, 302, 365, 366.
Kṛṣṇā *gs.* 490, 494.
Kṛṣṇā *q.* (=Draupadī) 3, 19, 23.
Kṛṣṇā-dvīpa *dt.* S. 365.
Kṛṣṇa-veṇā *r.* C. 300.
Kṛta *Age*, 224, 226, 272, 347, 387, 388, 437.
Kṛtamālā *r.* S. 303.
Kṛtasmara *mt.* NW.? 290.
Kṛtavīrya *k.* 101, 106.
Kṛti *k.* 39.
Kṛtraka? *p.* N. 347.
Kṛttika *cst.* 169, 355.
Kṛtyā *r.* 306.
Krumu *r.* NW. 298.
Kṣamā *w.* 249, 270.
Kṣānti *k.* 442.
Kṣatodara? *p.* N. 320.
Kṣatriya *caste*, 36, 317–319, 323, 336, 350, 351, 370, 380, 594–596, 671, 672.
Kṣatriya *virtue*, 124, 144, 145, 148, 188, 212, 246, 442, 591, 596–601, 627–634, 642, 663, 671, 672, 677.
Kṣemadhūrta? *p.* N. 381.
Kṣemadhūrti *k.* 381.
Kṣemaka *k.* and *c.* 273.
Kṣetra-jña, 220, 223; *see* Puruṣa.
Kṣiprā *r.* W.? 299.
Kṣiprā *r.* 306.
Kṣudraka *p.* M. 377.
Kṣudravīṇa? *p.* N. 377.
Kṣupa (*son of* Brahmā) *k.* 617, 618.
Kṣupa (*son of* Khanitra) *k.* 615–618.
Kṣurādri *h.* NW. 370.
Kubhā *r.* NW. 291.
Kuca-harā *gb.* 266.
Kuhu *r.* NW.? 291.
Kuhaka *p.* N. 324.
Kuhu *p.* NW. 324.
Kuhuka? *p.* N. 324.
Kujṛmbha *d.* 604–609.
Kukkuṭa *mt.* N. 279.
Kukṣi *prs.* 272.
Kul tr. 27.
Kulaṭa, Kulati *p.* NE. 382.
Kulattha *pt.* 84, 244, 245.
Kulattha *p.* N. 375.
Kulinda *p.* N. 316, 317, 323.
Kuliṅga *p.* N.? 316
Kulīra *mt.* N. 278.
Kulīya *p.* W. 338.
Kulu dt. N. 316, 382.
Kulūta *c.* N. 375, 381, 382.
Kulya *p.* N. 307.
Kulya *p.* S. 331, 332.
Kulya (*semi-divine race*?) 559.
Kumana *p.* S. 332.
Kumaon dt. N. 29, 286, 320.
Kumāra *k.* and *c.* 273.
Kumāra *g.* 502–505, 509, 514.
Kumāra *dg.* 232.
Kumārī *r.* C. 285.
Kumārī *r.* 305.
Kumud *pt.* 29.
Kumuda *mt.* W.? 332, 365, 445.
Kumud-vatī *r.* E.? 300.
Kumud-vatī *prs.* 627.

Kūṇa? *p.* NW.? 315.
Kuṇaha? *p.* NW.? 375.
Kuṇapa *p.* NW.? 375.
Kuṇḍalā *w.* 113, 116–118, 120.
Kuṇḍikera? *p.* C.? 371.
Kuṇḍina *t.* C. 336, 673.
Kunet p. N. 316.
Kuninda? *p.* N. 316.
Kuñjara *h.* S. 367.
Kuñjara-darī *pl.* S. 367.
Kuntala *p.* S. 308, 337.
Kuntala *p.* M. 308.
Kuntala *p.* W.? 308.
Kuntaprāvaraṇa *p.* N. 346.
Kunti *bd.* 6.
Kuntī *q.* 23.
Kuntila *dt.* M. 308.
Kunyatālaḍaha? *p.* NW. 375.
Kūpā *r.* 306.
Kupatha *p.* S. 332.
Kuram r. NW. 298.
Kurattee r. E. 294, 383.
Kurnool dt. S. 290.
Kurru tribe, S. 332.
Kuru *k.* and *c.* 274.
Kuru *k.* 354, 355, 461, 567, 652, 677.
Kuru *f.*, see Kaurava.
Kuru *p.* M. 308, 309, 333, 345–349, 353–355, 359, 377.
Kuru, Uttara (*Northern*), *p.* N. 282, 345, 376, 387–390, 457–460, 567, 575.
Kuruba *p.* S. 332.
Kuru-jāṅgala *dt.* M. 309, 354.
Kuru-kṣetra *dt.* M. 8, 293, 307, 354, 378, 655.
Kurumba *p.* S. 332.
Kurumin *p.* W. 339.
Kururvāhya? *p.* M. 354.
Kuruṭa *p.* N. 382, 383.
Kuruvinda *gr.* 245.
Kuśa *k.* 352.
Kuśa *k.* 328, 330.
Kuśa *gr.* 31, 67, 118, 161, 258.
Kuśa-dvīpa, 272–275.
Kuśala *k.* and *c.* 273.
Kuśa-sthalī *t.* (=Dvārakā), 289.
Kuśāvartta *b.* 612.
Kuśeruka *p.* N. 321.
Kuśika *rs.* 31, 45, 60, 61.
Kuṣmāṇḍa *gb.* 262.
Kuśottara *k.* and *c.* 273.
Kusuma *p.* S. 332, 366.
Kūṭa-śaila *mt.* 290.
Kutch dt. W., see *Kachh.*
Kuthaprāvaraṇa *p.* N. 346.
Kuvalaya *pt.* 29.
Kuvalaya, *horse*, 109, 113.
Kuvalayāśva *k.* 109–127, 133–142, 145, 186.
Kuvera *g.* 6–10, 460, 474, 475, 489, 494, 531, 562, 574, 638, 680.
Kyah partridge, 86.

Laḍaha *p.* NW. 375.
Laḍaka? *p.* NW. 375.
Lagenaria, pt. 118.
Lag-Goose, 30, 409, 410.
Lajjā? *r.* M.? 297.
Lakuca *tr.* 25.
Lakṣmī *gs.* (=Srī), 101–105, 249, 255, 269, 416, 419, 515, 522, 638.
Lalittha *p.* NW. 374.
Lambādi p. S. 333.
Lambagæ p. NW. 321.
Lambana *k.* and *c.* 273.
Lamghān dt. NW. 321.
Lampāka *c.* NW. 321.
Lāmūlinī *r.* E. 305.
Lāṅgalī *r.* E.? 305.
Lāṅgūlinī *r.* E. 305.
Lanius bd. 28.
Laṅkā *t.* S. 346, 362.
Lapis lazuli, 366.
Lapwing bd. 394.
Laśa *pr.* 670.
Laśuna *pt.* 165.
Lāu pt. 118.
Lauhi *b.* 357.
Lauhita *f.* 357.
Lauhitya *r.* NE. 357, 370.
Lauhitya *c.* NE. 357.
Lava *k.* 352.
Lavaṇa *k.* 352.
Laya (*music*), 131.
Lekha *gods*, 454.
Lentil pt. 165.
Lepa-bhuja *pitṛs*, 157, 158.
Leprosy, 443.
Light (*element*), 128, 129, 217, 221, 230.
Līka *d.* 266, 267.
Līla *dg.* 418 (=Nīla).
Lilajan r. M. 297.
Līlāvatī *prs.* 627.
Līlāyudha *p.* W. 334.
Limbu p. N. 322.

Lizard, 181, 210.
Locust, 8.
Lohinī *r*. NE. 293.
Lohita *r*. NE. 293, 357.
Lohita *pl?* 357.
Lohita *f*. 357.
Lohitya *pl*. M. 357.
Lohityā *r*. NE. 357.
Loka, *see World*.
Lokāloka *mts*. 275.
Loka-pāla *dg*. 55, 277.
Lola *k*. 439, 441.
Lolana *p*. NE. 383.
Loma-pāda *k*. 325, 464.
Lopāmudrā *prs*. 293.
Lotus, 1, 2, 18, 24, 29, 30, 97, 147 255, &c.
Lotus Water-lily, *pt*. 29.
Love, 2, 15, 115, 119, 170–172, 185, 188, 198, 215, 264, 430, 467.
Love-god, *see* Kāma.
Lūsatī *r*. 305.
Lute, 132, 135, 396, 417, 571, 647.

Madālasā *q*. 114, 115, 118–126, 133, 136–145, 148, 151, 155, 157, 160, 164, 168–171, 180, 181, 186–188, 214.
Madanikā *fem. d*. 7.
Madayantī *q*. 336.
Madgu *bd*. 31, 85, 86.
Madguraka *p*. E. 324.
Madhu *mt*. N. 279.
Madhu *k*. 352.
Madhu *rs*. 454.
Madhu *d*. 465, 469–472, 519.
Madhumatta *p*. NW.? 375.
Madhu-pura *t*. M. 352.
Madhu-vana M. 352.
Madhya-deśa *c*. 309, 333, 345, 351–355.
Madra *c*. and *p*. NW. 311, 315–317, 347–350, 372, 373, 377–380, 665, 670.
Madra? *p*. E. 329.
Madrā *r*. C. 299.
Mādra *p*.,=Madra.
Madraka *k*. 311, 315.
Madraka *p*.,=Madra.
Madras, 332.
Mādrī *q*. 23.
Madura t. and *dt*. S. 331.
Magadha *c*. and *p*. M. 308, 330, 337, 341, 357, 358.
Māgadha *p*. M. 330, 664.
Maghā *cst*. 168, 169.
Magic, 79, 201, 392–395, 554, 555, 614.
Magician, 174.
Mahā-bhadra *l*. N. 278, 282.
Mahā-bhadra *mt*. N. 279.
Mahā-deva *g*. 268.
Mahā-druma *k*. and *c*. 273.
Mahā-gaurī *r*. E.? 301.
Mahā-grīva *p*. SE. 360.
Mahā-hanu *d*. 476, 479.
Mahā-kāla *t*. C. 521.
Mahā-kālī *gs*. 521.
Mahā-Kosala *c*. 308, 342, 371.
Mahā-mārī, *disease*, 519, 521.
Mahā-Māyā *gs*. 465, 469, 515.
Mahā-nada *r*. SE. 295, 298.
Mahā-nāda *pr*. 670, 672.
Mahā-nadī *r*. SE. 284–286, 295–298, 300, 305.
Mahānanda *pr*. 672, 673.
Mahā-nīla *mt*. N. 278.
Mahā-padma *dg*. 408, 416, 494.
Mahā-rāṣṭra *c*. and *p*. W. 333, 363.
Mahā-ratha *k*. 612.
Mahā-raurava *hell*, 54, 71, 72.
Mahar-loka, 227, 553.
Mahārṇava *p*. W. 370.
Mahā-śaila *mt*. N. 279.
Mahat, 217, 220–223, 231.
Mahatī *r*. W. 294.
Mahāvīta *k*. 272.
Mahendra *mts*. E. 284–286, 305, 334, 362.
Maheśvara *g*. 504, 505, 514.
Maheswar t. C. 333.
Māheya *p*. W. 339.
Mahī *r*. W. 294, 339.
Māhika *p*. W. 340.
Mahindra mts. SE. 284.
Mahiṣa *d*. 473–487, 519, 524.
Māhiṣaka *p*. S. 333.
Māhiṣika *p*. S. 333.
Māhiṣikī *r*.? C. 334.
Māhiṣmaka *p*. C. 333.
Mahiṣmat *k*. 333, 371.
Māhiṣmatī *t*. C. 310 333, 336, 344, 371.
Mahitā *r*. W. 295.
Mahraṭṭa p. W. 333.
Mahyuttara *p*. E.? 327.
Mainā bd. 49, 58–61, 84.
Maināka *mt*. N. 269, 287, 376

Maināka *mt.* W. 288.
Maināka *mt.* S. 288.
Maināka-prabha ? *r.* C. 288.
Maitra *cst.* 370.
Mākandī *t.* M. 353.
Makara *dg.* 416, 417.
Makarī *r.* M. ? 298.
Makruṇā *r.* M. ? 298.
Makṣaṇā *r.* M. ? 298.
Māl p. E. 330.
Malada *p.* E. 326.
Mālada *p.* E. 326.
Malaja *p.* M. 309, 325.
Malaka *p.* M. 308.
Mālatī *pt.* 27, 152.
Mālava *p.* M. 341, 354, 377, 379.
Mālavānaka *p.* C. ? 326.
Mālavartin *p.* E. 326.
Malaya *mts.* S. 285, 287, 304, 362.
Mālda dt. E. 326.
Mālē *p.* E. 330.
Malignant spirits, 250-268.
Mālika ? *p.* NW. 318.
Mālinī *t.* E. 325.
Mālinī *aps.* 538.
Malla *p.* E. 330.
Malli p. 318.
Mallikā *pt.* 24, 25, 425, 426.
Mallikārjuna *temple,* S. 290.
Māl Pahāṛiya p. E. 330.
Mālwa c. 286, 312, 338, 341, 354, 361.
Mālya ? *p.* NW. 315.
Māna-bhūmi dt. E. 326.
Mānada *p.* E. 326.
Māṇaka, 178.
Mānakalaha ? *p.* N. 379.
Manas (*Mind*), 221.
Mānasa *l.* N. 278, 281, 288, 322, 376, 384.
Mānasa *k.* and *c.* 273.
Manasvinī *w.* 269.
Mānavācala *h.* E. 356.
Mānavarjaka *p.* E. 326.
Mānavartika *p.* E. 326.
Mānbhūm dt. E. 326, 327.
Mandagā *r.* 305.
Manda-gāminī *r.* 305.
Mandākinī *r.* N. 296, 298.
Mandākinī *r.* S. 302.
Manda-pāla *b.* 8.
Mandār tr. 27, 494.
Mandara *mts.* N. 277-280, 310, 316, 322, 351, 381, 382, 402.
Mandara *mt.* E. 287.
Mandāra *tr.* 27.
Mandāra *dg.* 402, 407.
Manda-vāhinī *r.* 305, 306.
Māṇḍavya *m.* 91, 94, 97.
Māṇḍavya *p.* NW. 349, 374, 380.
Māṇḍavya *rs.* 374.
Māṇḍavya-pura *t.* S. 374.
Mandhātā t. C. 334.
Māndhātṛ *k.* 655.
Maṇḍika *p.* NW. ? 374.
Mango tr. 24, 197.
Maṇijālā *r.* C. 302.
Maṇimat *mt.* NW. 370.
Maṇi-megha *h.* NW. ? 370.
Maṇiṅgā *r.* C. ? 302.
Māninī *q.* 578, 584-586.
Maṇipur t. C. 371.
Maṇi-śaila *mt.* M. 278.
Manīvaka *k.* and *c.* 273.
Mañjirā r. S. 289, 302.
Mañjulā *r.* M. ? 297.
Mān-kachu pt. 178.
Mankind, Primeval, 231–247.
Man-lion incarnation, 21, 503, 504.
Mano-java *g.* 454.
Mano-ramā *r.* M. 290, 306.
Mano-ramā *demi-gs.* 401, 402, 411.
Manus, *The,* 226, 227, 271, 408, 411-415, 432, 435–437, 441, 449, 455, 461–465, 535, 549, 550, 684, 686. *See* Svāyambhuva, Svārociṣa, Auttama, Tāmasa, Raivata, Cākṣuṣa, Vaivasvata, Sāvarṇi, Raucya, *and* Bhautya.
Manuga *k.* and *c.* 273.
Manvantaras, *The,* 218, 224, 227, 271, 549, 550, 685.
Mānya-vatī *prs.* 627.
Maraka ? *p.* NE. 383.
Marathī ? *r.* S. 302.
Mārīca *dg.* ? 462, 465, 535.
Marīci *rs.* 246, 249, 269, 558, 559.
Mārkaṇḍeya *rs.* 1–7, 11, 16–19, *and passim* 217–237, 247, 256, 268–283, 348, 349, 387, 391–467, 522–689.
Mārkaṇḍeya Purāṇa, 219, 684–688.
Markaṭaka *pt.* 165, 245.
Markaṭi ? *pt.* 245.
Marking-nut tree, 25.
Marriage, 118, 119, 149, 155, 166, 170, 176, 177, 252, 526, 527, 594–596, 670–672.

Mars, planet, 431, 626.
Mārtaṇḍa *g*. 455, 550, 551, 563–566 574–576.
Mārttikāvata *t*. W. 349.
Maru-dhanvan *dg*. 402.
Maru-bhūmi *c*. W. 354.
Marut *g*. 55, 461, 645, 648.
Māruta *pl*. 246.
Māruta *p*. M. 353.
Māruta *g*. 474.
Marutta *k*. 146, 644–649, 652–656, 672.
Marutta *k*. 653.
Māṣa *pt*. 84, 85, 165, 244.
Māsh-kalāy pt. 84.
Masūra *pt*. 165, 244.
Mātariśvan *g*. 100, 539.
Māṭhara ? *p*. NW. 317.
Mathurā *t*. M. 21, 307, 351, 352.
Mathurā *t*. S. 331.
Mātrā 128, 194, 205, 470.
Matsya *k*. 359.
Matsya *c*. and *p*. 307, 329, 347, 351, 354, 359, 360, 377, 382.
Mattā *gb*. 264.
Matter (element), 221.
Mauleya *p*. S.? 336.
Mauli? *p*. NW. 388.
Maulika *p*. S. 336.
Maunika *p*. S. 336.
Maurya *demons*, 501.
Maya *d*. 416.
Māyā *gs*. 250; *see* Mahā-Māyā.
Mayūra *mt*. N. 279.
Maxims, see Custom.
Measures of length, 240; *of time*, 226–228.
Meat, 164, 167, 168, 174, 175.
Medhas *b*. 466.
Medhātithi *k*. 272, 273.
Medhāvin *k*. and *c*. 273.
Megha-parvata *mt*. N. 279.
Mekala *hills* C. 288, 327, 341.
Mekala *c*. and *p*. C. 327, 341, 357.
Mekalā *t*. or *r*. C.? 358.
Mekhalāmuṣṭa ? *p*. E. 357, 358.
Menā *demi-gs*. 269.
Menā *ps*. 270.
Menā *aps*. 287.
Menakā *aps*. 4, 8, 571.
Merchant, see Trade.
Mercury, planet, 431, 626; *see* Budha.
Meru *mt*. 22, 223, 244, 269, 275–282, 345, 351, 390, 391, 478, 576, 582.
Meru-nanda *k*. 411.
Metempsychosis, see Transmigration.
Metres, 235, 236.
Michelia tr. 26, 326, 364.
Micitā *r*. M. 292.
Midnapur dt. E. 301, 327, 330.
Mimusops tr. 26.
Mind, 190, 221.
Mithila *p*. M. 330.
Mithilā *t*. and *c*. M. 329, 356, 358.
Mitra *g*. 588, 589.
Mitra-vindā *sf*. 433.
Mleccha *p*. 290, 312, 313, 317–320, 328, 335, 346, 350, 636.
Modāgiri *pl*. E. 324.
Mohammedans, 284.
Mohana r. C. 297.
Mohanī *gb*. 264.
Mokṣa-śāstra, 2.
Momordica pt. 114.
Monghyr t. and *dt*. E. 324, 325, 356.
Monkey, 49, 84, 208, 235.
Monkey-jack tr. 25.
Moon, planet and *g*., 147, 280, 431, 447, 448, 473, 474, 562, 626.
Moon-worship, 80, 173, 264.
Morning-star, 207.
Mosquito, 72, &c.
Mothers, goddesses, 504–506, 524; *see* Sakti.
Mountains, 275–289, 356, 357, 362, 370, 376.
Mṛga-śiras *cst*. 355.
Mṛkaṇḍa *dg*. 269.
Mṛṣika *p*. SE. 332, 359.
Mṛttikāvatī *t*. W. 342, 349.
Mṛtyu *pfn*. 247, 250, 263.
Mucukunda *k*. 333, 336.
Mudakara *p*. E. 324.
Mudāvasu? *k*. (=Udāvasu).
Mudāvatī *prs*. 604–609.
Mudga *pt*. 84, 165, 244.
Mudga-giri *pl*. E. 324.
Mudgala *p*. E.? 325.
Mudgalapuri *t*. E. 324.
Mudgalāśrama *t*. E. 324.
Mug pt. 84.
Mug-kalāy pt. 84.
Mujavant *pl*. N.? 655.
Mūka *p*. C. 309.

Mukhya *gods*, 464, 465.
Mukti, *see Final emancipation.*
Mukti-matī *r.* C. 298.
Mukuṭā *r.* M.? 298.
Mukunda *dg.* 416, 417.
Mūla *cst.* 170, 374.
Mule, 235.
Mūli *dg.* 394, 395.
Mūlī *r.* SE. 305.
Mūlinī *r.* SE. 305.
Muṇḍa *p.* C. 329.
Muṇḍa *d.* 494–501.
Muṅgīr t. E. 324, 325.
Muni *k.* and *c.* 273.
Muni *demi-gs.* 559.
Muñja *gr.* 192.
Muñja-pṛṣṭha *mt.* N. 655.
Muñjavat *mt.* N. 655.
Muñjavaṭa *ti.* M. 655.
Muñjāvaṭa *mt.* N. 655.
Mura, *see* Muru.
Mūrchanā (*music*), 131.
Murshidabad dt. E. 326.
Muru *k.* 328, 383, 501.
Mūṣaka *p.* S. 332.
Musi r. S. 366.
Music, 100, 107, 109, 130–132, 135, 138, 251, 571.
Mūṣika *p.* S. 332, 366.
Musk-rat, 87.
Mustard pt. 84, 162, 165, 181, 258–261, 266.
Muttra t. M. 307, 351, 352.
Myna bd., *see Mainā.*
Myrobalan tr. 25, 26.
Mysore c. S. 286, 332.

Nābhaga, Nābhāga (*son of* Manu Vaivasvata) *k.* 462, 588.
Nābhaga, Nābhāga (*son of* Manu Vaivasvata); *see* Nābhāgādiṣṭa.
Nābhāga (*son of* Riṣṭa) *pr.* 593–604.
Nābhāgādiṣṭa, Nābhāgāriṣṭa *k.* 463, 588, 593.
Nabhakānana *p.* S. 337.
Nābhānediṣṭha *k.* 588, 593.
Nābhi *k.* 271, 273, 274.
Nāciketa 159.
Nadia dt. E. 326.
Nāga, *race*, 7, 55, 109–111, 115–117, 125, 127, 130–140, 201, (232, 234), 238, 279, 288, 362, 379, 395, 429–435, 495, 516, 531, 542, 559, 571, 644, 645, 648, 653, 657–664, 677.
Nāga-dvīpa *c.* 284.
Nāga-giri *mt.* C.? 288.
Nāgāhva, Nāga-pura, Nāga-sāhvaya *t.* M. 355.
Nāgpur t. C. 288.
Naimiṣa *for.* M. 306.
Nairṇika *p.* S. 337.
Nairṛta *p.* S.? 337.
Naiṣadha *p.* W. 337, 341, 343.
Naiṣika *p.* S. 337.
Naiwal *r.* N. 291.
Nakula *k.* 312, 322, 342.
Nala *k.* 299, 343, 362.
Nala *pr.* 597, 600–602.
Nala candanodaka-dundubhi ? *pr.* 647.
Nalakālika *p.* S. 337.
Nalakānana *p.* S. 337.
Nala-nābha *dg.* 404.
Naldrug t. S. 289.
Nalina *tr.* 25.
Nalinī *pt.* 30.
Nāmavāsaka *p.* S. 333.
Nanda *p.* N. 383, 412.
Nanda *m.* 517.
Nandā *r.* N. 369, 383, 412.
Nanda-ka *dg.* 416, 418.
Nandana *pl.* 4, 487.
Nandana *for.* N. 278, 281.
Nanda-vatī *t.* N. 411.
Nāndīmukha *pitṛs*, 155, 179.
Nandinī *q.* 446.
Nandinī *q.* 618.
Nara 2.
Nara *k.* 442.
Nārā, *waters*, 20, 229.
Nārada *rs.* 4, 571, 654.
Naraka *k.* 328, 383.
Naraka 47–49, 54, 57, 69–72, 158, 247, 250; *see Hell.*
Nara-siṁha *incarnation*, 21, 503, 504.
Nārāyaṇa *g.* 2, 20, 55, 228, 229, 269, 280, 386.
Nārāyaṇī *gs.* 513–515.
Nārikela *p.* SE. 360.
Nārikela *isl.* 360.
Narikhorsum dt. N. 324.
Nariṣya *k.* 350, 463.
Nariṣyanta (*son of* Manu Vaivasvata) *k.* 463, 588, 666.
Nariṣyanta (*son of* Marutta) *k.* 577, 665–668, 673–676, 680–682.

Narmadā (*Nerbudda*) *r.* C. and W. 19, 286, 296, 298, 333, 338, 339, 343, 344, 365, 368, 371, 600.
Nāsatya *g.* 460, 575; *see* Asvins.
Nasik t. W. 289, 337, 339, 365.
Nāsikya *p.* W. 337, 339, 365.
Nāsikyāva ? *p.* W. 337, 339.
Nature (Prakṛti), 192, 193, 196, 224, 225, 231, 232.
Nauclea tr. 25, 277, 565.
Nava *k.* 333.
Nava-rāṣṭra *c.* and *p.* M. 333.
Nebu tr. 25.
Nediṣṭha, *see* Nābhānediṣṭha.
Nelumbium pt. 29, 30, 147; *see Lotus.*
Nepāl *c.* N. 316, 321, 322, 345–347, 360, 376.
Nerbudda r.; *see* Narmadā.
Newar p. N. 345.
Nibhā ? *prs.* 627.
Nioitā *r.* M. 292.
Nidhi *dg.* 408, 409, 415–419, 494, 638.
Nigarhara ? *p.* N. 345.
Nighna *gb.* 264.
Nightshade pt. 166.
Nīhāra *p.* N. 345.
Nikaṭa *p.* S. 362.
Nikṛntana, *hell*, 71, 72.
Nīla *mts.* N. 275–279, 388.
Nīla *k.* 334, 344.
Nīla *dg.* 416, 419.
Nīlāyudha *p.* W. 334.
Nilgiri mts. S. 285, 363.
Nīlī *q.* 353.
Nīlotpala *pt.* 29, 30, 104.
Nīpa *k.* 350, 598.
Nīpa *rs.* 597–599.
Nīpa *p.* 350, 353, 598.
Nīpa *tr.* *see* Kadamba.
Nirāhāra ? *p.* N. 345.
Niraya, *hell*, 68, 70.
Nirbandhyā *r.* C. 299.
Nirbindhyā *r.* C. 299.
Nir-mārṣṭi *d.* 257.
Nirṛti *gs.* 250, 263, 490.
Nirvindhyā *r.* C. 299, 605, 606.
Nirvindhyā *r.* S. 299.
Nirvīrā *r.* M. 292.
Nirvṛti-cakṣus *rs.* 440.
Niṣāda *p.* C. 360, 361.
Niṣadha *c.* and *p.* W. 300, 343, 360.
Niṣadha *mts.* N. 275–277.
Niṣadha *mt.* NW. 278.
Niṣadhā *r.* W. ? 300.
Niṣadhāvatī *r.* W. ? 300.
Niścara *rs.* 415.
Niścīrā *r.* M. 292.
Niścitā *r.* M. 292.
Niṣpāva *pt.* 86, 165, 244.
Niśumbha *d.* 488, 494–497, 500, 503, 506–509, 517–521, 524.
Nisvīrā *r.* M. 292.
Nitya-naimittika *sf.* 95.
Nīvāra *cer.* 165.
Nīvārā *r.* M. 292.
Niveśa, 318.
Niyati *gs.* 269.
Niyojikā *gb.* 257, 259, 264.
Nṛsiṁha ? *p.* NW. 375.
Nūpī *r.* M. ? 295.
Nymphæa pt. 29, 30.

Oceans, 275.
Ocymum pt. 164, 532.
Oḍra *p.* and *c.* E. 329.
Ogha-vatī *r.* M. 290, 306.
Okhalakiya p. 366.
Om, 128, 195, 205, 206, 550–554, 557, 561.
Omens, 207–211, 263.
Onion pt. 165.
Organs of sense (indriya), 15, 16.
Orissa c. E. 284, 301, 327, 334, 335, 360, 361, 365.
Ortygornis bd. 28, 86.
Osmotreron bd. 28.
Ougeinia tr. 28.
Owl, 72, 263.
Oxalis pt. 25.
Oxus r. NW. 292, 324.
Oxydraci p. N. 377.

Paddy, 84.
Paddy-bird, 59, 86.
Padgama *p.* C. 343.
Padma, *flower*, 30.
Padma, *seat*, 195.
Padma *dg.* 416.
Pādma mahā-kalpa, 228.
Padmāvata *c.* W. 289.
Padminī *pt.* 30.
Padminī, *science*, 408–411, 415, 416, 419.
Pahlava *p.* W. 314, 320, 350, 353, 368, 371, 383.

Pahoj r. W. 299.
Pairi r. C. 285.
Paisuni r. M. 297.
Paitrya *cst.* 361.
Pāka-saṁsthā *sf.* 128.
Palāṇḍu *pt.* 165.
Palāsh tr. 28.
Palaśinī *r.* 306.
Pallava ? *p.* N. 314.
Pallava *p.* S. 332.
Palmyra palm, tr. 27.
Pāṁśa-pāla ? *p.* NE. 381.
Pāṇ p. SE. 361.
Panasa tr. 25.
Pañcadaka *p.* NW. 372.
Pañcajana ? *dt.* NW. 312.
Pañcāla *c.* and *p.* M. 308, 309, 350–355, 382.
Pāñcāla *p.*,=Pañcāla.
Pañcana r. M. 330.
Pañcanada *c.* and *p.* NW. 312, 372, 378.
Pañcāpsaras *l.* C. ? 342.
Pañca-śaila *mt.* N. 279.
Pañcodaka ? *p.* NW. 372.
Pandanus, shrub, 26.
Pāṇḍara *mt.* M. ? 288.
Pāṇḍava *f.* 6–9, 19–24, 341, 344–347, 355, 365, 377, 416, 461, 669, 670.
Pāṇḍaveya *pr.* 31, 37.
Pandhawa mt. M. ? 287.
Pāṇḍu *k.* 3, 19, 20, 37, 146, 345.
Paṇḍua t. E. 326.
Pāndua h. M. 288.
Pāṇḍura *mt.* N. 279.
Pāṇḍura *mt.* M. ? 288.
Pāṇḍya *p.* S. 287, 304, 331, 332, 344, 370.
Pāṇḍya ? *p.* W. 369.
Panicum cer. 165, 203, 244.
Pañjāb 311–318, 321, 324, 333, 347, 351, 373, 377–380.
Paṅkaja, *flower,* 30.
Paṅkajinī *l.* W. 445.
Paṅkinī *r.* M. ? 298.
Para *p.* S. 365.
Para *period,* 224, 228.
Parā *r.* M. 295.
Pāra *rs.* 402, 407.
Pārā *r.* M. 295, 299.
Pārada *p* NW. 312, 317, 319, 369, 382.
Parakṣara *p.* W. 339.
Parāśara *rs.* 669, 677.
Pāraśava *p.* W. 339, 369.
Pāraśava *f.* 369.
Paraśu-Rāma *rs.* 310, 338, 339, 369, 371, 464.
Para-taṅgaṇa *p.* N. 323.
Pārāvata *tr.* 25.
Pārāvata *gods,* 415.
Pārbati r. M. 295, 299.
Pārijāta *tr.* 27, 494.
Parīkṣit *k.* 379.
Pāripātra *mts.* M. 285, 286, 295, 354.
Pāripātra *mts.* N. 277, 279.
Parita *p.* NW. 317.
Parivarta-ka *gb.* 257, 258, 263.
Pāriyātra *mts.* M.;=Pāripātra.
Parjanya *g.* 178, 539, 618.
Parjanya *rs.* 449.
Parṇā *r.* M. 294.
Parṇāsā *r.* M. 294.
Parṇa-śālāgra *mt.* NE. 388.
Parṇa-śavara *p.* SE. 361.
Parrot, 28, 87.
Parsaroni r. M. 297.
Partridge, 28, 86.
Pārul tr. 27.
Pārvaṇa śrāddha 157.
Parvata *rs.* 269.
Pārvatī *gs.* 290, 488, 493, 494.
Parwan r. M. 299.
Pāṣaṇḍa *p.* M. 354.
Pāśinī *r.* 306.
Paspalum cer. 244.
Passion (rāga), 15, 16.
Passion (rajas), *see Qualities.*
Paśu-pāla *c.* NE. 381.
Paśu-pati *dg.* 268.
Paṭaccara *p.* M. 309, 343.
Pāṭala *tr.* 27.
Pātāla, *world,* 47, 55, 60, 110–115, 119, 120, 125, 132–137, 429–435, 465, 475, 503, 518, 521, 531, 604–608, 645, 648, 656–661, 664, 677.
Pātāla-ketu *d.* 109, 113–116, 119–122.
Pātandhama *mt.* M. ? 287.
Pataṅgaka *mt.* N. 279.
Pathar mts. M. 286.
Patna t. and *dt.* M. 330.
Pattiāla dt. N. 321, 347.
Paṭu *p.* C. 343.
Paudanya *t.* C. ? 337.
Pauṇḍra *p.* and *c.* E. 329.

Pauṇḍraka, Pauṇḍrika *p.* E. 329.
Paunika *p.* W. ? 336.
Paurava; *race,* 331, 350, 360, 369, 374, 384, 461, 598, 677.
Paurava ? *p.* NE. 384.
Paurika *p.* S. 336.
Pauṛṇamāsa *rs.* 269.
Pauṣkala *cer.* 165.
Pāvaka *dg.* 270.
Pāvamāna *dg.* 270.
Pāvanī *r.* NE. 323.
Payolli ? *r.* C. ? 299.
Payoṣṇī *r.* W. 299, 335, 365.
Payoṣṇī *r.* M. 299.
Pea, 84, 86, 244, 245.
Peacock, 87, 147, 260, 394.
Pearl, 304, 366, 475.
Peepul, see Pipal.
Pelican, 30.
Pelicanus, bd. 30.
Pen-gaṅga r. C. 299.
Penner r. S. 303.
Perdix bd. 28, 86.
Peri r. S. 304.
Persia, 314.
Peyārā tr. 25.
Phala-giri *mt.* W. 373.
Phalgu r. M. 297.
Phalguluka *p.* W. 373.
Phalgunaka *p.* W. 373.
Phalgunī *cst.* 169, 361, 367.
Phaseolus pt. 84.
Phasianus bd. 29.
Phena-giri *mt.* W. 373.
Pheasant, 28, 29.
Phyllanthus tr. 25, 26.
Physician, 160, 180, 261.
Pīḍika *p.* N. 322.
Pig, see Boar.
Pigeon, 28, 84, 86, 87, 208, 263.
Pīna ? *p.* N. 319.
Pināka, *bow,* 403, 474.
Pinākā ? *r.* S. 303.
Piṇḍa, *cake,* 144, 155–158, 162, 167, 179, 183, 255, 532, 683.
Piṇḍa-mūlaka *pt.* 165.
Piṅgākṣa *bd.* 3.
Pingala *mt.* N. 279.
Pingala *p.* NW. 379.
Piñjalā *r.* 379.
Piñjara *mt.* N. 279.
Pinus tr. 27.
Pipal tr. 33, 277.
Pipāṭhaka *mt.* N. 279.
Pipīlika, *ant,* 86.
Pipīṛā, large ant, 86.
Pippala *tr.* 33, 277.
Pippalā *r.* M. 297.
Pippaliśroṇī *r.* M. 297
Pipṛā, large ant, 86.
Pipyalāśroṇī *r.* M. 297.
Piśāca *d.* 46, 47, 158, 207 232 236, 238, 308, 520, 533.
Piśācikā *r.* M. 297.
Piśika *p.* S. 366.
Piśuna *gb.* 263.
Pitṛs, 14, 75, 79, 80, 85, 88, 96, 119, 128, 133, 135, 144, 150–172, 176–183, 218, 232, 233, 236, 247, 249, 253, 254, 270, 272, 483, 526–538, 555, 561, 576, 619, 620, 639, 680, 686 : *their* 31 *classes,* 533–535.
Pitṛsomā *r.* SE. 304.
Pīvara *rs.* 442.
Pīvarī *q.* 76.
Plakṣa-dvīpa, 272–275.
Plakṣāvataraṇa *ti.* N. 127.
Planet, 168, 259, 278, 385–387, 431, 535, 581, 626.
Plantain tr. 25.
Plava *bd.* 30.
Podiceps bd. 31.
Pole-star, 112, 207.
Polyandry, 3, 19, 21, 23.
Pomegranate tr. 25.
Ponani r. S. 304.
Poona t. W. 336.
Porcupine, 49, 181.
Pota-ka *p.* NW. 388
Potter's wheel, 72.
Prabhākara *rs.* 320.
Prabhāsa *ti.* W. 338, 340.
Prabhāva *k.* 411, 412.
Prabhā-vatī *q.* 664.
Pracaṇḍa *d.* 266, 267.
Pracaṇḍa *pr.* 610.
Pracīra *pr.* 610.
Pracodikā *gb.* 264.
Pradhā *demi-gs.* 369, 559.
Pradhāna, 217, 220, 225.
Prādheya *p.* W. 368, 369.
Pradyumna *g.* 21.
Prāgjyotiṣa *p.,* *c.* and *t.* NE. 319, 328, 357, 383, 501.
Prajāni *k.* 611.
Prajāpati, 22, 70, 96, 99, 152, 153, 178, 179, 219, 233, 234, 238, 248, 258, 272, 273, 415, 436, 453, 455,

465, 470, 473, 474, 494, 526, 534–536, 551, 560, 566, 572, 582, 608, 685.
Prājāpatya *pl.* 246.
Prajāti *k.* 610, 611.
Prajā-vatī *q.* 272.
Prākara *k.* and *c.* 273.
Prākara *k.* and *c.* 273.
Prakāśaka *gb.* 267.
Prākṛt, 352.
Prakṛti, 217, 220–225, 228, 231, 232, 483, 489.
Pralolupa *bd.* 6.
Pramathā *q.* 618.
Pramati *rs.* 586, 597, 600–603.
Pramati *k.* 611.
Pramati *b.* 612.
Pramattā *gb.* 264.
Pramlocā *aps.* 538.
Prāṁśu (*son of* Manu Vaivasvata) *k.* 463, 588.
Prāṁśu (*son of* Vatsaprī) *k.* 610.
Pramuca *rs.* 443, 445.
Prāṇa (*vital air*), 203.
Prāṇa *dg.* 269.
Prāṇa *rs.* 415.
Prāṇāyāma, 194–196.
Pranhita r. S. 300, 302.
Prāpta *p.* N. 378.
Prāpti (*faculty*) 195.
Prasandhi k. 611.
Prasātika *cer.* 165.
Prasthala *p.* 320, 321, 347.
Prasuhma *c.* and *p.* 327.
Praśupāla *c.* NE. 381.
Prasūta *gods*, 454.
Prasūti *demi-gs.* 247–249.
Pratardanākhyagods, 436.
Pratilomā Sarasvatī *r.* 31.
Pratīpa *k.* 350.
Pratiṣṭhāna *t.* M. 93, 587, 590.
Pratyāhara, 196.
Pratyaya-sarga, 231.
Prauṣṭhapadā *cst.* 381.
Pravaṅga *p.* E. 325.
Prāvāra-karṇa *m.* 346.
Pravijaya *p.* E. 327.
Pravīra *m.* 44.
Prāvṛṣeya *p.* E. ? 327.
Prayāga *t.* M. 310, 361.
Prīti *w.* 269.
Priyalaukika ? *p.* N. 319.
Priyaṅgu *cer.* 165, 203, 244, 245.
Priya-putra *bd.* 28, 29.
Priya-vrata, 247, 248, 271–274, 445.
Proṣaka *p.* N. 320, 321.
Pṛṣadhra *k.* 463, 588–592.
Pṛṣata *k.* 350, 353.
Pṛthā *q.* 23; *see* Kuntī.
Pṛthu *rs.* 442.
Pruṣadhru, *see* Pṛṣadhra.
Psidium tr. 25.
Pterospermum tr. 27.
Pudukota dt. S. 332.
Pukkasa, *tribe*, 47–50, 68, 85, 87, 159.
Pulaha *rs.* 246, 249, 270, 274.
Pulastya *rs.* 246, 249, 269, 533.
Puleya *p.* W. 338.
Pulinda *p.* N. 315, 316, 321–323.
Pulinda *p.* C. 317.
Pulinda *p.* S. 335, 359.
Pulinda *p.* W. 338.
Pulse, 84, 86, 165, 244, 245.
Punarvasu *cst.* 169, 358.
Puṇḍarīka *pt.* 29; *see Lotus.*
Puṇḍra *k.* 325.
Puṇḍra *p.* and *c.* E. 327, 329, 331, 334, 358.
Puṇḍraka *p.* E. 329.
Punica tr. 25.
Puñjikā-stanā *aps.* 407.
Punnāga *tr.* 26.
Puṇya *isl.* S. ? 390.
Pura, *town*, 241, 242.
Purāṇas, 108, 219, 247, 685–689.
Purandara *g.* 494, 623.
Purandara-pura *t.* 113, 114.
Purandhra ? *p.* NW. 313.
Purañjaya *ps.* 146.
Purantāla ? *t.* S. 412.
Pure articles, 181, 182.
Puri t. E. 336.
Purification, 180–185.
Purikā *t.* S. 336.
Purṇa r. W. 289, 299, 335, 365.
Pūrṇa *p.* N. 324.
Purṇotkaṭa *h.* E. 357.
Puru *k.* 454.
Pūru *k.* 384.
Purūravas *k.* 146, 167, 587, 589.
Puruṣa, 220–224, 248.
Pūṣadhra, *see* Pṛṣadhra.
Puṣan (*Sun*), 582.
Puṣkala *p.* N. 320, 321, 378.
Puṣkalāvatī *t.* NW. 321.
Puṣkara *t.* and *p.* W. 306, 685.
Puṣkara *rs.* ? 538.

Puṣkara-dvīpa, 272, 275.
Puṣkara-mālin *m.* 116.
Puṣkarāvatī *t.* NW. 321.
Puṣpa *mt.* 288.
Puṣpajā *r.* S. 288, 303.
Puṣpa-jāti *r.* S. 304.
Puṣpaka *mt.* N. 279.
Puṣpa-vāhinī *r.* S. 304.
Puṣpa-vatī *r.* S. 304.
Puṣpa-vatī *ti.* E. 304.
Puṣpa-veṇī *r.* S. ? 304.
Puṣya *cst.* 169, 358.
Put, *hell,* 444.

Qualities (guṇa), 3–6, 16, 19–21, 220, 221, 224, 225, 229–239, 247, 251.
Querquedula bd. 30.
Quince tr. 25, 425.

Raddhakaṭaka *p.* NW. 317.
Rādheya ? *f.* 369.
Raghu *k.* 304.
Rāi pt. 84.
Raivata *mt.* W. 289, (445).
Raivata *for.* W. ? 23, 24.
Raivata, Manu *and* manvantara, 271, 443, 449, 549.
Raivataka *mt.* W. ? 445.
Rāja-gṛha *t.* NW. 318.
Rāja-gṛha *t.* M. 286, 330, 357.
Rāja-māṣa *pt.* 165.
Rājanya *p.* N. 380.
Rajas *rs.* 270.
Rāja-śaila *mt.* N. 279.
Rājasūya *sf.* 34, 35, 39, 58, 61, 366, 541.
Rāja-śyāmāka *cer.* 165.
Rājgir t. M. 331, 357.
Rājmahall hills, E. 325, 330.
Rājputāna c. W. 286, 333, 354.
Rājya-vardhana *k.* 577–579, 583–586, 684.
Rākṣasa *d.* 6–8, 42, 47, 84, 89, 162, 166, 201, 232–238, 255, 258, 279, 346, 367, 402–405, 425–434, 516–520, 533, 541, 559, 571, 641, 677, 682, 683.
Rākṣasa *marriage,* 596, 671, 672.
Rakta-kanchan tr. 27, 165.
Rakta-vīja *d.* 501, 504–506, 524.
Raktotpala *pt.* 29, 30.
Rāma (Candra), *k.* 309, 351, 352, 655.
Rāma Jāmadagnya, *see* Paraśu-Rāma.
Rama (Bala-), *see* Bala-Rāma.
Rāma *p.* NW. ? 317.
Ramaṇa *p.* NW. ? 317.
Ramaṭa *p.* NW. 317.
Rāmaṭha *p.* NW. 317.
Rambhā *w.* 647.
Rambhaka ? *p.* NW. 388.
Rām-gaṅgā r. M. 292, 354.
Rāmgaṛh c. C. 296.
Rāmgaṛh h. E. 330.
Ramyaka *c.* N. 390, 391.
Raṇavanya ? *k.* 551.
Raṅgeya ? *p.* E. 326.
Raṅkṣu ? *r.* N. 292.
Rantideva *k.* 363.
Rapti r. M. 294, 329.
Rasā *r.* NW. 377.
Rasālaya *p.* N. 377.
Rasātala, *world,* 109, 110, 115, 133, 430, 435, 531, 605–608, 644, 659.
Rāṣṭra-vardhana *k.* 577.
Rat, 85, 86, 184, 210.
Rati *gs.* 114.
Ratnadhāra ? *p.* N. 320.
Ratna-vāhinī *r.* M. ? 298.
Ratnavat *mt.* N. 279.
Rātrī *r.* M. ? 298.
Raucya, Manu *and* manvantara 271, 524, 526, 536–538, 550.
Raudra *d.* ? 32.
Raudrāśva *k.* 320.
Raudrī *cst.* 358.
Raurava, *hell,* 54, 62, 68, 72, 87, 250.
Rāvaṇa *d. k.* 362.
Raven, 81, 208.
Rāvi r. NW. 291, 292, 313–318.
Ṛc *hymns,* 20, 64, 458–460, 484, 553–557, 561, 565, 570, 581.
Ṛcīka *rs.* 310, 462, 595.
Ṛddhi *w.* 247, 248.
Ṛddhi *demi-gs.* 248.
Rechna doab, NW. 315.
Religion, 119, 120, 124, 170–173, 178, 179.
Religious devotion (yoga), 92, 167, 190–207, 210, 213–216.
Rer r. C. 296, 297.
Rest-house, 81.
Reur r. C. 296.
Revanta *dg.* 460, 461, 575, 576.

Revatī *cst.* 170, 384, 443–448.
Revatī *q.* 24.
Revatī *q.* 443–449.
Revenue, 422, 423, 593, 617, 618, 657.
Rewa dt. C. 297, 341.
Ṛg-Veda, 152, 206; *see* Ṛc *hymns.*
Rhinoceros, 164, 168, 181, 532.
Rice, 84, 165, 244, 245.
Riches, see Wealth.
Righteousness (Dharma), 21, 36, 39, 41, 53, 54, 66, 88, 96, 108, 124, 138, 144, 148, 170–172, 185, 187, 198, 215, 264, 273, 282, 400, 422, 424, 430, 442, 459, 575, 578, 595–598, 629, 630, 657, 671, 672.
Riṣṭa *k.* 588, 593.
Riṣṭā *demi-gs.* 559.
Ṛkṣa *mts.* C. 285, 286, 298–302, 336, 345.
Rocana *mt.* 288.
Rohi *rs.* 294.
Rohiṇī *cst.* 169, 355.
Rohiṇī *demi-gs.* 269, 420.
Rohita *k.* and *c.* 273.
Rohitāsya *pr.* 42, 51, 58.
Rope and jar at the well, 70, 71.
Rottleria tr. 26.
Ṛṣabha *k.* 271, 274.
Ṛṣabha ? *mts.* N. 275, 277.
Ṛṣabha *h.* S. 366.
Ṛṣabha *p.* S. 366.
Ṛṣabha *rs.* 415.
Ṛṣabhā *r.* C ? 300.
Ṛṣi-giri ? *h.* M. 357.
Ṛṣika *p.* N. 332.
Ṛṣika *p.* S. 332, 366.
Ṛṣikā *r.* S. 366.
Ṛṣīkā *r.* 305.
Ṛṣikulyā *r.* E. 285, 304.
Ṛṣikulyā *r.* 305.
Ṛṣis, *Seven,* 22, 226, 246, 270.
Ṛṣyamūka *mt.* S. 289, 365.
Ṛṣyaśṛṅga *rs.* 464.
Ṛta-dhvaja *k.*; *see* Kuvalayāśva.
Ṛta-vāc *rs.* 443, 444, 447, 448.
Ṛtu-hārikā *gb.* 257, 261, 266.
Ṛtukulyā ? *r.* SE. 304.
Ṛtu-mālā *r.* S. 303.
Ṛtvij, 160, 178.

Rucaka *mt.* N. 279.
Ruci *dg.* 247, 248.
Ruci *rs.* 526–538.
Rudra *g.* 10, 55, 168, 225, 232, 246, 247, 268, 269, 403, 461, 525.
Rules, various, 170–185.
Rumex pt. 25.
Rūpā *r.* 306.
Rūpapa *p.* W. 339.
Rūpasa *p.* W. 339.
Rūpavāhika p. W. ? 339.
Rūpnarain r. E. 300, 301, 330.
Ruru, *deer,* 164, 211.
Rutha *k.* 452.

Sabala *rs.* 270.
Sābandhanā *r.* M ? 294.
Sabar p. C. and S. 335.
Śabara *ps.* 18.
Sabindu *mt.* N. 278.
Saccarum gr. 192.
Śacī *gs.* 4, 90, 102, 420, 489.
Sacrifices, 170, 203, 433, 434, 621; *see* Śrāddha, &c.
Sad-ācāra, *see Custom.*
Sadānīrā *r.* W. 294.
Sadānīrā *r.* M. 294, 329.
Sadānīrā-mayā *r.* M.? 294.
Sadātīrā *r.* M. ? 294.
Sādhya *dg.* 55, 461.
Sagara *k.* 314, 317–320, 332, 346, 350, 362, 371, 656.
Sāgarānūpa *c.* E. 328, 344.
Saha-deva *k.* 346, 364, 367.
Sahaja *k.* 359.
Sahajanyā *aps.* 571.
Sahasa ? *p.* W. 340.
Sahasrākṣa *g.* 524.
Sahasra-patra *pt.* 30.
Sahasra-śikhara *mt.* N. 279.
Sahiṣṇu *rs.* 270.
Sahiṣṇu *rs.* 454.
Sahodaka *kinsman,* 157, 184, 185, 255.
Sahya *mts.* 285, 289, 303, 310.
Śaila *c.* S. 332.
Śailika *p.* S. 332, 362.
Śailodā *r.* N. 351, 381, 382.
Śailodakā *r.* N. 351, 382.
Sailūṣa *p.* S. 332, 362.
Saindhava *p.* NW. 315.
Sainika ? *p.* N. 322.
Sairandhrī *g.* 665.
Sairīṣaka *pl.* M. 383.

Sairiṣṭha? *p.* NE. 382.
Saivāla *mt.* N. 388.
Saivyā *q.* 35, 38, 47–52.
Saka *p.* NW. 314–320, 346, 353, 371, 463.
S'aka *p.* M. 350.
S'āka *p.* NW. 388.
S'ākabhava *k.* and *c.* 273.
S'āka-dvīpa, 272–275, 569.
S'ākala *t.* NW. 316, 364, 372, 373.
S'ākala-dvīpa *dt.* NW. 364.
S'ākambharī *gs.* 518.
Sāketa *t.* M. 353.
S'ākhā, 129.
S'ākhā-nagaraka, *city*, 241, 242.
S'akra *g.* 482, 503.
S'akṛdgrāha *p.* N. 346.
Sakṛdgrāha *p.* N. 346.
Sakri r. E. 285, 286, 298.
Sakṛn-nandā *r.* NE. 347.
Sakṛtraka *p.* N. 346.
S'akti *gs.* 129, 501–509, 512–514, 520.
S'akti, S'aktri *rs.* 669, 677.
S'akuli *r.* E.? 285, 298.
S'akuni *gb.* 257, 258, 263.
S'ākya-muni, 350.
S'āl tr. 27.
S'ala *pr.* 670.
S'āla *tr.* 27.
Salem t. and *dt.* S. 332, 365.
Salik bd. 58.
S'ālmali *tr.* 82, 147.
S'ālmali-dvīpa, 272–275.
S'ālmaveśmaka *p.* W. 373.
Salt, 166, 175, 182.
S'ālva *c.* and *p.* W. 309, 315, 347–350, 373, 595.
S'ālveya *p.*; *see* S'ālva.
S'alya *k.* 311.
S'alya-kīrtana *pl.*? M. 378.
Samādhi *m.* 467.
Sāman *hymns*, 20, 64, 235, 236, 458–460, 484, 554–557, 561, 581.
Samāna, (*vital air*) 203.
Samānodaka, 157; *see* Sahodaka.
Samarkand c. 314.
Sāma-Veda, 152, 206, 235.
S'ambara *d.* 10, 139.
S'ambaraṇa, *see* Saṁvaraṇa.
S'ambhu *g.* 408.
Sambhūti *w.* 249, 269.
S'amīka *rs.* 6, 9, 11, 17.
Sampāti *bd.* 6.
Saṁrāj *prs.* 272.
Samūla *mt.* N. 279.
Saṁvaraṇa *k.* 461, 567.
Saṁvarta *rs.* 653, 654.
Saṁvarta-ka, *weapon*, 658, 662.
S'aṇa *pt.* 245.
Sānandinī *r.* M. 294.
Sanatkumāra, 232.
Ṣaṇḍa *tr.* 390.
S'aṅgala t. NW. 316.
Sañjñā *gs.* 455–460, 566–569, 575.
Saṅkalana, 7.
Saṅkalpa *pfn.* 246, 247.
S'aṅkara *g.* 460.
Saṅketa? *p.* M. 353.
S'aṅkha *h.* S. 365.
S'aṅkha *dg.* 416, 419.
S'aṅkha-kūṭa *mt.* N. 279, 282.
S'aṅkhāvatī *r.* NE. 388.
Sāṅkhya, 129, 231, 588, 688.
Saṅkrandana *k.* 670, 675, 681.
S'aṅku *d.* 636.
Sannati *w.* 249, 270.
S'ānta *k.* 442.
S'ānta *k.* 446.
Santāl Parganas dt. 325, 356.
S'āntanu *k.* 9.
S'ānti *b.* 539–541, 546–548.
S'āntika *p.* NW. 372.
Sānumat *mt.* N. 279.
Sānumat *mt.* .N 279.
Sapiṇḍa 156–158, 184, 185, 255.
Sapiśika? *p.* S. 366.
Saptalā *pt.*=Mallikā.
Sapta-parṇa *tr.* 27.
S'arabha (*beast*), 49.
Saraca tr. see Aśoka.
S'aradvat *ps.* 464.
Saraja *p.* C. 341.
S'arāli *bd.* 58.
Sārasa *k.* 333, 364.
Sārasa *bd.* 647.
Sarasi-ja *pt.* 30.
Sārasvata *p.* M. 340, 351.
Sārasvata *p.* W. 340.
Sarasvatī *gs.* 2, 17, 18, 125–132, 434, 435, 515.
Sarasvatī *r.* M. 23, 127, 290, 310, 312, 320, 351, 354, 377, 378.
Sarasvatī *r.* W. 340.
Sarasvatī, Prati-lomā, *r.* 31.
Sarasvatī (*other rivers*), 290, 306.
S'arava *p.* S.? 362.
S'aravā? *r.* SE. 305.

S'arāvatī r. SE.? 305.
Sarayū r. M. 323, 376.
Sārdana? p. N. 378.
Sārgiga? p. W. 368.
S'ārikā bd. 49, 58, 84.
Sariṣā pt. 84.
Sarju r. M. 376.
S'arkara p. NW. 373.
S'ārkarākṣya b. 373.
S'ārkarāvartā r. S.? 373.
S'armāti, *see* S'aryāti.
S'armiṣṭhā q. 669.
S'ārṅga, *bow*, 108, 514.
Sarpa? p. C. 362.
Sarṣapa pt. 84.
Sarson pt. 84.
Sarva dg. 268.
Sarva q. 460.
Sarva p. S. 362.
Sarvaga? p. N. 345.
Sarva-hārī gb. 265.
S'arvāṇī gs. 490.
Saryāta k. 368; *see* S'aryāti.
S'āryāta p. W. 368, 371.
S'aryāti k. 368, 462, 463, 588, 600.
S'āśaka p. W.? 372.
Saśa-vindu k. 653.
S'āiśka p. W.? 340, 372.
S'āstras, *Wicked*, 79, 252.
Sasurasa mt. 288.
S'āśvata p. W. 340.
Sasya-han-tṛ gb. 257, 259, 264.
S'atabalā r. E.? 301.
S'ata-bhiṣaj cst. 170, 381.
S'atadru r. NW. 291, 316.
S'ata-dyumna k. 454.
S'ātaka p. N. 380.
S'atamālā r. S. 303.
S'atamūlī pt. 165.
S'ata-patha? dt? M. 309.
Satāra dt. W. 362.
S'ata-rūpā, 247, 248.
S'ata-śṛṅgin mt. N. 279.
S'ata-vāhana p. SE. 361.
Satī gs. 269, 408.
Satīrā r. M. 294.
Sātpura mts. C. 286, 287, 299, 343, 345, 362, 365.
S'atru-ghna pr. 352.
S'atru-jit k. 109-113, 117, 119, 135, 139, 140.
S'atru-mardana pr. 142, 143.
Ṣatsura p. C. 343.
Sāttvata f. 629.
Saturn, planet, 431, 461, 567, 576, 626.
Satya *gods*, 436, 437, 442.
Satyaka k. 449.
Satyākhya *gods*, 436, 437.
Sātyaki pr. 629.
Satya-loka, 553.
Satya-vat pr. 349, 350.
Satya-vatī q. 677.
Satya-vatī prs. 595.
Saubha t. W. 349.
Saudāsa k. 336.
Saumya c. 284.
Saumyā cst. 355.
S'aunaka rs. 591.
Saunanda, *club*, 606–609.
Saunandā q. 604.
S'auṇḍikera? p. C. 344.
Saur p. C. *and* S. 335.
Saurāṣṭra p. W. 370.
S'auri pat. 31.
S'auri k. (*son of* Prajāti), 612, 615.
Sauvīra p. and c. 315, 368.
Sauvīrī q. 664.
S'avadhāna? p. N. 378.
Savana k. 272.
S'avara p. C. and S. 319, 335, 361, 362.
Sāvarṇa-ka, Manus *and* manvantaras, 524, 525, 549, 550.
Sāvarṇi-ka, Manu *and* manvantara, 458, 461, 463–466, 522–524, 549, 567, 576.
Savitṛ (*Sun*), 282, 582.
Savitṛ d. 262.
Sāvitra for. N. 278, 282.
Sāvitrī prs. 349, 350.
Sāvitrī, *hymn*, 470.
Scythians, 350.
Scorpion rp. 172, 81, 85.
Screw-pine, *shrub*, 26.
Self, *see Soul.*
Self-existent, The, 225; *see Supreme Being.*
Self-repression, 194–200.
Sélye r. E. 300.
Semecarpus tr. 25.
Seemul tr. 82, 147, 191.
Senses, *see Organs of Sense.*
Seonath r. C. 285.
Serpents, The, 232, 234, 531, 577, 681, 683; *see* Nāga.
Seṣa (*Serpent*) k. 1, 21, 469, 475, 609, 648, 681.

Sesamum pt. and *seed*, 84, 86, 156, 162–168, 181, 224, 244, 245, 260, 261, 532.
Setuka *p.* S. 332.
Shadow-Sañjñā *gs.* 456–461, 464, 566–569, 576.
Shāhābād dt. M. 309.
Shāh-dheri t. NW. 379.
Sheep, 164, 166, 235.
Shieldrake bd. 30; *see* Cakravāka.
Shorea tr. 27.
Shrike bd. 28.
Sibi *p.* NW. 377.
Siddha *dg.* 55, 58, 78, 229, 393, 395, 403, 511, 530, 542, 581, 679, 682.
Siddha-vīrya *k.* and *rs.* 441.
S'īghrā *r.* C.? 299.
S'īghrodā r. C. 299.
S'ikhara *mt.* N. 279, 281.
S'ikhi *g.* 442.
S'ilavatī ? S'ilāvatī ? *r.* E. 300.
Silk, 86, 423.
Silk-cotton tree, *see Seemul.*
Silk-worm, 86.
Siṁhala *p.* S. 366.
Siṁhikā *d.* 367.
Simla t. N. 316.
Sin (*particular*), 78–88.
Sinapis pt. 84.
Sindh c. W. 313, 315, 373.
Sindh r. M. 293.
Sindh-sāgar doab, NW. 315.
Sindhu *r.* NW. 290, 370.
Sindhu *r.* M. 293.
Sindhu *p.* and *c.* W. 315, 347, 368, 370, 665.
Sindhu-kālaka-vairata ? *p.* W. 369, 370.
Sindhūttama *ti.* M. 293.
Sindhūttama *ti.* W. 293.
Sindhu-vīrya *k.* 665.
S'inibāhu *r.* E. 300.
S'inibālī *r.* E. 300.
S'iprā *r.* N. 285.
S'iprā *r.* C. 299.
Sirāla *p.* W. 338.
Sirmour dt. N. 320.
Sirsa dt. N. 321.
S'iśira *k.* and *c.* 273.
S'iśirakṣa *mt.* N. 279.
S'iśu-pāla *k.* 350.
Sītā *r.* NE. 281, 388.
Sitāmbuja *pt.* 30.
S'ītānta *mt.* N. 278–281
S'ītārtta *mt.* N. 278.
Siterajā *r.* M.? 297.
S'itibāhu *r.* E. 300.
S'ītodā *l.* N. 278, 281
S'iva *g.* 5, 17, 32, 38, 55, 98–100, 112, 125, 132, 133, 178, 206, 219, 224, 225, 249, 258, 262, 280, 281, 343, 356, 460, 471–474, 501–503, 509, 515, 521, 545, 555, 572, 574, 582, 588.
S'iva *k.* and *c.* 273.
S'ivā *r.* 299.
S'iva-dūtī *gs.* 503, 504, 507–509, 514, 524.
S'ivi *k.* 377.
S'ivi *p.* NW. 333, 354, 377–380.
S'ivākhya *gods*, 436, 437.
Skanda *g.* 269.
Slavery, 42–45, 323, 674.
Smell (*element*), 217, 221, 222.
Smṛti *w.* 249, 269.
Smṛti-hārikā *gb.* 257, 261, 266.
Snake, 76, 85.
Snātaka, 178.
Snowy Mountains, *see* Himavat.
Social rules, 170–184.
Solanum pt. 166, 167.
Solar Race, *dyn.* 43, 45, 683.
Soma (*Moon*), *g.* 153, 162, 420, 535, 561, 582, 589, 626.
Soma *rs.* 99, 269.
Soma, *juice*, 259, 262, 545, 655.
Somā *r.* N. 282.
Soma-datta *pr.* 629.
Soma-pā *pitṛs*, 533.
Soma-pā *gb.* 262.
Soma-saṁsthā *sf.* 128.
Someśvarī r. NE. 306.
Somnath t. W. 338, 340.
S'oṇa *r.* C. and M. 286, 288, 295, 298, 341.
Sone r.=S'oṇa.
Sorrel pt. 25.
Soul, 15, 142, 143, 150, 187, 190–194, 200, 206, 211, 220–225, 422, 459, 527, 542, 587.
Sound (*element*), 217, 220–222, 238.
Sparrow bd. 6, 28, 210.
Spirituous liquor, 32, 83 86, 100, 103, 106, 107, 136, 260, 573, 600, 603; *see Intoxication.*
Spondias tr. 24.

Sprite, 250–268, 533, 545.
S'rāddha, 79, 83, 133, 151, 154–171, 181, 185, 199, 203, 264, 266, 530, 531, 536, 537, 566, 686.
S'ravaṇa *cst.* 170, 376.
Sreewacolum t. SE. 361.
S'rī *gs.* 249, 269, 290, 484; *see* Lakṣmī.
S'rī-kākula *t.* SE. 361.
S'rī-parvata *mt.* S. 290, 366.
S'rīphal tr. 25, 425.
S'rī-śaila=S'rī-parvata.
S'ṛṅgavat *mts.* N. 277.
S'ṛṅgavat *mts.* N. 279.
S'ṛṅgin *rs.* 12.
S'ṛṅgin *mts.* N. 275, 276.
Sṛñjaya *k.* 353.
Sṛñjaya *f.* 353.
S'ruta-devā *q.* 361.
Stanapa *p.* N. 321.
Stanayoṣika *p.* N.? 321.
Star-worship 80.
Sterna bd. 86.
Stośala *p.* C. 342.
Strī-loka *pl.* NW. 375.
Strī-rājya *c.* and *p.* N. 375.
Strī-vāhya *p.* NW. 375.
Su-bāhu *pr.* 142, 143, 187–190, 207, 212–215.
Su-bāhu *k.* 322, 323.
Subalāśva *k.* 623.
Subarṇa-rekhā r. E. 301, 327.
S'ubhā *r.* C. 302.
Subhadrā *q.* 446.
Subhadrā *prs.* 627.
S'ubhra? *p.* E. 356.
Su-cakra pr. 610.
S'uci *dg.* 270.
Sūcī-mukha *bd.* 80.
Sudāman *dg.* 581.
Su-darśana *rs.* 378.
Su-deva *k.* 597, 600–602.
Su-deva *k.* 600.
Su-deva *k.* 627.
Sudhāman *rs.* 449.
Sudhī *gods*, 442.
S'ūdra, *caste* 85, 116, 123. 183, 318, 531, 591, 671, 676; *their duties*, 149.
S'ūdra *p.* W. and NW. 312–314, 368.
Sudrakæ p. NW. 314.
Su-dyumna *k.* 587–590.
Sugar-cane, 175.
Su-grīva, *monkey k.* 289, 333, 356.
Su-grīva *d.* 495.
Suhma *k.* 325.
Suhma *p.* E. 327, 329, 334, 356.
Suhmottara *p.* E. 327.
Su-hotra *b.* 612.
Su-hotra *k.* 670.
Suicide, 621.
Suir p. C. 335.
Sujaraka *p.* E. 324.
Sujātā *q.* 446.
Sujātya *p.* M. *or* W. 371.
Sukālin *pitṛs*, 531.
Sukaṇkavat *mt* N. 278.
Su-kanyā *prs.* 368, 600.
Su-keśī *q.* 664.
Sukhodaya *k.* and *c.* 273.
S'ukra *dg.* 58, 269, 650.
S'ukra (=Agni), 541, 544.
Sukṛṣa *rs.* 11, 12.
S'ukta *rs.* 270.
S'ukti *h.* S. 365.
S'uktimat *mts.* 284, 285, 306.
S'uktimatī *r.* M. 285, 297.
S'uktimatī *t.* M. 298, 359.
S'ukti-sāhvayā *t.* M. 359.
Su-kumāra *k.* and *c.* 273.
Su-kumārī *r.* 305.
Sukuṭya *p.* 307.
Sulaiman mts. W. 347.
S'ūlakāra *p.* N. 321.
Sūlika *p.* N. 323.
Sumahā-drumā *r.* M.? 296.
Sumanā *q.* 670, 674–676.
Su-mati *b.* 62, 69, 74, 76; *see* Jaḍa.
Su-mati *k.* 274.
Su-mati *k.* 361.
Su-mati *pr.* 605.
S'umbha *d.* 116, 488, 494–500, 503, 506–510, 517–521, 524.
Sumbha *p.* E.? 356.
Sumedhas *gods*, 449.
Sumedhas *rs.* 454.
Su-megha *mt.* W.? 370.
Sumerujā *r.* M.? 297.
Sumīna *p.* W. 338.
Su-mukha *bd.* 3.
Sun (Sūrya &c.) *g.* 147, 178, 280, 431, 455–461, 465, 466, 473, 474, 522, 535, 543, 550–553, 560–567, 580–588, 621, 626, 680.
Sunanda, *club*, 604, 609.
Su-nandā *q.* 604, 609, 611.
Su-naya *k.* 612.

Sunī? *r.* M. 297.
Su-nīti *pr.* 605.
Sunuwār p. N. 321.
Sun-worship, 80, 173.
Supara t. W. 338.
Su-pārśva *bd.* 6.
Supārśva *mts.* N. 277, 282.
Su-patra *bd.* 3.
Su-prabhā *r.* N. 290, 306.
Su-prabhā *w.* 597, 600, 601.
Supratīka, *elephant*, 9.
Suprayogā *r.* S. 303.
Supreme Being or *Soul* or *Spirit*, 55, 63–65, 92, 198, 201–206, 210, 216, 217, 229, 414, 459, 532, 552–555, 558, 570, 587, 588, 687; *see* Brahman.
S'ūra *k.* 24.
Surā *r.* M.? 295.
Sūra? *p.* NW. 313.
S'ūra (*son of* Vatsaprī) *pr.* 610.
Surabhi *dg.* 116, 117.
Surahādrumā *r.* M.? 296.
Surakṣa *mt.* N. 279, 281.
Surāla *p.* W. 338.
Surasa *mt.* N. 279.
Surasā *r.* M.? 296.
S'ūrasena *k.* 351.
S'ūrasena *c.* and *p.* M. 307, 309, 351–354, 371, 377.
Surāṣṭra *c.* and *p.* W. 288, 309, 340, 342, 344, 370, 446.
Surat t. W. 340.
Su-ratha *k.* and *c.* 273.
Su-ratha *k.* 465, 466, 522, 523
Su-ratha *k.* 601, 602.
Surathā *r.* M. 296.
Su-reṇu *r.* M. 290, 306.
Sūrpakarṇa *h.* E. 356.
S'ūrpāraka *c.*, *t.* and *p.* W. 289, 338.
Sursooty, *see* Sarasvatī *r.* M.
Su-ruci *q.* 420.
Su-rūpa *gods*, 442.
Sūrya, *see Sun.*
Sūrya *h.* S. 365.
Sūryā? *r.* M.? 295.
Sūrya-kānta *mts.* N. 389.
Sūryāraka? *see* S'ūrpāraka.
Sūrya-vaṁśa *dyn.* 308.
Su-śānti Manu;=Auttama.
Susarasa *mt.* 288.
Su-śarman *k.* 321.
Su-śarman *b.* 426.
Su-śobhanā *q.* 665.
Sūta, 23, 31.
Sutapa *gods*, 464.
Su-tapas *rs.* 270.
Su-tapas *b.* 440.
Sūta-viṣaya *dt.* E. 326.
Sūtika? *p.* S. 332.
Sutlej r. NW. 291, 292, 311, 312, 316, 324, 378–380.
Sūtpalāvatī *r.* S. 304.
Su-varcas *rs.* 540.
Su-varcas *k.* 623.
Suveṇā *r.* C. 300.
Su-vikrama *pr.* 610.
Suvīra *k.* 311, 315.
Suvīra *p.* NW. 370.
Suvīra *k.* 664.
Su-vrata *rs.* 605.
Su-yaṣṭavya *k.* 449.
Svadhā, 94, 151, 152, 163, 178, 249, 269, 270, 470, 483, 515, 527, 530–532, 542.
Svadhāman *gods*, 436.
Svāhā, 94, 151, 152, 162, 249, 269, 270, 470, 483, 527, 542.
Svakambalā *r.* NW. 389.
S'vapaca *p.* W.? 339.
Svāpada *p.* W. 339.
S'vapāka *p.* W.? 339.
Svar, 71, 206, 218, 227, 553.
Svara, 130.
Svarakṣu *mt.* N. 281.
Svarakṣu *r.* N. 281.
Svarasa *mt.* 288.
Sva-rāṣṭra *k.* 438.
Svar-bhānu (*Sun*), 582.
Svarga 36–41, 50, 57–61, 69–71, 75–78, 88–90, 147, 152, 168, 169, 279, 280, 283, 284, 310, 409, 443, 460, 462, 473, 513, 530, 652, 687, 688.
Svarga-bhaumānavadyaka? *p.* NE. 383.
Svarṇa-śṛṅgin *mt.* N. 279.
Sva-rocis *ps.* 401–415.
Svārociṣa, Manu *and* manvantara, 271, 391, 392, 398, 401, 406, 408, 411–415, 449, 466, 549.
Sva-rūpa *pr.* 610.
Svastika *posture*, 195.
Svāti *cst.* 169, 370.
Svayam-bhū *g.*, *see Self-existent.*
Svāyambhuva, Manu *and* manvantara, 247, 248, 270–274, 403, 424, 448, 449, 549.

Svayaṁ-hārikā *gb.* 257, 260, 265.
S'veta *k.* and *c.* 273.
S'veta *mts.* N. 275, 276.
S'veta-giri *mt.* N. 287, 381.
S'veta-parṇa *mt.* NE. 388.
S'veta-parvata, *see* S'vetagiri.
S'vetodara *mt.* N. 279.
S'yāmā *cer.* 165.
S'yāmā *r.* NW. 389.
S'yāmā *r.* NW. 389.
S'yāmaka *p.* N. 380.
S'yāmāka *cer.* 165, 245.
S'yeni *demi-gs.* 559.

Tailaṅga *p.* S. 367.
Taittirika *p.* W. 339.
Takka p. NW. 379.
Takṣaka *d. k.* 379, 648.
Takṣa-śilā *t.* NW. 379.
Tāla *tr.* 27.
Tāla (*music*), 131.
Tāla *t.* S. 411, 412.
Talagāna? *p.* N. 321.
Tālajaṅgha *p.* M. 371.
Tāla-ketu *d.* 121, 122, 125.
Tamaḥ-pracchādaka *gb.* 265.
Tamāla *tr.* 28.
Tāmalipta-ka *p.* E. 330, 357, 358.
Tāmarasa *pt.* 30.
Tamas, *hell*, 71, 72, 152.
Tamasā *r.* M. 296, 298.
Tāmasa *mt.* N. 278.
Tāmasa. Manu *and* manvantara, 271, 437, 438, 442, 549.
Tāmasa *p.* N. 323, 347.
Tāmasī *r* M. 296.
Tamba *rs.* 415.
Tamil p. S. 370.
Tāmisra, *hell*, 152.
Tamluk t. E. 301, 327, 330.
Tāmra *d.* 479.
Tāmrā, *demi-gs.* 559.
Tāmrāhvaya-dvīpa *c.* 367.
Tāmraka *mt.* N. 279.
Tāmralipta-ka *c.* and *t.* E. 301, 329, 330.
Tāmraparṇa *c.* 284.
Tāmraparṇī *r.* S. 303, 367.
Tāmraparṇī? *r.* SE. 305.
Tāmraparṇī *t.* and *isl.* S. 367.
Tāmraparṇī *h.* S. 367.
Tāmraparṇī dt. S. 367.
Tāmravarṇa *c.* 284.
Tanapa *p.* N. 321.
Tanaya *p.* N. ? 321.
Taṅgaṇa *p.* N. 316, 317, 322, 323, 346, 375, 381, 382.
Tañjor dt. S. 332.
Taṅkaṇa *p.* N. 323.
Tan-mātra, 231.
Tāpasa *p.* W. 339.
Tāpasāśrama *p.* S. 339, 366.
Tapatī *q.* 461, 567, 576.
Tāpī *r.* C. and W. 299.
Tapo-loka, 553.
Tapo-rati *b.* 590.
Tapo-vana *for.* 669.
Tapta-kumbha, *hell*, 71, 74, 83.
Tapti r. C. and W. 285, 286, 299, 335, 336, 340, 344, 365, 368.
Tārakṣati, Tārakṣiti, *dt.* W. 372.
Tārakṣura *p.* NW. ? 372.
Tārkṣī *bd.* 6, 8.
Tārkṣya *p.* NW. ? 372.
Taru-jit *d.* 663.
Taste (*element*), 217, 221, 222.
Tauṇḍikera? *p.* C. ? 371.
Taxila t. NW. 379.
Teal bd. 30.
Teesta r. NE. 293.
Teliṅga *c.* and *p.* SE. 334, 337, 367.
Telugu p. S. 334, 337, 367.
Tendukhera t. C. 344.
Tephrodornis bd. 28.
Terminalia tr. 26.
Tern bd. 86.
Tetrao bd. 28.
Tewar t. C. 343, 371.
Thāmi p. N. 322.
Thibet c. 319, 323.
Thunder-bolt, 2, 75.
Til pt. 84.
Tila *pt.* 84; *see Sesamum.*
Tilaṅga? *p.* N. 308.
Tilaṅga *p.* S. 367.
Tilottamā *aps.* 4, 571.
Time, measures of, 224-228, 459 543, 580.
Tindaka *tr.* 24, 25.
Tindu-ka *tr.* 24, 26.
Tinnevelly dt. S. 331.
Tippera hills, E. 306.
Titir bd. 86.
Tittira *p.* 339.
Tittiri *bd.* 86.
Tochari p. N. 320.
Todya (*music*), 132.
Tomara *p.* N. 323.

Tons r. M. 296.
Tortoise, 30, 49, 84, 85, 181, 195, 278, 348, 349, 355, 358, 367, 374, 376, 381, 384–387, 417.
Tortures, 48, 49, 66-68, 72–90.
Tośala *p.* C. 342.
Touch (element), 217, 221, 222.
Towns, 240–242.
Toyā *r.* C. 301.
Trade, 101, 108, 214.
Traigarta *p.* N. 347.
Traipura *p.* C. 343, 360.
Transmigration, 3, 5, 8–18, 38, 48–50, 54, 66–71, 77–88, 91, 158, 280.
Travancore dt. S. 367.
Tretā *age*, 32, 224, 226, 235, 239, 243, 272, 347, 387, 388, 437.
Tribhāgā *r.* E. 304.
Trichinopoly dt. S. 332.
Tridivā *r.* C. 298.
Tridivā *r.* E. 305.
Tridivācalā *r.* E. 305.
Trigarta *c.* N. 321, 324, 346–349, 372, 377–382.
Triḥ–srotasī *r.* NE. ? 293.
Triliṅga *c.* and *p.* SE. 367.
Tri-netra *p.* NE. 384.
Tripiṣṭapa *dt.* M. 290.
Tripurā *t.* C. 343, 360, 371.
Trisāmā *r.* SE. 304, 305.
Triśaṅku *k.* 339.
Tri-śikha *mt.* NW. 281.
Tri-srotas *r.* NE. ? 293.
Tri-suparṇa *hymns*, 160.
Tritīyā *r.* E. ? 293.
Triyāmā *r.* SE. 304.
Truthfulness, 14, 15, 35, 39, 41, 66, 68, 88, 122, 151, 568, 640.
Trumpet-flower tr. 20.
Tryambakā *gs.* 513.
Tukhāra *p.* N. 320, 350, 353.
Tulsi pt. 164.
Tumba *pt.* 118.
Tumbara *p.* C. 343.
Tumbhadra r. S. 303
Tumbula *p.* C. 343.
Tumbuma *p.* C. 343.
Tumbura *p.* C. 343.
Tumburu *rs.* 12, (118), 571, 647, 648.
Tumura *p.* C. 343.
Tunaya *gdh.* 646, 648.
Tuṇḍikera *p.* C. 344.
Tuṅga r. S. 303.
Tuṅga-bhadrā *r.* S. 303.
Tuṅgana *p.* N. 323.
Tuṅga-prastha *mt.* 288.
Turasita *p.* W. 339.
Turdus bd. 49, 58.
Turk p. 372.
Turkestan c. N. 324, 372.
Turmeric pt. 165.
Turuṣka *p.* W. 372.
Turvasu *k.* 623, 653.
Tuṣāra *p.* N. 319, 320.
Tuṣita *gods*, 415.
Tuṣṭikāra ? *p.* C. 344.
Tvaṅgana p. NE. 382.
Tvaṣṭṛ *g.* 21, 22, 120, 455–460, 569, 605.

Uccaiḥ-śravas, *horse*, 494, 495.
Udagra *d.* 476, 479.
Udāna, *air*, 66, 204.
Udāra *cer.* 244.
Udāvasu *k.* 612.
Udaya-giri *h.* M. 357.
Udaya-giri *h.* E. 356.
Udbhida *k.* and *c.* 273.
Udbhida *p.* S. 337.
Uddhata *d.* 479.
Udgītha, 484.
Udumbara *p.* M. 355.
Udumbara *c.* W. 355.
Udumbara *tr.* 182, 192, 255.
Udumbarāvatī *r.* S. 355.
Ugra *dg.* 268.
Ugra *k.* 454.
Ugra-darśana *d.* 476, 480.
Ugrāsya *d.* 479.
Ugra-vīrya *d.* 479.
Ugrāyudha *k.* 350, 598.
Ujhani t. M. 351.
Ujjain t. C. 295, 345, 521.
Ujjayanta *mt.* W. 288.
Ujjayinī *t.* C. 295, 345.
Ujjihāna *p.* M. 350, 351.
Ukti *gb.* 257, 258, 262.
Ulūka *p.* N. 346, 375.
Umā *gs.* 132, 269.
Umbilical cord, 70.
Unmattā *gb.* 264.
Unnata *rs.* 454.
Upa-giri *dt.* N. 325, 328.
Upaniṣad, 259.
Upaniveśa, 318.
Upaplava, -vya, *t.* M. 307.
Upupa bd. 80.

Urdamaru *p.* N. 376.
Ūrdhva-bāhu *rs.* 270, 449.
Ūrdhva-karṇa *p.* SE. 342, 360.
Ūrja *rs.* 415.
Ūrjā *w.* 249, 270.
Ūrjasvin *g.* 462.
Urjihānā *t.* M. 351.
Ūrṇa *p.* and *c.* N. 324, 346, 376.
Urū, Ūru, *k.* 454.
Urukarma ? *pl.* N. 376 .
Urvaśī *aps.* and *q.* 4, 571.
Uśanas *dg.* 9, 10, 58.
Uśīnara *k.* 333, 377–380.
Uśīnara *p.* M. 377.
Uśīra *gr.* 79.
Uśīra-vīja *rs.* 653.
Uṣṇa *k.* and *c.* 273.
Utkala *k.* 589.
Utkala *p.* and *c.* E. 299, 327. 329, 334, 341, 589.
Utpala *pt.* 29.
Utpalā *r.* S. 304.
Utpalāvata-ka *for.* 425.
Utpalāvatī *r.* S. 304.
Utpalāvatī *q.* 439.
Utsarga *oblation,* 151, 153.
Utsava-saṅketa *p.* N., W. *and* S. 319, 337.
Uttama *p.* C. ? 342.
Uttama *k.* 419, 420, 423–425, 429, 432, 435, 436.
Uttamarṇa *p.* C. 342.
Uttānapāda *k.* 247, 248, 419, 420, 423.
Uttānapāla *k.* 112.

Vābhravya *pat.*, *see* Bābhravya.
Vabhru, *see* Babhru.
Vācaspati *dg.* 626.
Vadana-dantura *p.* E. 356, 357.
Vadantika ? *p.* N. 379.
Vāḍhadhāna ? *p.* NW. 312.
Vadhra *p.* N. 378.
Vahirgira *p.* E. 325.
Vahir-giri *p.* E. 325.
Vahir-giri *dt.* NE. 325, 328.
Vāhlīka *k.* 311.
Vāhlīka *p.* NW. 311, 315, 375.
Vāhya ? *p.* M. 354.
Vāhyā *r.* S. 303.
Vāhyatodara ? *p.* N. 320.
Vaibhāra *mt.* M. 286.
Vaibhrāja *for.* N. 278, 281.
Vaibhrāja *mt.* M. 286.
Vaidehaka *p.* M. 352.
Vaidika ? *p.* C. 343.
Vaidiśa *p.* M. 343, 627, 630.
Vaidūrya *mt.* W. *and* C. 279, 287, 299, 365.
Vaidyanātha *h.* E. 287.
Vaidyuta *k.* and *c.* 273.
Vaidyuta *mt.* 287.
Vaigai r. S. 304.
Vaihāra *mt.* M. 286.
Vaikārika, 221.
Vaikuṇṭha *k.* 449.
Vaiṇava *k.* and *c.* 273.
Vaiṇī *r.* S. 303.
Vaippar r. 304.
Vaipracitta *pat. d.* 517.
Vairāṭa *c.* M. 288, 307.
Vairocani *d.* 465.
Vaiśāli *pat.* 426.
Vaiśālī *t.* M. 329, 600.
Vaiśālinī *prs.* 625, 627.
Vaiśikya *p.* S. 334.
Vaiṣṇava *sect,* 108.
Vaiśya *caste,* 74, 318, 671 ; *its duties, &c.*, 148, 591, 594, 597.
Vaitaraṇī *r.* E. 300, 334.
Vaitariṇī, *fabulous r.* 54.
Vaivasvata, Manu *and* manvantara, 271, 341, 350, 368, 454–463, 517, 549, 551, 566, 568, 575, 576, 587–590, (600), 617, 666.
Vāji-keśa *p.* NW. 374.
Vājivāsika ? *p.* S. 333.
Vajra-ketu *d.* 115.
Vaka *bd.* 58.
Vaka *p.* N. 376.
Vakṣu *r.* NW. 292, 324.
Vakula *tr.* 26.
Vala ? *pl.* NW. 375.
Valaka *rs.* 442.
Valāka *d.* 425, 426.
Valāva ? *pl.* NW. 375.
Vamana *p.* NW. 372.
Vāmana *incarnation,* 21.
Vaṁśa-dharā *r.* SE. 305.
Vaṁśa-dhāriṇī *r.* SE. 305.
Vaṁśa-karā *r.* SE. 305.
Vaṁśa-varā *r.* SE. 305.
Vanadāraka *p.* S. 337.
Vānaprastha, 149, 150, 216, 616, 675, 681.
Vana-rāṣṭra-ka ? *p.* and *c.* NE. 382.

Vānava *p.* NW.? 372.
Vanavāhyaka *p.* NE. 383.
Vanavāsaka *p.* S. 333, 364.
Vanavāsi, *c.* S. 333.
Vanavāsika *p.* S. 333.
Vanavāsin *c.* S. 333, 364.
Vanāyu, Vānāyu, *c.* and *p.* NW. 372.
Vaṅga *k.* 325, 326.
Vaṅga *p.* and *c.* E. 324–329, 334.
Vaṅgeya *p.*=Vaṅga.
Vanitā-mukha *p.* W. 368.
Vañjukā *r.* M. 297.
Vañjula *tr.* 28.
Vañjulā *r.* M. 297.
Vañjulā *r.* S. 302, 303.
Vaṅkṣu *r.* NW. 292, 389.
Vapantī? *r.* C. 295.
Vapu *aps.* 1, 2, 5–8.
Vapuṣ-mat *k.* 272, 273.
Vapuṣ-mat *pr.* 670, 673–683.
Vapuṣ-matī *q.* 665.
Vara *sf.* 433.
Varā *prs.* 627.
Varadā *r.* C. 300.
Varadā *r.* S. 303.
Varāha *incarnation,* 21.
Varāha *g.* 505, 509.
Vārāha kalpa, 228.
Varāhādri *mt.* N. 279.
Vāraṇāhvaya *t.* M. 355.
Vāraṇa-sāhvaya *t,* M. 355.
Vārāṇasī (*Benares*) *t.* M. 308, 654
Vārāṇasī *t.* E. 360.
Vāraṇa-sthala *t.* M. 351, 355.
Vāraṇāvata t. M. 347, 355.
Vardhamāna *mts.* NW. 388.
Vardhamāna *p.* E. 358.
Vāri-cara *p.* S. 365.
Varmavat (*town*), 242.
Varṇā *r.* S. 303.
Varṇāśā *r.* M. 286, 294.
Vārtāki *pt.* 167.
Vartula *pt.* 84.
Varuṇa *g.* 10, 122, 125, 153, 473, 474, 489, 494, 535, 538, 545, 562, 588, 589, 621, 680.
Varuṇā *r.* N. 392.
Vāruṇa *c.* 284.
Vāruṇa *cst.* 381
Varuṇoda *l.* N. 278, 381.
Varūtha *k.* 446.
Varūthinī *aps.* 391, 394–402.
Varva *p.* N. 376.
Varvara *p.* NW., NE. *and* S. 319, 369, 372.
Vaṣaṭ, 151, 152, 444, 470, 545.
Vasati (*village*), 242.
Vaśa-vartin *gods,* 436, 437.
Vāsika *p.* W. 339.
Vasiṣṭha *rs.* 59, 246, 249, 270, 289, 314, 336, 462, 570, 590, 615.
Vaśiṣṭha *rs.* 449.
Vaśiṣṭha *dg.* 403.
Vāsiṣṭha *pat. b.* 612.
Vāskala *d.* 476, 479.
Vasu *g.* 129, 168, 460, 461, 474.
Vasu *k.* (*of* Cedi), 330, 359.
Vasu *k.* (*of* Magadha), 330.
Vāsudeva *k.* and *g.* 3, 19–21, 55.
Vasu-dhāra *mt.* N. 279.
Vasu-homa *k.* 655.
Vāsuki, Nāga *k.* 648.
Vasu-mat *k.* 463.
Vasu-mat? *mt.* N. 376.
Vasurāta *pr.* 599.
Vaśya *k.* and *c.* 273.
Vaśyatā? *r.* S. 302.
Vāṭadhāna *k.* 312.
Vāṭadhāna *p.* NW. 312, 378.
Vātā-rūpā *gb.* 267.
Vātasvana *mt.* 277.
Vatsa *k.* 307.
Vatsa *c.* and *p.* M. 307, 341, 351.
Vatsa-prī *k.* 604, 607, 610.
Vatsarī? *r.* S. 302.
Vātsya *c.* and *p.* M. 307, 341.
Vāyu (*Wind*) *g.* 6, 10, 22, 23, 147, 178, 473, 474, 489, 562, 582, 648.
Veda-bāhu *rs.* 449.
Vedamali r. S. 303.
Veda-mantra *p.* M. 349.
Vedānta 129, 683.
Veda, 553–557, 685–687.
Vedasinī *r.* M. 293.
Veda-śiras *rs.* 269.
Veda-smṛtā, -ti, *r.* M. 293.
Veda-śrī *rs.* 449.
Veda-trayī? *r.* M. 295.
Veda-vatī *r.* N. 293.
Veda-vatī *r.* S. 303.
Vedi-pālā *r.* C.? 300.
Vegetables, 165, 166, 244, 245.
Vega-vāhinī *r.* M.? 298.
Veṇa *k.* 146, 320, 588.
Veṇā *r.* S. 300.
Veṇā *r., see* Veṇvā *and* Veṇyā.
Veṇī *r.* S. 362.

Veṇika *p.* W.? 373.
Veṇṇā *r.* S. 303.
Veṇu *mt.* N. 278.
Veṇugradha *pt.* 245.
Veṇuka *p.* N. 379.
Veṇu-matī *r.* W. 373.
Veṇu-matī *r.* NW.? 375.
Venus, planet, 9, 207, 431, 626.
Veṇvā *r.* N. 286, 294.
Veṇvā *r.* N.? 294.
Veṇvā *r.* W. 289.
Veṇvā *r.* S. 294, 300.
Veṇyā *r.* C. 300, 362.
Veṇyā *r.* S. 303, 362.
Veṣṇāpāśā? *r.* C.? 300.
Vetāla *gb.* 46, 47.
Vetasinī *r.* M. 293.
Vetra-vatī *r.* M. 295, 343.
Vetra-vatī *r.* W. 295.
Vibhāvarī *demi-gs.* 402, 406–408, 411.
Vibhītaka *tr.* 26.
Vibodha *bd.* 3.
Vibhu *g.* 449.
Vibhūti *k.* 623.
Vicia pt. 165.
Vīcī-kāka *bd.* 86.
Viḍāla *d.* 476, 479.
Vidarbha *c.* C. 76, 293, 299, 335, 343, 359, 360, 365, 618, 664, 670.
Vidarbha *k.* 335.
Vidarbhā *t.* C. 335.
Vidarbhā *q.* 454.
Videgha *pr.* 330.
Videha *c.* and *p.* M. 75, 294, 329, 330, 352, 356, 374.
Vidhātṛ *g.* 10, 153, 154, 269.
Vidiśā *t.* M. 295, 342, 343, 625, 627.
Vidiśā *r.* M. 295.
Vidūratha *k.* 578.
Vidūratha *k.* 604, 605, 677.
Vidūratha *k.* 677.
Vi-dveṣaṇī *gb.* 257, 261, 267.
Vidyā (*Science*), 128.
Vidyādhara *dg.* 115, 279, 401–404, 407, 460, 571, 679.
Vidyud-rūpa *d.* 6–8.
Vighna-rāj *dg.*? 32.
Vigna pt. 165.
Vīja-hāriṇī *gb.* 257, 261, 267.
Vijalpā *gb.* 262.
Vījāpahāriṇī *gb.* 261.
Vīja-pūraka *tr.* 25.
Vijaya *k.* 411.
Vijaya *t.* NE. 411.
Vikāra 228, 231, 232.
Vikrama *pr.* 610.
Vikrama-śīla *k.* 445.
Vikrānta *pr.* 140–143.
Vikrānta *k.* 449–452.
Vikṛti *gs.* 263.
Village, ancient, 242.
Vilolā *r.* M. 455 (=Yamunā)
Vimalā *r.* N. 305.
Vimalā *r.* E.? 305.
Vimalodā *r.* N. 305, 306.
Vimalodakā *r.* N.? 290, 306.
Vimāṇḍavya *p.* M. 349.
Vimarda *k.* 438.
Vimba *pt.* 114.
Viṁśa *k.* 618.
Vīṇā *r.* S.? 303.
Vinaśana *t.* M. 290, 310, 312.
Vinata *k.* 589.
Vinatā *demi-gs.* 559.
Vinatāśva *k.* 589.
Vinaya *k.* 589.
Vinda *k.* 345.
Vindhaculaka *p.* N. 374.
Vindhya *mts.* C. 3, 11, 12, 17, 19, 285, 286, 298, 299, 310, 331, 340–344, 360, 517.
Vindhya-mauleya *p.* C. 335.
Vindhya-mūlika *p.* C. 335.
Vindhya-pūṣika? *p.* C. 335.
Vindhyavat *m.* 116.
Vinnā *r.* C. 300.
Vipāśā *r.* N. 292.
Vipāśā *r.* C. 297.
Vipaścit *g.* 415.
Vipaścit *k.* 75, 76, 83.
Vipāṭhā *q.* 446.
Vipracitti *d.* 21, 102, 517.
Vipraśastaka *p.* W. 372.
Viprāṣika *pt.* 165.
Vipula *mts.* N. 277, 281.
Vipulasvat *rs.* 12.
Vīra *k.* 618.
Vīra *k.* 627.
Vīrā *q.* 625, 631, 632, 637, 639, 652, 653, 658, 664.
Vīrā *r.* 297.
Vīra-bhadra *k.* 627.
Vīrahotra? *p.* C. 344.
Vīrajā *r.* M.? 297.
Virajākṣa *mt.* N. 279.
Virajas *rs.* 269.

Virajas *rs.* 454.
Vīraṅkarā *r.* 297.
Virāṭa *k.* 353, 382.
Vīra-vatī *r.* 297.
Virodhinī *gb.* 257, 260, 265.
Virtue (*see Righteousness*), 2, 14, 34, 36, 468.
Virūpa *gb.* 263.
Vīrya-candra *k.* 625.
Vīrya-hārī *gb.* 265.
Viśākhā *cst.* 169, 370.
Viśākha-vat *mt.* N. 279.
Viśāla *mts.* NW. 388.
Viśāla *b.* 426.
Viśāla *k.* 627, 630–636, 641–646, 650.
Viśālā, *village*, 452, 453.
Viśālā *r.* E. 290, 297, 306.
Viśālā *t.* M. 345.
Viśālā *r.* C. 297.
Viṣṇu *g.* 1, 2, 10, 17, 20, 21, 40, 70, 98–102, 106, 108, 112, 130, 206, 219, 224, 225, 278, 290, 348, 349, 387, 389, 460, 465, 469–474, 489, 490, 502–505, 509, 512, 514, 522, 545, 555–558, 572, 574, 582, 588, 686.
Viśoka *mts.* NW. 388.
Viśvācī *aps.* 571.
Viśva-garbha *k.* 669.
Viśva-karman (=Tvaṣṭṛ) *g.* 455–460, 475, 566, 569, 572, 574.
Viśva-kṛt *g.*=Viśva-karman.
Viśva-mālā *r.* E. ? 301.
Viśvāmitra *rs.* 32–47, 50, 55–60, 309, 314, 347, 357, 462, 464, 591.
Viśvāvasu *d.* 113, 115.
Viśva-vedin *m.* 612–615.
Viśve Devās, *gods*, 32, 37, 153–156, 161, 163, 168, 178, 253, 461, 462.
Vītahavya *f.* 371, 600.
Vītahotra *p.* C. 344.
Vital airs, 66, 197, 202–204.
Vitastā *r.* N. 291, 438.
Vītihotra *k.* 344.
Vītihotra *p.* C. 344, 371.
Vivasvat (*Sun*) *g.* 455, 457, 523, 566, 576, 577, 586.
Viviṁśa, -śati, *k.* 618, 619.
Vizagapatam t. SE. 334, 335.
Vraja *dt.* and *p.* M. 308.
Vrata-ghnī *r.* M. ? 293.
Vṛhad-ratha *k.* 330.
Vṛhaspati 10, 50, 101, 102, 109.
Vṛhaspati *rs.* 654.
Vrīhi *cer.* 165.
Vṛji *dt.* M. 309.
Vṛka *k.* 309.
Vṛka *p.* M. 309.
Vṛṣabha *mt.* N. 279–282.
Vṛṣa-dhvaja *h.* E. 356.
Vṛṣaparvan *k.* 669.
Vṛṣavat *mt.* N. 278.
Vṛṣṇi *p.* W. 336.
Vṛtra *d.* 4, 22, 514.
Vṛtra-ghnī *r.* M. ? 293.
Vulture bd. 46, 53, 72, 74, 85, 208, 263, 680.
Vyāghra-grīva *p.* SE. 360.
Vyāghra-mukha *h.* E. 356.
Vyāna (*vital air*), 204.
Vyañjana-hārikā *gb.* 266.
Vyāsa *rs.* 2, 18, 20, 464, 677, 686.
Vyuṣitāśva *k.* 316, 350.

Wages, 43, 46–50.
Wain-gaṅgā r. C. 300, 305, 363.
Warangal t. S. 337.
Warda r. S. 300, 364.
Water (*element*), 217, 221, 222.
Water-fowl, 30.
Water-lily, 29, 30, 104, 115.
Wealth (Artha), 2, 119, 128, 170–172, 185, 187, 198, 252, 264, 430.
Well-rope and jar, 70–73, 91.
Wheat, 84, 165, 181, 244, 245.
Wind, *see* Vāyu.
Wine, 421.
Wolf 72, 82, 85.
Wood-pecker bd. 28.
Wool, 40.
Worlds (Loka), 20, 22, 55, 57, 71, 89, 95, 96, 102, 103, 110, 111, 116, 124, 128, 144, 151, 201, 206, 218, 223, 225, 227, 229, 246, 397, 462, 574, 662.

Xanthochymus tr. 28.

Yādava *race*, 309, 336, 342, 351, 352, 359, 371.
Yadu *k.* 26, 364, 371.
Yajña *pfn.* 247, 248.
Yajur-Veda, 152, 206, 235.
Yajus *hymns*, 64, 235, 458–460, 484, 554–557, 561, 581.
Yak bt. 166.

Yākhā p. N. 322.
Yakṣa *dg.* 46, 115, 232, 234, 236, 246, 272, 279, 460, 497, 541, 559, 571, 581, 648, 679.
Yakṣma, 179.
Yama *g.* 7, 10, 23, 48, 50, 66–68, 71–77, 80–83, 88–90, 147, 153, 162, 209, 215, 263, 420, 455, 457, 460, 473, 474, 489, 533, 562, 566–568, 574, 575, 579, 680, 683.
Yāma *gods*, 248.
Yamī *demi-gs.* 566.
Yamunā *r.* M. 121, 122, 125, 291, 377, 378, 455, 461, 566, 576, 590.
Yāmuna *hills* N. 377, 378.
Yāmuna *p.* N. 377.
Yāmya *cst.* 384.
Yaśodā *q.* 517.
Yaśo-matī ? *r.* N. 380.
Yaśomatya *p.* N. 380.
Yati (*music*), 132.
Yātudhāna *gb.* 262.
Yaudheya *p.* NW. 333, 380.
Yauna *p.* (=Yavana), 381.
Yavana *p.* NW. 284, 311, 314, 318, 319, 328, 350, 371, 377, 384, 466, 677.
Yayāti *k.* 316, 336, 371, 384, 623, 653, 669.
Year, 224–228, 271.
Yena ? *p.* NE. 381.
Yoga, 91, 92, 100, 133.
Yojana, 240, 275–277, 284.
Yudhiṣṭhira *k.* 9, 23, 353, 366.
Yuga, 226.
Yuñjavat ? *mt.* N. 655.
Yūthaga *gods*, 454.

Zizyphus tr. 27.
Zodiac, 169, 348, 387, 580.

BIBLIOTHECA INDICA;

A

COLLECTION OF ORIENTAL WORKS

PUBLISHED BY THE
ASIATIC SOCIETY OF BENGAL.
NEW SERIES, No. 700.

THE

MÁRKANDEYA PURÁNA.

TRANSLATED BY

F. E PARGITER, C. S.

FASCICULUS I.

CALCUTTA:
PRINTED BY G. H ROUSE, AT THE BAPTIST MISSION PRESS,
AND PUBLISHED BY THE
ASIATIC SOCIETY, 57, PARK STREET.
1888.

LIST OF BOOKS FOR SALE

AT THE LIBRARY OF THE

ASIATIC SOCIETY OF BENGAL,

No. 57, PARK STREET, CALCUTTA.

AND OBTAINABLE FROM

THE SOCIETY'S LONDON AGENTS, MESSRS. TRÜBNER & CO.

57 AND 59, LUDGATE HILL, LONDON, E. C.

BIBLIOTHECA INDICA.

Sanskrit Series.

	Rs.	
Advaita Brahma Siddhi, (Sans.) Fasc. I—II @ /6/ each	0	12
Agni Puráṇa, (Sans.) Fasc. I—XIV @ /6/ each	5	4
Aitareya Áraṇyaka of the Rig Veda, (Sans.) Fasc. I—V @ /6/ each	1	14
Aṇu Bháshyam, (Sans.) Fasc. I	0	6
Aphorisms of Sáṇḍilya, (English) Fasc. I	0	6
Aphorisms of the Vedánta, (Sans.) Fasc. III, V—XIII @ /6/ each	3	12
Ashṭasáhasriká Prajñápáramitá, (Sans.) Fasc. I—VI @ /6/ each	2	4
Asvavaidyaka, (Sans.) Fasc. I—V @ /6/ each	1	14
Asvalayana Gribya Sutra, Fasc. II—IV @ /6/ each	1	2
Átharvaṇa Upanishad, (Sanskrit) Fasc. I—V @ /6/ each	1	14
Avadána Kalpalatá by Kshemendra (Sans. and Tibetán) Vol. I, Fasc. I	1	0
Brahma Sútra, (English) Fasc. I	0	12
Bhámatí, (Sans.) Fasc. I—VIII @ /6/ each	3	0
Bṛihad Áraṇyaka Upanishad, (Sans.) Fasc. VI, VII & IX @ /6/ each	1	2
Ditto (English) Fasc. II—III @ /6/ each	0	12
Brihaddharma Puráṇam, Fasc. I	0	6
Bṛihat Saṃhitá, (Sans.) Fasc. II—III, V—VII @ /6/ each	1	14
Chaitanya-Chandrodaya Náṭaka, (Sans.) Fasc. II—III @ /6/ each	0	12
Chaturvarga Chintámaṇi, (Sans.) Vols. I, Fasc. 1—11; II, 1—25; III, 1—19, @ /6/ each Fasc.	20	10
Chhándogya Upanishad, (English) Fasc. II	0	6
Daṣarupa, Fasc. II and III @ /6/	0	12
Gopatha Bráhmaṇa, (Sans.) Fasc. I and II @ /6/ each	0	12
Gobhilíya Gṛihya Sútra, (Sans.) Fasc. I—XII @ /6/ each	4	8
Hindu Astronomy, (English) Fasc. I—III @ /6/ each	1	2
Kála Mádhaba, (Sans.) Fasc. I—IV @ /6/	1	8
Kátantra, (Sans.) Fasc. I—VI @ /12/ each	4	8
Kathá Sarit Ságara, (English) Fasc. I—XIV @ /12/ each	10	8
Kaushitaki Brahmanapanishads, Fasc. II	0	6
Kúrma Purana, (Sans.) Fasc. I—VIII @ /6/ each	3	0
Lalitá-Vistara (Sans.) Fasc. II—VI. @ /6/	1	14
Lalita-Vistara, (English) Fasc. I—III @ /12/ each	2	4
Madana Párijáta, (Sans.) Fasc. I—IV @ /6/ each	1	8
Manutiká Sangraha, (Sans.) Fasc. I—II @ /6/ each	0	12
Mímáṃsá Darṣaṇa, (Sans.) Fasc. II—XIX @ /6/ each	6	12
Márkaṇḍeya Puráṇa, (Sans.) Fasc. IV—VII @ /6/ each	1	8
Márkaṇḍeya Puráṇa (Eng.) Fasc. I	0	12
Nayavártikum, (Sans.) Fasc. I	0	6
Nṛisiṃha Tápaní, (Sans.) Fasc. I—III @ /6/ each	1	2
Nirukta, (Sans.) Vol. I, Fasc. I—VI; Vol. II, Fasc. I—VI; Vol. III, Fasc. I—VI; Vol. IV, Fasc. I—V @ /6/ each Fasc.	8	10
Nárada Smṛiti, (Sans.) Fasc. I—III @ /6/	1	2
Nyáya Darśana, (Sans.) Fasc. III	0	6
Nítisára, or The Elements of Polity, By Kámandaki, (Sans.) Fasc. II—V @ /6/ each	1	8
Nyáya Kusumánjali Prakaranam (Sans.) Vol. I, Fasc. I and II @ /6/ each	0	12
Narada Puncharatna, (Sans.) Fasc. IV	0	6
Pariśishṭaparvan (Sans.) Fasc. I—IV @ /6/ each	1	8

(Continued on third page of Cover.)

	Rs.	
Pingala Chhandaḥ Sútra, (Sans.) Fasc. II—III @ /6/ each ..	0	12
Prithiráj Rásau, (Sans.) Fasc. I—VI @ /6/ each	2	4
Ditto (English) Fasc. I	0	12
Páli Grammar, (English) Fasc. I and II @ /6/ each	0	12
Prákṛita Lakshaṇam, (Sans.) Fasc. I	1	8
Parásara Smṛiti (Sans.) Fasc. I—VII @ /6/ each	2	10
Paráśara, Institutes of (English)	0	12
S'rauta Sútra of Ápastamba, (Sans.) Fasc. I—XII @ /6/ each ..	4	8
Ditto Áśvaláyana, (Sans.) Fasc. I—XI @ /6/ each ..	4	2
Ditto Láṭyáyana (Sans.) Fasc. I—IX @ /6/ each ..	3	6
Ditto S'ánkháyana (Sans.) Fasc. I—VI @ /6/ each ..	2	4
Sáma Véda Saṃhitá, (Sans.) Vols. I, Fasc. 1—10; II, 1—6; III, 1—7 IV, 1—6 V, 1—8, @ /6/ each Fasc.	13	14
Samkhya Sutra vritti (Sans.) Fasc. I and II @ /6/ each	0	12
Sáhitya Darpaṇa, (English) Fasc. I—IV @ /6/ each	1	8
Sánkhya Aphorisms of Kapila, (English) Fasc. I and II @ /6/ each ..	0	12
Sarva Darśana Sangraha, (Sans.) Fasc. II	0	6
Sankara Vijaya, (Sans.) Fasc. II and III @ /6/ each	0	12
Sánkhya Pravachana Bháshya, Fasc. III (English preface only) ..	0	6
Sánkhya Sára, (Sans.) Fasc. I	0	6
S'ri Bháshyam, (Sans.) Fasc. I	0	6
Suśruta Saṃhitá, (Eng.) Fasc. I and II @ /12/ each	1	8
Taittiríya Áraṇya (Sans.) Fasc. I—XI @ /6/ each	4	2
Ditto Bráhmaṇa (Sans.) Fasc. I—XXIV @ /6/ each	9	0
Ditto Saṃhitá, (Sans.) Fasc. II—XXXIV @ /6/ each	12	6
Ditto Prátiśákhya, (Sans.) Fasc. I—III @ /6/ each	1	2
Ditto and Aitareya Upanishads, (Sans.) Fasc. II and III @ /6/ each	0	12
Táṇḍyá Bráhmaṇa, (Sans.) Fasc. I—XIX @ /6/ each	7	2
Tattva Chintámaṇi, Fasc. I—X (Sans.) @ /6/ each	3	12
Tul'sí Sat'saí, (Sans.) Fasc. I	0	6
Uttara Naishadha, (Sans.) Fasc. III—XII @ /6/ each	3	12
Uvásagadasáo, (Sans.) Fasc. I—V @ /12/	3	12
Varáha Purána, (Sans.) Fasc. I—VIII @ /6/ each	3	0
Váyu Puráṇa, (Sans.) Vol. I, Fasc. I—VI; Vol. II, Fasc. I—VII, @ /6/ each Fasc.	4	14
Vishṇu Smṛiti, (Sans.) Fasc. I—II @ /6/ each	0	12
Vivádáratnákara, (Sans.) Fasc. I—VII @ /6/ each	2	10
Vrihannáradiya Purána, (Sans.) Fasc. I—V @ /6/	1	14
Yoga Sútra of Patanjali, (Sans. & English) Fasc. I—V @ /14/ each ..	4	6
The same, bound in cloth	5	2

Tibetan Series.

Sher-Phyin— Fasc. I	1	0

Arabic and Persian Series.

'Álamgírnámah, with Index, (Text) Fasc. I—XIII @ /6/ each ..	4	14
Áín-i-Akbarí, (Text) Fasc. I—XXII @ 1/ each	22	0
Ditto (English) Vol. I (Fasc. I—VII)	12	4
Akbarnámah, with Index, (Text) Fasc. I—XXXVII @ 1/ each	37	0
Bádsháhnámah with Index, (Text) Fasc. I—XIX @ /6/ each ..	7	2
Beale's Oriental Biographical Dictionary, pp. 291, 4to., thick paper, @ 4/12; thin paper	4	8
Dictionary of Arabic Technical Terms and Appendix, Fasc. I—XXI @ 1/ each	21	0
Farhang-i-Rashídí (Text), Fasc. I—XIV @ 1/ each	14	0
Fihrist-i-Ṭúsí, or, Ṭúsy's list of Shy'ah Books, (Text) Fasc. I—IV @ /12/ each	3	0
Futúḥ-ul-Shám Waqídí, (Text) Fasc. I—IX @ /6/ each	3	6
Ditto Azádí, (Text) Fasc. I—IV @ /6/ each ..	1	8
Haft Ásmán, History of the Persian Mansawi. (Text) Fasc. I ..	0	12
History of the Caliphs, (English) Fasc. I—VI @ /12/ each ..	4	8
Iqbálnámah-i-Jahángírí, (Text) Fasc. I—III @ /6/ each ..	1	2
Iṣabáh, with Supplement, (Text) 49 Fasc. @ /12/ each	36	12
Maásir-ul-Umara, Vol. I, Fasc. I—IX, Vol. II, Fasc. I—V @ /6/ each	5	4
Maghází of Wáqidí, (Text) Fasc. I—V @ /6/ each	1	14
Muntakhab-ul-Tawáríkh, (Text) Fasc. I—XV @ /6/ each ..	5	10
Muntakhab-ul-Tawáríkh (English) Vol. II, Fasc. I—IV @ /12/ each ..	3	0

(Turn over.)

	Muntakhab-ul-Lubáb, (Text) Fasc. I—XIX @ /6/ each .. Rs.	7	2
	Mu'áṣir-i-'Álamgírí (Text), Fasc. I—VI @ /6/ each	2	4
	Nokhbat-ul-Fikr, (Text) Fasc. I	0	6
	Niẓámí's Khiradnámah-i-Iskandarí, (Text) Fasc. I and II @ /12/ each ..	1	8
	Suyúṭy's Itqán, on the Exegetic Sciences of the Koran, with Supplement, (Text) Fasc. II—IV, VII—X @ 1/ each	7	0
	Ṭabaqát-i-Náṣirí, (Text) Fasc. I—V @ /6/ each	1	14
	Ditto (English) Fasc. I—XIV @ /12/ each	10	8
	Táríkh-i-Fírúz Sháhi, (Text) Fasc. I—VII @ /6/ each	2	10
	Táríkh-i-Baihaqí, (Text) Fasc. I—IX @ /6/ each	3	6
	Táríkh-i-Fírozsháhí, Fasc. I—IV @ /6/ each	1	8
	Wís o Rámín, (Text) Fasc. I—V @ /6/ each	1	14
	Zafarnámah, Vol. I, Fasc. I—IX, Vol. II. Fasc. I—VIII @ /6/ each ..	6	6

ASIATIC SOCIETY'S PUBLICATIONS

1.	ASIATIC RESEARCHES. Vols. VII, IX to XI; Vols. XIII and XVII, and Vols. XIX and XX @ /10/ each .. Rs.	80	0
	Ditto Index to Vols. I—XVIII	5	0
2	PROCEEDINGS of the Asiatic Society from 1865 to 1869 (incl.) @ /4/ per No.; and from 1870 to date @ /6/ per No.		
3.	JOURNAL of the Asiatic Society for 1843 (12), 1844 (12), 1845 (12), 1846 (5), 1847 (12), 1848 (12), 1850 (7), 1851 (7), 1857 (6), 1858 (5), 1861 (4), 1864 (5), 1865 (8), 1866 (7), 1867 (6), 1868 (6), 1869 (8), 1870 (8), 1871 (7), 1872 (8), 1873 (8), 1874 (8), 1875 (7), 1876 (7), 1877 (8), 1878 (8), 1879 (7), 1880 (8), 1881 (7), 1882 (6), 1883 (5), 1884 (6), 1885 (6) 1886 (8). @ 1/ per No. to Subscribers and @ 1/8 per No. to Non-Subscribers,		
	N. B. The figures enclosed in brackets give the number of Nos. in each Volume.		
4.	Centenary Review of the Researches of the Society from 1784—1883 ..	3	0
	General Cunningham's Archæological Survey Report for 1863-64 (Extra No., J. A. S. B., 1864)	1	8
	Theobald's Catalogue of Reptiles in the Museum of the Asiatic Society (Extra No., J. A. S. B., 1868)	1	8
	Catalogue of Mammals and Birds of Burmah, by E. Blyth (Extra No., J. A. S. B., 1875)	3	0
	Sketch of the Turki Language as spoken in Eastern Turkestan, Part II, Vocabulary, by R. B. Shaw (Extra No., J. A. S. B., 1878) ..	3	0
	Introduction to the Maithili Language of North Bihár, by G. A. Grierson, Part I, Grammar (Extra No., J. A. S. B., 1880)	1	8
	Part II, Chrestomathy and Vocabulary (Extra No., J. A. S. B., 1882) ..	3	0
5.	Anis-ul-Musharrahin	3	0
6.	Catalogue of Fossil Vertebrata	2	0
8.	Catalogue of the Library of the Asiatic Society, Bengal	3	8
9.	Examination and Analysis of the Mackenzie Manuscripts by the Rev. W. Taylor	2	0
10.	Han Koong Tsew, or the Sorrows of Han, by J. Francis Davis ..	1	8
11.	Iṣṭiláhát-uṣ-Ṣúfíyah, edited by Dr. A. Sprenger, 8vo.	1	0
12.	Ináyah, a Commentary on the Hidayah, Vols. II and IV, @ 16/ each ..	32	0
13.	Jawámi-ul-'ilm ir-riyáẓí, 168 pages with 17 plates, 4to. Part I ..	2	0
14.	Khizánat-ul-'ilm	4	0
15.	Mahábhárata, Vols. III and IV, @ 20/ each	40	0
16.	Moore and Hewitson's Descriptions of New Indian Lepidoptera, Parts I—III, with 8 coloured Plates, 4to. @ 6/ each	18	0
17.	Puraṇa Sangraha, I (Markandeya Purana), Sanskrit	1	0
18.	Sharaya-ool-Islám	4	0
19.	Tibetan Dictionary by Csoma de Körös	10	0
20.	Ditto Grammar " "	8	0
21.	Vuttodaya, edited by Lt.-Col. G. E. Fryer	2	0

Notices of Sanskrit Manuscripts, Fasc. I—XXIII @ 1/ each ..	23	0
Nepalese Buddhist Sanskrit Literature, by Dr. R. L. Mitra	5	0

N.B. All Cheques, Money Orders &c. must be made payable to the "Treasurer Asiatic Society" only.

BIBLIOTHECA INDICA;

A

COLLECTION OF ORIENTAL WORKS

PUBLISHED BY THE

ASIATIC SOCIETY OF BENGAL.

NEW SERIES, No. 706.

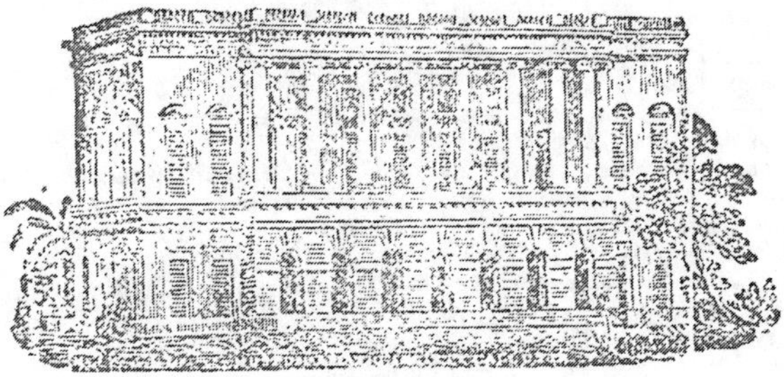

THE

MARKANḌEYA PURAṆA.

TRANSLATED BY

F. E. PARGITER, B. A.

BENGAL CIVIL SERVICE.

LATE BODEN SANSKRIT SCHOLAR, OXFORD.

FASCICULUS II.

CALCUTTA:

PRINTED BY G. H. ROUSE, AT THE BAPTIST MISSION PRESS,

AND PUBLISHED BY THE

ASIATIC SOCIETY. 57, PARK STREET.

1889.

LIST OF BOOKS FOR SALE

AT THE LIBRARY OF THE

Asiatic Society of Bengal,

No. 57, PARK STREET, CALCUTTA.

AND OBTAINABLE FROM

THE SOCIETY'S LONDON AGENTS, MESSRS. TRUBNER & CO.
57 AND 59, LUDGATE HILL, LONDON, E. C.

BIBLIOTHECA INDICA.

Sanskrit Series.

	Rs.	
Advaita Brahma Siddhi. Fasc. I—II @ /6/ each	0	12
Agni Puráṇa, (Sans.) Fasc. II—XIV @ /6/ each	4	14
Aṇu Bháshyam, Fasc. I	0	6
Aitareya Araṇyaka of the Rig Veda. (Sans.) Fasc. I—V @ /6/ each	1	14
Aphorisms of Sáṇḍilya, (English) Fasc. I	0	6
Aphorisms of the Vedánta, (Sans.) Fasc. III, V—XIII @ /6/ each	3	12
Ashṭasáhasriká Prajnápáramitá, Fasc. I—VI @ /6/ each	2	4
Asvalayana Grihya Sutra, Fasc II—IV @ /6/	1	2
Asvavaidyaka, Fasc. I—V @ /6/ each	1	14
Avadána Kalpalatá by Kshemendra (Sans. & Tibetan) Vol. I Fasc. I	1	0
Bhámatí. (Sans.) Fasc. I—VIII @ /6/ each	3	0
Brahma Sútra. (English) Fasc. I	0	12
Brihaddharma Puráṇam, Fasc. I—II @ /6/ each	0	12
Bṛihat Araṇyaka Upanishad. (Sans.) Fasc. VI, VII & IX @ /6/ each	1	2
Ditto (English) Fasc. II—III @ /6/ each	0	12
Brihat Saṃhitá. (Sans.) Fasc. II—III, V—VII @ /6/ each	1	14
Chaitanya-Chandrodaya Náṭaka, (Sans.) Fasc. II—III @ /6/ each	0	12
Chaturvarga Chintámaṇi. (Sans.) Vols. I. Fasc. 1—11; II, 1—25; III, Part I Fasc 1—18. Part II. Fasc. 1—2 @ /6/ each	21	0
Chhándogya Upanishad. (English) Fasc. II	0	6
Dasarupa, Fasc. II and III @ /6/	0	12
Gobhiliya Grihya Sútra. (Sans.) Fasc. I—XII @ /6/ each	4	8
Hindu Astronomy, (English) Fasc. I—III @ /6/ each	1	2
Kála Mádhava, (Sans.) Fasc. I—IV @ /6/	1	8
Kátantra. (Sans.) Fasc. I—VI @ /12/ each	4	8
Kathá Sarit Ságara. (English) Fasc. I—XIV @ /12/ each	10	8
Kaushitaki Brahman Upanishads, Fasc. II	0	6
Kúrma Purana, (Sans.) Fasc. I—VIII @ /6/ each	3	0
Lalitá-Vistara (Sans.) Fasc. II—VI. @ /6/	1	14
Lalita-Vistara, (English) Fasc. I—III @ /12/ each	2	4
Madana Párijáta, (Sans.) Fasc. I—V @ /6/ each	1	14
Manutiká Sangraha, (Sans.) Fasc. I—II @ /6/ each	0	12
Márkaṇḍeya Puráṇa, (Sans.) Fasc. IV—VII @ /6/ each	1	8
Márkaṇḍeya Puráṇa (Eng.) Fasc I—II @ /12/ each	1	8
Mimámsá Darsana, (Sans.) Fasc. II—XIX @ /6/ each	6	12
Nárada Pancharátra, (Sans.) Fasc. IV	0	6
Nárada Smriti, (Sans.) Fasc. I—III @ /6/	1	2
Nayavártikam, (Sans.) Fasc. I	0	6
Nirukta (Sans.), Vol. I. Fasc. I—VI; Vol. II. Fasc. I—VI; Vol. III, Fasc. I—VI; Vol. IV, Fasc. I—IV @ /6/ each Fasc.	8	4
Nitisara, or The Elements of Polity, By Kámandaki, (Sans.) Fasc. II—V @ /6/ each	1	8
Nyáya Darsana, (Sans.) Fasc. III	0	6
Nyáya Kusumánjali Prakaranam (Sans.) Vol. I, Fasc. I and II @ /6/ each	0	12
Parisishṭa Parvan (Sans.) Fasc. I—IV @ /6/ each	1	8

(*Continued on third page of Cover.*)

	Rs.	
Pingala Chhandaḥ Sútra, (Sans.) Fasc. II—III @ /6/ each ..	0	12
Prithiráj Rásau, (Sans.) Part I. Fasc. I, Part II, Fasc. I—V @ /6/ each	2	4
Ditto (English) Part II Fasc. I	0	12
Prákrita Lakshaṇam. (Sans.) Fasc. I	1	8
Parásara Smriti (Sans.) Fasc. I—VII @ /6/ each	2	10
Paráśara. Institutes of (English)	0	12
S'rauta Sútra of Ápastamba. (Sans.) Fasc. I—XII @ /6/ each ..	4	8
Ditto Áśvaláyana. (Sans.) Fasc. I—XI @ /6/ each ..	4	2
Ditto Látyáyana (Sans.) Fasc. I—IX @ /6/ each ..	3	6
Ditto Sánkháyana (Sans.) Fasc. I—V @ /6/ each ..	1	14
Sáma Veda Samhitá. (Sans.) Vols I. Fasc. 2—10; II, 1—6; III, 1—7; IV, 1—6; V, 1—8. @ /6/ each Fasc.	13	8
Sankhya Sutra Vritti (Sans.) Fasc. I and II @ /6/ each	0	12
Sáhitya Darpaṇa. (English) Fasc. I—IV @ /6/ each	1	8
Sánkhya Aphorisms of Kapila. (English) Fasc. I and II @ /6/ each ..	0	12
Sarva Darśana Sangraha. (Sans.) Fasc. II	0	6
Sankara Vijaya. (Sans.) Fasc. II and III @ /6/ each	0	12
Sánkhya Pravachana Bháshya. Fasc. III (English preface only) ..	0	6
S'ri Bháshyam, (Sans.) Fasc. I	0	6
Suśruta Samhitá. (Eng.) Fasc. I and II @ /12/ each	1	8
Taittiríya Áraṇya (Sans.) Fasc. I—XI @ /6/ each	4	2
Ditto Bráhmaṇa (Sans.) Fasc. I—XXIV @ /6/ each	9	0
Ditto Samhitá. (Sans.) Fasc. II—XXXIV @ /6/ each	12	6
Ditto Prátiśákhya. (Sans.) Fasc. I—III @ /6/ each	1	2
Ditto and Áitareya Upanishads. (Sans.) Fasc. II and III @ /6/ each	0	12
Táṇḍyá Bráhmaṇa, (Sans.) Fasc. I—XIX @ /6/ each ..	7	2
Tattva Chintámaṇi. Fasc. I—X (Sans.) @ /6/ each	3	12
Tul'sí Sat'saí, (Sans.) Fasc. I	0	6
Uttara Naishadha. (Sans.) Fasc. III. V—XII @ /6/ each	3	6
Uvásagadasáo. (Sans.) Fasc. I—V @ /12/	3	12
Varáha Purána, (Sans.) Fasc. I—VIII @ /6/ each	3	0
Váyu Puráṇa. (Sans.) Vol. I, Fasc. I—VI; Vol. II, Fasc. I—VII, @ /6/ each Fasc	4	14
Vishṇu Smriti. (Sans.) Fasc. I—II @ /6/ each	0	12
Vivádáratnákara. (Sans.) Fasc I—VII @ /6/ each	2	10
Vrihannáradiya Purána, (Sans.) Fasc. I—V @ /6/	1	14
Yoga-Sútra of Patanjali. (Sans. & English) Fasc. I—V @ /14/ each ..	4	6
The same, bound in cloth	5	2

Tibetan Series.

Sher-Phyin—Fasc. I—II @ /1/ each	2	0
Rtogs brjod dpag bsam hkhri S'iṅ (Tibetan & Sans.) Fasc. I. ..	1	0

Arabic and Persian Series.

'Álamgírnamah. with Index. (Text) Fasc I—XIII @ /6/ each ..	4	14
Áin-i-Akbarí, (Text) Fasc. I—XXII @ 1/ each	22	0
Ditto (English) Vol. I (Fasc. I—VII)	12	4
Akbarnámah. with Index. (Text) Fasc. I—XXXVII @ 1/ each.	37	0
Bádsháhnámah with Index. (Text) Fasc. I—XIX @ /6/ each ..	7	2
Beale's Oriental Biographical Dictionary. pp 291. 4to., thin paper ..	4	8
Dictionary of Arabic Technical Terms, and Appendix, Fasc. I—XXI @ 1/ each	21	0
Farhang-i-Rashídí (Text). Fasc. I—XIV @ 1/ each	14	0
Fihrist-i-Túsí. or, Túsy's list of Shy'ah Books. (Text) Fasc. I—IV @ /12/ each	3	0
Futúh-ul-Shám Waqidí. (Text) Fasc. I—IX @ /6/ each	3	6
Ditto Azádí. (Text) Fasc. I—IV @ /6/ each	1	8
Haft Asmán. History of the Persian Mansawi (Text) Fasc. I ..	0	12
History of the Caliphs. (English) Fasc. I—VI @ /12/ each ..	4	8
Iqbálnámah-i-Jahángírí. (Text) Fasc. I—III @ /6/ each ..	1	2
Isabáh. with Supplement. (Text) 49 Fasc. @ /12/ each	36	12
Maásir-ul-Umará. Vol. I, Fasc. I—IX, Vol. II, Fasc. I—V @ /6/ each	5	[illegible]
Maghází of Wáqidí. (Text) Fasc. I—V @ /6/ each	1	[illegible]
Muntakhab-ul-Tawáríkh. (Text) Fasc. I—XV @ /6/ each ..	5	[illegible]
Muntakhab-ul-Tawáríkh (English) Vol. II. Fasc. I—IV @ /12/ each ..	3	

(*Turn over.*)

Muntakhab-ul-Lubáb. (Text) Fasc. I—XIX @ /6/ each Rs. 7 2
Ma'asir-i-'Alamgiri (Text), Fasc. I—VI @ /6/ each .. 2 2
Nokhbat-ul-Fikr. (Text) Fasc. I 0 6
Nizámi's Khiradnámah-i-Iskandari. (Text) Fasc. I and II @ /12/ each .. 1 8
Suyúty's Itqán, on the Exegetic Sciences of the Koran, with Supplement, (Text) Fasc. II—IV, VII—X @ 1/ each 7 0
Tabaqát-i-Náṣiri, (Text) Fasc. I—V @ /6/ each .. 1 14
Ditto (English) Fasc. I—XIV @ /12/ each .. 10 8
Táríkh-i-Fíróz Sháhi of Zia-al-din Barni (Text) Fasc. I—VII @ /6/ each 2 10
Táríkh-i-Baihaqi (Text) Fasc. I—IX @ /6/ each 3 6
Táríkh-i-Firozshahi of Shams-i Siraj Afif. (Text) Fasc. I—IV @ /6/ each 1 8
Wis o Rámin. (Text) Fasc. I—V @ /6/ each 1 14
Zafarnámah, Vol. I, Fasc. I—IX, Vol. II. Fasc. I—VIII @ /6/ each .. 6 6

ASIATIC SOCIETY'S PUBLICATIONS.

1. Asiatic Researches. Vols. VII, IX to XI: Vols. XIII and XVII, and Vols. XIX and XX @ /10/ each .. Rs. 80 0
   Ditto Index to Vols. I—XVIII .. 5 0
2. Proceedings of the Asiatic Society from 1865 to 1869 (incl.) @ /4/ per No.; and from 1870 to date @ /6/ per No.
3. Journal of the Asiatic Society for 1843 (12), 1844 (12), 1845 (12), 1846 (5), 1847 (12), 1848 (12), 1850 (7), 1851 (7), 1857 (6), 1858 (5), 1861 (4), 1864 (5), 1865 (8), 1866 (7), 1867 (6), 1868 (6), 1869 (8), 1870 (8), 1871 (7), 1872 (8), 1873 (8), 1874 (8), 1875 (7), 1876 (7), 1877 (8), 1878 (8), 1879 (7), 1880 (8), 1881 (7), 1882 (6), 1883 (5), 1884 (6), 1885 (6) 1886 (8), @ 1/- per No. to Subscribers and @ 1/8 per No. to Non-Subscribers.
   N. B. The figures enclosed in brackets give the number of Nos. in each Volume.
4. Centenary Review of the Researches of the Society from 1784—1883 .. 3 0
   General Cunningham's Archæological Survey Report for 1863-64 (Extra No., J. A. S. B., 1864) .. 1 8
   Theobald's Catalogue of Reptiles in the Museum of the Asiatic Society (Extra No., J. A. S. B., 1868) .. 1 8
   Catalogue of Mammals and Birds of Burmah, by E. Blyth (Extra No., J. A. S. B., 1875) 3 0
   Sketch of the Turki Language as spoken in Eastern Turkestan, Part II, Vocabulary, by R. B. Shaw (Extra No., J. A. S. B., 1878) 3 0
   Introduction to the Maithili Language of North Bihár, by G. A. Grierson, Part I, Grammar (Extra No., J. A. S. B., 1880) .. 1 8
   Part II. Chrestomathy and Vocabulary (Extra No., J. A. S. B., 1882) .. 3 0
5. Anis-ul-Musharrahin .. 3 0
6. Catalogue of Fossil Vertebrata .. 2 0
8. Catalogue of the Library of the Asiatic Society, Bengal 3 8
9. Examination and Analysis of the Mackenzie Manuscripts by the Rev. W. Taylor 2 0
10. Han Koong Tsew, or the Sorrows of Han, by J. Francis Davis .. 1 8
11. Iṣṭiláhát-uṣ-Ṣúfiyah, edited by Dr. A. Sprenger, 8vo. 1 0
12. Inayah, a Commentary on the Hidayah, Vols. II and IV, @ 16/ each .. 32 0
13. Jawami-ul-'ilm ir-riyazi, 168 pages with 17 plates, 4to. Part I. .. 2 0
14. Khizánat-ul-'ilm .. 4 0
15. Mahabhárata, Vols. III and IV, @ 20/ each .. 40 0
16. Moore and Hewitson's Descriptions of New Indian Lepidoptera, Parts I—III, with 8 coloured Plates, 4to. @ 6/ each .. 18 0
17. Purana Sangraha, I (Markandeya Purana), Sanskrit .. 1 0
18. Sharaya-ool-Islam .. 4 0
19. Tibetan Dictionary by Csoma de Köros .. 10 0
20. Ditto Grammar .. 8 0
21. Vuttodaya, edited by Lt.-Col. G. E. Fryer .. 2 0

Notices of Sanskrit Manuscripts, Fasc. I—XXIII @ 1/ each .. 23 0
Nepalese Buddhist Sanskrit Literature, by Dr. R. L. Mitra 5 0

N.B. All Cheques, Money Orders, &c. must be made payable to the "Treasurer Asiatic Society" only.

BIBLIOTHECA INDICA;

COLLECTION OF ORIENTAL WORKS

PUBLISHED BY THE

ASIATIC SOCIETY OF BENGAL.

NEW SERIES, No. 810.

THE

MÁRKAṆḌEYA PURÁṆA.

TRANSLATED BY

F. E. PARGITER, B. A.,

BENGAL CIVIL SERVICE.

LATE BODEN SANSKRIT SCHOLAR, OXFORD.

FASCICULUS III.

CALCUTTA:

PRINTED AT THE BAPTIST MISSION PRESS,

AND PUBLISHED BY THE

ASIATIC SOCIETY, 57 PARK STREET.

1891.

LIST OF BOOKS FOR SALE

AT THE LIBRARY OF THE

Asiatic Society of Bengal,

No. 57, PARK STREET, CALCUTTA

AND OBTAINABLE FROM

THE SOCIETY'S LONDON AGENTS, MESSRS. KEGAN PAUL, TRENCH, TRUBNER & CO., LD.

Paternoster House, Charing Cross Road, London, W. C

BIBLIOTHECA INDICA.

Sanskrit Series.

	Rs.	
Advaita Brahma Siddhi, (Text) Fasc. I—IV @ /6/ each	1	8
*Agni Puráṇa, (Text) Fasc. II—XIV @ /6/ each	4	14
Aitaréya Áraṇyaka of the Rig Veda, (Text) Fasc. I—V @ /6/ each	1	14
Aniruddha's Commentary (English) Fasc. I	0	12
Aṇu Bháshyam, (Text) Fasc. I	0	6
Aphorisms of Sáṇḍilya, (English) Fasc. I	0	6
*Aphorisms of the Vedánta, (Text) Fasc. VII—XIII @ /6/ each	2	10
Ashṭasáhasriká Prajnápáramitá, (Text) Fasc. I—VI @ /6/ each	2	4
Aśvavaidyaka, (Text) Fasc. I—V @ /6/ each	1	14
Avadána Kalpalatá by Kshemendra (Sans. & Tibetan) Vol. I, Fasc. 1—3; Vol. II, Fasc. 1 @ 1/	4	0
Bhámatí, (Text) Fasc. I—VIII @ /6/ each	3	0
Brahma Sútra, (English) Fasc. I	0	12
Brihaddevatá, (Text) Fasc. I—III @ /6/ each	1	2
Brihaddharma Puráṇa, (Text) Fasc. I—II @ /6/ each	0	12
*Brihat Áraṇyaka Upanishad, (Text) Fasc. VI, VII & IX @ /6/ each	1	2
* Ditto (English) Fasc. II—III @ /6/ each	0	12
*Brihat Saṃhitá, (Text) Fasc. II—III, V—VII @ /6/ each	1	
*Chaitanya-Chandrodaya Náṭaka, (Text) Fasc. II—III @ /6/ each	0	12
Chaturvarga Chintámaṇi, (Text) Vols. I, Fasc. 1—11; II, 1—25; III, Part I, Fasc. 1—18, Part II, Fasc. 1—8 @ /6/ each	23	4
*Chhándogya Upanishad, (English) Fasc. II	0	6
*Daśarupa, (Text) Fasc. II and III @ /6/ each	0	12
Gopatha Brahmana, (Text) Fasc. I—II @ /6/ each	0	12
*Hindu Astronomy, (English) Fasc. II—III @ /6/ each	0	12
Kála Mádhaba, (Text) Fasc. I—IV @ /6/ each	1	8
Kátantra, (Text) Fasc. I—VI @ /12/ each	4	8
Kathá Sarit Ságara, (English) Fasc. I—XIV @ /12/ each	10	8
*Kaushitakí Brahman Upanishads, (Text) Fasc. II	0	6
Kúrma Puráṇa, (Text) Fasc. I—IX @ /6/ each	3	6
Lalita-Vistara (Text) Fasc. III—VI. @ /6/	1	8
Ditto (English) Fasc. I—III @ /12/ each	2	4
Madana Párijáta, (Text) Fasc. I—IX @ /6/ each	3	6
Manuṭíká Sangraha, (Text) Fasc. I—III @ /6/ each	1	2
*Márkaṇḍeya Puráṇa, (Text) Fasc. IV—VII @ /6/ each	1	8
Ditto (English) Fasc. I—II @ /12/ each	1	8
Mímáṃsá Darśana, (Text) Fasc. II—XIX @ /6/ each	6	12
*Nárada Pancharátra, (Text) Fasc. IV	0	6
Nárada Smṛiti, (Text) Fasc. I—III @ /6/ each	1	2
Nayavártika, (Text) Fasc. I	0	6
Nirukta, (Text) Vol. I, Fasc. 4—6; Vol. II, Fasc. 1—6; Vol. III, Fasc. 1—6; Vol. IV, Fasc. 1—8 @ /6/ each	8	10
*Nítisára, or The Elements of Polity, by Kámandaki (Text) Fasc. II—V @ /6/ each	1	8
Nyáyabinduṭika (Text)	0	10
Nyáya Kusumánjali Prakaraṇa (Text) Vol. I, Fasc. 1—6, Vol. II, Fasc. 1—2 @ /6/ each	3	0
Pariśishṭa Parvan (Text) Fasc. I—IV @ /6/ each	1	8

(*Continued on third page of Cover.*)

Title	Rs.	As.
Muntakhab-ul.l-Tawáríkh (English) Vol. II, Fasc. I—V @ /12/ each	5	10
Muntakhab-ul-Lubáb. (Text) Fasc. I—XIX @ /6/ each	7	4
Muntakhab-ul-Tawáríkh (English) Vol. II, Fasc. I—V @ /12/ each ..	3	12
Mu'ásir-i-'Alamgírí (Text), Fasc. I—VI @ /6/ each	2	4
Nizámí's Khiradnámah-i-Iskandarí, (Text) Fasc. I and II @ /12/ each ..	1	8
Nokhbat-ul-Fikr, (Text) Fasc. I	0	6
Riyazu-s-Salátín, (Text) Fasc. I—IV @ /6/ each	1	8
Suyúty's Itqán, on the Exegetic Sciences of the Koran, with Supplement. (Text) Fasc. II—IV; VII—X @ 1/ each	7	0
Tabaqát-i-Náşirí, (Text) Fasc. I—V @ /6/ each	1	14
Ditto (English) Fasc. I—XIV @ /12/ each	10	8
Táríkh-i-Baihaqí, (Text) Fasc. I—IX @ /6/ each	3	6
Táríkh-i-Fírozshâhí, of Shams-i-Siráj Aif, (Text) Fasc. I—V @ /6/ each	1	14
Táríkh-i-Fírúz Sháhí of Zia-al-dín Barní (Text) Fasc. I—VII @ /6/ each	2	10
Ten Ancient Arabic Poems, Fasc. I	1	0
Wís o Rámín, (Text) Fasc. I—V @ /6/ each	1	14
Zafarnámah, Vol. I, Fasc. I—IX, Vol. II. Fasc. I—VIII @ /6/ each ..	6	6
Túzuk-i-Jahángírí (English) Fasc. I	0	12

ASIATIC SOCIETY'S PUBLICATIONS.

No.	Title	Rs.	As.
1	ASIATIC RESEARCHES. Vols. VII, IX to XI; Vols. XIII and XVII. and Vols. XIX and XX @ /10/ each .. Rs.	80	0
	Ditto Index to Vols. I—XVIII	5	0
2	PROCEEDINGS of the Asiatic Society from 1865 to 1869 (incl.) @ /6/ per No.; and from 1870 to date @ /8/ per No.		
3.	JOURNAL of the Asiatic Society for 1843 (12), 1844 (12), 1845 (12), 1846 (5), 1847 (12), 1848 (12), 1850 (7), 1851 (7), 1857 (6), 1858 (5), 1861 (4), 1862 (5), 1864 (5), 1865 (8), 1866 (7), 1867 (6), 1868 (6), 1869 (8), 1870 (8), 1871 (7), 1872 (8), 1873 (8), 1874 (8), 1875 (7), 1876 (7), 1877 (8), 1878 (8), 1879 (7), 1880 (8), 1881 (7), 1882 (6), 1883 (5), 1884 (6), 1885 (6) 1886 (8), 1887 (7). 1888 (7), 1889 (10), 1890 (11), @ 1/8 per No. to Subscribers and @ 2/ per No. to Non-Subscribers.		
	N. B. The figures enclosed in brackets give the number of Nos. in each Volume.		
4.	Centenary Review of the Researches of the Society from 1784—1883 ..	3	0
	General Cunningham's Archæological Survey Report for 1863-64 (Extra No., J. A. S. B., 1864)	2	0
	Theobald's Catalogue of Reptiles in the Museum of the Asiatic Society (Extra No., J. A. S. B., 1868)	2	0
	Catalogue of Mammals and Birds of Burmah, by E. Blyth (Extra No., J. A. S. B., 1875)	4	0
	Sketch of the Turki Language as spoken in Eastern Turkestan, Part II, Vocabulary, by R. B. Shaw (Extra No., J. A. S. B., 1878) ..	4	0
	Introduction to the Maithili Language of North Bihár, by G. A. Grierson, Part II, Chrestomathy and Vocabulary (Extra No., J. A. S. B., 1882) ..	4	0
5.	Anis-ul-Musharrahin	3	0
6	Catalogue of Fossil Vertebrata	3	0
7.	Catalogue of the Library of the Asiatic Society, Bengal	2	8
8.	Examination and Analysis of the Mackenzie Manuscripts by the Rev. W. Taylor	2	0
9.	Iştiláhát-uş-Şúfíyah, edited by Dr. A. Sprenger, 8vo.	1	0
10.	Ináyah, a Commentary on the Hidayah, Vols. II and IV, @ 16/ each ..	32	0
11.	Jawámi-ul-'ilm ir-riyáşí, 168 pages with 17 plates, 4to. Part I ..	2	0
12.	Khizánat-ul-'ilm	4	0
13.	Mahábhárata, Vols. III and IV, @ 20/ each	40	0
14.	Modern Vernacular Literature of Hindustani by G. A. Grierson. (Extra No., J. A. S. B., 1888)	4	0
15.	Moore and Hewitson's Descriptions of New Indian Lepidoptera, Parts I—III, with 8 coloured Plates, 4to. @ 6/ each	18	0
16.	Purana Sangraha, I (Markandeya Purana), Sanskrit	1	0
17.	Sharaya-ool-Islám	4	0
18.	Tibetan Dictionary by Csoma de Körös	10	0
19.	Ditto Grammar " "	8	0
20.	Vuttodaya, edited by Lt.-Col. G. E. Fryer	2	0

Title	Rs.	As.
Notices of Sanskrit Manuscripts, Fasc. I—XXIV @ 1/ each ..	24	0
Nepalese Buddhist Sanskrit Literature, by Dr. R. L. Mitra	5	0

N. B. All Cheques Money Orders &c. must be made payable to the "Treasurer, Asiatic Society" only.

Parásara Smriti (Text) Vol. I, Fasc. 1—8, Vol. II, Fasc. 1—4, Vol. III. Fasc. 1—3 @ /6/ each .. .. Rs.	5	10
Paráśara, Institutes of (English)	0	12
*Pingala Chhandaḥ Sútra, (Text) Fasc. II—III @ /6/ each ..	0	12
Prákrita Lakshaṇam, (Text) Fasc. I	1	8
Prithiráj Rásau, (Text) Part I, Fasc. I, Part II, Fasc. I—V @ /6/ each	2	4
Ditto (English) Part II, Fasc. I	0	12
Sáhitya Darpaṇa, (English) Fasc. I—IV @ /6/ each ..	1	8
*Sáma Veda Saṃhitá, (Text) Vols. I, Fasc. 5—10; II, 1—6; III, 1—7; IV, 1—6; V, 1—8, @ /6/ each	12	6
*Sankara Vijaya, (Text) Fasc. II and III @ /6/ each	0	12
Sánkhya Aphorisms of Kapila, (English) Fasc. I and II @ /6/ each ..	0	12
*Sánkhya Pravachana Bháshya. Fasc. III (English preface only) ..	0	6
Saṇkhya Sutra Vritti (Text) Fasc. I—IV @ /6/ each	1	8
Ditto (English) Fasc. I	0	12
*Sarva Darśana Sangraha, (Text) Fasc. II	0	6
Srauta Sútra of Ápastamba, (Text) Fasc. I—XII @ /6/ each ..	4	8
Ditto Látyáyana (Text) Fasc. I—IX @ /6/ each ..	3	6
Ditto Sánkháyana (Text) Vol. I, Fasc. 1—7, Vol. II, Fasc. 1—3, @ /6/ each	3	12
S'ṛi Bháshyam, (Text) Fasc. I—III @ /6/ each	0	12
Suśruta Saṃhitá, (English) Fasc. I and III @ /12/ each	2	4
Taittiríya Áraṇya (Text) Fasc. I—XI @ /6/ each	4	2
* Ditto Saṃhitá. (Text) Fasc. IX—XXXV @ /6/ each	10	2
Ditto Prátiśákhya, (Text) Fasc. I—III @ /6/ each	1	2
* Ditto and Aitareya Upanishads, (Text) Fasc. II and III @ /6/ each	0	12
Táṇdyá Bráhmaṇa, (Text) Fasc. I—XIX @ /6/ each	7	2
Tattva Chintámaṇi, (Text) Vol. I, Fasc. 1—9; Vol. II, 1—3 @ /6/ each	6	8
Tul'sí Sat'saí, (Text) Fasc. I—III @ /6/ each	1	2
*Uttara Naishada, (Text) Fasc. III, V—XII @ /6/ each	3	6
Uvásagadasáo, (Text and English) Fasc. I—VI @ /12/	4	8
Varáha Puráṇa, (Text) Fasc. I—XIII @ /6/ each	4	14
Váyu Puráṇa, (Text) Vol. I, Fasc. 1—6; Vol. II, Fasc. 1—7, @ /6/ each	4	14
Vishṇu Smriti, (Text) Fasc. I—II @ /6/ each	0	12
Vivádáratnákara, (Text) Fasc. I—VII @ /6/ each	2	10
Vrihannáradíya Puráṇa, (Text) Fasc. 1—6 @ /6/	2	4

Tibetan Series.

Pag-Sam Thi S'iñ, Fasc. 1—2 @ 1/ each	2	0
Rtogs brjod dpag hkhri S'iñ (Tibetan & Sans.), Vol. I, Fasc. 1—3, Vol. II, Fasc. 1 @ 1/	4	0
Sher-Phyin Vol. I, Fasc. 1—5, Vol. II, 1—2 @ 1/ each ..	7	0

Arabic and Persian Series.

Áín-i-Akbarí, (Text) Fasc. I—XXII @ 1/ each	22	0
Ditto (English) Vol. I, Fasc. 1—7, Vol. II, Fasc. 1—3 ..	17	8
Akbarnámah, with Index, (Text) Fasc. I—XXXVII @ 1/ each	37	0
'Álamgírnámah, with Index, (Text) Fasc. I—XIII @ /6/ each ..	4	14
Arabic Bibliography by Dr. A. Sprenger	0	9
Bádsháhnámah with Index, (Text) Fasc. I—XIX @ /6/ each ..	7	2
Catalogue of the Persian Books and Manuscripts in the Library of the Asiatic Society of Bengal, Fasc. I	1	0
Dictionary of Arabic Technical Terms, and Appendix, Fasc. I—XXI @ 1/ each	21	0
Farhang-i-Rashídí (Text), Fasc. I—XIV @ 1/ each	14	0
Fihrish-i-Ṭúsí, or, Ṭúsy's list of Shy'ah Books, (Text) Fasc. I—IV @ /12/ each	3	0
Futúḥ-ul-Shám Waqídí, (Text) Fasc. I—IX @ /6/ each	3	6
Ditto Azádí, (Text) Fasc. I—IV @ /6/ each	1	8
Haft Ásmán, History of the Persian Mansawi (Text) Fasc. I ..	0	12
History of the Caliphs, (English) Fasc. I—VI @ /12/ each ..	4	8
Iqbálnámah-i-Jahángirí, (Text) Fasc. I—III @ /6/ each ..	1	2
Iṣabáḥ, with Supplement, (Text) Fasc. I—V @ /12/ each ..	38	4
Maásir-ul-Umara, Vol. I, Fasc. 1—9, Vol. II, 1—9, Vol. III, 1—9 @ /6/ each	10	2
Magházi of Wáqidí, (Text) Fasc. I—V @ /6/ each	1	14

* The other Fasciculi of these works are out of stock, and complete copies cannot be supplied.

(*Turn over.*)

BIBLIOTHECA INDICA:

A

COLLECTION OF ORIENTAL WORKS

PUBLISHED BY THE

ASIATIC SOCIETY OF BENGAL.

NEW SERIES, No. 872.

THE MÁRKAṆḌEYA PURÁṆA.

TRANSLATED BY

F. E. PARGITER, B. A.,

BENGAL CIVIL SERVICE.

LATE BODEN SANSKRIT SCHOLAR, OXFORD.

FASCICULUS IV.

CALCUTTA:

PRINTED AT THE BAPTIST MISSION PRESS,

AND PUBLISHED BY THE

ASIATIC SOCIETY, 57, PARK STREET.

1896.

LIST OF BOOKS FOR SALE

AT THE LIBRARY OF THE

Asiatic Society of Bengal,

No. 57, PARK STREET, CALCUTTA,

AND OBTAINABLE FROM

THE SOCIETY'S AGENTS, MESSRS. LUZAC & CO.

46, Great Russell Street, London, W. C., and Mr. Otto Harrassowitz, Bookseller, Leipzig, Germany.

*Complete copies of those works marked with an asterisk * cannot be supplied—some of the Fasciculi being out of stock.*

BIBLIOTHECA INDICA.

Sanskrit Series.

Title	Rs.	As.
Advaita Brahma Siddhi, (Text) Fasc. 1–4 @ /6/ each	Rs. 1	8
*Agni Puráṇa, (Text) Fasc. 2–14 @ /6/ each	4	14
Aitareya Áraṇyaka of the Rig Veda, (Text) Fasc. 1–5 @ /6/ each ...	1	14
Aitareya Brahmana, Vol. I, Fasc. 1–5 and Vol. II, Fasc. 1–5 @ /6/ ...	3	12
Anu Bháshyam, (Text) Fasc. 1–2 @ /6/ each	0	12
Aphorisms of Sáṇḍilya, (English) Fasc. 1	0	6
Ashtasáhasriká Prajnapáramitá, (Text) Fasc. 1–6 @ /6/ each ...	2	4
Aśvavaidyaka, (Text) Fasc. 1–5 @ /6/ each	1	14
Avadána Kalpalatá, (Sans. and Tibetan) Vol. I, Fasc. 1–5; Vol. II. Fasc. 1–4 @ 1/ each	9	0
*Bhámati, (Text) Fasc. 2–8 @ /6/ each	2	10
Brahma Sútra, (English) Fasc. 1	0	12
Brihaddevata (Text) Fasc. 1–4 @ /6/ each	1	8
Brihadharma Puráṇa, (Text) Fasc. 1–5 @ /6/ each	1	14
Brihadaranyaka Upanishad (English) Fasc. 2–3 @ /6/ each ...	0	12
Chaitandya-Chandrodaya Náṭaka, (Text) Fasc. 2–3 @ /6/ each ...	0	12
*Chaturvarga Chintamaṇi (Text) Vols. II, 1–25; III. Part I, Fasc. 1–18. Part II, Fasc. 1–10 @ /6/ each	19	14
*Chhándogya Upanishad, (English) Fasc. 2	0	6
*Hindu Astronomy, (English) Fasc. 2–3 @ /6/ each	0	12
Kála Mádhava, (Text) Fasc. 1–4 @ /6/ each	1	8
Kátantra, (Text) Fasc. 1–6 @ /12/ each	4	8
Kathá Sarit Ságara, (English) Fasc. 1–14 @ /12/ each	10	8
Kúrma Purana, (Text) Fasc. 1–9 @ /6/ each	3	6
*Lalita-Vistara, (Text) Fasc. 3–6 @ /6/ each	1	8
Ditto (English) Fasc. 1–3 @ /12/ each	2	4
Madana Párijáta, (Text) Fasc. 1–11 @ /6/ each...	4	2
Manutiká Sangraha, (Text) Fasc. 1–3 @ /6/ each	1	2
*Márkaṇḍeya Puráṇa, (Text) Fasc. 4–7 @ /6/ each	1	8
Márkaṇḍeya Puráṇa, (English) Fasc. 1–4 @ /12/ each	3	0
Mímáṃsá Darśana, (Text) Fasc. 3–19 @ /6/ each	6	6
*Nárada Smṛiti, (Text) Fasc. 1–3 @ /6/	1	2
Nyayavártika, (Text) Fasc. 1–3 @ /6/	1	2
*Nirukta, (Text); Vol. III, Fasc. 1–6; Vol. IV, Fasc. 1–8 @ /6/ each	5	4
*Nítisára, or The Elements of Polity, By Kámandaki, (Sans.) Fasc. 2–5 @ /6/ each	1	8
Nyayabindutika, (Text)	0	10
Nyaya Kusumánjali Prakarana (Text) Vol. I, Fasc. 1–6; Vol. II, Fasc. 1–3 @ /6/ each	3	6
Pariśishṭa Parvan, (Text) Fasc. 1–5 @ /6/ each...	1	14

Prithiráj Rásau, (Text) Part I, Fasc. 1, Part II, Fasc. 1–5 @ /6/ each Rs. 2 4
Ditto (English) Part II, Fasc. 1 ... . 0 12
Prákṛita Lakshaṇam, (Text) Fasc. 1 ... ... 1 8
Parásara Smriti, (Text) Vol. I, Fasc. 1–8; Vol. II, Fasc. 1–6; Vol. III, Fasc. 1–4 @ /6/ each 6 12
Parásara, Institutes of (English) 0 12
S'rauta Sútra of Ápastamba, (Text) Fasc. 1–12 @ /6/ each ... 4 8
Ditto Láṭyáyana, (Text) Fasc. 2–9 @ /6/ each 3 0
Ditto S'ánkháyana, (Text) Vol. I, Fasc. 1–7; Vol. II, Fasc. 1–4, Vol. III, Fasc. 1–3 @ /6/ each 5 4
*Sáma Veda Saṃhitá, (Text) Vols. I, Fasc. 5–10; II, 1–6; III, 1–7; IV, 1–6; V, 1–8, @ /6/ each Fasc. 12 6
Saṇkhya Sutra Vritti, (Text) Fasc. 1–4 @ /6/ each 1 8
Ditto (English) Fasc. 1–3 @ /12/ each 2 4
*Sankara Vijaya, (Text) Fasc. 2 and 3 @ /6/ each 0 12
*Sánkhya Pravachana Bháshya, Fasc. 3 (English preface only) ... 0 6
S'ri Bháshyam, (Text) Fasc. 1–3 @ /6/ each 1 2
Suśruta Saṃhitá, (Eng.) Fasc. 1 & 2 @ /12/ each 1 8
*Taittiríya Áraṇya, (Text) Fasc. 2–11 @ /6/ each 3 12
* Ditto Saṃhita, (Text) Fasc. 9–39 @ /6/ each 11 10
Táṇḍya Brahmaṇa, (Text) Fasc. 1–19 @ /6/ each 7 2
Tattva Chintámaṇi, (Text) Vol. I, Fasc. 1–9, Vol. II, Fasc. 1–10, Vol. III, Fasc. 1–2, Vol. IV, Fasc. 1, Vol. V, Fasc. 1–2 @ /6/ each ... 9 0
Tul'sì Sat'saí, (Text) Fasc. 1–4 @ /6/ each 1 8
Uvásagadasáo, (Text and English) Fasc. 1–6 @ /12/ 4 8
Varáha Purána, (Text) Fasc. 1–14 @ /6/ each 5 4
*Váyu Puráṇa, (Text) Vol. I, Fasc. 2–6; Vol. II, Fasc. 1–7, @ /6/ each 4 8
Vishṇu Smṛiti, (Text) Fasc. 1–2 @ /6/ each 0 12
Vivádaratnákara, (Text) Fasc. 1–7 @ /6/ each 2 10
Vrihannáradiya Purána, (Text) Fasc. 1–6 @ /6/ 2 4
Vrihat Svayambhu Puran, Fasc. I to IV 1 8

Tibetan Series.

Pag-Sam Thi S'iṅ, Fasc. 1–4 @ 1/ each 4 0
Sher-Phyin, Vol. I, Fasc. 1–5; Vol. II, Fasc. 1–3; Vol. III, Fasc. 1, @ 1/ each 9 0
Rtogs brjod dpag hkhri S'iṅ (Tib. & Sans.) Vol. I, Fasc. 1–5; Vol. II. Fasc. 1–4 @ 1/ each 9 0

Arabic and Persian Series.

Álamgírnámah, with Index, (Text) Fasc. 1–13 @ /6/ each 4 14
Áin-i-Akbarí, (Text) Fasc. 1–22 @ 1/ each 22 0
Ditto (English) Vol. I, Fasc. 1–7, Vol. II, Fasc. 1–5, Vol. III Fasc. 1–5, @ 1/12/ each 29 12
Akbarnámah, with Index, (Text) Fasc. 1–37 @ 1/ each 37 0
Arabic Bibliography, by Dr. A. Sprenger 0 6
Bádshánámah, with Index, (Text) Fasc. 1–19 @ /6/ each 7 2
Catalogue of the Persian Books and Manuscripts in the Library of the Asiatic Society of Bengal. Fasc. 1–3 @ 1/ each 3 0
Dictionary of Arabic Technical Terms, and Appendix, Fasc. 1–21 @ 1/ each 21 0
Farhang-i-Rashídí, (Text) Fasc. 1–14 @ 1/ each 14 0
Fihrish-i-Ṭúsí, or, Ṭúsy's list of Shy'ah Books, (Text) Fasc. 1–4 @ /12/ each 3 0
Futúḥ-ul-Shám Waqidí, (Text) Fasc. 1–9 @ /6/ each 3 6
Ditto Azádí, (Text) Fasc. 1–4 @ /6/ each 1 8
Haft Ásmán, History of the Persian Mansawi, (Text) Fasc. 1 ... 0 12
History of the Caliphs, (English) Fasc. 1–6 @ /12/ each 4 8
Iqbálnámah-i-Jahángirí, (Text) Fasc. 1–3 @ /6/ each 1 2
Iṣabáh, with Supplement, (Text) 51 Fasc. @ /12/ each 38 4
Maásir-ul-Umara, Vol. I, Fasc. 1–9, Vol. II, Fasc. 1–9; Vol III, 1–10 Index to Vol. I Fasc. X & XI & Index to Vol. III, Fasc. XI & XII @ /6/ each 12 0
Magházi of Wáqidí, (Text) Fasc. 1–5 @ /6/ each 1 14

* The other Fasciculi of these works are out of stock, and complete copies cannot be supplied.

	Rs.	
Muntakhab-ul-Tawáríkh, (Text) Fasc. 1–15 @ /6/ each ...	Rs. 5	10
Muntakhab-ul-Tawáríkh, (English) Vol. I, Fasc. 1; Vol. II, Fasc. 1–5 @ /12/ each	4	8
Muntakhab-ul-Lubáb, (Text) Fasc. 1–19 @ /6/ each	7	2
Mu'áṣir-i-'Álamgírí, (Text), Fasc. 1–6 @ /6/ each	2	4
Nokhbat-ul-Fikr, (Text) Fasc. 1	0	6
Niẓámí's Khiradnámah-i-Iskandari, (Text) Fasc. 1 and 2 @ /12/ each	1	8
Riyáẓu-s-Salatin, (Text) Fasc. 1–4 @ /6/ each	1	8
*Suyúṭy's Itqán, on the Exegetic Sciences of the Koran, with Supplement, (Text) Fasc. 7–10 @ 1/ each	4	0
Ṭabaqát-i-Náṣirí, (Text) Fasc. 1–5 @ /6/ each	1	14
Ditto (English) Fasc. 1–14 @ /12/ each	10	8
Táríkh-i-Fírúz Sháhi of Zia-al-din Barni (Text) Fasc. 1–7 @ /6/ each ...	2	10
Táríkh-i-Baihaqí, (Text) Fasc. 1–9 @ /6/ each	3	6
Táríkh-i-Fírozsháhi, of Shams-i-Siráj Aif, (Text) Fasc. 1–6 @ /6/ each...	2	4
Ten Ancient Arabic Poems, Fasc. 1 & 2 @ 1/8/ each	3	0
Wís o Rámín, (Text) Fasc. 1–5 @ /6/ each	1	14
Zafarnámah, Vol. I, Fasc. 1–9, Vol. II, Fasc. 1–8 @ /6/ each ...	6	6
Tuzuk-i-Jahángirí, (Eng.) Fasc. 1	0	12

ASIATIC SOCIETY'S PUBLICATIONS.

1.	ASIATIC RESEARCHES. Vol. VII, Vols. XIII and XVII, and Vols. XIX and XX @ 10/ each	Rs. 50	0
	Ditto Index to Vols. I—XVIII	5	0
2.	PROCEEDINGS of the Asiatic Society from 1865 to 1869 (incl.) @ /6/ per No.; and from 1870 to date @ /8/ per No.		
3.	JOURNAL of the Asiatic Society for 1843 (12), 1844 (12), 1845 (12), 1846 (5), 1847 (12), 1848 (12), 1850 (7), 1851 (7), 1857 (6), 1858 (5), 1861 (4), 1862 (5), 1864 (5), 1866 (7), 1867 (6), 1868 (6), 1869 (8), 1870 (8), 1871 (7), 1872 (8), 1873 (8), 1874 (8), 1875 (7), 1876 (7), 1877 (8), 1878 (8), 1879 (7), 1880 (8), 1881 (7), 1882, (6), 1883 (5), 1884 (6), 1885 (6), 1886 (8), 1887 (7), 1888 (7), 1889 (10), 1890 (11), 1891 (7), 1892 (8), 1893 (11), 1894 (8), @ 1/8 per No. to Members and @ 2/ per No. to Non-Members.		

N. B.—The figures enclosed in brackets give the number of Nos. in each Volume.

4.	Centenary Review of the Researches of the Society from 1784–1883 ...	3	0
	General Cunningham's Archæological Survey Report for 1863–64 (Extra No., *J. A. S. B.*, 1864)	2	0
	Theobald's Catalogue of Reptiles in the Museum of the Asiatic Society (Extra No., *J. A. S. B.*, 1868)	2	0
	Catalogue of Mammals and Birds of Burmah, by E. Blyth (Extra No., *J. A. S. B.*, 1875)	4	0
	Introduction to the Maithili Language of North Bihár, by G. A. Grierson, Part II, Chrestomathy and Vocabulary (Extra No., *J. A. S. B.*, 1882)	4	0
5.	Anis-ul-Musharrahin	3	0
6.	Catalogue of Fossil Vertebrata	3	0
7.	Catalogue of the Library of the Asiatic Society, Bengal, by W. A. Bion	3	8
8.	Iṣṭiláhát-uṣ-Ṣúfíyah, edited by Dr. A. Sprenger, 8vo.	1	0
9.	Ináyah, a Commentary on the Hidayah, Vols. II and IV, @ 16/ each ...	32	0
10.	Jawámi-ul-'ilm ir-riyáẓí, 168 pages with 17 plates, 4to. Part I ...	2	0
11.	Khizánat-ul-'ilm	4	0
12.	Mahábáhrata, Vols. III and IV, @ 20/ each	40	0
13.	Moore and Hewitson's Descriptions of New Indian Lepidoptera, Parts I–III, with 8 coloured Plates, 4to. @ 6/ each	18	0
14.	Sharaya-ool-Islám	4	0
15.	Tibetan Dictionary, by Csoma de Körös	10	0
16.	Ditto Grammar " "	8	0
17.	Vuttodaya, edited by Lt.-Col. G. E. Fryer	2	0

Notices of Sanskrit Manuscripts, Fasc. 1–26 @ 1/ each	26	0
Nepalese Buddhist Sanskrit Literature, by Dr. R. L. Mitra ...	5	0

N.B.—All Cheques, Money Orders, &c., must be made payable to the "Treasurer, Asiatic Society," only.

BIBLIOTHECA INDICA:

A

COLLECTION OF ORIENTAL WORKS

PUBLISHED BY THE

ASIATIC SOCIETY OF BENGAL.

NEW SERIES, No. 890.

THE

MARKAṆḌEYA PURAṆA.

TRANSLATED BY

F. E. PARGITER, B. A.,

BENGAL CIVIL SERVICE.

LATE BODEN SANSKRIT SCHOLAR, OXFORD.

FASCICULUS V.

CALCUTTA:

PRINTED AT THE BAPTIST MISSION PRESS,

AND PUBLISHED BY THE

ASIATIC SOCIETY, 57, PARK STREET.

1897.

LIST OF BOOKS FOR SALE

AT THE LIBRARY OF THE

Asiatic Society of Bengal,

No. 57, PARK STREET, CALCUTTA,

AND OBTAINABLE FROM

THE SOCIETY'S AGENTS, MESSRS. LUZAC & CO.

46, Great Russell Street, London, W. C., and Mr. Otto Harrassowitz, Bookseller, Leipzig, Germany.

*Complete copies of those works marked with an asterisk * cannot be supplied—some of the Fasciculi being out of stock.*

BIBLIOTHECA INDICA.

Sanskrit Series.

Title		Rs.	
Advaita Brahma Siddhi, (Text) Fasc. 1–4 @ /6/ each ...	Rs.	1	8
*Agni Purāṇa, (Text) Fasc. 2–14 @ /6/ each		4	14
Aitarēya Āraṇyaka of the Ṛg Veda, (Text) Fasc. 1–5 @ /6/ each ...		1	14
Aitarēya Brāhmaṇa, Vol. I, Fasc. 1–5 and Vol. II, Fasc. 1–5 Vol. III, Fasc. 1–5 @ /6/		5	10
Aṇu Bhāṣyam, (Text) Fasc. 1–3 @ /6/ each		1	2
Aphorisms of Sāṇḍilya, (English) Fasc. 1		0	12
Aṣṭasāhasrikā Prajñāpāramitā, (Text) Fasc. 1–6 @ /6/ each ...		2	4
Açvavaidyaka, (Text) Fasc. 1–5 @ /6/ each		1	14
Avadāna Kalpalatā, (Sans. and Tibetan) Vol. I, Fasc. 1–5; Vol. II. Fasc. 1–5 @ 1/ each		10	0
*Bhāmatī, (Text) Fasc. 3–8 @ /6/ each		2	4
Brahma Sūtra, (English) Fasc. 1		0	12
Bṛhaddēvatā (Text) Fasc. 1–4 @ /6/ each		1	8
Bṛhaddharma Purāṇa, (Text) Fasc. 1–5 @ /6/ each		1	14
Bṛhadāraṇyaka Upaniṣad (English) Fasc. 2–3 @ /12/ each		1	8
Caitanya-Chandrōdaya Nāṭaka, (Text) Fasc. 2–3 @ /6/ each ...		0	12
*Çaṇkara Vijaya, (Text) Fasc. 2 and 3 @ /6/ each		0	12
*Caturvarga Chintāmaṇi (Text) Vols. II, 1–25; III. Part I, Fasc. 1–18. Part II, Fasc. 1–10 @ /6/ each		19	14
*Chāndōgya Upaniṣad, (English) Fasc. 2		0	12
Çrauta Sūtra of Āpastamba, (Text) Fasc. 1–13 @ /6/ each...	Rs.	4	14
* Ditto Lāṭyāyāna, (Text) Fasc. 2–9 @ /6/ each		3	0
Ditto Çānkhāyana, (Text) Vol. I, Fasc. 1–7; Vol. II, Fasc. 1–4, Vol. III, Fasc. 1–3 @ /6/ each		5	4
Çrī Bháshyam, (Text) Fasc. 1–3 @ /6/ each		1	2
Kāla Mādhava, (Text) Fasc. 1–4 @ /6/ each		1	8
Kātantra, (Text) Fasc. 1–6 @ /12/ each		4	8
Kathā Sarit Sāgara, (English) Fasc. 1–14 @ /12/ each		10	8
Kūrma Purāṇa, (Text) Fasc. 1–9 @ /6/ each		3	6
*Lalita-Vistara, (Text) Fasc. 4–6 @ /6/ each		1	2
Ditto (English) Fasc. 1–3 @ /12/ each		2	4
Madana Pārijāta, (Text) Fasc. 1–11 @ /6/ each...		4	2
Manuṭīkā Saṇgraha, (Text) Fasc. 1–3 @ /6/ each		1	2
*Mārkaṇḍēya Purāṇa, (Text) Fasc. 4–7 @ /6/ each		1	8
Mārkaṇḍēya Purāṇa, (English) Fasc. 1–4 @ /12 each		3	0
*Mīmāṁsā Darçana, (Text) Fasc. 3–19 @ /6/ each		6	6
Nārada Ṣmṛti, (Text) Fasc. 1–3 @ /6/		1	2
Nyayavārtika, (Text) Fasc. 1–3 @ /6/		1	2
*Nirukta, (Text); Vol. III, Fasc. 1–6; Vol. IV, Fasc. 1–8 @ /6/ each		5	4

Work	Rs.	As.
*Nītisāra, or The Elements of Polity, By Kámandaki, (Sans.) Fasc. 2–5 @ /6/ each	1	8
Nyayābindoutīkā, (Text)	0	10
Nyāya Kusumāñjali Prakaraṇa (Text) Vol. I, Fasc. 1–6; Vol. II, Fasc. 1–3 @ /6/ each	3	6
Padumawati	1	8
Pariçiṣta Parvan, (Text) Fasc. 1–5 @ /6/ each	1	14
Prithivirāj Rāsa, (Text) Part I, Fasc. 1, Part II, Fasc. 1–5 @ /6/ each ...	2	4
Ditto (English) Part II, Fasc. 1	0	12
Prākṛta Lakṣṇam, (Text) Fasc. 1	1	8
Parāçara Smṛti, (Text) Vol. I, Fasc. 1–8; Vol. II, Fasc. 1–6; Vol. III, Fasc. 1–4 @ /6/ each	6	12
Parāçara, Institutes of (English)	0	12
*Sāma Vēda Saṁhitā, (Text) Vols. I, Fasc. 5–10; II, 1–6; III, 1–7; IV, 1–6; V, 1–8, @ /6/ each Fasc.	12	6
Sāṅkhya Sūtra Vṛtti, (Text) Fasc. 1–4 @ /6/ each	1	8
Ditto (English) Fasc. 1–3 @ /12/ each	2	4
*Sāṅkhya Pravacana Bhāṣya, Fasc. 3 (English preface only) ..	0	12
Suçruta Saṁhitā, (Eng.) Fasc. 1 & 2 @ /12/ each	1	8
*Taittirīya Āraṇyaka, (Text) Fasc. 2–11 @ /6/ each	3	12
* Ditto Saṁhitā, (Text) Fasc. 9–40 @ /6/ each	12	0
Tāṇḍya Brāhmaṇa, (Text) Fasc. 1–19 @ /6/ each	7	2
Tattva Cintāmaṇi, (Text) Vol. I, Fasc. 1–9, Vol. II, Fasc. 1–10, Vol. III, Fasc. 1–2, Vol. IV, Fasc. 1, Vol. V, Fasc. 1–4 @ /6/ each ...	9	12
Tul'si Sat'sai, (Text) Fasc. 1–4 @ /6/ each	1	8
Uvāsagadasāo, (Text and English) Fasc. 1–6 @ /12/	4	8
Varāha Purāṇa, (Text) Fasc. 1–14 @ /6/ each	5	4
*Vāyu Purāṇa, (Text) Vol. I, Fasc. 2–6; Vol. II, Fasc. 1–7, @ /6/ each	4	8
Viṣṇu Smṛti, (Text) Fasc. 1–2 @ /6/ each	0	12
Vivādaratnākara, (Text) Fasc. 1–7 @ /6/ each	2	10
Vṛhannāradīya Purāṇa, (Text) Fasc. 1–6 @ /6/	2	4
Vṛhat Svayambhū Purāṇa, Fasc. 1 to V	1	14
Tibetan Series.		
Pag-Sam Thi S'in, Fasc. 1–4 @ 1/ each	4	0
Sher-Phyin, Vol. I, Fasc. 1–5; Vol. II, Fasc. 1–3; Vol. III, Fasc. 1, @ 1/ each	9	0
Rtogs *brjod dpag hkhri* S'in (Tib. & Sans.) Vol. I, Fasc. 1–5; Vol. II. Fasc. 1–5 @ 1/ each	10	0
Arabic and Persian Series.		
'Ālamgīrnāmah, with Index, (Text) Fasc. 1–13 @ /6/ each	4	14
Āīn-i-Akbarī, (Text) Fasc. 1–22 @ 1/ each	22	0
Ditto (English) Vol. I, Fasc. 1–7, Vol. II, Fasc. 1–5, Vol. III Fasc. 1–5, @ 1/12/ each	29	12
Akbarnāmah, with Index, (Text) Fasc. 1–37 @ 1/ each	37	0
Arabic Bibliography, by Dr. A. Sprenger	0	6
Bādshāhnāmah, with Index, (Text) Fasc. 1–19 @ /6/ each	7	2
Catalogue of the Persian Books and Manuscripts in the Library of the Asiatic Society of Bengal. Fasc. 1 3 @ 1/ each	3	0
Dictionary of Arabic Technical Terms, and Appendix, Fasc. 1–21 @ 1/ each	21	0
Farhang-i-Rashīdī, (Text) Fasc. 1–14 @ 1/ each	14	0
Fihrist-i-Ṭūsī, or, Ṭūsy's list of Shy'ah Books, (Text) Fasc. 1–4 @ /12/ each ... ... Rs.	3	0
Futūḥ-ush-Shām of Waqidī, (Text) Fasc. 1–9 @ /6/ each	3	6
Ditto of Azádí, (Text) Fasc. 1–4 @ /6/ each	1	8
Haft Āsmān, History of the Persian Masnawi, (Text) Fasc. 1 ...	0	12
History of the Caliphs, (English) Fasc. 1–6 @ /12/ each	4	8
Iqbālnāmah-i-Jahāngīrī, (Text) Fasc. 1–3 @ /6/ each	1	2
Iṣābāh, with Supplement, (Text) 51 Fasc. @ /12/ each	38	4
Maāṣir-ul-Umarā, Vol. I, Fasc. 1–9, Vol. II, Fasc. 1–9; Vol III, 1–10 Index to Vol. I Fasc. X & XI & Index to Vol. III, Fasc. XI & XII Index to Vol. II, Fasc. X & XI @ /6/ each	12	12

* The other Fasciculi of these works are out of stock, and complete copies cannot be supplied.

Maghâzi of Wāqidī, (Text) Fasc. 1–5 @ /6/ each 1 14
Muntakhab-ut-Tawārīkh, (Text) Fasc. 1–15 @ /6/ each 5 10
Muntakhab-ut-Tawārīkh (English) Vol. I, Fasc. 1–3; Vol. II, Fasc. 1–5 @ /12/ each 6 0
Muntakhab-ul-Lubāb, (Text) Fasc. 1–19 @ /6/ each ... 7 2
Ma'āṣir-i-'Ālamgīrī, (Text), Fasc. 1–6 @ /6/ each 2 4
Nukhbat-ul-Fikr, (Text) Fasc. 1 ... ... 0 6
Niẓāmī's Khiradnāmah-i-Iskandari, (Text) Fasc. 1 and 2 @ /12/ each 1 8
Riyāẓu-s-Salātīn, (Text) Fasc. 1–4 @ /6/ each 1 8
*Suyūṭy's Itqān, on the Exegetic Sciences of the Koran, with Supplement, (Text) Fasc. 7–10 @ 1/ each 4 0
Ṭabaqāt-i-Nāṣirī, (Text) Fasc. 1–5 @ /6/ each 1 14
Ditto (English) Fasc. 1–14 @ /12/ each 10 8
Tārīkh-i-Fīrūz Shāhi of Ẓiyān-d-dīn Barnī (Text) Fasc. 1–7 @ /6/ each... 2 10
Tārīkh-i-Baihaqī, (Text) Fasc. 1–9 @ /6/ each 3 6
Tārīkh-i-Fīrūzshāhi, of Shams-i-Sirāj Aif, (Text) Fasc. 1–6 @ /6/ each... 2 4
Ten Ancient Arabic Poems, Fasc. 1 & 2 @ 1/8/ each 3 0
Wís o Rāmīn, (Text) Fasc. 1–5 @ /6/ each 1 14
Ẓafarnāmah, Vol. I, Fasc. 1–9, Vol. II, Fasc. 1–8 @ /6/ each . 6 6
Tuzuk-i-Jahāngirī, (Eng.) Fasc. 1 ... ... 0 12

ASIATIC SOCIETY'S PUBLICATIONS.

1. Asiatic Researches. Vol. VII, Vols. XIII and XVII, and Vols. XIX and XX @ 10/ each ... ... Rs. 50 0
2. Proceedings of the Asiatic Society from 1865 to 1869 (incl.) @ /6/ per No.; and from 1870 to date @ /8/ per No.
3. Journal of the Asiatic Society for 1843 (12), 1844 (12), 1845 (12), 1846 (5), 1847 (12), 1848 (12), 1857 (6), 1858 (5), 1861 (4), 1866 (7), 1867 (6), 1868 (6), 1869 (8), 1870 (8), 1871 (7), 1872 (8), 1873 (8), 1874 (8), 1875 (7), 1876 (7), 1877 (8), 1878 (8), 1879 (7), 1880 (8), 1881 (7), 1882, (6), 1883 (5), 1884 (6), 1885 (6), 1886 (8), 1887 (7), 1888 (7), 1889 (10), 1890 (11), 1891 (7), 1892 (8), 1893 (11), 1894 (8), @ 1/8 per No. to Members and @ 2/ per No. to Non-Members.

N. B.—The figures enclosed in brackets give the number of Nos. in each Volume.

4. Centenary Review of the Researches of the Society from 1784–1883 ... 3 0
General Cunningham's Archæological Survey Report for 1863–64 (Extra No., *J. A. S. B.*, 1864) 2 0
Theobald's Catalogue of Reptiles in the Museum of the Asiatic Society (Extra No., *J. A. S. B.*, 1868) 2 0
Catalogue of Mammals and Birds of Burmah, by E. Blyth (Extra No., *J. A. S. B.*, 1875) 4 0
Introduction to the Maithilī Language of North Bihár, by G. A. Grierson, Part II, Chrestomathy and Vocabulary (Extra No., *J. A. S. B.*, 1882) 4 0
5. Anis-ul-Musharrahin 3 0
6. Catalogue of Fossil Vertebrata 3 0
7. Catalogue of the Library of the Asiatic Society, Bengal, by W. A. Bion 3 8
8. Iṣṭilāhāt-uṣ-Ṣūfiyah, edited by Dr. A. Sprenger, 8vo. 1 0
9. Ināyah, a Commentary on the Hidayah, Vols. II and IV, @ 16/ each... 32 0
10. Jawāmi-ul-'ilm ir-riyāẓī, 168 pages with 17 plates, 4to. Part I ... 2 0
11. Khizānat-ul-'ilm 4 0
12. Mahābāhrata, Vols. III and IV, @ 20/ each 40 0
13. Moore and Hewitson's Descriptions of New Indian Lepidoptera, Parts I–III, with 8 coloured Plates, 4to. @ 6/ each 18 0
14. Sharaya-ool-Islām 4 0
15. Tibetan Dictionary, by Csoma de Körös 10 0
16. Ditto Grammar " " 8 0

Notices of Sanskrit Manuscripts, Fasc. 1–26 @ 1/ each 26 0
Nepalese Buddhist Sanskrit Literature, by Dr. R. L. Mitra ... 5 0

N.B.—All Cheques, Money Orders, &c., must be made payable to the "Treasurer, Asiatic Society," only.

Books are supplied in V-P. P.

BIBLIOTHECA INDICA:

A

COLLECTION OF ORIENTAL WORKS

PUBLISHED BY THE

ASIATIC SOCIETY OF BENGAL.

NEW SERIES, No. 947.

THE MÁRKAṆḌEYA PURÁṆA.

TRANSLATED BY

F. E. PARGITER, B. A.,

BENGAL CIVIL SERVICE.

LATE BODEN SANSKRIT SCHOLAR, OXFORD.

FASCICULUS VI.

CALCUTTA:

PRINTED AT THE BAPTIST MISSION PRESS,

AND PUBLISHED BY THE

ASIATIC SOCIETY, 57, PARK STREET,

1899.

LIST OF BOOKS FOR SALE

AT THE LIBRARY OF THE

ASIATIC SOCIETY OF BENGAL,

No. 57, PARK STREET, CALCUTTA,

AND OBTAINABLE FROM

THE SOCIETY'S AGENTS, MESSRS. LUZAC & CO.,

46, GREAT RUSSELL STREET, LONDON, W. C., AND MR. OTTO HARRASSOWITZ, BOOKSELLER, LEIPZIG, GERMANY.

*Complete copies of those works marked with an asterisk * cannot be supplied—some of the Fasciculi being out of stock.*

BIBLIOTHECA INDICA.

Sanskrit Series.

Advaita Brahma Siddhi, (Text) Fasc. 1–4 @ /6/ each ...	Rs.	1	8
*Agni Purāṇa, (Text) Fasc. 4–14 @ /6/ each ...		4	2
Aitarēya Āraṇyaka of the Ṛg Vēda, (Text) Fasc. 1–5 @ /6/ each ...		1	14
Aitarēya Brāhmaṇa, Vol. I, Fasc. 1-5 and Vol. II, Fasc. 1-5 Vol. III, Fasc. 1-5 Vol. IV, Fasc. 1-5 @ /6/ ...		7	8
Aṇu Bhāṣyam, (Text) Fasc. 1–5 @ /6/ each ...		1	14
Aphorisms of Sāṇḍilya, (English) Fasc. 1 ...		0	12
Aṣṭasāhasrikā Prajñāpāramitā, (Text) Fasc. 1–6 @ /6/ each ...		2	4
Açvavaidyaka, (Text) Fasc. 1–5 @ /6/ each ...		1	14
Avadāna Kalpalatā, (Sans. and Tibetan) Vol. I, Fasc. 1–5; Vol. II. Fasc. 1–5 @ 1/ each ...		10	0
*Bhāmatī, (Text) Fasc. 4–8 @ /6/ each ...		1	14
Bhāṭṭa Dīpikā Vol I, Fasc. 1 ...		0	6
Brahma Sūtra, (English) Fasc. 1 ...		0	12
Bṛhaddēvatā (Text) Fasc. 1–4 @ /6/ each ...		1	8
Bṛhaddharma Purāṇa, (Text) Fasc. 1–6 @ /6/ each ...		2	4
*Caturvarga Chintāmaṇi (Text) Vols. II, 1–25; III. Part I, Fasc. 1–18. Part II, Fasc. 1–10 @ /6/ each ...		19	14
*Çrsuta Sūtra of Āpastamba, (Text) Fasc. 3–14 @ /6/ each ...		4	8
Ditto Āçvalāyana (Text) Fasc. 1 to 11 @ /6/ ...		4	2
* Ditto Lāṭyāyana, (Text) Fasc. 1–9 @ /6/ each ...		3	6
Ditto Çānkhāyana, (Text) Vol. I, Fasc. 1–7; Vol. II, Fasc. 1–4, Vol. III, Fasc. 1–4 @ /6/ each ...		5	10
Çrī Bhāshyam, (Text) Fasc. 1–3 @ /6/ each ...		1	2
Kāla Mādhava, (Text) Fasc. 1–4 @ /6/ each ...		1	8
Kāla Viveka, Fasc. 1 to 3 ...		1	2
Kātantra, (Tetx) Fasc. 1–6 @ /12/ each ...		4	8
Kathā Sarit Sāgara, (English) Fasc. 1–14 @ /12/ each ...		10	8
Kūrma Purāṇa, (Text) Fasc. 1–9 @ /6/ each ...		3	6
Lalits-Vistara, (English) Fasc. 1–3 @ /12/ each ...		2	4
Madana Pārijāta, (Text) Fasc. 1–11 @ /6/ each ...		4	2
Manuṭīkā Saṅgraha, (Text) Fasc. 1–3 @ /6/ each ...		1	2
*Mārkaṇḍēya Purāṇa, (Text) Fasc. 4–7 @ /6/ each ...		1	8
Mārkaṇḍēya Purāṇa, (English) Fasc. 1–5 @ /12 each ...		3	12
*Mīmāṃsā Darçana, (Text) Fasc. 7–19 @ /6/ each ...		4	14
Nārada Smṛti, (Text) Fasc. 1–3 @ /6/ ...		1	2
Nyāyavārtika, (Text) Fasc. 1–4 @ /6/ ...		1	8
*Nirukta, (Text) Vol. III. Fasc. 1–6; Vol. IV, Fasc. 1–8 @ /6/ each ...		5	4

Title	Rs.	As.
Nyayabindutīkā, (Text)	Rs. 0	10
Nyāya Kusumāñjali Prakarana (Text) Vol. I, Fasc. 1–6; Vol. II, Fasc. 1–3 @ /6/ each		
Padumawati Fasc. 1 and 2 @ 2/	8	6
Pariçista Parvan, (Text) Fasc. 1–5 @ /6/ each	4	0
Prithivirāj Rāsa, (Text) Part II, Fasc. 1–5 @ /6/ each	1	14
Ditto (English) Part II, Fasc. 1	1	14
Prākrta Laksanam, (Text) Fasc. 1	0	12
Parāçara Smrti, (Text) Vol. I, Fasc. 1–8; Vol. II, Fasc. 1–6; Vol. III, Fasc. 1–5 @ /6/ each	1	8
Parāçara, Institutes of (English)	7	2
*Sāma Vēda Samhitā, (Text) Vols. I, Fasc. 5–10; II, 1–6; III, 1–7; IV, 1–6; V, 1–8, @ /6/ each Fasc.	0	12
Sānkhya Sūtra Vrtti, (Text) Fasc. 1–4 @ /6/ each	12	6
Ditto (English) Fasc. 1–3 @ /12/ each	1	8
Suçruta Samhitá, (Eng.) Fasc. 1 @ /12/	2	4
*Taittereya Samhitā, (Text) Fasc. 11–42 @ /6/ each	0	12
Tāndya Brāhmana, (Text) Fasc. 1–19 @ /6/ each	12	0
Tattva Cintāmani, (Text) Vol. I, Fasc. 1–9, Vol. II, Fasc. 1–10, Vol. III, Fasc. 1–2, Vol. IV, Fasc. 1, Vol. V, Fasc. 1–5, Part IV, Vol. II, Fasc. 1–7 @ /6/ each	7	2
Trikānda-Mandanam, (Text) Fasc. 1 & 2 @ /6/	12	12
Tul'si Sat'sai, (Text) Fasc. 1–5 @ /6/ each	0	12
Uvāsagadasāo, (Text and English) Fasc. 1–6 @ /12/	1	14
Varāha Purāna, (Text) Fasc. 1–14 @ /6/ each	4	8
*Vāyu Purāna, (Text) Vol. I, Fasc. 2–6; Vol. II, Fasc. 1–7, @ /6/ each	5	4
Visnu Smrti, (Text) Fasc. 1–2 @ /6/ each	4	8
Vivādaratnākara, (Text) Fasc. 1–7 @ /6/ each	0	12
Vrhannāradīya Purāna, (Text) Fasc. 1–6 @ /6/	2	10
Vrhat Svayambhū Purāna, Fasc. I to V	2	4
	1	14

Tibetan Series.

Title	Rs.	As.
Pag-Sam Thi S'în, Fasc. 1–4 @ 1/ each	4	0
Sher-Phyin, Vol. I, Fasc. 1–5; Vol. II, Fasc. 1–3; Vol. III, Fasc. 1 to 4, @ 1/ each	12	0
Rtogs brjod dpag hkhri S'în (Tib. & Sans.) Vol. I, Fasc. 1–5; Vol. II. Fasc. 1–5 @ 1/ each	10	0

Arabic and Persian Series.

Title	Rs.	As.
'Ālamgīrnāmah, with Index, (Text) Fasc. 1–13 @ /6/ each... ...	4	14
Al-Muqaddasi (English) Vol. I, Fasc. 1	0	12
Āīn-i-Akbarī, (Text) Fasc. 1–22 @ 1/ each	22	0
Ditto (English) Vol. I, Fasc. 1–7, Vol. II, Fasc. 1–5, Vol. III Fasc. 1–5, @ 1/12/ each	29	12
Akbarnāmah, with Index, (Text) Fasc. 1–37 @ 1/ each	37	0
Ditto English Fasc, I–III @ 1/ each	3	0
Arabic Bibliography, by Dr. A. Sprenger	0	6
Bādshāhnāmah, with Index, (Text) Fasc. 1–19 @ /6/ each	7	2
Catalogue of the Persian Books and Manuscripts in the Library of the Asiatic Society of Bengal. Fasc. 1–3 @ 1/ each	3	0
Dictionary of Arabic Technical Terms, and Appendix, Fasc. 1–21 @ 1/ each	21	0
Farhang-i-Rashīdī, (Text) Fasc. 1–14 @ 1/ each	14	0
Fihrist-i-Ṭūsī, or, Ṭūsy's list of Shy'ah Books, (Text) Fasc. 1–4 @ /12/ each	3	0
Futūh-ush-Shām of Wāqidī, (Text) Fasc. 1–9 @ /6/ each	3	6
Ditto of Āzādī, (Text) Fasc. 1–4 @ /6/ each	1	8
Haft Āsmān, History of the Persian Masnawi, (Text) Fasc. 1 ...	0	12
History of the Caliphs, (English) Fasc. 1–6 @ /12/ each	4	8
Iqbālnāmah-i-Jahāngīrī, (Text) Fasc. 1–3 @ /6/ each	1	2
Iṣābah, with Supplement, (Text) 51 Fasc. @ /12/ each	38	4
Maāsir-ul-Umarā, Vol. I, Fasc. 1–9, Vol. II, Fasc. 1–9; Vol III, 1–10 Index to Vol. I Fasc. X & XI & Index to Vol. III, Fasc. XI & XII Index to Vol. II, Fasc. X, XI & XII @ /6/ each	13	2

* The other Fasciculi of these works are out of stock, and complete copies cannot be supplied.

Maghāzi of Wāqidī, (Text) Fasc. 1–5 @ /6/ each ... Rs. 1 14
Muntakhabu-t-Tawārīkh, (Text) Fasc. 1–15 @ /6/ each 5 10
Muntakhabu-t-Tawārīkh, (English). Vol. I, Fasc. 1–7; Vol. II, Fasc. 1–5 @ /12/ each 9 0
Muntakhabu-l-Lubāb, (Text) Fasc. 1–19 @ /6/ each 7 2
Ma'āṣir-i-'Ālamgīrī, (Text), Fasc. 1–6 @ /6/ each 2 4
Nukhbatu-l-Fikr, (Text) Fasc. 1 ... ... 0 6
Niẓāmī's Khiradnāmah-i-Iskandari, (Text) Fasc. 1 and 2 @ /12/ each 1 8
Riyāẓu-s-Salāṭīn, (Text) Fasc. 1–5 @ /6/ each 1 14
*Suyūṭy's Itqān, on the Exegetic Sciences of the Koran, with Supplement, (Text) Fasc. 7–10 @ 1/ each 4 0
Ṭabaqāt-i-Nāṣirī, (Text) Fasc. 1–5 @ /6/ each 1 14
Ditto (English) Fasc. 1–14 @ /12/ each 10 8
Ditto Index 1 0
Tārīkh-i-Fīrūz Shāhi of Ẓiyāu-d-dīn Barni (Text) Fasc. 1–7 @ /6/ each... 2 10
Tārīkh-i-Fīrūzshāhi, of Shams-i-Sirāj Aif, (Text) Fasc. 1–6 @ /6/ each... 2 4
Ten Ancient Arabic Poems, Fasc. 1 & 2 @ 1/8/ each 3 0
Wīs o Rāmīn, (Text) Fasc. 1–5 @ /6/ each 1 14
Ẓafarnāmah, Vol. I, Fasc. 1–9, Vol. II, Fasc. 1–8 @ /6/ each .. 6 6
Tuzuk-i-Jahāngīrī, (Eng.) Fasc. 1 ... ... 0 12

ASIATIC SOCIETY'S PUBLICATIONS.

1. Asiatic Researches. Vol. VII, Vols. XIII and XVII, and Vols. XIX and XX @ 10/ each 50 0
2. Proceedings of the Asiatic Society from 1865 to 1869 (incl.) @ /6/ per No.; and from 1870 to date @ /8/ per No.
3. Journal of the Asiatic Society for 1843 (12), 1844 (12), 1845 (12), 1846 (5), 1847 (12), 1848 (12), 1866 (7), 1867 (6), 1868 (6), 1869 (8), 1870 (8), 1871 (7), 1872 (8), 1873 (8) 1874 (8), 1875 (7), 1876 (7), 1877 (8), 1878 (8), 1879 (7), 1880 (8), 1881 (7), 1882 (6), 1883 (5), 1884 (6), 1885 (6), 1886 (8), 1887 (7), 1888 (7), 1889 (10), 1890 (11), 1891 (7), 1892 (8), 1893 (11), 1894 (8), 1895 (7), 1896 (8), 1897 (8), @ 1/8 per No. to Members and @ 2/ per No. to Non-Members.

N. B.—The figures enclosed in brackets give the number of Nos. in each Volume.

4. Centenary Review of the Researches of the Society from 1784–1883 ... 3 0
   General Cunningham's Archæological Survey Report for 1863–64 (Extra No., *J. A. S. B.*, 1864) 2 0
   Theobald's Catalogue of Reptiles in the Museum of the Asiatic Society (Extra No., *J. A. S. B.*, 1868) 2 0
   Catalogue of Mammals and Birds of Burmah, by E. Blyth (Extra No., *J. A. S. B.*, 1875) 4 0
   Introduction to the Maithilī Language of North Bihār, by G. A. Grierson, Part II, Chrestomathy and Vocabulary (Extra No., *J. A. S. B.*, 1882) 4 0
5. Anīs-ul-Musharraḥīn 3 0
6. Catalogue of Fossil Vertebrata 3 0
7. Catalogue of the Library of the Asiatic Society, Bengal, by W. A. Bion 3 8
8. Iṣṭilāhāt-uṣ-Ṣūfiyah, edited by Dr. A. Sprenger, 8vo. 1 0
9. Ināyah, a Commentary on the Hidāyah, Vols. II and IV, @ 16/ each... 32 0
10. Jawāmlu-l-'ilm ir-riyāẓī, 168 pages with 17 plates, 4to. Part I ... 2 0
11. Khizānatu-l-'ilm 4 0
12. Mahābhārata, Vols. III and IV, @ 20/ each 40 0
13. Moore and Hewitson's Descriptions of New Indian Lepidoptera, Parts I–III, with 8 coloured Plates, 4to. @ 6/ each 18 0
14. Sharaya-ool-Islām 4 0
15. Tibetan Dictionary, by Csoma de Körös 10 0
16. Ditto Grammar " " 8 0
17. Kaçmīraçabdāmṛta, Parts I & II @ 1/8/ 3 0

Notices of Sanskrit Manuscripts, Fasc. 1–26 @ 1/ each 26 0
Nepalese Buddhist Sanskrit Literature, by Dr. R. L. Mitra ... 5 0

N.B.—All Cheques, Money Orders, &c., must be made payable to the "Treasurer, Asiatic Society," only.

1-2-99.

Books are supplied by V-P. P.

BIBLIOTHECA INDICA:

A

COLLECTION OF ORIENTAL WORKS

PUBLISHED BY THE

ASIATIC SOCIETY OF BENGAL.

NEW SERIES, No. 1058.

THE

MÁRKAṆḌEYA PURÁṆA.

TRANSLATED BY

F. E. PARGITER, B.A.,

BENGAL CIVIL SERVICE.

LATE BODEN SANSKRIT SCHOLAR, OXFORD.

FASCICULUS VII.

CALCUTTA

PRINTED AT THE BAPTIST MISSION PRESS,

AND PUBLISHED BY THE

ASIATIC SOCIETY, 57, PARK STREET,

1903.

LIST OF BOOKS FOR SALE

AT THE LIBRARY OF THE

Asiatic Society of Bengal,

No. 57, PARK STREET, CALCUTTA,

AND OBTAINABLE FROM

THE SOCIETY'S AGENTS, MESSRS. LUZAC & CO.,
46, GREAT RUSSELL STREET, LONDON, W.C., AND MR. OTTO
HARRASSOWI, BOOKSELLER, LEIPZIG, GERMANY.

*Complete copies of those works marked with an asterisk * cannot be supplied—some of the Fasciculi being out of stock.*

BIBLIOTHECA INDICA.

Sanskrit Series.

Title	Rs.	As.
Advaita Brahma Siddhi, (Text) Fasc. 1-4 @ /6/ each ...	Rs. 1	8
Advaitachinta Kaustubha, Fasc. 1	0	6
*Agni Purāṇa, (Text) Fasc. 4-14 @ /6/ each	4	2
Aitarēya Brāhmaṇa, Vol. I, Fasc. 1-5 and Vol. II, Fasc. 1-5; Vol. III, Fasc. 1-5, Vol. IV, Fasc. 1-5 @ /6/	7	8
Aṇu Bhāṣyam, (Text) Fasc. 1-5 @ /6/ each	1	14
Aphorisms of Sāṇḍilya, (English) Fasc. 1	0	12
Aṣṭasāhasrikā Prajñāpāramitā, (Text) Fasc. 1-6 @ /6/ each ...	2	4
Açvavaidyaka, (Text) Fasc. 1-5 @ /6/ each	1	14
Avadāna Kalpalatā, (Sans. and Tibetan) Vol. I, Fasc. 1-5; Vol. II. Fasc. 1-5 @ 1/ each	10	0
*Bhāmatī, (Text) Fasc. 4-8 @ /6/ each	1	14
Bhāṭṭa Dīpikā Vol. I, Fasc. 1-4	1	8
Bṛhaddēvatā (Text) Fasc. 1-4 @ /6/ each	1	8
Bṛhaddharma Purāṇa, (Text) Fasc. 1-6 @ /6/ each	2	4
Bodhicaryavatara of Cantidevi, Fasc. 1-2	0	12
Catadusani, Fasc. 1	0	6
Catalogue of Sanskrit Books and MSS., Fasc. 1-3 @ 2/ each ...	6	0
Çatapatha Brāhmaṇa, Vol. I, Fasc. 1-7; Vol. II, Fasc. 1	3	0
Catasahasrika Prajnaparamita, (Text) Fasc. 1-5 @ /6/ each ...	1	14
*Caturvarga Chintāmaṇi (Text) Vols. II, 1-25; III. Part I, Fasc. 1-18. Part II, Fasc. 1-10 @ /6/ each	19	14
Çlokavartika, (English) Fasc. 1-4	3	0
*Çrauta Sūtra of Āpastamba, (Text) Fasc. 4-17 @ /6/ each ...	5	4
Ditto Çāṅkhāyana, (Text) Vol. I, Fasc. 1-7; Vol. II, Fasc. 1-4; Vol. III, Fasc. 1-4 @ /6/ each	5	10
Çrī Bhāshyam, (Text) Fasc. 1-3 @ /6/ each	1	2
Dan Kriya Kaumudi, Fasc. 1-2	0	12
Gadadhara Paddhati Kālasāra, Vol I, Fasc. 1-6...	2	4
Kāla Mādhava, (Text) Fasc. 1-4 @ /6/ each	1	8
Kāla Viveka, Fasc. 1-5	1	14
Kātantra, (Text) Fasc. 1-6 @ /12/ each	4	8
Kathā Sarit Sāgara, (English) Fasc. 1-14 @ /12/ each	10	8
Kūrma Purāṇa, (Text) Fasc. 1-9 @ /6/ each	3	6
Lalita-Vistara, (English) Fasc. 1-3 @ /12/ each	2	4
Madana Pārijāta, (Text) Fasc. 1-11 @ /6/ each...	4	2
Mahā-bhāṣya-pradīpōdyōta, (Text) Fasc. 1-9 & Vol. II, Fasc. 1-9 @ /6/ each	6	12
Manuṭikā Saṅgraha, (Text) Fasc. 1-3 @ /6/ each	1	2
Mārkaṇḍēya Purāṇa, (English) Fasc. 1-7 @ /12 each	5	4
*Mimāṁsā Darçana, (Text) Fasc. 7-19 @ /6/ each	4	14
Nyāyavārtika, (Text) Fasc. 1-5 @ /6/	1	14
*Nirukta, (Text) Vol. III, Fasc. 1-6; Vol. IV, Fasc. 1-8 @ /6/ each ...	5	4
Nityacarapaddhati Fasc. 1-7 (Text) @ /6/	2	10
Nityacarapradiph Fasc. 1-2	0	12
Nyayabinduṭikā, (Text)	0	12
Nyāya Kusumāñjali Prakaraṇa (Text) Vol. I, Fasc. 1-6 Vol. II, Fasc. 1-3 @ /6/ each ...	0	10

	Rs	
Padumawati, Fasc. 1-4 @ 2/	8	0
Pariçişta Parvan, (Text) Fasc. 1-5 @ /6/ each	1	14
Prākrita-Pningalam, Fasc. 1-7 @ /6/ each	2	10
Prithivirāj Rāsa, (Text) Part II, Fasc. 1-5 @ /6/ each	1	14
Ditto (English) Part II, Fasc. 1	0	12
Prākṛta Lakṣaṇam, (Text) Fasc. I	1	8
Parāçara Smṛti, (Text) Vol. I, Fasc. 1-8; Vol. II, Fasc. 1-6; Vol. III, Fasc. 1-6 @ /6/ each	7	8
Parāçara, Institutes of (English)	0	12
Prabandhaointāmaṇi (English) Fasc. 1-3 @ /12/ each	2	4
*Sāma Vēda Saṁhitā, (Text) Vols. I, Fasc. 5-10; II, 1-6; III, 1 7; IV, 1-6; V, 1-8, @ /6/ each Fasc.	12	6
Sāṅkhya Sūtra Vṛtti, (Text) Fasc. 1-4 @ /6/ each	1	8
Ditto (English) Fasc. 1-3 @ /12/ each	2	4
Sraddha Kriya Kaumudi, Fasc. 1-3	1	2
Suçruta Saṁhitā, (Eng.) Fasc. 1 @ /12/	0	12
*Taittereya Saṁhitā, (Text) Fasc. 14-45 @ /6/ each	12	0
Tāṇḍya Brāhmaṇa, (Text) Fasc. 1-19 @ /6/ each	7	2
Trantra Vartika (English) Fasc. 1	0	12
Tattva-Cintāmaṇi, (Text) Vol. I, Fasc. 1-9, Vol. II, Fasc. 2-10, Vol. III, Fasc. 1-2, Vol. IV, Fasc. 1, Vol. V, Fasc. 1-5, Part IV, Vol. II, Fasc. 1-12 @ /6/ each	14	4
Tattvarthadhigama Sutrom, Fasc. 1	0	6
Trikāṇḍa-Maṇḍanam, (Text) Fasc. 1-3 @ /6/	1	2
Tul'si Sat'sai, (Text) Fasc. 1-5 @ /6/ each	1	14
Upamita-bhava-prapañca-kathā (Text) Fasc. 1-6 @ /6/ each ...	2	4
Uvāsagadasāo, (Text and English) Fasc. 1-6 @ /12/	4	8
Varāha Purāṇa, (Text) Fasc. 1-14 @ /6/ each	5	4
Varsa Krya Kaumudi, Fasc. 1-6 @ /6/	2	4
*Vāyu Purāṇa, (Text) Vol. I, Fasc. 2-6; Vol. II, Fasc. 1-7, @ /6/ each	4	8
Vidhano Parigata, Fasc. 1-3	1	2
Viṣṇu Smṛti, (Text) Fasc. 1-2 @ /6/ each	0	12
Vivādaratnākara, (Text) Fasc. 1-7 @ /6/ each	2	10
Vṛhannāradīya Purāṇa, (Text) Fasc. 1-6 @ /6/	2	4
Vṛhat Svayambhū Purāṇa, Fasc. 1-6	2	4
Tibetan Series.		
Pag-Sam Ṭhi S'iā, Fasc. 1-4 @ 1/ each	4	0
Sher-Phyin, Vol. I, Fasc. 1-5; Vol. II, Fasc. 1-3; Vol. III, Fasc. 1-5 @ 1/ each	13	0
Rtogs brjod dpag hkhri S'iā (Tib. & Sans.) Vol. I, Fasc. 1-5; Vol. II. Fasc. 1-5 @ 1/ each	10	0
Arabic and Persian Series.		
'Ālamgīrnāmah, with Index, (Text) Fasc. 1-13 @ /6/ each... ...	4	14
Al-Muqaddasi (English) Vol. I, Fasc. 1-3 @ /12/	2	4
Āīn-i-Akbarī, (Text) Fasc. 1-22 @ 1/ each	22	0
Ditto (English) Vol. I, Fasc. 1-7, Vol. II, Fasc. 1-5, Vol. III, Fasc. 1-5, @ 1/12/ each	29	12
Akbarnāmah, with Index, (Text) Fasc. 1-37 @ 1/ each	37	0
Ditto English Fasc. 1-8 @ 1/ each	8	0
Arabic Bibliography, by Dr. A. Sprenger	0	6
Bādshāhnāmah, with Index, (Text) Fasc. 1-19 @ /6/ each	7	2
Catalogue of Arabic Books and Manuscripts	1	0
Catalogue of the Persian Books and Manuscripts in the Library of the Asiatic Society of Bengal. Fasc. 1-3 @ 1/ each	3	0
Dictionary of Arabic Technical Terms, and Appendix, Fasc. 1-21 @ 1/ each	21	0
Farhang-i-Rashīdī, (Text) Fasc. 1-14 @ 1/ each	14	0
Fihrist-i-Ṭūsī, or, Ṭūsy's list of Shy'ah Books, (Text) Fasc. 1-4 @ /12/ each	3	0
Futūḥ-ush-Shām of Wāqidī, (Text) Fasc. 1-9 @ /6/ each	3	6
Ditto of Azādī, (Text) Fasc. 1-4 @ /6/ each	1	8
Haft Āsmān, History of the Persian Masnawi, (Text) Fasc. 1 ...	0	12
History of the Caliphs, (English) Fasc. 1-6 @ /12/ each	4	8
Iqbālnāmah-i-Jahāngīrī, (Text) Fasc. 1-3 @ /6/ each	1	2
Iṣābah, with Supplement, (Text) 51 Fasc. @ /12/ each	38	4
Maāṣir-ul-Umarā, Vol. I, Fasc. 1-9, Vol. II, Fasc. 1-9; Vol. III, 1-10; Index to Vol. I, Fasc. 10-11; Index to Vol. III, Fasc. 11-12; Index to Vol. II, Fasc. 10-12 @ /6/ each	13	2
Maghāzi of Wāqidī, (Text) Fasc. 1-5 @ /6/ each	1	14

* The other Fasciculi of these works are out of stock, and complete copies cannot be supplied

Muntakhabu-t-Tawārīkh, (Text) Fasc. 1-15 @ /6 each ... Rs. 5 10
Muntakhabu-t-Tawārīkh, (English) Vol. I, Fasc. 1-7; Vol. II, Fasc. 1-5 and 3 Indexes; Vol. III, Fasc. 1 @ /12/ each 12 0
Muntakhabu-l-Lubāb, (Text) Fasc. 1-19 @ /6/ each 7 2
Ma'āṣir-i-'Ālamgīrī, (Text), Fasc. 1-6 @ /6/ each 2 4
Nukhbatu-l-Fikr, (Text) Fasc. 1 ... ... 0 6
Niẓāmī's Khiradnāmah-i-Iskandarī, (Text) Fasc. 1-2 @ /12/ each 1 8
Riyāẓu-s-Salāṭīn, (Text) Fasc. 1-5 @ /6/ each 1 14
Ditto Ditto (English) Fasc. 1-3 ... ... 2 4
Tabaqāt-i-Nāṣirī, (Text) Fasc. 1-5 @ /6/ each 1 14
Ditto (English) Fasc. 1-14 @ /12/ each 10 8
Ditto Index 1 0
Tārīkh-i-Fīrūz Shāhi of Ẓiyāu-d-dīn Barni (Text) Fasc. 1-7 @ /6/ each... 2 10
Tārīkh-i-Fīrūzshāhi, of Shams-i-Sirāj Aif, (Text) Fasc. 1-6 @ /6/ each... 2 4
Ten Ancient Arabic Poems, Fasc. 1-2 @ 1/8/ each 3 0
Wis o Rāmīn, (Text) Fasc. 1-5 @ /6/ each 1 14
Ẓafarnāmah, Vol. I, Fasc. 1-9, Vol. II, Fasc. 1-8 @ /6/ each .. 6 6
Tuzuk-i-Jahāngīrī, (Eng.) Fasc. 1 ... ... 0 12

ASIATIC SOCIETY'S PUBLICATIONS.

1. ASIATIC RESEARCHES. Vols. XIX and XX @ 10/ each 50 0
2. PROCEEDINGS of the Asiatic Society from 1865 to 1869 (incl.) @ /6/ per No.; and from 1870 to date @ /8/ per No.
3. JOURNAL of the Asiatic Society for 1843 (12), 1844 (12), 1845 (12), 1846 (5), 1847 (12), 1848 (12), 1866 (7), 1867 (6), 1868 (6), 1869 (8), 1870 (8), 1871 (7), 1872 (8), 1873 (8) 1874 (8), 1875 (7), 1876 (7), 1877 (8), 1878 (8), 1879 (7), 1880 (8), 1881 (7), 1882, (6), 1883 (5), 1884 (6), 1885 (6), 1886 (8), 1887 (7), 1888 (7), 1889 (10), 1890 (11), 1891 (7), 1892 (8), 1893 (11), 1894 (8), 1895 (7), 1896 (8), 1897 (8), 1898 (8), 1899 (8), 1900 (7) & 1901 (7), 1902 (9), @ 1/8 per No. to Members and @ 2/ per No. to Non-Members.

N.B.—The figures enclosed in brackets give the number of Nos. in each Volume.

4. Centenary Review of the Researches of the Society from 1784–1883 ... 3 0
A sketch of the Turki language as spoken in Eastern Turkistan, by R. B. Shaw (Extra No., *J.A.S.B.*, 1878) 4 0
Theobald's Catalogue of Reptiles in the Museum of the Asiatic Society (Extra No., *J.A.S.B.*, 1868) 2 0
Catalogue of Mammals and Birds of Burmah, by E. Blyth (Extra No., *J.A.S.B.*, 1875) 4 0
Introduction to the Maithilī Language of North Bihār, by G. A. Grierson, Part II, Chrestomathy and Vocabulary (Extra No., *J.A.S.B.*, 1882) 4 0
5. Anīs-ul-Musharrahīn 3 0
6. Catalogue of Fossil Vertebrata 3 0
7. Catalogue of the Library of the Asiatic Society, Bengal, by W. A. Bion 3 8
8. Ināyah, a Commentary on the Hidāyah, Vols. II and IV, @ 16/ each... 32 0
9. Jawāmiu-l-'ilm ir-riyāẓī, 168 pages with 17 plates, 4to. Part I ... 2 0
10. Khizānatu-l-'ilm 4 0
11. Mahābhārata, Vols. III and IV, @ 20/ each 40 0
12. Moore and Hewitson's Descriptions of New Indian Lepidoptera, Parts I–III, with 8 coloured Plates, 4to. @ 6/ each 18 0
13. Sharaya-ool-Islām 4 0
14. Tibetan Dictionary, by Csoma de Körös 10 0
15. Ditto, Grammar " " 8 0
16. Kaçmīraçabdāmṛta, Parts I and II @ 1/8/ 3 0
17. A descriptive catalogue of the paintings, statues, &c., in the rooms of the Asiatic Society of Bengal by C. R. Wilson... ... ... 1 0
18. Memoir on maps illustrating the Ancient Geography of Kaśmir by M. A. Stein, Ph.D., Jl. Extra No. 2 of 1899 ... ... 4 0

Notices of Sanskrit Manuscripts, Fasc. 1-29 @ 1/ each 29 0
Nepalese Buddhist Sanskrit Literature, by Dr. R. L. Mitra ... 5 0

N.B.—All Cheques, Money Orders, &c., must be made payable to the "Treasurer, Asiatic Society," only.

2-11-03.

Books are supplied by V.-P P.

BIBLIOTHECA INDICA:

A

COLLECTION OF ORIENTAL WORKS

PUBLISHED BY THE
ASIATIC SOCIETY OF BENGAL.
New Series, No. 1076.

THE

MÁRKAṆḌEYA PURÁṆA.

TRANSLATED BY

F. E. PARGITER, B.A.,
BENGAL CIVIL SERVICE.
LATE BODEN SANSKRIT SCHOLAR, OXFORD.

FASCICULUS VIII.

CALCUTTA:
PRINTED AT THE BAPTIST MISSION PRESS,
AND PUBLISHED BY THE
ASIATIC SOCIETY, 57, PARK STREET,
1904.

LIST OF BOOKS FOR SALE

AT THE LIBRARY OF THE

ASIATIC SOCIETY OF BENGAL,

No. 57, PARK STREET, CALCUTTA,

AND OBTAINABLE FROM

THE SOCIETY'S AGENTS, MESSRS. LUZAC & CO.,

46 GREAT RUSSELL STREET, LONDON, W.C., AND MR. OTTO HARRASSOWI, BOOKSELLER, LEIPZIG, GERMANY.

*Complete copies of those works marked with an asterisk * cannot be supplied—some of the Fasciculi being out of stock.*

BIBLIOTHECA INDICA.

Sanskrit Series.

Title	Rs.	As.
Advaita Brahma Siddhi, (Text) Fasc. 1-4 @ /6/ each ...	Rs. 1	8
Advaitachinta Kaustubhe, Fasc. 1 ...	0	6
*Agni Purāṇa, (Text) Fasc. 4-14 @ /6/ each ...	4	2
Aitarēya Brāhmaṇa, Vol. I, Fasc. 1-5 and Vol. II, Fasc. 1-5; Vol. III, Fasc. 1-5, Vol. IV, Fasc. 1-5 @ /6/ ...	7	8
Aṇu Bhāṣyam, (Text) Fasc. 2-5 @ /6/ each ...	1	8
Aphorisms of Sāṇḍilya, (English) Fasc. 1 ...	0	12
Aṣṭasāhasrikā Prajñāpāramitā, (Text) Fasc. 1-6 @ /6/ each ...	2	4
Açvavaidyaka, (Text) Fasc. 1-5 @ /6/ each ...	1	14
Avadāna Kalpalatā, (Sans. and Tibetan) Vol. I, Fasc. 1-5; Vol. II. Fasc. 1-5 @ 1/ each ...	10	0
Bāla Bhaṭṭi, Vol. I, Fasc. 1 ...	0	6
Baudhāyana Sautra Sūtram, Fasc. 1-2 @ /6/ each ...	0	12
*Bhāmatī, (Text) Fasc. 4-8 @ /6/ each ...	1	14
Bhāṭṭa Dīpikā Vol. I, Fasc. 1-4 ...	1	8
Bṛhaddēvatā (Text) Fasc. 1-4 @ /6/ each ...	1	8
Bṛhaddharma Purāṇa, (Text) Fasc. 1-6 @ /6/ each ...	2	4
Bodhicaryavatara of Cantidevi, Fasc. 1-2 ...	0	12
Catadusani, Fasc. 1 ...	0	6
Catalogue of Sanskrit Books and MSS., Fasc. 1-4 @ 2/ each ...	8	0
Çatapatha Brāhmaṇa, Vol. I, Fasc. 1-7; Vol. II, Fasc. 1-2 ...	3	6
Çatasahasrika-projnaparamita, Part I, Fasc. 1-2 @ /6/ each ...	0	12
*Caturvarga Chintāmaṇi (Text) Vols. II, 1-25; III. Part I, Fasc. 1-18. Part II, Fasc. 1-10 @ /6/ each ...	19	14
Çlōkavartika, (English) Fasc. 1-4 ...	3	0
*Çrauta Sūtra of Āpastamba, (Text) Fasc. 4-17 @ /6/ each ...	5	4
Ditto Çānkhāyana, (Text) Vol. I, Fasc. 1-7; Vol. II, Fasc. 1-4; Vol. III, Fasc. 1-4 @ /6/ each ...	5	10
Çri Bhāshyam, (Text) Fasc. 1-3 @ /6/ each ...	1	2
Dan Kriya Kaumudī, Fasc. 1-2 ...	0	12
Gadadhara Paddhati Kālasāra, Vol I, Fasc. 1-6 ...	2	4
Kāla Mādhava, (Text) Fasc. 1-4 @ /6/ each ...	1	8
Kāla Vivēka, Fasc. 1-6 ...	2	4
Kātantra, (Text) Fasc. 1-6 @ /12/ each ...	4	8
Kathā Sarit Sāgara, (English) Fasc. 1-14 @ /12/ each ...	10	8
Kūrma Purāṇa, (Text) Fasc. 1-9 @ /6/ each ...	3	6
Lalita-Vistara, (English) Fasc. 1-3 @ /12/ each ...	2	4
Madana Pārijāta, (Text) Fasc. 1-11 @ /6/ each ...	4	2
Mahā-bhāṣya-pradīpōdyōta, (Text) Fasc. 1-9 & Vol. II, Fasc. 1-11 @ /6/ each ...	7	8
Manuṭīkā Saṅgraha, (Text) Fasc. 1-3 @ /6/ each ...	1	2
Mārkaṇḍēya Purāṇa, (English) Fasc. 1 8 @ /12 each ...	6	0
*Mīmāṁsā Darçana, (Text) Fasc. 7-19 @ /6/ each ...	4	14
Nyāyavārtika, (Text) Fasc. 1-6 @ /6/ ...	2	4
*Nirukta, (Text) Vol. III, Fasc. 1-6; Vol. IV, Fasc. 1-8 @ /6/ each ...	5	4
Nityacarapaddhati Fasc. 1-7 (Text) @ /6/ ...	2	10
Nityacarapradiph Fasc. 1-3 ...	1	2
Nyayabinduṭika, (Text) ...	0	10
Nyāya Kusumāñjali Prakara 1-3 @ /6/ each ...		6

Padumawati, Fasc. 1–4 @ 2/ ... ... Rs. 8 0
Pariçiṣta Parvan, (Text) Fasc. 1–5 @ /6/ each 1 14
Prākrita-Paingalam, Fasc. 1–7 @ /6/ each 2 10
Prithivirāj Rāsa, (Text) Part II, Fasc. 1–5 @ /6/ each 1 14
Ditto (English) Part II, Fasc. 1 ... ... 0 12
Prākṛta Lakṣaṇam, (Text) Fasc. 1 ... ... 1 8
Parāçara Smṛti, (Text) Vol. I, Fasc. 1–8; Vol. II, Fasc. 1–6; Vol. III, Fasc. 1–6 @ /6/ each 7 8
Parāçara, Institutes of (English) 0 12
Prabandhacintāmaṇi (English) Fasc. 1–3 @ /12/ each 2 4
*Sāma Vēda Saṁhitā, (Text) Vols. I, Fasc. 5–10; II, 1–6; III, 1–7; IV, 1–6; V, 1–8, @ /6/ each Fasc. 12 6
Sāṅkhya Sūtra Vṛtti, (Text) Fasc. 1–4 @ /6/ each 1 8
Ditto (English) Fasc. 1–3 @ /12/ each 2 4
Sraddha Kriya Kaumudi, Fasc. 1–5 ... ... 1 14
Suçruta Saṁhitā, (Eng.) Fasc. 1 @ /12/ 0 12
*Taittereya Saṁhitā, (Text) Fasc. 14–45 @ /6/ each 12 0
Tāṇḍya Brāhmaṇa, (Text) Fasc. 1–19 @ /6/ each 7 2
Trantra Vartika (English) Fasc. 1–2 @ /12/ 1 8
Tattva Cintāmaṇi, (Text) Vol. I, Fasc. 1–9, Vol. II, Fasc. 2–10, Vol. III, Fasc. 1–2, Vol. IV, Fasc. 1, Vol. V, Fasc. 1–5, Part IV, Vol. II, Fasc. 1–12 @ /6/ each 14 4
Tattvarthadhigama Sutrom, Fasc. 1 ... ... 0 6
Trikāṇḍa-Maṇḍanam, (Text) Fasc. 1–3 @ /6/ 1 2
Tul'si Sat'sai, (Text) Fasc. 1–5 @ /6/ each 1 14
Upamita-bhava-prapañca-kathā (Text) Fasc. 1–6 @ /6/ each ... 2 4
Uvāsagadasāo, (Text and English) Fasc. 1–6 @ /12/ 4 8
Vallala Caritam, Fasc. 1 ... ... 0 6
Varāha Purāṇa, (Text) Fasc. 1–14 @ /6/ each 5 4
Varsa Krya Kaumudi, Fasc. 1–6 @ /6/ 2 4
*Vāyu Purāṇa, (Text) Vol. I, Fasc. 2–6; Vol. II, Fasc. 1–7, @ /6/ each 4 8
Vidhano Parigata, Fasc. 1–4 ... ... 1 8
Viṣṇu Smṛti, (Text) Fasc. 1–2 @ /6/ each 0 12
Vivādaratnākara, (Text) Fasc. 1–7 @ /6/ each 2 10
Vṛhannāradiya Purāṇa, (Text) Fasc. 2–6 @ /6/ 1 14
Vṛhat Svayambhū Purāṇa, Fasc. 1–6 ... ... 2 4

Tibetan Series.

Pag-Sam Thi S'iñ, Fasc. 1–4 @ 1/ each 4 0
Sher-Phyin, Vol. I, Fasc. 1–5; Vol. II, Fasc. 1–3; Vol. III, Fasc. 1–5 @ 1/ each 13 0
Rtogs brjod dpag hkhri S'iñ (Tib. & Sans.) Vol. I, Fasc. 1–5; Vol. II, Fasc. 1–5 @ 1/ each 10 0

Arabic and Persian Series.

'Alamgīrnāmah, with Index, (Text) Fasc. 1–13 @ /6/ each... ... 4 14
Al-Muqaddasi (English) Vol. I, Fasc. 1–3 @ /12/ 2 4
Āīn-i-Akbarī, (Text) Fasc. 1–22 @ 1/ each 22 0
Ditto (English) Vol. I, Fasc. 1–7, Vol. II, Fasc. 1–5, Vol. III, Fasc. 1–5, @ 1/12/ each 29 12
Akbarnāmah, with Index, (Text) Fasc. 1–37 @ 1/ each 37 0
Ditto English Fasc, 1–8 @ 1/ each 8 0
Arabic Bibliography, by Dr. A. Sprenger 0 6
Bādshāhnāmah, with Index, (Text) Fasc. 1–19 @ /6/ each 7 2
Catalogue of Arabic Books and Manuscripts 1 0
Catalogue of the Persian Books and Manuscripts in the Library of the Asiatic Society of Bengal. Fasc. 1–3 @ 1/ each 3 0
Dictionary of Arabic Technical Terms, and Appendix, Fasc. 1–21 @ 1/ each 21 0
Farhang-i-Rashīdī, (Text) Fasc. 1–14 @ 1/ each 14 0
Fihrist-i-Ṭūsī, or, Ṭūsy's list of Shy'ah Books, (Text) Fasc. 1–4 @ /12/ each 3 0
Futūḥ-ush-Shām of Wāqidī, (Text) Fasc. 1–9 @ /6/ each 3 6
Ditto of Azādī, (Text) Fasc. 1–4 @ /6/ each 1 8
Haft Āsmān, History of the Persian Masnawi, (Text) Fasc. 1 ... 0 12
History of the Caliphs, (English) Fasc. 1–6 @ /12/ each 4 8
Iqbālnāmah-i-Jahāngīrī, (Text) Fasc. 1–3 @ /6/ each 1 2
Iṣābah, with Supplement, (Text) 51 Fasc. @ /12/ each 38 4
Maāṣir-ul-Umarā, Vol. I, Fasc. 1–9, Vol. II, Fasc. 1–9; Vol. III, 1–10; Index to Vol. I, Fasc. 10–11; Index to Vol. III, Fasc. 11–12; Index to Vol. II, Fasc. 10–12 @ /6/ each 13 2

The other Fasciculi of these works are out of stock, and complete copies cannot

Maghâzi of Wâqidi, (Text) Fasc. 1–5 @ /6/ each 1 14
Muntakhabu-t-Tawārīkh, (Text) Fasc. 1-15 @ /6 each ... Rs. 5 10
Muntakhabu-t-Tawārīkh, (English) Vol. I, Fasc. 1–7; Vol. II, Fasc. 1-5 and 3 Indexes; Vol. III, Fasc. 1 @ /12/ each 12 0
Muntakhabu-l-Lubāb, (Text) Fasc. 1–19 @ /6/ each 7 2
Ma'āṣir-i-'Ālamgīrī, (Text), Fasc. 1-6 @ /6/ each 2 4
Nukhbatu-l-Fikr, (Text) Fasc. 1 ... ... 0 6
Niẓāmī's Khiradnāmah-i-Iskandarī, (Text) Fasc. 1-2 @ /12/ each 1 8
Riyāẓu-s-Salātīn, (Text) Fasc. 1–5 @ /6/ each 1 14
Ditto Ditto (English) Fasc. 1–4 ... ... 3 0
Tabaqāt-i-Nāṣirī, (Text) Fasc. 1–5 @ /6/ each 1 14
Ditto (English) Fasc. 1–14 @ /12/ each 10 8
Ditto Index 1 0
Tārīkh-i-Fīrūz Shāhi of Ẓiyāu-d-dīn Barni (Text) Fasc. 1–7 @ /6/ each... 2 10
Tārīkh-i-Fīrūzshāhi, of Shams-i-Sirāj Aif, (Text) Fasc. 1–6 @ /6/ each... 2 4
Ten Ancient Arabic Poems, Fasc. 1-2 @ 1/8/ each ... 3 0
Wis o Rāmīn, (Text) Fasc. 1–5 @ /6/ each 1 14
Ẓafarnāmah, Vol. I, Fasc. 1–9, Vol. II, Fasc. 1–8 @ /6/ each ... 6 6
Tuzuk-i-Jahāngīrī, (Eng.) Fasc. 1 ... ... 0 12

ASIATIC SOCIETY'S PUBLICATIONS.

1. Asiatic Researches. Vols. XIX and XX @ 10/ each 50 0
2. Proceedings of the Asiatic Society from 1865 to 1869 (incl.) @ /6/ per No.; and from 1870 to date @ /8/ per No.
3. Journal of the Asiatic Society for 1843 (12), 1844 (12), 1845 (12), 1846 (5), 1847 (12), 1848 (12), 1866 (7), 1867 (6), 1868 (6), 1869 (8), 1870 (8), 1871 (7), 1872 (8), 1873 (8) 1874 (8), 1875 (7), 1876 (7), 1877 (8), 1878 (8), 1879 (7), 1880 (8), 1881 (7), 1882, (6), 1883 (5), 1884 (6), 1885 (6), 1886 (8), 1887 (7), 1888 (7), 1889 (10), 1890 (11), 1891 (7), 1892 (8), 1893 (11), 1894 (8), 1895 (7), 1896 (8), 1897 (8), 1898 (8), 1899 (8), 1900 (7) & 1901 (7), 1902 (9), @ 1/8 per No. to Members and @ 2/ per No. to Non-Members.

N.B.—The figures enclosed in brackets give the number of Nos. in each Volume.

4. Centenary Review of the Researches of the Society from 1784–1883 ... 3 0
   A sketch of the Turki language as spoken in Eastern Turkistan, by R. B. Shaw (Extra No., *J.A.S.B.*, 1878) 4 0
   Theobald's Catalogue of Reptiles in the Museum of the Asiatic Society (Extra No., *J.A.S.B.*, 1868) 2 0
   Catalogue of Mammals and Birds of Burmah, by E. Blyth (Extra No., *J.A.S.B.*, 1875) 4 0
   Introduction to the Maithilī Language of North Bihār, by G. A. Grierson, Part II, Chrestomathy and Vocabulary (Extra No., *J.A.S.B.*, 1882) 4 0
5. Anīs-ul-Musharrahīn 3 0
6. Catalogue of Fossil Vertebrata 3 0
7. Catalogue of the Library of the Asiatic Society, Bengal, by W. A. Bion 3 8
8. Ināyah, a Commentary on the Hidāyah, Vols. II and IV, @ 16/ each... 32 0
9. Jawāmiu-l-'ilm ir-riyāẓī, 168 pages with 17 plates, 4to. Part I ... 2 0
10. Khizānatu-l-'ilm 4 0
11. Mahābhārata, Vols. III and IV, @ 20/ each 40 0
12. Moore and Hewitson's Descriptions of New Indian Lepidoptera, Parts I–III, with 8 coloured Plates, 4to. @ 6/ each 18 0
13. Sharaya-ool-Islām 4 0
14. Tibetan Dictionary, by Csoma de Körös 10 0
15. Ditto Grammar " " 8 0
16. Kaçmīraçabdāmṛta, Parts I and II @ 1/8/ 3 0
17. A descriptive catalogue of the paintings, statues, &c., in the rooms of the Asiatic Society of Bengal by C. R. Wilson... ... ... 1 0
18. Memoir on maps illustrating the Ancient Geography of Kaśmīr by M. A. Stein, Ph.D., Jl. Extra No. 2 of 1899 ... ... 4 0

Notices of Sanskrit Manuscripts, Fasc. 1–29 @ 1/ each 29 0
Nepalese Buddhist Sanskrit Literature, by Dr. R. L. Mitra ... 5 0

N.B.—All Cheques, Money Orders, &c., must be made payable to the "Treasurer Asiatic Society," only.

Books are supplied by V.-P.P.

BIBLIOTHECA INDICA:

COLLECTION OF ORIENTAL WORKS

PUBLISHED BY THE

ASIATIC SOCIETY OF BENGAL.

NEW SERIES, No. 1104.

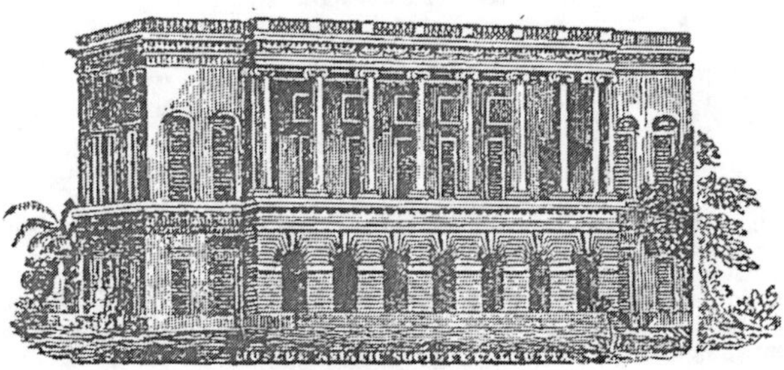

THE

MÁRKAṆḌEYA PURÁṆA.

TRANSLATED BY

F. E. PARGITER, B.A.,

BENGAL CIVIL SERVICE.

LATE BODEN SANSKRIT SCHOLAR, OXFORD.

FASCICULUS IX.

CALCUTTA:

PRINTED AT THE BAPTIST MISSION PRESS,

AND PUBLISHED BY THE

ASIATIC SOCIETY, 57, PARK STREET,

1905.

LIST OF BOOKS FOR SALE

AT THE LIBRARY OF THE

ASIATIC SOCIETY OF BENGAL,

No. 57, PARK STREET, CALCUTTA,

AND OBTAINABLE FROM

THE SOCIETY'S AGENTS, MR. BERNARD QUARITCH, 15, PICCADILLY, LONDON, W., AND MR. OTTO HARRASSOWITZ, BOOKSELLER, LEIPZIG, GERMANY.

*Complete copies of those works marked with an asterisk * cannot be supplied—some of the Fasciculi being out of stock.*

BIBLIOTHECA INDICA,

Sanskrit Series.

		Rs.	As.
Advaita Brahma Siddhi, (Text) Fasc. 1–4 @ /6/ each	...	1	8
Advaitachinta Kaustubhe, Fasc. 1–2	... ...	0	12
*Agni Purāṇa, (Text) Fasc. 4–14 @ /6/ each	... ...	4	2
Aitarēya Brāhmaṇa, Vol. I, Fasc. 1–5 and Vol. II, Fasc. 1–5; Vol. III, Fasc. 1–5, Vol. IV, Fasc. 1–5 @ /6/	... ...	7	8
Aṇu Bhāṣyam, (Text) Fasc. 2–5 @ /6/ each	... ...	1	8
Aphorisms of Sāṇḍilya, (English) Fasc. 1	... ...	0	12
Aṣṭasāhasrikā Prajñāpāramitā, (Text) Fasc. 1–6 @ /6/ each	...	2	4
Açvavaidyaka, (Text) Fasc. 1–5 @ /6/ each	... ...	1	14
Avadāna Kalpalatā, (Sans. and Tibetan) Vol. I, Fasc. 2–5; Vol. II, Fasc. 1–5 @ 1/ each	... ...	9	0
Bāla Bhaṭṭi, Vol. I, Fasc. 1	... ...	0	6
Baudhayana Srauta Sutra, Fasc. 1–2 @ /6/ each	... ...	0	12
*Bhāmatī, (Text) Fasc. 4–8 @ /6/ each	... ...	1	14
Bhāṭṭa Dīpikā Vol. I, Fasc. 1–5	... ...	1	14
Bṛhaddēvatā (Text) Fasc. 1–4 @ /6/ each	... ...	1	8
Bṛhaddharma Purāṇa, (Text) Fasc. 1–6 @ /6/ each	... ...	2	4
Bōdhicaryavatara of Cantidevi, Fasc. 1–3	... ...	1	2
Catadusani, Fasc. 1–2	... ...	0	12
Catalogue of Sanskrit Books and MSS., Fasc. 1–4 @ 2/ each	...	8	0
Çatapatha Brāhmaṇa, Vol. I, Fasc. 1–7; Vol. III, Fasc. 1–5	...	4	8
Çatasahasrika-prajnaparamita (Text) Part I, Fasc. 1–8 @ /6/ each	...	3	0
*Caturvarga Chintāmaṇi (Text) Vols. II, 1–25; III. Part I, Fasc. 1–18. Part II, Fasc. 1–10 @ /6/ each; Vol IV, Fasc. 1–3	... ...	21	0
Çlokavartika, (English) Fasc. 1–5	... ...	3	2
*Çrauta Sūtra of Āpastamba, (Text) Fasc. 4–17 @ /6/ each	...	5	4
Ditto Çāṅkhāyana, (Text) Vol. I, Fasc. 1–7; Vol. II, Fasc. 1–4; Vol. III, Fasc. 1–4 @ /6/ each; Vol 4, Fasc. 1	... ...	6	0
Çrī Bhāshyam, (Text) Fasc. 1–3 @ /6/ each	... ...	1	2
Dan Kriya Kaumudi, Fasc. 1–2	... ...	1	2
Gadadhara Paddhati Kālasāra, Vol I, Fasc. 1–7	... ...	0	12
Kāla Mādhava, (Text) Fasc. 1–4 @ /6/ each	... ...	2	10
Kāla Viveka, Fasc. 1–6	... ...	1	8
Kātantra, (Text) Fasc. 1–6 @ /12/ each	... ...	2	4
Kathā Sarit Sāgara, (English) Fasc. 1–14 @ /12/ each	... ...	4	8
Kūrma Purāṇa, (Text) Fasc. 1–9 @ /6/ each	... ...	10	8
Lalita-Vistara, (English) Fasc. 1–3 @ /12/ each	... ...	3	6
Madana Pārijāta, (Text) Fasc. 1–11 @ /6/ each	... ...	2	4
Mahā-bhāṣya-pradīpōdyōta, (Text) Fasc. 1–9 & Vol. II, Fasc. 1–12 @ /6/ each	... ...	4	2
		7	14
Manutīkā Saṅgraha, (Text) Fasc. 1–3 @ /6/ each	... ...	1	2
Mārkaṇḍēya Purāṇa, (English) Fasc. 1–8 @ /12 each	... ...	6	0
*Mīmāṁsā Darçana, (Text) Fasc. 7–19 @ /6/ each	... ...	4	14
Nyāyavārtika, (Text) Fasc. 1–6 @ /6/	... ...	2	4
*Nirukta, (Text) Vol. III, Fasc. 1–6; Vol. IV, Fasc. 1–8 @ /6/ each	...	5	4
Nityacarapaddhati Fasc. 1–7 (Text) @ /6/	... ...	2	10
Nityacarapradiph Fasc. 1–5	... ...	1	14
Nyayabinduṭikā, (Text)	... ...	0	10
Nyāya Kusumāñjali Prakaraṇa (Text) Vol. I, Fasc. 1–6 Vol. II, Fasc. 1–3 @ /6/ each		3	6

	Rs	
Padumawati, Fasc. 1-4 @ 2/	8	0
Pariçista Parvan, (Text) Fasc. 1-5 @ /6/ each	1	14
Prākrita-Paingalam, Fasc. 1-7 @ /6/ each	2	10
Prithivirāj Rāsa, (Text) Part II, Fasc. 1-5 @ /6/ each	1	14
Ditto (English) Part II, Fasc. 1	0	12
Prākṛta Lakṣaṇam, (Text) Fasc. 1	1	8
Parāçara Smṛti, (Text) Vol. I, Fasc. 1-8 Vol. II, Fasc. 1-6; Vol. III, Fasc. 1-6 @ /6/ each	7	8
Parāçara, Institutes of (English	0	12
Prabandhacintāmaṇi (English) Fasc. 1-3 @ /12/ each	2	4
*Sāma Vēda Samhitā, (Text) Vols. I, Fasc. 5-10; II, 1-6; III, 1-7; IV, 1-6; V, 1-8, @ /6 each Fasc.	12	6
Sāṅkhya Sūtra Vṛtti, (Text) Fasc. 1-4 @ /6/ each	1	8
Ditto (English) Fasc. 1-3 @ /12/ each	2	4
Sraddha Kriya Kaumudi, Fasc. 1-6	2	4
Suçruta Samhitā, (Eng.) Fasc. 1 @ /12/	0	12
*Taittirēya Samhitā, (Text) Fasc. 14-45 @ /6/ each	12	0
Tāṇḍya Brāhmaṇa, (Text) Fasc. 1-19 @ /6/ each	7	2
Tantra Vartika (English) Fasc. 1-3 @ /12/	2	4
Tattva Cintāmaṇi, (Text) Vol. I, Fasc. 1-9, Vol. II, Fasc. 2-10, Vol. III, Fasc. 1-2, Vol. IV, Fasc. 1, Vol. V, Fasc. 1-5, Part IV, Vol. II, Fasc. 1-12 @ /6/ each	14	4
Tattvarthadhigama Sutrom, Fasc. 1-2	0	12
Trikāṇḍa-Maṇḍanam, (Text) Fasc. 1-3 @ /6/	1	2
Upamita-bhava-prapañca-kathā (Text) Fasc. 1-7 @ /6/ each ...	2	10
Uvāsagadasāo, (Text and English) Fasc. 1-6 @ /12/	4	8
Vallala Carita, Fasc. 1	0	6
Varāha Purāṇa, (Text) Fasc. 1-14 @ /6/ each	5	4
Varsa Krya Kaumudi, Fasc. 1-6 @ /6/	2	4
*Vāyu Purāṇa, (Text) Vol. I, Fasc. 2-6; Vol. II, Fasc. 1-7, @ /6/ each	4	8
Vidhano Parigata, Fasc. 1-6	2	4
Viṣṇu Smṛti, (Text) Fasc. 1-2 @ /6/ each	0	12
Vivādaratnākara, (Text) Fasc. 1-7 @ /6/ each	2	10
Vṛhannāradīya Purāṇa, (Text) Fasc. 2-6 @ /6/	1	14
Vṛhat Svayambhū Purāṇa, Fasc. 1-6	2	4
Tibetan Series.		
Pag-Sam Thi S'iñ, Fasc. 1-4 @ 1/ each	4	0
Sher-Phyin, Vol. I, Fasc. 1-5; Vol. II, Fasc. 1-3; Vol. III, Fasc. 1-6 @ 1/ each	14	0
Rtogs brjod dpag hkhri S'iñ (Tib. & Sans.) Vol. I, Fasc. 1-5; Vol. II. Fasc. 1-5 @ 1/ each	10	0
Arabic and Persian Series.		
'Ālamgīrnāmah, with Index, (Text) Fasc. 1-13 @ /6/ each... ...	4	14
Al-Muqaddasi (English) Vol. I, Fasc. 1-3 @ /12/	2	4
Āīn-i-Akbarī, (Text) Fasc. 1-22 @ 1/ each	22	0
Ditto (English) Vol. I, Fasc. 1-7, Vol. II, Fasc. 1-5, Vol. III, Fasc. 1-5, @ 1/12/ each	29	12
Akbarnāmah, with Index, (Text) Fasc. 1-37 @ 1/ each ...	37	0
Ditto English Vol. I, Fasc. 1-8; Vol. II, Fasc. 1 @ 1/ each ...	9	0
Arabic Bibliography, by Dr. A. Sprenger	0	6
Bādshāhnāmah, with Index, (Text) Fasc. 1-19 @ /6/ each	7	2
Catalogue of Arabic Books and Manuscripts 1-2	2	0
Catalogue of the Persian Books and Manuscripts in the Library of the Asiatic Society of Bengal. Fasc. 1-3 @ 1/ each ...	3	0
Dictionary of Arabic Technical Terms, and Appendix, Fasc. 1-21 @ 1/ each	21	0
Farhang-i-Rashīdī, (Text) Fasc. 1-14 @ 1/ each	14	0
Fihrist-i-Ṭūsī, or, Ṭūsy's list of Shy'ah Books, (Text) Fasc. 1-4 @ /12/ each	3	0
Futūḥ-ush-Shām of Wāqidī, (Text) Fasc. 1-9 @ /6/ each	3	6
Ditto of Āzādī, (Text) Fasc. 1-4 @ /6/ each	1	8
Haft Āsmān, History of the Persian Masnawi, (Text) Fasc. 1 ...	0	12
History of the Caliphs, (English) Fasc. 1-6 @ /12/ each	4	8
Iqbālnāmah-i-Jahāngīrī, (Text) Fasc. 1-3 @ /6/ each	1	2
Iṣābah, with Supplement, (Text) 51 Fasc. @ /12/ each	38	4
Maāsir-ul-Umarā, Vol. I, Fasc. 1-9, Vol. II, Fasc. 1-9; Vol. III, 1-10; Index to Vol. I, Fasc. 10-11; Index to Vol. II, Fasc. 10-12; Index to Vol. III, Fasc. 11-12 @ /6/ each	13	2
Maghāzi of Wāqidī, (Text) Fasc. 1-5 @ /6/ each	1	14

* The other Fasciculi of these works are out of stock, and complete copies cannot be supplied.

Muntakhabu-t-Tawārikh, (Text) Fasc. 1-15 @ /6/ each	Rs. 5	10
Muntakhabu-t-Tawārikh, (English) Vol. I, Fasc. 1-7; Vol. II, Fasc. 1-5 and 3 Indexes; Vol. III, Fasc. 1 @ /12/ each ...	12	0
Muntakhabu-l-Lubāb, (Text) Fasc. 1-19 @ /6/ each ...	7	2
Ma'āṣir-i-'Ālamgīrī, (Text), Fasc. 1-6 @ /6/ each ...	2	4
Nukhbatu-l-Fikr, (Text) Fasc. 1	0	6
Niẓāmī's Khiradnāmah-i-Iskandari, (Text) Fasc. 1-2 @ /12/ each	1	8
Riyāẓu-s-Salātīn, (Text) Fasc. 1-5 @ /6/ each	1	14
Ditto Ditto (English) Fasc. 1-5 ...	3	12
Tabaqāt-i-Nāṣirī, (Text) Fasc. 1-5 @ /6/ each	1	14
Ditto (English) Fasc. 1-14 @ /12/ each ...	10	8
Ditto Index	1	0
Tārikh-i-Fīrūz Shāhi of Ẓiyāu-d-dīn Barni (Text) Fasc. 1-7 @ /6/ each...	2	10
Tārīkh-i-Fīrūzshāhi, of Shams-i-Sirāj Aif, (Text) Fasc. 1-6 @ /6/ each.	2	4
Ten Ancient Arabic Poems, Fasc. 1-2 @ 1/8/ each ...	3	0
Wīs o Rāmīn, (Text) Fasc. 1-5 @ /6/ each	1	14
Ẓafarnāmah, Vol. I, Fasc. 1-9, Vol. II, Fasc. 1-8 @ /6/ each	6	6
Tuzuk-i-Jahāngirī (Eng.) Fasc. 1	0	12

ASIATIC SOCIETY'S PUBLICATIONS.

1.	Asiatic Researches. Vols. XIX and XX @ 10/ each ...	20	0
2.	Proceedings of the Asiatic Society from 1865 to 1869 (incl.) @ /6/ per No.; and from 1870 to date @ /8/ per No.		
3.	Journal of the Asiatic Society for 1843 (12), 1844 (12), 1845 (12), 1846 (5), 1847 (12), 1848 (12), 1866 (7), 1867 (6), 1868 (6), 1869 (8), 1870 (8), 1871 (7), 1872 (8), 1873 (8) 1874 (8), 1875 (7), 1876 (7), 1877 (8), 1878 (8), 1879 (7), 1880 (8), 1881 (7), 1882, (6), 1883 (5), 1884 (6), 1885 (6), 1886 (8), 1887 (7), 1888 (7), 1889 (10), 1890 (11), 1891 (7), 1892 (8), 1893 (11), 1894 (8), 1895 (7), 1896 (8), 1897 (8), 1898 (8), 1899 (8), 1900 (7) & 1901 (7), 1902 (9), 1903 (8), @ 1/8 per No. to Members and @ 2/per No. to Non-Members.		
	N.B.—The figures enclosed in brackets give the number of Nos. in each Volume.		
4	Centenary Review of the Researches of the Society from 1784-1883 ...	3	0
	A sketch of the Turki language as spoken in Eastern Turkistan, by R. B. Shaw (Extra No., *J.A.S.B.*, 1878)	4	0
	Theobald's Catalogue of Reptiles in the Museum of the Asiatic Society (Extra No., *J.A.S.B.*, 1868)	2	0
	Catalogue of Mammals and Birds of Burmah, by E. Blyth (Extra No., *J.A.S.B.*, 1875)	4	0
5.	Anīs-ul-Musharrahīn	3	0
6.	Catalogue of Fossil Vertebrata	3	0
7.	Catalogue of the Library of the Asiatic Society, Bengal	3	8
8.	Ināyah, a Commentary on the Hidāyah, Vols. II and IV, @ 16/ each...	32	0
9.	Jawāmiu-l-'ilm ir-riyāẓi, 168 pages with 17 plates, 4to. Part I ...	2	0
10.	Khizānatu-l-'ilm	4	0
11.	Mahābhārata, Vols. III and IV, @ 20/ each	40	0
12.	Moore and Hewitson's Descriptions of New Indian Lepidoptera, Parts I-III, with 8 coloured Plates, 4to. @ 6/ each	18	0
13.	Sharaya-ool-Islām	4	0
14.	Tibetan Dictionary, by Csoma de Körös	10	0
15.	Ditto Grammar " "	8	0
16.	Kaçmīraçabdāmṛta, Parts I and II @ 1/8/	3	0
17.	A descriptive catalogue of the paintings, statues, &c., in the rooms of the Asiatic Society of Bengal, by C. R. Wilson...	1	0
18.	Memoir on maps illustrating the Ancient Geography of Kaśmir, by M. A. Stein, Ph.D., Jl. Extra No. 2 of 1899	4	0

Notices of Sanskrit Manuscripts, Fasc. 1-29 @ 1/ each	29	0
Nepalese Buddhist Sanskrit Literature, by Dr. R. L. Mitra ...	5	0

N.B.—All Cheques, Money Orders, &c., must be made payable to the "Treasurer Asiatic Society," only.

12-12-04.

Books are supplied by V.-P.P.

Published by

Facsimile Publisher
Ashok Vihar, Delhi-110052 (India)
Website: www.facsimilepublisher.com

Distributed by

Gyan Books Pvt. Ltd.
5, Ansari Road, Daryaganj, New Delhi-110002 (India)
E-mail: books@gyanbooks.com, Website: www.gyanbooks.com

2 222000 003739